THE HORTICULTURIST:

OR,

THE CULTURE AND MANAGEMENT

OF THE

KITCHEN, FRUIT, & FORCING GARDEN.

BY

J. C. LOUDON, F.L.S., H.S., &c.

EDITED AND REVISED BY

WILLIAM ROBINSON,

AUTHOR OF "ALPINE FLOWERS," "HARDY FLOWERS," "MUSHROOM CULTURE,"
ETC. ETC.

ILLUSTRATED WITH NUMEROUS ENGRAVINGS.

LONDON:
FREDERICK WARNE AND CO.
BEDFORD STREET, COVENT GARDEN.
NEW YORK: SCRIBNER, WELFORD AND CO.

LONDON:
SAVILL, EDWARDS AND CO., PRINTERS, CHANDOS STREET,
COVENT GARDEN.

Printing Statement:

Due to the very old age and scarcity of this book, many of the pages may be hard to read due to the blurring of the original text, possible missing pages, missing text, dark backgrounds and other issues beyond our control.

Because this is such an important and rare work, we believe it is best to reproduce this book regardless of its original condition.

Thank you for your understanding.

THE HORTICULTURIST.

PREFACE.

AMONG the various standard books of the late Mr. Loudon others are more expensive, elaborately illustrated, and comprehensive in aim, but none are so worthy of a re-issue as this volume. The excellent original plan has not been deviated from, but a good many sections treating of matters of but slight importance in connexion with practical gardening have been omitted; such as the "analogy between plants and animals," the "classification of plants with a view to Horticulture," the "nomenclature of plants with reference to Horticulture," &c., &c. The undue prominence, indeed, given to such matters might be considered the only faults in a book before its time in most other respects. A great number of the old illustrations, and a good deal of the more technical portions of the old matter, have also been omitted, and such alterations made in all parts as, it is hoped, bring it down to the present time, and within the reach of a much wider circle of readers. The changes made have mostly been in matters of detail. In consequence of the considerable variation in the practice of the culture of the Grape Vine and Pine Apple since the first appearance of the book, it was considered desirable to entirely re-write these chapters. The book was very rich in illustrations originally, so that it required little improvement in this way, but new ones have been added wherever necessary. The article on Pine culture was written by Mr. D. T. Fish, who also furnished valuable assistance in reading a considerable part of the book, and we have to thank Mr. Barnes, late of Bicton, for looking over several chapters in the culinary department. To Mr. Pearson, of the Chilwell Nurseries, we are indebted for some of the cuts illustrating his little book on the Orchard-house.

W. R.

July, 1871.

TABLE OF CONTENTS.

CHAPTER I.

	PAGE
Soils considered with reference to Horticulture	1
Origin and kinds of soils	1
The improvement of soils	7

CHAPTER II.

Manures considered with reference to Horticulture	13
Organic manures	13
Inorganic manures	18
Mixed manures	22

CHAPTER III.

The Atmosphere considered with reference to Horticulture	25
Heat	26
Atmospheric moisture	33
Circulation of the atmosphere	38
Light	42

CHAPTER IV.

Worms, Snails, Slugs, Insects, Reptiles, Birds, &c., considered with reference to Horticulture	46
The Earthworm	46
Snails and Slugs	50
Insects	52
Birds	68
Animals injurious to gardens	70

CHAPTER V.

The Diseases and Accidents of Plants	74

CHAPTER VI.

	PAGE
Implements of Horticulture	78
Tools used in Horticulture	81
Instruments	90
Utensils	98
Machines	111
Miscellaneous articles	115

CHAPTER VII.

Structures and edifices of Horticulture	130
Portable, temporary, and moveable structures	130
Fixed structures	137
Walls, espalier-rails, and trelliswork	137
Fixed structures with glass roofs	151
Various accessory garden structures	193

CHAPTER VIII.

Operations of Horticulture	196
Labours on the soil	196
Garden labours with plants	202
Operations of Culture	205
Propagation	205
,, by seed	206
,, by cuttings	214
,, by leaves	228
,, by layers	233
,, by sucker, slips, offsets, runners, and simple division	239
,, by grafting	241
,, by budding	265
Transplanting and planting	274
Potting and repotting	294
Pruning	299
Thinning	310
Training	313
Weeding	348
Watering	351
Manuring	356
Blanching	357
Sheltering	357
Accelerating vegetation	359
Retarding ,,	363
Resting ,,	364
Operations of gathering, preserving, keeping, and packing	368
Selecting and improving plants in culture	371
Operations of order and keeping	376

TABLE OF CONTENTS.

CHAPTER IX.

	PAGE
Operations of Horticultural Design and Taste	379

CHAPTER X.

Operations of General Management 379

CHAPTER XI.

The Culture of the Kitchen and Fruit Garden 383
    Laying out the kitchen-garden 383
    Distribution of fruit trees in a kitchen-garden 388
    Fruit trees for espaliers and dwarfs 392
    Fruit shrubs 400
    Selection of fruit trees adapted for an orchard 402

CHAPTER XII.

Cropping and General Management of a Kitchen-garden 406
    Rotation of crops 408
    Planting, sowing, cultivating, and managing 413

CHAPTER XIII.

The Forcing Department 416
    Culture of the Pine-apple 416

CHAPTER XIV.

Culture of the Grape Vine 440

CHAPTER XV.

Culture of the Peach, Nectarine, &c., under glass 476
    „   Cherry under glass 483
    „   Fig under glass 488
    „   Plum, Apricot, &c., and other fruit trees and shrubs
          under glass 492

CHAPTER XVI.

		PAGE
Culture of the Melon, Cucumber, &c.		492
,,	Melon	492
,,	Cucumber	498
,,	Banana	511
,,	Strawberry	513
,,	Asparagus	516
,,	Sea-kale	517
,,	Rhubarb and Chicory	517
Forcing the Potato		518
,,	Kidney-beans and Peas	519
,,	Salads, Pot-herbs, Sweet-herbs, and other culinary plants	521
,,	the Mushroom	522

CHAPTER XVII.

Catalogue of Fruits, with Summary of Culture, &c.

HARDY OR ORCHARD FRUITS:—

The Apple	526
The Pear	542
The Quince	548
The Medlar	549
The True Service	549
The Cherry	550
The Plum	554
The Gooseberry	557
The Currant	562
The Raspberry	563
The Strawberry	566
The Cranberry	570
The Mulberry	571
The Walnut	571
The Sweet Chestnut	572
The Filbert	572
The Barberry, Elder-berry, and Cornelian Cherry	573

HALF-HARDY AND WALL FRUITS:—

The Grape	574
The Peach and Nectarine	576
The Almond	583
The Apricot	584
The Fig	585
The Pomegranate	586
The Peruvian Cherry	587

TABLE OF CONTENTS.

TROPICAL OR SUB-TROPICAL FRUITS:—

	PAGE
The Pine-apple	587
The Banana	588
The Melon	588
The Cucumber	589
The Pumpkin and Gourd	589
The Tomato, Egg-plant, and Capsicum	591
The Orange Family	593
The Guava, Loquat, Granadilla, and other Fruits little known in British Gardens	597
Remarks applicable to Fruit-trees and Fruit-bearing Plants generally	599

CHAPTER XVIII.

Catalogue of Culinary Vegetables	602
The Cabbage Tribe	605
The Pea	613
The Bean	618
The Kidney-bean	619
The Potato	623
The Jerusalem Artichoke	631
The Turnip	631
The Carrot	633
The Parsnip	635
The Red Beet	635
The Skirret, Scorzonera, Salsify, and Œnothera	636
The Hamburgh Parsley	637
The Radish	637
Oxalis Deppei, O. crenata, and Tropæolum tuberosum	639
The Common Spinach	640
The Orache or French Spinach	641
New Zealand Spinach	641
Perennial Spinach	642
Spinach Beet and Chard Beet	642
Patience Spinach	642
The Sorrel	643
The Onion	643
The Leek	649
The Shallot	649
The Garlic	650
The Chive	650
The Rocambole	650
The Asparagus	651
The Sea-kale	655

TABLE OF CONTENTS.

Culinary Vegetables:— PAGE
   The French Artichoke 657
   The Cardoon 658
   The Rampion 660
   Substitutes for Asparagus 660
   The Lettuce 661
   The Endive 664
   The Succory and Chicory 665
   The Celery 667
   The Lamb's Lettuce, Burnet, Garden Cress, Winter Cress, American Cress, and Water Cress 670
   Small Salads 672
   The Parsley 672
   The Chervil, Coriander, Dill, Fennel, Tarragon, and Purslane 673
   The Indian Cress, Borage, and Marigold 675
   The Horse-radish 675
   The Rhubarb 677
   The Angelica, Elecampane, Samphire, and Caper 677
   Aromatic Esculents 679
   Fungaceous Esculents 681
   Odoraceous Herbs 682
   Medicinal Herbs 683
   Poisonous Herbs 684

Monthly Calendar of Operations 687
Index 697

THE HORTICULTURIST.

CHAPTER I.

SOILS CONSIDERED WITH REFERENCE TO HORTICULTURE.

The term soil is applied to that thin stratum on the surface of the ground which is occupied by the roots of the smaller herbaceous vegetables; on uncultivated surfaces it varies in depth with its nature and the character of the plants growing on it; but on lands in cultivation, the soil extends to the depth usually penetrated by the implements of culture. The principal materials of which soils are composed are earths formed of the débris of different kinds of rocks, combined with organic matter derived from decomposed vegetables or animals. Earths without organic matter will only support plants of the lowest grade, such as Lichens and Mosses; and where soils are found supporting the higher classes of plants, endogens and exogens, the vigour of these will generally be found to be greater or less according to the proportion of organic matter which the soil contains. This organic matter, when supplied by art, is called manure. The subject of manures will be most conveniently treated in our next chapter. Here we shall confine ourselves to the consideration of soils, and treat, first, of their origin and kinds, and secondly, of their improvement.

Origin and Kinds of Soils.

The earthy part of all soils must necessarily have been derived from the *débris* of rocks, and the organic part from the intermixture of decayed vegetable or animal matter. The earthy mass so produced varies in colour, but, from containing humus and mould, it is always darker in a greater or less degree than subsoils, which in general are without organic matter. Soils also contain mineral salts and metallic oxides, some of which are beneficial, others harmless, and some few injurious, to plants. The chemical constitution of a soil can only be known by analysis, which cannot, in general, be depended on, unless performed by professional or experienced chemists.[*] The me-

---

[*] It is now becoming a general custom for landed proprietors to send a pound or more of soil to an experienced chemist, to obtain an analysis of it, so as to know what mineral manures it may be best to use, in order to supply the constituents the land may stand in need of.

chanical state or texture of a soil is ascertained by digging up a portion of it; and its actual fitness for plants, by examining the species growing on its surface. The rock, or geological formation, the earth of which forms the basis of any soil, will frequently be found to constitute the substratum on which that soil rests; but this is frequently not the case, because the earths of many soils have been held in suspension by water in a state of motion, and by that means have been transported to a great distance from the rocks of which they are the débris. From this suspension of the earths of soils in water, and their transportation to a distance, we are able to account for the circumstance of several different kinds of earths being almost always found in the same soil. Thus in alluvial deposits on the banks of rivers, we find the earth of various rocks of the country through which the river has taken its course; and as such soils are always the most fertile, we may conclude that a mixture of various earths in a soil is to be preferred to any one kind of earth alone. From the earth of the alluvial deposits of every country being formed of the débris of the various rocks of that country, and from every country containing nearly the same kinds of rocks, the alluvial deposits on the banks of all the large rivers of the world consist nearly of the same earths. But as the rocks or geological formations from which the earths of soils are washed away still remain in their places, and are of many different kinds, it follows that there must be as great a variety in the upland soils of a country as there is uniformity in those of the lowlands, and of the banks of rivers. Thus there are between twenty and thirty geological formations in England, which form the substrata or bases of soils, and each of which must consequently be more or less different in its composition.[*] For all practical purposes, however, soils may be characterized by their prevailing primitive earths; and, hence, they are reduced to sands and gravels, clays, chalky and limestone soils, alluvial soils, and peatbogs.

Sandy Soil.—Silica, which is the basis of sandy soils, is, perhaps, the most universal of all earths: and there is scarcely a species or variety of rock in which it does not abound more or less. Silica is found perfectly pure in rock crystal, and tolerably so in what is called silver sand, and also in the sand of some rivers and of the sea. The practical test of this soil, when tolerably pure, is, that when moistened, it cannot be formed into a plastic mass, or consolidated by pressure, whether in a moist or dry state, so as to form a compact solid body. Hence all sandy soils are loose, never present a firm surface, and are seldom covered with a compact clothing of grass or other herbaceous plants. Such soils, from being without cohesion, are incapable of retaining moisture, and, as they are readily permeable by both moisture and air, they powerfully promote the putrefaction of organic matter, whilst they as readily permit it to be washed away from them by rains, or to escape in the form of gas. Hence, in manuring sandy soils, no more should be applied at once than can be consumed by the crop

---

[*] See Morton 'On Soils,' 4th edit. 8vo, 1843.

of the current year; and hence, also, they should be cultivated to a greater depth than other soils, in order that there may be a greater mass of material for retaining moisture. One great advantage of a sandy soil over all others is its natural warmth. This arises from its greater looseness and porosity, in consequence of which the atmosphere penetrates into it more rapidly, and to a greater depth, than in the case of any other soil. Hence, in the absence of sunshine, a sandy soil will be raised to the temperature of the atmosphere, to the depth of several inches, by the mere penetration of the air among its particles; while a firm, compact soil, the earthy basis of which is clay or chalk, could not be heated to the same depth without the direct influence of the sun's rays. Sandy soils are also more easily penetrated by water than any others, and hence they are sooner raised or lowered to the temperature of the rains which fall on them than a clayey or calcareous soil. As the water never rests on sandy soils, they are never cooled down by evaporation; the reverse of which is the case with clayey and calcareous surfaces. Sandy soils being much less cohesive than soils in which clay or lime prevails, they are much more easily laboured; and being always loose and friable on the surface, they are better adapted for the germination of seeds. Sandy soils may be made to approach alluvial soils by the addition of clay and calcareous earth, either taken from clayey or calcareous surfaces, or from subsoils in which these earths abound; but the former source is greatly preferable, from the earths being already in combination with organic matter.

Whatever has been said of sandy soils is applicable to gravelly soils; in some particulars in a greater, and in some in a less degree. The small stones of which the greater part of gravel consists being better conductors of heat than the particles of sand, it follows that gravels are both more easily heated and more easily cooled than sands; they are also more readily penetrated by rain, and more readily dried by filtration and evaporation. Like sands, they are improved by the addition of clay and chalk, or by alluvial soil; and they require also to be cultivated to a greater depth than clays or chalks. A gravelly soil, isolated so as not to be supplied with water from higher grounds, is of all others the most suitable for a suburban villa ('Sub. Arch. and Landscape Gard.,' p. 16); and therefore, though not so suitable for a kitchen-garden as a sandy or loamy soil, yet as a sufficient portion of soil, whatever may be its earths, may always be improved so as to render it fit for the cultivation of vegetables, a gravelly or sandy soil for building on should never be rejected.

Clayey Soil.—Alumina, which is the basis of clayey soil, is the most frequent of earths next to sand. It is found nearly pure in the ruby and sapphire, tolerably so in the blue or London clay, but more so in the white plastic clay which is found between the London clay and the upper chalk, and which is used for making tobacco pipes. This soil, relatively to water, is the very reverse of sand; for while in nature sand and water are never found chemically combined, in clay they are never found chemically separate. Hence, though clay when prepared by the chemist, and kept apart from water, appears as a light dry powder, scarcely different to the eye from pure sand or pure lime, yet in soils it forms an adhesive mass, the particles of which cannot be permanently separated except by burning to expel the water held in fixation. When clay is burnt and reduced to powder, it becomes for all practical purposes sand, and in that state it may be employed to great advantage for reducing the cohesive properties of stiff clay. Relatively to heat, clays do not admit the atmosphere between their particles, and an unimproved clayey soil is generally a cold one; partly because the heat penetrates with difficulty into it, and partly from the evaporation which during great part of the year is going on from its moist surface. The obvious way to improve clays is by the addition of sand or gravel; and when the clay does not contain lime, by the addition of that material, either in a caustic or a mild state, or as chalk.

Lime, or the basis of chalk and limestone rock, is much less common as a soil than either clay or sand; though there are scarcely any soils which are naturally fertile that are absolutely without it. Lime is found in a state of carbonate in white or statuary marble, and more or less so in chalk-rock and in some limestone-rocks. Lime is never found pure in a state of nature, but always combined with carbonic or sulphuric acid and water, which are driven off from it by burning, leaving the earth in the caustic state called quicklime. In this state lime rapidly reabsorbs water and carbonic acid from the atmosphere, or from any other material which comes in contact with it containing these elements. Hence its use in a caustic state in promoting the putrefaction of imperfectly decomposed organic matter in soils, and in attracting carbonic acid and moisture from the atmosphere. Relatively to the retention of water, a limy or chalky soil may be considered as intermediate between a sandy and a clayey soil, without becoming so tenacious as clay on the one hand, or parting with water so readily as sand on the other. Hence the use of lime or chalk in reducing the tenacity of stiff clays, and increasing the absorbent powers of sandy soils, and improving their texture. A calcareous soil is improved by sand and clay, especially if laid on in sufficient quantity to destroy the tenacity and compactness of its texture.

Magnesia is not very common in soils, and is said to be inimical to vegetation, under some circumstances. Magnesian limestone, when burned as lime, should not be used for manuring purposes.

The iron of soils is mostly in a state of rust, or oxide. There is scarcely any soil without it; but it is never very abundant in soils naturally fertile. In a dry state the oxide of iron is insoluble in water, and not injurious to vegetation; but when, in consequence of saline substances in the soil or applied to it, a salt of iron is produced, the iron becomes soluble in water, is taken up by the roots of plants, and is very injurious to them. Iron in this state is termed hydrate, and its evil effects are to be counteracted by caustic lime, with which it forms an insoluble compound.

Alluvial soils have been already described as composed of very fine particles of the débris of several kinds of rocks, which have been held in suspension by water, and deposited in plains, or along the banks of rivers, along with organic matter also held in suspension. The earthy character of this soil must necessarily always partake of the character of the rocks of the country in which it is found.

Peat or bog is composed of partially decayed vegetable matter, soft, light, and spongy to the touch; and is the very reverse of sand with respect to water, holding that element like a sponge, so as, in its natural state, to be totally unfit for the growth of vegetables, except those of a very low grade.

The organic matter in soils in its solid state may be considered as carbon, which is found pure in the diamond, and tolerably so in the charcoal of wood. In soils it is found in various states of decomposition, from recent woody fibre to humus, which is woody fibre in a state of decay. The proportion of organic matter varies exceedingly in different soils. In barren sands there is scarcely a trace of it, while in fertile soils it varies from 10 to 30 per cent.; and peat-bogs which have been drained and cultivated contain often 80 or 90 per cent. Humus, according to Professor Liebig, exercises its influence on vegetation " by being a continued source of carbonic acid, which it emits slowly. An atmosphere of carbonic acid, formed at the expense of the oxygen of the air, surrounds every particle of decaying humus. The cultivation of land, by stirring and loosening the soil, causes a free and unobstructed access of air. An atmosphere of carbonic acid is, therefore, contained in every fertile soil, and is the first and most important food for the young plants which grow in it. The property of humus, or woody fibre, to attract from the surrounding air its carbonic acid, diminishes in proportion as its decay advances; and at last a certain quantity of a brown coaly-looking substance remains, in which this property is entirely wanting. This substance is called mould; it is the product of the complete decay of woody fibre, and constitutes the principal part of brown coal and peat." ('Organic Chemistry,' p. 47.)

For practical purposes, all the soils ordinarily met with may be reduced to the following :—

Loose naked sands or gravels, without either clay or calcareous matter, and almost destitute of vegetation on the surface; exemplified on some parts of the sea-shore, and on Hounslow and other extensive heaths.

Calcareous soils or gravels, containing little or no clay or organic matter, and almost without vegetation on the surface; found on the sea-shore in some places, and on the surface of chalky districts.

Loams.—Rich sandy loams consist of sand, clay, and more or less of calcareous soil, with organic matter; they never become hard on the surface after rains followed by drought, and never retain water to such an extent as to prove injurious to vegetation. Vegetation commences some weeks earlier in sandy loams than in clayey loams, in the same climate, or even in the same garden; and during summer, plants on such soils will be in advance of those on clays; so much so, as Mr. Lymburn has observed, as to attain maturity a month earlier. Clayey loams consist of clay with a proportion of sand and organic matter; they produce large crops, but become hard and baked on the surface after heavy rains followed by drought. Stiff adhesive clays contain in their composition little or no sand or lime, and are almost without organic matter. All clayey loams are later than sandy loams.

Loams are the best soils, and are characterized according to the earths which prevail in them, as a sandy loam, &c.; according to their degree of friability, as a free loam, a stiff loam, &c.; or according to both, as a free calcareous loam, &c. These soils, with reference to geology, are generally found on the sides of valleys, along the bases of hills or mountains, or on the banks of upland rivers. Mechanically, they are of a texture easily penetrated by all the implements of culture, and not liable to become hard on the surface, and crack after heavy rains followed by drought; chemically, they contain clay, sand, calcareous matter, and humus; and with reference to vegetation, produce abundant crops in all ordinary seasons, with moderate supplies of manure.

In general, much more depends on the texture of a soil and its capacity for retaining or parting with water and heat, than on its chemical composition. Soils have been found consisting chiefly of clay, others chiefly of calcareous earths; some in America, without calcareous earths; and all producing good crops for a series of years. Nevertheless, it has been found that no soil will remain fertile for many years that does not contain lime in some form naturally, or is not liberally supplied with manure containing animal matter, one ingredient of which is lime in a state of phosphate.

Subsoils.—Next in importance to the texture of a soil, is the nature of the subsoil or substratum on which it rests; because on the texture and other circumstances of this subsoil depends, in a great measure, the capacity of the surface-soil for retaining or parting with water or heat. The worst subsoils are those of clay kept moist by subterraneous water; and the best, those of clay resting on gravel or porous rock; because these retain a useful degree of moisture, and admit of increasing the surface-soil to any depth which may be required for culture. Sandy and gravelly subsoils, with but a thin coating of surface-soil over them, are not sufficiently retentive of moisture; and chalky subsoils are generally cold.

The surface of soils has, perhaps, as powerful an influence on their natural fertility as the subsoil; because on the inclination of the surface depends, in a considerable degree, the moisture retained by the soil, and consequently its fitness for the growth of plants. Too steep a slope throws off the rain with too great rapidity, and thus deprives the soil of a sufficient supply of water during dry seasons; while a flat surface will retard its drainage and occasion loss of heat by evaporation. These natural results of a steep incline and a flat surface may be greatly modified by the depth of the soil and surface stirring, the colours, &c. The colour of the surface of a soil exercises some influence on its heat. A dark-coloured soil will be sooner heated by the rays of the sun than a light-coloured soil; but it will also part with its heat more rapidly when the sun does not shine. A white soil, such as we sometimes find on chalky or marly subsoils, is the longest of all soils in being warmed, because by all white surfaces the rays of light and heat are reflected, while by all black surfaces they are absorbed. Hence, taking into consideration colour, texture, and aspect, a dark sandy soil, on a surface exposed to the south or south-east, must be the warmest of all soils; and a moist white clay of compact texture, similarly exposed, the coolest. The aspect is not only of importance with reference to the influence of the sun in warming or cooling the soil, but also as to its effects in maturing the produce which grows on it.

The plants which grow on a soil are the surest indications, to a practical botanist and cultivator, of the actual state of that soil with reference to culture; though they do not always indicate the improvement of which the soil is susceptible. Marshy soils are indicated with considerable certainty both by herbaceous and ligneous plants, as are also very dry soils; but the earths of fertile soils cannot be so readily inferred from the plants growing on them. Thus thorn hedges will be found growing vigorously alike on clays, sands, and chalks; though never on these soils, or on any other, when they are either very dry, or saturated with water. Some few plants, when found in their native stations in considerable quantities, may be considered absolute in respect to the earths of the soil in which they grow; such as the Tussilago Farfara, which always indicates clayey soil; Clematis Vitalba, calcareous soil; Arenaria rubra, sandy soil; Rumex Acetosa, ferruginous soil; Vaccinium uliginosum, peaty soil; Salicornia herbacea, saline soil; Caltha palustris, marshy soil, &c.: but by far the greater number of plants only indicate the state of a soil relatively to water and organic matter. In short, nature may be said to have only three kinds of soil relatively to plants; the dry, the moist, and the fertile.

The Improvement of Soils, with a View to Horticulture.

Having seen, in the preceding section, that the permanent fertility of a soil depends mainly on its condition relatively to water and heat, it follows that the improvement of soils must be principally directed to increase their capacity for absorbing and retaining these elements in the degree most suitable for vegetation. The principal operations for this purpose are: draining, to withdraw superfluous water from soils; and mixture and pulverization for improving their texture, in order to admit more readily the moisture and heat of the atmosphere.

Draining is the principal means for altering the condition of a soil with reference to water. Soils are affected by rains from above and springs from below; the former are carried off by open gutters, and the latter by covered channels. All draining is founded on the well-known hydrostatic law by which all fluids have a constant tendency to arrange themselves in a horizontal position. Hence, to carry off water, either from a surface or a subsoil, it is only necessary to form channels above or under ground in an inclined position. The kind of drains, and the number employed in any given case, will depend on the texture of the soil and the inclination of the surface. Flat surfaces and retentive clays require the greatest number of drains, and inclined surfaces and porous soils the smallest number. There are very few soils that may not be improved by draining; and it is almost unnecessary to observe, that, where draining is requisite and not performed, the application of other modes of improvement will be made in vain.

Altering the texture and composition of soil by the addition of other soils is the improvement next in importance to that of draining, and requires only to be mentioned to be understood. Too sandy soils will be improved by the addition of clay, and the contrary; and both clay and sand by the addition of lime; because without alkaline matter no soil can be permanently fertile. Though on a large scale the expense of this kind of improvement is too great to be generally adopted, yet in the case of the grounds of small country residences it is practicable at a moderate expense. The proportion of any particular soil that must be added to any other soil so as to perfect its texture, can only be determined by experiment. The first thing to fix on is the depth to which the soil is to be cultivated. In kitchen gardens this may be between two and three feet; but in pleasure-grounds, where the surface is to be chiefly in grass, nine inches or one foot in depth will suffice. "It is astonishing," Mr. Rham observes, "how small a portion of pure alumina will consolidate a loose sand, and convert it into a good loam, the parts of which, when moistened, will adhere and form a clod in drying." ('Jour. Agr. Soc.,' vol. ii. p. 51.) If we take an extreme case, and suppose that any given soil is so sandy as to require the addition of one-sixth its bulk of clay, or so clayey as to require one-sixth its bulk of sand, then, in the case of kitchen gardens where the soil is three feet deep, every square foot of the clayey surface will require the addition of half a cubic foot of sand; and in the case of a lawn where the soil is a foot in depth, every square foot of sand will require the sixth of a cubic foot of clay. To cover a statute acre with soil to the depth of one inch requires 121 cubic yards. Hence, to add two inches to the soil of a garden of one acre, exclusive of the space occupied by the walks, would require 242 cubic yards or cartloads, which, at 2*s*. each, amount to 24*l*. 4*s*. The cost, however, will depend chiefly on the distance from which the soil is to be brought. A case is mentioned in the 'Journal of the Agricultural Society of England,' vol. ii. p. 67, in which a white sand varying in depth from one to four feet, and so barren that it never had been cultivated to profit, had the surface improved to the usual depth penetrated by the plough (nine to twelve inches), by laying on clay at the rate of 150 cubic yards to the acre. The clay being dug from the subsoil, the expense was not more than 5*l*. 10*s*. per acre. It frequently happens that a sandy or gravelly soil is incumbent on a bed of clay, and the contrary; in either of which cases the supply of the required soil may be obtained by digging pits, or sometimes even by deep trenching. The earth thus obtained will generally be without organic matter, but that can be supplied afterwards by manuring. Where the soil required for the improvement of another soil can be obtained in the state of surface soil, the effects produced will be more immediate from the organic matter which such soil contains; but even when it is obtained from the subsoil, the change in the condition of the soil to which the new soil is applied will soon be rendered obvious; though not so much so the first year, as it will be in two or three years afterwards, when the amalgamation of the two soils is more complete. Much of the effect of adding one soil to another will depend on their intimate mixture; and this can be best effected by repeated trenchings or diggings in dry weather, when both soils are as nearly as possible in a state of dry powder. This point is of great importance, particularly when the soils mixed together contain a good deal of organic matter, because if a very intimate mixture of both soils is not effected, they will, from the difference in their specific gravities, in a few years separate into two different strata. There is, indeed, a constant tendency to do this in all soils under culture, and more especially in all such as have been improved by admixture. This takes place in consequence of the softening of the soil by rains, by which the particles are in a manner held for a time in suspension, and the heaviest gradually take a lower place than those which are lighter. Hence the necessity of digging or trenching such soils frequently to the depth to which they have originally been improved. This is required even in artificial soils laid down in grass; for supposing a clayey soil to have received a considerable admixture of lime or chalk, and sand, with rotted stable-dung, and the whole to have been incorporated in a state of fallow, and afterwards sown with grass seeds, then in seven years the black matter or mould remaining from the dung will be found among the roots of the grass at the surface, the sand in a stratum three or four inches below the surface, and the lime at the bottom of the artificial soil. By placing the same mixture in a flower-pot, and watering it frequently during a year, the pot being plunged in the soil, the same result will take place sooner, and be more conspicuous. If the pot be kept constantly immersed in water to within an inch of the brim, the result will take place in the course of a few days. These facts ought to be kept constantly in mind by whoever would improve soils by admixture; if they are not, disappointment is very likely to ensue. When soils mixed together are comparatively without organic matter, and when the particles of which they are composed are very small, the mixture becomes more intimate; the particles of the one soil filling up the interstices among the particles of the other, and the amalgamation as it may be termed is then so complete that the earths will never afterwards separate. In this way pure sands may be improved by the admixture of pure clays, or by marls or chalks. The words pure and amalgamated are here used, not in a chemical, but in a popular sense.

Changing the inclination of the surface of soils is a mode of improvement that may frequently be adopted on a small scale, by arranging a steep slope into narrow terraces, and a broad slope into level platforms. The former mode has been practised from time immemorial in the Land of Canaan, and in other countries of the East, and the latter is common in France and Italy, in order to admit of surface irrigation without waste of water. By this last mode, a field or garden is arranged into different platforms, which may either be on the same or on different levels. In the former case, the water is let into one platform after another; or, if there is an abundant supply, into several at the same time; in the latter case the supply of water is conducted to the highest platform, which is first watered, and the others follow in the order of their elevation. Arrangements of this kind are not so important in British gardens as they are in those of warmer climates; but still they might in many cases be advantageously introduced with a view to watering summer crops.

Burning of soils has been resorted to as a means of altering their texture, destroying injurious substances, and changing or forming others which may act as a manure. Burning is useless on siliceous sands containing little or no vegetable matter; but on all soils containing chalk, lime, or clay, it may be practised with advantage. By burning calcareous or chalky soils, the same effect is produced as if quicklime had been procured and added to the soil; and by burning clayey soils the same result is obtained as if sand had been procured and mixed with them. The effect of burning clay is totally different from that of burning sand or lime. On sands and gravels burning can have no effect, except that in some cases it renders the particles smaller. Burning lime drives off the carbonic acid and the water, and renders the lime caustic and well adapted for decomposing organic matter; but the lime has no sooner lost its water than it begins to attract it again, and after a certain period will be found in the same state of combination with water and carbonic acid as it was before. Clay, on the other hand, when once the water is driven off by burning, will never regain it, but remains for ever afterwards in a state which, with reference to its mechanical effect on a soil, is exactly the same as that of sand. This is a fact, the great importance of which in the improvement of clayey soils, and indeed of all soils which are of too compact a texture, is not duly appreciated. It is evident that, by means of draining and burning, any clayey soil may have its texture as much improved as can be desired; and though the expense of this may, in many cases, be too great for application on an extensive scale, yet it may always be adopted in kitchen gardens; and often over the entire surface of the grounds of small villas. It is indeed only by this kind of improvement that the heavy clayey soils of many of the small villas in the neighbourhood of London can be at all rendered comfortable to walk on after rains in summer, and throughout the whole of the other seasons, or suitable and agreeable for the cultivation of culinary vegetables and flowers. Clayey soils often contain iron, and the operation of burning them, by forming an insoluble compound of iron and alumina, lessens the risk of the iron ever becoming noxious to the plants. Burning also destroys the inert vegetable fibre; and thus it at once produces ashes containing vegetable alkali, and supplies the soil with a portion of humus; without both of which, according to Liebig, no soil can bring plants to maturity. Where a strong clayey soil is covered with a healthy vegetation, as of pasture or wood, it may not be desirable to burn the surface soil, on account of the quantity of organic matter which it contains; but it may still be very desirable to burn such a portion of the clayey subsoil as may be sufficient, when reduced to a sandy powder, to render the surface soil of a proper texture. In this case the surface soil should be removed to the depth to which it has been cultivated, and a portion of that below taken up in lumps, and dried and burned. The burning is performed on the spot by the aid of faggot-wood, or any description of cheap fuel. The burned lumps being reduced to a powder, and scattered equally over the soil when also in a dry and powdery state, the whole should then be intimately mixed together by repeated diggings and trenchings. As an example of the strong clayey soil of a garden having been improved by burning, we may refer to that of Willersley Castle, near Matlock, which the gardener there, Mr. Stafford, has rendered equal in friability and fertility to any garden soil in the country. "When I first came to this place," says Mr. Stafford, "the garden was for the most part a strong clay, and within nine inches of the surface; even the most common article would not live upon it; no weather appeared to suit it—at one time being covered by water, at another time rendered impenetrable by being too dry. Having previously witnessed the good effects of burning clods, I commenced the process, and produced in a few days a composition three feet deep, and equal, if not superior, to any soil in the country." ('Hort. Reg.,' vol. i. p. 210.) The success was here greater than can be expected in every case, because the clay contained a large proportion of calcareous matter.

Pulverizing soils comes next in the order of improvement, and is effected by trenching, digging, and other modes of reversing the surface and mixing and transposing all the different parts. By changing the surface, fresh soil is exposed to the action of the weather; by changing the position of all the parts, new facilities for chemical changes are produced; and by loosening the whole mass of the soil, air and rain are more readily admitted, and greater freedom is given to the growth of the roots. By loosening soil the air is admitted among its particles and confined there, and hence it becomes a non-conductor of heat, and is consequently warmer in winter and cooler in summer than if it were in one firm mass. By the confinement of air in the soil, the heat imparted to it by the sun during the day is retained, and accumulates in all free open soils to such a degree as sensibly to raise their temperature over that of the air, especially during night. From thermometrical observations made at different places, it appears that the mean temperature of the soil, at about one foot below the surface, is somewhat higher naturally than the mean temperature of the atmosphere on the same spot; and hence we may reasonably suppose that, by draining and pulverization, the temperature of the soil may be permanently increased as well as that of the atmosphere. From experiments made by Mr. Thompson, in the garden of the Horticultural Society of London, it appears, that "in the valley of the Thames, the maximum mean of terrestrial temperature, at one foot below the surface, has been found to be $64.81°$ in

July, which is the hottest month in the year: but that the greatest difference between the mean temperature of the earth and atmosphere is in the month of October, when it amounted, in the two years during which the observations were made, to between three and four degrees; and that, in general, the mean temperature of the earth, a foot below the surface, is at least one degree, and more commonly a degree and a half, above the mean of the atmosphere. In these cases, if the terrestrial temperatures be compared with those of the atmosphere, it will be found that in the spring, when vegetation is first generally set in motion, the temperature of the earth not only rises monthly, but retains a mean temperature higher than that of the atmosphere by from one to two degrees; and that in the autumn, when woody and perennial plants require that their tissue should be solidified and their secretions condensed, in order to meet the approach of inclement weather, the terrestrial temperature remains higher in proportion than that of the atmosphere, the earth parting with its heat very slowly." (Lindley's 'Theory of Hort.,' p. 97.) In hot countries the sun often heats the soil to such a degree as to be injurious to the roots of cultivated plants, and pulverization is there resorted to to diminish the force of its rays, which, as it is well known, are less effective on a porous and spongy than on a solid substance. This, as Chaptal informs us, is one of the uses of pulverization even in the south of France.

The free admission of atmospheric air to soil is also necessary for the nourishment of the plants; as it is now found that plants derive a great portion of their carbon and nitrogen from the air penetrating into the soil in which they grow, and being taken up by the spongioles of the roots. The soil also, when loosened, becomes a rapid conductor of water; and, supposing the texture of the soil to be suitable for culture, it will retain a sufficient quantity of moisture for the purpose of vegetation, and allow the escape of what is superfluous by filtration into the subsoil, or into the underground drains which have been formed as a substitute for a porous substratum. The mere act of pulverizing any soil has a tendency to improve its texture, more especially if the operation be frequently repeated. In summer, by exposure of a soil to the air, the particles are separated by the evaporation of the water in their interstices by heat; and by exposing a soil to the frosts of winter, the particles are separated by the expansion of the water in the form of ice. Clayey soils containing iron are in an especial manner improved by exposure to the atmosphere; the iron being still farther oxidized, and thus acting like sand in separating the particles, as well as being less likely to be rendered soluble by the addition of saline matters.

Soils are improved by the modes in which they are cultivated; as for example, by the order in which crops are made to succeed each other, by fallowing, by resting, and by the manner in which water is applied to growing crops; but these subjects will come under notice when we are treating of the practice of Horticulture.

CHAPTER II.

MANURES CONSIDERED WITH REFERENCE TO HORTICULTURE.

The improvement of the composition and the texture of a soil, and of its condition with reference to water and heat, will have but little effect on the plants cultivated in it, without the addition of manure. In order to determine what substances are suitable for becoming manures, it is useful to know what are the constituent elements of plants. Of these we shall find that some elements are common to all plants whatever, such as carbon, with oxygen and hydrogen in the proper relative proportions for forming water, and nitrogen; while some elements are only found in particular plants, such as certain salts, earths, and metallic oxides. Every plant, therefore, may be said to have its general or common food, and its specific or particular food; and hence, in this point of view, manures may be classed as common and specific. The most perfect manure for any plant would therefore seem to be, that plant itself in a state of decomposition; but as the purpose for which plants are cultivated is to supply food, clothing, and various other necessaries for men and animals, hence, in a state of civilization, it is among these, and from animals themselves, that we must seek for the most suitable manure for plants. The various substances which have been used for manures may be classed, with reference to their effect on plants, as general and specific; and with reference to the soil, as improving, enriching, and stimulating. Improving manures are such as, while they afford positive nourishment or stimulus, add some permanent matter to the soil; such as lime, chalk, marl, bones, &c. Enriching manures are such as supply only nourishment to plants; such as stable manure, and every description of organic matter; and stimulating manures are such as serve to aid in the decomposition of, or otherwise operate on, the organic matter. As some manures, however, partake in an equal degree of more than one of these properties, such as lime, which is both a stimulating and improving manure, the most convenient arrangement of manures will be organic, inorganic, and mixed.

Organic Manures.

Organic manures must obviously be either of animal or vegetable origin. Purely vegetable manure is exemplified in leaf-mould, malt-dust, rape-cake, spent tanner's bark, some kinds of peat, and green vegetables when they are buried in the soil in a living state.

Leaf-mould is perhaps the most universal manure for garden plants, because, when thoroughly decomposed, the most tender kinds will live in it, and all the more vigorous-growing vegetables will grow in it most luxuriantly if it be mixed with fine sand. The sand seems essential, not only for growing many of the Cape and Australian shrubs, but also for general use.

Fresh and tender vegetables dug into the soil, produce an immediate effect, from the facility with which they undergo fermentation, and thus supply soluble matter for the spongioles. Sea-weed is still more readily decomposed than recent land or garden plants, in consequence of the mineral alkali which it contains; and hence this manure is stimulating as well as enriching. Malt-dust is valuable for the saccharine matter which it contains, and rape-cake for its albumen and oil; but these manures are only occasionally to be met with. Straw, haulm, and in general all the stems and leaves of herbaceous plants, and the shoots, with their leaves on, of trees and shrubs, form valuable manure when decayed; more especially if, from the saccharine matter which they contain, or the addition of stable manure or of animal matter, they can be made to heat and promote fermentation. Nevertheless, without fermentation, they form useful garden manures, or moulds, which, like leaf-mould, may often be substituted for heath-soil.

The least valuable truly vegetable manure is spent tanner's bark, which, consisting entirely of woody fibre impregnated with tannin, not only contains no soluble matter, but the tannin, in as far as it can be taken up by the spongioles, seems to prove injurious. Nevertheless, even spent tanner's bark may be rendered fertile, by mixing it with sand, clay, lime, or some other earthy substance which will supply the plants grown in it with the necessary salts, and also keep its particles sufficiently open to admit the air. From the porosity and lightness of tanner's bark, it is an excellent non-conductor of heat; and hence, when laid on the surface of the ground as a covering to the roots of tender plants, it protects them better from the frost than a more compact covering, such as coarse sand, or than coverings which are great absorbents of moisture, such as leaves or half-rotten litter, or any other covering of this kind which does not act as thatch. Rotten tan, however, being peculiarly favourable to the growth of fungi, should be used with great caution when applied about young trees, and more especially Coniferæ.

Peat soil is of two kinds, that formed in peat bogs by the growth of mosses, and that found in valleys, or other low tracts of country, which, being formed of overthrown and buried forests, consists of decayed wood. The latter being the remains of a much higher class of plants than the former, must contain a greater variety of the constituent elements of plants, and must consequently be a better manure. Peat from bogs cannot be used till it has been reduced, either by time or fermentation, to a fine mould or a saponaceous mass; the former result is obtained by exposure to the air, and repeated turnings during several years, and the latter by fermentation with stable dung. A load of this material, mixed with two loads of partially dried peat, will commence the putrefactive process, in the same manner as yeast commences fermentation in dough; and, in the one case as in the other, additions of any quantity may be made by degrees, so that two loads of stable-dung may be made to produce twenty, a hundred, or in short an unlimited number of loads of fermented peat. The peat of decayed wood is commonly reduced to mould by exposure and turning, and then applied to the soil, with or without lime. Both kinds of peat are frequently burned for the sake of their ashes. The ashes of the peat of wood are always found richer in alkaline matters than those of the peat of moss, and on this account they form an article of commerce in the neighbourhood of Newbury in Berkshire, and in Holland. A third kind of peat, more properly called heath-soil, is much used in the culture of all fine hair-rooted plants, such as heaths. It is the result of the decay of vegetation and the decomposition of rocks, and is generally sweet and ready for present use, because found only on upland districts, where there is no standing water. We associate peat with the morass; this heath-soil, with the upland moor or heath.

The principal vegetable manures which are formed in suburban villas are: the mould of collected leaves swept up in autumn, and in all seasons when they fall; the mould of grass mown from lawns, and either rotted by itself, or on dung-casings to forcing-pits; and the mould from the common vegetable rubbish heap; that is from a heap on which all decaying or refuse vegetable matters are thrown as taken from the garden, and sometimes, also, including the leaves of trees and short grass. This heap is, or should be, placed in the reserve ground of all gardens. The grass mown from lawns, however, is most economically added to casings of dung to aid in producing heat by fermentation, as it is laid on dug surfaces round the roots of plants during summer to retain moisture. The leaves also are generally best kept by themselves, for the purpose of decaying into leaf-mould. In whatever way these vegetable materials are made use of, the gardener ought to have a vigilant eye to see that none of them are lost; and one of the simplest and best means of doing so, is to cover all such rubbish heaps frequently with thin layers of soil, to prevent the escape of the nutritive gases.

Animal manures require much less preparation than those derived from plants, from their greater tendency to the putrefactive process. The kinds of animal manures are chiefly excrement; urine; coverings of animals, such as skins, wool, feathers; entrails of animals; entire animals of small size and not otherwise useful, such as fish, vermin, &c.; parts of animals, such as skins, bones, &c.; or articles manufactured from parts of animals, such as woollen rags, old leather; or any article manufactured from skins, hair, wool, feathers, horn, bone, &c. Of all these manures by far the most valuable is nightsoil, the next urine, and thirdly bones. The different excrements and urines of animals rank in value according to the kind of food with which the animal is nourished, and within this limit according to its grade; and hence the most valuable animal manure is that of man, the next that of horses as abounding with ammonia and nitrogen. The manure of the horse ranks before that of the cow or the sheep; and the manure of highly-fed animals before that of those which are lean.

Excrementitious manures, including urine, should never be applied to crops in a recent state, because from the abundance of ammoniacal salts which they contain, or perhaps from some other reason not understood, they are found in that state injurious to vegetation; but when these manures are fermented they are the most powerful of all, producing an immediate effect on the plants. It is a remarkable fact that the recent urine of sheep is not injurious to grass lands, while that of horses and cows commonly injures the grass on the spot where it falls, which however recovers and becomes of a darker green than before in the year following. The loss of excrementitious manures in the large towns in England is immense, and while they are lost to the soil, they are poisonous to the fishes of our rivers, and injurious to those who drink their water. The great advantage of urine or other liquid manure is, that its nutritive elements are consumed by the plants in a few months, and hence an immediate return is made on the capital employed; whereas, when solid excrementitious manures are employed, a period of two or three years must elapse before complete decomposition ensues. (See Sprengel 'On Animal Manures,' in 'Jour. Eng. Agr. Soc.,' vol. i. p. 473.) Liquid manure, also, from the ammonia which it contains, when poured on the soil destroys worms, snails, &c., as effectually as lime-water.

In every suburban villa, arrangements should be made for collecting all the liquid manure into two adjoining tanks, and mixing it there with water; one tank to be kept filling and mixing, while the other is fermenting and being emptied. Where urine cannot be got, excrement and water form the best substitute. The fermented liquid may either be poured direct on the soil of the garden, among growing crops, at the roots of fruit trees, or on the naked soil, with or without other manure, and more especially with straw, or other vegetable matters for the purpose both of enriching them and promoting fermentation. Fresh liquid manure may however be used at once, if sufficiently weakened, as by adding to pure urine five times its quantity of water. By this means are saved the nutritive properties thrown off by fermentation. The liquid manure tank that is supplied from a house, where water is used in cleaning and washing, will seldom be too strong to apply to strong growing plants in the open air at once.

Hair, wool, feathers, leather, horn, rags, &c., decompose much more slowly than excrementitious or vegetable manures; but they are exceedingly rich in gelatine and albumen, and are therefore very desirable where the object is duration of effect, as well as luxuriance. Dead animals of every kind, including fish, make excellent manure; and when there is any danger anticipated from the effluvia which arises during decomposition, it is readily prevented by covering or mixing the putrid mass with quicklime. In this way nightsoil and the refuse of the slaughter-houses in Paris, Lyons, and other continental towns, are not only disinfected, but dried under the name of *poudrette*, and compressed in casks, so as to form an article of commerce. Sugar-bakers' scum, which is obtained from sugar refineries, consists of the blood of cattle and lime; it can be sent in a dried and compressed state to any distance, and forms a manure next in richness to bones. In gardens it may be used as a top-dressing to culinary vegetables, and as an ingredient in the composition of vine borders. Animalized carbon consists of nightsoil of great age; it is sent to different parts of Europe from Copenhagen, where it has accumulated during ages in immense pits and heaps, which some years ago were purchased from the city by an Englishman. It is an exceedingly rich manure. Dry earth is the cheapest and most effectual disinfectant and deodorizer.

Bones, though a manure of animal origin, depend for their effects a good deal on their mineral constituents. Next to nightsoil, bones are perhaps the most valuable of all manures. Chemically they consist of gelatine, albumen, animal oils, and fat, in all about 38 per cent.; and of earthy matters, such as phosphate of lime, carbonate of lime, fluate of lime, magnesia, carbonate of soda, and a small quantity of common salt. In consequence of the animal matters which they contain, crushed bones when laid in heaps very soon begin to ferment, and when buried in the soil previously to being fermented in heaps, the putrescent fermentation goes on with great rapidity. In gardens they should seldom be used without being broken small and fermented in heaps for several months. Bones are valuable as a specific manure, because they contain phosphate of lime, which is an ingredient common to a great many cultivated plants both of the field and of the garden. Bone manure, if used on the same soil for a number of years, is found to lose its effect; the reason of which is inferred from one cause of its excellence, viz., that the animal matter which it contains acts as a ferment or stimulus to the organic matter already in the soil, by which means this organic matter becomes sooner exhausted than otherwise would be the case. A dressing of bone manure every fourth or fifth year will suffice for most soils.

Vegeto-animal manures consist of a mixture of animal and vegetable substances, such as the straw used as litter in stables or farmyards, and the excrements and urine of the animals which are kept in them. It may be classed according to the kind of animal to which the litter is supplied; and hence we have horse-dung, cow-dung, the dung of swine, sheep, rabbits, poultry, &c. All these manures require to be brought into a state of active fermentation, and reduced to a soft, easily separated mass, before being applied to the soil. This is effected by throwing them into heaps, and occasionally turning these heaps till the manure becomes of a proper consistence. When it is desirable that these manures should act as mechanical as well as enriching agents, then they should be applied before they are much decomposed.

In horticulture, advantage is generally taken of the heat produced by manures of this kind, in forming hotbeds, and in supplying heat to forcing-pits by what are called linings, but which are properly casings, of dung placed round a bed of dung, tan, or soil, supported by walls of open brickwork. The dung so placed can be taken away at pleasure, and applied to the soil when it has undergone a proper degree of fermentation; whereas, the dung of which a hotbed is formed cannot be removed without destroying the bed and the crop on it; and hence it is generally kept till the fermenting process is carried much further than is necessary, and often so far as to be injurious. Hence, in gardens, wherever economy of manure is an object, common hotbeds ought never to be made use of, but recourse should be had to exterior casings, such as those already mentioned, or to other modes of heating.

In many suburban villas, almost as much manure is lost as would suffice for enriching the kitchen-garden, and producing vegetables for the whole family. To save every particle of fluid or solid matter capable of becoming manure, the first step is to construct two or more large tanks for the liquid manure, and to form a system of tubes or gutters for conveying to these tanks all the soapsuds and other liquid refuse matters furnished by the mansion and offices, including the stables, unless they are at a distance. Similar tanks should be formed adjoining every cottage and dwelling belonging to the villa; such as the gardener's house, gatekeeper's lodge, and also in the back-sheds and in the frame and reserve ground of the kitchen-garden. In short, no water ought to be allowed to escape from the manure tanks but such as is perfectly pure; for all dirty water is more or less valuable as a manure, and will ferment in a degree of heat not much greater than that of the subsoil, even in winter; and all fermented liquids contain one or more of the constituent elements of plants. The second step to be taken with a view to saving manure is, to form a vegetable rubbish heap, on which all waste parts of plants and the remains of all crops, including mown grass when not otherwise used, clippings of hedges, summer prunings of trees, &c., are to be thrown as collected, left to ferment, and turned over occasionally. To this heap, lime, dung, sewage, or rich earth may be added, and the whole frequently turned over and well mixed. The third step is, to collect the cleanings of ponds, wells, ditches, hedge-banks, and similar earthy matters, and mix them with quicklime, turning the heap occasionally, as directed in the next section.

Inorganic Manures.

Inorganic or mineral manures are chiefly: lime in a state of chalk or carbonate, gypsum or sulphate, marl in which carbonate of lime is mixed with clay, saltpetre, kelp, mineral alkali, and common salt. The organic manures, as we have seen, act by supplying plants with the elements of which they are constituted, viz., carbon, oxygen, hydrogen, and azote or nitrogen; but the mineral manures contain none of these elements, and hence, according to most agricultural chemists, they must act beneficially on some other principle. This principle may be stated to be the rendering more soluble of the organic matters already in the soil in most instances, and in some cases rendering soluble matters insoluble, so as to diminish excessive fertility, and prepare a reserve of the fertilizing principle for future use. Quicklime, for example, effects the first of these objects, and slaked lime the second. According to some writers, inorganic manures also act specifically; alkaline matters being found in all, and some sorts in many plants.

Lime.—This is by far the most important of all the mineral manures. It is applied to soil in the form of quick or hot lime, mild or slaked lime, and chalk or carbonate. Quicklime is procured by burning chalkstone or lime rock till the water and the carbonic acid gas are driven off. Immediately after burning, it forms what is called quicklime; and in this state, when laid on the soil, having a powerful attraction for water, it assists in the conversion of woody fibre and other organic matters into the substance called humus, forming humate of lime, which again is rendered soluble and fit for supplying the food of plants by the action of the carbonic acid gas in the soil, or supplied to it by water or the atmosphere.

Mild lime.—When water is thrown on quicklime, it becomes what is called slaked, falls down into a fine white powder, and re-absorbing great part of the water which had been driven off by burning, it becomes what chemists call hydrate of lime; and soon after, from the absorption of carbonic acid gas, it becomes what is called mild lime. The use of lime in this state is partly the same as that of caustic or quicklime; and partly, also, when there is a superabundance of soluble manure, which would cause crops to become too rank, to lessen the putrescence of organic matter by the formation with it of humate of lime. In short, quicklime may be said to increase the solubility of inert organic matter, and mild lime to render less soluble organic matter already in a state of solubility.

The application of lime to soil may also be useful in cases where there is not already a sufficient portion of that earth; but, to ascertain this, a chemical analysis of the soil should be previously made. A small quantity of quicklime added to a soil in which little or none previously existed, will effect a great permanent improvement; and the same may be said of a small quantity of clay added to a soil in which that ingredient did not previously exist.

Carbonate of lime, or chalk, in its native state, differs from unburnt limestone in being of a much softer texture, and more easily acted on either mechanically or by the weather. When burned, it of course becomes lime, and may be used either in a caustic or mild state; but in chalky countries it is most commonly laid on land in its natural state, and left to pulverize by the influence of the weather. It is supposed to have no effect upon inert vegetable fibre, and to be incapable of generally uniting with humic acid; so that it appears to be destitute of the two properties of caustic and mild lime, viz., that of rendering insoluble matter soluble, and the contrary. Its beneficial effects are attributed to its altering the texture of soil, and to its property of retaining water without at the same time becoming adhesive. Hence it may be used both on sands and clays, to render the latter more friable without diminishing its retentive powers, and the former more absorbent without adding to its tenacity. Chalk, also, may be considered as a specific manure, since carbonate of lime is an ingredient in almost all the plants which have hitherto been analysed by chemists.

Marl is carbonate of lime mixed with clay at the rate of from twenty to eighty per cent. of carbonate, with alumina, silica, and more or less of the oxide of iron. Its action on the whole is similar to that of chalk, though it is more adapted for sandy and peaty soils than for clays. It is found from experience that it is injurious when spread on soil before being exposed for some months to the action of the atmosphere; though the reason of this has not yet been explained.

Gypsum, which is sulphate of lime, is a calcareous compound which occasionally produces extraordinary effects as a manure, though the rationale of its action does not appear to be thoroughly understood. All animal manures contain more or less of sulphate of lime as one of their constituents; and this mineral compound has also been found in wheat, in clover, saintfoin, lucern, and many other leguminous plants, and in various pasture grasses. Hence it may in part be considered as a specific manure, and it has been so treated by Grisenthwaite in his very ingenious 'Essay,' who contends that no manure that does not contain gypsum is fit for wheat. It is said to have little effect except upon light sandy, gravelly, or chalky soils.

Sea shells are very abundant on some shores, and may be either burned into lime or laid on without burning. Immense quantities are collected on the shore at Whitstable in Kent, and are laid on the soil without burning between Canterbury and Dover, where the soil is chiefly clayey. They are so much preferred to chalk or lime that they are fetched three times the distance.

The rationale of the action of lime in its different states is thus given by Sir Humphry Davy: "When lime, whether freshly burned or slaked, is mixed with any moist fibrous vegetable matter, there is a strong action between the lime and the vegetable matter, and they form a kind of compost together, of which a part is usually soluble in water. By this kind of operation, lime renders matter which was before comparatively inert nutritive; and as charcoal and oxygen abound in all vegetable matters, it becomes at the same time converted into carbonate of lime. Mild lime, powdered limestone, marls or chalks, have no action of this kind upon vegetable matter; by their action they prevent the too rapid decomposition of substances already dissolved; but they have no tendency to form soluble matters. It is obvious from these circumstances that the operation of quicklime, and marl or chalk, depends upon principles altogether different. Quicklime, in being applied to land, tends to bring any hard vegetable matter that it contains into a state of more rapid decomposition and solution, so as to render it a proper food for plants. Chalk, and marl, or carbonate of lime, will only improve the texture of the soil, or its relation to absorption, acting merely as one of its earthy ingredients. Quicklime, when it becomes mild, operates in the same manner as chalk; but in the act of becoming mild, it prepares soluble out of insoluble matter. It is upon this circumstance that the operation of lime in the preparation for wheat crops depends; and its efficacy in fertilizing peats, and in bringing into a state of cultivation all soils abounding in hard roots, or dry fibres, or inert vegetable matter. The solution of the question, whether quicklime ought to be applied to a soil, depends upon the quantity of inert vegetable matter that it contains. The solution of the question, whether marl, mild lime, or powdered limestone, ought to be applied, depends upon the quantity of calcareous matter already in the soil. All soils are improved by mild lime, and ultimately by quicklime, which do not effervesce with acids; and sands more than clays." ('Agricultural Chemistry,' 6th edit., p. 304.)

In the case of suburban villas, the most important uses of lime are, first, the formation of lime-water for the destruction of insects, snails, worms, &c.; and secondly, the formation of lime composts to be used as manure. For both these purposes lime must be obtained in its caustic state. In preparing lime-water, a very small quantity of lime in powder will be found to saturate many gallons of water; and, by letting this settle a few minutes till it becomes clear, the plants or the soil may be watered with it without leaving any coating of lime, which only takes place when the lime is applied in a state of mixture and solution. The causticity of the liquid, owing to the alkali which it contains, destroys the tender skins of caterpillars, earth-worms, snails, and slugs.

Lime compost is formed of caustic lime, at the rate of from sixteen to twenty-four bushels of lime to three times that quantity of earth taken from hedge-banks, cleanings of ditches or ponds, scrapings of roads, or even from the surface of any soil which is somewhat different in its nature or texture from the soil on which the compost is to be laid. Even the substratum of any soil, where good, may be used, and afterwards laid on the surface soil. The compost should lie from nine to twelve months, and be turned over in that time twice or thrice. In every part of Britain this manure may be formed at a moderate expense; and though it is better adapted for fields than gardens, yet in many cases, and particularly where manure is scarce, it will be found a valuable resource, and one to be recommended from the readiness and simplicity of its composition.

Saltpetre, or nitrate of potash, when analysed, consists of oxygen, nitrogen, and potassium. Saltpetre is found in almost all plants, and especially those which are cultivated in rich soils. As a manure it sometimes produces extraordinary effects on grass lands and corn crops; but its action is not understood, and it has been but little used in horticulture. Nitrate of soda produces nearly the same results as saltpetre. From some experiments with this salt lately detailed in the 'Journal of the English Agricultural Society,' vol. i. pp. 418 and 423, it appears to have increased the produce of corn crops, but not more so than saltpetre. In general both salts tell more on growth than on seeds. In many soils they make the straw of grain crops too luxuriant, and liable to fall before the grain is ripe.

Common Salt, or the chloride of sodium, consists of nearly equal parts of chlorine and sodium; but when dissolved in water a portion of the water is decomposed, its hydrogen unites with the chlorine to form muriatic acid, and its oxygen with the sodium to produce soda. Hence salt in a dry state is chlorate of soda, and dissolved in water it becomes muriate of soda. Its action in the soil depends on the effect which the muriate of soda has on the carbonate of lime; the latter, as we have before observed, being found in almost all soils. By the contact of these two salts, their acids and bases are interchanged, and the compounds which are the result are carbonate of soda and muriate of lime. Hence, as chalky soils abound more in carbonate of soda than any others, salt is supposed to be most beneficial to them. Salt applied in large quantities, it is well known, destroys plants; and hence it has been used in gardening, both in a dry and liquid state, to kill weeds and worms in gravel-walks, which it does most effectually. It has been used also for washing salads and other vegetables when gathered for the kitchen, when they are supposed to contain snails, worms, or insects. It forms a direct constituent of some marine plants, and plants of saline marshes or steppes; and, applied in small quantities, it appears to hasten the decomposition of organized matter in the soil. As a manure, however, it requires to be applied with very great caution; and, in gardens, is perhaps safest when used in walks for the purpose of killing weeds and worms—unless when given as a top dressing to asparagus and seakale, or other plants that are found by the sea shore.

In suburban villas calcareous manures are often required for the improvement of lawns and other grass lands; and a stock of quicklime, unslaked, should always be kept in a cask, or other closed vessel, to be ready for use with water. Where lime is not at hand, common potash or American pearlash dissolved in water, or urine—especially that of cows—will have the same effect on insects as lime-water; but potash and pearlash are more expensive.

Mixed Manures.

Mixed Manures include coal ashes, vegetable ashes, street manure, soot, and vegetable or vegeto-animal composts.

Coal Ashes are of very different natures in different parts of the country; the constituents of coal varying in the quantity of clay and lime, and also of sulphur and iron, which it contains. Many persons object entirely to coal ashes as a manure, considering them poisonous rather than beneficial. The portions of coal which contain iron or other metallic ores are converted by burning into hard porous masses, which, when buried in the soil, absorb moisture, and consequently soluble organic matter: and as the spongioles of the roots cannot be supposed to penetrate into cinders or scoriæ, that soluble matter must remain there till it is washed out by rains or set free by the disintegration of the cinder. Supposing this to be the case, the principal benefit to be derived from coal ashes would appear to be that of increasing the friability of stiff clayey soils.

Vegetable Ashes are obtained by burning weeds, leaves, prunings, or roots of woody plants, and in general all kinds of vegetable matter not readily decomposed by fermentation. The burning of vegetable substances must necessarily dissipate the whole of the oxygen, hydrogen, and nitrogen which they contain, together with more or less of the carbon, according to the degree in which the burning mass is exposed to the action of the atmosphere. Hence in burning wood for charcoal, the pile of logs is covered with earth or mud to prevent the production of flame, and consequent decomposition of the carbon, by the action of the oxygen of the atmosphere. The burning of vegetables, however, does not destroy the fixed saline ingredients which they contain; and hence vegetable ashes, as manure, will be valuable as containing salts which are either of general or specific use to plants, and also as containing more or less carbon. If one kind of plant only were burnt at a time, then the ashes of that plant would form a specific manure for plants of the same kind; but as a number of kinds are generally burned together, their ashes must contain salts of various kinds, and they may be considered as being useful to plants generally. Among these ashes there is always a large proportion of vegetable alkali (carbonate of potass); and this, when mixed with soil, combines with insoluble organic matter and renders it soluble; and hence vegetable ashes form a useful manure for all soils, since potass is of almost universal existence in plants. It is therefore not only a general manure by its action on organic matter, but a specific constituent of plants. Soda, which exists but in few plants, differs from potass in not being a specific manure, its action being limited to increasing the solubility of organic matter already in the soil; and in performing this office, it is found to be more efficient than potass.

Soot is composed of the various volatile matters derived from the burning of coal or wood, together with carbon, and earths which have been mechanically carried up the chimney with water in the form of smoke. From experiment it appears that soot owes its value as a manure to the saline substances which it contains; and these are chiefly the carbonate and sulphate of ammonia, together with a small quantity of bituminous matter. The fact of carbonate of soda proving useful as a manure is undoubted, though it is difficult to explain in what manner it acts, unless, like saltpetre, it stimulates the roots. Soot when applied in gardens is generally strewed on the surface, and it is considered offensive to snails, slugs, and worms; though by no means killing them, as is frequently supposed. Its effects are rarely perceptible after the crop to which it is applied: and therefore, like liquid manures, soot affords a quick return for the capital employed in it.

Street manure, or that which is swept up in the streets of towns, consists of a great variety of matters, animal, vegetable, and mineral. In the manner towns are now kept, it is smaller in quantity and of less value than formerly, when it was among the richest of all manures. When collected in quantities, even though containing a large proportion of earth and coal ashes, it ferments powerfully, and will continue giving out heat throughout a whole summer. For this purpose it has been used in forcing-gardens as a substitute for tanners' bark and stable-dung; and it has the advantage of not subsiding so much as those materials. Wherever it can be obtained, it may be applied to all soils; and when obtained from towns still under the old system, it may rank next to nightsoil and bones.

Composts of vegetable or vegeto-animal matter and earth are of various kinds. The most common in gardens is that produced by rotten leaves or vegetable refuse mixed with sand or with some other earth, or with stable-dung: composts of bones are likewise formed in this manner, and also of peat, where that material abounds. Peat composts have been already mentioned.

Mixed manure in a liquid state consists of the urine of animals, soap-suds, the foul water of kitchens and other offices, waste surface or rain water, and drainings of dunghills. The most advantageous way of employing it is by applying it, after being properly diluted and fermented, directly to growing crops. It may also be profitably employed by throwing it on heaps of vegetable matter, such as moss, leaves, straw, or any vegetable refuse matter whatever not containing woody matter of several years' growth. In this way, Jauffret, a French agriculturist, proposed to create immense quantities of manure by fermenting weeds and other refuse collected by hedge-sides, or on commons or wastes. The fermentation of such matters does not take place without the aid of animal manure or stable-dung; but, when once commenced, it can be continued for an indefinite period by adding to the heap. If the liquid manure and the excrementitious matter accumulated in every large establishment, independently altogether of the stable manure, were collected and fermented, we have little doubt it would suffice for all the kitchen-garden crops; the refuse of these crops and the weeds of the garden being added and fermented. It is highly probable that every individual animal produces as much manure as would raise the vegetables necessary for its support, because in the nourishment of animals, as of plants, nothing is annihilated, but merely changed: what escapes into the atmosphere is counterbalanced by what is absorbed from it; and what is embodied in the animal during life, is restored to the soil at its death.

Application of Manures.—Too much manure is injurious to all crops whatever, by increasing the proportion of watery matter, and by producing such an exuberance of growth as to prevent the maturation of the parts, the formation of blossom-buds, and the setting of fruit. It is particularly injurious to corn-crops; producing more sap than can be properly elaborated in the leaves, and hence disease. In this case the evil is counteracted by the application of lime or common salt.

All mineral manures ought to be employed in a dry and powdery state, and if possible, when the soil is equally dry and powdery; and all moist manures, when the soil is somewhat drier than the manure. Other circumstances being the same, spring is better than autumn for applying manures, because the rains of winter might wash them away, &c.; but, as a rule, the proper time is immediately before sowing or planting the crop. Calm weather is better than windy weather, and bulky manure ought no sooner to be laid on than buried in the soil.

Exhausting land of the manure which it contains by over-cropping, is like depriving a commercial man of his capital.

In consequence of the great value of manures in increasing the amount of the produce of land, many ingenious persons have contrived mixtures, which, in small bulk, they allege will produce extraordinary effects; and this idea seems to have been long since indulged by some writers. Lord Kaimes, nearly a century ago, thought the time might come when the quantity of manure requisite for an acre might be carried in a man's coat-pocket; a recent author speaks of "a quart of spirit sufficient to manure an acre;" and even Liebig says, that "a time will come when fields will be manured with a solution of glass (silicate of potash), with the ashes of burned straw, and with salts of phosphoric acid prepared in chemical manufactories, exactly as at present medicines are given for fever and goître." ('Organic Chemistry,' p. 188.) To those who believe in the homœopathic hypothesis of medicine such speculations will not appear unreasonable; and there may be some truth in them, on the supposition that these small doses of spirit, or of silicate of potash, are to act as stimulants to the organic matter already in the soil; but to ordinary apprehensions it seems difficult to conceive how bulk and weight of produce can be raised without the application of a certain degree of bulk of manure. Since the introduction of guano, and the more general manufacture of artificial manures, in the shapes of phosphates, sulphates, &c., we have daily proofs, however, of what can be effected by small quantities of concentrated manures.

With the exception of such manufactured manures, easily applied as to their bulk, but to be used carefully and sparingly owing to their strength, all the manures mentioned in this section are easily obtained by the possessors of suburban gardens. Soot and ashes are produced on their own premises; compost may be formed by the mixture of various articles collected or procured; liquids abound, and have only to be collected and properly fermented; and street manure may in general be purchased from the nearest town. It cannot be too strongly impressed on the possessor of a country residence who wishes to make the most of it, that no particle of organic matter, whether animal or vegetable, and no drop of water, with whatever it may be discoloured, ought to be left uncollected or allowed to run to waste.

CHAPTER III.

THE ATMOSPHERE, CONSIDERED WITH REFERENCE TO HORTICULTURE.

THE atmosphere on every part of the globe consists of the same constituent parts, to wit, nitrogen 78 parts, oxygen 21 parts, and carbonic acid gas and vapours of water about 2 parts. It likewise contains slight traces of ammonia and other gases. Its main constituents are always the same, but the percentage of aqueous vapour and carbonic acid gas varies, and certain modifications take place in the air as it is affected by heat, moisture, motion, and perhaps light.

Heat.

Heat, like light, is found to be capable of radiation, reflection, transmission through transparent media, and refraction; but it is radiated, reflected, transmitted, and refracted, in a different manner and degree from light. Thus it appears that both light and heat can be transmitted through either gaseous, fluid, or solid media, provided they are transparent. Any opaque body is to light, however, an impenetrable barrier; but to heat, or to its conduction, neither opaqueness nor solidity affords resistance. On the contrary, heat is conducted more rapidly by solid than by fluid or gaseous bodies; a fact which will be noticed in treating of artificial coverings for protecting plants. A solid body will obstruct the radiation of heat, as is familiarly exemplified in the case of the common fire-screen. The diffusion of heat by conduction and radiation is what chiefly concerns the horticulturist.

The conduction of heat is effected by the contact of bodies heated in different degrees, when the tendency to equal diffusion immediately raises the temperature of the one body and lowers that of the other. This takes place with different degrees of rapidity, according to the nature of the bodies in contact. If thermometers be placed on metal, stone, glass, ivory, and earth, all heated from the same source, we shall find that the thermometer placed on the metal will rise soonest; next, that placed on the stone; next, that on the glass; then that on the wood; and lastly, that on the earth. The conducting power of bodies is generally as their density. The greatest of all conductors of heat are metals; and the least so, spongy and light filamentous bodies. Silk, cotton, wool, hare's fur, and eider-down, are extremely bad conductors of heat, and hence their value as clothing. They give us a sensation of warmth, not by communicating heat to the skin, but by preventing its escape into the air, in consequence of their non-conducting properties. The power which these bodies have of stopping the transmission of heat depends on the air which is stagnated in their vacuities; for when the air is expelled by compression, their conducting power is increased. Hence, in covering plants or plant structures with leaves, litter straw, mats, or other light, porous bodies, the less they are compressed the more effective will they be found in preventing the escape of heat by conduction. All tight coverings, whether of animals or plants, retain very little heat, when compared with loose coverings; and hence mats, when drawn tightly round bushes, or nailed closely against trees on walls, are much less effective than when fastened over them loosely, and do not retain nearly so much heat as a covering of straw. Coverings of sand, ashes, or rotten tan, applied to the ground, or to the roots of herbaceous plants, are, for the same reason, much less effective than coverings of leaves so applied; and these, again, are much less so than coverings of litter or long straw. The heat of the trunks of trees is prevented from escaping to the extent it otherwise would do by their bark, which is a powerful non-conductor, and the heat of the ground by a covering of snow, which, by its spongy, porous nature, contains a great deal of air. Without this covering, the herbaceous plants of the northern regions could not exist; nor would spring flowers, such as the aconite, snow-drop, crocus, daffodil, &c., in the climate of Scotland, come nearly so early into bloom.

Heat is diffused amongst bodies not in contact by the process called radiation, in consequence of which property a person standing near any body heated to a higher temperature than himself will experience a sensation of warmth. The radiation of heat from any body proceeds from its surface in every direction in straight lines, in the same manner as the divergent rays of light from an illuminated body, as for example, a lighted candle; and rays of heat, like rays of light, may be reflected from polished surfaces, and transmitted and refracted through transparent substances, and even polarized. But though it be true that heat, in proceeding from a body, begins by radiating from it at right angles and in straight lines, yet this can only be strictly said of heat which is radiated perpendicularly into the atmosphere. Thus, from a pipe of water equally heated, the heat tends to radiate at right angles from its surface in all directions; yet none but those rays which proceed from the uppermost part of the convex surface of the pipe will preserve their perpendicularity. All the other rays, from their first contact with the air, will be deflected upwards, being in fact carried in that direction by the heating effect which those rays themselves produce upon the particles of air on which they impinge. The property of radiation, however, is that which chiefly concerns the horticulturist; and the following description of this phenomenon is given by Mr. Daniell, the author of by far the best essay which has yet appeared on climate, as connected with horticulture.

Radiation of heat is the "power of emitting it in straight lines in every direction, independently of contact, and may be regarded as a property common to all matter. Co-existing with it, in the same degrees, may be regarded the power of absorbing heat so emitted from other bodies. Polished metals, and the fibres of vegetables, may be considered as placed at the two extremities of the scale upon which these properties in different substances may be measured. If a body be so situated that it may receive just as much radiant heat as itself projects, its temperature remains the same; if the surrounding bodies emit heat of greater intensity than the same body, its temperature rises, till the quantity which it receives exactly balances its expenditure, at which point it again becomes stationary; and if the power of radiation be exerted under circumstances which prevent a return, the temperature of the body declines. Thus, if a thermometer be placed in the focus of a concave metallic mirror, and turned towards any clear portion of the sky, at any period of the day, it will fall many degrees below the temperature of another thermometer placed near it out of the mirror; the power of radiation is exerted in both thermometers, but to the first all return of radiant heat is cut off, while the other receives as much from the surrounding bodies as itself projects. This interchange amongst bodies takes place in transparent media as well as in vacua; but in the former case the effect is modified by the equalizing power of the medium." This description is clear and satisfactory; but it must not be supposed, that though the balance of temperature will not be disturbed from the effects of radiation when the body is completely enclosed, yet that it may not be so by the other law of heat, conduction.

"Any portion of the surface of the globe which is fully turned towards the sun receives more radiant heat than it projects, and becomes heated; but when, by the revolution of the earth on its axis, this portion is turned from the source of heat, the radiation into space still continues, and, being uncompensated, the temperature declines. In consequence of the different degrees in which different bodies possess this power of radiation, two contiguous portions of the earth will become of different temperatures, and if on a clear night we place a thermometer upon a grass plat, and another upon a gravel walk or the bare soil, we shall find the temperature of the former many degrees below that of the latter. The fibrous texture of the grass is favourable to the emission of the heat, but the dense surface of the gravel seems to retain and fix it. But this unequal effect will only be perceived when the atmosphere is unclouded, and a free passage is open into space; for even a light mist will arrest the radiant matter in its course, and return as much to the radiating body as it emits. The intervention of more substantial obstacles will of course still more prevent radiation, and the balance of temperature will not be disturbed in any substance which is not placed in the clear aspect of the sky. A portion of a grass plat under the protection of a tree or hedge will generally be found, on a clear night, to be eight or ten degrees warmer than surrounding unsheltered parts; and it is well known to gardeners that less dew and frost are to be found in such situations than in those which are wholly exposed. There are many independent circumstances which modify the effects of this action, such as the state of the radiating body, its power of conducting heat, &c. If, for instance, the body be in a liquid or aëriform state, although the process may go on freely, as in water, the cold produced by it will not accumulate upon the surface, but will be dispersed by known laws throughout the mass; and if a solid mass be a good radiator but a bad conductor of heat, the frigorific effect will be condensed upon the face which is exposed. So upon the surface of the earth absolute stillness of the atmosphere is necessary for the accumulation of cold upon the radiating body; for if the air be in motion, it disperses and equalizes the effect with a rapidity proportioned to its velocity." ('Hort. Trans.,' vol. vi. p. 10.)

All the phenomena connected with dew or hoarfrost have been explained by Dr. Wells on these principles. The deposition of moisture is owing to the cold produced in bodies by radiation, which condenses the atmospheric vapour on their surfaces. The deposition of dew takes place upon vegetables, but not upon the naked soil, because the latter is a bad radiator as well as a bad conductor of heat. The fibres of short grass are particularly favourable to the formation of dew. Moisture, including that modification of it called dew, is deposited more or less on all bodies in absolute contact with the air, whenever the temperature of the air is higher than that of the body with which it is in contact.

"The formation of dew is one of the circumstances which modify and check the refrigerating effect of radiation; for, as the vapour is condensed, it gives out the latent heat with which it was combined in its elastic form, and thus, no doubt, prevents an excess of depression which might in many cases prove injurious to vegetation."

"The vegetation of this country is liable to be affected at night from the influence of radiation, by a temperature below the freezing point of water, ten months in the year; and even in the two months, July and August, which are the only exceptions, a thermometer covered with wool will sometimes fall to 35°. It is, however, only low vegetation upon the ground which is exposed to the full rigour of this effect. In such a situation, the air which is evolved by the process lies upon the surface of the plants, and from its weight cannot make its escape; but from the foliage of a tree or shrub it glides off and settles upon the ground."

"Anything which obstructs the free aspect of the sky arrests in proportion the progress of this refrigeration, and the slightest covering of cloth or matting annihilates it altogether. Trees trained upon a wall or paling, or plants sown under their protection are sheltered from a large portion of this evil, and are still further protected if within a moderate distance of another opposing screen."

Almost all the modes in practice of protecting plants are designed to check radiation, and hence the gardener should keep constantly in his mind the fact, that all bodies placed in a medium colder than themselves are continually giving out their heat in straight lines, and that these straight lines, when the body is surrounded by air, may always be reflected back on the body from which they emanate by the slightest covering placed at a short distance from them, while, on the other hand, if this slight covering is applied close to the body, instead of reflecting back the heat, it will carry it off by conduction: that is, the heat will pass through the thin covering closely applied, and be radiated from its surface. Hence in covering sashes with mats, a great advantage is obtained by laying straw between the mats and the glass, or by any other means of keeping the mat a few inches above the frame. Hence also when the branches of trees are to be protected by mats, they will be rendered much more secure if first surrounded by straw, fern, or some other light body which contains in its interstices a good deal of air. "It should be borne in mind," Mr. Daniell observes, "that the radiation is only transferred from the tree to the mat, and the cold of the latter will be conducted to the former in every point where it touches. Contact should therefore be prevented by hoops or other means properly applied, and the stratum of air which is enclosed will, by its low conducting power, effectually secure the plant. With their foliage thus protected, and the roots well covered with litter, many evergreens might doubtless be brought to survive the rigour of our winters which are now confined to the greenhouse and conservatory."

"A very slight motion of the air suffices to break or check the force of radiation. The mere act of walking through a mist in a meadow has often been found sufficient to dissolve and dissipate it. A valley surrounded by low hills is more liable to the effects of radiation than the tops and sides of the hills themselves; and it is a well-known fact that dew and hoarfrost are always more abundant in the former than in the latter situations. It is not meant to include in this observation places surrounded by lofty and precipitous hills which obstruct the aspect of the sky, for in such the contrary effect would be produced. Gentle slopes, which break the undulations of the air without naturally circumscribing the heavens, are most efficient in promoting this action; and it is worthy of remark and consideration, that by walls and other fences, we may artificially combine circumstances which may produce the same injurious effect.

"But the influence of hills upon the nightly temperature of the valleys which they surround is not confined to this insulation; radiation goes on upon their declivities, and the air which is condensed by the cold, rolls down and lodges at their feet. Their sides are thus protected from the chill, and a double portion falls upon what many are apt to consider the more sheltered situation. Experience amply confirms these theoretical considerations. It is a very old remark, that the injurious effect of cold occurs chiefly in hollow places, and that frosts are less severe upon hills than in neighbouring plains. The leaves of the Vine, the Walnut-tree, and the succulent shoots of Dahlias and Potatoes, are often destroyed by frost in sheltered valleys, on nights when they are perfectly untouched upon the surrounding eminences; and the difference, on the same night, between two thermometers placed in the two situations, in favour of the latter, has amounted to thirty degrees.

"The horticulturist can effect but little in the way of raising the temperature of the climate in the open air, except by the choice of a sunny elevated situation, thorough drainage, the concentration of the sun's rays upon walls, and furnishing shelter. The natural reverberation of heat from walls and the earth itself is, however, very great, and generally effective in enabling the plants to resist the exhaustive force of radiation. Few of the productions of the tropical regions are exposed to a greater heat than a well-trained tree upon a wall in summer. It has been proved by experiment that the power of radiation from the sun, like that of radiation from the earth, increases with the distance from the equator; and there is a greater difference between a thermometer placed in the shade and another in the solar rays in this country, than in Sierra Leone or Jamaica. This energy of the sun is at times so great, that it often becomes necessary to shade delicate flowers from its influence; and it would at times be desirable to try the same precaution with the early blossoms of certain fruit trees. The greatest power is put forth in this country in June, while the greatest temperature of the air does not take place till July."

The construction of houses for growing the plants of warm climates, or for forcing, is founded chiefly on the doctrine of radiation, as well as on that of producing heat by combustion or fermentation. The roof and sides of a frame or a hothouse serve the purpose of reflecting back the heat of the bodies within, whether that heat is only such as the soil enclosed naturally affords, or whether it is generated artificially. But though the roofs of hothouses reflect back great part of the heat which is radiated to them, yet a great part also is conducted through the glass to its outer surface, and thence radiated into the free air. To prevent this waste of heat, without diminishing the quantity of light transmitted through the glass, is a desideratum in hothouse building. In Russia, double sashes are used, and might be more generally adopted in this country. A thin opaque screen of bunting or matting thrown over the transparent face of the glass would likewise reduce the loss by radiation to a minimum.

The power of man over the heat of the free atmosphere is comparatively limited. Nevertheless, as heat is carried off from the surface of the ground, and from all other objects, by wind, by radiation, and by evaporation, it follows that heat may be saved by shelter from the wind, and from being radiated into the air by a partial covering of the ground, on a large scale, by scattered standard trees, or, on a smaller scale, by covering beds or borders with straw; and it may be saved from being carried off by evaporation by under-draining, surface-draining, and by such a composition of the soil as will readily admit the infiltration of water, so as to render it at all times, except during rains, tolerably dry. The drier the earth the less water will be evaporated from its surface. The evaporation of water simply means its being lifted up by the agency of heat or wind. For every drop removed a certain measure of warmth is lost.

It takes above 200° of heat to convert water into steam; and though vapour does not require so much, part of the vapour being chemically attracted by the atmosphere, still the consumption is great. From these causes the earth and plants by degrees get so cold, from having parted with their heat, that their temperature descends below the freezing point. In spring and autumn the air is comparatively warm, and the nights not so long; and hence spring and autumn frosts seldom take place till near sunrise: and if a cloud happens to settle above any portion of the earth about that time, before the earth has been cooled down to the freezing point, it prevents the farther radiation of the heat upwards; and hence we often find places lying contiguous and below the cloud to be saved from frost at one time, while at another they will be much hurt. Where plants partially cover one another, they help to prevent radiation; and when one plant is more covered with moisture than another, more full of watery sap, and the bark more tender, from these and other causes it is often, to all appearance unaccountably, killed, while another is left unhurt.

In order to protect plants from frost, we should study to have the plants themselves and the earth around them as dry as possible towards the evening. The situation for plants liable to be hurt by spring and autumn frosts should be as much elevated as possible, in order to have the benefit of the wind in dispersing the cold heavy air and bringing forward the warmer. Wherever it is possible, when the clearness and coldness of the air indicate a tendency to frost, plants that are worth the expense should be carefully covered with the best non-conducting substances, such as straw, dry fern, mats, &c.

Whatever covering is used, whether straw mats, bast mats, cloth, wool, or wood, it should be elevated above the surface to be covered, so as to contain as much confined air as possible. Confined air is one of the worst conductors of heat; the covering will not radiate or give out heat till the confined air and covering are both heated above the state of the atmosphere; and the transmission of heat will take place more slowly through the confined air than anything else. Thus, with very little trouble, by elevating our coverings, we surround our plants or plant-structures with a substance which is very retentive of heat, and increases the protection of the covering in an immense degree. In doing so, however, the sides will have to be blocked up, or the heat will rapidly escape at the vacuum between the cover and the glass covered, both by radiation and conduction.

Wall-trees should have a broad coping of wood on the wall, to prevent the ascent of heat; and woollen nets or canvas, drawn down before tender peaches, &c., in cold nights, and carefully removed in good weather through the day, are a great help, when not left on in all weathers. The wall, for tender fruit-trees, or other tender plants, is best built of porous materials, as bricks, which retain the heat from the confined air better than stone; and they should be built with hollow chambers for the same purpose. Where painting is needed, white is the best colour. To prevent the bad effects of cold east winds in the spring, causing the sap to descend in standard fruit-trees, and destroying the blossom when expanded by the check it gives to the ascent of the sap that should nourish it, the stems and branches should be bound with straw ropes, and the ground mulched.

Various situations should be chosen to protect tender shrubs and trees, according to the nature of the plant. For those that grow early, and are apt to be nipped by spring frosts, a north border and cold soil are best to retard their time of starting till the danger from frost is less: for those that suffer from want of the wood being ripened sufficiently, as many American plants which have a warmer summer in their native situation to ripen the wood, as also for those that suffer by autumn frosts before the wood is ripened, a south exposure, and warm dry early soil are best: in dry soils there is not so much wood made, but that which is made is more easily ripened; and the more sun, the more likelihood that the wood will be ripened before frost sets in. In some late wet autumns, some of the hardiest of our trees have been killed: transplanted Birch, after being some years transplanted; Oaks, that were apparently sound, dying down half their length in the ensuing spring; and seedling American Oaks dying off in the ensuing summer, after having begun to grow ; thus showing that even the hardiest of our trees may be affected, from their wood not being sufficiently ripened in a cold wet autumn.

The presence of a stream or river increases the tendency to slight frosts in spring and autumn. The surface of the water, as it condenses by cold, descends to the bottom, and a warm stratum succeeds to the surface; and so far the tendency is towards heating rather than cooling the air : but the great evaporation that takes place through the day, and early in the evening, robs the air of so much caloric, that fields situated near shallow rivers, streams, or bogs, have generally been found most liable to frost ; near the sea, or near great bodies of deep water, the first-mentioned effect of a succession of warmer strata to the surface prevails, and we have less tendency to freezing.

Cold water applied to frozen plants early in the morning, before the sun touches them, by gradually thawing them, will frequently restore them, especially if they are shaded from the sun until the process of thawing is complete. But no power on earth can recover the plant if the juices have been exposed to freeze till the vessels are burst, which may be known by the change of colour in the leaves caused by the suffusion of the sap. If some of the most tender leaves only are hurt on the young growths, the plant may survive ; if the wood is chiefly young and succulent, as in seedlings, Dahlias, &c., the whole plant generally perishes, unless where there is an old ripened root or wood to renew vegetation.

It appears from these various considerations that the best mode of increasing or preserving the heat of the earth and of the atmosphere is to check the loss of heat from evaporation by drainage, and from radiation by coverings or shelter.

Atmospheric Moisture, considered with reference to Horticulture.

The existence of water in air, even when the latter is in its driest, coldest, and purest state, is easily proved ; and the quantity of aqueous vapour which it holds in suspension has been ascertained by experiment. It varies with the temperature, increasing as the heat is greater, in something like a geometrical ratio. "At 50° Fahr. air contains about 1-50 of its volume of vapour ; and as the specific gravity of vapour is to that of air nearly as 10 to 15, this is about 1-75 of its weight. At 100°, and supposing that there is a free communication with water, it contains about 1-14 part in volume, or 1-21 in weight." Water is also held in the atmosphere in a grosser form than that of elastic vapour; for example, as mist, fog, or clouds, which three forms only differ in their appearances, and not in their nature. It will be found afterwards that it is of some importance to bear in mind the distinction between water held in suspension in the atmosphere in the state of invisible elastic vapour, and water held in suspension in the state of steam, mist, or fog.

The simplest mode of measuring the amount of vapour in the air is by means of the wet and dry bulb thermometer, which is the best hygrometer for horticultural purposes.

Having denoted the means which may be resorted to in order to ascertain the hygrometric state of the atmosphere, we shall now give an example of the utility of that knowledge for horticultural purposes. We shall suppose that the grape is to be forced in a vinery; and we shall first imagine the plant growing under the most favourable circumstances in its native country, at the time of its flowering, and enjoying a temperature of 70° or 80° through the day, with 8° or 10° of dryness, according to the hygrometer of Mason or Daniell. At night, whilst the air has still a genial warmth, it is also charged with a refreshing moisture, or, in other words, it is in a state of saturation. The leaves expand, and the shoots become rapidly extended. The conditions under which this takes place, in the native country of the grape, we would wish to imitate in its artificial culture in our vineries. In a vinery we can, even in cold weather, command heat, and the degree of dryness through the day will not be much in excess; but when night comes, although we can still keep up the heat, the moisture is diminished instead of being increased. More fire-heat being required, the air in contact with the hot flues, or hot-water pipes, ascends upwards in consequence of its increasing elasticity, till it reaches the cold glass; the latter condenses the vapour which the air contains, just as the refrigerator of a still condenses, by its coldness, the spirituous or other vapour contained in the worm; and the condensed vapour may be seen trickling down the glass roof. The portions of air thus successively drained of moisture being also cooled by contact with the glass, become specifically heavier, sink and give place to a fresh supply of warmer air, which in its turn descends, likewise deprived of its moisture. Herein we have discovered the source of an evil, the amount of which may be accurately ascertained by means of the hygrometer; and it will sometimes, under such circumstances as are stated, indicate as much as 20° of dryness, or double what the vine naturally had in the day, instead of being in the natural state of saturation at night.

Over the state of saturation the horticulturist has little or no control in the open air; but over its velocity he has some command. He can break the force of the blast by artificial means, such as walls, palings, hedges, or other screens; or he may find natural shelter in situations upon the acclivities of hills. Excessive exhalation is very injurious to many of the processes of vegetation, and no small proportion of what is commonly called blight may be attributed to this cause. Dr. McNab, of Cirencester, has proved by numerous experiments that "in the sun plants transpire most in a saturated atmosphere; in the shade transpiration ceases when the atmosphere is loaded with watery vapour," so that "plants in the warm moist air of a hothouse will give off very large quantities of fluid by transpiration, unless this is modified and regulated by proper shading." Evaporation increases in a prodigiously rapid ratio with the velocity of the wind, and anything which retards the motion of the latter is very efficacious in diminishing the amount of the former: the same surface which, in a calm state of the air, would exhale 100 parts of moisture, would yield 125 in a moderate breeze, and 150 in a high wind. Under pressure, moreover, it has been established that absorption is greater than evaporation, but when the pressure is diminished, the rate of evaporation exceeds that of absorption.

When trees are trained upon a wall with a southern aspect, they have the advantage of a greatly increased temperature; but this temperature, in spring, differs from the warmth of a more advanced period of the year, or of a more southern climate, in not being accompanied by an increase of moisture.

In this country the sun is frequently sufficiently powerful in summer to raise the thermometer in the free air, at a distance from the wall, to 101°, whilst the heat in the shade may, perhaps, be only 60°, and the dew-point 50°. In early spring, with an east wind, a warm sun, and a parched air, it is often useful, and ensures a crop of tender fruit on walls, to check the loss of sap from tender leaves and flowers by a temporary shade. Under such circumstances the degree of dryness would be 20°.

Over the absolute state of vapour in the air we are almost powerless; and by no system of watering can we affect the dew-point in the free atmosphere. This is determined in the upper regions of the air, and it is only by temporary expedients, such as shelter and shade, that we can modify the effects of excessive exhalations.

Over rain we may be said to have little influence, though the planting of trees often causes it to fall, and the denudation of forests prevents it from doing so. We can likewise prevent it from falling upon particular plants or objects. By copings we can protect fruit-trees against walls from perpendicular rain, and thus preserve the bloom on the surface of fruit which would otherwise be washed off. The roofs of plant-structures of every kind, and even the surface of the ground, may be protected from rain by thatching or covering with any body that will carry off the rain at particular points, or channels, whence it may be conveyed away in underground drains. By these and other means the soil of a garden in a wet climate may be kept much drier, and consequently warmer, than it otherwise would be. Some situations are more liable to rain than others, such as the vicinity of woods and hills, and places exposed to the Western Ocean generally. Those, on the other hand, which are exposed to the Eastern Ocean have rains less frequently; but these rains have a better effect on vegetation, because the soil, from the less frequency of rain, being generally drier, is warmer to receive them.

Though we have little or no power over the moisture of the free atmosphere, we may be said to have the perfect command of the atmospheric moisture of hothouses. Till within the last twenty or thirty years the principal points attended to in the atmosphere of hothouses were heat and light; but meteorological and chemical researches having proved that with every increase of temperature in the open air there is always an increase of aqueous vapour, this condition began to be imitated in hothouses in which tropical plants were cultivated. " Capt. Sabine, in his meteorological researches between the tropics, rarely found, at the hottest period of the day, so great a difference as 10 degrees between the temperature of the air and the dew-point; making the degree of saturation about 730, but most frequently 5 degrees, or 850; and the mean saturation of the air could not have exceeded 910." In our hothouses as commonly managed, he observes, "it would be no uncommon thing to find in them a difference of 20° between the point of condensation and the air, or a degree of moisture falling short of 500."

The causes of this unnatural dryness in our artificial climates are the condensation of moisture on the glass, and the escape of heated and damp air through the crevices of the building, the space which it occupied being constantly supplied by dry external air. A third drain of moisture formerly existed in the absorbing surfaces of brick flues, which drank up the moisture of the air in contact with them, and carried it off with the smoke into the outer air. The very general use of hot water in iron pipes has removed this nuisance, and we have now only to contend with the other two robbers of moisture.

Some idea of the drain of moisture by the escape of heated air may be formed from the following considerations. The capacity of air for moisture, that is to say, the quantity of water which a cubic foot of air will hold in invisible suspension, depends upon its temperature, and increases with it in a rapid ratio. It is doubled between 44° and 60°. The consequence is, that every cubic foot of air which escapes at the latter temperature carries off with it twice as much moisture as it brought in. Where the difference of temperature is greater, the drain becomes greater also: air entering at 44°, and escaping at 80°, carries off three times as much as it brought in; escaping at 90°, four times. The amount of moisture thus abstracted cannot be very easily estimated, as it varies exceedingly according to the height and construction of the building heated, and the disparity between the temperature of the external and internal atmospheres.

There exists, however, another drain of moisture, constantly affecting all hothouses, however perfectly constructed, and however cautiously ventilated: viz., the condensation on the glass. In this case the expenditure is capable of pretty accurate calculation. It has been ascertained by experiment, that each square foot of glass will cool $1\frac{1}{4}$ cubic feet of air as many degrees per minute as the temperature of inner air exceeds that of outer air; that is to say, if the temperature of the outer air be 44°, and of the house 66°, for every square foot of glass $1\frac{1}{4}$ cubic feet of air will be cooled 22° per minute; and the moisture which this air held in suspension, in virtue of its 22° of heat, will be deposited on the glass, and will either drain away out of the house or fall in drip.

In a parched atmosphere the roots of plants are apt to suffer, as well as the tops, from rapid evaporation through the sides of the pots, and over active exhalations through the leaves.

The custom of lowering the temperature of fluids in hot climates, by placing them in coolers of wet porous earthenware, is well known, and the common garden pot is as good a cooler for this purpose as can be made. Under the common circumstances of the atmosphere of a hothouse, a depression of temperature, amounting to fifteen or twenty degrees, may easily be produced upon such an evaporating surface. But the greatest mischief will arise from the increased exhalations of the plants so circumstanced, and the consequent exhaustion of the powers of vegetation. Some idea may be formed of the prodigiously increased drain upon the functions of a plant, arising from an increase of dryness in the air, from the following consideration. If we suppose the amount of its perspiration, in a given time, to be 57 grains, the temperature of the air being 75°, and the dew-point 70°, or the saturation of the air being 849, the amount would be increased to 120 grains in the same time if the dew-point were to remain stationary and the temperature were to rise to 80°; or, in other words, if the saturation of the air were to fall to 726.

Such facts explain why plants in living rooms do not thrive so well as those which are kept in plant structures, the dry air of the living room constantly draining root and top alike of moisture. Hence the fibres in the inside of the pots are alternately moistened and dried, and cooled and heated, and the leaves are deprived of their water by evaporation faster than it can be renewed.

Excessive dryness of the air likewise interferes with the absorbing and transforming functions of plants, by which new matter is added to them, growth promoted, and all their secretions formed. Plants vary in their power of resisting the evil effects of a dry atmosphere. As a rule, it may be stated that the thinner their leaves the less their ability to withstand it, and *vice versâ;* hence the great fitness of leathery-leaved plants such as palms, orchids and ficuses, for the decoration of living rooms.

It is equally or more important to imitate the natural atmosphere of tropical or temperate climes in our hothouses, in regard to moisture than in reference to heat, and with care and attention the one is as easy as the other. The simplest means are generally the best. It is specially so in this matter. By sprinkling the leaves and stems of the plants, the floor, sides, and roof of the house, and placing evaporating pans on the heating apparatus, and covering the roof during severe weather, sufficient moisture may generally be preserved in the air. In vineries these means are often supplemented by the introduction of some sweet fermenting dung, which distils moisture and distributes food at the same time. This, however, would prove fatal in plant houses, and needs skill and caution in using it. An extra dose of ammonia is death to tender plants or young leaves, and there is no difficulty in supplying the air with moisture apart from fermenting materials. To give an idea of the amount required, it may be well to remember that the heat of the glass of a hothouse at night cannot exceed the mean of the external and internal air, and taking these at 80° and 40°, 20° of dryness are kept up in the interior, or a degree of saturation not exceeding 528. To this, in a clear night, we may add at least 6° for the effects of radiation, to which the glass is more or less exposed, which would reduce the saturation to 434°, and this is a degree of drought which must be nearly destructive. No kind of protection would be so effective as double glass, including a stratum of air. When it is considered that a temperature at night of 20° is of no very unfrequent occurrence in this country, the saturation of the air may, upon such occasions, fall to 120°; and such an evil can only at present be guarded against by diminishing the interior heat in proportion. But, by materially lowering the temperature, we communicate a check which is totally inconsistent with the welfare of tropical vegetation. It is, however, more natural, and consequently better for the health of the plants, to maintain a night temperature of from 10° to 15° lower than the day. This checks the loss of heat, and consequently of moisture, and brings down a natural dew on the leaves.

" The skilful balancing of the temperature and moisture of the air," said the late Dr. Lindley, "in cultivating different kinds of plants, and the just adaptation of them to the various seasons of growth, constitute the most complicated and difficult part of a gardener's art. There is some danger in laying down any general rules with respect to this subject, so much depends upon the peculiar habits of species, of which the modifications are endless. It may, however, I think, be safely stated that the following rules deserve special attention :—

(1.) Most moisture in the air is demanded by plants when they first begin to grow, and least when their periodical growth is completed.

(2.) The quantity of atmospheric moisture required by plants is, *cæteris paribus*, in inverse proportion to the distance of the countries which they naturally inhabit from the equator.

(3.) Plants with annual stems require more than those with ligneous stems.

(4.) The amount of moisture in the air, most suitable to plants at rest, is in inverse proportion to the quantity of aqueous matter they at that time contain. Hence the dryness of the air required by succulent plants when at rest." ('Theory of Hort.,' p. 153.)

The Circulation of the Atmosphere, considered in its relation to Horticulture.

The motion of the air is essential to life. It is the great carrier of the world's food and drink, the great remover of its filth and poison. It brings the food of plants from afar, and places it within reach of the open mouths of roots and leaves. Many have thought that by the motion it imparts it likewise helps plants to digest or assimilate their food, while the mechanical force of moving air is supposed to give strength and stability to their closely packed fibres and tissues. Moving air likewise sucks up the watery matter of plants, and increases the power and activity of their perspiring and absorbing functions. The wind dries and moves all bodies exposed to it, and doubtless each of these in moderation is essential to the full development of the life and beauty of plants. But, while exposure to air in motion is beneficial, the air very often moves faster, and the wind proves stronger, than desired. For this reason shelter may often be needed to break the force or change the direction of large volumes of air in motion. The most effectual mode of sheltering any surface of ground, whether level or hilly, is by planting groups or belts of trees. In this way a park or pleasure-ground in the most exposed situation may be sheltered in every part of its surface. In the same way, an orchard or plantation of fruit-trees, the trees being equally distributed over the ground, produces its own shelter; but as a kitchen-garden, if planted with standard fruit-trees so as to produce shelter, would be unfit for the culture of culinary vegetables, the best mode of sheltering it is by crossing it with walls and hedges at such distances as may produce the desired shelter in the given situations.

The renewal and agitation of the air in plant-houses is a subject which is still but imperfectly understood. It has been long known in practice that plants cannot be kept in a healthy and growing state in any houses that are not supplied with ample means of ventilation; and yet, admitting the external air into houses for tropical plants, and for forcing fruits, is often found to be decidedly injurious. The injuries sustained by the admission of the external air into a hothouse are greater or less according to the difference of temperature, and, consequently, of moisture. When the external air enters a hothouse in which the air is at a high temperature, it rushes in with considerable velocity, driving out by the pressure of the atmosphere the hot and vaporous air by which the plants are surrounded, and becoming heated and charged with moisture, at the expense of the enclosed air, the earth in the pots, and the foliage of the plants.

The best remedy for this evil is to heat the air, and to saturate it with moisture, before it is admitted among the plants; and this has been done first by Mr. Penn's mode of heating, and since by the Polmaise system and other modes of heating and ventilating. Both systems are founded on the well-known principle that hot air is lighter than cold air; and the object sought to be obtained by both is to make air circulate in the atmosphere of a plant house as water does in hot-water pipes. This is done by admitting hot air at one end of the house, and having an underground drain to draw off the cold air at the other. Mr. Penn's plan is shown in fig. 1, in which a is a chamber containing hot-water pipes, b a small opening for occasionally admitting fresh air, and c a drain or tunnel under the house, the bottom of which is kept covered with water. The principal objection to this plan is the great expenditure of fuel which is required to heat the air sufficiently; and this objection is so serious in the eyes of most cultivators that Penn's mode of heating is now scarcely ever heard of. The Polmaise system, on the contrary, is very generally

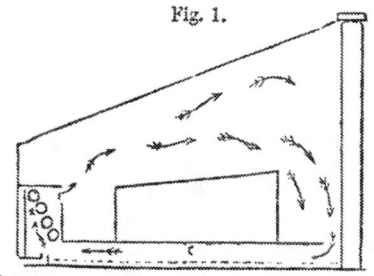

Fig. 1.

Section of a hothouse heated by hot water, according to Mr. Penn's mode.

known. There are several modifications of this system, but the best appears to be that by which a constant stream of fresh air is admitted to a chamber outside the hothouse, where it is heated by passing over the iron plate of a stove, and afterwards charged with moisture by passing over a tank of hot water. It then enters the house, through which its heat makes it rise and diffuse itself; but as it becomes cold it sinks, and is finally conveyed by a cold-air drain to feed the fire of the stove, the smoke being carried off by a chimney or flue. A similar, though not so perfect a circulation is established in most hothouses—without a drain at all. The roof and the floor are both converted into drains for the circulation from or return to the pipes or other sources of heat of the hot or cold air. Improved modes of admitting fresh air below the heating apparatus in front or at the back of houses are also general.

The great point connected with the admission of cold air to hothouses in cold weather is to charge it with moisture before it comes into direct contact with the plants.

Fig. 2.

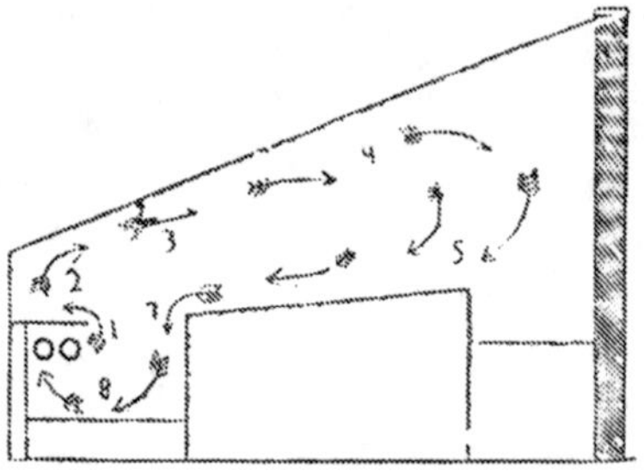

Section of a hothouse, heated by hot water in the ordinary manner.

The sketch, fig. 2, is the section of a house heated by pipes in the ordinary manner, under the front shelves. The arrows (numbered) indicate the course of the current of air. At No. 1 the air comes heated from the pipes *p*, and extremely thirsty; at No. 2 it finds moisture among the plants, and rising from the damp and warm shelf (slate, of course); at No. 3 it has parted with some of its heat; it is now supersaturated, and is parting with the moisture deposited on the glass; at No. 4 it is in the same state; at No. 5 it has ceased to lose heat or moisture; at Nos. 6 and 7 the same; at No. 8 it again comes within the influence of the pipes, and is heated, becoming again very dry. Now the air which descends to the floor (8) in the first place, is a small and feeble current, and secondly, is nearly saturated, so that it can take up little moisture; and what little it does get is because the floor, being slightly warmed by the radiation of the pipes, warms, and at the same time moistens, the air; but, nevertheless, the air at No. 1 is anything rather than saturated. By placing evaporating pans on the top of the pipes, to be filled or emptied at pleasure, the air would start from above it, nearly saturated with water, and provide the plants with a moist instead of an arid atmosphere. If fresh air were admitted on the ground lines under the pipes at 8, it would be warmed and watered at the same time, and intermixed with ascending currents of heated air. While, however, plant structures kept at high temperatures require such expedients for charging the air with moisture, they would prove simply mischievous in greenhouses, pits, or other cool structures for the storage of half-hardy plants. In all such structures it is more desirable to introduce dry air than moist. Some of the great uses of fire heat in such structures is to cause a motion or circulation of the air, to expel damp, and prevent the growth of fungi, &c.

Pits and cucumber frames, which are kept at a high temperature during winter, frequently have the air within surcharged with moisture to such a degree at that season as to endanger the health of the plants. The ordinary remedy for this evil is to admit a portion of the external air during bright sunshine; but a safer mode, if it can be adopted, is to admit the external air through tubes heated by being bedded in dung or tan, or by being placed in contact with the flues or hot-water pipes by which the pit is heated. By this means, the admitted air has its capacity for moisture greatly increased, and it will absorb and change the steam contained in the atmosphere of the pit, and the dew-drops on the glass and framework, into elastic invisible vapour.

In all plant structures change of air and ventilation are least necessary when the plants are at rest, and most so when they are in full growth. The more leaves there are upon a plant, or rather the wider the area they occupy, the more air is required to enable them to perform their respiratory functions. It is also found that increased ventilation and a drier air are of great advantage to the maturation of the fruit; but by dryness of the air must be here understood, not so much the absence of invisible elastic vapour, as of steam, or watery exhalations not held in a state of combination. "When grapes begin to colour, it is of as much importance to obtain a dry atmosphere, as it was, previously, to have a moist one; because the change effected in grapes while ripening is produced under the full influence of light, heat, and dryness: and it is well known that grapes grown in dry heat, in properly managed houses, acquire a flavour superior to those grown in plant-houses where the air is kept moist for the sake of the plants."

It is certain that, in all countries, the climate during the growing season is moist, and at the ripening season comparatively dry; and hence the practice of withholding water from fruit-bearing plants under glass, when the fruit is ripening, is in direct imitation of nature. It is also natural to suppose, that in the ripening season in the open air, when the surface of the soil is dry, the atmosphere over it will be less saturated with vapour than when the soil is moist; and, hence, the recommendation of dry air for the maturation of fruits is also natural. The effect of this air must be greatly to increase the perspiration of the leaves, which is probably auxiliary to the increased action of solar light, in the production of the saccharine matter and the peculiar odoriferous properties of fruits.

While, therefore, a free circulation of air is desirable at all times, it is essential to the ripening of wood and finishing of fruit. Cold draughts must, however, be avoided. Indeed, cultivators may lay it down as a general principle, that neither water nor air ought to be given to plants at a much lower temperature than that of the soil in which they grow, or the air by which they are surrounded.

Light, considered with reference to Horticulture.

Light is one of the most important agents in the growth of plants. It strengthens the colour and matures the growth of both wood and fruit. When plants are grown in the dark they are blanched white, and become an inodorous, insipid mass that can yield no flame when burned.

Plants suffer most at a distance from light, when the light is only from the top, or one-sided. This has been called the attraction of light, but is no explanation. In the one-sided light it may be the greater solidifying of the side next the light which draws. In the top-light of frames, the want of direct light at the sides may cause partly the greater elongation of the top; but plants elongate below glass, even though surrounded by light. The want of motion is a great cause of this: plants uniformly elongate more in a sheltered than in an exposed place. If there is any such thing as attraction between light and plants, like that which determines roots to follow the direction of their food, it will be, like the attraction of gravitation, more easily perceivable in its effects than capable of explanation. Refraction will disperse the light: it is difficult to understand how it should weaken what does pass through. The chemical power of light, however, is so much connected with electricity, that it may be weakened in a way we cannot account for. The chemical power of light is greatest in the least luminous part of the rays; and yet, as the quantity of light is equal, that at the equator must have most power. There is a connexion between heat, light, and electricity, not yet explained. The optical qualities of light have been much more attended to than the chemical. The red rays are less refracted than the blue; thus causing the red of the rising and setting sun, and the grey blue of the dawn. Perhaps more of the blue or chemical portion of the sun's rays may thus be lost in refraction. The carbon contained in all plants, and which of course is in greatest abundance in such as have woody stems, is entirely the result of the action of light on the leaves, by which plants are enabled to decompose carbonic acid, liberate oxygen and appropriate the carbon of the atmosphere to themselves. Fruits before they are ripe are acid; that is, their hydrogen and carbon are combined with an excess of oxygen; but they are rendered saccharine by the action of light, which occasions the evolution of the oxygen, and the fixation of carbon, by which the vegetable acid is converted into sugar. In a word, no plant, nor any part of a plant, can be brought to perfection without light; but it deserves also to be remarked that, in the cultivation of plants for the use of man, it is sometimes not desirable to bring all the parts of a plant to perfection; and, in these cases, the absence of light is as necessary as its presence is in others. For example, in the case of the Celery and other plants, the stalks of these, when rendered green by light, are disagreeable to the taste and even poisonous, but by excluding the light, they are rendered wholesome and agreeable: the same may be said of the tubers of the Potato, and of the stalks and leaves of Cardoons, Endive, &c.

Light, to a certain extent, follows the same laws as heat. It is received by radiation from the sun, reflected by smooth surfaces, transmitted and refracted by transparent bodies, such as water and glass; concentrated by reflection from concave surfaces, and dispersed by reflection from surfaces which are convex. All these properties of light are rendered more or less available in horticulture. Light, however, differs from heat in the impossibility of retaining it after the absence of the sun; whereas heat can be retained by enclosing heated bodies in non-conducting mediums, and by reflecting it back to the surfaces from which it is radiated.

The reflection of light is most direct when the impinging rays strike the surface at a right angle, and least so when the angle is most oblique: because, in the former case, the rays are reflected straight back, and consequently the objects in front are illuminated proportionately; but in the latter case the greater number of rays pass off at one side, and illuminate less effectively the objects in front. The reflected rays are always returned from the surface on which they fall, at an angle equal to the angle of incidence; if the reflecting surface be a plane, the reflected rays will be parallel to each other: if the surface be convex, they will be divergent, and consequently dispersed; and, if it is concave, they will be convergent, and hence concentrated. Smooth and shining surfaces reflect most light, and rough and dark surfaces least; and, with respect to colour, white reflects almost all the rays of light which fall on it, and black absorbs them all.

When light falls on a transparent medium, a portion of the rays is transmitted through it, and a portion is reflected from its surface. The latter portion follows the same laws as the light which is reflected from opaque surfaces; and the portion which passes through it is refracted—that is, it leaves the transparent medium at a different angle from that at which it fell upon it; and by this change the light is also weakened, so as at a very short distance from the surface of the transmitting medium, as of glass for example, to be dispersed and transfused in the atmosphere, in which state, in hothouses, it has no longer the same power on the vital energies of plants. We are not aware that the cause of the inefficiency of light, after it has passed through glass and reached a certain distance, has been fully explained; but the fact is well known to gardeners, who, in hothouses, invariably place the plants which they wish to thrive best at the shortest distance from the glass. As the quantity of light which passes through glass at the roof of hothouses is, all other circumstances being the same, greatest when the plane of the roof is at right angles to the plane of the sun's rays; hence, the slope of the roof is, or ought to be, adjusted to the direction of the sun's rays at that season of the year when its light is most wanted. As in houses for early forcing, the greatest deficiency of solar light is in the winter season, when the sun is low, so the roofs of such houses are made steep, in order that the sun's rays may be received at a smaller angle. Summer forcing-houses, on the other hand, have less steep roofs, so as to receive most benefit from the sun in April, May, and June, when forced fruits are ripening. A greenhouse, in which no fruit is ripened, but in which abundance of light is required all the year, has commonly perpendicular glass to receive a maximum of light during winter; and a sloping roof of glass at an angle of 45°; which is found favourable for the admission of light at every season, as well as for throwing off rain, &c. This subject, however, will be more fully discussed when we treat of the construction of hothouses.

The light of the sun, after it has passed through the clouds, is refracted, to a certain extent, in the same manner as when it passes through glass or water; and if plants were kept constantly under a cloud, but at some distance from it, and if the space in which they grew were enclosed by clouds on every side, we believe the effect on the plants thus enclosed would not be materially different from that produced by an enclosure of glass. In the open air, however, clouds are not stationary; and even where a succession of clouds covers growing plants for several days together, the space on which the plants grow is open on every side for the access of reflected and transfused light. This prevents the etiolation and want of colour which are found in plants in the back parts of hothouses having shed-roofs; but which are never found in nature, even on the north side of walls, except to a very small extent. Hence plant structures which are enclosed by glass on every side, and which are circular in the plan, are more likely to produce an equalization in the growth and appearance of the plants within, than such as have glass on one side, and a wall or opaque body on the other.

As an isolated body, such as a cone or small hill, disperses light most extensively when the sun shines, so when the sun is obscured by clouds the cone or hill receives most of the reflected light transfused in the atmosphere, because it is exposed to the atmosphere on every side. For the same reason the summits of all bodies in the free atmosphere receive more light than their sides; and hence the trees in dense forests, and the thickly-standing corn plants in cultivated fields, continue to grow and thrive though they receive little benefit from light, except from that which strikes on the tops of the plants. Hence the great importance of perpendicular light to plants under glass, and the advantages of conical, dome-like, angular, or ridge-and-furrow roofs to plant-structures; because they receive from the atmosphere the transfused light on every side.

Though art is quite powerless to increase the sum total of solar light, whether direct from the sun or transfused in the atmosphere, yet it possesses a considerable degree of power in increasing the efficiency on plants of such light as may be transfused in the atmosphere. Thus, by spreading out the branches of a tree against a wall exposed to the south, much more light as well as heat is brought to act upon the leaves, than if the tree were a standard in the free air; because, in the latter case, there would be neither the benefit of the reflection of the wall, nor that resulting from the circumstance of every leaf being exposed to the direct influence of the sun's rays when it shone. In like manner, herbaceous plants or shrubs may be planted or trained on surfaces sloping to the south; and on surfaces elevated and freely exposed, rather than in low and confined situations, in which light is obscured by surrounding objects or by aqueous vapour. The light thrown on the leaves of a plant in the open air may be increased by surrounding it on the north, and part of the east and west sides, by a wall or other upright surface painted white, or covered with glazed tiles or tinned iron. Practically, however, the grand means of increasing the efficiency on plants of such light as there may be in any given situation, is by training them against walls, espaliers, or on the surface of the ground; or, for those that cannot be conveniently so trained, by removing all other plants and objects which are so near them as either to obstruct the sun's rays or to interfere with reflection. To insure the full effect of the reflection of transfused light upon a plant, it ought to have a free space around it, in width on every side at least equal to its own height. No timber tree which has not at least this space can receive from light the full influence which it ought to have on its horizontal branches; and hence the trees in dense forests must necessarily produce timber inferior in bulk to those of the same kinds, in the same climate and soil, which are grown as single trees in parks, or in hedgerows.

In plant-structures a due proportion between light and heat ought, as much as possible, to be preserved, because this is always the case in nature, where both depend on the sun. It is not in our power to increase the natural light of the atmosphere, for the great disadvantage to which horticulture is subject in this climate is the uncertainty of clear weather; but artificial warmth can be supplied or withheld at pleasure.

The absence of light, as we have before mentioned, is necessary to render certain bitter or unwholesome parts of plants fit for culinary purposes; and the diminution of light is frequently had recourse to, when the habitation of plants which grow in shady places is to be imitated, and when the perspiration from the leaves of plants is to be diminished. In all cases of rooting plants from cuttings which have the leaves on, the diminution of perspiration, by shading them from the direct rays of the sun, is necessary, till the cuttings have taken root; and this is also more or less the case with all rooted plants which are removed with the leaves on, for some days after transplanting. When plants are in a dormant state, and without leaves, no light is requisite to maintain them in a healthy state; and even such evergreens as are in a state of comparative rest require very little. Hence orange-trees and other greenhouse evergreens, may be kept through the winter in an opaque-roof conservatory; and deciduous plants, which have lost their leaves, may be kept through winter in houses or in cellars into which no light is admitted. In the absence of light, however, a low temperature must be maintained: with the clear glass and light roofs of the present day, more shading is needed. There are many plants cultivated that cannot bear the fierce glare of the sun, and a subdued light is essential to the prolongation of the blooming period of most plants.

CHAPTER IV.

WORMS, SNAILS, SLUGS, INSECTS, REPTILES, BIRDS, &c.,

CONSIDERED WITH REFERENCE TO HORTICULTURE.

THE natural uses of plants are for the support of animals, and hence every plant, whether in a wild state or in cultivation, is more or less liable to their attacks. The most universal enemies to plants in British gardens are insects, snails, slugs, and earth-worms; but they are also subject to be devoured or injured by reptiles, birds, and some quadrupeds. In consequence of the introduction of new species and varieties of plants, the refinements of garden cultivation in forcing-houses, and the cultivation of tropical plants in stoves, the attacks of ordinary insects have been more severely felt, and several new species have been introduced. Hence, to prevent the increase of insects and other garden vermin, or to destroy them after they have commenced their attacks, has become an important element in garden-culture.

Till about the end of the last century very little attention was paid to garden vermin by horticultural writers. Birds were considered to be the chief enemies of gardeners, and they were directed to be scared away or shot at, on account of the injury they did to the rising seeds, or the ripe fruit which they ate or destroyed. The injuries done by insects of whatever kind then passed under the general term of blight. The scientific study of insects had made little or no progress in this country; and it does not appear to have been then known that birds, though injurious to gardens to a limited extent, are yet on the whole, by living in great part on insects, slugs, worms, &c., the gardener's best friends. Neither does the use of certain reptiles, such as the frog and toad, and even of quadrupeds, such as the weasel, appear to have been understood in gardens by the gardeners of the past generation. In the present day, however, this branch of garden management, like every other, has been subjected to scientific inquiry, and the object of this chapter is to generalize the results; leaving details relative to particular species of garden vermin till we come to treat of the plants by which they are chiefly affected. The order which we shall follow will be that of worms, slugs, snails, insects, reptiles, birds, and quadrupeds.

The Earth-Worm, considered with reference to Horticulture.

The common earth-worm (lumbricus terrestris L.) has a long cylindrical contractile body, without eyes, tentacula, or any external appendages; the head being only distinguishable from the posterior extremities by being more narrow and pointed. The mouth is a small orifice at one extremity, formed by two lips, of which the upper one is the larger and more projecting. The alimentary canal extends from the mouth to the opposite extremity, where it ends in the vent. The stomach is composed of two pouches, of which the first is membranous, and may be compared to a crop; while the second is muscular, and is analogous to a gizzard. At about one-third of its length from the mouth there is a sort of belt (clitellum) encircling the body, consisting of from six to nine rings, which are more prominent and fleshy than the others, and which indicate the position of the organs required for the reproduction of the species. The worm being hermaphrodite, it follows that every individual is furnished with a similar belt. The earth-worm has a well-developed ganglionated nervous system, but it appears that it has only the senses of taste and touch; the latter it possesses to an exquisite degree, as every one must have observed when approaching a worm half-extended from its hole. The worm is sensibly alive to every influence of the season and of the atmosphere; burrowing in winter to the depth of three or four feet when the cold is at the greatest, and equally deep during the greatest heats of summer. On the approach of rain or of thaw, it comes up close to the surface; moderate rains being agreeable to the worms, but standing pools of water over their holes drowning them. The taste of the worm is probably much less acute than its touch, since it is doomed to feed upon the soil in which it burrows, swallowing the earth mixed with all its decaying organized remains, from which its nutriment is extracted. Worms often draw into their holes blades of grass, straws, fallen leaves, and young seedling plants of various kinds; but these are scarcely for the purpose of food, though they have been found occasionally in the stomach, as well as small stones or gravel.

Whether worms breed oftener than once a year is uncertain. They either produce their young already hatched, or lay eggs. The eggs are placed at a considerable depth in the soil, and in clusters; they are produced at every season of the year, but chiefly in spring; and those laid at this season are hatched in June and July. The eggs, when of full size, are as large as a pea, elliptical, with a tubular aperture at one end, through which the young escape, there being more than one worm produced by each egg. In fig. 3, *a* is an egg before the embryo is visible; *b* the same egg with the embryo coiled up; and *c* the embryo worm in the act of escaping. When worms are newly hatched from the egg, they are about an inch in length; but when they are produced alive, their length is not more than four lines, and they do not attain the size of those that are born from the egg for four months. Young worms do not gain their full size till after a year.

Fig. 3.

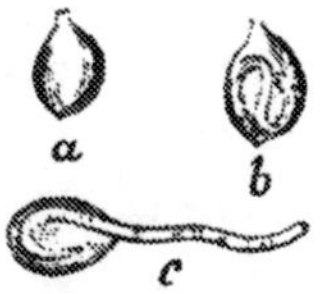

Eggs of the common earth-worm in different stages.

The popular belief, that if the earth-worm is cut into a number of pieces, every portion will in time become a perfect individual, is only true to a limited extent. The worm has the power of reproducing any part of the body cut off behind the belt; but if it is cut through in the middle of the belt, or between the belt and the mouth, the worm is killed. If the body is divided into two halves, the anterior containing the belt will reproduce a new tail; but from the posterior portion a perfect worm is never evolved, although it continues to live for a month or two, and grows in some degree. If the division is made into three parts, the middle and hinder ones die after some weeks' struggle for existence and some efforts at reparation. The mouth and lips are perfectly reproduced, provided the cerebral ganglions have not been included in the section.

The natural uses of the worm appear to be to serve as nourishment to moles, hedgehogs, frogs, toads, snakes, lizards, birds, fishes, and some kinds of insects. It is also said by naturalists that worms are useful to plants by penetrating the soil, loosening it, rendering it permeable to air and water, and even adding to the depth of the soil by bringing up their worm-casts to the surface. Soil is not loosened by boring through it, but rather rendered firmer in the parts not bored through; and so far from the surface soil being rendered permeable by water in consequence of the bores of worms, it is rendered less so, the worm-casts deposited on the orifices of the bores always being water-tight; so much so, indeed, that when lawns where worms abound are to be watered by lime-water in order to destroy them, the first step is to brush away the worm-casts with a long flexible rod, or remove them by a rake or stubby broom, in order to let the water enter the bores; it having been found from experience, that, when this operation is neglected, the lime-water sinks into the soil without producing much effect. With impervious loamy sub-soils, resting on gravel, the case is otherwise; and under such circumstances worms may be useful, by permitting the escape of water where it would otherwise be retained. The surface orifices of some burrows may also be left open, or perhaps partially closed; but this is not the case, as far as we are aware, except during those periods in the night, or in dull moist weather, when the worms have partially left their holes. With respect to worms adding to the depth of the soil (an opinion first promulgated, we believe, by Mr. Darwin, before the Geological Society in 1837, see page 505 of the Journal for that year, and still adhered to by him), it is extremely doubtful whether it takes place to any appreciable extent. According to this distinguished naturalist, however, the surface soil is raised by the agency of worms about the seventh part of an inch annually. This theory may well be questioned, and we may perhaps better attribute the undoubted growth of the thickness of surface soil, as proved by top dressings that had previously been applied to the surface, being found from six to twelve inches below it, to the action of gravitation, the decomposition of roots, and the deposit of an annual layer of carbon from the atmosphere.

The injury done by worms in gardens is much more apparent than their soil-deepening powers. By their casts they disfigure walks and lawns, and by cutting through the roots they injure more or less all plants whatever, and particularly those which are weak (to which worms always attach themselves more than to healthy plants), and plants in pots. Seedlings of all kinds are much injured by them, because when the point of the taproot is cut through, the seedling has no other resource, and, unless it be vigorous enough to throw out lateral roots, it dies.

To destroy worms is fortunately a very simple process; for such is the tenderness of their skin, that watering them with any caustic or bitter liquid deprives them of life in a few minutes. The cheapest caustic liquid is lime-water, which is made by dissolving quicklime, at the rate of half a pound of lime to twelve pints of water, and letting it stand a few minutes to clear. Before pouring it on the soil from a watering-pot with a rose on, the worm-casts ought to be removed, and the effects of the water will soon become obvious by the worms rising to the surface, writhing about there, and in a few minutes dying. To hasten their death, some more lime-water should be poured on them after they come to the surface. The quantity of lime-water required will depend partly on the depth of the soil and the number of worm-casts in a given space, and partly on the state of the weather. Least will be required in shallow soils moderately dry, and most in deep soils either very wet or very dry. Where lime is not at hand, corrosive sublimate, ammoniacal liquors, potash, soda, or urine, may be used; and a decoction of the leaves of Walnut-trees, of those of Hemp, Tobacco, or Potatoes, after being partially dried and fermented, will have the same effect. Hand-picking may also be resorted to; but this requires to be performed in the night-time, when the worms are on the surface of the ground, or immediately after rain. Rolling early in the morning—especially with a hollow iron roller weighted with hot water—speedily crushes the worms to death, as they lie in a sluggish state on the surface of grass or gravel. Worms in pots may either be removed by striking the sides of the pots, which will disturb the worms and cause them to rise above the surface; or by turning out the ball on one hand, and picking off the worms, which seldom fail to come to the outside.

To prevent worms from entering pots, a small cap (fig. 4, drawn to full size) has been invented by Mr. Barron, which, when placed over the hole in the bottom of the pot, will permit the escape of water and effectually prevent the entrance of worms. It has been in use in the gardens at Elvaston Castle for several years. All soil used for potting should be carefully prepared and examined, as prevention in this case is much better than cure. Among tropical plants another species of worm is sometimes found. The eel worm (Megascolex diffringes) has all the bad qualities of the common worm in an exaggerated form, and is much more difficult to catch or destroy. It resembles an eel in its rapidity and mode of motion, and when disturbed it rushes to the centre and not the extremity of the ball of the plants. It is most difficult to exterminate, and the soil must be entirely removed, and the roots washed clean, in collections where it has established itself. It is of tropical origin, and cannot live out of doors in this country, where,

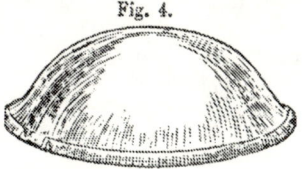

Fig. 4.

Cap for covering the holes in the bottoms of pots.

fortunately, it is not often met with, as the damage inflicted by it on pot-plants is tenfold greater than that caused by the common worm.

Snails and Slugs, considered with reference to Horticulture.

The only snail which interests the gardener is the Helix aspersa of naturalists; for that which they have named the garden snail (H. hortensis) is rather a field than a garden species. The former is much the larger of the two, and has a dull shell marked with three faint mottled brownish bands, and a white rim round the aperture; while the shell of the latter is glossy, distinctly banded with vivid colours, and the oral rim is brown.

The slugs which frequent the garden are the Limax agrestis, L. cinereus, and L. ater. The L. agrestis, the commonest, is of a greyish colour, and from one to two inches long; the L. cinereus is, on the contrary, from three to five inches in length, of a greyish or dusky colour, with darker spots and stripes; and the L. ater is easily known by the jet black and wrinkled skin of its back.

Both snails and slugs are furnished with tentacula placed in front of the head, and which, by a singular process, can be drawn entirely within it. The mouth is armed above with a semi-lunar horny jaw, having its outer or cutting edge furnished with one or several serratures. On the right side or neck of the snail and slug there are three apertures, that nearest the head being the respiratory orifice, the next the anus, and the third the exit for the organs of generation. Snails and slugs crawl on the flat sole which constitutes their foot and belly, and which is very muscular; but progression is principally performed by a pair of muscles which extend from the tail to the fore part of the belly, running along the middle of the foot.

Snails and slugs are hermaphrodite and oviparous. They deposit their eggs under clods of earth, loose stones, or in the ground, in which the parent digs, with its foot, a circular hole about an inch deep. The eggs vary from twelve to thirty in number; they are white, oval or round, about the size of a common shot, with a smooth soft skin, which is entirely membranous in the slug, but in the snail contains innumerable minute calcareous grains, always in a crystalline state, and usually of a rhomboid figure. They are, in ordinary seasons, hatched in about three weeks after being laid; but the time is regulated much by temperature, so that in cold seasons it is greatly retarded. The young issue from the egg in the likeness of their parents, active and furnished with every organ; and the young snails have even then a shell fitting their size and strength. The length of life of the snail or slug cannot be determined. The shell of the snail is usually completed before the termination of the second year, when the animal may have been said to have reached maturity. The snail and the slug are very patient of injury, often recovering from severe wounds; repairing their broken shells, and reproducing such parts of their bodies, posterior to the neck, as may have been cut away. In winter, snails and slugs retire under stones, clods, or into the crevices of walls: the slugs become merely less active than usual, but the snails hybernate; and to protect them from annoyance during this dead sleep of a winter's continuance, they seal up the apertures of their shells with a horny membrane.

The natural uses of the snail appear to be to serve as food for reptiles, birds, and the smaller quadrupeds, such as foxes, badgers, weasels, hedgehogs, &c. The blackbird and thrush are remarkably fond of them, and may be seen flying off with snails in their bills, and afterwards lighting on trees, and breaking the shells against the branches, or cracking them against stones on the ground.

The snail retires under the cover of foliage or some other protection from the sun and dry air during the day, and comes abroad to feed during the night, after rain, or when the weather is cloudy. It selects in preference tender seedling plants, or the leaves of maturer plants which have become tender and somewhat sweet by incipient decay. Snails are very fond of greasy matter; and where a snail has been killed by crushing, its remains are preyed on by living snails, which crowd to it in numbers. About the end of autumn, when the weather begins to grow cold, the snail retires into sheltered places, where it will be protected from the weather during winter. Where there are evergreens, such as the Box or the Ivy, it resorts to them; or if these be wanting, it will retire under loose stones, or rubbish of any kind, such as branches, spray, leaves, or litter; and if no other covering is at hand, it has a power of burying itself in any soil not too hard on the surface. Whatever has been said of the habits of the snail will apply to those of the slug; and the uses and the natural enemies of the two animals are exactly the same.

To destroy snails in gardens, the only effectual mode is hand-picking, either in the evening, early in the morning, or immediately after rain. Empty flower-pots reversed and distributed over the surface, if an opening under the rim is left on one side by making a small depression in the soil, will attract a great number of snails; and the more so if some greased cabbage-leaves or slices of turnip, carrot, &c., be placed under the pots. In the course of the autumn, winter, and early in spring, all their hiding-places should be searched, and the animals taken out and destroyed by crushing, or by giving them to swine, which are said to be very fond of them. Hedgehogs and weasels, being their natural enemies, may be kept in gardens, and poultry which do not scratch, such as the turkey, duck, &c., may be admitted occasionally. Blackbirds and thrushes likewise devour immense quantities. But all these natural means of reduction should be supplemented by hand-picking.

To destroy slugs in gardens, less labour is required than in destroying snails; because, their bodies being comparatively unprotected, they are liable to be operated on by any caustic or bitter liquid as readily as worms. Cabbage-leaves in a state of incipient decay, with the side which is to be placed next the soil rubbed over with greasy matter of any kind, or even with the bruised bodies of recently-killed slugs, distributed over any surface, will attract them in great numbers during the night: and if the leaves are examined every morning, and the slugs which are found destroyed, the piece of ground so treated will soon be freed from them. Pea-haulm being very sweet when in a state of incipient decay, forms a powerful attraction to slugs; and if handfuls of it are distributed over a piece of ground in the same manner as the cabbage-leaves, the little heaps of haulm may be examined every morning, and the slugs shaken from them and then destroyed by watering with lime-water. Thin slices of turnip or potato placed under inverted empty flower-pots form an excellent attraction, as do the dead bodies of slugs themselves, some parts or the whole of which are greedily devoured by the living animals. Where slugs are very abundant in a soil not covered with plants so large as to shelter them, as for example with rising seedlings, the slugs may be destroyed by watering the soil thoroughly with lime-water, or tobacco-water, late in the evening or early in the morning. Abundance of water should be applied, in order that it may sink into the soil, which the slugs penetrate a foot or more in depth, according to its state of pulverization. Quicklime has been laid round plants to protect them from snails and slugs; but it soon becomes mild and of no use as a protection. Coal-ashes, sawdust, and barley chaff annoy slugs by sticking to their foot, but they will not be deterred by this annoyance so effectually as to starve for want of food. Soot is also a great annoyance to slugs; but to keep them from a plant, it requires to be frequently and liberally renewed. Thorough drainage—trenching—and frequently dusting the surface of infected ground, with caustic lime, hot burnt earth, or ashes, will break up their haunts and exterminate them, and such radical measures are the cheapest in the end.

Insects, considered with reference to Horticulture.

The number of species of insects in the world greatly exceeds that of all other animals and plants put together, and the power which some insects have of multiplying themselves, such as the plant lice for example, is almost incredible. As by far the greater number of insects live on plants, some on several species, and others on only one, the importance of some knowledge of the natural history of insects to the gardener is sufficiently obvious.

Transformation of Insects.—The greater number of insects properly so called, with the exception of some without wings, change their form several times during their life in so striking a manner, that a person unacquainted with entomology would be inclined to consider one and the same insect, in different periods of its existence, as entirely different animals.

Insects, in general, are produced from eggs; a few species alone, in which the eggs are developed in the body of the mother, are viviparous; for example, the aphis. Shortly after pairing, the female lays her eggs, which are often stuck on, and covered with a sort of glue, to preserve them from the weather, in the place best adapted to their development, and which offers the proper food to the forthcoming brood. The white-thorn butterfly and the golden-tail moth lay their eggs on the leaves of fruit-trees or other leafy trees, and the latter covers them over with a gold-coloured covering of silk. The common lackey-moth (Bombyx neustria) fastens them in the form of continuous rings round the stems of fruit-trees; and the gipsy-moth (Bombyx dispar) fastens them in a broad patch on the stems of trees or on palings, and covers them with a thick coating of hair. The winter-moth (Geometra brumata) lays them singly on the buds of the leaves and flowers; the printer-beetle (Bostrichus typographus) introduces them between the bark and the albumen, &c.

Most insects are developed from the eggs in the shape of worms, which are called larvæ. The larvæ of butterflies, which are always provided with feet, are called caterpillars; those of beetles and other insects, grubs; and, when they have no feet, maggots. In this state, as their bodies increase, the insects often cast their skin, and not unfrequently change their colour. Many winged insects (*e.g.*, cimices, cicadæ, grasshoppers, and dragon-flies), in their larva state, very much resemble the perfect insect; they only want the wings, which are not developed till after the last change of the skin. The larva state is the period of feeding, and at this period insects are usually the destructive enemies of other productions of nature, and objects of persecution to farmers, gardeners, and foresters.

The nympha or pupa state succeeds that of larva. In this state insects for the most part take no nourishment (with the exception of the Orthopterous, Hemipterous, and part of the Neuropterous species, which vary but little in form from the larva), and repose in a death-like slumber. The body is covered with a skin more or less transparent, through which the limbs of the perfect insect are more or less apparent. To be safe from their enemies, or from the weather, the larvæ of many insects, particularly moths, prepare for themselves a covering of a silky or cottony texture; many burrow in the soil, or form themselves a nest of moss, leaves, grass, haulm, or foliage; many even go deep into the earth, or bury themselves in decayed wood, or conceal themselves under the bark of trees, &c.

After a certain period, which is fixed in every species of insects, and which can either be hastened or retarded according to circumstances, the perfect insect appears from the pupa. It is usually furnished in this state with other organs for the performance of its appointed functions. It is incumbent on the perfect insect to propagate its species, therefore the organs for this purpose are only perfected at this period of their lives. The male insect seeks the female, and the female the most suitable place for laying her eggs; hence most insects are furnished with wings. Food is now a secondary consideration, consequently, in many, the feeding organs are now less perfectly developed than in the larva state, or very much modified and suited for finer food, as for example in butterflies, which, instead of the leaves of plants, only consume the honey of their flowers.

Food of Insects.

Insects, like other animals, derive their nourishment from the vegetable and animal kingdoms; but a glance is sufficient to show, that they possess a much wider field of operations than the others. While the other animals make use for their subsistence of only a small portion of the inexhaustible treasures of the vegetable kingdom, and reject the rest as insipid or noxious, the insects leave perhaps no vegetable production untouched. From the majestic oak to the invisible fungus, or the insignificant wall-moss, the whole race of plants is a stupendous meal, to which the insects sit down as guests. Even those plants which are highly poisonous and nauseating to other animals are not refused by them. But this is not yet all. The larger plant-consuming animals are usually limited to leaves, seeds, and stalks: not so insects, to the various families of which every part of a plant yields suitable provender. Some which live under the earth attack roots, others choose the stem and branches, a third division lives on the leaves, a fourth prefers the flowers, while a fifth selects the fruit or seed.

Even here a still further selection takes place. Of those which feed on the roots, stem, and branches, some species only eat the rind, like the bee-hawkmoth (Sphinx apiformis); others the inner bark and the alburnum, like the Tortrix Wœberiana, and the injurious bark-beetle; and a third division penetrates into the heart of the solid wood, like the goat-moth (Cossus ligniperda), and the family of the long-horned beetles (Cerambycidæ).

Of those which prefer foliage, some take nothing but the juice out of the veins (aphides, in all their states); others devour only the substance of the leaves, without touching the epidermis (mining caterpillars); others only the upper or under surface of the leaves (many leaf-rollers, Tortrices); while a fourth division devours the whole substance of the leaf (the larvæ of many Lepidopterous insects).

Of those which feed on flowers, there are some which eat the petals (the larvæ of Noctua verbasci, the mullein-moth, N. linariæ, &c.); others choose the farina in a perfect state (bees, the rose-chafer, Cetonia, the Lepturidæ, &c., &c.); and a still greater number the honey from the nectaries (most perfect Lepidopterous insects, wasps, and flies). There are also insects which, not satisfied with any existing part of the plants as such, cause injury to one part or another, by occasioning a peculiar body or excrescence in which their young live, as the various sorts of gall insects and other sorts of flies. But insects are not confined to plants alone in their living and unused state. The death-watch, or ticking-beetle (Anobium), feeds on wood which for years has been used in our dwellings in various articles of furniture and utensils.

From what has been said it will appear, that a single plant can support a host of various sorts of insects on its different parts; whence it also appears, that the number of insects greatly exceeds that of plants.

An equal variety in the food of those insects which live on animal matter may also be pointed out. Some live as parasites on the skins of other animals, not excepting even insects themselves, suck their blood, and are a burdensome torment to the animals: to these belong the different sorts of lice (bird and sheep lice), ticks, and mites. Others attack man and the larger animals for only a short time, and draw blood—gnats, midges, autumn-flies, breeze-flies, bugs, and fleas. Some breeze-flies (Œstridæ) penetrate through the skin into the flesh of the red deer and horned cattle, others live in the stomachs of horses and asses, and one sort in the frontal sinus of sheep. The Ichneumonidæ feed on the flesh of the larvæ of other insects, and often greatly contribute to the extirpation of noxious insects.

The Carabidæ and other carnivorous beetles devour their prey entire, immediately after killing it; while the Cimices and Hemerobii only suck out the juices. The larvæ of the stinging-gnat and other flies which live in water devour whole swarms of infusoria alone. A great number live on carrion and the excrements of animals, and thus diminish and destroy the corruption proceeding from such matter: to these belong chiefly the blue-bottle fly, horse-beetle, carcase-beetle, and dung-beetle. Many feed upon prepared animal matter, and become very prejudicial to household economy. Many moths live entirely on hair, leather, wool, and feathers.

With the various transformations of insects their economy is changed, and consequently their abode is also varied: the caterpillar requires very different food from the butterfly; the maggot, from the beetle and fly. The larva of Sirex gigas feeds on wood, while the perfect insect preys on flies. The larva of the May-bug or cockchafer lives on roots and tubers; the beetle, on leaves.

Many insects are very gluttonous, and often consume more food in a day than is equal to the weight of their bodies. Thus the maggot of the flesh-fly, according to Redi, becomes 200 times heavier in the course of twenty-four hours. Caterpillars digest in one day from one third to one fourth of their weight; and hence it is apparent that a comparatively small number of caterpillars can entirely strip a tree in a few days.

Opposed to this gluttony of caterpillars, some insects in their perfect state appear to take no nourishment, such as the day-flies (Ephemeridæ), and the breeze-flies (Œstridæ); the latter of which, in their larva state, as maggots, feed on the flesh of horned cattle and red deer. Even among the Lepidoptera, many of those which spin cocoons, especially Bombycidæ, seem to take no nourishment in the perfect state.

Many insects only eat in the day, others in the evening, and a third division, such as the caterpillars of the night-moths, only in the night. Most of them seek their own food; but a few—namely, the larvæ of bees, which live in communities, humble bees, wasps, and ants, are fed by the perfect insect. Many stow away their food; others, indeed the greater number, live without making any previous supply of food. The larvæ of the caterpillar-killing kinds of wasps (Sphegidæ), of wild bees, and of a few other insects, are provided by their parents with a stock of provisions sufficient for their nourishment in the larva state.

Distribution and Habits of Insects.

The distribution of insects is in exact proportion to the diffusion of plants; the richer any country is in plants, the richer it is also in insects. The polar regions, which produce but few plants, have also but few insects; whereas the luxuriant vegetation of the tropical countries feed a numerous host of them. With respect to their habitation, insects are divided into those which live upon land or water.

Those which live in the water either never leave that element, or are able to live at will either in the water or on the earth, at least for a short time; for example, many water-beetles. Many live at certain periods of their development in water: at others, on land; such as many sorts of flies, and all the dragon-flies, which as larvæ and pupæ live in water, but as perfect insects on land, or in the air.

Land insects live in the earth, under stones, in decayed wood, in putrid animal substances, &c. Of these some pass their whole lives in these places, others only during a particular period of their development. The larvæ of the dung-beetle live deep under the ground, while the perfect insect inhabits the excrement of animals; many of the larvæ of flies live in carrion or excrement, while the perfect insect flies about in the open air. A very great number choose the different parts of plants for their abode, as the roots, bark, inner bark, alburnum, wood, pith, buds, flowers, leaves, and fruit. They change their abode in every new stage of development. Thus the bark-beetle, which in the larva state lived under the bark, swarms in its perfect state upon the trees; the curculio of the apple-tree, the larva of which infests the bottom of the apple-blossom, crawls on the trees, or on the surrounding ground; the mining-moth, which as a larva lives under the cuticle of the leaves, flutters in its winged state about the flowers and leaves.

A small number live upon other animals, on the skin, such as lice, or inside of the body, as the larvæ of ox and horse breeze-flies (Œstridæ). The two latter leave their first abode before entering the pupa state, which they effect in the earth, and hover as flies round the animals to deposit their eggs upon them.

Most insects live solitarily, either without any definite dwelling, or they construct for themselves a house composed of various kinds of vegetable or animal matter; for example, many caterpillars. A few species live in society, such as bees, ants, wasps, &c.

By obtaining a general knowledge of the abodes of insects, it is evident that the observer of the economy of insects will be able more satisfactorily to combat many that are injurious to him; as thus he can, with little trouble, greatly diminish or entirely annihilate those which he has ascertained to live in society, or in places of easy access.

Uses of Insects.

There are among insects no very inconsiderable number from which man derives, in many respects, immediate and important uses. We need here only to mention the bees and the silkworm. The different sorts of gall-nuts, ingredients so essential to dyeing and the manufacture of leather, are the productions of several insects, namely, the gall-flies, which wound with their ovipositor various parts of oaks, &c., in order to deposit their eggs in the cavity, and which produce these useful excrescences. The most durable and most beautiful red (cochineal) we owe to a small insect, the Coccus cacti. Another, nearly allied to the above-named insect, Coccus manniparus, is supposed to have saved the lives of the Israelites in their journey out of Egypt, for they would have died of hunger if they had not been provided with manna,—a sweet nutritive substance, which is regarded as identical with the material which, in consequence of a wound caused by this insect on the Tamarix gallica mannifera, trickles on the ground.

The Cantharides, or Spanish blister-flies, are an essential article of medicine. Many insects accomplish the fructification of different plants. (See the interesting and instructive work on the fertilization of orchids by Mr. Darwin.) Whole nations in other quarters of the globe live on locusts. Many mammalia, a number of birds, amphibious animals, and fishes, live entirely on insects.

A great number of these creatures even live upon other species of insects, and destroy them: thus preventing the hurtful from preponderating, and disturbing the balance in the economy of nature. To these belong chiefly the Ichneumonidæ and spiders.

Lastly, how many diseases are obviated, particularly in warm climates, by insects speedily consuming dead animal substances, and thereby preventing the generation of noxious gases!

Means contrived by Nature to Limit the Multiplication of Insects.

Many appearances in nature, even such as at first cause anxiety and care, on account of their injurious consequences, are found to be in many respects highly beneficial and salutary, although we may not always understand them. Thus continued rain, which in many respects is extremely hurtful, contributes greatly to diminish the number of noxious insects, and for a series of years renders them entirely innocuous. Thus in the spring of 1832, after incessant rain, Kollar saw the caterpillars of the white-thorn butterfly (Papilio cratægi), which for many years had not only stripped all the hedges, but also done considerable injury to the fruit-trees, dying by thousands, as if of a dropsy. The caterpillars swelled, became weak, and died. If they did attain the pupa state, they suffered from the same evil, and the perfect insect was very rarely developed, on which account the gardens in the following years were uninjured.

Late frosts are also very beneficial, as they entirely destroy many insects in their larva state. Kollar had an opportunity early in the summer of 1833 of observing great devastations on the fir-trees in the neighbourhood of Vienna, by a species of saw-fly (Tenthredo rufa, Klug). The larvæ of this insect had attacked certain parts of a young forest of Scotch pine, and the question was how their ravages were to be prevented from increasing next year. Fortunately, in the month of May, a moderate frost set in, and thousands of these larvæ were seen hanging to the twigs, as if scorched. In this manner their increase was limited for the time.

A multitude of insects are also destroyed by inundations, particularly such as undergo their transformations in the earth, or live upon it in all their stages, more especially if the inundation happens when they are near their final transformation. In meadows the different species of Maybugs (Melolonthidæ) suffer by this means; in kitchen gardens, the mole-cricket; in orchards, the pupa of the small winter-moth (Geometra brumata), when the water overflows the gardens late in the autumn, at the time when the moth is usually developed from the pupa lying in the earth. Besides the means of preserving an equilibrium by storms, and the effects of the elements, nature employs a multitude of others, although not so speedy and efficient, to the same end.

To these belong the enemies of the destructive insects, which we meet with in all classes of the animal kingdom. Among the mammiferous animals the bats hold a conspicuous place for their destruction of insects. We only see them flying about in the twilight, precisely at the time when many moths leave their hiding-places and hover round the flowers. As they live almost entirely on insects, they no doubt devour great numbers of the hurtful sorts; and perhaps it is to be ascribed to this circumstance that fruit-trees standing near houses, churches, barns, &c., suffer less from insects than isolated trees. Bats do not confine themselves to moths, but eat the beetles which fly about in the evening; and, among others, some of the weevils injurious to the flowers and buds of fruit-trees, as the Curculio (Anthonomus) pomorum, and pyri. These creatures, as they do no injury, should therefore be carefully preserved.

To the insectivorous mammalia also belong various sorts of mice, the mole, badger, hedgehog, squirrel, fox, and wild swine.

Birds contribute much more than the mammiferous animals to the destruction of injurious insects. Many caterpillars know instinctively how to conceal themselves from the birds which prey on them; in many their covering of stiff hair acts as a protection against their enemies; others remain all day between rolled-up or flatly-united leaves, and only go out to feed at night; others find sufficient protection in the buds, into which they soon penetrate. Gregarious caterpillars live while they are changing their skin, and when they are going into the pupa state, in webs, in which they are inaccessible to birds. Others live under the bark of trees, and even deep in the wood. Notwithstanding these and other obstacles, a great number are yearly devoured by the birds, particularly during the breeding season. In winter a multitude of birds, urged by hunger, diligently search the branches of trees for the eggs of many sorts of moths that are glued to them, and which yield a scanty sustenance to many of these animals. Réaumur states that the greenfinch tears open the strong nest of the yellowtail-moths (Bombyx chrysorrhœa), and consumes the young caterpillars.

Among the birds of the woodpecker race, the green and red woodpeckers (Picus viridis and major), the nut-hatch (Sitta cæsia), and the tree-creeper (Certhia familiaris), may be considered the most useful. Although these birds seek beetles chiefly, and consequently contribute to the diminution of the long-horned and weevil tribes of beetles, they also consume a number of caterpillars.

Among birds of the sparrow tribe, the starling deserves particular notice. It lives in summer chiefly in pastures, but comes in spring and autumn in large flocks to the meadows and orchards, where it devours a great number of insects, pupæ, and larvæ. The chaffinch is a determined consumer of caterpillars' and moths' eggs. The titmice are particularly useful—viz., the oxeye and tomtit; then the redbreast and redstart, and also the wagtails.

The cuckoo also particularly deserves to be spared; it not only devours many of the smaller smooth-skinned larvæ, but even consumes the hairy caterpillars of many moths, particularly of the Bombycidæ. On examining the intestines of a cuckoo, in the month of September, Kollar found therein, besides the remains of various insects, a great quantity of the skins of the caterpillar of the large Bombyx pini, which is one of the largest European species, and has very stiff hair. The inner coat of the stomach was entirely covered with hair, but a close inspection with the magnifying glass showed that the hair was not the hair of the stomach of the cuckoo, as some ornithologists suppose, but only the hair of the caterpillars. This bird may therefore be of very essential service when there is a superfluity of the caterpillars of the lackey or processionary moths (Bombyx neustria or processionea).

It is sufficiently known that great service is rendered by the whole race of crows to meadows and fields. Their favourite food consists of the larvæ of the cockchafer, which are thrown up by the plough, and which they also draw out of the earth with their strong beaks. It is a wonderful provision of nature, that exactly at the time that the insects injurious from their great numbers appear, the greatest number of the insectivorous birds have hatched their broods, and their voracious young are ready to be fed upon them.

Insectivorous birds are also sometimes granivorous, and feast readily on our fruit, particularly cherries; but the injury they cause in this respect is not to be compared to the use they are of in destroying insects.

Among amphibious animals which destroy insects, lizards hold a conspicuous place. Grasshoppers are the favourite food of many species. Frogs and toads also devour many insects.

Besides mammalia, birds, and amphibious animals, Nature, to

restore the equilibrium among her creatures, and particularly to prevent the preponderance of some sorts of insects, makes use chiefly of insects themselves, namely—those which feed upon others, and which by degrees obtain a superiority over those that are hurtful to us.

Thus many sorts of beetles, particularly of the family of ground-beetles (Carabidæ), destroy a multitude of the pupæ of moths lying in the earth. Many flies, allied to our house-fly, but much larger, lay their eggs in living caterpillars and destroy them. But the most useful are the Ichneumonidæ. The females of this numerous family, 1300 species of which Professor Gravenhorst has assigned to Europe alone, lay their eggs entirely in the bodies of other insects.

The manner in which these Ichneumonidæ accomplish their work of destruction is highly curious and interesting. All the species are furnished at the end of the body with an ovipositor, composed of several bristles attached together, with which they pierce the larvæ of other insects, and introduce their eggs into the flesh of the wounded animals. In some this sting is longer than the whole body, sometimes more than an inch long—namely, in those species which seek the objects of their requirements in the interior of trees or wood that has been much and deeply perforated by the insects which reside within. They perceive, either by their sense of smell or by their antennæ, that their prey is at hand, and introduce their eggs, not without difficulty, into the bodies of the larvæ living in the wood. Some attack caterpillars feeding openly on plants, others perforate the various excrescences, or gall-nuts, which also contain larvæ: there are even many species, scarcely visible to the naked eye, which lay their eggs in the eggs of other insects, such as butterflies, and thus anticipate their destruction. The eggs are hatched within the body of the living insect, and the young parasites, in the most literal sense, fatten on the entrails of their prey. At last the wounded caterpillar sinks, the enemies escape through the skin and become pupæ; or the caterpillar, notwithstanding its internal parasites, enters the pupa state, but instead of a butterfly, one or more Ichneumonidæ appear. To these wonderful animals we often owe the preservation of our orchards, woods, and grain.

Besides the above-mentioned Ichneumonidæ, ants, field or tree bugs, and many sorts of spiders, contribute greatly to the extirpation of various insects.

Means devised by Art for Arresting the Progress of Insects in Gardens, or of Destroying them there.

Insects may be destroyed in all their different stages; in some, however, with greater ease than in others. Some can only be taken or killed when in the perfect state, from the difficulty of discovering their eggs, or from their small size, or from the short period which elapses between the hatching of the insect and its maturity; for example, the aphides. Others can only be destroyed in the perfect state, with great difficulty; such as the different butterflies. A great number of the insects which infest British gardens are only to be destroyed in the larva state; while some, such as the gooseberry-moths, may be destroyed in every stage. We shall briefly indicate the different practices which may be had recourse to in different stages, for deterring or destroying insects, by the gardener; leaving particular details till particular insects come to be mentioned, when treating on the culture of the plants which they attack. We shall commence with operations connected with the perfect insect, and take in succession the eggs, the larvæ, and the pupæ.

Deterring the Perfect Insect.—The perfect-winged insect may, in some cases be deterred from approaching plants by covering them with netting or gauze, the meshes of which are sufficiently small to exclude the insect, but not too small to prove injurious to the plant by excluding light and air. Wasps and flies are in this manner excluded from vineries and peach-houses while the fruit is ripening. Bunches of grapes against the open wall are also protected by putting them in bags of woollen netting or gauze. Choice plants in pots are sometimes protected from wingless insects by placing the pot containing the plant in the midst of a saucer which surrounds the pot with water which it is found the insect will not cross. The stems of plants, such as dahlias and gooseberries, are sometimes protected by a zone of glutinous matter on wool, tow, or paper, over which the insect will not venture. A remarkable mode of deterring some insects from entering houses by the windows is described in the 'Architectural Magazine,' vol. ii., as practised in Italy, and known even in the time of Herodotus. This is simply to place before the openings of the window a net of white or light-coloured thread, the meshes of which may be an inch or more in diameter. The flies seem to be deterred from entering through the meshes by some inexplicable dread of passing through them. If small nails be fixed all round the window-frame at the distance of about an inch from each other, and thread be then stretched across both vertically and horizontally, the network so produced will be equally effectual in excluding the flies. It is essential, however, that the light should enter the room on one side of it only; for if there be a thorough light either from an opposite or side window, the flies pass through the net without scruple. (W. Spence in 'Transact. Entomol. Society,' vol. i.) It would appear to be a general principle, that winged insects may be deterred by meshes of such a size as will not admit them with their wings expanded, and also that insects will not enter from bright light into darkness, more especially if deterred by the slightest obstacle, such as the threads just spoken of.

Preventing the Perfect Insect from laying its Eggs.—Insects may be prevented from laying their eggs on plants within reach by surrounding them with a netting or other screen; or, in some cases, by sprinkling the plant with some liquid containing a very offensive odour. Thus moths are prevented from laying their eggs on gooseberry-bushes by hanging among them rags dipped in gunpowder and tar; and the watering of such plants as cabbages, peas, etc., overhead with lime or soot-water, weak sewage, and manure water, may deter butterflies from depositing their ova. A fine sprinkling of dry guano will cause ants to forsake their nests and prevent them from coming near ground so covered. Insects which deposit their eggs in the soil cannot easily do so when the soil is very hard, and may therefore be enticed to deposit them in portions of soil made soft on purpose. Thus boxes or large pots filled with rotten tan, sunk in the soil, form an excellent nidus for the eggs of the cockchafer, and will prevent that insect from laying them in the common soil of a garden. Hoeing or digging patches of soil here and there throughout the garden or plantation will have a similar effect, to a certain extent; and after some weeks, when the larvæ are some lines in length, the soil may be sifted, and the insects taken out and destroyed. While loosening the naked soil serves as a trap for the cockchafer, covering that soil with straw is found to act as a defence against them; and hence one of the principal uses of mulching rose-gardens, tree-nurseries, and other cultivated grounds.

Catching the Perfect Insect, so as to Prevent it from Depositing its Eggs.—Though this cannot be done to any great extent with winged insects, such as the butterfly, moth, and some flies, yet it may be employed in the case of the cockchafer, the rose-beetle, &c., which may be collected by children; and in the case of wingless insects, such as wood-lice, ants, and earwigs, which may be enticed into hiding-places by food, or by other means. A piece of boiled potato placed in a pot and covered with dry moss, is a capital trap for wood-lice, or earwigs. A piece of fruit similarly covered entices ants. Earwigs may also be caught by placing hollow bean-stalks in their haunts, to which they will retire in the day-time, when they can be shaken out of the stalks into a vessel of water. A simple and effectual trap for both wood-lice and earwigs is composed of two pieces of the bark of any soft rough-barked tree, such as the elm, placed inside to inside, so as to leave in the space between them a very slight separation, tying the two pieces of bark together by a piece of twig, part of which is left as a handle, and laying the trap where the insects abound. They will retire in the day-time between the pieces, which can be quickly lifted up by the twig and shaken over a vessel of water. No bait is required for this trap, the more tender part of the bark being eaten by the wood-lice and the earwigs. The same bark-trap will also serve for millipedes, beetles, and, to a certain extent, for ants. The most effective mode of destroying ants in frames or hothouses is by placing toads in them. One toad will be sufficient for a frame or a hothouse. The toad places himself by the side of an ant-path, and by stretching out his tongue as the insects pass him, draws them in and devours them. He is even fonder of wood-lice than of ants. Other such insects may likewise be destroyed wholesale by boiling water, crushing them with the back of the spade, &c.

Destroying the Perfect Insect.—This is effected in the open air by the use of washes or decoctions in the case of the aphides; or, in the case of the wasp, by hot water being poured into its nest, or sulphur or gunpowder being burnt in it, or by inserting a rag dipped in turpentine, or pouring tar into the hole, and digging the nest out; or by pouring salt and water into ants' nests; or by lighting a fire over the holes of burrowing insects, &c. In plant-houses, the perfect insect, such as the red spider, the green fly, &c., is destroyed by fumigation with tobacco smoke; dusting with tobacco dust, snuff, or other insect killer; syringing with tobacco juice, Gishurst's compound, a solution of smelling-salt, soot, &c., &c. The perfect insect is also destroyed in hothouses by the sublimation of sulphur, which may be mixed with lime or loam, and washed over the heating-flues and pipes, or placed on a hot stone or plate, or in a chafing-dish. Dusting the leaves of plants under glass with sulphur, in a state of powder, is found to destroy the red spider. Beetles, wood-lice, and other crawling wingless insects, are also destroyed by tempting them with food containing poison. A remarkable but very efficient mode of destroying the vine-moth in France has been discovered by Victor Audoin, which might in many cases, we have no doubt, be adopted in British gardens. This mode is founded on the practice of lighting fires during the night in vineyards, to which the moths are attracted, and burn themselves. M. Audoin has modified this practice in a very ingenious manner, which has been attended with the most effective results. He places a flat vessel with a light on the ground, and covers it with a bell-glass besmeared with oil. The pyralis, attracted by the light, flies towards it; and, in the midst of the circle which it describes in flying, it is caught and retained by the glutinous sides of the bell-glass, where it instantly perishes by suffocation. Two hundred of these lights were established in a part of the vineyard of M. Delahante, of about four acres in extent, and they were placed about twenty-five feet from each other. The fires lasted about two hours; and scarcely had they been lighted, when a great number of moths came flying around, which were speedily destroyed by the oil. The next day the deaths were counted. Each of the 200 vessels contained, on an average, 150 moths. This sum multiplied by the first number gives a total of 30,000 moths destroyed. Of these 30,000 insects, we may reckon one fifth females, having the abdomen full of eggs, which would speedily have laid, on an average, 150 eggs each. This last number, multiplied by the fifth of 30,000, that is to say, by 6000, would give for the final result of this first destruction the sum of 900,000. On the 7th of August, 180 lamps were lighted in the same place, each of which on an average destroyed 80 moths, or a total of 14,400. In these 14,400 moths there was reckoned to be, not only one sixth, but three fourths, females: but, admitting that there was only one half females, or 7200; and, multiplying this by 150 (the number of eggs that each would have laid), we have a total of 1,080,000 eggs destroyed. Two other experiments were made on the 8th and 10th of August, which caused the destruction of 9260 moths. ('Gard. Mag.,' vol. xiii. p. 487.)

Luring away the Perfect Insect.—Attracting the perfect insect from the plant or fruit by some other kind of food to which they give the preference and which is of less value to the gardener, may perhaps sometimes be effected. Wasps, hornets, and flies are easily entrapped in bottles filled with beer or honeyed water. The best bottles are so formed that the insect, once in, cannot get out again. The opening at the top is below the level of the sides (fig. 5), and not one insect in a thousand has sense enough to fly up in a perpendicular line: they constantly struggle to the highest point, and after a few attempts get their wings wetted, and perish. The bottle should be emptied daily, the liquor being passed through a sieve and saved, and the insects burned.

The side-opening is for emptying the contents, and is kept corked, unless when the bottle is emptied. The bottle is fixed to the wall or tree with wire. The top-opening is 1½ inches below the level of the top of the curved side, and is regularly bevelled down to the hole through which the wasps, flies, &c., enter. The body of the bottle is made of clear glass.

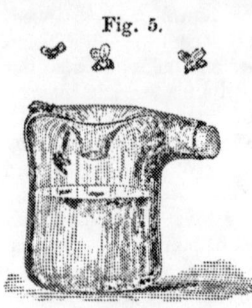

Fig. 5.

Wasp-trap bottle.

Though these bottles are the best traps, the hand-light trap is likewise very efficient. It is made as follows:—Take a common hand-glass,—the hexagonal or any other form will do (fig. 6); remove in the apex the whole or part of three of the panes, *a, b, c*. Then take a second hand-glass, which must be of the same form as the first, and place it on the roof of the first, so that the sides of the one may coincide with the sides of the other; next stop all the interstices between the bottom of the one and the eaves of the other, at *e, f, g*, with moss, wool, or any suitable substance, which will prevent the entrance or exit of flies. The bottom hand-glass must rest on three pieces of bricks (fig. 8), to form an opening underneath. The appearance of the trap when completed is simply that of one hand-glass above another (fig. 7). Fragments of waste fruit are laid on the ground, under the bottom hand-glass, to attract the flies, which, having once entered, never descend again to get out, but rise into the upper glass, and buzz about under its roof, till, fatigued and exhausted, they drop down, and are seen lying dead on the roof of the under glass. One of these traps, placed conspicuously on the ground before a fruit-wall or hothouse, acts as a decoy to all kinds of winged insects.

Fig. 6.

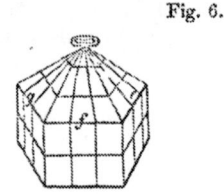

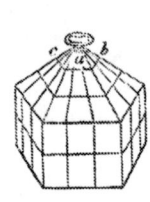

Hand-glasses prepared for making a fly-trap.

Fig. 7.

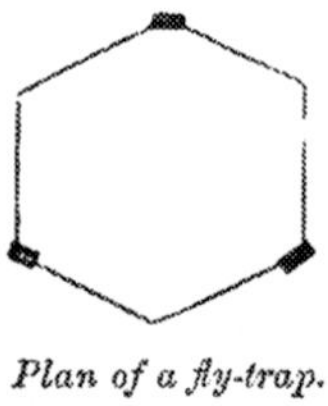

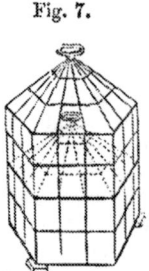

Hand-glasses arranged as a fly-trap.

Fig. 8.

Plan of a fly-trap.

Collecting the Eggs of Insects.—The eggs of insects, after being deposited on the bark or leaves of plants, may sometimes be collected by hand; for example, when they are laid in clusters or patches, so as to form a belt round the twig, as in the lackey-moth; or when they are covered with fibrous matter, as in the Bombyx dispar, which lays its eggs in large circular or oval groups, containing 300 or more each, on the bark of trees or hedges, and covers them with a yellow wool. The eggs of the yellow-tail moth are laid on the leaves of fruit-trees, in a long narrow heap, and covered with gold-coloured hair, whence the scientific name Bombyx chrysorrhœa, which makes them very conspicuous; but the leaves may easily be collected, and the eggs destroyed. The satin-moth, Bombyx salicis, which, in its larva state, feeds on the leaves of willows and poplars, often stripping entire trees, when it becomes a perfect insect, lays its eggs in July, in small spots like mother-of-pearl, on the bark of the tree; and as they are conspicuous, they may easily be scraped off. Practical men in general are too apt to undervalue the effects of hand-picking, whether of the eggs or larvæ of insects; not reflecting that every insect destroyed by this means, is not only an immediate riddance of an evil, but prevents the generation of a great number of other evils of the same kind. Circumstances have forced this on the attention of the French cultivator, and the following facts will place the advantage of hand-picking in a strong light. In 1837, M. V. Audouin, already mentioned, was charged by a commission of the Académie des Sciences, to investigate the habits of a small moth, whose larva is found to be exceedingly injurious in vineyards in France. During the month of August, women and children were employed during four days in collecting the patches of eggs upon the leaves, during which period 186,900 patches were collected, which was equal to the destruction of 11,214,000 eggs. In twelve days from twenty to thirty workers destroyed 482,000 eggs, which would have been hatched in the course of twelve or fifteen days. The number of perfect insects destroyed in a previous experiment, by an expensive process, was only 30,000. ('Gard. Mag.,' vol. xiii. p. 486.) Many insects, however, deposit their eggs singly or in very small quantities, or in concealed places; and the eggs being in these cases very small, they are not easily found.

Preventing Eggs from being Hatched.—Eggs, after being deposited, may sometimes be destroyed, or prevented from hatching, by the application of washes, or a coating of glutinous adhesive matter, such as gum, glue, paste, soft soap, sulphur and clay, or in some cases clay alone. A mixture of lime and water will not always have the effect of preventing the hatching of the eggs; because, when the egg begins to vivify and swell with the heat of the spring, the lime cracks and drops off. This, however, is not the case when the lime is mixed with soft soap and cow-dung, which render it adhesive and elastic. Water raised to the temperature of 200° will destroy the eggs of most insects; and when these are deposited on the bark of the trunk of an old tree, or the well-ripened branches of a young hardy tree, water at this temperature may be applied freely. For young

F

shoots in general the temperature should not exceed 130° or 150°. It should be remembered that insects, in depositing their eggs, always instinctively make choice of places where the newly-hatched insect will find food without going far in search of it. Hence they seldom lay them on walls, stones, glass, boards, or similar substances; and therefore the attention of gardeners, when searching for ova, should be directed much more to the plants which nourish the insects, than to the walls or structures which shelter the plants, though it is impossible to have the latter too clean.

Collecting or destroying Larvæ.—Insects in their larva state are much more injurious to plants than they are in any other; because, as we have already seen, it is in this stage of their transformations that they chiefly feed. With the exception, however, of several of the wingless or crawling insects, and certain bugs and beetles, larvæ are in general not difficult to discover, because, for the most part, they live on those parts of plants that are above ground; but some live on the roots of plants, and these are among the most insidious enemies both of the gardener and the farmer. The ver blanc, or larva of the cockchafer, in France, and that of the wire-worm, in England, are perhaps the most injurious of all underground larvæ, and those over which the cultivator has least power. Underground larvæ may be partially collected, but not without much care and labour, by placing tempting baits for them in the soil. As they live upon roots, slices of such as are sweeter and more tender may be deposited at different depths and at certain distances, and the places marked; then, the soil being dug up once a day, the insects may be picked off and the baits replaced. Slices of carrot, turnip, potato, and apple, form excellent baits for most underground larvæ. Such as attack leaves—as, for example, those of the gooseberry—may be destroyed in immense quantities by gathering the leaves infested by them, as soon as the larvæ become distinguishable from the leaf by the naked eye, and sprinklings of hellebore powder will likewise destroy the gooseberry caterpillar. Instead of this being done, however, it too frequently happens that the larvæ escape the notice of the gardener till they are nearly full grown, and have done most of the mischief of which they are capable. Hand-picking has been found most serviceable in preventing the injury caused by the black caterpillar on the turnip leaves, which, in certain seasons, has proved destructive of the entire crop. It may also be applied to the destruction of the cabbage caterpillars. Here, also, we may notice the beneficial effects of picking out and destroying young onion plants infested by the grub of the onion-fly. This ought to be done as soon as the plants appear sickly, because the grubs arrive at maturity in a very short time; and, by destroying the plant, future generations of the fly are prevented. Grub-eaten fruit ought also to be picked up as soon as it falls to the ground, before the enclosed grub has time to make its escape into the earth, and which it would do in a very short time, the fruit not falling until the grub has arrived at its full size. The larvæ of some kinds of saw-flies envelop themselves in a kind of web in the day-time, and only go abroad to feed during the night. Webs of this sort may be seen in great numbers, in the early part of summer, on thorn hedges, fruit-trees, spindle-trees, and a great many others; and they might readily be collected by children or infirm persons, and thus myriads of insects destroyed. The larva may be destroyed, both in its infant and adult state, by dashing against it water in which some caustic substance has been dissolved, such as quicklime or potass; or a bitter or poisonous infusion may be made, such as quassia or tobacco-water. While the larvæ are not numerous, or the plants infested by them are tender and highly valued, they ought to be collected by hand; and in the case of the larvæ of mining insects, in which the larva is concealed within the epidermis of the leaf, there is no way of destroying them but by gathering the leaves, or crushing the insects between the finger and thumb.

Collecting the Pupæ or Chrysalids.—Insects may be destroyed in the pupa state by collecting their chrysalids or cocoons, when these are placed above ground, as is most commonly the case with those of moths and butterflies. These are commonly deposited in crevices in the old bark of trees, or in sheltered parts of walls or buildings; rarely on young shoots or in the tender parts of plants, because, when the perfect insect comes forth, it no longer requires such food. Often the larva descends into the soil, there to pass through its pupa state; and in some cases it may be destroyed by watering the soil with boiling water, or by deep trenching; the surface soil, containing the insects, being placed in the bottom of the trench. As the eggs and chrysalids require the presence of air for their vivification and maturity no less than the seeds of vegetables, they are consequently, when deposited in the soil, always placed near the surface; and hence they may be destroyed either by heaping earth on the surface, or by trenching or digging down the surface soil, so that the eggs or pupæ may be covered at least to the depth of six inches. How long vitality will be retained under such circumstances is uncertain. In destroying the cocoons of insects, care should be taken not to destroy those of the insect's enemies, such as the cocoons of the spider, or those of the ichneumon flies. These are sometimes deposited in heaps on the bark of trees, and are individually not larger than the egg of a butterfly. The gardener ought to be able to recognise them, because they are his best friends.

This general outline will be sufficient to show the necessity of every gardener, who would be a master of his profession, studying the natural history of insects, and more especially of those which are known to be injurious or useful to him, whether in the open garden or in plant-structures. It is only by such a study that he can be prepared to encounter an insect which he has never heard of before, and that he will be able to devise new modes of counteracting the progress of, or destroying, insects already known.

Amphibious Animals, considered with reference to Horticulture.

The frog, Rana temporaria, L., and the toad, Bufo vulgaris, Flem., are found useful in gardens, because they live upon worms, snails, slugs, and terrestrial insects. The toad being less active than the frog, and being capable of living a longer period without food, is better adapted for being shut up in frames, or kept in stoves. Both prefer a damp and shady situation; and where they are intended to breed, they should have access to a shallow pond, or shady ditch. The ova of the frog is deposited in clusters in ditches and shallow ponds, about the middle of March; and the young, or tadpoles, are hatched a month or five weeks afterwards, according to the season: by the 18th of June they are nearly full-sized, and begin to acquire their fore feet; towards the end of that month, or the beginning of the next, the young frogs come on land, but the tail is still preserved for a short time afterwards. The common toad is a few days later in spawning than the frog. Its ova are deposited in long necklace-like chains in shallow water in shady ponds or ditches. There is one species, B. Calamita, Laurent, the Natter-Jack, which inhabits dry localities, and is a much more active animal than the toad, but much less common.

Birds, considered with reference to Horticulture.

Birds are, upon the whole, much more beneficial than injurious to gardens; and being also larger animals and more familiar to every person living in the country than insects, we shall only briefly notice the commoner kinds.

To give an idea of their usefulness to the horticulturist, it may be well to advert to the vigilance and voraciousness of the white or barn-owl (Strix flammea, L.), which feeds principally upon mice, snails, and slugs, and occasionally picks up rats, &c. Mr. Waterton points out, in his 'Essays on Natural History,' that when it has young it will bring a mouse to its nest about every fifteen minutes. But in order to have a proper idea of the number of mice which this bird destroys, we must examine the pellets which it ejects from its stomach in the place of its retreat. Every pellet contains from four to seven skeletons of mice. In sixteen months from the time that the retreat of the owl on the old gateway at Walton Hall was cleaned out, there had been a deposit of about a bushel of pellets. All the owls, hawks, ravens, crows, magpies, jays, and rooks are equally useful in their respective spheres, while the thrushes, blackbirds, &c., repay the value of the fruit they destroy by the great multitude of small worms and slugs they consume. The hedge-sparrow is about as useful in gardens as the house-sparrow is destructive; while the martins, swallows, wrens, and fly-catchers live wholly upon insects.

In destroying or reducing the number of birds, those that are wholly or chiefly insect-eaters must be spared, while such as bullfinches, chaffinches, and sparrows, that devour buds and seeds, should be thinned.

But most birds will eat fruit at certain seasons of the year, and it is therefore necessary to adopt various means of deterring or debarring them from their favourite fruits. Scarecrows of men or animals are of little use. The birds get accustomed to them, and will come and perch on them after a time. Wind and clapper-mills are better, as the noise and motion have a deterrent effect. Two bright pieces of tin, tied with a long string to the end of a pole, six feet or more high, and placed in a slanting direction, are effective. Rows of peas, crocuses in bloom, and other seeds and flowers, are preserved by having worsted, cotton, or linen threads run along singly or in pairs about six inches above them. No sooner does the bird alight for a meal than he looks up to see that the course is safe and clear. The string awakes suspicion, and he is off at once. The same remedy has been recommended to be used with fruit-trees on walls, a few inches in front of the leaves. The birds alight upon this, the thread turns round with the grasp of their feet, and pitches them suddenly to the ground. This plan is much recommended, as it is said that a few tumbles are sufficient to keep off the birds. Young cats, owls, and hawks are likewise occasionally tied up to guard particular crops, and if they are placed in sufficient numbers among the crops, they are effective, but not otherwise.

The different modes of deterring birds may be reduced to the following:—Excluding by netting, or other coverings, supported at a few inches' distance from the rising seedlings, fruit, flower, or plants to be protected; setting up scares, of different kinds, such as mock men or cats, mock hawks or other birds of prey, miniature wind-mills or clapper-mills; lines with feathers tied at regular distances, placed at a few inches' distance above the rows of newly-sown peas, or other seeds sown in drills; over rows of crocuses or other dwarf spring flowers, or over beds or entire compartments. A system of dark worsted threads, placed in front of wall trees at a few inches' distance from the leaves, will scare away most birds; because, taking the worsted string for a twig, and lighting on it, it turns round by the grasp, and sinking at the same time by the weight, the bird falls, and if this happens to him on a second attempt, he will be deterred for the future. The following scare is founded on an idea given by Mr. Swainson in the 'Encyclopædia of Agricul.,' 2nd edit., p. 1112:—Let poles, ten or twelve feet high, be firmly fixed in the ground, in conspicuous parts of the garden, each pole terminating in an iron spike six or eight inches long; pass this spike through the body of a dead hawk in the direction of the back-bone: it will thus be firmly secured, and give the bird an erect position; the wings being free, will be moved by every breeze, and their unnatural motion will prove the best scarecrow either for ravenous or granivorous birds, more particularly the latter. Cats are found useful in walled gardens as scares to birds, as well as for other purposes. R. Brook, Esq., of Melton Lodge, near Woodbridge, in Suffolk, had four or five cats, each with a collar and light chain and swivel, about a yard long, with a large iron ring at the end. As soon as the gooseberries, currants, and raspberries began to ripen, a small stake was driven into the ground, or bed, near the trees to be protected, leaving about a yard and a half of the stake above ground; the ring was slipped over the head of the stake, and the cat being thus tethered in sight of the trees, no birds approached them. Cherry trees and wall-fruit trees were protected in the same manner as they successively ripened. Each cat, by way of a shed, had one of the largest sized flower-pots laid on its side, within reach of its chain, with a little hay or straw in bad weather, and her food and water placed near her. A wall of vines between 200 and 300 yards long, in Kirke's Nursery, Brompton, the fruit of which, in all previous seasons, had been very much injured by birds, was one year completely protected from them, in consequence of a cat having constantly posted herself in the vicinity. ('Hort. Trans.,' 2nd series, and 'Gard. Mag.,' vol. xii. p. 429.) A stuffed cat has also been found efficacious. Crows and rooks are, in some parts of the country, deterred from lighting on sown wheat by pieces of rag dipped in a mixture of bruised gunpowder and tar, and stuck on rods, which are placed here and there over the field, and the rags renewed every three or four days. Of course this scare only operates where the birds have been previously accustomed to be shot at. The most certain mode of scaring birds, however, is to set boys or other persons to watch and sound a wooden clapper all round the fruit, or seeds, which may be ripening or germinating. Protection with wire or twine netting, bunting, or cheese-cloth is, however, the cheapest and most effective barrier to the ravages of birds. Unless where wire-netting is used, a framework of wood should always be employed, to keep perishable materials off the ground. This framework should be raised so high as to enable a man or boy to get underneath to gather the fruit as wanted. Such an arrangement will require more material in the first instance, but it will last treble the time, and add immensely to comfort and despatch in its use.

The destruction of birds is most judiciously effected by traps, or by poisoning, because neither of these modes operates like the gun in scaring away others. "The report of fire-arms is terrible to birds; and, indeed, it ought never to be heard in places in which you wish to encourage the presence of animated nature. Where the discharge of fire-arms is strictly prohibited, you will find that the shiest species of birds will soon forget their wariness, and assume habits which persecution prevents them from putting in practice. Thus the cautious heron will take up its abode in the immediate vicinity of your mansion; the barn-owl will hunt for mice under the blazing sun of noon, even in the very meadow where the haymakers are at work; and the widgeons will mix, in conscious security, with the geese, as they pluck the sweet herbage on your verdant lawn."

The smaller Quadrupeds, considered with reference to Horticulture.

A few of these deserve notice, partly as the enemies of gardens, and partly as the subduers of other garden enemies; and in order that none deserving notice may escape, we shall take them in scientific order.

Feræ (Wild Beasts).—The badger (Meles, Cuv.) burrows in the ground and comes abroad in the night to feed, devouring indiscriminately animal and vegetable substances. The marten (Mustela Foina, L.) inhabits the vicinity of houses, and preys on poultry, game, rats, moles, &c. It breeds in hollow trees. The polecat (M. putorius, L.) is a common inhabitant of woods and plantations in all parts of the country, and preys on game, poultry, eggs, and all the smaller quadrupeds, amphibiæ, snails, slugs, and worms. The ferret (M. Furo, L.), considered by some as the polecat in a domesticated state, is employed to destroy rabbits and rats. The weasel (M. vulgaris, Gmel.) is common in the vicinity of barns and outhouses. It devours young birds, rats, mice, moles, frogs, toads, lizards, snakes, snails, slugs, &c. Mr. Waterton, after recommending this animal to farmers, says: " But of all people in the land, our gardeners have most reason to protect the weasel. They have not one single word of complaint against it—not even for disturbing the soil of the flower-beds. Having no game to encourage, nor fowls to fatten, they may safely say to it, ' Come hither, little benefactor, and take up thy abode amongst us. We will give shelter to thy young ones, and protection to thyself, and we shall be always glad to see thee.' And fortunate, indeed, are those horticultural enclosures which can boast the presence of a weasel; for neither mouse, nor rat, nor mole, can carry on their usual depredations whilst the weasel stands sentinel over the garden. Ordinary, and of little cost, is the accommodation required for it. A cart-load of rough stones, or of damaged bricks, heaped up in some sequestered corner, free from dogs, will be all that it wants for safe retreat and a pleasant dwelling. Although the weasel generally hunts for food during the night, still it is by no means indolent in the daytime, if not harassed by dogs or terrified with the report of guns." ('Essays,' &c., p. 302.) The fox and the wild cat prey on birds and small quadrupeds. The domestic cat is too well known and too useful where rats, mice, or birds are to be deterred or destroyed, to require further notice. The mole (Talpa europæa, L.) burrows beneath the surface, but never to a great depth, throwing up hillocks at intervals. It feeds on worms and the larvæ of insects, and, according to some, on roots. It breeds twice a year, in spring and autumn; and as it carries on its operations chiefly in the night-time, the runs and hills may be watched early in the morning, and the animals dug out wherever they give signs of movement. They may also be taken by traps, of which there are several kinds. They may also be caught by sinking in their runs narrow-mouthed vessels of water, into which the animals will descend to drink without being able to get out again; or these vessels may have false covers similar to those set in the runs of rats.

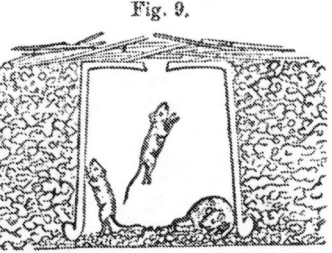

Fig. 9.

Inverted flower-pot for catching mice.

The shrew (Sorex, L.)

of which there are three species, inhabits gardens, fields, and hedgerows, and lives on insects, and also on vegetable substances. It may be caught by a water-trap in the same manner as the mole, or by an inverted flower-pot sunk in the soil, and slightly covered with litter or leaves, fig. 9, or checked by employing some of its natural enemies. The hedgehog is found in hedges, thickets, &c., remaining concealed in the daytime, but coming abroad at night in quest of worms, snails, slugs, and even frogs and snakes. It also lives on roots and fruits. Hedgehogs are occasionally kept in gardens for destroying frogs, toads, lizards, snails, slugs, and worms; and in kitchens, for devouring beetles, cockroaches, woodlice, and other terrestrial insects. Care is requisite, however, that they are not annoyed by cats, which, though they cannot devour them, will, if not prevented, soon force them to quit a habitation which is not natural to them. The spines of the hedgehog are soft at its birth, and all inclining backwards; but they become hard and sharp in twenty-four hours. The bat, of which there are several species indigenous, lives entirely on insects caught on the wing. It forms the natural food of the owl. The dog, which belongs to this order, is too well known and useful to be classed with such vermin. As the enemy of rats, rabbits, and other vermin, and by his faithful watchfulness, he renders important services to horticulture.

Glires (Dormice).—The common squirrel feeds on birds, acorns, nuts, and other fruits; and though he is very ornamental in woods, he should be but sparingly admitted into pleasure-grounds. The dormouse lives on similar fruits and roots, and builds his nest in the hollows of trees. The field-mouse may be caught and checked in the same manner as the shrew. The field-mouse in the Forest of Dean had become so destructive in 1813, that after trying traps, baits with poison, dogs, cats, &c. with little success, at last the plan of catching it in holes was hit upon. These holes were made from eighteen inches to two feet long, sixteen or eighteen inches deep, about the width of a spade at the top, fourteen or fifteen inches wide at the bottom, and three or four inches longer at the bottom than at the top. The object was to get the bottom of the hole three or four inches wider every way than the top, and the sides firm, otherwise the mice would run up the sides and get out again. The holes were made at twenty yards apart each way, over a surface of about 3200 acres: 30,000 mice were very soon caught, and the ground was freed from them for two or three years. As many as fifteen have been found in a hole in one night; when not taken out soon, they fell on and ate each other. These mice, we are informed, used not only to eat the acorns when newly planted, but to eat through the stems of trees seven and eight feet high and an inch and a half in diameter: the part eaten through was the collar or neck of the tree. (Billington's ' Facts on Oaks and Trees, &c.,' p. 43.) One of the simplest traps for mice is made of three bits of lath, supporting a brick or slate, with the bait just above the ground (fig. 10). No sooner do the mice nibble the bait than down comes the slate or brick and crushes them; the same trap of larger dimensions is almost equally effective for rats. It must be set lightly, the weight resting on the projecting part of the upper part of the trap; otherwise the perpendicular part of the trap will prevent the weight from falling. The black and the brown rat are omnivorous, and the latter takes occasionally to water and swims readily. Both are extremely difficult to extirpate, and the various modes of entrapping them are too numerous and well known to require description here. The hare feeds entirely on vegetables, and is very injurious when it finds its way into gardens and young plantations.

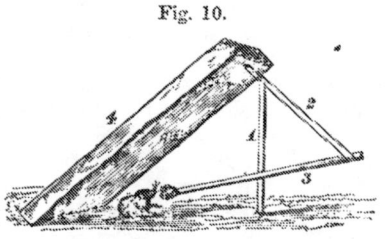

Fig. 10.

1. *Upright support.*
2. *Diagonal liner.*
3. *Bait stick, cut into to catch* 1, *and notched at the end to hold* 2 *fast.*
4. *Slate, brick, or stone crusher.*

It eats the bark of several trees, and is particularly fond of that of the Laburnum. Various mixtures have been recommended for rendering the bark of young trees obnoxious to the hare, and an ointment composed of powdered sloes and hogs' lard is said to prove effectual. Stale urine of any kind, mixed up with any glutinous matter that will retain it on the bark, has also been recommended. The rabbit is more injurious to gardens than the hare, because it is much less shy, and much more prolific. It may be deterred from injuring the bark of trees by the same means as the hare, and from eating pinks, carnations, and other evergreen herbaceous plants, by surrounding them with a tarred thread, supported by sticks

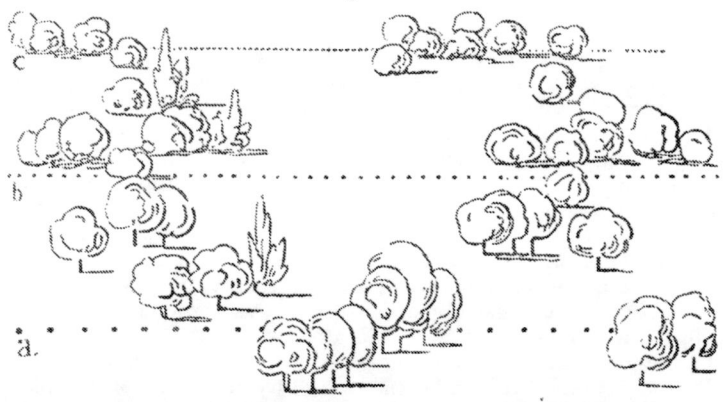

Fig. 11.

Triple fence: a, *for excluding cattle;* b, *sheep fence;* c, *hare and rabbit fence.*

dipped in sulphur, at the height of six or eight inches from the ground. The only effective barrier, however, is a strained wire fence, closely woven or set together, from 24 to 36 inches in height. To present a straight or wall-like boundary, three fences two or three yards apart are sometimes placed parallel to each other. The outer fence may consist of iron posts and rods, no closer together than is necessary to exclude horses, cattle, and deer; the second fence should be such as will exclude sheep; and between this fence and the outer one there may be several large bushes, or low trees, with branches reaching to within the height of a sheep from the ground. The third fence need not be more than two feet high, with an iron wire about a foot higher along the top, and with the wires sufficiently close together to exclude hares and rabbits; and between this fence and the sheep-fence there may be several shrubs with their branches resting on the ground. Thus, by the distribution into three fences of the materials which commonly form one fence, the outer margin of the plantation may be made to appear as free and irregular as if there were no fence at all. See fig. 11.

The chief objection to such a mode of breaking up a straight boundary line with picturesque beauty is the expensiveness of the fencing. The same object may often be gained by planting groups of trees and shrubs inside a single line of fence, or where a distant view is desired, a sort of ha-ha may be dug out the depth of the fence, which renders the boundary invisible.

CHAPTER V.

THE DISEASES AND ACCIDENTS OF PLANTS, IN THEIR RELATION TO HORTICULTURE.

There are various diseases and accidents to which plants are liable, some of which are beyond the control of the gardener, and others he can avert or subdue. The principal diseases which affect garden plants are the canker, mildew, gum, honey dew, and flux of juices.

The canker chiefly affects apple and pear trees, and of these some varieties of apples are constitutionally more liable to this disease than others—for example, the Ribston Pippin. The canker exhibits itself in small brown blotches, which afterwards become ulcerous wounds, on the surface of the bark, and soon extend on every side, eating into the wood, and sooner or later becoming so large as ultimately to kill the tree. The causes generally assigned are, the unsuitableness of the soil, the unpropitiousness of the climate, and the unfavourableness of the seasons; and here the matter generally rests. But soil and climate alike may be improved, and even the severity of the season modified, by drainage and proper cultivation. The chief causes of canker are a wet bottom, deep planting, and the use of rank manure.

To prevent canker all these conditions should be reversed. The soil should be a good friable loam, two feet or more in depth, resting on a dry bottom. Care must also be taken to keep the collar of the plant level with the surface, and to give the roots a horizontal direction. In cases where the good soil is only of very moderate thickness, and where the subsoil is a ferruginous gravel, or a stiff cold clay, it is not only necessary to drain the ground and plant upon the surface, but the trees should be set on the top of mounds from six inches to a yard above the surrounding level, and from four to eight feet in diameter; the bottom of these mounds being covered with some hard substance, such as stone, slate, &c., to prevent the roots descending, and to lead them out as it were in a horizontal direction. No manure whatever should be incorporated with the soil, unless it should be very poor indeed: but it may be applied as a mulching round the mound, which will tend to keep the roots sufficiently moist and also near the surface. If these points were attended to, we should hear little of canker, unless in places naturally very damp, where more than a fair average of rain falls; or where, from the prevalence of clouds, there is a deficiency of sunshine. In such places the shoots grow so luxuriantly during summer, that they are yet soft and spongy, and filled with crude juices in the end of autumn. The frost sets in, freezes these juices, bursts the sap-vessels, and the decay of the shoots, or brown blotches, and ultimate canker, are the consequence. The only preventive in such cases is to plant on hillocks, and in soil made light and poor: the wood will then be less luxuriant and better ripened.

What has been said respecting the prevention of canker will also apply to its cure. No scrubbing, scraping, or anointing will be of the least use. Cutting down the trees and allowing them to shoot afresh may be of benefit, if the canker has been produced by one very unfavourable season; grafting them with hardier sorts will succeed, if the evil arises from unfavourableness of climate; but neither of these methods will be of permanent benefit, when the evil proceeds from bad soil or planting. In such cases, where the trees are very bad, the best method is to destroy them gradually, and plant young ones in a proper manner, leaving some of the old trees until the young ones commence bearing. If the trees are not very old, nor yet too far gone, it will be advisable to take them up carefully, cut away all the cankered wood, plaster up all the wounds with a compound of clay and cowdung, plant them in fresh soil on hillocks, and give no manure unless what is supplied for mulching. Such trees will generally become quite free of disease and bear splendid crops. A number of years ago, in a large kitchen-garden in the neighbourhood of London, a great number of fruit-trees were found in the different quarters in a miserable state from canker. The gardener appropriated a quarter in the garden for the reception of these trees; had the ground thrown up into wide and high ridges: on the top of these ridges the trees were planted, and in a short time they presented a fine healthy appearance, and were well stocked with good fruit. The soil was a stiff clayey loam. Such radical measures are not only the best antidote to canker, but a certain cure for sterility.

The gum, by which is meant an extraordinary exudation of that secretion, takes place chiefly in stone-fruit trees, such as the Peach,

Cherry, Plum, &c., from a cut, bruise, bend, or other violent disruption of the tissue, or by injudicious pruning; often, however, without any visible cause. The gum on the young shoots of Peach-trees is analogous to the canker on Apple-trees, and seems to be caused by a cold wet soil, or a cold wet climate. Trees subject to this disease will live many years, and bear abundantly, though sometimes they are destroyed by it. For the gum we know of no remedy.

Mildew appears in the form of a whitish coating on the surface of leaves, chiefly on those of herbaceous plants and seedling trees. Deficiency of nutriment is favourable to the production of mildew; it seems also to prefer glaucous-leaved plants, as the Swedish Turnip, Rape, and Peas, which are particularly subject to it in dry weather. Some varieties of fruit-trees are more liable to mildew than others; for instance, the Royal George and the Royal Charlotte Peaches are often attacked, when other sorts, growing close by them, are free from the disease. Peaches with glands are mostly exempt from mildew, and ought to be planted where the disease is prevalent. The mildew is supposed to be produced by innumerable plants of a minute fungus, the seeds of which, floating in the air, find a suitable nidus in the state of the surface of the leaf, and root into its stomata. This favourable state for the appearance of the disease seems to be promoted by various circumstances. It sometimes proceeds from a tenderness in plants, produced from sowing or planting too thick. It exhibits itself in a season of dry weather, when the leaves become in a languid state, produced often by the roots being prevented, by injudicious surface watering, from drawing moisture from below. It also shows itself after a season of wet weather, if the drainage is defective, and the leaves have become surcharged with crude juices. More especially does it present itself in either of these circumstances, when the roots and branches of a plant are placed very differently relatively to moisture and temperature. For instance, it is very apt to make its appearance in a peach-house, if the border should be cold and wet, and the top of the tree in a warm arid atmosphere. The same effect will be produced when the atmosphere is genial and moist, and the border allowed to become too dry. Cucumbers grown in pine stoves, will often become much infested with mildew in the winter months; because unless the pines should be in fruit, they will neither enjoy the requisite temperature, nor a sufficiently moist atmosphere. In many cases also the disease proceeds from the soil being exhausted; from containing too much inert carbonaceous matter, or becoming soured or sodden from want of drainage. In such cases trees are often completely cured by replanting properly in fresh soil. The best temporary specific for arresting the disease, is washing the affected parts with a composition of water and flowers of sulphur. If the plants are tender, it will be advisable to shake the sulphur in a state of powder on the affected parts when dry. In both cases it will be necessary to guard against bright sunshine by partial shading. In some cases the labour of sulphuring may be dispensed with, by at once cutting off the affected leaves and shoots. Where the mildew is liable to be produced by drought, it may frequently be prevented by copiously watering the soil, by which means Mr. Knight prevented this disease from attacking his late crops of Peas. The rust in corn crops is produced by a fungus in the same manner as the mildew; but as it chiefly concerns the agriculturist, we refer the reader to Professor Henslow's Report on the Diseases of Wheat, 'Jour. Agr. Soc. Eng.,' vol. ii. p. 1, and the Rev. Edwin Sidney's little work, 'The Smut of the Wheat.'

Honey-dew is a sweet and clammy exudation from the surface of the leaves of plants during hot weather, and it is supposed to be occasioned by the thickening of the circulating fluids in the leaf, which being unable to flow back into the bark with their accustomed rapidity, the sugary parts find their way to the surface. The disease is common in the Oak, Beech, Thorn, and in many other plants. Hitherto no remedy has been applied to it in general cases, as, though it weakens plants, it seldom kills them. When, however, it appears on plants in a state of high cultivation, for instance, in a peach-house, or on a peach-wall, no time ought to be lost in applying the syringe or garden-engine, and even rubbing it off the leaves if necessary, otherwise the shoots or branches affected will be apt to be destroyed. Some persons suppose the honey-dew to be occasioned by the aphides, as the exuviæ of those insects are often found on leaves affected with this disease. This view of the case has recently been confirmed by writers in the 'Gardeners' Chronicle' for the year 1869. It has also been proved that ants are useful as antidotes to honey-dew. They eat both the honey-dew and the aphides, and in this way consume cause and effect together.

Blight is a term which is very generally applied to plants when under the influence of disease, or when attacked by minute fungi or insects. Any sudden disease or death of a plant, or part of a plant, is likewise termed a blight. Blight is often atmospherical or electrical; in some cases the continued action of dried air, and cold frosty winds, preventing the flow of the sap, may bring on a disease which might be called blight, exclusive of either the action of insects or of fungi or of electricity; but by far the greater number of instances of what is called blight are produced by these three causes. In general the fungi may be destroyed by the application of powdered sulphur, and the insects by some of the different means that have been already pointed out; but we have no panoply against the lightning, nor security against sudden changes of temperature.

Flux of Juices.—Under this term are comprehended the bleeding, or flow of the juices of the vine and other plants, when accidentally wounded, or pruned too early in autumn, or too late in spring; and the discharge of the descending sap, or the cambium, in a putrid state between the bark and the wood, which frequently happens in elm-trees, and is incurable. The flux of the rising juices seldom does much injury, and may generally be prevented by pruning before the sap is in motion, or after the leaf is fully expanded.

The accidents to which plants are liable are chiefly confined to the plants being broken or bruised, and the general remedy is amputation of the parts. When the section of amputation is large, it is best to cover the wound with some adhesive composition, which will exclude the weather, and not impede the growth of the bark over the wound; but this subject will be noticed more in detail when we come to treat of pruning. Some plants likewise require strong stakes to prevent their branches or stems from being broken, or their roots from being blown out of the ground by the wind.

A number of other plant diseases have been described and named by writers on Botany, but they are of very little interest to the practical gardener, because they rarely occur when plants are properly treated, or occur only in old age, or in a state of natural decay; or because, when they do occur, they seldom admit of any remedy. Those diseases to which some plants are more liable than others, will be mentioned when these plants are treated of; for example, the rot in the Hyacinth, the dropsy in Succulents, the blistering of the leaves in the Peach, the shanking of Grapes, fungi on the roots, etc., etc.

CHAPTER VI.

IMPLEMENTS OF HORTICULTURE.

WITH the progress of gardening a great many tools, instruments, utensils, machines, and other articles, have been invented and recommended: and some of these are without doubt considerable improvements on those previously in use; while, on the other hand, many would be rather impediments than otherwise in the hands of an expert workman. The truth is, that for all gardening in the open air, and without the use of pots for growing plants, or walls or espaliers for training trees, the only essential instrument is the spade. There is no mode of stirring the soil, whether by picks, forks, or hoes, which may not be performed with this implement. It may be used as a substitute for the dibber, or trowel, or perforator (in planting or inserting stakes); instead of the rake and the roller in smoothing a surface and rendering it fit for the reception of the smallest seeds; and after these are sown, the spade may be employed to sprinkle fine earth over them as a covering, in which way indeed that operation may be performed more perfectly than by "raking in." The only garden operation on the soil which cannot be performed with the spade, is that of freeing a dug surface from stones, roots, and other smaller obstructions, which are commonly "raked off;" but as the removal of small stones from the soil is of very doubtful utility, and as at all events these and other obstructions can be hand-picked, the rake cannot be considered an essential garden implement. The pruning-knife might in general be dispensed with in the training of young trees, by disbudding with the finger and thumb; but as the branches of grown-up trees frequently die or become diseased, and require cutting off, the pruning-knife may be considered the most essential implement next to the spade; and with these two implements the settler in a new country might cultivate ground already cleared so as to produce in abundance every vegetable which was found suitable to the climate and soil.

But though a garden of the simplest kind may be cultivated with no other implements than a spade and a knife, yet for a garden containing the improvements and refinements common to those of modern times, a considerable variety of implements is necessary or advantageous. Some of these are chiefly adapted for operating on the soil, and they may be designated as tools; others are used chiefly in pruning and training plants, and may be called instruments; some are for containing plants or other roots, or for conveying materials used in cultivation, and are properly utensils; while some are machines calculated to abridge the labour of effecting one or more of these different purposes, or reduce the cost of keeping ground in good order, such as the mowing machine.

General Observations on the Construction and Uses of the Implements used in Horticulture.

Implements may be considered with reference to the mechanical principles on which they act, the materials of which they are constructed, the saving of labour which they effect, their preservation and their repairs.

All tools and instruments, considered with reference to the mechanical principles on which they act, may be reduced to the lever and the wedge; the latter serving as the penetrating, separating, or cutting, and sometimes the carrying part; and the former, as the medium through which, by motion, force is communicated to the latter. All the different kinds of spades, shovels, and forks have their wedges in the same plane as the levers; all the different kinds of picks, hoes, and rakes have their wedges fixed at right angles to the levers. The blades of knives and saws are no less wedges than the blades of spades or rakes, only their actions are somewhat more complex; every tooth of the saw acting as a wedge, and the sharp edge of a knife consisting of a series of teeth so small as not to be visible to the naked eye, but in reality separating a branch by being drawn across it, on exactly the same principle as the saw. The series of combinations which constitute machines, when analysed, may be reduced to levers, fulcrums, and inclined planes; and utensils depend partly on mechanical construction, and partly on chemical cohesion. It is only by understanding the principles on which an implement is constructed that that part can be discovered where it is most vulnerable when used, or most liable to decay from age. In all tools and instruments the vulnerable point is the fulcrum of the lever, or the point where the handle is connected with the blade or head. Another reason why failure generally takes place in that part is, that the handle is there generally pierced with a nail or rivet, which necessarily weakens the wood by breaking off or separating a number of the fibres. In general, the power or efficiency of any tool or instrument, supposing it to be properly constructed, is as its weight taken in connexion with the motion which is given to it by the operator. Hence strongly-made implements of every kind are to be preferred to light ones, rotatory motion to any other kind; and this preference will be found to be given by all good workmen.

In the construction of implements, the levers or handles are for the most part made of wood, and the wedges or operating parts of iron or steel. The wood in most general use for handles in Britain is ash; and next to the ash, oak: but for lighter tools, such as the hoe, rake, the scraper, besom, &c., pine or fir deal is sufficient. Handles to implements are of four kinds: first, cylindrical and smooth from one extremity to the other, as in the hoe, rake, &c.; second, cylindrical, or nearly so, but dilated at one or at both extremities, as in the pick, hatchet, &c., such handles being called helves; third, cylindrical and smooth, but with a grasping piece at one end, as in the spade, shovel, &c.; and fourth, angular or rough throughout, as in the pruning-knife, hammer, hedgebill, &c. The reasons for these forms of handles are to be found in the manner of using the implements: one hand of the operator is run rapidly along cylindrical handles, as in the hoe and rake; in the dilated handles, one hand slides along between two extremities till it reaches the dilated part of the head, which wedges firmly into the hand; and, this dilated part being in the direction of the operating part of the tool, adds considerably to its strength. This is the case in the pick, and in the hatchet, in which implements, without the dilatations at both extremities of the handle, as well as in some degree in the middle part, it would be difficult for the operator to bring down an oblique blow with sufficient accuracy. Without the cross-piece or perforated handle of the spade, the operator could not easily lift a spitful or turn it over; and hence we find, that in using the Flemish and other Continental spades, that have no grasping piece at one end, the operator never attempts to turn over the spitful, but merely throws it from him in such a manner that the surface falls towards the bottom of the furrow. No pruning-knife or hedgebill could be grasped firmly in the hand if it were cylindrical; and unless these instruments are held firmly, it is impossible to cut obliquely with sufficient precision. The iron of all instruments should be of the best quality, and the cutting edges of blades, and sharp perforating points, should be of steel for greater hardness and durability.

Next to the importance of having implements properly constructed, is that of keeping them constantly in good repair. For this purpose the iron or steel parts require to be occasionally sharpened on a grindstone or by other means, or to have additions of iron or steel welded to them by the blacksmith or cutler. All implements, when not in use, should be kept under cover in an open airy shed or tool-house; some, as the spade, pick, &c., may rest on the ground; others, as the scythe, rake, &c., should be suspended on hooks or pins; and smaller articles, such as trowels, dibbers, &c., placed in a holster rail. This is a rail or narrow board fixed to the wall in a horizontal direction, an inch or two apart from it at the lower edge, and somewhat farther apart at the upper edge. Other small articles may be laid on shelves, and pruning-knives kept in drawers. No implement ought to be placed in the tool-house without being previously thoroughly cleaned; and all sharp-edged implements, such as the mowing-machine, scythe, hedgebill, &c., when laid by and not to be used for some time, should have the blades or knives coated over with grease or bees-wax, and powdered over with lime or chalk to prevent the grease being eaten off by mice, as well as by combining with it to render it more tenacious, of a firmer consistence, and less easily rubbed off. In coating the blades of a mowing-machine, scythe, or hedgebill, or the plate of a saw, with wax or grease, it should be first gently heated by holding it before a fire; and afterwards the wax or grease should be rubbed equally over every part of it, and the powdered chalk or lime dusted on before the grease cools. When the instruments are again to be brought into use, the blades should be held before the fire, and afterwards wiped clean with a dry cloth. The same operation of greasing should also be applied to watering-pots laid by for the winter, when these have not been kept thoroughly painted. Every implement ought to have its proper place in the tool-house, to which it should be returned every day when work is left off. In well-ordered establishments fines are agreed on between the master and his men, to be imposed on all who do not return the tools to their proper places in due time, and properly cleaned.

Tools used in Horticulture.

By tools are to be understood implements for performing the commoner manual operations of horticulture, and they may be included under levers, picks, hoes, spades, forks, rakes, and a few others of less consequence.

The common lever, fig. 12, is a straight bar of wood shod with iron, or of iron only, and is used for the removal of stones or large roots, which rest on, or are embedded in the soil. The advantage gained is as the distance from the power applied at *a*, to the fulcrum *b*; and the force of the power is greatest when it is applied at right angles to the direction of the lever. The handspoke, or carrying lever, belongs to this species of tool, and is simply a pole,

Fig. 12.

The common lever.

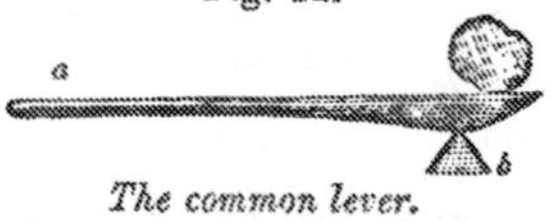

tapering from the two extremities to the middle, by means of one or two of which, tubs or boxes, or other objects, furnished with bearing hooks, can be removed from one place to another. Two of these poles, joined in the middle by cross-bars or boards, form what is called the hand-barrow—a carrying implement generally useful in gardening. Sometimes, to render a detached fulcrum unnecessary, the operating end of the lever is bent up, so that the elbow or angle, fig. 13, *c*, serves as a fulcrum. When the operating end terminates in claws, like those of a common hammer, it is termed a crowbar, *d*, and is extremely useful for forcing up stakes or props which have been firmly fixed in the ground. Sometimes the upper extremity of the bent lever and crowbar are made pointed and sharp, so as to serve at the same time as perforators, as shown in both the kneed lever and crowbar. Every garden ought to have one of these tools; and perhaps the most generally useful is the kneed lever, forked at the extremity, fig. 13, *c*.

Fig. 13.

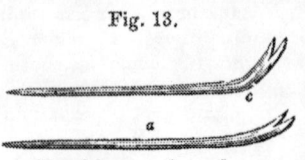

Kneed lever and crowbar.

Perforators, fig. 14, are straight rods of iron, or of wood pointed with iron, for making holes in the ground, in which to insert stakes for supporting tall or climbing herbaceous plants, standard roses, climbing roses, or other shrubs, and young trees. The pointed iron rod, with a solid ball at top, *e*, *i*, is most in use for inserting peasticks, and the smaller props in dug gardens, as well as for inserting branches in lawns to shelter tender shrubs in the winter time, or to prevent small plants from being trodden upon. The wooden stake, pointed with iron, *f*, is used for making holes for larger posts for protecting or supporting trees in parks and pleasure-grounds. It is driven in with a wooden mallet, and afterwards pulled out by passing an iron bar through the ring at *g*, one man taking hold of each end of the bar. The other bars are inserted by alternately lifting them up and letting them drop down, and they are pulled up either by hand or, in the case of fig. 14, *h*, by passing a stick or handle through the eye at the top. The solid ball *i* is for the purpose of adding to the weight of the rod, and which, of course, when lifted to a considerable height, adds greatly to its power in falling. The perforator, fig. 15, having a handle, *i*, and a hilt for the foot, *k*, is chiefly adapted for amateurs and ladies.

Fig. 14.

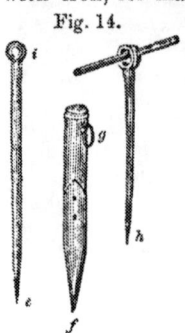

Perforators.

Fig. 15.

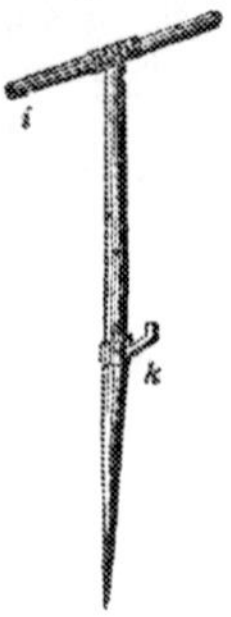

Perforator for amateurs.

The dibber, fig. 16, is a perforator for inserting plants, and sometimes also for depositing seeds or tubers in the soil. It is most suitable for planting seedlings, because these have a tap root, and few lateral fibres. Dibbers are very commonly formed of the upper part of the handle of a spade, as *l*, after the lower part has been broken, become decayed, or is no longer fit for use. This is sometimes shod with iron, which renders it more durable when it is to be used in stiff or gravelly soils. Sometimes a piece of a kneed branch is formed into a dibber, as shown at *m*. For planting cuttings of the shoots of shrubs or herbaceous plants, either in the open ground or under glass, small dibbers, *n*, are used, some

Fig. 16.

Dibbers.

TOOLS USED IN HORTICULTURE.

for inserting cuttings of heaths, not thicker than a quill; but these the gardener forms for himself. The potato-dibber, fig. 17, has a hilt for the foot, and a handle and shank as long as that of the spade. For the potato and other larger dibbers, cast-iron sheaths, fig. 18, are sometimes fitted to the lower extremities, to render them more durable.

Fig. 18.

Cast-iron sheaths for dibbers.

Fig. 17.

Potato-dibber.

Picks, fig. 19, combine the operation of perforating with that of separating, breaking, loosening, and turning over; and the pickaxe adds that of cutting. As the blow given by the pick on the soil, or on a root, is almost always given in a vertical direction, the helve is made cylindrical, excepting where it joins the head, and here it is dilated, so as to wedge into the hand of the operator, and serve to guide the direction of the stroke. The common pick is shown at *a*, the pickaxe at *b*, and the mattock at *c*. The narrow pointed end of the common pick is used for penetrating into the hardest soils; and the broad or chisel end for separating and turning over softer soils. The pickaxe *b* is for separating and turning over soft soils containing numerous roots of trees; those roots lying in a direction at right angles to the operator, being cut off with the chisel

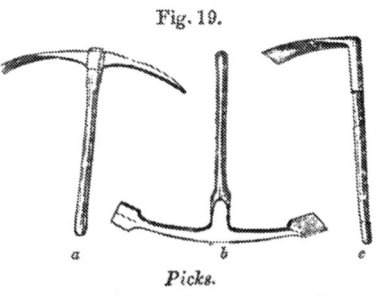

Fig. 19.

Picks.

at one end of the prongs, and those roots lying in the opposite direction by the chisel at the opposite end. The pick *c*, frequently called a mattock, and a grubber, or grubbing-axe, is principally used for grubbing up small trees or bushes. The pick *a* is essential to the toolhouse of the commonest garden, being frequently required for loosening gravel-walks, where repairs or alterations are to be made, or more gravel to be added.

The common draw-hoe, and its varieties, shown in figs. 20 and 21, are merely picks of a lighter kind, with the prongs dilated into blades. They are used for penetrating, moving, and drawing the soil, for the purpose of disrooting weeds, forming furrows in which to sow seeds, or drawing the earth up to plants. For light, easily-worked soils, the blade may be broad and narrow in depth; for stronger soils, it should be less broad, and the iron should be thicker; and for thin-

Fig. 20.

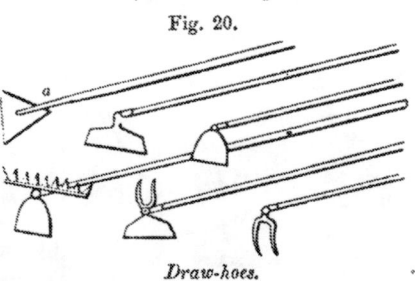

Draw-hoes.

ning seedlings, such as onions, lettuce, or turnips, the blade need not be more than two inches broad. The triangular hoe, fig. 20, *a*, is useful in light soils, and for separating, by its acute angles, weeds which grow close to the plants, to be left, and also for thinning out seedlings; but for loosening the soil among seedling-trees, or other plants growing close together on strong soil, the pointed or Spanish hoe or pick, fig. 21, deserves the preference. One of these tools has a short handle, and is used for stirring the soil in narrow intervals among the plants sown broadcast in beds; the other is worked with a long handle, like a common draw-hoe; and it has a cross-piece on the neck of the blade, which serves as a guide to the operator in directing the blade perpendicularly downwards, instead of to one side, when it might materially injure tap roots. In France and other parts of the Continent, there is almost an endless variety of hoes and hoe-picks, a number of which will be found figured and described in the 'Gard. Mag.,' and in the 'Encyc. of Gard.,' 3rd ed., 1832. Sometimes a draw-hoe and a rake, or a draw-hoe and a hoe-pick, are fixed back to back, as shown in fig. 20; but these instruments are not much used. The common draw-hoe, also shown in fig. 20, will suffice for most garden purposes.

Fig. 21.

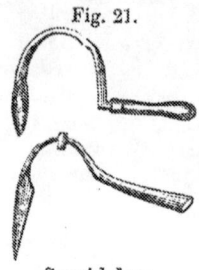

Spanish hoes.

Scrapers, fig. 22, are narrow pieces of board, or of sheet-iron, fixed to a long handle in the same manner as a draw-hoe, and used to scrape the worm-casts from lawns or walks. Where worms are kept under by the use of lime-water, or ammoniacal liquors, these tools are scarcely necessary.

Fig. 22.

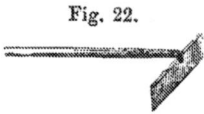

Lawn-scraper.

Thrust or Dutch hoes, fig. 23, may be considered as intermediate between the draw-hoe and the spade. The common form is shown at *a*, and a modification of it at *e*; but *b*, the blade of which is of steel, and sharp on every side, so as to cut either backwards or forwards, or on either side, is a more efficient implement; though in the hands of a careless operator it is liable to wound the plants, among which it is used for loosening the soil, or cutting up the weeds. Booker's hoe, *c*, is a very powerful implement, but liable to the same objection; as is Knight's hoe, *d*. Thrust-hoes are best adapted for light soils, and for cutting over annual weeds; they are also most suitable for hoeing between plants in rows, where the branches reach across the intervals; because no vertical stroke being ever given by

Fig. 23.

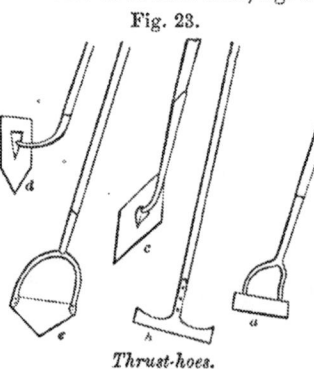

Thrust-hoes.

the thrust-hoe, as with the draw-hoe, the branches are less likely to be injured. The hoes *a* and *e* are, perhaps, the strongest and safest for general use.

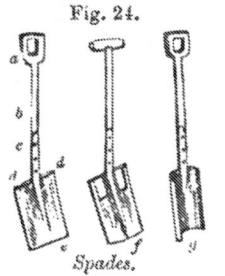

The spade in general use, fig. 24, consists of the grasping-piece or handle, or upper extremity, *a* ; the shaft, which joins the handle to the blade, *b*; the hose, or part of the blade into which the handle is inserted, *c;* the hilts, which are two pieces of iron which crown the upper edge of the blade for the purpose of receiving the foot of the operator, *d, d ;* and the blade *e*. As the hilt or tread projects over the blade, however useful it may be in saving the soles of the shoes of the operator, it is found in many soils to impede the operation of digging, by preventing the blade from freeing itself from the soil which adheres to it. Hence, in some parts of the country, instead of a hilt being put on the spade to save the shoes of the operator, a plate of iron about two inches broad, with leather straps, called a tread, is tied to his shoe, and effects the same purpose, while the spade requires much less cleaning. The spade *e* is for free easily worked soil, and is that most frequently used in gardens ; *f*, having the lower edge of the blade curved, enters more easily into stiff soil, while the upper part of the blade on each side of the hose being perforated, no soil can adhere there, and therefore spades of this form clean themselves, and in working are always quite free from soil. The spade *g* has a semi-cylindrical blade, and is without hilts ; it is chiefly used in executing new works, such as canals, drains, ponds, &c., in strong clayey soil. In consequence of the cylindrical form of the blade, and the lower extremity of it being applied to the soil obliquely, it enters the ground as easily as the blade of the spade *f*, while the spade separates the edges of the slice of earth from the firm soil ; and, after it is lifted up, serves as a guide in throwing it to a distance. There is a variety of this spade in which the blade, instead of being semi-cylindrical, is a segment of a cylinder, and rather broader at the bottom or cutting-edge than at the tread. This breadth at the entering edge diminishes friction on the sides of the upper part of the blade, by preventing them from pressing hard against the earth while passing through ; in the same manner as the oblique setting of the teeth of a saw prevents friction on the sides of the blade. This spade also, from the greater breadth of the lower part of its blade, lifts more completely the loose soil at the bottom of the furrow. It is chiefly used in engineering works, and in digging or trenching stiff soil. The handles of spades are almost always formed of sound root-cut ash, and their blades of good iron pointed with steel. Spades, however, made wholly of steel, are the best, and, in the end, the cheapest. The blade is not set exactly in the same plane as the handle, but at a small angle to it, in consequence of which, when the blade is inserted in the soil, the elbow formed between the blade and the handle serves as a fulcrum ; and the handle being thus applied to the lever at a larger angle, has considerably more power in raising up the spitful. In all spades designed for transplanting or other heavy works, the iron sheath should reach more than halfway up the handle, to give greater strength. Were the blade fixed to the handle in the same plane, and the blade inserted in the soil perpendicularly, the first exertion of the operator would be employed in gaining that angle, which, in the former, is produced for him by the manner in which the handle is joined to the blade. In the Flemish and other Continental spades, the blade is always fixed on in the same plane as the handle; but in these cases the blade is longer than it is with us, and it is always entered at a considerable bevel; and besides, the soil is generally lighter than in Britain, and requires less exertion to penetrate and separate it.

In ground works and for the removal of manure or light soil, shovels that may be described as lighter, wider spades, are most useful, and are used as substitutes for spades.

Turf-spades, fig. 25, are used for the purpose of paring very thin layers of turf from old pastures, for forming or repairing lawns or pleasure-grounds, laying grass-edgings, collecting turf for forming composts for plants, and for other purposes. One form, *h*, frequently called a breast-plough, from the handle being pressed on by the breast, has the edge of the blade turned up so as to separate the strip of turf to be raised from the firm turf: another form, *i*, is used after the turf has been cut or lined off into ribbons or bands, by the tool called a **turf-racer**.

Fig. 25.

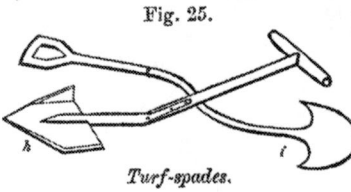

Turf-spades.

Turf-racers, or verge-cutters, fig. 26, are tools used either for cutting grassy surfaces into narrow strips to be afterwards raised up by the turf spade, or for trimming the grass edgings or verges of walks. The common verge-cutter, *k*, has a sharp reniform, or crescent-shaped blade; and the wheel verge-cutter, *l*, is a thin circular plate of steel, with a sharp-edged circumference, fixed to a handle by an axle, and operating by being pushed along before the workman. It is well adapted for cutting off the spreading shoots or leaves of grass edgings which extend over the gravel, without paring away any part of the soil. As the edges of these tools are very easily blunted, they require to be made of steel, and frequently sharpened.

Fig. 26.

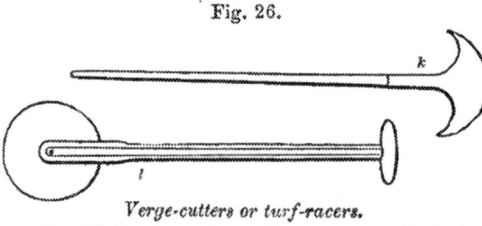

Verge-cutters or turf-racers.

*M'Intosh's wheel verge-cutter, fig. 27, is designed for cutting grass-verges on the sides of walks. With this instrument a man may cut as much in one day as he would cut in four or five days with the common verge-cutter without wheels. Bell's verge-cutter, instead of a wheel,

TOOLS USED IN HORTICULTURE.

has a broad bent plate of iron, through the middle of which the cutting coulters are inserted, and fixed and adjusted by screws. It is described and figured in 'Gard. Mag.,' vol. xiv. p. 177. In cutting turfs from a piece of grass land, the line is first stretched in order that the cutting may be performed in a perfectly straight direction. This is also the case in cutting the verges of straight walks, but in cutting those of curved walks the eye alone serves as a guide. In gardens and pleasure-grounds of moderate extent the common verge-cutter is the most useful, and it is also the most generally used in large establishments.

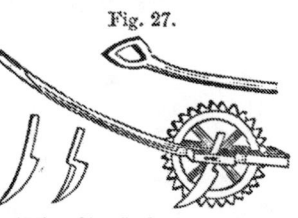

Fig. 27.

M'Intosh's wheel verge-cutter.

The trowel and the spud, the latter of which is also used as a spade-cleaner, belong to this group of tools. Though the spud, fig. 28, can hardly be considered as a fit tool for a professional gardener, yet with a suitable handle, it forms a most convenient walking-stick for the amateur gardener; because by it he may root out a weed, or thin out a plant, wherever he sees it necessary. The transplanting trowel, fig. 29, *a*, is a very useful tool wherever careful and neat gardening is practised; because by two of these, one in each hand, growing plants can be taken up with balls, put temporarily into pots, and carried from the reserve ground to the flower beds and borders, where they can be turned out into the free soil, without sustaining any injury. The trowel, *b*, is used for taking up plants and as a substitute for the hand to lift soil in potting plants. The best of all trowels for planting bedding or any other small plants, is not the concave garden trowel, but a rather small and flat steel trowel. The best I have had are those marked with a Crown and W. H. Much more work can be done in a given time than with the concave garden trowel, and with much greater pleasure and ease to the operator. A trowel with a flat blade and a forked point is sometimes used for raising up weeds from gravel or grass, and is called a weeding-trowel. The weeding-hook, which is a narrow strap of iron forked at the lower extremity, with a wooden handle at the other, is also used for raising weeds. There is a variety of this, with a fulcrum, for rooting daisies and other broad-leaved weeds out of lawns, fig. 30. The use of the fulcrum is to admit of a long handle which renders it unnecessary for the operator to stoop. Some of these tools have short handles, to adapt them for infirm persons and children.

Fig. 28.

Garden-spud.

Fig. 29.

a   b
Trowels.

Fig. 30.

Daisy-weeder.

Transplanters, figs. 31 and 32 (see also " Machines used in Horticulture").—These tools are used as substitutes for the transplanting trowel. In Saul's implement, fig. 31, the blades are opened by pressure on the lever, *a*; and in the spade trans-

88   TOOLS USED IN HORTICULTURE.

Fig. 31.

Saul's transplanter.

Fig. 32.

Transplanting spade.

Fig. 33.

Dung and tan forks.

Fig. 34.

Digging-fork.

planter, fig. 32, the blades are pressed together by moving the sliding-piece, *b*, downwards; and when the plant is carried to its place of destination, they are opened by moving it upwards. Both these transplanters are more adapted for amateurs than for professional gardeners, and the manner in which they are to be used is sufficiently obvious from the figures. Transplanters of this kind are generally supposed to be of French origin, but we are informed that the instrument of which fig. 31 is an improvement was an invention of the Rev. Mr. Thornhill, vicar of Staindrop, in the county of Durham, about 1820, who used it extensively on his farm for transplanting turnips.

The forks used in gardening are of two kinds; broad-pronged forks, for stirring the soil among growing plants, and as a substitute for the spade in all cases where that implement would be liable to cut or injure roots; and round-pronged forks, fig. 33, for working with littery dung, *a*, or for turning over tan, *b*. There are hand-forks of both kinds for working in glass frames, hotbeds, or pits. The digging-fork is almost as essential to every garden as the spade; and, wherever there are hotbeds, dung linings, or tan, the dung-fork with three prongs, fig. 33, *a*, and the tan-fork with five prongs, *b*, cannot be dispensed with. The three-pronged digging-fork is used for shallow digging, or pointing fruit-tree borders, and also for taking up potatoes. Parks's steel digging and manure forks are a great improvement on the old kinds, and one of the best aids to culture. After using them nobody would think of using the old forks. The American four-tined digging-fork, fig. 34, is perhaps the best known, and far superior to the kinds here figured.

Rakes, figs. 35 and 36, are used for freeing the surface soil from stones and other obstacles, for raking off weeds, or mown grass, or fallen leaves, and for covering in seeds. The common garden rakes, used for raking soil and gravel, differ chiefly in size. See fig. 36. The daisy-rake, fig. 35, *a*, has broad teeth, lancet-pointed, sharp at the edges, and set close together; and it is used for tearing off the heads or flowers of daisies, plantains, dandelions, and other broad-leaved plants, which appear in grass lawns, in the early part of the season; and thus it renders the necessity of mowing less frequent. The short grass-rake, fig. 35, *b*, is formed of a thin piece of sheet-iron, cut along the edge so as to form a sort of comb, and riveted between two strips of wood, as shown in the figure. It serves for raking off cut grass, and also, to a certain extent, as a daisy-rake.

Fig. 35.

Fig. 36.

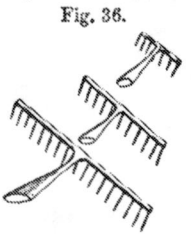

Besoms are used in horticulture for sweeping up mown grass, fallen leaves, and for a variety of purposes. The head or sweeping part is formed of a bundle of the spray of birch, broom, or heath, and lately the suckers of the snowberry, fibres of the cocoa-nut, strips of gutta-percha, &c., have come into use for this purpose. The handle is formed of any light wood, such as willow, poplar, or deal. A number of besoms are essential to every garden, though the general use of mowing machines has reduced their number and importance. For lifting matters collected together by the broom or grass-rake, two pieces of board are used by the operator, one in each hand, by which the smallest heap of leaves or grass can be quickly and neatly lifted up, and dropped into a basket or wheelbarrow. The pieces of board may be about 18 in. long, from 6 in. to 9 in. broad, and $\frac{3}{4}$ in. thick.

Daisy and grass rakes.

Garden-rakes.

Beetles and rammers, fig. 37, are useful tools even in small gardens, for beating down newly-laid turf-edgings; for ramming and consolidating the soil about posts and foundations, and for a variety of other purposes. For example, where part of a gravel-walk is taken up and relaid, unless the newly-moved soil and gravel are consolidated, or rammed down, to the same degree as the old part, there will be a depression in that part of the walk, which will increase after the sinking in of rain, and thus require continual additions. In fig. 37, *a* is the common turf beater or beetle, the head or beating part of which is commonly made of a block of wood, though it would be better if it were a plate of cast iron, because that would be heavier; *b* is the common wooden beater, which is also used as a rammer, the whole of which is formed of wood; *c* and *d* are two rammers, in which the heads are formed of cast iron, and which are very superior tools, invented by Anthony Strutt, Esq. To retain the handle in the socket, a slit is made in the handle, and a small wedge entered in it, and afterwards it is driven home till it assumes the appearance shown in the section at *e*. The great art in consolidating turf or

Fig. 37.

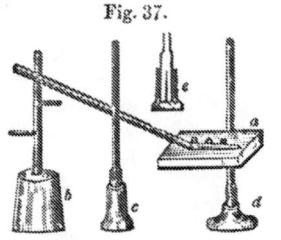

Beetles and rammers.

gravel with the beetle or rammer, is to bring down the tool in such a manner that the face of the head may be perfectly parallel to the surface to be acted upon. When the operator does not succeed in this, he will be warned of it by the jar which the tool will transmit through his hands.

The mallet, fig. 38, *a*, is formed of a piece of any tough wood, such as elm, or oak, or beech, and in any case it might have a ring at each end to prevent its splitting. It is used for driving posts, and there is a smaller or hand-mallet for using with the pruning chisel, and as a substitute for a hammer in driving in short stakes. In using a mallet, as in using the beetles, the centre of the striking part of the head should always be brought down on the centre of the stake or other object to be struck; otherwise the full power of the tool will not be obtained, and a jar on the hands of the operator will be produced.

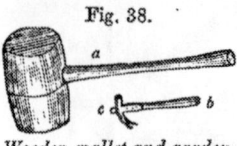

Fig. 38.

Wooden mallet and garden-hammer.

The garden-hammer, fig. 38, *b*, is used for nailing wall-trees, and for a great variety of purposes, and it differs from the common carpenter's hammer in having a projecting knob, *c*, in the head, to serve as a fulcrum in drawing out nails from walls, without injuring the young shoots. Since the wiring of walls or the covering them with wide-meshed netting for the training of wall-trees, the hammer is of less consequence; still it is an indispensable requisite in the garden. Considered by itself, the common hammer may seem an insignificant tool; but viewing it as including all the different kinds of hammers used in rendering metals malleable, and in joining constructions and machines of various kinds together, by means of nails and pins, it appears one of the most important of all implements. See Moseley's 'Illustrations of Mechanics,' p. 238.

Fig. 39.

Garden-pincers.

The garden-pincers, fig. 39, besides the pincing part, have a clawed handle for wrenching out nails, and are useful in gardens for this and a variety of other purposes. Some have a knob, which enables them to be used also as a hammer.

Instruments used in Horticulture.

Instruments are distinguished from tools by having sharp-cutting edges, and being adapted for operating on plants rather than on the soil; and they are also generally smaller than tools, and have for the most part handles adapted for grasping. Those used in horticulture are chiefly knives, bills, shears, and scythes.

Various kinds of knives are required in gardening operations: large long-handled knives for cutting and trimming vegetables, pruning, budding, and grafting-knives, and long curved ones, with teeth like a saw at the end, for cutting asparagus. Three kinds of knives are required in every garden—the cabbage-knife, a large rough-handled instrument, with a hooked blade, for cutting and trimming cabbages, cauliflowers, turnips, and other large succulent vegetables, when gathered for the kitchen; the pruning-knife, fig. 40, *a*, for cutting the branches and twigs off trees and shrubs, forming cuttings, &c.; the budding-knife, *b*, and the grafting-knife, *c*, used in performing the operations of budding and grafting, and also in making smaller cuttings. Where heaths and other small-leaved plants are propagated by cuttings of the points of the shoots, a common penknife is requisite, as well as a pair of small scissors for clipping off the leaves; but these instruments are so familiar to every one that it is unnecessary to describe them. Formerly garden-knives were distinguished from those in common use by having blades hooked at the points, for more conveniently hooking or tearing off shoots or leaves; but this mode of separating shoots or branches being found to crush that part of the shoot which was left on the living plant, and by that means render it liable to be injured by drought or by the absorption of water, a clean draw-cut has been resorted to as not liable to these objections; and this requires a blade with a straight edge like those of the pruning-knives now in general use. There are folding pruning-knifes combining in the same handle a saw, a chisel, a file, a screw-driver, &c., but these are for the most part more curious than useful. The asparagus-knife, fig. 41, has a blade about eighteen inches long, hooked and serrated, and is used for cutting the young shoots of asparagus when in a fit state for the table. It is thrust into the soil so as, when drawing it out, to cut the shoot from two to five inches under the surface, according to the looseness of the soil, and the taste of the consumer for asparagus more or less coloured at the points. Where green asparagus is preferred to what is thoroughly blanched, such a knife is hardly requisite, as the buds may be cut off at the surface with a common cabbage-knife. The asparagus-knife is less used now than formerly, as it was found to destroy many of the young shoots below the surface. A common knife or one shaped like a small chisel is a much safer, as well as a handier tool.

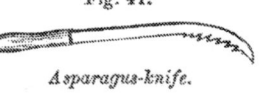

Ivory-handled budding-knives are now much used by gardeners for many kinds of light work as well as for budding. On the Continent, where the training of trees is so well understood, the use of the knife is not at all common with cultivators. It has been given up in favour of the sécateurs, described further on. Bill-knives or hedge-bills are large blades fixed to the ends of long handles for cutting off branches from young trees, and for cutting up the sides of hedges instead of shears. The advantage in using them in preference to shears is, that they have a clean smooth section instead of a rough one, which, as already observed, admits drought and moisture, and also stimulates the extremities of the branches to throw out numerous small shoots, and these, by thickening the surface of the hedge, exclude the air from the interior, in which, ultimately, the smaller shoots die, and the hedge becomes thin and naked. The most complete set of instruments of the bill kind is that used in Northumberland, and described by Blaikie in his 'Essay on Hedge-row Timber.' One of these instruments, fig. 42, ought to be in every

Fig. 42.

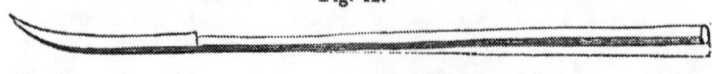

The scimitar bill-knife.

garden tool-house. The handle of this bill-knife, or scimitar, as it is called, is four feet in length, and the blade eighteen inches in length, the former deviating from the direction of the latter to the extent of six inches, as shown by the dotted line in the figure; this deviation is made in order to admit the free action of the operator's arm, while he is standing by the side of a hedge, and cutting it upwards. Fig. 43 is what is called a dress-bill, for cutting the sides of very small hedges, or such as are quite young.

Fig. 43.

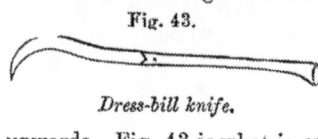

Dress-bill knife.

Pruning-saws are of different kinds, but they may be all reduced to draw-saws, fig. 44, *a*, and thrust or common saws, such as those in common use by carpenters. Draw-saws have the teeth formed so as to point to the operator, fig. 44, *b*, and only to cut when the blade is drawn towards him. Thrust-saws have the teeth or serratures formed at right angles to the edge of the blade, so as to cut chiefly when pushed or thrust from the operator, but partly also when drawn towards him. The draw-saw is always used with a long handle, and is very convenient for sawing off branches which are at a distance from the operator. In both these saws the line of the teeth is inclined about half the thickness of the blade to each side, as shown at *d*; the advantage of which is, that the blade passes readily through the branch without the friction which would otherwise be produced by the two sides of the section. Draw-saws being subjected to only a pulling-strain, do not require so thick a blade as thrust-saws; and, for that reason, they are also much less liable to have the blades broken or twisted, and are less expensive.

Fig. 44.

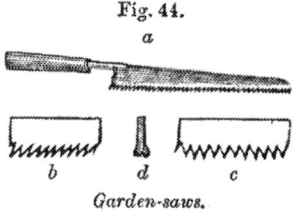

Garden-saws.

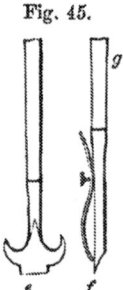

Fig. 45.

Pruning-chisels.

Pruning-chisels are chisels differing little in some cases, fig. 45, *e*, from those of the common carpenter, fixed to the end of a long handle, for the purpose of cutting off small branches from the stems of trees at a considerable height above the operator. The branch should not be larger than 1½ in. in diameter at the part to be amputated, otherwise it cannot be so readily struck off at one blow. In performing the

INSTRUMENTS USED IN HORTICULTURE.   93

operation two persons are requisite: one places the chisel in the proper position and holds it there, while the other, with a hand-mallet, gives the end of the handle a smart blow, sufficient to produce the separation of the branch. If properly performed, the section does not require any dressing; but sometimes there are lacerations of the bark, which require to be trimmed off with the hooked part, g, of the chisel, f.

The raidisseur is the ingenious " little wire-straining implement which plays such a very important part in the wiring of garden-walls, or erecting of trellises for fruit-growing in France. It is an implement which, though insignificant in itself, is calculated to make a vast improvement in our gardens and on our walls. It will save labour, time, and expense, and make walls and permanent trellises for fruit-growing infinitely more agreeable to the eye and useful to the cultivator than ever they were before.

"There are various forms, which I need hardly describe, as they are so well shown in the accompanying cuts. The first (fig. 46) is a reduced figure of one about three inches long, and of which I brought some specimens from Paris. The engraver has placed it in the best position to show its structure. The wire that passes in through one end is slipped through a hole in the axle; the other end is attached to the tongue, as shown in the engraving, and then by the aid of a key,

Fig. 46.

The raidisseur.

Fig. 47.

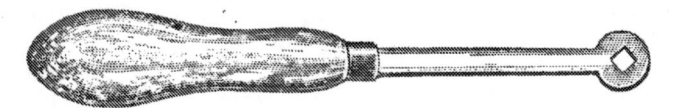

Key of raidisseur.

fig. 47, placed on the square end of the axle, the whole is wound much as a guitar-string is wound round its peg. The first form figured is very much used in the best gardens, and always seemed to me to do its work effectively.

"The next figure is that of the raidisseur invented by Collignon and recommended by Du Breuil. It does not differ much from the preceding. D shows the point of insertion of the wire that has to be tightened; B the fastening of the other end of the wire; and A the head on which the key is placed. Fig. 49 is a side view of the same

Fig. 48.

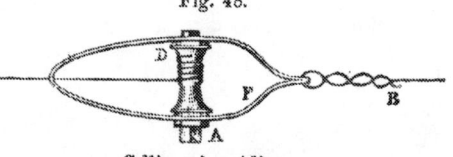

Collignon's raidisseur.

INSTRUMENTS USED IN HORTICULTURE.

implement. The foregoing kinds are galvanized, just like the wire. That shown by fig. 50 is a very simple one, not galvanized, which was much used in the fruit garden of the Paris Exhibition. This last form is so simple that it can be readily and cheaply produced in any of our manufacturing towns.

Fig. 49.

Side view of Collignon's raidisseur.

The best of these tighteners cost but a few pence; and if it were not so, it would still be profitable to employ them, in consequence of the great saving they effect, by enabling us to

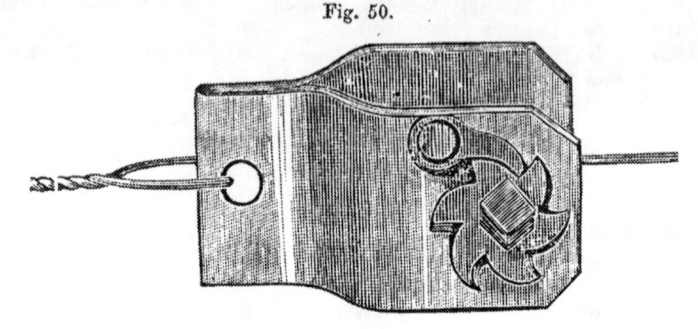

Fig. 50.

Raidisseur used in the garden of the Exhibition of 1867.

use a very thin wire, which is quite as efficient and infinitely neater than the ponderous ones now generally employed by us, wherever the nail and shred have given way to some costly system of wiring.

"Since writing the foregoing, I have found a much-improved and very simple raidisseur in use at Thomery. Fig. 51 represents its actual size. It is simply a little piece of cast-iron costing little more than a garden nail—so small that its presence on wall or trellis does not look awkward, as in the case of some of the larger kinds—and very effective. I never met with it except in the garden of M. Rose-Charmeux at Thomery. The walls there are very neatly wired by its help, and it is equally useful for espaliers. I have indeed never visited a garden in which the walls and trellises were so neatly done, and all by means of this simple strainer and the galvanized wire. Fig. 51 shows the wire strained tight, and is a little more than half the size I recommend. Messrs. J. B. Brown and Co., of 90, Cannon-street, have at my request cast a great number of these, and can supply them in any quantity and at a very low rate. They are made of malleable cast-iron, and are galvanized. The edges of the division in the head of this little implement being sharp, those of the specimen I brought from France were filed to prevent them cutting the wire in the straining; but any danger from this source is quite obviated by allowing the wire to be loose enough to permit of one coil being wound round the neck of the raidisseur before the real strain is applied. It is almost needless to add that the wire is simply placed in the groove in the head of the raidisseur, which is then turned, and finally tightened with a key like that for the other forms." ('The Parks, Promenades, and Gardens of Paris.')

Shears, in regard to their mode of cutting, are of two kinds: those which separate by a crushing cut, as in the common hedge-shears, fig. 52, the grass-shears, and verge-shears; and those which separate by a draw or saw cut, as in the pruning-shears, fig. 53. The common hedge-shears is used in gardens for topiary work, cutting hedges of privet, and other small-leaved, slender-twigged hedge-plants, which do not cut so readily with the hedge-bill; and it is more especially used for clipping box-edgings. The pruning-shears, fig. 53, have one blade, which, by means of a rivet, moves in a groove, by which means this blade is drawn across the branch in the manner of a saw, and produces a clean or draw-cut: that is, a cut which leaves the section on the tree as smooth as if it had been cut off by a knife. There are instruments of this kind of various sizes, from that of a pair of common scissors, for pruning roses or gooseberry bushes, to such as have blades as large as those of common hedge-shears, with handles four feet long, which will cut off branches from two to three inches in diameter. All of them may be economically used in gardens, on account of their great power and the rapidity and accuracy with which operations are performed by them. Fig. 53 shows two instruments commonly known as Wilkinson's shears, which are well adapted for pruning shrubs, and for the use of amateurs. Roses are better pruned by instruments of this kind than by knives, as unless the latter are kept very sharp, the softness of the wood and the large quantity of pith it contains, yield to the knife, and occasion too oblique a section, in consequence of which the shoot dies back much farther than if the section were made directly across.

The sécateur is a French instrument that every gardener should possess himself of. I know well the prejudice that exists in England among horticulturists against things of this kind, and their almost superstitious regard for a good knife. I also believed in the knife, but

Fig. 51.

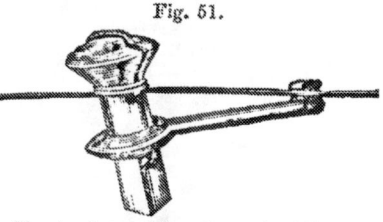

The simplest and best form of raidisseur.

Fig. 52.

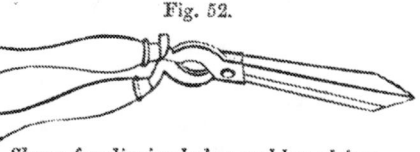

Shears for clipping hedges and box-edgings.

Fig. 53.

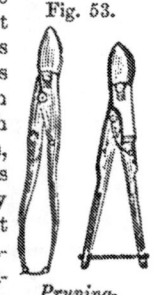

Pruning-shears.

when I saw how useful the sécateur is to the fruit-growers of France, and how easily and effectively they cut with it exactly as desired, I became at once converted. A sécateur is seen in the hands of every French fruit-grower, and by its means he cuts as clean as the best knife-man with the best knife ever whetted. They cut stakes with them almost as fast as one could count them; they have recently made some large ones for cutting stronger plants—such as the strong awkward roots of the briars collected by the rose-growers. Of these sécateurs there are many forms, two of the best being figured here.

First we have the sécateur Vauthier, a strong and handy instrument. Its sloping, semi-cylindrical handles have their outer side rough, which gives a firm hold; the springs, though strong, resist the action of the hand gently; the curvature of the blade and the adjustment are perfect; and lastly, the principal thing, the action is so easy as never to hurt the hand. "During the many years of my experience," observes M. Lachaume, a fruit-grower, who describes this implement in the 'Revue Horticole,' "I have used tools of all kinds, and the tools have also used me a little; but I have never met with anything which gave me so much satisfaction as the sécateur Vauthier. Every desirable quality is combined in it, and I recommend it with perfect confidence. The strongest branch will not resist its cutting, nor a single branch, however well concealed, be inaccessible to it. Moreover, the double notch on the back of the blade and hook will enable the operator when employed at his trellises to cut every wire without using the pincers."

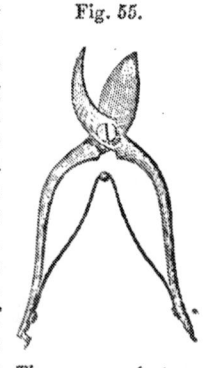

The sécateur Lecointe (fig. 54) is another variety recommended by the leading French horticultural journal. The inventor was led to devise this kind of spring in order to avoid the annoyance arising from the frequent breakage of the form usually employed. It is said that this form of spring secures an easy and gentle action of the instrument, and has the advantage of lasting longer than others, from not being so liable to break, while it secures a firmness and evenness in working which is not otherwise attained. A further improvement is pointed out in the fastening, which consists of a stop which catches when the two handles are drawn together, a projecting portion on the outside acting as a spring which is to be

Fig. 54.

The sécateur Lecointe.

Fig. 55.

The common sécateur.

pressed when the instrument is required to be opened. M. Lecointe of Laigle is the inventor.

Fig. 55 represents the sécateur of older date than the preceding, and one more generally used. It is much employed at Montreuil. There can be no doubt that where much pruning of any kind is done, and particularly pruning of a rather rough nature, the sécateur is a valuable implement. For pruning, in which great nicety of cutting is required, a good and properly-shaped knife is best. The sécateur was first invented by M. Bertrand of Molleville.

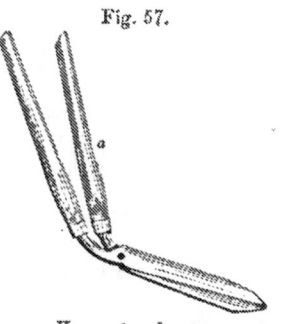

Fig. 56.

Garden-axe.

The axe, fig. 56, can scarcely be dispensed with in gardens, for the purpose of sharpening props or other sticks for peas, &c.; and a larger axe, as well as a common carpenter's saw, may be required where branches are to be broken up for fuel for the hothouse furnace, or other fires. The best axe is the American.

Verge-shears, fig. 57, are shears of the crushing kind used for clipping the edges of grass-verges, which they do without cutting the soil, as is commonly the case when any of the different descriptions of verge-cutters already described are used. The blades of these shears operate in a vertical plane, the handles being held edgewise.

Fig. 57.

Verge, &c. shears.

The short grass scythe, fig. 58, *c*, is now but little used in gardens; mowing-machines of all sorts and sizes have usurped its place, to the immense economy of labour and the better sweeping of the grass. Still as a scythe or two is indispensable in most gardens for cutting under trees, &c., the following instructions may be useful. The blade of the scythe cuts exactly on the same principle as that of the saw, and it requires to be frequently sharpened by a hand-stone or whetstone, as well as occasionally ground. The blade of the garden-scythe requires to be fixed to the handle in such a manner that when the handle is held by the operator standing upright, the plane of the blade shall be parallel to the plane of the ground. In the case of field-scythes, where the ground is rough, the plane of the blade may be very nearly in the same plane as that of the handle; by which means the inequalities of the ground's surface will chiefly be struck by the back of the blade, and never by its edge. The daisy-knife or daisy-scythe, fig. 58, *d*, is

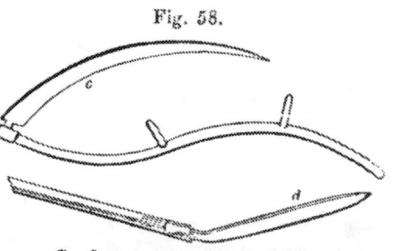

Fig. 58.

Garden-scythe and daisy-knife.

H

a two-edged blade, lancet-pointed, and is used for mowing off the heads of daisies, clover, and various other plants in lawns, which renders less frequent the necessity of mowing with the scythe. In using this instrument, the handle, which ought to be angular, is held firmly with both hands, and the blade, which ought to be at least four feet from the operator, is moved rapidly to the right and left parallel to the plane of the surface, the operator advancing as in mowing.

There are several other instruments which are only occasionally used, and chiefly by amateurs; such as the averruncator, which may be described as a cutting-shears fixed to the extremity of a long handle, and operated on by means of a cord and pulley. Its use is to enable a person standing on the ground to thin out branches in standard fruit trees, which it readily does, though frequently with a considerable loss of time. An amateur, however, who prunes his own orchard, will find this a useful instrument; though, if he has an attendant, the hooked pruning-chisel, fig. 45, *f*, is preferable. The grape-gatherer, or flower-gatherer, consists of a shears fixed at the extremity of a long handle, which clips and holds fast at the same time. It is occasionally useful for gathering flowers from the upper parts of stages in greenhouses, or from plants against walls, or on poles, that cannot be conveniently reached by hand; it is also used for gathering grapes which cannot be otherwise conveniently reached. There is also an instrument of this kind without a long handle, called a flower-gatherer, which clips off a flower and holds it at the same time, and is used by ladies in gathering roses. Scissors with long handles and sharp angular blades are required for thinning grapes. The fruit-gatherer is an amateur's instrument, of which there are several varieties; but they are very little used. Instruments for scraping the moss or bark off trees, gouges for hollowing out wounds in their trunks or branches, climbing-spurs, and some other instruments belonging to this section, and perhaps more fanciful than useful, will be found described in the 'Encyclopædia of Gardening,' edition of 1831.

Chests of tools and instruments for amateurs are made up by different ironmongers, and at prices varying with their contents. They are useful for ladies and amateurs, but are too delicate and small to be of much service to the practical gardener.

Utensils used in Horticulture.

Garden utensils are vessels for containing growing plants; for carrying different articles used in culture, such as soils, water, &c.; for preparing soil or other matters, such as the sieve; and for protecting plants. The principal are the plant-pot or box, the watering-pot, the basket, the sieve, and the bell-glass.

Earthenware pots for plants are made by the potter in what are called casts, each cast containing about the same quantity of clay, and costing about the same price, but differing in the size of the pots so

UTENSILS USED IN HORTICULTURE.

much, that while in the first size there are only two pots to a cast, in the tenth size there are sixty, as in the following table :—

					Inches diam.	Inches deep.
1st size has	2	to the *cast*, called	twos, being		18	12
2nd	4	,,	fours		12	10
3rd	6	,,	sixes		9	8
4th	8	,,	eights		8	7
5th	12	,,	twelves		7	6
6th	16	,,	sixteens		6	7
7th	24	,,	twenty-fours		5	6
8th	32	,,	thirty-twos		4	5
9th	48	,,	forty-eights		3	4
10th	60	,,	sixties		2	2½
11th	80	,,	thumbs or eighties		1½	2

These are the sizes of the London potters; but at Liverpool the sizes and the proportions are somewhat different. The sizes are from No. 1, which is 20 inches in height and diameter, to No. 37, which is 2 inches in height and diameter, as shown in fig. 59. About London the sizes of

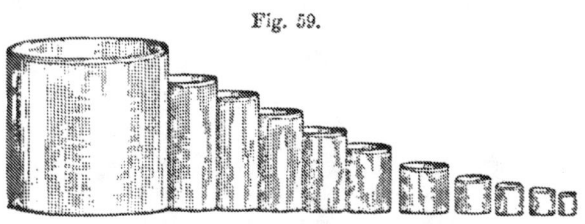

Fig. 59.

Relative Sizes of garden-pots at Liverpool.

pots in most general use are, twenty-fours, which are 5 inches in diameter and 6 inches deep; thirty-twos, which are 4 inches in diameter and 5 inches deep; and forty-eights, which are 3 inches in diameter and 4 inches deep.

So many complaints have been made about the uncertainty of size of the pots made by different makers, that an attempt was made by Dr. Lindley, in the 'Gardener's Chronicle' for 1845, p. 83, to remedy this evil. It was suggested by a correspondent that the term "cast" should be dropped, and the word "inch" substituted in its place. Every size to be henceforth named by the number of inches it measures across the top. This plan has now been generally adopted, and pots are ordered as 3, 6, 8, &c. inch pots, instead of sixties, forty-eights, thirty-twos, &c. The following table will make the matter plain, and will secure uniformity of size :—

UTENSILS USED IN HORTICULTURE.

Old Name.	Usual breadth in inches.	Usual depth in inches.	New Name.
Twos	18	14	18 in.
Fours	15	13	15 ,,
Sixes	13	12	13 ,,
Eights	12	11	12 ,,
Twelves	11½	10	11 ,,
Sixteens	9½	9	9 ,,
Twenty-fours	8½	8	8 ,,
Thirty-twos	6	6	6 ,,
Forty-eights	5	5	5 ,,
Sixties	3⅔	3½	3 ,,
Thumbs	2½	2½	Thumb.

When pots in which plants have been grown are to be laid aside for future use, they should be thoroughly cleaned within, because the smallest particles of earth adhering to the inner surface of the pot, when the pot is again filled with fresh soil, will, by the rough surface produced, cause that soil so to adhere to the sides of the pot, that the ball of earth, when the plant is to be shifted, cannot be turned out of the pot without being broken in pieces. The garden-pots in common use about London are generally made between a fifth or a sixth part

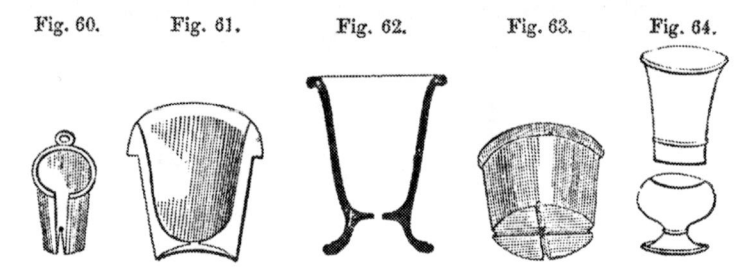

Fig. 60.   Fig. 61.   Fig. 62.   Fig. 63.   Fig. 64.

Fig. 60. *Propagating-pot.*
Fig. 61. *Pot with raised bottom, to prevent the entrance of worms.*
Fig. 62. *Pot with raised bottom, to prevent the entrance of worms.*
Fig. 63. *Pot with channelled bottom, to facilitate the escape of water.*
Fig. 64. *Ornamental pot, with the base serving as a receptacle for drainage water.*

narrower at bottom than at top; but for particular purposes, such as that of growing hyacinths, pots are made almost equally wide throughout, and deeper than usual in proportion to their width. For striking cuttings, or growing seeds, there are pots made broad and shallow, sometimes called pans or store-pots. There are also pots for aquatics, made without holes in the bottom to permit the escape of water; others for marsh plants, without holes in the bottoms, but with holes in the sides half way between the bottom and the top, so as to retain the lower half of the soil in a marshy state. There are pots made with a slit on one side (fig. 60), for the purpose of introducing the shoot of a plant to be ringed in order to cause it to produce roots—(a small wooden box is much better, as being less porous); others with a large hole in the side for the same purpose; some with concave bottoms, with the intention of putting the water-hole out of the reach of worms (figs. 61 and 62); others (fig. 63) with grooves in the bottom to prevent the retention of water by the attraction of cohesion, when the pot stands on a flat surface; and there are pots fixed within pots, so that the space within the outer and the inner pot shall be water-tight, in order to contain water or moist moss, so as to keep the soil in the inner pot in comparatively uniform moisture and temperature. There are pots made in two parts (fig. 64), the lower serving as an ornamental base—so as to give the pot a somewhat classical character—and at the same time as a receptacle for the water that drains through the pot. Pots are also made with rims pierced with holes, so as to construct on them a frame of wire-work for training climbers, as in fig. 65. There is also what is called a blanching-pot (fig. 66), which is placed over plants of sea-kale, rhubarb, &c., for blanching them, having a moveable top, which can be taken off at pleasure, to admit light or to gather the produce. Boxes of boards, however, are found more economical. There are also square-made pots, which, it is alleged, by filling up the angles left by round pots, allow of a greater quantity of room being obtained in a given space in beds or shelves under glass; and pots with one side flattened, and with a pierced ear or handle, to admit of hanging the pot against a wall or a trunk of a tree; and pots for orchids, for succulents, and hanging plants, made of all shapes and designs, and pierced with holes all over for the escape of the roots or shoots into the air. Many other fanciful pots might have been figured and described; but in the general practice of gardening all these peculiar pots may be dispensed with; and, in truth, with the exception of the last forms, they are only found in the gardens of some amateurs. It is useful, however, to know what has been done or attempted in this way, in order to prevent a waste of time in repeating similar contrivances.

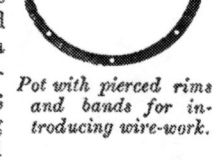

For ornamental purposes, pans of terra cotta, stone, marble, china, or iron are rapidly superseding common pots. And for common purposes, such as the storage of the thousands of plants required in the flower-garden, wooden boxes a foot wide, two feet long, and four inches deep, are largely used.

Fig. 65.

Fig. 66.

Blanching-pot.

Pot with pierced rims and bands for introducing wire-work.

From the porosity of the material of which common earthenware plant-pots are made, it is evident that when the soil within the pot is moist, and the pot placed in a warm dry atmosphere, the evaporation and transpiration through the sides must be considerable; and as evaporation always takes place at the expense of heat, this must tend greatly to cool the mass of soil and fibrous roots within. This may be prevented by glazing the exterior surface of the pot; but as this would add to the expense, and be chiefly useful in the case of plants in pots kept in rooms, it is seldom incurred. In many instances it has, likewise, been found that plants have not grown so well in glazed as in unglazed pots. To prevent evaporation in rooms the double pot is sometimes used, or single pots are surrounded by moss, or cased in woollen cloth or bark of trees: in plant-houses, the atmosphere is, or ought to be, so nearly saturated with moisture by other means, as to reduce the evaporation from the pots to a degree that cannot prove injurious. The advantage which earthenware pots have over boxes is, that they can be made round, by which means shifting is effected with much greater ease than it can be with any rectangular utensil.

Earthenware saucers for pots are made and sold on the some principle as pots—viz., in casts; a cast of saucers for sixties or thumbs costing as much as a cast for thirty-twos or sixes. Saucers are chiefly used in living rooms, or in other situations where the water which escapes from the hole in the bottom of the pot would prove injurious; and to prevent this water from oozing through the porous material of the saucer, it is sometimes glazed on the inside. There are also saucers, or flats, as they are called, made with raised platforms in the centre, for the pots containing the plants to stand in; in some cases, in order that they may stand dry and not be liable to be entered by earthworms; and in others, in order to surround them with water, and thus insulate them from the attacks of creeping insects, such as woodlice, ants, &c. Utensils of this kind are also used for supporting boards in the open garden, so as to isolate them, and of course the pots which stand on them, from wingless insects, snails, worms, &c. Fig. 67 shows one of these utensils, which might easily be substituted for a common saucer and inverted pot. An annular saucer, fig. 68, for containing water, is used either for protecting plants in pots or plants in the open ground; and if lime-water or salt-water is used, it will prove a very effectual protection from snails, slugs, wood-lice, ants, and other creeping wingless insects. A very ingenious substitute for this utensil has

Fig. 67.
Isolating-saucer.

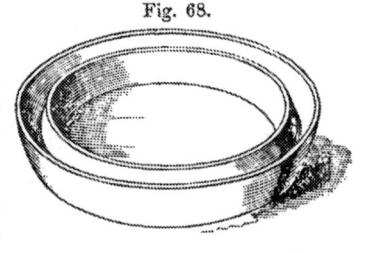

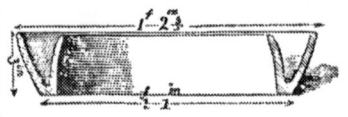

Fig. 68.
Annular water-saucer.

lately been invented by Mr. Walker, of Hull. It is founded on the galvanic principle of alternate plates of zinc and copper producing an electric shock, and is therefore called the Galvanic Protector. Take slips of zinc four or five inches in breadth, in order to enclose the plant or bed to be protected, as with a hoop; but in addition to the mere rim or frame of zinc, rivet to it, near the upper edge, a strip of sheet-copper one inch broad, turning down the zinc over this so as to form a rim, composed of zinc, copper, and zinc. The deterring effect is produced by the galvanic action of the two metals; and thus, when the snail or slug creeps up the rim of zinc, it receives a galvanic shock as soon as its horns or head touch the part where the copper is enclosed, causing it to recoil or turn back. A more beautiful application of science in the case of deterring insects is rarely to be met with, and it will not cost more than 6d. a linear foot. ('Gard. Chron.,' vol. i. pp. 115 and 165; and 'Gard. Mag.,' 1841.)

Rectangular boxes for growing plants are commonly formed of wood, but sometimes slate is substituted. Wood, however, as a better non-conductor both of heat and moisture, deserves the preference. A neat and most convenient plant-box was invented by Mr. M'Intosh, fig. 69, and used by him for growing orange-trees. It differs from the orange-boxes used in the gardens about Paris in having the sides tapered a little, and also in having all the sides moveable. Two of the sides are attached to the bottom of the box by hinges, and are kept in their places by iron bars hooked at each end, which slip into hasps fixed in the sides, as shown in the figure; the other sides, which are not hinged, lift out at leisure, being kept in their places at bottom by two iron studs, which drop into holes in the bottom. These boxes afford greater facilities than the French orange-boxes for the gardener to take them to pieces, without disturbing the trees, whenever he wishes to examine or prune their roots, to see whether they are in a proper state as regards moisture, or to remove the old, and put in fresh soil. The inside of these boxes can also be painted, or covered with pitch, as often as may be judged necessary; which will of course make them much more durable, and the trees may be removed from one box to another with greater facility.

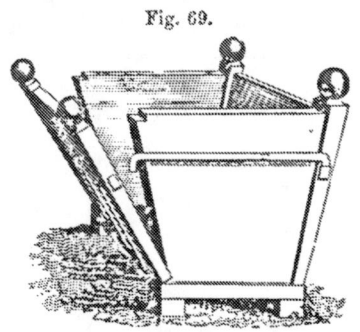

Fig. 69.

Plant-box.

Wooden tubs are very commonly made use of on the Continent to grow orange-trees, and they are made of different heights and diameters from one to two or three feet. When the roots of the trees are to be examined, or old soil to be removed and fresh soil added, the cooper is sent for, who separates the staves, and after the gardener has finished his operations, replaces them again and fixes the hoops. In the warm summers of France and Italy, it is found much better to grow plants in wooden boxes or tubs, than in any description of earthenware vessel. Round tubs, however, are neither so convenient nor so ornamental as the square plant-box.

Watering-pots are made of tinned iron, zinc, and sometimes of copper. There are a variety of sizes and shapes in use in British gardens: for plants under glass, which are placed at a distance from the operator, pots with long spouts are required; and for pots on shelves over the head of the operator and close under the glass, flat pots with spouts proceeding from the bottom, and in the same plane with it, are found necessary. Watering-pots have been contrived with close covers, containing valves to regulate the escape of the water through the spout, by the admission or exclusion of the atmosphere at pleasure; but these are only required for particular situations and circumstances, and are seldom or never used. The watering-pot very generally fails at the point where the spout joins the body of the pot, and the two parts ought therefore to be firmly attached together, either by separate tie-pieces, or by one continuous body, which may be so contrived as to hold the roses of the pot when not in use, as exemplified in Money's pot. The rose is generally moveable; but as, after much use, it becomes leaky, it is better, in many cases, to have it fixed, with a pierced grating in the inside of the pot over the orifice of the spout, as in metal tea-pots. This grating, Mr. Beaton suggested, should be moveable, by being made to slide into a groove like a sluice, in order that it may be taken out and cleaned occasionally. Fig. 70, *a*, represents a watering-pot with a kneed-spout, for watering plants, without spilling any water between pot and pot; because, by means of the knee or right angle made at the extremity of the spout, the running of the water is instantly stopped by quickly elevating it, which is by no means the case when the spout is straight throughout its whole length: *b* shows the face, and *c* the edge of a very fine rose of copper for screwing on the end of the kneed-spout, for watering seedlings. Fig. 70, *d*, shows a sucker watering-pot, by which the objects effected by the kneed-pot are attained more completely. There is a sucker or valve in the lid, by which the air is perfectly excluded; and when this valve is shut, not a particle of water can escape; but when it is slightly raised by the pressure of the thumb of the hand

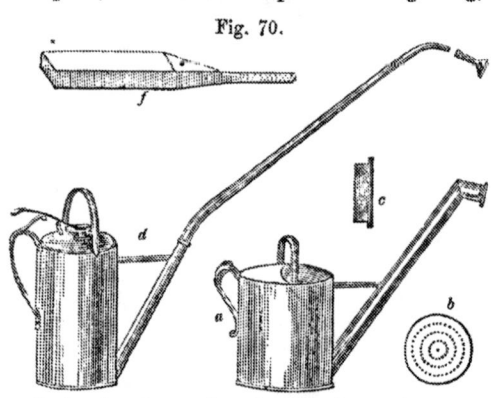

Fig. 70.

Sucker, kneed-spouted, and overhead watering-pots.

by which the operator holds the pot, the water instantly escapes, and can be stopped in a moment: *f*, an overhead watering-pot, for watering plants close under a glass roof, and above the head of the operator.

The best kinds of watering-pots for general use are those with tall and narrow bodies and large spouts, the roses having a great number of perforations. A very good type of watering-pot is that used by the market-gardeners of Paris. The pipe being very wide, and the rose broad and freely perforated with large holes, the water is discharged almost in an instant, and the workman again proceeds to his barrel close at hand, and always kept filled from the pump. Thorough watering is thus effected, but it involves a considerable expenditure for labour, one or two men being nearly always employed at it in each little garden during the summer months.

Fig. 71.

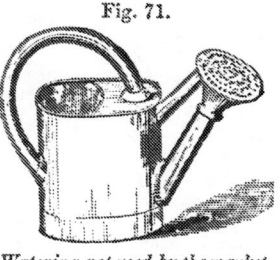

Watering-pot used by the market-gardeners of Paris.

In gardens where a force of water is at command, watering-pots are but little used. With a few lengths of gutta-percha tubing attached to the supply-pipe, a stream of water may be directed to each pot or plant with unerring certainty and great despatch. By the use of a rose on the end of the pipe, or a skilful employment of the finger, an overhead shower can likewise be given of the gentlest or heaviest character at will.

Sieves for sifting soil, and screens of wire for separating the larger stones and roots from soil to be used in potting, are required in most gardens, though much less used than formerly, as all soil is used much rougher for horticultural purposes. It has now become a common practice to screen or sift out the fine soil and use only the coarse. The screen, fig. 72, is not only used for mould, but also for gravel, and sometimes for tan. It consists of a wooden frame filled in with parallel wires half an inch apart, surrounded by a rim of three or four inches in breadth, and supported by hinged props, which admit of placing the screen at any required angle. The soil to be screened must be dry and well broken by the spade before it is thrown on the screen.

Fig. 72.

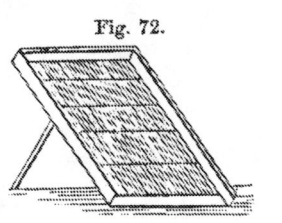

Wire-screen, for soil, old tan, or gravel.

For gravel two screens are sometimes required; one with the wires half an inch apart, to separate the sand and small gravel from the stones; and another with the wires one inch apart, to separate the larger stones from the smaller ones; those which pass through the screen being of the fittest size for approach-roads and carriage-drives; while the largest stones which do not pass through are adapted for common cart-roads. A barrel revolving-screen is likewise used for these purposes, as well as for separating cinders from ashes, &c. In small gardens sieves may be substituted for screens. The smallest may have the meshes a fourth of an inch in diameter, and the larger half an inch. The wire of the smaller sieves should always be of copper, but of the larger sieves and of screens it may be of iron.

Carrying utensils are sometimes wanted in gardens, though flower-pots, baskets, and wheelbarrows form very good substitutes. The mould-scuttle is a box of any convenient shape of wood or iron, with a hoop-formed handle, for carrying it; sometimes it is formed like the common coal-scuttle, but rectangular. The pot-carrier, fig. 73, is a flat board about eighteen inches wide and two feet long, with a hooped handle, by means of which, with one in each hand, a man may carry three or four dozen of small pots at once, which is very convenient in private gardens where there are many alpines in pots, and in nurseries where there are many seedlings or small cuttings.

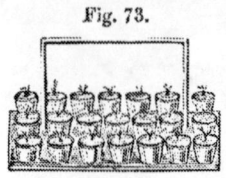

Fig. 73.

Pot-carrier.

But the hand-barrows carried by two men, or a wide frame mounted on wheels, are the carriers mostly used in large gardens. For light plants and short distances, sieves are likewise much used for carrying purposes. The spring-barrow should, where possible, be used instead of the hand-barrow for carrying plants.

Several different kinds of baskets are used in gardens. They are woven or worked of the young shoots of willow, hazel, or other plants, or of split deal or willow, or of twigs; but by far the greater number of baskets are made of the one year's shoots or wands of the common willow, Salix viminalis. They are for the most part used for carrying articles from one point to another, though some are employed as a substitute for a garden-wallet; others are used for growing plants; some for protecting plants from the sun or the weather, and others as utensils for measuring by bulk.

Details of basket-making will be found in the 'Arboretum Britannicum,' vol. iii. p. 1471, and the instructions will be sufficient to enable any person of ordinary ingenuity to construct every kind of wicker-work, whether baskets or hurdles, that can be required for a garden.

Carrying-baskets of different sizes are required in gardens for carrying plants for being transplanted, seeds, sets or roots for planting, vegetables or fruits from the garden to the kitchen, and for a variety of other purposes. A basket for hanging before the operator when pruning or nailing wall-trees, is sometimes made of wands, and occasionally of split wood; but a leathern wallet, to be hereafter described, is greatly preferable. Larger and coarser baskets than any of these are used for carrying soil, manures, tanner's bark, weeds, &c., and are commonly called scuttles, creels, &c.

Measuring-baskets are formed of particular dimensions, the largest seldom containing more than a bushel, and others half-bushels, pecks, and half-pecks. There are also pint baskets, punnets, pottles, and thumbs, which are utensils in use in the London fruit and vegetable markets for containing the more valuable vegetables, such as mushrooms, early potatoes, forced kidney-beans, and the more choice fruits. The bushel basket is generally made of peeled wands, but the others of split willow wood, or split deal. Fig. 74 represents a punnet manufactured in the latter manner, the construction of which will be understood by any person who understands the English mode of basket-making.

Fig. 74.

Punnet basket.

Baskets for growing plants were a long time in use in the open garden, being plunged in spring, and taken up in the following autumn; the object being to take up fruit-trees or other tender shrubs with a ball, and with most of the fibres. At present baskets for growing plants are chiefly used in orchid-houses, the basket being filled with moss; but as they are found to be of very short duration, wire baskets are substituted, earthenware pots with perforated sides, or a sort of open box formed of short rods laid over one another at the angles, somewhat in the manner of a log-house.

Portable glass utensils for plants are chiefly of two kinds: the bell-glass, fig. 75, and the hand-glass, fig. 76. Another kind of hand-glass is now in use in Messrs. Veitch's nursery, at Coombe Wood—one quite conical, and with a small piece of zinc forming one of its upper panes; in this there is a hole which enables the workmen to handle them conveniently. This answers its purpose perfectly. Bell-glasses vary in dimensions from the large green bell-glass, eighteen inches in diameter and twenty inches in height, used in the open garden for protecting cauliflowers in winter and cucumbers in summer, to the small crystal bell, three inches in diameter and two inches high, for covering newly-planted cuttings. Whenever the propagation of tender plants by cuttings, or by the greffe étouffé, is attempted, bell-glasses are essential. The French use large bell-glasses or cloches most extensively in the open ground. They are used by the thousand in most French gardens, and are capable of effecting great improvements in our kitchen gardens, while they are of much use indoors. The following description and figures are from the 'Parks, Promenades, and Gardens of Paris.'

Fig. 75.

Bell-glasses.

Fig. 76.

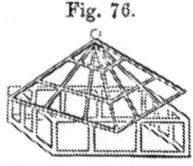

Cast-iron hand-glass in two parts, the roof and sides.

"The Cloche.—This is simply a large and cheap bell-glass, which is used in every French garden that I have seen. It is the cloche which enables the French market-gardeners to excel all others in the production of winter and spring salads. Acres of them may be seen round Paris, and private places have them in proportion to their extent—from the small garden of the amateur with a few dozen or score, to the large one where they require several hundreds or thousands of them. They are about sixteen inches high, and the same in diameter at the base, and cost in France about a franc apiece, or a penny or two less if bought in quantity.

"The advantages of the cloches are—they never require any repairs; they are easy of carriage when carefully packed; with ordinary care they are seldom broken; they are easily cleaned—a swill in a water-

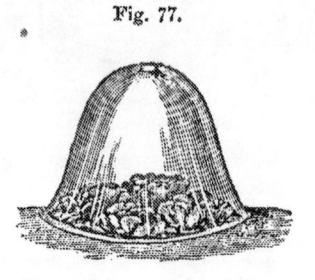

Fig. 77.

The cloche as used in winter-lettuce culture.

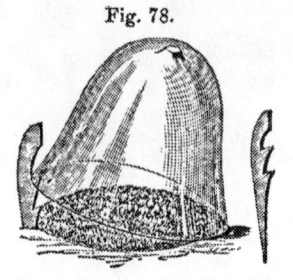

Fig. 78.

The cloche as used in the raising of seedling plants.

tank and a wipe with a brush every autumn clear and prepare them for their winter work. They are useful for many purposes besides salad-growing; for example, in advancing various crops in spring, raising seedlings, and striking cuttings; and finally, they are very cheap when bought in quantity. But of course it is only in market-gardens that they will be required in numbers; in some small gardens not more than a few dozen will be wanted. Every garden should be furnished with them according to its size; and when we get used to them and learn how very useful they are for many things, from the full developing of a Christmas Rose to the forwarding of early crops in spring, I have no doubt they will be much in demand. It is not only in winter that they are useful, but at all seasons, both in indoor and outdoor propagation and seed-sowing. In France seedlings of garden-crops likely to be destroyed by birds or insects are frequently raised under the cloche, and the same practice will occasionally be found advantageous in this country.

Fig. 79.

Cloche with knob.

"Usually the cloche is made without a knob, as that appendage renders their package a much greater difficulty and increases the cost, so that practical men use only the one without the knob, like the specimens first figured. One with a knob may, however, be had, but it is not to be recommended.

"In the Parisian propagating-houses may be seen small bell-glasses with openings at the top. It would be a great improvement if some cloches were made in like manner, and this particularly for propagation in tan-beds and hot-pits. The opening would afford very slight

UTENSILS USED IN HORTICULTURE. 109

though beneficial ventilation, and give a means of carrying or shifting the cloche with one hand only. I am informed that there will be no difficulty in making them thus without additional trouble or expense, as soon as the firm who will undertake their manufacture in England have full preparations made. When not in use the careful cultivator puts his cloches in some bye-place, in little piles of half a dozen in each, a piece of wood not more than half an inch thick and an inch and a half square being placed between each, so as to prevent them from settling down on each other. Workmen used to them carry two or three in each hand in conveying them from place to place, by putting a finger between each. In commencing to use them in our gardens it would be well to see that they are placed in some spot where they will not be in danger of breakage. The cloche must not be confounded with the dark and very large bell-glass that was in common use many years ago in our market-gardens, and which may yet be seen here and there. These were even dearer than the hand-

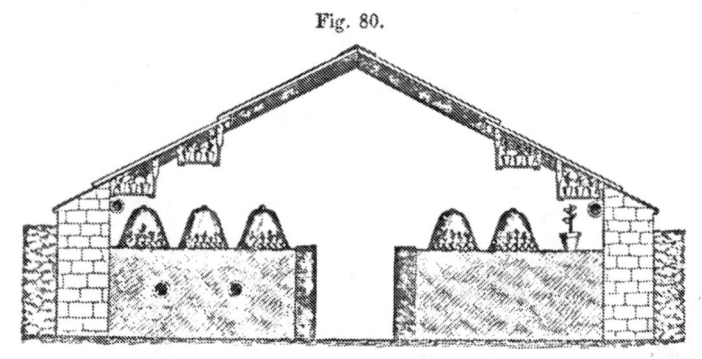

Fig. 80.

The cloche as used in the propagating-house.

glasses by which they were driven out of use. The French cloche does not cost one-fourth so much as a hand-light—and moreover does not require both painter, glazier, and plumber for keeping it in repair. It will prove a distinct improvement in every class of garden.

" How to procure these cloches has hitherto been the great difficulty. Many have been deterred from employing them by the trouble, expense, and loss consequent on ordering them from France, and I have always despaired of their becoming useful to cultivators generally till they are produced in England at a cheap rate. Even if the carriage was not as heavy as it is, the risk of conveying such very fragile articles across the Channel is such as would prevent us from getting them in a satisfactory way.

" I am pleased to announce that Messrs. E. Breffit and Co., proprietors of the Aire and Calder Glass Bottle Company's Works in Yorkshire, well known for its productions, are making preparations for their manufacture on an extensive scale. They will be able to supply them soon, and will have an abundant stock by the time it is necessary to employ them over next winter's crops of salads and other vegetables requiring their protection. They propose to sell them at from 10*d.* to 1*s.* each, according to the quantities required, and a small addition for package and carriage will put them down in every part of the kingdom. Messrs. Breffit and Co. have offices at 83, Upper Thames-street, E.C.; stores at Free Trade Wharf, Broad-street, Ratcliff, E., and 120, Duke-street, Liverpool—the seat of manufacture being at Castleford, near Normanton, Yorkshire."

The common hand-glass is formed either square, or of five or more sides of equal length and height, the latter commonly not more than eight or twelve inches. The framework is of lead, cast-iron, tinned wrought-iron, copper, or zinc; the last is much the cheapest, and also the lightest, and when kept well painted, it will last as long as cast-iron, which with the moisture of the soil soon becomes rusty at the lower edge. Cast-iron hand-glasses being very heavy, are commonly formed in two pieces; and when the form is square, air is very conveniently given by changing the position of the cover-part, so that its angles may project over the sides of the lower part.

The following substitute for bell-glasses may be readily adopted by any gardener who can get pieces of broken window-glass from his frames or hothouses, and who has a glazier's patent diamond, which

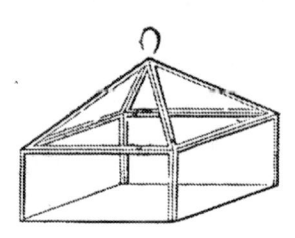

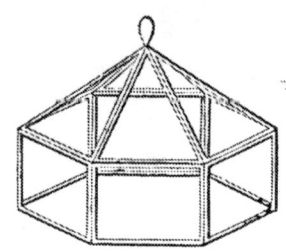

Fig. 81.

Substitutes for bell-glasses.

differs from the common diamond in this, that any person can cut with it. Having procured the diamond, and several pieces of broken window-glass, cut the latter into figures corresponding in size and form to the sides of four or six-sided prisms, as shown in fig. 81. When the pieces of glass are properly cut out by a wooden or card pattern, join them together with strips of tape, about three-eighths of an inch wide, made to adhere to the glass with india-rubber varnish. After the glass is formed, varnish over the tape, and the whole will be found firm and durable. A loop may be formed at top either of the tape or of wire, so as to lift them by. Glasses of this sort may be made from six inches to a foot in diameter, and will at all events be found useful for striking cuttings or protecting rising seeds. The cheapness of glass renders such expedients almost unnecessary. Even hand-glasses are being rapidly superseded by the use of Rendle's Fruit-tree and Plant Protectors. These have a base of tile, and a smooth glass top, and are thus endowed with a greater power of resisting cold than common bell-glasses. The tile base absorbs and stores up the sun's heat in the daytime, to be liberated during the night. The protectors are likewise made to lie closely to the ground, and are readily covered over in very severe weather. An excellent substitute for hand-glasses will be described under the section on structures.

Powdering-boxes for plants are required for dusting them with powdered lime, sulphur, coarse snuff, powdered charcoal, fine sand, &c. One of the most convenient forms is that of the common dredge-box, but for the light powders an appendage to be hereafter described may be added to the common bellows. All powders intended to rest on the leaves of plants should be dusted over them when they are moist with dew, or by having been previously watered.

We have omitted to mention some other utensils used in very extensive gardens, botanic gardens, and nurseries; such as the glazed packing-box; the earthenware shelter, which may be described as an inverted flower-pot, with the sides perforated with holes, or with a large opening on one side; plant-shades of various kinds; bulb-glasses; cast-iron pots for burning tobacco; and a few other articles not in general use, or readily substituted by others of a more simple and economical kind.

Machines used in Horticulture.

Machines differ from other horticultural implements in being less simple in their construction, and in their action enabling the operator to abridge labour. The principal gardening machines are the mowing-machine, water-carts, wheelbarrow, roller, watering-engines, garden-bellows, and transporting or transplanting machines.

The mowing-machine is indispensable in every garden. There are many kinds, but most of them are made on the same principle, and only differ in form and their mode of motion and delivery. The machine was originally modelled on the plan of the engine for shearing woollen cloth down to the required closeness of nap. By imparting rapid motion to 4, 6, or 8 bent knives, set at the proper angle on a round spindle, and bringing them into close contact with a steel plate that is carried close to the turf, the rapid revolution of these knives clips off all the grass between them and the plate, and lifts it into a receiving-box at the same instant, leaving the lawn short and smooth as a carpet. These machines have almost banished scythes from the garden, and are to be found everywhere. They are made of all sizes, from 10 inches to 4 feet in width, and are used by ladies as healthy exercise, while the larger ones are hard work for a full-sized horse. On their first introduction it was supposed that they could only cut the grass when it was dry, and where the surface was perfectly level. But they are now used in all weathers, and on all kinds of surfaces, with tolerable efficiency, though the smoother the ground the more perfectly they do their work. The chief makers are the Messrs. Shanks of Arbroath, Messrs. Ransome, Green, Brown, Milburn and Williams.

To do their work well they must be kept in good repair, geared with the utmost exactness, and the knives kept sharp and clean. They are readily and efficiently sharpened by simply reversing the motion against the bottom plate, and placing ebony-powder and oil between the two. One of the best mowing-machines is the Archimedean, recently introduced from America.

Wheelbarrows for gardens are of two kinds: one of large dimensions for wheeling littery dung, tan, short grass, leaves, haulm, or weeds; and another of moderate size (fig. 82), for wheeling soil and gravel. They are generally constructed of wood, with the wheel also of wood, and shod with iron; but some wheelbarrows are formed entirely of cast and wrought iron; they are, however, too heavy for wheeling anything excepting littery dung or other light matters, and they are far from being so durable as a wooden barrow, when the latter is kept well painted. Some dung and tan barrows have the body or box attached to the handles or levers (commonly called trams) by moveable iron bolts, so that it can be readily taken off and carried by two men into places where the entire barrow with its wheel could not be admitted; for example, in filling the bark pit of a stove with tan or leaves. There is a third kind of barrow, used by engineers in deep cuttings, which has shallow sides of an equal height on every side of the bottom of the barrow; it is well suited for carrying heavy subsoil, or stony materials, but is not required in gardens. For general purposes, a middle-sized barrow, between the dung-barrow and the mould-barrow, like that of which we have given a figure, is sufficient.

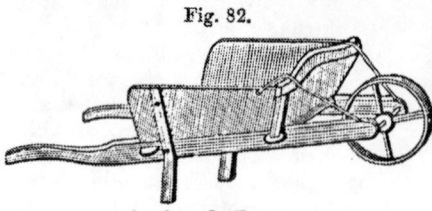

Fig. 82.

Garden wheelbarrow.

Rollers are essential in even the smallest garden, for compressing and smoothing gravel walks and lawns. They are formed of solid cylinders of stone, or hollow cylinders of cast iron, and a very convenient width is four feet. Cast-iron rollers are always easiest to draw, from the greater diameter of the cylinder. The operation of rolling is most effective after the soil or gravel has been softened by recent rains, but is at the same time sufficiently dry on the surface not to adhere to the roller. A roller has recently been invented in which the hollow cylinder can be filled with water, and reduced at pleasure. Thus it can be weighted or lightened according to the work required to be done. The mobility of the weighting fluid also throws the entire weight used upon the crushing portion of the roller, which increases to the utmost its crushing power. By filling the inside with hot water, this roller is one of the most efficient means of destroying slugs and worms on walks, lawns, roads, &c.

The watering engines used in gardens are the syringe, the hand-engine, and the barrow-engine. There are several kinds of syringe, but the best at present in use is decidedly that of Read (fig. 83). Its two points of superiority are, a ball-valve, *d*, which can never get out of repair, and an air-tube, *e*, which allows the air above the piston to escape during the operation of drawing in water, by which means the labour of syringing is greatly diminished. There is a cap, *a*, for

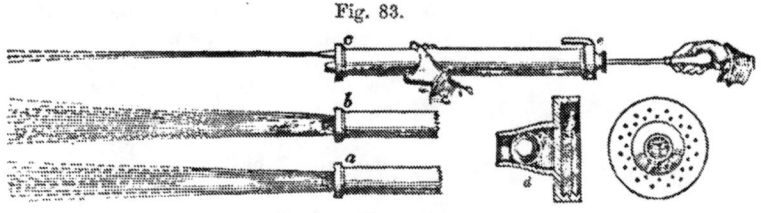

Fig. 83.

Read's garden-syringe.

washing away insects from wall-trees, and throwing lime-water on gooseberry-bushes and other standards in the open garden, and for watering pines overhead; a cap, *b*, for sprinkling plants in forcing-houses, which throws the fluid in a light and gentle moisture almost like dew, and which is also used for washing the leaves of trees and plants when frost-nipped in the cold nights that often prevail during the spring, and which operation should, of course, be performed before sunrise. There is also a cap, *c*, *d*, which is used when great force is required, more particularly in washing trees against walls; and this cap is also used in dwelling-houses for extinguishing fires. Trees against walls are frequently covered with netting, and when it becomes necessary to syringe these, the netting, when the cap, *b*, is used, requires to be removed, but with the cap *c d*, it may be kept on. For all small gardens this syringe will serve as a substitute for every other description of watering-engine.

The barrow-engine, fig. 84, is an oval copper vessel, containing about twenty-six gallons, particularly adapted for large conservatories and forcing-houses. It will pass through a doorway two feet wide, and is so portable that it may be carried up or down stairs by two men. The great power of this engine depends on the air-vessel, indicated by a dotted circular line, in the body of the engine, in which all superfluous force is employed in condensing air, so as to form a reservoir of power; and in the proximity of the bent fulcrum, *a*, to the handle or lever, *b*, by which the weight *c*, being brought near to the fulcrum, the power applied at *b* is proportionably increased. In most engines of this kind there is no pneumatic reservoir, and the distance between the weight, *c*, and the

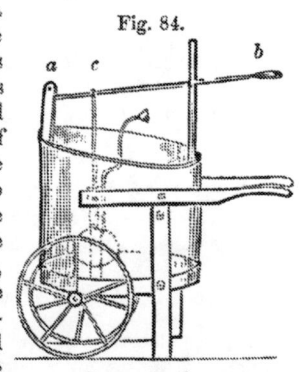

Fig. 84.

Barrow-engine.

fulcrum, *a*, is much greater. The construction of the piston-valves, &c.,

I

is on the simple ball-valve principle, so that this barrow-engine is not only a machine of great power, but not liable to get out of repair.

The hydronette is an instrument recently invented, which is very useful in syringing in glass-houses.

Fig. 85.

Garden water-barrow.

Water-carts or barrows (see illustration) are likewise much used in gardens for the conveyance of water on a large scale; gutta-percha tubing and other piping are, however, being rapidly substituted for these, and are of the highest value as labour-saving expedients. Nevertheless, there are few gardens where a number of two-wheeled hand water-carts are not necessary, and it is of great moment to the full enjoyment of a garden in dry weather that some of them should be furnished with spreaders for the watering of gravel walks, roads, &c.

When a large house is to be fumigated with tobacco or other smoke, a fumigating pot, such as fig. 86, may be used. It is made of sheet-iron, holds about three pounds of tobacco, and is placed on the outside of the house, with the smoke-tube entering it through a hole made on purpose in the front wall or front glass. In the figure a is the handle by which the pot is carried, b the pipe by which this smoke is introduced to the house, and which is attached to a moveable lid, and c, a tube to which the bellows is applied, and which enters the pot immediately under a perforated moveable bottom. A substitute for a pot of this kind is often formed by two flower-pots, a smaller one being placed upside down within a larger, and the tobacco placed in the former. Messrs.

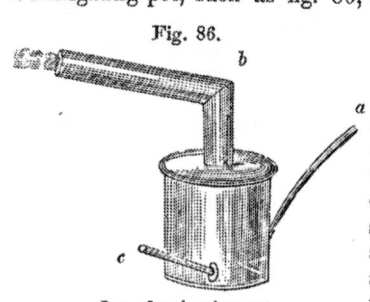

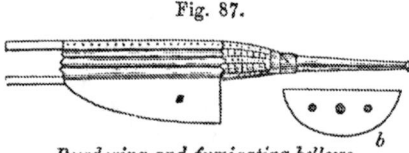

Fig. 86.

Iron fumigating-pot.

Fig. 87.

Powdering and fumigating bellows.

Dean and Appleby have recently invented a very simple and efficient fumigator. In fumigating plant-houses, the air should be as dry as possible, otherwise the aphides conceal themselves in the globules of water, and so escape destruction. A pair of common bellows may be rendered fit either for powdering plants or fumigating them, by substituting a piece of tinned iron, fig. 87, a, resembling in shape those tin scales used in the retail of meal, in the flat end of which, b, are two small valves $1\frac{1}{4}$ inch in diameter, with a hole between them, to which a screw-cap is fitted for introducing the dust or the tobacco to be burnt. It is evident that the air which enters through the valves by the upstroke of the bellows, raises the dust or smoke in the interior, which is ejected by the down-stroke; and, by repetition, all the powder introduced, or the whole of the smoke produced by the ignition of the tobacco-leaves, will be thrown out. The best contrivances for distributing sulphur are the very simple distributors made of a ball of india-rubber with a nozzle, which unscrews and permits the supply to be replenished.

In the 'Encyclopædia of Gardening' will be found described various machines for transporting large boxes or tubs containing plants, such as orange-trees; machines for transporting and for transplanting large trees, for regulating temperature, for entrapping or detecting the enemies of gardens, and for some other purposes; but few of these are adapted for the present work. It may be stated here, that the principle of all the best machines for transporting plants in large boxes or tubs, or transplanting large trees with balls to their roots, is the same—viz., two windlass axles are supported on four props, which rise out of two horizontal beams, and the box or tree being raised by means of the windlasses, is retained in that position till it is conveyed to its destination, either by means of two horizontal beams, by manual labour, as if they were the levers of a hand-barrow; or by placing wheels under them, in the manner of a cart or waggon. Mr. Barron, of the Borrowwash Nurseries, near Derby, is the inventor of an excellent transplanting machine, by which he has moved trees of almost any size hundreds of miles with unfailing success. The French have had much experience in the removal of trees, and understand it well; their best machines are described and illustrated in the 'Parks, Promenades, and Gardens of Paris.' A good machine of this kind for removing orange-trees in boxes, was that used at St. Margaret's, near London, and described in the 'Gardener's Magazine,' vol. x. p. 136. From the description of this machine it is obvious that it will answer either for transporting trees in boxes, or trees or shrubs with large balls; though, to convey the latter to any distance over rough roads, larger wheels would be requisite than those which belong to the machine referred to.

Miscellaneous Articles used in Horticulture.

In complete gardens, containing all the varieties of plant-structures, a number of articles are required for the purposes of cultivation and high keeping which can neither be classed as implements nor structures. Even in the smallest gardens, mats for protection, props for support, nails and ties for fastenings, and tallies for naming and numbering plants, are essential.

Bast mats, woven from ribands or strands of the inner bark of the lime and other trees, and imported from the Baltic and the West Indies, are in general use, both to protect from the cold by counteracting radiation, and to shade from the sun. Canvas, bunting, and netting of different kinds, and oiled-paper frames, are used for the same purposes, Netting of straw-ropes, formed by first stretching ropes as weft at regular distances, and then crossing them by others as woof, are sometimes used to protect wall-trees. Another mode of protecting trees by straw-ropes, is by placing poles against the wall, in front of the trees, at from four to six feet asunder: thrusting their lower ends into the earth about eighteen inches or two feet from the wall, and making them fast at top to the coping, or to the wall immediately under it; straw or hay ropes are then passed from pole to pole, taking a turn round each, and leaving a distance of about eighteen inches between each horizontal line of ropes. Straw ropes may also be used to protect early rows of peas or other plants, by first hooping over each row, and afterwards passing three or four ropes from hoop to hoop. Of course they act by checking radiation, and their influence will be greatest when they are placed between a foot and eighteen inches from the wall, the amount of heat reflected back diminishing in a geometrical ratio according to the distance of the covering from the body to be protected. Wisps of straw tied to a string, fig. 88, and hung in lines one above another in front of a wall, are also used for the same purpose as straw ropes, and in sheltered places are perhaps better.

Fig. 88.

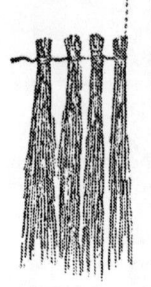

Wisps of straw for use as protectors.

Mats of straw or reeds are used for protecting plants in the open garden, and also for covering glazed sashes, whether of pits, frames, or hothouses. Every gardener ought to know how to construct these, in order to be able to employ his men within-doors in severe weather. The following directions are given by P. Lindegaard, late gardener to the King of Denmark, who used them extensively, and who states that they produce a considerable saving of fuel, afford a great security from accidents, such as breaking glass, and not only retain heat much better than bast mats, but, from their greater porosity, allow the steam of moist hotbeds to pass off more readily. When a heavy fall of snow takes place during the night, bast mats are not so easy to get cleaned and dried the next morning as straw mats, because they retain the moisture, and get frozen and stiff by the frost penetrating through them; and hence the next evening they cannot be put on again without the risk of breaking the glass. Mr. Lindegaard found four hundred straw mats sufficient to cover four hundred lights, for which if he had used bast mats, about twelve hundred would have been required. These mats are made of rye or wheat straw, or of reeds, and only in the winter time, when the weather is unfit for working out of doors. They are made in frames in the following manner:—An oblong frame (fig. 89) is formed of four laths, along the two ends of which, *a*, *a*, are driven as many nails as you wish to have binding cords, *b*, *b*, of which the usual number is six to a width of four feet, as the strength of the mat depends chiefly on the number of these cords. The cords are of tarred rope-yarn;

on these the straw, or reeds, is laid in handfuls, and bound to each longitudinal cord by other cords, which, for greater convenience, are

Fig. 89.

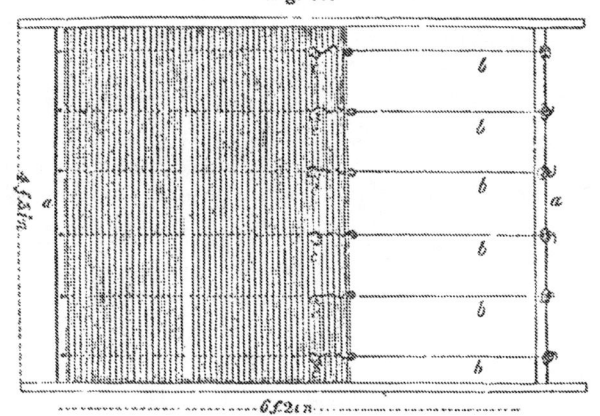

Mode of making straw mats.

made up in little balls, *c, c.* These cords are also of tarred rope-yarn. When a mat is finished, the cords are tied together at the top or finishing end, the mat is then detached from the frame, and its sides chopped straight with an axe. These mats are more conveniently made by two men than by one man; and by placing the frame upon a raised plank or bench, than by placing it on the ground, and obliging the men to stoop. When straw is used, that of rye is the best, and will last, even in Denmark, three years: reeds last longer. In the most severe weather these mats are rolled on the glass lengthways; that is, from top to bottom of the mat; by which the direction of the straw is at right angles to that of the sash-bar, which prevents the glass from being broken; and over this covering, in very severe weather, reed mats may be laid with the reeds in the same direction as the sash-bar, so that the water may run off them as it does off the thatch of a house, and keep the mats below quite dry. Where reeds cannot be got, mats of rye or wheat straw may be substituted; because it is evident that having the straws or reeds laid in the direction of the slope of the glass must be attended with great advantages by throwing off the rain instead of absorbing it. ('Gardener's Magazine,' vol. v. p. 416.) The usual dimensions of these mats are six feet by four feet, because that size answers for covering frames and pits of the ordinary dimensions; but when they are to be used for covering the sloping glass of hothouses, they should be made of sufficient length to reach from the coping to the ground, covering the front glass or front parapet. A ring of twisted wire should be placed exactly in the centre of the upper end of each mat, and to this ring a cord should be attached, for the purpose of being passed over a pulley to be fixed on the coping-board, or on the back wall immediately under it, or on the top rail of the uppermost sash of the roof. This cord must be at least twice the length of the mat, in order that, when the mat is drawn down and rolled up, the end of the cord may be within reach of the operator on the ground at the front of the house. Another ring ought to be fixed to the centre of the lower end of the mat, for the purpose of fastening it to the front sill when it is drawn over the roof. When the mats are removed from the roof, and rolled up during the day, the cord is loosened from the ring, and lies on the roof, ready to be re-fastened to it, to draw the mats up the next evening. A second layer of mats might be drawn up over the former, in a direction across the sashes, so as to throw off the rain in the manner of thatch, by attaching a cord to one corner of each end of the mat, passing these cords over two pulleys, and laying the mats on like tiles on a roof. Drawing up two mats, however, the one immediately over the other, would be much less trouble, and would, excepting in the cases of heavy rains or thawing snows, keep out the cold sufficiently well. Where the roof is divided by wooden rafters, the mats should be exactly the width of the sash, so as to fit in between them: but where it is not so divided, the mats should overlap one another in the manner of slates—that is, one-half the number of mats should first be drawn up, leaving half the width of a mat between each, and afterwards the remaining half should be drawn up so as to cover the intervening spaces, and overlap a foot over the mat at each side. It is much to be regretted that mats of this kind are so little used in England, especially in country places, where straw is abundant and cheap; for being made at a time when little other work can be done, and of a material of very little value, and retaining heat much better than any other covering, they would prove a great saving of fuel and of the labour of attending on fires, as well as ensure the safety of plants. Mr. Shennan, a gardener of great experience, who used these mats extensively, observes, in the 'Gardener's Magazine' for 1827, that he considers the revival of the old system of covering with straw or reeds, and the system of heating by water, as the greatest improvements that have been introduced into the forcing department in his time. Such mats are now in general use in many gardens. They are frequently made with the aid of wooden frames the size of the lights and space to be covered. Such reed, or straw, or felt coverings, are readily lifted off or on by two boys or men—one at top, and the other at bottom—and they form most efficient and durable barriers against cold. Neat straw mats are universally employed about Paris for covering frames, pits, and low houses; they are cheaper, neater, and in every way better than the bast mats used in England.

Wooden shutters form an excellent covering for the sashes of pits and frames; and though they are the most expensive at first, yet from their great durability when kept well painted, they are found by market-gardeners to be the cheapest of all coverings in the end. Boards do not retain heat so effectively as reeds or straw, but they exclude rain and wind better than those materials; and by being kept an inch or two above the glass by the cross-bars which bind the boards together, a space is left sufficient to check radiation, and to prevent the escape of heat by conduction. If boarded shutters could be kept about six inches from the glass, and air excluded from entering at top and bottom and at the sides, radiation would be effectually checked, and less risk of the escape of heat by conduction incurred than when the boards touch the sash-bar; but this would require great care in excluding the air from the sides and ends. All the frames and pits in the gardens at Syon are covered by boarded shutters, as are all those in the extensive forcing-ground of Mr. Wilmot of Isleworth. Narrow shutters of this kind might be contrived for hothouse roofs, so as to produce a great saving of heat. Canvas would, in many instances, repel wet and check radiation as well as deal boards, and might be put on much quicker; but the great objection to it is its liability to be disturbed by high winds—unless, indeed, it is attached to wooden frames, which occupy as much time in taking off and putting on as wooden shutters, and are much less durable.

Wicker-work hurdles are useful in gardens for sheltering low plants from high winds, for placing horizontally over seedlings to protect them from birds, and, in various positions, for shading plants. They are constructed of upright stakes fixed in the ground, or in holes in a board, at regular distances of from four inches to eight inches, according to the size of the materials and the dimensions of the hurdle, and these stakes are filled in or wattled with small rods, wands, or spray. When kept dry, they will last three or four years, if the stakes are made of willow, or of any of the soft woods; and from four to six or seven years, if they are made of hazel, oak, ash, or any of the hard woods.

Fig. 90.

Props for plants vary in form, dimension, and material, from the small wires used for supporting hyacinths in water-glasses, and the sticks of six inches in length used for supporting plants in pots, to cast-iron rods of six or eight feet in length, and pillars, arches, or houses for roses and other climbers, formed of the stems of young fir-trees, of from ten to twenty feet in length, as in fig. 90. All the varieties of wooden props may be reduced to four kinds:—1. Straight rods with the bark on, but with all the side branches cut off, varying in size from the shoot of one year to the stem of a fir of twenty years' growth. These are used for every purpose, from the tying up of plants in pots to the support of lofty climbers, including between these extremes tying up dahlias and standard roses. 2. Branches or stems, with all the side branches and branchlets retained, used for the support of climbing annual stems, such as peas, kidney-beans, tropæolums, &c., but only suitable when these plants are grown in the open ground;

Props for climbers.

when grown in pots, wire frames, or a regular framework of laths, are more in accordance with the artificial state in which the plants are placed. 3. Wooden rods, formed out of laths or deal by the gardener or carpenter, regularly tapered and pointed, and in some cases painted. These are chiefly used for choice plants in pots, but partly also in the open garden. 4. Iron rods, from short pieces of wire to rods of cast or wrought iron, for supporting dahlias, standard roses, and other plants, and with or without spreading heads for climbers. Fig. 91 shows a variety of these rods, which may be had of the principal London ironmongers. All iron work, before being used in the open

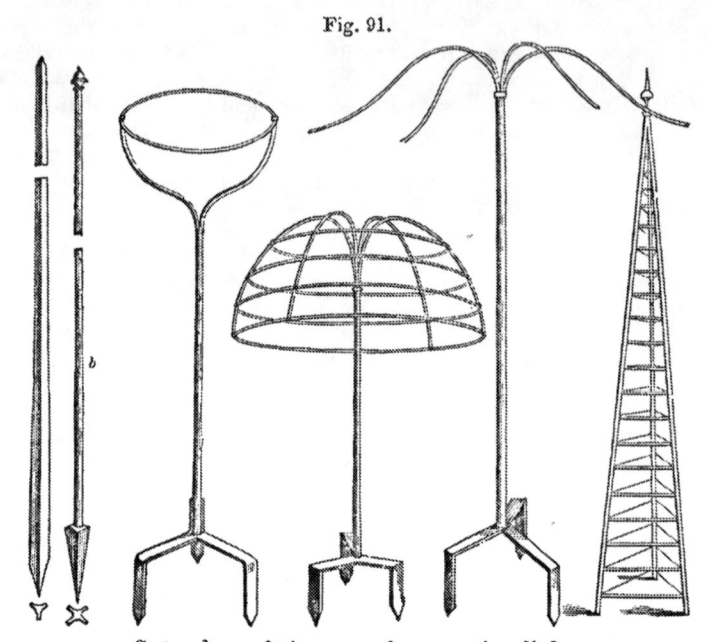

Fig. 91.

Cast and wrought iron props for supporting climbers.

air in gardens, would be rendered more durable if thoroughly heated and painted over with oil, the effect of which is, by carbonizing it, to prevent the action of the atmosphere on the surface of the iron. After this operation painting may be dispensed with, excepting for ornament. It is in general, however, better to paint them, and the colour should be some shade of green. All glaring and conspicuous colours had better be avoided; they are quite out of place here, and do not harmonize with the simple verdure of the foliage which the props support. The object should rather be to conceal the props as much as possible.

The durability of wooden props may, perhaps, be increased by soaking them in Burnett's anti-dry-rot composition; or if they are made of deal, by first kiln-drying them, and afterwards soaking them in linseed oil. After the oil is thoroughly dried, which will require two or three weeks, the sticks may be painted. Sticks of red deal, treated in this manner, will remain good for upwards of twenty-five years. ('Hort. Reg.,' i. p. 301.) Mr. Masters is of opinion ('Gard. Mag.,' xv. p. 321) that the duration of hop-poles may be doubled by kyanizing them; but little benefit has been yet derived from it in the case of props for garden plants. Mr. W. H. Baxter found kyanizing of little or no use.

Garden tallies and labels are articles by which names or numbers are attached to plants, and they are of many different kinds. The materials are wood, iron, zinc, lead, or earthenware, and the forms are still more various than the materials. The most durable are those of lead, with the name or number stamped with a steel punch or type, and rendered conspicuous by having the letters filled in with white lead paint. The most common are made of wood, with the numbers, in imitation of the Roman numerals, cut with a knife. To form tallies to receive numbers of this description, take firm ash-rods, about an inch or an inch and a half in diameter; saw them into lengths of ten or twelve inches; point the lower end rather abruptly, and either plane or cut with a knife a surface sufficient to receive the number required on the upper half. This kind of tally may be made during winter and wet weather, when little else can be done, and a stock kept on hand for use, if required. They are found to last eight or ten years, according to the situation in which they are placed. Sometimes the number is written or painted, and the writing is in ordinary cases done with a black-lead pencil on a smooth surface, on which a little white lead has been previously rubbed in with the finger, which, when written on in a moist state, is found greatly to increase the durability of the impression. Sometimes Indian ink is used on a white painted ground, and, being a body colour, presents a more conspicuous and durable impression than common ink, which is only a stain. The most durable letters, next to impressions stamped in lead, are those in black oil-paint on a white ground. For plants in pots, a label formed of wood, cut with a common knife from thin laths, rubbed with white lead, and written on with a black-lead pencil, is one of the most convenient and economical forms and materials. Fig. 92 shows one with a shank of wood; if wire is used it ought to be fixed to the rim of the pot, as the wire would injure the roots by corrosion. The plate is 2½ inches long and 1¼ inch broad, and about a quarter of an inch thick; the wooden or wire shank is about three-sixteenths of an inch thick, and is painted black, while the wooden plate is painted white. These tallies are very conspicuous and very durable. For herbaceous plants, or low shrubs or trees in the open air, the tally, fig. 93, is very neat and durable, and much more economical than would at first sight appear. It is formed of cast-iron, with a head of the same metal, in which is a sunk panel,

Fig. 92.

Wooden label, with a shank of iron wire or wood.

into which the label with the name is placed, and afterwards covered with a piece of glass neatly fitted in, and puttied like the pane of a window. The label should be a slip of wood, lead, pewter, or earthenware, as not being liable to rust, shrink, or warp, from drought or moisture. Previously to putting in the labels, the tally should be carbonized by heating it nearly red-hot and immersing it in oil, as is practised with gun-barrels to render them impervious to the action of the atmosphere. This being done, a coat of paint may be dispensed with, or the iron-work may be painted black, and the part on which the name is written white; or the label may be simply rubbed over with a little white lead, and the name written with a black-lead pencil. In the Glasgow Botanic Gardens this kind of label, with the slip of wood, has been extensively used for many years. For plants in greenhouses or stoves, very neat porcelain tallies are made at the potteries, and they are perhaps the handsomest of all. They cost from 2*d.* to 3*d.* each, and readily receive black paint, Indian ink, or common ink, without previous preparation: in the open air, however, they are very liable to be broken. Terra-cotta labels are, however, more durable, and the following are useful either for pots or out of doors.

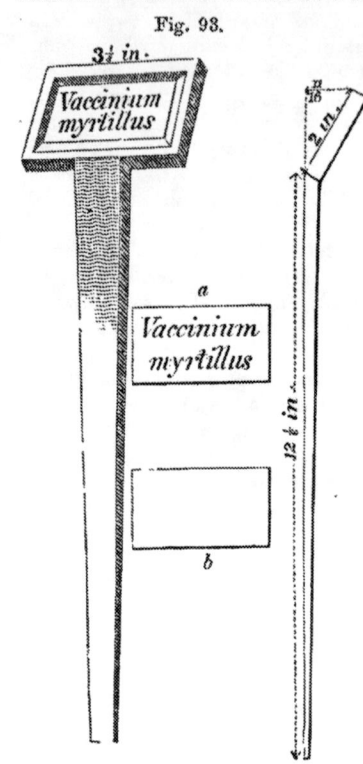

Fig. 93.

Cast-iron tally, with the label of wood placed in a sunk panel, and covered with a piece of glass secured by putty.

For alpine or other herbaceous plants in pots in the open air, no tally is better than strips of sheet lead, about an eighth of an inch thick, with the name at length stamped in with steel type—an operation which the gardener may perform in inclement weather. For large tallies for trees, bricks, moulded with a sloping face and a sunk panel to contain a label of lead, zinc, or wood, may be used; or tallies of heart-of-oak, previously steamed to draw out the sap, and afterwards boiled in linseed oil, painted black, with the name in white. The simplest of all labels for large trees are formed of pieces of zinc four or five inches long by about three deep, half an inch of the upper side being turned down to act as a small coping. This may be very conveniently fastened to the bole of the tree, at about six feet from the ground, by passing a wire through two holes formed immediately beneath the coping. The letters are best painted white on a black ground. Perhaps the most economical and durable tally for plants in pots is a small strip of zinc, about three-quarters of an inch broad and six inches long, on which the name may be written with a black-lead pencil, after rubbing on a little white-lead paint, or with Indian ink on dried white paint, or on the naked metal with prepared ink which is sold on purpose. The neatest, least obtrusive, and most durable tallies for this description of plants are undoubtedly strips of sheet lead, with the names stamped in, and the letters distinguished by being filled with white lead. Temporary labels for plants are written on strips of parchment, or narrow slips of wood, and tied to them with twine, or sometimes, when the plants are to be sent to a distance, with copper or metallic wire. In all cases of writing or painting names or numbers on permanent tallies, the words or figures may be rendered more conspicuous and durable by painting them over when dry with mastic varnish, or with boiled oil. Instead of painting tallies black, Mr. Nesfield prefers a very dark lead colour, composed of ivory black (not lamp black) and flake white, mixed with boiled linseed oil. His reason for disapproving of a pure black ground is founded on the fact that certain colours, having a greater affinity for water than for oil (such as blacks, umbers, and ochres), are liable to be affected by damp, unless they are held together by a powerfully oleaginous vehicle, with a small portion of white lead. The lettering Mr. Nesfield recommends to be done with Paris white, mixed with nearly equal parts of copal varnish and nut oil, avoiding turpentine, because it soon evaporates, and causes the colour to look dead and chalky. The white should be used as thick as it will flow from the pencil, because the letters in that case will be so much more opaque; and the varnish should be mixed with only a small quantity at a time, on account of its setting very rapidly. Turpentine must be entirely avoided, except for cleansing pencils, as it soon evaporates, while the varnish remains and hardens as it becomes older.

Nails, lists, and ties are wanted in every walled-in garden, though the wiring of walls with copper, zinc, or galvanized iron, or the covering of them with wide-meshed netting, has reduced the original importance of these requisites. Cast-iron nails, about an inch and a half in length, and the lists from the selvages of woollen cloth, are in general use for fastening the branches of trees to walls. Various preparations of canvas, warranted proof against insects of all kinds, are now offered instead of lists, which often prove harbours for them. Rope-twine is also frequently used in the place of shreds on the same principle of affording no hiding-place to insect pests. The nails, previously to being used, are heated nearly to redness, and thrown into oil, for the reason before mentioned; and old lists, before they are used a second time, are boiled in water, to destroy any eggs of insects that may be deposited on them. The most common material in use for ties are strands of bast matting, and these are rendered much more durable when previously steeped in soft soap and water. For large branches, ties of the smaller shoots of willows or of clematis are sometimes used; and on the Continent, the smaller branches are tied with rushes or the twigs of broom collected in the winter season, and preserved in bundles so as to retain a certain degree of moisture to prevent them from becoming brittle, and at the same time not to rot them. In this country tarred twine of different degrees of thickness, and bast matting procured by unravelling a mat, are almost the only ties in use. Metallic wire and small copper wire have been recommended, but they are only fit for tying labels to trees sent out of nurseries to a distance. A leathern wallet, fig. 94, is found of great use in pruning and nailing wall-trees, when the operator is standing on a ladder. It is suspended from his shoulder by straps, and contains a large pocket for the shreds, nails, and hammer, and two small pockets over it for a knife and sharpening-stone.

Fig. 94.

Fig. 95.

Wallet for putting on when nailing wall-trees from a ladder.

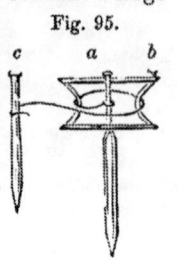

Iron reel and pin for a garden-line.

The garden-line, fig. 95, consisting of an iron reel, *a*, knob for winding it up, *b*, iron pin, *c*, and a hempen cord of any convenient length, is an essential article; as is a measuring-rod, marked with feet and inches, for laying off dimensions, and a Gunter's measuring-chain, for use on a large scale. A pocket foot-rule and a measuring-tape are also useful.

Ladders of different kinds and lengths are required for use in the open garden and in hothouses. Figs. 96 and 97 represent a light folding ladder, the sides of which may be constructed of yellow deal, and the rounds or treads of oak. It is used in hothouses, and also in the open garden, and may be of any length, from fifteen to thirty feet. When the ladder is open for use, it has the appearance shown in fig. 97, *d*; when half shut, of *e*; and when entirely shut, of fig. 96. The section of each of the sides, or styles, is a semi-oval; their junction, when the ladder is shut up, forms an entire oval in the section, as shown in fig. 96. The rounds, or treads, are cylindrical; and, when the ladder is shut up, they fall into grooves, hollowed out, of the same form; half of the groove of each round being in one style, and half in the other, as indicated by the dotted lines *a b*, in fig. 96. The ends of each of the rounds turn on iron pins; one end rests on a shoulder, as at *a*, while the other end is suspended from below the shoulder, and turns on an iron or brass pin, as indicated by *b*. The ends of the iron pins which pass through the styles are slightly riveted. In every description of plant-houses, vineries, verandahs, conservatories, aviaries, &c., a folding-ladder of this kind is a most convenient article; because, when shut up, it may be carried through a house much easier than a common ladder. For working among climbing plants under glass, it is found to be particularly useful, as it may be introduced in places where there is not room for a common ladder. For pruning standard trees out of doors, it is particularly convenient, because it can be thrust though the branches like a round

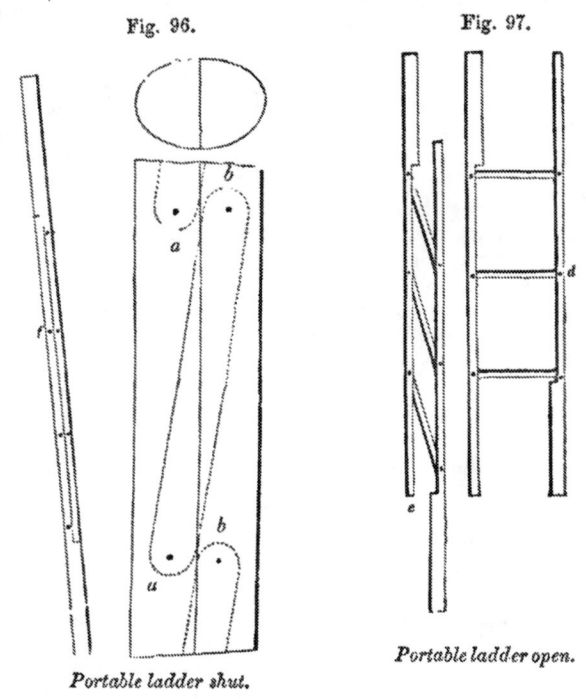

Fig. 96. Fig. 97.

Portable ladder shut. *Portable ladder open.*

pole, so as not to injure them; and when once it has got to the desired place or position, it can be opened, when the styles will press the branches on one side without injuring them. Orchard ladders for pruning standard fruit-trees, or gathering their fruit, are of various kinds—some with two legs to give them stability, and others forming a triangle, with horizontal pegs in each leg for supporting planks, which cross from one leg to the other, and on which the operators stand. Fig. 98 is what is called a rule-joint ladder, for painting and repairing curvilinear glass roofs. The ladder fig. 99 is in common use in the south of France and Switzerland, for gathering cherries.

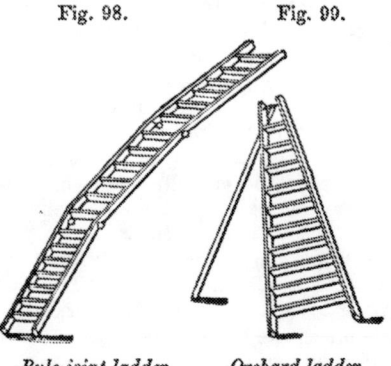

Fig. 98. Fig. 99.

Rule-joint ladder. *Orchard ladder.*

A levelling instrument of some kind is occasionally required in gardens; for example, when box-edgings are to be taken up and replanted, it is necessary to have the ground of exactly the same level on both sides of the walk, and this can only be done by levelling across. The use of the level implies also the use of poles, borning-pieces, and other articles belonging to surveying, which, as every one who can take levels must necessarily be familiar with, we do not stop to describe. Fig. 100 is a more convenient form for a garden level than that used by bricklayers; because, by the curvature on the under-side, the operator can more readily level across raised gravel-walks.

Fig. 100. 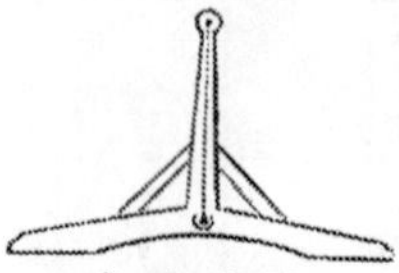
Garden-level.

Thermometers are requisite, more especially where there are plant structures of any description; and it will be very desirable to have terrestrial thermometers for ascertaining the temperature of the soil in the open garden, as well as of the soil, and of tan or dung beds, under glass. It is true that a knowledge of the temperature of the soil in the open garden will not often enable us to increase that temperature, but it will assist us in accounting for particular effects: and sometimes, as in the case of coldness produced from the want of drainage, or from a non-conducting covering repelling the rays of the sun, we have it in our power, by removing the cause, to remedy the evil. To ascertain the temperature of the soil with reference to plants growing in it, the bulb of the thermometer should be sunk to such a depth as may correspond with the great mass of the roots, or between eight inches and a foot. For plant-houses, a registering thermometer is a very desirable instrument, as a check upon the attendants in the absence of the master, and more especially in the night-time. Those of Six used to be considered the best; they are now, however, largely superseded by Negretti's, and other makers. For experimental purposes no thermometer should be used but those tested by the authorities at some of the Meteorological Observatories. For common garden use most of those sold by respectable makers are exact enough.

An hygrometer of some kind is almost as necessary as a thermometer, more especially now, when the importance of keeping the atmosphere of plant structures saturated with moisture to a certain degree is beginning to be understood. Perhaps Daniell's hygrometer is as good as any for garden purposes. It denotes the degree of moisture in the air with sufficient accuracy, and exhibits the amount in temperature of the dew-point, thus enabling the moisture to be read off as easily as an ordinary thermometer. Regnault's hygrometer is said to possess several advantages over Daniell's, but both of them are somewhat too sensitive and delicate for common use in hothouses. We are indebted to James Glaisher, Esq., for a much simpler mode of measuring the amount of vapour in the air. For this purpose a wet and a dry bulb thermometer are simply placed side by side, and it is most satisfactory to learn that Mr. Glaisher's mode of calculating the dew-point from their two readings of temperature, has been found substantially to agree with the best hygrometers, up to balloon elevations of 20,000 feet above the level of the sea.

The bulb of one thermometer is kept wet by being covered with thin muslin, round the neck of which is twisted a conducting thread of common darning-cotton, floss-silk, or lamp-wick; this passes into a vessel of water, with a conducting thread of about three inches long. The cup or glass should be placed on one side or a little beneath, so that the water may not be placed so close to the dry bulb as to affect its reading. The following minute instructions, and the position and precautions for using the wet and dry bulb thermometer, are taken from Mr. Glaisher's Tables.

"The instrument should be mounted in an open space with the bulb raised about four feet above the soil, in the shade, at some little distance from walls, trees, &c. The water-vessel or reservoir should always be supplied with rain or distilled water. If the temperature of the air be below 32°, it will frequently happen that the wet bulb thermometer will for a time read higher than the dry bulb; such observations must not be recorded; when the water surrounding the wet bulb has begun to freeze, the proper readings will take place. In frosty weather the water in the reservoir will be frozen, but this is no reason for suspending observations; if the water upon the muslin be frozen at the same time, the readings are perfectly available. If the muslin be dry it is necessary that it be wetted by means of a sponge or brush by the observer, who should leave it a sufficient time to allow the water to become frozen, and who (having satisfied himself of the fact) will proceed to take the reading in the usual way; unless this caution be attended to, the wet bulb will read higher than the dry. When the weather is frosty, the muslin should be wetted a sufficient time before the appointed hour of observation, and as a rule in frosty weather it is desirable to immerse the bulb and conducting thread in water after every observation. If the temperature of the air should have ascended above 32°, immerse the wet bulb thermometer for a short time in warm water, so as to melt any ice which may remain; unless this be attended to, the wet bulb will read 32° so long as any ice is in contact with it. Before use the cotton lamp-wick should be washed in a solution of carbonate of soda, and pressed while under water throughout its length. In use it should be of such extent that the water conveyed be sufficient in quantity to keep the muslin on the bulb as moist as when the air is saturated with vapour. The amount of water supplied can be increased or diminished by increasing or decreasing the extent of the conducting thread.

"In observing, the eye should be placed on a level with the top of the mercury in the tube; and the observer should be careful to abstain from breathing while taking the observation."

Temperature of the air and of evaporation are given by the readings of the two thermometers.

Temperature of the Dew-point.—If a mass of air be gradually cooled it will descend to a degree of temperature at which it will be saturated by the quantity of vapour then mixed with it. This temperature is called the dew-point. It can be found directly from observation, by the use of either Daniell's or Regnault's hygrometer. For calculating the dew-point from observations of the dry and wet bulb thermometers, we subjoin the following table of factors by which it is necessary to multiply the excess of the reading of the dry thermometer over that of the wet, to give the excess of the temperature of the air above that of the dew-point, for every degree of temperature from 10° to 100°.

Reading of Dry Bulb Thermometer.	Factors.	Reading of Dry Bulb Thermometer.	Factors.	Reading of Dry Bulb Thermometer.	Factors.
10°	8·78	41°	2·26	71°	1·76
11	8·78	42	2·23	72	1·75
12	8·78	43	2·20	73	1·74
13	8·77	44	2·18	74	1·73
14	8·76	45	2·16	75	1·72
15	8·75	46	2·14	76	1·71
16	8·70	47	2·12	77	1·70
17	8·62	48	2·10	78	1·69
18	8·50	49	2·08	79	1·69
19	8·34	50	2·06	80	1·68
20	8·14	51	2·04	81	1·68
21	7·88	52	2·02	82	1·67
22	7·60	53	2·00	83	1·67
23	7·28	54	1·98	84	1·66
24	6·92	55	1·96	85	1·65
25	6·53	56	1·94	86	1·65
26	6·08	57	1·92	87	1·64
27	5·62	58	1·90	88	1·64
28	5·12	59	1·89	89	1·63
29	4·63	60	1·88	90	1·63
30	4·15	61	1·87	91	1·62
31	3·70	62	1·86	92	1·62
32	3·32	63	1·85	93	1·60
33	3·01	64	1·83	94	1·60
34	2·77	65	1·82	95	1·59
35	2·60	66	1.81	96	1·59
36	2·50	67	1·80	97	1·59
37	2·42	68	1·79	98	1·58
38	2·36	69	1·78	99	1·58
39	2·32	70	1·77	100	1·57
40	2·29				

The numbers in this table have been found from the combination of all the simultaneous observations of the dry and wet bulb thermometers with Daniell's hygrometer, taken at the Royal Observatory, Greenwich, from the year 1841 to 1854, with some observations taken at high temperature in India, and others at low and medium temperatures at Toronto. The results at the same temperature were found to be alike at these different places, and therefore the factors may be considered as of general application.

By the numbers in this table the temperature of the dew-point in the general tables has been calculated, and these have been constantly checked by direct comparison with Daniell's hygrometer at the Royal Observatory, Greenwich, up to the year 1868, and found correct.

Other most useful tables follow of the expansion of air by heat—the elastic force of aqueous vapour—the weight and enlargement of a cubic foot of air and vapour, at different temperatures and different degrees of humidity, and a series of readings of the dry and wet bulb thermometers in relation to these and other points from 10° to 100°, and these tables are indispensable to all who would thoroughly master the subject. But it may be stated in general terms here that the nearer the reading of the wet and dry bulb thermometer approximate to each other, the more moist the air is, and the greater the disparity the drier the air. For instance, in a plant stove at a temperature of 70°, a genial atmosphere for the growth of plants would be secured by the wet bulb thermometer reading 62° or 64°. See 'Glaisher's Tables.'

Other articles of various kinds are required in gardens, of which it will be sufficient to enumerate those which are most important. A grindstone is essential in every garden; because, unless tools and instruments are kept at all times sharp, it is impossible that operations can either be properly performed, or a sufficiency of work done. Whetstones are also necessary for scythes and knives. Portable shoe-scrapers of cast-iron, for using when coming off dug ground in wet weather on the gravel walks. One or more bridge-planks, fig. 101, for wheeling across box-edgings. Common planks for wheeling on when the soil is soft, or when injury would be done by the sinking of the wheels; and trestles for raising them as scaffolding. Some hundreds of bricks and flat tiles for forming traps for birds or mice, and for a variety of purposes. A pair of leather bearing-straps for relieving the arms in wheeling or in carrying hand-barrows, fig. 102. Old fishermen's-netting, for protecting rising seeds from birds, and for covering currant or cherry-trees for the same purpose, or for protecting wall-trees, or for shelter. Finely-meshed wire frames are likewise much used for protecting purposes against birds, mice, &c. Live moss (commonly sphagnum) for packing plants and for other purposes. Lime unburned, but broken into small pieces, in order to be burnt in the hothouse fires, to supply quicklime as wanted for making lime-water: quicklime will answer, if kept compressed in a cask or box, so as to exclude the air. Potash, for using as a substitute for quicklime, in preparing a caustic fluid for destroying worms, snails, &c. Refuse

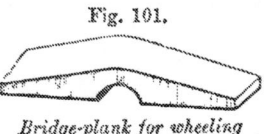

Fig. 101.
Bridge-plank for wheeling across box or other edgings.

Fig. 102.
Leather bearing straps.

tobacco, tobacco paper, or tobacco liquor, from the tobacconist's, or tobacco of home growth, for destroying insects. Quassia chips for the same purposes. Sulphur in a state of powder, for destroying the mildew, and for sublimation to destroy the red spider. Soft soap, tar, gum, glue, &c., for suffocating the scale, and for coating over the eggs of insects to prevent their hatching. Gunpowder, for bruising and mixing with tar to deter insects by its smell. Bird-lime, for entrapping birds. Baskets, hampers, boxes, and cases of various kinds, for packing vegetables and fruits, and sending them to a distance. A cabinet or case for the office, or for the seed-room, for containing seeds; another for bulbs, if collection of tulips, &c., are grown. Canvas for bags, which may be used as a substitute for boxes for containing seeds. Paper of different kinds, twine and cord, cotton, wool, hay, fern-leaves, the male catkins of the beech, or sweet chestnut, hair, charcoal, dust, and the chaff of buck-wheat, to aid in packing fruit. Straw, reeds, tan, common sand, pure white or silver sand, oyster-shells as coverings to the holes in bottoms of pots; pieces of freestone, for mixing with peat soil used in growing heaths; leaves and leaf-mould, grafting-wax, grafting-clay, common paint, and probably various other articles which we cannot recall to mind, might be enumerated under this head. But it is scarcely necessary to observe, that no gardener ought to confine himself to those implements of his art which have hitherto been in use, whether as regards the construction of particular instruments or utensils, or their number and kinds, for particular operations. Let him at all times think for himself; and if he can devise any tool, instrument, or utensil for performing any operation better than those hitherto in use, let him not fail to do so. Such is the variety of operations required in extensive gardens, where a great many different kinds of culture are carried on, that this power of invention in the gardener becomes essentially requisite, and is, in fact, called forth by the circumstances in which he is placed.

CHAPTER VII.

STRUCTURES AND EDIFICES OF HORTICULTURE.

STRUCTURES and edifices are required in horticulture for the more perfect cultivation of hardy plants, or for bringing them earlier to perfection; for the protection of exotics that will not endure our winters in the open air; for preserving and keeping horticultural articles; for the enclosure and defence of gardens, and for gardeners' dwellings.

Portable, Temporary, and Moveable Structures.

Portable structures are such as can be readily moved about by hand, such as the common hand-glass, cloches, wicker-work, protectors, &c.; temporary structures are such as are taken to pieces every time they are removed from place to place, such as temporary copings, canvas or glass screens, &c.; and moveable structures are those which can be removed entire, such as the common hotbed frame.

Wicker-work structures for protecting plants may be of any convenient form. Fig. 103 consists of a rim about two feet high, and a semicircular cover for taking off during fine days; it has been used at Britton Hall to protect half-hardy Rhododendrons. Fig. 104 shows various forms which have been used for protecting tender plants during winter, at Abbotsbury, in Dorsetshire: *a* is a semicircular hurdle, to protect plants trained against a wall, especially if newly planted and exposed to a sunny or windy quarter; *b* is a double semicircular hurdle or split cylinder, with loops on each side forming hinges or clasps. This is useful to put round the stems of young trees, whose branches are too spreading to allow of a circular hurdle being passed over them from above. It is used as a protection against hares and rabbits in a shrubbery; *c* is a large cylindrical basket to cover tall shrubs, with a vizor, or window, to be turned towards the sun or away from the wind, but to admit air. These three forms are chiefly adapted for permanent defences in the winter season. The following are for use in spring: *d* is the simple form of basket or circular hurdle, closed on every side and at top, intended to protect low bushes, or growing herbaceous plants coming into flower; *e* is a bell-shaped wicker case with a handle, for covering during the night plants that shoot early in spring. All these forms are constructed of stakes of hazel, oak, or other wood, strong and pointed so as to be firmly fixed in the ground, and the wattled work is of willow wands or young shoots of hazel, snowberry, or whatever can be most conveniently got from the woods. For newly planted conifers, square branches stuck round within a foot of the branches, and as high as, or higher than, the top of the trees, is an excellent protection. It is a good practice to leave these rustic protectors for one or two whole years, as

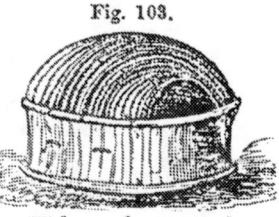

Fig. 103.

Wicker-work protector for low shrubs.

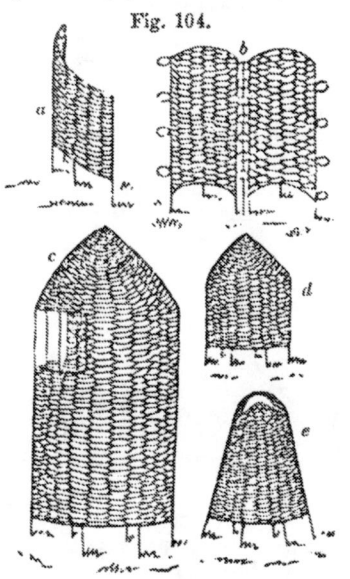

Fig. 104.

Wicker-work protectors of various kinds.

such trees often suffer as much from the glare of the sun and the force of driving winds as from frosts. Those structures used for the more tender plants may be filled with straw or hay, provided the plants are on a lawn where grass seeds dropping from the hay will not prove injurious; or they may be covered with mats or canvas. Besides these forms, which may be made of any size, according to that of the plants to be protected, small semi-globular, close-woven chip baskets, not above a foot high, are used at Abbotsbury as shades for delicate Alpine plants in sunny or windy weather. Where baskets of this kind cannot be conveniently procured, very good substitutes may be found in bast mats, canvas, or oil-cloth, supported by rods forming skeletons of suitable sizes and shapes.

As hand-glasses, from their great liability to breakage and the quantity of the glass they contain compared with the ground they cover, become very expensive articles, cheaper substitutes may be mentioned. A common square hand-glass, it has been shown by Mr. Forsyth, 'Gard. Mag.' 1841, contains seven square feet of glass to light or shelter two and a quarter square feet of ground, being a little more than three times as much as is really necessary for the plants usually cultivated under them: hence he proposes to substitute boards well painted, pitched or tarred, to increase their durability, in place of upright glazed sides to the hand-glass; and instead of a conical or pyramidal roof, to employ a square cast-iron sash, twenty-four inches on the side. Fig. 106 shows the sash glazed with small panes, say

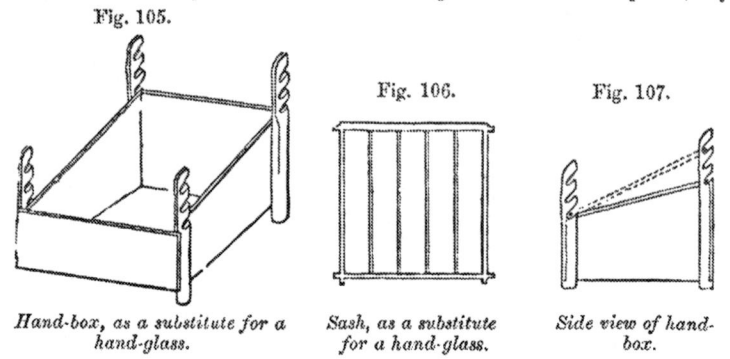

Fig. 105. Fig. 106. Fig. 107.

Hand-box, as a substitute for a hand-glass.   *Sash, as a substitute for a hand-glass.*   *Side view of hand-box.*

four inches and a half wide, on account of their cheapness and greater strength than larger-sized panes. The frame, fig. 105, may be six to nine inches high in front, and from fifteen to eighteen inches high at back. These small sashes, when not wanted for hand-glasses, or rather hand-frame coverings, Mr. Forsyth proposes to use as roofing to peach-houses, vineries, &c., and for various other purposes; and he anticipates, and we think with reason, great economy from their adoption in gardens. Fig. 107 is an end view of the box, showing the uprights at the angles for supporting the sash, either close over the box, or raised to different heights to admit more or less air. By means of the notched uprights, the sash may either be raised six inches above the box at top and bottom, or it may be raised three or six inches at the back, and not raised, or raised only three inches in front, so as to admit more or less air at pleasure, and yet throw off the rain; the sash being in any of these cases held firm in its place, so as not to be liable to be disturbed by wind. The pivots which fit into the notches are square, in order to admit of their being mounted on rafters of different kinds, so as to form coverings to frames, pits, or even forcing-houses. Supposing, says Mr. Forsyth, a bed of violets, running east and west, in the open air, twelve feet long and three feet six inches wide; drive seven notched pegs two feet apart down the centre of the bed to stand one foot above ground, and seven down each side at the same distance apart, but only four inches out of the ground; then, to make the sides and gable ends, take a piece of turf four feet by four feet, shaped out with the edging-iron, and taken up with the turfing or floating spade, an inch and a half thick, of the proper shape, so that it may be set on edge and kept so by a peg on each side, and having the green side out; when the lights are put on with every alternate one higher than and embracing the iron edges of the two under it, you will have a very elegant little flower-house, which a labourer might erect in an hour with sixpenny-worth of building materials, and the finished structure would have thus every other light hinged and ready to admit air or allow of water-ing and gathering flowers like a complete forcing-house. We regard this as promising to be one of the most useful and economical inven-tions that have been introduced in horticulture for some time. This box may be used in the open ground for forcing sea-kale, rhubarb, and for a variety of other purposes. The most efficient of all substi-tutes for hand-glasses are the common barless ground vinery and the cloche. The various "protectors" recently invented are decidedly inferior to these.

Canvas coverings for glazed structures or detached plants require for the most part to be in framed panels, as well to keep them tight as to throw off the rain, and to prevent them from being blown and beat about by the wind. To render the canvas more durable, it may be oiled, tanned, or soaked in an anti-dry-rot composition. When applied to cover the glass sashes of frames or pits, it should be in panels in wooden frames of the size of the sashes; and this is also a convenient and safe mode of forming temporary structures for protecting standard plants or trees; but by suitable arrangements, to be hereafter described, canvas or netting for protecting walls may be hooked on and fastened without wooden frames. This is done in a very efficient manner in the garden of the Horticultural Society of London, to pro-tect a peach-wall. The stone coping of this wall projects over it about an inch and a half, with a groove or throating underneath. Coping-boards nine inches broad, fitted to join at their ends by means of plates of iron, are supported on iron brackets built into the wall. Fig. 108 shows one of these brackets, in which *a* is an iron which is built into the wall, the thickness of a board below the stone coping; and *b*, the hole for the iron pin which secures the wooden coping. To these brackets the coping-boards are secured by broad-headed iron pins, passing through corresponding holes, *b*, in the board and bracket, a slip of iron, or "spare-nail," being then introduced through an eye in the lower end of the pin. The upper edge of the board is slightly bevelled, so as to fit as closely as possible to the under side of the coping of the wall, in order effectually to obstruct the radiation of heat, and the ascent of warm air. From this coping, woollen netting of various kinds, common netting, such as fishermen use, bunting, and thin canvas, have been let down, and tried experimentally, in the course of the last fifteen years; and we are informed by Mr. Thompson, that after repeated trials, the thin canvas was found the preferable article for utility, appearance, and duration. This description of fabric costs about 4*d*. per yard, procured direct from the makers. It requires to be joined into convenient lengths, or into the whole length of the wall to be covered, and bound with tape at top and bottom, and to have loops or rings sewed to it at top, by which it is secured to small hooks screwed to the upper side of the coping-boards. These hooks serve also for attaching the ends of pieces of twine, which are stretched down to pegs driven in a line four feet from the bottom of the wall. These twine-rafters are stretched at intervals of twelve feet, and support the canvas at a uniform slope, the appearance being that of an elegant light roof, reaching to within three feet of the ground. The coping-boards are put up before the blossom-buds of the peach-trees have swelled so much as to exhibit the tips of the petals; and before the most forward buds open, the thin canvas (or netting, if that should be preferred) should be attached to the hooks. The covering is generally put up about the beginning of March, and it remains on without being opened or altered, till all danger from frost is over, which is generally, in the climate of London, about the middle of May. The coping is entirely removed at the same time as the canvas, because the trees are found to thrive much better when exposed to perpendicular rains and dews. The canvas is found to be of great utility in bright sunny weather, when the trees are in full blossom; for the peach and other stone fruit, which in their native country blossom at an early period of the season, whilst the air is yet cool, do not succeed so well in setting when the blossoms are exposed to as much as 100°, which they frequently are, against a south wall. The thin canvas admits also plenty of air; while woollen netting, which it might be thought would admit still more air, was found to render the leaves too tender, in which case they suffer from the intensity of the light when the netting is removed. Common thread netting is not liable to produce this effect, being much more airy; and this netting has the advantage, when not placed farther than a foot from the wall, of admitting of the trees being syringed through it. Very little syringing, however, is required till the trees are out of blossom, and none while they are in blossom; and when the space

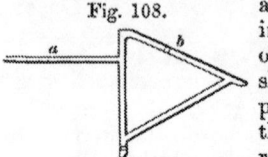

Fig. 108.

Iron bracket for supporting a temporary wooden coping.

PORTABLE, TEMPORARY, AND MOVEABLE STRUCTURES.   135

between the canvas and the wall is nine inches wide at top, and four feet wide at the bottom, as in the Horticultural Society's garden, the syringing can be very well performed in the space within.

(A broader coping would be far better. No temporary coping should be less than two feet in diameter, and it should always be inserted beneath a short permanent one. This is by far the best way of protecting fruit-trees, and the coping is so wide that it is seldom anything is required in front of the wall.)

A very simple and efficient apparatus for rolling up and letting down canvas shades over the roofs of hothouses was brought into use in the kitchen-garden at Syon by Mr. Forrest; and as it is equally well adapted for covering awnings for tulip-beds or other florists' flowers, and for a variety of other garden purposes, we shall here give

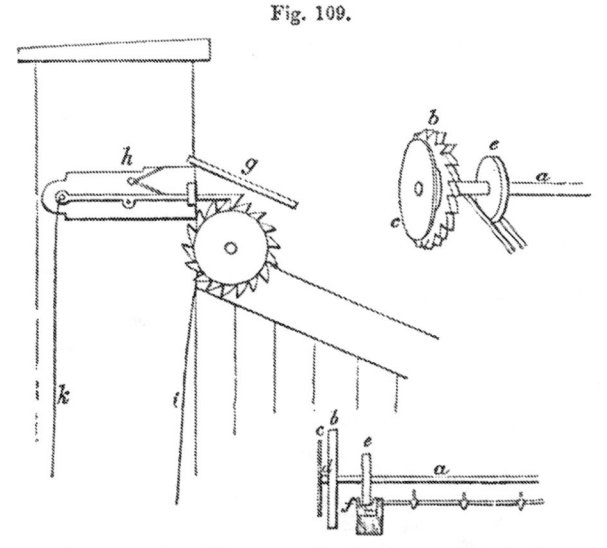

Fig. 109.

Apparatus for rolling up and letting down canvas shades.

such details as will enable any intelligent blacksmith or carpenter to construct the apparatus. The canvas is fixed to a roller of wood, fifty or sixty feet in length, the length depending on the diameter of the pole or rod, fig. 109, *a*, and the toughness of the timber employed, as well as the dimensions and strength of all the other parts. On one end of this rod, and not on both, as is usual, a ratchet wheel, *b*, is fixed, with a plate against it, *c*, so as to form a pulley-groove, *d*, between, to which a cord is fastened; and about three inches further on the rod is fixed a third iron wheel, about six inches in diameter and half an inch thick, *e*. This last wheel runs in an iron groove, *f*, which extends along the end rafter or end wall of the roof to be covered. The canvas or netting being sewed together of a sufficient size to cover the roof, one side of it is nailed to a slip of wood placed against the back wall—that is, along the upper end of the sashes; the other side is nailed to the rod, a. When the canvas is rolled up, it is held in its place under a coping, g, by a ratchet, h; and when it is to be let down, the cord, i, of the roll is loosened with one hand, and the ratchet cord, k, pulled with the other, when the canvas unrolls with its own weight. The process of pulling it up again need not be described. The most valuable part of the plan is, that the roll of canvas, throughout its whole length, winds up and lets down without a single wrinkle, notwithstanding the pulley-wheel is only on one end. This is owing to the weight of the rod, and its equal diameter throughout.

A very simple mode of placing canvas on roofs is to have it on rollers in the usual way. Then divide the roller space into three equal parts, nail a strong cord on to the top of the roof at each of these points, and bring the cord down under the roller to the front of the house. Then carry the cord back over the canvas, run it through a pulley at the point where it is fixed at top, return the two ends to the bottom, and join them together. The roller will bring the blind down the roof by its own momentum. All that is needed to roll it up is to pull the cord in front and hook the slacks on to a pin. To bring it down, unloose the cord, and give the blind a sudden jerk. This plan gets rid of all rack wheels, &c., and cannot fail to keep the canvas square.

The common hotbed frame is a bottomless box, commonly six feet wide, and three, six, or eighteen feet in length, formed of boards from one to two inches in thickness. The height at the back may be two feet, and in front one foot. The bottom should be level, so that the sides and the sashes laid on the frame may slope from back to front. A three-light or three-sashed frame is divided by two cross bars or rafters, so as to leave a space between them from two feet nine inches to three feet for the width of the sash. It is placed either on the open ground, or on a mass of heating material, according to the purpose for which it is wanted, and, excepting for particular purposes, facing the sun. As the great object of frames is to increase temperature without excluding light, the soil on which they are placed, or the dung-bed or other means of heating which they cover, ought to be as dry as possible, either naturally or by artificial drainage; and the glass ought to be clear, and so glazed as to permit as little air as possible to escape between the laps. When common crown glass is used, small panes are found to be less liable to breakage than large ones of this kind of glass; but when the sheet window-glass is used, from its greater thickness, the panes may be two or three feet in length, without much danger of breakage. The boards used for the frame should be of the best red deal; and if, after being prepared for fitting together, they are thoroughly dried on a kiln, and afterwards soaked with train-oil in the manner which we have before described for preparing wooden props, the duration of the frame will be greatly increased. All frames and sashes, when not in use, should be kept in an open airy shed, and there raised from the ground a few inches by supports of bricks or other suitable materials. In gardens where cucumbers and melons are grown extensively, there are commonly one or more small frames with single lights for raising seedlings, and others of two or three lights for winter or early spring crops; the smallness of the frame allowing a greater command of the heating material beneath it, by the application of outside casings of warm dung. The back, front, and ends of frames are generally permanently fixed together by tenons and mortices, and by being nailed to posts in the four inner angles; but in some cases the back and sides are fastened together by keyed iron bolts, which readily admit of separating the frame into pieces, and laying these away under cover, and in little space, when not required for use. From the short duration of frames, and from the great quantity of dung required to heat them, as well as from the waste of heat incurred in preparing the dung, frames are now, in most British gardens, being replaced by pits, which may be called fixed frames, with brickwork substituted for wood.

Fixed Structures used in Horticulture.

The fixed structures required in gardens are chiefly walls, espalier-rails, trellis and lattice-work, and structures for containing growing plants.

Walls, Espalier-rails, and Trellis-work.

Walls are used for the protection of gardens, and also as furnishing surfaces on which fruit-trees and ornamental plants may be trained, with a view to producing increase of temperature and protection from high winds: they may be considered in regard to direction, material, height, foundation, coping, and general construction.

Walls constructed merely for boundaries take the direction indicated by the form of the ground to be enclosed; but those built purposely for training trees, in the interior of a garden, are varied in direction according to the aspects which are considered most desirable. A wall in the direction of east and west, gives one side of the wall fully exposed to the sun for the finer fruits, or for fixing against it glass structures: while the north side of the wall may be employed for inferior fruits, for retarding crops, as well of fruit against the wall, as, in some cases, of vegetables on the border. A wall in the direction of north and south furnishes two good aspects for the secondary fruits, such as apricots, plums, and the finer pears. Walls have been built in a curvilinear direction, but no advantage has been found from them excepting a saving of material, in proportion to the length of the wall, the curves having the same effect in resisting lateral pressure as buttresses; but walls in situations exposed to high winds, built with projections at right angles, of the height of the wall and the width of the border, but somewhat sloped down from back to front, have been found beneficial in checking the course of the wind when in a direction parallel to the wall. Screen walls of this kind are frequently built at the exterior angles of the walls of kitchen-gardens; and sometimes they occur at distances of from 100 to 200 feet along walls having a south aspect; and in the case of east and west winds they are found very beneficial. Walls with piers at regular distances, allowing room for one trained tree between every two piers, have also been found beneficial from the shelter afforded by the piers, which at the same time greatly strengthen the wall, and admit of its being built thinner. In general, however, a straight wall, without projections of any kind, is most convenient, most suitable for training, and for protecting by temporary copings, and most agreeable to the eye.

The materials of walls are brick, stone, mud, earth, concrete, and wood; but the first is by far the best. Brick retains warmth, in consequence of its much greater porosity than stone; forms a very strong wall with comparatively little substance, from the rectangular shape of the bricks, and the firmness with which mortar adheres to them; and it is the best of all walls for training on, from the small size of the bricks and the numerous joints between them. Add also, that from the porosity of the bricks, nails may even be driven sufficiently far into them to hold branches, as securely as nails driven into the joints. Stone walls are good in proportion as they approach to brick walls. For this reason, if the stone is not naturally porous and a bad conductor of heat, the walls should be built of extra thickness, and the stones should not be large, nor so rough as to make coarse joints. The warmest walls of this kind are such as are of sufficient thickness to allow of the interior of the wall being built without mortar, in consequence of which much air is retained, and heat is not readily conducted from the warm side of the wall to the cold side. A stone wall, with a facing of bricks on the warm side, forms the next best wall to one entirely of brick; and, next to this, a stone wall stuccoed or plastered over with a mixture of stone lime and sharp sand, or coated over with Roman cement of good quality. Walls formed of earth or mud are still better non-conductors than brick walls; but though they are warm, yet as surfaces for training trees on they are attended with several disadvantages. They cannot conveniently be built high, and whatever may be their height, they require the coping to project farther than is beneficial to the plants trained on them at any other season than in early spring; and they require a trellis on which to fasten the plants. Nevertheless the vine and the peach have been successfully grown against such walls at various places in the neighbourhood of Paris, though they are now rapidly giving way to stone walls. These walls are commonly built without mortar, excepting to close the outside joints, or to plaster over the surface of the wall as a substitute for a trellis, which is always used when this is not done. The grapes at Thomery, near Fontainebleau, are chiefly grown on trellised walls of this kind; and the peaches at Montreuil, near Paris, are chiefly on stone walls stuccoed. Concrete walls are likewise used in different parts of France. Walls formed of boards are frequent in the north of Europe, where timber is abundant; but, except when the boards are five or six inches in thickness, they are very cold. In Holland, and more particularly in Sweden, when such walls form the backs to hothouses, they are thatched from top to bottom. In Britain, were it not for the expense of the material, boarded walls might, in many cases, be adopted instead of brick; more especially in the case of walls built in the direction of north and south, because in them the air is of nearly the same temperature on both sides; whereas in an east and west wall, the heat produced by the sun on the south side is being continually given out to the much colder north side. Boarded walls two or three centuries ago afforded the only means, in the neighbourhood of London, of forcing the cherry, the only fruit which at that time was attempted to be produced out of season. The boarded wall or fence was placed in the direction of east and west, the cherries planted against it on the south side, and casings of hot dung placed on the north, close to the boards. To derive the full advantage from the south side of an east and west wall, it ought to be of greater thickness than a south and north wall under the same circumstances; because, from the much greater cold of the north side, the south side is continually liable to have the heat abstracted from it in that direction. A south and north wall, on the other hand, can never become so hot on either side as an east and west wall does on the south side; and as it receives its heat equally on both sides, so it loses it equally. Where an east and west wall is thin, and consequently cold, it might become worth while, when it was desirable to retain as much heat on the south side as possible, to thatch it on the north side during the winter and spring months. The great advantage of covering with some protecting material the north sides of walls in spring, when trees are in blossom, may be inferred from the case of trees trained against dwelling-houses, which invariably set their blossoms better than trees against unprotected garden-walls.

The height of garden-walls may vary according to the object in view, but it is rarely necessary to be more than twelve or fifteen feet, or less than six feet. In kitchen-gardens the highest wall is generally placed on the north side, as well to protect the garden from north winds as to admit of a greater surface for training on exposed to the full sun, and to form, if necessary, a back sufficiently high for forcing-houses. The east and west boundary walls are commonly made two or three feet lower than the north wall, and the south wall somewhat lower still. The usual proportions in a garden of three acres are 17, 14, and 12; for gardens of one acre, 14, 12, and 10; that part of the north wall against which the forcing-houses are placed being in small gardens raised somewhat higher than the rest. Twelve feet is found to be a sufficient height for peach and apricot trees; but for pears and vines it may be one-half more; and indeed for vines there is scarcely any limit. An attempt has been recently made to introduce walls of glass, which the projectors conceived to possess such advantages as would cause them to supersede ordinary walls. This, however, they are not likely to do, as they reflect much less heat than a common brick-wall, or one of any kind of cement and with its surface whitewashed.

We now proceed to give the following instructions for the erection of walls:—

The foundations of garden-walls should be at least as deep as the ground is originally dug or trenched. The wall is sometimes supported on arches; but this is not in general desirable, more especially in walls built in the direction of east and west, because the roots of the trees planted on the one side of the wall are liable to extend themselves to the border on the opposite side, which not being exposed to the same temperature as that on the other side, the excitement which they receive from atmospheric temperature must necessarily be different, and consequently unfavourable to growth and the ripening of fruit and wood.

The permanent copings of walls should not, as a rule, project more than two or three inches, because a greater projection would deprive the leaves of the trees of perpendicular rains in the summer season; and in spring the trees can be protected from the frost by temporary wooden copings, as already mentioned. In order to admit of fixing these wooden copings securely, iron brackets should be built into the wall immediately under the coping, and these should in all cases be at least 2 ft. long, so as to support a wide temporary coping: or, where temporary rafters are to be fixed to the wall for supporting sashes, stones, such as fig. 110, may be built in, to which the rafters may be fitted and fixed by a tenon and pin, as indicated in fig. 111. Along the front border, a row of stone or iron posts, not rising higher than the surface, may be permanently fixed, on which a temporary front wall or plate, for the lower ends of the rafters, may be placed.

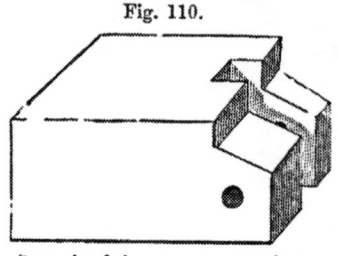

Fig. 110.

Stone for fixing temporary rafters.

The garden-walls for arrangements of this kind should be flued. Stones for fixing rafters can only be wanted on the south side of east and west walls, because glass is seldom placed before walls with any but a south aspect. The permanent coping is generally formed of flagstone, slate, artificial stone, tiles or bricks, and raised in the middle so as to throw the rain-water equally to each side; and in the case of stone, a groove or throating is formed underneath, an inch within the edge, to prevent the water from running down and rotting the mortar. Where the coping is very broad, and formed of flagstone, it is sometimes hollowed out along the middle, so as to collect the rain-water, from which it is conveyed to a drain along the foundation of the wall by pipes; but this mode is

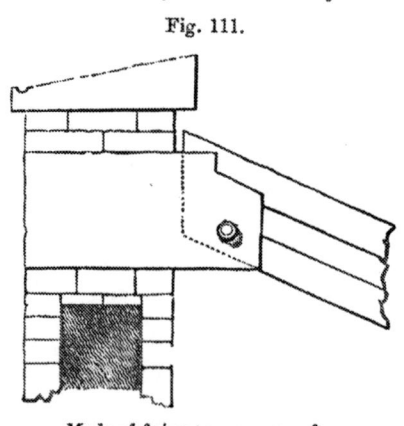

Fig. 111.

Mode of fixing temporary rafters.

only necessary in the case of conservatory walls. Where no trees are planted on the north side of an east and west wall, the coping is sometimes bevelled, so as to throw the rain-water to the north side as in fig. 111; but this can never be advisable when trees are trained there.

In the construction of walls they are generally built solid; but when the wall is formed entirely of brick, a saving of material is obtained, as well as a warmer wall produced, by building them hollow. There are various modes of effecting this, but one of the simplest is that shown by the plan fig. 112, in which a wall fourteen inches wide, with a vacuity of five inches and a half, may be built ten or twelve feet high with little more than the materials requisite for a solid wall nine inches wide. Such walls may be carried to the height of ten or twelve feet without any piers, and one advantage attending them is that they can be built with a smooth face on both sides, whereas a solid nine-inch wall can only be worked fair on one side. A still more economical wall may be formed by placing the bricks on edge, which will give a width of twelve inches that may be carried to the height of ten feet without piers. Walls of both kinds have been employed in the construction of cottage buildings, as well as in gardens. (See 'Encyc. of Cottage Architecture,' where several kinds of hollow walls are described.) A very strong wall, only seven and a half inches in thickness, may be formed of bricks of the common size, and of bricks of the same length and thickness, but of only half the width of the common bricks, by which means the wall can be worked fair on both sides. The bricks are laid side by side, as in fig. 113, in which a represents the first course, and b the second course. The bond, or tying together of both sides of the wall, is not obtained by laying bricks across (technically, headers), but by the full breadth bricks covering half the breadth of the broad bricks when laid over the narrow ones, as shown in the dissected horizontal section, fig. 113, at b, and in the vertical section, fig. 114. Besides the advantage of being built fair on both sides, there being no headers, or through and through bricks, in these walls, when they are used as outside walls the rain is never conducted through the wall, and the inside of the wall is consequently drier than the inside of a wall nine inches in thickness. These walls are adapted for a variety of purposes in

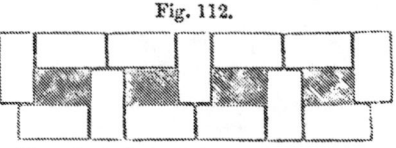

Fig. 112.

Plan of a hollow brick wall 14 inches wide and 12 feet high.

Fig. 113.

Plan of a brick wall 7½ inches thick.

Fig. 114.

End view of a 7½-inch thick brick wall.

house-building and gardening, in the latter art more especially. The only drawback that we know against them is, that the narrow or half-breadth bricks must be made on purpose. For the division walls of a large garden, or for the boundary wall of a small one, such walls with piers projecting eighteen inches or two feet, to enable the walls to be carried to the height of ten or twelve feet, might be economically adopted: the space between the piers ought not to be greater than can be covered by a single tree. The piers are an admirable position for growing cordons upon, which add greatly to the effect, and increase the produce. Conservatory walls may likewise be turned to good account, both as assisting in supporting the temporary copings or glass, and as heightening architectural effect. Walls are almost always built perpendicularly to the horizon, but they have been tried at different degrees of inclination to it, in order to receive the sun's rays at right angles when he is highest in the firmament during summer; but though some advantage may probably have been obtained from such walls at that season, yet the great loss of heat by radiation during spring and autumn would probably be found greatly to overbalance the gain during summer. Nicol informs us that he constructed many hundred feet of boarded walls which reclined considerably towards the north, in order to present a better angle to the sun, but he does not inform us of the result; a German gardener, however, has found advantage from them. (See 'Nicol's Kal.,' p. 149, and 'Hort. Trans.' vol. iv. p. 140.) Upon the whole, however, walls are better upright. An inclined surface is easily formed by raised banks of earth, which are cheaper and often warmer than walls.

Wherever the surface of a garden wall is found to be too rough, or is formed of too large stones to admit of conveniently attaching the branches of trees to it by nails and shreds, it becomes necessary to fix to the wall trellis-work of wood or of wire. The laths or wires are generally placed perpendicularly six or eight inches apart, because the branches are generally trained horizontally, or at some angle between horizontal and perpendicular. Wires stretched horizontally, however, and screwed tight, form the most economical description of trellis; and if occasionally painted, they will last a number of years. Trellis-work of wood is more architectural, and the branches are more readily fixed to them by ties, which are apt to slide along the small wire unless the double operation is performed of first attaching the tie to the wire, and then tying it to the shoot of the tree. The colour both of the wire and woodwork should not differ much from that of the stone of the wall, otherwise it will become too conspicuous. Undoubtedly the best kind of trellises for walls are those of galvanized wire.

"If there be any one practice of French horticulturists more worthy of special recommendation to the English fruit-grower than another, it is their improved way of placing wires on walls, or in any position in which it may be desired to neatly train fruit trees. So many have been the failures in British gardens as regards the placing of the wire

WALLS, ESPALIER-RAILS, AND TRELLIS-WORK. 143

to which to affix the trees, that the system has been given up as useless and too expensive, and many have said that the old-fashioned shred and nail are yet the best. But there is a very much better and sounder way, and I am completely converted as to the value of the French mode of wiring here illustrated. In the first instance, several strong iron spikes are driven into the brickwork at the ends—in the right angle formed by two walls—nails with eyes in them being driven in in straight lines, exactly in the line of direction in which the wire is wanted to pass. The wires are placed at about ten inches apart on the walls, and the little hooks for their support, also galvanized, are fixed at about ten feet apart along each wire. The exact distance between the wires must, however, be determined by the kind of tree and the form to be given to it. If horizontal training of the branches be adopted, the wires had better be placed to form the lines which we wish the branches to follow; if the branches are vertical, as in fig. 115, we need not be so exact. The wire—about as thick as strong

Fig. 115.

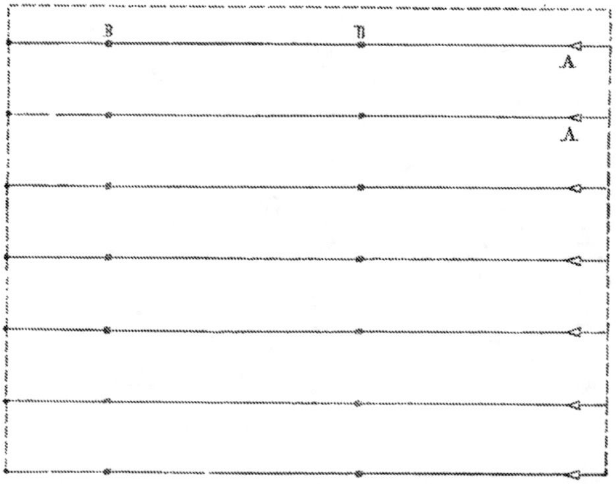

Mode of arranging wires on walls for training fruit-trees with vertical or horizontal branches. A, *Position of raidisseur;* B, *Nails with eyes, through which the wire is passed.*

twine—is passed through the little hooks, fastened at both ends of the wall into the strong iron nails, and then made as straight as a needle and as tight as a drum, by being strained with the raidisseur. The wires remain at about the distance of half an inch or three-quarters from the wall.

"If we consider the expense of the shreds and nails, the cutting of the former, the destroying of the surface of the walls by the nails, and the leaving of numerous holes for vermin to take refuge in; the great annual labour of nailing, and the miserable work it is for men in our cold winters and springs—it will be freely admitted that a change is wanted badly. The system of wiring a wall above described is simple, cheap, almost everlasting, and excellent in every particular: and it must before many years elapse be nearly universally adopted in our fruit-gardens. A man may do as much work in one day along a wall wired thus as he could in six with the old nail and shred. As to galvanized wire having an injurious effect on the fruit-trees trained on it, it is simply nonsense; I will not therefore waste space and the intelligent reader's time by discussing it. Given a concrete wall, smoothly plastered, and wired thus, what fruit-trees could be in a more excellent position than those upon it? The temporary coping taken off after all danger from frost was past, every leaf would be under the refreshing influence of the summer rains, all the advantages of walls as regards heat would be obtained, the syringing-engine would not be counteracted by countless

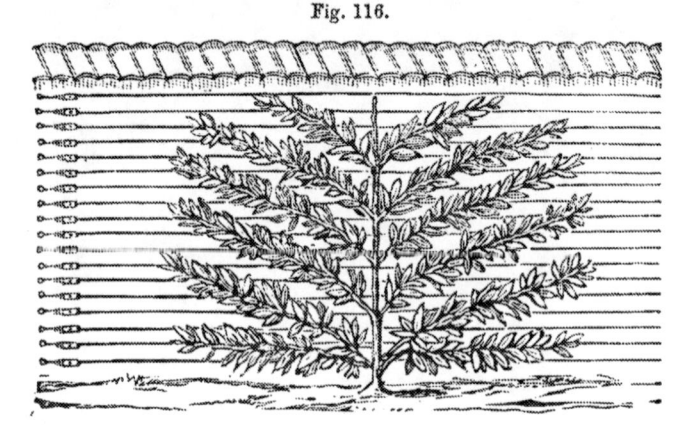

Fig. 116.

Wall with galvanized wires for training trees.

dens offering dry beds and comfortable breeding-places to the enemies of the gardener and the fruit-tree, while the appearance of the wall would be all that could be desired.

" The wire and the raidisseur are also efficiently used so as to do away with any necessity for nailing in training the peach and other trees, when trained as cordons, as shown in the accompanying figure. When the lines which the wires are to follow are fixed upon, bolts and eyes are driven in, the wire is fixed to and passed through them, and then made firm, as shown in the illustrations." ('The Parks, Promenades, and Gardens of Paris.')

Colouring the surface of walls black, with a view to the absorption of heat, has been tried by a number of persons, and by some it has been considered beneficial; but as the radiation during night and in cloudy weather is necessarily in proportion to the absorption during sunshine, the one operation neutralizes the other. If, indeed, we could ensure a powerful absorption from a bright sun during the day, and retain the radiation by a canvas or other screen during the night, a

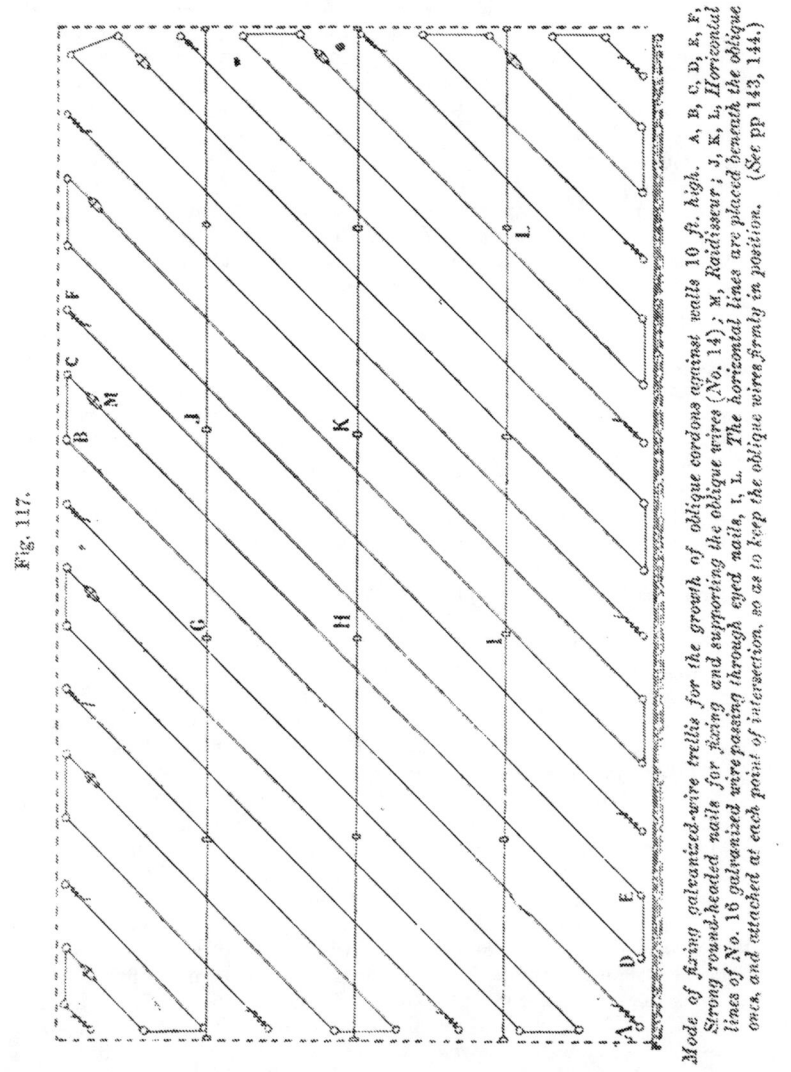

Fig. 117.

Mode of fixing galvanized-wire trellis for the growth of oblique cordons against walls 10 ft. high. A, B, C, D, E, F, Strong round-headed nails for fixing and supporting the oblique wires (No. 14); M, Raidisseur; J, K, L, Horizontal lines of No. 16 galvanized wire passing through eyed nails, I, L. The horizontal lines are placed beneath the oblique ones, and attached at each point of intersection, so as to keep the oblique wires firmly in position. (See pp 143, 144.)

considerable increase of temperature might probably be the result; but the number of cloudy days in our climate in proportion to those of bright sunshine is not favourable to such an experiment.

L

"No matter of what material the wall be made, it will be desirable to whiten its surface and keep it white. Black and dark-coloured surfaces absorb heat in the daytime, and give it out again during the night in the form of radiant heat; from which facts we might draw the conclusion that walls for training fruit-trees against should be black, or at any rate of a dark colour. Direct experiment was, however, necessary to settle this question, and M. Vuitry, who employs his leisure in arboriculture, has communicated the results of his experiments in this direction to M. du Breuil, which leave no doubt as to the proper colour to be chosen for walls against which fruit-trees are to be trained. He has proved—1st. That a thermometer hung during the day with its face turned towards a white wall, at a distance from it equal to that of a fruit-tree trained against it—*i.e.*, about an inch and a quarter—always showed a mean temperature of nearly 6 deg. Fahr. higher than one hung against a black wall under precisely similar circumstances. 2nd. That during the night the difference of temperature shown by these two thermometers was inappreciable. Contrary therefore to the opinions entertained by many persons, it seems to be evident that the walls must be whitened when we wish to give the trees trained against them the maximum amount of heat to be obtained from the particular climate and aspect. Indeed, it is precisely the plan that has already been pursued by the fruit-growers of Montreuil for peach-trees, and of Thomery for their vines, it having been frequently remarked that trees trained against white walls were healthier than those nailed to more or less dark-coloured ones. This result is easily explained, for not only does the lighter colour reflect more heat back to the trees, but by this means they receive a greater quantity of light; and it is well known how greatly vegetation is stimulated by these agencies. Walls of a light tint are advantageous in another way, for they not only reflect light and heat on the particular trees trained against them, but also on the others in their immediate neighbourhood." ('The Parks, Promenades, and Gardens of Paris.')

Flued walls are either built entirely of brick, or with one side of brick and the other of stone; the latter being the north side of east-and-west walls. In the case of north-and-south walls which are to be flued, the thickness is equal on both sides, and the wall is built entirely of brick. The flues, which are generally from six to eight inches wide, commence about one foot above the surface of the border; the first course is from two to three feet high, and each successive course is a few inches lower, till the last flue, within a foot of the coping, is about eighteen inches high. The thickness of that side of the flue next the south should, for the first course, be four inches, or the width of a brick laid flatways; and for the other courses it is desirable to have the bricks somewhat narrower, on account of the heat being less powerful as the smoke ascends. All the bricks, however, whatever may be their width, must be of the same thickness, in order to preserve uniformity in the external appearance of the wall. As, where garden walls are to be built, a large supply of bricks is requisite, no difficulty need occur in getting such a quantity as might be requisite for the flued walls made of any convenient width. To prevent the risk of overheating the trees by the flues, trellises are sometimes applied against them for training on; but where the wall is properly constructed, and only moderate fires kept, they are unnecessary. Flued walls may now, however, be almost considered things of the past, as they are, to a great extent, supplanted by the orchard-house.

Conservative or flued walls for growing half-hardy or greenhouse shrubs require a somewhat different arrangement from those intended for fruit trees; chiefly because in the former case it is necessary, in order to preserve the plants through the autumn and winter, to keep the border from perpendicular rains, at least to the width of three or four feet. For this purpose a temporary roofing is made to project over the border, immediately from under the fixed coping. This temporary roofing may be formed of hurdles thatched with straw, or reeds fixed by hooks close below the coping of the wall, and resting on a front rail, supported by posts at regular distances. The posts may either be poles with the bark on let into the ground, or prepared from sawn timber and let into fixed stone bases. The straw on the hurdles should be disposed lengthways in the direction of the slope, in order to throw off the rain; and the eaves ought to drop on a broad gutter of boards or tiles, or in a firm path from which the water may be carried off in drains, so as not to moisten that part of the border which is under the hurdles. The border should be thoroughly drained, and an underground four-inch wall may be built at the same distance from the wall as the bases to the posts, on which wall these bases may be placed. In order to enjoy the full advantage of flues to a conservatory wall, glass frames should be used during the autumn, instead of thatched hurdles, so as to admit the light at the same time that rain was excluded; and afterwards the glass might be covered so as to retain heat, or thatched hurdles might be substituted.

A protected trellis, with moveable glass sashes, for ripening early fruit, has been long in use at Hylands, Bulstrode, and Strathfieldsaye, having been originally imported from Holland. (See 'Gard. Mag.,' vol. ix. p. 675.) Some of these protected trellises are double, with reeds in the centre, so as to form a kind of wall. One erected at Hylands, in Essex, the plan of which is shown in fig. 118, and the section

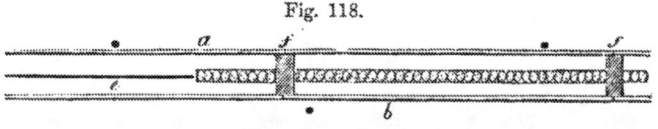

Fig. 118.

Plan of a reed wall.

in fig. 119, may be described as ten feet high, and consisting of a double trellis, *a, b*, composed of horizontal laths about eight inches apart; a coping-board, *c*, nine inches broad; the reeds placed endwise within the trellis, *d*, and supported about a foot from the ground to keep them from rotting; this interval of a foot being filled up with slates, placed on edge, *e*. The trellis rods are nailed to posts, fig. 118, *f*, and by

148   WALLS, ESPALIER-RAILS, AND TRELLIS-WORK.

taking off a few of these rods on one side, the reed mats can be taken out and removed. Russian mats would no doubt answer very well, and last a long time, and they might be taken out with still less trouble. Straw mats would also do, where reeds could not be got; and heath, as being of a dark colour and very durable, would make the best of all structures of this kind. Peaches, grapes, and other fruits, ripen just as well on these structures as on brick walls, both in Holland and England. The trellises at Strathfieldsaye resembled low pits when we saw them in 1833, with the glass on, and the peaches, apricots, and figs, ripened on them about a month sooner than on the open walls.

Fig. 119.

Espalier-rails are substitutes for walls, commonly placed in borders parallel to walks. The commonest form is nothing more than a row of perpendicular stakes driven into the soil, about eight inches apart, centre from centre, about five feet high, and connected by a rail at top. When the stakes are of larch with the bark on, or when they are of oak with their lower ends charred, they last five or six years; but in general they are of shorter duration, and continually requiring repair. Framework of prepared timber well painted, supported from the ground by sockets of stone, is much more durable, and still more so are espalier-rails formed entirely of cast iron. In every case, however, when either wooden or cast-iron framework is used, the stones which support it ought to be raised two or three inches above the surface of the ground, not only because this is more architectural, but because it contributes to the preservation of the iron or the wood. When the stone bases are to support timber, the posts should not be let into the stone, because in that case water is apt to lodge and rot them; but the stone should be bevelled from the centre, and a dowel of iron or wood inserted in it, so as to pass into the lower end of the post. If the post is let into the stone, it should be set in lead, pitch, or asphalte. In our 'Villa Gardener,' pp. 231 and 232, we have shown figures of two very economical espalier-rails formed of hoop iron and iron wire, which had been in use upwards of fifteen years, without requiring any other

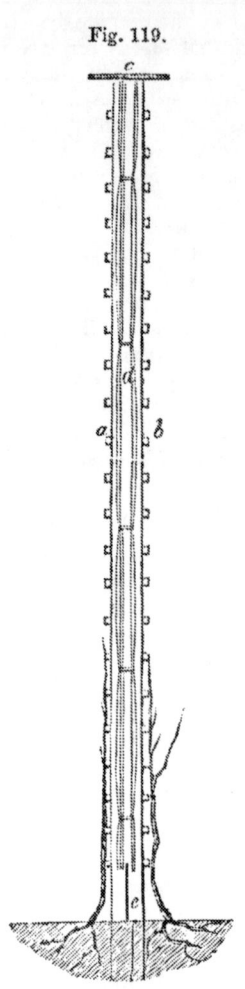

Section of a reed-wall.

repairs than that of being once coated over with gas liquor. A very light and elegant espalier-rail, and perhaps the most economical of any, consists of iron standards let into blocks of stone, strong wires being stretched through the standards; and at the extremities of each straight length the standards are braced by stay bars, and a connecting bar holding the two together; the upper end of the stay bar being screwed to the main post. The triangle thus formed at each end of a straight line of trellis admits of straining the wires perfectly tight. A structure of this kind was first used as an espalier for trees at Carclew, in Cornwall; but it has been frequently put up in various parts of the country in pleasure-grounds, to separate the lawn from the park, and is now almost the only espalier used. The chief difficulty in erecting this fence is to strain the wires perfectly tight; but this may be easily effected by means of the raidisseur described at pp. 93, 94, 95. Fences or espalier rails of this description are most easily erected when in a straight line; but by means of underground braces, either of iron, wood, or stone, they may be erected on any curve whatever. Where effect is any consideration, the braces should in every case be concealed under ground. When trellis-work is placed against walls, or against any object which it is desired to conceal, it may be wholly covered by the plants trained on it; but where it is placed in any position by which it will be seen on both sides (such as when it forms the supports to a verandah, or a summer-house, or a trellised arcade over a walk), the surface must not be entirely covered by the plants; because it is desirable that leaves and blossoms should be seen on both sides, and this can only be done effectively by the partial admission of direct light through the interstices or meshes of the trellis-work. A trellised walk closely covered with the most ornamental roses will show no more beauty to a person walking within, than if it were covered with the most ordinary plants; but let partial openings be made in the covering of roses, and their leaves and blossoms will be seen hanging down over the head of the spectator, forming a perspective of flowers and foliage, instead of one presenting only the branches, and the footstalks and backs of the leaves.

Trellises and lattice-work are constructed either of wood or iron, or of both materials combined; and though lattice-work, by which we mean trellis-work with the meshes or spaces between the intersections smaller than is usual for the purposes of training, is chiefly required in ornamental structures, yet it is occasionally used for supporting fruit-trees, and for culinary plants, such as cucumbers. In order to render trellis-work durable and architectural, it ought never to rise directly out of the soil, but always be supported either by the wall or frame against which it is placed, or when it is independent, by bases of stone. This is almost always neglected, both in kitchen and ornamental gardens, in consequence of which the construction is unsatisfactory to the artistical eye, and the posts, or other parts which rise out of the soil, decay long before the superstructure. Where espalier-rails of this, or of any other kind, are put up in flower-gardens for supporting shrubs which come early into flower, such as the Pyrus japonica, Wistaria sinensis, China and other climbing roses, &c., they may be easily protected by a moveable coping of boards, like an inverted gutter, which can be dropped on or taken off in a very few minutes. In order to economize space in small gardens, Mr. Alexander Forsyth proposes to cover the walks with trellis-work for the support of fruit-trees. "Every species of hardy fruit-bearing tree and shrub," he says, "may be trained on curvilinear trellises, as in figs. 120 and 121, over the walks and thoroughfares of the garden;

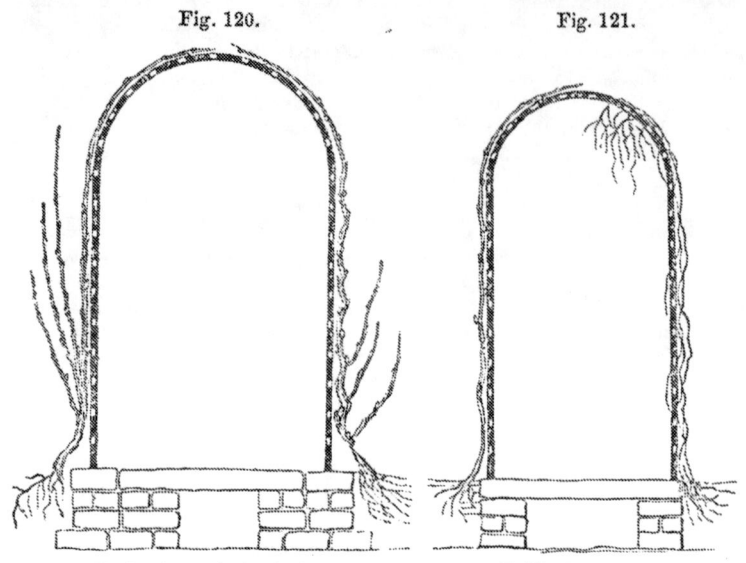

Fig. 120.   Fig. 121.

Trellised arcade for fruit-trees.   *Trellis for climbers.*

which walks, when once properly drained, paved, and trellised with cast-iron arches and wire rods, will remain cost free, painting excepted, for twenty years; at the end of which term, independently of the increase of fruit, and of the grateful shade and pleasing promenade that they will afford, they will be found cheaper than the walks made of gravel, in the same way that a slated roof is far cheaper in the long run than one thatched. Besides the difference in daily comfort and annual expenditure in walks paved with slate, slabs, or flagstone, at all seasons clean, and capable of being traversed by the foot or the wheelbarrow alike in frost and in thaw, there will be no more danger of dessert strawberries or garnishing parsley, when grown as edgings, being mingled with the coal-ashes in the walks; no more cleaning and rolling of gravel; and no planting and clipping of box." Fig. 122 shows the plan of the paving and pillars at the intersections of the walks, with the small footpaths outside, for conducting the culture of the compartments. In open, airy situations where hedges for shelter are desirable, trellises of this sort might frequently be adopted as substitutes both in kitchen and flower gardens. Single lines of trellis-work, or even of frames to be filled in with wire network, might also be adopted as sources of shelter in spring; and in summer they might be covered with kidney-beans, peas, gourds, tomatoes, nasturtiums, &c. The wire netting to fit into such framework can be made by common country workmen and their families, as is the case in various parts of Norfolk, both with hempen and wire netting, for hare and rabbit fences, and for folding sheep.—(See 'Gard. Mag.,' vol. xv. page 222.)

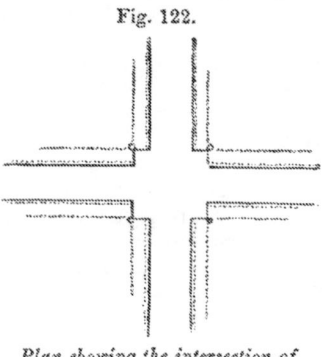

Fig. 122.

Plan showing the intersection of trellised walks.

Fixed Structures for Growing Plants, with Glass Roofs.

Plant-houses are required in gardens for forcing the productions of the open air into maturity earlier than would otherwise be the case; for retarding these productions, as in ripening grapes late and preserving them through the winter hanging on the tree; and for the growth of plants of warm climates. Hence it follows that all the requisites for growing plants in the open air in their natural climate must be imitated in plant-houses. As the grand difference between one climate and another lies in difference of their temperature, one principal desideratum in hothouses is to supply heat, without which little can be done either in forcing hardy plants, or in preserving those of warm climates. Next to heat, moisture is the most important agent in growth, and that element is readily supplied both to the soil and the atmosphere; but though heat and water are sufficient to induce growth, it cannot be continued or perfected without the influence of light, and fortunately this is now, in a great degree, at the command of art. Nearly the whole light of the climate is now admitted into our artificial plant-houses, without dilution or diminution, through our clear glass roofs. For growing certain fungi, and for forcing some roots, very little light is necessary; and where ripened crops of fruit are to be retained on the trees and retarded, light, at least direct solar light, may be in a great measure dispensed with. The retention or production of heat therefore, and the admission of light, are the great objects to be kept in view, in deciding on the situation, form, and construction of hothouses.

In the selection of a situation with reference to the surrounding country, the north side of a sheltered basin, on the south side of a hill and open to the south, with a dry warm soil, is to be preferred. The object of this choice is to have as little heat as possible carried off, either by the evaporation of surface water, or by N., N.E., or N.W. winds. If the surface of the soil is hard and smooth so as to carry off the winter rains and thawing snows, without allowing them to sink into and cool the soil, so much the better. It is seldom, however, that these conditions can be fulfilled to their utmost extent; because not only such situations are not frequent in nature, but that even where they do exist, the situation for the hothouses is determined by the artificial circumstances connected with the house, offices, and grounds. For ornamental structures the situation chosen is generally some part of the pleasure-ground, or flower-garden, not far from the dwelling-house; and forcing-houses are generally placed in the kitchen-garden, or in some place intermediate between it and the stable offices ('Sub. Arch. and Landscape Gardener,' p. 412). Wherever the situation may be, the soil and subsoil ought to be rendered perfectly dry by drains so placed as to intercept all subterraneous water, from whatever direction it may come; and by surface-gutters, or the surfaces of walks, &c., so arranged as to carry off the water of cold rains and thawing snows, without allowing it to sink into and cool the soil. The next point is to produce artificial shelter, by walls or other buildings, and plantations or hedges, so placed as to check the winds which blow from cold quarters without obstructing the south and south-east winds, and the morning and evening sun. The amount of heat carried off by winds which are at a lower temperature than the surface they pass over, is great in proportion to the velocity of the wind and the moisture of the surface, and hence the much greater ease with which the temperature of a greenhouse may be kept up when it is placed in a sheltered, rather than in an exposed situation; for example, in the concave side of a curvilinear wall, rather than against a straight wall.

The most perfect form of house for the admission of solar light and heat is that of a semi-globe of glass, because to some part of this form the sun's rays will be perpendicular every moment while he shines, and at every time of the year; and by it a maximum of light will be admitted at those periods when he does not shine; but this form, excepting under particular circumstances—that, for example, in which there was a double glass dome, or in which only a temperature of a few degrees above that of the open air was required to be kept up—would occasion too great a loss of heat, either for economy or the health of the plants; for when heat is rapidly conducted away and rapidly supplied by art, it is found extremely difficult to obtain a sufficient degree of atmospheric moisture for healthy vegetation. For these reasons a semi-dome is preferable to a semi-globe, because the glazed side being placed next the sun, the other side may be opaque, so as to reflect back both heat and light, and it may be made so complete a non-conductor as not to allow the escape of any heat. There is an objection, however, to the general adoption of the semi-dome, because it is found that the rays of light after passing through glass-roofs, lose their influence on the plants within in proportion to their distance from the glass and its clearness. Hence, for general purposes, span-roof or lean-to houses are the best; and hence also herbaceous plants are grown best in pots in frames; and were it not for the quantity of glass that would be required, all shrubby and climbing plants would be grown to the highest degree of perfection if trained on trellises parallel to the glass roofing, and at no great distance within it. In pits and frames, herbaceous or low plants are nearer the glass than they can ever be in large houses, in which, unless they are placed on shelves close under the roof, they are either at a distance from the glass, as in the body of the house, or they present only one side to it, as when they are placed near the front glass. There is another reason in favour of narrow houses where perfection of growth and economy is an object, which is,

Fig. 123.

Span-roofed forcing-house.

that the major portion of the heat by which the temperature of hot-houses is maintained, is supplied by the sun. The power of the sun therefore will be great on the atmosphere within, inversely as its cubic contents, compared with the superficial contents of the glass enclosing it. Thus, suppose one house to be twenty feet high and twenty feet wide, and another to be twenty feet high and only ten feet wide, the contents of the former will be exactly double that of the latter; at the same time, instead of containing double the surface of glass on its roof, it will contain scarcely one-third more; being nearly in the proportion of twenty-eight for the house of double volume, to not fourteen, or one-half, but twenty-two, for the one of half the internal capacity. In the wide house every square foot of glass has to heat upwards of seven cubic feet of air; in the narrow house only about four and a half feet ('Gardener's Magazine,' vol. xiii. p. 15). There are, however, plant-houses erected not merely for growing plants, but for walking into, in order to enjoy them; and in these, other considerations interfere with rigid economy, both in heating and lighting. The form of plant-houses, therefore, must be determined by the object in view, and the means at command. For early and for late forcing, narrow houses with upright glass, or glass at a very steep slope, are preferable, as giving but a small volume of air to be heated, and as admitting the sun's rays at a right angle, at those seasons when he is low in the heavens, and shines only for a short time. For summer forcing the angle of the roof may be larger, and of course its slope less steep; for greenhouses and plant stoves, in which plants are to be grown all the year, there should be a portion of the roof with the glass very steep, or upright front glass, for admitting the sun's rays in winter. The roofs of such houses may be at a large angle, say from 35° to 45° with the horizon, which is more favourable for throwing off rain, and also for resisting hail, than a flatter surface. For growing herbaceous plants and young plants, and for the general purposes of propagation, whether by seeds, cuttings, or layers, a low flat house, in which the glass shall be near to all the plants, as in pits and frames, is the most convenient form; though when fruits are to be ripened in such houses in the winter season, the flatness of the glass, and consequent obliquity of the sun's rays to it, is a great disadvantage. Hence, when such plants can be conveniently grown in pots, as in the case of strawberries, or bulbous or other flowers, it is desirable to have very steep glass, and to place the plants on shelves immediately within it, as practised by Mr. Wilmot, and other market-gardeners, in such structures as fig. 125; or, when the plants are climbers, as the cucumber and melon, to train them up trellises parallel to the glass, and at a short distance within it, as in Ayres' cucumber-house.

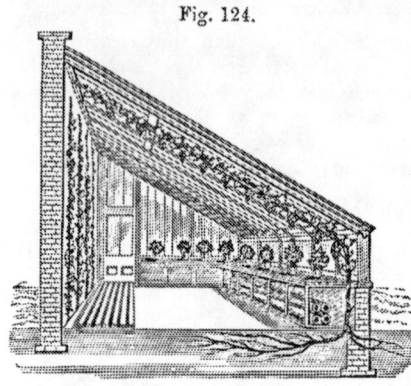

Curvilinear roofs.—The ordinary form of the roofs of plant-houses is that of a right-lined plane, like the roof of any other building, but they have been also formed with curvilinear roofs, which, as compared with roofs having upright glass with standards and wall-plates, more especially when the sash-bar is of iron, admit much more light. The ends of plant-houses are generally vertical planes, but in curvilinear houses they are sometimes of the same curvature as the front, which adds greatly to their beauty, as well as being favourable to the admission of the sun's rays, morning and evening, and to the transmission of diffused light when the sun does not shine. The only disadvantages attending curvilinear ends to plant-houses is, that the doors cannot be placed in these ends without some intricacy of construction; but when such houses are placed against walls, as in fig. 126,

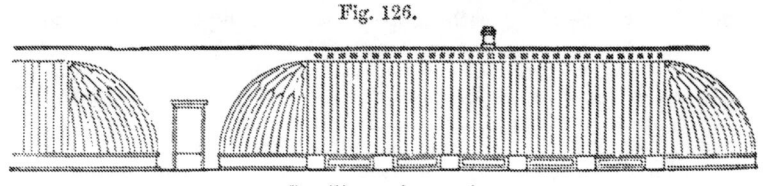

Fig. 126.

Curvilinear glass roofs.

they may be entered through a door made in the wall to a recess taken from the back shed, as shown by fig. 127, in which *a, a*, represent the plans of portions of two curvilinear houses; *b, b*, back sheds to these houses; and *c*, lobby common to both. These houses may be ventilated by openings in the upper part of the back wall, the orifice within being covered with pierced zinc, and wooden shutters moving

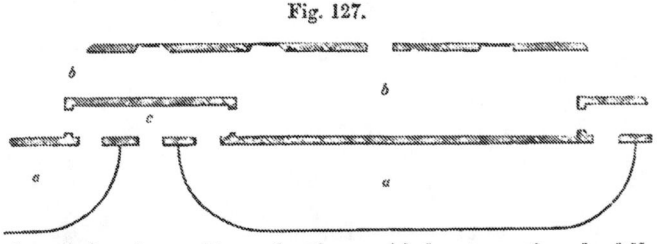

Fig. 127.

Ground plan of a curvilinear plant-house, with the entrance through a lobby in the back wall.

in grooves simultaneously. Where a lobby cannot conveniently be made in the back shed, one door may be made in the centre of the front of each house, as at Messrs. Loddiges'; and where the end is semicircular, a door might be made in it in a similar manner, or with a projection brought forward so as to form a porch; the mode represented in fig. 127 is, however, greatly preferable, as occasioning no obstruction to light.

Roofs of greenhouses, &c., formed in the ridge and furrow manner, and even glass sashes so formed for pits, were tried by us many years ago ('Encyc. of Gard.,' 1st edit.): and the idea has been improved on, and applied in the happiest manner, by Sir Joseph Paxton, at Chatsworth; and adopted by Mr. Marnock, in the Sheffield Botanic Garden; Jedediah Strutt, Esq., at Belper; William Harrison, Esq., Cheshunt; John Allcard, Esq., Stratford Green; and at various other places. The advantages of this description of roof are :—1. That the roof does not require to be raised so high behind, in proportion to its width, as in flat roofs; because the descent of the water does not depend on the general slope of the roof, but on the slope of the ridges towards the furrows; and the water in these furrows, being confined to a narrow deep channel, and in a larger body than it ever can be on the glass, passes along with proportionate rapidity. 2. That the morning and afternoon sun, by passing through the glass at right angles, produces more light and heat at these times of the day, when they are, of course, more wanted than at mid-day. 3. The rays of the sun striking on the house at an oblique angle at mid-day, the heat produced in the house at that time is less intense than in houses of the ordinary kind, in which it is often injurious, by rendering it necessary to admit large quantities of the external air to lower the temperature. 4. More light is admitted at all seasons, on the principle that a bow window always admits more light to a room than a straight window of the same width. 5. The panes of glass, if crown-glass be employed, may be smaller than in houses the roofs of which are in one plane, and yet, from there being a greater number of them, admit an equal quantity of light; from their smallness also, they will cost less, and be less liable to be broken by the freezing of water between the laps. 6. By the employment of sheet window-glass, which is much thicker than crown-glass, panes of three or four feet in length may be used, so that only one pane need be required for each division, and consequently no lap being required, no breakage by frost can take place, and no heated air can escape. And 7. That wind will have much less influence in cooling the roof, because the sides of the ridges will be sheltered by their summits. Sir J. Paxton, to whom the merit of this mode of roofing is entirely due, has also adopted an improvement in the construction of the sash-bar—viz., having grooves for the panes instead of rebates (see figs. 128 and 129); the advantages of which grooves are, that less putty is required, and that what is used does not so readily separate from the wood, and thus admit the wet between the wood and the putty. The roofs of such houses are entirely fixed, and ventilation is effected either by having the perpendicular ends of the ridges moveable on hinges, or by the front glass and ventilators in the back wall. The expense of this mode of roofing is doubtless greater than that of the common flat mode, but not so much

Fig. 128.

Section of an iron sash-bar, with grooves for the glass.

Fig. 129.

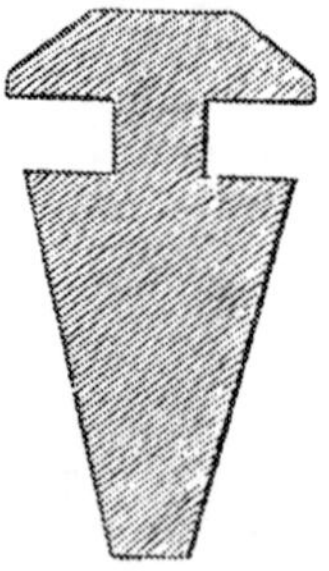

Section of a wooden sash-bar, with grooves for the glass.

so as might be expected, because the sash-bar can be formed lighter, and where crown-glass is used the panes may be much smaller. For plant-houses the advantage of admitting the sun's rays perpendicularly, early in the morning and late in the afternoon, will much more than compensate for any additional expense. In an architectural point of view the merits of this mode of roofing are perhaps as great as they are with reference to culture: the roofs being lower, are less conspicuous, and the common shed-like appearance is taken away by the pediments which form the ends of the ridges, and appear in a range as a crowning parapet to the front glass. Indeed, if it were desirable, the tops of the ridges might be made perfectly horizontal, and all the slope that is necessary for carrying the water from back to front, or to both the sides, given in the gutters between the ridges, as is done in roofing common buildings of great width. Fig. 130 is a

Fig. 130.

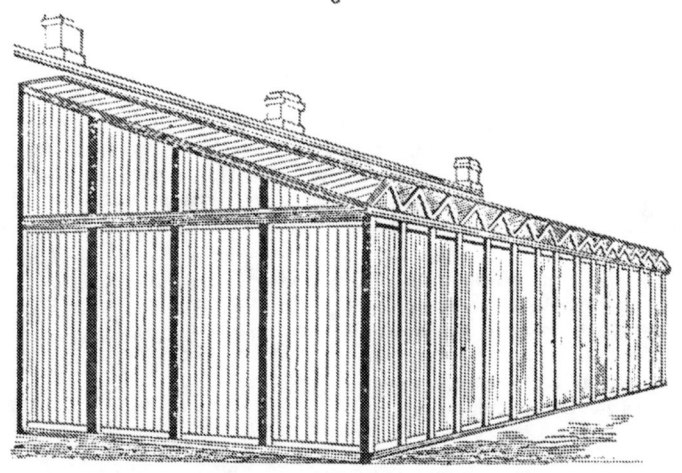

Perspective view of the original ridge and furrow house at Chatsworth.

perspective view of a house erected by Sir J. Paxton, at Chatsworth, and fig. 131 a vertical profile of part of two ridges of the roof. It will be observed that the sash-bar is not in a direction parallel to the pediments, but oblique to it. This is done to prevent the water from running down on one side of the glass, which it would do in consequence of the general slope of the ridge from the back to the front if the bars were placed at right angles to the ridge. The angle at which the bars are fixed will vary with that formed by the slope of the ridge, and the mode of determining it is to place the bars so that the lap of the glass, which is in square panes, may form, when the panes are fitted in their places, lines truly horizontal. There are many persons, however, who attach no great importance to causing the water to run down the middle of the glass instead of one side; and they will, of course, place the bars for holding the glass, parallel to the pediments, in order to avoid the short bars at the ends of the ridges, as seen in fig. 131. For more minute details respecting this mode of construc-

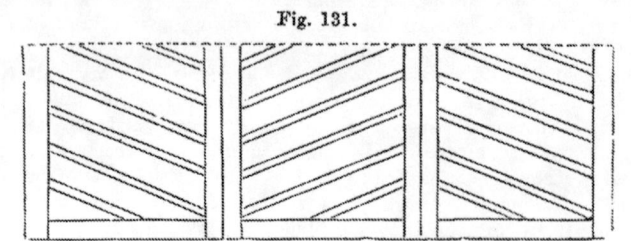

Fig. 131.

Vertical profile of part of a ridge and furrow roof.

tion, we refer to 'Paxton's Magazine of Botany,' vol. ii. p. 30; and 'Gard. Mag.,' vol. xv. p. 452, and also for 1841. The Great Exhibition Building of 1851 in Hyde Park, with the Crystal Palace at Sydenham, furnish magnificent examples of this mode of glazing.

The materials used in the construction of plant-houses differ in nothing from those used in other buildings, except that where as much light as possible is required to be admitted, the framework for containing the glass is formed of iron or other metal, as supplying the requisite strength with less bulk than wood. The proportion of opaque surface of an iron roof may be estimated at not more than 7 or 8 per cent., while in a wooden roof it is upwards of 20 per cent.; both roofs being in one plane and of the ordinary construction. Where sheet-glass is employed, and the panes made of more than ordinary length and width, as in the large conservatory erected in the Royal Horticultural Society's garden, the proportion of light admitted in the case of iron roofs will be found still greater. Ridge and furrow roofs, if we take the area of the bases of the ridges as the total area of the roof, and then deduct from it the space occupied by the bars forming the sides of the ridges, and the ridge-pieces and gutters, will not appear to admit the same proportion of light as a roof in one plane; but the practical result will be different, in consequence of the sun's rays being twice in the day perpendicular to one-half of the roof, the advantage of which to the plants will far more than compensate for the obscuration produced by the greater proportion of sash-bars, which, operating chiefly at mid-day and in very hot weather, is rather an advantage than otherwise. To prove this, it is necessary first to know the law of the reflection of light from glass.

The law of the reflection of light from glass was calculated by Bouguer, a French philosopher, in 1729, and is exhibited by the following figures; the first line representing the angles of incidence, and the second the number of rays reflected, exclusive of decimal parts:—

Angle of incidence . . . 85°, 80°, 70°, 60°, 50°, 40°, 30°, 20, 10°, 1°.
Per centage of rays reflected 50, 41, 22, 11, 5, 3, 2, 2, 2, 2.

Now, if we suppose a roof in one plane with the sun shining on it at six o'clock in the morning, and at six o'clock in the afternoon, at an angle of 85°, which would be the case in March and September, fully one-half the rays which fell on the roof would be reflected; while, in the case of a ridge and furrow roof, if he shone on half the roof, that is on one-half of each of the ridges, at any angle with a perpendicular not exceeding 30°, at the same periods, only two per cent. of the rays would be reflected. Suppose, then, the area of the entire roof, taken as one plane, to be 100 square yards, and, to facilitate calculation, that only 100 rays fell on each yard, then the total number which would enter through the roof in one plane would be 50,000, while those which would enter through the ridge and furrow roof would be 99,000, or very nearly double the number. If we compare a roof in one plane with the framework of wood, with a similar one with the framework of iron, and take the space rendered opaque by the wood at twenty-one per cent., and by the iron at seven per cent., then the greater number of rays admitted at all times by the iron roof over the wooden one will be as three to one.

Iron roofs have been objected to from their somewhat greater original expense, from their supposed liability to break glass by contraction and expansion, and from the iron being liable to conduct away heat in winter, and to become hot to such a degree as to be injurious to the plants in summer. With regard to expense, that is, we believe, now considered the chief objection; but though it may be heavier at first, yet it is amply compensated for by the great durability of iron houses, when properly constructed, and when the iron is never allowed to become rusty for want of paint. As a proof of the durability of iron houses, we may refer to the iron camellia-house, at Messrs. Loddiges', erected in 1818, and the iron houses in the Horticultural Society's garden, which were erected, we believe, in 1823. The breakage of glass supposed to result from the contraction or expansion of the metal was at one time considered a very weighty objection; but the severe winter of 1837–8 did not occasion so much broken glass in iron as it did in wooden houses. A bar of malleable iron, 819 inches in length, at a temperature of 32°, only increases in length one inch, when heated to 212°; but this difference of 180° of temperature is more than plant-houses are liable to; indeed 50° or 60° are as much as is necessary to be taken into account. If we suppose the iron-work is fitted at a period of the season when the temperature is 55°, then 50° lower would be within 5° of zero, and 50° higher would be 105°; extremes which the iron roof of a hothouse will seldom exceed. Now, according to the above data, a bar ten feet in length would extend or contract, by the addition or reduction of 50° of heat, 1-25th of an inch as nearly as possible. An iron sash-bar, half an inch thick between the two edges of the glass, would not expand in thickness, from 50° of heat, much more than one six-thousandth part of an inch. It may easily be conceived, therefore, that the lateral expansion of sash-bars, which are in general not quite half an inch in thickness, by any heat which they can receive on the roof of a hothouse, will never have any effect on the glass between them. To guard against all risk of breakage from this cause, however, it is only necessary not to fit in the panes too tightly. Indeed, the objection may now be considered as given up by all experienced hothouse-builders. The liability of iron to conduct away heat in winter, and to attract too much in summer, is also found to be an objection more imaginary than real. It is true that iron, from its being a powerful conductor, is liable to undergo sudden changes of temperature, which must, doubtless, render it less congenial to plants that come in contact with it than wood or brick; though plants do not appear to suffer when the iron is in small quantities, such as the rods to which vines are attached under rafters, wire trellis-work, &c.; but when the rafters are of iron, and when plants are trained round the iron pillars used in supporting hothouse roofs, it may readily be conceived that they will be injured by them. This will also be the case, more or less, when tender plants are grown close under the glass in hotbeds or pits covered with iron sashes. Indeed, when we consider the much greater weight of iron sashes than wooden ones, and the constant occasion that there is for moving the sashes of pits and hotbeds, we would recommend them in most cases to be made of wood. The injury done to plants in the open air by iron coming in contact with them, can only take place when the iron is of considerable thickness; because we do not find it in the case of cast-iron espalier rails, or of dahlias, roses, and other open-air plants tied to iron stakes. In plant-houses it probably takes place after the iron has been highly heated by the sun, and then watered, when the chill produced by evaporation will contract the vessels and chill the juices. The greatest objections that we know to iron roofs are the expense and the difficulty of forming them with sliding sashes which shall not rust in the grooves in which they slide; but this last objection can be obviated, either by forming the styles and rails, or outer frame of the sash, of wood, and the rafters of iron, or the reverse. In the greater proportion of plant-houses, however, sliding sashes in the roof may be dispensed with, air being admitted during winter through apertures in the upper angle of the house in the back wall, or by raising a hinged sash in the upper part of the roof; and in the hottest weather in summer, by these and the sliding sashes or other openings in front. The whole of the objections to iron roofs are now abolished by an improved mode of glazing, that dispenses with the use of putty, and improved methods of ventilation that supersede the necessity of moveable sashes.

The following description and illustration of Beard's patent metallic hothouses and sash-bars will exhibit most of the latest improvements in metallic hothouses. The foundation of the whole is the patent sash-bar (fig. 132), for which a is the bar; b, the covering bars; c, a white metal cap-nut; and d, the felt that acts as a buffer at all points between the iron and the glass. Under this arrangement no glass can possibly be broken by the contraction or expansion of the iron, and the iron bar becomes almost as narrow as a wooden one. Air is admitted at top and bottom in the most simple manner, by means of a mechanical contrivance that opens or shuts a part or the whole of the ventilating space at once with the utmost ease. These houses, as will be seen, admit a maximum amount of light, as those slim but strong rafters produce scarcely any shade. Numbers of them have recently been erected throughout the country, and cultivators speak highly of their cultural merits. The materials used in the interior of plant-houses, such as shelves for supporting pots of plants, pathways for walking on, walls for enclosing tan or other fermenting matter in pits, are bricks, flagstones, slates, wood, and cast iron. The paths are sometimes covered with open gratings of cast iron, which admit of the soil under

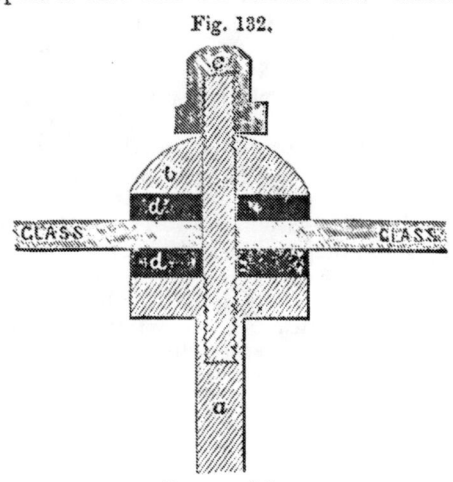

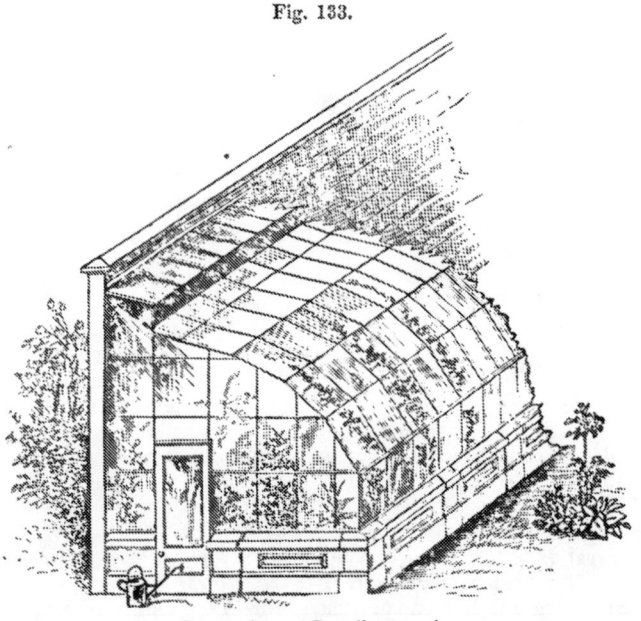

Fig. 132.

Patent sash-bar.

Fig. 133.

Lean-to house (Beard's patent).

them being occupied with the roots of vines, climbers, or other plants. Sir J. Paxton preferred a flooring formed of loose pieces of board laid across the path, each piece as long as the path is wide, and about four inches broad, with a one-inch space between. One advantage of this plan is, that the dust and other matters lying on the paths when they are swept descend immediately without raising a dust in the house to disfigure the leaves of the plants, and encourage the red spider, which dust deposited on the leaves is always apt to do.

Heat.—The natural heat of the locality is retained in plant-structures by the roof and sides forming a covering which checks radiation from the ground; and it is increased in them at pleasure, by fermenting substances applied within or externally, by the consumption of fuel, and the conveyance of the heat so produced in smoke and hot-air flues, by steam, or by hot water in pipes or cisterns. In every mode of supplying heat artificially, the following desiderata ought to be kept constantly in view:—1. To maintain a reservoir of heat which shall keep up a sufficient temperature for at least twelve hours, under ordinary circumstances, in the event of the supply of heat from the consumption of fuel, or the action of the sun, being discontinued through neglect or accident, or through cloudy weather. 2. To provide means of speedily increasing the supply of heat, when the sudden lowering of the external temperature, or the action of high cold winds, or a cold humid atmosphere among the plants, requires it. 3. To provide the means, by an adequate surface of flue, or steam, or hot-water pipes, of supplying a sufficiency of heat in every house, according to the temperature required, not merely under the ordinary external temperature, but when that temperature shall fall as low as $10°$, or in situations exposed to very high cold winds, to zero. 4. To make arrangements for supplying atmospheric moisture in proportion to the supply of heat, and for withdrawing this moisture at pleasure. 5. Where no means can be provided for supplying extra heat on extraordinary occasions, to provide the means of conveniently applying extra external coverings for the same purpose. It is proper to remark that in every plant-structure there is a reservoir of heat and of moisture, to a certain extent, in the soil in which the plants are grown, whether that soil is in pots or in a bed; and that all the paths, shelves, and other objects within the structure, being heated to the proper degree, part with their heat whenever the air of the house falls below the temperature of these objects. This source of heat might be considerably increased in houses where there is abundance of room: for example, below a greenhouse stage, by placing objects there of moderate dimensions and separated from each other—such as parallel walls of four-inch brickwork, flagstones set on edge two or three inches apart, or slabs of slate set on edge one inch apart. These, by presenting a great extent of surface, would absorb a powerful reserve of heat, and give it out whenever the other sources of heat were defective.

Fermenting substances, such as stable-dung, tanner's bark, leaves, &c., are either applied in masses or beds under the soil containing the plants, as in the common hotbed; or in casings or linings exterior to the soil or structure to be heated, as in M'Phail's and other pits. A steady reservoir of heat is thus provided, and instead of an extra supply for unexpected cold nights, extra coverings of bast mats or mats of straw are provided, for retaining heat that would escape through the ordinary covering. An additional supply of heat for extra cold weather may also be obtained by different means. Where exterior casings of dung are employed, if the heat of the dung is admitted through a pigeon-holed wall to an inside flue with thin covers; or if the dung is brought into close contact with thin plates of stone or slate, instead of the pigeon-holed wall, which, like the flues, are made to enclose the soil containing the plants; then, by keeping a part of these warm surfaces generally covered with soil, or with boards, or with any other material which shall operate as a non-conductor, when extra heat is wanted unexpectedly, all that is necessary is to take off the non-conducting covers. Even in the case of a common hotbed, heated only by the bed of dung beneath the plants, extra heat may be provided for by bedding a plate of stone, slate, zinc, or cast iron, on the dung, in one or more places of the interior of the frame, according to its size, and covering these with boards, supported at the height of two or three inches above them, so as to enclose a stratum of air, to act as a non-conductor; the sides being closed by a rim previously formed of cement, or brick-on-edge, on the stone or slate, or by a rim two or three inches deep, cast on the edges of the iron. By taking off the wooden covers, an extra supply of dry heat will immediately be obtained, which may be rendered moist at pleasure by pouring on water. Another mode of obtaining an immediate extra supply of heat from a dung-bed is, by bedding in it, when first made, an iron pipe of three or four inches in diameter, with the two extremities turned up, and covered by flower-pot saucers. The length of the tube may be nearly equal to that of the bed, and the one end must be sunk a few inches deeper than the other, as in fig. 134. It is evident that by taking off the covers of this pipe there will be a

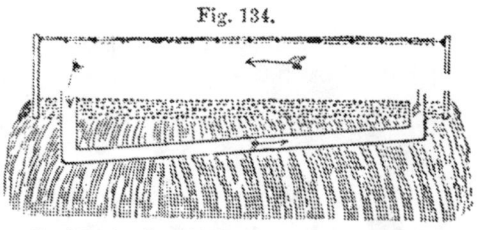

Fig. 134.

Section of a dung-bed, with a tube for supplying hot air.

draught created in it, in consequence of its sides being heated by the dung; and an extra degree of heat will by this means be brought into the atmosphere of the bed. This plan might also be adopted for putting the air of a plant-bed in motion, without the admission of the external air.

Fermenting Materials and Fire-Heat Combined.—In pits and low forcing-houses heated chiefly by dung, provision is frequently made for the supply of extra heat, by the addition of smoke-flues or hot-water pipes. Fig. 135 is a perspective elevation and section of a house, in which a bed of leaves within is heated by a dung-lining placed on the outside of a pigeon-holed wall, and extra heat is provided for by three turns of a flue, one above the other, in the back path: *a* is the pit in which the dung-lining is placed and covered with a hinged shutter;

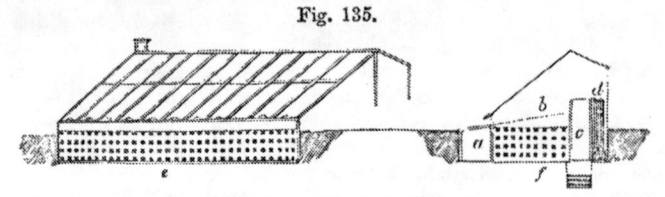

Fig. 135.

Pinery heated by dung-linings.

b, the surface of the bed of leaves, in which pine-apples, or cucumbers, or melons may be grown, or strawberry-plants or flowers forced; *c*, door; *d*, flues; *e*, front pigeon-holed wall; and *f*, end pigeon-holed wall. Fig. 136 shows a mode of applying dung under a bed of soil without coming in immediate contact with it, and by which no heat whatever produced by the dung is lost: *a* is the bed of soil in which the vines are planted, and which is supported by cast-iron joints and Welsh slates; and *b* shows the openings furnished with shutters by which the dung is introduced. Beds on the same plan, but wider, have been used for growing pine-apples and melons, and for various similar purposes. An extra supply of heat from the dung may be obtained by having panels of slate in the inside wall, *c*, to be kept covered by wooden shutters, except when extra heat is wanted; or by tubes, as in fig. 134; or it may be rendered unnecessary by extra coverings. The first forcing which we read of in the history of British gardening was effected, as Switzer informs us, by placing casings of hot dung against the north side of walls of boards, against the south side of which cherries were trained.

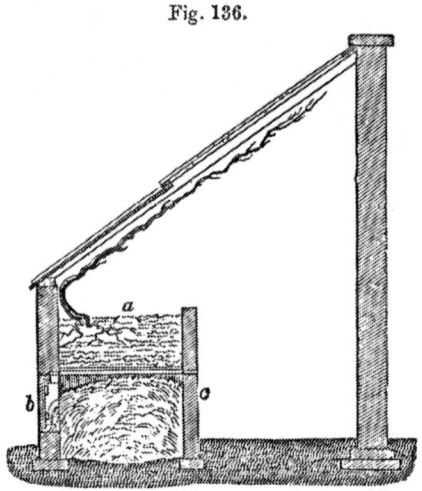

Fig. 136.

Section of a vinery heated by dung.

Heating from Vaults, or from Stacks of Flues.—The oldest and simplest mode of applying fire-heat to hothouses was by means of a pit in the floor, or a vault under it. In the 'Gardener's Chronicle' of Oct. 2, 1869, a full account of hypocaust heating is given. The plan has been successfully carried out by C. W. Martin, Esq., at Leeds Castle, Kent, to heat a range of glass-houses through the floor, as well as a large piece of ground in the kitchen garden. The vault was of the same length and breadth as the floor, with the chimney at one end; or it occupied a smaller space in the centre of the floor, with a stack of flues rising over it, and forming a mass of heated material in the body of the house. The fire was of wood and made on the floor; or of charcoal or coal, and made in an open, portable iron cage, like that used by plumbers when soldering joints in the open air, with a plate of iron over it to act as a reverberator, and prevent the heat from rising directly to the roof. The flue by which the smoke escaped had its lower orifice on a level with the floor of the vault, so that the air and smoke did not enter it until they had parted with most of their heat. These modes are capable of great improvement, and in various cases would perhaps be found more eligible and economical than any other, by a gardener who is aware of the importance of connecting with them an efficient means of supplying atmospheric moisture: by placing cisterns of water over the hottest part of the floor, or by having dripping fountains formed on the siphon principle, by inserting the ends of strips of woollen cloth in open vessels of water, and placing these in different parts of the house. The danger, however, from the escape of gas into the house is very great, and such modes of heating are but seldom resorted to for the growth of early vegetables, &c. One of the houses was devoted to pine-growing, and the heat was sufficient to maintain them in perfect health, planted out in a bed of soil on the floor.

Flues.—As the mode of heating by vaults could only be adopted when the plants were to be grown in pots or boxes, as soon as the practice of forcing fruit-trees trained against walls, and having their roots in the border or floor of the house, was introduced, flues in the wall against which the trees were trained, and afterwards detached flues along the front of the house, became necessary; and when these last are properly constructed, and the dry heat which they produce is rendered moist by placing water over them, they form a convenient and economical mode of heating. The flue is always most efficient when carried along the front and ends of the house, because the air immediately within these is more liable to be cooled by the external air than that next the back of the house, the back being generally a wall of brick or stone. Where the house is glass on every side, as well as on the roof, the flues will be most efficient if carried round it, for obvious reasons; while the air immediately under the roof, in every case, will be kept sufficiently warm by the natural ascent of the heated air from the flue, in whatever part it may be placed; though when the flues are placed in the lower part of the house there will be a greater circulation than when they are elevated; and this arises from the greater number of particles which must be put in motion by the ascent of warm and the descent of cold air. The quantity of flue requisite for heating a house to any required temperature has not been determined. One fire with a flue in front, and a return in the back, is generally found sufficient for a greenhouse of thirty feet or forty feet in length, and from twelve feet to fifteen feet in width, and two fires, one entering at each end, for a stove or forcing-house of similar dimensions; the flues in both cases being twenty inches high and twelve inches wide, outside measure. Perhaps one square foot of flue for every two feet in length of iron hot-water pipes, found according to the rule given on page 174, would be a near approximation to the quantity wanted, reckoning the top and sides of the flue, but not the bottom. The furnace or fireplace from which the flue proceeds should be one or two feet lower than the level of the bottom of the flue, in order to assist in creating a draught, as that depends on the length and height of the space allowed for the heated air to ascend before it is permitted to escape into the atmosphere; and the flue generally terminates on the top of the back wall, for the same reason. The fireplace is generally formed behind the back wall for the sake of concealment: but when this is not an object, the best situation is at one end of the house, in a sunken area, which can be covered with shutters; because, the smoke and heat not receiving the check given by a turn in the flue made so near the furnace as it must necessarily be when it enters from behind the house, the heat is more equally diffused along the front. A very desirable arrangement for flues, where it is practicable, is to have two from the same furnace, with the power of throwing the whole or any part of the smoke and heated air into either flue at pleasure, which is easily effected by a damper at the throat of the flue, close to the furnace, as shown in fig. 137, in which *a* is the upper or extra heat flue; *b*, the under or reserve flue; *c*, the damper; *d*, the furnace; *e*, the cover to the feeding hopper; and *f* is the ash-pit. One of the flues should be conducted through a solid mass of brickwork or masonry, or through a box or bed of sand, in order to produce a reservoir of heat; and the other flue should have thin covers and sides, and be quite detached, in order to furnish an extra supply of heat, when the external air suddenly became much colder than usual, or at particular times to dispel damp, &c. Both flues ought to be near the front of the house, and, in most cases, the one might be over the other. Wherever flues are sunk below the level of the floor, they will be found to give out their heat very slowly; or, if given out, to lose it in the adjoining ground, from the want of a current of air to carry it off. But this may generally be supplied by underground cross drains, as in fig. 138, in which *g* is

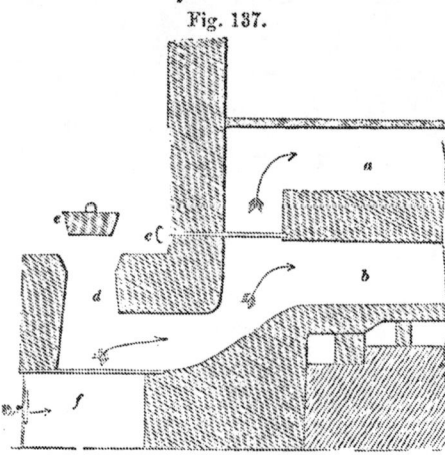

Fig. 137.

Section of a furnace and flue.

the floor of the house; *h*, the reservoir flue, three feet broad, which is sunk so that its top is on a level with the floor; *i*, an air-drain from the back of the house; *k*, an upper flue for additional heat; *l*, front path; *m*, front shelf; *n*, stage; and *o*, path on the upper part of the stage for watering the plants.

Fig. 138.

The best materials for building flues are bricks and paving tiles, the latter for the bottom and top, and the former for the sides. The advantages of bricks over stone are, their greater adhesion to the mortar; their narrowness, by which little space is occupied; and their

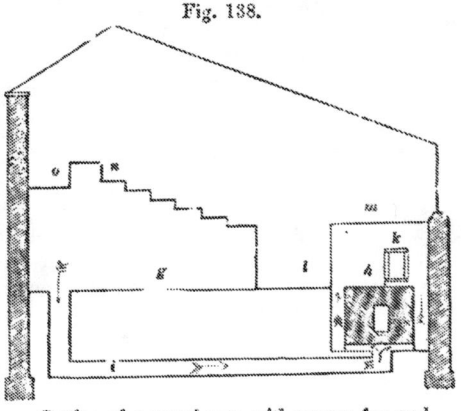

Section of a greenhouse, with reserve flue and common flue.

being better non-conductors than stone, by which means the heat is more equalized throughout the length of the flue than it would be by the use of that material. Stones are likewise very liable to split and burst into fragments when overheated. A slight disadvantage attending the use of bricks and tiles arises from the earth of which they are made; clay absorbing and entering into chemical combination with the moisture of the atmosphere, especially when the latter is at a high temperature. This evil, however, can always be counteracted by placing water over the flues, or in some other hot part of the house. For this purpose, the covers of flues, whether of tiles or stone, ought to be made with sunk panels to contain water; or, what is much better, a shallow cistern of iron, lead, or zinc, as in fig. 139, may be placed over them for the same purpose. In Germany the flues are sometimes entirely covered with plates of cast-iron; and if these were formed with turned-up edges, they would serve at once as covers and cisterns. Flues are always detached from the ground, by being built on piers, either connected by low flat arches, or so close together as to be joined by the square tiles which form the floor of the flue. Neither the inside of the flue nor its outside ought to be plastered, when it is desired that they should give out a maximum of heat at a minimum of distance from the furnace; but when the flue is to be of great length, plastering either in the inside or outside, or both, by rendering the walls of the flue greater non-conductors, tends to equalize the heat given out. Plastering is also useful to prevent the escape of smoke from the joints, which is liable to take place where the materials and workmanship are not of the best quality, and to prevent the absorption of moisture by the bricks. Narrow flues are preferable to broad ones, as occupying less horizontal space in the house, and also because as flues part with their heat chiefly from their upper surface, it is better equalized by a narrow flue than a broad one. Hence also narrow deep flues are found to "draw" better than broad shallow ones. The ordinary dimensions of narrow flues are eight inches in width and fifteen inches in depth; and they are formed by tiles one foot square for the bottom, and ten inches square for the covers, and three paving-bricks, which are only two inches thick, on edge, for each of the sides, as in fig. 139. The joints of the sides and covers are formed by lime putty, and the bottom tiles are set on bricks on edge. In fig. 139, *a* is the brick on edge, which supports the one-foot tile *b*, which forms the bottom of the flue; *c* is the smoke chamber, and *d* the zinc cistern over the ten-inch tile cover. The inside plastering should be of the best mortar, mixed with lime, but without sand, as being less liable to crack.

Fig. 139.

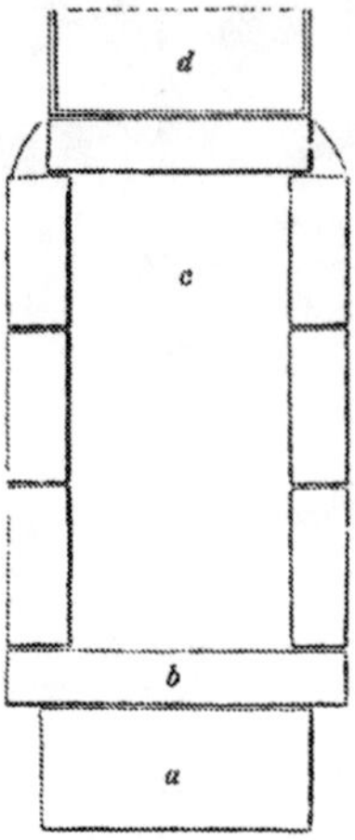

Section of a common brick flue, with a zinc cistern over it.

The furnace, when built in the usual manner, should have double iron doors to prevent the escape of heat; and the fuel-chamber should be about double the area of that portion of it which is occupied by the bar or grate, in order that the fuel not immediately over the grate may burn slowly. A damper in some accessible part of the flue, and as close to the furnace as is practicable, affords a convenient means of regulating the draught; and there ought always to be a register valve in the ash-pit door for the same purpose. Where cinders, coke, or anthracite coal only are burnt, no horizontal opening to the grate containing the fuel is necessary. It may be put in by an opening at the top, as in fig. 137, which will contain a supply for any length of time, according to the heat and width of the opening, and the bars of the grate can be freed from ashes with a hooked poker applied from the ash-pit. By this kind of construction less heat is lost than by any other. Indeed, this kind of fireplace, with a reserve flue, will be found by far the most economical mode of heating hothouses; but it will not answer where the practice is to depend on the sudden action of the flue, which is produced by stirring up the fuel: in lieu of this, the damper must be drawn so as to admit the heated current into the extra heat flue. Whatever may be the construction of the furnace, no air ought ever to be admitted to the fire, except through the grating below it; because air admitted over the fuel can serve no purpose but that of cooling the flue; unless in very rare instances, where it might assist in consuming the smoke. Where this object is a desideratum, Witty's smoke-consuming furnace, described in 'Gard. Mag.,' vol. vii. p. 483, which roasts or cokes the coal before it is put on the fire, may be had recourse to. This and various other details, however, must be left to the bricklayer or mason employed. All flues ought to have flag-stones of the width and height of the interior of the flue, or iron doors built into them at the extremities of each straight-lined portion, which may readily be taken out or opened in order to free the flue from soot; an operation which will require to be performed at least once a year in all houses, and in stoves twice a year, or oftener, according to the kind of fuel used.

As substitutes for smoke-flues, earthenware pipes or can-flues, as they are called, have long been in use in Holland and France; and as the fuel used in those countries is almost always wood, which produces little soot in comparison with coal, they are found to answer as perfectly as brick flues. When they are occasionally employed, the entire surface of the pipes is exposed; but when they are used constantly, as in houses for tropical plants, they are embedded in a casing of dry sand, which forms a reservoir of heat capable of being increased to any extent, even to that of the entire floor of the house, over which a flooring for plants may be placed. Pipes of this kind might also be conducted through a bed of small stones, so as to form a very effective mass of heated material as a reservoir, while a portion of naked pipe might serve for raising the temperature on occasions of extraordinary cold. Iron pipes would, however, be the safest for burying underground. In country situations, where wood for burning is not very dear, or where coke from coal could be readily obtained, such flues might be economically employed for drying up the cold damp of greenhouses, and for a variety of purposes. We have said more on the subject of smoke-flues than may be thought necessary at the present time, when they are being so generally relinquished for hot-water pipes; but our object is to prevent our readers from being so completely prejudiced against flues as not to have recourse to them in particular situations and circumstances. The principal reason why so much has been said against smoke-flues is, that gardeners till lately were not fully aware of the importance of supplying moisture to the atmosphere of planthouses in proportion to the supply of heat, and of having reserve flues, in consequence of which excessive heat would not become so frequently requisite, and noxious gases would have less chance of being driven through the top and sides of the flue into the atmosphere of the house. Flues may also still be combined with boilers to utilize much of that heat which is otherwise wasted up the chimney.

Steam was the first substitute for flues employed in this country; and, under some circumstances, it may deserve a preference to either flues or hot water. For example, where the heating apparatus must necessarily be at a great distance from the structure to be heated, steam can be conducted to it in a tube not more than an inch or two in diameter, which may be so encased in non-conducting matter as to occasion far less loss of heat than if either smoke or hot water were employed. The disadvantages attending the use of steam in ordinary cases are, the necessity of heating the water to the boiling-point, by which more heat is driven up the chimney and lost than if the water were raised to only half that temperature, and the want of a reservoir of heat when the steam is not in action. The last disadvantage has been supplied by passing the steam-pipes through brick flues filled with stones, through pits, or through other large masses of stones, or through tubes, cisterns, or tanks of water. By arrangements of this kind, steam can be made both to supply heat permanently and expeditiously. Waste steam from mills and factories might often be turned to excellent account by turning it into hot-water pipes. It forms a better circulating force than most boilers, the motion of the water being well-nigh instantaneous. The rate of the circulation and the degree of heat generated can be regulated at will by stop-cocks.

Hot water is the medium of heating plant-structures now generally adopted, and it is without dispute far preferable to any of the preceding modes. Water is such an excellent carrier of heat, that a house warmed by hot-water pipes is not hotter at one end than at the other, which is almost always the case when smoke-flues are employed: none of the heat which the water derives from the fuel is lost, as in the case of flues, which when coated internally with soot convey a great part of the heat out at the chimney-top; no sulphureous or other disagreeable effluvium is ever given out by hot-water pipes when they become leaky, as is the case with flues when they are not air-tight; and the hot water in the pipes serves as a reservoir of heat when the fire goes out; but smoke-flues, when the fire goes out, are rapidly cooled from within by the current of cold air which necessarily rushes through them till it has reduced the temperature of their tops and sides to that of the open air. Whether heating by hot-water is more economical than heating by smoke-flues, will depend chiefly on the kind of apparatus employed; but in general we should say that it is not attended with any advantages of this kind. Mr. Rogers is of opinion that with a well-constructed and well-managed apparatus, the saving of fuel may amount to twenty-five per cent. over well-constructed and well-managed flues; but he allows that in a large proportion of the hot-water apparatus now in use the consumption of fuel greatly exceeds that of common furnaces. The cause of the circulation of water in pipes is the same as that which produces the ascent of the air in flues— viz., difference of specific gravity produced by heat. In water, the particles at the bottom of the boiler being heated become lighter and rise to the surface, while their place is taken by cold particles from the water in the boiler itself, or in the pipes that communicate with it, which are heated in their turn, and ascend to the surface of the water in the boiler and the surface of that in the upper pipe. In like manner, the air heated by the consumption of the fuel in the furnace becomes lighter, and ascends along the flue, while its place among the fuel is supplied by cool air, which enters through the grating beneath it to supply combustion. Neither air nor water will move along readily in very small flues or pipes: for smoke-flues seven inches by ten inches are the smallest dimensions, and hot water does not circulate so rapidly in pipes under two inches in diameter as to give out heat equally throughout their whole length.

The modes of heating by hot water are very numerous, and it would occupy too much room in this work to enter into a detailed description of them, which, however, is the less necessary as the best modes are sufficiently known for all ordinary purposes by most ironmongers;

and those who wish to make themselves masters of the subject will have recourse to Hood's 'Practical Treatise on Warming Buildings by Hot Water.' The simplest form of applying this mode of heating is by having one boiler to each house in a recess in the back wall, or in some other situation where it will be out of the way, and an upper or flow-pipe proceeding from it on a level, with an under or return-pipe, also on a level. Fig. 140 will give an idea of this mode of circulation, *a* representing the boiler, *b* a cistern at the extreme end of the house to serve as a reservoir, and *c* the flue and return-pipes.

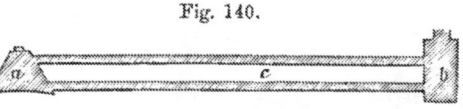

Fig. 140.

A hot-water apparatus for circulation on a level.

When the water is to be circulated in pipes or on different levels and above the level of the boiler, or on different levels but never below the level of the bottom of the boiler, then a closed boiler is requisite; or one open, but carried to a height equal to that of the highest point in the line of the pipes, as in fig. 141; and when water is to be circulated below the level of the boiler, a closed boiler with particular arrangements (see Hood's Treatise, figs. 10 and 11, pp. 44, 45) may be em-

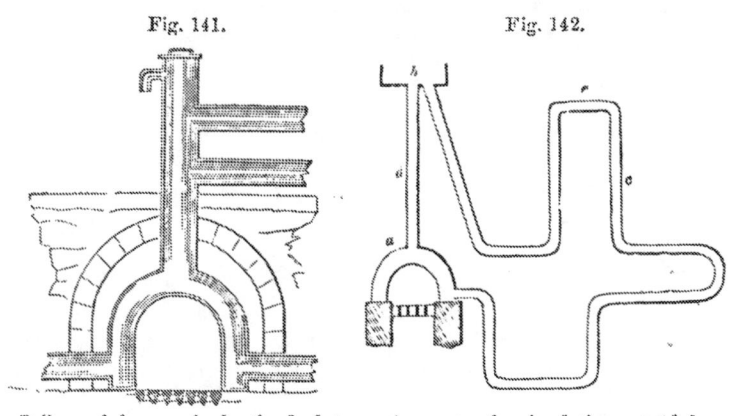

Fig. 141.

Fig. 142.

Boiler and furnace for heating by hot water in rising and falling pipes.

Apparatus for circulating water below and above the level of the boiler.

ployed, or the form of open boiler shown in fig. 142 may be resorted to. All depression below the level of the boiler should be avoided if possible. They involve a great loss of force, and frequently stop the circulation. In this figure, *a* represents the boiler, *b* an open cistern at its top, in which the orifice of the heating-pipe terminates. Now it is obvious that when the water passes from the orifice of the boiler into the orifice of the pipe, the circulation must go on from the difference in the specific gravity between the water in the pipe at *c*, and that at *d*, provided that a small open pipe be placed at *e*, to admit of the escape of the air which will accumulate in that part of the pipe. Hot water

172   *FIXED STRUCTURES FOR GROWING*

has also been circulated on the siphon principle with great success by Mr. Kewley; the advantage of which mode is, the rapid communication of heat along the whole length of the pipe, in consequence of which it is never necessary to raise the water in the boiler to so high a temperature as by any of the other modes; and hence this mode of heating is the most economical of all in the consumption of fuel. Fig. 143 will give a correct idea of the system: *a c e* represent the two legs of the siphon; the upper leg, commencing at *c*, being that

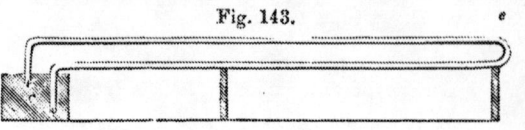

Fig. 143.

Siphon mode of circulating hot water.

through which the heated water ascends, and the lower leg being that by which it returns. The disadvantage of this system is, that after the pipes have been some time in use they become leaky, and the slightest leak, by admitting the air, instantly empties the siphon; nor is the leak easily discovered afterwards. The siphon mode of heating, were it not for this disadvantage, would deserve the preference over most others. Hot water has also been circulated in hermetically-sealed pipes by Perkins; but this mode is attended with great danger from the high temperature of the water. All these, and other modes of heating, will be found impartially examined in Hood's Treatise.

A reservoir of heat is very readily formed in heating by hot water, whatever may be the kind of apparatus adopted, by placing a cistern or series of cisterns at different parts of the house, either close to or at any convenient distance from the water-pipes, and connected with them by smaller pipes, having stop-cocks to interrupt the connexion at pleasure. When it is desired to heat the house with as little loss of time as possible, all connexion between the pipes and the reservoirs should be cut off by turning the stop-cocks; and as the house becomes sufficiently heated, the connexion ought to be restored by opening the upper and under stop-cock of one cistern at a time. In some cases, the cistern might be a long trough about the bulk of a common flue, placed parallel with and close to the pipe, as in fig. 144, in which *a* is the pipe, *b* the cistern, and *c* the connecting pipes with stop-cocks. Fig.

Fig. 144.

Hot-water pipe, and reserve cistern of hot water.

145 is a cross section of the pipes and reserve cistern, which requires no explanation. Where the circulating pipes are below the level of the floor of the house, and where there is to be a raised pit for containing plants, a tank or cistern might be formed under it of the length and width of the pit, and of a depth equal to the distance between the upper and lower heating-pipes; and with this tank the pipes might

communicate by means of stop-cocks; so that whenever there was more heat in the pipes than was wanted for heating the air of the house, it could be transferred to the reservoir tank. To save the expense of stop-cocks where the cisterns could be wholly or partially uncovered, the orifices of the connecting pipes might be stopped by plugs; and when the reservoir tank is above the level of the heating-pipes, the connexion between them might be made by means of siphons with stop-cocks.

Fig. 145.

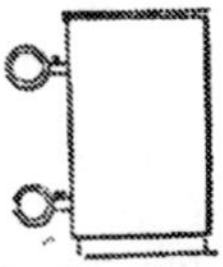

Section of reserve cistern and hot-water pipes.

The pipes employed are generally of cast-iron, and round, as being more conveniently cast; but any other metal and form will answer; and when there is no great pressure on the pipes, earthenware may be used, the joints being made good with cement; and at the angles, where elbow-joints would be necessary, small cisterns could be employed, or elbows of earthenware might be made on purpose. For obtaining a large heating surface, flat cast-iron pipes have been used, placed vertically in some cases, and in others horizontally; but round pipes of four inches in diameter are in most general use. When the object is to obtain a supply of heat in the shortest time, then the boiler and pipes should be of small capacity; and this is generally desirable in the case of greenhouses, where heat is occasionally wanted for a few hours in damp weather, not for the sake of raising the temperature, but for drying up cold damp: nevertheless, even in greenhouses it is desirable to have a reservoir of heat for supplies in very severe weather. In stoves in which fire heat is employed the greater part of the year, both boiler and pipes may be of large capacity; and this should also be the case in early forcing-houses. Whatever mode of heating or kind of pipes may be adopted, the pipes should always have a gradual ascent from the place where they enter the house, or are intended first to give out heat, towards the farther extremity; otherwise, the circulation will be less rapid, and consequently the heat less equally distributed. The quantity of pipe required to heat any house depends on various circumstances; such as the form and construction of the house, the temperature that is to be kept up in it, and the temperature of the external air. Various calculations have been made on the subject by different engineers, and more especially by Mr. Hood, who says: "It may be taken as an invariable rule, that in no case should pipes of a greater diameter than four inches be used, because, when they are of a larger size than this, the quantity of water they contain is so considerable, that it makes a great difference in the cost of fuel, in consequence of the increased length of time it will require to heat them, which is four and a half hours for four-inch pipes, three and a quarter hours for three-inch pipes, and two and a quarter hours for two-inch pipes, supposing the water to be at 40° before lighting the fire, and the temperature to which the water was raised 200°. Pipes of two or three inches diameter therefore are to be preferred for greenhouses and conservatories which only require fire-heat to be applied occasionally." After calculating the loss of heat from exposed surfaces of glass under different circumstances and situations, Mr. Hood gives the following rules for determining the quantity of pipe as a sufficient approximation for ordinary purposes:—"In churches and very large public rooms, which have only about an average number of doors and windows, and moderate ventilation, by taking the cubic measurement of the room, and dividing the number thus obtained by 200, the quotient will be the number of feet in length of pipe, four inches in diameter, which will be required to obtain a temperature of about 55° to 58°. For smaller rooms, dwelling-houses, &c., the cubic measurement should be divided by 150, which will give the number of feet of four-inch pipe. For greenhouses, conservatories, and suchlike buildings, where the temperature is required to be kept at about 60°, dividing the cubic measurement of the building by 30 will give the required quantity of pipe: and for forcing-houses, where it is desired to keep the temperature at 70° to 75°, we must divide the cubic measurement of the house by 20; but if the temperature be required as high as 75° to 80°, then we must divide by 18 to obtain the number of feet of four-inch pipe. If the pipes are to be three inches diameter, then we must add one-third to the quantity thus obtained; and if two-inch pipes are to be used, we must take double the length of four-inch pipe.

"The quantity of pipe estimated in this way will only suit for such places as are built quite on the usual plan." ('Treatise,' &c., p. 125.) The above calculations for heating are made on the supposition that the lowest external temperature will be 10°; but in situations "exposed to high winds, it will be prudent," Mr. Hood observes, "to calculate the external temperature from zero, or even below that, according to circumstances; and in very warm and sheltered situations, a less range in the temperature will be sufficient." Local circumstances, therefore, may require from 5 to 10 per cent. to be added to, or deducted from, the length of pipe found according to the foregoing rules. As a proof of the soundness of Mr. Hood's calculation, we may state that the great stove at Chatsworth is heated at the rate of one superficial foot of heated pipe to thirty cubic feet of air; and the temperature kept up during the severest weather of the winter of 1840-41 was 60°, though there were frequently from 20° to 35° of frost during the night. This house is sixty feet high, with glass on all sides, exposing a surface of 60,000 feet, and enclosing 1,050,000 cubic feet of air. The quantity of coal consumed was about two tons per night. ('Gard. Chron.,' April 17, 1841, p. 243.)

The situation in which the pipes are placed is, in general, what we have stated to be the most suitable for smoke-flues (p. 165)—viz., along the front and ends of houses placed against a back wall, and entirely round detached or span-roofed houses. In the case of pits or frames with flat roofs, the pipes may be either placed in front or in the middle, always bearing in mind that heated air ascends, and that the quantity heated in a given time will, all other circumstances being alike, depend on a regular supply to the heating body, by a current distinct from that by which the heated air escapes. Such a current is formed by the cross drains adopted by Mr. Penn, and exhibited in various sections of plant-structures given in this work. For the same reason it is desirable, when practicable, and under certain circumstances, to confine the pipes on each side, so that the air which passes up among them may not escape without being heated. To illustrate the effect of this arrangement, we may take Perkins' double boiler, and compare it with the common boiler. It would not occur to any person who had not reflected on the subject, that water could be boiled any sooner in one boiler than another, both boilers being of the same dimensions, made of the same material, set in the same manner, and with a fire beneath them of the same power. Yet such is the case; and this exactly on the same principle that we recommend confining the sides of hot-water pipes, and supplying the air to be heated from a distinct channel. Suppose we have a common boiler, such as is used in common wash-houses, then place another boiler within it, of such a size as to leave only a few inches between the inner boiler and the outer boiler all round, and support it in this position by stays, as shown in fig. 146; let this inner boiler have a hole in its bottom about one-third of its diameter, and let its rim be two inches below the level of the water to be heated. These arrangements being made, and the heat applied below, a circulation instantly takes place and continues, the water coming into contact with the heated bottom and sides of the outer boiler, rising rapidly to the surface, and descending through the inner boiler, which thus necessarily contains the coldest portion of the liquid. ('Gard. Mag.,' vol. xvi. p. 325.) The heat communicated by the fire to the bottom and sides of the outer boiler is rapidly carried off by the current that is created, exactly on the same principle that wind, which is a current of air, cools any body exposed to it more rapidly than air at the same temperature but quite still. The underground drains should either have vacuities at the sides and over the top to prevent them from absorbing much heat, or they may be carried through the bottom of the tan-pit, where there is one. In general, we would not cover the heating-pipes, nor would we adopt the upright tubes which Mr. Penn originally used, but has since dispensed with. There may be situations and circumstances where it would be more desirable to have the heat of the pipes or flues carried off by radiation with the usual degree of slowness rather than by conduction; such, for example, as when the attendant on the hothouse was likely be a long time absent, or when some danger from overheating was anticipated; and this can always be attained by covering the orifices by which the air enters to the cross-drains. It is proper to state, that at the present time the opinions of a number of persons are against the use of air as a carrier of heat in hothouses, on account, they say, of the difficulty of maintaining it in exactly the proper state of moisture. This, however, can be effected without difficulty, by keeping the bottoms of the cross-drains

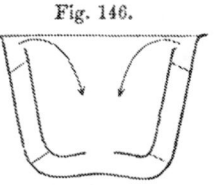

Fig. 146.

Perkins' double boiler.

covered with water, or by having cisterns of water over the pipes, or both. A few years' experience is probably required to set the matter at rest; in the meantime, the reader who wishes to examine both sides of the question, may consult the 'Gard. Mag.' for 1840-41, and the 'Gard Chron.,' more especially an article by Mr. Ainger, April 3rd, page 212. Our opinion is, that the power of producing motion in the air, even though it should be only wanted occasionally, and obtainable at an extra expense of heat, is of so much value for setting blossoms, equalizing heat and moisture in some cases, drying up damp in others, or producing a feeling of coolness, that no plant-structure of large dimensions, and where fire heat is employed, ought to be without it. To explain the manner in which the motion of heated air in hothouses produces a sensation of coolness, without being altered in its temperature, we make the following quotation from Lardner's 'Cyclopædia': "The air which surrounds us is generally at a lower temperature than that of the body. If the air be calm and still, the particles which are in immediate contact with the skin acquire the temperature of the skin itself, and having a sort of molecular attraction, they adhere to the skin in the same manner as particles of air are found to adhere to the surface of glass in philosophical experiments. Thus sticking to the skin, they form a sort of warm covering for it, and speedily acquire its temperature." Agitation of the air, however, "continually expels the particles thus in contact with the skin, and brings new particles into that situation. Each particle of air, as it strikes the skin, takes heat from it by contact, and being driven off, carries that heat with it, thus producing a constant sensation of refreshing coolness." Less importance is attributed to confining the pipes and underground drains than formerly. If the source of heat is placed mostly in one part—viz., the front of the house, the roof and cooler portion of the house will induce a rapid circulation of air, apart from drains or other expedients.

A boiler of small capacity, and with a large superficies for the fire to act on, will be the most economical in first cost and also in fuel. "The extent of surface which a boiler ought to expose to the fire should be proportional to the quantity of pipe that is required to be heated by it;" and Mr. Hood has calculated a table, which, like various others in his excellent work, will be referred to by the intelligent inquirer, or by the gardener who intends to direct the construction and putting up of his own heating apparatus. By this table it appears—

That $3\frac{1}{2}$ square feet of surface of boiler exposed to the fire will heat 200 feet of 4-inch pipe, or 266 feet of 3-inch pipe, or 400 feet of 2-inch pipe.

That 7 square feet of surface of boiler will heat 400 feet of 4-inch pipe, 533 feet of 3-inch pipe, and 800 feet of 2-inch pipe, and so on in the same ratio.

"A small apparatus," Mr. Hood observes, "ought perhaps to have rather more surface of boiler, in proportion to the length of pipe, than a larger one, as the fire is less intense, and burns to less advantage, in a small than in a large furnace" (p. 71).

The furnace for a hot-water apparatus has also been subjected to calculation by Mr. Hood. For generating steam, an extremely brisk fire and rapid draught are required; but a very moderate draught will suffice for heating a boiler where the temperature of the water is rarely required to be above 180°, or at most 200°. The following observations on the construction and management of furnaces are valuable both with respect to a hot-water apparatus and the furnaces to common smoke-flues. "The heat should be confined within the furnace as much as possible, by contracting the farther end of it, at the part called the throat, so as to allow only a small space for the smoke and inflamed gases to pass out. The only entrance for the air should be through the bars of the grate, and the heated gaseous matter will then pass directly upward to the bottom of the boiler, which will act as a reverberator, and cause a more perfect combustion of the fuel than would otherwise take place. The lightness of the heated gaseous matter causes it to ascend the flue, forcing its passage through the throat of the furnace with a velocity proportional to the smallness of the passage, the vertical height of the chimney, and the levity of the gases, arising from their expansion by the heat of the furnace" (p. 77). After giving a table of the area of bars required for pipes of different dimensions and lengths, Mr. Hood observes: "In order to make the fire burn for a long time without attention, the furnace should extend beyond the bars both in length and breadth; and the coals which are placed on this blank part of the furnace, in consequence of receiving no air from below, will burn very slowly, and will only enter into complete combustion when the coal which lies directly on the bars has burnt away."

The kinds of boilers are very numerous, and few things are more bewildering to the amateur than making a selection from them; it is nearly equally so to the gardener, as no proper trials have as yet been made to ascertain the best kind of boilers.

For a small house or a single house of any kind there is no better than the upright oval tubular boiler made by Mr. Gray, Danvers Street, Chelsea, which is the best where there is sufficient depth of stoke-hole. Where this is not the case, a very flat saddle-boiler, made by Mr. Lynch White of Blackfriars, is excellent. For large conservatories and extensive ranges of glass, Weeks's system has unquestionably been proved to be of great excellence, and very recently it has been much improved. Ormson, Green, and many other makers have also good boilers.

The one-boiler system, by which the whole of the glass of the largest gardens is heated by one fire, is often adopted, and there is doubtless a saving of both labour and fuel by this arrangement. A supplementary boiler should always form part of the one-boiler system, to guard against the tremendous risk of being wholly at the mercy of one boiler for the safety of an entire establishment. The patent duplex improvements of Weeks's, however, will probably go far to do away with the necessity for having two boilers.

Rain-water should, as we have just seen, always be used in hot-

178   FIXED STRUCTURES FOR GROWING

water apparatus; for hard water deposits a sediment or incrustation, which if not removed, will form a coating of several inches in thickness, which coating acting as a powerful non-conductor, will allow the bottom of the boiler to become red-hot without sufficiently heating the water it contains; and ultimately, from the cracking of the deposit in consequence of the greater expansion of the red-hot iron, the water comes in contact with the red-hot metal, and an explosion takes place. (See 'Gard. Mag.,' vol. ix. p. 206.) Hence the necessity of having all boilers where hard water is to be used constructed so as to admit of

Fig. 147.

Weeks's patent duplex boiler.

being readily cleaned out. As the deposit consists of calcareous matter, it may be removed by a weak solution of muriatic acid aided with a slight mechanical agitation: but it is much better to prevent its taking place by using only soft water.

To prevent the water in the apparatus from freezing, salt may be added to it; but this may be rendered unnecessary in the case of horizontal pipes by drawing off a portion of the water, so that they shall not be quite full, because in that case the water has room for that expansion which takes place when it passes into ice. The quantity of salt put into water to keep it from freezing, Mr. Hood observes, may vary from $3\frac{1}{2}$ per cent, the quantity contained in sea-water, which will not freeze when it is above 28°, to 35 per cent, the greatest amount of common salt which water will hold in solution. With 4·3 per cent of salt, water freezes at $27\frac{1}{2}$°; with 6·6 per cent of salt, at $25\frac{1}{2}$°; and with 11·1 per cent, at $21\frac{1}{2}$°. The effect which would be produced on cast-iron pipes and boilers by any of these quantities of salt, Mr. Hood states, would not be of much importance. As salt does not evaporate, when a sufficient quantity is once added for the purpose required, the waste which takes place can be supplied by fresh water. ('Hood's Treatise,' p. 167.) In severe weather it is much safer to empty the pipes or put on a little fire. All boilers should have a waste-pipe at their lowest part, to empty them thoroughly at pleasure.

Retaining Heat by Coverings.—Whatever mode of heating plant-structures may be adopted, it should be constantly borne in mind that it is incomparably better for the health of the plants to prevent heat from escaping by non-conducting coverings during the night, than to allow it to be continually given off into the atmosphere, and as continually supplied by fire-flues or hot-water pipes. Where coverings cannot be applied, and a high temperature must be kept up, reserve sources of heat, and abundant supplies of water to maintain atmospheric moisture, are the only means by which the plants can be kept healthy. "A weakly growth," Sir J. Paxton observed, "is the sure consequence of a high temperature maintained by fire-heat, whatever plan of artificial heating be adopted." He therefore recommends, in all cases where practicable, the use of external coverings, by which, at Chatsworth, a difference of from 10° to 15° is gained, and two-thirds of the fuel that would otherwise be necessary are saved.

Atmospheric Moisture.—The necessity of proportioning moisture to temperature, and the causes which render the climates of our plant-structures unnaturally dry, have already been pointed out. To give an idea of the quantity of moisture requisite for an atmosphere at a high temperature, Mr. Rogers has shown that a vinery twenty-five feet long by thirteen feet six inches wide in the roof, maintained at 65° when the outer air is 35°, will condense on the glass, in twenty-four hours, $35\frac{1}{4}$ gallons of water. ('Gard. Mag.,' 1840, p. 282.) In devising the best method of procuring a constant supply of moisture for the air of a hothouse proportionable to the expenditure, Mr. Rogers finds the end may be most effectually attained by placing cisterns on the heating-pipes. As the temperature of the water in these cisterns would vary with that of the pipes, the evaporation from them would be greatest when the pipes were hottest; when the greatest degree of artificial temperature was being obtained, and consequently the greatest drain upon it by condensation. The cisterns may be made of zinc, with their bottoms fitted to the curvature of the pipes, at least six inches deep to the top of the pipes, and of the same length as the space between the rings by which the pipes are joined. Where two pipes are placed side by side on the same level, the form shown in fig. 148 may be adopted, and a single pipe may have cisterns fitted to it in the same manner, or it may be made to embrace the sides of the pipe and cover it entirely with water, as in fig. 149. In some cases shallow cisterns are cast on the pipes, but their power is insufficient, and in general zinc cisterns may be considered the best. Cisterns so placed on pipes heated to 200° will contain water at 145° to 150°; but this will not be

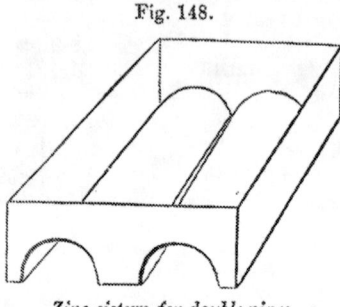

Fig. 148.

Fig. 149.

Zinc cistern for double pipes.   *Zinc cistern for a single pipe.*

the case unless they are properly fitted, and luted on the pipes with wet sand; for the smallest interstice is found to make a great difference in the heat transmitted. Mr. Rogers finds that cisterns fixed in this manner, with water at a temperature of from 120° to 145°, evaporate about three-quarters of a gallon per square foot of surface in twenty-four hours. The proportion which he employs in an orchidaceous stove is about one square foot of evaporating surface to ten square feet of glass; and, in stoves and forcing-houses, he is of opinion ('Proceedings of the Horticultural Society,' 1840, p. 149) that there ought to be one square foot of water for every fifteen square feet of glass. If houses heated by flues had this proportion of cistern placed over the flues, we should no longer hear so much of the dry disagreeable atmosphere produced by this mode of heating. It is almost unnecessary to observe that the cisterns will be most effective where the flues are most effective; or that, as the covers of flues have not interruptions like the joints of pipes, the cisterns may be made of any length. Slate cisterns placed above the pipes may be advantageously used for increasing the moisture, serving at the same time as a reservoir of heat, and of water for watering the plants, and also for growing aquatics; but as the water in such cisterns will seldom exceed the temperature of 80° to 85°, a much larger surface is required than in the case of zinc cisterns accurately fitted to the curvature of the pipes. On smoke-flues the water in such cisterns will rise to a much higher temperature than on pipes, because the slate bottoms will come in close contact with the entire surface of the covers of the flue. Much may be done towards keeping a wholesome degree of moisture in houses by covering the shelves, beds, and in fact every surface, with an inch of gravel or broken spar, which should be kept well moistened.

Ventilation and Aëration.—Till lately the subject of giving air to plant-houses has been very imperfectly understood; and, indeed, as it was generally supposed that a very small supply of air was sufficient for the growth of plants, ventilation was principally employed to lower the temperature of a hothouse when the heat was too great, or to let off sulphurous or other noxious gases which might be generated by the modes of heating employed. Now, however, that it begins to be well known that plants derive a great proportion of their carbon from the air, another and the most important use of ventilation has been discovered; and gardeners are become aware that a constant supply of fresh air is almost as necessary to plants as water, and, consequently, that without fresh air no plants can be kept in a perfectly healthy and vigorous state. The admission of air for the purpose of nourishing plants has been very properly distinguished by Dr. Lindley under the name of Aëration, from ordinary ventilation, and it requires to be regulated in quite a different manner. It has been already observed that if the sashes of a hothouse are opened in front and in the upper part of the roof at the same time, so as to create a thorough draught, when the atmosphere is colder than the temperature of the house, a great injury is done to vegetation, not only by the sudden chill, which the admission of a current of cool air produces, but by the quantity of moisture which it carries off. Hence, aëration should be effected by the circulation of a constant supply of warm moist air; and hence it is that plants grown in houses heated by the Polmaise system are generally in a state of vigorous health. Ventilation is, however, frequently necessary as well as aëration. In greenhouses, pits, and frames, where there is a large proportion of earthy and moist surface to a small volume of air, the latter may become too moist, and fresh air may be required to dry it; and in every description of plant-structure it may be required to lower the temperature. Hence, for houses heated by smoke-flues, and for pits and frames heated by fermenting dung, a greater power of ventilation becomes requisite than for houses heated by hot water, in which noxious vapours can rarely be produced, or the temperature raised much above 80° or 90°. For lowering the temperature of a hothouse, air is best admitted by opening sashes or ventilators in the upper part of the roof. In roofs with sliding sashes, the upper sashes along the whole line of roof may be let down uniformly, if the house be at an equal temperature throughout, and rather more at the hottest part, if it is of unequal temperature. The width opened need seldom exceed half an inch or an inch in the winter time; but in summer it may be much greater, according to the temperature to be kept up in the house, and other circumstances. If the roof should be a fixed one, then a narrow opening might be made in the upper angle of the roof along the whole length of the house, and the cover to this opening might be raised simultaneously and uniformly by simple mechanical means. A portion of the heated air of the house will escape by this opening, while a portion of the outer air will enter to take its place, mixed, as it descends, with the heated air, and becoming by this means heated to a certain extent before it reaches the plants. The great object in ventilating houses which are kept at a high temperature is to avoid thorough draughts, which are always produced when ventilators in the front and back are opened at the same time. Even in houses kept at a low temperature, such as greenhouses and conservatories, it is desirable in the winter season to admit the air from the roof only, and not from the sides. In summer, when the temperature of the outer air is as high as that of the house ought to be, openings may be made in every direction at pleasure. In stoves, the precaution of covering the openings of the upper part of the roof, by which air is given, with wire netting might be taken, which, while it excludes wasps and flies in summer, would in winter act like Jeffrey's Respirator in abstracting the heat from the heated air which escaped, and imparting it to the cold air which entered, or the double tube, recommended by Dr. Arnott in his 'Treatise on Warming and Ventilating,' might be adopted. The external air may be heated in the winter season before it is allowed to enter the house, by enclosing a part of the pipes or smoke-flues in a trunk or box, with a communication at the lower part of one end with the open air, and at the upper part of the other with the air of the house. So long as the pipes are kept at a temperature considerably above that of the house, fresh air will flow in, and a corresponding quantity will be displaced by the accidental crevices of the roof. In hotbeds it is customary to leave openings for the escape of moist vapour during the whole of the night; this is generally done by raising the sashes behind; but, as by this mode the steam from the dung is sometimes driven in, some gardeners have a narrow opening in the upper part of the sash, with a lid to fit to it, hinged along the upper edge.

Light is one of the elements of culture as essential as heat. The health, strength, and beauty of plants depend very much upon the amount of light to which they are subjected; hence the immense importance of cheap and good glass to horticulture. With heavy roofs of wood, and panes of glass five inches by three, all lapped, nearly a half of the old frames and roofs were opaque. With the abolition of the duty, these panes gave place to others a yard long by nearly half a yard wide. The results at first appeared somewhat disappointing. The plants were tender and the glass was uneven. Each inequality became a lens to burn the emaciated foliage, and large panes were for a time in bad repute; but again they are in the ascendant. It is found that with an even surface and healthy plants, burning is reduced to a minimum. The glare of the sun is broken by temporary shading or by the use of tinted glass, as in the great conservatory and new palm-house at Kew. Crown or sheet glass in large squares is the most generally used. This is occasionally butted, or placed end to end, on steep roofs, but it is more generally lapped. The laps should not exceed one-eighth of an inch. The broader the lap, the more liable is the glass to breakage, when the water so retained becomes frozen. This lap is sometimes entirely, and sometimes partially, rendered air and water tight by putty. In the former case it prevents the water which condenses on the inside of the glass from escaping to the outside; and in the latter, while it allows the condensed water to escape, it also retains, by the attraction of cohesion, as much as fills the space between the lap; and this water, in severe weather, is apt to freeze, and by its expansion when undergoing that operation, the glass is broken. By having the laps unputtied, not only is there great danger rom breakage by frost, but much heated air escapes during cold weather, and rain is apt to be blown into the house during high winds in certain directions. It is better, therefore, in the opinion of most scientific gardeners, to putty the laps and render them waterproof; to accomplish which in an efficient and economical manner, Mr. Forsyth proposes a lap three-eighths of an inch broad (in our opinion a greater breadth than is necessary), with the space between filled in with soft putty in the usual manner, and then carefully to paint the joinings of the glass, both the under lap and the over lap, and also the putty between, in the following manner:—Let the upper edge of the paint on both sides of the lap run in the direction of d, c, in fig. 150, thus directing all the water which condenses on the inside or falls on the outside down the centre of the squares. The only disadvantage attending close-puttying the lap is, that the condensed water, when the roof is very flat, sometimes drops on the plants; but

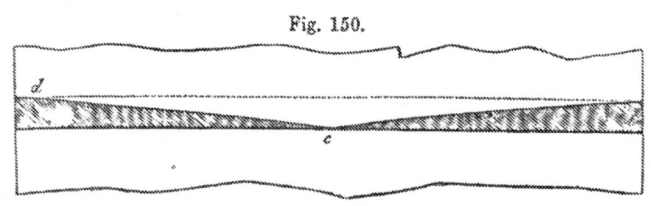

Fig. 150.

Lap of glass panes puttied and painted.

if the house is kept at a proper temperature, the water that drops in this manner will do little injury, and will be speedily taken up by the dry air which has just parted from it. In particular cases, where the drip falls on a plant, it may be directed to a point where it will do no injury, by a simple process pointed out by Mr. Rogers—viz., to fix at places where the drip will do no injury, small pieces of cobblers' wax or putty, which, by interrupting the descending current, will cause it to drop down. The drip, however, is much more common from the bars between the glass than from the glass itself, and to these Mr. Rogers's plan is peculiarly applicable. One great argument for puttying the laps is, that the moisture of the atmosphere, though it may be condensed on the glass, is not, if proper means are taken to retain it at the bottom of the sloping glass, allowed to escape from the house, but must be re-absorbed by the air which deposited it, somewhat in the same manner that takes place in growing plants in close glass cases. These cases being air-tight, when the temperature within is greater than that without, moisture is deposited on the glass, and after some time runs down and settles along the inside of the rim; whence, when the temperature within is raised to the same height as before, it is again taken up and held in suspension in the form of elastic vapour. In the case of air-tight stoves, nearly the same process must be constantly going on; but few have hitherto been built sufficiently air-tight for this purpose. One of the greatest improvements that have taken place in the glazing of plant-structures of every description, is the introduction of sheet-window-glass, which, while it is nearly as thick and strong as plate-glass, is not much dearer than crown-glass. The thickness of this glass varies from one-eighth of an inch to something more than one-sixteenth, and either thickness may be used in lengths of from two to five feet. In the grand conservatory at Chatsworth, the panes are three feet nine inches in length, that being the length of the side of the ridge, and they are six inches in width, so that there is no occasion for a lap. Ridge and furrow houses, when this kind of glass is used, may be made nearly air-tight. In the grand conservatory in the Horticultural Society's garden, the same kind of glass is used, and the panes are sixteen inches by twelve inches. This house is remarkably well glazed, and the laps are all puttied. Indeed, if this were not the case, it would be almost impossible to heat such a lofty structure with glass on all sides; but this glass being very even, as well as thick and strong, the laps are not more than three-sixteenths of an inch, and do not retain any water, which, indeed, from the temperature within being seldom greater than that without, is not often deposited on it. Most of the evils of drip and breakage, described in this chapter, are wholly avoided by cutting the glass, and the abolition of putty-glazing, as in Beard's system.

Water is commonly supplied to plants in hothouses by hand; but pipes, pierced with small holes, have been arranged under the roof, which, on turning on water from a cistern above the level, will throw down a shower at pleasure. For lofty houses, such as the palm-stoves of Messrs. Loddiges, the inventors of this system, this mode of watering is very eligible, and it might also frequently be adopted in conservatories attached to dwelling-houses, the cistern being in the upper part of the house. As a luxury, the noise of the artificial shower, like that of drops of rain in a warm summer's evening when all is arid without, will more than compensate for the expense. The evils incident to such modes of watering are, that all the plants, dry or not dry, get the same quantity. Such expedients are, therefore, not to be recommended, unless for watering the foliage nicely. A much better, because discriminate mode of root-watering is to screw a length or two of gutta-percha or india-rubber hose on to a water-pipe or tank, and then, with a conductor, direct a stream of water to any pot or root that requires it. A dexterous use of the finger to stop or regulate the flow, and an exact aim, renders this the most expeditious and efficient mode of watering. As water should never be applied to plants at a lower temperature than the mean of the atmosphere in which they grow, there should be a cistern in every house, of sufficient capacity to supply all the water which can be wanted at any one time, placed over the flues or hot-water pipes in such a manner as soon to be heated by them. In plant-houses these cisterns may be used to a certain extent for growing aquatics; but in this case only a small portion of water should be taken from the cisterns at a time, so that the addition of cold water may not chill the plants. To prevent the rose of the watering-pot from being choked by the leaves or other matters in such water, watering-pots with the grating described by Mr. Beaton (p. 104) should be used.

The different kinds of fixed structures for plants, are—the pit, the greenhouse, the orangery, the conservatory, the plant stove, the pine stove, the forcing-house, the orchid-house, and the orchard-house. We shall conclude by shortly noticing the characteristic features of these, and their varieties.

Pits are low buildings with glass roofs, but without glass in the sides or ends. The angle of the roof is between 15° and 25° with the horizon, and the surrounding walls are generally built of brick, and hollow, or in some kinds of pits they are pigeon-holed, or with thin panels to admit the heat of exterior casings. The provision for heating varies from the mere power of retaining natural heat by coverings of glass or other materials, to the obtaining of 70° or 80° or upwards of artificial heat, which may be supplied either by fermenting materials or fire-heat, or by both combined. The cold-pit is without any artificial source of heating, and in some its walls are of turf or earth; and instead of glass sashes, frames of reeds, or boards, or thatched hurdles, or other coverings, are substituted. The cold pit is used for protecting plants in pots not in a growing state, or for preserving culinary vegetables from the frost. In warm situations and dry soil, it has a thick mound of earth, or thick wall of turf, which in either case should be coped so as to be kept as dry as possible. Even in the case of brick pits, an outer casing of dry turf prevents to a very great extent the effects of frost and sudden changes of temperature. The casing may also be made of boards, where great neatness is an object, leaving a cavity to be filled with coal-ashes, charcoal, dry sand, or other non-conducting materials. In pits of this kind, with glass sashes instead of opaque covers, many hard-wooded greenhouse plants, such as camellias, myrtaceæ, heaths, &c., may be preserved through the winter without any artificial heat, care being taken to adapt the nightly coverings to the weather. The usual width of such pits is from six to eight feet; height of the back wall, three to five feet; and of the front wall, two to three feet. A pit to be heated by a bed of tan within, and exterior cases of dung, may be of the same or larger dimensions, with the back and front wall pigeon-holed or panelled (p. 164), and with boarded covers to protect the linings from rain and wind, hinged to the wall-plate. Instead of exterior linings for supplying extra heat, flues or hot-water pipes may be introduced along the front and ends, or entirely round the pit; sometimes with a platform of boards over them for plants in pots, or even for a bed of soil, but more frequently separated from the bed of tan by a narrow wall, or by a partition of slates or flag-stones. The width of the bark-bed in such pits is seldom less than five or six feet, and eighteen inches of additional width is necessary for the front flue, or four-inch pipes; and double these widths if the flues or pipes are carried round the house. For the more convenient management of pits, they are sometimes constructed sufficiently high behind to admit of walking upright there; and a passage for that purpose is left at the back, of three or four feet in width, and a door made in one end. The roof over the passage is generally opaque and sloping to the north, as in fig. 151. To the possessor of a small garden, and an amateur, this is a very desirable description of pit, as in it he may grow almost everything, provided he does not attempt too many kinds of culture at once. The form is very economical, from there being as much surface of pit as there is covering of glass; and the interior is very comfortable to work in, as the operator need not stoop. If the ends were made of glass, it would be an improvement, by admitting the morning and evening sun: it would then, however, be entitled to be called a small house, instead of a pit. The sashes of all pits used to be made to slide between rafters which are fixed to the plates of wood, which form, partially or wholly, the copings to the walls. Such pits as shown in fig. 151 are now often made with fixed roofs, ventilated above, and in the front and back walls. There should be a bolt to each sash for fixing it when shut, and also when let down for giving air, in order that there may be no risk of its being blown off by high winds; and all the sashes ought to admit of being readily taken off, for the purpose of taking out, and putting in dung, tan, or other materials. When the pit is ten or twelve feet in width the sashes may be in two lengths, the one sliding over the other; the upper sash sliding on ledges formed in the rafters, so as to render it independent of the lower sash. In general, short sashes for pits last much longer, and occasion much less breakage of the glass than long ones, from their leverage being so much less. The roofs of all pits ought to have coverings, and the best material, in our opinion, is boards, as, where glass is so flat as it generally is in pits and frames, it is apt to get dirtied by straw mats, unless these are put over a covering of bast mats. Fig. 152 is an excellent plan of a pit or small house, with a

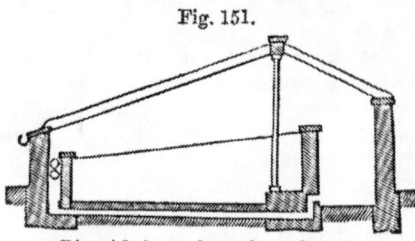

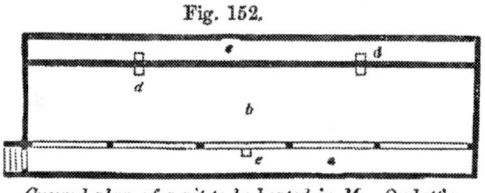

Fig. 151.

Pit, with the roof over the path opaque.

Fig. 152.

Ground plan of a pit to be heated in Mr. Corbett's manner.

a, Back path.
b, Bark pit, 50 ft. long in the clear.
c, Exterior pit for dung casing, to revive the heat.
d, d, Gratings to drains.
e, Stink-trap to drain.

span-roof all of glass, designed by Mr. Glendinning, for general purposes, and heated by Corbett's hot-water apparatus. Mr. Corbett's system appears to be better adapted for pits than for larger and longer houses, where its heating power would probably not be sufficient, or be unequal for the slowness of the circulation in consequence of the water-troughs being necessarily on a dead level. Mr. Glendinning's pit, however, may be heated by any mode, not even excepting a smoke-flue. Fig. 153 is a section of this pit, showing:—

f, f, Glass roof. *g*, Bark pit.
h, Back path.
l, Pit for dung casing. *k*, Drain. Hinged cover of ledged boards to protect the dung from the rain and wind.
m, Ground line.
n, Suspended shelf for strawberry pots.
o, Slate shelf for pots.
p, Stink-trap communicating with the cross-drain (*q*), which leads to the main or barrel-built drain (*k*).
r, Corbett's hot-water apparatus.
s, Hollow wall of bricks on edge.

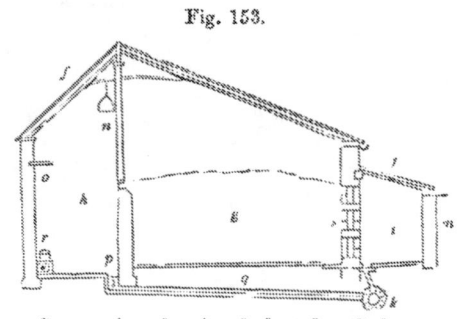

Cross section of a pit to be heated on Corbett's system, or by smoke-flues.

Pits or low houses have been formed with glass on all sides, and span roofs (see 'Gard. Mag.,' vol. vii. p. 290); but from the great quantity of glass in proportion to the surface of floor enclosed, they become too expensive for general purposes, and, unless furnished with a warm covering, the extensive surface of glass occasions an injurious degree of radiation.

The greenhouse is a light, airy structure, with a glass roof at an angle of 35° or 40° with the horizon, and upright glass in front and at the ends; and with the means of heating sufficient to keep out frost and in humid weather to dry up damp. The plants are grown in pots placed on a stage, or range of shelves rising one above another from a path in front, to within six or seven feet of the upper angle of the back wall. Between the front path and the upright glass, there is a broad shelf on a level with the lowest shelf of the stage, for small plants that require to be near the light. All the front and roof sashes are made to move, because it is frequently necessary to admit a free circulation of the external atmosphere; and coverings are seldom applied, because a very little fire-heat is found to exclude the frost. This is the common or normal form of the greenhouse, when it is placed against a wall, or the side or end of a dwelling-house, and facing the south or some point between south-east and south-west; but much more elegant forms, of the curvilinear or ridge and furrow kind, may be adopted, and where the expense of fire-heat is not an object, it may face the east or west, or be constructed of glass on all sides. For placing against a wall in a flower-garden, we should prefer a curvilinear structure, with ends of the same kind, and an architectural entrance, either in the back wall, as in fig. 127, p. 155, or in front; but against a dwelling-house, and on a small scale, we should recommend the ridge and furrow construction, as from the ease with which the roof may be partially or wholly concealed, it is the most easily rendered architectural.

Fig. 154.

Lean-to cool-house.

The orangery is an architectural building, more like a living-room than a plant-structure, with large windows and narrow piers in front and at the ends, and with an opaque roof. It is used for preserving orange-trees and other large plants which are in a dormant state during winter; and the power of heating is about the same as that for the greenhouse; but, from the roof being opaque, less extent of flue or hot-water pipe is required. Plant-structures of this description are chiefly wanted in large establishments; but as architectural appendages to a house they may sometimes be advantageously introduced in small villas, the area of the orangery being used in the summer time, when the orange-trees and other plants usually kept in it are set in the open garden, as a place for prolonging the beauty of plants in bloom, and for other purposes. Such houses are now but little used, as it is found that the perfect development of the orange requires all the light that can be secured for it in our climate. Still, where large orange-trees are grown in boxes out of doors in summer, as at Holland House, Kensington, and other places, such houses may prove useful winter dormitories — the object in such cases being simply to keep the plants at rest till the following season.

The conservatory differs from the orangery and the greenhouse in being more lofty and architectural, and in having the plants growing in a bed of soil which forms the floor of the house. As the plants in a conservatory are generally kept growing through the winter, a power of heating is required greater than that of the orangery; and when it is joined to a dwelling-house, and is to be frequently walked in by the inmates, greater than that of a greenhouse. The temperature during the night should not be under 45°, nor need it be raised higher during bright sunshine than 55° or 60°. The forms, and other particulars relative to the construction and adaptation of conservatories, have already been given in the 'Suburban Architect and Landscape Gardener.'

Botanic stoves are of various kinds; but with respect to temperature and moisture they may be reduced to the dry stove, the damp stove, and the intermediate or bark stove. The first requires abundance of light and a power of heating from zero to 60° in the winter season, and is chiefly used for growing succulents; the second requires less intensity of light, but a power of heating equal to 80° in the winter season above the external air; for although such will seldom be required, yet it is better to have too much than too little heating power. In the damp stove there must also be a power of saturating the atmosphere with moisture at all seasons; as it is chiefly used for growing orchidaceous plants and ferns. The intermediate or common botanic stove requires the same power of heating as the last, but more light and much more space, as it is used for growing the trees and shrubs of tropical climates. These are commonly kept in pots, and very frequently plunged in a bark-bed, whence this kind of house, before the use of damp-stoves, was called the barkstove, to distinguish it from the dry-stove.

The pine stove used to be a low structure, and with a bark or other bed in which the pots were plunged, and differing little from a large pit, excepting that it was generally arranged so as to admit of growing crops of grapes as well as pines. The glass roof was generally placed at some angle between 25° and 35°, and the power of heating should be equal to 70° during winter. Now, however, any good span roof or lean-to house is used for pines. In growing the succession plants, it is best to keep their tops within a foot or eighteen inches of the glass. But they are often fruited at a distance of one, or even two yards from it. The clear glass of the present day prevents them drawing. It is also common now to plant out the fruiting pines in a bed of soil, so that more head-room is needed. A power of communicating atmospheric moisture should be at command as in the common botanic stove.

Forcing-houses are chiefly employed for bringing forward early crops of grapes, peaches, cherries, or other fruits, and for producing early culinary vegetables of different kinds, or flowers. The power of heating varies with the season of forcing, and the kind of fruit to be forced; but it should not be less than 70°, with a command of atmospheric moisture. Sometimes the trees are trained on trellises one or two feet within the glass; and sometimes they are partly trained under the glass, and partly on the back wall. In either case, the narrower the house the more readily is it heated either by fire or the sun. As these details vary with the kind of trees and plants to be forced, they belong more properly to the following part of this work. See 'Practice of Horticulture, Forcing-Garden.'

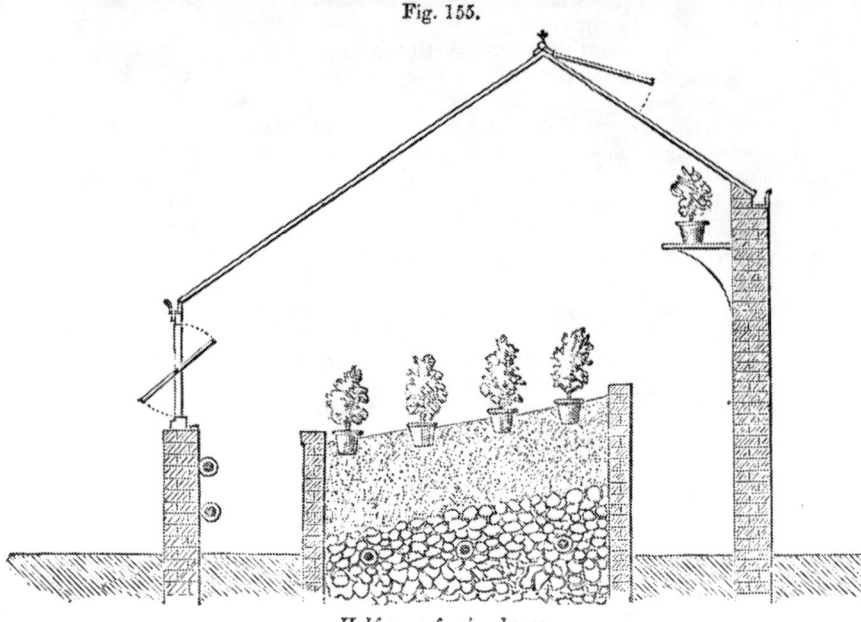

Fig. 155.

Half-span forcing-house.

A Plant-structure for all or any of the above Purposes.—The pit, fig. 151, or that shown in figs. 153 and 154, will answer for any one of the purposes for which orangeries, greenhouses, and stoves are erected. Orange-trees and similar plants, in a dormant state, may be preserved through the winter in such pits with ample coverings, and scarcely any artificial heat; greenhouse plants, with very little heat; dry stove-plants, with a little more heat; damp-stove plants, with increased temperature and moisture; other stove plants, till they attain a certain size; pine-apples, to the highest degree of perfection; and the fruit-trees trained to trellises under the glass may be forced, as may be also every description of culinary vegetable, not excepting mushrooms, which may be grown in a portion of the bark-bed, or in shelves against the back wall or in arched recesses, or cellars, or vaults under the tan of the pit. In short, there is nothing in the way of culture that may not be carried on to the highest degree of perfection in these pits, provided that all the large-growing plants are trained on trellises close under the glass; but the airy elegance of the greenhouse, the grandeur and picturesque luxuriousness of the conservatory, and the tropical aspect of the lofty botanic stove, are not to be expected from them. The low span-roofed house, with a sunk passage in the centre, combines the advantage of the best type of houses and pits for plant-growing purposes.

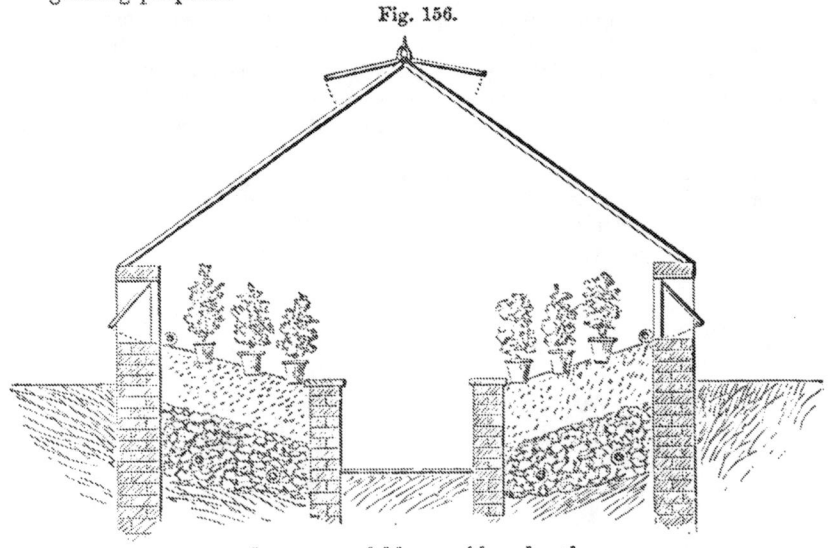

Fig. 156.

Low span-roofed house, with sunk-path.

The Orchard House.—This is a comparatively modern structure, first suggested by Mr. Rivers, and now a favourite with many amateurs. Those about constructing one would do well to provide themselves with Mr. Rivers's book, and also with Mr. Pearson's, both on the orchard house. The best orchard houses in England are undoubtedly those in Mr. Pearson's nursery at Chilwell, near Nottingham. Mr. Pearson's advice on the subject of building orchard houses is valuable. "Having had eighteen houses erected within the last few years, each being an improvement on the former ones—and seeing that Mr. Foster, who built them, and is largely engaged in their manufacture, is constantly making improvements in their construction—I have arrived at the conclusion that amateur building is a mistake. It appears advisable to take advantage of experience acquired at other people's expense rather than make mistakes at our own cost. The houses built by Mr. Foster, of Beeston, near Nottingham, are by far the best I have hitherto met with. They are constructed of all sizes, adapted to the requirements of the smallest or the largest establishments, and they are not only of an ornamental, but a durable character. The mode by which Mr. Foster ties the span of his houses, and renders them firm in their construction, is particularly meritorious, and far superior to anything I have yet seen for strength and elegance. It is perfectly novel in design, and has been secured by a patent. A conservatory or orchard house ought to be constructed so that ladies may enjoy a walk there with no more feeling of constraint than in an open garden; to be able to cut a flower, reach a peach, or water a plant without difficulty, is essential to the enjoyment of such houses. It is not sufficient to be able to get inside, exclaim, 'How beautiful!' and wish to be out again as soon as possible. Similar objections may be urged against covering peach-walls with glass; a covered wall is no place for enjoyment; but for the production of fruit, irrespective of all other considerations, no one can take exception to such houses as those erected at Dalkeith, which though they may be called covered walls, are wide enough for a row of dwarf trees in front, and a path down the middle. Having often heard the remark, 'If I were living on my own property I would have an orchard house imme-

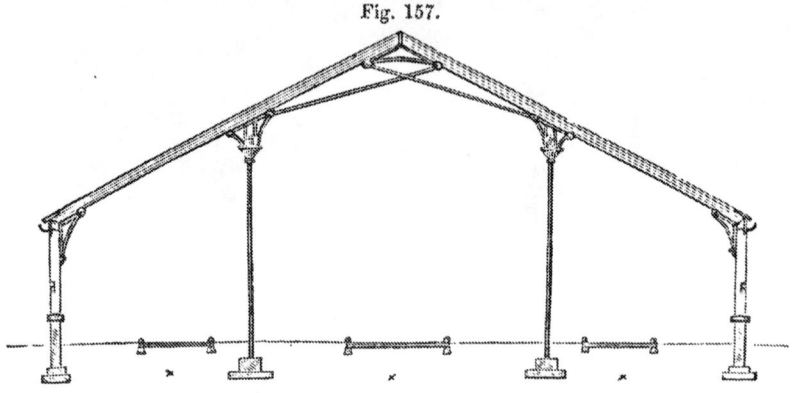

Fig. 157.

Section of Forster's orchard house.

diately,' I have great pleasure in calling attention to Foster's patent moveable house on iron supports. It is as strong as any house can be built, and yet may be taken in pieces and removed without difficulty. The feet, pillar, and bracket are all cast in one piece. The roof is made in separate lights, and also the ends and sides, so that there is no occasion to break a pane of glass in removing the whole structure. I have a house erected on this principle, 60 feet by 24, heated by six rows of pipes. It is used as a conservatory, and is a beautiful building. Many persons will remember a storm of wind from the west which occurred on the 3rd of December, 1863. In the neighbourhood of Nottingham it did a great amount of damage, blowing down timber trees and unroofing houses. By that storm many greenhouses were much injured, some having their sides blown quite in, others being partially unroofed. This moveable house proved so much stronger than any house merely resting on brickwork that, excepting the noise, no one could tell a storm was blowing. It will be easily understood that a house having iron pillars every 10 feet, forming part of its sides, must be of immense strength; and when we take into consideration the great pressure of wind on a house 90 to 100 feet long, stability is a matter of great importance." I can, from personal examination, testify to the great merit in every way of these houses recommended by Mr. Pearson. They are described in detail in Mr. Pearson's little book.

Edifices used in Horticulture.

The edifices required in horticulture are chiefly the head gardener's house, the journeyman gardener's lodge, the fruit-room, the seed and herb-room, the root-cellar, the tool-house, and the potting and working sheds.

The gardener's house, wherever there are many plant structures, should be as near the garden as possible; but it should by no means form an object in the scenery of the garden. Like what the house of every man ought to be, the occupant should possess it as his castle for the time being. It may be wholly or partially veiled by trees; but within whatever boundary it is placed perfect liberty should prevail; and this cannot be the case where the inmates are either constrained to remain in-doors, or when they go out are forced into contact with their superiors, to the annoyance of both parties. Besides a kitchen and sleeping-rooms, the gardener's house should contain at least one good parlour. All the fixtures and principal articles of furniture should be the property of the proprietor of the garden, and valued to the gardener on his entering on the situation, and again valued on his leaving it; he paying any difference in value which may have been occasioned by use. This is not the general practice, though it is fast spreading, and deservedly so, because it must occasion less pain to a considerate master to part with a married servant under such circumstances, and less inconvenience to the gardener when he leaves his place, without perhaps knowing where he shall find another.

The journeyman gardener's lodge, and all the other edifices mentioned, are generally included in the sheds behind the different plant-structures; because they tend to keep the latter warm, and because the high back wall of the hothouses existing at any rate, they can be erected there more economically than anywhere else. It has been observed, however, by a number of gardeners, both in England and Scotland, that living-rooms at the back of hothouses are not healthy; and that those that are situated at the back of stoves are still more unhealthy than those at the back of greenhouses or other plant-structures where less heat is required. Damp and want of ventilation are the probable causes; for which reason we should recommend the journeyman-gardener's rooms to be separated from the back wall of the plant-house against which they are built by a vacuity, communicating above and below with the open air. The floor should be raised at least a foot above the general surface, and should have an ample vacuity below it, which on the one side may communicate with the vacuity between the walls, and on the other with the open air. This will insure a current of air through both these vacuities, which will be sufficient to carry off damp, and to prevent the ill effects of the excessive heat from the plant-structure. Another point which ought to be attended to in the construction of living-rooms behind hothouses is, to have larger windows and more of them than is usual; and always to have them carried up to within a few inches of the ceiling, in order that air may be admitted from the top as well as from the bottom of the window. It would generally be better to build a cottage for the young men wholly detached from the back wall, and to have a good separate bedroom for each man. The sitting-room arrangements for cooking, cleaning, &c., should likewise be made comfortable and convenient.

The fruit-room should have a double roof, or roof with a ceiling, a hollow front wall, and double doors and windows, so as to maintain an equable temperature. It should be divided into at least two apartments, so completely separated from each other as to prevent the air of that in which the early ripening fruits are placed from contaminating that in which the late ripening sorts are deposited. Both apartments should be fitted up with broad shelves of open work of white deal, or of some wood without resin or other qualities that would give a flavour to the fruit; and there ought to be bins or portable boxes for preserving fruit packed in sand, fern, hay, bran, kiln-dried straw, leaves or blossoms of the beech or chestnut, or other materials. The fronts of the shelves should have a narrow ledge, on which temporary labels can be pasted, indicating the names of the fruits, and when they ought to be fit for use, &c. Where fruit is to be frequently packed for sending to a distance, there should be a third apartment for containing the packing materials, and for packing in. Where there is danger from damp or heat, the back wall and floor can have vacuities as in the journeyman's room, with stoppers to the outlets, to be used in severe weather.

The seed-room should adjoin the fruit-room at one end, and the tool-house at the other. It should contain a cabinet fitted up with drawers for seeds; an open airy case, with drawers for bulbs; shelves for catalogues, a book-case, partitioned off, because moths are apt to be introduced along with some kinds of seeds, for a garden library, unless this is kept in the head gardener's house as a part of his furniture; a press for compressing dried herbs into cakes, to be afterwards wrapped up so as to be air-tight in paper, and kept in drawers to be taken out as wanted for the kitchen; and a variety of minor articles, some of which have been mentioned (p. 80), and others will occur in practice.

Root-cellar and other Conveniences.—Underneath the fruit or seed-room, if the soil is dry, there may be a cellar for preserving dahlia-roots, bulbs, potatoes, &c.; though, on a small scale, the seed-room and some part of the sheds may serve as substitutes. A mushroom-house, and a house for forcing rhubarb and succory, and for producing early potatoes by a particular process which may be carried on in the dark, may also form part of the back sheds; and a supply of water by a pump or well, or by a large cistern, supplied by an hydraulic ram or other means; and conveniences for liquid manure, lime-water, &c., &c., must not be forgotten. In short, whatever is wanting for the cultivation and management of a garden, exclusive of plant-structures and the gardener's house, should be provided for in the back sheds; and, as a general principle, it may be laid down that every plant-structure that has a back shed should have a direct communication with it by means of a door in the back wall. By means of this communication much time is saved in conveying articles from the shed to the house, and the contrary; fires can be more promptly attended to, and above all, plants in pots can be taken into the shed and examined or shifted, without exposing them to the open air.

The tool-house should adjoin the seed-room, and should be fitted up as before indicated. The potting-shed should contain, facing the windows, benches for potting on, and ample space for pots, crocks, potting trowels, stakes, ties, tallies, bell-glasses, and a variety of other articles. It should, however, be well lighted alike from the front and the roof; sashes should likewise be placed here. Soils are in general fresher, and in a better state, when kept in the open air; but still there ought to be bins for sand, peat, leaf-mould, and some other kinds in constant use.

Open Sheds.—A portion of the sheds open in front ought to be set apart for tanner's bark, and other portions for hotbed-frames and such like portable structures, or articles that would be injured by exposure to the weather when not in use; one for sticks for peas, props for plants, mats, coal or wood for fuel, and for other purposes. In short, there can hardly be too much shed-room; for besides all the ordinary purposes mentioned, a portion of it may be sometimes required for preserving deciduous greenhouse plants through the winter for which there is not room in the plant-structures, such as large Fuchsias, Brugmansias, Pomegranates, and many other plants which are turned out into the open garden during summer. If there is no regular mushroom-house, that vegetable may be grown in the open shed, on dung ridges covered with hay and mats. Tart rhubarb and sea-kale may be forced there, protected by mats supported on hoops; peas and beans for early crops may be germinated before being transplanted into the open garden; and indeed there is no end to the objects that may be effected within open sheds, while on their roofs onions may be dried in wet seasons—a practice very general in Scotland and in the north of England.

CHAPTER VIII.

OPERATIONS OF HORTICULTURE.

Labours on the Soil.

THE objects for which the soil is worked, are pulverization, to render it more readily penetrated by the roots of plants, and by heat, air, moisture, and sometimes by frost; to allow superfluous moisture to escape into the subsoil ; to mix the upper and lower parts of the upper stratum of soil together ; to deepen the tilth; to mix the coarser and finer parts together ; to add or mix in earths or manure; to free the soil from roots or perennial weeds, stones, or other objects unfavourable to culture ; and to destroy surface or annual weeds. The grand sources of heat to the soil are the sun and the atmosphere, including rain at a higher temperature than the soil; and the sources of cold, or of the abstraction of heat are, rain at a lower temperature than the soil, frost, snow, ice, and where drainage has been neglected, subterraneous water and evaporation from the surface. The greatest degree of cold produced by these causes, excepting the last, will always be found on the surface of the soil, and the best mode of supplying the heat that has been abstracted will be by leaving the surface to the action of the sun and of the air. By digging or trenching down a cold surface such as ice, or a substance such as snow, heat is abstracted from the soil, the natural temperature of which will in that case be lowered; and thus a plant grown in a soil so treated, will be, in so far as bottom heat is concerned, worse than if it were in a state of nature, in which heat abstracted by the air is always restored by it. The average temperature of the surface soil in most countries is believed to be nearly the same as that of the atmosphere ; but by considering all the causes that contribute to the warmth of a soil, there can be little doubt but in many cases its average temperature might be increased. The colour and texture of some soils is better adapted for absorbing heat than others, and the inclination of the surface of the soil is of as much importance in deriving heat from the direct action of the sun's rays as the angles of glass roofs. Hence the advantage of laying up soil in narrow ridges, which, when in the direction of east and west, very soon become much drier and warmer on one side than on the other. Rain, though in the cold season it abstracts heat from the soil, yet in spring and summer, being of the temperature of the atmosphere, it communicates heat more effectually than air, because, under ordinary circumstances, it penetrates deeper, in consequence of its greater specific gravity ; and as it requires two hundred and eighty-nine times as much coal to heat one cubic foot of water as would be required to heat the same bulk of air to the same degree, so is the quantity of heat which water of a given bulk will give out to soil greater than what will be communicated by the same bulk of air. Water, in a frozen state, though injurious as abstracting heat, is in many cases favourable by contributing to the pulverization of stiff soils, which are laid up in a rough state, in order to expose as large a surface as possible to be cooled and frozen during winter, and to be thawed and heated during spring. The retention of moisture by pulverization is an important object of working the soil. All properly cultivated soils hold water like a sponge, while in untilled soils the rains either never penetrate the surface, or they sink into the subsoil and are lost, or are retained by it and prove injurious. Wind, like rain, will communicate heat or abstract it from soil, according to its temperature and the rapidity of its motion; but as in either case it carries off moisture in proportion to its dryness and velocity, it is in general in cold climates much more favourable than hurtful for soils, considered apart from the plants which grow in them. If possible no operation should be performed on the soil excepting when it is in a dry state, and when the weather is also dry. Moist soil cannot be dug without first treading on it, and thus making it into a kind of paste or mortar, which renders it unfit for being pierced by the fibres of plants, and prevents it from being penetrated either by moisture or air; and water in the form of ice or snow, if dug in, abstracts that heat from the soil which it ought to derive direct from the atmosphere. "A pound of snow (newly fallen) requires an equal weight of water heated to 172° to melt it, and then the dissolved mixture is only of the temperature of 32°. Ice requires the water to be a few degrees warmer to produce the same result. When the ice or snow is allowed to remain on the surface, the quantity of heat necessary to reduce it to a fluid state is obtained chiefly from the atmosphere; but when buried so that the atmospheric heat cannot act directly upon it, the thawing must be very slowly effected by the abstraction of heat from the soil by which the frozen mass is surrounded. Instances have occurred of frozen soil not being completely thawed at midsummer when so buried.

Digging.—The use of the lever and the pick, the former in moving large obstacles, such as stones, and the latter for perforating and raising up hard soils or subsoils, may be considered as preparatory operations for the more perfect pulverization and mixture of the soil by digging. Previous to performing this operation, if the surface is uneven, it should be levelled; but as we are treating of garden digging, we shall suppose that the surface is already in a fit state to be dug. The first step is to fix on those parts of the plot where the operation is to commence and finish; which being done, a trench is to be opened at the former place, and the earth wheeled or carried to the latter. In most gardens where there is to be a regular course of cropping, the compartments are rectangular, and these are easily divided into smaller figures of the same kind for temporary purposes, the number of which divisions, with a view to digging or trenching, for reasons which will presently appear, must always be even. For example, a piece of ground of a square form, fig. 158, a, b, c, d, may be thrown into two parallelograms, a, f, and e, d, and the soil taken from the trench opened from a to e can be laid down from e to b, where the operation will be finished. Had the plot been divided into three parallelograms, as in fig. 159, the soil must have been removed from *g* to *h*, which would have more than doubled the labour of wheeling. A fourfold division would not, however, have been liable to the same objection, which con-

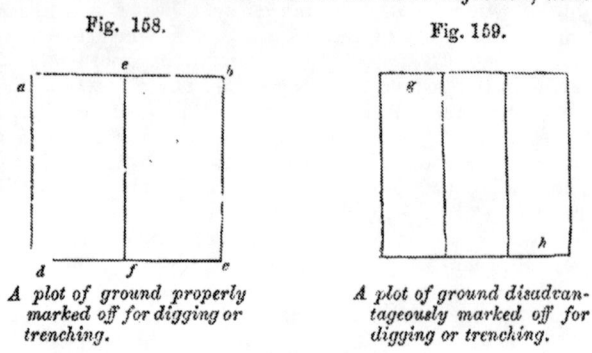

Fig. 158.

A plot of ground properly marked off for digging or trenching.

Fig. 159.

A plot of ground disadvantageously marked off for digging or trenching.

firms the rule, that the division ought always to be into equal numbers. Where a plot is circular or oval it may be divided into zones, and an irregular plot may be thrown into figures approaching as near as may be to regularity. In digging for pulverization and mixture, the surface is reversed by the operator, and left as rough as possible. When a crop is to be sown or planted, this surface is broken more or less fine according to the kind of crop. When the ground is not to be immediately cropped, it is commonly "rough dug," that is, laid up in broken spitfuls, so as to present as large a surface as possible to the action of the weather; and afterwards, when a crop is to be introduced on ground which has been "rough dug," it is "pointed," or slightly dug and smoothed on the surface with a rake. "Double digging," or trenching, is in horticulture what subsoil ploughing is in agriculture; the surface soil is kept on the surface, but the bottom of the trench is dug over as the work proceeds, and the soil turned over, a small portion of the subsoil being mixed with the top spit, the major portion of it being kept in the bottom of the trench. "Baulk digging" is an operation for rapidly exposing a large surface to the atmosphere, and consists in taking out a line of spitfuls and laying them on a line of firm ground, so that only half the ground is moved. It is only used where economy is a main object, and where the soil, being tenacious, will be much benefited by exposing a large surface to the frost. When soil, compost, or manure is to be dug in, it is previously distributed over the ground in heaps, by the aid of the wheelbarrow, and spread over the surface in moderate portions at a time, if loss will be sustained by evaporation; but if soil, such as sand or burnt clay, or a compost of lime and earth, is to be dug in, the whole may be spread over the soil at once; as the drier it becomes before being dug in, the better it will mix with the soil. In every description of digging the trench should be in a straight direction, from one side of the plot to the other, and equally wide throughout; or if curved, the same curvature should be maintained throughout; for if the trench is increased in length, it becomes lessened in capacity, and the soil can neither be moved to the proper depth nor sufficiently mixed. All roots of trees or bushes ought to be carefully picked out as the work proceeds, as they become fruitful centres for generating fungi. But small stones, brickbats, &c. should be left, as they tend to make heavy soils porous, and to consolidate those that are too light.

Trenching.—The object of deep trenching is to increase the depth of soil fit for plants, by which means it becomes a larger reservoir of air, moisture, and manure; and in the case of plants which do not permanently occupy the soil, it admits of entirely changing the surface, so as to bring up fresh soil every time the ground is trenched. The plot to be trenched is marked out by a line, exactly in the same manner as in digging; but instead of a narrow furrow, which suffices for that operation, a trench at least as broad as the depth to which the ground is to be moved, say from two to three feet, is marked off and opened, the soil being wheeled to the place of finishing, as in digging. The next point to determine is, whether the whole of the soil to be moved is to be equally mixed together; whether the subsoil only is to be mixed, and the surface soil still kept on the surface; or whether the surface is to be laid in the bottom of the trench, and the subsoil laid on the top.

In trenching ground that is to be cropped with culinary vegetables for the first time, the whole of the soil turned over should be equally mixed together, manure or compost being added and incorporated at the same time. When the ground of a kitchen-garden has been originally trenched in this manner to the depth of three feet, a fresh surface may be exposed for cropping every year, by trenching one year two spits, and the next three. Top and bottom and middle will thus exchange places in rotation.

In the operation of trenching, when the object is to reverse the surface, the firm soil is loosened, lifted, and thrown into the trench in strata, which, when completed, will hold exactly the reverse positions which they did in the firm ground; but when the object is to mix the soil throughout, or when the surface soil is to be kept uppermost, the face of the surface of the moved ground must be kept in a sloping position, in order that every spitful thrown on it may be deposited in the proper place, with a view to mixture. To secure space enough for the thorough admixture on the slope, a trench four feet wide will be used, as the soil should be bodily removed from one side and laid at the opposite side, ready to fill up the last trench. " Ridge trenching" is the term applied when the surface of the moved soil, instead of being smoothed and levelled, is laid up in the form of a ridge, in order to benefit by exposure to the atmosphere. Whatever mode of trenching may be adopted, it is of great importance that the bottom of the trenches should either be level, or form one or more regularly inclined planes, in order to carry off the superfluous water of the surface soil. In a very retentive subsoil, if the bottom is trenched irregularly, the places marked *a*, *b*, *c*, in fig. 160, would retain stagnant water injurious to the roots of trees, &c.; but if the bottom were loosened so as to form a regular slope, as from *d* to *e*, the water would gradually follow that direction.

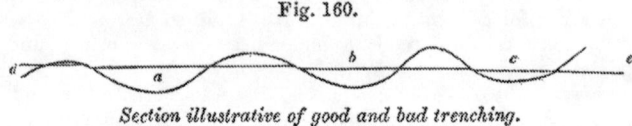

Fig. 160.

Section illustrative of good and bad trenching.

Forking soil is simply stirring the surface with the broad-pronged fork, which is greatly preferable to the spade for working among the roots of growing crops. For working with litter or dung, the forks with round, pointed prongs are used; the rotundity of the prongs diminishing friction, both in inserting the fork in the dung, and in discharging the forkful.

Hoeing is a mode of stirring the soil on the surface, and at the same time cutting up weeds or thinning out crops; and it is effected either by the draw-hoe or the thrust-hoe. Soil is also drawn up to, or taken away from, plants; and drills, or narrow furrows, are drawn by the former tool, of which there are several kinds, more or less adapted for these different purposes. In no kind of draw-hoe should the plane of the blade form a right angle with the handle, as at *a*, in fig. 161; but it should always be within a right angle, more or less, as at *b* or *c*. If the ground be soft the angle should be more acute than when it is hard, or when its surface is much matted with weeds. This

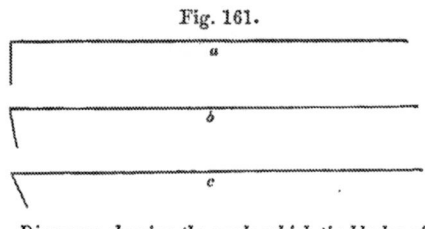

Fig. 161.

Diagrams showing the angle which the blades of draw-hoes ought to make with the handles.

variable angle should be provided for, partly in the formation of the eye or socket of the hoe, and partly by the application of a small wedge, the heel of which should be turned up, like those used for scythe-handles, in order that it may be driven out at pleasure. In short, the angle which the handle forms with the blade should be such, that when the latter is inserted in the soil to the required depth, the blade, in being drawn towards the operator, may retain that depth with the least possible exertion to his muscles in guiding it; for whatever muscular exertion is required in this way, beyond what is necessary for overcoming the resistance of the soil, is a waste of power. For the purpose of cutting weeds, or thinning out crops in light sandy soil, a hoe with a broad blade may be used; and of these the best that we know is the Leicestershire or shifting-blade hoe, the blades of which are pieces of the blade of an old scythe. This hoe is shown in fig. 162, in which *d* is the head, consisting of a socket for the blade, and a tubular socket or hose for the handle, without the blade; *b*, one of the blades not inserted in the socket; *c*, the socket with the kind of blade inserted which is used for general purposes, and more especially for hoeing between rows of drilled crops; and *a*, a socket with the blade, *b*, inserted, which is used chiefly for thinning turnips. For working in strong soil, a hoe with a narrow stout blade is required; and for very stiff soil, the Spanish hoe is the best tool. Some of these hoes are made with a small three-tined fork on the back, and are useful implements. For hoeing, with a view to cut weeds, the different descriptions of thrust-hoes are the most effective tools, especially among tall plants, but they are not calculated for stirring the soil to any depth. A thrust-hoe with a shifting blade, like the Leicestershire draw-hoe, would doubtless be a valuable implement.

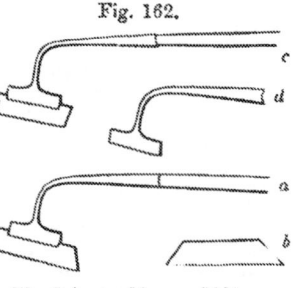

Fig. 162.

The Leicestershire or shifting-blade draw-hoe.

Raking is an operation used for separating the surface of soil from stones, roots, and other extraneous matters; for rendering even dug surfaces or gravel; for covering seeds; for collecting weeds, leaves, or mown grass; and, in general, for smoothing, covering, collecting, and finishing off surfaces. The teeth of the rake are placed at nearly a right angle to the bar to which they are riveted, and somewhat bent towards the handle, so that when the operator keeps the handle at an angle of 45°, the teeth will pass through the soil at nearly that angle, and consequently penetrate to nearly the whole length. The teeth of the iron rakes should be made with a small shoulder, neatly formed, so as to rest flatly against the under side of the bar in which they are riveted. The holes made in this bar for their reception should be widened below to admit a thickening next the shoulder of the tooth, as shown in fig. 163, for there the stress lies, and there, in nine cases out of ten, the breakage occurs in the teeth. The rest of the perforation should be narrow, in order not to weaken the head-bar, a slight countersink only being required for the rivet or clench on the upper side. The neck of the tooth is exposed to a force, tending to bend or fracture it across; but when once the neck is secured, the remaining part which passes through the head-bar has only a longitudinal tension. One of the most common purposes to which raking is applied, is covering small seeds sown broadcast; and this operation requires more care and skill in the operator than any other which is performed with the rake. If the ground has been raked previously to sowing the seeds, its surface will be ribbed or covered with very small furrows left by the teeth of the rake, at regular distances and of uniform depth: the seed being scattered evenly over the surface, will fall one-half in the furrows, and one-half on the small ridges between them: if in

Fig. 163.

Section of the head of a garden-rake, showing how the teeth should be inserted in it.

raking afterwards the teeth of the rake could be made to split the ridges between the furrows and do nothing more, the seed would be perfectly and equally covered; but owing to various causes, and principally to the unavoidable treading of the soil by the feet of the operator, it is next to impossible to effect this; and in consequence of more raking being required in the hard and depressed places than in the soft ones, as well to loosen the soil as to raise it to the proper level, the seed there becomes too deeply covered; and a part being drawn from the places from which the extra covering is taken, the seedling plants rise very irregularly. The best antidote to such evils is to sow all seeds either in narrow beds or drills.

Rolling is applied to walks to render their surface smooth, firm, and impervious to rain, and it is always most effective when the gravel is moist below and moderately dry above. When dry gravel is laid over the bottom of a walk that is in a very wet or puddled state, rolling should not be attempted till the whole is uniformly saturated, either by rain, which is preferable, or artificially; otherwise it will long remain unconsolidated. Grass lawns are also rolled to render the surface of the soil smooth and even, for which purpose they are previously raked or swept to destroy such inequalities as are produced by worm casts, or other accumulations that would interfere with the scythe, the uniform pressure of the roller, or the uniform smoothness and colour of the lawn. The general use of mowing-machines has superseded the use of the roller on grass, unless during winter and early spring.

Screening or lifting soil or gravel is best performed when these materials are dry; but excepting for sowing seeds, or planting very small or tender plants or cuttings, sifted soil is seldom wanted, it being found that pieces of turf, roots, and stones in soil are useful to plants, as forming vacuities for air, or for accumulations of decaying vegetable matter; or, more especially in the case of freestone, as sources of moisture.

Other labours on the soil consist in forming and cutting the edges of alleys or earth-walks, beating down, or rolling in seeds that require pressure, such as onions, moulding up celery, &c. &c.

Garden Labours with Plants.

Garden labours with plants may be reduced to sowing, cutting, clipping, mowing, and weeding; all of which may be performed at most seasons, and during moist weather as well as dry. In the first three of these labours, it must be borne in mind that growing trees and large shrubs should not be deprived of their branches when the sap is rising in spring, on account of the loss of the vital fluid which would be sustained at that season; that wounds can only be healed over when made close to a bud or shoot; and that the healing process proceeds from the alburnum and cambium, and not from the bark. For the operations of weeding and mowing with the scythe, wet weather is preferable to dry; but the grass cuts best if dry when the mowing-machine is employed. Clipping may be performed in wet weather.

Sawing is the most convenient mode of separating large branches, because it effects the separation with less labour than cutting with the axe or the bill, and also with less waste of wood. In sawing off large branches, whether close to the trunk or at a distance from it, it is advisable to cut a notch in the under side of the branch, or to enter the saw for a few inches in depth there, and in the same plane with the proposed saw-cut, in order to prevent the bark from being torn down when the branch is sawn through and drops off. It is also advisable to smooth over the section with a chisel or knife, in order that it may not retain moisture; and to cover the entire wound with a cataplasm of some sort, or with putty, or with paint, in order to exclude the air, and by that means to facilitate the process of healing.

Cutting and sawing are essentially the same operation; for the common saw is formed of a series of wedges cut in the edge of a thin plate of steel, and the knife only differs in having these wedges so small and so close together as not to be perceptible to the naked eye. In cutting living plants a smooth unbruised section will be more easily healed over than a rough one; hence, in all cutting or amputating, the rough or fractured section ought to be on the part amputated. In separating a branch, or cutting through a stem, with an axe, bill, or chisel, this result is effected by the obliquity of the strokes of the instrument to the direction of the body to be cut through, and with a knife by drawing it more or less obliquely across the shoot; but principally by the non-resistance offered by the part of the shoot to be cut off. Hence all shoots cut from living plants ought to have the cut made in an outward direction from the stem or root of the plant; because if the reverse of this practice were adopted, as is sometimes done in plashing hedges, the fractured section would be left on the plant. Every cut made in a living plant ought to be sufficiently near a bud or a shoot to be healed over by its influence, and the section made should never be more oblique than is necessary to secure its soundness and smoothness. In general, therefore, the separation of all branches from living plants ought to be made by cutting or sawing across at very nearly a right angle to the direction of the stem, or branch, in order that it may be the more rapidly healed over. When due attention is not paid to this rule, and the cut is made very obliquely to the line of the shoot, a wedge-like stump is left protruding beyond the bud or branch, as in fig. 164, *a*, which never can be healed over, and which, consequently, soon decays, and disfigures and injures the tree, by retaining water and bringing on the rot; but when the cut is made not more than the thickness of the branch above the bud or shoot, and nearly directly across, as at *b*, the wound is healed over completely and in the shortest possible time. It must be observed, however, that the distance of the cut above the bud must depend in a great measure on the porosity of the wood of the shoot, and the proportion of its diameter which is occupied by the pith; for if the raspberry and the vine

Fig. 164.

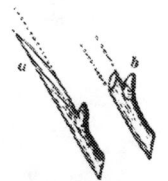

a, *a shoot improperly cut;* *b*, *a shoot cut properly.*

were cut close above the bud, the shoot would dry up beyond the bud, and prevent it from developing itself. Hence, in all such cases, and even sometimes in common fruit-trees, it is customary to make the first cut an inch or more above the bud; and when the shoot has grown and produced two or three perfect leaves, to cut off the remaining stump. This would be the best mode in every case, but as it occasions double labour, the risk of its not being attended to induces most persons to cut near to the bud at once.

Clipping in gardening is chiefly applied to hedges, and to the edgings of walks or beds, when composed of dwarf box or under shrubs. The common hedge shears differ from the pruning shears in crushing the shoot which is clipped on both sides of the section, and hence clipping is not a desirable mode of pruning plants in general; nor from the want of mechanical power are the common hedge shears applicable to any shoots, except those of one, or at most two years' growth. In clipping box or other edgings which are in a straight direction, a line is generally stretched close alongside the box at the height to which it is to be clipped. The top of the edging is then clipped down to the proper height, after which the line is taken up, and stretched along the centre of the top of the edging; and the width of the top being determined on, the sides are cut accordingly, leaving the edging somewhat wider at the bottom than at the top. The height and width of edgings vary according to the width of the walks, or beds, and the taste of the gardener; two inches wide and three inches high are ordinary proportions; but some gardeners prefer having their edgings smaller, as less likely to harbour vermin. The ordinary time for clipping edgings is the spring, before the shoots of the season are made; but many gardeners prefer waiting till the shoots have been completed, and clip in June, after which the plants put out one or two leaves at the points of most of the shoots, which thus obliterate the marks of the shears on the other leaves. With box this appears to be decidedly the best mode. Where lines of edgings are not straight, they are of course clipped by the eye without the application of the line; a matter of no difficulty to an expert operator.

Clipping hedges is generally performed by the eye, without the aid of the line; but in the case of architectural hedges in gardens laid out in the geometrical style, both the line and the plummet are occasionally resorted to, to prove the exactness of the work. Hedges are generally clipped in the summer season, immediately after the growth of the year has been completed. Hedges are better cut with the hedge-bill than shears, as it leaves a clean cut that is soon healed. The width of a hedge at the base need seldom exceed two feet in gardens; but where a strong fence is required, or where the height exceeds twelve or fifteen feet, three feet in width at least will be required at the base, for the closest and best clothed hedges are found to be those whose section forms the sides and base of a pyramid. If the sides are perpendicular, the hedge sometimes gets naked at the bottom; but if it is wider at top than at bottom, no art will prevent it from getting every year more naked, till at last plashing, or otherwise securing the gaps, must be resorted to, and then its beauty as a live fence is gone. Another advantage is gained by sloping the sides of hedges, and that is in respect of keeping them clean; for when so cut, the twigs at bottom, sharing in the dews and light, thrive and grow so close to the ground, that few weeds can rise below them. Again, in fields, the uniformity of surface which can be maintained with ease in hedges cut on the sloping principle, prevents animals from readily attempting to leap or make a breach in them.

Mowing, as done by machines, is so well understood in gardening, that it is useless to dwell upon it. All lawns and garden grass should be cut weekly, to keep them in the highest condition of beauty, verdure, and cleanliness.

Weeding by hand is now almost unknown in gardens. Nearly all crops being sown in drills, and the hoe destroying the weeds with far greater despatch, no weed, except in seed-beds, or patches of seed, should ever be allowed to grow large enough in gardens to permit of the hand laying hold of it. The moment weeds are seen, the hoe should be driven through them.

Other labours with plants, such as tying and training, might be enumerated, but these belong more properly to garden operations, and will be fully dealt with in their proper place.

Operations of Culture.

Garden culture may be arranged under the heads of Propagation, Rearing, Preservation, and Amelioration.

Propagation.

Plants are propagated either by seed, or by division. The latter mode, including cuttings, joints, leaves, layers, suckers, slips, budding, grafting, and inarching. All the modes of propagation by division are founded on the principle that a bud, whether visible or latent, is essentially the same as a seed, and will consequently produce a plant; and that, as there is a bud, either visible or in an embryo state, in the axil of every leaf, it follows that for every leaf a plant contains, a young plant may be originated by art. This, however, is not done with equal ease in every species, and perhaps with some it may be almost impracticable; but it holds good with the great majority of plants, and may therefore safely be laid down and acted on as a general principle. There is an important difference between propagating by seed and propagating by any of the other modes known to gardeners—viz., that in propagating by seed, the species in the abstract is propagated, while in propagating by any of the other modes, the species is continued with the habits of the individual parent. Thus, a shoot taken from a weeping-ash, and grafted on a common ash, will produce a tree like the parent; while a seed taken from the weeping-ash will not in general produce a weeping plant, but an upright growing one like the species. Nevertheless this does not always hold good, even in such trees as the weeping-ash and the weeping-oak; and it does not hold good at all in the case of trees in a high state of culture, such as fruit trees; or in the case of herbaceous plants in a highly artificial state, such as the culinary vegetables of our gardens, and the principal agricultural plants of our farms. The weeping-ash was an accidental sport; but notwithstanding this, out of many hundred plants raised from seed collected from a weeping tree by a nurseryman at Berlin, one or two were found to exhibit the weeping characters of the parent; and when we consider that all the common weeping-ash trees in Europe have been propagated from one tree, that at Gamblingay, in Cambridgeshire, and that this tree is a female, so that the blossoms, when fertile seeds have been produced, must have been fecundated by the male blossoms of some adjoining common ash, the small proportion of weeping plants raised is not surprising. The acorns produced by a celebrated weeping-oak at Moccas Court, in Herefordshire, produce plants almost all of which have the branches drooping, though this tree is not farther removed from nature than the weeping-ash, both having been found accidentally in a wild state. The stones of a greengage plum, and the seeds of a golden-pippin apple, will unquestionably produce plants, many of which will bear varieties of the greengage and golden pippin; and though these may vary from the fruit of their parents, yet they will not vary more than the produce of a wilding, such as a crab-apple, or a wild plum, will sometimes do from its parent. The seeds of the cultivated varieties of cabbage, peas, wheat, oats, &c., it is well known, produce plants in all respects like their parents, or, in horticultural language, " come true." The seeds of trees, however, are not so much to be depended on as those of herbaceous plants, and especially of annuals, in a high state of culture; for a kernel out of the same apple which produced the Ribston pippin produced another tree, the fruit of which proved little better than a crab. From these facts we consider it safe for the gardener to adopt it as a principle, that the seeds of trees, as well as of herbaceous plants, will not only reproduce the species, but, to a considerable extent, also the variety; though we cannot depend on this mode for reproducing the variety with the same certainty as we can on propagation by division.

On Propagation by Seed.

The seed is of a mucilaginous consistency when young, and it becomes more or less solid when matured. Before germination can take place, the solid part of the seed must be rendered again mucilaginous, and soluble in water; and this is effected by the moisture and heat of the soil, and the oxygen of the atmosphere. The absence of light, or at least of much light, is also favourable to germination, but not essential to it; for though when seeds are sown they are generally covered in proportion to their size, in order to maintain an equal degree of moisture and to keep them in darkness, we also sow the smaller seeds, such as those of ferns and heaths, on the surface, and maintain the requisite moisture by means of a close covering of glass, only moderating the light by placing them in the shade. That the want of moisture prevents the germination of seeds, though every other requisite should be present, is known to every gardener; and indeed, were it otherwise, it would be next to impossible to preserve seeds from one season to another, since, though it is in our power to keep them dry, it is scarcely practicable to prevent the access of air and heat. The presence of air and warmth are likewise necessary to the growth of seeds. That the want of air has an effect in preventing the germination of seeds is proved by the following experiment. If a number of seeds be put in a bottle with from ten to twenty times their bulk of water, and all communication with the surrounding atmosphere be cut off, so that the water may not absorb any oxygen from it, the seeds will not germinate, though placed in a temperature suitable for germination; but if the same experiment be repeated with a proportionately larger quantity of water, the seeds will find in the air which it contains sufficient oxygen to enable them to germinate. ('Gard. Mag.' for 1841, p. 482.) That seeds will not germinate without the presence of a certain degree of heat, is rendered evident by the fact of self-sown seeds lying in the soil all the winter, and only vegetating when the temperature becomes sufficiently high in the spring.

Process of Germination.—If the husks are hard or impenetrable, germination proceeds slowly. Various means have been adopted to hasten the growth of acacias and other hard seeds. Steeping in hot or boiling water has hastened the process; but it is safer to cut or file through the hard shell at one spot. From this spot the seed imbibes the requisite quantity of air and moisture, the radicle is quickly developed, and, with the help of the swollen tissue within it, bursts the sutures of the husk. In this way many hard-shelled seeds of monocotyledonous and dicotyledonous plants, such as canna, pæonia, acacia, abrus, erythrina, cassia, schotia, guilandina, adenanthera, bauhinia, and cæsalpinia, have been made to germinate in a short time, mostly in from ten to twenty days. If the seeds be old, they should, after cutting, be laid for a few days in lukewarm rain-water, and, if they have any life remaining, this will stimulate it. Something similar also takes place with seeds which, besides the testa, or husk, are also enclosed in a pericarpium, or outer-covering. They lie either in fours, at the bottom of a dry hollow cup, as in the labiatæ and boragineæ; or they are single, or several, surrounded with a thick fleshy cup, as in many species of the rosaceæ; or single, or in twos, covered with a dry cup, as in compositæ, umbelliferæ, and their allied species. Lastly, in the gramineæ, we find them only surrounded with the pericarpium, as true caryopses. Many of these germinate as easily as naked seeds; but this depends, in some measure, on the capacity or incapacity of the husk to absorb water in a natural state. We find seeds hard and stony only among the rosaceæ, as in rosa, prunus, cotoneaster, mespilus, cratægus, &c., and these require cutting or filing, if intended to germinate quickly. The remainder are divided, according to their formation, into two groups; those possessing albumen, in which the embryo lies, and those that do not. This division is useful, for the cotyledons always imbibe the water first and easiest, whereas the albumen is less capable of doing so; and hence the germination of those seeds which have none, but whose interior is entirely filled with the embryo and its cotyledons, as in the boragineæ, labiatæ, compositæ, &c., will be more easily effected. The gramineæ and umbelliferæ, on the contrary, possess albumen: in the former, the embryo lies outside of the albumen, on which account they easily germinate; whereas, in the latter, the embryo is entirely surrounded by the albumen, for which reason, with the exception of most of the annual or biennial sorts, they are more difficult to vegetate. As these seeds cannot be cut with advantage, it is usual to sow them late in autumn, with other difficult-growing sorts; so that when the universal period of germination comes, in the spring, they may be sufficiently permeated with moisture. This method is very well suited for sowing on a large scale; but as the seed often perishes during the winter, and the earth becomes soddened, or thickly covered with moss, the preferable way for valuable seeds which are to be raised in the open air, is to sow them in the spring, after they have been soaked for some days previously in warm water. Seeds that are to be raised under glass, with the aid of artificial heat, may be sown at any time.

The period necessary to complete the process of germination varies in different seeds, though all attendant circumstances may be alike. The grasses generally vegetate most rapidly, and they are quickly followed by some of the cruciferous and leguminous plants; umbelliferous plants are generally slower, and rosaceous plants still more so. Adanson gives the following table of the period of germination in several seeds tried by himself in France:—

	Days.		Days.
Wheat, millet	1	Purslane	9
Strawberry blite, beans, mustard, kidney-beans, turnips, radishes, and rocket	3	Cabbage	10
		Hyssop	30
		Parsley	40 or 50
Lettuce, and aniseed	4	Cow-wheat, almond, chestnut, peach, and peony	One year
Melon, cucumber, gourd, and cress	5		
Horse-radish, leek	6	Rose, hawthorn, hazel-nut, and cornel	Two years
Barley	7		
Orache	8		

('Fam. des Plantes,' vol. i. p. 84.) The same author found that the seeds which germinated in twelve hours in an ordinary degree of heat, might be made to germinate in three hours by exposing them to a greater degree of heat; and that seeds transported from the climate of Paris to that of Senegal, have their periods of germination accelerated from one to three days. On the same principle seeds transported from a warmer to a colder climate have their period of germination protracted till the temperature of the latter is raised to that of the former. The seeds of annuals generally germinate quicker and with more certainty than those of perennial plants; and they generally retain their power of germination much longer.

The quantity of moisture most favourable to germination must depend on various circumstances, such as the degree of heat with which it is accompanied, the vital power of the seed, and the nature of the species. The seeds of aquatic plants vegetate when immersed in water, and the plants live and attain maturity in that element; but those of land plants, though they will vegetate in water, yet if the plants be not removed immediately after germination, they will become putrid and die. In general, the most favourable degree of moisture for newly-sown seeds, is that which a free soil holds in its interstices. Clayey soil will retain too much moisture for delicate seeds, and sand too little; but an open, free loam will attract and retain the proper quantity for all seeds, excepting those which are very small and very delicate; and for these a mixture of peat loam and fine sand will retain just moisture enough, and no more. With all delicate seeds it is better rather to have too little moisture than too much; and with all seeds whatever, it is of great importance to preserve the degree of moisture uniform. For this purpose, in the open garden, newly-sown delicate seeds are shaded or covered by different means, such as sowing them on the north sides of hedges or walls, interposing hurdles placed upright or horizontally between the sown seeds and the sun, covering with mats, or branches, or litter, or, in the case of very small seeds, with moss. The more tender kinds are also sown in frames, or under hand or bell-glasses, by which evaporation is prevented or checked, and a steady degree of moisture effectually maintained.

The water requisite to cause old seeds to germinate should be more gradually given to them than that given to vigorous young seeds; because the power of absorbing water in old seeds is not diminished in the same proportion as their power of decomposing it. When old seeds are placed in moist soil, they are consequently very liable to rot; more especially if the temperature be not somewhat higher than new seeds of the same species usually require. Hence, old seeds should be sown in a much drier soil than new seeds, and should be supplied with water much more sparingly, or left to absorb it from the atmosphere.

The depth to which a seed is buried in the soil has, for its chief object, the maintenance of a due degree of moisture, but another purpose is to exclude the light, and to give the future plant a better hold of the ground; though there is no seed whatever that will not vegetate on the surface, if that surface be kept uniformly moist and shaded. It may be assumed that every seed will vegetate and establish itself in the soil, if buried to its own thickness; but the experience of gardeners proves, that some large seeds, such as leguminous seeds, nuts, &c., make better plants when buried much deeper.

The degree of heat most favourable for the germination of seeds may be considered as that best adapted for the growth of the parent plants; and hence if the native country of any plant is known, it may be assumed that its seeds will germinate best in the temperature of the spring, or growing season of that country. Some seeds of cold climates, such as those of the common annual grass, chickweed, groundsel, &c., will germinate in a temperature little above the freezing point; but, in general, few northern plants will germinate under

40°, and the most favourable temperature for germinating, Dr. Lindley states to be—for the seeds of cold countries, from 50° to 55°; for seeds of greenhouse-plants, from 60° to 65°; and for seeds of the plants of the torrid zone, 70° to 80°. ('Theory of Hort.,' p. 166.) It may be remarked that though the seeds of warm countries will not vegetate in the temperature of cold countries, yet that the reverse of this does not hold true, as may be observed in the germination of British weeds in our stoves; but the plants thus produced, unless immediately removed to the open air, remain weak and sickly.

The degree of heat which the seeds of plants will endure has already been slightly noticed. Certain leguminous seeds, as those of some acacias, may be subjected to the boiling point for a few minutes without injury; others may be allowed to steep and cool for twenty-four hours in water heated to 200°. The seeds of Acacia Lophantha were subjected to boiling water for five minutes, and the plants raised from them were exhibited before the Horticultural Society, some years ago, by Mr. Palmer of Bromley, Kent. Messrs. Edwards and Colin found that wheat, barley, and rye could germinate between 44° and 45°; that they were killed by remaining three days in water at the temperature of 95°; that in sand and earth, at 104°, they lived for a considerable time; but that at 113° most of them perished; and that at 122° all of them perished; but it was found that a higher temperature could be borne by these and other seeds for a shorter time. At 143°, in vapour, wheat, barley, kidney-beans, and flax retained their vitality for a quarter of an hour; in dry air these seeds sustained no injury at 167°; but in vapour, at this temperature, they all perished. Dr. Lindley mentions the very remarkable case of the germination of the seeds of a raspberry, which had been picked from a jar of jam, and which, consequently, must have been subjected to the temperature of the boiling point of the syrup, which is 230°.

The degree of cold which seeds will endure differs according to the species, their native country, and their condition in respect to moisture. Dry seeds stand so high a degree of cold, that even the lowest temperature of the frigid zone does not injure them; but if they have imbibed any moisture they freeze according to the degree of growth which may have been excited, and the degree of cold to which they had been accustomed in their native zone.

Atmospheric air is as necessary to the germination of seeds as moisture and heat; and this is the principal cause why seeds buried to a certain depth in the soil do not vegetate. It also affords a reason for having the surface of the soil, in which seeds are sown, porous, and exposed to the action of the atmosphere, and to rain-water, which contains more air than the water of wells. Hence the rapidity with which seeds spring up in the open ground after the first warm spring showers. Hence, also, the propriety of giving fresh air to hotbeds, and to hand and bell-glasses covering sown seeds, even though they have not come up.

Bright light is found to be universally unfavourable; because it has a tendency to decompose carbonic acid, and fix carbon; whereas, the first step in the progress of germination is to render carbon mucilaginous and soluble in water, and so to cause the evolution of carbonic acid gas.

Accelerating the Germination of Seeds.—In ordinary practice this is chiefly effected by the application of a higher degree of heat, as by placing pots of sown seeds in hotbeds, or by immersing seeds in tepid water, or by cutting or paring nuts, or gently fermenting them in heaps of sawdust, as is frequently done with chestnuts, walnuts, acorns, almonds, &c. On a large scale, both in the field and the garden, the most common resource is steeping in warm water for a few hours, which is found to bring up the seeds of barley, turnips, beets, parsnips, onions, &c., when the soil in which they are sown is very dry, much sooner than would otherwise be the case; this is found to prevent them from becoming a prey to insects or birds. The sowing of some seeds before they are perfectly ripe has also been found to promote their early vegetation.

Various experiments have been made to accelerate germination with different degrees of success. These all proceed on the principle that germination cannot take place until the carbon of the seed is changed into carbonic acid; and as this can only be done by extraordinary supplies of oxygen, the agents employed are such as have the power of supplying that substance in greater abundance than water or air, from which, under ordinary circumstances, the plant obtains it by decomposition. Humboldt was the first to observe that watering with chlorine induced speedy germination; and as, according to the observations of Göppert, iodine and bromine, in conjunction with hydrogen, produce a similar effect, it appears that both these matters, as well as the oxalic and other acids frequently applied for that purpose, hasten the process of assimilation. It cannot be denied that all these substances accelerate germination; but to the practical gardener they must be considered as experiments unfit for general practice, for the young plants thus called into existence most frequently become sickly through the excitement, and die off, which cannot surprise us, as the same effect is seen when plants of cold climates are reared too warmly, and are not placed in a cooler situation after germination.

Electricity and Alkalies as Stimulants to Vegetation.—It is conjectured that electricity causes or accelerates chemical decomposition. In experiments made some years since by M. Maltuen, it was found that seeds germinated sooner at the negative or alkaline pole of a galvanic battery than at the positive or acid pole, and following up these discoveries by enclosing seeds in phials of alkalies and acids, he found they germinated quickly in the former, and with difficulty, and sometimes not at all, in the latter. Connected with the same subject are the experiments of Dr. Horner and Mr. Hunt, on the differently coloured rays of the spectrum; the violet or deoxidizing end produces a chemical effect, similar to the negative or alkaline pole, and the red end produces the opposite or acid effect, by the retention of the oxygen. To test the nature of these theories, some very old spruce-fir-seed was treated as follows: It had been three years out of the cones, and some of it sown the year before this experiment only yielded one-sixth part of a crop. After damping the seeds they were sprinkled with quicklime, which, besides furnishing an alkaline, has a great affinity for carbonic acid, which is necessary to be extracted from the starch before it can be made soluble, and which produces heat by concentration of the oxygen and carbon when being extracted. The seed was thoroughly damped and sprinkled with powder of lime for ten or twelve days; at the end of which time it had swelled off plump, and had all the sweet smell of the sugar formed in healthy seed when malted in this way: and, when deposited in the ground, it was not long in pushing up its seed leaves, as healthy, upright, and dark green in the colour, as the first year it was sown; and the seedling plants were strong and healthy. The reasons why I preferred lime were its cheapness, and the affinity of quicklime for carbonic acid: as to its alkaline properties, soda is much more powerful, but lime seemed to be that which had produced most effect in other experiments on the same subject. The seed must be carefully kept damp till sown, as the dry powder is apt to corrode it; and seeds should never have their dormant powers brought into action without being sustained and carried forward. Lime has likewise been applied to magnolias and other weak-growing seeds difficult to start, and made them germinate sooner, and make stronger plants than usual.

The length of time during which seeds retain their vitality varies exceedingly in different species; and the difference in this respect, even in the plants in common cultivation, as every seedsman knows, is very considerable. It is remarkable that the seeds of annual plants not only germinate in general sooner and with more certainty than those of perennials, but also that they retain their power of germination much longer. The greater part of the seeds of perennial plants and trees, when well kept, preserve their germinating powers for a long time; while certain oily seeds, like those of dictamnus, magnolia, and myristica, &c., decay soon after ripening. Melon-seeds have been known to retain their vitality for nearly half a century, kidney-beans for a century, and the seeds of the sensitive-plant upwards of sixty years.

The length of time that seeds will lie in the ground without growing, is not less remarkable than the difference in their retention of vitality. Many seeds which, when sown in spring, come up soon afterwards, will not come up the same year if sown in autumn. This is the case with many common annuals, which when sown immediately after ripening either do not come up at all that year, or come up sparingly and sickly. On the other hand, the seeds of the greater portion of biennial plants, if sown immediately after ripening, come up freely, become strong plants before winter, and flower the following year. This is also the case with a great number of annual plants, especially those of California, which in their native country spring up before winter, and are preserved through that season by a covering of snow. The seeds of cratægus, mespilus, ilex, prunus, cerasus, and some others, if sown immediately after being gathered, will in part come up the following spring, but chiefly in the second spring, though some will not germinate till the third or fourth season. If these seeds, instead of being sown immediately after gathering, are dried and sown the same autumn, none will come up till the spring of the second year. This holds good also with the seeds of a number of trees and shrubs, among which may be mentioned daphne, ribes, rubus, rosa, potentilla, berberis, pæonia, &c. De Candolle mentions a sowing of tobacco which continued to send up plants in sufficient numbers to form a crop every year for ten years. It is a common occurrence to find plants, especially annuals, springing up in ground newly brought into cultivation, after it had been used many years for other purposes. Thus, a field of grass that was ploughed up near Dunkeld in Scotland, after a period of fourteen years in turf, yielded a considerable crop of black oats without sowing. Mustard-seed has sprung up in the fern lands, which must have lain there upwards of a century; and white clover, it is well known to every agriculturist, springs up, on the application of lime in soils, where it had not been before seen in the memory of man. In pulling down old buildings, seeds capable of germinating have been found in the clay used as mortar. The seed of Veronica hederæfolia, L., after heavy rains, has been known to spring up on the surface of fields where previously no trace of that plant was to be found.

The season for sowing seeds is, in nature, when they are ripe, but in artificial culture it varies according to the object in view. The spring, however, is the most favourable period for germination, because at this season the warmth daily increases, and the vegetable kingdom awakens from the sleep of nature. Seeds removed from foreign countries, and also the seeds of any rare indigenous plant, should be sown as soon as they are removed or gathered, in a soil and situation favourable for germination and growth. For a succession of crops of annual culinary plants, or annual flowers, the gardener sows at different periods; and in the case of biennial plants, he sows in the autumn. The time of sowing is very much determined by the time that it is desired to reap. It should be noted that all seeds, of whatever kind, should be sown in dry soil, and not watered till they begin to vegetate; in the case of old or sickly seeds, to water them at the time of sowing is to insure their destruction by rotting; that shading is to be preferred to watering; finally, that all seedlings, except bulbs, should be potted or transplanted as soon as they will bear handling.

The mechanical process of sowing is very simple; whether the seeds are sown broad-cast, that is, distributed equally over an even surface, or deposited in drills or regular furrows, they are delivered from the hand, or from small hand drills. Some rough seeds, such as those of the carrot, are mixed with sand, to separate them so that they may drop singly; and other very small seeds, such as those of rhododendrons, and other ericaceæ, are mixed with fine sand to prevent them from falling too thickly. The smallest seeds of all, such as those of the ferns, and of some of the hardy orchideæ, are sown on the surface of pots or pans filled with well-drained peat and sand, and placed in a shady place and covered with glass. American tree seeds of small size are generally sown in pans or boxes as soon as received, and kept under glass in a cold pit, and shaded during sunshine till they vegetate. Cape and Australian seeds, and in general all seeds from warm climates, are sown as soon as received, in a mixture of loam, peat, and sand, and placed in a temperature similar to that of the growing season in the country they came from.

Sowing seeds in powdered charcoal has been tried in the Botanic Garden at Munich with extraordinary success. Seeds of cucumbers and melons sown in it germinated one day sooner than others sown in soil, and plunged in the same hotbed; becoming strong plants, while the others remained comparatively stationary. Ferns sown on the surface of finely-sifted charcoal, germinate quickly and vigorously; and it seems not improbable, that this material may be found as useful in exciting seeds difficult to germinate, as it is in rooting cuttings difficult to strike. Ferns also do well sown on the surface of porous pots or stone, and on the dark sides of damp brick walls.

On Propagation by Cuttings.

A cutting is a portion of a shoot containing either leaf-buds, or leaves in the axils of which buds may be produced. It must at least be of sufficient length to have two buds or two joints—one at the lower extremity to produce roots, and another at the upper end to produce a shoot. A portion of a stem with only one bud is not considered a cutting, but is technically an eye or joint. It is almost unnecessary to state that the cause of success is to be found in the analogy between a cutting and a seed; the bud being the embryo plant, and the alburnum of the cutting containing the nutriment which is to support the development of the bud, till it has formed roots sufficient to absorb nutriment from the soil. The roots formed by the cuttings are protruded from the section at its lower extremity, and are, in fact, a continuation of the alburnous process, which, had the cutting not been separated from the plant, would have been employed in adding to its young wood and inner bark. Every cutting must either contain a stock of alimentary matter in its alburnum, as in the case of cuttings of ripened wood without leaves, or it must contain healthy leaves, capable of elaborating alimentary matter from the moisture absorbed from the soil joined to the alburnous matter already in the cutting. All cuttings may be divided into two kinds—deciduous, as the common gooseberry or willow; or evergreen, as most greenhouse plants, such as the camellia, the geranium, the fuchsia, heaths, &c. In both cases the cutting, after being planted, is excited by heat, and supported by the moisture absorbed from the soil. In the case of the leafless cutting the buds expand, and preceding, or simultaneous with, their development, roots are formed; while the leaves of evergreen cuttings continue to perform their function, and thus send down fresh supplies of organizable matter for the formation of new roots. In most species this organizable matter is first developed as a swelling or callosity between the bark and the wood, or over the whole base of the cutting. When this is fairly formed, roots are certain to follow. While possibly all leaf-bearing stems may be rooted, there are great differences as to the time and skill needed for their conversion into plants.

Selecting Plants from which the Cuttings are to be Taken.—Every plant from which cuttings are taken ought to be healthy, otherwise it will probably lack the power of forming roots, and will become a diseased plant. It is found from experience that cuttings taken from the lower branches of plants which are near the soil, root more readily than such as are near the summit of the plant and are surrounded by drier air; doubtless because the tissue of the wood which contains the nutriment is in a more concentrated and hardened state in the latter case than in the former. Hence the practice of putting plants which are difficult to strike into a warm moist atmosphere, and keeping them there till they have produced shoots sufficiently soft in texture to insure their rooting. Hence cuttings of evergreens, such as the holly and laurel, strike more readily after a wet season than after a dry one, and better in the Irish nurseries than in those of England or France. Hard-wooded plants, such as heaths, should make their young wood in a warm, close, moist atmosphere, and the propagating-house should have the same moist, still, unchanging atmosphere, as if it were under a bell-glass. The following are some of the expedients adopted by Mr. Cunningham, of the Comely Bank Nursery, Edinburgh, one of the most successful propagators. The more rare plants which are to be propagated are planted in a bed of sandy peat and leaf-mould, or of some such soil, where they are found to grow much more freely than in pots, and speedily to produce shoots, which are taken off in a young and tender state, and struck in sand. Various modes are adopted to induce the plants which are to be propagated from to protrude young shoots, such as when they have small leaves, like heaths, &c., by bending down, twisting them, &c.; and in the case of plants having larger leaves, such as the Statice arborea, or some of the more rare fuchsias, by cutting a notch in the stem above every bud, and inserting a wooden wedge in the notch to keep it open, in consequence of which the ascending sap being checked, every bud protrudes a shoot, which is taken off in a tender state, with or without the base of old wood from which it sprang, according to circumstances. In some cases the shoot is taken off, and the base left to produce other shoots from the latent buds; in other cases, the shoot and its base are taken off together, and occasionally, before taking off the shoot and its base, a notch is made below the bud as well as above it, and the lower notch as well as the upper one is kept open by a wedge, till a callosity is formed on the upper edges of the lower notch, from which roots are very readily protruded, after the cutting (with its base attached) has been taken off and planted in sand.

Selecting the Shoot.—The wood of the present or of the past year is almost invariably chosen for cuttings. In the case of plants which are not difficult to strike, a portion of the young shoot is cut off at any convenient distance from the branch from which it proceeded, and of such a length as may be considered most convenient for forming a plant. Thus in the case of willows, gooseberries, currants, &c., from nine to eighteen inches is considered a suitable length; and the points of the shoots of these and other kinds of easily-rooting plants are cut off, as not being sufficiently ripened to have strong buds, or as containing too many small buds. In plants somewhat difficult to strike, lateral shoots are chosen, and these are often drawn or "slipped" out of the wood, so as to carry with them the axillary formation of the bud and the vessels of the leaf. The plexus of vessels at the heel of the shoot or insertion of the branch in the stem, causes a peculiar activity of life there; and both buds and roots are much more easily formed and in greater quantity there than in any other part of the shoot. The insertion of the branch resembles in this respect the collar of the stem. If the heel of the gooseberry or currant-cutting is taken out completely by breaking off, not cutting, it is better than taking off a piece of the old wood. This is the only way in which shoots covered with a woolly tissue, such as several gnaphaliums and helichrysums, can be made to root. This method is also very successful with plants that are difficult to root, and that have leaves surrounded with prickles, such as Mutisia ilicifolia, Berkleya grandiflora, Logania floribunda, latifolia, &c.; also with those the leaves of which have stalks with very strong veins, or their circumference very strongly defined, such as Banksia grandis, Berkleya ciliaris, the different species of Daviesia, Chorozema ovata, &c.; or those that have winged stems, such as Acacia alata. The reason of the success is, that the heel being formed by the first growth of the lateral, consists of wood more or less ripened; and consequently, when it is planted, it is less likely to be damped off by the moisture of the soil than younger wood. When the heel is too ripe, the cutting will not strike.

Shoots which have formed blossom buds ought in general to be avoided; because it frequently happens that all the assimilated nourishing matter has been laid up for their future support, and no root formation can take place.

As general rules, it may be stated that cuttings made of the ripened wood of deciduous plants that have a large pith, succeed best when taken off with a portion of the preceding year's wood, such as the gooseberry, currant, vine, fig, honeysuckle, elder, hydrangea, spiræa, syringa, philadelphus, &c. Cuttings of hard-wooded plants, difficult to strike, such as Erica, Epacris, Burtonia, are best made from points of the shoots cut off where the wood is beginning to ripen, as in Erica pinguis, aristata, ferruginea, Hartnelli, cerinthoides, empetrifolia, picta, fasciculata, vernix, &c.; or from lateral shoots made from wood of the same year, as in almost all the more easily growing species of Erica; such are Erica margaritacea, rubens, ramentacea, mucosa, tenera, tenella, scabriuscula, persoluta, pellucida, and all those of a similar growth. Cuttings of soft-wooded plants, or of plants with woolly bark, such as Manulea, Mutisia, Gnaphalium, &c., are best made of lateral shoots beginning to ripen at the lower end, and drawn out from the main shoot with a heel. Cuttings of soft-stemmed plants which are easily rooted, such as Dahlia, Petunia, Geranium, &c., may be cut off from any growing shoots where the tissue is somewhat firm, but moderately strong shoots will be found the best. Cuttings of growing succulent wood have most active vitality, and strike root most quickly; but, from the unripened state of the wood, are most apt to die, and require to be kept more close and moist. There is danger in both extremes, and both must be guarded against in such as are difficult to strike.

The time of taking off cuttings depends much on the nature of the plant to be propagated. In the case of hardy deciduous trees and shrubs, such as the gooseberry, poplar, &c., any period between the falling of the leaf in autumn and the swelling of the buds in spring, will answer, but the autumn is preferable, because more time is given for the cutting to accommodate itself to its new situation and circumstances before the growing season. This it does by cicatrizing the wounded section, and thus preventing it from absorbing moisture in excess when the growing season commences. If the cutting be not taken off till spring, the buds on it will have been supplied with moisture from the root, and the sudden cutting off of this supply will materially check the growth of the buds. Cuttings of hardy evergreens not difficult to strike, such as those of the box, laurel, &c., may be taken off in the ripened wood in the autumn rather than in spring, for the same reason as given in the case of deciduous cuttings of ripened wood. Cuttings of house plants, whether deciduous or evergreen, such as Fuchsia, Aloysia, Camellia, &c., may be taken off at whatever season the wood ripens.

The length of cuttings is not material to their rooting. One eye in the ground and one out constitutes a cutting, and their length beyond this is determined by the height and form of plant desired.

The number of leaves which are left upon the cutting should be determined by its character and treatment. If the cutting is succulent, and has large leaves, one may suffice; otherwise the whole of the leaves may be left. The more that can be sustained without flagging, the sooner will roots be formed; hence the number of leaves left will depend mostly upon the atmosphere in which the cuttings are placed. Flagging must not be allowed, as the drooping leaves will drain the sap out of the cutting, instead of nourishing it with fresh supplies of food. The lower leaves of a cutting, when they can be kept on, have more influence on the formation of roots than the upper ones, because they expose a larger surface to the action of light; and hence, when from their long petioles, or any other cause, they are not likely to rot, they should always be kept on. The leaf on a level with the base of the cutting is the most valuable of all, as it excites life at the very point where all its energies are needed to form roots; but small and closely-set leaves, such as those of Erica, Brunia, &c., when covered with soil, soon begin to rot, and endanger the cutting, and they ought therefore to be taken off. This ought always to be done with a very sharp-pointed pair of scissors, and the greatest possible care should be taken not to lacerate the bark by the operation, or to bruise the end of the cutting in cutting it across with a knife. The cuttings of Pelargoniums, on the other hand, may be of any length, and covered with leaves. Pelargoniums, and most soft-wooded plants, strike freest full in the sun, out of doors. The danger to them is from damp, not exhaustion. The temporary fading of the leaves supplies the needed nutrition, and saves them from rottenness; but short cuttings make the handsomest plants. When the season is dry and warm, and little time can be spared to attend to keeping them moist, succulent cuttings, such as pinks, are most certain to strike by paring them close below the uppermost joint, and cutting them off above close to the joint, removing all the leaves, except those beginning to develop. Such a cutting is a mere joint in a vital, active, not ripened state, and will stand a great deal of heat; if covered with a hand-glass in sunny weather, or in a hotbed frame in cold weather, they seldom or never fail. The excitement of heat is all that is wanted.

In taking off a cutting, regard should be had to the healing of the section left on the plant, and therefore the cut ought to be made upwards or outwards, so as to leave a smooth unfractured section that will speedily heal over. The cut on the lower end of the cutting should be made with a very sharp knife, so as not to crush in any degree the vessels of the shoots, and thereby prevent them from cicatrizing and forming a callosity. The cut should not be made through the joint, because the roots seldom proceed from the joint itself, but rather from its base, beneath the point of insertion of the petiole of the leaf. Shoots that have opposite leaves should be taken off by cutting across at a right angle with the direction of the shoot, either immediately under the base of the petiole, or where its combined vessels distinctly reach the stem. Shoots that have alternate leaves should have the knife inserted on the opposite side of the bud, under the node, and the cut should be performed in a slanting upward direction from the base, or under that of the point of the insertion of the leaf, so as to convey away its combined vessels in as perfect a state as possible, which produces the same effect as when a lateral shoot is torn off and then cut clean. This practice is found very successful with many cuttings, such as those of Camellias, Banksias, and similar plants. The lower ends of stout cuttings of plants somewhat difficult to strike, such as the Orange, are sometimes cut direct across, so as to rest on the bottom of the pot, and sometimes they are in addition split up for an inch or two, and the wound kept open with a wedge. This has been

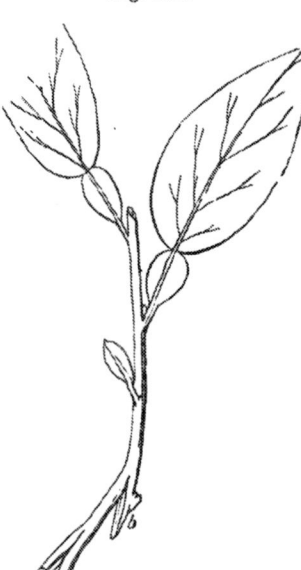

Fig. 165.

Prepared cutting of a shaddock.

found by long experience greatly to facilitate the rooting of such cuttings, probably by increasing the surface by which absorption of moisture takes place, and at the same time ensuring only a moderate supply of moisture, and perhaps creating a greater demand for the action of the leaves to cicatrize the wound with granular matter. When cuttings are tardy to strike, and have callosities formed, heat has a powerful effect in causing them to root. Those that have stood months, without any appearance of rooting, will strike in a few days in a strong heat.

Treatment of Cuttings from the time they are made till they are planted.—In general, cuttings are no sooner made than they are inserted in the soil where they are to remain till they strike root. If cuttings of Dryandra, some Banksias (B. integrifolia, B. Baueri, B. media, B. Caleyi, &c.), most of the long-leaved Acacias (A. longissima, A. pendula, A. brevifolia, A. glaucescens, A. longifolia, A. micracantha, &c.), and some sorts of Diosma (D. dioica, formosa, and umbellata), be stuck in the earth immediately after being taken from the parent plant, the inner bark will become black in from fourteen days to four weeks, and the cutting will perish. This phenomenon appears to be in close connexion with the form of the leaves of these plants, as those of the Acacias have very small stomata, while those of the Dryandras have none at all. In their stead, on the under side of the leaves of the latter plants are small dimples, lined with short hairs, which the Diosmas also possess. Now, as the crude nourishing matter is drawn up through the open wood in its existing state, and received by the cutting, while the spongioles of the roots only imbibe it in a very thin solution, it appears that the above-named plants, on account of the peculiar formation of their leaves, cannot elaborate in any great quantity this gross nourishing matter; and hence arise stagnation of the juices, and the before-mentioned appearances. The good effect of leaving these cuttings lying, and thus interrupting the growing process, appears to be the prevention of the superabundant rise of the crude nourishing matter; and this is the more probable, as it is usual, for the same purpose, to rub over the section with a piece of clay.

Cuttings of succulent, or fleshy, plants must also lie for a time before planting, and on no account in a moist atmosphere, that the surface of the cut may be sufficiently dried. The species of the families Melocactus, Echinocactus, Mammillaria, Opuntia, Cereus, &c., have an extremely thick bark, and a fine epidermis, with very few stomata; on which account the process of evaporation is so slow, that they remain alive for a long time without receiving external nourishment. The dried cuttings of these plants, therefore, are generally planted in dry earth, and set in a bed or house filled with warm air, and are not watered till they have formed roots from the nourishing matter accumulated in themselves. The roots are generally produced on the section between the wood and the bark. The other succulent and fleshy plants, such as the Aloe, Haworthia, Sempervivum, Mesembryanthemum, Crassula, Plumieria, and its congeners, as well as all the Cacti, which form side roots, may be watered as soon as they are planted. Lastly, plants with milky juice require similar treatment, as they are equally liable to damp off.

The kind of soil in which cuttings are planted depends on the greater or less facility with which they emit roots. Cuttings of hardy trees and shrubs that root easily are planted in common garden soil; those that are somewhat difficult, in sand or sandy loam on a base of garden soil; and those which are most difficult in sand or charcoal covered with a hand or bell-glass. Cuttings of house plants are almost always planted in pots or boxes well drained, and the drainage covered, first, with a layer of good soil, or leaf mould, or peat, according to the soil which the plants to be propagated naturally prefer; next with a stratum of sand, in which the cuttings are planted. The sand excludes the air and retains as much moisture as is necessary for the existence of the cutting, and no more, so that its lower end is not likely to rot; and the stratum of soil below the sand supplies nourishment to the roots as soon as they penetrate through the sand. The cuttings of Cape Heaths, and almost all plants whatever which are difficult to root, are planted in pure white sand, which is quite free from soil, metallic oxides, or salts.

Fig. 166.

A cutting of a Cape Heath, prepared and planted; the dotted line in this and the following figures of cuttings represents the surface of the soil in the pot.

Fig. 167.

A cutting of an Epacris prepared and planted.

The depth to which cuttings are planted varies according to the length and thickness of the cutting, but in general it should not be more than from half an inch to four inches. Willows may be inserted a foot deep; gooseberries and currants six inches; common trees and shrubs nine or ten inches.

Fig. 168.

A cutting of the young wood of Acacia alata, prepared and planted.

In planting cuttings it is of importance to make them quite firm at their lower ends, by pressing the sand or soil about them with the dibber used in planting them; or in the case of large cuttings, such as those of common laurel, which are planted in trenches, by pressure with the foot. In the case of Cape Heaths and similar cuttings planted in sand, the dibber or pricker, which need not be larger than a knitting needle, is taken in the right hand, while the cutting is held in the left, and, the hole being made, the cutting is inserted nearly as deep as the leaves have been clipped off, and the pricker is again applied to close the sand round it, as closely and compactly as possible, without bruising the cutting. Large cuttings are planted in precisely the same manner, but with a larger dibber. Large cuttings of kinds which are somewhat difficult to strike, when not planted in pure sand, are made to touch and press against the bottom or sides of the pot, which is thought to facilitate their rooting.

The distance at which cuttings are planted varies according to the size of the cutting, its leaves (either on the cutting, or to be produced from its buds), the season of the year, the length of time they require to root, and other circumstances. The object is to root as many cuttings as possible in a limited space, and consequently to plant them as close together as can be done without incurring the risk of rotting or damping them off. All cuttings whatever that are planted with the leaves on, require to be immediately well watered, in order to settle the soil about them; and all those that are in a growing succulent state, and are at all difficult to strike, should be immediately covered with a hand-glass or bell-glass; for, though the cutting receives as much moisture through the face of the cut as it loses in ordinary circumstances by evaporation, yet no sooner is it placed in very dry air or in a draught, or exposed to the sun's rays, than a disproportion takes place between the demand and supply.

After Treatment of Cuttings.—The hardiest sorts in the open garden, such as gooseberries, &c., require no particular treatment whatever, and need not even be placed in a shady situation; but those which root less freely, such as box, holly, juniper, &c., succeed best when planted in a shady border in a sandy soil. Cuttings planted in pots or boxes require to be placed not only in a shady situation, but for the most part under glass, in order to diminish evaporation from the soil as well as from the cuttings. All the more delicate sorts of cuttings, such as heaths, and most house plants, require to be covered with a bell-glass, and shaded during bright sunshine. All cuttings with the leaves on, require to be looked over frequently, supplied with water when it is required, and such leaves as decay taken off, as well as any dead or dying cuttings removed.

The most proper form of bell-glass for covering cuttings is that which gradually tapers from the base to the top, as from glasses of this shape the moisture, which adheres to the inside in the form of drops, runs gradually off, without the dropping so injurious to cuttings. This disadvantage is found in all other forms more or less, such as those that are round at the top, or cylindrical, with the top bluntly truncated. The enclosed air under the glasses will soon lose its oxygen through the respiring process of the plants within, and also be vitiated by other exhalations, and if it is not changed, it generates mouldiness, and the cuttings lose their fresh appearance. For this reason the glasses, if possible, should be daily ventilated and wiped; or, what is still better, as it will entirely renew the air, dipped in a vessel of cold water, and well shaken before being put on again, so that too many drops of water may not remain on the glass. The cloche, or large bell-glass, of the French market-gardeners, is very much used indoors by the Continental propagators, and might be advantageously used in this country.

Watering cuttings is an operation requiring great care and judgment. The object is, to maintain as uniform a degree of moisture in the soil as possible, without occasioning mouldiness on its surface, or rotting the leaves, hence the water is in some cases poured on the soil in such a manner as not to touch the leaves of the cuttings; and in others a reservoir of water is formed by placing a small pot in the centre of a larger one, the water being left to ooze slowly through the porous sides of the pot, as shown in fig. 169, in which *a d* is a No. 60 pot, with the bottom closed up with clay, put into one of larger size; *b*, the drainage in the larger pot; *c*, the sand or soil in which the cuttings are inserted; and *d*, the water in the inner pot, which is prevented from escaping through the bottom by the clay stopping at *a*. Mr. Forsyth, the inventor of this mode of striking cuttings, proposes it to be used with hardy plants, such as pinks and wallflowers, under hand-glasses or frames, in the open air, as well as for all kinds of houseplants. The advantages, he says, are the regularity of the supply of moisture, without any chance of saturation; the power of examining the state of the cuttings at any time without injuring them, by lifting out the inner pot; the superior drainage, so essential in propagating, by having such a thin layer of soil; the roots being placed so near the sides of both pots; and the facility with which the plants, when rooted, can be parted for potting off, by taking out the inner pot, and with a knife cutting out every plant with its ball, without the awkward but often necessary process of turning the pot upside down to get out the cuttings. No water but rain-water should ever be used, either for seeds or young cuttings.

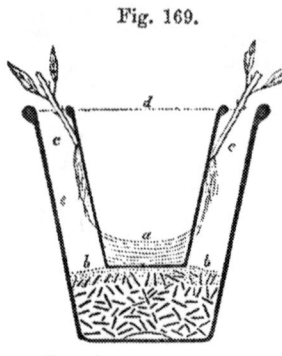

Fig. 169.

Forsyth's mode of striking cuttings.

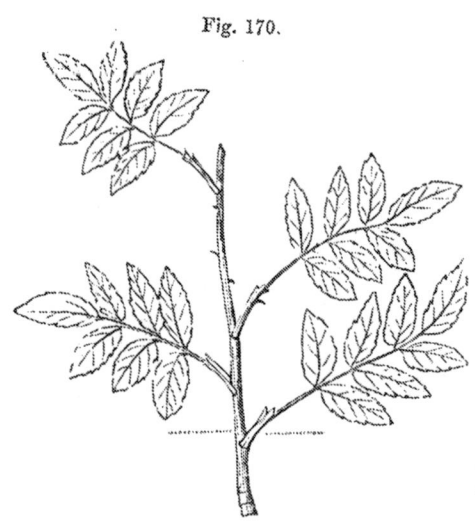

Fig. 170.

A cutting of Rosa semperflorens prepared and planted.

The temperature most suitable for cuttings may reasonably be expected to be that which is most suitable for the parent plants, when in the same state as to growth as the cuttings, or rather in advance of it. Hence, for all hardy plants the temperature of the open air will generally be found sufficient, though when they begin to grow a somewhat higher temperature than what is natural to them will be advantageous. This, however, will be of no use, but rather injurious, when cuttings are planted without leaves, or when evergreens with ripened wood are put in; for a certain time is required for every cutting to accommodate itself to its new situation. The bottom heat should slightly exceed that of the atmosphere. If the shoot has, however, been much excited into growth by heat, in order to obtain the cutting, the latter must have that heat kept up in its new situation, otherwise its vegetation will be checked. For cuttings of all the difficult-rooting greenhouse plants, the best heat for the soil is from 55° to 60° Fah.; for those of hothouse plants, from 65° to 75° Fah., which should be as regular as possible. This regularity is of great moment to ensure the success of the cuttings. Where the propagation of house-plants by cuttings is carried on extensively, a pit or house should be formed on purpose, in which there should be a bed of gently fermenting matter, such as tan or leaves, or, what will in general be found preferable, of sand, or coarsely-powdered charcoal, heated by the vapour of hot water from below. Where dung-beds are employed, great care is necessary to prevent the exhalations rising from the dung from entering into the house, as they would destroy most cuttings. Cuttings put in without leaves, or with leaves, but with ripened wood, will be much longer in rooting than those put in with leaves, and in a growing state, such as geraniums, petunias, dahlias, and even heaths.

Cuttings of the plants in common cultivation in British gardens may be classed as under:—

Cuttings of hardy deciduous trees, and shrubs, such as the gooseberry, currant, willow, poplar, &c., are easily rooted in the open garden, and the same may be said of the vine and fig. As it is desirable that the gooseberry and currant should not throw up suckers, and should have a clean stem, all the buds are cut clean out, except three, or at most four, at the upper end of the cutting. The cuttings are planted erect, with the dibber, or dug in with the spade, about six inches deep, and made quite firm at their lower extremity. Cuttings of honeysuckles, syringas, ampelopsis, artemisia, atragene, atriplex, baccharis, berchemia, bignonia, calycanthus, ceanothus, chenopodium, clematis, China roses, and the like, are rather more difficult to root, and succeed best in a shady border and a sandy soil.

Cuttings of hardy evergreens, such as the common laurel, Portugal laurel, laurustinus, arborvitæ, evergreen privet, and a few others, may be rooted in common soil in the open garden; being put in in autumn, and remaining there a year. Cuttings of buxus, juniperus, rhamnus, holly, sweet bay, aucuba, &c., require a shady border and a sandy soil. They are put in in autumn, the wood being well ripened; but young wood of these, and all the kinds mentioned in this and the preceding paragraph will root freely, if taken off in the beginning of summer when the lower end of the cutting is beginning to ripen, and planted in sand, and covered with a hand-glass.

Cuttings of all the Coniferæ and Taxaceæ may be taken off when the lower end of the cutting is beginning to ripen, and planted in sand, with a layer of leaf-mould beneath, in pots well drained, in the month

224   ON PROPAGATION BY CUTTINGS.

of August or September, and kept in a cold frame, from which the frost is completely excluded, till the growing season in spring, when they may be put into a gentle heat. It is not in general necessary to cover these cuttings with bell-glasses. The taxodium roots best in water.

Cuttings of hardy or half-hardy herbaceous plants, such as pinks, carnations, sweet-williams, wallflowers, stocks, dahlias, petunias, verbenas, rockets, and in general all herbaceous plants that have stems bearing leaves, root readily in sand under a hand-glass, placed in a shady border, or in a gentle heat, if greater expedition is required. All the cuttings must be cut through close under a joint, or in the case of pinks, carnations, or sweet-williams, the operation of piping may be performed.

Some plants, such as pinks, carnations, picotees, &c., are increased by pipings or layers. The operation is performed when the plant has flowered, or soon afterwards, when it has nearly completed its growth for the season. The shoot chosen is held firm by the left hand, to prevent the root of the plant from being injured, while with the right the upper portion of the shoot is pulled asunder at the joint above the part held by the left hand. A portion of the shoot is thus separated at the socket formed by the axils of the leaves, and the appearance is as in fig. 171. Some propagators shorten the leaves before planting, but others leave them as in the figure. The soil in which the pipings are to be planted being rendered very fine, mixed with sand and then well watered, the pipings are stuck in without the use of a dibber or pricker, and the operation is completed by a second watering, which settles and renders firm the soil at the lower end of the piping.

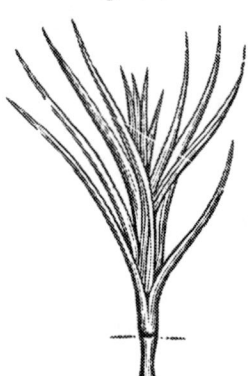

Fig. 171.

A piping of a pink prepared and planted.

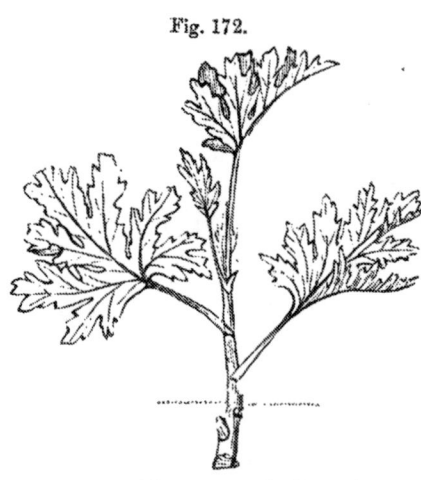

Fig. 172.

A cutting of the rose-scented pelargonium, prepared and planted.

Cuttings of soft-wooded greenhouse plants, such as pelargoniums, fig. 172, fuchsias, fig. 173, brugmansias, maurandyas, and all other soft-wooded plants, being cut off where the wood is beginning to ripen, and planted in sand or sandy loam, or sand and peat, root readily in the greenhouse or covered frame. Cuttings of these and all other soft-wooded plants may be divided into one or more lengths; it being only essential that there should be two joints, one for burying in the soil to emit roots, and the other kept above the soil to produce a shoot. The cuttings of soft-wooded plants which root best are laterals which are of average strength.

Cuttings of hard-wooded greenhouse plants, such as camellias, myrtles, evergreen acacias, and most Cape and Australian shrubs with comparatively broad leaves, are more difficult to root than soft-wooded greenhouse plants.

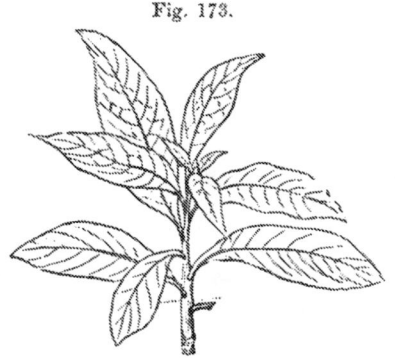

Fig. 173.

A cutting of a fuchsia prepared and planted.

The cuttings are made from the points of the shoots after the spring growth has been completed, and before the young wood is thoroughly ripened. If put in in February or March, such cuttings will be fit to transplant in July or August. Sometimes they are put in in autumn, or the beginning of winter, in which case they will not root till the following spring, and must be kept cool till that season. In either case, all the leaves must be kept on, except one, or at most two, on the lower end of the cutting, which need not be planted more than an inch in depth, and should in general be covered with a bell-glass.

Cuttings of the Underground Stems and Roots.—A great many plants, both ligneous and herbaceous, may be propagated by cuttings of the underground stems, as in the liquorice; and of the roots, as in the common thorn, and most of the Rosaceæ. The roots may be cut into

Fig. 174.

A cutting of the young wood of a camellia, prepared and planted.

lengths of from three to six or nine inches, and planted in free soil, with the tops just above the surface. Care must be taken that the upper end of the cutting, or that which was next the stem before it was separated from the plant, be kept uppermost, for if that is not done, the cutting will not grow so well. This is the case even with cuttings of the horse-radish and sea-kale; but if cuttings of the roots of these and similar plants are laid down horizontally, and but slightly covered with soil, they will protrude buds from what was the upper end before removal, and send out roots from the lower end. All roses may be propagated by cuttings, and all fruit-trees which are seedlings, or have been raised by cuttings or layers. The Robinia, Acacia, Gleditschia, Coronilla, Gymnocladus, and many other leguminosæ; Ailantus, Catalpa, the balsam Ontario and Lombardy poplars, the English elm, the mulberry, the Maclura, various other ligneous plants, and all plants whatever that throw up suckers, may be increased by cuttings of the roots; as may a great number of herbaceous perennials. The best mark for such as strike most readily by pieces of the root is an abundance of thick viscid juice, as in the genera Rhus, Papaver, Ailantus, Gymnocladus, &c., which strike more freely than Cydonia, roses, thorns, &c., which have less. The best time of taking them off is when the plants are in a dormant state, and all that is required is a clean cut at both ends.

Striking Cuttings in Water or Moist Moss.—All marsh plants having leafy stems, whether ligneous or herbaceous, will strike root in water, and still better in vessels containing moss kept thoroughly moist. Besides marsh plants, a great many others will root in this way, which, indeed, seems the most ancient mode of artificial propagation. Cuttings of narcissus, vines, figs, &c., have often been rooted in phials of water. The chief difficulty attending this mode of propagation is the transference of the rooted cuttings from the water to the soil, which can hardly be done without a severe check.

Propagation by Joints and Nodules.—This mode of propagation is founded on the principle, that every bud, whether visible or adventitious, is capable of being made to produce a plant; and it only differs from propagating by cuttings, in the buds or joints being taken off the plant with a smaller quantity of nutritive matter attached to them. Plants are also propagated by inserting the buds under the bark of other plants; but this mode, which is called budding, will form the subject of a separate notice. As bulbs are only buds, nature may be said to employ this mode of propagation in the case of some species of bulb-bearing plants, such as Allium and Lilium, in which the buds frequently drop from the stems on the soil, and root into it. All the offsets of bulbs are of course buds, and may be employed in propagation; the nutriment to the young plant being supplied from the scales, which eventually elongate into leaves, and the roots proceeding from the plate or base to which these scales are attached. The buds, with the exception of bulbs, which are taken from the stems, branches, or roots of plants, for the purpose of being rooted in the soil, always contain a portion of the stem or root, to supply them with nourishment till they are able, by the roots they form, to abstract it from the soil. In the case of the vine, a joint is commonly taken; but in that of the potato, a single bud, with a portion of the underground stem or tuber attached, is found sufficient. There are very few plants, besides the vine and the potato, which are at present propagated by rooting buds or joints in the soil, though there can be no doubt that this mode is applicable to a great number of plants with which it has not yet been tried. The late Mr. Brown, of the Hampstead Nursery, was very successful in striking camellias in this way. Plunged in a strong bottom-heat covered with bell-glasses, every leaf with its embryo distinct, produced a well-rooted plant. The advantage of propagating by buds or joints is, that a plant is produced from every bud or joint; whereas, in propagating by cuttings, at least two buds, and commonly several, are required.

A nodule is a concretion of embryo buds, such as may be frequently seen in the matter extravasated from the joints of pelargoniums and the stumps of old elms and poplars, olives and mulberries, occasioned by the returning sap not flowing freely to the root. These nodules are seldom used for the purpose of propagation, except in the case of the olive; but there can be no doubt that they might be employed for this purpose, and would answer, were it not that the plants which produce them are in general very readily propagated by cuttings. The only remarkable instance of propagation by this mode that is on record is practised in Italy with the olive. The old trees are commonly found to contain swellings or nodules in the trunk, called "uovole," and these being separated, are planted in the soil in the manner of bulbs, and produce plants.

In propagating by joints of the vine it is reasonable to suppose that the larger the portion of wood attached to the joint the stronger will be the plants produced. Mr. Knight found that the buds of the vine, wholly detached from the alburnum, were incapable of retaining life; but that a very few grains of alburnum were sufficient to enable a bud to form minute leaves and roots, such as would have been produced by plants raised from seeds. By increasing the quantity of alburnum, the shoots produced from the buds increased in the same proportion; and when the bud had a piece of two years old wood, a foot long, attached to it, the growth was nearly as strong as it would have been if the bud had remained on the parent tree. In preparing joints of the vine, about half an inch of the wood is left above and below the bud, as in fig. 175; but this and all other plants that are so propagated are found to root better when the shoot is cut through, so as to separate about one-third part of the pith, as shown in fig. 176. By this latter mode of treatment plants have been raised from buds and half-joints of camellia, poinsettia, euphorbia, brugmansia, and other species.

Fig. 175.

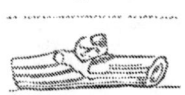

A joint of a vine prepared in the common manner, and planted.

Fig. 176.

A joint of a vine, in which two-thirds of the shoot and pith are removed previous to planting.

Propagation by bulbs, and entire tubers and tubercles, is effected simply by separating them from the parent plant, and inserting them in the soil about the same depth at which they are found on the parent plant, or a little deeper in very light soil, and not quite so deep if in very heavy soil. A phenomenon, De Candolle observes, common to all tubers is this: that while in the seed the radicle or descending part pushes first, in the tuber, on the contrary, the ascending part or plumule is first developed, and the roots appear a short time afterwards.

Propagating by Bulb-bearing Leaves.—The leaves of malaxis paludosa bear little bulbs at their extremities; several sorts of allium originate bulbs in the axils of the bracts; and in some ferns, such as asplenium bulbiferum, and Woodwardia radicans, bulbs are found at the extremities of the leaves, which when these touch the soil, grow, throw down roots, and produce young plants.

Propagation by Leaves.

This mode of propagation is of considerable antiquity. It is said by Agricola ('L'Agriculteur Parfait, &c.,' ed. 1732) to be the invention of Frederick, a celebrated gardener at Augsburg, and to have been first described by Mirandola, in his 'Manuale di Giardinieri,' published in 1652. Subsequent experiments by C. Bonnet, of Geneva; Noisette, Thouin, Neuman, and Pepin, of Paris; Knight, Herbert, and others, in England and Germany, have proved that there is probably no class of plants which might not be propagated by leaves. It has been tried with success with cryptogamous plants, with endogens and exogens; with the popular divisions of ligneous and herbaceous plants, annuals, biennials, and perennials, and with the leaves of bulbous plants and palms.

The conditions generally required for rooting leaves are, that the leaf be nearly full grown; that it be taken off with the petiole entire; that the petiole be inserted from an eighth to half an inch, according to its length, thickness, and texture, in sandy loam, or in pure sand on a stratum of rich soil; and that both the soil and the atmosphere be kept uniformly moist, and at a higher temperature than is required for rooted plants of the same species. The leaves of such succulents as cacalia, crassula, cotyledon, kalankoe, portulaca, sedum, sempervivum, cactus, gloxinias, begonias, and similar plants, root when laid on the surface of soil, with the upper side to the light, the soil and atmosphere being kept sufficiently close, moist, and warm. The first change that takes place is the formation of a callosity at the base of the petiole; after which, at the end of a period which varies greatly in different plants, roots are produced, and eventually, at an equally varying period, a bud from which a leafy axis is developed.

Rooting Portions of Leaves.—In 1839, M. Neuman, of the Paris Garden, saw the theophrasta latifolia (Clavija ornata, D. Don) growing so well from cuttings of leaves, that he conceived the idea of cutting several of them in two, and treating them in the same manner as entire leaves. Accordingly, he cut a leaf in two, and planted both parts in the same pot, treating them exactly alike. In about three months, the lower half of the leaf had made roots, but the upper half had none; though, some time afterwards, when it became necessary to separate the cuttings, M. Neuman found that the upper part of the leaf had also made roots, but that these roots were much shorter than those of the lower half. The rooting of the two halves of a leaf of the theophrasta, so hard and dry as every one knows these leaves to be, appearing to him an interesting circumstance, he continued to pay attention to them for six months.

He wished to ascertain if they would produce buds as in other cases, for he was in hopes they would, as he remarked that the roots increased in the pot. At last in the seventh month, for the first time, he saw at the extremity of his two half leaves, buds appearing, as well formed as those proceeding from the base of the petiole of an entire leaf. In June, 1840, these two cuttings had become beautiful and healthy plants, which it was impossible to distinguish from others produced from entire leaves.

We see from this experiment that it requires double the time to produce a bud from the upper part of some leaves, that it requires for the lower half to produce one; and that, in propagations by leaves, it is not always necessary to take the heel or lower end of the petiole with the leaf, which sometimes injures and deforms the shoots. M. Neuman's experiment proves further, that wherever cambium can be formed, there are at the same time a number of utricules or germs of buds formed, from which a new plant will be developed when the parent is placed in favourable circumstances. From this circumstance, in short, we may conclude that all the veins may serve for the reproduction of plants. The dots in fig. 178 show the parts of the upper half-leaf which were cut off to allow of its being put into a small pot; and this proves that it is only the middle rib (or prolongation of the petiole), which is required for reproduction. The smallest portion of such plants as begonias, gloxinias, &c. will form an independent plant.

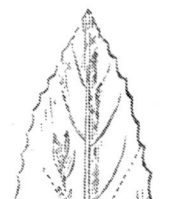

Fig. 177. *The lower half of the leaf of theophrasta rooted and sending up a shoot.*

Fig. 178. *The upper half of theophrasta rooted and sending up a shoot.*

Leaves of the orange, the hoya, the aucuba, ficus elasticus, the clianthus, the common laurel, and a few more, have been occasionally rooted, but more as matter of curiosity than for the purpose of increase.

Propagation by the leaves of bulbs has been successfully effected by the Hon. and Rev. W. Herbert, who first tried it, in 1809, by setting a cutting of a leaf of a Cape Ornithogalum. " The leaf was cut off just below the surface of the earth in an early stage of its growth, before the flower-stalk had begun to rise; and it was set in the earth, near the edge of the pot in which the mother plant was growing, and so left to its fate. The leaf continued quite fresh, and on examination (while the bulb was flowering) a number of young bulbs and radical fibres were found adhering to it. They appeared to have been formed by the return of the sap which had nourished the leaf. Thereupon two or three more leaves were taken off and placed in like situations; but they turned yellow, and died without producing any bulbs. It appeared to me then, and it was confirmed by subsequent experience, that in order to obtain a satisfactory result the leaf must be taken off while the plant is advancing in its growth. I found it easy thus to multiply some bulbs that did not willingly produce offsets. I afterwards tried, without cutting the leaf off, to make an oblique incision in it under ground, and in some cases just above ground, attempting, in fact, to raise bulbs by layering the leaf. This attempt was also successful, and some young bulbs were formed on the edge of the cut above ground as well as below. I tried cuttings of the stems of some species of Lilium, and obtained bulbs at the axil of the leaf, as well as from the scales of the bulb; and that practice has been since much resorted to by gardeners, though I believe it originated with me. I raised a great number of the bulbs of the little plant which has been successively called massonia, scilla, and hyacinthus corymbosus, by setting a pot full of its leaves, and placing a bell-glass over them for a short time. A bulb was obtained with equal facility from a leaf of a rare species of Eucomis; and experiments with the leaves of Lachenalias were equally successful. I apprehend that all liliaceous bulbs may be thus propagated; but the more fleshy the leaf, the more easily the object will be attained." ('Gard. Chron.' for 1841, p. 381.)

Rooting Leaves and Parts of Leaves in Powdered Charcoal.—Most cuttings will root as freely, and even more so, in this than in sand. Mr. Jas. Barnes, late of Bicton, used to mix charcoal with the soil in which he grew every kind of plant, from the cabbage and the onion to heaths, pine-apples, and orchideæ, and with extraordinary success. The charcoal was generally broken into small pieces, say an inch or more in length, and seldom thicker than a quill; but he also used it of a larger size, along with drainage materials, and, when sown along with seeds, in a state of powder.

Leaves with the buds in the axils root freely in the case of many species. The buds and leaves are cut out with a small portion of the bark and alburnum to each, and planted in sandy loam, so deep as just to cover the bud; the soil being pressed firmly against it, and the back of the leaf resting on the surface of the soil. Covered with a bell-glass and placed on heat, in a short time the buds break through the surface of the soil, and elongate into shoots. The late Mr. Knight tried this mode with double camellias, magnolias, metrosideros, acacias, neriums, rhododendrons, and many others, some of which rooted and made shoots the same season, and others not till the following spring.

Immature fruits have even been made to produce plants. M. Thouin planted fruits of the Opuntia Tuna, which were about three-fourths ripe, with their peduncles entire, in pots of sand almost dry, and covered them with a bell-glass, placing the pot on a hotbed. In eighteen days, callosities appeared at the base of the peduncles, which soon became roots, and a few days afterwards little protuberances appeared on the summits of the fruit, which, at the end of two months, became shoots. The same result took place in the case of the fruits of Opuntia polyanthos, and Mammillaria simplex. ('Cours de Culture,' &c., tome ii, p. 551.) Some or the whole of the parts of the flower

PROPAGATION BY LEAVES.

are frequently metamorphosed into leaves, and even shoots, in warm, moist seasons, and from these there can be no doubt plants could, in many cases, be raised by taking them off and treating them as cuttings.

The essence of all the different modes of forming plants from cuttings may thus be stated. Wherever a joint of the ripened wood of a plant, or of the unripened wood, with a leaf or leaves, can be procured, it is probable that a rooted plant may be produced by proper treatment; that in many cases, especially where the leaves are large, a bud with a leaf attached will produce a plant; that in a number of cases plants may be produced from leaves alone, and that in some cases they may be even produced from parts of leaves, from the calyxes, and other parts of flowers, and from immature fruits. That to render more certain the rooting of a cutting or a bud, or even a leaf, it is advisable partially to separate it from the parent plant some days, weeks, or, in some cases, months, before it is entirely taken off, by cutting a shoot half through immediately under a joint or leaf, and keeping the wound open, if necessary, with a wedge, as in fig. 179, *b*, or by ringing under each bud, as in fig. 180, *c*. That, in regard to soil, the safe mode is to plant in pure sand, with a layer of the soil in which the plant delights below; and, in regard to light, that the cuttings should in all cases, when they are under glass, be placed as close to it as possible. Finally, that in regard to woody plants, those with the leaves on, and the wood half-matured at the lower end of the shoot, will root more readily than shoots of ripened wood without the leaves. Camellia shoots of the season, put in in July or August, will be rooted by December, while those not put in till September, will not root till the following spring. That the rooting of cuttings with the leaves on depends very much on the action of light, is proved by the following experiment made by M. Caie:—A pot of cuttings of Monsoa incisifolia was placed in a close pit, at two feet from the glass; another at two feet three inches; and a third at two feet six inches. The cuttings in the first pot were rooted, but very little advanced in growth; those in the second were elongated in the tops, but had only callosities at the lower ends of the cuttings; and those of the third pot were grown as high or higher than those

Fig. 179.

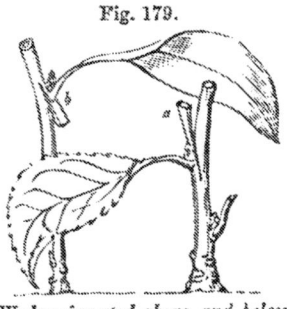

Wedges inserted above and below buds to check the flow of the sap, and excite them to produce shoots.

Fig. 180.

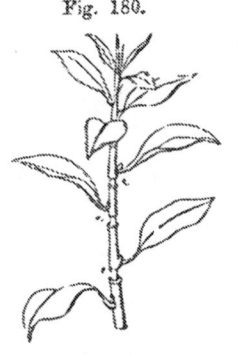

A shoot ringed to accumulate sap at the base of the buds, and prepare them for throwing out roots when they are taken off and planted.

of the second, but without either callosities or roots. ('Gard. Chron.,' vol. i. p. 782.)

To induce stems or shoots to produce leaves or growths from which cuttings may be formed, various modes have been adopted, the object of all of which is to stimulate the normal or latent buds. The most common mode with plants in pots or under glass, is by an increase of temperature and atmospheric moisture; but there are modes which are applicable to all plants whatever, the object of which is to interrupt the ascending or descending sap. When the ascending sap is accumulated by art at a joint, and can no longer pass freely onwards, it stimulates the buds which exist there, either normal or adventitious, to develope themselves, and the sap thus escapes organized into the form of leaves or shoots; while the interruption of the descending sap, more especially under a joint or bud, produces an accumulation or callosity there, which, sooner or later, is organized into roots. To accumulate the ascending sap at any point, the shoot may be bent to one side from that point; and it may be bent back again from a second point, and if the shoot is long, the operation may be repeated, so as to leave it in a serpentine or zigzag form from every exterior angle in which, as at *a, a*, in fig. 181, a bud will be developed. Where the shoot cannot conveniently be bent, a notch may be made in it immediately above a bud, so deep as to penetrate the alburnum; or in the case of more slender shoots, the knife may be merely inserted above the bud, or above several buds, so as to penetrate into the alburnum, and the wound kept open by inserting wedges in them, as in fig. 179, *a*. Some days or weeks afterwards, according to the nature of the plant, a notch or cut may be made under the bud, in order to interrupt the sap returned by the leaf, and thus form a callosity there for the production of roots. In this way all the buds or joints on a tree or shrub of almost any size may be prepared; and if a tree so treated could be covered with moss kept moist, leaving only the buds, or the joints, or points from which buds were expected, exposed to the light; or if it could be laid down on the surface of soil kept moist, and very slightly covered with soil, or laid down flat on the surface of water, so as just to touch it, a rooted plant, or at least a shoot, would be produced from every bud or joint. In preparing buds in this manner, however, it must always be borne in mind, either that the plants require to be kept in a close, moist atmosphere, or to have the wounds covered with moss or soil; for if they are exposed to dry air, they will frequently neither cicatrize, nor emit roots, in consequence of the excessive evaporation which will necessarily take place.

Even the petioles of large leaves may be prepared before they are taken off, by being cut half through near the base, by which means

Fig. 181.

A shoot bent to cause the buds at the angles to produce shoots.

they will form a callosity there, and root more rapidly when planted. The roots of plants which contain latent buds may be stimulated to develop them by the exposure of portions of them to the light, or by bending, or twisting, or cutting notches in them, in the same manner as in stems. Piercing the stems or roots by a longitudinal cut through a joint, and keeping the wound open with a wedge or splinter, or driving pegs or nails through them, will facilitate both the formation of roots and the development of buds; and various other modes of exciting buds, and causing the protrusion of roots, will occur to the gardener who understands what has been already said on the subject. It is only necessary to bear in mind that when the ascending sap is to be interrupted by cutting, the knife must penetrate into the alburnum, and that when roots only are the object in view, it is only necessary to penetrate the bark.

Propagation by Layers.

The theory of layering is founded on the following facts:—The sap absorbed from the soil by the roots rises to the buds and leaves chiefly through the alburnum; for though it has been proved, by the transmission of coloured fluids from the roots upwards, that a communication is maintained throughout the whole stem, yet the greatest flow of sap, whether ascending or descending, takes place through the youngest layers, whether of wood in ascending, or inner bark in descending. A decortication may therefore be made with little or no interruption resulting to the ascent of the sap. The elaborated fluid, in returning from the leaves, descends by the inner bark, depositing in its progress an organized layer of alburnum, a portion of this extending to the extremities of the roots, where it protrudes in the form of spongioles. From these facts it will appear evident that although ringing does not interrupt the upward flow of sap, because the incision does not reach the vessels in which it proceeds, yet that the descent is prevented by the chasm formed by the operation; on the brink of this chasm it accumulates, and under favourable circumstances a callosity is formed, or mass of cellular substance protruded, which by degrees assumes a granulated form, and these granulations ultimately elongate into spongioles; or the teguments above the incision, being rendered soft by the earth or other suitable moist covering, are ruptured, and afford egress to the nascent roots. From this the principle of the operation of ringing, applying ligatures, twisting, tonguing, or splitting the parts about to be laid, will be easily understood.

The operation of layering, like that of forming cuttings, is chiefly applicable to plants having leaf-bearing stems; and the advantage which a layer has over a cutting is that it is nourished, while roots are being formed, by the parent plant; whereas the cutting has no other resource than the nutritive matter laid up in it, or that produced by the functions of the leaves. Hence, layering is one of the most certain modes of propagation by division, though it is in general slower than any other mode. In whatever way layering is performed it consists in the interruption of the descending sap at a joint of a stem, or shoot, and placing it under circumstances favourable for the production of roots. The interruption is most successful when it takes place immediately under a bud or joint, when the shoot is more or less matured, and when it penetrates into the alburnum; though, if the alburnum is penetrated too far, the ascent of the sap will be interrupted, and the supply to the buds or leaves will be insufficient to develop them, or keep them from flagging. The descending sap may be interrupted either wholly by cutting off a ring of bark, or partially by a cut or notch, by driving a peg or nail through it, by a slit kept open, by twisting the stem at a joint, by strangling it there with a wire, by bending it so as to form an angle, by the pressure of a stone laid on it, or by attracting it by heat and moisture. The latter mode of causing a branch to protrude roots may often be observed in nature, in the case of the lowest branches of trees and shrubs that rest on the soil, and by their shade keep it moist, and, after some time, root into it. Whatever mode of interrupting the sap be adopted, the wounded part of the layer from which roots are expected to proceed must be covered with soil, moss, or some other suitable material kept moist, or it must be partially or wholly immersed in water. Layering, from the certainty which attends it, was formerly much more extensively employed as a mode of propagation than it is at present; the art of rooting cuttings being now much better understood, and being chiefly adopted in house and in herbaceous plants; and layering being confined in a great measure to hardy trees and shrubs, of which it is desired to multiply plants that will speedily produce flowers, or that cannot otherwise be so readily propagated.

The state of the plant most favourable for layering is the same as that most suitable for propagation by cuttings. The wood and bark should be soft and not over ripe, and this is most likely to be the case with lateral shoots produced near the surface of the soil or in a moist atmosphere. Layers, like cuttings, may be made either of ripe wood in the autumn or spring, or of growing wood any time in the course of the summer; the only condition, in the latter case, being that the part of the shoot where the sap is interrupted be somewhat mature, or firm in texture.

Hardy trees and shrubs, with reference to layering, may be divided into two kinds, those which, when cut down, throw up shoots from the collar, that is, technically, which stole, such as most kinds of deciduous trees and shrubs; and those which do not stole, such as all the coniferæ. The former are planted and cut down, and layers made of the young shoots which proceed from the collar; while the latter are either laid entirely down, and their branches extended along the surface of the soil, and the extremities of all the shoots layered, or such side branches as can be bent down to the soil are made fast there by hooked pegs, and their shoots layered. When the shoots to be layered are small, they are frequently twisted or slit through at the point where the roots are to be produced; but when they are strong the knife is entered beneath a joint, and the shoot cut half through, and the knife afterwards turned up half an inch or more, so as to form what is technically called a tongue (fig. 182, *a*), and the shoot being bent down and its point turned up, the wound is kept open as at *b*; the shoot being kept down by a hooked peg, or by a portion of a twig, first twisted to render it tough, and next doubled, as at *c*; one or more buds being left on the layer, *d*; and the wound being kept open by the bent position of the shoot. When the shoots are small or brittle, in order

Fig. 182.

Layering with the tongue made in the under-side of the shoot.

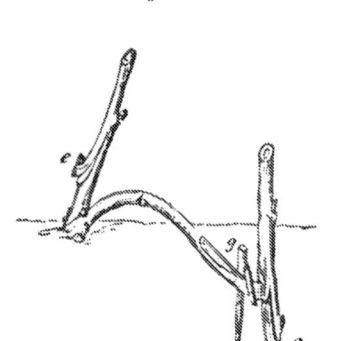

Fig. 183.

Layering with the tongue made in the upper side of the shoot.

to lessen the risk of breaking them by tonguing below, the incision is made above, and the tongue kept from uniting by giving the layer a twist when pegging it down, as shown in fig. 183, in which *e* is the tongue made in the shoot before being laid down, *f* the position taken by the tongue after the layer is fixed in its place, and *g* the peg which keeps the layer down. The dotted line in this and the preceding figure indicates the surface of the soil. Layers are always buried in the soil, and secured there, and the soil pressed firmly against them. The plant furnishing the shoots which are layered is called a stool, and as it generally furnishes a number of shoots, these are laid down radiating all round it, as in fig. 184, and the soil formed into a circular basin, the better to retain water about the rooted parts of the layers. Layers that are difficult to root are laid into pure sand with good soil beneath, as is done with cuttings difficult to strike; and the shoots laid down and layered are commonly shortened to one eye above the soil, in order that there may be only one stem to the plant to be produced. (See figs. 182 and 183.)

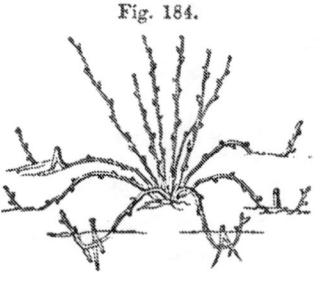

Fig. 184.

A stool with several of the shoots layered.

In former times, when few trees were propagated in nurseries, excepting limes and elms, the shoots produced from the stools were not laid down, but after two years' growth the shoots were earthed up, and after remaining on two years longer, they were slipped off and found to have a sufficient supply of roots to ensure their independent existence, after, however, being cut in and headed down.

Shrubs with very long shoots, such as clematis, tecoma, vitis, wistaria, honeysuckle, &c., are stretched along the surface, and every joint, or every alternate joint, prepared for rooting; so that one shoot produces half as many plants as it contains joints, or even a plant for every joint. The joint in this case is not tongued, but bruised, pierced, or slit, or simply pressed down to the moist soil by a hook, peg, or small stone—the latter having the advantage of retaining moisture, as well as checking the return of the sap. Shoots which continue growing all the summer, such as those of the wistaria, are laid as they extend in length; and when the parent plant is placed on moist heat, under glass, and near it, it is incredible the number of rooted layers that may thus be obtained in one season.

Layering by Insertion of the Growing Point.—Shoots of the bramble will emit roots by the usual mode of twisting and pegging down; but if the growing point of the shoot is merely inserted in the soil to the depth of an inch, an astonishing quantity of roots will be produced in the same season, more, in fact, than in two years by the other mode. The gooseberry, the Aristolochia, and the common nightshade, treated in the same way, succeed equally well; and doubtless many other species might in like manner be easily and quickly propagated.

Plum and Paradise stocks for fruit trees are raised in large quantities, by a somewhat similar mode. The shoots of the stool are pegged down flat on the surface, and covered entirely over, to the depth of half an inch, with loamy soil. This is done early in spring, and in the course of the summer every bud sends up a shoot which roots at its base, and at the end of autumn is fit to be taken off as a separate plant. The tree peony is sometimes propagated in this manner, but with this difference, that a ring of bark is taken off between each bud.

Roses, though mostly increased by budding, grafting, and cuttings, are also readily rooted by layers, which in the nurseries are made both in spring and autumn,

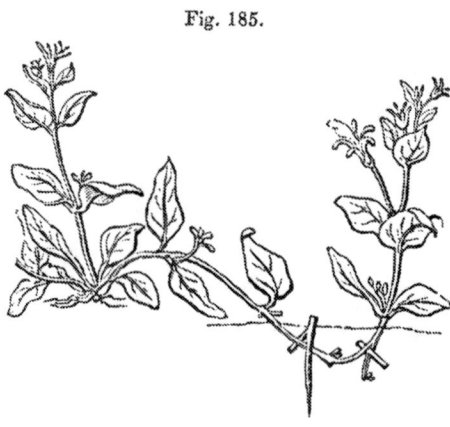

Fig. 185.

A petunia layered.

and sometimes at both seasons, on the same stool. The shoots being brittle are generally twisted, or slit through, and the slit kept open with a fragment of stick or stone. When they are tongued the tongue is generally made on the upper side of the shoot, fig. 183, which greatly lessens the risk of breaking the shoot when bending it down.

Hardy herbaceous plants, such as the chrysanthemum and the carnation, are frequently layered. The shoots are chosen when of sufficient length, the lower leaves cut off, and the shoot pegged down and covered with sandy loam, or sand and leaf-mould.

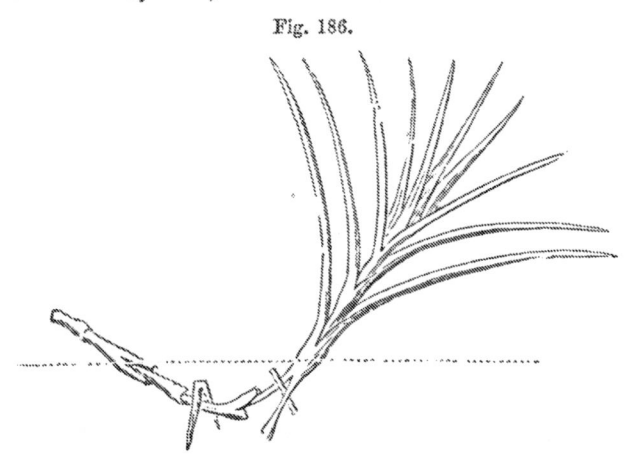

Fig. 186.

A carnation layered.

Shrubby plants in pots kept under glass may either be layered by laying down the entire plant on its side, or by placing pots under it, or raising pots among its branches, and layering the shoots into these. The shoot may either be laid down into the pot, or brought up through a hole in its bottom, or in its side; a tin case filled with soil or moss may be suspended from the plants, and the shoots ringed, as indicated in figs. 188 and 189, or a ring of bark being taken off, the wounded part may be enveloped in a mass of loam covered with moss, a mode practised by the Chinese. The moss, in either case, may be kept moist by suspending near it, and somewhat higher, a vessel of water with some worsted threads, connecting the water with the moss, and acting as a siphon.

Fig. 187.

Layering a cutting.

The soil in which plants are layered should, in general, be that in which the parent plants naturally thrive best, but with a mixture of sand, or with the wounded part entirely enveloped in sand or powdered charcoal, to prevent it from retaining too much water, which would prevent the wound from protruding granular matter, and cause it to rot. Plants which grow in heath soil, such as most of the Ericaceæ,

238   PROPAGATION BY LAYERS.

and all other hair-rooted plants, must be layered in sand or in heath soil, but almost all others will root freely in sandy loam. Where the soil and the season are not naturally moist, layers, even in the open gardens, require watering, or, at least, are much benefited by it. Mulching may also be advantageously employed in order to retain moisture.

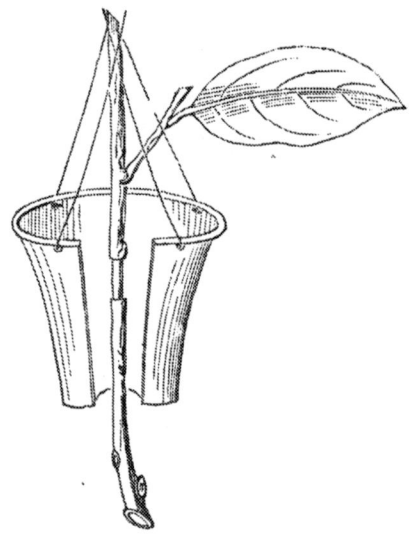

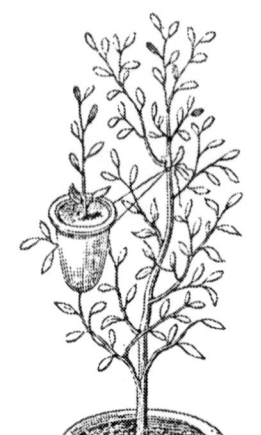

Fig. 188.

Fig. 189.

A branch ringed and prepared to be rooted in a tin case without separating it from the tree.

A branch layered in a tin case.

Hooked pegs were formerly considered as essential articles for fixing down the layers, but the general practice at present is to take a piece of the shoot from the stool, or any waste piece of shoot about a foot in length, or longer if the soil be very loose, and twisting it in the middle so as to prevent it from breaking when bent, to double it like a lady's hair-pin over the shoot, as shown at c, in fig. 182.

The time which layers require to produce roots varies in different plants, from one to two, and even, in some cases, three or four years. The process of rooting is facilitated by increased heat and moisture, and by ringing below the tongue, or wounded or bent part from which the roots are expected to protrude; but this operation can only be safely performed where the parent plant is in vigorous health, because, otherwise, it would weaken the root, and prevent it from sending up sap to nourish the layer. In taking off layers which are difficult to root, it is a safe mode not to cut through the layer at once, but by degrees, at intervals of several weeks. In the case of stools in the open air the butt ends of the shoots from which the layers have been taken are cut off close to the stool, to make room for a second succession of layers, which are made annually from the upright shoots produced during the preceding season. In the case of layers taken from plants in pots, the stumps left after the layer is taken off should be cut to a leaf-bud, in order that a shoot may be produced to supply the vacancy made in the head of the plant by the removal of the layer.

Propagation by Suckers, Slips, Offsets, Runners, and Simple Division.

A sucker is properly a shoot sent up from the underground part of the stem, from a latent bud there existing, or from an adventitious bud on that part of the stem, or on the horizontal roots. Many herbaceous plants are propagated by root-suckers; a number of shrubs, such as the lilac, the spiræa, the raspberry, &c., and some trees are occasionally so propagated, such as the white, trembling, and balsam poplars, the English elm, &c. The suckers of herbaceous plants are chiefly taken off in spring and autumn, when they are in a growing state, and those of ligneous plants late in autumn, when the sap is dormant; but suckers of both kinds may be taken off at any season, provided those which are in a growing state are put into a moist atmosphere and shaded.

Stem-suckers or slips may be described as shoots which proceed from the collar, or above it from the lower part of the stem, and which have few or no roots, unless the stem has been earthed up. Heading down plants, or otherwise rendering the top inadequate for the due appropriation of the supply of sap furnished by the roots, favours the production of stem-suckers. The tendency is also induced in consequence of any sudden check given to the foliage, such as that arising from excessive drought, or the depredations of insects, more especially if the roots are at the same time growing in rich, moist soil. These shoots, being drawn or slipped off, are planted and treated as cuttings, and they are found to root more readily than shoots taken from the plant at a greater distance from the root. To produce slips on the lower parts of stems they may be cut down, and in the case of plants in pots stimulated by an extra supply of heat and moisture. The stumps of pine-apple plants are sometimes so stimulated after the fruit has been gathered, and slips or suckers are in that case produced by the buds which had remained dormant in the axils of the leaves. When the bases of such plants as the banana, are treated in a similar manner, similar results will follow; and by destroying the growing point or central bud of such plants as Yucca, Dracæna, and Zamia, and also of Mammillaria, and other Cactaceæ, and of all bulbs, slips, suckers, or offsets will be produced from the latent buds in the axils of the leaves. By earthing up, these shoots may generally be made to emit roots before being separated from the parent plant; or they may be slipped off without roots, and treated as cuttings. Cuttings or layers from the branches of coniferous plants sometimes continue growing a number of years before they throw up a leading shoot; but this result may be obtained much sooner than it otherwise would be by pegging down the entire plants, when a stem-sucker will be produced, as in fig. 190, in consequence of the check given to the ascending sap by the acute angle formed by the bend, after which all the other branches of the plant may be cut off close to the stem-sucker. Cuttings of the side branches of Cunninghamia lanceolata have by this treatment made as good plants as seedlings; and we believe it has also been successful with Araucaria excelsa.

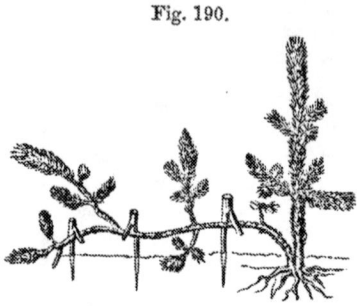

Fig. 190.

The branches of a coniferous plant pegged down to force it to throw up a stem-sucker as a leader.

Offsets.—An offset is a term for the most part confined to the small bulbs, corms, tubers, or underground stems, which are formed at the side of the base of large ones, and by which the plant producing them may be propagated. They are very readily observed in the hyacinth, tulip, and crocus, in which they afford the only means of propagation, excepting by seed. All offsets have a natural tendency to separate from the parent bulb, excepting when they are very small and young; in which case they are left adhering to the parent bulb or tuber for another growing season. When offsets are to be separated, the bulb, when it is in a dormant state, is taken up, and the offsets are removed and planted by themselves, at various depths, according to the size and nature of the offset; and bearing in mind that all bulbs are buds, and consequently that they would all grow if placed on the surface of moist soil, and pressed firmly against it, without any covering of soil. Offsets may be produced from bulbs, by searing or otherwise destroying their central bud by mutilation, or by cutting them over a little above the plate from which the scales proceed, as in the hyacinth, and the concentric coats, or rudiments of tubular leaves, as in the onion; the buds in both cases being in the axils of the members. Sometimes the frost destroying the outer scales of a bulb will stimulate the buds in their axils to develop themselves (fig. 191); and sometimes, when the scales are very closely compressed at top, the buds in their axils will be developed, and will protrude below (fig. 192). A bulb of Crinum canaliculatum, cut over a little above the plate, was found by M. Syringe to throw out no fewer than forty offsets.

Fig. 191.

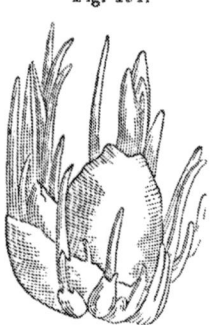

The buds in the axils of the scales of a bulb developed in consequence of injuries sustained by the scales from frost.

Runners are long slender shoots, with joints at distant intervals, which are protruded from the collar of perennial herbaceous or sub-herbaceous plants, such as the strawberry, many grasses, some saxifrages, potentillas, &c. The joints of these plants rest naturally on the ground, send roots downwards, and leaves or shoots upwards; and being separated from the internodi of the stolones, constitute rooted plants. Very little assistance from art is required in this mode of propagation; but the soil may be loosened and enriched, and the joint pressed firmly against the soil, by pegging it down with a hooked peg, or by laying a small stone on each side of the joint. The principal plant propagated in this manner in gardens is the strawberry.

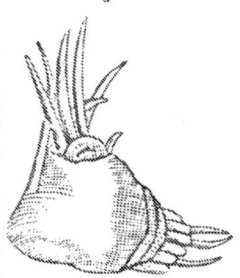

Fig. 192.

Simple division is an obvious mode of propagating all herbaceous perennials, not bulb-bearing, and all shrubs which produce numerous suckers. The most common mode is to take up the entire plant, and separate it into as many stems as have roots attached; or if only a few plants are wanted, these may be taken off the sides of the plant without greatly disturbing the interior of the root stock.

Buds developed below in consequence of the scales being closely compressed at top.

Propagation by Grafting, Inarching, and Budding.

The term graft is in England generally confined to one mode of performing that operation—viz., grafting with detached scions; but it is our intention in this article to use it, in the Continental sense, as a generic term, including also, inarching, or grafting with attached scions, and budding or grafting by means of a bud attached to a plate of bark. The principle on which all these operations are founded is the phenomenon of the union of newly-generated tissues when in the act of being generated. No union can take place between the parts of plants previously formed, but only when these parts are in the act of forming. Thus two shoots or branches may be selected, and by means of similar sections be most accurately joined, and placed under the most favourable circumstances for uniting, as in fig. 193, representing a stock and a scion; yet when the two are bound together, though a union ultimately does take place, not one particle of the existing tissue at the time of grafting becomes united with similar tissue brought in contact with it. Close contact is all that takes place with regard to these surfaces of the scion and stock, for a vital union only occurs when nascent tissues meet. The parts a, a, which are alburnum of the preceding year, never unite. The vital union is formed solely by the coalition of newly-generated tissues, thrown out by such parts as have the power of generating them. This power does not exist in the heart-wood, nor in the outer bark, but only in the alburnum, or rather the substance embedded between it and the inner bark, constituting the cambium, represented by the lines b, b. If the sections are placed against each other, so that the inner barks coincide, the scion may perhaps derive an immediate supply of moisture; but it

R

242   PROPAGATION BY GRAFTING, ETC.

does so only in a mechanical way, and a piece of dry sponge might as truly be said to have formed a connexion from its absorbing moisture, in consequence of being placed on the top of a stock, as the scion that only takes up moisture as above-mentioned. When, however, new tissue is formed by the parts, *b, b*, of the respective sections, and when the portions so formed protrude so as to meet, they immediately coalesce, forming a connecting chain of vessels between the buds of the scion and the roots of the stock. If an old grafted tree is cut down, and all the wood cut away to the original portions which existed at the time of grafting, it will be found that the sections similar to *a, a*, made by the grafting-knife, are only mechanically pressed together, and may be easily taken asunder. Instances frequently occur of the inner bark of the scion being placed out of contact with that of the stock, and a union nevertheless ensues; but this takes place in consequence of the cellular substance protruding from the respective alburnums over the surface of old wood, which it only covers. As soon as the new-formed tissue of stock and scion touch each other, a union is then formed.

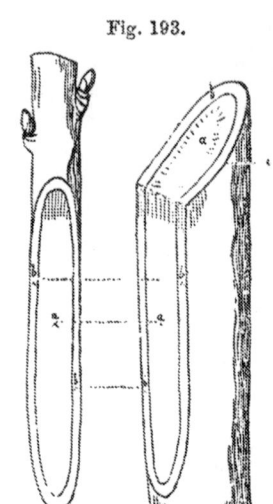

Fig. 193.

Scion and stock, to illustrate the principle on which they are united.

The origin of grafting is of the most remote antiquity, but whether it was suggested by the adhesions of the parts of two plants, frequently seen in a state of nature, or by the appearance of one plant growing on another, as in the case of the mistletoe, it is impossible to divine. Theophrastus and other Greek authors mention the graft; and upwards of twenty modifications of it have been given by the Roman Varro.

The phenomena of grafting are thus explained by De Candolle:— The shoots springing from the buds of the scion are united to the stock by the young growing alburnum, and, once united, they determine the ascent of the sap rising from the stock; and they elaborate a true or proper juice, which appears evidently to re-descend in the inner bark. This sap appears to be sufficiently homogeneous in plants of the same family to be, in the course of its passage, absorbed by the growing cellules near which it passes, and each cellule elaborates it according to its nature. The cellules of the alburnum of the plum elaborate the coloured wood of the plum; those of the alburnum of the almond the coloured wood of the almond. If the descending sap has only an incomplete analogy with the wants of the stock, the latter does not thrive, though the organic union between it and the scion may have taken place; and if the analogy between the alburnum of the scion and that of the stock is wanting, the organic union does not operate, and as the scion cannot absorb the sap of the stock, the graft does not succeed.

The conditions essential to the success of the graft are the exact coincidence of the alburnum and the inner bark of the scion with those of the stock. The graft is effected in two forms: that of a cutting or scion, which consists of wood and bark with buds (as in grafting and inarching), and that of a bud, which consists of a shield of bark, containing a bud or buds, but deprived of its wood, as in budding. In the case of the scion it is essential to success that its alburnum coincide exactly with that of the stock; and in the case of the bud it is essential that the disk of bark to which it is attached should be intimately joined to the alburnum of the stock by being placed over it, and gently pressed against it by means of ligatures. The buds of the scion and of the shield are supplied with sap from the alburnum of the stock, and develop themselves in consequence. As a proof that it is the ascending sap which supplies the nourishment in both cases, the scion and the bud succeed best when the stock is cut over almost immediately above the graft; and when the scion or the shield are placed immediately over a part of the stock which contained buds. The success of a scion or a bud placed in the internodia of the stock where no normal buds can exist, will therefore be much less certain than if it were placed on the nodia; because the vessels which conducted the descending sap to the original buds are ready to supply it to those which have taken their place. Hence, in the case of the graft, fig. 193, the stock is cut sloping, and so as to have a bud on or near the upper extremity of it, in order to prevent the stock from dying down behind the graft; and the section a, against which the scion is to be placed, is made at the lower part of the sloping section, in order to insure abundance of sap at its upper extremity as well as at its lower; for were there no bud to expend the sap, it would cease to be impelled through that part of the stock, which would consequently die. By the end of August the scion and stock will be united, and the section at the top of the latter healed over perhaps as far as e; and if the heel, or part above c, is then cut off, the part will probably be completely healed over by the end of the season.

Anatomical Analogy.—Plants can only be budded or grafted on one another within certain limits, and these depend on the anatomy or organic structure of the tissue, and the physiology or vital functions of the organs of the plant; but the anatomy of the cellules and the structure of the vessels are so delicate and difficult to observe, that the differences between plants in these respects are not sufficient to enable us to arrive at any practical conclusion from examining their organization, and hence our only guide in this matter hitherto has been experience. From this it is found that as plants of the same natural family have an analogous organization, they alone can be grafted on one another with any prospect of success; though the success of the operation even within this limit will not always be complete, partly, perhaps, from some difference in organic structure, as in the case of the apple and pear, which can only be united for a few years, but chiefly on account of the physiological differences which may and do frequently exist. As a proof that plants of the same natural family may be grafted on one another, De Candolle succeeded in grafting the lilac and the fringe-tree on the ash, the fringe-tree on the lilac, the lilac on the phillyrea, and the olive on the ash and the privet; and though these grafts did not live a long time, on account of the physiological differences of the species, yet their having succeeded at all sufficiently proves the anatomical analogy of plants within the same natural order. This analogy is greater between plants of the same genus; more so still between individuals of the same species, and most so between branches of the same individual.

Physiological Analogy.—In a physiological point of view, the epochs of vegetation are the principal points to be attended to, and hence no plant can be grafted on another which does not thrive in the same temperature. Two plants in which the sap is not in motion cannot be successfully united, because it is only when cellular tissue is in a state in which it can form accretions that a vital union can be formed, and a reciprocal activity must exist both in the stock and scion. Hence evergreen trees seldom succeed for any length of time when grafted on deciduous kinds. The analogy of magnitude is also of some importance, for if a large growing tree is grafted on one naturally of small stature, the graft, by exhausting the stock, will ultimately deprive it of life; and when a small or weakly growing species is grafted on a large vigorous one, it receives too much sap, and ultimately perishes from hypertrophy, as the other did from atrophy. The analogy of consistence also merits notice. Soft woods do not associate well with hard woods, nor ligneous plants with such as are herbaceous, nor annuals with perennials. An analogy in the nature of the sap is also requisite, experience having proved that plants with a milky sap will not unite for any length of time with plants the sap of which is watery. Thus the Acer platanoides—the only species of Acer which has milky sap—will not graft with the others; and, numerous as are the species of tree on which the mistletoe grows, it is never found on those which have a milky sap.

The modifications effected by the graft form a subject of great practical interest to the cultivator. The graft neither alters the species, nor the varieties, but it has some influence on their magnitude and habits, and on their flowers and fruit. The apple grafted on the paradise stock becomes a dwarf, and on the crab stock, or a seedling apple, a middle-sized tree. The size of the stock here seems to influence the size of the graft; but in the case of the mountain ash, which is said to grow more quickly when grafted on the common thorn, than when on its own roots, the stock is naturally a smaller plant than the tree grafted on it. The habit of the plant is sometimes altered by grafting. Thus Acer eriocarpum, when grafted on the common sycamore, attains in Europe double the height which it does when raised from seed. Cerasus canadensis, which in a state of nature is a rambling shrub, assumes the habit of an upright shrub when grafted on the common plum. Various species of Cytisus become greatly invigorated when grafted on the laburnum, as do the different varieties of Pyrus Aronia when grafted on the common thorn; the common lilac attains a large size when grafted on the ash; and Tecoma radicans, when grafted on the Catalpa, forms a round head with pendent branches, which are almost without tendrils. The hardiness of some species is also increased by grafting them, as in the case of the Eriobotrya japonica on the common thorn, and the Pistacia vera on the P. Terebinthus; the Quercus virens is rendered hardier by being grafted on the evergreen oak; but in other cases, the species are rendered more tender, as when the lilac is grafted on the phillyrea. Those species that are rendered hardier by grafting have probably tender roots, and by being placed on such as are hardier, they suffer only from the cold at top, instead of being injured by the effects of cold both at root and top; or if they grow more stunted, they will also be less susceptible of cold. The period of flowering is well known to be accelerated by grafting; and hence, both in the case of fruit-trees and ornamental trees and shrubs, the shoots of seedlings are frequently grafted on the extremities of the branches of old trees; in consequence of which they blossom several years sooner than if left on their own roots. The mountain-ash, and the different varieties of Pyrus Aria, produce double the number of fruits when grafted, to what they do on their own roots. The increase of the size of fruits, more especially of kernel fruits, is said by Thouin to be often from a fifth to a fourth part, but the number and size of seeds produced is diminished. The flavour as well as the size of fruit is said to be altered by the graft. Thus pears are said to become gritty on quince or thorn stocks; and the greengage plum to vary in flavour, according to the kind of plum-stock on which it is grafted; producing insipid fruit on some stocks, and fruit of the most delicious flavour on others; the cherry also, when grafted on the Cerasus Mahaleb, on the wild cherry, on the bird cherry, or on the common laurel, will produce fruit very different in flavour on each. The fertility or sterility of fruit-bearing trees is likewise greatly affected by grafting. The duration of trees is greatly altered in certain cases by the graft; the apple on the paradise stock is generally shorter lived than on the crab-stock; while the Pavia, grafted on the horse-chestnut, has its longevity increased. The period of leafing and flowering is also occasionally changed by the graft, the general effect of which is to produce a somewhat earlier vegetation; because the graft, by arresting the descent of the sap, produces in some measure the effect of ringing. So much for the influence of the stock upon the scion.

The influence of the scion on the stock is very limited, and as far as experience has hitherto gone, it consists only in communicating a change of colour; buds of the variegated common jasmine having been inserted in a species without variegated leaves, and having communicated its variegation to the entire plant, both above and below the graft. The common alstonia has likewise become variegated by A. Thompsoni being grafted upon it. Similar facts have been noticed in regard to other trees, such as the ash and the holly.

The uses of grafting in addition to those of all the other modes of increasing plants by extension are—

1. The propagation of varieties or species, which are not increased freely by any other mode; such as pears, apples, and other fruit-trees, oaks, and other forest-trees, and many species of shrubs.

2. The acceleration of the fructification of plants, more especially of trees and shrubs, which are naturally a number of years before they come into flower. For example, a seedling apple, if grafted the second year on the extremities of the branches of a full-grown apple-tree, or even on a stock or young tree of five or six years' growth, will show flowers the third or fourth year; whereas, had it remained on its own root, it would probably not have come into flower for ten or even twenty years. To obtain the same result with climbers that flower only at their extremities, the tips of the shoots of seedlings are taken off and grafted near the root; and when these have extended an inconvenient length, the tips are again taken off and regrafted; and after the operation has been performed several times, the plant at last produces flowers in a much shorter time than it otherwise would have done, and in a comparatively limited space.

3. To increase the vigour or the hardiness of delicate species or varieties, by grafting them on robust stocks, such as the Mexican oaks on the common oak, the China roses on the common dog-rose, the double yellow rose on the China or musk-rose, the Frontignan Muscat, Golden Champion, or other grapes, on the Syrian, Hamburg, Sweetwater, or Muscadine.

4. To dwarf or diminish the bulk of robust species, as in grafting the pear on the quince or medlar, the apple on the doucin or paradise stock, the cherry on the perfumed cherry, &c.

5. To increase the fruitfulness and precocity of trees. The effects produced upon the growth and produce of a tree by grafting, Knight observes, "are similar to those which occur when the descent of the sap is impeded by a ligature, or by the destruction of a circle of bark. The disposition in young trees to produce and nourish blossom-buds and fruit is increased by this apparent obstruction of the descending sap; and the fruit of such young trees ripens, I think, somewhat earlier than upon other young trees of the same age which grow upon stocks of their own species; but the growth and vigour of the tree, and its power to nourish a succession of heavy crops, are diminished, apparently by the stagnation in the branches and stock of a portion of that sap, which in a tree growing upon its own stem, or upon a stock of its own species, would descend to nourish and promote the extension of the roots."

6. To preserve varieties from degenerating, which are found to do so when propagated by cuttings or layers, such as certain kinds of roses and camellias.

7. By choosing a stock suitable to the soil, to produce trees in situations where they could not be grown if on their own roots; for example

the white beam-tree will grow in almost pure chalk, where no pear-tree would live; but grafted on the white beam-tree, the pear, on a chalky soil, will thrive and produce fruit.

8. To introduce several kinds on one kind. Thus one apple or pear-tree may be made to produce many different kinds of apple or pear; one camellia a great many varieties; one British oak all the American oaks; and even one dahlia several varieties of that flower.

9. To render diœcious trees monœcious—that is, when the tree consists of only one sex, as in Negundo, some maples, the poplar, willow, Maclura, Salisburia, &c., to graft on it the other sex, by which means fruit may be matured, a knowledge given of both forms of the species, both forms introduced into small arboretums, and in the case of fruit-trees and ornamental shrubs, such as the pistacia and aucuba, the necessity of planting males rendered no longer requisite.

10. The last use which we shall mention is that of renewing the heads of trees. For example, if a forest or fruit-tree is cut down to the ground, or headed in to the height of ten or twelve feet, and left to itself, it will develop a great number of latent buds, each of which will be contending for the mastery; and the strength of the tree, and the most favourable part of the season for growth, will be in some degree wasted, before a shoot is singled out to take the lead; but if a graft is inserted either in the collar or stool, or in the amputated head, it will give an immediate direction to the sap, the latent buds will not be excited, and the whole concentrated vigour of the tree will be exerted in the production of one grand shoot.

The different kinds of grafting may be classed thus:—grafting by detached scions or cuttings, which is the most common mode; grafting by attached scions, or, as it is commonly termed, by approach or inarching, in which the scion, when put on the stock, is not at all, or is only partially, separated from the parent plant; and grafting by buds, in which the scion consists of a plate of bark, containing one or more buds. The stock on which the scion is placed is, in every case, a rooted plant, generally standing in its place in the garden or nursery; but sometimes, in the case of grafting by detached scions, taken up and kept under cover while the operation is being performed. The two first modes of grafting are performed when the sap is rising in spring; and budding chiefly when it is descending in July and August. Under particular circumstances, however, and with care, grafting in every form may be performed at any period of the year.

The materials used in grafting are the common knife for heading down stocks; the grafting-knife and budding-knife (fig. 194); ligatures of different kinds for tying on the scions, and grafting clay or grafting wax for covering them. The ligatures in common use are strands of bast matting, or of other flexible bark; but sometimes coarse worsted thread is used, or occasionally shreds of coarse paper, or cotton cloth, covered with grafting wax. The dried stems of the common Sparganium ramosum, the Bur-reed, are now very generally used in France for grafting purposes—in fact, they are considered the best material for this purpose. When bast mat is used, it may be rendered waterproof, by passing it first through a solution of white soap, and next through one of alum; by which a neutral compound is formed insoluble in water. These prepared shreds, before being put on, are softened, by holding them over a small vessel of burning charcoal, which the

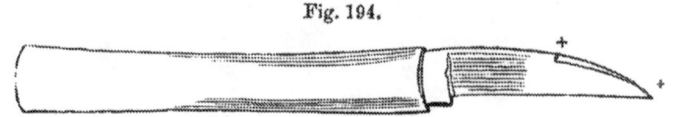

Fig. 194.

Grafting-knife, with the portion of the back of the blade from + to + ground to a cutting-edge, so as to make it serve also for a budding-knife.

grafter carries with him; and when grafting wax is employed instead of grafting clay, it is kept in an earthen pot, also placed over live charcoal, and the composition taken out and laid on with a brush. There are compositions, however, which become soft by the heat of the hand, or by breathing on them.

Grafting clay is prepared by mixing clay of any kind, or clayey loam, fresh horse or cow-dung, free from litter, in the proportion of three parts in bulk of clay to one of dung; and adding a small portion of hay, not, however, cut into too short lengths, its use being analogous to that of hair in plaster. The whole is thoroughly mixed together, and beaten up with water, so as to be of a suitable consistency and ductility for putting on with the hands, and for remaining on in wet weather, and also in dry weather without cracking. The beating is performed with a beetle or rammer, on a smooth hard floor under cover, turning over the mass, and adding water, and then beating afresh, till it becomes sufficiently softened and ductile. The process of beating must be repeated two or three times a day for several days; and it should be completed from three weeks to a month before the clay is wanted; care being taken to preserve it in a moist state, by covering it with mats or straw. The grafting clay used by the French gardeners is composed of equal parts of cow-dung, free from litter, and fresh loam, thoroughly beaten up and incorporated.

Grafting wax is very generally used on the Continent, instead of grafting clay. There are various recipes for composing it, but they may all be reduced to two kinds:—1. Those which, being melted, are laid on the graft in a fluid and hot state with a brush; and 2, those which are previously spread on pieces of coarse cotton, or brown paper, and afterwards wrapped round the graft in the same manner as strands of matting. The common composition for the first kind is one pound of cow-dung, half a pound of pitch, and half a pound of bees-wax, boiled up together, and heated when wanted in a small earthen pot. For the second kind, equal parts of turpentine, bees-wax, and rosin are melted together. Both these are now nearly superseded by the use of the composition called "Mastic l'Homme Lefort," which is fully described in Mr. Robinson's work on the "Parks, Pleasure-grounds, and Gardens of Paris," page 565. This substance can be bought in

England of Messrs. Hooper and Co., of Central Row, Covent Garden, London. It is of the consistence of common white lead, somewhat resembling half-melted gutta percha, and has an agreeable perfume. It is spread over the parts with the blade of a knife or a flat piece of wood, like butter on bread. While in a box, away from the air, it will keep pliable and moist for many years. It very soon hardens on the outside after being exposed thinly on the graft, and, as it were, hermetically seals up the point of junction, and thus prevents all access of air to the cuts. It is at the same time elastic, and easily removed when required. It has been largely used and highly approved by the late Mr. Thompson of Chiswick, and others. It is much more convenient than clay for tall trees, and is admirably adapted for vine-grafting. Clay and moss are objectionable, as the moist atmosphere of vineries causes the scion to root into them; the use of this mastic checks the formation of such roots, and ensures success. It is equally useful in healing wounds and bruises quickly. A sixpenny box will suffice for a hundred grafts, and the work can be finished without soiling the fingers. Its great advantage over all other mastics is, that it can be used cold, while they require heating.

Grafting by Detached Scions.

Grafting by detached scions is the most common mode, and it is that generally used for kernel-fruits, and the hardier forest-trees. It is performed in a great many different ways, as may easily be conceived, when we consider that the only essential condition is the close connexion of the alburnum of the scion with that of the stock. Upwards of forty modes of grafting by detached ligneous scions have been described by Thouin; but we shall confine ourselves to a few which we consider best adapted for general use. The time for grafting hardy trees and shrubs by detached scions in England is generally in spring, when the sap is rising; but the vine, if grafted before it is in leaf, suffers from bleeding. In Germany and North America, grafting is frequently performed in the winter time on roots or stocks which have been preserved in sheds or cellars; and the scion being put on and tied and clayed over, the grafted stock is kept till the spring, and then taken out and planted. Where scions are grafted on roots, this practice is sometimes followed in British nurseries, as in the case of pears and roses. Plants under glass may be grafted at almost any period; and herbaceous grafting, when and wherever performed, can, of course, only succeed when the shoots of the scion and stock are in a succulent or herbaceous state. In all the different modes of grafting by detached scions, success is rendered more certain, when the sap of the stock is in a more advanced and vigorous state than that of the scion; for which purpose the scions are generally taken off in autumn, and their vegetation retarded by keeping them in a shady place till spring; and the stock is cut over a little above the part where the scion is to be put on, a week or two before grafting takes place. The manual precautions necessary to success are: to fit the scion to the stock in such a manner that the union of their inner barks, and consequently of their alburnums, may be as close as possible; to cut the scion in such a manner that there shall be a bud or joint at its lower extremity, and the stock so that there shall be a bud or joint at its upper extremity; to maintain the scion and the stock in the proper position for growth, and in close contact, by a bandage of narrow shreds of matting or cloth; to exclude the air by a covering of clay or grafting-wax; and, in addition, when the graft is close to the surface of the ground, by earthing it up with soil; and when the scion is making its shoot, to tie it to a prop if necessary; to remove the clay or grafting-wax, when the scion has made several leaves; to remove the bandage by degrees, when it appears to be no longer necessary; and to cut off the heel on the upper part of the stock at the proper time, so as that it may, if possible, be healed over the same season. The modes of grafting detached scions adapted for general use, are: splice or whip-grafting, cleft-grafting, rind-grafting, saddle-grafting, side-grafting, root-grafting, and herbaceous-grafting.

Splice-grafting, tongue-grafting, or whip-grafting, is the mode most commonly adopted in all gardens where the stocks are not much larger in diameter than the scion; and it has the advantage of being more expeditiously performed than any of the other modes described in this work. The stock is first cut over at the height at which the scion is to be put on (fig. 195, *a*), and a thin slice of the bark and wood is

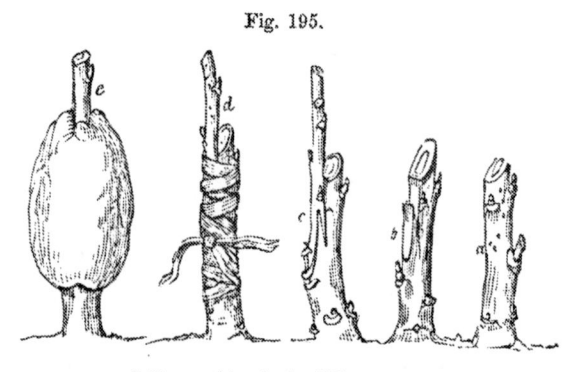

Fig. 195.

Splice-grafting in its different stages.

then cut off with a very sharp knife, so as to leave a perfectly smooth, even surface (*b*); the scion, which should at least have three buds, and need never have more than five (the top one for a leading shoot, the next two for side shoots, in the case of fruit-trees, and the lower to aid in uniting the scion to the stock), is next cut, so as to fit the prepared part of the stock as accurately as possible, at least on one side; then a slit or tongue, as it is technically termed, is made on the scion, and a corresponding one in the stock (*c*). All being thus prepared, the scion is applied to the stock, inserting the tongue of the one into the slit of the other (*c*); then the scion is tied on with matting (*d*); and, lastly, it is clayed over (*e*); and sometimes, in addition, it is earthed up, or covered with moss, to serve as a non-conductor of heat and moisture. In earthing up the graft, the loose surface soil should be used at the grafting season, as being drier and warmer than that which is less under the immediate influence of the sun. When the scion is placed on the stock with the right hand, the ribbon of bast by which it is tied, is brought round the graft from right to left; but when the scion is put on by the left hand, the bast is brought round from left to right; the object in both cases being to make sure of the exact coincidence of the inner bark of one side of the scion, with the inner bark of one side of the stock. The ball of clay which envelopes the graft should be about an inch thick on every side, and should extend for nearly an inch below the bottom of the graft, to more than an inch over the top of the stock, compressing and finishing the whole into a kind of oval or egg-shape form, closing it in every part, so as completely to exclude air, light, wet, or cold. The ball of clay will not be so apt to drop off, if the matting over which it is placed is rendered a fitting nucleus for solid clay, by previously smearing it over in a comparatively liquid state. This envelope of clay, with the earthing up, preserves the graft in a uniform temperature, and prevents the rising of the sap from being checked by cold days or nights; and, therefore, earthing up ought always to be adopted in the case of grafts in the open garden which are difficult to succeed. The next best resource is a ball of moss over the clay, or of some dry material, such as hay, tied on from within an inch of the top of the scion to the surface of the ground, so as to act as thatch in excluding rain and wind, and retaining heat and moisture. When the scion and the stock are both of the same thickness, or when they are of kinds that do not unite freely, the tongue is sometimes omitted; but in that case, more care is required in tying. In this, and also in other cases, the stock is not shortened down to the graft; but an inch or two with a bud at its upper extremity is left to ensure the rising of the sap to the scion, as in fig. 193; and after the latter is firmly established, the part of the stock left is cut off close above the scion, as shown in fig. 196. When the stock is not headed down till the scion is about to be put on, it is essentially necessary to leave it longer than usual, in order to give vent to the rising sap, which might otherwise exude above the scion, and occasion its decay. In the case of shoots having much pith, such as those of the rose, the scion is often put on the stock without being tongued into it, as in fig. 197, in which

Fig. 196.

The scion with its young shoots on, and the heel of the stock cut off.

the scion in the one case, *a*, is without a bud on its lower extremity, and is therefore less likely to succeed than *b*, which has a bud in that position. Sometimes a notch is cut on the scion immediately under a bud, and this notch is made to rest on the top of the stock, as in fig. 198; and in such cases, when the scion and the stock are about the same diameter, the summit of the latter is certain of being healed over the first season.

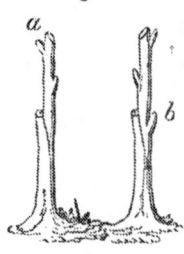

Splice-grafting the Peach. — In splice-grafting the shoots of peaches, nectarines, and apricots, and other tender shoots with large pith, it is found of advantage to have a quarter of an inch of two-year old wood at the lower extremity of the scion (fig. 199, *a*), and to have the stock cut with a dovetail notch (*b*). In the case of the fruit-trees mentioned, the buds of the scion on the back and front are removed, leaving two on each side, and a leader; and when these have grown six or eight inches, their extremities are pinched off with the finger and thumb; by which means each shoot will throw out two others, and thus produce in autumn a finely-shaped tree, with ten branches. Such trees will bear two or three fruits the second year from the graft.—'Gard. Mag.,' vol. iii. p. 150.

Cleft grafting, fig. 200, requires less care than splice-grafting, and seems to have been the mode in most general use in former ages. It is now chiefly adopted when the scion is a good deal larger than the stock, and more especially when grafting stocks of considerable height, or heading down old trees. The head of the stock being cut over horizontally with a saw (fig. 201), a cleft is made in it, from two to three inches in length, with a stout knife or chisel, or with the splitting-knife (fig. 202). The cleft being kept open by the knife or chisel, or the pick-end of the splitting-knife, one or two scions are inserted, according to the diameter of the stock; the scions being cut into long wedge shapes, in a double sense, and inserted into the slit prepared for them, when the knife or chisel being withdrawn, the stock closes firmly upon the scions, and holds them fast. The graft is then tied and clayed in the usual manner, and the whole is frequently

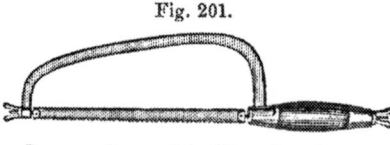

GRAFTING BY DETACHED SCIONS.

covered with moss. When the stock is an inch or more in diameter, three or more scions are frequently put on at equal distances from

Fig. 202.

Splitting-knife and opening-pick for using in cleft-grafting.

each other round the circumference, and this is called crown-grafting. Cleft-grafting with one scion is in general not a good mode, because if the split has been made right through the stock, it is in danger of being injured by the weather before it is covered with wood by the scion. If the cleft is made only on one side of the stock, the evil is mitigated; but there still remains the tendency of the scion in its growth to protrude the wood all on one side. In crown-grafting headed-down old trees, the scion is generally chosen of two-years old wood, and it is sometimes inserted between the inner bark and the alburnum, as in what is called rind-grafting (fig. 203). In rind-grafting, great care must be taken to open the bark of the stock without bruising it, which is done by the spatula-end of the grafting-knife. The scion is prepared without a tongue, and inserted so that its wood may be in contact with the alburnum of the stock. As in this case both edges of the alburnum of the scion come in close contact with the alburnum of the stock, the chances of success, other circumstances being alike, are increased. In cases of this kind also, a longitudinal notch is sometimes cut out, instead of a slit, and the scion cut to correspond. Sometimes also the scion is prepared with a shoulder, more especially when it consists of two-years old wood, and this mode is called shoulder-grafting.

Fig. 203.

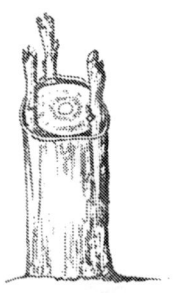

Rind-grafting.

Fig. 204.

Cleft-grafting the vine is shown in fig. 204, in which *a* is a bud on the scion, and *b* one on the stock, both in the most favourable positions for success. The graft is tied and clayed in the usual manner, excepting that only a small hole is left in the clay opposite the eye of the scion, for its development. In grafting the vine in this manner, when the bud, *b*, on the stock is developed, it is allowed to grow for ten or fourteen days, after which it is cut off; leaving only one bud and one leaf near its base to draw up sap to the scion till it be fairly united to the stock. The time of grafting is when the stock is about to break into leaf, or when it has made shoots

Cleft-grafting the vine.

with four or five leaves. By this time the sap has begun to flow freely, so that there is no danger of the stock suffering from bleeding; though if vines are in good health and their wood thoroughly ripened, all the bleeding that usually takes place does little injury. The best mode of grafting the vine, however, is by inserting a single bud with a piece of wood an inch or thereabouts in length attached to it. Cut half the under portion of the wood away, and fit it into the stock exactly at each end, and closely to one or both sides of the stock. Leave an eye or two on the stock beyond the graft until the eyes break, when they may be cut off, and the bud will form a strong healthy shoot. Mr. Stevens, at Trentham, also buds growing vines with the current year's wood, as roses are budded. In Flanders the rose is frequently grafted in the cleft manner, the scion, if possible, being of the same diameter as the stock (fig. 205, *a*); or the cleft in the stock is made so near one side of the cross section that the bark of the wedge part of the scion may fit the bark of the stock on both sides (*b*).

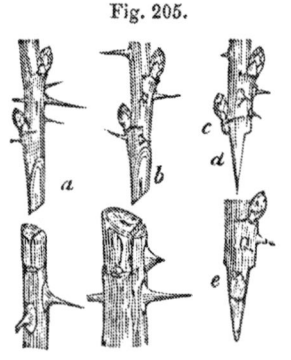

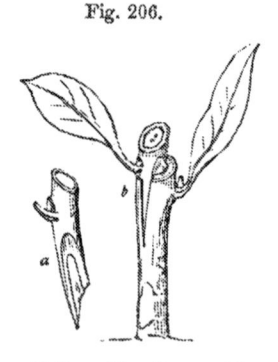

Fig. 205.   Fig. 206.

Cleft-grafting the rose.   Cleft-grafting the camellia.

Sometimes a shoulder is made to the scion (*c*), in order that it may rest with greater firmness on the stock; and the wedge part of the scion, instead of being part of an internode, as at *d*, is, when practicable, selected with a bud on it, as at *e*. The camellia is sometimes cleft-grafted, with only a single bud on the scion (fig. 206, *a*), which is inserted in the stock, *b*, just when the sap is beginning to rise, and being tied, it is found to take freely without claying. Epiphyllum truncatum is frequently cleft-grafted on Pereskia aculeata, as shown in fig. 207.

Fig. 207.

Epiphyllum truncatum grafted on Pereskia aculeata.

Saddle-grafting (fig. 208) is only applicable to stocks of moderate size, but it is well adapted for standard fruit-trees. The top of the stock is cut into a wedge shape, and the scion is split up the middle, and placed astride on it, the inner barks being made to join on one side of the stock as in cleft-grafting. The tying, claying, &c.,

GRAFTING BY DETACHED SCIONS.

are of course performed in the usual manner. Fig. 209 represents a mode of grafting practised in Herefordshire after the usual season for grafting is over, and when the bark may be easily separated from the stock. The scion, which must be smaller than the stock, is split up between two and three inches from its lower end, so as to have one side stronger than the other. This strong side is then prepared and introduced between the bark and wood, as in rind-grafting; while the thinner division is fitted to the opposite side of the stock. Mr. Knight, who describes this mode of grafting, says, that grafts of the apple and pear rarely ever fail by it, and that it may be practised with success either in spring, or with young wood in July, as soon as that has become moderately firm and mature. Saddle-grafting, in whichever way performed, has the advantage over all others of presenting the largest surface of the alburnum of the scion to receive the ascending sap of the stock, and at the same time without causing it to deviate from its natural course, which it is made to do to a certain extent, when the scion is put on one side of the stock only, as in splice-grafting and side-grafting.

Fig. 208. Saddle-grafting.

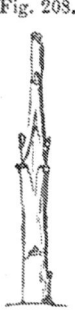

Fig. 209. Herefordshire saddle-grafting.

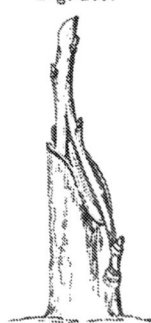

Side-grafting is nothing more than splice-grafting performed on the side of a stock, the head of which is not cut off. It is sometimes practised on fruit-trees to supply a branch in a vacancy, or for the sake of having different kinds of fruits upon the same tree; but it is better for the latter purpose to graft on the side branches, because, in consequence of the flow of the sap not being interrupted by being headed down, the success of this kind of grafting is more uncertain than almost any other mode. In grafting the lateral branches of fruit-trees, it is always desirable, in order to ensure success, to have corresponding buds in the scion and the stock, as in fig. 210. What the French call veneer-grafting, fig. 211, is a variety of side-grafting, in which the scion, e, is prepared to fit into the stock, f, which has a notch at the lower extremity of the incision, for the scion to rest on. This mode of grafting is practised with orange-trees, camellias, &c., in pots; and after the operation is completed, the grafted plant is plunged in heat, and closely covered with a bell-glass. Fig. 212 is a peculiar mode of side-grafting the vine, which is performed in November, when both scion and stock are in a dormant state, and in which the scions, a and b, being prepared, as in the figure, and inserted and bandaged

Fig. 210. Grafting the lateral branches of fruit-trees.

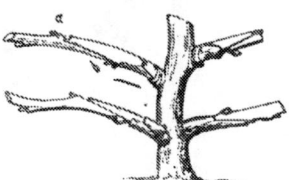

256 GRAFTING BY DETACHED SCIONS.

Fig. 211.

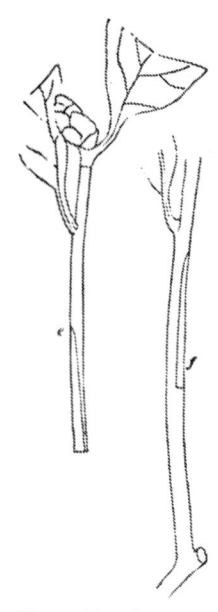

Side-grafting the orange.

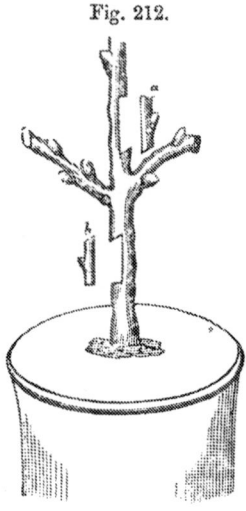

Fig. 212.

Side-grafting the vine.

instead of being clayed, are surrounded with a mass of mould. About a month afterwards the plant is plunged in a mild heat, and in about three weeks the buds from the scions will be seen emerging from the mould with which they are surrounded. This mode of grafting may also be adopted after the vine has started into full growth, and such grafts will take readily throughout the summer. Wedge-grafting (fig. 213), which is a modification of side-grafting, has been very successful in grafting Cedrus Deodara, on the cedar of Lebanon. The scions, c, are chosen of the preceding year's wood, from three to five inches in length, and they are inserted in wood either one or two years old, as may be convenient, and as near the top of the stock as is practicable, in order to gain height. The slit in the stock is cut through the pith, and from 1 to $1\frac{1}{2}$ inches in length; and the graft being tied, is coated over with grafting-wax, as being lighter than clay, and not so liable to bend down the shoot. Many cedars of Lebanon at Elvaston Castle have had the extremities of their shoots grafted in this manner with Cedrus Deodara, by Mr. Barron, the inventor of this mode. (See 'Gard. Mag.,' vol. xiv. p. 80.)

Grafting the mistletoe has been successfully performed in the wedge manner by Mr. Pit, farmer and grafter, near Hatfield, in Herefordshire. To be attended with success, there must be a joint let into the soft wood of the stock, or a scion taken off with a heel, and the heel of the preceding year's wood inserted.

Root-grafting is merely the union of a scion to the root, instead of to a stem. It is sometimes practised in nurseries, by grafting the apple and the pear on the roots of thorns, tree peonies on herbaceous peonies (see herbaceous grafting), stove passion-flowers, Japan clematises, &c., on the common sorts, and with various other stove and greenhouse plants,

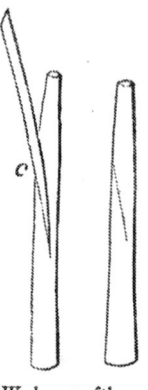

Fig. 213.

Wedge-grafting.

especially climbers. The greatest care is requisite to prevent any particles of soil from getting in between the scion and the stock, for which purpose the upper part of the latter is sometimes washed with water before the operation is performed. The roots of thorns, pears, and crabs, as already observed, are frequently grafted indoors, and taken out and planted so deep, that only the upper part of the scion appears above ground. Another mode where a thorn hedge is taken up, or a row of seedling pear or crab stocks is transplanted, and a portion of the roots left in the soil, is to graft on them where they stand, and afterwards to earth-up the graft—a mode which would doubtless be very successful.

Herbaceous-grafting is applicable either to the solid parts of herbaceous plants, or to the branches of ligneous plants when they are in a herbaceous state. By this method the melon has been grafted on the cucumber, the tomato on the common potato, the dwarf French bean on the scarlet-runner, potatoes on each other, the cauliflower on the broccoli and the borecole; and on the tender growing shoots of various forest trees, and of azaleas and other shrubs, hardy and tender, allied species have been successfully grafted. This mode has been extensively employed for many years past in the forest of Fontainebleau, in grafting the Pinus Laricio on the P. sylvestris; and many hundreds of plants of pines and firs of different kinds, and of Indian azaleas, have been so propagated at Fromont. Many trees were thus grafted by Baron Tschoudy in the botanic garden at Metz, and on his own estate in the neighbourhood; and these and the pines at Fontainebleau prove this mode of grafting to be particularly applicable to the Abietinæ.

Grafting the Pine and Fir Tribe.—The proper time for grafting pines is when the young shoots have made about three-quarters of their length, and are still so herbaceous as to break like a shoot of asparagus. The shoot of the stock is then broken off about two inches under its terminating bud, the leaves are cut or clipped off from twenty to twenty-four lines down from the extremity, leaving, however, two pairs of leaves opposite and close to the section of fracture, which leaves are of great importance to the success of the graft. The shoot is then split with a very thin knife between the two pairs of leaves (fig. 214), and to the depth of two inches; the scion is then prepared (*b*), the lower part being stripped of its leaves to the length of two inches is cut and inserted in the usual manner of cleft-grafting. They may also be grafted in the lateral manner (*c*). The graft is tied

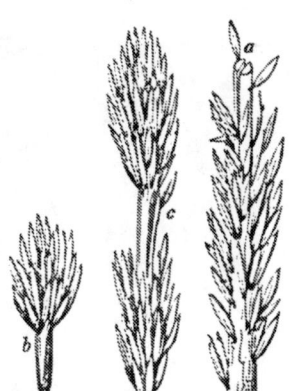

Fig. 214.

Herbaceous-grafting the pine and fir tribe.

with a coarse woollen thread, and a cap of paper is put over the whole to protect it from the sun and rain. At the end of fifteen days this cap is removed, and the ligature at the end of a month; at that time also the two pairs of leaves (*a*) which have served as nurses are removed. The scions of those sorts of pines which make two growths in a season, or, as the technical phrase is, have a second sap, produce a shoot of five or six inches the first year; but those of only one sap, as the Corsican pine, Weymouth pine, &c., merely ripen the wood grown before grafting, and form a strong terminating bud, which in the following year produces a shoot of fifteen inches or two feet.

We have described this mode of grafting at greater length than we otherwise should have done, because it is little known in this country, and because we think it ought to be adopted in a great many cases for the multiplication of plants now propagated with difficulty by cuttings, or reared, after being so propagated, so slowly as to exhaust the patience of the propagator or amateur. For example, though the pine and fir tribe may all be increased by cuttings, yet these cuttings grow very slowly, and though they ultimately become good plants,—many kinds as much so as if they had been raised from seeds—yet if the kinds to be propagated had been grafted on the points of the budding shoots of pines or firs of five or six years' growth, they would have grown with incomparably greater rapidity and vigour, and would have become trees of twenty feet in length, before cuttings had attained the height of three feet.

Fig. 215.

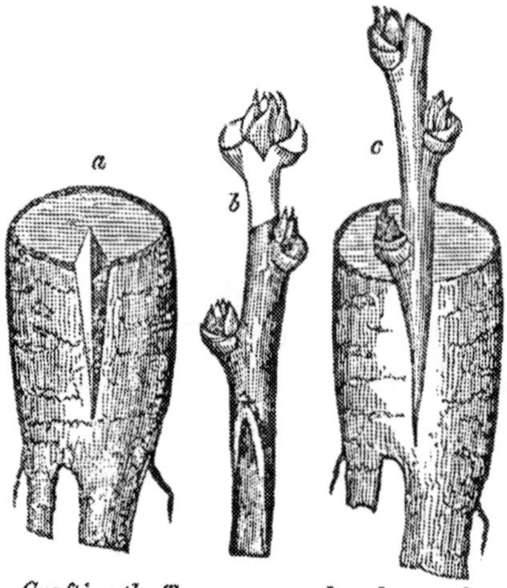

Grafting the Tree-peony on the tubers of the herbaceous peony.

Grafting the Tree-peony on the roots of the herbaceous species is performed from the middle of July to the middle of August, and will be easily understood from fig. 215, in which *a* represents a triangular space in the tuber or stock; *b*, the scion, the lower end of which is cut so as to fit the cavity in the stock; and *c*, the scion fitted to the stock. It is not necessary that there should be more than one bud on the scion, for which reason the upper part of *b* might have been inserted in *a*, in the cleft manner. The graft being tied with bast, and covered with grafting-wax, the whole is inserted into a bed of tan, leaving only about half an inch of the scion above the surface. The tubers throw out roots by the end of September or the beginning of October, and are then taken up and potted, and placed in a cold frame, where they remain through the winter.

GRAFTING BY DETACHED SCIONS.   259

The following kinds of herbaceous-grafting are in use in France and Belgium:—

Grafting on fleshy roots, as in the dahlia and peony, may be performed either with a growing shoot (fig. 216), or with a dormant eye, as in fig. 217. The former mode requires no explanation; by the latter, on the neck of a barren tubercle a small hole is made, in which the bud is inserted, but in such a manner that its base shall be perfectly on a level with the surface of the tubercle, and the edges are covered with grafting-wax. The tubercle is then planted in a pot, care being taken not to cover the bud, and the pot is plunged in heat under glass. When the plant has taken, it may, if hardy, be turned out into the open border. This mode of grafting, applied to Dahlia imperialis, dwarfs the rampant habit of that plant and causes it to flower more freely.

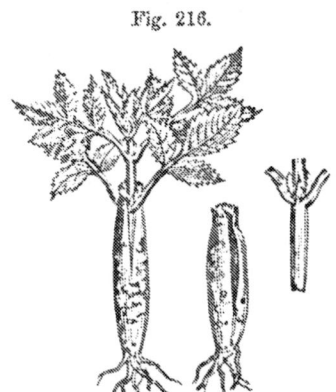

Fig. 216.

Cleft-grafting the dahlia on its own tubers.

Fig. 217.

Peg-grafting the dahlia on its own tubers.

Herbaceous wedge-grafting (fig. 218) is effected by paring the scion into a wedge shape, and inserting it into a corresponding slip in the stock. It succeeds well both with trees and herbaceous plants, more especially when the plants are in pots so that they may be plunged in heat and covered with a bell-glass.

Herbaceous-grafting for shoots with Opposite Leaves (fig. 219).—In the middle of the shoots, between two opposite eyes, an angular and longitudinal incision is made, and a small portion of the stem cut out from one side to the other. The scion is cut to fit this opening, and it is inserted as in the figure, and bandaged in the usual manner.

Fig. 218.

Herbaceous wedge-grafting.

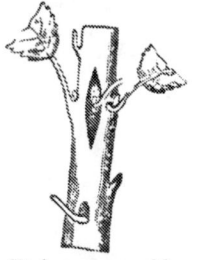

Fig. 219.

Herbaceous-grafting with stems having opposite leaves.

Herbaceous-grafting — Annual or Perennial Plants (fig. 220).—The period chosen for this mode of grafting is that of the greatest vigour of the plant, that is, some days before its going into flower. The stem of the stock is cut through above a leaf, as near as possible to its petiole, and a slit downwards is made in the section. A shoot is then taken off

s 2

near the root of the plant to be increased, the end of which is cut into a wedge shape, and is inserted in the slit made in the stock, taking great care of the leaf on the latter; for it is that which must nourish the scion until it has taken thoroughly, by keeping up the circulation of the sap. A bandage is applied at the junction, covered with grafting wax as before. When the graft has taken, which is ascertained by its growth, the ligature is removed, and also the old leaf, and the shoots from the stock below the graft.

Fig. 220.

Herbaceous grafting annuals or perennials.

Grafting Herbaceous Shoots of Succulents (fig. 221).—Take a young shoot, and cutting its base to a point or wedge, insert it in a hole or slit made in the stem or leaf of the stock.

Grafting the Melon (fig. 222).—On the stem of a cucumber, or any other plant of the family of Cucurbitaceæ, but having some analogy with the melon, choose a vigorous part of a shoot having a well-developed leaf. In the axil of this leaf an oblique cut is made, of half its thickness. The point of a melon shoot, so far developed as to have its fruit quite formed, is then cut off, and pointed at its end, two inches below the fruit. It is inserted in the cleft made in the stock, always taking care to spare the leaf until the scion has taken. The remaining part of the operation is performed in the usual manner, with ligatures and grafting wax. This mode of grafting succeeds pretty well; but it has not hitherto been applied to any useful end.

Fig. 221.

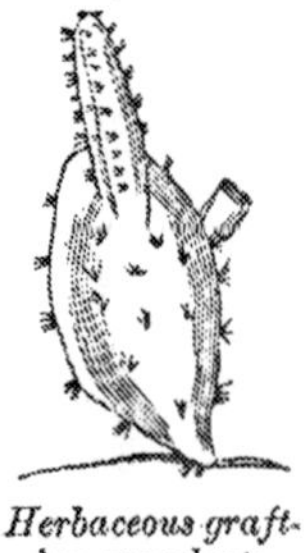

Herbaceous grafting succulents.

Fig. 222.

Herbaceous-grafting the melon.

The greffe étouffée, or stifled graft, is so named, not from any particular mode of performing the operation, but because the plants so grafted are closely covered with a bell-glass, so as completely to exclude the surrounding air, and placed in moist heat, while the union between the scion and the stock is going on. It is only applicable to plants of small size, and in pots; but for these, whether hardy, as in the case of pines, firs, and oaks, or tender, as in the case of orange-trees, camellias, rhododendrons, &c., it is the most expeditious of all modes of grafting. The operation is very commonly performed in the cleft mode, the stock being in a growing state with the leaves on, and being cut over close to a leaf which has a bud in its axil, and so as to slope away from it. Great care is taken not to injure the leaf and bud on the stock, as on these, in a great measure, depends the success of the operation. The stock is split to a depth equal to two-thirds of its thickness, and the scion prepared is inserted, made fast with a shred of mat, or with worsted threads; and the upper part of the stock, not covered by the scion, is coated over with grafting wax. The pot containing the plant is then plunged in heat, and closely covered with a bell-glass, which must be taken off and wiped every second day, and left off an hour or two, if at any time the plants appear too moist. Side-grafting and inarching are also employed by those who practise the greffe étouffée, more especially in autumn. After the scion is inserted and bound close to the stock, the pot containing the stock is half buried in a horizontal position, on a bed of dry tan, or dry moss; and the grafted part covered with a bell-glass, stuffed round the bottom with tan or moss, so as to prevent any change of air taking place within the bell-glass. The graft is kept thus closely covered for from two to four weeks, according to the season, when the scion will, in general, be found perfectly united to the stock. Air is now admitted by degrees; and after a week or two more, the glass is removed altogether, the pot set upright in a gentle heat, and the upper part of the stock neatly cut off close above the scion. There is yet another species of grafting, which may be denominated bud-grafting, and is the best for most evergreens, such as daphnes, &c. When the stock has begun to grow vigorously, cut the head off, and, making an incision in the bark a few inches down, open it on both sides, in the same way as for budding; prepare the graft without a tongue, and insert the lower part as you would a bud, leaving the herbaceous-growing top green above. Soft succulent evergreens, in which the bark opens freely, will do better in this way than any other.

Grafting by Approach or Inarching.

Grafting by approach differs from grafting by detached scions in the scion or shoot not being separated from the plant to which it belongs, and by which it is nourished, till a union takes place. For this purpose it is necessary that the two plants which are to form the scion and the stock be planted, or, if in pots, placed adjoining each other, so that a branch of the one may be easily brought into close contact with the stem, or with a branch of the other. A disk of bark and alburnum is then removed from each at the intended point of union, and the parts being properly fitted to each other, so that the inner barks of the respective subjects may coincide, as in the case of grafting by detached scions, they are bandaged and covered with clay or grafting wax. This being done, in a short time, in consequence of the development of cambium, the alburnum of the scion and that of the stock become united, and the scion may be cut off below the point where it is united with the stock, leaving the former to be nourished only by the latter. This kind of grafting is the only sort that takes place in nature, from the crossing of the branches of trees (more especially where they are crowded together in hedges), when, by the friction between them, the alburnum is laid bare, and if a season of repose takes place when the sap is rising, the parts adhere and grow together. This is not uncommon in beech-trees, and in beech and hornbeam hedges; and it is even occasionally imitated by art in young hedges of these, and of several other kinds of trees or shrubs, in order to make a very strong hedge. The principal use, however, of grafting by approach is to propagate plants of rarity and value, which it is found difficult to increase by any other means, and of which it is not desirable to risk the loss of any part by attempting an increase by means of detached scions or cuttings. It is also much employed in France for furnishing bare portions of fruit trees. Inarching may be performed with various organs of plants; but in horticulture it is chiefly confined to stems, branches, and roots; and all the different forms may be included under side-inarching, terminal inarching, and inarching by partially-nourished scions. The season for performing the operation is principally in spring, when the sap is rising; but it may be effected at every season, except during severe frost or extreme heat. No other instrument is necessary than the grafting-knife, and the graft may often be secured from the sun and air by bandages, without the aid of moss, clay, or grafting wax.

Fig. 223.

A scion and stock prepared for inarching.

Side-inarching may be effected either with or without tongueing. In the latter case, the incisions in the scion and the stock are of the simplest description (as shown in fig. 223 and in fig. 224 *a*), and the parts being bound together with matting, as at *b*, and covered by clay or moss, are left to form a union. Side-inarching with a tongue is represented in fig. 225, in which *a* is the stock prepared

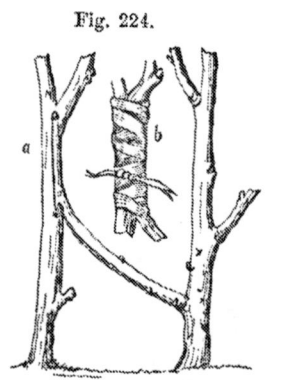

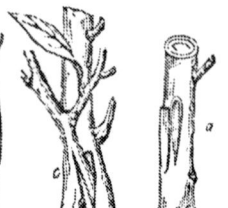

Fig. 224.

Fig. 225.

The scion inarched to the stock and bandaged with matting.

Inarching with the scion and stock tongued and united, but not bandaged.

with an under tongue, and *b* the scion, with an upper tongue for inserting into *a*; *c* is the scion and the stock united. One of the purposes, though perhaps more curious than useful, to which De Candolle and Thouin say that this kind of grafting may be applied, is to increase the number of roots to a tree. Thus, if a tree be planted in the centre of a circle, and three or more of the same, or of allied species, be planted in the circumference, so that their tops may be at a suitable distance for inarching to the centre tree; then, after the union has been effected, if the parts of the side trees be cut off above the graft, all the sap sent up by their roots will go to the nourishment of the tree in the centre. When the root of one tree is to be joined to another, with a view of strengthening the latter, this mode of inarching is the one generally adopted.

Terminal inarching consists in heading down the stock, and joining the scion to it, either in the manner of splice-grafting, cleft-grafting, or by saddle-grafting, as exemplified in figs. 226 to 228. The stock

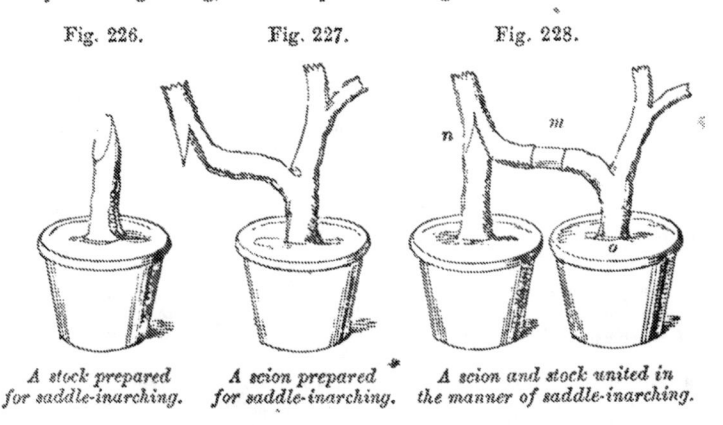

Fig. 226.   Fig. 227.   Fig. 228.

A stock prepared for saddle-inarching.   *A scion prepared for saddle-inarching.*   *A scion and stock united in the manner of saddle-inarching.*

is cut off in the form of a wedge, as in fig. 226, and the scion is cut upwards, half way through, for a sufficient length, as in fig. 227; then the scion is placed upon the stock as in fig. 228, and bound on with bast and clay as usual, a ring of bark being taken off between the graft and the root, as in fig. 228, m, which causes the returning sap to flow through the graft into the stock, n, instead of into its own root, o. This mode is recommended for grafting whenever the stock and the scion are of the same size, or very nearly so; but when the stock is twice the size of the scion, the following modification of it is preferable:—the top of the stock is cut off slanting from one side only, as in fig. 229; then a long tongue is made to the scion, about one-third of its thickness, as in fig. 230, and as much of the bark and wood is cut from the back and front of the stock as will correspond with the width of the tongue on the scion; when the stock is ready to receive the graft,

Fig. 229.

A stock cut over for inarching when it is twice the size of the scion.

it will appear like fig. 231, q; there is also a piece cut off the bark of the stock at r, fig. 231, but it is not seen in the figure. Then the scion is placed across the middle of the stock, as in fig. 232, and bound

264   GRAFTING BY APPROACH OR INARCHING.

with bast-mat and clay as usual; after which a ring of bark is taken off at *s*, in fig. 232, in the same manner as directed for fig. 228.

Inarching with partially-nourished scions appears, at first sight, to belong to the preceding section, but it is placed here because the scion has an auxiliary support from moist soil or water, till it adheres to the stock. This mode is applicable either to the side or crown manner of inarching, and it only differs from them in the inferior end of the scion being inserted in a vessel of water, as in figs. 233 and 234, or in a pot of moist earth. The vessel of water must be removed from time to time, and the base of the submerged scion renewed by paring a slice off its extremity, and replacing it again in the water. If the stock be headed down, a bud must be left on it at its upper extremity, in order to attract the sap to the graft. The finer sorts of camellias are sometimes grafted in this manner, as indicated in fig. 234. In

Fig. 230.

A scion prepared for inarching when it is only half the size of the stock.

Fig. 231.

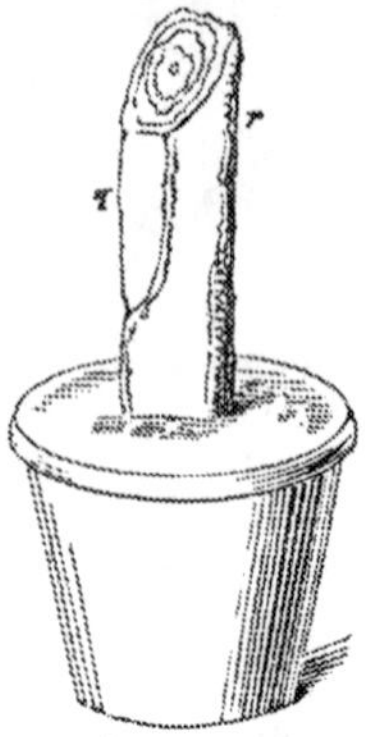

A stock prepared for inarching when it is twice the size of the scion.

Fig. 232.

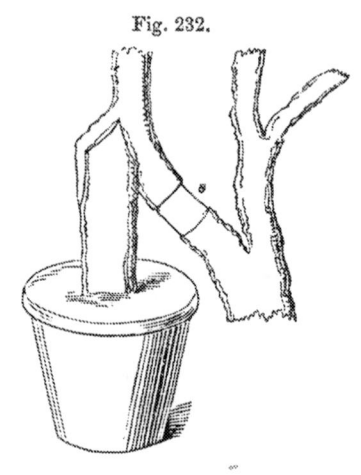

A large stock and a small scion united by inarching.

Fig. 233.

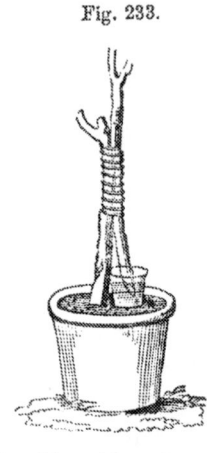

Inarching with a scion nourished by its lower extremity being inserted in a vessel of water.

some cases, when it is desired to prevent evaporation, instead of claying or mossing, the graft is covered with a piece of paper tied on below and above the parts operated on, so as completely to enclose them. Some persons, instead of a vessel of water, insert the lower part of the scion into a pot of soil kept moist, or into a potato or a turnip.

Fig. 234.

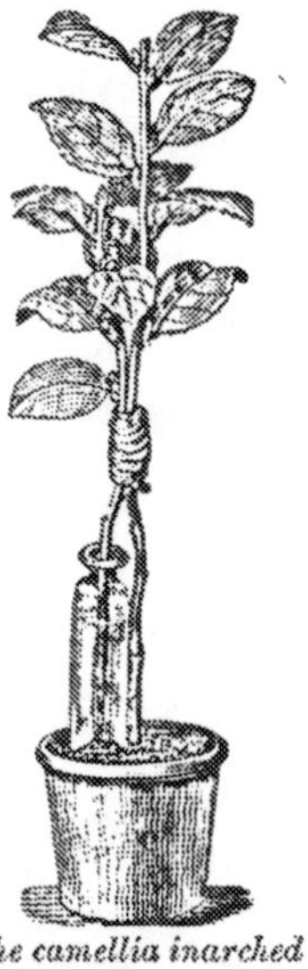

A great many different kinds of inarching have been described by M. Thouin, which, if not useful, are at least curious: such, for example, as uniting a number of different stems of different species of the same genus, and afterwards allowing only one shoot to expend all the sap drawn up by the different stocks; the object being to ascertain whether the different saps supplied would make any difference in that of the scion, which, however, was found not to be the case.

Budding or Grafting by Detached Buds.

Budding consists in transferring a portion of bark containing one or more buds, and forming the scion, to the wood of another plant forming the stock, a portion of the bark of the stock being raised up or taken off to receive the scion. The buds of trees are originated in the young shoots in the axils of the leaves; and when the bud begins to grow, its connexion with the medullary sheath ceases; or, at all events, the bud if detached and properly placed on the alburnum of another plant, will become vitally united to it.

The camellia inarched with a scion partially nourished by a phial of water.

On these facts the art of budding is founded. This mode of grafting is chiefly applicable to woody plants, and the scion may, in general, be secured to the stock, and sufficiently protected there, by bandages of bast-mat or thread, without the use of grafting clay or wax. The union between the scion and the stock takes place, in the first instance, in consequence of the exudation of organizable matter from the soft wood of the stock; and it is rendered permanent by the returning sap from the leaves of the stock, or from those of the shoot made by the bud. All the different modes of budding may be reduced to two :—shield-budding, in which the scion is a piece of bark commonly in the shape of a shield, containing a single bud; and flute-budding, in which the scion consists of a ring or tube of bark containing one or several buds. In both modes the bark of one year is chosen in preference; and the operation is more certain of success when the bud of the scion is placed exactly over the situation of a bud on the stock. The shield may, however, be placed on the internodes, or a piece of bark without buds may be put on as a scion, and yet a vital union may take place between the parts, because the cambium is diffused everywhere under the bark, and it is by it, during the process of organization, that the layer of wood of one year in a growing state is joined to that of the year before. A disk or shield from which the visible bud has been removed will also succeed, and the latent buds may remain dormant for years, and yet be developed afterwards. In the year 1824 several buds were placed on the branches of a fig-tree, and, from some accidental cause, though the shield adhered in every case, yet most of the visible buds were destroyed, and only one of the latent buds was developed. Twelve years afterwards, when the fig-tree received a severe check, in the winter of 1837-8, the development of a second latent bud from one of the shields took place. When the bud is placed on the stock, its point is almost always made to turn upwards, as being its natural position; but in budding the olive, and other trees which are liable to gum, the bud is made to point downwards, and the success is said to be greater than when the common mode is adopted. There are two seasons at which budding is practised, viz.:—when the sap rises in spring, when the bud inserted is developed immediately, in the same manner as in detached ligneous scions; and in the middle of summer, when the sap is descending, the operation being then performed with a bud formed during the same summer, which often forms a shoot at once and sometimes remains dormant till the following spring. The French often use the former method for inserting fruit-buds where they are scarce, and so skilfully is the operation performed, that the fruit generally comes to perfection. In budding, the stock is not generally cut over in the first instance, as in grafting by detached ligneous scions; but a tight ligature is frequently placed above the graft, with the intention of forcing a part of the ascending sap to nourish the graft.

The uses of budding, in addition to those of the other modes of grafting, are, to propagate some kinds with which the other modes of grafting are not so successful, as, for example, the rose, peach, plum, and all stone fruits. To perform the operation of grafting with greater rapidity than with detached scions, or inarching, as in the case of most fruit-trees and roses; to unite early vegetating trees with late vegetating ones, as the apricot with the plum, they being both in the same state of vegetation during the budding season; to graft without the risk of injuring the stock in case of want of success, as in side-budding, and in flute-budding without heading down; to introduce a number of species or varieties on the same stem, which could not be done by any other mode of grafting without disfiguring the stock, in the event of the want of success; to prove the blossoms or fruits of any tree, in which case blossom-buds are chosen instead of leaf-buds; and, finally, as the easiest mode of distributing a great many kinds on the branches of a tree, as in the case of roses, camellias, and fruit-trees.

In performing the operation, mild, cloudy weather should be chosen, because during hot, dry, windy weather, the viscous surfaces exposed to the air are speedily dried by evaporation, by which the healing process is retarded; besides, the bark never rises so well in very dry, windy weather as it does in weather which is still, warm, and cloudy, but without rain. The first step is to ascertain that the bark of the scion and that of the stock will separate freely from the wood beneath them; then procure the cutting from which the shields or tubes of bark are to be taken. If the budding is to be performed in spring, the cuttings from which the buds are to be taken should be cut from the tree the preceding autumn, and kept through the winter by burying their lower ends in the ground, in a cool, shady situation, as in the case of grafting by detached scions. When these cuttings are to be used, their lower ends should be placed in water, to keep them fresh, while the operation of cutting shields or rings from them is going on. If, on the other hand, the budding is to be performed in summer, which is almost always the case in Britain, then the cutting from which the buds are to be taken is not cut off the parent tree till just before the operation is to be performed. The cutting should be a shoot of the current year's wood, which has done growing, or nearly so, and its leaves should be cut off, to prevent the waste of sap by evaporation, as soon as it is taken from the tree; the end of the cutting should then be put in water to keep it fresh, and the buds taken off as wanted. When the leaves are cut off care should be taken to leave part of the petiole of each, to handle the shield or ring by when putting it on the stock. A slit is next made in the stock, or a ring of bark taken off; and the shield or ring from the cutting, containing a bud or buds which are ripe or nearly so, is introduced in the manner which will be described in treating of the different modes of performing the operation. Tying the bud on the stock generally completes the operation, though sometimes grafting wax is employed to cover the junction of the shield or ring.

Prepared wax for budding may be composed of turpentine, beeswax, resin, and a little tallow melted together. It may be put on in the same manner as grafting clay, but should not be more than a quarter of an inch in thickness; or it may be very thinly spread upon cotton cloth, and used in shreds, like sticking-plaster. In this last state it serves both as a ligature for retaining the shield of the scion in its place, and as a covering for excluding the air. In very delicate budding and grafting, fine moss or cotton wool are frequently used as substitutes for grafting clay or grafting wax, the moss or cotton being tied firmly on with coarse thread or with fine threads of bast matting.

Plastic wax, or grafting wax, which the heat of the hand, or breathing on, will render sufficiently soft for use, is thus prepared:—Take common sealing-wax, of any colour except green, one part; mutton fat, one part; white wax, one part; and honey, one-eighth of a part. The white wax and the fat are to be first melted, and then the sealing-wax is to be added gradually in small pieces, the mixture being kept constantly stirred; and lastly, the honey must be put in just before taking it off the fire. It should be poured hot into paper or tin moulds, and kept slightly agitated till it begins to congeal.

Shield-budding in the end of summer is almost the only mode in use in British nurseries, where it is generally performed in July or August. A cross cut and slit are made in the stock, in the form of the letter T, and if possible through a bud (fig. 235, *a*). From a shoot of the present year deprived of its leaves, a slice of bark and wood, containing a bud, *b*, is then cut out, and the wood is removed from the slice by the point of the knife. This is done by holding the shield by the remains of the leaf with one hand, and entering the point of the knife at the under extremity of the shield, and between it and the thumb;

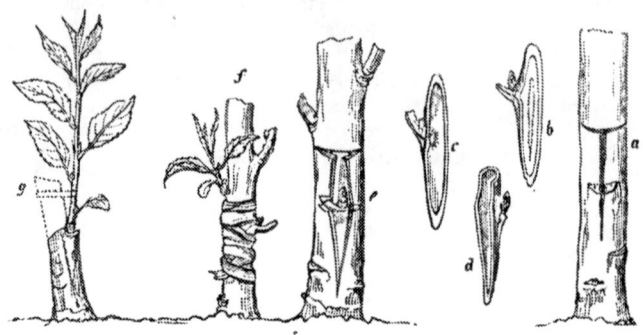

Fig. 235.

The different steps in the process of shield-budding.

and then raising and drawing out the wood by a double motion outwards from the bark, and upwards from the lower to the upper extremity of the shield. The bud being now prepared, as at *c*, the bark on each side of the slit in the stock is raised up by the spatula end of the budding-knife, and the shield inserted beneath it; its upper part being cut straight across, as at *d*, to admit of its joining accurately with the inner bark of the stock, as at *e*, so as to receive its descending sap. A bandage of soft matting is now applied, so as to exclude the air from the wounded parts, and to show only the bud and the petiole, as at *f*, and the operation is complete. At *f*, the bud is shown developing its leaves, and at *g* it has produced a shoot of some length, which is tied for a short time to the upper part of the stock; but that part of the latter which is shown by dotted lines is cut off in July.

The size of the shield or piece of bark attached to the bud is not a matter of very great importance; it is generally however from an inch to an inch and a half in length, and the eye should be situated about a third from the top. Spines, prickles, and leaves should be carefully cut off and shortened. Sometimes in taking out the splinter of wood from the scion, which is done with a quick, jerking motion, the base of the bud which is woody is torn out also, leaving a small cavity, instead of an even surface; the surface, when the bud is in a proper state, being either quite even, or only gently raised above the surrounding bark, in consequence of the woody base of the bud being left in. When the woody base of the bud has been torn out, so as to leave a cavity, it is safest not to use the bud, but to prepare another; though when the cavity left is not very deep, and a small portion of wood is seen in it, the bud will sometimes grow. Only those buds must be taken from the scion that are nearly mature; which is readily known both by the size of the bud and by the full expansion and firm texture of the disk of the leaf, in the axis of which it grows.

Shield-budding in June.—Roses of most kinds may be budded at almost any period from June to October. June is, however, the best month for budding; the shoots from these buds will mostly flower in the autumn of the same year.

Shield-budding in spring may be exemplified by the Belgian practice with the rose. For this purpose, scions are cut before winter, and stuck into the ground till the moment in spring when the bark of the stock will rise, or, technically speaking, run. To prepare the bud, a transverse cut should be first made into the wood, a little below an eye (fig. 236, *a*), which incision is met by a longer cut downwards, commencing at a short distance above the eye (*b*), care being taken that a portion of wood is removed with the bark (*c*). The bud is then inserted into the bark of the stock which is cut like an inverted T (*d*), and the horizontal edges of the cut in the stock and of the bud must be brought into the most perfect contact with each other (*e*), and then bound with waterproof bast (*f*), without, however, applying grafting clay. Eight days after the insertion of the bud, the stock is pruned down to the branch above on the opposite side, and this branch is stopped by being cut down to two or three eyes; all the side-wood is destroyed as it appears; and when the bud has pushed its fifth leaf, the shoot it has made is compelled to branch, by pinching off its extremity; it will then flower in September of the same year. The rose may also be budded in spring, without waiting till the bark separates, by placing the bud with some wood on it in a niche made in the stock as at (*g*), similar to what would be formed by taking an eye off it, for budding in the manner above described; the bud is fitted exactly in the niche, with a slight pressure, and then tied on as usual. The camellia may also be budded in this manner in spring by taking a bud with the wood in from the scion, and substituting it for a corresponding piece cut out of the stock, as in fig. 237.

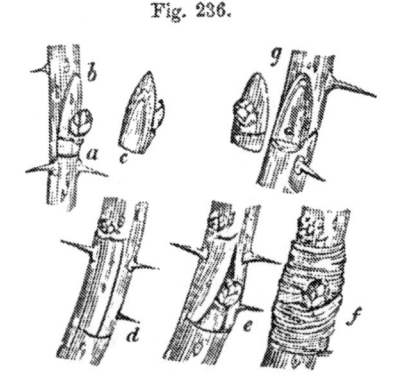

Fig. 236.

Shield-budding the rose in spring.

Fig. 237.

Shield-budding the camellia in spring.

Fig. 238.

Shield-grafting without a bud.

Shield-grafting without a bud or eye (fig. 238) is used simply to

270   BUDDING OR GRAFTING BY DETACHED BUDS.

cover a wound or blemish in one tree by a portion of the live bark of another.

Budding with a circular shield, with a portion of wood attached (fig. 239), is employed to equalize the flower-buds over a tree, by removing some from places where there are too many to other places in which there are too few. With the point of a penknife, in spring, cut a small cone of bark and wood containing a bud, and insert it in an orifice made in the same manner, securing the edges with grafting wax.

Fig. 239.
Budding with a circular shield.

Fig. 240.
Budding by the aid of a punch.

Budding with a shield stamped out by a punch (fig. 240) is considered excellent for budding old trees, the thick and rugged bark of which is not suitable for being taken off with the budding-knife. With a mallet the punch (fig. 241) is driven through the bark of the scion, and then through that of the stock, and the piece which comes out of the former is inserted in the cavity formed by taking the piece out of the latter.

Fig. 241.
Punch used for punching out shield-buds.

Fig. 242.
Budding with the shield reversed.

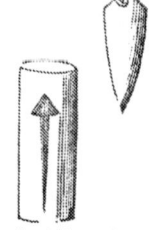

Fig. 243.
Budding with a pointed shield for resinous trees.

Budding with the shield reversed (fig. 242) is almost the only manner of budding used in the south of Europe, particularly at Genoa and Hières, to propagate orange-trees. It is said also to be suitable for trees having abundant and gummy sap.

Budding with the Eye turned Downwards. — By this method the buds are forced to grow in a direction opposite to that which they would have taken naturally; but they soon resume their usual position; and the desired end — viz., that of increasing the size of the fruit by stagnating the returning sap, is thus by no means attained. De Candolle says, that this mode of budding is used advantageously in the case of the olive, and of trees which produce a great deal of gum, but that he sees no reason for attributing to it any superiority over the ordinary mode.

Shield-budding for resinous trees (fig. 243) is said to succeed with the Abietineæ, and with all trees that have a gummy and very abundant sap.

Budding with the Shield Covered (fig. 244).—The shield being inserted in the usual manner, another with an orifice in it, to admit the bud of the first, is laid over it, and is bandaged in the usual manner, or covered with grafting wax. The object of the double shield is to lessen the effect of drying winds.

Fig. 244.

Fig. 245.

Budding with a square shield (fig. 245) is an old practice which has lately been revived with some modifications. When this mode is practised the bark raised up on the stock to make room for the shield is tied over it; the shield being previously shortened, so as to reach only to the under side of the bud; and between the two barks, the petiole of a leaf is inserted, the disk of which is intended to protect the bud from the sun. The strip of bark being peeled down from the stock, instead of being raised up from it by the spatula of the budding-knife, is found to lessen the risk of injuring the soft wood; and this appears to be the chief recommendation of this mode of budding.

Budding with a double shield.

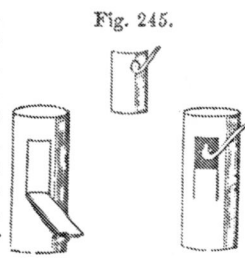

Budding with a square shield.

Shield-budding with a terminal bud (fig. 246) is supposed to produce a more vigorous shoot than when a lateral eye is used; and it is, therefore, recommended for supplying a leader to a shoot that has lost one. The stock is cut as at a, and the bud is prepared as at b, inserted as at c, and tied in the usual manner, as at d.

Fig. 246.

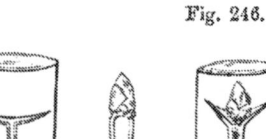

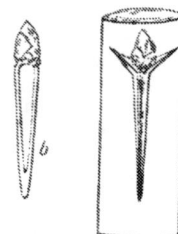

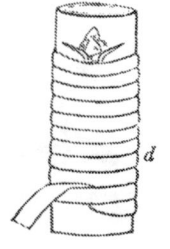

Budding with a terminal eye.

Flute-budding, or Tube-budding.—There are several modifications of this mode of budding, which is a good deal used on the Continent for trees which are difficult to take, such as the walnut and the chestnut; and for several oaks, as well as for the white mulberry. It is generally performed in spring; but it will also succeed in autumn. The shoot from which the buds are to be taken, and that on which they are to be placed, must be of the same diameter, or nearly so; and a ring being removed from each, that from the stock is thrown away, and the one from the scion put on in its stead. Sometimes this is done without shortening the stock or branch, when it is called annular, or ring-budding; and sometimes the stock is shortened, and the ring put on its upper extremity, when it is called flute-budding, or terminal tube-budding.

272   BUDDING OR GRAFTING BY DETACHED BUDS.

Flute-budding in Spring.—The scions are taken off in autumn, or early in winter, and preserved through the winter in a cool shady situation, in the same manner as is done in grafting by detached scions, and in spring shield-budding. Fig. 247, which requires no description, shows the mode of spring terminal flute-budding the white mulberry, as it is practised in the royal nurseries at Munich. When the ring of the scion is too large, a portion is cut out of it longitudinally, so as to admit of its being pressed closely and firmly to the stock; and when it is too small, it is slit up so as to admit of its being put round the stock. The tube is tied on with matting, and the summit of the stock is covered with grafting wax.

Fig. 247.

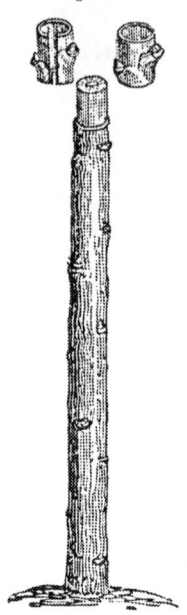

Flute-budding the mulberry in spring.

Terminal flute-budding in the South of France (fig. 248).—The head of the stock being cut off, a ring of bark, two inches or three inches long, is removed. A shoot is then taken from the tree to be increased, of exactly the same thickness as the stock, and a ring or tube of bark is taken off the thick end (without being split longitudinally), not quite so long as the piece of bark taken off the stock, but provided with several good eyes. The tube thus formed is placed upon the stock in the room of the one removed, and care is taken to make the two edges of bark join below. The part of the stock which projects over the ring of the bark is next split into shreds, and brought down over it all round, in the same manner as when secured by grafting wax or clay. This mode of budding is chiefly employed in the South of France for propagating walnuts, chestnuts, figs, mulberries, and other trees with thick bark and abundant pith.

Flute-budding with Strips of Bark (fig. 249).—The head of the stock is cut off, but instead of removing a ring of bark, as in the preceding mode, it is cut longitudinally into four or five strips, each two inches or three inches long, and turned down as in the figure, being left still attached to the tree. From a shoot of the tree to be propagated, a tube of bark is taken, furnished with four or five eyes, rather shorter than the strips, though longer than in tube-budding. When the tube of the scion is

Fig. 248.

Terminal flute-budding in spring or summer.

Fig. 249.

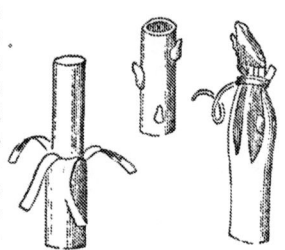

Flute-budding with strips of bark.

slipped on the stock, the strips of bark are raised over it, and fastened at the top by a ligature. Sometimes the end of the stock is cut obliquely, and the straps are brought up as at *a*, in which case the top of the stock is not cut into shreds, and turned down over the tube of bark, as in flute-budding in the South of France. A curious experiment by this mode of budding, consists in placing rings of the bark of different allied species, one above another, without allowing any of the buds to develop themselves. On cutting down the stem of a tree so treated, some years afterwards, it will be found that under each kind of bark is a portion of its proper wood, proving that the wood is deposited by the inner bark from the returning sap, and that the bark has the power of so modifying this sap, as to produce the particular kind of wood of the species to which it belongs, without the aid of any leaves of that species.

Annular budding (fig. 250) is performed either at the principal movement of the sap in spring, or at the end of its principal movement in August. In either case the top of the stock is kept on; and if the ring of bark containing a bud or buds taken from the scion is larger than the space prepared for it on the stock, a piece must be taken from it longitudinally, so as to make it fit exactly. In Belgium this mode is considered particularly suitable for hard-wooded trees, which are difficult to increase by any other mode.

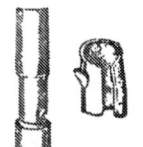

Fig. 250.

Annular budding.

The after-care of grafts by budding consists, in all cases, in removing the bandages or plasters as soon as it is ascertained that the buds or scions have adhered to the stock. This may generally be known in two or three weeks, by the healthy appearance of the bark and its bud or buds, and by the dropping off of the petiole, which in the case of the death of the bud withers and adheres. It is also of the utmost importance to attach supports or stakes firmly to the stock, and to tie the grafts or buds as they grow tightly to them, otherwise they will often be broken off by wind. The next operation is to head-down the stock to within an inch or two of the bud, the stump being left for a week or two as a prop, to which the shoot produced by the bud of the scion may be tied, till it acquires vigour enough to support itself. The stump is then cut off in a sloping direction, close above the bud. In general, any buds which develop themselves on this stump should be rubbed off; but in the case of very weak scions, one or more buds may be left on the stump to draw up the sap till the graft has taken. When budding is performed in spring, the stock should have been headed-down before the ascent of the sap; but in autumn-budding, as no shoot is produced till the spring following, heading-down is deferred till that season, and takes place just before the sap is in motion. Where a number of grafts by buds are introduced on one stem or on one branch, heading-down can, of course, only take place above the uppermost bud; and in terminal flute-budding, it is performed as a necessary part of the operation. Much of the success of budding depends on the stock and bud growing vigorously, to supply the juices or cam-

T

bium causing the union to take place; and allowing the bark to separate easily from the wood, so as to prevent laceration and bruising of the vessels in separating them. If the bark does not rise freely from the stock when the handle of the knife is inserted, it is not likely the bud will succeed; and the same if the shield of the bud does not part freely from its wood; if either of them has commenced ripening, or if the sap has not begun to run or flow, the labour will be in vain. In order to ensure the cut being smooth, and no laceration of the bark of the shield taking place, the best of all methods (especially for such barks as the cherry and plum, which will not bear handling, and are very apt to spoil) is to mark the size of the shield intended, all round the bud with the point of the knife, cutting into the wood, and then introducing the thumb at the side of the bud, and raising it off with a gentle squeeze. If the shoot is growing vigorously, it will spring out, without any difficulty, so clean and smooth on the edges, as greatly to facilitate the success of the operation. By the common method if the bark is much handled, the shield of the bud is apt to be spoiled at the edges before insertion.

Rearing.

The operations of rearing in horticulture are those which are required to bring plants to that particular state of bulk, succulence, colour, or flavour, for which they are cultivated in gardens and garden scenery. These operations may be included under transplanting, planting, potting, pruning, training, thinning, weeding, watering, stirring the soil, blanching, shading, sheltering, and protecting.

Transplanting and Planting.

To transplant is to take up a plant with its roots, and to replant it again in such a manner that it shall continue to grow. In some cases the roots are taken up enveloped in soil and entire, as in transplanting plants in pots; and in others they are divested of soil, and more or less mutilated, as is the case in all other modes. In whatever manner a plant has been originated, whether by seeds or by some modification of division, the first step in carrying on its cultivation is most commonly transplanting.

The uses of transplanting are:—1. To afford more room for the growth of the top, and for stirring and manuring the soil about the roots. 2. To produce immediate effect in scenery, by placing trees or shrubs in particular situations. 3. To supply deficiencies in plantations already made. 4. To limit the extent of the main roots, and to increase the number of fibrous roots, within a limited distance of the stem of the plant, and thus to fit it for being removed, with all its roots, when of a large size. 5. To retard the growth and flowering of certain plants, and by that means to increase the bulk and succulency of their foliage. 6. To inure plants to particular soils and situations, and to hasten and establish the fertility of fruit-bearing trees.

The theory of transplanting is founded on the tenacity of life common to all plants, their powers of adaptation to altered conditions, and their ability to replace portions of their structure that have been removed by accident or design. When plants are in a state of active growth, a constant perspiration is taking place from their leaves, which is supplied by the absorption of the moisture in the soil by the spongioles of the roots; and when this supply through the roots is cut off by the destruction of the spongioles, the leaves wither, and the plant dies or becomes greatly injured; but there is a period in the growth of every plant, in which the leaves either drop off, as in deciduous plants, or cease to be in a state of activity, as in evergreens; and it is chiefly when in this state that the operation of transplanting can be successfully undertaken with large plants. Even when trees are without their leaves, perspiration is going on to a certain extent through the bark, and absorption to supply this waste must necessarily be taking place at the same time through the spongioles; for though the functions of most plants are annually in a dormant state, yet they are never wholly inactive; and hence, even in transplanting trees without their leaves, the effects of more perspiration by the bark than the roots can supply must be guarded against. This is more especially the case in transplanting evergreens, in which the functions of the leaves, and, consequently, of the spongioles, are carried on through the winter. As the perspiration both of the leaves and bark is greatly dependent on the moisture or dryness of the atmosphere, it follows that on the state of the weather at and after transplanting, a good deal of the success of the operation must depend; and as the kind of weather bears close relation to the season of the year, that also requires to be taken into consideration. All plants, considered with reference to transplanting, may be divided into three classes—viz., those which can be transplanted in a state of active growth, and with their leaves on, which are chiefly seedlings, and other small plants, and plants in pots; those which can only be transplanted with success when without their leaves, as deciduous trees, and herbaceous perennials of more than a year's growth; and those which are transplanted when their leaves are on, but in a comparatively dormant state, as evergreens.

Seedlings and such small plants as can be taken up with all their fibres and spongioles uninjured, and planted immediately, may be removed at any season which admits of the progress of vegetation; though their success will be most certain when the atmosphere is warm and cloudy, and the soil moist rather than dry. The plants should be raised out of the soil with a spade, trowel, or flat-pointed stick, kept out of the earth as short a period as possible, firmly planted, and if the ground is dry, instantly watered overhead. Tender plants, when thus transplanted, are covered with a hand-glass or frame, to preserve a moist atmosphere around them; or if in pots, they are plunged into a hotbed for the same purpose, and also to stimulate their roots. The hardier annuals, on the other hand, such as seedlings of the cabbage tribe, may be transplanted with less care, since when they flag or fade, their leaves soon recover again, in consequence of fresh spongioles being emitted by the main or tap root. During moist weather, or where there is an opportunity, by means of coverings, of preserving a moist atmosphere round plants, and excluding the direct rays of the sun, herbaceous plants of considerable size, with the leaves on, may be transplanted; but in ordinary weather, and without the aid of protection, this is difficult in proportion to the number and size of the leaves, the thinness of their texture, and the number of their stomata. The evaporation, in cases of this kind, being greater than the absorption by the spongioles, it requires to be lessened by shading, by cutting off a portion of the leaves, by thinning them out, or by cutting them off altogether. In general, this latter treatment can only be practised with impunity in transplanting young plants that have fleshy roots, such as the Swedish turnip, the rhubarb, &c. In transplanting seedlings, the top or main perpendicular root is generally shortened to increase the number of lateral spongioles, more especially in the case of vigorous-growing plants. The object of this shortening is, in some cases, to cause the roots to derive their chief nourishment from the upper and richest part of the soil; and in others, that the plant by having abundance of roots in a limited space may be the better adapted for being again transplanted.

Deciduous trees and shrubs, and perennial herbaceous plants, can only be safely transplanted when in a dormant state. This dormant state is indicated by the fall of the leaf, at which period the roots, stem, and branches contain a greater accumulation of nutritive matter than they do at any other season of the year, and not being in a state of activity, they can exist in a great measure without the assistance of the spongioles. They are, therefore, in a fitter state for being transplanted than they can be at any other period, and the success will in general be in proportion to the number of roots that are taken up entire.

From October to the middle of December is the best period of the year for the transplantation of all deciduous trees and shrubs. With suitable weather, and if the ground is not too dry, the earlier after the fall of the leaf the tree is moved, the sooner will its normal condition be restored by the formation of fresh roots. Some even prefer transplanting before the whole of the leaves are shed, as " by the action of the mature leaves which remain, the injuries which the roots may have sustained will be speedily repaired; new roots will be immediately produced, and the plant will then become established before winter, and prepared to grow with nearly if not quite its usual vigour in the following spring. ('Gard. Chron.,' vol. i. p. 811.) In the neighbourhood of London, wall-fruit trees are frequently transplanted in this manner. In transplanting deciduous trees before the leaves are fallen, it is found in practice that the shoots are not ripened, and die back often to a considerable distance, in the same manner as if the leaves had been destroyed by early frost. The young fibres, also, will protrude spongioles more quickly in the spring from the fibre that has been well ripened, than from that lifted before ripened. It can only be when the distance of removal is very short, and the plants very small, and lifted with the earth adhering to the roots, that the transplanting of deciduous plants in autumn, before ripe, can be attended with any advantage. In the nurseries we have great experience of lifting and moving immense quantities of deciduous plants, and experience must say that, unless during mild winters, little root-growth is made until the spring season has commenced. Unless the winter is more than ordinarily mild, the spongioles are never seen to protrude, nor the buds to swell, till the spring begins to advance. Different plants commence their season of growth at different periods. Gooseberries, cherries, thorns, birch, larch, &c. may begin to move in February or March; beech, oaks, apples, &c. are later, and seldom begin to show much before April or May. Even the mezereon, which often flowers in February, is seldom found to protrude new roots before that period. Of course the period will vary as to localities; some soils and situations are more than a month earlier than others within very short distances. Autumn planting is preferable where the soil is dry, as it washes the soil closer to the root; where the soil is clayey, and the weather soft at planting time, it gets into a state of puddle and rots the roots in winter; and, unless the weather is dry at planting time in autumn, such soils had better be deferred till spring. A second argument in favour of autumn-planting is the dampness of the atmosphere which prevails at that season and during winter; by which the perspiration through the bark is lessened, and the demand made on the roots to supply the waste is consequently diminished. In spring, not only is the sun more powerful, but drying winds generally prevail, which have a constant tendency to drain the young branches of a tree of their moisture. These drying winds are much more injurious to newly transplanted evergreens than to deciduous trees, as will afterwards appear.

Different Modes of Transplanting Large Trees and Shrubs.—To lessen the injuries which every large tree must receive in transplanting, from the mutilation of its roots, six different modes of performing the operation have been adopted: viz., 1, by retaining large balls of earth attached to the roots; 2, by previously preparing the roots, so as to furnish them with new fibres and spongioles; 3, by previously shortening the roots, and treating them so as to heal over and granulate the wounds made in their extremities; 4, by simply thinning and pruning the roots and the branches at the time of transplanting; 5, by removal without previous preparation; and 6, by shortening the roots and heading in the branches.

Transplanting with Large Balls of Earth.—In this case the head of the tree is generally preserved entire, and the ball of solid soil is made so large as to include as many of the roots as possible. It is then carefully planted in fresh rich soil, consolidated by watering, and secured by stakes, by guy ropes, wires, iron rods, or by any other means that will render it immovable. This stability of the root is the first step to success, as, if the tree moves with every wind, the roots will undergo an alternate process of growth and destruction, and the tree must perish. A good deal likewise depends on climate, soil, and situation, and probably as much or more upon the completeness of the ball and the number of roots that are safely removed with it. No large tree taken up from a moist soil will thrive if transferred to a dry one; and, on the contrary, a tree taken up from a dry soil, that would do little good when transferred to another dry soil, will yet thrive if planted in a soil that is moist. This mode of moving trees entire, with the whole of their roots and branches complete, has been carried out with great success by Mr. Barron, of the Borrow-wash Nurseries, near Derby. With the assistance of his transplanting machines, and his skilful management, no tree can be pronounced too large to be safely removed. He has taken up trees from fifty to sixty feet high, transported them for hundreds of miles, and they have started into growth with full vigour and robust health. An illustration of a transplanting machine, much and successfully used by the French, who have now become great adepts in the transplantation of large trees, is given at pp. 287 and 288 of this work.

Transplanting by Shortening the Roots, so as to induce them to throw out Fibres.—This is effected by digging a circular trench round the tree, one or two, or even three or four years before transplanting, cutting off all the roots which extend as far as the trench, and filling it up with prepared soil, or with the surface soil and subsoil mixed. The distance of the trench from the stem of the tree may vary with its size, the kind of tree, and other circumstances; but a good general rule would be, where the tree is to stand from two to four years, to make the diameter of the circle included within the trench of as many feet as the diameter of the trunk of the tree at the surface of the ground is in inches. Thus, for a tree with a stem six inches in diameter, the trench should be made at the distance of three feet from it on every side; and for one of eighteen inches in diameter, the distance of the trench from the stem should be nine feet. The width and depth of the trench should also be proportionate to the size of the tree, and to the period which is to intervene between its preparation and removal. It is evident that where the tree is to stand three or four years after its roots are cut, more room should be left for the extension of the fibres, than when it is to stand only one year; unless, indeed, the roots could be confined, as if in a pot, by the hardness of the outer side of the trench; in which case they might after removal be spread out at length. It is evident also that when a tree is to stand only one year after making the trench, the trench should not only be made narrower, but at a greater distance from the stem, in order that a greater length of old root may be taken up to serve in lieu of the new roots made when the tree stands three or four years before removal. The width of the trench can never conveniently be made less than eighteen inches, and its depth should not be less than two feet, in order to cut through the lower roots; since it is chiefly by the fibres that will be produced by these that the tree will be supplied by fluid nutriment to support the perspiration of its leaves the first year after transplanting. In making the trench, it is not, in general, desirable to undermine the ball of earth, so far as to cut through the tap-root, because this main root is necessary as a source of nourishment, in the absence of so many lateral roots.

In selecting trees to be transplanted in this manner, it is well, if possible, to take only those which have been exposed to the free air and weather on every side; but as we cannot always get such trees, the next best are those which stand in the margins of plantations. Supposing one of these to be 25 feet high, a trench 30 inches wide should be opened round it at a distance of three and a half feet, if it is meant to stand for four years or upwards after the operation; and at a distance of six or seven feet, if it is meant to stand only two years. If the tree is to stand four or more years, the trench should be cut to the full depth of the subsoil, in order to get somewhat underneath the roots. If the subsoil be wet, a drain should be made from the trench, and the soil, if good, returned, or if inferior, a compost should be substituted for it. If the tree is to stand only two years, the same method may be followed, but with this difference—that on the sides most exposed to the wind, which in this island are generally the south-west, two or perhaps three of the strongest roots should be left uncut, and allowed to pass entire through the trench, to act as stays against the winds. In taking up the tree for removal, the greatest care must be taken to preserve the minutest fibres and the spongioles entire; and to accomplish this a new trench should be made exterior to the old one, so as not to injure any of the new fibres which have been protruded into the prepared soil. A fork or sharp pick is the best instrument for this purpose, and the utmost care must be exercised when removing the earth, not to cut or bruise the roots. The picking away the soil from the roots may reach within three, four, or five feet of the stem, according to the size of the tree; and a ball of earth, with two or three feet broad of the sward adhering to it, should be left undisturbed round the collar. The tree may now be pulled over, and raised out of the pit. The following was Sir Henry Steuart's mode of effecting these two operations:—

Pulling Down the Tree and Raising it out of the Pit.—" A strong but soft rope, of perhaps four inches in girth, is fixed as near to the top of the tree as a man can safely climb, so as to furnish the longest possible lever to bear upon the roots; taking care at the same time to interpose two or three folds of mat, in order to prevent the chafing of the bark. Eight or nine workmen are then set to draw the tree down on one side. Or it is a good way, if you have an old and steady-pulling horse, to employ him in this business. For it is plain that one stout horse, acting forcibly on the rope, will do more than twenty men, even if so great a number could get about it; and, moreover, he will save some manual labour in excavating, by giving an effectual pull at a much earlier period of the work. Next to an old and steady horse, heavy oxen are to be preferred, for these have been known to drag timber out of plantations where horses were defeated, in consequence of the rugged nature of the surface. Horses make one very spirited pull, but rarely a second, if they have been checked by the first. Oxen, on the other hand, appear less sensitive, and bear steadily and slowly onward by the mere force of gravity, and without recoiling like horses. The tree being drawn down, it is next forcibly held in that position, until earth is raised to the height of a foot or more, on the opposite side of the pit, so that, as soon as it is liberated, it springs up and stops against the bank thus formed. On this the workmen proceed to lighten the mass of earth with the picker, laying bare the roots as little as possible, but still necessarily reducing the mass to manageable dimensions. The tree is then pulled down on the opposite side, and a foot of earth forced up, in a similar manner; and the same thing being repeated once or twice, it is gradually raised to even a higher level than that of the adjoining surface. In this manner, by a method extremely simple, and not less expeditious, whatever it may appear in the narrative, it becomes quite an easy instead of a formidable undertaking to draw the tree from the pit." ('Planter's Guide,' 2nd ed., p. 243.)

Transporting and Replanting the Tree.—The machine used by Sir Henry Steuart consisted of a pole and two wheels, with a smaller wheel occasionally used, which is fixed at the extremity of the pole, and turns on a pivot. The pole operates both as a powerful lever to bring down the tree to a horizontal position, and in conjunction with the wheels as a still more powerful conveyance to remove it to its new situation. The wheels of the machine are brought close up to the body of the tree, and the stem laid along the pole, with the largest branches uppermost, in order that no branch or root of considerable length should be suffered to sweep the ground during the time of transportation. The tree thus attached to the pole is drawn to its destination by horses, and placed upright in a shallow pit, which is, if possible, opened and prepared a twelvemonth beforehand by trenching and mixing manure, and exposing the soil in the bottom of the pit to the influence of the weather. The transplanted tree, after being set upright, and the soil carefully rammed into all the cavities about the roots, is held in its position, either by posts or stakes above ground, by horizontal poles under it, or by forming a circular bank of earth on the extremities of the main roots. The great success which attended the operations of this distinguished planter may, we conceive, be chiefly owing to the care with which they were performed, to the circumstance that the trees were always prepared for three or four or more years beforehand, and the extraordinary moistness of the climate in that part of Scotland. It is a common practice in England to prepare the trees only one year before removal, in which case, as Sir Henry very justly observes, " the fresh fibres being nearly as tender as the roots of an onion or a cabbage, can neither be extricated nor handled without sensible injury." In the case of shrubs, however, one year will be found sufficient for many kinds that rapidly emit a great number of roots. The earth round a newly transplanted tree should always be consolidated by heavy waterings, and it is a good practice to cover the surface with a mulching four inches thick, for the double purpose of keeping the moisture in and the cold out.

Transplanting by Shortening the Roots, without permitting them to throw out Fibres at their Extremities.—This mode has not been much practised, but it is sound in theory, and has been successful. Take out a trench as before, at three, four, five, or six feet from the tree, and cut off any root that protrudes beyond the solid ball. Leave the trench unfilled for one or two years. Cover it over with board, slate, tile, branches, dung, or litter, to exclude light and air. The young roots, instead of being formed on the outside of the ball, will spread a network of fibres through it, which will bind the earth together, and enable the plant to be moved in safety. The cut roots will likewise be found to have callosed at their extremities, and will at once form roots into the fresh soil, as soon as the tree is transplanted. It is obvious that the growth of the tree must be greatly checked by this mode of preparation, which will consequently have the effect of rendering it capable of living on a limited quantity of food, and therefore much better adapted for removal. The only objection that occurs to us is, that in the case of previous preparation for two or three years, too many fibrous roots will be protruded into the ball, more, perhaps, than can be nourished in that limited bulk of soil, even after the tree is transplanted. If, however, the tree is prepared only one year previous to removal, the objection will not apply to the same extent, if at all.

Transplanting by thinning and pruning the roots and branches is the most common mode, and in a moist soil and climate it is generally attended with success. The trees are taken up by cutting a trench round the roots about the same distance as in preparing trees by the first mode; the ends of the roots are cut smooth, and the top is thinned of its branches, and pruned more or less, according to the reduction of the roots, the size of the tree, and the soil, situation, and climate in which it is to be planted. When the tree is of considerable size, say nine inches or a foot in diameter, it must necessarily be deprived of the greater number of its effective roots; and in this case, unless in a very moist climate and soil, the safest mode is to cut off at least half of the branches of the head, covering the sections left by amputation with grafting clay or grafting wax. In some cases large trees can be removed without preparing the roots, and without cutting off any, or at least very few, of the branches; but in such cases it will be found that, from some cause or other, the roots are mostly near the surface, and the soil moist, and that a great proportion of the roots can be taken up along with the tree. When this mode of transplanting large trees with the branches on is adopted in a dry soil, the success will be very different, even though the ground should be mulched round the transplanted trees, and the stem and main branches closely wrapped round with straw ropes to lessen evaporation. The most suitable trees for planting out, with no other preparation than thinning or pruning the branches, are those whose roots and heads have been properly thinned and pruned by cultivation in a nursery.

Transplanting by "Heading-in," that is, Cutting the Branches.—The trees, whether oak, ash, elm, poplar, or other leafy kinds, are taken from the nursery when they are fifteen feet or more in height, and about the thickness of a man's arm; the lateral branches are all cut off close to the stem, to the height of six or seven feet from the collar; the top is also cut off in a slanting direction, at about ten feet from the roots; and the remaining branches are shortened to from three to six inches, the cut being made close above a bud. The trees are taken up in November or December. The first year they grow but little; the second year they may be said to commence their growth, when the uppermost shoot is trained for the leader. As the tree progresses, it is pruned every year, if necessary, in winter or early in spring, cutting out all the cross and unequal branches, and thinning those that are or may become crowded. It may be thought that trees treated in this manner would all become round-headed, and that they would only have about ten feet of straight timber; but this does not necessarily follow, unless that form be really desired. On the contrary, the straightest and most beautifully attenuated timber is obtained by training the upper shoot in time to a stick tied to the stem; or if the uppermost shoot is emitted a few inches below the summit, which is sometimes the case, it may be tied to the dying point, till it is fixed in an unchangeable erect position. This is one of the cheapest and safest modes of transplanting trees in exposed, bleak situations in Britain, more especially on the sea-coast and in mountainous districts.

The staking or supporting of newly-transplanted trees, and the protection of their stems from cattle, require to be carefully attended to; and we shall therefore shortly notice the different modes of doing both. Fig. 251 shows the common modes of protecting trees which are to have clear stems to the height of eight or ten feet, from deer, horses, or cattle, the main posts being made of oak or of larch, or of any other wood, charred on the part which is buried in the soil, and for nine inches or a foot above the surface of the ground. Circular cradles of iron, made in two semicircles, bolted together, are now mostly used instead of wood. They are lighter, more elegant and durable, and in the end cheapest. For trees which grow with their lower branches sweeping on the ground, such as cedars, pines, silver firs, &c., circles of iron hurdles fastened together with bolts and nuts should be employed, enlarging the circle as the branches extend themselves, by introducing additional hurdles. These hurdles being always only a few feet from the branches, are scarcely perceptible at a very short distance, and therefore are no deformity in the landscape. Small trees, with the branches on, may be tied to stakes with bands of hay, and their stems protected with thorns or furze tied on. Trees of thirty or forty feet in height may be supported by guy ropes; or if the roots are strong and of some length, they may be kept in their places by horizontal poles placed over them, and tied to them, concealed under, or level with, or immediately above the surface of the ground; the ends

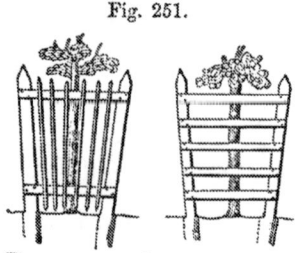

Fig. 251.

The most general modes of protecting recently-planted single trees from cattle and deer.

of those poles being made fast to stakes, so as to cross over the roots and hold them tightly down. Fig. 252 shows a plan and elevation of a newly-removed tree, the roots of which are fastened down in this manner by means of the rods, *a*, and stakes, *b*; the latter being securely nailed to the former, and the whole covered with soil, as shown by the dotted line *c*. Trees of moderate size may also be secured against high winds by inserting a stout stake in the soil in the bottom of the pit in which the tree is to be planted, of sufficient length to reach four or five feet above the surface, securing it firmly there before planting the tree, and afterwards placing the stem of the tree close to it, and fastening it by some soft tie. Three larch poles fixed in this manner, so as to form a triangle, converging at top to the thickness of the stem of the tree, the tree being planted in the centre, would serve at once as a firm prop, and as a protection from cattle. Another mode is to cover the surface of the ground for four or more feet round the tree with a number of large rough stones. The stones are not built up high, but packed close to each other, and set on edge, so as to meet and form a continuous, but very rugged surface round the foot of the tree. The stones are placed in ordinary cases to the distance of four feet, which is sufficient to keep off cattle and horses. Horses and cattle are also kept at a distance from the trees by a series of horizontal rails, forming a tabular polygon round the tree fifteen or eighteen inches in height, and ten feet in diameter (see ' Gard. Mag.,' vol. vi. p. 47). Fig. 253 shows the general appearance of a tree fenced round in this manner. Fig. 254 is a vertical profile of the horizontal frame-work; and fig. 255 is a cross section. In this section the posts are shown, inclined a little outwards, the better to resist pressure from cattle or sheep in that direction. The advantage of this fence is its economy in requiring only short pieces of not very stout timber, and its inconspicuousness when seen at a distance.

Fig. 252.

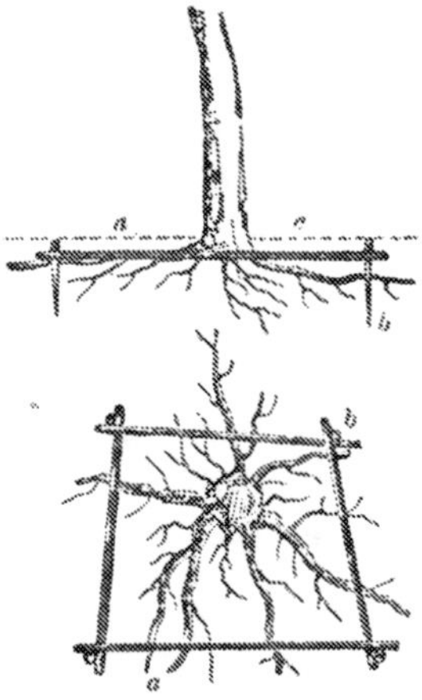

Plan and elevation of a newly-moved tree, secured from high winds by underground fastenings.

The machinery for moving large trees has been adverted to, to which it may be added that trucks or sledges, poles and ropes, require to be abundantly provided: though for ordinary purposes, a wood gin or a pair of high wheels and an axle for large trees without balls, and a sledge with an iron bottom, to be afterwards described, for shrubs with balls, is all that is essential.

Transplanting Evergreens.—There is scarcely any residence in the country in which it is not frequently necessary to transplant evergreen shrubs, sometimes from changes or new arrangements, and sometimes

284   TRANSPLANTING AND PLANTING.

on account of the plants crowding each other. Evergreen trees, such as those of the pine and fir tribe, are also occasionally transplanted,

Fig. 253.

Fig. 254.

Isometrical view of the tabular tree-guard.

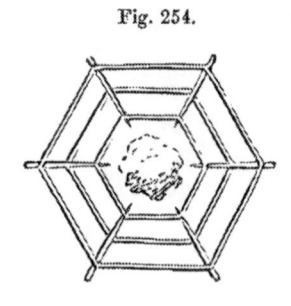

Vertical profile of the tabular tree-guard.

though much less frequently than shrubs. The most readily transplanted evergreen trees of large size, are the spruce-fir and the yew; the former having numerous fibrous roots near the surface, and the latter having also numerous fibrous roots growing together, and consolidating the soil immediately round the tree into a compact mass. Spruce-firs, yews, and hollies of large size were, some years since, transplanted at Elvaston Castle by Mr. Barron, with scarcely a single failure, though the spruce-firs were from sixty to eighty feet in height, and many of the yews were above a hundred years old. Evergreen shrubs of all sizes have also been transplanted with the greatest success in the new botanic garden of Edinburgh, by Mr. McNab.

Fig. 255.

Cross section of the tabular tree-guard.

The best season for transplanting evergreens is from April to June, or just before the old leaves drop off and the new ones begin to be formed; though with skill in their removal, and care in after treatment, evergreens may be moved with safety any day in the year. The reason why dull or moist weather is so essential a condition is, that the process of perspiration continues to go on in evergreens at all seasons, excepting, perhaps, in the most severe weather; and that when the atmosphere is saturated with moisture, the perspiration is reduced to its minimum. Evaporation also proceeds in an increasing ratio with the temperature, all other circumstances being the same. Thus, when the temperature is 80°, the quantity evaporated from a given surface will be three times greater than when the temperature is only 40°, the degree of dryness in the air being the same in both cases. So long as the leaves remain on a plant in a healthy state, their functions are performed in a greater or less degree, and they draw upon the roots accordingly; so that evergreens, as they never lose their leaves, may be said to be in a growing state all the year; and were the growth not much slower in autumn and winter than it is in summer, it would be as difficult to transplant evergreen trees, even at that season, as it is to transplant deciduous trees in summer with the leaves on. The first effect of separating a plant from the soil, is to cut off the supply of sap to the leaves; and as, notwithstanding this, perspiration and evaporation will still continue, it follows that these leaves must fade, unless the perspiration is either checked by a moist atmosphere, or supplied by watering the roots. That the atmosphere in Britain is nearly saturated with moisture from October to February inclusive, is satisfactorily proved by the tables drawn up by Mr. Robert Thompson, of the Horticultural Society's Garden. These tables show the atmospheric moisture for the different months of the year, as under:—

	Mean Temperature.	North.	N. East	East.	S. East.	South.	S. West.	West.	N. West.	Mean Moisture.
January	31·6	882	893	989	1000	982	1000	983	1000	966
February	39·0	815	657	992	1000	963	874	804	1000	888
March	39·0	815	688	752	1000	913	846	846	1000	857
April	53·2	747	778	870	775	711	846	752	902	797
May	60·0	718	687	574	767	798	1000	752	651	743
June	57·5	721	572	574	767	798	664	707	673	684
July	57·5	721	703	662	767	798	750	684	599	710
August	64·8	773	836	693	767	776	724	666	826	757
September	56·6	907	1000	723	767	813	853	761	905	841
October	56·6	907	1000	1000	904	885	862	939	905	925
November	56·6	907	1000	1000	1000	980	938	940	938	962
December	39·0	971	920	1000	1000	980	939	986	1000	974

As evergreens can hardly be said to have a season of rest, it is of the utmost importance that their roots be not dried, nor exposed to the air during their removal. As soon as the plant has been put into its place, the earth should be filled in, leaving a sufficient hollow round the stem, and as far out as the roots extend, to hold water, which should then be poured in, in sufficient quantity to soak the ground down to the lowest part of the roots; in short, the whole should be made like a kind of puddle. By this practice, which is particularly necessary in spring, summer, and autumn planting, the earth is carried down by the water, and every crevice among the roots is filled. Care must always be taken to have as much earth above the roots of the plants as will prevent them from being exposed when the water has subsided. After the first watering has dried up, the earth should be levelled round the stem of the plant, and as far out as the water has been put on; if the plants are large, a second, or even a third watering is sometimes necessary; but for ordinary-sized plants, one watering is quite sufficient, and after about twenty-four hours, more or less, according to the nature of the soil, the earth about the stem, and over the roots, should be levelled, smoothed, and made tolerably firm, and the surface mulched with littery dung, ferns, leaves, or cocoa-fibre refuse.

Transplanting Evergreens with Balls.—In transplanting evergreens it is desirable to leave as much earth about the roots as possible; but when treated in the way recommended, the greater part of the earth that may be about the roots is of importance, rather in preserving them from injury during the operation than for any value it may have after the plant has been put into the ground. With large plants it is a safe rule never to move them without keeping a large ball of earth about their roots, and keeping it as entire as possible.

The machines and implements for transplanting large shrubs with balls need not be on such a large scale as those for transplanting large trees. A contrivance formed of sheet-iron, fig. 256, is of the greatest service;- *a*, represents the upper side, *b*, the under side, and *c*, a longi-

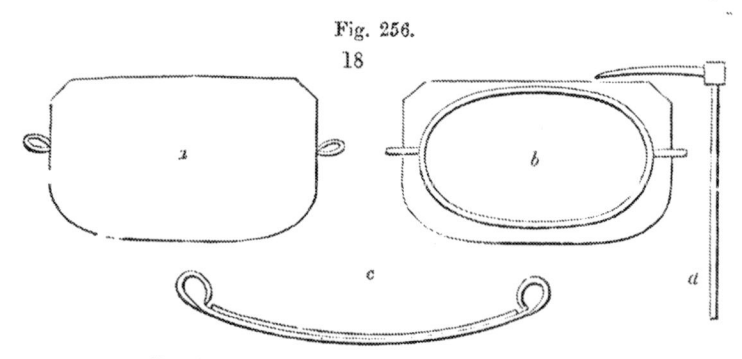

Fig. 256.

Contrivance for transplanting large shrubs with balls.

tudinal section. A truck with low wheels, and a common hand-barrow, with wooden levers and planks, some strong hay-forks, a mattock to sever any roots that may cross our path, and the pick, *d*, will also be useful. A pointed crowbar is often of great service in prizing the ball over, in order to get under it. The sheet-iron hand-barrow would be useful in three or more sizes—viz., four feet, by two feet six inches; three feet, by one foot nine inches; and two feet two inches, by one foot three inches; they should be rounded at the corners, a little turned up at the ends, and strengthened by flat iron bars underneath, carried round near the edges. These iron bars are welded into handles at each end, and the handles are kept above the ground by the ends of the irons being turned up. The ground is opened at a distance from the stem, regulated by the size and nature of the plant intended to be removed, and the fibres are carefully tied up,

TRANSPLANTING AND PLANTING.

as they are met with, to the stem of the plant. By the use of the pick, *d*, the plant is completely undermined on three sides, leaving the remaining side undisturbed till the iron, *b*, is put under the roots, when that side is cut down, and the plant falls upon the iron; and if not sufficiently in the middle, it is easily slipped into the centre. If the plant be large and heavy, an inclined plane is dug on the most convenient side of the hole, and a rope being put into the iron handles, the plant is hauled out. A short strong board is in some states of the ground used for this purpose, instead of the inclined plane. The plant may then, if not too heavy, be carried on a hand-barrow, which admits of the application of the strength of six men, two between the handles, and the other four on the outside. Heavier plants, which are to be carried any distance, are lifted on a truck with low wheels, or a sledge, made strong for the purpose; and if too heavy for this mode, as many boards as are wanted are laid down in succession, and the plant is hauled by the iron upon these boards to the place where it is to be planted. The plant is invariably hauled into the new hole on the iron, which is not removed till its proper position is ascertained; this pre-

Fig. 257.

Small machine for lifting specimen shrubs and conifers.

vents the disturbance of the ball of earth or roots. The plant is then lifted a little on one side and the iron drawn out, earth is then filled in to the level of the fibres, which are untied and laid out straight, and the plant is earthed up. The heaviest plants, Portugal and other laurels, eight feet and nine feet high, and six feet or seven feet in diameter, which cannot be lifted by any strength that can be applied without injury to the ball of earth and roots, are thus moved with great ease and expedition, with large balls of earth, and without any disturbance of the roots; and, consequently, the plants invariably proceed in their growth, often without experiencing the slightest check. The following mode of transplanting trees is much practised in Paris, and well worthy the attention of planters in this country. "Round each tree a circular trench is opened large enough for a man to move about in it at his ease. The depth should be equal to that of the deepest large roots, and a ball of earth large enough to ensure the safe removal of the tree should be left. All the smaller roots found in the trench should be carefully preserved. The ball is shaped into the form of a truncated cone, with its smallest portion below. It is next surrounded with light deal boards, separated from each other by the distance of three-quarters of an inch or so, like the staves of a barrel. These are next secured temporarily by a suitable rope. A man then descends into the hole and fixes the rope by means of the screw apparatus shown in fig. 258, so as to press the planks firmly against the soil of the ball. The press

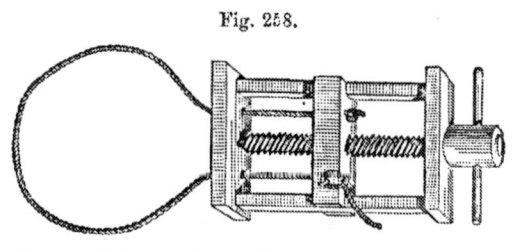

Fig. 258.

Screw used in preparing specimens for removal, as shown in the preceding figure.

is then removed and the same thing done higher up, within say four inches of the top, an ordinary cask hoop being first nailed round the planks before the screw is unfixed. The ball being firmly fixed in its proper position, it is hove over so as to get to its underneath part. The bottom of a cask, having its boards fastened together with a circular piece of sheet-iron rather larger than itself, is passed under, the iron being pierced with two or three holes and turned up so that it may be nailed against the planks. In some cases the stem of the tree should be fixed by iron wire to the sides of the improvised cask.

"When it reaches its destination it is gently inclined to one side, the bottom boards removed, and the roots carefully arranged in their natural position, some good earth being spread over them. The amount of success capable of being attained by this method may be seen throughout the squares of Paris, hardly a single tree having been killed during the plantation of the myriads planted so successfully in the squares and public gardens of that city."

Packing Evergreens.—In removing evergreens, even of small size, and whether they are of the pine and fir tribe, or shrubs, the same care is requisite not to expose their roots to the air, and to plant them as soon as possible after they have been taken up. When evergreen shrubs are to be sent to a distance, they ought to be packed in such a way as to prevent the roots from becoming dry, by surrounding their balls or pots with moist sphagnum, and leaving their tops as loose as possible. The top of the hamper being formed with strong stakes into a roomy cover, and the whole enclosed with a mat.

Methods of Planting Small Plants.—We have seen that in transplanting all large plants, a pit is opened of dimensions proportionate to the size of their roots, and this is also the case in planting single plants of small size; but when small plants are planted in large numbers, different modes are adopted for the sake of expedition, and to save labour. Such of these modes as are in general use, we shall shortly describe, premising that in almost every case when plants are planted in considerable numbers in gardens, they are placed in rows, but that in plantations and shrubberies they are generally planted irregularly or in groups. The rows should in almost every case be placed in the direction of north and south, for reasons easily understood, when we consider the influence of the sun on the soil between the rows and on the sides of the plants in this case, as compared with rows in the direction of east and west. No trees or shrubs should be inserted deeper in the soil than they were before being taken up. The burying up of the collar of the plant is a fruitful source of weakness, disease, and death.

Planting with the Dibber is adapted for seedlings and very small plants. The soil ought to have been previously dug, or stirred by some other means, so that the fibres of the young plant may strike readily into it. In performing the operation, a hole is made with the dibber with one hand, then the root of the plant is inserted to the proper depth, and held there by the leaves, or stem, with the other hand, while, by a second movement, the dibber is inserted by the side of the hole in such a manner as to press in one of its sides to the root of the plant, taking care that the pressure on the roots shall be greatest at its lowest extremity, and that it should be such as to hold the plant so fast that when slightly pulled by one of its leaves it does not come up. Large seeds, bulbs, and cuttings of tubers, or of roots without leaves, as of the potato, Jerusalem artichoke, &c., are frequently planted with the dibber, which, in these cases, is furnished with a blunt point. Newly-rooted small-cuttings, on the other hand, are planted with small pointed sticks. All common seedlings, such as those of the cabbage tribe, are planted with the large dibber, and most small seedlings with the small one.

Planting with the Trowel.—The trowel is entered in the soil perpendicularly, so as to open a hole, against one side of which the plant is placed, and the soil returned and firmly pressed against it if the soil be dry, or gently if it be moist. The majority of plants in the flower-garden are planted in this manner.

Planting in Drills.—The drill is drawn with a draw-hoe, and large seeds, such as beans, or sets such as cuttings of the potato, are placed along the bottom at regular distances, pressing them against the soil, and drawing the soil over them with the hoe. Root-stocks such as those of the asparagus, and root-cuttings such as those of the sea-kale and horse-radish, are sometimes planted in this manner.

Laying in by the heels is a temporary mode of planting, in which a notch or trench is made in the soil, sufficiently deep to cover the roots of the plants which are to be laid in it, but not their tops. An opening or trench is made, as if the land were to be dug, and the roots of the plants are laid in the furrow, with their tops standing out in a sloping direction; after which the digging is continued till the roots are covered, and the soil is then pressed down with the foot, and another trench prepared. This mode of planting is employed wherever more plants are taken out of the ground than can be immediately planted, and it is founded on the necessity of avoiding the great injury which the fibres and spongioles of plants sustain by exposure to the air.

Trench-planting is the most common mode, next to planting with the dibber. It is used in transplanting most kinds of trees in the nursery, and most kinds of edgings of single lines of plants. The spade is inserted perpendicularly along the line, and a trench is opened of the required depth, perpendicular on one side and sloping on the other; and the plants are placed against the perpendicular side with one hand, while, with a spade in the other hand, or by the foot, some soil is drawn over their roots; after which the trench is filled up by the spade, the surface levelled, and the line lifted and placed at a suitable distance, for a second trench. In general, this mode of planting is carried on simultaneously with digging or trenching; trenching being used for plants having very large roots, such as rhubarb, seakale, horse-radish, &c. In planting box and other edgings to walks in shallow trenches, the ground along the line of the intended edging is first dug to a uniform depth and width, and the soil is well broken, so as to be of an equal degree of fineness; it is then compressed by treading or beating, so as to be rendered uniformly firm along the intended line of plants. The line being now stretched, a notch or trench is made along it, generally on the side next the walk, perpendicular to the surface, and of the depth of the roots of the box or other plants. The box is now laid in against the perpendicular side of the trench, using both hands, while the roots are covered with soil by drawing it up against them, with a spade or the foot, so as to keep the plants in their place. The remaining quantity of soil necessary to support the plants, and to earth them up as high on the walk side as on the border side, is then brought forward with the spade, and the work is completed by firmly treading the soil to the plants with the foot.

Slit-planting is effected by inserting the trowel or the spade perpendicularly, moving it backwards and forwards an inch or two, and then withdrawing it. In the open slit thus left a plant is inserted, and the sides brought together, when the slit is not deep, by treading with the foot; but, when it is deep, by inserting the trowel or spade on one side, so as to press one side of the slit against the other throughout its whole depth. Young forest-trees are frequently planted in this manner on unprepared soil, and sometimes seedlings with long tap-roots in gardens.

Hole-planting.—Two men, or a man and a boy, are required for this operation. The ground being dug or trenched, and the width of the rows and the distance between the plants in the rows fixed on, a hole is opened by the man, and the soil thrown aside; a plant is then placed in the hole by the boy, and held there till its roots are covered by a spadeful of soil which is taken out in forming the second hole. The plant is held upright, while the soil is being thrown in over the roots, and it is afterwards fixed by pressure with the feet. A third hole is opened, and a second plant inserted in the same manner till the work is completed.

Planting in Pits.—A pit is dug somewhat larger than the estimated size of the roots which are to be placed in it; and, if in garden or trenched soil, it may be made immediately before planting; but if in firm uncultivated soil, as is frequently the case in forest-planting, it should be made some months, or even a year or more before, in order that the soil in the bottom or sides of the pit, and that which has been taken out, and is to be returned to it, may receive the benefit of the weather. When the pit is dry, the soil in the bottom is loosened; and before planting, a portion of the surface soil taken out is thrown in and mixed with it, and raised up so as to form a long slightly convex surface in the centre of the pit, the apex of which shall be nearly level with the surface of the ground. On this cone the plant is placed, with its roots spread out regularly on every side; the soil is then thrown in over them, and in doing this the soil should be made to fall either perpendicularly, or spread so as not to reverse the direction of the fibres, as is too frequently done when the soil is thrown with force from the circumference of the hole towards the stem. The plant being gently shaken, if necessary, to settle the soil among the fibres, the whole is finished in the form of a cone, rising a few inches above the adjoining surface, having been previously consolidated by treading with the feet. This is the most general mode of planting transplanted trees of from five feet to ten feet in height, whether in the garden, the orchard, the pleasure-ground, or a plantation of forest-trees. In all these departments great care is requisite that the collar of the plant, when the operation is finished, should stand somewhat above the general surface of the ground; because, otherwise, the sinking of the soil, which must inevitably take place, would bury it underneath the surface.

Hole-planting and fixing with Water.—Pits are prepared as in the last mode; and while one man holds the tree in the proper position, the roots having been previously spread out, a second man throws in soil, and a third pours in water from the spout of a watering-pot, held as high above his head as his arms will reach, in order to add to its force in falling on the soil, and settling in about the roots of the tree. This is an admirable mode of planting those trees that have numerous fibrous roots; particularly if the trees be from ten feet to twenty feet, or twenty-five feet in height.

Planting in Puddle.—The pit having been dug in the usual manner, water is poured into it, and soil stirred in till the pit is half full of mud, or puddle. The roots of the tree are then inserted, and worked about, so as to distribute them as equably as possible through the watery mass. More puddle, previously prepared, is then thrown in, the roots again shaken, and the whole finished with dry soil. This mode is well adapted for trees of from ten feet to twenty feet in height, when planted in a dry sandy soil; but it is not suitable for a soil with a retentive bottom, as that would retain the water, and rot the roots.

Planting out Plants which have been Grown in Pots.—In preparing the pit, regard should be had to the probable length of the roots coiled round the inside of the pot; and a sufficient surface of soil should be prepared on which to stretch them out. Unless this is carefully done, the plant, if it has numerous roots matted together, will make little more progress in the free soil than what it did in the pot; because the check given to the descending sap by the numerous convolutions of the fibres, prevents them, so long as they remain in that state, from acquiring the strength of underground branches, which they would otherwise do. This attention to spreading out the roots of plants transplanted from pots is more especially necessary in all those kinds which do not make vigorous tap-roots, such as the pine and fir tribe; but it should not be neglected in any class of plants whatever. It frequently happens that the roots of pines and firs, which have been three or four years in pots, are six or eight feet in length when stretched out; and these ought to be planted in a shallow pit, not less than from twelve to sixteen feet in diameter. Unless the roots are carefully removed, and thus spread out, the tree will either continue unhealthy and die, or it will by a great effort throw up the whole of the spiral roots above the level of the ground, and make a fresh start with new roots. No trees should ever have their roots confined long enough in pots to become matted.

Watering, mulching, and staking newly-planted subjects should, in general, never be neglected where the plants are of large size; not so much to supply moisture to the fibres as to consolidate the soil about the roots; and in the case of evergreens, which are all the year in a growing state, it should be copiously supplied for both purposes. Where it is considered requisite to continue the watering after the plant has been planted, a pan or basin should be formed round it, of somewhat larger diameter than the pit in which the plant was placed, into which the water may be poured so as to ensure its descent to the roots. To lessen evaporation from this basin, or from the soil round newly-planted subjects, it may be mulched, that is, covered with any loose open material, such as litter, leaves, or spent tanners' bark; or, in firm soil, with reversed turf, small stones, large gravel, or tiles. In watering box edgings, &c., newly planted in dry weather, it is of great moment, when the earth is trod firmly to the roots, and before levelling the remainder of the earth, to saturate the soil completely all round the roots with water, with an unsparing hand, and then finish by spreading the dry soil above. When water is poured on the surface of the soil in dry weather, the deluge of water runs the surface of the soil into a paste, which again hardens by the sun into a cake, obstructing thus the free entrance of the atmosphere into the soil, without which no plant will thrive. When straw or moss, or any other kind of mulching is spread on the surface, it obviates this fault. Where this cannot be done, it is better to open holes in the soil, or pare up a portion of the surface, saturating the soil below, and then adding the dry soil when the moisture begins to subside. One such watering will be better than ten surface waterings, which often do more harm than good. Where none of these plans can be adopted, the direct beams of the sun should be kept from the surface by a covering of branches closely spread over it.

Taking up previously to Planting.—It must be constantly borne in mind that the food of plants is taken up by the delicate extremities or spongioles of their fibres, which the slightest tear or bruise will destroy; that these mouths will only act when the soil in which they are placed is in a moist state, and that they are easily rendered useless to the plant by being kept for any length of time exposed to dry air. Hence, in taking up trees, and particularly those of small size, such as are grown for sale in the nurseries, the roots should be separated from the soil with the greatest care, by previously loosening it at a distance from the stem, and never forcibly drawing the roots out of the soil till this has been done, as is too commonly practised in nurseries. It is true we cannot expect to remove all the fibres of a plant of any size uninjured, but by great care we may save the principal part of them. For this purpose a round-pronged blunt fork should generally be used for taking up trees instead of a spade, and the roots, as soon as they are out of the soil, should be covered with a mat, or some other protecting material, to prevent them from being dried by the air. Young trees in nurseries should be frequently and regularly transplanted; this fits them for their final removal by keeping the roots near at home, and causing them to become fibrous. Care should be taken in spreading out the roots to allow none to cross another; and if this cannot be avoided by any other means, recourse must be had to amputation. Cross roots do little harm when young, but, as in the case of branches, they gall one another as they get large.

As a summary of general rules for planting, it may be stated that early in autumn, when the soil has not parted with its summer heat, is the best time for deciduous trees and shrubs, and open-air plants generally, but that evergreens are better planted late in spring or early in summer; that roots should be placed by art as much as possible in the same position in which they would be by nature, that is, with the collar at the surface, and the points of the roots and fibres more or less under it, and in a descending rather than in an ascending direction, excepting for fruit trees, when these conditions should be reversed, as fruit and not wood is the object with these; that the hole or pit in which plants are placed should always be made larger than the roots which it is to contain; and in the case of large plants, convex at the bottom and not concave, that the plant being placed on the centre of this convexity, and the roots spread out in every direction, the soil, finely pulverized, ought to be gently thrown over them, either by dropping it perpendicularly, or throwing it in a direction from the centre to the circumference; that the plant should not be pulled from side to side or up and down, in order to settle the earth about the roots, as was formerly practised with that view, but the effect of which was to break, bruise, or double the fibres; and finally, that the soil should be settled about the roots by one thorough watering at the time of planting, and that this watering, in the case of deciduous trees at least, need not in general be repeated.

Potting and Repotting or Shifting.

To pot a plant is to sow or plant it in a pot, box, or tub; and to repot or shift it, is to turn it out of one pot or box and replace it in the same or in another, with the addition of fresh soil. The mass of soil and roots which is to be shifted is termed a ball. If the object is to add fresh soil, without using a larger pot, then a proportionate quantity must be removed from the ball or mass containing the roots of the plant to be repotted; but if the object be to add fresh soil without disturbing the roots, the mass or ball of soil and roots is simply placed in a pot a size larger than that from which it was taken, and the vacant space between the ball and the pot filled up with soil. If the object should be to grow the plant in a smaller pot than that in which it was before, then the ball must be considerably reduced, so as to be somewhat smaller than the pot in which it is to be placed, in order to allow room for some fresh soil. The implements, utensils, &c., necessary for potting are: a bench or table, either fixed or portable, and which must be perfectly level; pots, tubs, or boxes; broken pots, oyster-shells, or other materials for drainage; proper soils, a trowel, a small dibber, a spade, and a watering-pot and water.

Potting.—Plants are either sown in pots, planted in them when newly originated from seeds, cuttings, or other modes of propagation, or removed to them from the free soil when of considerable size. When a rooted plant, placed in a pot, has begun to grow, its fibres extending in every direction, soon reach the sides of the pot, where, being checked, they are compelled to follow its sides till, after a short time, they form a net-work between the pot and the earth which it contains, so firmly enveloping the latter, that when turned out, it remains entire as one solid body, or, as it is technically called, "ball." As the plants advance in growth, they are moved into larger pots, and thus derive the full benefit of the fresh soil.

The same soil which is suitable for the open garden is not always suitable for using in pots.—Every gardener must have observed that soil that will remain sufficiently open for the roots of plants in the quarters of a kitchen garden, or even when placed in a hotbed, becomes too compact when used in pots, even though it receives as much watering in the one case as in the other. The fact has been thus explained. When the nature of the soil is such as that the cohesion of its particles is greater than that which is formed between the soil and sides of the pot, it loses hold of the latter, and becomes concentrated by every withdrawal of moisture, leaving an almost clear cavity between it and the sides of the pot, and this cavity being readily filled with water, the soil is prevented from expanding in a degree proportionate to the force that would be necessary to displace the water. In addition to this, the fibres of the plant tend to bind it together, and it ultimately becomes so much solidified that it either refuses to take in sufficient moisture, or, if it does, it retains it so as to prevent the ingress of a fresh supply; whilst, at the same time, the water so retained becomes impure, and consequently injurious to the health of the plant. A similar quantity of soil in the quarter from which the above soil is supposed to be taken will be found in a very different state; for there it is kept from contracting on any central portion by its cohesion with the soil in the circumference. Hence the necessity of using such soil for plants in pots as is not too cohesive; or, at all events, weakening its cohesive power by mixture with sand, peat, turf, or other substances that may be found to answer the purpose, and at the same time afford congenial nourishment to the plants. The evils arising from the cohesion of soil in pots, have been well nigh neutralized by the use of rough filling, composed of a mixture of charcoal, broken bones, freestone, &c.

Bottom Drainage.—Whether plants are put in small or large pots, the first point which requires to be attended to is, to cover the hole in the bottom of the pot with some description of material which will readily allow of the escape of water, and if possible prevent the entrance of earth-worms. One crock, somewhat larger than the hole, is placed over it, and over that is placed a layer of smaller pieces, in depth more or less according to the size of the pot and the degree of drainage wanted; and to prevent the soil which is to be placed above from being washed down into this drainage, it is commonly covered with a layer of fibrous or turfy matter, obtained from turfy soil, or with live or dead moss, or cocoa-fibre refuse. In the case of small plants, requiring nothing more than ordinary care, a single crock, or in large pots a single oyster-shell, placed over the hole in the bottom of the pot, is generally found sufficient; but in very delicate plants, a fourth, a third, or even half the pot is filled with drainage material.

The mode of sowing or planting in a pot is so simple and well known as to require no description here. After crocking or draining the pot, a little soil is put in with the right hand, and the seedling or plant held in the left, the roots being spread out carefully while putting in the plant, if a seedling, and the soil applied till level with the rim. A gentle pressure with the hand, or tap on the bench, will lower the soil an inch. The plants should be carried at once to their place, carefully watered with a rose, and should be kept close and shaded for a few days.

In transplanting from the free soil into a pot or box, the plant, if in leaf, is commonly taken up with a ball adjusted to the size of the pot; and to fit such plants for removal, their main roots are frequently cut by the spade, a week or two before taking up, at a short distance from the stem, so that the wounded parts may be within the limits of the ball. This lessens the check to vegetation which would otherwise be given by taking up the plant, and may be usefully applied in the case of many plants which are removed from the open border to the greenhouse late in autumn.

Care of Plants Newly Potted from the Open Ground.—As the absorption of moisture by the spongioles is necessarily checked by the disturbance of the roots, occasioned by taking up the plants and replanting them, so must also be the perspiration of the leaves by the diminished supply of moisture. To lessen this perspiration, therefore, where there is danger of its proving injurious, the plants must be placed in a still humid atmosphere, by watering the surface on which the pots are set, and then covering them with mats, or by placing them in a close frame, and if necessary, shading them from the sun, and supplying extra heat. The more delicate kinds may be placed for a short time on a hot-bed, but the hardier plants will succeed very well if merely sheltered by being hooped over and shaded by any slight covering for a day or two, taking care to remove it at night, and during still, cloudy weather; while the hardiest merely require the shade of a hedge or a wall. The most difficult plants to manage, after being potted, are large herbaceous plants, or large-leaved free-growing greenhouse plants, which have been grown during summer in the open garden, such as stocks, dahlias, brugmansias, &c. These are very apt to lose their leaves after being taken up and potted, whether kept in the open air or in a frame or pit. The best mode of preventing this evil is to check their growth by cutting their roots early in the autumn, as already described.

Shifting or Repotting.—In repotting in the same pot, the ball or mass of soil and roots being turned out of the pot, the soil is shaken away from the roots either wholly or in part, without, however, breaking or injuring the fibres and spongioles any more than can be helped. In shifting from a small pot into a larger one, the larger pot being drained and prepared, the ball is turned out of the smaller pot by turning it upside down, and while holding it in that position, with the ball resting on the palm of the left hand, with the stem of the plant between two of the fingers, striking it gently against the edge of the potting bench, so as to cause the ball to separate from the pot. The ball being now in the left hand, and turned upside down, remove the drainage from it with the right, then reverse it, and place it in the larger pot, filling in the vacant space all round with fresh soil, gently compressing it by working it in with the hands. In shifting from a large pot to a smaller, the ball being taken out of the large pot must either be reduced equally on every side and on the bottom, by picking off a portion of the roots and soil, including of course almost all the spongioles, or the soil must be shaken off from the roots entirely, the roots cut in, and the plants inserted in the smaller pot among fresh soil. In shifting plants from one pot to another, care should in general be taken not to place the collar of the stem deeper in the new pot than it was before in the old one, excepting in the case of plants which root readily from the stem, such as balsams and a few others; but in general, in pots as in the open ground, the stem should rise from a gentle eminence, and the ramifications of the upper roots, where they depart from the stem, should be seen above the soil.

Seasons and Times for Potting and Shifting.—Small plants may be potted at any growing season; but the most favourable are spring and autumn, and the least so mid-winter, even under glass, owing to the absence of light. Shifting also may be performed at any season; but the most suitable for established plants is just before they commence their annual growth, or just after completing it; while young rapidly-growing plants may be shifted from time to time as long as they continue growing. Slow-growing woody plants are seldom shifted oftener than once a year, unless it is desired to accelerate their growth; but rapid-growing plants, such as pelargoniums, and such annuals as the balsam, cockscomb, &c., are shifted many times in a single season, beginning, more especially in the case of the balsam, with a pot of the smallest size, and gradually increasing the size as the plant advances in growth, till from being 2 inches high in a pot of the same height in April, it is 3 feet or 4 feet high in a pot 1 foot in diameter in June or July. By heat and frequent shifting for upwards of a year, pelargoniums are grown so as to form bushes 3 feet or more in diameter in pots of not more than 8 inches or 10 inches across. Pine-apples are grown to a large size in comparatively small pots, but the soil employed is rich and frequently supplied with liquid manure.

The most difficult plants to manage in pots are the hair-rooted kinds, such as all the Ericaceæ, and many Cape and Australian shrubs requiring sandy peat soil, which must be well drained, and kept uniformly moderately moist, but never either soaked with water or very dry. The drainage must be so perfect as to prevent the possibility of water stagnating in the soil; and while the nature of this soil, sand and peat, readily permits the water to pass through it to the drainage below, the porous sides of the pot incessantly carry off moisture by evaporation, and the more so as heaths require to be kept in a rather dry atmosphere. The roots of heaths, and indeed all hair-like roots, are as readily destroyed by over-dryness as by moisture, and hence the continual risk of danger to this description of plants when grown in pots. To guard against the extremes of dryness and moisture, the pots when small are sometimes plunged in sand or moss, or placed in double pots; or when the plants are large, shifted into wooden boxes or slate tubs. To provide against excess of moisture on the one hand, and the want of it on the other, two very ingenious and useful practices have been introduced into the culture of heaths and heath-like plants in pots, by Mr. M'Nab. The first is, always to keep the collar of the stem of the plant a few lines above the general surface of the pots, in consequence of which it is always dry, and not liable to be chilled by evaporation, or rotted off by the stagnation of moisture; and the second consists in mixing with the soil fragments of any coarse, porous stone, such as freestone, from one inch to three inches in diameter, which retaining more moisture than the soil, gives it out to the latter when it becomes too dry; and thus a temporary neglect of watering is not attended with the sudden destruction of the plant, which without these reservoirs of moisture it often is.

Mr. Barnes, late of Bicton, has been in the habit of using rough, rooty, unsifted soil for upwards of twenty years, and of introducing a portion of charcoal among such soil for more than twelve years. He was led to use charcoal from observing, in a wood where charcoal had been burned, the great luxuriance of the weeds around the margins of the places where the charcoal heaps had been, and where a thin sprinkling of charcoal dust had got amongst the weeds. He got a basketful of this dust, and tried it first among cucumber soil. He found it improved the plants in strength and colour, and then began trying it with other soft-growing plants; and he has continued trying it ever since with thousands of plants under pot-culture, and with most kitchen-garden crops. Mr. Barnes finds the following a good plan to make a rough sort of charcoal for use in the kitchen-garden. When made, it must be kept dry; and when seed is sown in the open garden, the charcoal must be put into the drills along with it, at the rate of three or four pints of powdered charcoal to a drill of a hundred feet in length.

Collect a quantity of rubbish together, such as trimmings of bushes, cabbage and broccoli stalks, old pine-apple stems, and such other parts of plants as will not readily rot; put these together, laying some straw beneath them, and set the straw on fire. The straw must be so laid, that the fire can run into the middle of the heap. When the heap is completed, cover it over with short, close, moist rubbish, such as short grass, weeds, and earth, from the rubbish-heap, in order to keep the flame from flaring through at any one place for any length of time. As soon as the fire breaks through in a blaze, throw on more short rubbish, so as to check the flames. It is necessary to thrust a stake or broom-handle into the heap in different places, in order to encourage the fire to burn regularly through it; but as soon as the flames burst through these holes, stop them up, and make others where you think the heap is not burning. When it is all burned, collect the whole of the charred rubbish, ashes, &c., sift it through different-sized sieves, and put the sizes separately into old casks or boxes, keeping these boxes constantly in a dry place. In Mr. Barnes's potting-shed we observed four different sizes of charcoal (considering charcoal dust as one size); sods of heath-soil; different kinds of loam; leaf-mould; pots filled with four different sizes of pebbles, from the size of a grain of wheat to the width of the palm of the hand; four different sizes of broken freestone; four different sorts of sand; two sizes of bone—one of half-inch pieces, and the other of bone-dust; four different sizes of broken pots for draining; different sizes of shards for putting over the holes of pots, previously to laying on the drainage; a basket of live moss, a box of soot, and one of rotten cow-dung.

Growing hardy plants in pots, and especially the more rare kinds of trees and shrubs, for the purpose of transport, is one of the most useful purposes to which the practice of potting can be applied. Great care must, however, be taken not to keep the plants so long in the pots as to cause the roots to become matted.

Pruning.

Pruning consists in depriving a plant of a portion of its stem, branches, buds, leaves, bark, or roots, in order to produce particular effects on the part of the plant which remains. There are different kinds of pruning, named after the manner, extent, and implement used, such as knife-pruning, lopping, clipping, disbudding, disleafing, disbarking. pinching, &c. The instruments necessary for these operations are chiefly the pruning-knife, the bill, the saw, the cutting-shears, and the clipping-shears; but there are some other instruments, such as the pruning-chisel, the averruncator, the girdling-machine, &c., which are occasionally used.

The specific principles on which pruning is founded, and its general effects, are these :—The nutriment of plants is absorbed from the soil by their roots, and formed into branches, flowers, and fruit, by their buds and leaves. If the stem and branches of a plant contain a hundred buds, by removing half of these the shoots or fruits produced by the remainder will be supplied with double their former supply of nourishment; and if all the buds be removed but one, that one may be able to monopolize the major portion of the sap that has been distributed into a hundred channels, consequently the one bud must be developed into a very strong shoot. One of the specific principles of pruning is the stimulus given to vitality. When the leading branch of a small tree, which, perhaps, has not been growing well, but has got the roots fully established, is cut back to one bud, not only is the flow of sap which should have supplied all of the buds diverted into this one, and the shoot made thus more vigorous, but the vitality of the tree has acquired an impetus that it did not formerly possess. From a lazy slow-growing plant it has been converted into one of a quick, healthy, vigorous growth, a stimulus is given to the roots also to increase, and the tree is entirely renovated. The benefit is lasting, not temporary, and will continue, if circumstances are favourable, and no check of bad soil or bad weather ensues to counteract its vigour. It is thus that the forester cuts back his oak plants in the forest, after being a few years planted, and trains a single shoot from the bottom, knowing well that the vigour of this one shoot will be lasting; that the impetus given to the growth of the tree will continue; and that, in a few years, the cut-over tree will be many times larger than those allowed to stand uncut. It is thus that nurserymen increase the vigour of their young plants by pruning; and that gardeners, when pruning for wood, cut farther back than when pruning for fruit. On the other hand, when the whole of the buds of a tree are so abundantly supplied with sap from the roots as to produce chiefly leaves or shoots without blossoms, then by cutting off a portion of the roots the supply of sap is lessened, a moderate degree of vigour is produced, and instead of barren shoots, blossom-buds appear. By these means the growth of plants is controlled by pruning. We can lessen the size, control the form, and direct the energies of plants into either wood or flowers, by the use of the knife upon either root or branch. One of the most useful effects of pruning is to cause the development of dormant or adventitious buds, which is effected by amputating the shoot, branch, or stem, close above any point where visible buds are usually situated, though they may now be wanting there.

For forest-trees pruning is of the greatest use in modifying the quantity of timber produced. Thus by commencing when the tree is quite young, and shortening the side branches and encouraging the leading shoot, the whole of the timber produced is thrown into a main stem; whereas had no pruning been employed, great part of the wood might have been distributed in branches of little use, excepting as fuel. On the other hand, should crooked timber be desired, pruning by destroying the leading shoot, and encouraging those that have a suitable direction, tends to attain the end in view; and by the aid of training this end can be completely effected. Trees which are stunted in their growth from being hide-bound (a disease which is brought on by the sudden exposure of trees to the weather after they have been drawn up by shelter, and in the case of young trees by being planted of too large a size in proportion to their roots), may in general be made to shoot vigorously by being cut down or headed-in. On the other hand, trees which are in particular situations, where it is feared they will grow too large, may be arrested in their growth, or stunted by amputating the larger roots.

For ornamental trees pruning is chiefly employed to remove diseased branches, because much of the effect of these trees depends on the development of their natural form and character, which pruning with a view to timber has in general a tendency to counteract; but for all ornamental trees, grown chiefly for their flowers or fruit, pruning can be as usefully applied as in the case of fruit trees; and where ornamental hedges and other verdant architectural structures are to be grown, pruning by the bill or the shears is essential.

For ornamental shrubs pruning cannot be dispensed with, since many of them are grown for their flowers, which are produced much stronger and of brighter colours when the shoots are thinned out, or shortened, or both; and when the plants are prevented from exhausting themselves by the removal of decaying blossoms, so as to prevent them from maturing their seeds. Every one knows the value of pruning to the rose, and to all shrubs with double blossoms, and shrubs with large blossoms, such as the Magnolia or the Passion-flower.

Fruit trees and shrubs are above all other plants benefited by pruning, which is indeed by far the most important part of their culture. The most general object of pruning is to create an abundant supply of sap during summer by the production of leaf-shoots, by which the general strength of the tree is augmented, and to limit the distribution of this sap when it ascends from the roots in the following spring, by diminishing the number of buds. The effect of this is to increase the vigour of the shoots or fruits produced by these buds; and if this be done in such a manner as to obtain also the greatest advantages from light and air, the pruning will have answered its purpose. If a fruit tree were not deprived every year of a part of the wood or the buds which it produces, its shoots and fruits would gradually diminish in size, and though the fruit would be more numerous it would be deficient in succulence and flavour, as we find to be the case in old neglected orchard trees. The application of pruning to fruit trees differs so much according to the species of tree that the subject can only be properly treated by taking each class separately. Thus kernel fruits which are produced on wood of two or more years' growth, require to be pruned in a different manner from such fruits as the peach, which is produced from the shoots of the preceding year.

To herbaceous plants pruning is applicable, not only when they are being transplanted, when both roots and top are frequently cut in, but also to fruit-bearing kinds, such as the melon tribe, the tomato, &c. The topping of beans, and the picking off of potato blossoms, are operations belonging to pruning; as is the cutting off of withered flowers for the sake of neatness, or to prevent the production of seed. Having noticed the uses of pruning in culture, we shall next shortly describe the different kinds in use in British gardens and plantations. These may be included under close-pruning, shortening-in, foreshortening, spurring-in, heading-in, lopping, snag-lopping, lopping-in, stopping, pinching out, disbarking, disbudding, disleafing, slitting, bruising or tearing, root pruning, girdling, and felling.

Close pruning consists in cutting off shoots close to the branch or stem from whence they spring, leaving as small a section as possible in order that it may be speedily healed over. In performing the operation care should be taken to make the wounded section no larger than the base of the shoot, in order that it may be healed over as quickly as possible; and at the same time to make it no smaller, because this would leave latent buds which would be liable to be developed, and thus occasion the operation to be performed a second time. This mode of pruning is only adopted where the object is to produce stems or trunks clear of branches or of any kind of protuberance, as in the case of standard trees in gardens, especially fruit trees, and in the case of forest trees, grown for their timber. If the branch cut off is under an inch in diameter, the wound will generally heal over in two seasons, and in this case the timber sustains no practical injury; but if it is larger, it will probably begin to decay in the centre, and thus occasion a blemish in the timber. Mr. Cree's mode of pruning forest trees grown with a view to the production of straight timber, which appears to us to be decidedly the best, is an application of this mode.

Mr. Cree commences his operations before the tree has been taken from the nursery, and continues them till he has obtained a clear trunk, of such a height as he thinks the kind of tree will produce of a useful timber size, in the climate and soil where it is planted. He cuts off no branches whatever till the tree has attained the height of from sixteen to twenty feet, with a stem from fifteen to eighteen inches in circumference at the surface of the ground; but during the growth of the tree to that height he shortens in the side branches whenever they extend farther than between three and four feet from the trunk. In consequence of being thus shortened, these shoots do not, so long as they are allowed to remain on the tree, attain a greater diameter at their departure from the trunk than about an inch. The tree having attained its sixteenth, eighteenth, or twentieth year, its head forms a narrow cone, clothed with branches from the ground to the summit. Its pruning is now commenced by taking off one tier of branches annually, commencing with the lowest, cutting close to the stem, generally just before midsummer, that the wound may be partially healed over the same season, and continuing to do this annually till the stem has grown and been cleared to the required height. While the process of clearing the stem is going on below, that of shortening in the side branches is going on above, so as to preserve the narrow conical shape, and prevent any of the branches which are to be cut off from attaining a greater diameter than an inch. The trunk being at last cleared to the proper height, the head over the cleared part is left in the form of a cone, and no longer touched with the averruncator. The head now, by degrees, takes its natural form, and continues growing in that form till the tree is felled. The quantity of timber produced will not be so great as in the case of a tree standing alone, and throwing out its branches uncontrolled on every side, because the quantity of foliage produced, and properly exposed to the light, will not be nearly so great; but it must be recollected, that the timber produced will be in a more useful form, and that more trees may be grown on the same area by this than by any other mode of training.

Shortening-in is the term applied when shoots are shortened at the distance of from two to four or five feet from the stem, the cut being always made to a bud. Exceeding that distance it is called fore-shortening, and is chiefly applicable to timber trees in hedgerows; and under that distance it is called spurring-in. We have seen the use of shortening-in in connexion with close pruning, in the case of forest trees, in the preceding paragraph. In the culture of fruit trees it is applied in connexion with spurring-in, to produce trees of conical forms with branches which, never being allowed to attain a timber size, are prolific in fruit-bearing spurs.

Fore-shortening.—When the lateral branches of a standard tree extend farther than is desirable, a portion of their extremities is cut off, the cut being always made close above a branch of sufficient thickness to form a leader of sufficient strength to keep the branch alive and healthy, but not so strong as to cause it to produce much timber, or in any way to come into competition with the trunk of the tree. The object is to prevent the lateral branches of the trees from injuriously shading the plants under them; and hence it is chiefly used in the case of trees in hedgerows.

Spurring-in.—The apple, the pear, the cherry, the plum, and other fruit trees, or fruit shrubs, produce what are called spurs, or very short shoots or knobs, covered with blossom-buds naturally, and the object of spurring-in pruning is to produce these knobs artificially. This can only be done with lateral shoots, to which the sap is not impelled with the same vigour as to the growing point, because the great object in producing spurs is to obtain blossom-buds, and these are never produced on the most vigorous shoots. A lateral shoot of the present year being produced, may be shortened to two or three visible buds, either in the beginning of summer after that shoot has grown a few inches in length, or the following winter; but the former is in general the better season, because it is not desirable to encourage the production of wood, and consequently of sap, but rather to lessen their production, so as to produce stunted branches, which are in fact the spurs. In the second and third years the shoots produced are shortened in the same manner as they were in the first, and it will generally be found that the leaf-buds left on the lower ends of the shoots when cut down will, the year after, become blossom-buds. As by the process of continually shortening the shoots, the spurs in a few years become inconveniently large, they are from time to time cut out and new spurs formed by the same process as before; and finally, after a certain time, the entire branch bearing the spurs is cut out close to the main stem of the tree, and renewed, as spurs are, by a young shoot produced from its base. The laying-in of small shoots, in place of cutting back to naked branches and spurs, should be more encouraged. More distance than usual should be left between the leading branches, and plenty of young wood nailed in, after the manner of peach-trees. It diminishes the quantity of breast-wood, which is an evident practical anomaly and serves no good purpose, being annually renewed and annually cut out. The growth would be much better spent in producing young wood and fruit, which will not require so much slashing of wood.

Heading-in is cutting off all the branches which form the head of a tree close to the top of the stem, leaving, however, their base to produce buds. This is done with what are called polled or pollard-trees periodically, for the sake of the branches produced as faggot or fence wood, and with fruit trees when they are to be re-grafted.

Lopping.—This term is very generally applied to heading-in, but it is also as generally used to signify the cutting off large branches from the sides of stems, and in this sense we shall here treat of it. Lopping is performed by foresters in three manners, two of which are highly injurious to the timber of the trunk of the tree, and the other not so. The first injurious practice is that of—

Close lopping, by which a large wound is produced, the surface of which not only never can unite with the new wood which is formed over it, because, as we have seen, growing tissue can only unite to growing tissue, but the wood in the centre of the wound will, in all probability, begin to rot before it is covered over, and consequently the timber of the trunk will be more or less injured. The second injurious mode of lopping is, that of cutting off side branches at from six inches to a foot, or even two feet, from the trunk, which is called—

Snag Lopping.—By this mode there can be no efficient source of returning sap, the wounds can never heal over, and are certain, in connexion with the stumps on which they are made, to rot and disfigure and deteriorate the timber much more than in the case of close lopping.

Lopping-in.—The only mode of lopping large branches from the sides of the trunks of trees, without injuring the timber in these trunks, is to shorten them to a branch of sufficient size to heal the wound at its base, or at all events to maintain the growth of the whole of the part of the branch left, and prevent any decay from reaching the trunk. Clean timber, that is, timber free from knots, will not be produced by this mode, but sound timber will be the result, which is much more valuable than the apparently clean and sound timber that would have been produced by close lopping, and letting the tree stand till the wounds were covered with new wood and bark. If the branch had not been lopped, it would have continued to increase in diameter in as great a ratio as the stem; but when lopped so as to produce only as much foliage as keeps the part left alive, such part will increase very little; and as the stem increases, the proportion which the diverging sound knot bears to the straight timber of the stem will be less and less.

Cutting down the stem or trunk of a tree to the ground is an important operation, because in some cases, such as that of resinous or needle-leaved trees, it kills the tree; while in others, or what are called trees that stole, which is a property of most broad-leaved trees, it affords the means of renewing the tree. Thus coppice-woods, which consist of trees and shrubs cut down periodically, have their stems and branches repeatedly renewed from the same root or collar. Thorn hedges are also frequently renewed by cutting down to the ground; but perhaps the most valuable application of the practice is to young stunted forest trees when finally planted out. The slow growth of a tree which is stunted appears to depend on the thinness of the alburnum, and consequent smallness of its sap channels, the result of which is, that the sap rises slowly and in smaller quantities than it otherwise would do; and hence, that a proportionately smaller quantity is returned from the leaves through the bark. But by cutting over the stem just above the collar, the whole force of the sap accumulated in the roots will be employed in the development of some latent buds in the collar, and one of the shoots produced by these buds being selected, and the others slipped off, an erect stem will be produced of five or six feet the first season, and the sap vessels in this shoot being large, and abundantly supplied from the root, the plant will grow freely ever afterwards. A tree may be renovated though not cut back to the collar, and part of the old stem with its thin alburnum left. The vigour of the new growth will give a thicker coating of alburnum;

though old hardened bark will not swell up so quickly as the new bark on a young shoot.

Stopping and Pinching out.—When the point of a shoot is cut off or pinched out, while that shoot is in a growing state, it is said to be stopped; that is, the shoot is prevented from extending in length, and the sap which was before impelled to its growing point, is now expended in adding to the largeness or succulence of the leaves or fruits which may be on the shoot, or in swelling or developing the buds, or, in some cases, changing them from leaf-buds into flower-buds. The principal uses of stopping, however, are to promote the setting and swelling of fruit, either on the shoot of the current year, as in the case of the vine and the melon, or at its base, as in the case of the peach. By stopping the stem of the tobacco-plant, and of the basil, above the third or fourth leaf, the leaves acquire an extraordinary degree of magnitude and succulence, and the same result is sometimes produced with common spinach and the curled parsley. By stopping flower-bearing shoots after they have shown their flower-buds, and removing these, as in the case of annual flowers, the strawberry, the raspberry, the rose, &c., the blossoming and fruit-bearing seasons are retarded, as they are accelerated by stopping all the shoots on a plant that are not blossom-bearing. This stopping has been carried to great lengths in the cultivation of fruit trees in pots, or in the training of them as cordons. (See Training.) Much of the winter pruning of trees might be prevented by stopping the shoots early in summer, provided the state of the tree did not require that the shoots should be allowed to grow their full length in order to send down nutriment to the increase of the roots, in consequence of which greater vigour is in turn imparted to the stem and branches.

Disbarking.—Disbarking the living tree used to be practised for two purposes: one to clear the trees of moss, lichens, or insects, and permit more freedom of growth to the young bark and alburnum; and the other to induce fruitfulness. The latter was effected by ringing or removing a band of bark, of more or less width, entirely, and thus checking the flow of the sap. This practice is now abolished, as fertility may readily be secured by skilful root-pruning. Disbarking for the tanner consists in removing the whole of the bark, and is best performed in spring, when in consequence of the abundance of ascending sap, the bark separates easily from the wood.

Disbudding is the removal of buds early in spring, just when they are beginning to develop their leaves, and is commonly performed with the finger and thumb; the object being to lessen the number of shoots or of blossom-buds to be produced. By lessening the number of blossom-buds, it will add to the strength and probability of setting of those which remain, and the same increase of strength will take place in respect to the shoots, whilst, at the same time, the number of these is reduced to an approximation of that which can ultimately be retained for training. By applying this mode of pruning judiciously to such trees as the peach, apricot, and plum, especially when trained against walls, the use of the knife may be in a great measure dispensed

x

with, excepting for cutting out diseased or decaying shoots. Disbudding is one of the most important summer operations in the management of wall-trees. By disbudding in summer, we prevent the necessity of much shortening and thinning at the winter pruning. In removing the buds care should be taken not to injure the bark of the shoot. The buds ought not all to be disbudded at the same time; the fore-right ones should be first removed, and the others successively, at intervals of several days, in order not to check the circulation of sap by a too great privation of foliage at once. Extent should likewise be given to the wall-tree to exhaust itself by growth, and so bring on maturity. If the border is not too rich, this would be better than tearing off a great mass of breast-wood. More young shoots should be laid in, and they should be left longer at pruning-time in the strongest-growing sorts. Weak-growing sorts, apt to fruit, should be encouraged with manure, or we may have dry mealy, in place of large succulent fruit.

Disleafing.—By taking the leaves off a growing shoot as fast as they are unfolded, no buds are matured in their axils; and thus while the superfluous vigour of the tree is expended, no sap is returned to the root. The practice consequently rapidly reduces the strength of over-luxuriant trees. If trees are not very luxuriant indeed, one year of this treatment will reduce them to a moderate degree of strength. As buds are only formed in the axils of leaves, probably much disbudding and pruning might be saved by disleafing as soon as the leaves are developed; but it must always be borne in mind that every leaf has not only the particular office to perform of nourishing the bud in its axil, but the general one of contributing to the nourishment of all that part of the tree which is between it and the farthest extremities of the roots. Hence, in particular cases, where it is desirable to give additional vigour to the roots, instead of disleafing or disbudding a weak tree, all the leaves and shoots which it produces, even the breast-wood and upright shoots, which the French call gourmands, ought to be encouraged within certain limits. Disleafing is therefore not to be generally commended. It may, however, be usefully applied in various instances to the destruction of perennial weeds, both on the ground and in water, by cutting their leaves off the moment they appear, and before they are even partially developed. Docks, thistles, rushes, horse-tails, and such weeds in pastures, might be destroyed in this mode at less expense than by any other. Even couch-grass, that pest of gardeners in a superlative degree, may be so destroyed, notwithstanding its creeping underground stems, if no green leaves are allowed to be formed; as might the bulrushes, bur-reeds, common reeds, and other weeds which rise up from the bottom of ponds; care being taken to repeat the operation as long as the weeds continue to grow, and never to let them exceed an inch or two in height.

Slitting and splitting the bark of hide-bound trees may also be classed under a mode of pruning; it is now, however, but seldom done, the practice being of doubtful utility. It consists of a number of longitudinal slits, right through the bark, from the branches to the bottom of the bole.

Bruising, or breaking down the branches of trees, has sometimes been adopted as a means of inducing their fruitfulness. The lowest wood of pear-trees on walls is frequently bent or broken down as in fig. 259, with good results, the buds at the base being developed into fruit, and with less risk of their breaking into leaf in the autumn than if they had been cut off at once. They are of course removed at the winter pruning.

Clipping is a species of pruning that was formerly much in vogue when the antique style of gardening was general. Clipping is now mostly confined to the dressing of hedges and box-edgings.

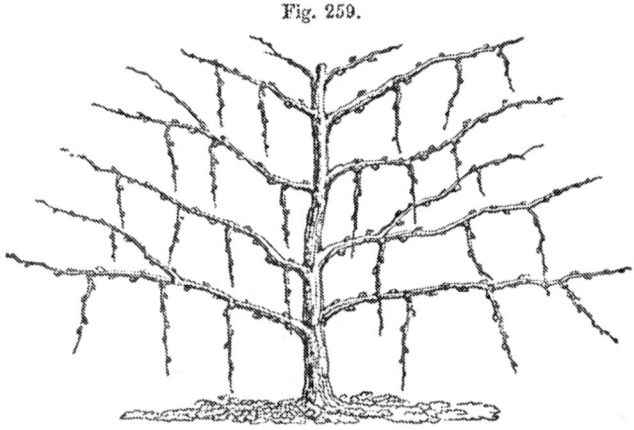

Fig. 259.

A pear-tree with the young shoots twisted, broken, and fastened down, to cause them to produce blossom-buds.

Root-pruning.—As the nourishment of a plant is absorbed from the soil by the roots, it is evident that the supply will be diminished by partially cutting off its source. The operation may be performed so as to effect a twofold result. Its immediate effect is to check the luxuriance of wood shoots, and induce the formation of fruit-buds. If judiciously performed, the operation will not be carried so far as to reduce too much the vigour of the tree, and prevent the second result, that of pushing a number of fibrous roots from those amputated; for in defect of these the health of the tree must decline under the load of, in that case, imperfectly nourished fruit. With a view to the production of a greater number of fibrous roots, old trees may be subjected to a cautious root-pruning; but it must not be performed on subjects unable to bear the shock, or on those in which the power of throwing out fresh roots is very weak. If, however, it is found that fresh roots have been emitted from one amputation, others may be performed as the roots resulting from each preceding operation come into action. Some, again, root-prune their trees annually or biennially. This operation should be performed with a sharp knife, and the cut be clean and slanting outwards. A whole network of fibres then proceeds from the wound, and no decay of the root takes place.

Though root-pruning is chiefly employed to check the luxuriance of young fruit trees, and throw them into blossom, yet it may be employed for these purposes with all trees and shrubs whatever, and even with some kinds of herbaceous plants. The dahlia may be rendered more productive in blossoms, either by ringing the stem just above the root-stock, or by cutting through some of the main roots just beneath it. The Chinese, it is well known, are celebrated for their dwarf or miniature trees, and these are formed of the extremities of the branches of very old trees, rooted by the process shown in fig. 189, and afterwards planted in shallow pots in very poor soil, and as the roots are produced, they are cut or burnt, so as to cramp the growth to any degree required.

Girdling and Felling.—Girdling consists in the cutting out clean a ring of the bark, about four inches in width, close to the ground; which, in larches, seems to cause the turpentine to be wholly incorporated in the wood, instead of passing down to the roots, and, in fact, it so totally alters the condition of the trees, that the workmen complain of their being much more difficult to saw. Another result appears also very interesting. On February 9, 1831, a section was cut from a larch that had been girdled, as above mentioned, in the spring of 1830, and which then weighed 6540 grains. On March 21 it weighed 4990 grains, having lost 1550 grains. A similar section, cut at the same time from an ungirdled larch, weighed on February 9, 5610 grains, and, if it had lost by evaporation only in the same proportion as the other, should have shown, when weighed on March 21, a loss not greater than 1330 grains, instead of which, it then weighed only 3330 grains, thus showing a loss of 2280 grains, nearly double the proportion of the former. The effect of this process in establishing the straightness of the wood is, moreover, very beneficial. A ladder made from a larch so treated will be useful, whilst one not so seasoned will twist so as to be quite worthless. The testimony of a gentleman of great experience is: " Before I girdled, I never could have a ladder made of larch that would continue straight for a month; but now I have them made durably perfect." The common Scotch fir is equally improved by the girdling process. It prevents the wood from warping. A door made of home-grown pine has stood in a very exposed place as well as the best foreign deal. Girdling seems to change what would otherwise be mere alburnum into timber resembling heart-wood; and this may be one reason why the boards made from such trees are found not to warp.

The Girdling Machine.—Figure 260 will give some idea of the girdling machine. *a* is a piece of wood two feet long, four inches wide, and two inches thick, having two saws screwed on it, one on to the top, and the other at the bottom, so as to be perfectly parallel at the distance of six inches from each other, and projecting about three-quarters of an inch; *b* shows the uppermost saw; *c* is another piece of wood of the same dimensions, having four small rollers projecting opposite to the saws; *d d* show the uppermost two of these rollers; *e* is a slip of tempered steel, fixed to *a* at one end, and set to *c* at any requisite point, by a screw-nut *f*, passing through different holes made in *e*, at about one inch distance; *g* is a leather strap, fixed at one end to *c*, and fastened to *a* by a button *h*, by suitable holes. Fig. 261 is a perspective view of this machine. The bark, after being girdled by the saws, may be taken off with any chisel about three or four inches broad.

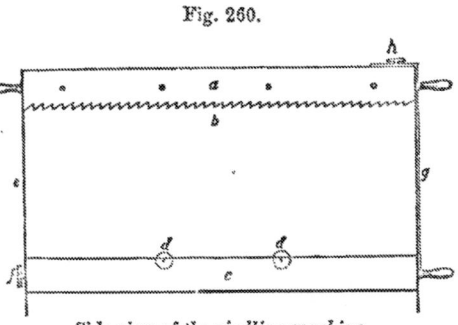

Fig. 260.

Side view of the girdling machine.

The seasons for pruning vary according to the object in view. Where wood is to be cut out or buds removed, so as to throw strength into the remaining parts of the tree, the sooner the operation is performed after the fall of the leaf the better; because as the sap is more or less in motion, and consequently impelled to all the buds

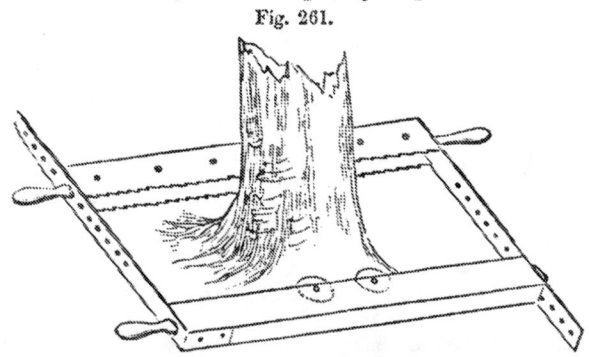

Fig. 261.

Perspective view of the girdling machine.

throughout the whole of the winter, that which would have been employed on the shoots and buds cut off is saved, and those which remain are invigorated by it. Next to autumn, winter is to be preferred for the same reason; but in this season mild weather should always be chosen, because the frost, if severe, will seize on the moisture of newly-made wounds, and rupture their surface. In pruning forest trees, large branches should never be cut off in autumn, because as they cannot heal over till the following summer, decay will commence on the surface of the wound. Spring, just before the rising of the sap, is a better season; but better still, a fortnight before midsummer, at which period the returning sap will commence to deposit a coat of alburnum on the lips of the wound. The worst season in which any description of wood-pruning can be performed is the spring, just before the expansion of the leaves, when the sap is rising with the greatest vigour. The slightest wound made in many plants, either ligneous or herbaceous, at this season, especially young vigorous ones where the sap-vessels are large, occasions a great loss of sap, which must necessarily weaken the plant, unless speedily checked by the only effectual mode in which this can be done, the expansion of the leaves. For disbudding, spring is the most suitable season, though it should not be done all at once, but gradually at different times up to the end of June. By this time the buds will have grown into shoots, and the practice might be called disbudding. Disleafing may be practised to a greater or less extent throughout the whole season of growth. It is not, however, a practice to be commended. The advantages of pruning just before midsummer are, that the wounds may be partially healed over the same season, and that the sap which would have been employed in maturing the shoots cut off is thrown into those which remain. The disadvantages are, that the sap which would have been elaborated by the leaves cut off, and which would have added to the strength of the tree and its roots, is lost. In the case of trees already sufficiently strong this is no disadvantage, but in the case of those which are too weak it is a positive loss. The summer season is found better than any other for pruning trees which gum, such as the cherry and the plum, provided too much foliage is not thereby taken away; and it is also considered favourable for resinous trees. The autumn, on the other hand, is considered the best time for trees that are apt to suffer from bleeding, such as the vine, the birch, and some species of maple. The best season for pruning evergreens is just before midsummer.

Thinning.

Thinning is an operation founded on a general knowledge of the laws of vegetation and on the habits and bulk of particular plants. Its object is to allow sufficient space to entire plants, or to the parts of plants, to attain certain required dimensions and particular properties. When plants stand too close together for attaining those purposes, whether from want of nourishment at the root, or light and air at the top, they are thinned out; and when branches, leaves, flowers, and fruit are too numerous on an individual plant to be properly nourished, and exposed to the sun and air, they also are thinned out. As this last operation is effected by pruning, it requires no farther notice in this article, which is confined to the thinning out of entire plants by uprooting them. Thinning by uprooting is performed by the hand alone, when the plants are small; and when they are larger, by the aid of the trowel, spade, pick, or other implements. The subject may be considered with reference to seedling crops in gardens, and transplanted crops in plantations. Transplanted crops in gardens, being generally of short duration, are placed at such distances at first as mostly to render future thinning unnecessary. One general rule in thinning is that the plants to be removed, when they cannot be taken away all round the plant to be left, should be taken from the east and west sides of it, in consequence of which it will receive the sun and air on two sides instead of on one, which would be the case if thinning took place only on the south side; while if it were limited to the north side, air would be admitted, but no sun.

Seedling Crops in Gardens.—To make sure of a sufficient number of plants, and of their distribution over every part of the surface, much more seed is sown than is required for the number of plants requisite for a crop. As soon as the plants from these seeds make their appearance, and are considered safe from accidents or insects, all or the greater part of those which are not judged necessary for producing a crop are pulled and thrown away, hoed up and left to die on the spot, or in some cases taken up by the trowel or spade and transplanted elsewhere. The distance at which the remaining plants are left depends on their nature and habit, on the richness or poverty of the soil, and on the kind of crop required. For example, in thinning out an autumnal crop of turnips, the distance between the plants left will be much less than in thinning out a spring crop; because in the latter case, the plants being destined to benefit by the warmth and light of summer, their roots will attain a much larger size than those of the autumn-sown crop. It will readily be conceived that crops that have few or narrow leaves and perpendicular roots, such as the onion, require less thinning than such as have broad-spreading leaves, such as the turnip; and that those which have tap-roots, like the carrot, do not require so much surface soil as those which have spreading roots, and creeping or trailing shoots, such as the New Zealand spinach. Thinning seedling herbaceous plants may take place at any season; but when they are to be cut out with the hoe and left to die on the spot, dry weather and a dry state of the soil are necessary; and when they are to be pulled up by hand, or taken up by the roots with a tool for transplanting, a moist state of the soil and cloudy or rainy weather are essential, in order that the fibres may receive as little injury as possible in parting from the soil.

Thinning Plantations.—Timber trees when planted in masses are placed much closer together than they are intended to be finally, partly to shelter one another, and partly to profit by the trees which are to be from time to time thinned out. By planting moderately thick, the nutriment contained in the soil is much sooner turned into wood than it would be if only the few trees were planted which are finally to remain; and by these trees standing near together they are drawn up with straight stems, so that the timber produced, even by young trees so treated, is of some use. By increasing the distance between these trees by thinning, the source of nourishment to the roots of the trees which remain is increased, and the space round the branches for light and air enlarged, so that by degrees, with every successive thinning, larger timber is produced. At what time the thinning of a plantation ought to commence, how long it ought to be continued, and at what distances the trees ought finally to stand, will depend on the sort of tree, the kind of plantation, the soil and situation, and the climate. In the case of a plantation where the object is to produce straight timber, the first point to determine is the probable height to which the kind of tree to be planted will attain in the given locality; and then to obtain from the experience of others, or from observation of natural woods in similar localities, the distance required to enable a tree to attain that height. A tree in a sheltered valley and on deep rich soil not much above the level of the sea will attain double or triple the height which it will on a hill at a distance from the sea; the temperature in the latter situation being much lower, the soil generally poorer, and the wind stronger. The subject of timber plantations not forming a prominent feature in this volume, we shall only add that experienced planters have laid down certain rules for thinning timber plantations, and that the best of these we consider to be those of Mr. Cree, published in the 'Gardener's Magazine' for 1841, and applicable to every situation from the level of the sea to an altitude of 1800 feet. Supposing the height which the trees in a plantation of round-headed kinds are supposed to attain is 85 feet, and that they have been planted at the distance of about 4 feet, tree from tree; then the first thinning should commence when the trees are 13 feet 6 inches high, and the trees thinned so that those that remain may stand at twice the former distance from each other, or 8 feet apart each way. The second thinning should take place when they are about 24 or 25 feet high, when the trees should be left so as to be 16 feet apart each way, thus leaving 170 to the acre. The third thinning should take place when the trees are about 47 or 48 feet high, when only 42 trees should be left to the acre to attain the height of 85 feet; and these must accordingly stand at the distance of 32 feet apart each way. It is not pretended that these rules should in all cases be exactly followed; on the contrary, they are only given as approximations, the result of extensive experience and scientific reasoning, for round-headed trees; for poplars and coniferous trees, the final distance is much less. (See Mr. Cree's table in the 'Gardener's Magazine' for 1841, p. 553, and also some excellent observations on the subject in the 'Gardener's Chronicle' for 1842, p. 19, and in various other parts of that journal and in the 'Gardener's Magazine.') A forester should be well impressed with the importance of light, air, moisture, and shelter as regards vegetation; and he should closely observe the density which the various trees that are under his charge will bear. In all extensive plantations some trees will be seen suffering from being too close: he should learn from cases of the kind how to proceed to thin others that he can easily foresee are approaching a similar condition. As a guide to the time when to commence thinning, we should say— Always when the trees are about to touch, but not yet touching.

Thinning Ornamental Plantations.—As the object of these is to display the natural character of the trees, either of their heads at a distance, as in masses of groves or trees only, or singly, or in groups of trees among under growths, or on smooth turf, it is obvious that thinning is of as much importance to the desired result as in timber plantations. It is equally so in plantations of shrubs, especially flowering shrubs, where the object is to show the individual character of the shrub, and also the beauty of its blossoms and fruit. Every tree and shrub has two characters, both of which are natural to it; the one when it grows up in a mass of other trees or shrubs of the same kind, or of other kinds, and the other when it grows up singly. In the former case the stem or stems are always straight and comparatively free from branches to some height, while in the latter it is generally clothed with branches from the ground, or a short distance above it, upwards. The thinning, therefore, of an ornamental plantation will depend on the natural character to be imitated. An open grove where the trees have clear trunks to half or two-thirds of their height, affords a delightful retreat for walking in in the hottest weather of summer; and this is also the case with an avenue where the trees have been properly thinned and pruned to the height of fifteen or twenty feet; while a lawn studded with trees and shrubs singly or in small groups, and with their lower branches resting on the ground, affords views from a gravel-walk or a drawing-room window peculiarly characteristic of an English pleasure-ground.

Training.

To train a plant is to support or conduct its stem and branches in some form or position, either natural or artificial, for purposes of use or ornament. It is effected partly by pruning and thinning, but chiefly by pegging down to the ground, tying and fastening to rods, stakes, or trellises, or nailing to walls. The articles more immediately required are hooked pegs, ties, nails, and lists, wire-netting, with props of various kinds, arched espaliers, and ladders.

The principles upon which training is founded vary according to the object in view, but they all depend more or less on these facts:—that the sap of a plant is always impelled with the greatest force to its highest point; that, in general, whatever promotes this tendency encourages the production of leaves and shoots, and whatever represses it, promotes the formation of blossom-buds. When a plant is to be trained over the surface of the ground, it must be borne in mind that, as the tendency of the sap is always to the highest bud, the shoots pegged down should be allowed to turn up at the points, in order to promote their extension. When the object is to induce blossoms or fruitfulness, a contrary practice should be followed, and the points of the shoots kept down, or in the case of upright-grown plants, trained horizontally, or even in a downward direction. This should also be done when the object is to restrain over-luxuriance, and a contrary practice when a weak or sickly plant or tree is to be invigorated. When the object is to economize space, the plants are trained against a trellis, as occupying length, but very little breadth; and when it is to increase temperature, they are trained or spread out against a wall, which prevents the conduction of heat and moisture from the branches, by acting as a screen against winds; and increases heat by reflecting the rays of the sun during the day, and giving out heat during the night and whenever the atmosphere is at a lower temperature than the wall.

Manual Operations of Training.—The tie or the list, by which the shoots are fastened to the trellis or wall, should be placed in the internode, and always immediately behind a bud or joint; because when tying or nailing takes place in the summer season, and near the points of the growing shoots, the latter sometimes elongate after being fastened, and if this elongation is prevented from taking place in a straight line by the fastening being made immediately before a bud or leaf, instead of being made immediately behind it, the shoot will be forced into a curved direction, and the bud and its leaf injured. Ties, which in this country are commonly of bast, or woollen, linen, or cotton, twine, osier, &c., are gently twisted before being tied into a knot, in order that it may be the firmer, and the tie not liable to be torn during the operation of tying. Osier-ties, which are sometimes used for espalier trees, are fastened by twisting together the two ends, and turning them down in a manner sooner and easier done than described. In fastening shoots with nails and shreds, when any restraint is required to retain the shoot in its position, the pressure must always be against the shred and never against the nail, as the latter would gall the shoot, and in stone-fruits generate gum. The shred ought never to be placed in the hollow of a bend in the branch to be attached; for there it is worse than useless. On the contrary, the shreds should be put on so as to pull the external bends inwards towards the direct line, in which it is desirable the branch should be trained. In fig. 262, the straight direction in which it is desired to

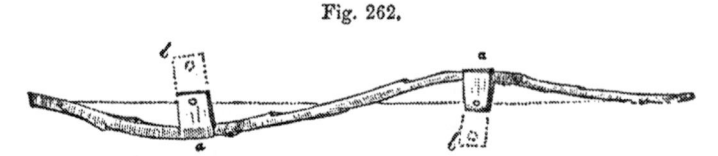

Fig. 262.

Bringing a bent shoot into a straight direction by nails and shreds.

train the shoot is indicated by the dotted lines; *a* represents the shreds and nails put over the shoot to bring it to its place over the dotted lines, and *b*, dotted lines indicating the points which will be covered by the shreds and nails when the shoot has been rendered straight, by drawing both shoots from *a* to *b*. The nails used, whether of cast or wrought iron, should have round shanks and small round heads, as being less likely to injure the branches than sharp-angled nails. Nails an inch in length are sufficient for ordinary branches, but twice that length is necessary for very large ones. Cast-iron nails are most generally employed, and they are so cheap, and, besides, not liable to bend in the points, that they are generally preferred to nails of wrought iron. They seldom break when being driven into mortar joints; and if they do so when drawing them out, it is perhaps cheaper to buy new cast-iron nails than to point and straighten wrought-iron ones. Boiling nails in linseed-oil prevents, or, at all events, greatly lessens their rusting. Nails should in general be driven into the joints, and not into the bricks, because the joints are easily repaired. They should never be driven far in, and in summer training a much slighter hold of the wall will suffice than in winter-training, because in the latter case the shoots will not be moved for a year; for if they hold at the time of nailing, they become faster as they begin to rust; the oxide requiring an additional space to that required by the metal on which it is formed. Before a nail which has been some time in a wall is attempted to be drawn out, it should receive a tap with the hammer, by which it will be loosened, and be more likely to separate without breaking. Shreds of woollen are preferred to those of any other cloth or to leather, as being softer and less influenced by the weather. Their length should be such as to contain a shoot double the size of that for which they are intended, in order that they may never compress the shoot so much as to impede the returning sap, and their breadth may be from a quarter to three-quarters of an inch. They should be folded up a little at each end, so that in driving the nail through the shred it will pierce four times its thickness, and be in no danger of tearing, as it often does when the nail passes through only twice its thickness. Medicated insect-proof shreds of various kinds of linen are now offered, which afford less harbour for insects, and are altogether neater and cleaner than woollen lists. When a shoot is merely to be nailed to the wall, without requiring constraint on either side, then the nails are placed alternately; but when a crooked branch is to be nailed in, two or more nails in succession will frequently be required on the same side. In driving the nails, they should incline with their heads downwards to prevent water as much as possible from hanging on them, as the rust produced is often injurious, especially to fruit. The branches should be fastened quite close to the wall, in order not to lose the benefit of its heat. Brown or grey lists are best, not being too conspicuous. Trained fruit trees are generally loosened from the wall at the time of winter or spring pruning, when the wall can be cleaned and coloured if necessary, and the tree washed with a composition for the destruction of insects. The re-nailing is in general performed immediately afterwards; though some, in order to retard the blossoming of the tree next spring, tie the branches to stakes at some distance from the walls. This, however, can only be safely performed with the very hardiest kinds of trees, and even with them must be attended with danger during severe winters, unless in very sheltered situations. In re-fixing a trained tree, place all the leading branches in their proper positions first, beginning at the lower part of the tree, so as to make sure of covering the bottom of the wall. The main branches being placed, lay in the young wood, beginning also at the bottom of the wall, and at the further extremity of the branch, and working up to the main stem. We shall now describe the different kinds of training, commencing with the simplest, and concluding with the different forms employed in training fruit trees.

Training herbaceous plants in beds or borders is in some kinds effected by fastening them down to the surface of the ground, or to rock-work or a surface of pebbles, by means of pegs, loops of matting, hair-pins, or other material; or by laying on the shoots small stones. Twining flowers, such as the common convolvulus, or twining esculents, such as the scarlet-runner, only require straight rods, or branches with upright shoots, such as those of the beech, placed close by the plants. Branches are in general to be preferred to straight branchless rods for herbaceous climbers, because by offering a number of interruptions to the ascent of the climbing stem, they encourage it to divaricate, and consequently to produce a greater number of flowers and fruit within a limited space. Tendrilled climbers, such as sweet peas, and those with rambling stems, such as the nasturtium, are also supported by branches placed in a circle round each patch, or along each side of a row, of the height to which the plants are expected to grow; or straight hazel rods are inserted in the soil obliquely so as to touch at top and bottom, and cross in the middle, so as to form lozenge-work; or wires may be supported by iron or wooden rods in any desired form. Tall-growing plants with stems having terminal flowers, and which do not branch, such as some asters, when they cannot support themselves, require to be loosely enclosed by three or four rods placed close to the roots at bottom, and spreading outwards at top, and connected by twine; or, in some cases, a slender rod may be placed to each stem. On no account should such clusters of stems be tied together in bunches, a common practice among slovenly gardeners, as the compression rots the leaves and lessens the size of the flowers.

Fig. 263.

Wire-framework for climbing-plants in pots.

Plants having branchy stems, such as Lupines, should, if staked at all, have a stake to each stem, thinning them out where they are so numerous as to produce a crowded appearance. Florists' flowers, such as the carnation, the dahlia, &c., require particular kinds of stakes, and the greatest care in tying.

Herbaceous and shrubby plants in pots being in a highly artificial state, when they require training should have straight rods, or symmetrical frames of laths, or of wire-work. Pelargoniums when of large size are trained by means of straight terminal shoots of willow or hazel, so as to radiate their branches from the pot, and form a regular hemisphere of foliage and flowers, close but not crowded. Various training frames have been adopted for ornamental climbers in pots, which are formed of rods and rings of stout wire,

TRAINING. 317

the whole being painted green, or of the colour of bark, according to the taste of the gardener or his employer. Globular, balloon-shaped, half-spherical, flat, round, and square trainers of wire or iron are so common as to need no description. In training slender climbers or twiners, such as Kennedia rubicunda, nails may be driven into the wall near the ground (fig. 266, *a*), and three or four feet above it (*b*), close to which the plant is placed; strings are drawn from the lower nails to those above, and the stems of the plant twined round them.

Fig. 264.

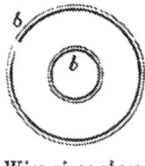

Fig. 265.

Wire standard for supporting rings, so as to form the framework shown in fig. 263.

Wire-rings shown in fig. 263.

Training Hardy-flowering Shrubs in the Open Ground.—Trailing and creeping shrubs seldom require any assistance from art, excepting when they are made to grow upright on posts, trellises, or walls. In general all creepers that are trained upright, and all climbers, whether by twining, tendrils, hooks, root-lets as the ivy, or mere elongation as in the Lycium and the climbing roses, when they are to form detached objects, should be trained umbrella fashion, see fig. 268, next page. Fig. 267 is a portrait of a climbing rose, trained down from a ring which forms the top to an iron rod. This is called the balloon manner of training, and was first applied to apple-trees. When the rod is fixed in the ground, the ring at the top should stand an inch or two higher than the graft at the top of the stock, or than the head formed on the stem of the plant, if it should not have been grafted. Six or eight of the strongest shoots are then to be selected, and tied to the ring with tarred twine; and if, from their length, they are liable to blow about, their ends are attached to twine, continued from the wire to pegs stuck in the ground, as shown in the figure. When it is desired to cover the stem of a spreading-headed climber with the foliage and flowers of a different plant, the taste of which is questionable, as they never grow so freely in such a situation where they are shaded and the roots of the plants starved, fig. 268 may be used. Climbing roses may also be advantageously displayed on such props, and more slender climbers, as well as standard roses, and other shrubs, trained to single stems, may be tied to stakes of larch, oak, ash, or sweet chestnut, or to cast-iron stakes. When climbers or other flowering plants are trained on arched trellises covering walks, it must be borne in mind that if

Fig. 266.

Mode of training herbaceous climbers on a brick wall.

318   TRAINING.

the display of the flowers is an object, the trellis-work must not be continuous, but rather of arches springing from piers of trellis-work, or

Fig. 267.

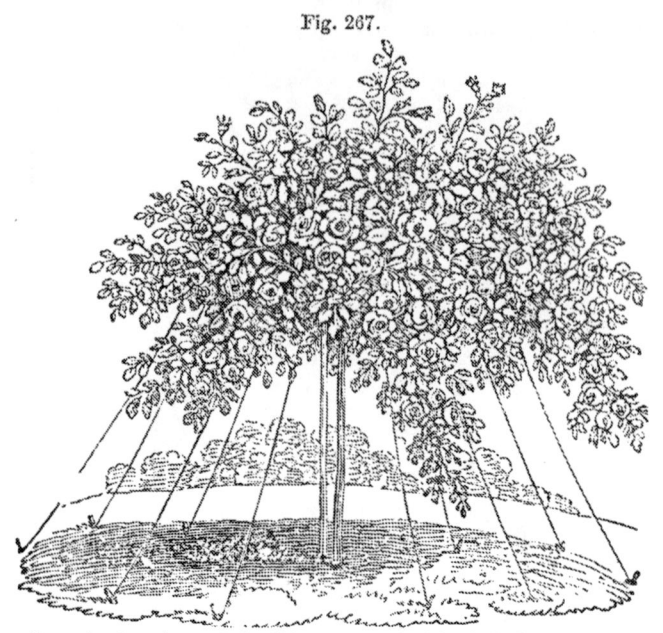

Portrait of a Bizarre de la Chine rose, trained in the balloon manner.

pilasters, at short distances from each other, so as to admit the light between. When this is neglected, the plants will only look well on their outer surface. The laburnum, when trained over an arched trellis of this kind, has a splendid effect when in flower; but when the trellis is continuous, the blossoms have a pale, sickly appearance, as we witnessed some years ago at a country seat, where the trellis of which fig. 269 is a section was covered with laburnum; the low table trellis, *a, a*, being clothed with ivy. The contrast between the dark green ivy and the yellow blossoms would have been effective, had the latter enjoyed the benefit of light.

Fig. 268.

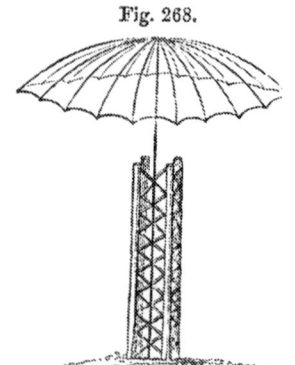

Prop with umbrella-top for spreading headed climbers, and for training other plants round their stems.

Evergreen shrubs require very little training, excepting in the case of fastigiate-growing species in situations exposed to high winds, or shrubs that are to be shorn into artificial shapes. The evergreen cypress, and the upright variety of arbor vitæ, are apt to have the side-shoots displaced by high winds or heavy snows, for which reason these branches are frequently tied loosely to, or rather connected by tarred twine with the main stem. If, however, the side branches are carefully cut-in as the tree increases in growth, no such tying will be needed. When evergreen shrubs are to be shorn into common shapes, such as cones, pyramids, piers, pilasters, &c., little or no training is required; but when they are to be grown into more artificial shapes, such as those of men or animals, the figure required is constructed of wire or trellis-work, and being placed over the plant, the shoots are confined within it; and if the plants are healthy, and in a good soil and situation, the figure is speedily formed. The best shrubs for this kind of ornament are those which have narrow leaves, such as the yew, the juniper, the arbor vitæ, and the spruce-fir. One of the figures, the most readily formed by any of these plants, is a hollow vase, which only requires a series of hoops tied to ribs, and the latter attached to a stake placed close by the main stem of the plant. In selecting plants for being trained into figures of men and women, it was usual to use variegated varieties to represent the female forms. The best examples of this kind of training are to be found at Elvaston, near Derby. It is now considered old-fashioned and barbarous.

Fig. 269.

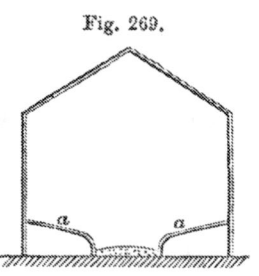

Section of a laburnum trellis over a walk, with table trellises, a, a, *for ivy.*

Training Fruit Trees.—By far the most important application of training is to fruit trees, whether for the purpose of rendering them more prolific, improving the quality of the fruit, growing fruit in the open air which could not otherwise be grown except under glass, or confining the trees within a limited space. Fruit trees are trained either as ordinary bushes or trees in the open garden, or spread out on flat surfaces against walls or espaliers, or trained to single branches on walls, espaliers, or within a few inches of the ground as cordons. In either case the operation is founded on the principle already mentioned—that of suppressing the direct flow of the sap, by which it is more equally distributed over the tree, the tendency to produce over-vigorous shoots from the highest part is diminished, and the production of flowers from every part increased. We find that trees in a state of nature always produce their first flowers from lateral branches, to which the sap flows less abundantly than to those which are vertical; and the object of training may be said to be, to give all the parts of a tree the character of lateral branches. With a view to this, certain rules have been derived from the principle of the suppression of the sap, which it may be useful to notice as of general application to every mode of training:—

1. Branches left loose, and capable of being put in motion by the wind, grow more vigorously than those which are attached; and hence the rule to nail or tie-in the strongest shoots first, and to leave the

weaker shoots to acquire more vigour. Hence also the advantage of training with fixed branches against walls, as compared with training with loose branches in the open garden, when greater fruitfulness is the object.

2. Upright shoots grow more freely than inclined shoots. Therefore when two shoots of unequal vigour are to be reduced to an equality, the weaker must be elevated and the stronger depressed.

3. The shoots on the upper side of an inclined branch will always be more luxuriant than those on the lower side; therefore preserve, at the period of pruning or disbudding, only the strongest shoots below, and only the weakest above. Some have practised the system of only preserving the upper branches and removing the whole of the under ones, with a view of securing uniformity of growth and a maximum of strength.

4. The lower branches of every tree and shrub decay naturally before the upper branches; therefore, bestow the principal care on them, whether in dwarf bushes in the open garden, or with trees trained on espaliers or walls. When they are weak, cut them out, and bring down others to supply their place, or turn up their extreme points, which will attract a larger portion of sap to every part of the branch.

The different modes of training bushes and trees in the open garden are chiefly the conical for tall trees or standards, and some modification of the globe or cylinder for dwarfs. The flat, horizontal, or table form, and the cordon, have also been tried successfully. But it may be remarked that unless these and all other artificial forms are constantly watched to check the tendency to return to nature, they are much better dispensed with. By careful attention, some of these artificial forms will bring trees sooner into a bearing state, and a greater quantity of fruit will also be produced in a limited space; but if the continued care requisite for these objects is withdrawn for two or three years, the growth of the tree, while returning to its natural character, will produce a degree of confusion in the branches that will not be remedied till all the constrained branches have been cut away. Wherever, therefore, fruit is to be grown on a large scale, and in the most economical manner, in orchards or in the open garden, it is found best to let every tree take its natural shape, and confine the pruner and trainer to such operations as do not greatly interfere with it. These are chiefly keeping the tree erect with a straight stem, keeping the head well balanced, and thinning out the branches where they are crowded or cross each other, or become weak or diseased.

The different modes of training fruit trees against walls or espaliers, may all be reduced to three forms or systems:—the fan or palmate form, which is the most natural mode, and that most generally applicable; the horizontal system, which is adapted to trees with strong stems, and of long duration; and the perpendicular system, which is chiefly adapted to climbers, such as the vine. Trees trained by any of the above modes, against a wall or espalier, are much more under the control of art than can ever be the case with trees or bushes in the open garden; because, in the latter case, the whole tree, as well as its branches, are at all times more or less liable to be put in motion by the wind, whereas against a wall they are fixed, and have not the aid of motion to increase their thickness. For these reasons, and also because flat-training is applied to trees which, as ordinary bushes in the open garden, would scarcely produce fruit at all, flat-training cannot be dispensed with. In making choice of a mode of flat-training, the nature of the tree, the climate, soil, and the object in view, must be jointly taken into consideration. Trees of temporary duration, which naturally produce numerous divergent branches, such as the peach and the apricot, are best adapted for fan-training, where the climate is favourable; but in a cold climate, an approach to the horizontal manner may be preferable, by lessening the quantity of wood produced, and thus facilitating its ripening. The horizontal system of training produces the greatest constraint on nature, and is therefore adapted for fruit trees of the most vigorous growth, and of large size, such as the pear and apple, which are almost always trained in this manner, whether on walls or espaliers. For plants producing shoots having little or no tendency to ramify, and which are of short duration, such as the vine, climbing roses, &c., the perpendicular manner is the most natural and the easiest; nevertheless, by disbudding and training, plants of this kind can be made to assume the fan form, and thus be rendered more productive in blossoms and fruit than if trained in a manner which is more natural to them; and in the case of the vine, even the horizontal system may be adopted, because its shoots are of great duration. We shall first describe the methods of training dwarfs and standards in the open garden, and next the different modes of flat-training on walls and espaliers.

Dwarfs in the open garden are trained in the form of hollow bushes, concave, or shaped like cups, urns, goblets, or barrels, the form being in every case produced by training the shoots to a frame-work of rods and hoops. Dwarfs are also trained in the form of globes, balloons, cylinders, low cones, pyramids, triangles, and sometimes with the branches in regular stages like a chandelier. Most of these forms are also capable of being varied by training the shoots which compose their form vertically, horizontally, obliquely, or spirally; and also by tying down the current year's shoots as soon as they have ceased elongating, in the manner of quenouille training, to be afterwards described. All dwarfs, whether to be left to nature or trained artificially, are grafted on stocks naturally of humble growth, such as the quince or the mountain-ash for the pear, the doucin or the paradise for the apple, the Mahaleb for the cherry, the Myrobolan or the sloe for the plum, &c.

Spiral Cylinders.—Of all these different modes of training dwarfs, that which best deserves adoption in a small garden is the spiral cylinder, the training of which is thus described by Mr. Hayward:—
" Prune and manage the tree so that it shall form from three to six branches of as nearly equal size as possible, within about six or eight inches of the ground, as in fig. 270; and as soon as the branches are grown from three to five feet long, fix six rods or stakes into the earth

for supporting them, in a circle about the root, as in fig. 271, the centre dot marking the root, and the others the rods. Each branch is then to be brought down, and being fixed to the rod near its base, the branch is to be carried round in a spiral manner, on such an elevation as will form an inclination of about fifteen degrees, and each branch is to be fixed in the same manner, one after another; thus all will move in the same direction, one above another, like so many corkscrews following in the same course, as shown in fig. 272. As from this position of the branches the point-bud of each leader will present the most vertical channel for the sap, the strongest shoot will form there, and thus afford the means of continuing the leaders to a great height and for a great length of time, without crossing or obstructing each other, or throwing out useless collaterals; at the same time, by the depressed position of the leading branches, enough sap will be pushed out on their sides to form and maintain vigorous fruiting spurs. As trees trained in this manner need never exceed the bounds allotted them on a border or bed, a greater number of trees may be planted, and a greater quantity of fruit produced, in a given space, than can be the case when they are trained in any other manner. But as pear and apple-trees on free stocks may be found to grow too rude and large after a few years, those best answer which are grafted on dwarf-growing stocks; that is, pears on quince stocks, and apples on paradise stocks. However, to keep dwarf trees from growing too luxuriant and rude, it is a good practice to take them up and root-prune them every three or four years.

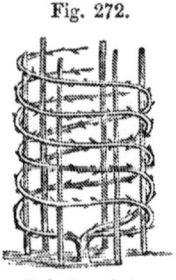

Standards in the open garden are, in France, sometimes trained with heads in similar shapes to those we have mentioned as adopted for dwarfs; but those in most general use, where the natural form is departed from, are the spurring-in system, the conical or pyramidal system, to either of which may be applied the quenouille system; a term which is sometimes applied to the distaff or conical form of the tree, and sometimes to the mode of tying down the current year's shoots, like the fibres of flax on a distaff, so as to stagnate in them the returning sap. Trees trained in any of these manners are generally grafted on dwarfing stocks, so as to keep their growths within moderate bounds.

The Spurring-in System.—Choose a tree that has a leading shoot in an upright direction, fig. 273, *a*; having planted it, shorten the side shoot, leaving only two or three buds, and shorten also the leading shoot, according to its strength, so that no more buds may be left on

TRAINING. 323

it than will produce shoots, as at *b*. The first summer the produce in shoots will be as at fig. 274, *c*; and if before Midsummer the leading shoot be shortened as at *d*, it will probably throw out side shoots the same season, as at *e*. At the winter pruning all the side shoots may

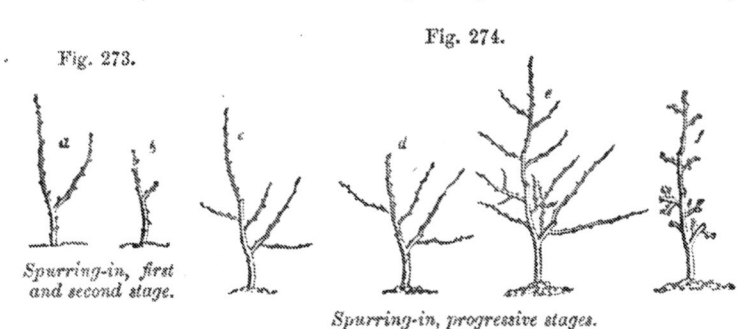

Fig. 273.

Spurring-in, first and second stage.

Fig. 274.

Spurring-in, progressive stages.

be shortened to two or three buds, and the leading shoot to such a number as it is believed will be developed. The tree will then appear as at *f*; and the process of shortening is to be repeated every year till the tree has the appearance of fig. 275; or until it has attained the height required, or which the kind of tree is calculated to attain.

Fig. 275.

Spurring-in completed.

Conical Standards, or, as they are erroneously called, pyramidal standards, may be produced from trees partially spurred-in; but the most general mode is to cut in the side branches, as shown in fig. 276, which represents several successive stages; while fig. 278 shows the tree brought to its regular shape; and fig. 279,

Fig. 276.

Quenouille training, progressive stages.

the same tree with the branches of the current year tied down in the quenouille manner. The best example of this mode of training which we have seen in England, was in the Horticultural Society's garden in 1830; and in France, in the Royal Kitchen Garden at Versailles, in 1840. There were in the latter garden, in that year, two hundred

y 2

324 TRAINING.

trees trained in the conical manner with the current year's shoots tied down *en quenouille.* They had attained the height of from six to

Fig. 277.

Fig. 278.

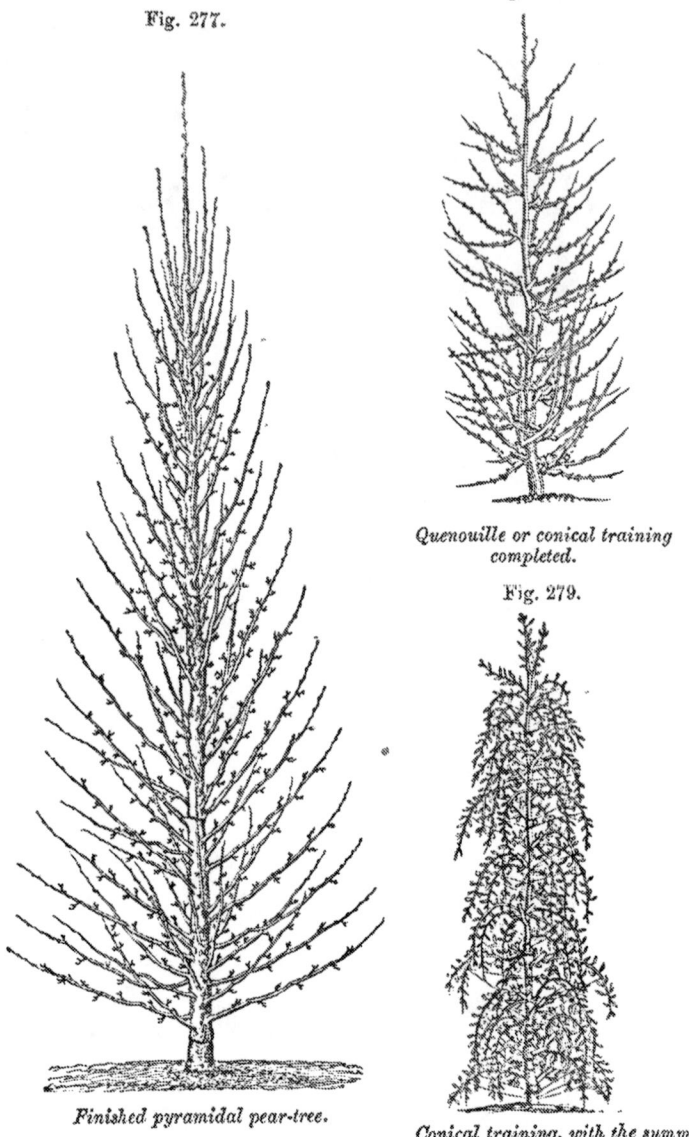

Quenouille or conical training completed.

Fig. 279.

Finished pyramidal pear-tree.

Conical training, with the summer shoots tied down.

twelve feet before the branches were bent down; but the effect of this was to cover the shoots with blossom-buds, and to produce most extraordinary crops. From the experience of French gardeners, it would appear that trees trained in the conical manner and *en quenouille* do not last longer than ten or twelve years. Copper wire is used for tying down the branches, and the lower ends of the wires are attached to the stouter branches, to the main stem, to hooked pegs stuck in the ground, or to a wooden frame fixed a few inches above its surface.

Hayward's Quenouille Training.— Take a plant with four or five strong shoots of three feet or four feet long, on a stem of four feet or more high (fig. 280); let a small hoop be bent round the bottom of the trunk, and all the branches brought regularly down and fixed to it, as in fig. 281. Several of the uppermost buds on the base of each branch will probably throw out strong wood shoots, one of them, that is placed in the best situation to admit of being bent down to supply the place of the parent branch when worn out, should be selected, and all the rest rubbed off close; and as the shoot that is left will grow large and strong, in order that it may be better adapted for bending, it should, as soon as it is five inches or six inches long, be brought gently down and affixed to the old branch, as in fig. 282, *a, a*, marking the young shoot which has been tied down. Trained in this manner, whenever it may be found necessary to cut out the old branches, these, by a half-twist, may be brought down without danger of breaking, and the bend will be less abrupt and unsightly. By the same rules, trees may be trained in the same manner, with two or more tiers, as in fig. 283. The success of this mode of training depends upon due attention being paid to the disbudding or rubbing off useless shoots in the spring, and taking due care of those which are intended either to carry on and extend the tree, or to succeed and occupy the place of the old bearers. It, however, requires great attention, and is almost too formal to be generally adopted.

Fig. 280.

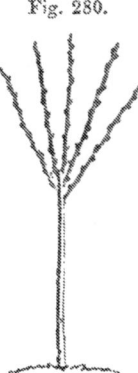

Hayward's quenouille training, first stage.

Fig. 281.

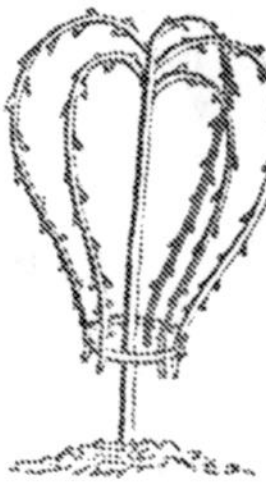

Hayward's quenouille training complete.

Fig. 282.

Hayward's quenouille training, showing two successional shoots.

Fig. 283.

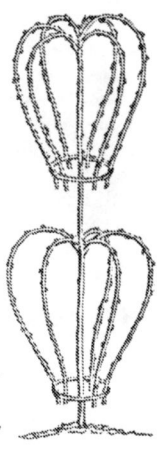

Hayward's double quenouille training.

Fan-training is chiefly adapted for trees trained

against walls, and more especially for the peach, apricot, nectarine, plum, and cherry. There are several modifications of the fan form, and five different varieties may be pointed out. The first is the equal fan, in which there are a number of main branches all radiating from the graft of the tree; in the case of dwarfs, all the branches radiate from the horizontal line upwards, but in the case of standards against walls, or what in Scotland are called riders, they radiate downwards as well as upwards; and this forms the second, or what is called the stellate-fan manner of training. The third mode is called the open fan, or the Montreuil training, in which there are two main branches laid into the right and left of the centre, at an angle of 45°, and the wall is covered by subordinate branches from these and their laterals. The great advantage of this mode of training is, that whenever the wall gets naked below, it can be covered by bringing down the two main branches and their subordinates. An improvement on this mode of training as applied to the peach-tree was made by Dumoutier, and is described by Lelieur, in his 'Pomone Françoise;' another, by Sieulle (a cultivator at Montreuil, to whom we were introduced, in 1819, by M. Thouin), is described in Neill's 'Horticultural Tour,' and in the first edition of our 'Encyclopædia of Gardening;' and a third improvement has been recently made in the Montreuil training, by F. Malot, a cultivator at Montreuil, which consists in first covering the lower part of the wall, by preventing any shoots from being produced from the upper sides of the two main branches till the part of the wall below them is covered. This mode is described in the 'Annales d'Horticulture de Paris' for 1841, and in the 'Bon Jardinier' for 1842. A fourth mode of fan-training, is what is called Seymour's, which, on principle, appears to be the most perfect of all modes of training, and to which the nearest approach made by the French gardeners is that called the "Palmette à la Dumoutier," alluded to above. A fifth mode is the curvilinear fan-training of Mr. Hayward, which is good in principle, but which has not yet been much adopted, notwithstanding some excellent points which it exhibits. If we describe the common English mode of fan-training, Seymour's mode, and Hayward's mode, the other variations will be readily understood. In fact, there can be no difficulty with any mode of training, provided the operator possesses beforehand a clear conception of the form to be produced, and bears in mind the function of buds, and the influence of elevation and depression on their development.

Fan-training in the common English Manner.—The maiden plant is to be headed down to four eyes, placed in such a manner as to throw out two shoots on each side, as shown in fig. 284.

Fig. 284.

Fan-training, first stage.

Fig. 285.

Fan-training, second stage.

The following season the two uppermost shoots are to be headed down to three eyes, placed in such a manner as to throw out one leading shoot, and one shoot on each side; the two lowermost shoots are to be headed down to two eyes, so as to throw out one leading shoot, and one shoot on the uppermost side, as shown in fig. 285. We have now five leading shoots on each side, well placed, to form our future tree. Each of these shoots must be placed in the exact position in which it is to remain; and as it is these shoots which are to form the leading character of the future tree, none of them are to be shortened. The tree should by no means be suffered to bear any fruit this year. Each shoot must now be suffered to produce, besides the leading shoot at the extremity, two other shoots on the uppermost side, one near to the bottom, and one about midway up the stem; there must also be one shoot on the undermost side, placed about midway between the other two. All the other shoots must be pinched off in their infant state. The tree will then assume, at the end of the third year, the appearance shown in fig. 286. From this time it may be allowed to bear what crop of fruit the gardener thinks it able to carry; in determining which he ought never to over-rate the vigour of the tree. All of these shoots, except the leading ones, must at the proper season be shortened, but to

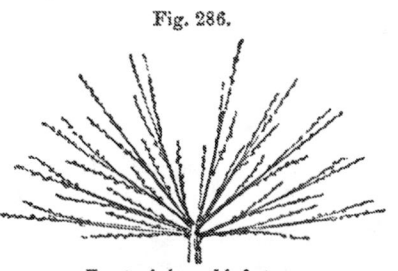

Fig. 286.

Fan-training, third stage.

what length must be left entirely to the judgment of the gardener, it, of course, depending upon the vigour of the tree. In shortening the shoot, care should be taken to cut back to a bud that will produce a shoot for the following year. Cut close to the bud, so that the wound may heal the following season. The following season each shoot at the extremities of the leading branches should produce, besides the leading shoot, one on the upper and two on the under part, more or less, according to the vigour of the tree; whilst each of the secondary branches should produce, besides the leading shoot, one other, placed near to the bottom; for the grand art of pruning, in all systems to which this class of trees are subjected, consists in preserving a sufficient quantity of young wood at the bottom of the tree; and on no account must the gardener cut clean away any shoots so placed, without well considering if they will be wanted, not only for the present, but for the future good appearance of the tree. The quantity of young wood annually laid in must depend upon the vigour of the tree. It would be ridiculous to lay the same quantity of wood into a weakly tree as into a tree in full vigour. But if any of the leading shoots manifest a disposition to outstrip the others, a larger portion of young wood must be laid in, and a greater quantity of fruit than usual suffered to ripen on the over-vigorous branch. At the same time a smaller quantity of fruit than usual must be left to ripen on the weaker branch. This will tend to restore the equilibrium better than any other method. Fig. 287 presents us with the figure of the tree in a more advanced state, well balanced, and well calculated for an equal distribution of sap all over its surface. Whenever any of the lower shoots have advanced so far as to incommode the others, they should be cut back to a yearling shoot: this will give them room, and keep the lower part of the tree in order. Whatever system of training is pursued, the leading branches should be laid in in the exact position they are to retain; for whenever a large branch is brought down to fill the lower part of the wall, the free ascent of the sap is obstructed by the extension of the upper and contraction of the lower parts of the

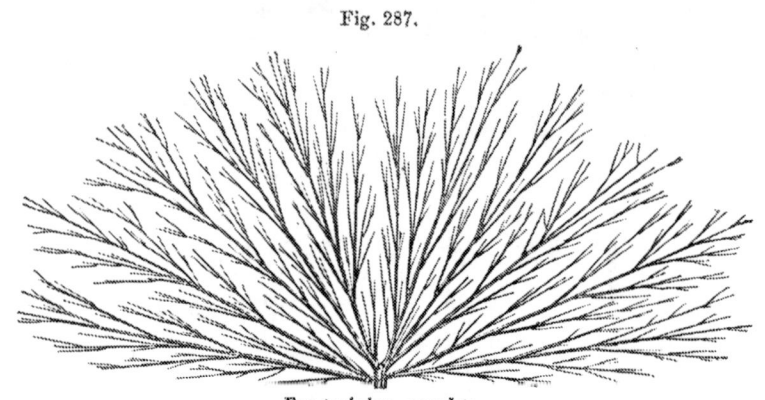

Fig. 287.

Fan-training, complete.

branch. It is thus robbed of part of its former vigour, whilst it seldom fails to throw out immediately behind the part most bent one or more vigorous shoots. To assist the young practitioner in laying in the leading branches of the tree, the following method may perhaps be acceptable:—Drive a nail into the wall, exactly where the centre of tree is to be, then with a string and chalk describe a semicircle of any diameter, divide the quadrant into 90°; the lower branch will then take an elevation of about 12°, the second of about 27°, the third of about 43°, the fourth 58°, and the fifth about 74°. A nail should then be driven into each of these points, and the chalk rubbed off.— ('Gard. Mag.,' ii. p. 144.)

Fan-training according to Seymour's Mode.—Head down the maiden plant to the three eyes, as shown in fig. 288, *a*. Three shoots being produced, the second year head down the centre one to three eyes, and leave the two side shoots at full length, as at *b*. Rub off all the buds on the lower side of the two side branches, and leave only on the upper side a series of buds from nine inches to twelve inches apart. When these buds have grown five inches or six inches, stop the shoots produced, but still allowing the leading shoot to extend itself. At the end of the summer of the second year, there will be

TRAINING. 329

four side shoots, and six or more laterals, as at *c*. In the following spring, the laterals, *d*, which had been nailed to the wall, are loosened and tied to their main shoot, as at *e*, and the upright shoot or main leader shortened to three buds, as at *f*, or if the tree be very vigorous, to five buds. At the end of the third summer, the number of laterals

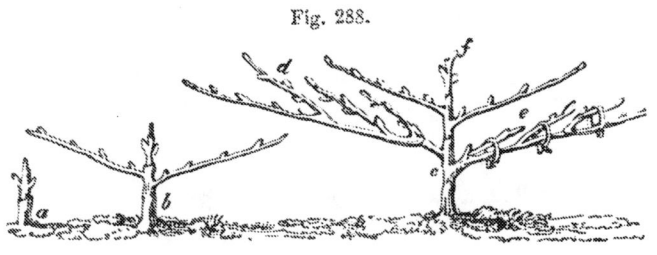

Fig. 288.

Seymour's fan-training, progressive stages.

will be doubled on the two lower branches, as shown in fig. 289: a new lateral having sprung from the base of the one tied in, as at *g*, and another from its extremity, as at *h*. In the pruning of the spring of the fourth year, the original laterals, now of two years' growth, which had borne fruit, are cut off close to the branch, and the young

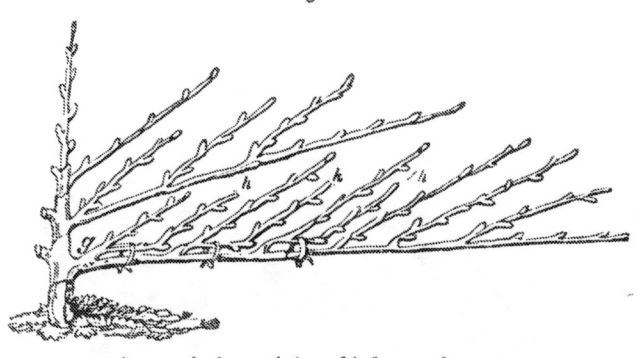

Fig. 289.

Seymour's fan-training, third stage, in summer.

laterals which had sprung from their base are loosened from the wall, and tied down to succeed them, as at fig. 290, *i*. The other laterals produced are tied in, as at *k*, and the upright shoots shortened, as at *l*, as before. This method of pruning and training the peach, its author, Mr. John Seymour, describes as truly systematical, as all the principal leading shoots are trained by a line stretched from the setting on or origin of the shoot to beyond its extreme length, and the distance of the leading shoots from one another is regulated by a semicircular line, at about ten feet from the stem, as shown in fig. 291. On this line is marked off the distances between the shoots, which are ten inches each. The lateral shoots are laid in about a foot asunder, as at *a*, in this figure. In the third or fourth year, and sometimes in the second, instead of laying in all the side shoots at full length, some of

Fig. 290.

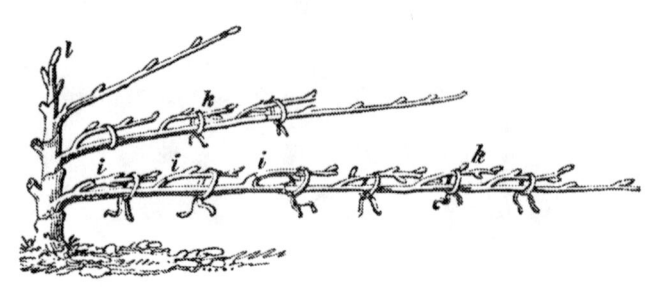

Seymour's fan-training, third stage after the winter pruning.

them are shortened, so as to get two leading shoots from as many side shoots as may be necessary to fill the wall, as shown at *b*, *b*. If the double side shoots thus produced are strong, they may be laid in their

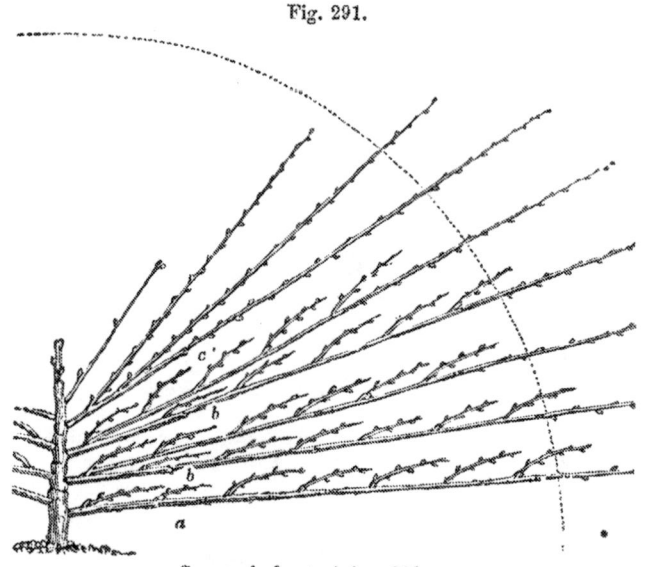

Fig. 291.

Seymour's fan-training, fifth year.

whole length; but if weak, they must be cut short to give them strength. Occasionally a side shoot may be made to produce three others, as at *c*; so that there never can be any difficulty in producing a sufficient number of leading shoots to furnish the wall. Fig. 292 is a portrait of one-half of a Vanguard peach of six years' growth, taken

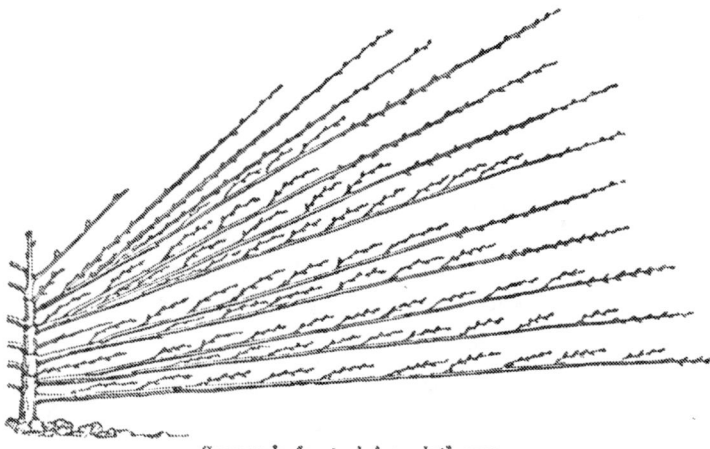

Fig. 292.

Seymour's fan-training, sixth year.

in March, 1826. This tree, which very possibly still exists in Carlton Hall Gardens, covered nearly eight hundred square feet of wall, and was universally admired. For high walls it is recommended

Fig. 293.

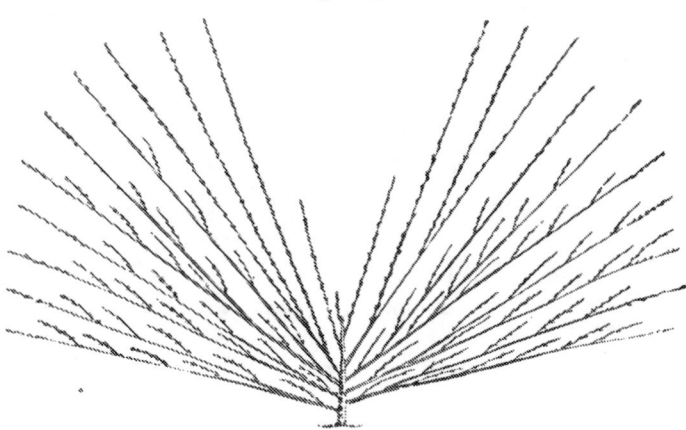

Seymour's fan-training, in progress for a low wall.

to train the tree in form of the fig. 293, till it reaches the top of the wall, and afterwards to change the position of the shoots in the manner shown in fig. 294, encouraging the shoots produced from *a, a,* to throw out branches to fill the centre of the tree. There can be no doubt that this is a very systematic and beautiful mode of training, and its perfect symmetry ought strongly to recommend it to the amateur who has leisure.

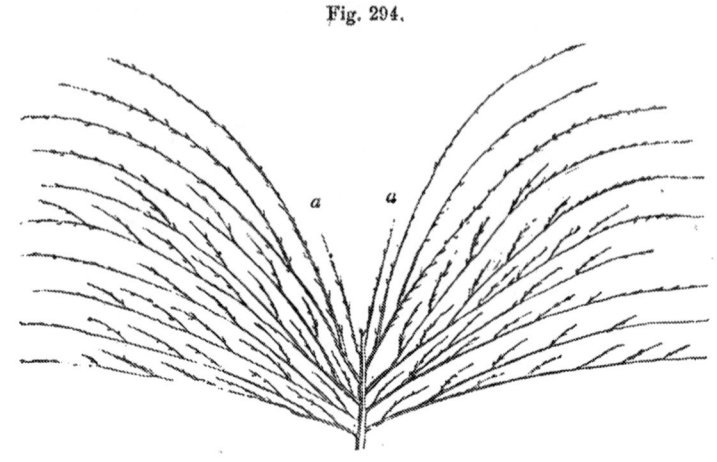

Fig. 294.

Seymour's fan-training, suited to a low wall.

Fan-training in the wavy or curvilinear manner is founded on the fact, that the sap will always flow in the greatest quantity to the most vertical buds; so that on a branch bent like an inverted siphon, however low the centre may be, yet if the extreme point be turned upwards, the buds there will produce vigorous upright shoots, however distant they may be from the main stem. If a branch be fixed in a vertical position, the strongest shoot will be produced at the point-bud *a,* in fig. 295, as it will also if the shoot should be bent, as shown at *b* and *c* in the same figure. Again, if a branch be fixed in a horizontal position, as in fig. 296, the strongest shoot will be produced from the most vertical bud near the base of the shoot, as at *d,* and the shoot produced from *e* will be the weakest; but by turning up the point of this horizontal shoot, as at fig. 297, *f,* nearly as strong a shoot will be produced as if the branch had been fixed in a vertical position, even though the bud at *g* should be at a considerable distance from the main stem of the plant. The bud at *f,* in this example, will also make a strong shoot. It is easy to conceive how these facts may be taken

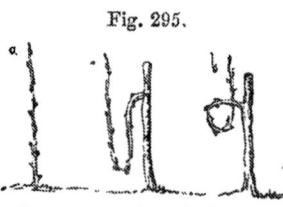

Fig. 295.

Illustrating the principles of wavy-training.

Fig. 296.

Illustrative of wavy-training.

advantage of in training trees on flat surfaces. All the main branches, which in the common mode of fan-training, and also in Seymour's mode, are laid in at an angle of 45°, are by Hayward's mode laid in much nearer the horizontal position, but always with their extreme points turned up. Trees

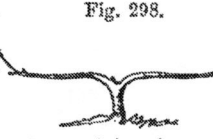

Fig. 297.

Illustrative of wavy-training.

Fig. 298.

Wavy-training, first stage.

may be trained in this manner either without a main stem, with one main stem, or with two main stems.

Wavy Fan-training with Two Stems.—Suppose that the object is "to cover a space of wall of sixteen feet in length and twelve feet high, we must obtain a plant with two equal stems, growing from the same base, of four feet each; and in order to bring the fruiting part of the tree as near the earth as possible, and to fill the lower part of the wall or trellis, we must bend each of the stems down, as in fig. 298; and all the buds being removed, but three at each extremity, *h, h*, those will take the full quantity of sap supplied by the root, and form shoots of proportionate strength, and those shoots during the summer may be trained upwards, as in fig. 299. The following winter the side branches must be brought down to their proper position to the right and left, as in fig. 300. If the horizontal branches are four feet long, or of the full length required to fill the space of sixteen feet allowed, the points of those branches must be laid flat, as at *i*, on the right-hand side of 300; but if they are required to grow longer, the points must be turned up, as on the left-hand side, *k*. The next object must be to manage the centre shoots, or stems, which are to furnish horizontals, so as to cover the upper part of the wall. There are two modes of effecting this: the one to bend the leading branch in a serpentine form, as represented at *k*, in fig. 300, and form the bends so that they may present a wood bud on the upper side of each, at from four inches to nine inches apart, which will place the horizontals from nine inches to eighteen inches apart on each side; all other buds but these being removed, they will be furnished with sufficient sap to form horizontals of due length the following year, and also a centre shoot to form the stem, to be managed in the same

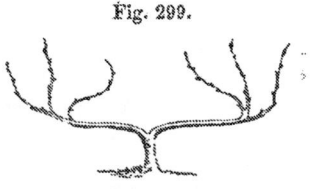

Fig. 299.

Wavy-training, second stage.

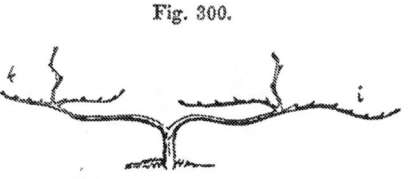

Fig. 300.

Wavy-training, third stage.

manner to produce horizontals the following year; and so on every year, until the tree has attained the height of the wall. The other mode of proceeding with the stem is to train it in an upright direction, and to cut it off, or shorten it, as at *i*, in the last figure, from nine inches to eighteen inches every year; rubbing off all the buds, except the three which are best placed at the end to furnish two horizontals and a leader for the following year. This is not only the most simple, but perhaps the most certain, mode of providing horizontals of due strength, and at the distances wanted. Indeed this mode of shortening the centre branch must be adopted with all fruit trees, except the peach. The peach-tree, with care and attention, may be trained on the serpentine plan, so as to place the horizontals with great regularity. When it is thus trained, there is this advantage—the current of the sap being checked in the buds, a larger portion is sent into the horizontals, and the sap is more equally divided; they are thus sustained in greater luxuriance at the lower part of the tree, and sometimes two tiers of horizontals may be obtained in one year. But as almost all other trees are prone to form their shoots at the ends of the last year's shoots, the bending will not always force out shoots where wanted. In order to secure this, therefore, the leading shoots must be shortened every year, down to the place where it is desired to form the horizontals; and even in this mode of forcing out branches (by shortening) the upright flow of the sap may be checked by bending the leader each year from one side to another, on an inclination of about 45°, as in fig. 301, which, as indicated by the numbers 1 to 5, is of five years' growth. Proceeding in this manner, a tree will advance in height only by a tier of horizontals each year, and hence it will appear to fill the upper part of the wall but slowly; but it must be considered, that the time you lose in covering the upper part of the wall, you gain in width on the lower part. Moreover, by laying down the first branches to such lengths, you obtain a space sufficient, the second or third year, to dispose of every inch of wood the tree makes, without crowding it too closely together; and indeed the means of appropriating to a profitable purpose all the nutriment extracted from the soil by the tree. From a tree trained in this manner above seven hundred perfectly ripened peaches have been gathered the fifth year of training, all growing within six feet of the surface of the border. When a tree is full grown, it will have the appearance of fig. 302. Particular attention must be paid to the rubbing off all or most of the "shoots, as soon as they appear in the spring, from the front and under sides of the horizontals, as well as from all other parts of the

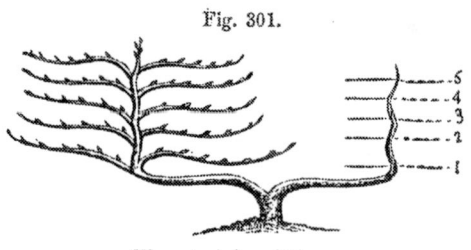

Fig. 301.

Wavy-training, fifth year.

TRAINING. 335

tree where young wood is not wanted." (Hayward, 'On the Fruitfulness and Barrenness of Plants and Trees, &c.,' 1834). Moreover, our own experience from the observations which we have made on some trees trained in this manner enables us to suggest, that a sufficient number of shoots and leaves should be left on the main stems, to strengthen them and the roots. This is an approximation to the "Palmette Verrier" of the French. (See M. Dubreuil's book. The stems, when bared of covering leaves, are also liable to be scorched by the rays of the sun, unless they are protected, either by a covering or screen of some kind, or by training down some of the shoots, so that the foliage may overhang them.

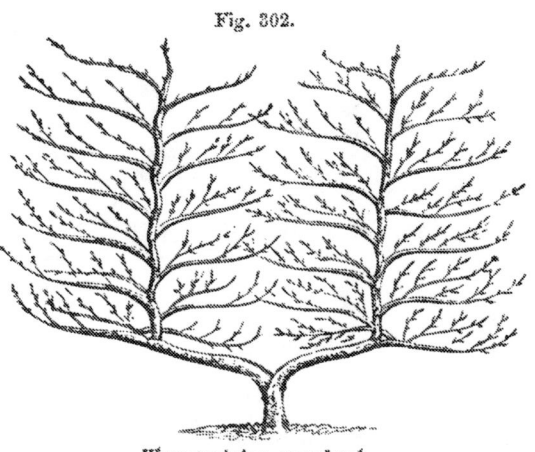

Fig. 302.

Wavy-training, completed.

Wavy fan-training with a single stem will readily be understood. On planting, if the stem is without branches, cut it back to three buds; but if it has already three shoots, shorten the centre one to nine inches or a foot, according to the kind of tree, and leave only three buds at its upper extremity, laying in the side shoots as in fig. 303. In like manner after next year's growth, shorten the centre shoot, and lay in the two side shoots as before, and proceed in this manner till the wall is filled, or till the tree has the appearance of fig. 304. It is

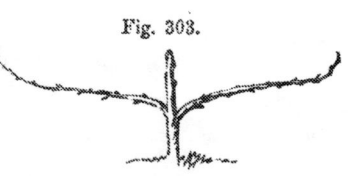

Fig. 303.

Wavy-training with a single stem, first stage.

necessary to observe, with reference to this figure, that the length of stem is for the purpose of admitting a single shoot of a vine, to be trained horizontally below it. In wavy fan-training with a single stem which is short, Mr. Hayward observes, "It will be difficult to prevent the horizontal branches near the centre of the tree from becoming naked of bearing wood, because the sap cannot pass through a sufficient space of bark to prepare it for fructification, until it is a great distance from the trunk. But this defect may in a great measure be remedied, if, instead of being cut back to make it throw out branches from a short stem to form the tree, a stem of four or five feet be bent

336 TRAINING.

down as in fig. 305; and if all the buds, as they push out, be rubbed off, except the three at the end, these may be trained up in the same manner as if the stem had been cut back or shortened, and afterwards the stem or centre may be treated in the same manner as the one that is cut back; the difference will then be, that the centre of the tree will be formed four feet on one side of the root, instead of being immediately over it; but as the sap will thus have a space of four feet of bark to pass, the tree will produce its bearing wood in greater abundance near the stem, and fill the wall more equally with fruit." This idea of fertility is now exploded; but root-pruning, &c., enables plants to fruit close down to root or stem.

Fig. 304.

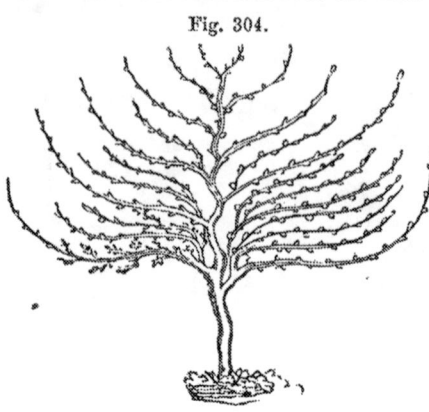

A half rider trained in the wavy manner.

Horizontal training is in a great measure confined to apples and pears. It is but little used for stone-fruit trees. It is compatible either with one or two stems, and with the upright stem either straight or in a zigzag direction, to stimulate the lateral buds to develop themselves. From this upright stem the branches proceed at right angles, generally at nine inches apart for apples, cherries, and plums, and from ten inches to a foot or eighteen inches for pears. A maiden plant with three shoots having been procured, the two side ones are laid in horizontally, and the centre one upright, as in fig. 306; all the buds being rubbed off the latter but three—viz., one next the top for a vertical leader, and one on each side as near the top as possible, for horizontal branches.

Fig. 305.

Illustrative of wavy-training with a long stem.

Fig. 306.

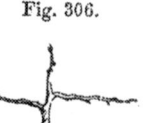

Horizontal training, first stage.

In the course of the first summer after planting, the shoots may be allowed to grow without being stopped. In the autumn of the first year the two laterals produced are nailed in, and also the shoots produced from the extremities of the lower laterals; the centre shoot being headed down as before, as shown in fig. 307. But in the second summer, when the main shoot has attained the length of ten inches, or twelve

Fig. 307.

Horizontal training, second stage.

inches, it may be stopped, which, if the plant is in proper vigour, will cause it to throw out two horizontal branches, in addition to those which were thrown out from the wood of the preceding year. The tree will now be in its second summer, and will have four horizontal branches on each side of the upright stem, as in fig. 308, and by persevering in this system four horizontal branches will be produced in each year, till the tree reaches the top of the wall, when the upright stem must terminate in two horizontal branches. In the following autumn the tree will have the appearance of fig. 309.

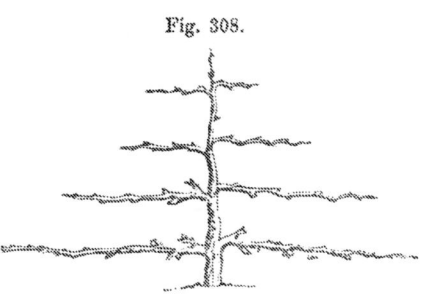

Fig. 308.

Horizontal training, third stage.

Fan-training and Horizontal-training combined.—In training trees horizontally, we have seen that a considerable period must elapse before the wall is filled. It is alleged also that heading-down does not always produce two lateral shoots, and also that it has a tendency to make the shoots already produced grow more rank than is desirable. By the following method this inconvenience is avoided, and the wall is much sooner filled in height with shoots. Let us suppose the wall to be under twenty feet long, and that it is intended to train a pear-tree a-

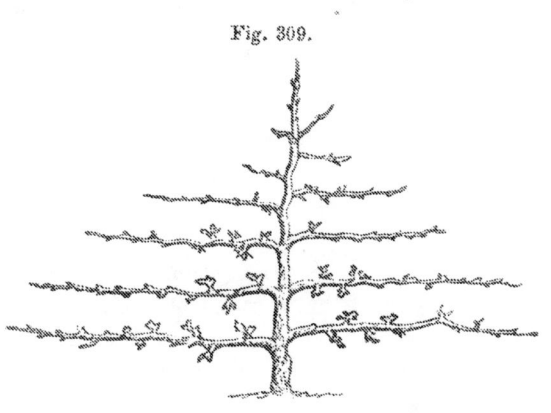

Fig. 309.

Horizontal training, fourth year.

gainst it; plant the tree at one end of the wall, and then proceed as follows:—Let the situation of the tree be at *a*, in fig. 310; stick a nail in the wall at *b*, and another nail at *c*, and strike a line on the wall from *b* to *c*; then train all the shoots to one side, after the fan manner, and bend the whole of the shoots into a horizontal position, as soon as they reach the line that is drawn from *b* to *c*; after which continue to train them horizontally. If the wall is from thirty to forty feet in length, plant the tree in the middle of it, as at *d*, in fig. 311, and proceed as follows:—Stick a nail in the wall in the centre, near the top, at *e*; stick another nail at *f*, and

z

another at *g*; then strike a line from *e* to *f*, another line from *e* to *g*; train the tree in the fan manner until the shoots reach the lines drawn upon the wall, and then bend them horizontally. If the wall is higher than it is wide, proceed as follows :—Plant the tree in the middle of the wall as at *h*, in fig. 312; stick one nail at *i*, one at *k*, and one at *l*; strike the lines as before; but instead of spreading out the shoots horizontally,

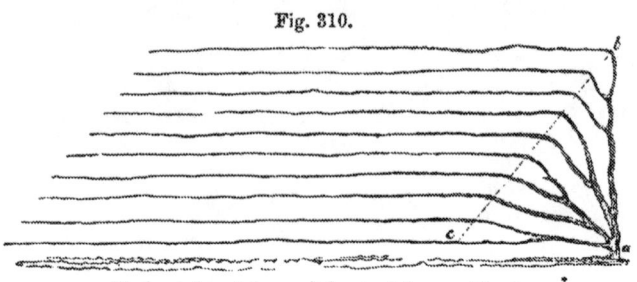

Fig. 310.

Horizontal training and fan-training combined.

train them perpendicularly. The chief objection to this mode of training is that the centre of the tree will run away with the strength from the sides. To prevent this, the sides might be raised and the centre depressed. A similar mode of training has been adopted for the finer apples and best late pears : fig. 313 represents a tree one year from the graft, newly planted, and afterwards cut down to two buds on each

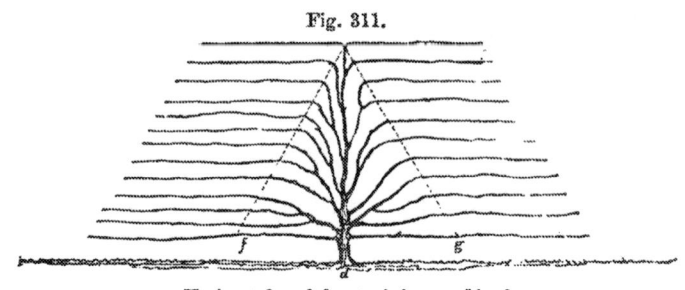

Fig. 311.

Horizontal and fan-training combined.

shoot. Fig. 314 represents the same tree two years old, and fan-trained. Fig. 315, the same tree three years old, cut back and fan-trained. Fig. 316, the same tree six years old, fan-trained; the shoots brought down in a curvilinear form to the horizontal direction, and different years' growth marked one, two, three, four, five, six. The centre is still trained in the fan form, and the branches brought down yearly, until the tree reaches to the top of the wall, where the fan-training terminates, and the branches are trained forward horizontally.

Perpendicular training is comparatively little used, excepting on espaliers and for climbing shrubs, such as roses, the vine, and the gooseberry and currant, when trained against a wall or espalier rail.

TRAINING. 339

The principle is to have two horizontal main stems on the lowest part of the wall or trellis, and to train from these upright shoots at regular distances. Sometimes four horizontal main stems are used—two at the bottom, and the other two half way up the wall or espalier; but this mode is chiefly adopted with the vine. With the exception of the latter plant and the fig, when trained in this way, the main horizontal branches are very short, seldom in the case of the rose, gooseberry, or currant, extending more than two feet or three feet from each side of the stem. A young plant with two shoots may have these shortened to one foot each in length, and tied to the lower bar or wire of the trellis, as in fig. 317. This being done in autumn, next year two upright shoots will be produced, and an addition made to the horizontal shoots, as in fig. 318. The third year two other upright shoots, or if the plant is in a vigorous state, four will be produced, as in fig. 319; and this will generally be found sufficient horizontal extension for a gooseberry, currant, or rose. (See fig. 320.) The six upright shoots now established will advance at the rate of from nine inches to a foot in a year, if the plants are gooseberries or currants, but a great deal faster if they are climbers of any kind. This mode of training is frequently combined with the fan manner, when vines, roses, Wistarias, or other luxuriant climbers, are to be trained against the gable-ends of houses, as shown in fig. 312.

Fig. 312. 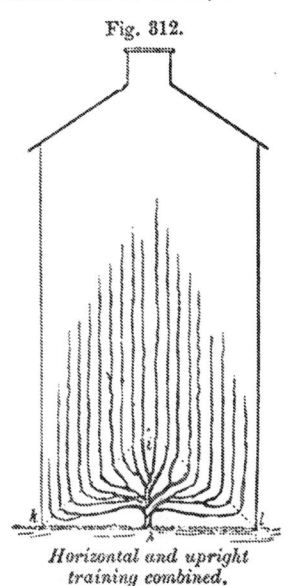
Horizontal and upright training combined.

Fig. 313. 
Half-fan training, first stage.

Fig. 314. 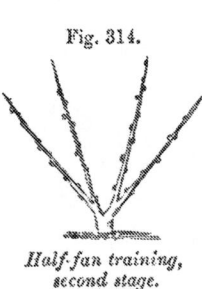
Half-fan training, second stage.

Fig. 315. 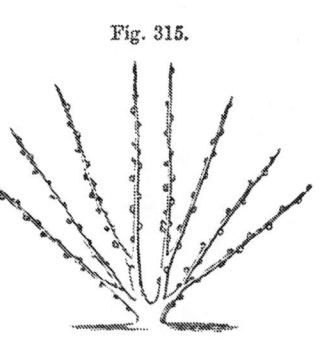
Half-fan training, third stage.

Perpendicular training is often beautifully done on the Continent. This mode, in the hands of a careful trainer, is very favourable to a regular distribution of the energy of the tree, so to say. A simple modification of this form leads to no little improvement in the training of ornamental climbers against walls. Much the best result from

z 2

climbers may be attained by allowing them to run wild over stumps, banks, common shrubs, &c.; but when they are trained against walls, they should be trained differently from what is usually the case to secure a good result. We frequently see all the vigorous shoots allowed to start up from the base and rush towards the top of the wall, the only training given being annually to back away all these vigorous shoots. A space of wall that should be devoted

Fig. 316.

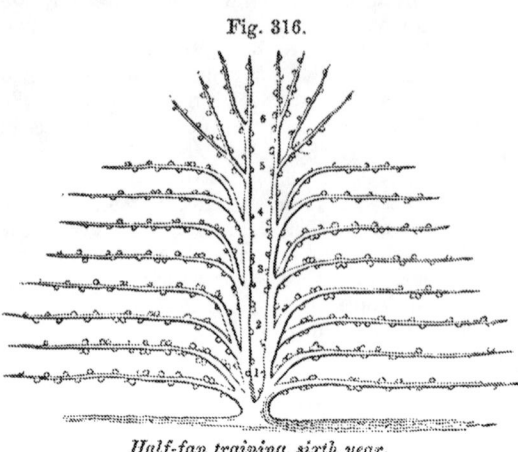

Half-fan training, sixth year.

to one tree is often occupied by half a dozen; the walls are seldom well and regularly covered. Those, however, who first take a strong main shoot to each side, and from these train erect a number of shoots, obviate the bad results we deprecate, and perfectly cover the wall with foliage, flowers, and fruit. A contracted variety of the same form is admirable for the pear trained against walls, especially when grafted on the pear-stock, and, therefore, less likely to remain within fertile limits as a cordon. Four, five, or six shoots trained erect form a handsome and easily-trained tree.

Fig. 317.

Perpendicular training, first stage.

Fig. 318.

Perpendicular training, second stage.

Fig. 319.

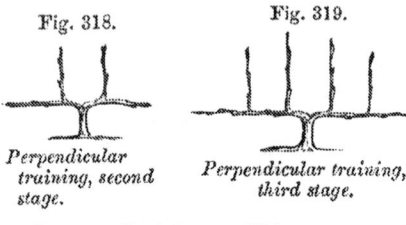

Perpendicular training, third stage.

Fig. 320.

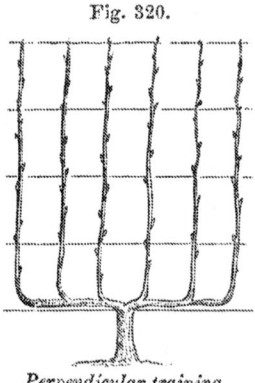

Perpendicular training, complete.

Cordon Training. — This system, about which so much has recently been written, is, in this country, chiefly valuable for the production of the finer apples and pears: the kinds that do not attain perfection in this country. The following account, which treats of it as applied to the apple, will serve to explain its merits.

Whatever may be the merits of this system applied to other fruits, it is most certain that the cultivation of the apple as a horizontal cordon grafted on the true French paradise stock, is one of the most pleasant and profitable things that can occupy the attention of the amateur gardener. The following description of it is from the 'Parks, Promenades, and Gardens of Paris,' and the figures will serve to put it fairly before the reader. As it is purely a Continental plan, and has not up to the present time been much used in our gardens, cultivators should not be deterred from attempting it because they may not find examples of it in their immediate neighbourhood.

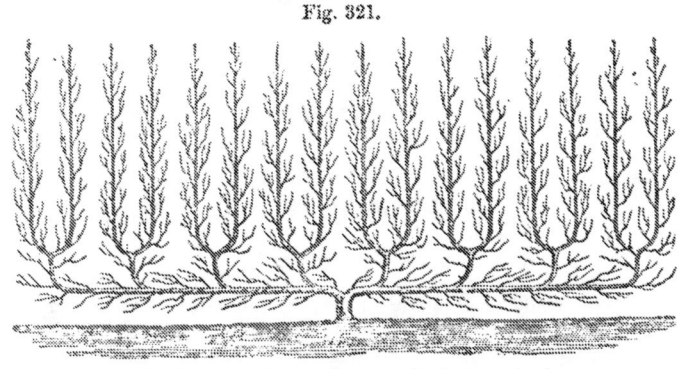

Fig. 321.

Peach-tree at Montreuil perpendicularly trained.

"The first thing we have to settle is, What is a cordon? There has been some little discussion on this point—discussion that was utterly needless, and even mischievous, as tending to prevent the public knowing exactly what the term is used for. It simply means a tree confined to a single stem; that stem being furnished with spurs, or sometimes with little fruiting branches nailed in, as in the case of the peach when trained to one stem. Some contended that it meant any

Fig. 322.

The apple trained as a simple horizontal cordon, grafted on the French paradise stock, and in full bearing.

form of branch closely spurred in; but this is quite erroneous. The term is never applied to any form of tree but the small and simple-stemmed ones. The French have no more need of the word to express a tree trained on the spur system than we have, and they have trained trees on that system for ages without ever calling them by this name.

"A simple galvanized wire is attached to a strong oak post or bit of iron, so firmly fixed that the strain of the wire may not disturb it. The wire is supported at a distance of one foot from the ground, and tightened by one of the handy little implements known as raidisseurs. This raidisseur will tighten several hundred feet of the wire, which need not be thicker than strong twine, and of the same sort as that recommended for walls and espaliers. The galvanized wire known as No. 14 is the most suitable for general use. At intervals a support is placed under the wire in the form of a bit of slender iron with an eye in it, and on this the apple on the French paradise is trained, thus forming the simplest and best and commonest phase of the cordon system. This is the kind best suited for making edgings around the squares in kitchen gardens, &c.

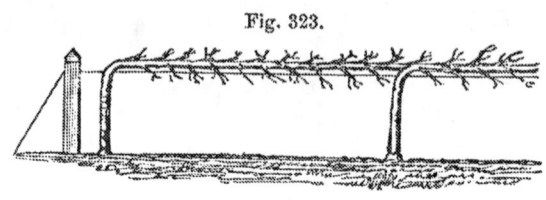

Fig. 323.

The simple horizontal cordon.

"Cordons are trained against walls, espaliers, and in many ways, but the most popular form of all, and the best and most useful, is the little line of apple-trees acting as an edging to the quarters in the kitchen and fruit garden. By selecting good kinds and training them in this way, abundance of the finest apples may be grown without having any of the large apple-trees or those of any other form in the garden to shade or occupy its surface. The bilateral cordon is useful for the same purposes as the simple one, and especially adapted to the bottoms of walls, bare spaces between the fruit trees, the fronts of pits, or any low naked wall with a warm exposure. As in many cases the lower parts of walls in gardens are quite naked, this form of cordon offers an opportunity for covering them with what will yield a certain and valuable return. It is by this method that the finest-coloured and best French and American apples, sold in Covent Garden and in the Paris fruit shops at such high prices, are grown. I have seen them often in Covent Garden and in Regent Street marked two and three shillings each, and M. Lepère fils, of Montreuil, once told me that they have there obtained four francs each for the best fruit of the

Fig. 324.

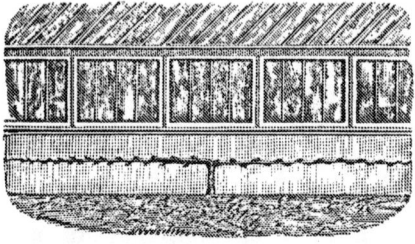

The cordon on low sunny wall of plant-house. In this way Calville Blanc, Reinette du Canada, the Lady Apple, the Melon, Mother, Newtown Pippin, and all the finer and tenderer French, American, and British apples may be grown to perfection.

Calville to send to St. Petersburg, where they are sold in winter for as much as eight francs each! Why should we have to buy these from the French at such a high rate? Considering the enormous number of walled gardens there are in this country, there can be no doubt whatever that by merely covering, by means of this plan, the lower parts of walls now entirely naked and useless, we could supply half a dozen markets like Covent Garden with the very choice fruit referred to, and be entirely independent of the French.

"Doubtless many think that these very fine fruit require a warmer climate than we have for them. But by treating them as the French do we may produce as good or a better result, and may, in addition, grow tender but fine apples, like the Calville Blanc, that do little good when grown as standards. The climate in most parts of England will be found to suit them quite as well as that of Paris, if not better, because the sun in France is in some parts a little too strong for the perfect development of the flesh and flavour of the apple. There is no part of the country in which the low cordon will not be found a most useful addition to the garden—that is, wherever first-rate and handsome dessert fruit is a want. So great is the demand in the markets for fruit of the highest quality that sometimes the little trees more than pay for themselves the first year after being planted. In any northern exposed and cold places where choice apples do not ripen well, it would be desirable to give the trees as warm and sunny a position as possible, while the form recommended for walls should be used extensively. In no case should the system be tried except as a garden one—an improved method of orcharding being what we want for kitchen fruit, and that for the supply of the markets at a cheap rate.

"When lines of cordons are perfectly well furnished the whole line is a thick mass of bold spurs. Some keep them very closely pinched in to the rod, but the best I have ever seen were allowed a rather free development of spurs, care being taken that they were regularly and densely produced along the stem. If anybody will reflect that as a rule the best vigour of the ordinary espalier tree flows to its upper line of branches, he will have no difficulty in seeing at a glance the advantages of the horizontal cordon, particularly if he bears in mind that the system as generally applied to the apple is simply a bringing of one good branch near the earth, where it receives more heat, where it causes no injurious shade, and where it may be protected with the greatest efficiency and the least amount of trouble. It is just a carrying further of the best principles of grafting and pruning—a wise bending of the young tree to the conditions that best suit it in our northern climate. The fact that by its means we bring all the fruit and leaves to within ten inches or a foot of the ground, and thereby expose them to an increase of heat, which compensates to a great extent for a bad climate, will surely prove a strong argument in its favour to every intelligent person.

"The form is so definite and so simple that anybody may attend to it, and direct the energies of the little trees to a perfect end, with much less trouble than is requisite to form a presentable pyramid or bush.

It does not, like other forms, shade anything, and beneath the very line of cordons you may have a slight crop. They are less trouble to support than either pyramid or bush; always under the eye for thinning, stopping, &c.; easy of protection, if that be desired; and very cheap in the first instance.

"A few words are necessary as to the best method of planting and managing the apple trained and planted around the quarters or on borders. In a garden in which particular neatness is desirable it would be better to plant them within whatever edging was used for the walks, but in the rough kitchen or fruit garden they may be used as edgings. The reason of supporting the cordon at one foot from the surface is to prevent the fruit getting soiled by earthy splashings. By having something planted underneath which would prevent this, we

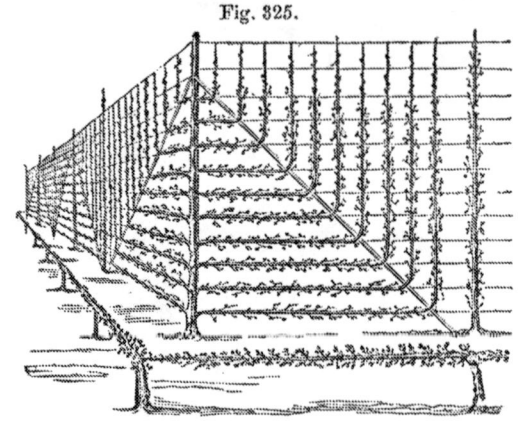

Fig. 325.

Edgings of cordons in French fruit-garden. These are three years old. When older, if well managed, they ought to regularly present a wider array of spurs.

might bring the cordon lower down; but, though I have thought of several things likely to do this, none of them are very satisfactory. Doubtless, however, we shall yet find something that may be cultivated with profit immediately under the cordon and prevent the splashings, and then be able to bring it within six inches of the earth.

"As regards the planting and treatment of the apple trained in this form some remarks are necessary. In planting keep the union of stock and scion just above the surface of the ground, to prevent the apple grafted on the paradise emitting its own roots, and consequently becoming useless for such a mode of training. The trees should never be affixed down to wire or wall immediately after being planted; but allowed to grow erect during the winter months, and until the sap is moving in them, when they may be tied down. Some allow them to grow erect a year in position before tying them down. They should in all cases be allowed to settle well into the ground before being tied to anything. For general plantings the best and cheapest kinds of plants to get are those known as "maidens"—*i.e.*, erect growing trees about a year from the bud or graft. These can be readily trained down to the wire, or to the wall, in spring. In training the young tree the point with its growing young shoot of the current year should always be allowed to grow somewhat erect, so that the sap will flow equably through the plant, drawn on by the rising shoot at its end. To allow gross shoots to arise at any other parts of the tree is to spoil any prospect of success. If the tree does not break regularly into buds, it must be forced to improve by making incisions before dormant eyes.

"A chief point is not to pinch too closely or too soon. The first stopping of the year is the most important one, and the first shoots should not be cut in immediately; but when the wood at their base is a little firm, so that the lower eyes at the bases of the leaves may not break when the shoot is checked. Pinch at five or six leaves, as the object is not to have a mere stick for the cordon, but a dense bushy array of fruit spurs quite a foot or more in diameter, when the leaves are on in summer. All the after pinching of the year may be shorter, and as the object is to regularly furnish the line, the observant trainer will vary his tactics to secure that end—in one place he will have to repress vigour, in another encourage it. About three general stoppings during the summer will suffice, but at all times when a strong soft "water shoot" shows itself well above the mass of fruitful ones, it should be pinched in, though not too closely. I have even in nurseries seen things called "cordons" with every shoot allowed to rise up like a willow wand—utterly neglected and on the wrong stock, and I have in other cases seen them so pinched in as to be worthless sticks. Of course success could not be expected under the circumstances, and I must caution the public against taking such things as examples, or the opinions of their managers as to the merits of the cordon system.

"As the paradise keeps its roots quite near the surface of the ground, spreading an inch or two of half-decomposed manure over the garden, or in gardening language, mulching it, could not fail to be beneficial."

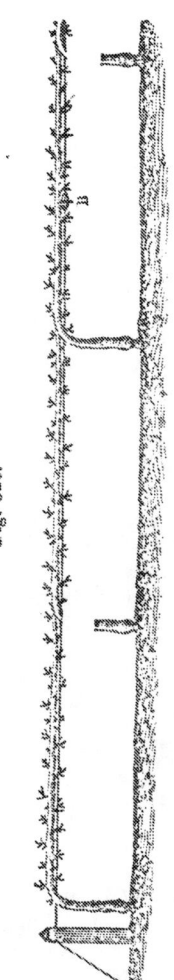

Fig. 326.

The horizontal cordon trained as an edging to the quarters in the fruit and vegetable gardens. Originally the trees represented here were planted too thickly, and after all had been securely grafted together, every second stem was cut away. B *shows the position of the ruidisseur.*

A full account of the cordon system as applied to other trees will be found in the 'Parks, Promenades, and Gardens of Paris,' from which the above extract is taken. The wire and implements necessary for making the supports of these cordons, and also for erecting the neat, permanent, and cheap trellises shown in fig. 325 may be had from Messrs. J. B. Brown and Co., of 90, Cannon Street, E.C., and are described and figured in the catalogue of that firm."

The varieties of apples to be grown on the cordon system should be most carefully chosen. As the system is chiefly valuable for the production of superb dessert fruit, only the finest kinds should be selected; but, as some apples are of high value both for kitchen and dessert, some of the finer kitchen apples are included in the following list. All the following will be found very suitable: Reinette du Canada, Reinette du Canada Grise, Reinette Grise, Reinette de Caux, Reinette d'Espagne, Reinette très Tardive, Belle Dubois, Pomme d'Api, Mela Carla, Calville St. Sauveur, Coe's Golden Drop, Newtown Pippin, Calville Blanc, Northern Spy, The Melon, Cox's Orange Pippin, Duke of Devonshire, Kerry Pippin, Lodgemore Nonpareil, White Nonpareil, The Mother, Early Harvest, Lord Burleigh, Beauty of Kent, Bedfordshire Foundling, Lord Suffield, Cox's Pomona, Hawthornden, Tower of Glammis, Winter Hawthornden, Betty Geeson, and Small's Admirable. Some of the best of the above are valuable keeping apples. The Reinette Grise is in fine condition in the markets at Rouen in June, and Reinette très Tardive is good in July. Those who wish to plant good early apples might try Borovitsky, and a few of the best early kinds; but it is best to devote most of our horizontal cordons to the growth of the finer, later, and most valuable fruits. Of the above selection, Calville Blanc, Reinette du Canada, and Mela Carla must be grown on a warm wall; Newtown Pippin, The Mother, Melon, and several of the other later and finer apples will also be grateful for the same protection.

Instruments and Materials.—In addition to those required for training in general, we may add for training against walls and trellises—a pair of scissors for clipping the shreds; a hammer, with a shaft of sufficient length, that when hung on one round of the ladder by the head, the other may rest on the round below, so as not to fall through; a leather wallet or basket, fig. 327, about twelve inches long, six inches broad, and six inches deep, with loops to put a belt through on one side, that it may hang before the operator, having the side on which the loops are made bending, to rest the better against his body, and a division in the middle for two different sorts of shreds; a deal plank to tread upon, with a strap at each end to drag it along either way, or to lift it with one hand; a small pair of pincers for drawing out nails in places where the hammer cannot be so conveniently employed, and a pair of pliers, if wire is used as ties, the raidisseur, sécateur, and sundry other instruments and materials already described; a narrow saw for taking off old branches; a mallet, and a chisel about two inches

Fig. 327.

Trainer's basket.

broad at the mouth, for the same purpose; to which we may add, a couple of step-ladders, on which a plank may be placed at different heights, parallel to the wall, for the operator to stand on, by which he will do much more work, and with much greater ease to himself. In cutting branches of trees trained against walls, the cut or wounded section should always, if possible, be on the under side of the branches, or next the wall; and in the case of espaliers, it ought to be on the under side.

Comparative View of the Different Modes of Training.—It is well to understand the various methods of training detailed in the foregoing pages; and, knowing them, any modification may be adopted which circumstances may require, provided the general principles are kept in view. Ornamental shrubs are easily managed, because they have not a tendency to rear themselves by forming a strong stem; but with regard to fruit trees the case is otherwise. These, it is well known, if left to nature, form one strong stem, supporting a top which reaches the height of twenty, thirty, or forty feet, or more. In order to attain this, the sap rushes, whilst the tree is young and vigorous, towards the leading shoot; and if lateral branches are occasionally produced, the flow of sap is not strongly directed towards them compared to that which is impelled towards the more upright part. At length, however, a ramification does take place, in comparison with which the leading shoot becomes less and less predominant, till it becomes ultimately lost amongst its compeers. A tolerably equal distribution of sap then results, and a conical or spherical top is formed bearing fruit, not generally in the concavity, where it would be greatly excluded from light, but at the external surface, where the fruit itself and the leaves immediately connected with the buds producing it can be fully exposed to light, air, and dews. It was remarked that lateral branches were occasionally produced on the stem in the progress of its ascent. When the top is formed, these are placed at great disadvantage, owing to their being overshaded, and they are then apt to decay, the tree assuming the character of a large elevated top, supported on a strong naked stem. This is the natural disposition of trees, and to this it is necessary to attend, in order that it may be counteracted where the natural form of the tree cannot be admitted. It should be borne in mind that the disposition to form an elevated naked stem is still strongly evinced in dwarf trees, in which, although subdivided, each branch possesses its share of the original disposition, and its lower and horizontal shoots are left to become weak in comparison with the upper ones and those that are vertical.

A standard tree, from its being least restrained from attaining its natural habit, requires least management in regard to training, as has been already explained. When trained in any dwarf form, attention is in the first place required towards counteracting the disposition to form one large elevated stem by stopping the leading shoot. In this and other processes in pruning and training, it is necessary to be aware of the nature of the buds on different parts of the shoot, and the effect of cutting near or at a distance from the base. Where a shoot is shortened, the remaining buds are stimulated, and those immediately below the section seldom fail to produce shoots, even although they would have otherwise remained dormant. The lowest buds on the base of a shoot do not generally become developed, unless the shoot is cut or broken above them. They remain endowed with all their innate vital power, although comparatively in a state of repose; but should the shoot on the base of which these buds are situated be destroyed or amputated, very soon they are called into vigorous action, producing supplementary shoots quite as strong as could be obtained from any other buds more remote from the base. Were these buds as prone to development as others, a mass of shoots and foliage would be produced in the central parts, where the foliage could not have a due share of light, an arrangement that would prove bad. They must be looked upon as being placed in reserve for furnishing wood shoots, whenever the pruner chooses to stimulate their development by amputating the portion of shoot above them.

From this view of the properties belonging to the lowest-growing buds, it is evident they are the most unlikely to become fruit-buds. These are formed towards the extremities. In some cases they are terminal; but generally about two-thirds from the base is the situation where fruit-buds are first formed, and in some kinds of fruit trees are developed into blossom the following season, while in others the basis of a spur is established. This spur sometimes continues slowly to elongate for years before it produces fruit. According to the principles of Seymour's training, the originating of the side branches from buds near the base of the vertical central shoot is well provided for, and this ought to be kept in view in every mode of training adopted. In order to furnish well the lower part of a tree, it is necessary to procure strong branches, and these can be best obtained from the lower part of a strong central shoot; and in order that this shoot may have sufficient strength, it must have a vertical position. Trees commenced to be trained in nurseries have often the objectionable form imposed upon them of an open centre, being deprived of an upright shoot and set off like a V; and similarly objectionable are the Montreuil U's and other modes on the same principle. With skilful management, these modes do succeed in France; but in the rich soil and humid climate of Britain, the flow of sap cannot be equalized by any mode that admits of a competition between vertical and horizontal branches.

Weeding.

A weed is any plant which comes up in a situation where it is not wanted. It may be either an absolute weed, such as are all plants of no known use; or a relative one, such as a useful plant where it comes up and is not wanted among other useful plants, or on walks, walls, &c. Weeds are injurious by depriving the soil of the nutriment destined for other plants; by depriving other plants of the space they occupy, as in the case of weeds in beds of seedlings, and of broad-leaved plants on lawns; by their shade, when they are allowed to grow large; and by their mere existence, as when they appear on gravel-walks. In those parts of gardens where the soil is kept constantly pulverized on the surface, the most numerous weeds consist of annual plants; but among the grass of lawns, and sometimes among crops which remain in one place for more than a year, perennial weeds also make their appearance. The seeds of weeds are brought into gardens by stable dung, by birds, by the wind, by fresh soil brought in for the renewal of borders, for compost, &c., and by some other sources; and they are perpetuated there by being allowed to come to maturity and shed their seeds. The obvious mode of preventing the existence of all absolute weeds, whether annual or perennial, would be to prevent all weeds, whether in gardens or fields, from ripening seeds, by cutting them down before they come into flower; and this, we think, ought to be made an object of national concern for the sake of the agriculture of the country, even more than for its gardening. Prices per peck or per bushel might be offered for the unopened flower-buds of different weeds, according to their bulk or frequency, to be paid by parish-officers to such children and infirm persons as might find it worth while to collect them, nothing being paid for those buds which have been suffered to expand. This practice, we are informed, exists in some parts of France and Bavaria; but to be effective in any country it ought to be general. In the meantime, all that can be done is to destroy weeds as fast as they appear.

Annual weeds among growing crops are readily destroyed in dry weather by hoeing, and leaving them to die where they have grown; but if large, they may be raked off and wheeled to the compost ground, where mixed with soil or with other putrescent matters, they will be speedily decomposed and rendered fit for manure. Weeds among broadcast crops which stand thick on the ground, such as onions, spinach, &c., require to be pulled up by hand; and for this purpose a moist state of the soil is preferable, but not so much as to occasion poaching by the feet of the weeder, unless indeed the plants should be in beds, where they may be weeded immediately after the heaviest rains.

Perennial weeds, except when they are quite young and not far advanced beyond the seed-leaf, when they may be treated as annuals, require more care to eradicate than annual weeds. Their roots generally must be raised up by a fork, weeding hook, spade, trowel, or some other implement, which penetrates deeper than the hoe; and great care must be taken with underground stems, such as those of the couch-grass, the small field convolvulus, the hedge-nettle, and others, to take up every joint, otherwise the result will merely be the propagation of these weeds by division.

Weeds in gravel-walks should be removed by weeding, or by hoeing and raking. Salt, either sprinkled on them, or better still applied as hot brine, likewise destroys all weeds, and so do sulphate of copper and other substances; but these should commonly be used to walks that have no living edgings, such as box, &c., and they must not be applied very heavily in kitchen gardens where the roots of trees run under the gravel-walks. In pleasure-ground walks there are no easier methods of keeping them clear of weeds than by the use of Fleming's salting-machine. Walks have likewise been made of concrete, which is so hard as to prevent the weeds laying hold of them. Asphalte, with a sprinkling of bright shingly gravel rolled into it before it has quite cooled down, makes one of the cleanest and brightest weed-proof walks.

Weeds in lawns or grass-walks include all the broad-leaved plants which spring up among the proper grasses, not even excepting the clovers, commonly sown with them to give the grass a better hold of the scythe in mowing. All these broad-leaved plants, and even all broad-leaved grasses, such as the cocksfoot, ought to be weeded out if it is intended to have a perfect lawn, which to be so ought to resemble a piece of cloth in uniformity of texture and appearance. The worst weeds in lawns are those which have very broad and flat reclining leaves, which the scythe is apt to pass over, leaving them to feed the roots, such as a certain species of plantain, dandelion, &c.; and these are the more difficult to eradicate, because they have tap-roots, furnished with adventitious buds which seldom fail to be developed, unless the roots are cut over two or three inches beneath the surface. The best remedy for plantains, dandelions, dock, thistles, &c., on lawns, is to pickle their crowns with a patch of salt, or scorch them with a drop of vitriol. The common daisy is very troublesome in lawns from the breadth of the tuft formed by its leaves; but being a fibrous-rooted plant it is easily eradicated, and provided none are allowed to ripen seed, a lawn may soon be cleared of them.

Weeds in Shrubberies and Plantations.—It used to be customary to dig shrubberies annually to destroy weeds, or hoe and rake them many times during the summer for the same purpose. But it is much better to smother them by the close planting of the shrubs and by covering all the earth beneath taller shrubs with a thick carpet of low evergreens, such as ivy, berberis, periwinkle, laurel, &c. The shrubs should constantly come right down to the turf, and not show a raw edge of earth. Still, in their young state, shrubberies will need both hand-weeding and a vigorous use of the hoe to keep them clean.

Weeds in woods and park scenery are chiefly destroyed by mowing; and it has been found that bruising and tearing off the stems often destroy the root more effectually than cutting with the scythe. In thick woods consisting of trees and under growths, the ground is generally so effectually covered with the bushes that no weeds can make their appearance; but in groves of trees, and in thin plantations, there will always be spaces more or less liable to throw up rampant weeds, which in merely useful plantations ought to be mowed and left to decay on the spot, for the sake of the manure which they will afford to the trees. In cultivated or smooth park scenery, all coarse weeds should be got rid of, so as to present a smooth turf; but in rough forest park scenery, all the plants which it produces should be allowed to grow as being appropriate: of these, the large fern or brake (pteris aquilina) is peculiarly characteristic.

Weeding ponds, rivers, and artificial waters, in garden and park scenery, is often very expensive from its being necessary to empty and clean out the bottom and sides of the excavation. Much of this trouble and expense might be rendered unnecessary in many cases by mowing over the weeds in the bottom of the water, when they first make their appearance there in early spring, and repeating the operation at short intervals till the roots are destroyed from the want of elaborated sap sent down by the leaves.

Watering.

Water, whether as a source of nutriment or as a medium of effecting various other objects, is one of the most important agents of culture. A certain degree of moisture in the soil is essential to the existence of plants; because no food can be absorbed by the roots that is not held in solution by water, and because the decomposition of water, and its perspiration from the leaves and bark, are continually going forward. Plants require a certain degree of moisture at their roots, not only when in active growth, but when in a state of comparative rest, because even then perspiration is going on from those parts which are above the ground, and from the roots themselves when plants are taken up for transplanting. In the season of growth the demand for water is greatly increased, and it diminishes as the period of growth declines, and the power of decomposition and evaporation ceases. If water in excess is given at this period of the growth of a plant, its parts become distended in consequence of the absorption by the spongioles still going on, while the power of decomposition and perspiration by the leaves is diminished; it becomes sickly, its leaves assume a yellow colour, and if the excess of water is not soon withdrawn from the soil, death ensues. By pulverizing soils and increasing their depth, their capacity for holding water is increased, while by underground draining it cannot be retained in excess. By these means, and by the addition of manure acting mechanically and keeping the soil open, a great facility is afforded to the extension of the roots, and the vigour of the plants is increased in proportion, but at the same time the power of the roots to exhaust the soil of water becomes greatly increased. If under such circumstances a proportionate supply of water is not afforded at the proper time, either by nature or art, the growth of the plant will fall much short of what it might be; of which examples may be seen both in garden and field crops, by comparing the crops of a moderately wet summer with those of a very dry one. It may be concluded, therefore, that the full benefits of stirring the soil, draining, and manuring, cannot be obtained without a command of water.

The specific purposes for which water is used in horticulture are numerous. In general it may be applied wherever a stimulus is wanted to growth, unless indeed the soil be already sufficiently moist. It is given to newly-sown seeds, or newly-planted plants; for the purpose of setting blossoms, swelling fruits, increasing the number and succulency of the leaves; conveying manure held in suspension; conveying matter for destroying insects, or parasitic fungi, such as the mildew; or poisoning weeds on walls or gravel-walks; for causing substances in powder to adhere to plants, as in applying sulphur and other articles; for clearing the leaves and stems of plants from dust or other foreign matters; for accelerating vegetation when the water is warmer than the soil; for retarding it when it is cooler; for thawing frozen plants; for forming steam or dew in plant structures; for rooting cuttings of some kinds of plants; for growing aquatics; for heating plant structures, and for supplying fountains and other aquatic ornaments. Water in the form of snow, forms a valuable protection to low plants when they can be covered by it, acting as a non-conductor of the heat of the soil, and preventing it from escaping into the atmosphere; and water as ice is an object of the gardener's care, the filling of the ice-house being generally committed to him.

The ordinary sources from which water is obtained in gardens are chiefly wells, and the collection of rain water in cisterns; but it occasionally happens that a natural stream passes through or near the garden, or that water is conveyed to it by pipes or drains from some abundant source. In whatever way water is supplied, it ought always to be exposed in a pond or basin, so as to be warmed by the sun to the same temperature as the surface of the soil before being used; unless indeed the object be to retard vegetation by its coldness, which can very seldom be the case. Some very interesting experiments were made by Mr. Gregor Drummond, in 1826, on the comparative effects of spring water and pond water, in lowering or raising the temperature of the soil of a peach border, which it may be useful to quote:—

1. "The first experiment was made on the 10th of May. At the depth of 18 inches the temperature of the border was 64°, and that of the spring-water used 46°. In twenty-four hours after, the temperature of the border was reduced to 52°, or had lost 12°. At the same time the temperature of the soil being 64° as above, and heat of the pond water 67°, the soil at the close of twenty-four hours was 66°, or instead of losing 12° had gained 2°.

2. "June 20th the second watering was given. The temperature of the border at the depth of 18 inches was now 74°, and that of the spring water 52°. In twenty-four hours the border was reduced to 58°, or had lost 16°.

"At the station where the pond water was used the temperature of the border at the above-mentioned depth was 77°, and that of the water 82°. In twenty-four hours the temperature of the border was 80°, or had gained 3°.

3. "The third and last watering was performed on the 28th of July. The temperature of the border at 18 inches below the surface was 72°, and that of the spring water 57°. In twenty-four hours the border was reduced to 61°, or had lost 11° of temperature. At the pond water station the border at the depth of 18 inches was 78°, and the water itself 74°. In twenty-four hours the temperature of the

border was still 78°, or had suffered no change of temperature from the watering it had undergone.

"It is very clear from these facts, that whilst spring water greatly cooled the soil, that from the pond exerted no such influence, but on the contrary often raised the temperature." ('Hort. Trans.,' vol. ii. 2nd series, p. 57.)

Hence in our opinion every complete kitchen garden, and every flower garden whatever, ought to have a basin, or basins of water in a central situation fully exposed to the sun. In every plant structure there ought to be a cistern to receive the rain water which falls on the roof; and if convenient, another for pond or well water, which should only be used when there is a deficiency of rain water.

The distribution of water in gardens is in some cases effected by open surface gutters of hewn stone, running streams, lead or iron pipes, open basins, elevated lakes or reservoirs at a distance, flexible tubing fixed on town mains, portable engines, water-barrows, pails, water-pots, leather hose, &c. It is of the utmost importance to have the source of the water so high as to enable it to distribute itself through any kind of pipe by the force of gravity, instead of having to raise, carry, and distribute it by steam, horse, or man power. In some gardens it is only needful to screw on a hose at any point, and with a rose or spreader pour a stream on any crop, or over the highest trees at will. The Parisians have displayed considerable ingenuity in arranging contrivances for watering their gardens. The chief feature of the system is that each length of perforated hose is supported upon two pairs of small wheels. The choicer gardens are, however, watered with watering-pots with wide spouts; the operator using two pots at once, and the water being pumped up into tanks or barrels. A well is indispensable in French market gardens, as the dry climate renders copious waterings so essential.

The ordinary mode of giving water to plants is by watering-pots of different sizes, and hand or horse barrows. On a large scale it is sometimes conveyed in barrels on carts, and distributed over lawns, and plantations of strawberries or other low plants in rows, by the same means as in watering roads. To such moveable barrels or other contrivances a length or lengths of gutta-percha tubing can be attached with a common spreader, which enables a man to water with great rapidity. When the leaves of plants are to be cleaned from dust or other matters that water alone will bring off; or when liquid compositions, such as lime-water, tobacco-water, soapy water, &c., are to be thrown on them, the syringe or engine is used, and when water is applied to small plants, or very small seeds newly sown, recourse is had to a small watering-pot with a very fine rose.

When it is proper to water, and how much water to give, must be determined by the circumstances in which the plant is placed. In nature the atmosphere is very rarely otherwise than saturated with moisture, when it rains; but as artificial watering is a substitute for rain, it must not be withheld when the plant requires it, on account of atmospheric dryness. As the nearest approach to the state of the atmosphere in which nature supplies water, the afternoon or evening may be chosen, when the air is both cooler and somewhat moister than during sunshine. As in soils that are stirred on the surface, the greater part of the roots are always at some depth, the quantity of water given should be such as will thoroughly moisten the interior of the soil, and reach all the roots. A slight watering on the surface, unless the soil is already moist below, will not reach the fibres, and will soon be lost by evaporation. Such driblets do more injury than good to plants; for when in want of water the roots penetrate deep, and under such circumstances a small quantity of water on the surface checks the capillary attraction of moisture from below; and thus the roots that are grown deep, which are those on which the plant is made to depend in times of great drought, are deprived of their supply of water, and the plant exerts its efforts to throw out horizontal fibres; by the time these fibres are formed, and the young shoots extended, the supply of water on the surface again fails, and they are again checked, and perhaps destroyed: thus the efforts of the plant being uselessly exhausted between the two extremes of a supply and a deficiency of water, it naturally declines in its growth, and hence arises the general opinion that watering in dry weather injures more than it benefits plants. Most water is required by plants that are in a vigorous state of growth and have a large breadth of foliage; least by those which have nearly completed their growth; and in general none by plants in a dormant state, excepting in such cases as that of watering grass lawns in summer to stimulate vegetation, or irrigating meadows after they have been mown for the same purpose. In the case, however, of excessive dryness, some degree of moisture must be afforded to such plants as are liable to become desiccated even though dormant. Succulent plants, for example, will bear a great degree of dryness, through a protracted period; whereas others that perspire more through the bark would be completely dried up if equally exposed to drought. An excess of water to plants in pots, and especially to those having suffruticose stems, such as the pelargonium, or to hair-rooted plants, such as heaths, and to many bulbs, is extremely injurious, and often destructive of life. In the first case more water is absorbed by the roots than can be decomposed by the leaves; in the second case the roots are suffocated and rotted from their delicacy; and in the third, rotting takes place from mere organic absorption; for when the leaves of bulbs decay, their roots decay also, and consequently they cannot absorb water by their spongioles; while absorption by the tissue still going on, the vessels become surcharged and burst, and the bulb rots. Hence in the case of bulbs, and similar plants in pots, the soil in which they are kept should contain no more moisture than what is necessary to keep the bulb, tuber, or corm, in a succulent state; but in proportion to the dryness in which bulbs are kept at this season, should be the abundance of the supply of water when they begin to grow. All bulbs will be found to flower in their natural habitats, either during or immediately after a rainy or moist period of the year, as is the case with our wood hyacinths in spring, and with the colchicum in autumn; and much more strikingly so with the bulbs and corms of Africa, which grow and flower only in the rainy season. When plants are ripening their fruit, a diminished supply of water increases the flavour, because at that period of growth the power of decomposing it is diminished; and if it is absorbed without being decomposed, the effect will be to render the fruit watery without flavour; to crack it in some cases, to burst it in others, and in the case of all keeping fruits to shorten the period for which they may be kept. The same effects are produced by excess of water on bulbs, such as those of the onion; on roots and tubers (underground stems), such as the turnip and the potato; and even on leaves, such as those of the lettuce and the cabbage, which in wet cloudy seasons are never so highly flavoured as in seasons moderately moist, when succulency and flavour are combined.

Whether plants should be watered over the leaves or only over the soil in which they grow depends on the state of the plant, the temperature in which it is placed, the time of the day, the season of the year, and other circumstances. Plants in a state of vigorous growth, in a suitable temperature in spring or summer, and in the afternoon or during cloudy weather, are better watered over the top, in order to make certain of clearing their foliage; but late in autumn or during winter, when growth even in hothouses is or ought to be slow, owing to the deficiency of light, plants should be watered only at their roots. In general, all plants, whether in the open air or in plant structures, ought to be watered overhead during spring, summer, and the early part of autumn, unless they are in a dormant state, or in flower. On the other hand, all plants in houses not undergoing forcing, and all plants whatever in the open air during the latter part of autumn, during winter, and in the early part of spring, should be watered only at the root. Watering over the top should in general never be performed during bright sunshine. Watering in summer should be performed in the afternoon or evening, because at these periods less will be carried off by evaporation than during the day; while during winter and spring, watering ought to take place during the morning, that during the day the surface of the ground may be warmed and dried by evaporation and infiltration.

One of the chief difficulties in watering plants in pots is to ascertain that the water given has penetrated the whole of the soil in the pot. The ball or mass of soil is frequently so filled with roots, or from its nature and treatment is so compact, as not to be readily permeable by water, which in that case, after merely moistening the surface, escapes between the ball and the pot; while the operator, seeing the water escaping from the bottom of the pot, concludes that the mass of soil has been thoroughly penetrated and saturated by it. To ascertain when the water has penetrated the mass of soil in a pot, it is common to thrust into it, not far from the stem of the plant, a round pointed stick, and to make sure of moistening the interior, to pour water into the hole so formed. In loamy soils, or soils containing a large proportion of sand, this mode will suffice for saturating the ball; but in the case of heath-soil, it becomes necessary to immerse the pot and the plant in a vessel of water, so that the soil shall be six inches or a foot under its surface, and thus receive a pressure sufficient to cause the escape of the contained air. Another class of evils in watering plants in pots arises from their not being sufficiently drained, which may follow either from the operation having been improperly performed in potting or shifting, or from the crevices among the drainage having become choked up by the washing down of the soil. The obvious manner of preventing this evil is, whenever there is the slightest suspicion of over-watering, to turn the plant out of the pot, examine the drainage, which will come out with the ball, and take it off and replace it with fresh materials. It would be well also, in the case of all plants that are likely to be over-watered, to use a larger proportion of sand in the soil, and to put extra drainage in the bottom of the pot, and also to introduce among the soil a considerable proportion of fragments of freestone.

Aquatic and marsh plants form exceptions to the treatment required for plants in general; but even these sometimes suffer through looseness of soil when kept in pots.

Watering with liquid-manure is of the greatest importance to plants in pots and in the free earth. It provides them with food and drink by one and the same means, and the rule in applying it should be "*Weak and often.*" It is most advantageous when given to plants in a growing state; because, though at other seasons a portion of it would still be absorbed by the roots, yet the greater part would be washed into the subsoil.

To economize the water given to plants, more especially in the open air, the surface is sometimes mulched with fibrous or littery matter, or even with small stones or pebbles. Both materials retain moisture and heat; while stones or pebbles, by becoming soon dry, prevent surface-damp, and reflect much heat during sunshine. The strawberry is sometimes mulched with straw, and sometimes with tiles or slates, or pebbles, for the double purpose of retaining moisture and keeping the ripening fruit clean; and the surface of the ground in the rose nurseries about Paris and in different parts of England is sometimes mulched with straw or littery dung, to save watering, and prevent the rose-beetle from depositing her eggs in the soil.

Stirring the Soil and Manuring.

So much has already been said on these subjects that it is only necessary here to advert to them.

Stirring the soil is advantageous as the means of admitting air, rain, and heat to the roots of plants, of promoting evaporation in moist soils, and of retaining moisture in such as are dry. In the latter case the dry loose soil on the surface acts as a mulching or non-conductor to the soil below; and in the former it acts by exposing a greater number of moistened particles to the air than could be the case if these particles were consolidated.

Manuring.—Permanent manures, such as stable-dung and other solid substances, are for the most part incorporated with the soil when it is dug or trenched before being cropped, and it is generally thought that most advantage may be obtained from them when they are deposited near the surface. Temporary manures, such as soot, bone-dust, and other powders, waste yeast (one of the richest of manures), and liquid manures, such as drainings of dung, and solutions of salts of different kinds, and town sewage (which is one of the best fertilizers), are most advantageously applied on the surface of the ground, and to growing crops. The unusually heavy crops which have been raised from town sewage are proofs of its enormous force as a producer of food.

Blanching.

The operation of blanching, or depriving the leaves and stems of plants of their green colour, is effected by excluding light from the growing plant, in consequence of which it is produced without colour, and without that portion of its flavour which depends on colour. The tubers of potatoes are blanched naturally, because in general they are produced under the surface of the soil, or they are shaded by the foliage of the plant. Celery is blanched as it grows, or after it has grown, by drawing up earth so as to cover the petioles of the leaves. The leaves of the cardoon are blanched in a similar manner, and sometimes by tying them round with ropes of hay or straw. The interior leaves of the common cabbage, and of the cabbage-lettuce and endive, are blanched naturally, but the process is sometimes heightened by tying up the leaves, and sometimes by coverings. In general, perennial plants in which the nutriment for the leaves of the coming year has been deposited in the roots during the year preceding, such as the asparagus, sea-kale, chicory, &c., may be blanched by covering them entirely either with soil or some kind of utensil; while annual plants, the leaves and every part of which are the produce of the current year, require to have the operation performed by degrees as the leaves advance in size, whether by tying up, earthing up, or by both modes. By the operation of tying up, two effects are produced: the inner leaves as they grow, being excluded from the light, are blanched; and being compressed, in proportion to their number and the degree of growth which takes place after tying up, the head of leaves becomes at once tender and compact. Perennial and biennial plants with branching roots may be blanched on a large scale, by placing the roots in soil in a cellar or dark room; but this cannot be done with annual plants, which must be grown in light, and blanched as they grow.

Protection from Atmospherical Injuries.

The great number of plants cultivated in this country, even in the open air, many of them from climates very different from ours, have given rise to a variety of contrivances to protect them from atmospherical injuries. The most effective of these is without doubt that of forming for such plants artificial climates, as in the different kinds of hotbeds and hothouses; but there are also various contrivances for protecting plants growing in the open air or against walls, and it is to these that we at present intend to confine our attention. They may be included under shading from the sun, sheltering from wind, and protecting from rain or from cold.

The object of shading is to lessen evaporation from the soil or from plants, or to exclude light or heat. It is effected by interposing some opaque medium, or glass, the purest of which, as we have seen, excludes a certain portion of light, between the objects to be shaded and the direct rays of the sun, and this medium differs in its texture and other properties according as it is intended to be temporary or permanent. Mats and canvas are the common articles for temporary shading in the case of plants under glass; but for plants in the open garden, hurdles of wickerwork, or frames filled in with beech or birch branches, or screens of reeds are used, or the plants are placed on the north, east, or west sides of walls or hedges. Sometimes also they are planted under trees: but as this kind of shade excludes rain and dew, it is only adopted in particular cases. A slight degree of shade is produced by forming the surface of ground into narrow ridges in the direction of east and west, and sowing or planting the crop on the north side of the ridge. On the same principle, crops in rows in an advanced state are made to shade seedling crops sown between them, when shading them is desirable. Oil paper-caps, and other articles for shading individual plants have been figured and described, and also canvas shades for hothouse roofs. Some of the most severe injuries which plants trained against walls sustain in this country are from the powerful action of the sun in early spring, succeeded by extreme cold; but by judicious shading such evils may be greatly mitigated or altogether avoided.

Sheltering from wind, the principles of which have been pointed out, is effected on a large scale by plantations, and in gardens by walls, hedges, hurdles, wickerwork covers, hand-glasses, cloches, moveable frames, and other articles.

The principles of protecting from cold have been described at length in our chapter on the atmosphere, and the different materials and contrivances for this purpose have been enumerated. Coverings for the surface of the ground include dead leaves, litter, straw, sawdust, spent tan, rotten dung, coal ashes, coarse sand, spray and branches of trees or shrubs, &c. Coverings for standard plants in the open garden include temporary roofs of thatch, boards, canvas, wickerwork, bark, or manufactured materials, such as pitched paper, asphalte sheeting, &c. Coverings for walks include glass, branches with the leaves on, such as those of the silver or spruce-fir, of the beech, birch, or hornbeam, cut before the wood is ripened, in consequence of which the leaves will adhere to the shoots, and being dead and without moisture, they are better non-conductors than green leaves, straw or hay ropes, rope-netting, canvas, bunting, woollen-netting, oiled paper-frames, wickerwork, hurdles, &c.

Protecting from rain requires the application of some description of temporary roofing impervious to water. For beds or borders in the open garden, frames, or hurdles, thatched with drawn wheat-straw or reeds, may be employed, and these will also protect standard plants; or projected from the tops of walls, and supported by props in front, they will protect from rain both the trees and the border in which they are planted.

Accelerating Vegetation.

The acceleration of the growth of plants may be effected by the position in which they are placed relatively to the rays of the sun, by withdrawing moisture, by sheltering from cold winds and rains, by the choice of early varieties, by pruning, and by the application of artificial heat. For crops of herbaceous vegetables in the open garden, the most general modes of acceleration are to cover with hand-glasses, Rendle's Protectors, or other portable frames with glass roofs, and to sow or plant in borders on the south side of east-and-west walls, and as near to the wall as circumstances will permit. Next to walls, the south sides of hedges or espalier rails are selected; or, in default of either of these, ridges in the open garden, in the direction of east and west, are thrown up, their sides forming an angle of 45°, and on the south side of these the crop is sown or planted. The growth of early peas and early potatoes is frequently accelerated in this manner, and also the ripening of strawberries, as well as the early production of spinach, lettuce, and other culinary plants; and dry warm soil, culture in pots by which the plants are rendered portable, and the selection of the earliest sorts, are obvious adjuncts.

Artificial heat, for the purpose of acceleration, is applied by means of fermenting substances, as in hotbeds; the combustion of fuel, as in hotwalls and hothouses of various kinds, whether heated by flues, hot water, or steam. The different kinds of hothouses and pits, and their general management, have already been given, and we shall here confine ourselves to what concerns hotbeds and pits heated by fermenting materials.

Hotbeds are chiefly made of stable-dung, but tanners' bark, cocoa fibre and cotton refuse, leaves of trees, and especially oak leaves, mown grass, weeds, clippings of hedges, and almost every other article capable of putrescent fermentation, may be used either alone or with stable-dung. Tanners' bark, cocoa fibre, or oak leaves, are found the preferable fermenting materials for hotbeds in hothouses, because they undergo less change in bulk, and retain their heat longer than dung or any other fermentable substance that can be readily obtained in equal quantities. Leaves do not produce such a powerful heat as bark, but they have this advantage, that when perfectly decayed, they form a rich mould, which is useful both as soil and as manure; while rotten tanners' bark is found rather injurious than useful to vegetation, unless it be well mixed with lime or with earth, or left till it is thoroughly decayed into mould. When it ceases, therefore, to be used in the hothouse or hotbed, it is employed in the open garden as a surface-mulching, to keep in heat or moisture.

Preparation of Materials for Hotbeds.—The object being to get rid of the violent heat which is produced when the fermentation is most powerful, it is obvious that preparation, whether of leaves, tan, or stable-dung, must consist in facilitating the process. For this purpose a certain degree of moisture and air in the fermenting bodies are requisite; and hence the business of the gardener is to turn them over frequently, and apply water when the process appears impeded for want of it, and exclude rain when it seems chilled and retarded by too much water. Recent stable-dung generally requires to lie a month in ridges or beds, and to be turned over in that time thrice before it is fit for cucumber-beds of the common construction; but for linings or casings to any description of hotbed or pit, no time at all need in general be given, the dung being formed at once into linings. Tan and leaves require in general a month to bring them to a proper degree of heat; but much depends on the state of the weather and the season of the year. Fermentation is always most rapid in summer; and if the materials are spread abroad during frost, it is totally impeded. In winter, the process of preparation generally goes on under cover from the weather, in the back sheds, which situation is also the best in summer, as full exposure to the sun and wind dries the exterior surface too much; but where sheds cannot be had, it will go on very well in the open air.

M'Phail's hotbed or pit consists of two parts, the frame and lights of which are of wood, and not different from those used for growing cucumbers, or other ordinary purposes, and the basement on which the frame is placed, which is flues of brickwork, with the outer wall uniformly perforated, or, as it is commonly called, pigeon-holed. Against these perforated flues, linings of dung are formed, the steam of which enters the flue, and heats the earth enclosed. The chief objections to this plan are the first cost and the greater consumption of dung which is required to keep up the proper heat. Its advantages are, that hot dung may be used without any preparation, by which much heat is gained; and that in the winter months, when a powerful artificial heat is required, which (in the case of common hotbeds) is apt to burn the plants, they are here in the coldest part of the soil, and cannot possibly be injured by any degree of heat which can be communicated by dung. Fig. 328 is a section of a pit on this principle, with some improvements: *a a* is the surface of the ground; *b b*, excavations for the dung-casings, 2½ feet deep, 18 inches wide at bottom, and 2 feet wide at the ground's surface; the greater width at top being to prevent the dung from shrinking from the sides of the excavation as it sinks; *c* is the outer perforated wall, a brick in width; *d*, the inner wall of brick set on edge, and tied to the outer wall with occasional cross bricks; *e* is a layer of billet-wood, one foot in thickness, to admit of the heat penetrating from each side, or the same object may be effected by a layer of loose stones: *f*, a covering of faggot-wood, over which a layer of turf or litter is placed to prevent the soil from sinking into and choking up the interstices in the layer of billet-wood; *g*, the bed of soil; *h*, a trellis for vines, melons, or other plants, at one foot from the glass; *i*, a gutter for receiving the water from the glass, and which should conduct it through a small pipe, either at one end or in the middle, to a barrel,

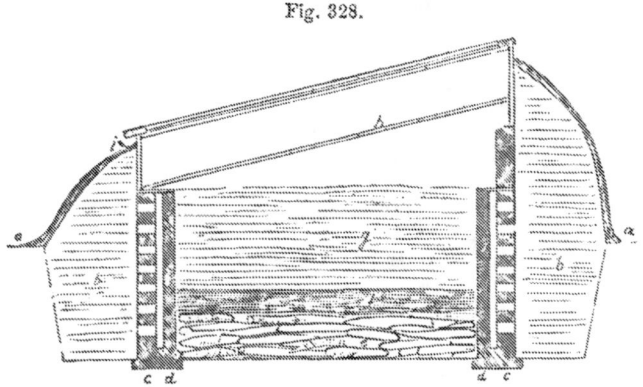

Fig. 328.

Cross section of a pit on M'Phail's principle, with variations.

or to a cistern of slate or of other material sunk in the soil of the pit in front. The preferable situation is midway between either end, in order that the vapour of the water may be equally diffused in the atmosphere of the pit. By keeping the upper surface of the dung in the form shown in the figure, it will throw off the rain, which may be conducted away in small surface gutters.

The formation of common hotbeds is effected by first marking out the dimensions of the bed, which should be six inches wider on all sides than that of the frame to be placed over it, and then, by successive layers of dung laid on by the fork, raising it to the desired height, pressing it gently and equally throughout. In general such beds are built on a level surface; but Mr. Knight forms a surface of earth as a basis, which shall incline to the horizon to the extent of 15°; on this he forms the dung-bed to the same inclination; and finally the frame, when placed on such a bed, if, as is usual, it be deepest behind, will present its glass at an angle of 20° instead of six or eight, which is undoubtedly of great advantage in the winter season. This seems a very desirable improvement where light is an object, which it must be, in a high degree, in the case of the culture of the cucumber and melons, as well as in forcing flowers. Sometimes a stratum of faggots or billet-wood is placed on the ground as a foundation for the dung, which keeps it from being chilled; and if here and there the stratum is carried up vertically for a foot in width and eighteen inches in height, it will facilitate the entrance of heat when casings are applied, or of cold air, if the heat of the bed should be found too great. The ends of these vertical strata, when not to be used, should be covered with litter to prevent the escape of heat through them.

Ashes, Tan, and Leaves.—Ashes are often mixed with the dung of hotbeds, and are supposed to promote the steadiness and duration of their heat, and to revive it if somewhat decayed. Tan and leaves have also been used for the same purpose; and it is generally found that about one-third of tan and two-thirds of dung will form a more durable and less violent heat than a bed wholly of dung. The heat of dung-beds is revived by linings, or collateral and surrounding walls, or banks of fresh dung, the old dung of the bed being previously cut down close to the frames. These linings, as before observed, require less preparation than the dung for the beds. The dung-bed being formed, and having stood two or three days with the frame and lights placed over it to protect it from rain, is next to be covered with earth, of such quality and quantity as the purpose to which it is to be applied requires. In severe weather, the sides of the bed are often protected by hurdles of straw or faggots, which tend to prevent the escape of heat.

The nightly covering to hotbeds and pits may be of boards, or of bast-mats, or reed or straw mats; and the following mode of securing the covering will be found neat as well as economical: — Three pieces of iron of the form of fig. 329, *a*, are screwed on to the end of the frame, one piece at the top, another at the bottom, and the other in the middle, so that the top of the iron is about two inches above the light; on the opposite end three pieces of the form of *c*, are screwed on at the same distances as *a*; *b* is a side view of *a*, and *d* is a side view of *c*. A wire, three-eighths of an inch in diameter, and rather longer than the frame it is intended for, must be made with a loop at one end (*f*) to place over the iron *d*; the other end must be fitted with a thumb-screw (*e*), to screw up the wire when it is placed in the notch *g*, which should be countersunk in the centre. Small hooks should be driven in the frames, either in front or back, to lay the wires in when not in use. A much simpler and more common method is to lay a piece of wood of sufficient height on to the front and back of the frame.

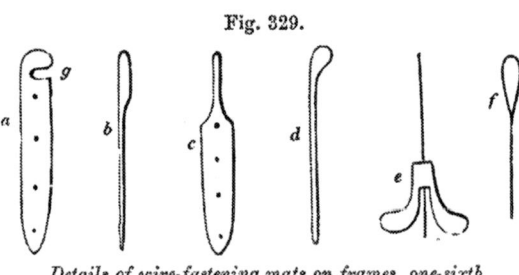

Fig. 329.

Details of wire-fastening mats on frames, one-sixth of the full size.

Management of Hotbeds and Pits Heated by Dung.—As the body of air enclosed is small, its temperature is easily raised too high by the sun, and depressed too much by high winds or very cold nights. The artificial supply of heat from the fermenting material not being under control is another cause of overheating, and hence the constant attention required to give or take away air during the day, and to regulate the coverings put on at night. Much mischief is produced by over-covering, and yet, for the reasons we have just mentioned, it would be very unsafe to leave a hotbed uncovered during any of the nights of winter or early spring; though later in the season, or where plate-glass is used, covering at night might be dispensed with. The covering should not be drawn over the linings so as to confine the steam; which in that case would find its way into the frame to the injury of the plants. The temperature and moisture to be kept up in hotbeds vary with the kinds of plants and the object in view.

Retarding Vegetation.

The different modes of retarding vegetation being in many cases the opposite of those for its acceleration, the subject may be similarly arranged. As on the south side of ridges of ground, in the direction of east and west, plants are accelerated by meeting the rays of the sun at a larger angle, so on the north side of such ridges, as well as on the north side of walls and hedges, they will be retarded by the exclusion of the sun's direct influence. Opaque coverings put on in winter or in early spring, are also effective, more especially when of some thickness, by excluding the stimulus of light, and presenting a thicker mass to be penetrated by atmospheric heat. Thus herbaceous perennials, such as asparagus, rhubarb, sea-kale, and other plants which do not retain their leaves during winter, may, by a thick covering of leaves or litter put on in January, when the soil is at the coldest, be prevented from vegetating for a week or a month later than the same plants on a surface sloping to the south, without any covering, and with the soil dry and loosened about the collars of the plants. The production of blossoms and fruit may in many cases be retarded by taking off the flower-buds at their first appearance in spring or early summer, as is often done with roses, strawberries, and raspberries, which, when so treated, flower and fruit a second time in the autumn. Currants and gooseberries, and even pears and apples on dwarfs, are preserved on the trees till Christmas, by matting them over; and the season of wall-fruits and of grapes in hothouses is prolonged by excluding the sun and preserving the air dry. In general, all exogenous perennial herbaceous plants, when cut over as soon as their flower-buds are formed in spring, will spring up again and produce flowers a second time in autumn; but this does not happen with endogens, excepting in the case of grasses and a few other plants. Retarding no less than accelerating may be effected by changing the habits of plants; and thus, as plants which have vegetated early one season are likely also to vegetate early the season following, so plants which have continued to grow late in autumn one year, will be later in vegetating in the following spring, and continue to grow later in the autumn. There is a considerable difference in the natural earliness and lateness of vegetation in all plants of the same species or variety raised from seed, and hence, early and late varieties may always be procured by selection from the bed of seedlings. By this means have been obtained all the earliest and latest varieties in cultivation both in fields and gardens. Seeds or plants procured from cold and late soils and situations, and brought to earlier ones, continue for a time to be late from habit, and the contrary; and hence the practice of farmers in cold, late districts procuring their seed-corn and potato-sets from low, warm districts, and the contrary. When plants are grown in pots, they can generally be more effectually either accelerated or retarded than by any other means; because they may be at pleasure transferred to a cold cellar, to an ice-house, or to a forcing-house. Thus fruit trees and flowering shrubs in pots, put into an ice-house in January, will have their vegetation retarded for any length of time, as no growth can take place where the temperature is under the freezing point. Plants so treated, if not retained too long, may be made to vegetate at any season that is desired, but the transition from the temperature of the ice-house to summer-heat must be very gradual, in order that the buds may be fully distended with sap before they are developed. Fruit or vegetables which would spoil or advance too far if left on the plants, such as peas, cauliflowers, cucumbers, peaches, &c., may be retained several days in the state required in the ice-house, or in a room adjoining it, and even for a certain period in a cool cellar or shed. The earliest potatoes are obtained by some gardeners by keeping them in a place so cool as to prevent vegetation for two seasons: that is, the produce of the summer of one year is to be planted in the December of the year following. The German gardeners, by retarding the roots of the ranunculus in this manner, are enabled to produce it in flower all the year, and the same thing might be effected with various bulbs. The flowering of annual plants is easily retarded by sowing them late in the year; and on this principle the gaiety of the flower-garden is preserved in autumn, and culinary productions, such as spinach, lettuce, &c., obtained throughout winter.

Resting Vegetation.

In the natural state of vegetation all plants experience a more or less low degree of temperature during the night than during the day. In the tropics the difference is but little, particularly as regards plants that grow in the shade. It, however, increases from the torrid to the frigid zone; and therefore artificial temperature should be regulated accordingly. Tropical plants are injured by a greater discrepancy of temperature than occurs in their native regions. There the temperature independent of direct sun heat is almost uniform. But in the case of such plants as the vine, the fig, and the peach, the natural habit of which extends to a latitude as high as 45°, a considerable range of temperature is necessary. They enjoy, in summer, a long day of high temperature—indeed, a tropical heat; but at night a tropical temperature is not maintained. These plants, and others having corresponding habitats, require not only a temperature lower by night than by day, but also lower in winter than in summer. Tropical plants, on the contrary, are injured by having a wintering imposed upon them, a condition they are never naturally placed in. In particular situations, even in extra-tropical countries, plants may be found growing where the temperature varies little, owing to shade and shelter, the vicinity of springs, &c., but these are only the exceptions.

Nightly temperature requires to be considered chiefly with reference to plants under glass. The fear of too low a temperature within being produced by the cold without, has naturally led gardeners to bestow particular care on covering up hotbeds, and raising the temperature of the air in hothouses in the evenings. In consequence of this, it often happens that when the temperature of the external air has not fallen so low during the night as was expected, the temperature under glass becomes greater than was intended. The consequences of this excess of heat during the night are highly injurious to the fruit trees of temperate climates, and not at all beneficial to those of tropical climates; for the temperature of these is, in many instances, low during the night. In Jamaica, and other mountainous islands of the West Indies, the air upon the mountains becomes soon after sunset chilled and condensed, and, in consequence of its superior gravity, descends and displaces the warm air of the valleys; yet the sugar-canes are so far from being injured by this sudden decrease of temperature, that the sugars of Jamaica take a higher price in the market than those of the less elevated islands, of which the temperature of the day and night is subject to much less variation. Plants, it is true, thrive well, and many species of fruit acquire their greatest state of perfection in some situations within the tropics where the temperature in the shade does not vary in the day and night more than seven or eight degrees; but in these climates, the plant is exposed during the day to a full blaze of a tropical sun, and early in the night it is regularly drenched with heavy wetting dews; and consequently it is very differently circumstanced in the day and in the night, though the temperature of the air in the shade at both periods may be very nearly the same. A high night temperature often causes a large portion of the blossoms of cherries and other fruit trees to prove abortive, because they are forced to expand before the sap of the tree is properly prepared to nourish them. Under a lower night temperature, the blossoms advance with more vigour, and expand to a larger size. Another evil effect of a high temperature at night is that it exhausts the tree rather than hastens the growth or accelerates the maturity of the fruit. The Muscat of Alexandria, and other late grapes, are, probably owing to this cause, often seen to wither upon the branch in a very imperfect state of maturity; and the want of richness and flavour in other forced fruits is often attributable to the same cause. There are few peach-houses, or indeed forcing-houses, of any kind in this country, in which the temperature does not exceed during the night, in the months of April and May, very greatly that of the warmest valley in Jamaica in the hottest period of the year: and there are probably as few forcing-houses in which the trees are not more strongly stimulated by the close and damp air of the night, than by the temperature of the dry air of the noon of the following day. The practice which occasions this cannot be right; it is in direct opposition to nature.

What the night temperature of a hotbed or hothouse ought to be as compared with that of the day, can only be determined by experience; because plants under glass are so far removed from plants in the free air, that the same difference which takes place in the latter case may not in the former case be advisable. Nevertheless it is clear from the experience of gardeners that a very great fall during the night is seldom or never attended with bad effects, provided there has been sufficient heat and light during the day. Much of the evil of a high temperature during night, especially where opaque coverings are used, must be owing to the absence of light. A fall of from 10° to 15° at night under the maximum maintained by day, would seldom be injurious, and as a rule might be safely and advantageously adopted.

Double glass roofs would evidently form the least objectionable nightly covering to plant structures of every kind; and next to these the use of plate-glass, instead of common crown glass, as from the much greater thickness of the former far less heat would be allowed to escape by conduction. The use of plate-glass in cucumber and melon frames, and also in greenhouses and forcing-houses, has of late years been adopted by several persons, and the glass being much less liable to be broken, and requiring no covering during night, it is found to be on the whole more economical than common glass, and much better for the plants.

The annual resting of plants is effected, as we have seen, either by cold or by dryness, and both these causes can be imitated in a state of culture, either separately or combined. Plants in the open garden may be safely left to the influence of the seasons; but half-hardy plants against walls, or in borders by themselves, may be brought to a state of rest by thatching the ground so as to prevent what rain may fall on it from sinking in; the lateral supplies being cut off by surface gutters or underground drains. The supply of sap by the roots being thus reduced, growth will gradually cease, and the parts will be matured, and at once enabled to resist the winter and vegetate with redoubled vigour the following spring. It may be observed here that the shoots of a tree which is to be protected from frost during winter, do not require to be ripened to the same degree as shoots which are to be exposed to the action of frost in the free atmosphere; because buds, like seeds, will vegetate provided the embryo be formed, even though they should not be matured. Plants which have been forced have their period of rest brought on naturally by the maturation of the plant; and hence peach-trees which have been forced, have almost always better ripened wood, containing more blossom-buds, than peach-trees on the open walls. In the case of peach-houses, vineries, &c., by withholding water and applying dry heat, maturation is easily effected. Greenhouse plants, such as natives of the Cape of Good Hope and Australia, are brought to a state of rest, partly by lowering the temperature of the greenhouse and partly by withholding water. The last mode is that which is most to be depended on, because in most greenhouses there are some plants in flower at every period of the year, and for these a greater degree of heat must be kept up than would merely suffice for throwing greenhouse plants into a state of rest. All tropical plants are brought to a state of repose by dryness, and this is readily imitated in hothouses, in consequence of the plants being in pots. There are some tropical plants, however, which though in certain localities they have what almost amounts to a short cessation of growth, yet in a state of culture will succeed better without it.

The natural period of rest in hardy plants may be varied or changed by withholding moisture, even without reference to temperature. We see this taking place both with trees and herbs in dry seasons: when wood is ripened, leaves drop off; and grass fields become brown in July and August, which in moist seasons would have continued growing till October or November. By imitating these effects in gardens, the operation of accelerating and retarding may be greatly facilitated; and the imitation is easy when plants are kept in pots. Even pruning after the leaves drop in autumn, as we have seen, has a tendency to produce an earlier development of the buds than when that operation is deferred till spring; because the number of buds to be nourished during winter being smaller, they are swelled to a larger size, and are more ready to be developed. In general, whatever tends to ripen the wood in ligneous plants, and mature the leaves in herbs, tends to bring the plant into a state of repose; and hence the value of walls, dry borders, dry soils, and warm exposures.

The advantages of putting trees that are to be forced into a state of rest, and thus rendering them as excitable as possible previously to the application of artificial heat, are now well understood by gardeners. The period of maturity, under any given degrees of temperature and exposure to the influence of light in the forcing-house, will be regulated to a much greater extent than is generally imagined by the previous management and consequent state of the tree, when it is first subjected to the operation of artificial heat. Every gardener knows that when the previous season has been cold and cloudy and wet, the wood of his fruit trees remains immature, and weak abortive blossoms only are produced. In the autumn, the plants have just sunk into their winter sleep; in February they are refreshed and ready to awake again: and wherever it is intended prematurely to excite their powers of life into action, the expediency of putting these powers into a state of rest early in the preceding autumn appears obvious. Mr. Knight placed some vines in pots in a forcing-house, in the end of January, which ripened their fruit in the middle of July; soon after which the pots were put under the shade of a north wall in the open air. Being pruned and removed in September to a south wall, they soon vegetated with much vigour, till the frost destroyed their shoots. Others, which were not removed from the north wall till the following spring, when they were pruned and placed against a south wall, ripened their fruit well in the following season in a climate not nearly warm enough to have ripened at all, if the plants had previously grown in the open air. Peach-trees somewhat similarly treated unfolded their blossoms nine days earlier, " and their fruit ripened three weeks earlier than in other trees of the same varieties." Pots of grapes which had produced a crop previously to midsummer were placed under a north wall till autumn; on the 12th of January they were put into a stove, and ripened their fruit by the middle of April. Early resting is the best preparation for early forcing, and indeed is almost essential to its success.

Operations of Gathering, Preserving, Keeping, and Packing.

Gathering.—The productions of horticulture are in part enjoyed as scenery, and in part as articles of food, and other uses of domestic economy; and the gathering of articles for the latter purposes forms a part of the duty of the gardener. All crops are taken from the plant when mature, as in the case of ripe fruit or roots; or they are cut from it when the plant is in a growing state, as in gathering herbs or cabbages; or the entire plant is taken up, as in the case of turnips, carrots, &c. In all these cases the part of the plant to be gathered should not have been moistened by rain, and the weather at the time should be dry. Wherever the knife requires to be used in gathering, the operation may be considered as coming under pruning, and should be performed with the same care in respect to buds and wounded sections. In gathering fruit, care should be taken not to rub off the bloom, particularly from cucumbers, plums, and grapes. When ripe seeds are gathered, the capsules or pods should be perfectly dry, and they should be spread out afterwards in a shaded, airy shed or loft, or on a seed-sheet in the open air, till they are ready to be rubbed out, cleaned, and put up into paper bags till wanted.

Preserving.—Culinary vegetables may be preserved in a fresh state by placing moveable covers, such as thatched hurdles, over them in the open garden, as indicated in fig. 330; or by planting them in soil, in pits or frames, to be covered during severe weather; or they may be planted in soil, in light cellars, the windows being opened in the daytime—a practice common in the colder countries of the Continent. Aromatic herbs, such as mint, thyme, &c., may be preserved by first drying them in the shade, and next compressing each kind into small packets, and covering these with paper. Aromatic herbs, and also pot-herbs, such as parsley, celery, leaves, chervil, &c., may be preserved by drying in an oven, rubbing or grinding them to powder, and stowing them away in wide-mouthed closely-corked bottles. The ripe fruit may be preserved in dried sand, dry bran, chaff, &c., in the following manner. Wrap any ripe fruit round with tissue-paper, and pack them in barrels or pots with layers of such substances between them to exclude the air, and keep the fruit from bruising each other. Roots, tubers, and bulbs are preserved in soil or in sand, moderately dry, and excluded from frost; and some kinds, which have coverings which protect them from evapo-

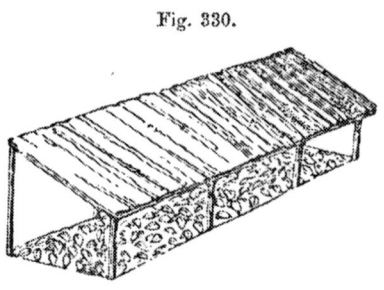

Fig. 330.

Low-roof thatched hurdles for protecting plants in the open garden.

ration, such as the tulip and the crocus, are kept on cool dry shelves or lofts, or in papers till the planting season. Parsnips, turnips, carrots, &c., are preserved with most flavour by leaving them where they have grown, covering the ground with litter, so as to exclude frost and admit of their being taken up daily as wanted. Towards the growing season they should have a thicker covering to exclude atmospheric heat; or a portion should have been taken up in autumn, and buried in sand or soil, in a cool cellar, in order to retard vegetation as long as possible. The potatoes and onions will keep upwards of a year without rotting or vegetating, if mixed with sand and buried in a pit in dry soil, the upper part of which shall be at least five feet under the surface of the ground, so as effectually to exclude air and change of temperature. Ice-houses also prove valuable for retarding the growth of vegetables in spring, and prolonging their season at all times. Henderson, an eminent gardener at Brechin, makes use of the ice-house for preserving roots of all kinds till the return of the natural crop. By the month of April, the ice in the ice-houses is found to have subsided four or five feet; and this empty space may be filled with vegetables to be preserved. After stuffing the vacuities with straw, and covering the surface of the ice with the same material, case-boxes, dry-ware casks, baskets, &c., filled with turnips, carrots, beetroot, celery, and potatoes, may be placed upon it. By the cold of the place, vegetation is so much suspended that all these articles may be thus kept fresh and uninjured, till they give place to another crop in its natural season.

Keeping-fruits, such as the apple and pear, are preserved in the fruit-room, on shelves, placed singly so as not to touch each other; the finer keeping-pears may be packed in jars and boxes, with dried fern, or with kiln-dried barley-straw; and baking apples and pears may be kept in heaps or thin layers on a cellar floor, and covered with straw, to retain moisture and exclude the frost. But the subject of keeping-fruits will be recurred to in treating of the fruit garden.

Packing and Transporting Plants and Seeds.—Rooted plants and cuttings, and other parts of plants intended to grow, may be preserved for weeks, and, under certain circumstances, even for months, in damp or dry moss, the direct action of the air and sun being excluded; and in this medium also they may be packed and sent to any distance within the temperate hemispheres, but not in tropical regions, on account of the extreme heat. Plants that are to pass through these regions are planted in soil, in boxes with glass-covers, Wardian cases, etc., and being occasionally watered, they are transferred from India to England with a very moderate proportion of loss. Seeds are in general most safely conveyed from one country to another in loose paper packages, kept in a dry airy situation, so as neither to be parched with dry heat nor made to vegetate by moisture; but some seeds which are apt soon to lose their vitality, such as the acorns of American oaks, may be packed in moist moss, in which they will germinate during the voyage; but if planted in soil as soon as they arrive, they will suffer little injury. Nuts and other large seeds should be packed in sandy earth or chaff.

B B

The roots or root-ends of plants or cuttings are enveloped in a ball of clayey loam, wrapped up in moist moss, or in the case of cuttings or scions of ligneous plants, stuck into a potato, turnip, or apple, and sent to any distance; or, they may be enclosed in moistened brown paper, or wrapped up in oiled paper, and sent by post. Scions of fruit trees have been sent considerable distances with safety by being carefully wrapped in cabbage-leaves, the lower side of the leaf being turned toward the scion, as the outer side is impervious.

Packing Fruits and Flowers.—Firm fruits, such as the apple and pear, and flowers either in a growing state in pots, or cut for nosegays, are easily packed; but grapes, peaches, strawberries, &c., are with more difficulty sent to a distance without being injured. To pack such fruit, and also the more delicate flowers, a box is suspended within a box, in such a manner that the inner case can never touch the outer one. This mode is "found better than any other for ensuring the safe transport of delicate philosophical instruments, and is equally adapted to ripe fruit. Having packed the fruit in an inner case with soft cotton, or whatever may be deemed best for the purpose, let that inner case be suspended within an outer one by lines or cords. Suppose, for instance, that the outer case is two or three inches clear all round the inner case, and the eight cords proceeded from the eight outer corners of the one, and were fastened to the eight internal corners of the other case. In this way, whatever side was uppermost, the inner case would be suspended from the four upper cords, the four lower ones serving only to steady it and to prevent its swinging against the outer case. If the whole be turned upside down, the functions of the cords become reversed, so that they must all be strong enough to perform either office, about which, however, there is no difficulty. A still better plan, for those who have frequently very choice specimens of fruit to transmit, would be to insulate the inner case by spiral springs, with the addition of small portions of felt or woollen cloth to limit the vibrations; the springs would be very cheaply made, and would avoid the repeated trouble of packing or tying; but the cords will do extremely well." ('Gard. Chron.,' vol. i. p. 485.) It is likewise common now to have a number of shallow trays of wood or tin, made to fit one above another, to be all enclosed in a larger box. The depth of these trays is that of the circumference of the fruit sent, with a little to spare for packing material: two inches for strawberries, four or five for peaches, four for apples, and eight or ten for grapes. These trays are again subdivided into spaces about the same size. Each fruit has thus a space for itself. Wrapped round with tissue-paper, packed tight with cotton wool, fruits can be sent anywhere without risk of bruising. Grapes, perhaps, travel best fixed to a board, lined with a thick layer of cotton wool, the upper portion of the branch and its sides being left wholly free; this board, with the grapes attached, is then placed inside a box, securely and immovably fixed in its place, and a lid, which does not bruise the grapes, placed on. Others place tissue-paper over the grapes, and fill the entire space with chaff, bran, or cotton wool.

Selecting and Improving Plants in Culture.

All the plants in cultivation that are remarkable for their value as culinary vegetables, fruits, or flowers, are more or less removed from their natural state; and the three principal modes by which this has been effected, are:—increasing the supply of nourishment, selection from seedlings or accidental variations, and cross-breeding. It has been well observed that nature "has given to man the means of acquiring those things which constitute the comforts and luxuries of civilized life, though not the things themselves; it has placed the raw material within his reach, but has left the preparation and improvement of it to his own skill and industry. Every plant and animal adapted to his service is made susceptible of endless changes, and as far as relates to his use, of almost endless improvement. Variation is the constant attendant on cultivation, both in the animal and vegetable world; and in each the offspring are constantly seen, in a greater or less degree, to inherit the character of the parents from which they spring." (Knight's 'Physiological Papers,' &c., p. 172.) See also Darwin's 'Improvement of Plants and Animals.'

Cultivation, then, is the first step in the progress of improving vegetables. It is almost needless to state that this consists in furnishing a plant with a more favourable soil and climate than it had in a wild state; supplying food by manure to as great an extent as is consistent with health and vigour; allowing an ample space for its branches and leaves to expand and expose themselves to the action of the sun and the air; guarding the plant from external injuries, by the peculiar kind of shelter and protection which it may require, according as the object may be the improvement of the entire plant, of its foliage only, of its flowers, or of its fruit. All cultivation is founded on the principle that the constitution and qualities of plants are susceptible of being influenced by the quantity and quality of the food with which they are furnished, and that the constitution and qualities so formed can be communicated to their offspring. The seeds of plants abundantly supplied with food, and growing in a favourable climate, will produce plants of luxuriant foliage, and larger than usual in all their parts; while the contrary will be the case with seeds produced by plants grown in a meagre soil, and in an unfavourable climate. Seeds produced in a hot climate will produce plants better adapted for that climate than seeds from a climate that is cold, and the contrary; and hence also the seeds of plants grown in a poor soil and ungenial climate will succeed better in that soil and climate than plants raised from seeds produced under more favourable circumstances. Almost every species of fruit acquires its greatest state of perfection in some peculiar soils and situations, and under some peculiar mode of culture. The selection of a proper soil and situation must therefore be the first object of the improver's pursuit; and nothing should be neglected which can add to the size, or improve the flavour, of the fruit from which it is intended to propagate. The improver, who has to adapt his productions to the cold and unsteady climate of Britain, has still many difficulties to contend with: he has to combine hardiness, robustness of character, and early maturity with the improvements of high cultivation. Nature has, however, in some measure pointed out the path he is to pursue; and if it be followed with patience and industry, no obstacles will be found which may not be either removed or surmounted. If two plants of the vine, or other tree of similar habits, or even if obtained from cuttings of the same tree, were placed to vegetate during several successive seasons in very different climates; if the one were planted on the banks of the Rhine, and the other on those of the Nile, each would adapt its habits to the climate it which it was placed; and if both were subsequently brought in early spring into a climate similar to that of Italy, the plant which had adapted its habits to a cold climate would instantly vegetate, whilst the other would remain torpid. It appears that the powers of vegetable life in plants habituated to cold climates are more easily brought into action than in those of hot climates; or, in other words, that the plants of cold climates are most excitable: and as every quality in plants becomes hereditary to some extent, it follows that their seedling offspring have a constant tendency to adopt or exaggerate the peculiarities of their recent or remote parentage.

Selection.—An individual wild plant being thus improved, the next step is to sow its seeds under the most favourable circumstances of soil and situation, and from the plants so produced to select such, or perhaps only one, or even a part of one, which possesses in the highest degree the qualities we are in search of. This plant being carefully cultivated, its seeds are to be sown, and a selection made from the plants produced as before. By such means, most of our garden plants have been improved. Plain-leaved parsley has become superbly curled; plain Scotch kail beautifully variegated; and cauliflowers, peas, potatoes, turnips, &c. enlarged in size and improved in quality. The same means have been used with fruits, and with equal success. Many of our varieties of grapes, Hambro's especially, probably owe their origin to selection; and it is doubtless to a careful selection of the best parents that we owe the many splendid new peaches and nectarines that Mr. Rivers has given us of late years.

Selecting from Accidental Variations, or, as they are technically termed, Sports.—Among a great number of seedlings raised in gardens, or of plants in a wild state, some entire plants, or parts of plants, will exhibit differences in form or colour from the normal form and colour of the species. Among these peculiarities may be noticed double flowers, flowers of a colour different from those of the species, variegated leaves, leaves deeply cut where the normal form is entire, as in the fern-leaved beech; and even the entire plant may be of more diminutive size, or its shoots may take a different direction, as in fastigiate and pendulous-branched trees. All these, and many other accidental variations, which cannot generally be reproduced from seed, may be perpetuated by cuttings, or some other mode of propagating by division.

Cross-breeding.—This process is effected by fecundating the stigma of a flower of one plant with the pollen from the flower of another of the same species, but of a different variety. Sometimes fecundation may be effected with the pollen of a different species, and in that case the produce is said to be a hybrid, while in the other the result is merely a cross or a cross-bred variety. The following is the best mode of proceeding:—Choose the varieties possessing between them the qualities from which to develop them just as the blossoms of the seed-bearing plant are on the point of opening, or just after they have opened; when one is just on the point of opening and exposing the anthers, take a pair of scissors and cut off the stamens, and remove the anthers, and then leave the blossoms thus operated upon for a day or two, or until the petals are quite expanded, and the pistil arrived at a state of maturity; when it is in this state, select a blossom of the plant with which it is desired to impregnate the prepared female blossom, and when this is in a state of maturity, and in a state to part with its pollen or farina freely, take a small camel's-hair pencil, collect the farina on the point, and place it on the stigma or crown of the pistil of the prepared blossom. "New varieties of every species of fruit," Mr. Knight observes, "will generally be better obtained by introducing the farina of one variety of fruit into the blossom of another, than by propagating from any single kind. When an experiment of this kind is made between varieties of different size and character, the farina of the smaller kind should be introduced into the blossoms of the larger, for, under these circumstances, I have generally (but with some exceptions) observed in the new fruit a prevalence of the character of the female parent; probably owing to the following causes. The seed-coats are generally generated wholly by the female parent, and these regulate the bulk of the lobes and plantule: and I have observed, in raising new varieties of the peach, that when one stone contained two seeds, the plants raised were much inferior to others. The largest seed, obtained from the strongest plants, and that which ripens most perfectly and most early, should always be selected. It has generally been found too, that the seed-bearing plant imparts strength and constitution, while the male parent gives colour and quality.

Precautions against promiscuous fecundation require to be taken both in the case of flowers the seeds of which are to be sown for the purpose of selection, and in those which have been cross-fecundated. In the former case, the plants should as much as possible be isolated from all others of the same or of allied kinds; and in the latter something more should be done. The reasons are, that in both cases the farina of adjoining flowers of the same kind is in all probability floating in the atmosphere, and will adhere to whatever stigmas of its own species it may light on; and secondly, that bees and other insects which frequent flowers carry off the pollen from one to another, and thus produce accidental cross-fecundation, which would render nugatory that which was attempted by art. The only mode to guard against pollen floating in the atmosphere is by placing the plants far from all others of the same kind, though what distance is required is uncertain. For the cruciferæ generally most space is required; varieties of cabbages and turnips having been adulterated when at a distance of upwards of a mile, in an open country and in the direction of the prevailing winds. To guard against the effects of bees and other insects, the blossoms when selected and fecundated by art may be surrounded by coarse gauze, or enclosed in a case of glass, till the blossom begins to fade. To strengthen the embryo seeds, the plant may be pruned in such a manner as to throw an extra share of sap into the branch, stem, or pedicel on which the flower is situated. Thus, if the fecundated flower form part of a spike, the upper part of the spike may be cut off; a corymb or an umbel may be thinned out; the suckers may be taken from a sucker-bearing plant, such as the raspberry; the runners from the strawberry; the offsets from a bulb, the tubers from a potato, and so forth.

Fixing and rendering permanent the variety produced is effected in general by one or other of the modes of propagation. Improved varieties of fruit trees are generally perpetuated by grafting; fruit shrubs, such as the gooseberry, and flowering plants, such as the fuchsia, pelargonium, &c., by cuttings; perennials, by division, offsets, or suckers, &c.; improved annuals and biennials, and some perennials, are perpetuated by seeds. Numerous means are adopted, such as those named above, to keep the stock of improved varieties true or pure. There is one practice common among cultivators, the rationale of which it is difficult to explain. This is the transplantation of culinary biennials, such as the turnip, carrot, parsnip, beet, cabbage, cauliflower, onion, and many such plants, after they are full grown, previously to their being allowed to send up their flower-stems. By this practice the variety is said to be prevented from degenerating; and if so, it may probably be on account of the greater part of the nourishment to the seeds being furnished by the store laid up in the plant, and but only a small portion taken from the soil. It is certain that transplanted plants do not produce nearly so much seed as they would have done if not transplanted; and it is equally certain that in the case of the turnip, when the bulb is of a moderate size, and even small rather than large, much stronger flower-stems are sent up, and more seed produced, than when it is large. The reason probably is that the roots below the unswelled bulb are stronger, not having yet fulfilled their functions, and hence are enabled to draw a larger proportion of nourishment from the soil.

The production of double flowers is a subject not yet thoroughly understood by physiologists. As double flowers are seldom found in a wild state, they appear to be the result of culture, and yet there is scarcely any well-authenticated instance of culture having produced them. It is certain, however, that double flowers degenerate into single ones when culture is withdrawn, and that extraordinary supplies of nourishment and moisture, as in moist and warm seasons, seem to produce flowers more double than in dry seasons. It has also been said that by concentrating the strength of the plant one season into two or three seed-pods, instead of allowing it to expend itself through a greater number, double flowers will be produced, and scarlet stocks so reduced produced nearly all double flowers, while those kept to ripen all the seed shown were mostly single. De Candolle states cases in which the fixing a ligature round the collar of the plant produced double flowers. Seeds from semi-double flowers are likewise likely to originate those that are wholly double; and it has likewise been asserted that single flowers grown among double ones are likely to be the parents of double flowers. What is positive is, that some varieties or strains of seed yield a much larger percentage of double flowers than others, and that in finally planting such plants as stocks into their flowering quarters, those of medium strength are more likely to prove double than the strongest plants. Others suppose that the food provided, and even the age of the seed, affects the production of flowers. It is well known, and has often been proved, that calyx, corolla, stamens, and pistils are only more highly organized leaves, and each in the order in which they are mentioned is more highly organized than the preceding. While liberal culture seems to favour this transformation of the leaves into these portions of flowers, over-feeding may reverse them back again to leaves. When the branch is highly gorged with crude sap, the pistil is often lowered back again into a shoot, as seen in the case of roses and other flowers. Alternate starving and natural feeding, or a check, is often productive of double flowers. Old seed is likewise much more prolific of double flowers than that which is new.

Duration of Varieties.—The permanence of the duration of varieties, so long as man wishes to take care of them, is evident from the continued existence of varieties, the most ancient of those which have been described in books. A great deal however depends upon constitution in vegetable as in animal life. The victory is to the strongest. By negligence, or by a series of bad seasons, they may become diseased, like some of our varieties of apple or potato, but by careful culture they may be restored and retained to all appearance for ever. The species might be recovered, but we question whether in many instances that will be the case with the variety. Improved varieties, as they are understood in a horticultural point of view, are doubtless prone to decay in proportion to their degree of departure from that physiological perfection which enables the wild variety to maintain itself continually on the surface of the globe, independent of the care of man. A wild variety will produce seed under favourable circumstances, but many highly improved varieties, in a horticultural sense, do not perfectly mature their seeds under any circumstances whatever, and therefore must be physiologically imperfect, and being so, à priori, if it be admitted that imperfection is a principle of decay, it will not be denied that no plant imperfectly constituted can carry on its functions but for a more or less limited time, even under the most favourable circumstances.

We have dwelt longer on this subject than may appear necessary, because we consider the civilization of wild plants by cultivation, the originating of new varieties of those already in our gardens from seed, or of wild plants from accidental variations, among the most interesting and rational amusements which can engage the amateur, as well as one of the most important that can command the attention of the horticulturist. There is a great deal of enjoyment in displaying our power over plants in propagating them by cuttings, leaves, and the different modes of grafting and budding; but greater still is that of creating new kinds of fruits or flowers by cross-fecundation, or improving a wild plant so as entirely to change its character. As examples of what may be done, we may refer to the common carrot, which in five generations from seed was brought from a wild state to be fit for the table, by M. Vilmorin; and among flowers to the heart's-ease, which in the course of the last twenty years has, by cross-breeding and selection, been raised from a flower with thin crumpled petals and irregular shape, to one of our most symmetrical and flat firm-petalled florists' flowers. In more recent varieties we would point to the wondrous improvements in pelargoniums, especially the variegated varieties, fuchsias, begonias, vegetables, grapes, peaches, nectarines, &c. We conclude by reminding the amateur that the blossoms or fruit produced by newly-originated plants the first or second year, are often inferior to what the same plant will produce when it has acquired a greater degree of vigour; and that to do justice to new varieties of herbaceous plants, they should be allowed to flower at least two years, and ligneous plants to flower and fruit, three, or even four years before they are rejected. Seedlings often sport and manifest the most extraordinary vagaries before they settle down into their true characters.

Operations of Order and Keeping.

By order is to be understood that relation of objects to one another, which shows that the one follows the other as an obvious or natural consequence. Thus, suppose that on entering a kitchen garden we observe a border along the walk separated from the larger compartment by a continuous espalier rail; this rail we naturally expect will be continued all round the garden, or if interrupted it will be by some obvious and satisfactory cause. Suppose the line of railing discontinued without any obvious reason; in that case we should say there was a want of order. Still more so should we be struck with a want of order, if the walk were bordered by dwarf fruit trees, not in a straight line or in a line parallel to that of the walk, but sometimes nearer and sometimes farther from it, and with the trees also at irregular distances in the line. Again, a striking want of order is sometimes seen in the disposition of crops. Five or six patches of onions, carrots, potatoes, cabbage, &c., all scattered here and there, as if they had been shot out of a dung-cart in motion, instead of each being in a break or breadth by itself. There is a secondary meaning in which the word order is used among gardeners, which has reference to keeping; and thus a border of flowers or other plants confused with weeds would be said to be disorderly, or not in order. In the former case the term refers to design, and in the latter to management; and it may be easily conceived that the unfavourable impression on a stranger is much graver in the case in which it is of a permanent nature, than in the other where it is only temporary. Neatness, as applied to horticultural scenes and objects, may be considered as synonymous with cleanliness.

The term keeping in horticulture relates to the degree of order and neatness which are maintained in management; and hence the expressions, badly kept, highly kept. A garden that is in high order and keeping must have been correctly laid out and planted at first, and cultivated and managed with great care afterwards. This care must not be devoted merely to some particular department, or to some object under the gardener's charge, but must extend to everything according to its importance. In a kitchen garden the system of managing the wall and espalier fruit trees, and of cropping the compartments, demands the first attention, because the result will not only influence the most conspicuous features in the garden, but also increase or diminish the quantity or quality of the produce.

The following rules may perhaps be of some use, if impressed on the mind of the young gardener, and if the master or the amateur insist on their being kept by the workmen:—

1. Perform every operation in the proper season and in the best manner, on the principle that "whatever is worth doing at all is worth doing well." Nothing can be more annoying to a person who is desirous of having his garden kept in the highest order, than to see the slovenly manner in which some gardeners thrust plants into the soil, tie them up when they require support, and hack and cut at them when they require pruning. "Cut to the bud" is a precept too often disregarded by such persons; among whom we have known excellent growers of crops, both in the open air and under glass.

2. *Complete every operation consecutively.*—The neglect of this is a very common fault. For example, the wall-trees are receiving their summer pruning, and as this occupies a day or two, or is necessarily performed at intervals, so as not to deprive the trees of too much foliage at once, the shoots cut off are left on the ground till all the trees have been gone over. The same mode of proceeding is followed in every other operation. We allow that, on the principle of the division of labour, this is the most economical mode, but on the principle of high keeping it is most objectionable.

3. *Never, if possible, perform one operation in such a manner as to render another necessary.*—It is a common practice with many gardeners, when weeding borders or trimming plants, to throw the weeds or trimmings on the gravel-walks, thereby occasioning the labour of sweeping them up, as well as soiling the gravel of the walk. There is scarcely a practice more to be condemned than this, both with reference to economy of time and to high keeping. The walk is disfigured by the weeds and trimmings perhaps for a whole day, and when they are swept off it is found that the gravel has been disturbed and is discoloured. In all cases of weeding borders and pruning shrubs, or hedges, close to walks, the weeds and prunings should be put at once into a wheelbarrow or basket.

4. *When called off from any operation, leave your work and your tools in an orderly manner.*—Do not leave a plant half planted, or a pot half watered, and do not throw down your tools as if you never intended to take them up again. Never leave a hoe or a rake with the blade

or the teeth turned up, as if you intended them as man-traps. Never stick in a spade where it will cut the roots of a plant; but if you must stick it in among plants, let its blade be in the direction of the roots, not across them.

5. *In leaving off work, make a temporary finish, and clean your tools and carry them to the tool-house.*—Never leave off in the midst of a row. Never leave the garden-line stretched. Never show an eagerness to be released from work. Never prune off more shoots, pull up more weeds, or make more litter of any kind than you can clear away the same day, if not the same hour. Never leave heaps of anything on grass or gravel, as it will take as much time to clear them up as to form them. Let all grass, leaves, or other rubbish be put into a hand-cart or barrow as the work proceeds.

6. Never do that in the open garden or in the hothouses, which can be equally well done in the reserve ground or in the back sheds: potting and shifting, for example.

7. Never pass a weed or an insect without pulling it up or taking it off, unless time forbid. Much might be done in this way towards keeping down weeds, were it not for the formality of some gardeners, who seem to delight in leaving weeds to accumulate till a regular weeding is required.

8. In gathering a crop, take away the useless as well as the useful parts. Never leave the haulm of potatoes on the ground where they have grown. Take up all the cabbage tribe by the roots, unless sprouts or second crops are wanted; and carry every kind of waste to the reserve or the frame ground, to rot as manure or mix with dung-linings.

9. Let no plant ripen seeds, unless these are wanted for some purpose useful or ornamental, and remove all the parts of plants which are in a state of decay. The seed-pods of plants should not be allowed even to swell, unless the seeds are wanted for some purpose, because being the essential result of every plant, they exhaust it more than any other part of its growth, and necessarily always more or less weaken it for the following year.

To these rules many others might be added, but it is not our wish to render gardeners mere machines. One great object of the young gardener ought to be to cultivate his faculty of seeing, so that in every garden he may be able to detect what is worth imitating, and what ought to be avoided. There is nothing tends more to this kind of cultivation than seeing the gardens of our neighbours, in which we may often detect those faults which exist in our own, but which, from having become familiar to us, we had not been able to see in a similar light. Without a watchful and vigilant eye, and habits of attention, observation, reflection, and decision, a gardener will never be able to become a complete master of his profession.

CHAPTER IX.

OPERATIONS OF HORTICULTURAL DESIGN AND TASTE.

Such matters are treated of fully in the 'Suburban Architect, and Landscape Gardener,' Price 'On the Picturesque,' M'Intosh's 'British Gardener,' Kemp's 'How to Lay out a Garden,' Loudon's 'Gardener's Magazine,' and other works; and it is not intended to enter into matters of landscape art in this volume, as it would unduly extend the work. But the work of taking plans of gardens, garden-buildings, or of any part of them, or of garden implements, or of modes of performing operations, ought to be understood by every gardener who aspires to eminence in his profession, and by every amateur who wishes to improve his own garden by what he sees in those of others.

Carrying plans into execution by transferring them from paper to ground, or in whatever manner they require to be realized, is equally necessary to be understood by both the gardener and the amateur; and for this purpose, and that of the preceding paragraph, some knowledge of geometry, land-surveying, and drawing is requisite. We would recommend Pasley's 'Practical Geometry and Plan-drawing,' 8vo, 16s., Crocker's 'Land-surveying,' 8vo, 12s., and Loudon's 'Self Instruction for Young Gardeners.'

Reducing a surface to a level, or to a uniform slope, is one of the most common operations required of a gardener in forming a garden or laying out grounds. For this purpose he must have learnt the use of the spirit-level or of the common mason's level, borrowing pins, &c., so as to be able to stake out level or regularly sloping lines on irregular surfaces. We recommend, as the best work on this subject for the practical gardener, Jones's 'Principles and Practice of Levelling.'

The designing and laying out of walks, roads, lawns, and the formation of pieces of artificial water, fountains, rockwork, and various other works that fall more or less under the superintendence of the gardener, are given at length in the volumes referred to.

CHAPTER X.

OPERATIONS OF GENERAL MANAGEMENT.

The general management of a garden, whether it includes the pleasure-ground, and all the scenes which come under the gardener's department in an extensive country residence, or merely a few rods of ground for growing culinary crops and flowers, requires such constant attention throughout the year, that gardeners have wisely invented calendars to remind them of their duty, monthly and even weekly. An abbreviated calendar of this kind will be found at the end of our volume, and we shall here confine ourselves to giving some hints on general management.

On undertaking the charge of a garden, the first point to determine is, the number of hands required for its cultivation, and how many of these men are to be professional gardeners, as journeymen or apprentices, and how many common country labourers or women. It is scarcely possible to keep a garden in the highest order, however small it may be, without a professional gardener in constant attendance; or without a garden-labourer, directed by the amateur, who in this case may be supposed to perform all the more delicate operations of propagating, pruning, training, &c., himself. Where only one professional gardener is kept, he will frequently require the help of a labourer to assist in operations that cannot well be done by a single person, or that require to be done quickly; or of one or more women, to assist in weeding, gathering crops, or keeping down insects.

The books to be kept by a gardener in a small place need not be more, as far as the business of the garden is concerned, than an inventory-book of the tools, &c.; a cash-book, in which to enter what he pays and receives; and a memorandum-book, to enter the dates and other particulars of orders given to tradesmen, &c., of sowing main crops, of fruit-ripening, and such other particulars as his master may require, or as he may think useful. Such books should be furnished by the master, and consequently be delivered to him when they are filled up. In some gardens a cropping-book is kept, in which on one page is registered the date, and other particulars of putting in the crops; the page opposite being kept blank, to enter the dates when they begin to be gathered, and how long they last. In all large gardens a produce-book is kept, in which every article sent to the kitchen every day in the year is recorded. There are various modes of keeping books of this kind, but one of the simplest and best appears to us to be the following:—A list, or kitchen-bill, is printed of all the culinary articles which the garden is supposed to produce in the course of the year; and a similar list, or dessert-bill, of all the dessert articles. On these lists, every morning, the gardener marks such articles as are in season, or as he can supply, and sends the kitchen-bill to the cook or steward, and the dessert-bill to the housekeeper, who put their marks to every article which is wanted for that day. The bills are carried back to the gardener, who puts them into the hands of his foreman; who sends the articles to the kitchen in the course of the forenoon with the bills, which are signed by persons receiving the articles, and returned to the gardener; who preserves them, and has them bound up in a volume at the end of the year. This book forms an excellent record of garden-produce for future reference.

The ordering of seeds and plants is one of the most important duties of the head-gardener; the difficulty being to determine the exact quantity of seed required, which is of some importance when the garden is at a considerable distance from the seedsman. A little practice, however, will soon make any gardener familiar with the exact quantities of the different kinds of seeds required for the garden in which he may be employed, especially if he is careful to make memoranda for this purpose.

The management of men and the distribution of work are the great points to which a head-gardener ought to direct his daily attention.

The work of every day ought to be foreseen the day before, subject, however, to changes in the weather, to meet which other work should be provided. A general idea of the labours and operations of the coming week should be formed the week before, and communicated to the foreman, who ought to receive his directions every evening for what is to be done the following day. For this and all other matters of general management, gardeners' calendars are of the greatest use as remembrancers; but the gardener's principal dependence must be on his own knowledge and experience. Unless he think and act for himself, as if no calendar had been in existence, he will never succeed; and if this may be said of a professional gardener, it applies still more forcibly to the amateur.

The Wages of a Gardener.—Something may here be expected to be said on this subject, and we shall observe :—(1) That there cannot be a greater mistake than to suppose that the products and enjoyments of a garden, however small, can be obtained without the services of a really good professional gardener; and (2) that all the difference between a garden-labourer, who perhaps can barely read or write, and who can neither spell nor pronounce botanical names, is not above 20*l.* or 30*l.* a year. No man would think of giving a garden-labourer, to whom he committed the management of his garden, less than a guinea a week, with his lodging, and some other perquisites, such as spare vegetables, fuel, &c. Now, for 70*l.* or 80*l.* a year, a scientific professional gardener may be engaged; one who can understand and reason upon all that is written in this volume, as well as carry all the practices described into operation, and who in consequence will elicit more enjoyment from a quarter of an acre than a man who has no scientific knowledge will do from any extent of ground, and means without limits. We by no means set down 70*l.* or 80*l.* as adequate wages for such a person; we know many gardeners who receive 100*l.*, and some 150*l.* and 200*l.* a year, with house, coals, candles, and various other perquisites. We merely state that such is the salary at which a scientific gardener may be engaged at the present time. It is a common notion that it requires a much less skilful gardener to manage a small place than a large one; but this only holds true where the variety of products required is small in proportion to the extent of the ground on which they are to be grown. If all the kinds of produce are required from a small garden that are required from a large one: if, for example, forcing in all its departments is to be carried on in both; if there are to be small crops in the cottage garden of all those plants which are grown in the mansion garden on a large scale ; then we affirm that a more skilful, experienced, and attentive gardener is required for the former than for the latter. More skill is necessary, because more is required with less means; more experience is requisite, because it is only by experience, joined to skill and knowledge, that success can be rendered tolerably certain ; and more attention is required to watch the progress of favourable or unfavourable circumstances, because, on a small scale, these circumstances are more immediate in their operations, and their results, if unfavourable, are more severely felt. The wages of a professional gardener, it must be allowed, are but small, compared with the amount of knowledge and the steady attention which the exercise of his profession requires; but wages in this, as in every other case, depend on demand and supply, and it would serve little purpose here to discuss the subject of increasing the one or diminishing the other. This much it may be useful to observe, that gardening, when studied scientifically, is a profession which tends to elevate the mind, and confer intellectual enjoyments of a much more exalted character than mere money-making can ever do. This, we think, is proved by the excellent moral character of almost all professional gardeners, and by the high degree of intelligence and scientific knowledge which many of them acquire. There are few persons, we believe, who have a more extensive personal knowledge of British master-gardeners than we have, and we also know a good many on the Continent; and we must say that, as a body, we have the very highest respect for them. They are almost all great readers; and in consequence of this, the intellectual and moral powers of many of them have been developed in a manner that commands our utmost veneration. There is scarcely a science or an art which some master-gardener of our acquaintance has not of his own accord taken up and studied from books, so as to obtain a respectable degree of knowledge of it. We know a number who have taught themselves several languages, and one of the best Hebrew scholars in Scotland, as we are informed by a clergyman (a good judge), is a gardener, who taught himself that language without the assistance of a master. We know gardeners that excel in almost every department of mathematics and geometry. Some are scientific meteorologists, naturalists in all the departments, and a number are good draftsmen. Many Scotch gardeners dip into metaphysics, and we have long known one whose library contains all the best English works on the subject, including those of Reid, Kames, Stuart, Monboddo, Drummond, and many others, besides translations. The development of so much talent among gardeners is no doubt owing to the nature of the profession, which excites thought; to the isolation of their dwellings and the necessity of their staying at home in the evenings to look after hothouse fires, and very much also to the kind indulgence of their masters, who, with very few exceptions, allow them the use of whatever books they want from their own libraries. Most employers also make presents of books to their gardeners; and some have established in their gardens, libraries, with mathematical instruments, globes, and maps. Another more recent yet great cause of the development of the minds of gardeners is the practice, which has become general among them within the last twenty years, of writing for the press. The 'Transactions of the Horticultural Society of London,' and the 'Memoirs of the Caledonian Society,' first called forth this talent, which, as the gardening books in existence previously to the first edition of our 'Encyclopædia of Gardening' will show, had been confined to very few persons. The grand stimulus to writing, however, was given by the 'Gardener's Magazine,' a work most liberally supported by the contributions of gardeners; and how generally this has called forth the talent of writing among both masters and journeymen will appear by the abundance of communications which continue not only to be supplied to that periodical, and several others which appear monthly, but to several gardening newspapers. Amateurs also have very generally become writers on horticultural subjects; and from the views which many of them take different from those held by practical men, the discussions they often elicit prove highly instructive to all parties. What we greatly admire in all this intellectual progress is, that gardeners still maintain their modesty of deportment and that high moral character which command the respect of their employers and of all who know them.

CHAPTER XI.

THE CULTURE OF THE KITCHEN AND FRUIT GARDEN.

Laying out the Kitchen-Garden.

The situation, relative to the other parts of a residence, should be as near the house as is consistent with other details. In general the kitchen, stable offices, and kitchen-garden should be on one side of the mansion or dwelling, and so placed as to admit of intercommunication without bringing the operations or operators into the view of the family or their visitors. As the stable offices are generally near the kitchen offices, so the kitchen-garden may be near the stables; and in such a situation it will generally be found that the kitchen-garden is less seen from the windows of the mansion, than if it were placed at a much greater distance. A very little reflection will convince anyone that this must necessarily be the case. Relatively to surface, one which is level, open, and airy, is the best; because it is least liable to be affected by high winds. The next best surface is one gently sloping to the south, or south-east; and the worst is one sloping to the north-east. The surface of a hill is to be avoided on account of its exposure to high winds; and equally so one in a valley, on account of the cold air which descends from the adjoining heights and settles there. The extent is regulated by the wants of the family, and may vary from a quarter of an acre to several acres; everything depending on the quantity and quality of the produce required. The best soil is a loam, rather sandy than clayey, on a subsoil moderately retentive. The form of the garden should be rectangular, as better adapted than any other for the operations to be carried on within. The area is enclosed by walls, in general forming a parallelogram with its longest side in the direction of east and west, in consequence of which the greater length of walling has a surface exposed to the south. When the situation is such as to require artificial shelter, plantations are formed exterior to the garden for this purpose, but they should never, if practicable, be nearer the walls than 100 or 150 feet; for though science has not yet satisfactorily assigned the reason, yet it is certain that nothing is more injurious to culinary vegetables and fruits, than the exclusion of a free current of air in every direction. The sole object of shelter ought to be to break the force of high winds. Water should never be wanting in a garden, and it should always be exposed in a basin for some time before being used. The garden walls should if possible be of brick; or if they are formed of stone, or of mud or compressed earth, which in some parts of the country make excellent walls, retaining much heat and lasting a long time, they ought to be covered with a wooden trellis on which to train the trees. It has been recommended by Hitt and others to build the walls on piers, for the sake of allowing the roots of the trees to extend themselves on both sides of the wall. But, as there are generally trees on both sides of every garden wall, it does not appear that, under ordinary circumstances at least, anything would be gained by this mode of building walls, excepting the saving of a small proportion of materials. Where walls are not built of brick, stone, or earth, they may be formed of boards, which, when properly seasoned and afterwards saturated with boiling tar, will endure many years, and produce as much heat in the summer season as brick or stone. They are indeed colder in winter and spring, but that circumstance is often an advantage by retarding the blossoming of the trees, and lessening the risk of their being injured by spring frosts. If a cavity were formed beside the boarding, and filled with pounded clinkers, or charcoal, or coke, much heat would be absorbed from the sun's rays, and thus form a source for giving out heat at night. Reed walls have likewise been used, and even fresh-cut furze, closely packed together, will stand eight or ten years and form a good shelter. Concrete again is very commonly employed for walls in France, and sometimes in this country. It is cheap, strong, durable, and warm. Where the walls are formed of brick they may always be built hollow, to save material; and as very little additional expense will be required to form the hollows into flues or channels for hot-water pipes, such an arrangement should not be neglected in the colder parts of the island. The walks in the interior of the garden are laid out in a direction parallel to the walls, and espalier-rails are commonly formed parallel to the walks. Exterior to the walls, a narrow portion of ground is enclosed which is technically called the slip, the object of which is to admit of getting the full benefit of the wall on the outside as well as within.

In trenching and levelling the surface of the kitchen garden, care must be taken to form a complete system of underground drainage; not only by having drains formed of tiles to carry off subterraneous water, but by having the surface of the subsoil parallel to the exposed surface, both being inclined towards the situation of the drains; so that the water on sinking down from the surface may not rest in hollows. The best situation for these drains will generally be under the walks. The depth of the soil of a garden should seldom be less than from two to four feet, this depth being penetrated by the roots of even the smallest kinds of culinary vegetables when growing vigorously. The depth of the soil, however, ought to bear some relation to its quality, and to the climate. A loamy or a clayey soil in a humid climate need not be trenched to the same depth as if it were in a warm and dry climate; because one use of the soil to plants being to retain moisture, a small body, not liable to lose by evaporation, may be as effective as a larger one so constituted as to lose a great deal. The borders for fruit trees form an important part of the kitchen garden, and should always be prepared with a due regard to the soil, the climate, and the kinds of trees to be planted. The bottom should generally be prepared so as to prevent the roots from penetrating into the subsoil: though as this naturally limits the supply of water to the roots in dry seasons, and consequently gives occasion for artificial waterings, a better mode than making the borders very shallow, is never to dig them, and to spread the manure always on the surface. By this means the roots will not be forced downwards, as they necessarily must be when the surface is loosened and exposed to the drying influence of the sun and winds, or the exhaustion of crops of vegetables. The subsoil of the borders, however, ought in every case to be drained. In planting fruit trees in the kitchen garden, we would on no account whatever introduce standards, or any description of fruit tree, in those parts of the open garden which are to be cropped with herbaceous vegetables; because such trees injure the surrounding crops by their shade, and seldom produce much fruit, or fruit of good quality, in consequence of their roots being forced down into the subsoil by the necessary stirring of the soil among the herbaceous crops. We recommend no fruit trees to be planted in the kitchen garden excepting against the walls, against espalier-rails, in rows along the walks, or in compartments by themselves. A forcing department, a frame ground, and a reserve ground, are accompaniments to every complete kitchen garden, and even the smallest has at least a reserve and frame ground. The two latter accompaniments are generally placed exterior to the walls of the garden, in that part of the slip which is nearest the stables, and the forcing department is sometimes placed there also; though more generally it consists of glass structures placed against the north wall of the garden. The best outer fence for a garden is a sunk wall, the ditch in which it is built serving as a main drain, into which all the drains in the interior may discharge themselves. The wall of this fence may be carried up three feet or four feet above the surface of the ground, to render it more effectual as a fence, without at the same time producing too much shelter and shade in the slip. In many places it is customary to surround the slip with a shrubbery bounded by a hedge, which has a very good effect for a few years while the trees are young, but when they grow large they produce an injurious degree of shelter and shade. The main entrance to a kitchen garden should always be so placed as to look towards the main feature within, this feature necessarily being the south side of the north wall, not only because that wall supports the hothouses when there are any within the garden, but because on it are grown the finest fruits. As an example of a kitchen garden arranged agreeably to the foregoing observations, but combining also a flower garden, which is frequently required in a suburban villa, we refer to fig. 331. It contains one acre within the walls, and half an acre in the slips; and the following references will explain the details:—

386   LAYING OUT THE KITCHEN GARDEN.

Fig. 331.

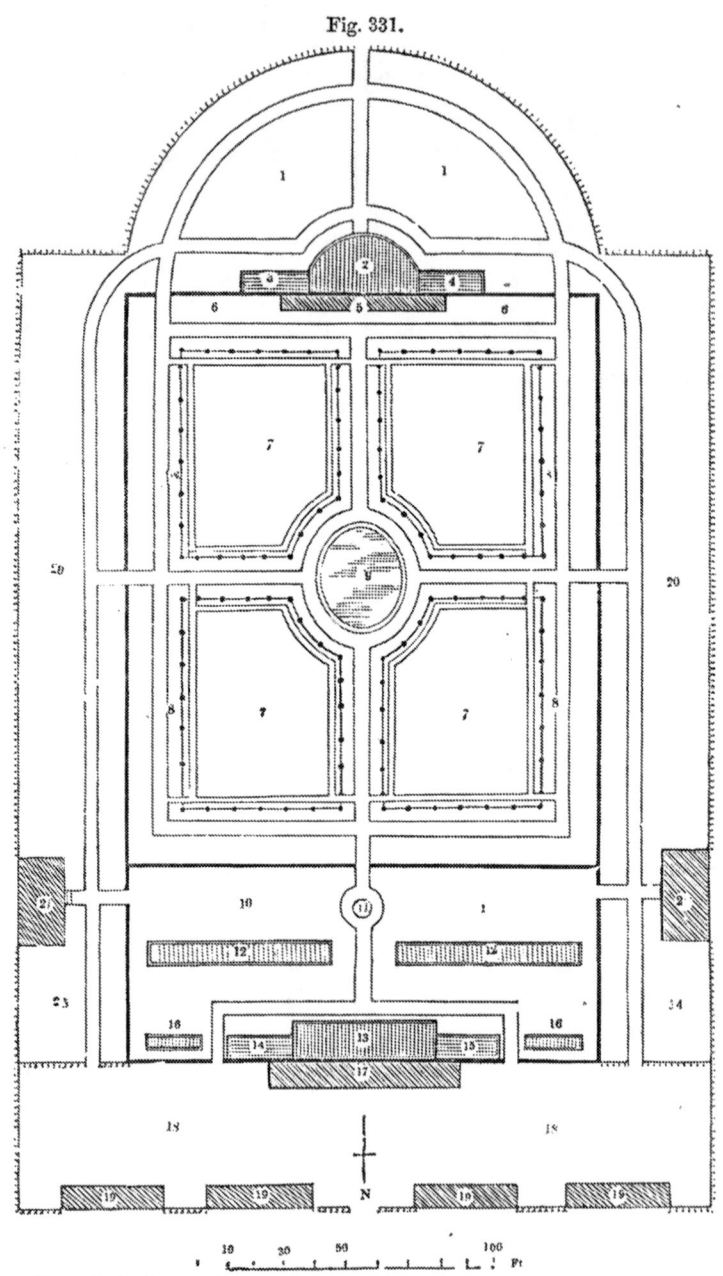

Plan of a kitchen garden containing one acre within the walls, and half an acre in the surrounding slips.

1. Flower garden.
2. Conservatory.
3. Greenhouse.
4. Forcing-house for flowers.
5. Back-shed.
6. Area for setting out greenhouse plants in summer.
7. Culinary departments with espaliers.
8. Espalier-borders.
9. Pond, surrounded with a stone margin.
10. Forcing department.
11. Water basin.
12. Ranges of pits for melons, cucumbers, &c.
13. Pine stove.
14. Peach-house.
15. Vinery.
16. Pits.
17. Back-shed.
18. Department for compost, mixing dung, &c.
19. Mushroom-sheds, tool-house, wintering vegetables, &c.
20. Slips, bounded by a sunk wall fence, surrounded by an open iron railing.
21. Gardener's house.
22. Fruit and onion-room, with lodging-room for under-gardener, and seed-room over.
23. Yard to gardener's house.
24. For pot-herbs.

Supposing the flower garden and hothouses are to be omitted, then the references may stand as under:—

1. Fruit garden.
2, 3, 4, 5. To be omitted if not desirable.
6, 7, 8. Culinary departments, with espaliers.
9. Pond.
10. Forcing department.
11. Water-basin.
12. Ranges of pits for melons, cucumbers, &c.
13. Pine-stove.
14. Peach-house.
15. Vinery.
16. Pits.
17. Back-shed.
18. Department for compost, mixing dung, &c.
19. Mushroom-sheds, tool-house, wintering vegetables, &c.
20. Slips as before.
21. Gardener's house.
22. Fruit and onion-room, with lodging-room for under-gardener, and seed-room over.
23. Yard to gardener's house.
24. For pot-herbs.

The following plan, fig. 332, contains an acre within the walls, and is without a gardener's house, or slips at the sides, the situation being supposed to render it necessary to conceal the walls by a plantation of evergreen shrubs made close to them. To prevent the roots of these shrubs from penetrating to the borders inside of the walls, their foundations must be at least three feet deep in the most impervious subsoil, and deeper still on soil that they will readily penetrate. The following are references:—

a, a, Fruit-garden, the border next the outer fence for pot herbs.
b, b, Culinary departments with espaliers.
c, c, Forcing department.
d, d, Department for compost, mixing dung, &c.
e, e, Ranges of pits for melons and cucumbers.
f, Pine-stove.

388 DISTRIBUTION OF FRUIT TREES IN A KITCHEN GARDEN.

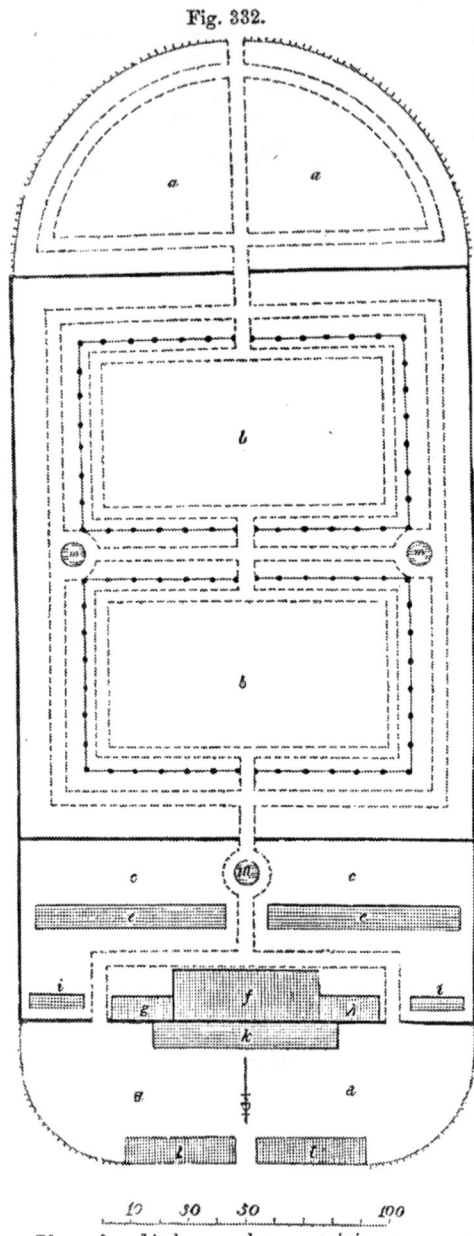

Fig. 332.

Plan of a kitchen garden, containing one acre within the walls, and three-quarters of an acre in the slips, at the two ends.

g, Peach-house.
h, Vinery.
i, i, Pits.
k, Back-shed.
l, l, Sheds for mushrooms, or for other purposes.
m, m, Water-basins.

The Distribution of Fruit trees in a Kitchen garden.

The more delicate fruit trees are always placed against walls, and those which are less so are planted in the open garden as standards, dwarfs, or espaliers. South of London the trees planted against walls are chiefly the grape, fig, peach, nectarine, and apricot. Sometimes there are planted against walls of a south aspect, one or two choice plums, or a few cherries to come into early bearing; and on the north side of an east-and-west wall, some Morello cherries and sometimes currants, to come in late; the fruit being covered with netting, to preserve it from birds, and so retain it on the trees till Christmas. North of London, pears, and apples of the finer kinds, are trained against walls; and north of York, even the mulberry, which in Scotland never ripens fruit as a standard. Nuts, such as the walnut and filbert, are almost always grown as standards; but the crops of the two former are very precarious north of York, and but rarely ripened in Scotland. All kinds of nuts are best grown outside the garden, as they tempt the squirrels and other vermin, who not only devour the nuts but feast upon other fruits as well. The only suggestions that can be given for selecting the trees which require a wall in any given situation are, to observe what has been done in gardens in the same locality or in similar localities. The lists given consist of varieties which have all been proved to be of first-rate excellence, and have been extensively cultivated for many years in most of the best gardens in England, Scotland and Ireland. In choosing from these lists for a garden in the north of Scotland, the grapes and the figs must be rejected altogether for the open walls, because they would not ripen there; while for a garden in the south of England the apples and pears should be rejected, because there the fruits would ripen sufficiently well in the open garden, on espaliers, dwarfs, or standards. We shall here give only the names of the kinds selected; other particulars will be found in Dr. Hogg's Fruit Manual.

Wall Fruit Trees.

Select List of Fruit Trees adapted for walls of different aspects, those marked * deserving the preference :—

Apples.
*Golden Pippin, S., S.E., or S.W.
*Ribston Pippin, E. or W.
*Nonpareil, S., S.E., or S.W.
*Herefordshire Pearmain, E. or W., or S.E.
Court of Wick, E. or W.
Reinette du Canada, E. or W., or S.E., or S.W.
Newtown Pippin, S.E. or S.W.
*Cornish Gillyflower, S.E. or S.W.
*Court-pendu-plat, S.E. or S.W., or E. or W.
*Golden Harvey, S.E. or S.W., or E. or W.
Scarlet Nonpareil, E. or W.
Hughes's Golden Pippin, E. or W.
*Pearson's Plate, E. or W.
Irish Peach, W., S.
Aromatic Russet, E.
Golden Reinette, S.
King of the Pippins, W.
Cox's Orange Pippin, E., W.
Devonshire Pippin, S.
Red Ingestrie, W.
The Mother Apple, W.
The Melon Apple, S.
Lord Burleigh, S.
Calville Blanc, S.

Pears.
*Jargonelle, S.E. or W.
*Marie Louise, E., W.
Gansel's Bergamot, E., W.
Duchesse d'Angoulême, E., W.
*Beurré Diel, E., W.
*Glou Morceau, S.E. or W.
*Passe Colmar, S.E. or S.W.
Nélis d'Hiver, S.E. or W.
Beurré d'Aremberg, S.E. or W.
Colmar, S.E. or W.
*Easter Beurré, S.E. or W.
*Beurré de Ranz, S.E. or W.
Williams' Bon Chrétien, W.
Chaumontel, S.
Huyshe's Prince Consort, W.
Do. Prince of Wales, W.
Do. Victoria, W.
Josephine de Malines, E., W.
Monarch Knight's, W.
Van Mon's Léon Le Clerc, E.

Cherries.

*May Duke, S., E., W.
*Royal Duke, S., E., W.
*Knight's Early Black, S., E., W.
*Elton, S., E., W.
*Florence, E. or W.
*Early Purple Guigne, S., E., W.
Black Tartarian, S., E., W.
Late Duke, E., W., N.
*Morello, E., W., N.
Bigarreau, E.
Dr. Jabouldy, S., W.
Bigarreau, Black, W.
Werder's Early Black, W.
Transparent, E.

Plums.

*Royale Hâtive, S.E.W.
*Green Gage, S., E., W.
*Coe's Golden Drop, S., E., W.
*Washington, S., E., W.
*Purple Gage, S., E., W.
Ickworth Impératrice, E. or W.
Kirke's Plum, E. or W.
Drap d'Or, S., E., W.
Jefferson, E., W.
Reine Claude Martelle, S.
Reine Claude de Bavay, W.
Transparent Gage, W., S.
Reine Nectarine, E., W.
Nectarine, E.
Pond's Seedling, E., W.
Rivers's Early, E.
Victoria, E.

The four last are kitchen plums.

Apricots.

*Large Early, S., E., W.
*Moorpark, S., E., W.
*Royal, S., E., W.
*Turkey, S., E., W.
Breda, E. or W.
Kaisha, W., S.
Large Red, W.
Peach Apricot, S.

Peaches.

Early Anne, S.
*Grosse Mignonne, S.
Royal George, S.
*Noblesse, S.
*Malta, S.
*Bellegarde, S.
*Barrington, S.
*Late Admirable, S.
Crawford's Early, S.
Early York, S.
Raymacker's, S.
Dr. Hogg, S.
Rivers's Early, S.
Lord Palmerston, S.
The Nectarine, S.

Nectarines.

*Elruge, S.
*Violette Hâtive, S.
White, S.
Pitmaston Orange, S.
Duc de Tello, S.
Rivers's New White, S.
Rivers's Pine Apple, S.
Rivers's Orange, S., W.
Rivers's Early, S.

Figs.

*Blue or Black Ischia, S.E., S., or S.W.
*White or Brown Ischia, S., S.E., or S.W.
Black Genoa, S.E., S., or S.W.
White Genoa, S.E., S., or S.W.
*Brown Turkey, S.E., S., or S.W.
*Brunswick, S.E., S., or S.W.
Castle Kennedy.
Early White.
White Marseilles.

Grapes.

*The Early Black, S.
*White Muscadine, S.
Grove-end Sweet-water, S.
Pitmaston White Cluster, S.

Esperione, S.
Black Hamburgh, S.
Grizzly Frontignan, S.

The last two grapes ripen remarkably well on the open wall in the climate of London in fine seasons.

The mulberry is sometimes planted against a west wall.

Of all these different kinds of fruits, with the exception of the fig and the grape, both dwarfs and riders may be procured in any of the nurseries. The former, that is, the dwarfs, are for filling up the lower parts of the wall, and ultimately also the upper part; and the latter, the standards or riders, are for filling up the upper part till the dwarfs are so far advanced as to take their place, when the riders are taken up and used elsewhere. The plants may be procured either one year grafted, or one, two, or three years trained, the latter trees being double or treble the price of the former, but filling the wall much sooner. As riders are but of temporary duration, it is customary to procure them three or more years' trained, that they may bear fruit immediately. When the walls are under twelve feet high, it is scarcely necessary to plant riders; for if three years' trained trees are planted, the wall will be covered to the top in seven years.

The distance from each other at which the trees should be planted depends on the species of tree, its size, the mode of training adopted, the climate, the height of the wall, and to a certain extent also on the width of the border. The following distances are calculated for common dwarfs on a wall twelve feet high, with a border twelve feet wide, in the climate of London:—Peaches, nectarines, and figs, fifteen feet to twenty feet; apricots, fifteen feet for the early sorts, and eighteen feet to twenty-four feet for the late strong-growing sorts, as apricots and plums do not bear pruning so well as other wall-trees; cherries and plums, fifteen feet to twenty feet, or the stronger-growing plums, such as the Washington, twenty-four feet; apples on dwarfing stocks, fifteen feet—if on free stocks, from twenty-five feet to thirty feet; mulberries, from fifteen feet to twenty feet. These distances are calculased for the common fan or horizontal modes of training. If cordon trees are used, the trees may be planted from three to four feet apart, and trained either perpendicularly to the top of the wall, or more obliquely. The wall will thus be covered much sooner, and more fruit may be gathered from a given space in less time. Vines may be planted among the other trees at thirty feet or forty feet distance, and a single stem from each plant trained up to the coping of the wall, and then horizontally close under it, where, if pruned in the spurring-in manner, it will bear abundantly, and produce more fruit than if it had been treated like a fruit tree. If however the situation is favourable for vines, they may be planted from ten feet to fifteen feet apart, and trained either in the perpendicular manner, or horizontally with upright laterals, or in the fan or other modes to be afterwards described. One rider, peach, cherry, or plum, may be introduced beside every dwarf, if the latter should be maiden plants; but if they are three or four years' trained, riders are unnecessary excepting on walls above twelve feet high.

For low walls, the distances above given may be increased one-fourth, when the height of the wall is nine feet, and one-half when it is only six feet. It is more profitable however to plant the trees thickly on dwarf walls, so as to cover them at once, and then thin out every other tree or two trees, and leave one, as they advance in age. The mode of training for walls under nine feet should generally be the half-fan manner, shown in fig. 293. By thus having only one shoot from a plant, the top of the wall will be reached by that shoot in three or at most four years; and as the permanent trees encroach on the temporary ones on each side, the latter can be taken out one at a time, so as never to leave an unseemly blank on the wall.

Training, in the case of walls twelve feet high and upwards, should be the fan manner for the peach, nectarine, early apricots, and figs; the half-fan for the stronger apricots, plums, cherries, the more delicate pears, and the mulberry; and the horizontal manner for the apple and the greater number of pears.

Planting.—The plants should be placed on hillocks higher or lower according to the depth to which the ground has been moved in preparing the border, in order that in two or three years, when the ground shall have finally settled, the collar or part of the stem whence the first roots proceed shall be between two inches and four inches above the general surface of the ground. The distance of the collar from the wall, when newly planted, should be for the more delicate-growing trees, such as the peach, from six inches to nine inches; and for the more vigorous-growing kinds, such as the apple, pear, and cherry, from nine inches to a foot. We say nothing as to the season of planting, or the mode of performing the operation, these and every part of culture generally applicable to ligneous plants, having been treated of in detail in those parts of the work with which the reader is supposed to be already familiar.

Fruit Trees for Espaliers and Dwarfs.

Espaliers are commonly planted in lines parallel to the main walks in kitchen gardens. There is commonly an espalier-rail on both sides of all the walks, excepting the surrounding one next the wall-border. On that border espalier-trees are not generally planted, and the border should be wholly devoted to the roots of the wall-trees, with the exception of a line of horizontal cordons carried along within a foot of the walk. The espalier-rail is generally placed from two to four feet distant from the walk, and on the inner side of the rail there is commonly a footpath one or two feet wide, at a distance of two or three feet, so that these trees have a space of from five to eight feet wide, which may be considered as exclusively devoted to their roots. If the main walks are of flagstone, supported on piers, or if they are formed of a thin layer of gravel on good soil, then we may add half the width of the walk, in addition to that already mentioned. If the border is not dug and cropped, but only slightly manured on the surface, and once a year gently stirred with the three-pronged fork, the trees will bear abundantly; but if the ground is dug and cropped, or if flowers are grown on it, the roots of the fruit-trees being forced to descend to the subsoil, and to produce more wood than they can properly ripen, and the trees being thus forced to take a habit of luxuriance rather than of fruitfulness, the fruit produced will be few and without flavour.

The trees should be planted from three to five feet from the walk, and the path at the inside should be at an equal distance from them. This will give a border of from six to ten feet in width, besides the width of the path; and if the ground is not dug and the trees are carefully trained, an immense quantity of fruit will be produced. Many prefer conical, pillar, or bush-formed trees to espaliers, and when tastefully arranged, and laden with flowers or fruits, they impart a great beauty and dignity to a kitchen garden, either in lines or in compartments by themselves. As the spurred-in trees will grow twelve feet high, and if on dwarfing-stocks, and the border be not dug, will bear abundantly, we know no mode in which so much fruit can be produced on so limited a surface of ground, excepting always the espalier mode, in which the trees do not occupy above a foot in width.

Espalier-rails are variously constructed. The simplest mode is to drive in stakes, which may be of young larch trees, or of any other young wood disbarked and steeped in Burnett's composition, at two feet apart, with temporary stakes of a slight description between; the latter being for the purpose of training forward the growing shoot of each horizontal branch from one permanent stake to another, during the growing season. Thus in fig. 333, Nos. 1, 2, 3, and 4, represent permanent stakes, and *a*, *b*, temporary ones. These latter may be removed from between Nos. 1 and 2 when they are no longer of any use there, and placed between Nos. 2 and 3 till the growing shoots obtain a bearing on the stake No. 3, when they may be removed to the space between Nos. 3 and 4, and so on.

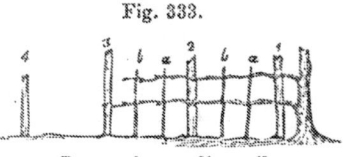

Fig. 333.

Progressive espalier-rail.

Another mode is to drive in stakes of the proper height, and eight inches or nine inches apart, beginning at the centre of each tree, and extending them on each side as the tree advances in growth. In the first stage of training, the stakes require to stand as close together as twelve inches or fourteen inches, and to be arranged in regular order to the full height of five feet, with a rail slightly fastened on the top of them for neatness' sake, as well as to steady them. If stakes of small ash, Spanish chestnut, or the like, from coppices or thinnings of young plantations, be used, they will last for three or four years, provided they are from one and a half to two inches in diameter at a foot from the bottom. They need not be extended further, in the first instance, than the distance it is considered probable the trees may reach in three years' growth: at that period, or the following season, they will all require to be removed, and the new ones may be placed on each side, to the extent that the trees may be thought to require while these stakes last, finishing the top, as before, with a rail. As the trees extend their horizontal branches and acquire substance, the two stakes on each side of the one that supports the centre leader of the tree can be spared, and removed to any of the extremities where wanted. And as the tree extends further and acquires more substance, every second stake will be found sufficient; and the centre stake can be spared also, after the leader has reached its destined height and is of a sufficient substance to support itself erect. When such a form of training is completed, and the branches are of sufficient magnitude, about six, eight, or twelve stakes will be sufficient for the support of the horizontal branches, even when they have the burden of a full crop of fruit. At any other time, about six stakes to each tree will be all that are necessary.

Espalier-rails of cast-iron consist of a top and bottom horizontal rail, into which upright nails are fixed at from six inches to nine inches apart, with standards at every ten or twelve feet, which are let into

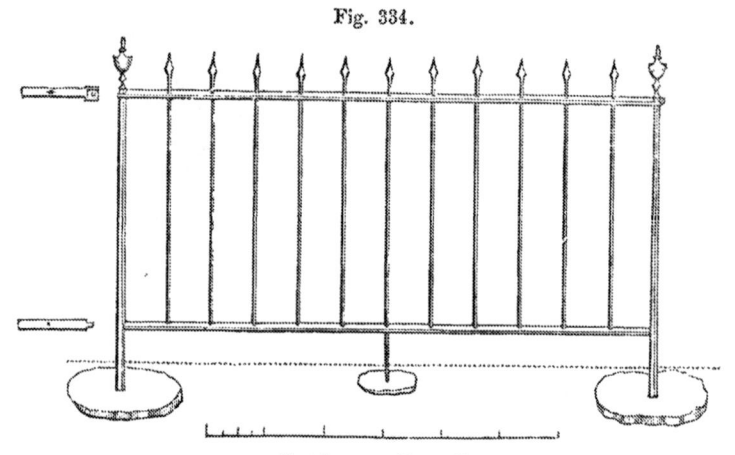

Fig. 334.

Cast-iron espalier-rail.

blocks of stone, firmly fixed in the soil, as shown in fig. 334. Wooden espalier-rails are also formed in the same manner as cast-iron rails, and the standards let into iron sockets, which are fixed in stone blocks or supports.

Espalier-rails of wrought-iron may be formed of hoop and wire iron of any height or degree of strength, and are neat, durable, and serviceable. Fig. 335 is a representation of an espalier of this description, erected in the kitchen garden at Carclew, and a full account of the manner of putting it up will be found in the 'Gardener's Magazine' for 1839. The total cost at Carclew was from 1$s.$ 6$d.$ to 2$s.$ per linear yard. Strained wire may be put up in this manner, either for espaliers or pleasure-ground fences,

FRUIT TREES FOR ESPALIERS AND DWARFS.

not only in straight lines, but in curves of every description. This is effected by means of underground braces, or underground perpendicular posts, and these posts may be either of stone or of cast-iron, and they may be built into masses of masonry where the soil is soft, or has been moved several feet in depth. No brace need ever appear above ground, as at *b*, in fig. 335; nor should the posts ever appear

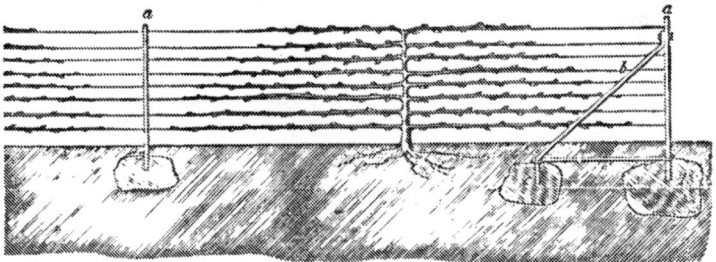

Fig. 335.

Strained wire espalier-rail.

to rise out of the naked soil, as do *a, a,* in the figure, but always out of a block of stone. Where the soil is on turf, this block, which may be six inches square, need not rise more than an inch above the surface; but where the ground is to be dug as in a kitchen garden, the upper surface of the block may be nine inches, or a foot square, and may rise two inches or three inches above the surface of the soil.

The reasons for a stone base are as follow:—All materials which have been prepared for the purposes of construction are considered as thus rendered subject to the laws of architecture; and the first law is, that every superstructure must have an architectural base, on which it is placed. Thus, speaking with reference to design, every perpendicular line must rest upon a horizontal one; and speaking with reference to materials, this horizontal line must be of the same, or of a kind analogous to that of the perpendicular; of a kind which must at all events be equally, if not more, firm and durable than it is. Live wood, that is, growing trees, may rise out of soil, but never architectural wood, that is, squared posts, which ought always to rise out of stone. If this be true of wood, of course it must be much more so of iron, which, though harder than either wood or stone, yet is not nearly so durable as the latter material, which consequently forms a proper base for it to rest on.

Some of the preceding remarks merely serve to show how rude and awkward is the system of trellising employed in British gardens. "The French are far before us in this respect. So satisfactory is the system adopted, that I am certain if English cultivators generally could get an idea of its excellence it would lead to a revolution in our fruit culture, and a great improvement in the appearance of our gardens. I know of no way whereby we may so highly improve the garden culture of the pear than by paying more attention to it as an espalier tree. This is also the opinion of many of the best fruit-growers in Britain, who agree that there is no finer fruit than that gathered from well-managed espalier trees. It is well known that some pears lose quality by being grown against walls. It is equally certain that a fuller degree of sun and exposure than the shoots and fruit get on a pyramidal tree is very desirable in many parts of this country, especially for particular kinds. Many sorts grow beautifully as pyramids; others, to be had in perfection, must be grown upon walls; but by means of the improved espalier system the majority of the finer kinds may be grown to the highest excellence. If the French can teach us nothing else they can certainly give us a lesson as to the improvement in appearance, cheapness, and utility of the espalier mode of growing fruit, especially as regards the finer varieties of pear-trees.

"It should be borne in mind that the good opinion of espalier trees given by British cultivators has been won by them under great disadvantages, for nothing can be uglier or more inefficient than the usual mode of supporting and training espaliers in our gardens. It is generally so costly and disagreeable to the eye, that it has been done away with for these reasons alone in many gardens. I know some important ones near London, and indeed in many parts of Britain, where the espalier support is the most unworkmanlike and discreditable affair to be seen in the place. Great rough uprights of wood, which soon rot and wabble out of position, thick and costly bolt-like wire, cumbrous and expensive construction, and, in a word, so many disadvantages as would suffice to prevent the prudent cultivator from attempting anything of the kind. The form of tree used, too, is such that the lower branches become impoverished, and often nearly useless.

"To support his espalier fruit trees the Emperor's gardener, M. Hardy, has largely adopted a system which is at once cheap, neat, and almost everlasting. Instead of employing ugly and perishable wooden supports he erects uprights of T-iron, and connects these with slender galvanized wire. These are tightened with the little raidisseurs before alluded to, and then there is an end of all trouble. He manages to erect this trellising nine feet high for less than a shilling a yard run; but it could not be done so cheaply in smaller quantities. Then, instead of adopting the common form of espalier tree, with horizontal branches, he more frequently uses trees of which each branch ascends towards the top of the trellis, and thus secures an equable flow of sap through the tree. The accompanying figure (fig. 336) will give a better idea of both trellis and tree than any description. There is no more important matter connected with our fruit culture than this very point, and therefore I should be much obliged to all my readers, both amateur and professional, if they will give the subject attention, as I am sure that by doing so they will be led to adopt it largely, and will much improve their fruit culture. The finest stores of pears I have ever seen were in gardens with a good length of trees trained in this manner; and I know few places in France where the espalier system is so extensively and so well carried out as here. The form here represented is much better than the cordon or single-branched pear tree, because a more free and natural development is allowed to the tree, and at the same time the trellis is covered quickly, and a considerable variety of fruit may be obtained from a small space. It is very extensively adopted by M. Hardy, upon walls as well as on the neat and elegant trellis of which he has constructed so much. Of course the Palmette Verrier, the fan, or any other form, may be trained on these trellises, but decidedly the best are such as combine the advantages of quick covering and early productiveness claimed for the cordon, and the fuller development and more pleasing appearance of the larger forms. It should be borne in

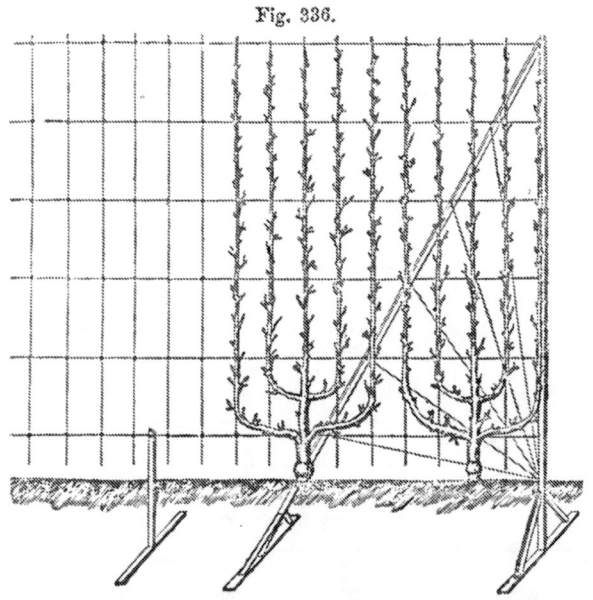

Fig. 336.

Trellis for pear-trees, ten feet high. Uprights and stays of T-iron, horizontal lines, slender galvanized wire; vertical lines, pine-wood half an inch square and painted green; to these the ascending branches are trained.

mind that planting erect cordons close together, as they must be planted, involves a great expense, which is avoided by using trees of a fuller development. It takes a good many years to form the large style of tree usually adopted, and therefore I advise the general planting of these intermediate forms.

"Nothing can be neater alongside garden-walks than lines such as these trained on the trellis alluded to. There is no shaking about of rough irons or wooden beams, no falling down or loosening of the wires; the fruit is firmly attached and safe from gales, the wood is fully exposed, and the trellis when well covered forms an elegant dividing-line in a garden. The best way to place them is at from

398   FRUIT TREES FOR ESPALIERS AND DWARFS.

three to six feet from the edge of the walk, and if in the space between
the espalier and the walk a line of the cordons elsewhere recommended
be established, the effect and result will prove very good indeed. In
some cases where large quantities of fruit are required, it may be
desirable to run them across the squares at a distance of fifteen or

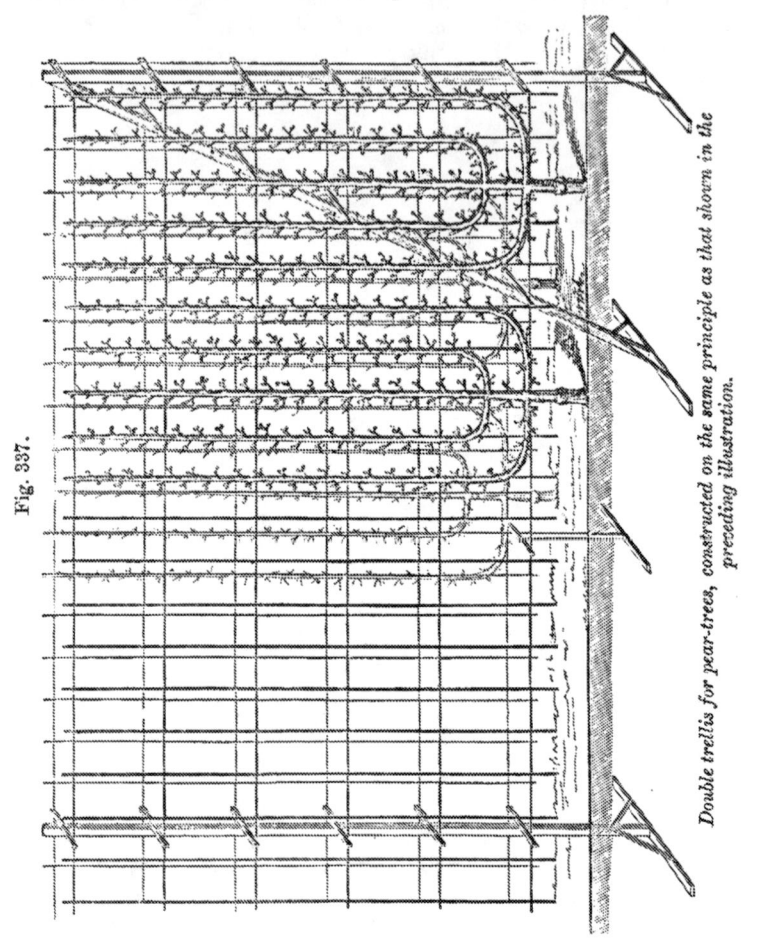

Fig. 337.

Double trellis for pear-trees, constructed on the same principle as that shown in the preceding illustration.

eighteen feet apart. The principle is quite simple, the proof of which
is that the trellises at Versailles were erected by the garden workmen.
M. Hardy, the head gardener at Versailles, is the son of the celebrated
writer on fruit trees of that name, and has had much experience in
fruit-growing. 'These trellises,' says he, 'are the cheapest as well
as the most ornamental that we have yet succeeded in making, and the
trees which I plant against them are of the form that I prefer to all

others, for promptly furnishing walls and trellises, and for yielding a great number of varieties in a comparatively restricted space.' The mode of employing the uprights of pine wood painted green and reaching from the top of the trellis to within six inches of the ground, is not a common one, though very desirable where the erect way of training the shoots is practised. The reader will readily perceive that this system combines the advantages of the cordon and the large tree. Of course many other forms, or any form, may be used with this system of trellising, with slight modifications to suit different kinds of trees or different forms. The double trellis shown is simply a modification of the preceding, and is not only desirable where space is limited, but also for its economy, for one set of uprights supports the two sets of wires simply by using cross bits of iron about eighteen inches long, and at the desired distance apart. However, the engraving (fig. 337) shows this at a glance." (Robinson's 'Parks, Promenades, and Gardens of Paris.')

Select list for espaliers, dwarfs, or standards trained conically or spurred in :—

Dessert Apples.

Oslin.
King of the Pippins.
Wormsley Pippin.
Golden Reinette.
Hughes' Golden Pippin.
Court of Wick.
Ribston Pippin.
Adams's Pearmain.
Pearson's Plate.
Golden Harvey.
Court-pendu-plat.
Reinette du Canada.
Braddick's Nonpareil.
Old Nonpareil.
Scarlet Nonpareil.
Boston Russet.
Downton Nonpareil.
Reinette Grise.
Reinette Golden.
Scarlet Crofton.
Belle Dubois.
Pomme d'Api.
Newtown Pippin.
Melon Apple.
Cox's Orange Pippin.
American Mother.
Early Harvest.
Cockle Pippin.
Claygate Pearmain.

Kitchen Apples.

Dumelow's Seedling.
Royal Russet.
Alfriston.
Brabant Bellefleur.
Keswick Codlin.
Calville Blanc.
Lord Suffield.
New Hawthornden.
Manks Codlin.
Waltham Abbey Seedling.
Tower of Glammis.
Bedfordshire Foundling.

Pears.

Dunmore.
Seckle.
Beurré de Capiaumont.
Flemish Beauty.
Duchesse d'Angoulême.
Marie Louise.
Beurré Superfine.
Jean de Witte.
Beurré d'Amanlis.
Williams' Bon Chrétien.
Ligne de Naples.
Suffolk Thorn.
Van Mon's Léon le Clerc.
Louise Bonne (of Jersey).

Napoléon.
Glou Morceau.
Nélis d'Hiver.
Beurré Clairgeau.
Beurré Giffard.
Passe Colmar.
Ne plus Meuris.
Beurré Diel.
Easter Beurré.
Beurré Rance.
Huyshe's Prince of Wales.

Cherries.

May Duke.
Morello.
Kentish.
Royal Duke.
Elton.
Knight's early Black.

Bigarreau.
Late Duke.
Florence.
Black Eagle.
Black Heart.

Plums.

Royale Hâtive.
Greengage.
Orleans.
Fotheringham.
White Magnum Bonum.
Blue Perdrigon.
Purple Gage.
Washington.
Coe's Golden Drop.
Kirke's.
Denyer's Victoria.
Jefferson.

Other Fruit Trees, the mulberry, quince, medlar, service, and filbert, are sometimes introduced as espalier trees or dwarf standards, especially where there is no orchard; but all such trees do best trained in a more natural form.

The plants may be procured either one year grafted or some years trained. All those to be planted on espaliers should be trained in the horizontal manner; and in planting, the greatest care must be taken to place the plants on hills, so that when the ground has finally settled, their collars may be an inch or two above the surface. The distance at which they are placed from the espalier-rail may be from six inches to nine inches, and the distance from plant to plant may be from five to fifteen feet. All plants grown on espaliers should be on dwarfing stocks, and the thicker they are planted the sooner the space is covered. If large trees are preferred, it is very easy gradually to cut away those that are in the way, and allow the permanent plants to occupy the space of two or three temporary trees.

Fruit-Shrubs.

Gooseberries and Currants are frequently planted as espaliers or dwarfs along the margins of walks; but to train these fruits on espaliers is to produce them at an unnecessary expense, unless the saving of room is a material object; and as dwarfs they are in general too low to make an effective separation of the walk and its border from the interior of the compartment. They are, however, very effective as pyramids, either in rows by the sides of walks, or otherwise. They are, however, mostly cultivated in plantations by themselves. The distance may be ten feet between the rows, and six feet between the plants in the row. Goose-

FRUIT SHRUBS.

berries and currants require an open airy situation, and a cool moist loamy soil.

Raspberries prefer a situation somewhat shaded, as in a west or east border; or, for a late crop, in a north border.

The Cranberry, where it is grown as a fruit shrub, requires a peat soil kept somewhat moist, and with the bilberry and some other wild fruits may be conveniently placed in the slip.

Gooseberries, Red Small Sorts.
Red Champagne.
Raspberry.
Rough Red.
Red Turkey.
Small dark rough Red.
Scotch Nutmeg.
Ironmonger.
Warrington.
Wilmot's Early.

Large Sorts.
Boardman's British Crown.
Melling's Crown Bob.
Conquering Hero.
Clayton.
King Cole.
Hartshorn's Lancashire Lad.
Leigh's Rifleman.
Farrow's Roaring Lion.
Slaughterman.
London.

Gooseberries, White, Small Sorts.
White Crystal.
White Champagne.
Early White.
White Damson.
White Honey.
Woodward's Whitesmith.
Bright Venus.
Snowdrift.
Coppice Lass.

White, Large Sorts.
Snowdrop.
King of Trumps.
London City.
Careless.
Antagonist.
Freedom.
Hero of the Nile.

Yellow, Small Sorts.
Champagne.
Golden Hero.
Early Sulphur.
Perfection.
Glory.
Yellow Ball.
Goldfinder.

Yellow, Large Sorts.
Peru.
Rodney.
Trumpeter.
Catherina.
Broom Girl.
Husbandman.
Marigold.
Sovereign.
Leveller.

Gooseberries, Green, Small Sorts.
Early Green Hairy.
Hepburn Green Prolific.
Glenton Green, or York Seedling.
Pitmaston Green Gage.
Gascoigne.
Green Walnut.

Large Sorts.
General.
Queen Victoria.
Thumper.
Turn Out.
Stockwell.
Hopley's Lord Crewe.
Parkinson's Laurel.
Collier's Jolly Angler.
Briggs's Independent.
Massey's Heart of Oak.
Edwards's Jolly Tar.

D D

Currants, Red.

Red Dutch.
Champagne.
Cherry.
Jackson's Mammoth.
Raby Castle, or Victoria.
Knight's Early Red.
Knight's Sweet Red.

Currants, White.

White Dutch.
Cut-leaved variety of White Dutch.

Currants, Black.

Naples.
Grape.
Carter's Prolific.

Raspberries.

Early Prolific.
Red Antwerp.
Yellow Antwerp.
Double Bearing, or Rivers's Victoria.
Fastolf.
October Red.
October Yellow.
Barnet.

Plants of gooseberries and currants may be procured from the nurseries, of one, two, or three years' growth; care should be taken not to plant them too deep; if against espaliers, they are trained in the perpendicular manner; but if in compartments or long walks, as dwarfs, they are best left to take their natural shapes; thinning out the branches so as to give free access of light and air to the interior of the bush. Raspberries being suffruticose plants, the wood formed in one year dying down the next, can only be procured of one year's growth, and they require little pruning except that of shortening the shoots.

Selection of Fruit Trees adapted for an Orchard.

Few kitchen-gardens can produce a sufficient supply of apples, pears, and nuts within the walls, and therefore it commonly happens that a plantation or orchard is formed either in the slip, or in some spot adjoining the kitchen-garden. This plantation should always be separated from the culinary departments by some appropriate line of demarcation. This may frequently be a dwarf wall, on which, if the aspect is suitable, young fruit trees may be trained for the purpose of removal, to fill up occasional blanks in the principal walls. In the plan, fig. 331, the semicircular plot at the south end of the garden might be separated from the walled garden by a dwarf wall, at the same distance from the main wall as the side fences are distant from the main side walls, and the space so walled-off would form a very convenient area for the orchard; provided it were suitable in all other respects. Sometimes the trees are distributed in groups over a lawn or paddock, so as to constitute the main part of the woody scenery of a small villa. They are also occasionally mixed in with ornamental trees and shrubs; a most incongruous assemblage in our opinion, and one which can never form an efficient substitute for an orchard. In whatever situation standard fruit trees are planted, the subsoil should be rendered dry, and the surface if very poor put into good heart by manure. This must, however, be applied in a rotten state, as rank manure is most injurious. It is better, when practicable, to select a rich loamy soil on a dry firm clayey, loamy, or rocky subsoil, and to give no manure. Sandy or gravelly subsoils should be kept especially for apples and cherries; but pears or quinces will thrive on most dry and light soils, provided they be of good depth. Wherever the common hawthorn grows luxuriantly with a clear healthy bark, there orchard fruit trees will thrive.

The plants may be dwarfs, if the plantation is to be exclusively devoted to fruit trees, and the ground neither cropped nor laid down in grass; but standards are preferable, as admitting more light and air. A very convenient and economical mode is to plant rows of standards and dwarfs alternately: the dwarfs, being on dwarfing-stocks, come first into bearing, and may be removed as the branches of the standards extend themselves. Gooseberries, currants, and raspberries may be planted in the intervals, and retained there for two or three years; but they ought to be removed as soon as they are in the slightest degree shaded by the trees. As this is very generally neglected, we should prefer having no fruit shrubs at all, but leaving the surface naked, to be occupied entirely by the roots of the dwarfs and standards. All the plants ought to be set on little hills, more especially if the subsoil is such as to be readily penetrated by the roots, or if the ground has been previously trenched; the great object being to preserve the roots near the surface. The distances at which the trees may be planted are:—For standards, apples, and pears, from thirty feet to forty feet in a medium soil; or in a thin soil and exposed situation, from twenty-five feet to thirty feet; and in a rich soil, from forty feet to fifty feet. Cherries and plums, from twenty-five feet to thirty-five feet, according to soil and situation. For dwarfs on free stocks, one-half the above distances will suffice; and where dwarfs on dwarfing-stocks are to be planted among standards, three dwarfs may be planted for every standard: that is, there may be a row of dwarfs between every two rows of standards, and a dwarf alternating with every standard in the row. The standards, if they have been two or three years grafted, will probably require to be supported by stakes, to which the stems a short distance below the head ought to be carefully tied with haybands. Sheathing the stems of standard trees, especially when they have been planted late or have not abundance of roots, should not be neglected, for reasons already given. The sheathing, which may be of moss, fern, or straw, tied on with matting, or simply of straw or hay ropes wound round, may be left on till it drops off itself. Mulching is also of great use in keeping out the frost and keeping in the moisture.

Select list of standard fruit trees, adapted for an orchard or plantation subsidiary to a kitchen garden:—

Apples.—Early Red Margaret, Summer Golden Pippin, Oslin, Duchess of Oldenburgh, White Astrachan, Kerry Pippin, Dutch Codlin, Kilkenny Codlin, Manks Codlin, Keswick Codlin, Alexander, Hawthornden, Hollandbury, Wormsley Pippin, King of the Pippins,

SELECTION OF FRUIT TREES ADAPTED FOR AN ORCHARD.

Blenheim Pippin, Golden Reinette, Fearn's Pippin, Hughes' Golden Pippin, Claygate Pearmain, Hicks's Fancy, Gravenstein, Court of Wick, Pearson's Plate, Beachamwell, Dutch Mignonne, Scarlet Pearmain, Ribston Pippin, Golden Pippin, Margil, Syke House Russet, Sam Young, Barcelona Pearmain, Maclean's Favourite, Pennington's Seedling, Adams's Pearmain, Hubbard's Pearmain, Herefordshire Pearmain, Golden Harvey, Coe's Golden Drop, Court Pendu Plat, Boston Russet, Lamb Abbey Pearmain, Reinette du Canada, London Pippin, Newtown Pippin, Braddick's Nonpareil, Downton Nonpareil, Old Nonpareil, Scarlet Nonpareil, Cornish Gilliflower, Dumelow's Seedling, Royal Russet, Alfriston, Bedfordshire Foundling, Brabant Bellefleur, Sturmer Pippin, Rhode Island Greening, Gloria Mundi, Crofton Scarlet, Easter Pippin, Emperor Napoleon, Gravenstein, Kentish Fill Basket, King of Pippins, Lemon Pippin, Lord Burleigh, Lord Suffield, Nonesuch, Norfolk Beaufin, Cox's Orange Pippin, Russet, Watson's Dumpling, New Hawthornden, Tower of Glammis.

Pears.—Citron des Carmes, Ambrosia, Dunmore, Althorp Crasanne, Summer St. Germain, Flemish Beauty, Marie Louise, Duchesse d'Angoulême, Doyenné Blanc, Doyenné Gris, Beurré de Capiaumont, Fondante d'Automne, Autumn Colmar, Beurré Diel, Bon Chrétien Fondante, Louise Bonne (of Jersey), Beurré Bosc, Hacon's Incomparable, Thompson's, Napoleon, Winter Nélis, Glou Morceau, Passe Colmar, Knight's Monarch, Ne Plus Meuris, Easter Beurré, Beurré de Ranz, Suffolk Thorn, Beurré de Malines, Croft Castle, Doyenné d'Eté, Swan's Egg, Comte de Lamy, Beurré Superfin. Such varieties as Easter Beurré, Passe Colmar, Glou Morceau, and Winter Nélis should be planted in greater quantity than most of the others, as they keep well and come in at a time when good fruit are scarce.

Cherries.—May Duke, Royal Duke, Knight's Early Black, Elton, Downton, Bigarreau, Black Eagle, Early Purple Guigne, Late Duke, Kentish, Morello, Belle Agathe, Black Circassian, Werder's Early Black, Belle d'Orleans, Büttner's Blackheart.

Plums.—Royal Hâtive, Green Gage, Pond's Seedling, Gisborne's Victoria.

Dessert Plums.—Purple Gage, Washington, Coe's Golden Drop, Ickworth Impératrice, Kirke's, Coe's fine late Red, Drap d'Or, Diaprée Rouge, Nectarine, Rivers's Early, Gisborne's Victoria, Prince Englebert, Perdrigon Violette Hâtive, Reine Claude de Bavay, Woolston Black Gage, Guthrie's late Green.

Kitchen Plums.—Shropshire Damson, Orleans, Early Orleans, Mirabelle, Goliath, Diamond, Belle de Septembre, Pond's Seedling.

Figs.—In many situations the following may be tried as bushes in the orchard:—The Black and Brown Ischia, Brown Turkey, Brunswick, and White Marseilles.

Apricots.—The best for orchards are the Roman, Breda, Turkey, Moorpark, and Alsace.

Medlars.—The Dutch and the Nottingham are the best; the former large, and the latter small and better flavoured.

Of Quinces, the Portugal is the most useful.

Mulberries will likewise fruit well in sheltered localities. Only two varieties, the black and large white fruited, are grown.

The Prolific is far superior to the common Walnut, inasmuch as it bears freely, even in a young state.

There are a great many varieties of Cob-nuts and Filberts. Probably the following are among the best:—The red and white skinned Cobnuts, Lambert Filbert (Kentish Cob), Purple Filbert, Prolific, or Northamptonshire, and the thin-skinned Cosford.

Training.—All the trees may be allowed to take their natural shapes, taking care, by pruning them for some years after they are planted, to give their main branches an upright direction, diverging from the main stem at an angle not greater than 45°, that they may be the better able to support a load of fruit. With many kinds, however, such is the divergent or pendulous character of the branches that this direction cannot be given to them, in which case the object should be to increase the number of main branches so as to lessen the load to each. This is particularly necessary in the case of apples and pears.

Culture of the Soil.—Where fruit is the main object, the soil ought never either to be cropped with vegetables or laid down in grass, because in both cases the trees are deprived of nourishment. In the case of grass, air is excluded; and in orchards where culinary vegetables are grown, the roots are prevented from coming up to the surface and, being forced into the subsoil, feed there on a more watery nutriment, which produces shoots of spongy wood without blossom-buds and in many cases infested with canker. Where the surface is kept in grass there is less danger from canker and spongy shoots, provided the trees have been planted on hillocks; but in this case, from want of nourishment, the fruit will be smaller and less succulent. If, however, the soil is naturally good, and occasionally manured on the surface, more and better flavoured fruit will be produced in such an orchard than in one cropped with culinary vegetables. As no orchard can be pastured unless each separate tree is enclosed, which, where the ground is properly covered with trees, would probably cost more than the pasture is worth, it will in general be found better, where grass must be introduced, to mow it and supply manure, till the stems of the trees are so large as to be able to protect themselves. It is almost unnecessary to observe, that as soon as the branches of the trees approach within two feet or three feet of each other, the branches of the temporary trees should be shortened in, and soon after removed by degrees, so as at all times to leave a clear space of five feet or six feet round the head of every tree.

CHAPTER XII.

CROPPING, AND GENERAL MANAGEMENT OF A KITCHEN GARDEN.

The fruit trees and fruit shrubs being planted, the former against the walls and espalier-rails, and the latter in plantations by themselves in the compartments, or in rows between the fruit trees, or along the secondary walks, the remaining part of the garden is devoted to herbaceous vegetables. The number of these required to be grown in every kitchen garden is considerable, and the soil ought to be managed and the crops sown or planted according to some preconceived system. With respect to the soil, this consists in changing the surface, in stirring and manuring it, weeding, watering, &c., on the principles already detailed; and we shall now explain the system of cropping and rotations.

Cropping.

The herbaceous vegetables grown in kitchen gardens are of two kinds: perennials which remain several years in the ground, such as asparagus, sea-kale, rhubarb, horse-radish, artichokes, perennial sweet herbs, and strawberries. The first of these crops remains on the same piece of ground from six to twelve years, and the others are renewed generally in about half that time or oftener. The other and by far the more numerous crops are annuals or biennials, and many of them only remain on the ground during a part of the year. The proportion of the perennials being fixed on, little more trouble is required with them; but the annuals being numerous and of short duration, the proportionate quantities that require to be sown or planted to supply the demands of the kitchen, and yet to be in due proportion to the extent of the ground to be cropped, and the kinds of crops which ought to succeed each other, require the constant exercise of the gardener's judgment. The first point is to determine the proportion of different crops, and the next is their succession: though the proportions will depend to a certain extent on the peculiar taste or wants of the family, and whether they reside on the spot or at a distance—whether they have a farm for growing the winter supply of potatoes, &c., yet some rules or hints may be devised which are generally applicable.

General Proportions of Crops.—The greatest breadth of surface in almost every garden requires to be sown with peas; but as this crop only lasts at an average about six months, a second crop may be planted on the same ground in the same year. The cabbage tribe, including cauliflower, broccoli, savoys, Brussels sprouts and borecoles, occupy the next greatest space in most gardens, and they very generally succeed the crops of peas. Turnips are perhaps the next most extensive crop, unless indeed the main summer crops of potatoes are grown in the kitchen garden, which is not desirable where they can be grown on the farm; the potato being a crop that, for some reason or other which we do not pretend to explain, is seldom found so mealy and high-flavoured when grown in a garden as when grown in a field. There are next several crops, each of which has nearly an equal claim for space, viz.—carrots, parsnips, onions, beans, kidney-beans, celery, and winter spinach. Jerusalem artichokes and red-beet crops may come next in the order of space required; and then leeks, garlic and shallots, salsafy and scorzonera. In some gardens salading is a most important consideration, requiring almost more space and attention than all other crops. In others, such plants as lettuce, endive, radish, cress, mustard, chervil, parsley, and other summer salading, garnishings or herbs, may in general be grown among other crops, or a very small surface of ground suffices.

In determining the extent of each crop, the nature of the produce must be taken as a guide. It would be of little use to have a less quantity of any crop than would not at a single gathering produce a dish sufficient for a family of several persons. This for such articles as asparagus and peas requires considerable breadth of ground; but this breadth once planted and in bearing, will afford several or perhaps many gatherings during the time it is in season. On the other hand, where a succession of crops of turnips or carrots is wanted, if only two or three square yards were sown each time, that space would afford one or two dishes. For such articles as salsafy and scorzonera, which in most English families may perhaps not be asked for above two or three times in a season, a very small surface will be sufficient. When a gardener enters on a new place, before he determines on the extent of particular crops, he ought to consult the cook or housekeeper as to the style of cookery, the ordinary amount of company, and the seasons when extraordinary supplies are wanted, with the periods when vegetables and fruits require to be sent to a distance, and other particulars bearing upon the kind of crops to be grown. Having formed general ideas on the extent of each crop, he will next be able to determine on a system of succession, or, as it is called, rotation.

The quantity of seed for crops, proportioned as above described for a garden of an acre and a quarter, may be as follows:—Peas, from fifteen to twenty quarts; white cabbage of different kinds, three oz.; savoys, two oz.; Brussels sprouts, two oz.; cauliflowers, three oz.; broccoli, seven oz.; borecoles, two oz.; red cabbage, one oz.; kohl rabi, one oz.; turnips, white, six oz.; yellow, two oz.; early potatoes, from one bushel to four, according to demand; carrots, five oz.; onions, eight oz.; beans, broad, four qts.; kidney beans, three qts.; scarlet runners, two qts.; celery, one oz.; Flanders spinach, one qt.; summer spinach, two qts.; Jerusalem artichoke, one peck; red beet, four oz.; parsnips, four oz.; leeks, two oz.; garlic, half lb.; shallots, three lbs.; salsafy, half oz.; scorzonera, half oz.; lettuce, Cos, three oz.; cabbage do., two oz.; endive, two oz.; radish, three pts.; cress, one pt.; mustard, one qt.; parsley, two oz.

The following are the actual quantities used in Bicton, a first-class garden, by Mr. Barnes:—

Peas.—Carter's First Crop, four qts.; Dillistones, one qt.; Sangster's No. 1, two qts.; Laxton's Prolific; Maclean's Advancer, two qts.; Auvergne, one qt.; Maclean's Wonderful, one qt.; Dixon's Favourite, one qt.; Harrison's Glory, one qt.; Nonpareil Wrinkled, one qt.; Napoleon, one qt.; Veitch's Perfection, six qts.; Champion of England, one qt.; Defiance, one qt.; the Prince, one qt.; British Queen, one qt.; Ne Plus Ultra, one qt.; Ringwood Marrow, one qt.; Mammoth Tall Green Marrow, one qt.; Knight's Tall Marrow, one qt.

Beans.—Monarch (long-pod), two qts.; Johnson's Wonderful, two qts.; Green Pod, two qts.; Green Windsor, two qts.

Broccoli.—Early Purple Cape Broccoli, one oz.; Cornish White, one oz.; Walcheren, one oz.; Snow's Early, one oz.; Knight's Protecting, one oz.; Malta, half oz.; Early Purple Sprouting, half oz.; Wilcove's, half oz.; Cattell's Eclipse, one oz.

Garnishing Kale, one oz.; Improved Brussels sprouts, one oz.; Rosebud ditto, half oz.; best red beet, one qt.; Nonpareil cabbage, four oz.; Atkin's Matchless, four oz.; Paragon, four oz.; Little Pixie, one oz.; Enfield, two oz.; Shilling's Queen, two oz.; dwarf red Dutch, one oz.; Guernsey parsnips, two oz.; Hollow Crown, two oz.; Early Dutch carrot, four oz.; Early Horn carrot, four oz.; white mustard, two qts.; common cress, one qt.; Normandy curled cress, half pint; American cress, half pint; best curled endive, one oz.; Batavian ditto, one oz.; Victoria cabbage lettuce, two oz.; Hardy Hammersmith, half oz.; Deptford onion, four oz.; Reading ditto, four oz.; Brown Globe ditto, four oz.; White Globe ditto, four oz.; Prickly spinach, one qt.; Round ditto, one qt.; New Zealand ditto, one oz.; Early Dutch turnip, one qt.; Early Stone, one oz.; Veitch's Early Red Globe, one qt.; Early short-top radish, one qt.; red turnip ditto, one qt.; white turnip ditto, one qt.; thyme, half oz.; savory, half oz.; sweet marjoram, half oz.; sweet basil, half oz.

Potatoes.—Myatt's Early Ash-leaved, one bushel; Milky-White, two pecks; Smith's Early Wandsworth, two pecks.

Rotation of Crops.

Crops in horticulture are made to follow each other according to two distinct plans or systems, which may be termed successional cropping and simultaneous cropping; the former is generally followed in private gardens, and the latter in market gardens.

Successional cropping is that in which the ground is wholly occupied with one crop at one time, to be succeeded by another crop, also wholly of one kind. For example, onions to be followed by winter turnips, or potatoes to be followed by borecole. Simultaneous cropping is that in which several crops are all coming forward on the ground at the same time. For example, onions, lettuce, and radishes, sown broadcast; or peas, potatoes, broccoli, and spinach, sown or planted in rows.

The object to be attained by a system of cropping is that of procuring the greatest quantity and the best quality of the desired kind of produce at the least possible expense of labour, time, and manure; and in order that this object may be effectually obtained, there are certain principles which ought to be adopted as guides. The chief of these is to be derived from a knowledge of what specific benefit or injury every culinary plant does to the soil, with reference to any other culinary plant. It ought to be known whether particular plants injure the soil by exhausting it of particular principles, or whether the soil is rendered unfit for the growth of the same, or any allied species, by excretions from the roots of plants, while the same excretions, acting in the way of manure, add to the fitness of the soil for the production of other species. The excretory theory is now generally abandoned, and it is believed that plants exhaust the soil generally of vegetable food, particularly of that kind of food which is peculiar to the species growing on it for the time being. For example, both potatoes and onions exhaust the soil generally, while the potato deprives it of something that is necessary to ensure the reproduction of good crops of potatoes, and the onion of something which is necessary for the reproduction of large crops of onions. According to the theory of De Candolle, both crops exhaust the soil generally, and both render it unfit for the particular kind of crop; but this injury, according to his hypothesis, is not effected by depriving the soil of the particular kind of nutriment necessary for the particular kind of species, but by excreting into it substances peculiar to the species with which it has been cropped, which substances render it unfit for having these crops repeated. Both these theories are attended with some difficulty in the case of plants which remain a great many years on the same soil, as, for example, perennial-rooted herbaceous plants and trees. The difficulty, however, is got over in both systems. By the first, or old theory, the annual dropping and decay of the foliage are said to supply at once general nourishment and particular nourishment; and by the second, or new theory, the same dropping of the leaves, by the general nourishment which it supplies, is said to neutralize the particular excretions. A wood of the pine or fir tribe standing so thick that their roots will form a network under the surface, will not poison each other; but remove these trees, and place a new plantation on the same soil and they will not thrive, owing, as we think, to the principles most conducive to the growth of coniferous trees being exhausted, as is explained by Liebig. The practical inference from either theory is much the same—that is, a change of crops, the rules for which adopted by the best gardeners are as follows :—

1. Crops of plants belonging to the same natural order or tribe, or to the natural order and tribe most nearly allied to them, should not follow each other. Thus, turnips should not follow any of the cabbage tribe, sea-kale, or horse-radish, nor should peas come after beans.

2. Plants which draw their nourishment chiefly from the surface of the soil should not follow each other, but should alternate with those which draw their nourishment in great part from the subsoil. Hence, carrots and beets should not follow each other; nor onions and potatoes.

3. Plants which draw a great deal of nourishment from the soil should succeed, or be succeeded by, plants which draw less nourishment. Hence a crop grown for its fruit, such as the pea; or for its roots or bulbs, such as the potato or the onion, should be followed by such as are grown solely for their leaves, such as the common borecole, the celery, the lettuce, &c.

4. Plants which remain for several years on the soil, such as strawberries, rhubarb, asparagus, &c., should not be succeeded by other plants which remain a long time on the soil, but by crops of short duration; and the soil should be continued under such crops for as long a period as it remained under a permanent crop. Hence, in judiciously cropped gardens, the strawberry compartment is changed every three or four years, till it has gone the circuit of all the compartments; and asparagus beds, sea-kale, &c., are renewed on the same principles.

5. Plants, the produce of which is collected during summer, should be succeeded by those of which the produce is chiefly gathered in winter or spring. The object of this rule is to prevent two exhausting crops from following each other in succession.

6. Plants in gardens are sometimes allowed to ripen their seeds, in which case two seed-bearing crops should not follow each other in succession.

These rules, and others of a like kind, apply generally to both systems of the successional crops, and they are independent altogether of other rules or principles which may be drawn from the nature of the plants themselves, such as some requiring an extraordinary proportion of air, light, shade, moisture, time, &c., or from the nature of the changes intended to be made on them by cultivation, such as blanching, increase of succulency, magnitude, &c. We shall now notice the two systems separately.

Successional Cropping.—The plants calculated for this mode of cropping are such as require, during almost every period of their growth, the fullest exposure to light and air, and remain a considerable time in the soil: these are, the turnip, the onion, the potato, the carrot, &c. If any of these crops are raised and brought forward under the shade of others, they will be materially injured both in quality and quantity; though at the same time, while they are merely germinating, shade will not injure them. Hence successional cropping may be carried on in breadths of twenty or thirty feet between rows of tall-growing plants without injury, thus approximating this manner of cropping to the simultaneous mode, which, wherever the soil is rich, is by far the most profitable.

The simultaneous mode of cropping is founded on the principles that most plants, when germinating, and for some time afterwards, thrive best in the shade; and that tall-growing plants, which require to receive the light on each side, should be sown or planted at some distance from each other. Hence, tall-growing peas are sown in rows ten, twelve, or twenty feet apart, and between them are planted rows of the cabbage tribe; and again, between these are sown rows of spinach, lettuce, or radishes, &c. Hence, also, beans are planted in the same rows with cabbages (an old practice in the cottage gardens of Scotland), and so on. The great object in this kind of cropping is to have crops on the ground in different stages of growth, so that the moment the soil and the surface are released from one crop, another may be in an advanced state, and ready, as it were, to supply its place. For this purpose, whenever one crop is removed, its place ought to be instantly supplied by plants adapted for producing another crop of the proper nature to succeed it. For example, where rows of tall marrow-fat peas have rows of broccoli between them, then the moment the peas are removed, a trench for celery may be formed where each row of peas stood; and between the rows of broccoli, in the places where lettuces were produced early in the season, may be sown drills of winter spinach.

Of these two modes of cropping, the first is the one best calculated for poor soils, or for gardens where the supply of manure is limited; the second cannot be prosecuted with success, except in soils which are light and extremely rich. It may be proper to observe here, that a system of cropping can be carried to a much higher degree of perfection in a commercial garden, on a large scale, than in a private one; because in the former whenever one crop is in perfection, it is removed and sent to market at once; whereas, in a private garden, it is removed by driblets. Hence in small gardens, where labour and manure are of less consequence than economizing the extent of surface, it will often be found desirable to have a small reserve garden, with several frames, pots, and other requisites. As soon as one plant, or a few plants of any crop in a condition for gathering, are removed, the soil should be stirred, and a plant or plants (which should have been some days before potted in preparation) should be turned out of the pot, its fibres being carefully spread out, and water supplied, so as to make it commence growing immediately. The use of potting is to prevent the plant from experiencing the slightest check in its removal; and in autumn, as is well known, the loss of a single day, by the flagging of a plant, is of the utmost consequence.

Successional and Simultaneous Cropping Combined.—The following is from an excellent article on cropping, published in the 'Gardener's Chronicle.' The writer divides kitchen-garden crops into (1) Perennial or stationary crops; (2) Rotation crops, which include all the principal annual crops; and (3) Secondary crops, such as salads, spinach, &c., which are usually sown in vacancies between rotation crops.

Order of Rotation.—1st year, peas and beans, succeeded by broccoli, savoys, winter-greens, coleworts, spring cabbage; 2nd year, carrots, parsnips, beet, scorzonera, and salsafy; 3rd year, onions, cauliflowers, turnips, succeeded by spinach, spring onions, and other secondary crops; 4th year, savoys, broccoli, winter-greens, red cabbage, leeks; 5th year, potatoes; 6th year, turnips, cabbage, broccoli; 7th year, celery; 8th, French beans, &c. ('Gard. Chron.,' 1841, p. 180, with additions.)

Secondary crops are those of the shortest duration, such as lettuce, radishes, small salads, annual herbs, and very early peas and beans (sown in November), very early cauliflowers, very early turnips, and early potatoes, all of which will require a warm south border, or sloping banks, or Plant Protectors.

Times of Sowing and Planting.—Peas and beans should be sown from February to June; the first crop of peas will be cleared for early broccoli in the end of June, and for the other seasons until September for later broccoli, savoys, borecole, Brussels sprouts, coleworts, and spring cabbage; this crop should have a slight coat of manure. Broccoli ground will be cleared of early sorts by winter, and should be ridged up all winter for a crop of carrots, which should be sown as early as possible; the later broccoli, colewort, sprouts, &c., will make way by April or the beginning of May for beet, parsnips, scorzonera, and salsafy. Carrots, beet, and parsnips, will be cleared in the beginning of November, when the ground must be again ridged up for winter, and have a good coat of dung, ready for cauliflowers, onions, garlic, and shallots; the two latter being planted in November, and also the principal crops of turnips sown in the end of March and April. Cauliflowers, onions, and turnips will be cleared from July to September; the cauliflowers and shallots, &c., in July for autumn spinach and endive; the onions for winter spinach, and the turnips for spring onions, winter lettuce, and other secondary crops. Spinach, endive, and spring onions will be cleared by the end of May for savoys, winter-greens, red cabbage, cauliflowers, and leeks, all of which require a moderate coat of manure. Savoys, winter-greens, red cabbage, &c., will be ready for early potatoes in April and May. Potatoes will make way in July and August for turnips, spring cabbage, late broccoli, and such crops, if wanted. Turnips, cabbage, broccoli, may be cleared in May for celery and cardoon trenches—if all the ground is wanted; but if not, the cabbage may be allowed to remain for sprouts during all the summer. The intermediate spaces between the trenches may be planted with lettuce, or any other secondary crops; dung must be given for celery, of course. Celery and similar crops will in part make way in autumn, when the ground should be ridged up for winter, and the remainder as soon as the entire crop is cleared; the ground will then be ready for French beans, scarlet runners, cauliflowers, cucumbers, and tomatoes, in the end of April or beginning of May. French beans will be cleared by November, when the ground should be again ridged up all winter to be ready for peas and beans, as at first begun. This will make eight or ten years between the return of the principal crops to the same place; and by judicious management of the secondary crops among the rotation crops, every space of ground between one crop and another may be occupied to advantage during the intervals of cropping. ('Gard. Chron.' for 1841, p. 180.) This is doubtless a very good rotation, but in small gardens the ground is always under crop. The whole of the potato and early pea ground is planted with cauliflowers, and this is again succeeded by broccoli and other winter stuff when the potatoes and cauliflowers are both used. Winter cabbages again constantly succeed onions, and onions celery. Strawberries are dug down as soon as the fruit is gathered, and then a crop of winter broccoli taken. Then potatoes, followed by, or intermixed with, peas, and so on. All the secondary crops become catch crops on this hard system of cropping; but deep tilths will bear it for years with plenty of feeding.

Planting, Sowing, Cultivating, and Managing.

In general all crops should be planted or sown in rows from south to north, in order, as already observed, that the sun may shine on every part of the soil between the rows, and equally on every side of the plants in the row. Beds, also, such as those of asparagus, should be made in the same direction and for the same reasons. When asparagus, sea-kale, and rhubarb are to be forced in the open garden by hot dung, the alleys or paths between the beds should be of double the usual width, and all the beds intended to be subjected to a course of forcing should be placed together. The secondary perennial crops, such as mint, thyme, sage, savory, perennial marjoram, rue, &c., should always be planted together, and in an open airy situation, forming a garden of herbs. This saves much time, and gives the charm of order in small matters.

Management of the Dwarf or Pyramid Fruit-tree Borders.—The wall-borders in which the espaliers are planted, and the ground among plantations of fruit shrubs or fruit trees, should on no account be cropped or even deeply dug, for reasons which we need not repeat. The soil may be loosened on the surface in spring with a three-pronged fork, and in autumn a top-dressing of well rotted manure may be given and slightly turned in with the spade, or left on the surface till the spring-stirring. If the border is narrow, and the trees, after having filled it with their roots, appear to require additional nourishment, a trench may be cut along the front of the wall-border next the walk, three feet or four feet in width, and of such a depth as to cut through all the roots, not, however, deeper than eighteen inches. A part of the soil taken out of the trench may be removed altogether, and a rich compost of rotten dung and leaf-mould mixed with the remainder and filled in; or, better still, with good turfy maiden loam, used in a rough fresh state. This is in imitation of a plan long followed with success by the Lancashire growers of prize gooseberries; all the difference being that they use an excessively rich compost, which would not be suitable for fruit trees generally. It might be advisable to do this work by degrees rather than all at once, by taking out every third yard, in the case of wall and espalier borders, and the third part of a circle in the case of dwarfs and standards. The second yard might be taken out in two years, the third in two years more, and at the end of the sixth year the operation might be recommenced, because the rich soil would very soon be filled with fibrous roots. In this operation, as in every other of the kind, the gardener or the amateur must exercise his own judgment, bearing in mind that the object is not to produce luxuriant branches, but blossom-buds. It is better, however, generally to renew the productive power of the soil with liquid manure, or town sewage, than with such dressings of composts.

Management of the Culinary Crops.—All culture must necessarily consist in the application of general practices, or in the performance of such operations as are required by particular species or for particular objects. The former are already given, and the latter will be found when treating of the culture of each particular culinary plant in our catalogue of Culinary Vegetables.

Gathering, Storing, and Keeping of Fruit.—" The chief requirements of a good fruit-room are, darkness, a low and steady temperature, dryness to a certain point (for apples are found to keep best, as regards appearance, in a rather damp atmosphere, but for flavour a moderately dry air is preferable), and exclusion of the external air. If the light of the sun strikes upon a plant, the latter immediately parts with its moisture by perspiration, in proportion to the force exercised on it by the sun, and independently of temperature. The greatest amount of perspiration takes place beneath the direct rays of the sun, and the smallest in those places to which daylight reaches with most difficulty. Now, the surface of a fruit perspires like that of a leaf, although not to the same amount. While growing on the tree, it is perpetually supplied by the stem with water enough to replace that which is all day long flying off from its surface; but as soon as it is gathered, that source of supply is removed, and then, if the light strikes it ever so feebly, it loses weight, without being able to replace its loss. It is thus that fruit becomes shrivelled and withered prematurely. Light should therefore have no access to a good fruit-room."

" Temperature should be uniform. If it is high, the juices of the fruit will have a tendency to decompose, and thus decay will be accelerated; if, on the contrary, it is below 32°, decomposition of another kind is produced, in consequence of the chemical action and mechanical effects of freezing. In any case, fluctuations of temperature are productive of decay. A steady temperature of from 40° to 45°, with a dry atmosphere, will be found the best for most kinds of fruit. Some pears of the late kinds are better for being kept in a temperature as high as 60°, for this ripens them, renders them melting, and improves their quality very essentially. The general construction of the fruit-room ought not, however, to be altered on their account; such fruits can readily be placed in a hothouse or hot closet. The air should be kept moderately dry, but ventilation should not be used except for the purpose of removing offensive smells, arising from the putrefaction of the fruit. Ventilation by continual currents of air carries off from fruit the moisture which it contains, and thus acts in the same way as light, in producing shrivelling, and destroying that plump appearance which gives its beauty to fruit." ('Gard. Chron.,' vol. i. pp. 611, 61.)

Great care should be taken in gathering, handling, and storing the fruit, and placing each kind by itself. Gather in baskets, and place them on the shelves side by side with their eyes downwards. When gathering and stowing are completed, shut the room as close as possible, and only open it when the fruit is wanted. The best modes of packing fruit which is to be sent to a distance have been already given. (See p. 370.)

Gathering the Fruit and Management of the Fruit-room.—No fruit ought to be allowed to drop from the tree, nor should it be beaten down or shaken off. Except in wet or late seasons, it ought not to be gathered till it is quite ripe, which in stone fruits and berries is known by its softness and fragrance, in kernel fruit by the brown colour of the seeds, and in nuts by the opening of the husks. It ought in every case to be gathered by hand; and in addition to ladders of different kinds, there is the orchardist's crook, fig. 338, the use of which is to

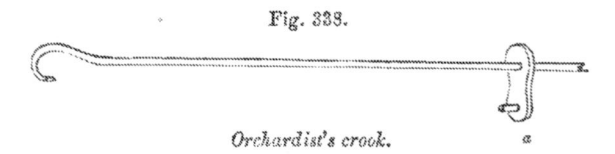

Fig. 338.

Orchardist's crook.

take hold of one branch with the hook, and draw it towards the operator; and then, by putting the sliding-piece, *a*, over another branch, that branch is held in that position by the obliqueness of the line of pressure, which prevents the sliding-piece from moving: thus leaving the operator free to use both hands in gathering the fruit. The fruit ought to be put into baskets, placing each kind in a basket by itself, and laying it in so gently as to run no risk of bruising it; and not only keeping each kind of fruit by itself, but keeping wall fruit apart from standard fruit, because the former will be soonest fit for the table. The fruit laid on shelves should be placed with their eyes downwards, and so as not to touch each other; but baking apples and pears may be spread on a cool floor. In whatever manner fruit is placed in the fruit-room or fruit-cellar, the doors and windows of the apartments should be kept closely shut, so as to keep the atmosphere of as uniform a temperature and moisture as possible. It should, as we have already observed, never be lower than 40°, nor higher than 45°, if possible in close mild weather to keep it so low, with the dew point indicating a very slight degree of dryness occasionally. There are, however, exceptions, such as in the case of ripening off, or keeping such kinds in that temperature which experience proves to be most conducive for producing fine consistence and flavour. This requires one or more separate compartments having a command of heat, wherein the temperature may be graduated as circumstances may require. The external air ought only to be admitted when that within is rendered offensive by the decomposition of the fruit. If at any time the temperature should fall below 32°, still no artificial heat ought to be applied, but thawing allowed to take place in the dark, by which precaution injury will be avoided. Table apples and pears which are expected to keep for some months, are kept on shelves singly, or in shallow drawers, or packed in boxes, jars, or pots, with dried fern or dry sand. New garden-pots are found to answer remarkably well for keeping fruit, any damp being readily absorbed by the dry, porous, unglazed materials of which they are usually composed. Fruits which are thus packed do not require to be examined till the time when they are expected to be fit for the table, which should always be marked, along with the name, on the label attached to the jar or box; but fruits exposed to the air on the open shelves require to be examined almost every day, in order to remove those which exhibit symptoms of decay. Walnuts, sweet chestnuts, and filberts, may be kept in boxes or casks, placed in the fruit-cellar on account of its low but uniform temperature. Summer fruit, such as peaches, nectarines, plums, are seldom kept more than a day or two in the fruit-room, but they are sometimes kept in the ice-house for a week or more, which causes some loss of flavour.

CHAPTER XIII.

THE FORCING DEPARTMENT.

The principles of constructing houses for plants, together with their culture in artificial climates, having been already given, we proceed to show their application to the pinery, vinery, peach-house, fig-house, cherry-house, cucumber and melon pits and frames, and the forcing in frames and pits of such culinary vegetables as it is desired to have produced out of season. We have already seen that artificial heat may be applied in plant-structures by dung or other fermenting substances, by hot water, by steam, or by smoke-flues; or by two or more of these modes of heating combined. Fermenting substances are almost always the safest, and hot water generally the best; but the same result may be obtained by smoke-flues, and is still obtained in many parts of the country, though not without extra care on the part of the gardener. With respect to the form of house where low plants, such as pines, melons, cucumbers, strawberries, or kidney-beans are to be grown or forced, low structures, such as pits or frames, are most eligible; but where trees, such as the vine, peach, fig, &c., are to be grown, houses of the ordinary height of garden-walls are preferred, at least for general crops. The reasons are obvious in both cases.

Culture of the Pine-apple, and Management of the Pinery.—The pine-apple has long been considered the king of the dessert. It also makes an admirable sweet preserved in sugar, or made into a jam. In the East Indies it takes the place of our common apple or other fruits; and pine-apple sauce and fritters are as common in Calcutta as apples are in England. Its fibre is made into thread, twisted into cordage, or woven into linen.

We shall first give the natural data on which the culture of this plant is founded, and next a thoroughly practical and original treatise founded on the best practice up to the year 1870.

Natural Data on which the Culture of the Pine-apple is Founded.

The pine-apple is an evergreen monocotyledonous plant, a native of countries tropical or bordering on the tropics, and found in low situations on or near the sea-shore, or near wide rivers. It grows almost always on sandy soil, dry on the surface, but moist at the depth of a foot or two beneath. It is indigenous or cultivated in various similar situations, as in South America, at Rio Janeiro; in the West Indies, at Grenada; and in Africa, at Sierra-Leone. As an evergreen monocotyledonous plant, it is without buds, and consequently not intended by nature to be long, if at all, in a state of repose; as a native of the sea-shore, it is not calculated for enduring a great difference of temperature between summer and winter; and as a native of countries within the tropics, it is calculated for growing in a high temperature throughout the year. The temperature of various places at or near the equator, as given by Humboldt, exhibits an average of about 83° for the warmest month, and 72° for the coldest; thus giving a difference between the summer and winter heat adapted for the pine-apple of only 11°. But in the small island of Grenada, in the West Indies, where the pine-apple luxuriates, the temperature in the shade never exceeds 85° and never falls below 80°; thus giving a difference of only 5°. It is clear therefore that there ought to be very little difference between the summer and winter temperature of the pine-apple house. In practice, however, it is found that this difference may range from 15 to 20 degrees. The temperature of the soil in Grenada during summer, and at one foot beneath the surface, we are assured on good authority is 85°. With respect to the water of the atmosphere in the countries where the pine-apple thrives, there is generally a dry season and a rainy season—the latter much shorter than the former. In the dry season there are heavy nightly dews; and the rainy season, which is like the spring of temperate climates, produces such an exuberance of growth as to throw the plants into fruit. In the neighbourhood of Rio, there are heavy rains at intervals from October to April; the suckers from the roots are taken off in April or May, which is about the end of their summer, and planted in the fields from one foot and a half to two feet from each other. The strongest of them produce fruit in the following year, which weigh between 3 lbs. and 4 lbs. each; and those which do not fruit the second year, produce the third year, the fruit often weighing from 10 lbs. to 12 lbs. each.

The conclusions to be drawn from these data, and which are at the same time confirmed by the experience of successful and unsuccessful growers in England, are, that the temperature of the pine-stove ought never to be more than a few degrees lower than 70° in summer, or a few degrees lower than 60° in winter. As our days are much shorter in winter than they are between the tropics, a lower tempera ture ought to be allowed for that season, because growth in the absence of light would be of no service to the plant, but rather the reverse. In winter, therefore, 65° may be adopted as the standard heat of the atmosphere, and in summer the temperature may vary between 70° and 80°, or in the fruiting-house from 75° to 85°. With respect to the temperature of the soil, as the soil in all countries, at a short distance under the surface, is found to average 2° or 3° higher than the atmosphere, owing to earth having a greater capacity for heat than air, and parting with it more slowly, if we allow a bottom heat of between 70° and 75° in winter, and between 75° and 80° in summer, we shall probably be acting in accordance with what takes place in nature.

With respect to soil, it is almost unnecessary to say that plants in a wild state are not always found in the soil that is best adapted for bringing them to a high degree of perfection, but rather in one that is best adapted for their propagation, or the continuance of the species. It has been found by experience that almost any porous soils will grow pines. In a growing state pines likewise require a liberal supply of water, which should always be applied at a temperature of 75° to 80°.

Culture of the Pine-apple in British Gardens.

From the earliest times the successful cultivation of the pine-apple has been looked upon as the highest manifestation of horticultural skill. It seems to have been known in England for more than two hundred years. There is a picture in Kensington Palace of Mr. John Rose, then gardener to the Duchess of Cleveland, presenting a pine-apple to Charles II. It is doubtful, however, whether this pine was grown in England. If so, the art of pine-growing does not seem to have taken root. The next authentic information comes from Flanders; from thence, Miller observes, our gardens were furnished with plants. In 1718 the culture of the pine-apple was first successfully established in England, in the garden of Sir Matthew Decker, at Richmond, Surrey. In that year Bradley reports he saw forty plants in fruit. The suckers were planted in August, bloomed in April, and were ripe in September. The pits were heated with bark, the plants watered with tepid water, a thermometer was used that he might be certain about the heat, and Bradley recommends at that early time that a hygrometer and barometer should be added as guides to the gardener. Mr. George M. Johnson, from whose compilation of the history of the pine most of these facts are collected, adds that in the Fitzwilliam Museum at Cambridge, there is a Landscape painting, in which a pine-apple is introduced, and it is said to be the first pine grown in England at Sir Matthew Decker's. The pine is said to have been introduced into Ireland by Mr. Buller, in the reign of Queen Anne, 1712-1714, and into Scotland by James Justice, Esq., of Crichton, near Dalkeith. With the art of pine-growing the literature of this subject arose and spread. Everyone who could grow a pine-apple was fired with a noble ambition to tell all how it was done. Miller, Nicol, and McPhail had written before; but their directions were short and imperfect. In

1769 Mr. John Giles, the gardener to Lady Boyd at Lewisham, in Kent, published the first formal treatise on the culture of the pine-apple in England, which also contained a plan of a pinery heated with tan and flues. This treatise was followed by another in 1769, by Mr. Adam Taylor, of Devizes. Pine-growing was reckoned of such importance that it was brought before the Royal Society by W. Bastard, Esq., of Shotley, Devon, in 1779. Speechley's treatise followed two years later. This was followed by another from Mr. W. Griffin in 1806, and by that of Mr. J. Baldwin in 1818. Loudon, with his usual industry, collected all that had been previously written upon this matter, and offered his contribution to pine culture in 1822, in the form of a volume on the different modes of cultivating the pine-apple. Mr. Knight about the same period treated the subject in the 'Horticultural Transactions.' About twenty-five years later the modern authors, Glendinning, Hamilton, Mill, Barnes, Forsyth, and others appeared, ending with Mr. David Thomson, the last of the list of famous authors on this subject.

With such a formidable list of authors the modern pine-grower is in some danger of foundering his cultural barque, boldly launched to reach the fair haven of success, and may be grateful to us for classifying and arranging the matter for him with a fulness and a distinctness that has probably not yet been reached by any single writer. The subject may be conveniently and perspicuously arranged and treated of in the following order:—

Soils.
Houses and pits.
Modes of heating.
Times and manner of potting.
Watering of root and top.
Manures.
Shading.
Temperature (day and night, summer and winter).
Propagation.
Selection of varieties.
Age of the fruiting-plants.
Pot *versus* the open-bed system.
The Hamiltonian system.

Expedients for enlarging the size and improving the quality of the fruit.
Making the plants show fruit.
Retarding of the fruit.
Preservation of ripe pines.
What constitutes a good pine.
Weight of the finest fruit.
Insects—to prevent and destroy.
Diseases and malformation, and their remedies.
Monthly doings amongst pines throughout the year.
Pine-growing in the open air.

Selection of Soils.—Though the pine-apple is found in very sandy soils, it may not be always best to choose such soils for growing or fruiting the plants under cultivation. The plant will grow well in almost any soil, as is sufficiently proved by the fact that almost every grower and writer has recommended some particular mixture for it. Amid these endless nostrums, pure peat in France and pure fibrous loam in England have been the most popular and most generally used. The former is too light, and the latter too heavy. Between these two extremes everything has been tried. Hamilton used nothing but half-decayed tan; Oldacre grew pines in powdered bones; Brown in pure peat and a mixture of sand and lime. Others have used half charcoal and loam, vegetable earth and powdered oyster-shells, moss mixed with earth and by itself. "White soils and red, black soils and grey— mingle, mingle, mingle; let all mingle as they may who grow pines," seemed to be the motto of old cultivators. Hence after the current had fairly set in in favour of turfy loam, almost a generation had passed away before horticulturists learned the useful lesson of employing it pure and simple in a rough turfy state, made porous by the mixture of a liberal percentage of sharp sand and broken charcoal, and enriched with one-inch or half-inch bones. Speechley advises to take good turf of a strong, rich, loamy texture, turn it topsy turvy in a sheepfold to be trodden on for two or three months, until the quantity of sheep's dung equals about one-third that of the loam, and stack for six or twelve months, turn, and make fine with the spade. Then the receipt is:—three barrow-loads of this rich material, one of decayed leaf-mould, and half a barrow-load of coarse sand, for crowns, suckers, and young plants. For fruiting-plants three barrow-loads of the enriched turf, two ditto of vegetable mould, one ditto of coarse sand, and one-fourth of a barrow-load of soot.

Mr. Griffin, another writer, recommends four barrow-loads of light-brown pasture loam, one barrow-load of sheep's dung, and two of swine's dung. This is to be thrown into a heap, and frequently turned for a year before being used. Mr. Baldwin recommended stripping a good old pasture meadow six inches deep, mixing it with one-half good rotten dung, leaving it to mellow a year before being used. Mr. Dodemeade's receipt for fruiting-pines was, one-half fine fibrous loam, and one half fowls' or sheep's dung, well incorporated. Mr. Hamilton recommended old pasture loam, stripped three inches deep, one-third well-decomposed stable or hotbed dung, and one-tenth of the whole mass wood-ashes. Coming down to more modern growers, we find Mr. Glendinning recommends two parts of turfy loam to one of fresh sheep's or deer's dung, and four of vegetable mould, the mixture to be three months old before use. Mr. Mills used three-fourths strong loam and heath mould in equal proportions, and one-fourth fresh horse-droppings—the whole used in a fresh state. Mr. Forsyth, a great authority in pine-growing, used six parts of turfy loam, chopped up into pieces about the size of walnuts, night soil one part, leaf-mould one part, silver-sand one part. Mr. James Barnes, late of Bicton, used turfy loam, pure and simple, with all the roots and natural vegetation upon it, mixed with a few lumps of charcoal, never breaking nor turning it till it came to the potting bench, and thrusting into the pots heath and grass altogether, with no kind of manure. The loam is taken off dry, about three inches thick, turned upside down, and left a few days to dry. It is then built up like a haycock on a rough foundation of wood, and thatched over to exclude the rain. Mr. David Thomson, of Drumlanrig, almost the latest authority upon the subject, likewise recommends turfy loam from a rocky crag.

It is somewhat singular that all our best modern pine-growers should have come back to what one of the first cultivators advocated as the best soil. Mr. Giles, one of the earliest writers on the pine in England, says, that "the soil should be a rich stiff loam, taken from a well-pastured common, or what is called virgin earth." And adds, notwithstanding the directions given by several authors to make compositions of various soils, "this answers much better, not only for pine-apple plants, but for most other vegetables." Thus after three or four generations, we arrive, by an exhaustive method of trying all else, at the very point where Mr. Giles started in the olden times. Theory and practice alike declare that a rich, light, fibry, sandy loam, used in a fresh rough state, is the best possible soil for pine-growing.

Pine-houses.—The heated pit, or house for pine-growing, is a subject that has received an exaggerated amount of attention for many years past. Most cultivators have had their favourite shapes and sizes. Some of the best, however, have cared but little about such matters. There is a general concurrence of opinion that the houses for

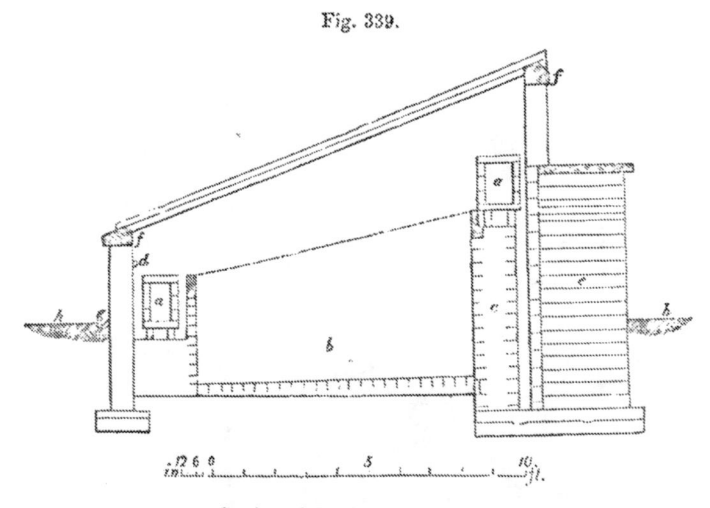

Fig. 339.

Section of the pine pit at Oakhill.

a, a, Pipes.　　b, Bark-bed.
d, Steam pipe for occasional use.
e, Arches, supporting the pathway, occasionally filled with fermenting matter.

f, f, Coping stones to the walls.
g, Gutter to receive the water from the sashes.
h, h, Ground line.

pines should be small and low, rather than large and lofty. But there are also exceptions to this rule. Notably, Mr. Ward, of Bishop's Stortford, who grows his succession pine-plants close to the glass in lean-to houses, and then fruits them in a lofty span-roofed house, from four to six feet clear of the glass. It is necessary to have separate compartments or houses for the growing and fruiting-plants. Many forward all the former in pits and only use houses for the fruiting-pines. Small houses or close pits are certainly best adapted for the rapid strong growth of the young stock. Fig. 339 shows the section of a pit very generally used for the growth of succession-plants, as well as the fruiting of pines. It is the same as those so successfully used at Oakhill many years ago. But any common pit about seven feet deep and six to nine feet wide will grow pines. . If the tank system or hot-water pipes

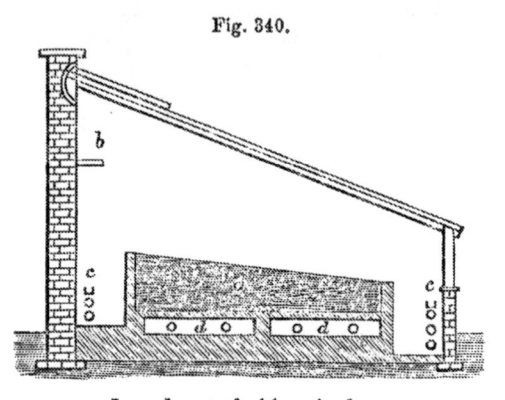

Fig. 340.

Large lean-to fruiting pine-house.

a, a, Bed for planting or plunging the fruiting-plants in. *b,* Shelf for strawberries. *c, c,* Vapour troughs. *d, d,* Pipes for bottom-heating.

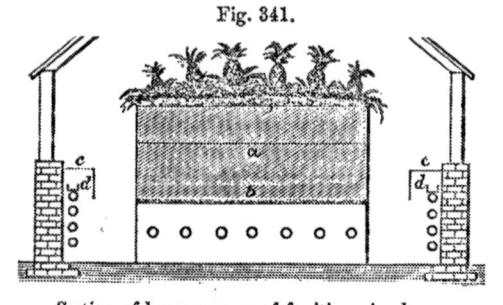

Fig. 341.

Section of large span-roof fruiting pine-house.

a, Bed in which the fruiting-plants are either planted out or grown in pots. *b,* Caithness pavement forming bottom of bed. *c, c,* Shelves for French beans or pot-vines. *d, d,* Vapour troughs.

are used for bottom heat, a less depth will be needed. A clear space of from three to four feet should be left from the surface of the plunging material to the glass. For fruiting-houses this distance must be greater, and may be regulated by the size of the plants.

Figs. 340, 341 are good forms of houses for fruiting-pines. But any other form, provided it is sufficiently lighted and heated, will probably answer equally well.

Success does not depend upon the house, provided it is air-tight and water-proof, but upon the skill of the cultivator. The roofs of pineries are generally rather flat. In a house twelve feet across, a fall of four feet may be given. About 35° is a good pitch. Under a steep roof the plants are in more danger of being scorched by the sun.

Modes of Heating.—Now that the flue is abolished, and steam given up, there are but three means of heating generally used—the tank, hot water, and fermenting materials. Each has its advocates, and success has been obtained by all. The commonest mode of applying fermenting material is illustrated by the accompanying woodcut. Or

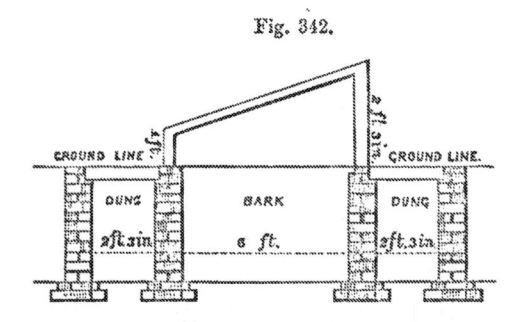

Fig. 342.

the walls of the pit may be pigeon-holed, in the same way as melon and cucumber pits. Perhaps the most scientific mode of applying fermenting materials is that employed at Meudon, near Paris, fig. 343, in which it will be seen the bed of soil is heated by a mass of fermenting dung underneath, and provision is made for the escape of any excess of heat at the sides. Generally pine-growers prefer the heat from fermenting materials. It is kindly nourishing and moist, and the gases generated are cleansing and feeding. Perhaps no heat can be better for application outside. For a plunging medium it is all that can be desired, if it can but be moderated and kept from rising to excess. This is managed by a cautious introduction of fresh plunging materials. Perhaps oak-leaves and tanner's bark are the best and safest fermenting material for growing the roots of pines in. The bed should be partially renewed at the spring potting in February or March. The best mode of proceeding is to turn over the whole bed, still keeping the leaves chiefly at the bottom and the tan at the top. Remove the most rotten part of the leaves by passing them through a rough sieve, then add a foot or two of fresh leaves, and incorporate them with the old; or place the new layer wholly in the bottom of the pit. The tan should be thrown bodily out of the pit, run through a fine sieve, and only the finest rejected; the coarse, with about six inches of fresh tan, to be returned and spread carefully over the leaves. In arranging the tan, keep the bulk of the fresh towards the sides, as it is in the centre that the greatest danger of an excess of heat arises. Half-spent tan, or that which has previously heated, should likewise be employed if it can be had. Notwithstanding all these precautions, over-heating will sometimes occur. This renewal of the materials is a cause of great anxiety to the pine-grower, as an excess of bottom heat is fatal. It must never exceed 90°, 85° being better and safer. Great watchfulness is needed for a few weeks. Thermometers should be plunged in the bed, and if the heat rises, the pot must be instantly shaken from side to side, and the tan drawn away from it. It is well only to half-plunge the pots at first where there is danger, or to insert another pot under the pine pot. When all danger of excess has passed over, re-arrange, and plunge the pots up to the rims. The pine bed may again be renewed, with even more caution and care, in October. These instructions, which are absolutely necessary, reveal the superiority of the tank or hot-water methods of heating the plunging-beds. With these, the bottom and top heat are equally under perfect control. The Meudon mode of applying the fermenting materials

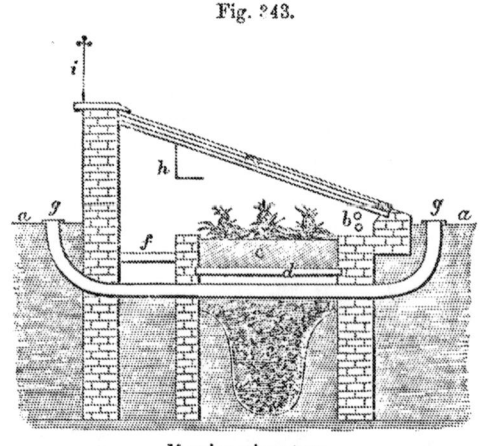

Fig. 243.

Meudon pine stove.

a, a, Ground line. *b,* Hot water-pipes for top-heat. *c,* Bed of peat soil in which the pine-apples are planted. *d,* One of the iron bars for supporting the boarded flooring on which the bed of soil rests. *e,* Vault filled with stable-dung and leaves. *f,* Footpath. *g, g,* Air-holes. *h,* Shelf for strawberries. *i,* Iron rail over which the strawberries are hung when the house is uncovered.

underneath and outside the plunging-beds, is almost as safe as the hot-water method; but the latter, as shown in our sections of fruiting-houses, is undoubtedly the best, and taking into account the labour involved in the management of bark-beds, it is also perhaps the cheapest. It is easy also to retain most of the supposed advantages of plunging in fermenting material without its risks, by having the plunging-beds heated with hot water. Tan or spent leaves, one foot or eighteen inches in depth, for plunging the pots in, may be spread over tanks or pipes. These will wrap the pots or roots in a genial warmth, which will prove most conducive to their health. Tanks may be used in lieu of pipes; their heat is even more genial. The choice between the two may be determined by their relative cost. Wooden tanks soon rot, slate or cement are in danger of cracking and breaking, and iron tanks are dearer than pipes. For surface-heat there is nothing like four-inch hot-water pipes, and the law for pineries should be a large surface of pipes and plenty of boiler power. The heat given off at a high temperature is drier and less genial than that diffused from iron of lower temperature. The upper pipe should either be cast with a trough for the reception of water throughout its whole length, or close-fitting pans may be placed upon it and removed at pleasure. We greatly prefer this to a perforated steam-pipe carried above the pipes to water them, and also steam the house when required; whilst the latter may at times be serviceable, the former is the best mode of maintaining a genial atmosphere.

The Times and Modes of Potting.—The time of potting pines used to be definitely laid down in the treatises upon the subject. March and October were the two seasons; some, again, included May; two or, at the most, three days in the year were devoted to this purpose. On these occasions the pines were potted whether they needed it or not, and those that needed it in the interval had to wait till these charmed seasons. More marvellous, at the March shifting most of the plants were potted backwards—that is, they were taken out of large pots and put into smaller; hence it came to pass that good growers had to pot again in May; otherwise the plants rooted into mattedness before October.

Now, although with pines it is well to have set times for examining them and for general arrangement, especially where fermenting materials are used for bottom heat, the plants should be potted as they require it. Few now adhere strictly to set seasons for potting. Indeed, such seasons are not only injurious to the plants, but are also the means of producing one of the great evils of pine-growing — a glut of fruit at one time, and a scarcity at another. Pot a hundred plants on the same day, and treat them in the same way afterwards, and the chances are that twenty-five of them will ripen together. Therefore, and also for the welfare of the plants, treat pines as most other plants are now treated, and pot them when they want it. Were it practicable to pot two pines every day in the year, it is probable that one might likewise be cut every day. As to the mode of potting, nothing can be more simple. Shift a pine-plant as you would a palm, or any other plant, with equal care of leaf and root. The old practice of tying up the leaves was most injurious; it saved them from breakage at the time, and bruised them for ever afterwards, as sturdy pine-plants cannot be tied up without serious injury, and a weak, drawn-up, flaccid plant is not worth a fresh pot. Suckers should be carefully detached from the old stem; the rugged point of junction smoothed off with a sharp knife; the small scaly bottom-leaves removed by hand for about four or five inches, or as far as sound brown roots appear; then proceed to pot them firmly in 6-inch or 8-inch pots according to their size. The pots should be scrupulously clean, and carefully drained, thus: place one large piece of broken pot, or an oyster-shell, over the hole of the pot, then from one and a half to two inches of drainage of broken bricks, pots, charcoal, or freestone, finished with some oyster-shells broken fine; over this place two inches of the roughest of the turfy loam; then turn the plant carefully out of the pot, and place it in its new quarters, and fill in firmly with the rough loam, using a strong stick, two inches square, to press it firm all round. The soil cannot be rendered too firm. Mr. Barnes recommends the entire rejection of all the soil but the fibre. Every piece of turf as it is placed on the potting-bench receives a violent blow from a stout piece of wood; it is then briskly shaken till all the fine soil is removed, and the fibre is mixed with some rubbly charcoal as the operation of potting proceeds; then the whole soil is an open porous mass of material, readily admitting a free circulation of air and water. We would use exactly the same sort of soil for planting out. As to the size of the pots, only two sizes are now generally used for suckers and for fruiting-plants. The strongest plants are at once shifted from 8-inch pots into 12-inch; the weaker ones from 6-inch into 11-inch pots. It is found that these sizes are large enough to carry the finest fruit. After potting, the plants are immediately plunged in their newly-made bed.

Watering at Root and Top.—This should be at once attended to. As soon as the plants are plunged, they should be watered with soft rain or pond water at the temperature of 80°. Enough should be given to penetrate the ball and moisten the entire soil. It is needless to add that no plant should ever be shifted in a dry state. After the first watering, no more may be needed at the roots for two or three weeks. There is great danger of over-watering newly potted pines. The ball will be surrounded with a mass of new or moist soil, and will draw water from thence. Until the fresh earth is occupied, partially at least, caution must be the signal held over the watering-pot. In fact, in all stages of growth, excess of water must be avoided. Like all other plants, pines should only be watered when the soil is dry, and then thoroughly. For some time after potting, clean water is best. Until the roots "bite" and occupy the new soil, manure-water can do little good and may prove injurious. After they have advanced so far, manure-water only should be given. It has been made of the dung of sheep, cows, deer, and pigeons, and any or all of these, if applied clear and weak, are useful. But the best manure-water for pines is that formed by putting a handful of soot or guano into a four-gallon pot of water. Superphosphate of lime is sometimes used in preference to soot, and probably Meredith's Vine Manure would be equally good. It is also a common practice to place some guano, soot, or liquid manure in the evaporating pan on the hot-water pipes, thus distributing food along with the vapour for the leaves of the plants. This, with the rich odours arising from fermenting materials, has always been valued by pine-growers as imparting that hue and substance to the leaves which is the sure index of robust health. Some even recommend syringing the plants with manure-water overhead. As roots form in the axils of the leaves, there is no doubt that pines may be fed in this manner. It is, however, better to diffuse such chemical fertilizers through the air than apply them directly, in a grosser manner, through the syringe. To a great extent, the same rule will hold good as to sprinkling the leaves of plants with water. Some growers sprinkle incessantly, and others but little. All, however, agree on the importance of a moist atmosphere, unless in the depth of winter and at the flowering and finishing stages. The fruit sets most freely in a tolerably dry atmosphere, and it ought to be flavoured off in the driest air consistent with health. At all other times an atmosphere bordering on saturation may be maintained. Some provide this moisture by its direct application to the leaves and stems, others by filling the houses with steam, while more generate the aqueous vapour by sprinkling the walls, pipes, floor, and every available surface with water. By such means the whole air is slowly, but surely, charged with vapour. The time for this general watering of the air or surface of pine-houses is from four to five o'clock in the afternoon. The houses are then shut up, and the increased heat raises the water, and gives the plants a stimulating vapour bath. During the swelling of the fruit, water is generally applied directly to its surface for several of the summer months. And as, immediately after potting, or during the bright days and frosty nights of March, there is a double drain upon the water of the pine-pits or houses, that of the sun by day, and of the cold glass at night, the sprinkling of paths, walls, &c. should be repeated many times during the day. Double glazing or the slight covering at night of such houses or all houses at high temperature, would not only preserve their heat, but husband their moisture. Such expedients should therefore be adopted for pine-houses.

Manures.—None to be given to the soil, with the exception of bones, roots of grasses, and charcoal, if indeed the latter should be so called. In a liquid state, any stimulating manure, applied clear and weak, such as sewage, animal excrements, and especially guano, and soot-water, may be used. Carbonate of ammonia, at the rate of one ounce to four gallons of water, has likewise been recommended.

Ventilation.—More or less air should be given every day, if the weather will permit of it. In fact, the air of the house should move night and day if possible, and a gradual exchange between the exhausted air within and the free strong air without be constantly going on, so gradually as to renew and move the air without creating draughts. This circulation of air may be carried on without greatly affecting the temperature. It is best effected by admitting a modicum of outside air in front, beneath the hot-water pipes. Before it reaches the level of the plants, it will be warmed and saturated; still it is fresh new air, and will supply the place of that which is exhausted.

Ventilation on a larger scale, to control and regulate temperature, should be provided at the highest point of the house. This provision should be ample, and readily controlled, so as to regulate the heating power of the sun with the utmost facility. During the last or fruiting stages, the flavour of the fruit is improved by thorough ventilation. At other times, unless on the sultriest days, it will be seldom or never desirable to open top and bottom ventilators at once. We would recommend, however, a reversal of the usual order. During the coldest weather give air only in front, and not only at the back.

Shading.—Closely allied to ventilation is the question of shading. In the olden times pines were shaded to excess. Possibly that was the dark penalty paid for disrooting. With the glare of light on large sheets of glass and sashless roofs, some have gone to the opposite extreme, and cried " shade not at all." Of two evils, however, it is wise to choose the least. In this case we must elect either to shade or burn. For an hour on each side of noon it will mostly be useful to break the full force of the sun with thin bunting or matting, or have the leaves of free-growing pines browned or scorched. There is indeed another alternative, the placing of the plants a good way from the glass. Early ventilation, so as to dry the leaves before the sun shines upon them, is likewise a preventive of burning. Still, with all these precautions, slight shading may be necessary for a few hours, for the four hottest months in the year; the less shading, however, the better.

Temperature.—A few general remarks have already been made upon this subject. We propose here giving the temperature of the air at Calcutta, where pines are grown and gathered all the year round, though the heaviest fruit may be said to ripen from April to September. The following are average temperatures, and the extremes range from 53° to 129°:—

Temperature at Calcutta.

	Maximum.	Minimum.
January	84·5	60
February	90	65
March	90·5	71
April	97	77·5
May	95	78·5
June	91·5	81
July	88	80
August	87	80
September	90	80
October	91	75
November	85·5	64
December	81·5	57

The following are the night temperatures recommended by Mr. Glendinning:—

CULTURE OF THE PINE-APPLE.

Monthly Tables of Night Temperatures.

	Succession pits.	Fruit stove.
January	54	65
February	56	68
March	57	71
April	59	73
May	60	75
June	61	76
July	62	78
August	62	78
September	60	76
October	58	73
November	56	69
December	54	65

The following Tables are the day and night temperatures recommended by Mr. Errington:—

	FRUITING PINES.					SUCCESSION PINES.			
	Day Max.	Day Min.	Night Max.	Night Min.		Day Max.	Day Min.	Night Max.	Night Min.
January	70	60	62	55	January	60	50	55	51
February	73	64	65	58	February	63	53	57	53
March	80	70	70	60	March	66	60	62	56
April	84	70	70	62	April	71	62	65	59
May	86	70	72	65	May	75	65	68	63
June	88	70	73	66	June	80	68	70	65
July	90	73	74	67	July	85	70	70	65
August	88	70	73	66	August	83	68	71	63
September	80	68	71	63	September	75	60	66	59
October	75	65	67	62	October	68	58	60	57
November	70	62	65	60	November	62	56	57	54
December	66	60	60	54	December	56	50	55	50

The temperatures recommended by Mr. David Thomson do not greatly vary from these. To succession-plants, for the first four months in the year, he allows a range of from 55° to 75°. For fruiting-plants the range for the same period is 65° to 75°. The summer temperature is higher, reaching for fruiting-plants to much more in May, when from 80° to 100° may be permitted for these plants, only however for a few hours after shutting up, falling to 70° or 75° by midnight. After September, for which month 65° to 70° is given for succession-plants, and, doubtless, at least 5° more allowed to those in fruit, 60° to 65° is quoted for October, and 55° to 60° for November and December. The bottom heat is allowed a range of from 75° to 90°, the latter, however, being the utmost limit; 85° is permitted just after potting, to sink soon after to 80°, which is a good growing average. From 65° to 70° is sufficient bottom heat for succession-plants in winter, and 70° to 75° to fruiters, unless, like the Black Jamaica or Cayenne, they are ripening or swelling fruit, when 80° or 85° may be maintained. Some of the best growers raise the fruiting-plants up to 100° for a few hours on the afternoons of bright days, with a saturated atmosphere, permitting it to fall to 80° or 75° during the night.

Propagation.—This is effected by crowns, gills, suckers, and the old stems. The two first are never resorted to now, unless for the increase of scarce varieties. The same remark is applicable to the last mode of increase. For all practical purposes, the mode of propagating pines is by suckers only. These are produced so numerously, and grow so rapidly, forming strong plants in a few months, that in practice suckers alone are used as a rule to perpetuate or increase the stock. The mode of potting them has been already described. It is best for the suckers not to remove them until the fruit is nearly ripe. For the sake of the fruit, however, they are often taken much earlier, and only one, or two at most, should be left on each plant. They ought to be carefully twisted or cut out at their base, without bending or breaking their higher or softer parts, and potted immediately. Some varieties, however—notably the smooth-leaved Cayenne—are shy in making suckers, and as this is a valuable variety, it is often increased by plunging the old stem, bereft of its leaves, in a horizontal position, in a strong bottom heat. Suckers may thus be forced forth from the axil of each leaf, and a good stock of new plants be got out of the old parent stem.

Varieties.—Modern pine-growers mostly confine themselves to a few varieties: those who value quality chiefly, and are content with ripe pines only during the summer and autumn, grow only Queens and Charlotte Rothschilds. If pines must be had throughout the winter and early spring, the Black Jamaica and smooth-leaved Cayenne must be added to these. Beyond these four it is vain to look for the highest quality. Many, however, grow other sorts for variety and size. For the latter the White Providence is the grandest and heaviest variety. A well grown fruit of this, from 12 to 14lbs. in weight, is a magnificent ornament for the dinner table. The Blood Red is likewise a showy variety, a few of which are often grown for their unique colouring, and when well finished the quality is second or third rate. The chief other varieties are Globes, Sugar-loafs, Envilles, and Antiguas, of various sizes and colours, all of which have been favoured in turn by different growers, and which may be grown by units, while the first four are grown by tens or hundreds. There are several other sorts, such as the prickly Cayenne, which is, however, inferior to the smooth-leaved variety; the Trinidad, which has been grown of good quality and large size, and the Montserrat, which is, however, but another name for different varieties of the Black Jamaica. It is well also to bear in mind that there are several varieties of Queen pine, perhaps the very best being the broad-leaved common Queen, which, when well grown, is the highest flavoured of all pines, unless it be a Charlotte Rothschild full of golden juice.

In purchasing pines it is most important to know something also if possible of the previous history of the plants purchased. The clean stocks of a successful pine-grower are worth their weight in gold. Weak dirty plants are only fit for the rubbish-heap.

Good growers cultivate only the best varieties in each class, and by the double process of constant selection and superior culture, their plants are freighted as it were at starting with all the elements of future success. No operation within the range of horticulture requires more judgment, skill, and caution than the selection of the right varieties of pines, in the best possible condition to start with. Cleanliness and sturdiness are the chief desiderata. To begin with weak, drawn, dirty plants, is to court vexation, failure, and defeat. To the novice we would say, get a pine-grower in whom you can trust to select your plants.

Age of the Fruiting-plants.—In nothing have modern pine-growers so much improved upon those of the past as in the saving of time. From twelve to eighteen months from the suckers most fruit are now cut. Strong suckers alone are chosen to start with, and they are pushed on without let or hindrance until the fruit is perfected; or if checked at all, it is simply to throw them into a fruiting state. Every root and leaf formed is carefully treasured, and becomes the nucleus for other and stronger ones. In one word, pines are now grown by express: rapidity and strength are the main ideas worked up into a rich harvest of luxurious fruit by modern pine-growers.

The Pot versus *the Open-bed System.*—Nearly all our best growers lean to pot culture. The plants are more manageable, and more fruit can be cut from a given space. Even those who plant out their fruiting-plants grow the successional ones in pots. The plan practised at Meudon was to grow the plants in pots in winter, and plant them out on dung-beds for the summer. They were planted out in March and potted again in October. The fruiting-plants were finally planted out in a bed of ten inches of peat in March, and perfected their fruit in that position. At Versailles and other places in France, and at the Royal Gardens at Munich, a similar system is adopted. One of the chief advantages claimed for this system is that suckers are produced in all stages of growth, and that consequently fruit may be cut at all seasons of the year. From pines planted out in low pots at Munich, ripe fruit were cut every month for a period of five years. In several French gardens the suckers are not potted at all. The suckers produced by the fruiting-plants of the previous season are allowed to remain on the old stools till the following March, when they are taken off and planted out in a gentle hotbed. About the month of August they are removed to their fruiting quarters, and planted out in borders of earth about eighteen inches deep, placed over a hotbed of dung or leaves. Good results are thus obtained in France, and it is difficult to see why, with the aid of hot water for bottom heat, the best soil, abundant surface-manuring, and earthing up, a greater weight of fruit might not be grown in a limited space and time by this mode than by any other. The source of bottom heat might be a tank of water or of liquid manure, of the same length and breadth as the interior of the pit, and over this the soil might be supported on a flooring of pierced tiles, so as to admit of the roots passing through them into the liquid manure; or, it might be a bed of stones or coarse gravel, heated by pipes, a mode which has been successfully employed in various parts of the country. The planting-out system is or used to be extensively practised in the Royal Gardens, Frogmore. A bed of leaves was used for bottom heat; the suckers were planted out into beds of soil, and finally transplanted into the fruiting-pots, at distances of two feet apart in the rows.

The Hamiltonian system is admirably adapted for open-bed culture, though it can likewise be practised in pots by using hoops of zinc, or lumps of turf, to enable the stem of the parent plant to be earthed-up to the base of the sucker. The object of the system is to make the new plant of the sucker draw as much strength as possible out of the old magazine of growing force. Hence the sucker is not removed, but a few of the bottom leaves of the old stem are stripped off, until the bottom of the sucker is bared. New soil is then heaped up against it, into which it roots rapidly. The result is that a second fruit is often cut from the same stool within a period of eight or ten months from the first. Another sucker is again left as before, which will produce another plant, and so on in succession until the bed becomes so much elevated or the bottom so exhausted that it must be renewed. In pot-culture it is seldom possible to take more than four fruit from one stool. But plant out, and there seems no limit to the number of fruit that may be cut from each centre of life. Sometimes, even two suckers are left to fruit at once. In the ordinary course, by this system, two fruit may be cut within a year, and another the following year from a sucker produced from the second fruiter. Yet this system can hardly be said to have taken deep root among pine-growers. It has not the neat and orderly appearance so much valued by the craft, and can hardly be expected to produce fruit of such large size as the single-plant system. But, for a constant succession of serviceable fruit, the Hamiltonian system, carried out in beds heated with hot water, is probably unrivalled. There is yet another system—a sort of hybrid between the pot and open-bed—that is, to plant out the fruiting-plants when they are arranged for fruiting. We have seen some splendid pines grown in this manner. Still, take it for all in all, the pot system is the most popular, and probably the best.

Enlarging the Size and Improving the Quality of the Fruit.—This is chiefly done by the highest culture between the flowering and the ripening periods, but the foundation of it all is laid in the sturdy habit and robust health of the plant from the very beginning. Assuming, however, that this has been attended to, a good deal may be done within the time prescribed alone. The fruit should be kept moist when swelling, and the root well fed with manure-water. All suckers not needed should likewise be removed. Any undue development of crown should be arrested by squeezing out its tops. No gills should be allowed at the base of the fruit. Every means must be taken to concentrate the whole power of the plant into the development of the fruit. Having obtained size, the next step is to develop quality. All excess of water, both at top and bottom, must be avoided, and every form of manure vapour weak or rich carefully kept out of the pine-house atmosphere. A dry heat, with abundance of light and air, are the physical and chemical conditions for the manufacture of luscious quality.

Making the Plants show Fruit.—The best general means are great strength of base and short thick leaves. Drawing up long leaves is the readiest means of ensuring sterility. Hence, the opposite condition may be accepted as the preliminary of fertility. The practised eye can generally tell at a glance if the plant means fruit. " Coming events cast their shadows before." It is so with growing pines. A thick stem, short central leaves, a black eye, and deep colour in the heart, all proclaim the coming fruit. Still at times they come forth provokingly slowly. Then a few special aids can be given. Keep the air of the house dry, and the roots warm, venturing even on 90° or 100° bottom heat. Keep the roots without water for a month or six weeks, until the leaves exhibit visible signs of distress. Then suddenly reverse the treatment, and the chances are, that the change will throw the plants into fruit. The air may also undergo great changes of temperature from 55° to 80°. All this will check, and as it were, directly agitate the plants, and sooner or later they will discover what is meant, and throw up their fruit. Should this, however, fail, we have one more powerful means of forcing a show. Cut off the head of the pine-plant at the level of the pot, remove a few of the bottom leaves, put it in a 10-inch pot, plunge in a bottom heat of 85°, and very soon it will throw up a fruit, and often a fine one too.

Retarding of the Fruit.—It is sometimes of the utmost importance to be able to keep back pines for particular occasions, or to avoid a glut. Pines may safely be removed from their fruiting quarters when they are half-coloured, and placed in vineries, or even in a cool, dry room for a month without injury. Mr. Barnes is of opinion that slow-ripening develops quality, and it is well known that pines ripened slowly in vineries are often the very highest flavoured.

The preservation of ripe pines is perhaps best effected by removing the plants with the fruit upon them into a dry and rather warm room, the suckers, if wanted, being of course previously taken off. The fruit alone may also be kept good for six weeks in a fruit-room after they are cut. If required to keep longer than this, the crown should be removed, as any attempt at growth in the latter could only be made at the expense of the fruit.

What Constitutes a Good Pine-apple.—The points of merit are chiefly these :—Respectable size, depth and fulness of pips evenly swelled out from base to summit, a small, sturdy, perfectly upright crown of from three to four inches in height; fruit bright and golden in colour, and heavy in proportion to its bulk; scent strong and flavour exquisite, rich and juicy, or as Mr. Barnes puts it, the juice oozing from the rind as thick as

F F

honey. Queens, with 12 pips deep, and 12 inches high, and 20 round weighing 6 or 8 lbs., with crowns 3 inches high; Black Jamaicas, 7 or 8 pips, 9 or 10 inches deep, and 22 round, with crowns 3 inches high, and the fruit round and well-shaped; and Providences, weighing 12 lbs., with crowns only 4 inches high, are models of excellence in form, size, and quality.

Weights of the Finest Fruits.—The following have been reached by Mr. Barnes, late of Bicton, and though they may have been equalled by others, have seldom or never been exceeded:—

Queens, above	8 lbs.	Green Olive Montserrat	7 lbs.
Providences	14 „	The Trinidad or Russian Globe	10 „
Smooth Cayenne	10 „		
The Black Antigua	11 „	The Old Globe	11 „
Prickly Cayenne	9 „	Black Jamaica	6 „
The Brown Antigua	8 „	The Enville	11 „
Copper Montserrat	8 „		

Insects, to Prevent and Destroy.—"Prevention is better than cure," is never more applicable than as regards the insects on pines. Under good culture, and starting with clean plants and pine-houses, no insects should ever appear. The steam arising from dung and other fermenting materials is looked upon as a specific against insects, and it seems certain that neither scale, white and brown, nor mealy bug, the three great pests of pines, relish a vapour bath heavily charged with ammonia. It must, however, be admitted that these strong fumes will not kill them, unless made too powerful for the well-doing of the plants. The white scale is the worst of the two, and is difficult to eradicate after it is established. Hand-picking, rubbing, and washing, syringing with hot strong soapsuds, at a temperature of 130°, and dipping in various mixtures, are prescribed as certain remedies. Perhaps one of the simplest, and one said to be perfectly efficient, is to syringe the plants over with water, and then, while wet, dust them over, above and below, with equal parts of dry soot and sulphur, and leave the mixture on for three weeks. If this is done at the dead season the plants will not be injured by their medicated coat of penetrating dust. The brown scale may certainly be destroyed by the hot-water remedy. The mealy bug is the worst of all pests of insects on pines. Dustings of strong Scotch snuff, common and Cayenne pepper, on wet foliage, hot water, and a host of other things have been tried for it. One of the best dips for infected plants is three gallons of water, two pounds of soap, eight ounces sulphur vivum, and two ounces of camphor, boiled together for an hour; add three ounces of turpentine to the mixture when it falls to a temperature of 130°; then turn the plant out of the soil, wash the roots clean, prune away any superfluous roots or leaves, and immerse the pine plant, top and bottom, in this hot poison-bath for five minutes. Others add to this mixture two ounces of nux vomica and a quart of strong tobacco-water. Of course plants so treated will look queer for a time, unless the mixture is washed off at once with clean water—which it ought not to be. But they will soon outgrow this effect of the bath, and anything is better than mealy bug. An equally efficient, and more cleanly remedy, is to wash the whole plant over with spirits of wine, diluted with half water. With a long-handled paint-brush in skilful hands, this may be done with considerable despatch. Part of the liquid must be allowed to penetrate the axils of the leaves. This mixture will not disfigure the most tender foliage, and kills every bug that it touches. Red spider is sometimes seen on pines, but never where the culture is skilful. It is readily destroyed by sulphur fumes from hot-water pipes.

Diseases and Malformations.—The pine-apple is singularly free from disease; in fact, under the conditions here prescribed, no plant is more easily grown, or more healthy. Occasionally, however, when suckers are removed too early from the parent plant, and potted before they have become firm, a species of canker will be developed which will cripple, if not ruin, the plant, running right through its centre, and causing even the fruit-stalk to wither up before the fruit is ripe. The best preventive is never to pot immature suckers; remedy for canker there is none.

Another peculiar disease occasionally affects the fruit : all is fair and beautiful outside, but when cut open, instead of the viscid rich juice so much prized, out rushes a mass of semi-putrid-looking water. This may be called fruit-dropsy; it arises perhaps from an excess of moisture during the flowering period, or a plethora of water at either root or fruit during the swelling or ripening period. Its cause, however, is not certainly known, and there is no cure for the disease once it is developed. A dryish atmosphere, free ventilation, and plenty of sunlight during the entire period of flowering, are the likeliest antidotes to fruit-dropsy.

Malformation may be classified under an excess of suckers, the multiplication of gills, double or cockscomb crowns, excessively large crowns, and irregular development of the pips. Most of these evils are simply remedied; the first two by timely thinning, or their entire removal if not needed for increase. The gills, as a rule, should be taken off. A cockscomb crown can never be changed into a regular crown, but its sides may be shortened by twisting out the centre, and their numbers reduced, or the grotesque form stamped out of a collection by never propagating from plants that have once formed such crowns. The crown may be kept small by inserting a small sharp knife into its centre shortly after the pine has flowered, and turning it sharply round, when the centre will be cut out. Plants with many crowns may have the worst-set ones removed in an early stage, leaving one only in the best position. The best means of securing a regular development of all the pips is to take every care against drip, cold draughts, an excess of vapour, and scorching, during the period of inflorescence.

Doings among Pines for every Month in the Year.

JANUARY.

Start the first batch of Queens for ripening in June. These will succeed the winter-fruiting varieties. About half of the stock of Queens should be started now. If a few Black varieties or Cayennes are started with them, they will prolong the fruiting season and give a pleasing variety. Choose the strongest plants for the first batch of fruiters; attend to coverings, &c.; water with care, and be sparing with water in the atmosphere; maintain a brisk genial heat for the fruiting-plants and a low temperature for the main stock of successions; keep, however, the winter stock of these moving on.

FEBRUARY.

Most of the fruiting-plants started last month will show now; as soon as they have done so, water more freely, increase the heat, and diffuse more water throughout the atmosphere. Keep Black pines that are changing colour by themselves, or remove them to a vinery or other forcing-house to finish; cut and preserve ripe fruit; give the succession-stock more warmth as the sun strengthens; prepare material for the renewal of the beds, potting, &c.; shift the most forward plants; turn the beds; attend to covering and watering; see that no plant is potted dry; let all such be soaked thoroughly with manure-water two or three days before potting, to soak every portion of the ball; attend to covering; give more heat and moisture.

MARCH.

Start a second batch of Queens; pot the strongest of the winter fruiters into their fruiting-pots, that they may be filled with roots at starting time in September and October; keep up the heat; fill steaming troughs, and maintain a genial moisture; renew the bed for the fruiting-plants; water freely, but avoid excess; cut ripe fruit; pot the general stock of succession-plants, Queens, Blacks, Cayennes, &c.; if practicable, give the Black pines 5° more heat than the others; renew the beds; attend to coverings.

APRIL.

Push on the fruiting-plants; give water more freely at the roots; guard against any excess of bottom heat; sprinkle paths, plunging bed, or any vacant space frequently on bright days. Charge the evaporating troughs with manure-water; remove all gills from the bottom of the fruit and the stems; take off and pot superfluous suckers from plants swelling their fruit; water with guano-water; encourage a free steady growth among succession-plants; cover and water with care; renew or turn the linings.

MAY.

Rest, if possible, the Black pines intended to fruit in winter; they ought now to have a cool house for themselves. As this is the great growing month for the general stock of pines, fruit swells and plants grow more freely in May than in any other month; hence all our growing forces of heat, moisture, and stimulants should be applied most fully during this month. The temperature of fruiting-houses may be run up to a hundred for a few hours in the afternoon and evening; the atmosphere may be kept saturated in fruiting-houses; manure-water may be sprinkled everywhere, and the syringe freely applied overhead; some of the plants started in January will begin to change colour towards the end of the month, these must be at once removed to a cooler and airier house; the most of the first batch of Queens will ripen next month; if wanted earlier, they must be started in December or November; if later, in February or March; the second batch of Queens are mostly started in March. By starting a batch of Queens every two months from December to April, a succession of fruit can readily be had from June to November; two startings will generally suffice for the summer and autumn supply, as the plants will seldom all fruit together. If a few Blacks are introduced with each lot of Queens, the supply of ripe fruit will with greater certainty be rendered continuous. The first batch of fruiters will yield a crop of suckers for fruiting in from twelve to fifteen months after they are potted; the later batches will yield suckers to succeed them; the winter and spring fruiters will succeed these, and thus the season of ripe pines may be made to meet at both ends. March and April are the most likely months for blanks to occur. The succession-plants must also make hay while the sun shines in May. Pot any plants that require it, and push all on to a maximum of strength throughout the month.

JUNE.

Cut and remove the first batch of Queens; start the first batch of Black Jamaicas, Cayennes, or other similar sorts; keep a genial heat to the second lot of Queens; water freely and saturate the air with manure-water; syringe the fruit as soon as it is out of flower; grow on succession-plants sturdy and strong; give all the light and air possible; avoid scorching by free ventilation and partial shade; pot any plants that require it.

JULY.

Remove any ripe fruit to a cooler house; attend to gills and crowns, remove the former, and regulate the latter; keep a high moist atmosphere, and shut up early in the afternoon, syringing freely; push on succession-plants; pot suckers.

AUGUST.

Start the second lot of winter and spring fruiting-pines, the smoother-leaved Cayenne being the best for the season, either in the end of the month or the beginning of the next; top-dress the fruiting Queens with rich soil; water constantly with manure-water; shift succession-plants; pot the general stock of Queens and other suckers; gradually lessen the amount of moisture in the air of pits to ripen growth already made.

September.

Shift some of the strongest succession-plants into their fruiting-pots; pot another batch of winter-fruiters to be shifted into their fruiting-pots in March and started in September and October, to succeed those started in June and July; keep up a regular genial temperature; water still with manure-water; cut and remove ripe fruit; pot suckers, and gradually mature the growth of succession-plants.

October.

Pot all the suckers of the winter sorts that can be got; push them on rapidly till the end of April; rest them in May and June, and start them into fruit in July; prepare for renewing, or lessen the fruiting-bed; keep the plants near to the light; keep the plants quite dry when in flower, and reduce the summer moisture considerably; water them, however, freely at the root; reduce the temperature of the general stock of succession-plants, with the exception of the growing Black varieties.

November.

Keep up the temperature of the fruiting-houses; water more sparingly; allow the steaming-pans to become dry; sprinkle the paths when requisite, and thereby nourish the swelling fruit; cut and remove those that are ripe; renew the bed, if not already done; allow the general stock of succession-plants to rest quietly or advance slowly.

December.

Start the first batch of Queens, if required early in May; attend to the watering of swelling fruit; cut and remove ripe ones; cover at night if the weather should prove severe, and avoid excessive firing, which is injurious to the plants and robs the air of its moisture; keep succession-plants quiet, with the exception of the winter-fruiters, which must be kept growing without being driven fast throughout the winter; renew beds and make up linings.

We have advisedly refrained from specifying temperatures or adverting to ventilation. For the former we refer to the Tables, pp. 428, 429; for the latter to the section on Ventilation, page 427.

Pine-growing in the Open Air in England.—The honour of originating this bold idea, and embodying it in successful practice, belongs to the veteran pine-grower, Mr. James Barnes, late of Bicton, Devon. Over twenty years ago, this distinguished cultivator startled the gardening world by sending up to London pine-apples grown and ripened out of doors, for which he was awarded the large silver medal by the Royal Horticultural Society; this was on the 7th of September, 1847, when Mr. Barnes exhibited a Montserrat pine 5 lbs. weight, and an Antigua 5 lbs. 5 oz., both grown and ripened in the kitchen-garden at Bicton. In the next year the following fruit were cut:—

July	7.	Two Queens, whose united weights were		8 lbs.	6 oz.
,,	18.	One Queen, whose weight was		4 ,,	0 ,,
,,	28.	,, ,, ,,		4 ,,	8 ,,
Aug.	11.	,, ,, ,,		4 ,,	0 ,,
,,	24.	,, ,, ,,		4 ,,	7 ,,
,,	21.	,, Enville ,,		6 ,,	2 ,,
,,	24.	,, Queen ,,		4 ,,	8 ,,
,,	31.	,, ,, ,,		4 ,,	8 ,,
Sept.	26.	,, Enville ,,		6 ,,	0 ,,
,,	4.	,, Montserrat ,,		4 ,,	8 ,,
,,	8.	,, ,, ,,		5 ,,	0 ,,

Others were cut at intervals from 3 lbs. to 4 lbs. each. The method of procedure was as follows:—About the middle of May a place was prepared for the plants on a south border; a trench was formed from five to six feet wide at top and about two feet at bottom, of sufficient depth to protect the plants from the wind. Three bricks on edge were then placed at regular distances in the trench in the form of a triangle for the pots to stand upon to ensure efficient drainage. Then the pine plants, which had finished blooming, and had been wintered in a pit heated with dung and leaves, at a temperature of from 50° to 60°, were brought out and placed on the bricks. The spaces between the pots and the sides of the trench were then filled up to the rims of the pots, with half-spent leaves. Owing to the cold rains, however, these leaves never heated. A layer of charred hay or grass was then spread over all to absorb and retain the solar heat. The plants received no other protection whatever. The weather continued dark, stormy, and rainy. On the 1st of July ice was actually found at 6 A.M. Such plants as heliotropes, dahlias, French beans, and even pelargoniums, were blackened by frost in September; but the pines received little check, and swelled well. The suckers also were clean and strong, and were potted in the first week of October; several of them fruited in the open ground next year. Some of the fruit cut out of doors in 1848 were produced by suckers taken from the plants grown out of doors the previous year. All the out-of-door fruit had pretty little crowns, and the fruit was of good quality. Mr. Barnes continued the practice for many years with similar success. We do not advance it as a system that can be generally adopted; still it proves what can be done, and is interesting and instructive. Possibly even more could be accomplished by giving the plants a hotbed to grow upon. This much seems certain, that the amateur or suburban gardener who can command a strong fruiting-plant to start with, a barrow-load of hot dung, and one of Rendle's Round Plant Protectors, need never despair of enjoying a pine-apple.

CHAPTER XIV.

THE GRAPE VINE.

The grape vine is a deciduous climber, indigenous or cultivated in a considerable portion of the temperate parts of the northern hemisphere. It is found wild in Greece, Turkey in Asia, Persia, the Morea, near the Black and Caspian Seas, and in many other places; but the countries in which it is found in the highest degree of perfection are Armenia and Syria. In Armenia and Syria, judging from their latitudes, the mean temperature of the coldest winter month in the region of vine culture is probably between 45° and 50°, and the mean temperature of the warmest summer month between 75° and 80°. It is certain, however, that the vine will bear a much lower winter temperature than 45°; for on the hills in Germany, where several kinds are cultivated with success, and the vines are every winter buried under the snow, the temperature for two or three months cannot be much above 32°. It is also found in our forcing-houses that the vine will bear a summer temperature of between 70° and 80°. It may, we think, be assumed that the vine is not calculated to sustain uninjured a winter temperature much below 40°; and this is confirmatory of the excellence of the practice of British gardeners, in wintering the shoots of vines grown under glass under some kind of protecting cover: such as between outer and inner front sashes, or tied loosely up in mats or in thatch, so as to keep them quite dry without excluding the air.

What interests us most is the ground temperature of the countries where it flourishes best; and taking the country of the Muscats, the kinds which require the most heat to bring them to maturity in this country, we find in Sicily the ground temperature to be 66° for the season of growth, 80° for the season of ripening, and 55° for the season of rest; while in Paris, which may be considered the country of the more hardy varieties, such as Muscadines, Sweetwaters, Hamburgs, and the like, we find the ground temperature to be for the season of growth 58°, for the season of ripening 66°, and for the season of rest 41°. With such incontestable facts as these before us, it seems almost irreconcilable with fact that there should be gardeners in this country, and clever grape-growers too, who contend that ground heat is not only unnecessary for the early-forced vine in this country, but that artificially applied it is positively injurious to its well-being. Before any reliable opinion can be pronounced upon this subject, it is necessary that the ground temperature of the soil and subsoil in which and over which the plant is growing should be accurately ascertained, and then no doubt it will be discovered that some soils are much warmer than others, and hence, though artificial ground temperature may not be needed in one place, it may be indispensable in another. Now, the ascertained average ground temperature of London, as established by the careful experiments of the late Mr. R. Thomson, is for the season of growth 55°, for that of ripening 62°, and for the season of rest 42°. Compare these figures with the temperatures before given for Sicily and Paris, and we find that the natural conditions of the soil of this country, so far as temperature is concerned, are not suitable to the cultivation of the vine; and hence the reason why it so rarely attains anything like maturity in the open air.

If, then, the ground temperature of the soil of Britain is unsuitable to the growth of the vine in its natural season, when the solar influences of light and heat are in its favour, it certainly seems unreasonable to expect, when we reverse the order of cultivation and force the vine into growth in the dead of winter rather than in the spring, that it will progress so satisfactorily as it would with a genial natural ground temperature. But we have bottled up in the body of the earth a constant source of heat. We know that beyond the influence of atmospheric changes the temperature of the ground generally increases, and that the deeper we go the greater the heat becomes; hence the late Mr. Archibald Gorrie, a gentleman of no mean authority in horticultural matters in his day, utilized the head of a well by keeping greenhouse plants in glazed frames over the mouth of it; and Mr. Loudon recommended that pits for the protection of half-hardy plants should be connected with a series of tunnels, through which the ground heat could be carried to protect them. Hence, upon the sandstone formation, the oolite, and even the worked coal measures, it is not unreasonable to assume the ground temperature is naturally greater than upon the London clay or similar formations. Four years ago, a gentleman on the Peak of Derbyshire had a vinery erected, and, wishing to have grapes grown in the best possible manner, he called to his assistance Mr. Speed, now gardener at Chatsworth, to make the border and plant the vines; and the extraordinary progress which those vines have made is something to call for special remark by relating a circumstance which bears upon the subject of ground temperature. In excavating for the border the workmen came upon the mouth of worked coal mines, which was taken advantage of to form a complete drain for the border. We, however, think it is something more than a drain, and that the latent heat, which is ever escaping from the shaft and permeating the drainage substratum of the border, plays a much more important part in promoting the complete luxuriance of those vines than even the drainage itself. From these vines Muscat bunches 3lb. to 5lb. in weight are not an unusual occurrence; while Barbarossas of 9lb., and Hamburgs and black Alicantes of proportionate size are not unusual. These weights, be it observed, are the result of amateur cultivation, so that larger results might be fairly anticipated from skilled professional management.

As has been before remarked, vine roots in the valley of the Thames, if not prevented by paving or concreting the bottom of the borders, go at once into the gravel beneath. There they find a congenial temperature, free from atmospheric influences, and hence the vines may be forced year after year without sustaining much injury.

Other vines, where the necessity for bottom heat is ignored, may be similarly situated—that is, with the roots deep in the earth—and hence beyond injury; but make one of the modern fashionable borders eighteen inches to two feet deep, leave that unprotected through the winter or early forcing season, and blind and spindled bunches will probably be the result. However, the vine is a generous plant that will endure almost any amount of ill-treatment and yet produce fruit; but if the best fruit is desired, why, then the best means to secure it—the means which deserve success—must be carried out. Now ground heat, in its application to the production of early grapes, is not a modern discovery. Perhaps the man who first thought of growing early grapes from plants established in pots was the first to give it practical application. He could not introduce the plant into a warmed atmosphere without something approaching the natural conditions being realized, and those who were the most successful growers of pot grapes soon ascertained that bottom heat, carefully applied, was the main hinge of success in their cultivation. Thus we progressed, until with thinking and advanced grape-growers the most economical means of applying bottom heat became the feat to be accomplished.

The first step in this direction was the husbanding of the heat stored in the earth by the summer sun, by covering the vine border early in the autumn, so as to prevent its escape; the second, by forcing the heat of the leaves, dung, and other fermenting material placed upon the border to travel contrary to its natural bent—viz., downwards; and the third, by instituting artificial means, such as inside and covered borders, and sub-heated borders, to secure the means of obtaining the desired ground temperature. Here it is not necessary to detail the various ways which were resorted to. The Dutch gardeners, with their dung-heated pits, were not the least successful—of which examples might be seen at Highlands, near Chelmsford, at Lord Hill's in Shropshire, and at Wolverstone Park, near Ipswich.

Means to secure bottom heat, but of a rather secondary nature, were devised in connexion with Mr. Mearn's chambered borders at Welbeck, nearly forty years ago. The first really grand scheme for sub-heating a vine border was that of Sylvester, as carried out for Edward Strutt, Esq., now Lord Belper, at Kingston Hall, in Nottinghamshire. Here the borders are formed entirely upon brick arches, heated by hot-water pipes, the spaces underneath them being sufficient for a man to walk upright. The cost of this arrangement was something enormous, many thousands of pounds being expended; but the results, though enormous crops of grapes have been produced, have not been so satisfactory as to the quality of the crop as could be desired. So convinced was Mr. George Westland, who had the charge of these vineries for about eight years, that the isolating of vine borders was not the best plan that could be adopted, that he has propounded a counter-scheme, which will be mentioned hereafter, and which appears to possess many elements of success. Then we have the plan adopted by Mr. William Thomson, and recommended in his 'Practical Treatise on the Grape Vine.' This consists of a vault some eighteen inches deep, covered in with paving stones supported by brick walls, and traversed by hot-water pipes about a yard apart, according to the width of the border. These are heated, when forcing commences, so as to raise the temperature of the soil of the border to about 60°, and at that it remains until such time as the vines are in bloom, when it is gradually increased, until during the ripening process it attains, according to the kind of grape grown, 70° to 80°, the latter temperature being necessary for the full maturation of the Muscats.

Now, the objections to this kind of heating are threefold. First, unless the pavement be cemented and made perfectly impervious to the roots of the vines, they pass through into the chamber beneath, and so long as the moisture is kept up they increase and multiply to a great extent, and the vines grow vigorously; but directly the moisture is withdrawn, a process necessary to the proper maturation of the crop, the grapes begin to " shank and spindle," and the crop never attains full maturity. Secondly, without very careful management, there is the danger of the border becoming over-heated, and the crop suffering in that way. Thirdly, if the hot-water pipes get out of order, it is next to impossible to get to them for repairs. Under these circumstances, Mr. Westland, who has had practical illustration of all that we have said against the plan of isolating and sub-heating, recommends that the heating pipes, instead of being placed beneath the border, should be placed in a trench in front of it, from which, at right angles, earthenware socket pipes properly jointed in cement shall be placed thirty inches apart, through which the heat will pass into the house, and thus keep up a constant circulation of warmed air into the house, and at the same time give the necessary heat to the border. An arrangement of this kind will admit of easy management at all times, and the heat of the border may be increased or decreased accordingly as the valves connected with the pipes inside the house are opened, partly opened, or shut. It is also proposed that this arrangement shall act as a system of ventilation, by which a stream of warmed air shall at all times, night and day if necessary, be forced into the house. This system we consider as near perfection as possible, and by it an expensive apparatus is not used for a few months in the forcing season, but may be used throughout the year if considered expedient; in fact, by this system the sub-heating of the border becomes a part, and a very important one, of the atmospheric heating of the house.

Going to the practical application of the system, the bottom of the border space is supposed to be concreted; the conduits are laid, and over them, in ridge-and-furrow style, the draining material of the border, through which the heat circulates and warms the overlying soil. Of course it is necessary that a border of this kind should be protected from cold rains through the winter, and for that purpose either glass frames, wood shutters, or thatch may be used, the first of course being the most desirable material, and perhaps the cheapest, inasmuch as it may be used to forward other crops when not required for the border.

One other system of heating may be named, and, as it is practised by Mr. M. Henderson, of Coleorton, Leicestershire, the most successful exhibitor of early grapes in England, it is not without its merits, and it is of cheap and easy application where other systems could not be practised. The system presupposes the complete protection of the borders from cold rains, and then, at the time of commencing to force, it receives a thorough soaking of weak manure-water at the temperature of 80°: the first watering will raise the temperature to 60°, and the second and third, following some weeks afterwards, will increase it to 70° or more if necessary. In this way Mr. Henderson has succeeded in exhibiting grapes at the early metropolitan shows with almost undeviating success, and with the further advantage that few of his compeers have been able to bring their fruit to the table at that early season in such a state of complete finish. Of course this is not entirely attributable to the use of warm water for raising the temperature of the soil, though no doubt it played an important part.

Vine Soils and Vine Manures.—Few plants in cultivation are more pliable than the vine; for, whether perched upon the side of a mountain, or with its roots lying in the bed of a sewer, it will, so long as those roots are not in stagnant water or a cold ungenial soil, produce fruit. It may not be the best in the world, or, judged by a proper standard, any credit to the grower; but still with the majority the produce may pass as grapes, to which too frequently the estimate of sour may be applied without any stretch of imagination. But for the production of grapes of the finest quality certain conditions must be complied with, and those are—first, that the soil in which the plants are growing, and if possible the subsoil also, shall be free from stagnant water; secondly, that mechanically its qualities shall be free and porous; and thirdly, if grapes of superior quality are desired, it shall be free from rich, raw, and stimulating manures, and yet contain sufficient stimulant of a permanent character, such as bones, charcoal, and burnt earth, to yield the food necessary for the proper and permanent sustenance of the vine.

Within the last quarter of a century various nostrums have been prescribed for the growth of this plant, some recommending one mixture, some another; but, in plain truth, the more simple the compound—so long as the right ingredients are used—the more certain the success. If we go to the valley of the Thames or the Mersey, or if we procure the alluvial deposit of any of our great rivers, more especially where the "tidal wave" serves, and it is rich in vegetable matter, we may make sure the vine will grow in it. We mention the tidal wave, and we do so because we have a conviction that the vine does not object to, but rather luxuriates in, a "taste of the brine." Go to Brighton, to Garston, or, for a more recent example of success, to Glammis Castle near Forfar—where the grapes were grown which attracted so much attention at the last International Fruit Show (1869) at Edinburgh—or go to many places which we could name on the coast of England and Wales, and you will find good grapes, and that almost independently of any attention that may be devoted to them. It would be easy to name a place near Bangor, where grapes in the most extraordinary quantities are grown year after year, and where, too, at times we have seen them of very superior quality. And what are the conditions of their cultivation? Why, first, that the substratum of the border is a dried rivulet, from which the tiny mountain stream has been diverted for the purpose of building the vinery, though in storm times it overflows and floods the border, laying it under water two or three times in the season for a day or two together; and secondly, that the drainage of the border is of the most complete description—not an ounce of superfluous water hanging for many hours in the soil after the storm has abated. Indeed, it may almost be laid down as a rule that you cannot over-water the vine, so long as the water is not cold and can have free egress from the border.

In an indirect manner the evidence above cited shows the indispensable necessity of complete drainage for the vine border. You may make it on the bed of an occasional rivulet, so long as the water is not dammed back, so as to become stagnant; but let the water once hang in the soil, and every chance of success in the cultivation of the grape is at an end. Now in the valley of the Thames—and in that term we include its course from Oxfordshire to the Nore—you may make vine borders as elaborately as you please, you may procure the finest soils and the best manures, and yet, if you do not confine the roots by concreting the bottom and walling the sides of the border, they will immediately pass through it into the red sand and gravel beneath. So convinced was the late Mr. John Willmot of Isleworth of this fact, that for many years prior to his death he abandoned the making of vine borders altogether; and, merely trenching the ground over and adding a barrow-load of fresh compost to each vine at the time of planting, he grew, if not "sensational" grapes, such as commanded the best price at all times in Covent Garden Market, which may be regarded as a complete proof of the success of his plan. Journey we now to the confines of Hertfordshire, to the hills adjoining Barnet, Finchley, and Colney Hatch; and there nothing more is often necessary than to provide proper drainage, trench the ground, dig out a hole, and plant the vine, and success is certain. These may be considered the natural conditions of the vine; and yet there are other soils, to external appearance equally suitable, in which the vine will not grow at all, or so indifferently as to be almost worthless. The gardener of a nobleman in Gloucestershire, a person of considerable intelligence, at the recent (1869) Horticultural Congress at Manchester, endeavoured to account for this by attributing the failure to the presence of magnesian limestone in the soil; but, unfortunately for this theory, the vine in its natural state delights in the calcareous rock, while some of the finest grapes in Britain are growing in the soil taken from the side of a limestone rock. In the face of such evidence of course the theory falls to the ground, as being altogether untenable.

In the formation of the vine border, however, we cannot always procure the soil we would like, and therefore we must use what we can get. For choice, we should take the turfy loam of a sheep walk skinned not more than four inches thick from the face of the rock, and this so rich in fibrous matter as to form a complete mat of roots; then next to that we would take old turf from any dry elevated spot, the conditions approaching those before described as nearly as possible; and thirdly, we would take old turf from the bank of a river, always premising that the fibre of the turf shall be thick and dense, and the spot from which it is taken is high and dry, except at flood tides. In point of quality, the loam should be what is called medium—that is, neither too light nor yet containing much clay, though the latter element may be corrected by an additional admixture of lime-rubbish and burnt earth at the time of forming the border.

For a vine border to retain its active qualities for a long series of years, light sandy soil should never be used; for, though the vines may maintain a strong and even luxuriant habit for seven or ten years, they will generally, at the expiration of that time, begin to fail; while a border properly prepared from good sound loam will retain its invigorating properties for a century or more.

The soil selected, the next thing is to cart it home, and that should be done either in the autumn before the rains set in, or otherwise during the dry weather of April or May. In either case, convey it to some convenient spot where it can be charred and laid up until it is desired to form the border.

When we speak of charring, we do not mean that operation to be carried out in the full acceptation of the term; but it is of the first importance that the soil of a vine border should be submitted to sufficient heat to destroy all insects and their ova that may be in it, and also the roots of all perennial weeds. This will be best effected by providing such garden refuse as old pea sticks, the prunings of trees, roots, weeds, &c., and forming them into a conical heap, with provision for lighting in the centre. These fire cones should be of considerable size, say, not less than 4ft. in diameter at the base, and as much in height, and they should also contain some large pieces of wood, that will burn for some time, and throw out a strong heat. These cones being provided, proceed to build up the turf over the wood to the thickness of a foot or fifteen inches, packing it close together, but not breaking it any more than can be avoided. Then light the fire, making a hole somewhere near the top of the cone for a draught, and vents may be made in other parts of the heap with a crowbar or similar implement, so as to cause the fire to spread regularly through the mass. Let it, however, be thoroughly understood that nothing more than a thorough heating of the soil is necessary, and therefore the fire need not burn briskly, and fresh turf may be added so long as it can be heated to the proper temperature. When the fire has subsided, pack the soil into a narrow ridge, so that it may be exposed to atmospheric influences, but at the same time be protected from heavy rain until such time as the border is to be formed. Then to every six cubic yards of the turf it will be necessary to add one load of dry horse-dung, two yards of brick or plaster-rubbish—the latter being the best—two quarters of oyster-shells, and one quarter of each of charcoal and inch bone. These ingredients should be intimately mixed together by turning twice or thrice for a fortnight before the time the vines are to be planted; but at the same time let it be remembered it is not desirable to break the loam into pieces less than the size of the fist, neither should it be trampled upon during the operation any more than can be avoided. As a rule, the last turning should take place about a week before the vines are to be planted, and then, if it is April or May, and the soil is in proper condition, the mass will heat sufficiently to yield a very nice bottom heat, a circumstance upon which the vigorous growth of the vines when planted is in some measure dependent.

A border thus prepared would be as good as could be desired, as it would not only be a suitable chemical combination of manures, but also a mechanical arrangement of parts which would secure perfect porosity for any series of years, and at the same time be in a slowly decomposing state. This is the great secret of forming the vine border, and those materials are the best which for the longest period shall maintain a slow process of decomposition. So long as decomposition is going on, so long will the elements necessary for vegetable nutrition be formed, and so long will the vines prosper; but directly decomposition ceases, the feeding properties of the soil are exhausted, and to the plant the natural consequences follow.

To the component parts of the border which we have indicated, there is only one addition that we should like to make, and that is, after the soil has been charred, lay it six or nine inches thick in a covered shed, and let sheep be folded upon it for a fortnight or three weeks. This is going back to the days of Speechley, for he recommended that sheep should be folded upon the turf for some time before it was taken from the pasture, and he was not wrong in the recommendation. So far we have spoken of a vine border, such as we should prefer, and fortunately, all the parts except the turfy loam can be easily procured; and if that cannot, why then the best that can be met with must be made use of. The sides of roads and old commons, building sites, and similar places, yield fair turfy loam, but rarely such as will come up to the quality we should select. If, however, the best that can be procured is taken and prepared as we have directed, adding more lime-rubbish and charcoal if the soil is heavy, or less if it is light, a good approximation to our standard may be ensured. Of all things avoid a light sandy soil without fibres and rich stimulating manures. With such a border you may grow strong rampant vines for a few years, but their vigour will be of short duration, and the grapes of inferior quality. To produce grapes of really superior quality, a sound loam is indispensable, securing its porosity and mechanical action by such ingredients as we have recommended to be mixed with it.

Propagating and Planting.—Having prepared the border, our next duty will be to get ready the young vines so as to have them in vigorous health at the most suitable time for planting. Some good cultivators plant strong two or three-year-old vines when they are in a dormant state, as at that time the roots may be shaken clean out of the soil, and spread in the most uniform manner in the newly-prepared border. This is a very good plan, especially if the border at the time of planting is of a genial temperature, say 70° to 80°, or if fermenting material can be so placed at the commencement of the growing season as to bring it to that temperature. Then the plants will start vigorously; but if not, the check consequent upon the shaking is one which the vine in a cold border takes a long time to recover. Again, the vine may be cut down and started in the pot in which it had grown the previous season; and then when it has made a strong shoot, two or three feet long, it may be planted out, loosening so many of the roots as will enable you to distribute them in the new soil without subjecting the plant to any very severe check. Still a check occurs, and though such a proceeding may be sanctioned by custom, it is much better for the present and permanent well-being of the plant that it should be avoided.

Apart from these checks at the time of planting, we have the conviction that a properly treated young vine makes a greater quantity of young roots the first season than at any subsequent period of its history; and therefore, not to make use of them by the most careful nursing is as absurd as to shake the plant out of the soil, and thus destroy them. We have tried the experiment on many occasions, and have invariably found that a properly managed young vine in the first season's growth would make as strong a plant, and we believe an infinitely better rooted one than a yearling or two-year-old plant cut down and treated in the usual manner. Those who feel sceptical about the profuseness of the roots in the first season's growth, have only to take a yearling plant and a spring-rooted plant, and grow them on together, and if, when both have attained the height of three feet, the young plant has not the best and most vigorous roots, their experience will be different from our own. The fact then being established, it follows as a natural consequence, that it must be better to plant a vine the first season of its growth, than by keeping it to run the risk of losing that "wig" of roots which is so essential to its permanent success. Hence we say, take the young vine. This we know is contrary to received opinion. But never mind—we speak from experience extending over a practice of nearly forty years.

The grape vine is propagated in several different ways: by eyes or cuttings, by layers, by grafting and budding, and also (for raising new varieties) by seed. The first step, however, towards complete success is to prepare a bed of fermenting material, such as properly sweetened dung, or dung and leaves, or in their absence, sweet tan. The bottom heat should not be less than 80°, nor should the atmospheric temperature fall much below 70°, while it may rise to 85° or 90° with advantage with sun heat.

As a rule, more plants are raised from eyes or cuttings than in any other manner, and they are thus prepared: selecting vigorous shoots, which should be of the previous season's growth, and thoroughly matured, take the shoot in the left hand, and with a sharp knife make a cut from the underside upwards, one inch above the bud, and then, holding the bud firmly between the thumb and finger, make another clean cut in the same direction, the same distance below the bud. In this manner, with a good knife, a quantity of eyes may soon be prepared. Then make ready a quantity of 3-inch pots, placing in the bottom of each a piece of turf and a pinch of soot to check the worms, fill up the pot with rich sandy half-decayed loam, press in the eye half an inch below the finished surface of the soil, and the work is done. So proceed, of course naming or numbering the different varieties as you go on, until the requisite number of pots have been provided. Then take the pots to the hotbed, and placing them in a regular and systematic manner, cover them over an inch deep with cocoa-nut fibre, or in the absence of that, with fine ashes or leaf-mould. If the mould with which the pots are filled is in a proper state, no water, beyond a mere sprinkling on sunny days, will be required until the plants start into active growth, which will be in a month or six weeks, according to the time the eyes were started or the parent vines might have been forced the preceding season. When the young plants get into free growth, encourage them in every manner by maintaining the necessary bottom heat, and also a sweet brisk atmospheric temperature.

Planting the Vines.—Supposing the cuttings to be started into growth in January, the best season, the plants by April should be in a vigorous healthy state, with roots filling six-inch pots. Then, if you wish to prepare plants for permanent planting, procure a quantity of oak or deal scantling, each piece being thirty inches long by an inch and a quarter square; bore these at each end with a centre-bit sufficiently large to take a quarter-inch or three-eighths pin; and procuring four of these for each basket, proceed to form them just the same as you would to receive orchids. Each of the pins should be a foot long, and formed with a head at one end and a screw and nut at the other, so that the baskets may be put together with strength and firmness. When the baskets are formed, line them with fresh turf, and fill up with properly-prepared loam and bone-dust, to which a handful of rotten manure or leaf-mould may be added. In each of these baskets place two plants, at about nine inches apart, and close to the side, so that when the vines are permanently planted out, the plants will fit close to their place without any need for shifting. These baskets should, if possible, be placed upon a bed of nice fermenting material, not necessarily for the bottom heat they may obtain, but so that the atmosphere surrounding the roots may be moist and genial. It is important that the roots should not pass through into the bed beneath; and for that reason, after the roots begin to fill the baskets, it will be necessary that they be moved once or twice a week, or be raised upon bricks a few inches above the bed.

So planted, with the roots regularly laid out and properly watered, the vines will grow with great vigour, so that the baskets in a few weeks will become a mass of fine healthy roots. Then prepare to plant them out, either by making the border up quite fresh, so that it may ferment and give the necessary bottom heat, or by laying hot dung upon it to impart the required temperature. This obtained, clear away the soil to the proper depth, always planting shallow, so as to allow for the border sinking, and then carrying the baskets out, place them as they are to remain. Then removing the nuts from the pins, carefully withdraw the latter, so that the basket may fall to pieces and be removed almost without injuring a root. Here then we have a compact ball of earth, densely filled with roots; and we have only to fill in round it with congenial soil, and to maintain the proper earth heat, to ensure vigorous growth, and have canes by the end of the season twenty to thirty feet long, and properly matured.

And here let us remark, we are not advocates for extraordinary luxuriance in the vine, for a nice short-jointed, thoroughly-matured cane, three-quarters of an inch in diameter, or less, is better than a shoot double that size, with pith in the centre as large as a cedar-pencil. It is the moderately large, close, dense, thoroughly-matured wood, with compact, prominent, well-rounded buds, that gives compact, handsome, well-formed bunches, and large highly-coloured berries; while, on the contrary, gross immature branches produce loose ill-shaped bunches, and too frequently berries defective in colour. Too much attention cannot be paid to these facts by those who require grapes of first-class excellence. It is easy to grow vines that may be wonders of luxuriance, but not so easy to establish good permanent vines. We recommended that two vines should be placed in each basket, but we did not say why. The object is that one plant may be allowed to produce a small crop of bunches the season after planting, and then be cut away, and that the other may be cut down and have a pair of branches taken from it to carry the crop in the third season.

We have now carried the vine from its cutting state to the final planting, and must turn to other systems of propagation. Increase by layers is not much practised, at least not in this country, for the vine strikes very readily from cuttings, which are much less troublesome than layers. Still, if any person wishes to practise that system, it is only necessary to cut a tongue in the old wood, an inch or two below its junction with the shoot of the previous season, and lay it in the earth or bend it into a pot of good soil, and, the season being congenial, it will quickly strike root. Layers should not be severed from the parent plant until the wood is ripe in the autumn, and then what have we? A fine vigorous branch without a proportionate quantity of roots, and though possibly much stronger, not so suitable for planting as a well-grown plant from a cutting. Hence we say, avoid layers.

The object of grafting the vine is to provide a vigorous-growing stock for those varieties which are constitutionally delicate, and hence do not grow properly upon their own roots. Among these may be mentioned the Black Muscat, or Muscat Hamburgh, as it is commonly called, a variety which sets irregularly upon its own roots, and produces but very small berries, but grafted upon the Hamburgh, it grows vigorously, is not less prolific than that variety, and sets its fruit equally well. We have in the same border four vines of this variety growing upon its own roots, and four grafted upon the Hamburgh. The latter are remarkable for the size and finish of bunches and berries —the former for their shabby appearance, we might say uselessness.

No proof could be clearer than this of the behaviour of this variety upon the new red sandstone formation, and we believe many who condemn this superb variety do so because it is growing upon its own roots. Grafted, it kept with us as well as the Hamburgh until Christmas, while upon its own roots, the berries were all damping before the end of October. Some keep it long in this way.

Among the varieties which are improved by grafting we would mention the Frontignans, Chasselas Musqué, and that fine new grape, the Golden Champion, for though it grows tolerably well upon its own roots, we find it does much better grafted upon a well-established stock. Of the kind of stock used, the Hamburgh is perhaps the best for the black varieties, and the Muscat of Alexandria for the white ones. Some have tried a stronger stock, such as the Barbarossa, Syrian, &c., but they are not so good as those which we have before mentioned.

The stocks, which should be established plants in 6-inch pots, being selected, the stems not being less than half an inch in diameter at the base, select the grafts of nearly the same size, and put them on in the whip-fashion, fitting stock and scion neatly together, and tying them securely. Then immediately coat them round with the French cold grafting wax, sold by Messrs. Hooper in Covent Garden, and the work is done. The grafting may be performed while the plant is in a dormant state, cutting it down to the necessary height six inches to nine inches at the end, then placing it in a moderately close place where the temperature does not exceed 50° until such time as the buds of the graft begin to swell. Then the temperature may be gradually increased up to 70°, and if at the same time the pots can be placed in a nice gentle bottom heat, the progress of the plants will be much accelerated. Once fairly established with a young growth of six inches, loosen the bandages and let the plants have free scope, repotting or preparing them for planting out as has been previously directed. Some people prefer to plant below the junction of the stock and graft. We do not, as, if the stock is of any use at all, it is important that its influence should be kept intact.

In grafting upon the old stock—that is, to put a new kind upon an established vine—it is usual to cut the old plant down to within two feet of its base, leaving at the winter pruning a certain number of buds to draw the sap until such time as the graft or grafts are established; then, a fortnight or three weeks before the vines are to be started into growth, and while they are quite dormant, take some strong, well-ripened shoots of the previous season's growth, hold each quite firm, and an inch above and below the bud; with a sharp knife cut from the upper side downwards, split the graft through the pith, paring the part quite smooth, and it will be fit for use. Cut a notch into the old vine of a size suitable to take the graft, making it fit most accurately; tie it securely down, and then cover the bandage with grafting wax, so as to make the wound quite air-tight. No further attention will be necessary, except to protect the bud from injury. Tie the young shoot as it progresses, and gradually reduce the shoots upon the old vine until the whole resources of the plant are concentrated upon the young shoot. Sometimes this kind of grafting or budding is deferred until the sap begins to rise; then the bark is raised in the same way as in budding, and the bud is inserted and tied down in the same manner. The only objection to the practice is that the vines are frequently injured by bleeding; and hence we prefer to graft in the dormant season, as being safer from injury, and we think more certain.

Another kind of grafting or budding is now becoming fashionable. A new vine is sent out in the autumn, and you are anxious that you should fruit it in the following season. To do this, cut grafts of the half-ripened wood near the base of the plant, retaining the petiole or leaf-stalk, but removing the leaf. Then cut a corresponding incision in the established vine intended for a stock; fit the graft accurately, making it quite secure, then cover with the grafting wax as before directed. It is best that the graft or bud should be placed close under a leaf, so that it may have the advantage of its nursing, and, if desired, a number may be placed upon each vine. To ensure success, the house should be kept close until such time as the grafts have taken, and they may be shaded for the first fortnight. Strong grafts thus carefully put on will generally produce fruit the following season; indeed, they are much more sure of doing so than those worked in the spring.

The scions grafted, or the eyes rooted, planted out, and in a vigorous-growing state, the next thing is the care of the young vines. These, in the earth-bed to which we have before referred, will progress with great rapidity; but it is essential that the growth should be strong and healthy, the joints strong and short, and the buds plump and well rounded up. To this end the temperature of the house should not exceed 70° by fire heat, but it may rise to 80° or 90° with sun heat and plenty of moisture in the atmosphere. Give a free circulation of air throughout the day, but avoid cold draughts, especially in dull weather. The vines will require to be syringed morning and evening in fine sunny weather, and in the evening on dull days, until such time as the full growth is made, and then the syringing may be gradually discontinued.

Budding the vine has been most successfully practised by Mr. Z. Stevens, the able gardener at Trentham. The best time to perform the operation is in the end of August or beginning of September, when the wood of the vine to be worked will be in a half-ripe condition, that of the scion being also in a somewhat green and pliable state. The bud to be inserted is cut out as shown on a reduced scale in the engraving, the small layer of wood not being cut out as in the case of the rose. A corresponding piece is cut out of the stock, a small nick being made at the lower part of the incision, so that the bud may rest firmly in its position, as shown in the illustration. A small corresponding cut is made in the bud. Care is of course taken that the surfaces of bud and stock fit as evenly as possible. Afterwards, a slender strand of bast mat is passed round both bud and stem; then a bandage of cotton wool is closely and neatly wrapped round the stem, from an inch or so below to an inch above the ends of the incision, exposing the point of the bud, and allowing the leaf-stalk (which should not be removed from the bud) to project. This bandage should also be firmly bound with bast mat, and kept moist for

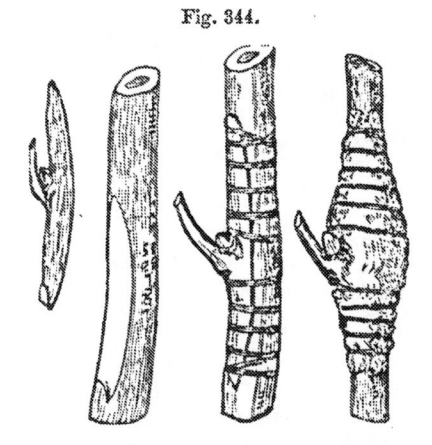

Fig. 344.

Budding the vine:—The bud—Cut in scion—Bud in position—Bud enveloped in cotton wool.

several weeks after the operation is performed. Managed in this way, Mr. Stevens finds that "every eye will take, and show fruit as freely as the natural buds of the vine." We have no doubt that the operation would be simplified, and success rendered even more certain, by the application of a little of the French cold grafting mastic after the bud has been secured; and with its aid there would be little necessity for any attention as regards moistening the outer covering. Apart altogether from the advantage it gives us in securing early bunches of a new variety, we believe this to be superior for general purposes to grafting the vine, inasmuch as, performed in early autumn, the union is effected before the winter, and thus time is gained as compared with the practice of grafting in early spring. The union of the bud is also more complete than that of the graft. It is scarcely necessary to suggest how useful it is to the vine-grower in enabling him rapidly to test the merits of the various kinds of stocks, &c. It need hardly be added, that when a spur is successfully budded in this way, it will be necessary to remove all the other shoots and buds from it. The operation may be performed on main as well as lateral shoots. By mistake the engraver has not shown the leaf-stalk attached to the tied-up bud. It should not be removed.

Watering at the root will have to be governed by circumstances, such as the dryness of the situation and the influence of the sun. With a well-formed border properly mulched, watering twice in the season— say in the end of June and early part of August—will be quite sufficient; but let these be really waterings—that is, use water at the proper temperature, and give sufficient each time to saturate the soil wherever the roots have penetrated. After this last watering, and when the vines have reached the top of the house or the distance you intend them to fill the first season, begin gradually to ripen the wood by giving more air, so as to allow a free circulation both day and night. The laterals which have been stopped at the first or second joint may be allowed to ramble, and the plant must be encouraged to thoroughly mature its growth, so as to make the young shoot as firm and hard as possible. This accomplished by the end of August, leave the vines to themselves for the remainder of the season, merely protecting them from early and severe frost. With a properly ripened vine, the leaves should hang on until they attain a golden yellow hue, and then it is a sign of maturity if the leaves drop leaving the petiole still adhering to the young shoot. Through the winter the young vines may be left to the care of nature; but we do not like to expose them to atmospheric changes, and therefore we should protect them from rain, snow, or severe frost. A slight frost after the leaves have fallen will not injure the canes.

In the second season pruning should take place not later than the middle of January, and then, if two vines have been planted in each space, the weakest may be cut down to the bottom of the rafter, and the other to half, or if very strong to two-thirds, of its length. This, according to its strength, will carry four to six, or if strong ten bunches of grapes; while the one that has been cut down will produce two shoots, which will be trained right and left of the fruiting plant. The vines should not be started in the second season earlier than from the end of February to the middle of March, and then as gradually as possible. Begin by giving sufficient heat to maintain a temperature of 45° to 50° for the first fortnight, and increase the temperature gradually two or three degrees weekly until it gets up to 60°, and at that, with an increase of 10° to 15° by sun heat, keep the temperature until the leaves begin to show. Then give the inside border a soaking of weak manure-water at 80° to 85°, and for this purpose water equal to a rainfall of three or four inches over the whole surface should be given. Less than that will be a mere driblet, and will not answer the purpose intended, that of ensuring moisture to the roots, and at the same time considerable warmth. After this the young shoots will progress with great rapidity; and when the earliest leaves are fairly developed, say two or three inches across, go over the plants and remove the superfluous shoots, retaining such only as may be necessary to furnish the vine with fruit and make wood for a succeeding crop. As a rule, if for the spur system of pruning—of which we do not approve, for reasons which will be explained in the proper place—shoots left at a foot apart all up the vine will be enough for that purpose, of course leaving the leader to again make its way to the top of the house, and perhaps a little further. As the side shoots progress from the fourth to the sixth joint, they will show the incipient bunches, and perhaps, according to the kind of grape grown, three or four bunches upon each shoot. These when fairly formed, so as to discriminate which is likely to make the most compact and handsome bunch, must be reduced to one bunch, and those retained may be allowed to grow on until the fruit is set, when another selection may be made, retaining, according to the strength of the vine, the bunches necessary to produce a fair crop. As the young shoots and bunches progress and the leaves develop themselves, it will be necessary to stop them, so as to concentrate the force of the vine in the young bunch. The general rule is to stop up two joints beyond the bunch; but if there is sufficient room between the main branches to allow the laterals to form themselves, stopping at the third joint will be near enough. With a broad development of foliage, which stopping at the third leaf enjoins, the stopping of the secondary lateral shoots may be performed regularly at the first leaf. Let it, however, be always recollected that the stopping of the vine, or in fact of any tree, should never be performed in a rough and wholesale manner. It is better to remove a few shoots twice or thrice a week than to allow them to grow for a fortnight or three weeks, and then, as some do, cut them out by the barrow-load. Such treatment, though not unusual, is most injurious to the plant, as it necessitates a complete check to the system, and checks to the growing plant are always injurious.

All the time until the flowers begin to open upon the young bunches continue to dew the vines over morning and evening with tepid water, and sprinkle the border and the floor of the house many times during the day. Some think it necessary to maintain a dry atmosphere during the time the vines are in bloom, fancying the fruit sets better in consequence. We have never found any decided advantage from so doing, and hence, though we cease to syringe the foliage from the time the bloom begins to open, we continue the sprinkling of the entire surface of the house until such time as the ripening process sets in and the berries begin to change colour. Then moisture is gradually withdrawn from the atmosphere, so that during the final maturation of the crop the house contains little more moisture than what is in the natural atmosphere. This complete ripening and high finish of colour depends upon a free circulation of air, night and day, from the time the berries begin to change until they are fully matured; and therefore, if the weather should be dull or damp at the time, it is better to increase the fire heat to maintain the temperature than to decrease the circulation of air.

In thinning the grapes, especially for the summer crop, we do not advocate the extreme measure of thinning for large berries only. On the contrary, we consider a handsome bunch, sufficiently compact to retain its form when placed upon the dessert dish, to be the standard of good grape-growing; so that loose bunches, however large the berries, have no charm for us. Therefore in thinning be guided by this rule, and it will be better to take out a few berries later in the season than have a loose straggling bunch.

All this time we have been devoting our attention to the crop, and now we must have a peep at the young vines that were cut down, and from which two shoots have been carried to the top of the house. These have had their lateral shoots regularly stopped, and are fine handsome canes, nearly an inch in diameter. Encourage the ripening process by every means in your power, and do not be satisfied until, on cutting the top of the vine, you find the pith in the centre has almost disappeared. This is the true test of perfect ripening, and with such wood fine grapes are almost certain.

If the season should be dry, twice or thrice during the brightest weather the outside border must receive a drenching of warm weak manure-water, and the inside border, according as the soil may be heavy or light, may receive at five or six separate waterings eighteen to twenty-four inches of water, always using it warm, and if manure-water, let it be weak.

One of our vines has carried a crop of fruit, and the other made two shoots from the starting point to the top of the rafter; and the next consideration is, what shall we do with them next year? Now it is quite certain that if the young fruiting vine has been fairly used—that is, if it has not been overcropped, a fault not unusual—it will carry a second crop, perhaps not quite so good as in the preceding year, but still good enough for a reason why the permanent vines should not be allowed to bear a crop until the fourth season after planting. Thus, then, the fruiting vines may have their leading shoots shortened to about three feet, and the side branches may be cut to the best eye or bud, because, as the object is to obtain good bunches of fruit, and as the vines will be cut out altogether at the end of the season, systematic training is of no consequence. Hence the advantage of planting duplicate vines; it enables you to leave the permanent ones until such time as they get thoroughly established—a point of great importance in their welfare. Those vines will have made two shoots, each reaching perhaps to the top of the house, and these will have to be shortened back so as to form the foundation of the permanent plants. For that purpose the branches will be laid down horizontally, parallel with the wall plate of the house, and each will be shortened to five feet in length. At the distance of eighteen inches from the centre on each side, a shoot will be taken up to form permanent rods, and at three feet from these two more rods will be taken up for the same purpose; while the leading bud upon each branch may be permitted to grow to the length of six feet or more. The three shoots being secured upon each of the horizontal branches to form the permanent rods, the fruit bunches must be removed from them directly; but if from the secondary shoots it is desired to take a few bunches, that may be done; but certainly not more than six medium or four good-sized bunches should be taken; and, to speak the truth, the vine will be much benefited if those are not taken. If such a determination should be arrived at, then remove the bunches as fast as they show, stopping these secondary branches at the fifth or sixth leaf, while the permanent shoots will be allowed to grow to their full length, or, at any rate, the length of the rafter, and may then be stopped, though if they go a yard or two beyond the length of the rafter there will be no harm in it, but rather an advantage. Through the growing season, the laterals upon these main shoots will be stopped weekly at the first leaf; and, beyond keeping the plants perfectly free from insects, with a moist, growing temperature, and a free admission of air upon all favourable occasions, no further care will be necessary.

It is August, the vines have made fine rods, and it is important that they should be ripened thoroughly. Upon this point too much cannot be said, for it is the point upon which success in grape cultivation hinges. If the wood is not thoroughly ripened in the autumn, it is impossible that it can produce first-class fruit in the following season. To that end it will be necessary to withdraw the moisture from the atmosphere—that is, no more syringing or sprinkling of the house must be indulged, but, on the contrary, a fair amount of heat must be maintained in the house (say 60° by night and 70° during the day) by artificial means, at the same time admitting a free circulation of air through the house both day and night. When the wood is thoroughly ripe the bark will be of a reddish-brown, varying according to the vines grown, and the leaves should ripen off a golden yellow. If the wood is thoroughly ripened—which may be told by the almost entire absence of pith in the centre—the leaves should be allowed to hang on as long as they will, and it is a sign of complete maturity to see them drop from the leaf-stalk; and a short time after, the latter will fall from the vine. Far too little importance is paid to the maturing of the wood, and frequently the crop of the following season is lost from the want of a little extra fire and trouble in the autumn. This is especially the case in late vineries and greenhouses, particularly in the latter, where the vines form a secondary object compared with the regular plants.

Well, the growth has been completed, the leaves have fallen, and the vines are ready to be pruned; so before we leave them we will perform that operation.

If all has gone well, the fruiting vines will be removed entirely—that is, they will be cut out at the root—and the permanent vines will occupy the entire space. The rods at the end of the third season should be in every respect perfect in their growth, and, presuming that they are so, each may be cut back to half its length, while the leading horizontal shoot may be shortened to three or four eyes, and the secondary shoots cut out altogether. Trim off the laterals in a neat and workmanlike manner, always cutting close to the bud, and making the wound quite smooth.

For the purpose of pruning, we prefer good clean-cutting shears to the knife—the spring shears that make the draw cut being the best. These do not bruise, but the common ones, unless very sharp, generally do. From the fact that we have provided four main shoots to each vine, it will be perceived that we do not approve the restriction or spur system of training the vine. We grant that under ordinary circumstances fine crops have been and may be grown in that way; but at the same time we deny that it is either a natural or rational system of training the vine.

To take a plant which, properly planted and unrestrained, would in a few years cover with vigorous branches an area of fifty to one hundred or more yards; to prepare for it a rich and perfect border; to confine it to a single rod of fifteen feet to twenty feet in length; to thin out the grapes, and part of the side branches as fast as they are produced; and from the time that those branches retained have each made half-a-dozen leaves to keep them regularly stopped; and at the same time to expect that a plant so treated can take vigorous root-hold of the soil in which it is planted—is just as reasonable as it would be to tie a horse's tail to the rack or manger where the food is placed, and then blame him for not getting fat. Plants live and thrive and have their being by the reciprocal action of roots and branches. Without the latter roots cannot flourish, because there is no storehouse of organizable matter from which they can draw the material necessary for their formation.

We have therefore given each of our vines four branches to begin with, having three instead of twelve permanent vines in each house, supposing the houses to be forty feet long; but we have also provided for the horizontal branches to extend themselves, so that, should it seem desirable, the centre or the two end vines shall, at the will of the cultivator, fill the house.

It will have been seen that we do not advocate the whip-stick or single rod system of training the vine; for, though we know that some wonderful examples of cultivation have been produced by that system, another fact must be noted, and that is that the remarkable bunches have been produced during the first seven or ten years of the vine's life, the produce afterwards sinking into comparative mediocrity, while at twenty, or twenty-five years of age, the vines are completely "used up." Nor can it be otherwise; no plant of free and vigorous growth like the vine can be unnaturally cramped into a very limited area, without in the course of years being enfeebled in constitution. The perpetual pinching of the orchard-house system of torturing fruit trees into a bearing state is nothing more nor less than inducing premature old age. We induce fruitfulness by subverting the constitution of the plant; and the more robust a plant is naturally disposed to grow, the more must it suffer from the practice. The system of excessive restriction in the vine originated with the Crawshays of Norwich. Something like thirty years ago it was adopted almost without thought, because of its neatness and simplicity.

By establishing our vines the four or more branches to each, we seek to lay a broader basis of constitutional vigour; in fact, we wish to establish the plants upon something like a natural foundation, and not from infancy to old age keep them perpetually dwarfed. Assuming each rod to be twenty feet long, they will be at the top of the rafter by the end of the third year. We then divide each rod into five equal portions of four feet each; at the bottom two spurs will be formed, and two more at each four feet up to sixteen feet, and all the rest of the spurs or branches will be removed for the whole length of each stem. From these spurs on alternate sides shoots will have been made that will carry the crop this year, and from the spurs on the opposite sides shoots will be carried this year that will produce next year's crop. Thus these bearing branches are not allowed to bear any fruit in the first year of their growth, but they carry a full crop in the second year. In the autumn pruning the bearing branches are entirely cut away, merely leaving a spur or two at their base, from which the shoots of the next year will be made, while the other shoots are shortened to three feet each. Thus we have annually a continuous series of young, vigorous, well-nurtured buds from the bottom to the top of each main rod—not the last and least bud upon a branch which has produced fruit the previous season, as in the spur or "whip-stick" system of pruning, but a young, vigorous branch, which throughout the year preceding has had nothing to do but take care of itself.

If we needed any proof of the success of this system, we have only to appeal to the experience of Mr. Montgomery Henderson, gardener to Sir G. Beaumont, Bart., of Coleorton, Leicestershire, the veteran exhibitor of grapes at the London exhibitions for nearly thirty years; and what does he say?

"The vines here are thirty-nine years old, and have been pruned upon the extension system for more than twenty years. I began to compete at Chiswick in 1841, and at the Royal Botanic Garden in 1848. I took the first prize the first time I exhibited at the latter place—the first time I showed black Hamburghs; I took it on June 30, 1869, and have seldom missed the first prize during the whole time. I know I took it every show at the Botanic for three years without intermission, and, if I remember rightly, for twelve pounds as well as for the single dish. I have had four prizes for grapes in one day, and I exhibited Hamburghs eight times in one season, and was first each time. I have exhibited at the Crystal Palace and many local shows, but have no conception of the number of prizes I have taken altogether."

Here then we have vines nearly forty years old, the produce of which has stood in the fore rank of the battle for thirty years, and still they stand, being very rarely beaten; and yet during that time we could point to scores of exhibitors that have come out with a rush, discharged a volley of big bunches, and then have fallen into obscurity. To this rule there has been no exception. Exhibitors who have stood in the fore rank, and maintained their positions as grape-growers, are those who have had a succession of young vines to fall back upon. And so it ever will be upon the restrictive plan of management; while Mr. Henderson, without a single young vine to aid him, continues the even tenor of his way for a lifetime, and is rarely beaten. We grant that much of this results from the matchless colour and exquisite finish of his productions; but still the fact remains.

He has done that which no other man has done, and he has accomplished it by the extension system of managing the vine.

Now, upon this system of training the vine, it will be manifest that, after the apportioning of the crop and the management of the bunches—always bearing in mind that a thoroughly matured medium crop is preferable to an ill-ripened large one—the main care of the summer's treatment should be concentrated in attention to the branches which are to produce the following year's crop. These must have their leaves fully exposed to light; each will be stopped at the length of four feet, and the lateral branches will be stopped at each leaf. The branches which are carrying the crop will be stopped at two or three leaves beyond the bunches, and their laterals regularly at one leaf; but in case of crowding and insufficient exposure to light, then all but the two leading laterals upon each branch may be removed, to make room for the principal leaves. This is a practice not to be generally recommended, but it is of less consequence upon branches that will be entirely cut away than it would be upon others from which a crop would be expected the following season. These laterals or secondary branchlets from the fruiting branch have their use, and that is to provide food for and mature the buds at the base of each. This they will do so long as the foliage is fully exposed to light; but if not, then it is better to remove the laterals than to allow an amount of shade that must be detrimental to the plant and the crop.

Should any readers fail to understand the previous directions as to pruning on the extension system, the diagram on the opposite page may serve to explain it.

The vine in the winter of the first year of planting, is cut down to three buds, or if not to three buds they are reduced to that number, and form the pruned plant of the second year. In the third year the lower part of the central shoot has formed its side branches as shown in the second illustration, and also the spurs, from which the bearing branches of the following year will be taken; those that have produced a crop being cut close back. In the fourth year the central shoot is shown fully developed, and all the other shoots as they attain age will be treated in the same manner, each forming a base (or rather a reservoir) of stored organizable matter, upon which the young shoots can draw in case of need. In this manner there will be a constant succession of young wood from the bottom to the top of each main branch, each young shoot being, when pruned, from two to three feet long. It will be perceived that at the winter pruning each bearing branch is cut close out to its base, care being taken to encourage another branch from the same point the following spring. The main shoots are supposed to be laid in at three feet apart, and in this manner a single vine may fill a whole house, or it may be confined to three or more shoots, at the will of the cultivator. As branches make roots, it is clear that the larger the vine the greater must be its quantity of roots, the greater its store of nourishment, and consequently the greater its power to resist changes arising from unnatural conditions, such as a scarcity of moisture at the root, or extreme cold. In a word, by this system of training the vine we lay the foundation of a vigorous old age, and secure that soundness of constitution which is impossible under the close-pruning or restrictive system.

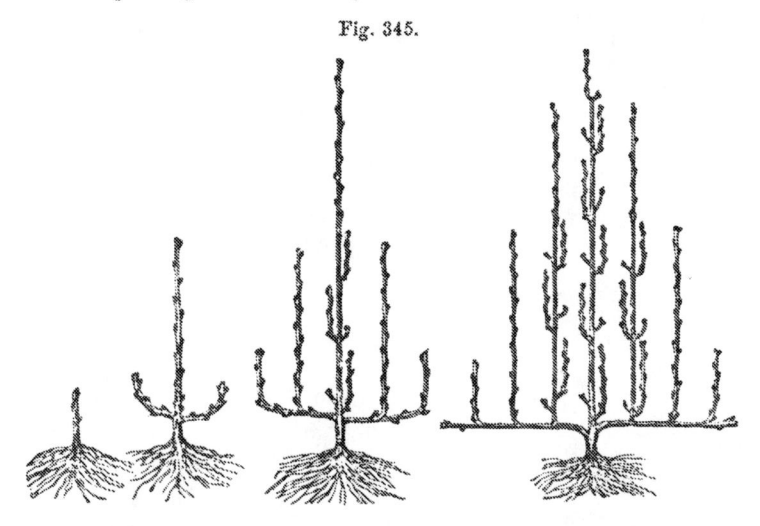

Fig. 345.

Diseases and Pests of the Vine.—Of these the most formidable is certainly the new disease which has recently played sad havoc among the vineyards of the Continent, decimating them completely, and leaving scores of acres entirely devoid of plants. This disease, which might at first sight be mistaken for an attack of fungi, is found to originate in a small insect so minute that it can only be discovered by the use of the microscope, and then it may be seen in myriads. They attach themselves to and live upon the root of the plant, from which they suck every vestige of sap, until at last the plant is obliged to succumb from exhaustion. All remedies which have been tried are found to be useless, except those which destroy the plants, and the only check upon the progress of the pest appears to be a soil which contains more than the usual proportion of salt, the plants being less liable to be attacked upon such a soil than upon others. The only real remedy appears to be the fire; and the best plan is not only to burn the plants, but also to subject the soil in which they have been growing to sufficient heat to destroy animal life.

Fortunately, this pest is not much known in this country, though it is said to exist in one or two vineries. This report we hope is not true; but if it is, then the pest ought to be stamped out at once, whatever may be the sacrifice to be made in doing so. For a long time the French vine-growers could not decide what the pest really was, but at last M. Planchon obtained a clue, by which he determined it to be a new and extremely minute species of aphis, of a dirty yellow colour, which attaches itself to the roots of the vines, and is the cause of all the evil. To this insect the name of Phylloxera vastatrix has been given. So far as its habits are at present ascertained, it appears to attach itself to the roots. Only the young are to be found, says M. Planchon, small in size, hidden away amongst the rootlets and crevices in the bark. With the approach of spring they awaken up from their semi-dormant condition, increase in size, and select their positions for depositing their eggs. The roots are always the portions first attacked; the malady from thence spreads throughout the body of the plant. For this pest there appears to be no remedy, mineral oils, gas tar, ammoniacal applications, sulphur, quicklime, arsenious acid, having all been equally unsuccessful. Let us, while we commiserate the fate of our neighbours, hope we may never have to combat the enemy in this country.

Next to this pest, which we know only by report, we think the root fungus is the most troublesome disease. A few years back we had occasion to plant some vines for a gentleman who had provided himself with a quantity of the parings and raspings of horses' feet from the shoeing-smith's shop. To such an article there did not appear to be the slightest objection, and we used it in about the same proportion that bone-dust would be used, taking care to incorporate it thoroughly with the soil. The vines were planted late in the season, and made tolerable growth. Being cut down at the autumn pruning, they started into growth the following spring, progressed for a few weeks, and then came to a standstill, drooping under bright light, until at last it was clear something was wrong somewhere. An examination of the soil revealed the fact that the border was full of fungi, and the roots of the plants quite dead. Upon closer examination we found the fungus the most plentiful where pieces of the "frog," or inner part of the hoof, were lying, and from these it spread in a direct line through the soil. So convinced were we of the cause of the failure, that we directly removed the soil and made a new border. Last spring we found upon another border that had been top-dressed with soil which contained the parings a quantity of fungi, which spread very rapidly, though we removed it, and sulphured and sooted the soil wherever it appeared. However, upon examining the vines a few days back, we found that wherever the fungus had shown itself the surface rootlets were destroyed, quite black and dead; so that we have removed the soil with the greatest care, dusting the old soil with lime, soot, and sulphur, and replacing with fresh soil, to which soot and lime have been added. When we begin to force we shall give a good soaking of lime and soot water, and in that way we hope to conquer the pest. Until this experience convinced us of our error, we had looked upon root fungi as more terrible in theory than in practice; but now we have reversed our judgment, and find it a most formidable plague, which must be guarded against at every point. Hence, we say again, avoid nostrums in making vine borders, and, above all things, do not put half-decomposed leaves or sticks into your borders.

The vine mildew will rarely put in an appearance if the atmosphere of the house is kept right, and free ventilation is indulged in. Localities, however, make a great difference to the attacks of this disease; low, damp, ill-ventilated places, badly drained and surrounded by trees and stagnant water, are much more liable to the attacks of mildew than those gardens which lie high and dry. Free ventilation and the copious use of sulphur are the great and sure remedies, but they must be used at the first appearance of the disease, and continued until it is quite destroyed. If taken in time, we have always found steaming twice or thrice with sulphur vapour, as prescribed for the destruction of red spider, to be a certain remedy. If the fungus is destroyed, the specks upon the leaves will turn quite black.

Then again we have what is called the rust in grapes—a disease which attacks the fruit, and may invariably, we think, be put down as the result of bad management. It shows itself as a brown spot upon the delicate skin of the grape. Frequently it is induced by careless handling with a heated and sweaty hand, and many times we have known it to originate through a man rubbing his head and hair against the bunches of young grapes. More generally, however, it originates in careless ventilation. Air is given in April or May when there is a keen cutting north-east wind, which, rushing through the young bunches, chills the tender skin and stops the growth; then rust is the consequence, and most ugly bunches it induces. The preventives—for we need not speak of remedies—are these: Never touch a bunch with the hand or hair, but in thinning or regulating use a small clean stick; or if you must touch, take a single berry between the finger and thumb, and afterwards cut that berry away. Secondly, ventilate cautiously in cold windy weather, and use the precautions which we have previously recommended, especially perforated zinc, to break the force of cold wind.

Sometimes upon young and vigorous vines small warts may be seen, both upon the upper and under side of the foliage. These are generally induced by a vapour-loaded and close atmosphere; and the remedy, as for most of the ills the vine is heir to, is a healthy atmosphere, which implies proper ventilation.

And now we come to that trouble of troubles, "shanking." Volumes have been written upon this disease, but its frequent cause may be written down in two words—bad management; its cure the reverse. We are quite willing to admit the truth of much that has been written respecting sour, ill-drained borders, and the want of activity in the roots; but, at the same time, we know that grapes shank sometimes in well-drained and properly-prepared borders, and then what is the cause? An acquaintance of ours had to manage a garden where several early vineries had borders inside as well as outside the houses, and the grapes which they had produced for years previously had been nearly half shanked. The vines were fine old fellows, with many branches, and had been formed upon the close-pruning system. The gardener took charge in April, at which time the crops in three early houses would not number a bunch to each vine. He conceived the vines were debilitated by over-pruning, and the roots crippled in consequence; and accordingly, he gave orders that the shoots should be allowed to run wild for the remainder of the season. He also, upon examining the border, found it for more than a foot from the surface as dry as dust; and therefore he determined to remove the surface soil down to the healthy roots as quickly as possible, to give the under soil a thorough soaking of warm weak manure water, and when he replaced the soil with fresh compost, to bring some of the young roots as near to the surface of the border as possible. This was done; the houses were kept close until the roots had taken good hold in the new soil; and so effectual was the remedy, that scarcely a shanked berry could be seen the following season in the whole of the houses. Here, it will be seen, the cause was not a cold, ill-drained border, but its opposite—a dry, poor one. Here the vines failed from exhaustion consequent upon the want of water and nutriment, and the remedy was as certain as it was simple and natural. In the open border, wholly exposed, and where the roots are not so much under control, it is difficult to deal with shanking. The first step, however, to a remedy, it is certain, must be the removal of stagnant water, and, as far as possible, of the sour and stagnant soil. Do this carefully, replace with fresh, properly-prepared compost, and the result is almost certain to be satisfactory. If, however, in low situations, the roots are allowed to ramble where they please, shanking is sure to be the consequence. An example of this came under our notice very recently. A gentleman who had several vineries, and who grew good grapes, found that the fruit upon two or three of the vines shanked immoderately. The situation was scarcely above the level of an adjoining river; the bottom of the border had been concreted, and the front walled in, so that it was thought the roots could not get out. However, upon digging to the bottom of the wall opposite the failing vines, it was found that the roots had pierced the brickwork, and were luxuriating three feet deep in the stagnant subsoil of some asparagus beds. These were taken up and returned to the proper border, and the following season the shanking ceased. At Trentham, Mr. Fleming, when gardener there, found that directly the vine roots passed the concrete border and got into the cold soil beneath, the grapes began to shank. A cold wet border, and the debilitating influence of excessive stopping under the restrictive system of training the vine, may be considered the main causes of shanking. With a warm, well-drained, and not over-rich border, we never hear of shanking; but, planted in rich, highly-manured borders, with restricted growth, shanked grapes, after the first flush of growth is over, are almost as certain as day precedes night. The cause of shanking is almost invariably in the border. The roots fail, and then the fruit, as being the most recent and delicate production of the vine, must fail also. Bad or defective atmospheric treatment, such as cold and unseasonable draughts, may increase the evil; but as a rule, if the roots are right, and the plants receive fair atmospheric treatment, there will be no shanking to complain of.

Adventitious roots rarely occur upon healthy vines, unless they receive some check or injury, and then, if the proper roots are thrown out of action, nature will endeavour to repair the damage by throwing out roots to feed upon the atmosphere. Thus vines are started to force early, the border is not protected, and the roots are in consequence very cold—so cold that they lie quite dormant, and are unable to answer the call for assistance when the swelling buds or growing branches require it. In such a case air roots will be thrown out, and may assist the vine in the time of need. Again, as I remarked when speaking of shanking, a border may be too dry, or too wet and cold, and then air roots may be made; but as a rule it may be allowed that air roots will never be produced except the plant receives a check from some cause or other. Of course some kinds of grapes are less hardy than other kinds, and those, under the circumstances we have named, are the first to produce air roots.

Once (many years ago) two houses of first-rate vines were started into growth, and when the shoots had attained the length of two inches they came to a stand-still. A moist atmosphere was maintained, which had the effect of inducing the profuse production of air roots all over the vines; but still the shoots made no progress, and the incipient bunches withered and died. In this emergency the border was examined, when it was found that the principal roots of all the vines had been eaten off by field-mice, and every plant was ruined. Can there be any doubt as to the cause of air roots in this case? I think not. Air roots, then, may be considered the result of feeble or suspended root action, arising from any of the causes which I have mentioned, or from others which may readily occur to the cultivator. In no case can they be regarded as a sign of health, and though vines that produce these roots may, under judicious management, bear fair grapes, that does not alter the fact that their presence is not a sign of health.

Among the absurdities with which unthinking custom has rendered vine-growers familiar, that which is called winter dressing is the most mischievous; we allude to the annual custom of stripping the loose bark from the stem of the vines at the winter pruning. If the stripping was confined to the bark actually loose, there would be less room to complain; but this scarifying is carried to such an extent that many cultivators actually scrape the branches, so as to leave the plants in a state of perfect nudity. In a state of nature we find no such sloughing of the skin, but, on the contrary, the aged vine if left to itself has a soft spongy covering of bark, which we really believe has not been placed there except for some end. If we are asked what those purposes are, we would say a shade from scorching sunbeams, a shelter from cold draughts. and above all a sponge which sucks up water from the shower, the syringe, or the saturated atmosphere, and gives it off for the sustenance of the plant, when the sun may be scorching and the atmosphere parched. Expose the main stem of an early-forced vine to a cold draught, the sap ceases to flow, and the leaves will droop and quickly wither; protect the stem from the cold, and the economy of the plant is immediately restored. With such facts before us, are we to conclude the rough bark is an incumbrance which must be removed? To the removal of any loose hanging bark there can be no great objection, but to strip vines of their bark, as is the practice with some, is a time-losing barbarism which cannot be too much reprobated. Of course it may be said this excoriation is carried out for sanitary reasons—the bark is a harbour for insects and their ova. To such a plea we will say, Remove the cause, give your vines such treatment as insects cannot live under, and then you will have no reason to scarify them annually to remove an enemy which ought not to have been allowed to establish itself upon them. Prevention is better than cure, and that most notably in dealing with insect life in the garden.

"It is not always practicable to prune the vines in late houses before the sap has commenced to circulate; therefore we are bound to adopt some means to prevent the loss of sap and injury to the vines that result from excessive bleeding of the sap when they are cut late. For several years past I have paid much attention to this matter, and during that time, by way of experiment, have tried every known remedy to test their respective merits, most of which are either useless or so expensive as to prevent their being used where there are large numbers of vines, or by amateurs with limited incomes. One, however, quite superseded all those hitherto known, so that I have hesitated whether I ought not to turn an honest (?) penny by distributing it to the public at so much per bottle; but I have decided instead to make the matter public in this way, so that all who have late vineries may have a simple and effectual remedy at hand when required. Knowing the drying nature of the 'Patent Knotting' used by painters for dressing knots in wood previous to applying the usual coat of paint, I fancied it would make a good styptic, and tried it accordingly. It was first tried upon some vines the crop from which was not gathered until the sap was in active circulation, and it was found to be very effectual. The wounds caused by cutting the lateral shoots back were painted with it, and the vines scarcely lost a drop of sap. The "Patent Knotting" can be obtained from any oilman, and sufficient for dressing a large house of vines can be had for a few pence. Styptics ought not to be required where very early forcing is not carried on, or where the whole of the grapes are cut before Christmas, because if the vines are pruned, as they should be, before the sap begins to move, there is no danger of 'bleeding,' and therefore no styptics for its prevention are wanted."—Mr. G. Fairbairn, in the 'Gardener's Magazine.'

Grapes in Pots.—This is a very convenient method of producing early grapes, and sometimes later crops are obtained in such quantities as to render their production in this manner really profitable. Of this a remarkable example came under our notice in the autumn of last year in the garden of Newstead Abbey, in Nottinghamshire, where a span-roofed house, twenty-five feet long by thirteen feet wide, produced from thirty vines growing in thirteen-inch pots the enormous quantity of three hundred bunches, the average weight of each bunch being one pound. The annexed engraving shows a section of the house in question, which was contrived and erected by Mr. G. Messenger, horticultural builder, of Loughborough. The section will almost speak for itself, but we may remark that over the hot-water pipes slate slabs are placed, supported by cross walls of dry bricks, so that the slates may be raised to the height of the inner retaining wall, or they may be lowered to the level of the heating pipes. This is a

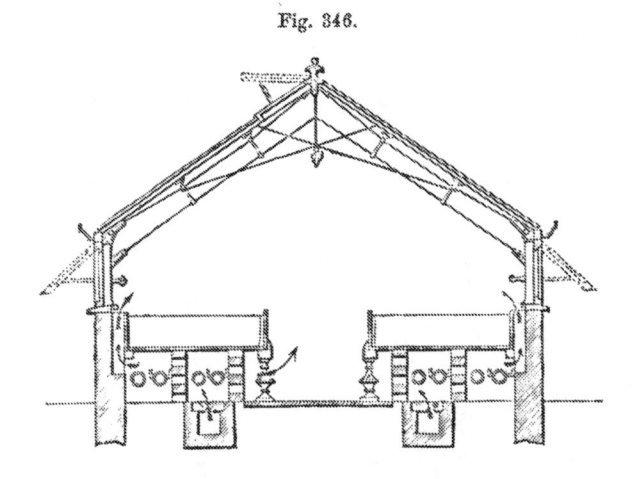

Fig. 346.

great convenience in working, as the gardener may stand his plants upon the slates, or he may have a bed two feet deep if he requires it.

In the case of the grapes in question the bed had been used the previous season for growing melons, and hence the soil was levelled down, and the vine pots were placed upon it. Of course the roots passed through into the bed, which was very material to the perfecting of the crop.

Now, in selecting vines for cultivation in pots, it is necessary that the most vigorous and healthy should be chosen, that they be grown on without the slightest check to their progress, and that they should be thoroughly ripened early in the autumn. To this end, therefore, select the most vigorous young vines from your earliest-struck stock, and grow them on with a special view to attaining the utmost vigour. Presuming the vines to be potted from the cutting pot into three-inch pots, they will, when nine inches to one foot high, be shifted into six-inch pots, and when these are full of roots the plants will be removed to thirteen-inch pots, which, as a rule, may be considered as large enough, though some good growers use pots of the eighteen-inch and twenty-one inch size. There is, however, really little to be gained by this, for we have always found the thirteen-inch pots to finish six or eight bunches as well as they could be finished, and to grow more than that quantity upon a single vine is no gain.

The best compost for pot vines is rich turfy loam, about a sixth of fresh dry horse-droppings, and about one pint of bone-dust to each vine, mixing the whole intimately together, using it when comparatively dry, and at the time of potting making the soil as firm as possible, not only by compression with the hand, but also by ramming it with a blunt stick. The best drainage is oyster-shells, using them three or four deep, and some crushed up and mixed with the soil will not do any harm, but, on the contrary, much good.

In the earlier stages of their growth the young plants will be much benefited if they receive the assistance of a bottom heat of 75° to 80°; but more than that is not desirable. The secret of complete success is to start a plant vigorously, and never let it know any check until the growth necessary for fruiting purposes is completed; then bring it gradually to a state of maturity and final rest. Do not, however, believe that maturity is attained when you see brown bark and yellow leaves; but maturity means that stage of growth when the pith in the centre of the young shoot has given way to hard matured wood, and when the leaves drop from the leaf-stalk, leaving the latter attached to the wood. Such may be considered a matured, well-ripened plant; and such a plant, with proper management, in the second season is sure to produce fine, well-matured fruit. To grow vines to this state of perfection, it is necessary that they be trained close to the glass, allowing each sufficient room for the development of its foliage (say eighteen inches apart), and that they be kept clear from insect enemies of all kinds. With the most genial atmosphere and daily syringing necessary for the successful growth of the vine, this is sure to be the case. If the vines attain maturity early in the autumn, then they may be set out of doors, with the branches nailed up to a south wall, with advantage, the object being to bring them early to rest; but, unless the wood is thoroughly ripened, a fruiting pot vine should not be set out of doors at all.

For very early forcing, to produce ripe grapes the vines should be ripe by the end of July; and, if such is the case, then they may be placed in a south aspect for a month, and dried off by giving them no more water than may be necessary to keep the leaves from drooping, and then during September the pots may be laid down under a north wall and kept as cool as possible; and this will be the only winter or dormant season which they will get.

Forcing the Grapes in Pots.—Pruning is a very simple matter, and consists in removing the lateral or secondary branches and shortening the vine to a given length. If the wood is thoroughly matured to the top, the best plan is to leave the vine the full length, say seven feet or eight feet, and then, as the finest buds are at the point, coil the lower part down into the pot, so that four feet to five feet of bearing wood may be left out. For this purpose it will be wise to pot the vines rather low at the last shift, not only to facilitate the coiling, but also to admit of a liberal top dressing of fresh soil over the roots. The coiling will be found a very simple matter if a few strong pegs are provided to fasten the shoot down as the work proceeds, and it will enable you not only to secure the best buds at the top of the vine, but will also add materially to the strength of the plant by the new roots that will be made from the coiled part of the shoot.

Well-ripened grapes are wanted in March and April, and therefore it will be necessary to commence forcing the first week in October. The first thing then will be to collect some leaves, or leaves and dung, sufficient to fill the bed and produce a nice bottom heat; then take the plants and place them upon the bed, but do not press the fermenting material around the pots until such time as the buds begin to break. To ensure their doing so at this early season it will be necessary to tie or peg the shoots down quite horizontally, or if they are tied to a straight lath they will be none the worse. At the commencement of the forcing the temperature of the house should not exceed $50°$ to $55°$, while if the bottom heat can be kept $10°$ to $15°$ in excess of that temperature the roots will take precedence of the branches, which is a sure presage of their breaking regularly and well. As the shoots progress increase the temperature $3°$ or $4°$ a week until a minimum of $58°$ by night and $65°$ by day, with a rise of $10°$ to $15°$ by sun heat is attained. This will be sufficient until the bunches begin to assume their proper form, and then $60°$ to $65°$ by night and $10°$ more on bright days will be sufficient. From the moist heat that will be generated by the fermenting material much syringing will not be required over the vines; but it will be wise to sprinkle the bed and walls, and a little over the vines on bright mornings up to the time of their coming into bloom will not do any harm. During the winter it is not wise to train the branches nearer than fifteen inches from the glass, and in very cold weather they may be lowered to eighteen inches from the glass with decided advantage. Water at the roots will not be required in any great quantity, and whatever is used must be warm.

In treating the vines it will be necessary to thin out the branches directly the strongest bunches of fruit can be seen, of course retaining the best and casting the others away. Do not leave more than one branch upon a shoot, and stop about three leaves before the bunch. During the time the vines are in bloom, the sprinkling at that dark season must be discontinued; however, after the fruit is set, the sprinkling must be resumed, but there must be no more syringing of the vines. Your bunches being fairly set, reduce them to the required number, and thin out the berries directly they are the size of very small peas.

Of course when the grapes are set there is nothing to do but to force away, maintaining a brisk moist temperature until such time as the fruit begins to colour: then more air must be given, but even then do not run to the other extreme of a dry arid atmosphere. From vines started the first week in October we have cut ripe, well-matured grapes the last week in March; but it is severe work, and the same vines, started a month or six weeks later, would produce a much finer crop. After the crop is set and swelling, weak manure given at each alternate watering is a material element in the production of fine fruit, and a light crop is the secret of large bunches and finely coloured and matured berries. Vines forced early are rarely fit to force a second season, but we have occasionally used them, and obtained a fair crop of fruit. In such cases we always allow the leading shoot to grow to the length of four feet, and then shift into a large pot, cut off the lateral shoots, and coil the old wood into the pot as in the preceding season.—(W. P. Ayres, in *Field*.)

The Ground Vinery.—This simple mode of cultivating grapes has attracted some attention of late. The best ground vinery is the barless ground vinery, so called from being glazed with a single row of large panes of glass without any sash bars as in the original ground vinery. To permit of slipping in the glass with ease a rather deep groove is made at the top, into which the glass slips and falls back again into its appointed bed, and no putty is used except at the bottom, the panes fitting closely to each other. One side of these vineries does not open with a hinge, as in the patent kind, but being made in seven feet lengths, there is no difficulty in quickly taking them off when anything requires to be done to the grapes, and that is only likely to happen when they want thinning, or the vines stopping at wide intervals. Ventilation being free, and syringing or watering not being required, it will not often be necessary to take off the vinery from the bricks, which raise it a little from the earth. They are much neater-looking than ground vineries with bars, while of course the flow of light to the vine, or whatever crop may be inside, is perfectly uninterrupted.

Mr. Rivett, Railway-bridge, Stratford, Essex, is the maker of these, and the scale of prices is very reasonable indeed. The frames are usually sent by goods train, and the glass packed in boxes; but the manufacturer informs us that some people get their own glass and glaze the frames, as the glass may be obtained in some places as cheap as by having it sent from London. To send the frames glazed to any distance would, of course, be anything but wise, and they would most likely all get broken; but to places immediately around London, or within easy distance of the manufactory, they could be sent with safety, though here too it is doubtful if it would not be better to send the frames unglazed, and have them finished when placed in position, as the panes are large.

Apart from grape-growing, even in the largest gardens in the land they will be found most useful during our wretched winters and cutting springs, for the protection of such stuff as small salading, &c., and not a few other uses which will soon suggest themselves to the amateur when once he makes the acquaintance of this simple ground vinery. Parsley, for instance, is often taken up and potted, to ensure having a supply in case of hard weather; but placing one of these over it will quite suffice for the usual run of our winters, while numerous batches of seedlings and half-hardy things will be the better for their protection; and of course they may be taken off the vines when they have had their fruit removed and wood ripened in autumn if it be desired to do any of these things with the ground vinery. Strawberries may be nicely advanced by placing one or more ground vineries over the rows, which their size just adapts them to fit. They seem, in fact, as well adapted for gently forwarding the strawberry as for the sure fruiting of good grapes without artificial heat; and the longer we can prolong the season of the strawberry the better. Lettuce, and endive too, in winter will be very thankful for the protection, and with the aid of the ground vinery (by keeping snails and such vermin from devouring them) we may enjoy salad, which in winter is usually only for those who have pits and frame to spare, and who, moreover, manage them well. The engraving represents two ground vineries,

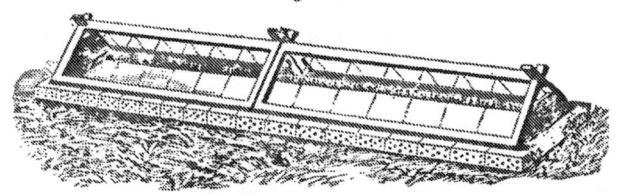

Fig. 347.

The barless ground vinery.

each seven feet long, two feet six inches wide at base, and the glass twenty inches deep at each side. The open aperture at each end provides, with the wide openings all round between the bricks, quite sufficient ventilation at all times. When the structures are placed in twos in this way, only one end of each need be filled, and this is likely frequently to be the case, as the vine which fills one will soon fill two, or even more, if it be desired.

One thing would be a considerable improvement in the arrangement of ground vineries—though it is not practised by any of those who use them—and that is to place the frame on complete rows of the common drilled or perforated brick (fig. 347), instead of on isolated bricks. The floor of the vinery should also be covered with large slates. Sufficient ventilation would flow through the holes in the bricks, and rats, birds, &c. would be effectually excluded. As we have seen the vineries arranged, these vermin have full opportunity to do as they like. We have seen rats climb up straight trellises against a back wall, and cut down fine bunches of grapes as readily as monkeys; and it is not to be hoped that they will spare the grapes when once they discover them in one of these simple structures. The following are the prices:—No. 1 (the usual size)—7 ft. long, 2 ft. 6 in. wide, 1 ft. 3 in. high inside; woodwork, 5s. 6d. each; 21 oz. glass and putty, packed, 7s. 6d. each. No. 2 (large size for two vines)—7 ft. long, 3 ft. wide, 1 ft. 6 in. high inside; woodwork, 6s. 6d. each; 21 oz. glass and putty, packed, 9s. 6d. each. Painting, 1s. 6d. each; closed ends, 1s. each. It should be added that these ground vineries are so simply made that any village carpenter should be able to construct them.

Growing the Grape on open Walls, and on Cottages.—South of London this may be practised to a great extent, and the grapes brought to a high degree of perfection. In the southern counties of England, where vines are grown on cottages, Mr. Hoare was of opinion that five times the quantity of grapes of superior flavour might be annually produced on the same extent of surface; and that for every square foot of cottage wall on which vines are now trained, there are twenty that are either entirely vacant, or occupied in a useless manner. As a general result of his calculations, he says, that for every pound of grapes now grown, one hundred pounds might be annually produced on the existing surface of walling. "Every moderate-sized dwelling-house having a garden and a little walling attached to it, may, with ease, be made to produce yearly, a quarter of a ton weight of grapes, leaving a sufficient portion of its surface for the production of other fruit." The grand error which prevails in the culture of the vine on walls and cottages consists in the mode of pruning, which is far from being sufficiently severe. Nine parts out of ten of the current year's shoots, and all those of the preceding year, should if possible be cut off; and this is so different from what is required for other fruit trees, that few persons have the courage to attempt it.

Warmth and shelter are the grand requisites. The perspiration of the foliage of the vine is so great that it is carried to an injurious extent by the slightest wind. Mr. Hoare has found that, during the space of twenty-four hours, when the wind has blown briskly, the shoots exposed to its influence have not perceptibly grown at all, while, shortly afterwards, the wind having entirely sunk away, the same shoots have grown upwards of three inches in the same space of time, the temperature of the air in a sheltered situation being alike during each period. The best aspects for vines on the open wall in the south of England are those which range from E. to the S.E., both inclusive; and the next best from S.E. to S. Those which range from S. to W. are good, provided they are sheltered; but N. or W., though they may sometimes produce tolerable grapes, yet are very uncertain both for the ripening of the grapes and of the wood. E. by N. Mr. Hoare found a very good aspect. On a wall facing this point the sun shines till about eleven o'clock in the morning, and Mr. Hoare for many years past brought several sorts of grapes, including the Black Hamburgh, to great perfection in this aspect. It would thus appear that if a cottage, the general outline of the ground-plan of which is a square or a parallelogram, is placed so that a south and north line shall form a diagonal to it, vines may be planted against every part of the walls and trained over the whole of the roof. We have shown in the Supplement to the Encyclopædia of Cottage Architecture the immense importance of placing every cottage so as to have the diagonal a south and north line, without reference to the front or any of the sides being parallel to the adjoining road or street. "We wish it to be distinctly understood, that it forms no part of our plan to have either the front or the back of the cottage next to, and parallel with, the road; on the contrary, we prefer, in almost every case of single cottages, to have next the road, an angle of the building, by which the views across the road will be oblique, instead of being direct; as the former, in every case, exhibits a longer perspective, which must consequently contain a greater number of objects." The walls and roofs of cottages so placed, north of London, may be covered with the apple, pear, cherry, plum, and, in some cases, the apricot; and those south of London may be covered with the grape vine.

Light, rich, sandy loam, not more than eighteen inches in depth, on a dry bottom of gravel, stone, or rock, forms the most desirable soil and subsoil for the vine. Mr. Hoare truly observes, that " one of the principal causes of grapes not ripening well on the open wall in this country is the great depth of mould in which the roots of vines are suffered to run, which, enticing them to penetrate in search of food below the influence of the sun's rays, supplies them with too great a quantity of moisture; vegetation is thereby carried on until late in summer, in consequence of which the ripening process does not commence till the declination of the sun becomes too rapid to afford a sufficiency of solar heat to perfect the fruit." It is hardly possible to form the vine border of materials too dry or porous. Stones, brickbats broken moderately small, lumps of old mortar, broken pottery, oystershells, and other materials which retain air and heat, and permit heavy rains to pass quickly through, should be mixed up with two-thirds of light rich soil, such as the sweepings of roads, or the top spit of a field of good arable land. The border should never be cropped or digged, and only stirred occasionally with a fork to the depth of two inches, to admit the sun and air. Where borders cannot be prepared for vines, they may be planted in pits eighteen inches square, and eighteen inches deep, filled up with suitable soil; and if the situation is dry, the roots will soon push themselves into some suitable place; for, as Mr. Hoare observes, the roots of the vine possess an extraordinary power of adapting themselves to any situation in which they may be planted, provided it be a dry one.

As the vine border once properly made ought never to be disturbed, it follows that the manure incorporated with the soil at making should be of a permanent nature, decomposing from time to time to supply the nutriment extracted by the plants. Top-dressings and liquid manure may also be added when the border is made, or at any subsequent period. Some of the best permanent manures are bones, horns and hoofs of cattle, bone-dust, cuttings of leather, woollen rags, feathers, and hair. Bones Mr. Hoare considers by far the most valuable manure that can be deposited in a vine border, and he recommends their being buried in the soil whole, and as fresh as possible, and of every size from the smallest bone of a fowl to the largest bone of an ox. Excess of manure deteriorates the flavour of grapes, and produces an excessive and unnatural growth of long-jointed wood, with nothing but leaf-buds.

Walls.—In an unsheltered situation, exposed to W. and S.W. winds, Mr. Hoare has never seen prime grapes produced much higher than eight feet from the ground; but in sheltered situations, and in S. and S.E. aspects, grapes may be matured at any height from the ground.

The lower part of the wall, however, will always enjoy an increased degree of warmth from the reflected heat of the ground. Hence grapes growing within two or three feet of the bottom of a wall facing the south will, in general, ripen from ten days to a fortnight earlier than those growing on the upper part of it. It may be observed, that the higher the wall the warmer will its southern aspect be, and the colder its northern aspect. There is a disadvantage, however, in training grapes near the ground, as it respects their remaining on the vine after being ripe. If grapes can be kept perfectly dry, they will hang on the vine and improve in flavour for a long time after they are ripe; but if dampness or moisture of any description reach them, the consequences are quickly seen in the decay of the berries. After the middle of October, therefore, it will be found a difficult matter to preserve grapes that hang within two feet of the ground, on account of the damp exhalations that continually arise from the soil at that period of the year. Projecting copings to vine walls preserve the shoots from late frosts in spring, and the blossoms from cold dews and heavy rains; they also keep the grapes in good condition for some time after they have become ripe; they prevent the escape of heat, and are convenient for fastening netting, bunting, &c. to, when it is necessary to protect the fruit from birds and insects. The disadvantages of copings are, that they exclude light, air, dew, and rain, which are very beneficial from the time the fruit has set till it begins to ripen. The width of the projecting part of the coping Mr. Hoare regulates by the height of the wall and its aspect. "If the height be less than four feet, and the aspect south, the coping ought not to project at all, as the light and solar heat excluded by it will be a serious drawback on the healthy vegetation of the vines. But if the wall be four feet high, then the coping may project as many inches; and if this width be increased an inch for every foot that the wall increases in height up to twelve feet, the principal advantages arising from the protection which a coping affords will be secured, in conjunction with the smallest portion of its disadvantages." If the aspect be east or west, the coping must be as narrow as possible, as every inch of projection in these aspects causes a considerable diminution in the duration of sunshine on the face of the wall. At the same time a coping that projects less than four inches is calculated to do more harm than good, as the drip will fall on the blossoms and the fruit. Moveable wooden copings produce, Mr. Hoare observes, all the benefit of fixed copings, without any of their disadvantages. All garden walls whatever should have iron brackets built in immediately under the stone coping, in order to admit of temporary wooden copings being applied at pleasure. Temporary copings should be applied, from the 21st of March to the middle of May, to protect the young shoots, from the first expanding of the buds until the berries are well set; and again from the berries showing symptoms of ripening till the fruit be all cut from the vines. Prune as soon after the 1st of October as the gathering of the fruit will admit; and never prune in March, April, or May. The best system of pruning and training is the common or spur-pruning.

The appearance of a portion of the front of a house covered with vines is shown in fig. 348, in which there are seven different plants, marked *a* to *g* in the figure. The plant *a* has a long stem, and arms rather shorter than usual for covering a portion of the wall equal to the height of the bed-room windows; *b* covers a space equal to the height of the parlour windows; *c* covers the space between the parlour and the bed-room windows: it has arms exceeding the usual length, every shoot bearing shoots in the Thomery manner; *d* has a very short

Fig. 348.

The front of a plain house, covered with grape vines on the left side, and other fruit trees on the right side.

stem, and long arms, with short bearing shoots, for covering the space between the sill of the parlour windows and the plinth; *e* has a stem which reaches above the bed-room windows, with very long arms and short shoots, in the Thomery manner, for covering the space between the bed-room windows and the roof. The other half of the front is shown covered with fruit trees; *h* may represent an apple, a cherry, or a plum; *i* and *k*, pears; and *l* may be the same as *h*.

Vines may be planted against houses in the streets, and we see in many villages and country towns, the roots running under the foot pavement, and even under the street, for no fruit tree is less particular in regard to soil, provided that it be on a perfectly dry bottom. Of course the bearing arms of vines grown in streets should be at such a height from the ground as to be out of the reach of mischievous persons.

The walls and roof of a cottage of the most irregular architecture may be covered with vines or fruit trees on the same principle as we have just exhibited on the front of a plain house. In the perspective view, fig. 349, thirty-five plants are shown, with stems and arms so

Fig. 349.

Two sides of a cottage, covered with vines, trained in Mr. Hoare's manner.

adjusted as to cover two sides of the building. To avoid confusion, only the stems and arms are shown, and the position of the spurs whence the bearing wood is produced.

It will be observed that the stems *a, a,* are long for the purpose of covering the upper part of the roof; and *b, b,* for covering the upper part of the gable; *c, c,* are for covering the lower part of the roof; *d, d,* the upper part of the wall; and *e, e,* the lower part. The other stems speak for themselves.

CHAPTER XV.

THE PEACH, NECTARINE, ETC.

Culture of the Peach and Nectarine under Glass.

THE peach (Amygdalus persica, L.) is indigenous in Persia, where it attains a high degree of perfection, and where, Dr. Royle informs us, both the free and cling-stone varieties are known. It is also found in various parts of Turkey in Asia, in India in different parts of the

Himalayas, and it is cultivated in China, Japan, North America, and in most parts of Europe. Our data for the culture of the peach must chiefly be taken from the practice in countries where it is successfully cultivated, and in no country is it more so in the open air than in the neighbourhood of Paris, or under glass than in England.

Natural and Experimental Data.—If the mean temperature of February amount to 40° and that of March to 44° or 45°, the peach-tree will be in full flower against a wall with a south aspect about the last week in March; and the general crop will be ripe in the last week of August, or first week of September, provided the mean temperature of April be 49°, May 55°, June 61°, July 64°, and that of August 63°. The period required for the maturation of the fruit from the time of flowering is, on the open wall, five months; but it may be reduced to four by means of fire-heat and the protection of glass. It cannot, however, be advantageously diminished any further. This fact being borne in mind, it is easy for the gardener to know at what time to commence forcing his peaches in order to obtain a crop in a given month.

From the natural climate and habit of the peach-tree, it is obvious that when forced it must be flowered under a comparatively low degree of temperature. It cannot therefore be well forced simultaneously with the vine; for the temperature of March, which in this climate serves to bring the peach into flower, does not unfold the buds of the vine, this being only effected a month or six weeks farther in the season by a mean temperature of 55°. The peach may be subjected at first to a temperature of 45°, but not exceeding 55° till the flowering is over, after which it may be gradually raised to 60°, and not exceeding 65°, till the substance of the stone is indurated; and after this crisis from 65° to 70° may be allowed. This is to be understood as referring to the application of fire-heat. Even in the total absence of the latter, sun-heat will frequently raise the temperature much higher; but in such cases air is mostly freely admitted, and even apart from this, an elevation of temperature by sun-heat is not so injurious as the same amount of fire-heat. Air should, however, be always freely admitted during the day when the weather is at all favourable.

Light is so essential, that unless peaches be trained near the glass, the fruit will neither acquire due colour nor flavour. Vicissitudes of dryness and moisture must be avoided. The roots should be well supplied with water before the fruit begins to ripen off, because at a later period none can be applied without deteriorating the flavour.

The management of the peach-tree can only be correctly understood by those who are aware of the disposition of its buds and its mode of bearing. The leaves on the shoots of the current season are produced either singly, in pairs, or in threes from the same node. In the course of the summer, or early part of autumn, a bud is formed in the axil of every individual leaf, and these are termed single, double, or triple eyes, or buds, according as one or more are produced at each node. In the following season, these buds develop themselves, either as flower-buds or young shoots; and, previously to pruning, it is necessary to distinguish the one description from the other. The flower-buds are plump and roundish; the wood-buds are more oblong and pointed, and one of these is generally situated between two flower-buds in the case of triple buds occurring at the same node. It is therefore expedient in pruning to shorten a shoot to these triple eyes, or in their absence to a leaf-bud. The mode of bearing is solely on shoots of the preceding summer's growth.

Culture of the Peach under Glass in British Gardens.

Construction of the Peach-house.—The form of the peach-house need not differ much from that of the grape-house, but in general it is made narrower and not so high at the back wall. It may, however, be made of any height or width, with either a lean-to or a ridge-and-furrow roof; from ten to fifteen feet, are good widths for lean-to peach-houses, with a height in front of four feet, and at back of ten feet. Of much more consequence than the form of the houses is the keeping of the trees near to the glass, and the provision for ventilation. There is no better mode of training peach-trees, so as to gather the finest, highest-coloured, best-flavoured fruit, than that of spreading them over a roof trellis, at a distance of fifteen inches to thirty inches from the roof, though under clear glass they will do well as bushes or standards, or trained on the back wall, or bent over arches.

Peaches best adapted for Forcing.—The sorts of peaches best adapted for forcing are: Grosse Mignonne, Royal George, Red Magdalen, Bellegarde, Early York, Stirling Castle, Chancellor, Noblesse, Rivers' Early New White, Dr. Hogg, Lord Palmerston. To these may be added such sorts as the Salway, Late Admirable, and the Barrington, when it is desired to prolong the succession under glass. These sorts ripen in the order in which they are placed; the two latter kinds being late peaches, are only proper to be planted where a prolonged succession is required. The Bellegarde is not so subject to the attack of mildew as many others are that have serrated glandless leaves.

Nectarines.—Among the best varieties of nectarines for forcing are the Violet Hâtive, Elruge, Pitmaston Orange, Downton, Rivers' Orange, Victoria, Pine-apple, and Murray.

Plants and Modes of Training.—Time is gained by procuring from the nurseries, or from the open walls of the same garden trees which have been three or four years trained, which may be removed in November. The fan mode of training is unquestionably the best for forced peaches. In lofty or wide houses it may be necessary to introduce riders in order more speedily to cover the upper part of the trellis or walls, and these also should be three or four years trained; but where the peach has been properly treated on a garden-wall, and its roots encouraged to run near the surface of the border, trained trees of almost any size may be transferred from the open wall to the forcing-house at once, so as even to bear a tolerable crop of fruit the first year.

Pruning.—The winter pruning of the peach under glass should take place immediately after the fall of the leaf. The young shoots on the lower branches should be cut back so as to ensure that the trellis may be furnished from the bottom with young wood. The shoots on the upper or farther extended branches may be shortened back to half or one-third of their lengths, according to their strength, provided they have been well ripened, and are free from canker; but if the tree be at all diseased, they should be cut so far back as to get rid of the cankered or mildewed parts. The riders need not be pruned so much as the dwarfs, the object being rather to throw them into a bearing state, than to cause them to push very strong shoots, which would not be fruitful. If they make moderately strong shoots, and if these be well ripened in autumn, a good crop may be expected on them next year. "Unless peach-trees be very strong," Mr. Thompson observes, "the shoots should be more or less shortened, according to the vigour of the tree. If this be not attended to, it will be impossible to prevent the bearing wood from becoming naked at the base. The setting and stoning of fruit, situated at or near the extremity of a three-year-old branch, which has perhaps only leaves on the part produced during the last season, is, indeed, very precarious."

The summer pruning consists in pinching off all foreright shoots as they appear, and all such as are ill-placed, weakly, watery, or deformed, leaving a leader to every shoot of last year, and retaining a plentiful supply of good lateral shoots in all parts of the tree. If any blank is to be filled up, some conveniently-placed strong shoot is shortened in a very early stage of its growth to a few eyes, in order that it may throw out laterals. All luxuriant shoots should be stopped as soon as their tendency to over-luxuriance is observed, in order that the sap, which would otherwise be wasted, may be forced into the adjoining shoots, or expended in forming two or three fruit-bearing branches, or in nourishing the fruit.

The Fruit is thinned before and after the Stoning Season.—There should be a preparatory thinning soon after the fruit is set, leaving of course a sufficient number in case of imperfection that may only become apparent at the period of stoning; because most plants, especially such as have overborne themselves, drop many fruit at that crisis. When this is over, the thinning should be effected with great regularity, leaving the fruit retained at proper distances—three, four, or five on strong shoots, two or three on middling, and one or two on the weaker shoots, and never leaving more than one peach at the same eye. The fruit on weakly trees should be thinned more in proportion.

The peach-border will be partly within the house, but chiefly on the outside, where it may extend ten feet or twelve feet from the front wall. The usual depth of the border in medium soils and situations is from two to three feet. The bottom should be previously thoroughly drained, and covered with a stratum of gravel, broken bricks, or other similar materials, to conduct away superfluous water. The best soil is a fresh strong loam from an old pasture, mixed with a few fragments of freestone. The part of the borders on the outside may be covered with dung, and, after forcing is commenced, those in the inside may be occasionally watered with liquid manure; but no manure whatever is required till such time as the trees are in a bearing state.

General Treatment.—From the rise of the sap, it occupies in some sorts about four months to make mature fruit; in the later varieties, five months; and when much of the winter is included in the course of forcing, the time is proportionally lengthened. To ripen moderately early kinds by the end of May, begin to force on the 21st of December. Little is gained by commencing sooner. Begin with a temperature of 45° maximum, from fire-heat, and rise in a fortnight to 50° maximum, from fire-heat, giving plenty of air. In the progress of the second fortnight, augment the temperature from three to eight degrees, so as to have it at the close up to 53° minimum, 56° maximum, from sun-heat, admitting air in some degree daily. When the trees are in blossom, let the heat be 55° minimum, 60° maximum. Continue this treatment till the fruit is set and swelling. When the fruit is set, raise the minimum to 60°, the artificial maximum to 65°, in order to give fresh air; when the sun shines, do not let the maximum from collected heat pass 70°, rather employing the opportunity to admit a free circulation of air. While the fruit is in blossom, heavy syringing over head should be avoided, but a slight drenching at night refreshes and strengthens the flowers, and probably causes them to set more freely. The roots at this period must neither have an excess nor suffer from a scarcity of water, as either extreme is apt to cause the trees to shed their blossoms. An important point to be attended to in watering is to let the water be warmed to the same temperature as the air of the house. When the fruit is ripening, its flavour is improved by direct exposure to the sun and air, and too much air can hardly be given. When it is quite ripe, the border should be covered with moss, or some soft substance, or nets suspended under the trees, to prevent those which drop off from being bruised; but the best flavour is obtained by gathering the fruit a day before it is quite ripe, and ripening it for twenty or thirty hours in the fruit-room.

Insects and Diseases.—The red spider is the grand enemy to the peach-tree; but it is also attacked by mildew, the aphis, thrips, ants, and sometimes even by the coccus. Their ravages become apparent by the leaves curling up, and often by the ends of the shoots becoming bunched and clammy, which retards their shooting. In this case it is advisable to pick off the infected leaves, and cut away the distempered part of the shoots. Further to check the mischief, if the weather be hot and dry, give the trees a smart watering over head with a garden engine. It should be applied two or three times a week, or even once a day. The best time of the day is the afternoon, when the power of the sun is declining. These waterings will clear the leaves, branches, and fruit from any contracted foulness, refresh and revive the whole considerably, and conduce greatly to exterminate the insects. Washings with soot or quassia-chip water, will likewise exterminate the fly, and dustings with sulphur and lime, either on the shoots or floors, extirpate mildew and red spider. Tobacco dust or smoke will also be needed to clear off thrips and aphides, should they get a strong hold of the trees.

Peaches are now extensively grown in pots, either in orchard-houses, vineries, peach-houses, or even plant-stoves, and, with care in the flowering and stoning periods, good results are obtained from very small space. It may be well to observe that the peach to be grown in pots, or to be transplanted when of two or more years' growth, must be worked on plum-stocks, on account of the much greater number of fibrous roots which these stocks produce than almonds; the latter are generally employed as stocks to the peach in France and Italy, being found to answer well in these countries, where the peach is seldom transplanted, and where the soil and climate are much drier and warmer than in Britain. Mr. Rivers has carried this mode of cultivating the peach and other stone-fruits to great perfection, and pyramidal trees, dwarf bushes, and standards may be had in a fruiting state from all the leading nurseries. Plants in pots require the same general treatment as those out of them, with more care in feeding them with water and manure, and great caution in not giving them severe checks from an excess or a paucity of either, or by sudden changes of temperature. But with these increased risks there are several advantages, the chief being that the confinement of the roots favours fertility. It is no uncommon thing to see peach or nectarine trees in pots carry from four to eight dozen of fruit to perfect maturity. Peaches and nectarines in pots are generally trained in such a contorted and scrubby fashion, that we give an illustration to show they may be trained as gracefully and correctly as many plants supposed to be much more tractable. This is from a photograph taken in the Royal Horticultural Gardens at Chiswick, and is a shape very easily attainable. The tree was presented to the society, with others, by Mr. Pearson, of Chilwell, in whose magnificent orchard-houses at Chilwell, near Nottingham, are many specimens trained in like manner. Where trees are grown in pots, and these pots have to be stored in houses, everything that tends to allow of the plants enjoying the greatest amount of light, while not wasting space, is a decided gain to the cultivator; and it need scarcely be said that while two sets of trees, the different outlines of which may be roughly suggested by the following, △△△——▽▽▽,

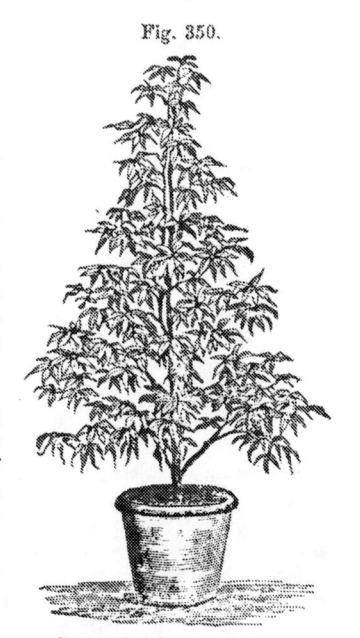

Fig. 350.

Pyramidal Peach-tree in pot.

occupy about the same amount of space in a house, trees approaching the former shape will enjoy the light over nearly all their parts. Besides, trees pyramidal in outline are much more presentable. The general tendency is too much towards squat-headed trees, which have been allowed to develop their primary branches much as they liked, and which frequently betray no trace of any attempt at judicious training. Yet nothing is easier than to secure this desirable form in the case of the peach: first, by securing a broad furnished base secondly, by repressing those parts that grow too vigorously at the expense of weak and ill-furnished ones; and thirdly, by first pinching the upper parts of the tree, so as to prevent it running to a head. Once fairly trained into this form, there is little after-trouble beyond routine pinching. But to get the broad well-furnished base it is necessary to cut the young tree at first down, instead of allowing the first erect shoot it makes to form the pyramid. Neither has the pot-culture of fruit trees been confined to peaches and nectarines, but apricots, cherries, plums, and even apples and pears and grapes are now extensively grown under glass in this manner.

Orchard-houses or glass structures, wholly devoted to the cultivation of fruit trees, either in pots or planted out in the border, are to be met with frequently. The most common form is a lofty span-roofed house, with a wide border down the centre for pyramidal trees in pots or planted out, and borders at the side for smaller trees of similar character, or in the form of bushes at the sides. Such structures are either heated or not heated, and have all the characteristics of a miniature orchard under glass. Many of our stone-fruits, such as cherries and plums, set and finish their fruit better in such structures than in peach or any other fruit-houses, chiefly from there being more light and a freer, fuller ventilation.

The routine of culture under glass does not differ from that on walls. Attention to cleanliness, disbudding, pruning, stopping, and tying in the young wood is required in both cases. Ventilation is the chief difference, and this is of great moment. Air should always be admitted early in the morning, and before the sun has raised the temperature of the house more than five degrees. Sudden or extreme changes of temperature must be guarded against, and the fruit must not be overhung by the leaves in the last or ripening stages, else its flavour will be injured. The winter treatment consists in excluding frost only, at least from the roots.

Applying a Preventive Composition.——Previously to tying the trees to the trellis, the whole of their stems, but not the bearing wood, should be washed with a composition, formed of one pound of soft-soap, one ounce of tobacco, and a little flowers of sulphur, mixed with as much boiling water as will make the whole of the consistence of paint. This composition is carefully applied with a painter's soft brush whilst it is milk-warm. The process of cleaning should never be omitted at the pruning season, as it clears the trees of brown scale. When the trees are tied to the trellis, the borders may be slightly forked over and top-dressed with fresh soil, or well-rotted manure if the trees are weak.

The culture of the nectarine varies in no degree from that of the peach, and it may be grown with equal ease and success either in the peach-house or the orchard-house, or in pots in any other glass-house or large pit.

Succession Crops.—Where peach-forcing begins in December, a second house ought to be started in February, and a third in March, to keep up the supply of peaches, until those grown on the walls come in. Where there is only one house, it will be best not to start it till the middle of January, or there will be a long season in summer or early autumn without fruit. Besides, the later the forcing begins the greater the probability of complete success. By planting early and late sorts, peaches may, however, be gathered from one house for six weeks or two months.

Culture of the Cherry under Glass.

The cherry in its wild state being indigenous to Britain, and as a cultivated fruit brought to as high a degree of perfection in our climate as in any other, very little requires to be said on the subject of natural data for culture. The cherry is cultivated in Italy and the fruit attains a large size, but in point of flavour it is inferior to the fruit of the same varieties grown in England or in central Germany. The cherry is forced in all the northern countries of Europe, and as it matures fruit in the open air in three months from the time of blossoming, it is ripened earlier in forcing-houses than the fruit of any other tree. The temperature and moisture to be imitated are those of April, May, and June. The general practice in British gardens is to begin at 40°, and throughout the first week to let the minimum be 40°, and the maximum 45°, giving plenty of air. By gradual advances in the second, third, and fourth weeks, raise the heat to 45° min. 50° max. In strong sunshine, admit air freely, rather than have the temperature above 60° by confining the warm air. In the fifth and sixth weeks, the artificial minimum may be gradually extended to 50°, but the maximum should be limited to 55° from fire-heat, and to 60° from sun-heat, until the plants are in flower. It is safest not to exceed these temperatures, though five degrees more may be allowed in the finishing stage, say 60° minimum and 65° maximum.

The practice of forcing cherries has now become general, and is carried to a high degree of perfection in many gardens.

The practice of Cherry Forcing in British Gardens.

When cherries are required at the earliest period at which they can be produced in a forcing-house, which is about the middle of March, it is desirable to have a stock of plants in pots; because the entire plant being under the command of the forcer, can be excited much more effectually than if its roots were in the cold soil, and only its head exposed to the action of the warmth of the house.

The cherry-house may be thirty feet long, fourteen feet wide, twelve feet high at the back, and seven feet high in front, or any other convenient size. The ends should be of glass, and both ends and front should be placed on brick walls two feet high supported by arches. The front sashes may either be hung on hinges at the tops, or at the sides, to open outwards. The roof sashes should be in two lengths; the lower ones to pull up, and the upper ones to let down. As cherries require a great deal of air, and this often during wet weather, above the upper sashes there should be a projecting flashing of lead, to exclude the rain when the sashes are let down an inch or two. The heating may either be by flues or by hot water; and in either case one furnace or one boiler, with the flues or pipes going round the house immediately within the front and ends, will be sufficient.

Kinds of Cherries for Forcing, Potting Plants, &c.—Hardly any fruit has been more improved, or more rapidly, than the cherry. A few years ago it could be truly written that the best forcing cherry was the May Duke, and indeed it was the only one generally used; now there are over one hundred varieties of more or less merit. We will endeavour to select a few of the best:—Werder's Early Black, Knight's Early Black, Bowyer's Early Heart, Bigarreau, Napoleon, Belle d'Orleans, Florence, Black Eagle, Noir précoce, Early Purple Guigne, Downton, Elton, and White Heart. The plants for potting should have been three or four years worked, and should be such as are well furnished with blossom-buds. The soil used in potting may be a stiff, almost clayey loam, such as that in which melons are grown; to which, if necessary, one-fifth part of thoroughly rotten dung may be added; bearing in mind that too rich a soil makes the shoots too luxuriant, and causes them to gum. The season for potting is September and October, and success is rendered more certain if the trees have been in pots one year before they are forced. While the trees remain out of doors, it is necessary to watch the operations of the sparrows, which are very apt to pick off the buds of cherries in the winter season, probably in search of the eggs or larvæ of insects. If the trees potted are standards, they may be set on the ground, or on a low stage; and if they are dwarfs, upon a higher stage, so as, in either case, to bring their heads within eighteen inches of the glass. They may be set so close together that their heads may be within a few inches of touching each other.

Time of Commencing to Force.—For the first crop shut up the house and begin lighting fires about the middle of December. Proceed cautiously with the temperature, as already indicated. During the whole period of forcing air must be admitted more or less, both during mild nights and by day; but especially in the daytime and during sunshine. The cherry is most impatient of a stagnant atmosphere. When fine weather prevails at the time the trees are coming into bloom, a comparatively greater heat is required at night than during the day; because if they are kept cool at night, the heat of the day is apt to expand the flowers before the stalks have grown to their natural length; and if so, although all the flowers might set (which is not the case when they are short-stalked), it would be impossible for a full crop to swell off, as there would not be space enough for the cherries to expand. Watering must be withheld from the tops of the trees during the time they are in blossom, but given as required for their roots, and the floor kept moist by sprinkling it morning and evening.

Progress.—Trees begun to be forced in the middle of December will come into blossom in the middle of January, set their fruit about the end of the month, and stone it about the middle of February.

Insects.—After the leaves expand, it very often happens that a caterpillar, or some black fly, makes its appearance; these are sometimes scarcely to be met with in the daytime, but on going into the house at night the caterpillar will be found crawling on the leaves and eating them. Fumigation with tobacco, and hand-picking, are the only remedies for these pests. Ants too sometimes make their appearance when the trees are in blossom; and though they are not so injurious to the cherry as they are to the peach, they ought to be at once destroyed by pouring tobacco-water or sprinkling guano upon their nests. Till the ants' nests are destroyed, the insects may be prevented from getting at the blossoms by tying pieces of paper round the stems of the trees, and coating them over with a mixture of tar and grease: the paper should be of a coarse spongy kind, so as to absorb the tar, and prevent it from running down the bark of the stem when the temperature of the house is high—or yarn may be used instead of paper. In either case, as soon as the tar becomes hard, the ants will walk over it, and in that case it must be renewed. When the trees are in blossom, it will facilitate the setting of the fruit if bees can be introduced, which may easily be done, by bringing in a hive, or, what is preferable, by fixing a hive immediately in front of the lower part of one of the front sashes, and so as to touch it, and having an entrance for the bees at the back of the hive, as well as the usual one in front of it. Corresponding with this back entrance, a small hole may be cut in the bottom rail of the sash, and a stopper or slide fitted to it, through which the bees may be admitted to the cherry-house at pleasure.

Thinning and Stoning, &c.—When the fruit is fairly set, it should be thinned out with the grape scissors, removing from one-fourth to one-third of the cherries, according the vigour of the tree, and the number of fruit it has set. When once the fruit is set it is not liable to be injured by cold, as in the case of peaches and grapes. On the contrary, cherry-trees in pots have been turned out into the open garden, by way of experiment, after the fruit was set; and the frosts, which damaged the leaves, had no effect at all upon the fruit, except to retard its growth. After the fruit has begun to stone (which is generally about a fortnight after it is set), the trees should be watered freely at the roots, but in eight or ten days, when the kernel begins to harden, the quantity of water may be diminished. The temperature of the house, except in sunshine, should never exceed 60°, either by night or by day, from blossoming up to the time of stoning; but in three weeks after setting, when the stoning will generally be found completed, and the pulp of the fruit beginning to assume a pale red, the temperature may be raised to 65° at night, and even to 70° or 75°

in the day, during sunshine, and when abundance of air is given. After the fruit is ripe, water should be withheld till it is gathered. In every stage of the progress of the cherry in a forcing-house, the plants may be watered with liquid manure, which is found to strengthen their leaves and buds without injuring the flavour of the fruit.

Treatment of the Plants in Pots after they are taken out of the House.—Immediately after the crop is gathered the trees should be taken to a cool, rather shady situation, set on the ground, and the pots surrounded up to the rim with rotten tan, sawdust, or any similar materials, to keep them cool, and in an equable degree of moisture. If, on the other hand, a second crop of cherries should be wanted late in autumn, the soil in the pots should be allowed to be quite dry for a month; and, by afterwards watering it freely, and placing the trees in the house about the end of August, and treating them in the same manner as was done in early spring, they will ripen their fruit in October or November. Such trees, however, will not be again fit to force for two or three years to come; and they should, therefore, be turned out of the pots into the free soil, and allowed at least two years to recover themselves, when they may be again re-potted and forced. While in the open ground, all the blossoms produced should be picked off as soon as they appear, to prevent them from weakening the trees. In the cherry, as in most trees that produce their blossoms on the wood of the preceding year, or on spurs, the blossom-buds expand first, and next the barren or wood-buds. The latter continue growing till the petals of the flowers drop off, when they receive a check, and scarcely grow at all, till the fruit is set and begins to swell; after which they grow rapidly, and complete the shoots of the year, by the time the fruit is stoned.

To have a constant succession of cherries from the middle of March till July, as soon as the trees of one house have come into blossom, those of the next should have artificial heat applied, and the temperature and management will be in every case the same as that which has been above described. It may be observed here, that cherry-houses, with the trees planted in the ground, are much less suitable, not only for early forcing, but for main and late crops, than cherry-trees grown in pots. The cherry cannot, like the peach and nectarine, be forced for a number of years together; and hence, as a house in which the trees are planted in the ground must, every three or four years, have a season of rest, the house during that season, having the sashes taken off, is in a great measure of no use.—(See 'Gard. Mag.,' vol. xiv. p. 41.)

Forcing Cherries by a Temporary Structure.—Where a portion of wall (especially with a southern aspect), already well furnished with cherries, perfectly established, and in a bearing state, can be spared for forcing, a temporary glass case may be put up against it; the flue may be built on the surface of the border, without digging or sinking for a foundation; neither will any upright glass or front wall be requisite; the wooden plate on which the lower ends of the rafters are to rest may be supported by piles, sunk or driven into the soil of the border, one pile under every, or every alternate, rafter. The space between the plate and the surface of the soil should be filled by boards nailed against the piles, to exclude the external air, for the plate must be elevated above the level of the surface from eighteen to thirty inches, or whatever height may be sufficient to let the sashes slip down, in order to admit fresh air. This structure, or one formed of Beard's patent sashes, will suit well for cherries, for such structures have been erected for forcing peaches with great success, as well as for maturing and preserving a late crop of grapes.

German Practice.—In the Royal Gardens at Potsdam, cherries are frequently forced so as to be ripe at the end of February. The plants are potted a year before they are forced. They are potted in autumn, and the roots protected from frost through the winter by being covered with litter.

In the following spring the blossom-buds are broken off as soon as they appear; and, by the end of June, all the shoots which have pushed freely have their points pinched off, so as to leave not more than six buds, which buds by that operation become blossom-buds.

Before the plants are taken in they must at least have sustained 14° Fahr. of cold, otherwise they are found to break very irregularly. The blossoms are thinned out; so much so, that where fifteen have appeared, not more than three have been allowed to expand. The construction of the house in which the forcing is commenced varies according to the season. When the trees are taken in, in December and January, the glass of the roof must be much steeper than when they are not taken in till February and March.

Heat is communicated by flues, commencing with 46° Fahr. The trees are frequently sprinkled with lukewarm water; and the roots, which ought to have been kept quite dry for some time before the plants are taken in, are well soaked with warm water. Boiling water is mixed with equal quantities of cold, and water of this temperature is used till within fourteen days of the trees coming into blossom.

When the buds break out into bloom, watering overhead with lukewarm water is left off, but the stems are kept moist by rubbing them two or three times a day with a wet brush. During the blooming season the temperature is raised from 46° to 67°, every third day, $2\frac{1}{4}°$ more heat being added. Abundance of air is given, and shade during bright sunshine. In boisterous weather gauze is placed over the openings through which the air is admitted, of the advantage of which in moderating the violence of the wind, the Royal gardener has expressed himself well assured after eight years' experience. To cause the blossoms to set, the branches and spray are frequently put in motion, but care is taken not to move the main stem, by which the fibrous roots might be injured. When the fruit is setting and swelling, the temperature must be kept between 54° and 65°.

When the fruit is stoning, the temperature is lowered to 59° for two or three weeks, during which period the house must be shaded in bright sunshine, and the plants watered overhead once or twice a day.

When the stoning is completed and the fruit begins to swell, the temperature is again raised to 65°, and no more shade given, in order that the fruit may acquire a high flavour through the operation of the sun's rays, to facilitate the action of which on the fruit, the superfluous leaves are removed. By this practice, plants begun to be forced in December commonly produce ripe cherries in February, and sometimes even in January, though without a good flavour.

It must be borne in mind, that the atmosphere in Prussia, and on the Continent generally, is much clearer than in Britain, and that there are few days when the sun during the short time in which he is above the horizon does not shine brightly. Hence as far as light is concerned in forcing, the British gardener can never contend with the German one.

Culture of the Fig under Glass.

The fig (Ficus Carica, L.) is a native of Asia and the sea-coast of Africa, and it is cultivated on the shores and islands of the Mediterranean, in Italy, and in the south of France; but, like the olive, never far from the sea-side, or at great elevations. The soil is generally light, but resting on a subsoil which is supplied with water within the reach of the roots. It would thus appear that the fig is not intended by nature to endure a severe winter, a great degree of drought, or a very hot summer; and this conclusion is in accordance with the succulence of its wood, the retention of young fruit on its shoots throughout the winter, and its broad succulent leaves. The spring and summer temperature suitable for the grape vine has been found to answer for the fig, but the latter requires a moister atmosphere, and more water at the root when in a growing state, and the temperature should not be below 40° during winter. It is the nature of the fig to produce two crops in the year, both when it is cultivated in the open air, and when it is under glass. The first crop, which is produced on the points of the shoots of the last year, ripens in Italy in May and June; and on the walls in the climate of London in September and October. The second crop is produced on the shoots of the current year, and ripens in Italy in October; but in the open air in this country it never ripens at all, excepting a few of small size, which remain on through the winter, and constitute the first crop, just mentioned, of the following summer. Under glass, the first crop ripens at various periods between March and June, according to the time of commencing to force; and the second crop, which in the open air never attains maturity, is under glass that which is most to be depended on. The first crop under glass ripens in four or five months from the time of commencing to force, and the second crop in six or eight months. The fruit of the fig is what is called a common receptacle for the flowers, but turned up in a turbinate or top shape, so as to enclose the florets and completely exclude them from view. The fig, both in fig countries and in British gardens, is apt to drop its fruit prematurely; and in Italy and Greece the process of caprification is employed to counteract this tendency. It consists in placing among the branches of cultivated fig-trees, branches of the wild fig, or even fruit that has dropped off wild trees, in which a kind of gnat abounds, and which enters the fruit on the cultivated tree, and passing over the anthers distributes the pollen over the stigma. The utility of this practice is doubted by many; at all events, it is neither practised in France nor Britain, but as a substitute for it, ringing the branch immediately behind the fruit has been found successful in some instances; but the best antidote to the dropping of the fruit is abundant supplies of water at the root.

The Forcing of the Fig as practised in British Gardens.

The fig is daily growing in favour with the British public, and the demand for green figs is becoming general. It is most generally forced in pots, either placed in pits, or in peach-houses, vineries, or even pine-stoves; and as the plants bear two or more crops in a year, it is not difficult to have a supply of fruit at most seasons; the chief dependence, however, is on the second crop, or that produced on the wood of the current year.

The construction of the fig-house may be the same as that of the peach-house; but the leaves being large, the trellis may be placed from six inches to a foot farther from the glass. The soil of the border should be light, sandy, liberally mixed with lime or broken bricks, and thoroughly drained.

The varieties best adapted for forcing are White Marseilles and Black Marseilles, Early Violet, White, Brown, and Black Ischia, Singleton, Castle Kennedy, Golden or Ligne d'Or, and Brown Turkey. Close pruning is to be avoided, and the best form of tree for securing a large crop is a sort of half-standard with a mass of young wood standing out two feet or more from the roots. The plants may be trained in the fan manner, and the mode of pruning should be such as to favour the production of young wood over every part of the tree. Very little pruning is required for the fig; but by pinching out the points of the shoots after the fruit appears, its progress is hastened, and the chances of its setting increased.

The time of beginning to force the fig is commonly the same as that for forcing the grape or the peach, and the temperature is also much the same as that for the vine, or somewhat intermediate between it and the peach. The apricot, peach, plum, and cherry, vegetate in March or the beginning of April; but the vine and the fig require the temperature of May to bring them into vegetation even when growing against a south wall. Hence, when forced, they require a proportionately higher temperature to bring them into leaf.

The first crop of figs, which is that produced on the points of the shoots of the last year, will ripen in May or June; but the second crop will not ripen before September, though, as it does not ripen all at once, it will last till December. The only difficult point in forcing the fig is to preserve the embryo fruit formed on the points of the shoots of the current year, so that they may ripen as a first crop in the next year. The fig will thrive at a greater distance from the glass than either the vine or the peach, and also with less air than any other fruit tree. It is very subject to the red spider, which should be kept under by watering copiously over the leaves; or, if that is not sufficient, by washing the flues or hot-water pipes with a mixture of flowers of sulphur and lime. Brown scale, and even mealy bug, are also partial to the fig, and the best way of exterminating such pests is by dressing the whole tree with a similar mixture to that recommended for the peach; or to wash every portion of the tree with spirits of wine.

The forcing of fig-trees in pots is perhaps the best mode, at least for small establishments, because, by having an abundant stock of plants, fruit may be obtained nine months in the year, as indeed it is at Preston-hall, in East Lothian, where forty varieties are cultivated under glass. "The plants should be low and bushy, so that they may stand on the kerb of the tan-bed, or they may be plunged in a gentle tan heat, or in a bed of leaves of trees. The best way to propagate plants for this purpose is to take layers or slips which have good roots: plant them in pots in good earth, one plant in each pot, and plunge them in a bed of tan or of leaves of trees, in which is a very gentle heat: a brick bed will answer the purpose very well; or they will do in the forcing-house, if there be room for them. Let them be put into the house in the latter end of February or beginning of March, and keep them sufficiently watered. When they are two years old, they will be able to bear fruit; the pots in that time having become full of roots. In the month of November or December, turn the plants out of the pots, and with a sharp knife pare off the outside of the ball, by which the plant will be divested of its roots matted against the inside of the pot; then place them in larger pots, filling up the vacancy round the balls with strong loamy earth. During the winter, let them be kept in the greenhouse, or in a glazed pit of a like temperature, till the month of February, which will be a means of preventing the fruit from falling off before it comes to maturity. In this manner let them be treated every year, till the plants become too large for the pots; then move them into the forcing-house, where it is intended they shall ripen their fruit."—('Gard. Rem.')

Of figs in pots, Mr. Pearson, of Chilwell, writes as follows to the 'Field':—" The cultivation of the fig is evidently on the increase. This is not at all to be wondered at. Though there are some persons who do not like the large black or purple figs the first time they eat them, yet I have often noticed these very persons acquire a taste for them after a little time; and those who do like them soon get to like them very much. This may be accounted for, perhaps, on the principle that we like what agrees with our constitutions, and soon, as a rule, dislike what disagrees with us. Now the fig, from the absence of acid, is a peculiarly wholesome fruit to most persons, and even people subject to gout can eat it with impunity, I believe. Then, though the peculiar flavour of some of the dark-coloured figs makes them distasteful to some till a taste for them has been acquired, yet few fail to appreciate a fine white fig in good condition. The absence of any strong flavour, and its peculiar luscious sweetness, is liked by almost every one the first time, unless a bad specimen is tasted. Then, again, the fruit ripening in succession almost the whole season is a great advantage. Unlike many crops which all ripen at once, and are only in perfection for a short time, the owner of a fig-house can gather fresh-ripened fruit every day for a long period.

"The very superior varieties lately introduced from the south of France have no doubt given an impetus to this cultivation. And lastly, there is no doubt the culture is better understood, and success more generally follows. Whatever the reason, no one can doubt that there is an increased desire to grow figs. The cultivation of figs in pots, being very simple—more so perhaps than that of any other fruit tree—has made great progress. This plan, when well carried out, has its advantages—the principal one being that a great variety can be grown in a given space. Indeed, a plant in a large pot may be often seen carrying a larger crop than a huge fan-trained tree on a back wall; these latter generally making more wood than is consistent with fruitfulness.

Fig. 351.

Fig in pot.

"The object of this paper is to call attention to a mode of growing figs I have seen carried out for several seasons at Worksop Manor by Mr. Miller, which is more successful than any method I have seen practised. His trees are grown in large pots and plunged in the borders, so as just to cover the rims of the pots. A circle of small turfs is placed round them, and some rich soil and manure is given as a top-dressing. The plants are also supplied with manure-water. The shoots are pinched much the same as in pot culture. In the autumn the soil is removed from around the pots, and all the roots which have grown over the rims of the pots or through the bottoms are cut off, and fresh soil placed round the pots. These trees, though highly fed during the fruiting season, make no more wood than is desirable, and the annual root-pruning renders them very fruitful; indeed, there are almost as many fruits as leaves, and these of first-rate quality. I have seen no plan of growing figs which appears so good as this."

There is no fruit which bears pot culture so well as the fig. Plants such as that shown in the cut, and about eighteen inches in diameter, afford a succession of first-class fruit.

Winter Treatment.—The glass of the fig-house should not be taken off during winter, because it is an important object to preserve the embryo fruit that are to produce the first crop in the following year. Hence, wherever it can be accomplished, the sea-side temperature of Genoa or Naples, which is rarely under 38° or 40°, ought to be maintained in the fig-house throughout the winter months. This is most conveniently and economically done when the plants are kept in pots or tubs, as they can then be removed to a shed or cellar, as is the practice in Germany.

On Forcing the Plum, Apricot, Gooseberry, and other Fruit Trees and Fruit Shrubs.

In Germany, and more especially in Russia, it is customary to force all our hardy fruit trees and fruit shrubs, including even the currant and raspberry. The plants are invariably kept in pots; and, when the fruit is ripe, the pot with the entire plant is placed on the dessert-table. The forcing is generally carried on in the same house with various culinary vegetables, and being ripened without the natural quantity of light and air, it is, as far as we have tasted it, when in these countries in 1813 and 1814, without much flavour. Plums and apricots are occasionally forced in Britain; they are planted in pots, and placed in pits, or in any forcing-house where there is room. The temperature and treatment of a cool peach-house, it will readily be conceived, is most suitable for them.

CHAPTER XVI.

CULTURE OF THE MELON, STRAWBERRY, ETC.

The melon (Cucumis Melo, L.) is an herbaceous trailing or climbing annual, indigenous or cultivated in great part of the warmer districts of Asia or Africa from time immemorial. In the warmer parts of Europe, it has been cultivated at least from the time of the Romans. The melon is extensively cultivated in Armenia, Ispahan, and Bokhara, and very generally in Greece, Italy, and other Mediterranean regions. It succeeds in the open air as far as 43° N.; and its culture extends within the tropics, but only when it is abundantly supplied with moisture. Its extremes of temperature may be 70° and 80° for atmospheric heat, and from 75° to 90° for the soil. The atmosphere in the countries where the melon is most successfully cultivated is so dry that the plants depend almost entirely on surface irrigation and on dews. The soil in which the melon is found to thrive best is a fresh loam, rather strong than light, such as may be obtained from an alluvial meadow which is flooded during the winter season. In Persia, pigeon's dung is used; and in Britain stable dung, thoroughly rotted, is sometimes mixed with the soil; but it is not desirable to introduce rank manure to such an extent as to produce the same degree of luxuriance in the shoots which might be desirable under a tropical sun. The melon in this country requires all the light which it can receive, and therefore the plants must have their shoots trained close under the glass, for which purpose a trellis is found superior to the surface of the soil; for unless this is the case, and abundance of air is admitted, the fruit produced will be of very inferior flavour.

Early crops of the melon are with difficulty obtained in Britain, on account of our cloudy atmosphere. Late crops are less liable to be affected with disease from the greater degree of light and heat admitting of more abundant ventilation. The varieties of the melon belong to two races: the Persians and the Cantaloups. The former are the most difficult to cultivate, requiring a very high temperature, a dry atmosphere, and an extremely humid soil. The Cantaloups, which are so named from a place of that name in the neighbourhood of Rome, are cultivated throughout Europe with great success, although from being generally inferior in flavour they are not so much grown in England as the green-fleshed varieties, which have sprung in endless numbers from the Persian stock.

Summary of Culture of the Cantaloup or Scarlet-fleshed Melons.— "About four months may be allowed, on an average, for the period between the sowing of melons and the ripening of the fruit. The middle of January is found to be early enough to sow; and the young plants are so exceedingly tender that accidents are then very likely to occur to them. It is on this account necessary to make successive sowings, in order to be prepared for replacement, if requisite, and also for continuing the supply throughout the summer. A sowing for the latest crops will require to be made in April. Melons may be grown by means of frames on hotbeds, or in pits, heated according to some of the various modes of hot-water application, now so generally adopted; or, best of all, in low lean-to or span-roofed houses. But whatever be the form of the pits or houses, or the mode of heating adopted, one point of essential importance is to have the sashes glazed with British sheet glass, in large sheets, to admit as much light and have as few laps as possible. The seeds are sown in pans, or in small pots, and transplanted into other small pots when their seed-leaves are about half an inch broad. It is best to put only a single transplanted melon into each pot. In the process of potting, carry the stalk of the melon up to the first leaves, and lay it along the side of the pot, and plunge the pot up to the rim in a smart bottom heat. Meanwhile, a separate frame, that which is intended for their future growth and fruiting, is prepared for their reception by placing small hills, rather more than a foot high, of light rich mould below each sash, and nearer to the back of the frame than the front. Care must be taken that this mould be of the proper temperature before the young plants are introduced, which is to take place when they have made a few rough leaves. As the roots extend, more soil should be added, of a gradually stronger nature; and ultimately the roots should have a depth of from nine to eighteen inches of such soil. The soil should never be introduced in a cold state; and if there be no means for previously bringing it to the temperature of at least 70°, it should be put into the frame in small quantities. When water is required, it should be given at a temperature of 80°. It should not be applied when the air of the frame is at a high temperature from sun-heat, nor until the heat of the sun begins to decline—say at four o'clock in the afternoon. With regard to pruning and training the runners or vines of melon plants, it is necessary that a sufficient number of these for filling the frame—say four or six to a plant—should be made to ramify as close to the base of the main stem as can be conveniently effected, by pinching off the top of the latter when it has made a few joints, or four leaves above the cotyledons. The laterals should then be permitted to reach the sides of the frame or pit without stopping. When they have done so, pinch out their heads; blossoms of a monœcious character will soon after make their appearance. The male blossoms, or at least a portion of them, must be retained for the purpose of fertilizing the female ones which will appear later. To effect this, it is only needful to see that the pollen is in a powdery state, that can be dispersed with a breath or a touch. Then place the male flower on the stigma of the female, and fertilization is accomplished. As soon as the requisite quantity of fruit is fairly set, the male blossoms are picked off as they appear. The extremities of the fruit-bearing vines are stopped by pinching at the second or third joint above the fruit. The vines must afterwards be kept regulated so as not to overcrowd the frame with more foliage than can be duly exposed to the light. The regulation should be early and frequently attended to, so as not to have occasion to remove many vines from the plant, or divest it of much foliage at any one time. A piece of slate or tile is placed under each fruit, for the purpose of keeping it from the damp soil. The heat must be fully maintained, or even considerably increased, as the fruit approaches maturity, in order to allow the admission of a more free circulation of air; but if, at the same time, the bottom heat be allowed to decline, the plants will become diseased, and fall a prey to the mildew or to the red spider."

When a trellis is used it should be raised from a foot to eighteen inches above the soil, and within from ten inches to fourteen inches of the glass. The trellis is formed in panels of the same size as the lights, and rests on projections from the front or back of the frame, or pit, or is suspended by hooks. The trellis may either be formed of wire fixed to a wooden frame, and forming meshes five inches square to admit passing the hand through to the soil beneath; or it may be formed of laths three-quarters of an inch broad, and half-an-inch thick, also formed into squares, and nailed at the intersections. In general laths are preferable to wires, on account of their forming a flat surface for the fruit to rest on. The trellis is not introduced into the frame or pit till the plants are grown sufficiently high to admit of their tops being brought through it. The shoot having been brought through the middle of the trellis, and grown three joints above it, remove two joints with the finger and thumb, which will cause the plant to throw out fresh shoots. When those retained get sufficiently long, they must be tied down to the trellis with care. Similar treatment may be given to the garden varieties—green-fleshed Persian, Ispahan, and other more delicate sorts. In general four shoots, trained towards the four corners of the trellis till they reach within a foot of the outer edge of the bed, will be sufficient. There they must be stopped. They will now produce laterals, which should be thinned, three or four only being left on each of the four main shoots, and the others should be taken off close to the main stem out of which they grew.

Varieties.—The following are among the best varieties grown in British Gardens:—Queen Emma, Bromham Hall, Pine Apple, Trentham Hybrid, Bailey's Eclipse, and Princess Alexandra, among green-fleshed; and Moreton Hall, Turner's Gem, and Lady Sefton among scarlet.

Very early melons may be grown in pots, one plant in each, to mature one fruit, in the pine-stove, or in a house or pit on purpose, where a wholesome high temperature is maintained of 75° or 80°; the fruit may be supported by being laid on a small earthenware saucer, inverted into a larger one suspended from the roof.

Seedlings.—Melons planted out on a ridge, on a bed of tan, dung, or leaves, under glass, may be advantageously cultivated in the following manner. In any house, pit, or frame, where an atmosphere as above described is maintained, sow some seeds in thumb-pots, one seed in each pot, which must be kept near the glass after the plants are above ground, and be allowed a free circulation of air, in order to rear the plants as robust and short-stemmed as possible. Some prefer this mode of cultivation: short cuttings taken off the leading or side-shoots, and plunged in a strong bottom heat, under bell-glasses, root in a week or a fortnight; and plants so raised fruit sooner, and some cultivators think more finely than seedlings.

Planting Out.—Plants being reared, either from seeds or cuttings, healthy and robust, are, let us presume, in 32-sized pots, about nine inches high, with leaves as large as the palm of the hand. The hotbed being made up to within eighteen inches of the glass, and a ridge of loamy turf, mixed with one-fourth its quantity of dung, pulverized to a mould, being laid along the centre of the bed, about twelve or fourteen inches deep, a day or two previous to the planting of the melons, and all fears of offensive steam from the bed or linings being guarded against, the plants may be turned out of the pots along the centre of the ridge, about one foot apart for a bed nine feet wide, or for a six-feet bed about fifteen inches apart, with a fine sweet moist heat, such as could be breathed comfortably, about 75° to 85°. Excess in quantity of heat is not so much to be feared as inferior quality of heat. A strong heat will rarify the air and cause ventilation; to facilitate which, a small aperture should be left open, say a quarter of an inch, at the top of every light, and this for eighteen or twenty hours out of the twenty-four.

General Treatment.—Plants raised from cuttings show fruit with less vine than those reared from seeds; and this is the best remedy, in conjunction with keeping them rather dry at the roots, for the ever-crying evil, that the "vines have run all over the bed without showing fruit." When fruit appears, they must be carefully managed to prevent sudden atmospheric changes; and, during the time that they are in flower, water overhead must be dispensed with, and gentle vapour only occasionally raised, to nourish the leaves, for it would be injurious to keep the flowers too moist at this time. Every female blossom must now be carefully impregnated; and, as soon as the fruits are set and beginning to swell, plenty of moisture and a closer atmosphere will be of the greatest service till they are swelled full size, when moisture at the root, and also vapour on the leaves, must be finally dispensed with. As soon as a reasonable number of fruits are swelling favourably, say three to six on a plant, the rest, with every leaf and lateral that can be dispensed with, must be discarded, leaving always one leaf, or perhaps two, beyond every fruit; and let every fruit be elevated on an inverted earthen saucer. In setting a crop, as it is called, the proper number of fruit should be set on the same day, as if one fruit gets far ahead of the others, the whole of the latter drop off or refuse to swell together. To grow very early melons dry heat is indispensable, as every leaf, in moist weather, ought to be carefully dried once every day; and, in hot weather, every leaf ought to be as carefully moistened, by means of vapour or syringing. Before the fruit appears, and also when it is ripening off, a well ventilated atmosphere is best; but, whilst the fruits are swelling, closeness and humidity will be found to answer the purpose best. An occasional dusting of powdered charcoal and lime, mixed with sulphur and Scotch snuff, will go far to prevent the ravages of insect enemies.

The bed must be soiled over to the same depth as the ridge was originally made, at different times, as the progress of the roots shall dictate; and the roots must be supplied with soft well aërated water, as the firmness or the flaccidity of the leaves must determine. As little shading as possible should be given, as the plants should be inured to the full sun as soon as possible; the minimum heat may be 70°, and the maximum 90°, though 100° would do no harm, even with the lights closed, or with the lights not closed, provided the transition were not rapid.

Melons of delicate texture, such as many of the Persians, are very liable to burst, and care must be taken not to give too much water; and it is good practice to raise the point of the fruit higher than the stems. Such melons, however, succeed best growing in narrow houses heated with tanks or hot-water pipes, and trained up the roof of the glass within two feet from it. In such houses fewer of them rot off or burst, and the flavour is superior to those grown in common pits or frames.

Culture of the Melon in the Open Air.—In the climate of London a late crop of melons may be raised on beds of dung in the open air, the plants when newly turned out being protected by hand-glasses. The customary mode is to have the beds flat, about four feet wide and two feet and a half high; and when the heat declines, casings of hot dung are applied, first on one side, and, when that casing has ceased to be effective, on the other. The better mode, however, is to form the bed in the direction of east and west, with the north side supported by boards, so as to be perpendicular, and three feet six inches or four feet high, and the south side sloping at an angle about 40° east and west, and open to the south. The situation must be well sheltered from the north. Whichever description of bed is used, the plants may be raised from seeds or cuttings in April or May, and turned out the first week in June. The plants should not be raised on bottom heat, because the transition to the open air is found to give them such a check as to turn the leaves yellow, and the entire plant sickly. There are two decided advantages in growing the melon in ridges sloping to the south: the sun's rays are received at a much larger angle, in consequence of which the temperature is raised from $10°$ to $15°$ higher than it is in the shade; and a larger, and consequently a more effective, casing can be applied behind. The only disadvantage is the difficulty of maintaining a uniform degree of moisture in the soil, which must, therefore, be frequently watered, and always with water at a temperature of $70°$ to $90°$. When the plants are first inserted in the bed they are closely covered with hand-glasses, but as soon as they have begun to grow the glasses are raised on bricks, so as to allow the shoots to advance from beneath them; and these shoots are carefully pegged down to preserve them from being deranged by the wind. The first fruit from such beds is generally cut in August, and they will continue productive till the plants are destroyed by frost in October. The hand-lights should remain over the crowns of the plants, to save them from canker. Some of the hardier rocky melons, or coarse scarlet-flesh melons, are most suited for this mode of culture.

Insects and Diseases.—The aphis, the red spider, and the thrips, are the greatest enemies to the melon, and if once the plants are overrun with any of them, it is scarcely possible to restore them to health. The aphis may be destroyed by fumigating with tobacco. The best method of doing it is with the fumigating bellows, the muzzle being introduced through a perforation in the front of the frame or pit, nearly on a level with the surface of the mould; the sashes should be covered with mats at the same time, to prevent the escape of the fumes. The operation should always be performed in the evening, and renewed the following one; not a drop of water, from any source, should be allowed to touch the plants the next day. The frames are to be kept closed and shaded, and not opened, if it can be avoided, for twenty-four hours. Prevention is, however, not only better, but easier than cure, and with a moist atmosphere and a free ventilation most of these pests may be kept down. The wood-louse is a constant enemy to the melon, and is most effectually kept under by keeping a toad or two in the frames. If they should become exceedingly numerous, a flower-pot, laid on its side, with a cooked potato and some dry hay in it, renewing it when it becomes damp, is an excellent trap. The canker is a frequent disease in the melon, generally occurring at the point where the plants emerge from the soil. A little air-slaked lime, as fresh as can be obtained, to the wounded part, though it does not cure the disease, for it is incurable, retards its progress. The rotting of the stems from damp, want of light, or too free a use of the knife, is nearly as fatal as the canker, and, like it, is incurable; but where it takes place at a distance from the root, an increase of heat and the free admission of air and light, will cause new shoots to be produced. Mildew may always be checked by powdering with flowers of sulphur.

The red spider can be best fought with a moist atmosphere and a vigorous unchecked growth.

Culture of the Cucumber.

The cucumber (Cucumis sativa, L.) is an annual, climbing by tendrils, or trailing on the surface of the ground, a native of the East Indies, and probably of many parts of Asia and Africa. It has been cultivated in the old world from time immemorial for its fruit, which is used in an unripe state, alone, or in salads, and for salting and pickling. The cucumber will bear a tropical heat, for it grows abundantly in many tropical countries. In the lower regions of India, the mean annual temperature may be reckoned as high as 80°; the thermometer seldom sinking below 70° in the hottest period of the season. The cucumber thrives well where the heat of the nights is more oppressively felt by Europeans than that of the days. As a wide difference does not occur in the diurnal and nocturnal temperatures of tropical countries, where the cucumber grows spontaneously, it is not necessary that a great variation should, in this respect, be imposed upon it when under artificial treatment. In order to be tender when cut for use, it requires to be grown rapidly, and, therefore, requires as much heat and moisture as can be safely applied. If the native plants of colder climates are forced night and day in a uniformly high temperature, a drawing, or weakness, soon becomes evident; but no such signs are exhibited by the rigid leaves of the pine-apple, although grown in a uniform temperature of 80°, provided they have not less than eleven or twelve hours' light out of the twenty-four. The cucumber will grow side by side with the pine-apple; and also naturally in a much higher latitude; but in that case its growth is limited to the summer season, when nearly a tropical heat is maintained. If the nights are cold, although the days may be warm, cucumbers growing on ridges in the open air, in this climate, invariably become diseased and attacked by mildew. A temperature ranging between 70° and 80° of artificial heat is suitable for the growth of the cucumber; if sun-heat is likely to raise the temperature much higher, air should be copiously, yet gradually, afforded; and presuming that the plants are in good health, and their roots well established, enough of moisture being present, they will bear from 90° to 110° of sun-heat without injury.

In cultivating the cucumber in British gardens, the object is to have a supply of fruit throughout the year. This may be effected in dung-beds, but more conveniently by some description of pit heated by flues or hot-water, or by a house constructed on purpose, with a steep glass roof. The plants may be raised either from seeds or cuttings. The soil cucumbers prefer is light and rich, but they will grow in poor soil watered with liquid manure. Sandy-peat has been found suitable for dung-beds in the winter season, because water passes rapidly through this soil, without so much being retained by it, especially on the surface, as to cause the plants to damp off. The shoots of the cucumber are commonly allowed to trail on the ground; but they are much less likely to damp off when trained on trellises within one foot or eighteen inches of the glass. To concentrate the vigour of the plant, the shoots are stopped repeatedly as they advance in growth, by pinching out the growing point with the finger and thumb. Shoots bearing fruit are generally stopped at the second joint beyond the fruit, as soon as its blossom has begun to fade, in order to throw more of the sap into the fruit. The cucumber will live either in the open air or under glass, at a temperature of 50°, and it will grow and produce fruit at 60°, but not vigorously and abundantly at a lower temperature than between 75° and 80°—and with this the bottom heat should correspond. With abundance of light, air, and frequent watering, it will grow vigorously in an atmosphere of from 85° to 90°, saturated with moisture for at least a portion of every twenty-four hours. The foliage of the plants ought always to be kept pretty close to the glass; and in the winter season the more light they can have the better the plants will thrive. For this reason the glass over cucumbers (and melons also) should never be covered till it is nearly dark, and always be uncovered at daybreak. The cucumber requires an ample supply of water, which should be pond or rain-water, and always of the same temperature as the soil in which the plants grow. Liquid manure may be advantageously used when the soil is poor, or when it is limited in quantity, as in the case of cucumbers grown in pots. As the cucumber, like the melon, has the stamens and pistils in different flowers, artificial fecundation is by most gardeners considered necessary, or at least conducive to the swelling of the fruit; but by others, and among these some of the best cultivators, it is considered of no use, excepting when seed is required. Without abundance of seeds cucumbers for pickling or stewing would be good for nothing. Cucumbers grown for seed are of course always allowed to attain maturity, in which state they are of a yellow colour. The seed is taken out, washed and dried, and preserved for use, and it is generally considered that, for early crops, seeds which are several years old produce plants less likely to run to foliage, and consequently more prolific in blossoms. The cucumber is liable to the same insects and diseases as the melon, which are to be subdued by the same means. Want of sufficient bottom heat, and watering with cold hard water, are the general causes which produce the mildew, canker, and spot; and want of atmospheric moisture encourages the red spider and the thrips, and to a certain extent also, the aphides.

Culture of the Cucumber in a Dung-bed.

The formation of a dung-bed for general purposes has been already given. For the purpose of growing cucumbers in mid-winter, great care is necessary to prepare the dung properly, so that by reducing its heat there may be no danger of an excess, or what is termed a "burning heat," after the bed is made up. When this burning heat takes place, the bed becomes dry and mouldy to within a few inches of its surface, from which a noxious vapour arises, which, together with the excessive heat, speedily destroys the plants. The best antidote to this state is to turn the dung used twice a week for six or eight weeks, before it is finally made up.

The seed-bed requires to be first formed. It should be three feet high at the back, and two feet six inches in front; and when the lights are put on, eight or ten days should elapse before sowing the seeds. In order to prove whether or not the bed be sweet, shut the lights down close for three or four hours; then take a lighted candle in a lantern, push down one of the lights, and put the candle and lantern into the frame, and if the candle be not put out by the excess of moisture or amount of gas, but should continue to burn, the bed will be in a fit state to receive the plants or seeds.

Soil.—Some use leaf-mould, others loam and rotten dung, some chopped turf, and others peat alone; but the best soil is a sandy loam, enriched with a fourth part rotten dung. For winter growth, dispense with the dung.

Sow the seeds, one, or six, or a dozen in a pot, and plunge in a bottom heat of 80°. The plants will appear in four or five days, and when they are clearly above the soil, the pot may be lifted up and set on the surface of the bed. When the plants show the third leaf, reckoning the cotyledons two, they may be potted off singly into two or three-inch pots. The soil used should be moderately fine but not sifted, and a piece of turf should be placed over the crock at the bottom of the pot for drainage. The plants should be inserted so deep in the pot that the seed-leaves should just be a little above the level of the rim, and the soil should be within an inch of the rim, in order to allow of adding a little more when the roots show themselves above the surface. The tops of the plants, when set in the bed, should be within six or eight inches of the glass, and as they increase in height the pot should be lowered, so as always to keep the plants at about the same distance. Water may be applied whenever it appears wanting, there being much less danger in watering peat-soil than in watering leaf-mould, because the former only retains a very moderate quantity. When the heat of the bed falls below 70° some fresh lining may be added. When the third leaf gets perfectly developed, a leading shoot will rise from the base of its petiole, which, as soon as it is clearly formed, should be pinched off; its removal will cause it to throw out fresh shoots from the base of the seed-leaves. These shoots are allowed to grow until they are two joints in length, when they must be pinched back to one joint. As soon as the pots are filled with roots, the plants may be either shifted into a six-inch pot or transferred to their fruiting quarters.

As every two joints of a cucumber will form roots, nothing can be simpler than striking them from cuttings. It is much easier than the striking of melons, and if done in the frame or pit no bell-glass will be needed.

Fruiting Bed.—The dung should be prepared as for the seed bed. The size of the frame may be twelve feet long and four feet wide, the height at the back two feet, and in front one foot six inches; the lights should be glazed with sheet glass, one pane to each division. If the bed is made in an excavation, it should be sufficiently large to allow of the dung being three inches wider than the frame all round; with an additional space of eighteen inches in width for linings, which will require a space fifteen feet six inches long by eight feet wide. Where there is a proper melon ground, however, such an excavation will be unnecessary. Commence the erection of the bed by laying on the ground, nine inches or a foot thick, brushwood, or the loppings of trees, four feet six inches wide, and twelve feet six inches long; on the wood lay a little long litter to keep the dung from falling into it, as this would stop the drainage, and prevent the bottom heat from working under the bed. Upon the litter place your manure, carefully shaking it as you proceed, and keeping the surface regular, by beating it down with a fork as you advance, but do not tread it. The manure should be four feet or five feet high at the back, independently of the wood, and six inches lower in front. When the bed is finished, put on the frame, and keep the lights carefully closed till the heat rises, then give air, in order that the rank steam may pass off; fork over the surface every other day, as directed for the seed-bed, and as the heat decreases give less air. If the dung with which the bed has been made has undergone the preparation directed, it will be fit to receive the plants in about fourteen days. Before transplanting, however, prove the sweetness of the manure with a candle and lantern, as pointed out for the seed-bed; and, if satisfied on this important point, from twelve inches to eighteen inches thick of the chosen soil may be put on, to form the hillocks for the reception of the plants.

Ridging out the Plants.—After the mould has been in the frame twenty-four hours, it will be sufficiently warm for the plants to be ridged out. To do this, make a hole in the top of each hillock, and place the pot containing the plant in it; you will then be able to judge as to the proper distance it should be from the glass, which may vary from six inches to nine inches. Carefully turn out the plants, insert them into the holes, press the earth more firmly around them, and water the whole overhead with water at a temperature of 80°.

Air.—A little air may be given during twenty hours out of the twenty-four, to allow of the escape of steam and noxious gases, being careful to admit it only on the sheltered side of the frame or pit, and to prevent draughts. Should the heat of the bed be low, and an increased warmth be requisite, let the unoccupied surface of the bed be forked over, about six inches or eight inches deep, either back or front, and from this a fine steam will arise, which will be very beneficial to the plants; and, when air is afterwards given, it will materially assist in drying them, which it is well to do, if possible, during the day. In an hour or two after uncovering in the morning, a little more air may be given, reference being had to the state of the weather; and again let it be gradually increased, after the lapse of a similar period, up to twelve o'clock in the day. About one, lower in part; and at three or four o'clock shut down till six, when you should again give air; the heat then should be about 70° and the plants dry. At eight or nine regulate for the night, according to the heat, and so let it remain until the next morning, unless there should be a sudden change in the weather, when the lights may be shut down.

Earthing-up.—The hillocks of earth being small, every part of them will be filled by the roots in the course of a week or ten days, and the roots will show themselves on the surface. They should therefore be covered with about two inches of fresh soil, previously warmed to the temperature of the bed, by being spread out on the parts not occupied by hillocks. The linings must be occasionally turned to keep up the heat; and when the inside of the frame becomes dry it should be sprinkled with water when the air is taken away in the evening, by which a healthy steam will be generated for the plants during the night. When a dry bottom heat prevails, and the dung looks white and mouldy on the surface of the bed, it should be forked over, and watered with water about the same temperature as the bottom heat ought to be, and cold should be carefully guarded against immediately afterwards, by giving air sparingly, so as not to promote too rapid an evaporation. The heat of the dung will then escape freely, and as the roots in the hillocks are above the dung they will not easily be injured by the heat.

Linings of Cucumber Beds, and their Management.—Linings should be turned over once in eight or ten days, to keep them in a regular state of fermentation, especially from November to February, inclusive. They should not, however, be all turned at once: the front should be done one week, and the back the next, and so on. The ends will not require turning so often, provided the heat keeps up to what is necessary, according to the season. To dry the inside of the frame in December, January, and February, let the linings be one foot above the level of the surface of the bed, which will be sufficient; in March and April they may be lowered in proportion to the increased power of the sun's heat. During the operation of turning, should there appear any part too much decayed, let it be removed, and its place filled with fresh linings, which should be put on the top of the old, in order to draw up the heat from it, and to keep up a good warmth round the frame; besides, when the new linings are above the bed, there will be no danger of their rank steam getting to the plants. New linings should never be allowed to mix with the old ones until they have become quite sweet; for you must, on no account, allow rancid heat to be confined at the bottom of your linings. Attention to these directions must be continued until June, if it is desired to keep the plants in a healthy state; and although after the month of March the turnings need not be quite so frequent, a good warmth must be kept up, or the plants will not swell off their fruit kindly.

Water.—In the winter months, from the moisture of the fermenting material, and of the outer air, and the absence of solar heat, they will require but little from the water-pot. The surface of the bed, near the frame, will occasionally become dry from the heat of the linings passing upwards through it; and when that occurs, let it be sprinkled with water through a fine-rosed pot, just before covering up; and on fine mornings, about ten o'clock, give to the soil in which the plants are growing a little water in a tepid state. In November, December, and January, little water will be wanted, but in February, March, and April, more may be given; always, however, in the morning, and only when there is a prospect of the plants becoming dry by covering-up time. In dull weather never water the plants, but the mould only.

Stopping.—The shoots should never be suffered to get into a crowded state, otherwise they will become weak and unfruitful; and their fruit, such as they will bear, will be of a small and inferior kind. After the plants are thoroughly established, stop at a leaf beyond each fruit as it appears.

Moulding-up.—As the roots show themselves through the hillocks of earth, let them be covered with an inch or two of the soil recommended, placing more between the hillocks than elsewhere. This is done in order that the hillocks may meet and form a ridge along the middle of the bed by the end of December; but care should be taken to keep the sides clear of mould, to admit of the heat of the linings rising through them, to give that lively heat within the frame which is usually called top-heat, and which is necessary for the plants, as it causes them to dry in the day, during the most unfavourable weather, and yet gives them steam moisture by night. The whole of the bed should not be covered with earth until the end of March.

The covering at night must be carefully managed, so as to allow the mats or other material to overlap on to the linings at any point, otherwise the rank steam will be drawn in to the destruction of the plants. The covering should be thickened as the cold increases; and when the weather is very severe, double mats, with a layer of straw or hay between them, should be used. When the season turns, the days lengthen; and as the sun's heat, during the day, aids in warming the bed within the frame, discontinue the covering by degrees down to a single mat, to be finally dispensed with at the end of May.

Setting or impregnating the fruit is considered helpful to their swelling, and may be practised with the earlier crops.

To procure seed from the large varieties is often difficult. It is well to impregnate every blossom several times when seed is desired, and then to watch for any irregularity of growth in the fruit, and save those for seeds with such tendencies. They should not be cut until they are quite ripe, then put into a warm, dry vinery for a month, when they may be opened, the seed taken out, washed and dried; those only which sink being retained.

When extraordinary fine fruit is desired, allow the plant to mature only; but a succession may be permitted, so that the after-fruit do not follow too closely on the first. By this plan the growth will be rapid, provided the plants are in health; and the fruit be much better flavoured than if grown slowly. When long in swelling off, the fruit frequently becomes hard and bitter, and is therefore worthless. From $75°$ to $80°$ are as high as the plant will bear to advantage; and in that temperature fruit will grow faster than in a higher one. It will be seen from these directions respecting preparing the dung, making the beds, applying and working the linings, &c., that the mode of growing the cucumber on dung-beds is exceedingly troublesome and expensive, so much so that it has been almost superseded by the use of brick pits or houses heated with water at top and bottom. Most of the cultural instructions given here will, however, be almost equally applicable to cucumber-growing by any of the following methods.

Culture of the Cucumber in Pits Heated by Dung-linings, Flues, or Hot Water.

Of pits heated wholly or in part by dung-linings, there are a great variety of forms, chiefly differing in the construction of the exterior wall through which the heat is communicated to the bed of soil or fermenting material within. One of the most common, and most generally useful, is that known as M'Phail's pit. The principal advantage of these pits is, that dung-casings may be applied with little or no previous preparation, and thus much heat, that in the preparation of dung for common hotbeds is lost, is here turned to account.

Pits to be heated by flues or hot water, are as various in their construction as those to be heated by dung-linings; some forms have already been given, and we shall here describe some other forms.

Pits heated by flues have grown very good cucumbers; the dry heat is rather favourable than otherwise for winter work. The following are the dimensions of a pit of this description used by the late Mr. Knight for the culture of Persian melons. Such a pit would be equally or more useful for cucumber-growing, and as it may prove within reach of some who could not afford hot water, we give it a place here at the risk of being called antiquated. The back wall is nine feet high, and the front six feet high, the width nine feet, and the length thirty feet. The fireplace is at the east end, very near the front wall, and the flue passes to the other end of the house within four inches of the front wall, and returns back again, leaving a space of eight inches only between the advancing and returning course of it; and the smoke escapes at the north-east corner. The front flue is composed of bricks laid flat, and the returning flue of bricks standing on their edges, as is usual; the space between the flues is filled with fragments of burned bricks, which absorb much water, and gradually give out moisture to the air of the house. Air is admitted through apertures in the front wall, which are four inches wide, and nearly three inches in height; and which are situated level with the top of the flues, and are eighteen inches distant from each other. The air escapes through similar apertures near the top of the back wall. These apertures are left open, or partially or wholly closed, as circumstances require. Thirty-two pots are placed upon the flues described above, each being sixteen inches wide at least, and fourteen inches deep; but they are raised by an intervening piece of stone and brick out of actual contact with the flues. Into each of these pots one melon plant is put, which in its subsequent growth is trained upon a trellis, placed about fourteen inches distant from the glass, and each plant is permitted to bear one melon only. This pit was used by Mr. Knight for the culture of Persian melons, but it is evidently well adapted for the culture of cucumbers, underneath which seakale, rhubarb, or various other articles, might be forced.

A pit to be heated by hot water and by a flue from the fire which

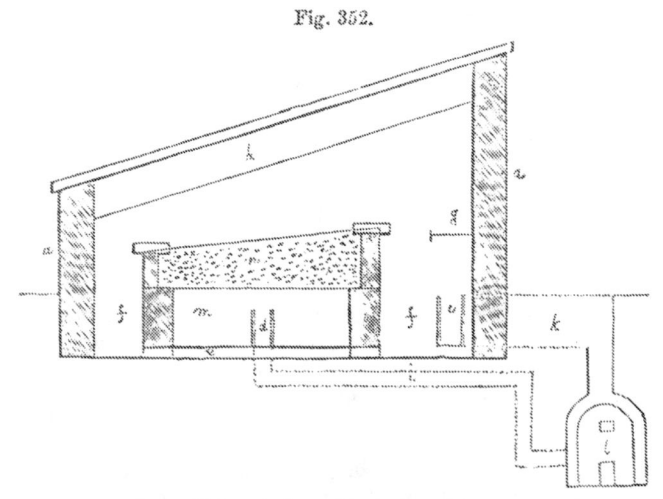

Fig. 352.

Cucumber or Melon-pit, heated by hot water in open troughs.
(The scale ¼ of an inch to a foot.)

a, Outer walls.
b, Walls of the pit.
c, Gutters, or troughs for heating the atmosphere.
d, Troughs under the soil in the open chamber (*m*), which is air-tight, resting on the openings (*e*), which convey the cooled air from the front walk to the trough at the back, to be heated; these openings being introduced at regular distances of 4 ft. or 5 ft.

f, Walks round the bed.
g, Shelf for plants.
h, Trellis for training the plants.
i, Descending return-pipe, which is a common 6-inch pipe.
k, The trough at entering, which is closed from the boiler till it reaches *c*.
l, Boiler.
m, Air-chamber; the air of which is always at the point of saturation.
n, The soil, or other material, in which the plants are planted.

heats the boiler, is thus described by Mr. Torbron. It is almost unnecessary to add that it will answer as well for melons as for cucumbers, and indeed if the pit was filled with proper soil and vines planted in it, there could not be a better house for an early crop of grapes. Length, thirty feet; width, eight feet; height at back, seven feet; at front, four feet. A flue to run first to the front, and return under the back wall, with cavities of two inches and a half. The space between the flues to have gutters for the pipes from a boiler, with a power of filling and emptying the gutters at pleasure; so as to have a command of either dry or moist air, as either may be wanted. The floor of the pit may be supported on arches, or it may be made of planks, or of slates or tiles resting on joists. The pit to be filled with mould, sand, or sawdust, according as it may be desired to grow the plants in pots or in the free soil. A trellis may be made to hook on the rafters, on which to train the plants. The upper surface of the pit to be two feet from the glass, and the trellis to be one foot from the glass.

Corbett's cucumber-pit (fig. 352) is heated with hot water circulated in open troughs, which, however, have covers for being put on when a dry heat is wanted. The mode of heating by water in open gutters, as we have seen, is strongly recommended by Mr. Glendinning, as it is by Mr. Lymburn, on account of the great radiating powers of water, which are equal to those of lampblack, which is to polished iron as 100 is to 15. Mr. Duncan, from whose 'Treatise on Cucumber Culture' the section (fig. 352) is taken, also says Corbett's mode is "the most economical plan of heating yet discovered, and deserving the support of every one interested in horticulture, especially the cucumber-grower." This seems to have been the parent of what has long been known as Rendle's system of tank heating which has been extensively used in cucumber, melon, and plant-houses, and for many purposes is still equal, if not superior, to hot-water pipes.

The troughs are arranged so as to produce both bottom and top heat, accompanied with proper moisture, or a dry air at pleasure, by putting on the covers to the troughs. The air in the confined chamber under the bed is always at the point of saturation, and a circulatory movement of the air of the pit, exterior to the chamber, is always maintained by drains, passing from the front path, under the troughs in the chamber, to the troughs in the back path, at the bottom of the back wall, as shown in the section.

Green's cucumber-pit is thus described by himself: "The walls are built of nine-inch brickwork, five feet high in the back, and two feet and a half in front, and the space enclosed is five feet wide in the clear, and thirty-six feet long, covered with nine lights, and divided into three compartments. A trough of brickwork is carried along the middle of the bottom from end to end. This trough is constructed by first laying a bottom of two bricks thick, one foot wide, and then forming the two sides of the trough with bricks on edge; the whole being so cemented as to hold water. The pit is heated with hot water by means of a branch of two-and-a-half-inch pipes proceeding from the boiler which heats a stove at a short distance. The hot water flows along the back and front of the pit, above the level of the bed of soil, but the return pipes are placed beneath the bed in the trough just described, which is filled with water, or partly so, as circumstances may require, by means of a small pipe that leads to the outside. Another small pipe is laid in the bottom of the trough for letting off the stagnant water, and for emptying the trough occasionally; for in very dark damp weather, a drier heat is required. In order to have a succession of fruit, it is requisite to sow the seed at three different times: the 1st and 20th of September, and the 5th of November. The first and second sowing are fruited in No. 2 pots, and the third are planted out. The branches are trained on a temporary trellis, and the fruit is allowed to hang down.

Messrs. J. Weeks and Co., who erected Mr. Green's pit, have obligingly furnished us with a section of it (fig. 353) to a scale of one-sixth of an inch to a foot.

Fig. 353.

a a, Outer walls.
b, Hot-water pipes, laid in a trough of brickwork (*c*), which can be filled with water, and emptied at pleasure.
d d, Ground level.
e, Joists of wood or iron, forming the floor of the pit.
f, Bed for planting or plunging, in which there may be upright tubes, chimney pipes, or flower-pots with the bottoms out, at regular distances, so as to admit at pleasure the moist air from the chamber below.
g, The trellis.
h h, Hot-water pipes for top-heat.

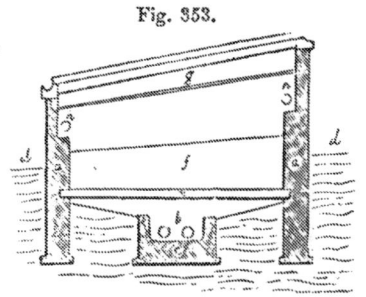

Mr. Green's Cucumber-pit.
(Scale ⅙ of an inch to a foot.)

Culture of the Cucumber in Pots, in a Pinery, Vinery, or in a Cucumber-house.

The culture of the cucumber in pots has become common, and is the cheapest of all modes of growing winter fruit. The fruit will not generally be so fine as by other methods; but small fruit rapidly grown are the best and the most useful.

To cut cucumbers through the winter, from November to February, in pits or frames heated by fermenting materials only, is almost an impossibility, let them be attended ever so closely. The reason of this is, the atmosphere of the pit being too moist, the plants absorb more aqueous matter than they can decompose and assimilate, and consequently, their digestive energies being impeded, the leaves become covered with mildew and other fungi, which consume their juices, choke their respiratory organs, and general debility, if not death, ensues. This is the cause of so many young plants damping off in dull weather; but keep them in an atmosphere which can be kept moist or dry, in accordance with the absence or presence of light, and no such effect will be produced; thus proving the superiority of a heating apparatus that will place the hygrometric state of the atmosphere under the control of the attendant, and explaining the reason of cucumbers growing so much better in houses heated by fire, than in dung-pits, in the winter season.

Construction of the Cucumber-house.—The grand point to determine is the slope of the glass, so as to obtain a maximum of solar influence in mid-winter. To obtain the perpendicular rays of the sun in December, it would be necessary in latitude 53° to place the glass at an angle of 75° 28'; in January, 71° 52'; in February, 62° 29'; and in March, 51° 41'.

Fig. 354, to scale of a quarter of an inch to a foot, is a copy of the section given by Mr. Ayres; in which *a* is the tan-bed in which the pots containing the plants are plunged; *b* is the trellis to which the plants are trained; *c* is the pathway under which is a flue, with the pipe of an Arnott's stove, or, better still, hot-water pipes passing through it, and *d* is the ground line. The flue should be divided into four equal compartments, the first and third of which, by keeping the pipes wholly or partially immersed in water, might be made to produce moist heat, while the others will produce dry heat; so that by tilting or removing the covering tiles of any of the compartments, the humidity of the atmosphere will be placed quite under the command of the attendant.

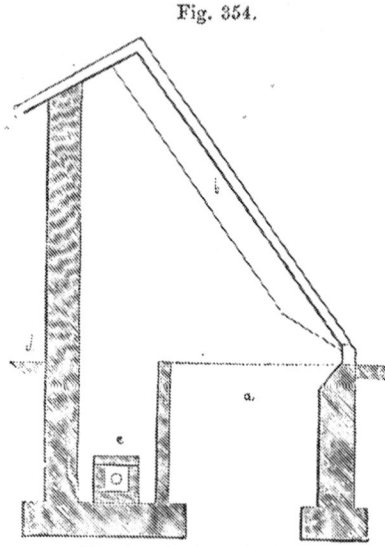

Fig. 354.

Mr. Ayres's Cucumber-house.
(Scale ¼ of an inch to a foot.)

Such a house as fig. 354 might be heated by hot-water pipes by Corbett's open gutters or iron tanks at very little expense. The pit might be filled with tan or leaves for plunging the pots in in winter and spring, and in summer with soil in which the plants might be grown without pots. The great advantage of this house is, that, let the weather be what it will, the plants can always be properly attended to and treated.

Treatment of the Plants. — The cucumber, Mr. Ayres observes, will grow in any soil, even old tan or brick-rubbish, provided liquid manure is supplied. For pot-culture use turfy loam two parts, thoroughly decomposed dung two parts, leaf-mould two parts, and very sandy turfy peat two parts. The whole thoroughly incorporated immediately before using, but not sifted. Manure-water is prepared by steeping two pecks of sheep or deer dung, one peck of pigeons' dung, and half a peck of soot, in a hogshead of boiling rain-water; in two days it will be fit for use. When applied, it is diluted with rain-water, and used alternately with clear water from March to October. The great secret of keeping the cucumber in vigorous growth in pots, Mr. Ayres continues, is the use of manure-water. The plants should be raised from seed sown on the first of August, so as to be fit for planting in fruiting pots in the first week of September. These pots should not be less than sixteen inches wide, and eighteen inches deep. Two plants should be placed in each pot, but the leading shoot must not be stopped, but be allowed to grow until it reaches the top of the house. "On this, success in pot-culture mainly depends, for if the plants are stopped, they are thrown into a bearing state before they are sufficiently established, and the consequence is early fruit, but a short-lived plant; but if the plants are allowed to grow to the length of ten or fifteen feet before the leading shoot is stopped, a great quantity of true sap will be generated, and the plant will consequently be better able to support a crop than if it had been allowed to bear fruit before it was properly established." The temperature which Mr. Ayres approves of is 60° through the night, 65° in dull, and 70° in clear weather, by fire heat; and 80°, 90°, or even 100° with plenty of atmospheric moisture and air in sunny weather. The two shoots from the two plants in each pot are to be trained to the trellis at one foot nine inches apart; and when they begin to send out laterals these must be stopped at one joint above the fruit. Impregnation or setting the fruit, Mr. Ayres believes, does neither good nor harm, for he has cut scores of fruit, the flowers of which never expanded. If the fruit grows crooked, he places it in glass tubes or narrow troughs, which mould it into the proper form; or he suspends a small weight by a piece of bast to the end of each fruit, a practice which appears to have been first adopted by Mr. Robert Fish.

Culture and Treatment of the Cucumber for Prize Exhibitions.

Choose the best-formed longest varieties, such as Dale's Conqueror, Hamilton's Invincible, and Blue Gown. The plants must not be allowed to set fruit till they have attained considerable strength. The fruit is put into cylinders of glass or tin to protect the prickles and bloom. Every means is employed to encourage vigorous growth, and rather a higher temperature is maintained than in ordinary culture. "In the event of fruit being ready to cut before the time wanted, they should be divided three parts across their foot-stalk, and secured to the trellis to prevent falling. By this means they will keep fresh and stationary several days, much better than by cutting or entirely separating them from the plant. If necessary to carry or send them to a distance, they should be packed nicely in a box made for the purpose, in the largest nettle-leaves that can be got, or in cucumber-leaves, but by no means in smooth leaves, which are certain to rub off the bloom. They may then be folded in tissue-paper, and wrapped in wadding, and placed in narrow boxes of well-thrashed moss. By these means the spines, powdery bloom, and partially withered blossom at the end of the fruit are preserved, without which no cucumber can be considered handsome, or well grown. In being exhibited they should be put in dishes in pairs or leashes, on a little clean moss, or on vine-leaves, and the brace or leash should always be of the same sort, and if possible of the same length.

Cultivation of the Cucumber in the Open Air.

Cucumbers grown in the open air are commonly protected by hand or bell-glasses. The seeds are sown some time about the middle of

April in a cucumber or melon bed, and when they come up, they are potted out into small pots, two or three plants in each pot, and are kept properly watered, and stopped at the first or second joint. About the middle of May, a warm situation, where the mould is very rich, is pitched on, and a trench is dug out about two feet deep and three feet broad, and the length is proportioned according to the number of glasses it is intended for. The bottom of this trench is covered with prunings of bushes, or coarse vegetable rubbish of any kind, and it is then filled with good warm dung, and when the dung is come to its full heat, it is covered over with eight, ten, or twelve inches deep of rich mould. The glasses are then set upon it about three feet distant from each other, and when the mould gets warm under them, the plants are turned out of the pots with their balls whole, and plunged in the mould under the glasses, and a little water given them to settle the mould about their roots, the glasses set over them, and after they have made roots, and begin to grow, in fine days they are raised a little on one side to let the plants have the free air; and as the weather gets warmer and warmer, air is given more plentifully, to harden the plants, so that they may be able to bear the open air, and run from under the glasses. When the plants begin to fill the glasses, they are trained out horizontally, and the glasses are set upon bricks or such like props, to bear them from the plants. After this the plants require nothing more but to be supplied with water when the summer showers are not sufficient, and to stop them when they become deficient of branches, and thin them of leaves or branches when they are likely to be overcrowded. In warm summers and in warm situations, by this mode of management the plants will bear plentifully for about two months, provided they be not attacked by insects or weakened by diseases. If the situation should require shelter, a row of runner beans four feet from the bed at the north side and ends, and a row of some crop that will not grow more than three feet high, on the south side of the bed, and about the same distance from it, will attain this object. The surface of the ridge, for some time after it is made, should be covered with straw to shoot off the wet, and the leading branches must be pegged to the soil, but not stopped.—(Ayres.)

Increasing the Atmospheric Heat of the Soil.—When cucumbers are grown on the natural ground, as they are extensively at Sandy in Bedfordshire, a considerable portion of heat may be worked into it by artificial means. Thus, when the bed has been marked out, let the soil be dug over in the evening of every sunny day, and then either raked perfectly smooth, or covered with mats or litter; in this way the radiation of accumulated heat being nightly intercepted, a sufficient quantity of heat will in a week or ten days be collected to raise the temperature 8 or 10 degrees above that of the adjoining soil.—(Ayres's 'Treatise,' p. 40.)

Cucumbers against a South Wall.—" Cucumbers will succeed beautifully, trained against a south wall, if planted in a little good soil to start them; afterwards they will flourish in the soil of the border, without further trouble, especially if the summer should be warm."—(Duncan's 'Cucumber Culture,' p. 83.) Warm coverings at night, so as to prevent the radiation of heat acquired through the day, would, in this case, and also in that of cucumbers grown in ridges, prove very beneficial.

Growing Cucumbers on Balconies, or in Court-yards.—"Those who have no garden ground, but have yards or balconies on a south, east, or west exposure, may plant them in very rich compost, in large pots, or boxes eighteen inches or two feet square, and train the plants to the wall. They will require precisely the same treatment in watering, stopping, &c., as directed for pots in the cucumber-house. In this way those who have no garden may have the pleasure of growing their own cucumbers."—(Ayres's 'Treatise,' p. 41.)

Watering Cucumbers in the Open Garden.—During the time the plants are under the glasses, they may be watered in the same way as if they were under frames; but after the glasses are raised, and the plants permitted to extend themselves over the bed, water, on a warm day, as seldom as possible, but when it is done do it effectually; that is, saturate the ground to the depth of a foot at least, and with water which, either by admixture with warm water, or by exposure to the solar influence, has attained the same temperature as the soil in which the plants are growing, choosing if possible a dull day for the purpose.—(Ibid., p. 40.)

Cucumber and Melon Culture Compared.—Much of what has been advanced on the culture of the cucumber may be applied to the culture of the melon, but their treatment differs in the following particulars. The melon cannot be ripened in this country in the winter-time, and therefore the seeds need never be sown before February. The soil for the melon should be of a firm texture, loamy, and should lie solid in the bed rather than loose like that of the cucumber. It is often covered with gravel, pebbles, tiles, or slates. When the fruit of the melon is advancing to maturity, water must be gradually withheld so as not to deteriorate the flavour; whereas in cucumber culture the supply of water must be uninterrupted. The melon, in hot dry seasons, can be brought to a higher degree of perfection than the cucumber, because the atmosphere cannot in general be kept sufficiently moist for the latter fruit. In the highest state of cultivation the cucumber requires as much heat as the melon; but it may be grown in a much lower temperature, more especially as compared with that required by the Persian varieties of the melon, for these require a greater heat than the Cantaloups.

Culture of the Banana.

The banana (Musa sapientum, L.) is a Scitamineous herbaceous evergreen, a native of Asia, in forests, in soil formed of rich masses of vegetable matter, kept moist by the shade of trees. There are many varieties cultivated in India and other warm regions of the East, varying in height from three feet to twenty feet; but those which are in most esteem in British gardens are the Musa Cavendishii, from the Isle of France, and the M. Dacca, from the East Indies, neither of which exceed the height of from three feet to six feet. The culture of these plants for their fruit in British stoves is of very recent date, but as the fruit is excellent, and the plant easily grown, it may be well briefly to describe its culture. All the varieties of banana are propagated by suckers; they are grown in large pots or tubs, eighteen inches or two feet in diameter, in a mixture of sand, loam, and thoroughly rotten dung, and watered with liquid manure. The same temperature that suits the pine-apple will suit the banana. Suckers will fruit within a year or eighteen months, according to their strength, and they may be retarded or accelerated so as to ripen their fruit at almost every season. The following mode of cultivating the banana is from the pen of the late Sir Joseph Paxton, who first grew this fruit for dessert at Chatsworth, in 1836:—

"A banana-house, thirty feet long, fifteen feet wide, twelve feet high at the back and six feet high at the front, heated by flues or by hot water, will hold about ten full-grown or fruiting plants, with room between for different-sized successional ones, to be tubbed successively as the large plants ripen off their fruit, these being shaken out of their tubs as soon as the fruit is gathered, and potted, to produce suckers; by judicious management in tubbing and in administering water, a supply of fruit may be had the greater part of the year. I have had at one time ten fruiting plants nearly of the same size and age, being suckers produced the same spring, and receiving similar treatment; yet no two of them produced their spadix at the same time; and even if they are disposed to do so, it may be prevented, different treatment being given them. As their approach to fruiting is easily ascertained by their leaves decreasing in size, soon after which the embryo fruit-stalk may be detected by the sudden swelling of the lower part of the stem, if more than one should show these indications at one time, the one it is desired to fruit first must have abundance of water and the warmest situation, and the others be retarded by opposite treatment. The period between them may be still further lengthened a considerable time, if the whole spadix of fruit of one approaching too close upon another in ripening be cut off with a portion of the stem attached, when the upper tier of fruit is just ripening, and suspended in a dry and airy room, in the way that late grapes are often kept. I have cut excellent fruit from a spadix, two months after it had been separated from the plant; and they may be made to ripen fast or slowly in this manner, according to the temperature to which they are exposed. The sooner the flower-stem is made to develope itself, the longer the spadix will be, and the greater quantity of fertile flowers it will produce; consequently the greater weight of fruit, which will vary from fifteen to thirty pounds, according to the plant's strength, the season, and other circumstances. I need hardly add that the soil can scarcely be too rich, and that it should be rather light than retentive, in order that abundance of water may be given, and readily pass off. A pit forty feet long, fifteen feet broad, and five feet high, will produce several hundredweight of fruit in a year, with no other care or attention than that of giving plenty of manure to grow in, and a good supply of heat and water. The banana will fruit at all seasons, and no doubt with easier culture than any kind of fruit grown under glass. The Musa Cavendishii is by far the best variety to cultivate for its fruit; the plant is not only more showy, but the fruit is the largest and best flavoured. They do best and are least trouble planted out in a border, provided with bottom heat. English-grown fruit are very superior to those imported, as in our stoves the fruit can be gathered daily as it ripens, and the delicious aroma and delicate flavour, so unlike that of any other fruit, are generally relished and much liked."

Forcing the Strawberry.

Data on which the Forcing of the Strawberry is Founded.—The strawberry (Fragaria, L.) is a genus of herbaceous perennials or biennials, of which some species are natives of Europe, and others of North and South America. They all grow in woods, and in soil more or less loamy and moist; but the kinds have been so changed by culture in British gardens, and this culture has been so successful both in the open garden and under glass, that we shall adopt it as a guide. Almost all the kinds of strawberry in cultivation will bear forcing; but the kinds preferred are chiefly the Black Prince, Keen's Seedling, British Queen, Carolina Superb, Dr. Hogg, Sir Charles Napier, Mr. Radcliffe, Trollope's Victoria, Sir Harry, Sir Joseph Paxton, President, Prince Arthur, Princess Alice, Maud, Pathfinder, and Prince Imperial. As the flavour of strawberries is seldom good when they are ripened before the middle or end of March, forcing is seldom commenced till the middle of January, and those excited about that time, and properly treated, will ripen fruit in about nine weeks. The plants should be previously well established in pots; though in default of this they may be taken up with balls, and potted, and at once placed in the forcing-house; or the balls may be set close together on the surface of a bed of fermenting material, or heated by a flue or hot-water pipes underneath. The crown of the plants, whether in pots or on a bed, should not be more than a foot from the glass. The temperature at first should not exceed 45° or 50°, with fire-heat, and abundance of air should be given, even when the temperature is as low as 40°. After the fruit is set, the temperature may be raised from 55° to 60°, with fire heat, and 65° or 70° with sun-heat, provided abundance of air is given. Strawberries may be forced with great advantage in the peach-house, vinery, orchard-house, the cherry-house, or in warm pits. They may be also forced in the open garden by having pipes of hot water laid a foot under the surface of the soil, between the rows of the plants, and covering them with glass or with canvas during nights and in stormy weather.

Routine Practice in Forcing the Strawberry.—As soon as the runners are fit for the purpose, layer each in a sixty-sized pot in good strong loam, with a portion of well-decayed manure. Place a stone on each runner, for the double purpose of keeping the plant in a fixed position, and preserving moisture to the roots. The first runners are preferable. As soon as the plants are well rooted, re-pot them in thirty-two-sized pots, still using the same strong soil; then place them in the hottest part of the garden, fully exposed to the direct rays of the sun, but not under a wall; or by giving them merely the shelter of glass alone, the season may be hastened a month or six weeks. Here they should be left exposed to the elements most conducive to bring them rapidly to a state of maturity: a free circulation of air, abundance of moisture, which they should be liberally supplied with, and a full share of solar heat. In this situation the plants grow freely, forming well-matured crowns, to send up fine stems of bloom in the forcing-house, with strong and vigorous roots to support them. A few of the most vigorous may have a second shift into twenty-four-sized pots, but the majority should remain in thirty-twos, as they flower and fruit best when root-bound. One plant to each pot is preferable to a great number. If the autumnal rains are heavy, lay the pots on their sides, and about the middle of December place them in pits or houses, or pack them up out of doors, so as to keep the frost from injuring the roots, till they are placed in the forcing-house.

Thus grown and protected, the strawberries may, any time between December and March, be brought into the forcing-pit, previously filled with tan, dung, or leaves, to about eighteen inches of the glass. On this bed the plants are set, and a gentle temperature of from 50° to 55° is maintained in the pit, or house. From this time till the plants have perfected their fruits, a leaf should never be allowed to droop for want of water: yet an excess is equally destructive, more especially before the flower-stems appear; as soon, however, as these are up, a liberal supply of water is necessary till the fruits get to their proper size; when it must again be supplied sparingly, only just enough to keep the leaves from flagging, till the strawberries are gathered. Whilst in flower, a temperature of from 60° to 65°, with a free circulation of air, is best. The fruit once set, the plants will do very well in a stove where the minimum temperature is as high as 75°, provided abundance of air can be admitted. Plants treated in this manner, introduced into the forcing-house in the middle of December, will generally perfect their fruit about the middle of March. The fruit ought to be thinned out: all the deformed ones should be cut clean away, and the more promising ones should be pegged to the sunny side of the pot, and if there are too many leaves the footstalks of a number of them may be broken or twisted, so as to check the flow of sap and throw it into the fruit. Dry heat and free air are indispensable to their being well-flavoured. These conditions are likewise most favourable for the setting of the fruit during dull weather. This may also be assisted by the admission of bees, or the use of a camel's-hair pencil.

After forcing, turn the plants out of the pots, and plunge them in rows, at moderate distances, in a piece of spare ground in the garden, well exposed to the sun and a free circulation of air. From these a late gathering will be obtained after the natural crops are over;

and well-established plants for forcing may be obtained from their runners, the latter being produced so much earlier than they are from plants in the open ground. In the autumn take the plants up with good balls of earth, and plant them in rows in a melon-pit or cold frame, placing them rather thick, to economize the rows, and press the mould firmly to their roots. The pit need have neither bottom-heat nor pipes, but be simply covered with mats. As soon as the frosts set in, place the lights on, but do not begin to cover up with mats before March. If warm showers come in April, take the lights off, and let the plants have the benefit of the showers (which is better than watering from a pot), to forward them. When the sun is shining hot in the afternoon, shut up close, and cover up directly with double mats. These plants will bear abundantly, coming in at a very seasonable time, just before the out-door strawberries, which are very often retarded by late frosts, and after the forced ones are completely exhausted. After the fruit is gathered, the plants are dug up and thrown away, and the pit planted with melons. By following this simple routine, year after, or reserving a number of fresh potted plants for this purpose, and also by covering a few rows out of doors with hand-lights, or Rendle's Plant Protectors, the strawberry season may be prolonged and made continuous from first to last at a very trifling expense.

The Alpine strawberry continues bearing in the open air till it is checked by frost, and if a month previously to this a number of plants have been planted in a bed of soil on heat, or potted and placed in a frame, pit, or strawberry-house, quite near the glass, and a temperature kept up of from 45° to 55° during night, and from 55° to 60° during day, the plants will continue bearing during winter; and they may be succeeded by other plants kept through the winter in cold frames, and put into heat about the middle of February. This mode is very successfully practised in the neighbourhood of Paris; but Alpine strawberries are seldom thought worthy of forcing, or of so much attention, in England.

Forcing Asparagus, Sea-kale, Rhubarb, Chicory, and other Roots.

All these vegetables may be forced where they stand in the open garden, by placing hot dung over them; or when they are planted in rows or beds, by digging out trenches between eighteen inches or two feet wide, and two feet deep, and filling up these trenches with hot dung. Or the plants may be taken up before the forcing season, with as many of the roots as possible, and planted close together in a house, frame, pit, or cellar, or placed in the mushroom-house on a bed of fermenting matter, or of soil heated artificially, at first to 40° or 50°, and gradually raised to 60°, 65°, or 70°. Nothing can be more simple or easy than this kind of forcing, since it is merely the excitement by heat and moisture, without, or with but very little, light and change of air, of the mass of vegetable nutriment laid up in the plant during the previous season.

Asparagus.—In the beginning of winter, begin six weeks before it is proposed to have a crop; when the days are longer, five weeks, or about a calendar month before. Those who wish to have asparagus on the table at Christmas should prepare for forcing it in November. The temperature at night should never be under 50°. In the daytime keep the maximum down to 62°. If by the heat of the bark or dung, and the use of mats or canvas covers at night, the thermometer stands as high as 50°, fire-heat will be unnecessary; but otherwise recourse must be had to the flue or hot-water pipes. A very moderate degree of fire-heat, however, will be sufficient; and a small fire made in the evening will generally answer the purpose. Air must be freely admitted every day, in some cases, to allow any steam to pass off and for the sake of the colour and flavour of the plants. As the buds begin to appear, as large a portion of air must be daily admitted as the weather will permit. When the asparagus bed has stood two or three days after planting, and when the heat has begun to warm the roots, give the plants a sufficient watering. Repeat such waterings as the soil becomes dry, using water at a temperature of 70°. By the time the buds have come up three inches above the surface, they are fit to gather for use, as they will then be six or seven inches in length. In gathering them, draw aside a little of the mould, slip down the finger and thumb, and twist them off from the crown. This is a better method than to cut them; at least it is less dangerous to the rising buds, which come up in thick succession, and might be wounded by the knife, if cutting were practised. The roots, after they have furnished a crop, are considered useless for future culture, because no leaves having been allowed to develop themselves, of course no buds could be formed for the succeeding year. If the pit in which asparagus is forced be twenty-five feet to thirty feet long, it will be enough for the supply of an ordinary family to fill one-half at a time. If the second half be planted when the shoots in the first half are fit for use, and so on, a constant succession may be kept up in the same pit for any length of time required. In some gardens asparagus is grown in beds cased with pigeon-holed brickwork, with alleys between two feet wide and two feet deep, which are filled with hot dung, and frames are put over the beds; it is a good plan, and answers well. In other cases the alleys are simply dug out to a depth of three or four feet and filled up with hot dung, and the beds are covered with frames, or hooped over with mats, or, better still, shutters or waterproof-tarpaulins. Beds treated in this manner in December will produce a crop in four or five weeks, which will last for five or six weeks. After the crop is gathered, the dung is removed from the alleys, which are then filled to the brim with rich soil, for the roots to strike into. Asparagus plants forced in this manner are injured, but in three seasons they will be restored, and may be forced again successfully. When asparagus is forced in this manner later in the season, much less dung is required, and the plants are proportionately less injured. Perhaps the simplest and surest, though not the cheapest mode of forcing asparagus, is to run three or four hot-water pipes along under a six-feet bed; fill in for two feet with rich soil. Plant five rows of plants on such beds, and cover them with moveable frames. With another pipe or two for surface-heat, asparagus may be thus had as plentifully and good at Christmas as in May. By a liberal summer treatment, and the use of salt and strong manure during its growth, such beds may be safely forced every year.

Sea-kale.—This may be forced exactly in the manner above described for asparagus, but a less degree of heat is required; for the sea-kale naturally shoots up early in spring, while the buds of the asparagus are much later in appearing. The asparagus requires to be grown three or four years from the seed before it is fit to force; but as the sea-kale can be forced at two years' growth, and the plants are consequently less valuable, there is less objection to taking them up, forcing them, and throwing them away. It is good practice to plant so many rows of sea-kale every spring, three feet apart, and the plants fifteen inches distant in the rows; the plants being raised from seed the previous year. The roots are taken up for forcing as soon as the leaves are decayed, with much care; and as much as possible removed entire, as the root is a magazine of nourishment for the incipient bud. The main stock is then "laid in by the heels," and covered with litter until wanted. In the mushroom-house a pit or trench may be sunk below the level of the floor-line about four feet: this furnishes room in the length of the house for about four successions of plants: the second lot of roots being introduced the moment the first begin to bud, and so on with the rest. Fermenting matter—viz., dung and leaves mixed, is placed about two feet six inches deep, under the roots. The roots are placed upon this as thickly as they will stand, and some fine old tan or rich soil mixed with water poured in to fill the crevices between the roots completely. The surface of the crowns when finished is a foot or so below the floor-line; and a row of trusses of straw should be laid side by side over the whole to shut in the steam, and keep the pit completely dark, which is one of the main points.

No vegetable is more easily or cheaply forced than sea-kale, whether in the open air in beds or drills, or by covering the plants with pots or boxes surrounded by hot dung; or by taking up the plants and potting them, and placing them in cellars, frames, or pits, or on a bed of heated materials. A temperature of from 40° to 45° will excite vegetation, after which it may be raised to 50° or 55°. Great care must be taken never to exceed 55°. Plants of sea-kale in the open ground may be forced every year; but much the cheapest mode is to take up the roots and force on beds heated artificially. The best crop is generally obtained by simply blanching the crop under pots as they come naturally into growth in the open ground.

Rhubarb and Chicory.—What has been said of sea-kale, in the preceding paragraph, will apply equally to rhubarb and chicory. They may both be forced in the open ground in trenches filled with hot dung, or by placing over them pots or boxes surrounded by that material; or, what is by far the most economical mode, the plants may be taken up and potted, and placed in a cellar; or, like the sea-kale, they may be planted close together on a bed of material heated artificially, or laid side by side in the floor of a vinery, or between the flue and wall, and covered with tan, peat, or leaf-mould. The rhubarb should be grown at least two years from the seed, in the same manner as the sea-kale, before being taken up for forcing; but the chicory should be sown the same year. The leaves of the chicory require to be blanched, and therefore it ought always to be forced in the dark; but as most people prefer the rhubarb only partially blanched, a certain degree of light may be admitted. In Belgium the roots of chicory are taken up on the approach of winter, and stacked in cellars in alternate layers of sand, so as to form ridges with the crowns of the plants on the surface of the ridge. Here, if the temperature is a few degrees above the freezing-point, the crowns soon send out leaves in such abundance as to afford an ample supply of salad during the whole winter. Mushroom-houses are invaluable for these purposes; and during winter the beds on the ground line are often reserved for such purposes in the forcing of rhubarb, sea-kale, chicory, &c.

Forcing other Roots.—The common dandelion (Leontodon Taraxacum, L.) affords a salad in all respects equal to that of the chicory, and may be similarly treated. Hamburg parsley, the common parsley, burnet, fennel, wild spinach (Chenopodium Bonus Henricus, L.), wild beet, as a substitute for spinach, and the common turnip, for the leaves as greens, and various other plants having fleshy roots, and of which the foliage or leaf-stalks are used in salads or cookery, may be forced on the same principle as asparagus, sea-kale, &c.; the practice being founded on the physiological fact that the root of every perennial herbaceous plant contains within itself, during winter, enough matter to enable it to develop its leaf-stems and unfold its leaves in a genial warm atmosphere without the aid of either light or food.

Forcing the Common Potato.

The common potato (Solanum tuberosum, L.) is forced in a great variety of ways. The best varieties for this purpose are the Ash-leaved kidney, the Rufford kidney, Champion, Handsworth, Myatt's Prolific, and Rivers's Royal Ash-leaf. They may be forced in pots or boxes on shelves in a peach-house or vinery, or in frames or pits moderately heated, the plants in every case being kept quite near the glass, as few plants suffer more when placed at a distance from the glass than the potato. The first crop may be planted on the 1st of November, either in a peach-house or vinery at work, or in a small house or pit devoted to them. Plant sets or whole tubers that have been thoroughly greened, and have the young shoots starting into growth; keep them near the glass, and maintain a temperature of from 50° to 60°, and good potatoes may be had in March. Though the crop may not be so heavy in pots, a few weeks may be gained in time by pot-culture. Care must be taken to earth-up the tubers as they swell, or the tops of pot-grown potatoes will be apt to become green. Time may also be gained by starting the tubers in pots, and when they have reached a height of about six inches transfer them to frames. Distance from plant to plant one foot each way. Give water occasionally, and admit as much air as possible at all times. The general mode is to plant in frames or pits, on a bed of fermenting material, sufficient to produce a gentle heat, for the potato will not bear rapid forcing, a high temperature, or a dry atmosphere. They, however, cannot have too much light, being natives of a high table-land with a clear sky. Some gardeners plant them on old hotbeds and supply the heat by linings; and many plant them on beds unprotected by glass, but covered with hoops and mats during nights and very severe weather. Six weeks may likewise be gained in the ripening of early potatoes by planting them in light dry soils in front of south walls.

A substitute for new potatoes is obtained by placing layers of potatoes alternately with sawdust in a box, and placing them in a moderate temperature in a room or cellar. The potatoes vegetate and produce tubers in December and January, about the size of walnuts, and sometimes larger, without any leaves having been protruded. This plan is most successful when potatoes of the growth of the season-before-last are used. By this treatment no leaves will emerge above the soil, and, consequently, as no nutritive matter can be deposited by them, the new potatoes, which may be produced at any required period by burying the old potatoes three weeks before, are nothing more than a recomposition of the old tuber, in consequence of the application of heat and moisture. Few persons, however, will be satisfied with this kind of a substitute for a new potato formed by the aid of light and foliage. Another mode of producing a substitute for new potatoes is, by retarding the tubers of early varieties by keeping them in a cool dry cellar till June or July, and then planting them. Being early sorts, they produce, even when planted thus late, a crop of young potatoes which possess in a great degree the flavour peculiar to potatoes taken fresh from the stem. By covering the ground with litter, so as to exclude the frost, young potatoes may thus be obtained throughout the winter. In the mild climate of Cornwall, where the winters frequently pass with little or no frost, the planting of sets can be deferred till autumn; and with a little protection, the plants, although pushed above ground, are preserved through the winter, and in consequence afford an early supply of genuine young potatoes.

Forcing Kidney-beans and Peas.

The kidney-bean (Phaseolus vulgaris, L.), being a native of India, may be forced in the same heat as that required for the pine-apple; but although it will bear this extreme, it will succeed in a temperature very much lower. The varieties generally preferred are—the Early Speckled, Early Negro, and Dun-coloured Dwarf, the latter being thought the best. They are planted in equal parts of rotten dung reduced to a soil, and loam, in shallow 24-sized pots: place in the bottom of each pot one inch of crocks, and above these two inches of soil; then plant six beans, covering them with one inch more of soil. These pots may be stowed away in any corner of the house or pit till the plants appear above ground, when they must be brought near the glass, and thinned out to two or three of the best plants. As they advance, they must be earthed-up. When they come into flower, air must be admitted, to set the fruit; and every pod must be gathered as soon as it is fit for the table. The plants may be grown in a house at any temperature from 45° to 75°; from 60° to 65° being preferable. They succeed well when planted out in a pit or frame, with a bottom heat, in rows eighteen inches apart, and three inches apart in the row; and, as they advance, they may be topped and sticked. Planted at Christmas, they require about eight weeks to bear fruit fit for the table, in a temperature of 60° or 65°. To have kidney-beans all the year, the first sowing for forcing should be made in August, and sowings should be made every fortnight till April, after which the crop in the open air from plants which have been raised in heat will come into use. Forced kidney-beans will continue bearing for a considerable time; but it is best only to keep them for two or, at the most, three gatherings, and then throw them out, as more fruit of higher quality can thus be gathered from a given space, and insects are less troublesome on young plants. The aphis and thrips often attack the French bean when grown under glass, but these insects may be readily destroyed by fumigation, by tobacco-water, or by quassia-water.

The common garden pea (Pisum sativum, L.), may be forced, but being a native of a colder climate (the South of Europe), not so successfully as the kidney-bean. The best varieties for this purpose are such classes as Beck's Gem, Tom Thumb, &c., First Crop, and Early Frame. It is necessary to begin at a low temperature, and not to exceed 50° or 60° with sun-heat, and from 40° to 50° during the night, till the fruit is set. Afterwards the temperature may be increased, so as to vary during the day from 55° to 70°. The peas may be sown in pots or boxes, and either fruited in them, or transplanted into other pots or boxes, or a pit. In general the best mode is to grow them in pots or boxes, because these admit of being kept well ventilated and close to the glass. Without abundance of light and air it is in vain to attempt forcing the pea. For the earliest crop the seeds may be sown in October, and these will produce pods in February or March, from which time by successive sowings, peas may be obtained till they are produced in the open ground from plants which have been raised in heat, and transplanted into a warm sheltered situation. Whatever description of forcing is adopted, transplanting is found to check luxuriance, concentrate growth, and produce a greater amount of blossom in a limited space. The front borders of orchard-houses have been found admirably adapted for early peas, and such varieties as Carter's First Crop sown in them in November may be gathered in April.

Forcing Salads, Pot-herbs, Sweet-herbs, and other Culinary Plants.

Lettuce, chicory, radish, cress, mustard, rape, parsley, chervil, carrot, turnip, onion, and similar plants, may be raised in pots or in beds, in a gentle heat, and quite near the glass. In general it will be of little use beginning to sow sooner than January; and, indeed, with the exception of the carrot, parsley, and onion, February will be soon enough, on account of the light required. Young carrots being much used in soups, some families require a supply all the year, which is to be obtained by successive sowings in the open air and on heat. The first sowing on heat may be made in January, to succeed the autumnal sowing in the open garden; and the second may be made in February or March, to serve till the first crop in the open air comes into use.

Small salading, such as cresses, mustard, rape, radish, chicory, lettuce, &c., to be cropped when in the seed-leaf, or in the third or fourth leaf, may be sown in boxes or in beds, and kept in a warm, moist atmosphere, near the light. As the plants forming small salading are always cut beneath the seed-leaf, as soon as one portion of salading is gathered, the soil may be stirred and a second crop sown. Where there is a constant demand for small salading, a sowing should be made every week.

Radish.—To obtain the earliest spring radishes, sow on a hot-bed, of dung or leaves, some of the early dwarf short-top varieties, such as Beck's Superb Scarlet and Early Breakfast, in December, January, or the beginning of February. Having made a hotbed two or three feet high of dung, place on the frame; earth the bed at top six inches deep; sow on the surface, covering the seed with fine mould about half an inch thick; and put on the lights. When the plants have come up, admit air every day in mild or tolerably good weather, by tilting the upper end of the lights, or sometimes the front, one, two, or three inches, that the radishes may not draw up weak and long-shanked. If they have risen very thick, thin them in young growth, moderately at first, to about one or two inches apart. Be careful to cover the lights at night. Give gentle waterings about noon, on sunny days. If the heat of the bed declines much, apply a moderate lining of warm dung or stable litter to the sides, which, by gently renewing the heat, will forward the radishes for drawing in February and March. Remember, as they advance in growth, to give more copious admissions of air daily, either by tilting the lights in front several inches, or, in fine mild days, by drawing the glasses mostly off; but be careful to draw them on again in proper time. Small turnip-radishes of the white and red kinds may be forced in the same manner. For raising early radishes on ground not furnished with frames, a hotbed made in February may be arched over with hoop-bends or pliant rods, which should be covered with mats constantly at night, and during the day in very cold weather. In moderate days turn up the mats at the warmest side, and on a fine mild day take them wholly off.

To produce full-grown cabbage-lettuces throughout the winter is a desideratum on the Continent, where the higher classes have cabbage-lettuces on their tables every day in the year. The seed is sown on the 1st of September, and when the plants have produced their fourth leaf they are transplanted into a melon-bed which has done bearing; and as soon as they have taken root, abundance of air is given night and day. In October, when the air grows cold, and the heads of the cabbage-lettuce begin to get close and hard, air is no longer given, and the lights are entirely closed; but the leaves must be prevented from touching the glass, as, if they do, the least unexpected frost will hurt their edges, and the consequence will be that the plants will rot. In this case the frame will have to be lifted every now and then. When the nightly frosts commence, generally in October, great attention must be paid to covering the beds with a single layer of bast mats, and adding slight linings; yet too much covering is to be avoided before the plants are grown to perfect heads. Watering is quite out of the question, and even very hurtful; care, indeed, should be taken to prevent moisture as much as possible. Cover more or less, according to the severity of the weather, and keep the lights uncovered in the day, whenever and as much as the weather will permit. In this way the Dutch gardeners produce cabbage-lettuce during the whole winter till April, when they are succeeded by the plants which have been early forced. Perhaps the most successful of all cultivators of winter lettuce are the French, who grow them in frames and under the cloches elsewhere described in this book. The cloches, when used for forcing, being always placed on a gentle hotbed, while by the use of the cloche alone, without the hotbed, beautiful crops of early lettuce are annually raised round Paris.

Perennial pot and sweet herbs, such as mint, sage, tarragon, savory, thyme, tansy, scurvy-grass, and similar plants, may be taken up from the open ground, potted, and transferred to the forcing-house, where they will soon produce abundance of foliage; care being taken to let the heat with which forcing is commenced be low, in proportion to the coldness of the country of which the plant is a native, and that of the season at which it naturally expands its leaves. Thus, in forcing scurvy-grass, which is a native of Denmark, a much lower temperature ought to be commenced with than in forcing sage, which is a native of Greece; and again, a plant which naturally springs up in April will bear commencing with a higher temperature than one which makes considerable progress in the previous colder months.

Forcing the Mushroom.

The mushroom (Agaricus campestris, L.) is indigenous to Britain, appearing "in the fields chiefly after Midsummer, in the months of July, August, and most abundantly in September. On a ten years' average, the temperature of these months respectively in the neighbourhood of London has been found to be 64°, 62°, and 57°; and in the same periods the temperature of the earth one foot below the surface is a few degrees higher; but at the depth of two or three inches, where the vegetating spawn is situated, the temperature in hot sunny weather is frequently as high as 80°. Whilst such hot weather continues, mushrooms are rarely met with; but when the atmosphere changes to a humid state, and when the earth becomes sufficiently moistened and lowered in temperature, in consequence of rain and absence of sun-heat, to be between 60° and 65°, mushrooms become plentiful. Hence it may be concluded that spawn will not be injured by a heat of 80° during what may be termed its underground state of progression. This is corroborated by the fact that spawn introduced into melon-frames when the beds are moulded, increases whilst the melons are grown in a heat of about 80°; and when the melon crop is over, the frame cleared, and the heat of the bed naturally abated, a gentle watering, with shade, is all that is necessary to bring up an excellent crop of mushrooms from the spawn so deposited. It is evident, from what has been stated, that the spawn requires a high temperature for its diffusion; but, when this has taken place, a declining temperature is requisite, till gradually the bottom heat is lowered to 60° or 65°, and the temperature of the air limited between 55° and 65°, when the mushrooms first appear above the soil.

"With regard to moisture, it may be observed that a dry atmosphere is injurious, not only to artificial crops, but also to those in the fields; for the latter, warm foggy mornings are most favourable, and these should be imitated as closely in cultivation as circumstances will permit. A gentle steam is more easily maintained in mushroom-houses than in structures adapted for other subjects of cultivation where light is an object of importance: but mushrooms do not require its agency, and consequently a glass roof is unnecessary: on the contrary, the roof and walls where they are intended to be grown should be composed of such substances as will cause the least possible condensation of the internal vapour, and which are in other respects eligible for the purpose.

"A thatched roof of a good thickness is very proper; a slated or tiled one is, on the contrary, objectionable, unless a ceiling be formed under it. If the cavity between the ceiling and the external covering were filled with dry moss, a more complete protection would be formed against any sudden vicissitudes of cold and heat, an object of importance towards success either in the cold winter months or during the greatest heat of summer."—('Penny Cyc.,' vol. xvi. p. 19.)

Forcing the Mushroom in British Gardens.

The ordinary form of a mushroom-house is a lean-to shed, at the back of a south wall, or of a range of hothouses, about nine feet wide, eight feet or nine feet high at front, and twelve feet or fifteen feet at the back. Along the middle there is a path three feet wide over a flue, or hot water-pipes, or in some cases a trench of two feet wide, and the same depth, for a bed of fermenting manure. Planks, in this latter case, are placed over the dung for the purpose of walking on. The space between the walls and the path is occupied by shelves of slate or flag-stone, three feet broad, eighteen inches or two feet apart in the height; each shelf having a slate or stone curb nine inches deep. The manner in which mushrooms are grown in such a house is as follows:—

The spawn may be either made or purchased. Cake or brick spawn is the sort best worth making, and the best sort of materials to make it of are, equal portions of horse-droppings, cow-droppings, and loam, well mixed, and pounded or beaten, adding only as much water as will bring the materials to the consistence of brickmakers' moulding clay. Then let a circular mould without a bottom, nine inches in diameter and three inches deep, be placed on a table, with the wide end uppermost, and filled with this mortar and straked level; before it is turned out of the mould, let three holes be made in each cake with an ironshod dibber, one inch and a half deep: the mould must be shaped like the frustum of a cone, that the cakes may easily part with it. When the cakes are all but hand dry, let them be spawned, by putting a piece of spawn about the size of a pigeon's egg in each hole, closing it up with a little of the original mortar. Then pile the cakes in pairs, with their spawned ends together, resembling a cask; and in this state let them be cased up in brick-shaped batches, and sweated and kept up to about 85°, by placing a layer of sweet dung all around and over the batch, varying it in quantity, to obtain the desired heat. The spawn must be examined as it runs in the cakes, and when one is broken and appears mouldy all through, and smells of mushroom, it is mushroom spawn in the highest state of perfection. It must not be allowed to run so far as to form a thread-like substance. To preserve it, it must be thoroughly dried in an airy loft, and kept dry for use. It will retain its properties for several years.

To Grow the Mushroom.—Collect a quantity of horse-droppings; lay a little in an open shed. Allow the moisture to evaporate; and to facilitate this, turn the heap several times. Let the condition of the droppings be the same throughout, as, if a portion of the mixture be sweetened and other parts sour, the bed will give an irregular fermentation, and will be less congenial to the mushroom. Then lay a stratum of turfy loam, two inches or three inches deep, in the bottom of the bed, and over this three layers of droppings, each about two inches deep, rendered as compact as possible, by giving each layer a good pummelling with a hand-mallet. When the last layer is made up, thrust a few "watch sticks" into the bed, in order to ascertain when it begins to heat. When the heat has declined to about 80°, the spawn may be inserted. If the heat is violent a few deep narrow holes may be made to let it escape; and if too slight it may be aided by a covering of dry hay, or a layer of warm dung; and when all danger of violent heat is gone by, and the spawn beginning to run, put on the upper stratum of loam, mixed with a little cut hay or dry horse-droppings to make a tough firm crust, about one inch deep. A temperature of from 55° to 60° is found best for the atmosphere in the house, and about 80° of bottom heat will set the spawn actively to work.

Growing the mushroom in a cellar may be readily accomplished where the temperature does not fall below 45°, or rise above 70°. Take a quantity of fresh manure, with short litter intermixed, from a stable where the horses are fed on hay and corn, but not on green food. Spread the manure on the floor of the cellar about four inches deep, and beat it firmly down with a mallet. After a few days repeat this operation, and again do so at intervals, till the bed becomes about fourteen inches deep, and of such a breadth as may be most convenient. To ascertain the degree of heat, put two or three sharp-pointed sticks into the bed, and when, upon being drawn out the next day, they feel about milk-warm, or between 80° or 90°, it is time to put in the mushroom spawn. Observe, however, that when this operation is performed, the heat should be rather on the decline than on the increase.

Having purchased or otherwise procured the spawn, break it into pieces about the size of a hen's egg. Place the pieces all over the bed, about a foot apart, and two inches below the surface. Beat the whole down hard. Be careful not to let the heat increase above the degree mentioned above, otherwise the spawn will be destroyed, and the bed must be stocked again with fresh spawn. Indeed, for security's sake, it is always best to repeat the spawning when the heat is on the decline. After all danger of increased heat is past, cover the bed with light soil about two inches deep, then beat it down hard. Mushrooms always do best in a firm hard soil: however hard, they will find their way through it. They have even been known to raise the pavement of a cellar floor.

Management of the Bed.—Examine the sticks which were originally placed in the bed; if they are lukewarm all is right. A few days afterwards cover the bed with hay or straw; but if it increases the heat, remove it for a time. If the place is warm and dark this covering may be dispensed with. In five or six weeks the mushrooms ought to appear. A gentle watering now and then will hasten their growth; but too much will cause the spawn to rot, and then, of course, the bed will be unproductive, whereas it ought to produce for five or six weeks.

Mushroom spawn, planted in loam and dung, or in either, and screened from sun and rain in summer, will produce this vegetable in abundance; and the same materials will produce the same effect in winter under favourable circumstances, such as being placed in boxes or baskets in a stable or warm cellar. Mushrooms may be grown remarkably well on dung-beds, covered with frames, having thatched hurdles or boards instead of glass; the surface of the bed being covered with hay, litter, or dried shorn grass.

Half-dried droppings of highly-fed horses, good spawn, and a gentle moist atmosphere, are the principal things to be attended to in cultivating the mushroom.

In gathering mushrooms for present use, they may be cut; but if they are to be kept a few days, they must be got with the stem entire, which is easily done by slipping them off with a gentle twist.

The duration of a crop of mushrooms varies from three to six months, so that it is always safe to make up a bed or a couple of shelves every three or four months.

The subject of mushroom culture is very fully treated of in 'Mushroom Culture,' published by Warne.

CHAPTER XVII.

CATALOGUE OF FRUITS.

Hardy or Orchard Fruits.

The hardy fruits include all those which arrive at maturity in the open garden without the aid of glass or artificial heat. These are the apple, pear, quince, medlar, the true service, cherry, plum, gooseberry, currant, raspberry, strawberry, cranberry, bilberry, cornel, elder, barberry, winter cherry, buffalo berry, chestnut, walnut, hickory, and mulberry.

The Apple.

The Apple (Pyrus Malus, L.; Malus communis, Dec.), is a deciduous tree, under the middle size, with spreading branches, which form in general an irregular head. In its wild or crab state, it is indigenous in most parts of Europe, and as a fruit tree, it is cultivated in all civilized countries, more especially in those of temperate climate. It flowers in May, and ripens its fruit at various periods from July to November, and some sorts of apple may be kept throughout the year or longer. The tree is naturally of considerable hardiness and durability, but the cultivated varieties are comparatively delicate and short-lived. Trees of the more hardy varieties, however, have been known to endure for two or three centuries; but it is presumed that individual trees of such varieties as the Hawthornden and the Ribston pippin would scarcely live a century. The apple, like every other plant, accommodates itself more or less to the climate and soil in which it is placed, but still it attains a higher degree of perfection in some climates and soils than in others. The climate of England and the north of France, and the loamy soils on limestone rock that are found in these countries, appear to bring the apple to the highest degree of perfection. Italy and Spain are much too warm, and the north of Germany and Sweden too cold and sunless. Several kinds of apples were introduced into Britain by the Romans, who possessed, according to Pliny, twenty-two varieties; but, in all probability, these were lost in the interval between the Roman dominion in Britain, and the power of the Church, though many wildings might doubtless spring up, when the trees established by the Romans began to be neglected. Some of the varieties, it may be reasonably supposed, were introduced by the Roman clergy, but the greater number of sorts which have not been raised in Britain have doubtless been introduced from Normandy, either when that country was subjected to England, or previously at the Norman conquest. The apple is not indigenous in North America, but nevertheless it flourishes in all the temperate parts of the United States, and the flavour of some varieties grown in America, for example the Newtown pippin, is thought by many to be superior to that of any kinds grown in the north of France or England. The number of varieties now in cultivation has been greatly increased within the present century, partly from importations, but chiefly from seedlings raised in this country. In consequence, we have varieties suitable for different soils and situations, from the warm moist climate of Devonshire and Cornwall, to the cloudy and stormy atmosphere of Orkney. There are varieties which ripen as early as July, and others which are not fit to eat till the following spring; and which, with proper care, will keep till apples come again, and even longer. No fruit tree is more prolific than the apple when in a suitable soil and situation, and no fruit is applied to a greater variety of useful purposes.

The use of the apple in pies, tarts, sauces, the dessert, or boiled or roasted, is familiar to every one. The expressed juice fermented forms cider—that of the crab verjuice; and when both these liquids are mixed, and properly managed, a very good wine, it is said, may be produced. One-third of boiled apple-pulp, baked with two-thirds of flour, and fermented for twelve hours, is said to make an excellent bread, very palatable and light. In confectionery the apple is used for comfits, compôtes, marmalades, jellies, pastes, tarts, fritters, and various other purposes. To form a jelly, the apples are "pared, quartered, and the core removed, and put in a closely-covered pot, without water, in an oven, or over a fire. When well stewed, the juice is squeezed through a cloth, a little of white of an egg is added, and then sugar; and lastly it is skimmed, and by boiling reduced to a proper consistence." Medicinally, boiled or roasted apples are considered laxative and at the same time strengthening. In perfumery, the pulp of the apple beat up with lard forms pomatum; and by mixing apples with elder-flowers, in a close vessel, an odour of musk is said to be communicated to them. The juice of the apple concentrated by boiling will keep fresh for several years, and may be used to form a liquor similar to cider, by adding a little to water as it is wanted for use. The apple-tree when in flower is very ornamental, particularly some varieties which have their petals tinged with pink, such as the Hawthornden; and the tree is still more beautiful when covered with fruit, especially with such as are highly-coloured, such as the red Astrachan, the tulip-apple, &c. The bark of the tree may be used for dyeing yellow; and the wood of the tree being fine-grained and very compact, is well adapted for turning and for staining, so as to be used as a substitute for ebony. We have dwelt thus fully on the uses of the apple because we regard it as a fruit of more use and benefit to society at large than all the other fruits cultivated in Britain, and it ought be much more extensively grown as an article of food for the masses of the people.

Properties of a Good Apple.—Apples for table are characterized by a firm juicy pulp, high flavour, regular form, and beautiful colouring; those for kitchen use by the property of falling, as it is technically termed, or forming in general a pulpy mass of equal consistence when baked or boiled, and by a large size. Some sorts of apples have the property of falling when green, as the Keswick Codlin, Hawthornden, and other codlins; and some only after being ripe, as the russet varieties. Those which have this property when green are particularly valuable for forming sauces to geese early in the season, and for succeeding the gooseberry in tarts. For cider an apple must possess a considerable degree of astringency, with or without firmness of pulp or sugariness of juice. The best kinds, Knight observes, are often tough, dry, and fibrous; and the Siberian Harvey, which he recommends as one of the very best cider apples, is unfit either for culinary purposes or the table. The same eminent pomologist has found that the specific gravity of the juice of any apple recently expressed, indicates, with very considerable accuracy, the strength of the future cider.

Varieties.—The varieties of apple in cultivation previous to the time of Henry VIII. do not appear to have been numerous; but Evelyn informs us, that Harris, the fruiterer to that monarch, introduced many sorts of apples and other fruits from Flanders, and distributed them in the neighbourhood of thirty towns in Kent only, to the great and universal improvement of this fruit. In the time of Charles I., Lord Scudamore introduced a number of cider apples from Normandy into Herefordshire. Hartlib, during the Commonwealth, in 1650, "believes there are nearly 500 sorts in this island." Some were introduced from Holland in the time of William III., and the number would doubtless gradually increase till the commencement of the present century, when it has been greatly enlarged by the growing taste for gardening, and the great stimulus given by Mr. Knight to raising new fruits from seed. The Horticultural Society of London have collected varieties of fruit from every part of the world, and the number of sorts of apples, that have been proved in their gardens to be distinct, is believed to be nearly 1500; the number of names exceeding twice that amount, many varieties having more than one name. Thousands of seedlings also exist, of more or less merit, without names. The great difficulty, where the choice is so ample, is to make a selection, and this, with the assistance of the late Mr. Thomson, of Chiswick—perhaps the best practical pomologist in Europe—and other authorities, combined with our own experience, we have endeavoured to make as useful, complete, and choice as possible.

Early Dessert Apples, ripening from July to September.

Early Red Margaret, Early Harvest, Early Strawberry, Oslin, Kerry Pippin, Summer Golden Pippin, Irish Peach, Red Quarrenden, Early Shrewsbury, Reinette Jaune, Hâtive, White Juneating, Chromatic Beauty, Red Astrachan.

Dessert Apples to succeed Early Kinds, in season from October to December.

Wormsley Pippin, King of the Pippins, Golden Reinette, Silver or Pine Russet, Cellini, Pine Golden Pippin, Mother Apple, Fearn's Pippin, Margil, Red Ingestrie, Golden Reinette, Early Nonpareil, Stamford Pippin, Sam Young, Adam's Pearmain, Cox's Orange Pippin.

DESSERT, KITCHEN, AND CIDER APPLES.

Winter Dessert Apples, in season from January to March.

Adams's Pearmain, Hubbard's Pearmain, Mannington's Pearmain, Claygate Pearmain, Golden Pearmain, Herefordshire Pearmain, Scarlet Nonpareil, Old Nonpareil, Braddick's Nonpareil, Cox's Orange Pippin, Cockle Pippin, King of the Pippins, Golden Pippin, Pitmaston Golden Pippin, Hughes' Golden Pippin, Downton Pippin, Wyken Pippin, Keddleston Pippin, Newtown Pippin, Forfar Pippin, Pitmaston Nonpareil, Boston Russet, Sykehouse Russet, Brownlow's Russet, Pearson's Plate, Pine-apple Russet, Ashmead Kernel, Court of Wick, Melon Apple, Maclean's Favourite, Winter Peach, Northern Spy, Duke of Devonshire, Pomme Royale.

Latest of all Dessert Apples, in season from April to June.

Allen's Everlasting, Spring Ribston Pippin, Victoria, Wellesley, Lord Burleigh, Court Pendu-Plat, Reinette Van Mon's, Reinette du Canada, Prince Albert, Sturmer Pippin, Court of Wick, Golden Harvey, New Rock Pippin, Golden Pippin, Wanstall, Lodgemore Nonpareil.

Early Kitchen Apples, from July to October.

Dutch Codlin, Keswick Codlin, Hawthornden, Nonesuch, Alexander, Lord Burleigh, Carlisle Codlin, Nelson Codlin, Lord Suffield, Cox's Oldenburg, Stirling Castle.

Kitchen Apples for Winter Use, from November to January.

Calville Blanc, Gloria Mundi, Gravenstein, Waltham Abbey Seedling, Golden Noble, New Hawthornden, Flanders Pippin, Mère de Ménage, Beauty of Kent, Kentish Fill Basket, Black and Orange, Monstrous Leadington, Small's Admirable, Betty Geeson, Wadhurst Pippin, Alfriston, Tower of Glammis.

Kitchen Apples for Spring and Summer Use, from January to June.

Green Apple, Dumelow's Seedling, Green Beefing, Red or Striped Beefing, Baldwin, London Pippin, Greenup's Pippin, Rymer, Bedfordshire Foundling, Brabant Bellefleur, French Crab, Hanwell Souring, Winter Majeting, Forge Apple, Winter Pearmain, Bess Poole, Fearn's Pippin, Northern Greening.

Cider Apples.

Siberian Bitter Sweet, Foxley, Red Streak, Fox Whelp, Golden Harvey, Hagloe Crab, Cooper's Red Streak.

Kitchen Apples which may be used as Dessert Apples.

Gravenstein, Blenheim Pippin, Orange Pippin, Manks Codlin, Alfriston, Nonesuch, London Pippin, Northern Greening, Rhode Island Greening.

While this distinction between kitchen and dessert apples is preserved, it may be well to state that nearly the whole of the dessert apples cook admirably, while sorts like the Pearmains and the larger pippins, such as Ribston, Blenheim, Sturmer, &c., are admirable either in tarts. pies, or compôtes. For fritters likewise the firmer flesh of the dessert varieties gives them a special value. Such varieties as the Golden Pippin and Golden Harvey are admirably adapted for stewing whole, as are the smallest Nonpareils. The following are among the best dessert apples for cooking: Sugarloaf Pippin, Wormsley Pippin, Autumn Pearmain, King of the Pippins, Fearn's Pippin, Ribston Pippin, Old Pearmain, Herefordshire Pearmain, Reinette du Canada, Dutch Mignonne, Downton Nonpareil, Newtown Pippin, Boston Russet.

Apples for Cottage Gardens, where the Soil and Situation are favourable, and which may be used either for the Table or the Kitchen.—Where the space will admit of only one tree, the best is the Ribston Pippin; where two, the Ribston Pippin and the Blenheim Pippin; where three, or more, add successively to those previously named, the Sturmer Pippin, King of the Pippins, Herefordshire Pearmain, Wormsley Pippin, Reinette du Canada, Bedfordshire Foundling, Downton Nonpareil, Waltham Abbey Seedling.

Apples for Training against the Walls or on the Roofs of Cottages, or on the Walls of Cottage Gardens.—Ribston Pippin, Old Nonpareil; and if a large kitchen apple be required, the Bedfordshire Foundling, Nonesuch, and Calville Blanche on the south gable end.

Apples for Cottage Gardens in situations liable to Spring Frosts.—The Court Pendu-plat, as expanding its blossoms later in the season than any other apple; and the Northern Greening.

Apples for a Cottage Garden in an unfavourable Climate.—The Claygate Pearmain and Sturmer Pippin are considerably hardier than the Ribston Pippin. The Northern Greening is a hardy and late kitchen apple; and the Keswick Codlin is a hardy autumn kitchen apple. The Hawthornden comes earlier into bearing than any other variety generally cultivated; the New Hawthornden having the same peculiarity, and it would be preferable to the Old Hawthornden or to the Keswick Codlin, were it not that it is liable to canker in some soils.

Apples adapted for walls of different aspects are enumerated on p. 389.

Apples adapted for espaliers, dwarfs, or conical standards, are enumerated on p. 399.

Apples suitable for an orchard are enumerated on p. 403.

Apples remarkable for the form of the Tree, or the beauty of the Blossoms or Fruit.—The Red Astrachan has the fruit of a bright red, with a fine bloom like that of a plum. The white Astrachan, or transparent crab of Moscow, has the fruit of a wax colour, with a fine bloom, and is almost transparent. The black crab has small fruit which is of no use, but it is so dark as almost to be black The Lincolnshire Holland Pippin is remarkable for the large size of its blossoms, and the fruit keeps till February. The Tulip apple has fruit of a very bright red, and is a great bearer. The Violet apple has fruit of a violet colour, covered with a bloom like that of the plum. The Cherry crab is a spreading tree with drooping branches, and numerous fruit about the size and colour of a large cherry. The Supreme crab is a more erect tree than the Cherry crab, with larger fruit. Big's Everlasting crab is a vigorous-growing, round-headed tree, the fruit and leaves of which remain on long after Christmas, in sheltered situations.

General Principles of selecting Varieties of the Apple.—The first requisite in forming a selection is to determine how far the climate, soil, and situation, differ from those of the central counties of England, which may be taken as those for which most of the selections above given are adapted. A number of varieties, which may be grown as standards in the centre or south of England, require a wall in various parts of the north of England and of Scotland. The winter and spring table apples may require a south wall in one district, while in another they may attain equal maturity as standards or espaliers. Where there is ample room, a selection of large sorts, as the Alexander and Blenheim Pippin, or of such as are the most beautifully coloured, as the Violet, Hollandbury, &c., may be made to gratify the eye; where room is wanting, useful sorts and great bearers are to be preferred—such, indeed, as are enumerated in the above selection, which has been made with a view to both quality and abundance of produce. In general, small-sized fruit are to be preferred for standards, as less likely to break down the branches of the trees, or be shaken down by winds; middling-sized and high-flavoured sorts for walls; and the largest of all for espaliers. Such sorts as the Calville Blanc depend on walls, or the shelter of glass, in England, to bring them to the highest excellence or full size.

Propagation.—The apple may be propagated by seeds, cuttings of the branches or roots, by layers, suckers, inarching, grafting, or budding; but the two last modes are most generally adopted for continuing varieties, and seeds are seldom resorted to, except when new varieties are the object. Only a few sorts, such as the Burknott, some of the codlins, and the Creeping-apple, can be increased readily by cuttings; but this mode is resorted to occasionally, when these kinds are wanted as stocks for grafting on. Suckers from a grafted tree should only be used as stocks; but from kinds of apple which are used chiefly as stocks, such as the Paradise apple, suckers are not an uncommon mode of propagation. Thus the first step in the propagation of the apple by grafting or budding, is the propagation of the stock. Crab stocks are raised from seeds of the wild crab, and are used when the object is strong and durable trees; wildings or seedling apple stocks are used for strong trees in good soils, and are raised from seeds of apple-trees, most commonly of free-growing seedlings, which have grown in hedges in cider counties, or from cider apples; dwarfing stocks, such as the Paradise, Doucin, Creeping-apple, and some codlins, are commonly raised from layers and suckers. Seedlings, after one year's growth in the seed-bed, are transplanted in rows, three feet apart and eighteen inches distance in the row; and they are commonly grafted the third or fourth spring from the seed, when they are from half an inch to one inch in thickness. Both dwarfs and standards are commonly grafted within a few inches of the ground, and the standards are formed by encouraging the leading shoot, which is commonly cut over at the end of the second year at the height of five or six feet from the ground, and after it has grown another season in the nursery, the side-shoots being cut off about midsummer, it is fit for being transplanted to where it is finally to remain. If the tree should not be sold or transplanted the first year after the head is formed, the shoots are shortened, technically "headed in," to one or two buds, and this operation is repeated every spring till the plant is sold or transplanted to where it is finally to remain. The same heading-in takes place with dwarfs, the reason in both cases being that it is desirable to have no more wood left on the tree than the root, after undergoing the mutilation consequent on transplanting, can readily support. This severe heading-in is likewise practised to economize space. But it is less practised than it used to be, as the demand has increased for trained trees alike as standards, dwarfs, espaliers, cordons, bushes, and pyramids; consequently instead of the usual heading back in the winter, summer training and pinching is adopted to form the trees into shape and produce early fruitfulness. The more frequently trees are transplanted in the nursery before being finally removed, the greater will be the number of their fibrous roots; and as these must necessarily be within a limited space, the quantity of nourishment they take up will be limited also. Hence by their number of fibrous roots, they will suffer little from removal, while by the concentration of these roots they will only absorb the nourishment obtained within a very limited space, and thus keep the tree dwarf, and throw it early into a fruit-bearing state, or at least prevent it from growing so vigorously as if it were furnished with a number of ramose roots, which by extending their fibres to a distance have a proportionately greater command of nourishment. Hence maiden plants one year grafted on free stocks that have not been transplanted, are to be preferred in every case in which the object is large and vigorous trees; and when the object is dwarf trees, plants on dwarfing stocks, such as the Doucin or Paradise that have been several times transplanted, should be chosen.

Soil and Situation.—The apple-tree acquires the largest dimensions in a deep strong loam, or marly clay, on a rocky bottom, or on a subsoil that is not retentive of moisture, and in a situation which is neither very high nor very low. "It will grow tolerably well in any common soil, neither extremely sandy, gravelly, nor clayey, on a dry subsoil, and with a free exposure. On wet subsoil, it will do no good; but, after being planted a few years, will become cankered, and get covered with moss. Where fruit trees must be planted on such soils, they should first be rendered as dry as possible by under-draining; next, provision made for carrying off the rain-water by surface-gutters; and lastly, the ground should not be trenched above a foot deep, and the trees planted rather in hillocks of earth, above the surface, than in pits dug into it. There is no point of more importance than shallow trenching and shallow planting in cold wet soils, in which deep pits and deep pulverization only serve to aggravate the natural evils of moisture and cold." A good mode of planting on such soils is to form ridges of litter about three or four feet high, quite above the natural level, and plant the trees on these continuous mounds, as they may be termed.

Mode of Bearing, Pruning, and Training.—The apple bears invariably on the old wood, often on that of the preceding year, and the blossoms continue being produced from terminal and lateral spurs, or short robust shoots, for a great number of years. These spurs require to be thinned out when they become crowded, to be shortened when they become too long, and to be cut in when they become so old as to produce smaller fruit than is desirable.

The treatment of spurs is that part of the pruning of the apple when trained against walls or espaliers, on which the production of fruit chiefly depends, and it requires greater skill and care than any other part of the pruning. For this reason, and as the spur-pruning of the apple corresponds exactly with the spur-pruning of the pear against walls or espaliers, and in a great measure also with that of all other fruit trees that bear on spurs, we shall enter into it here at some length, as this will save repetition in treating of the pear, cherry, plum, apricot, mulberry, and even the gooseberry and currant. We shall commence with an apple-tree one year grafted, just taken from a nursery and planted at the base of a wall or espalier-rail. We shall give the winter and summer pruning for ten years, commencing every year with the beginning of the winter pruning, which should always be performed as early in the winter as possible. We have supposed the tree to be trained in the horizontal manner, but the mode of treating the spurs is equally applicable to every other kind of training, and to standard trees or bushes as well as to those against walls or espaliers. We quote the substance of this article from the 'Gardener's Magazine,' vol. iii.

Spurring-in Pruning.—First Year.—Winter Pruning.—The tree is headed down before it begins to push; in doing which, the foot is placed upon the soil, and close to the bole, in order to prevent it from being drawn up by the force which is used in the operation. The cut is made in a sloping direction towards the wall, and about half an inch above the bud which is selected for the leading shoot. The tree is cut down so that seven buds remain.

Summer Pruning.—If all the buds push (which will generally be the case), they are all permitted to grow until they have attained three inches in length, when two of them are rubbed off; those rubbed off are the third and fourth buds, counting upwards from the origin of the tree. The uppermost shoot is trained straight up the wall for a leading stem, and the remaining four horizontally along the wall, two on each side the stem of the tree. These shoots are trained nine inches apart, for when they are much nearer than this they exclude the sun and air from operating upon the buds and wood in such a manner as is required to keep the tree productive. When the leading upright shoot has attained about fifteen inches in length, the end is pinched off so as to leave it about eleven inches long. This causes shoots to be produced from the upper part of the leader thus stopped, three of which are trained in, the uppermost straight up the wall, and the others one on each side the stem of the leader. This stopping of the leading shoot is not performed later than the end of June or early in July; for, when it is done much later, those shoots which push afterwards in that season do not arrive at a sufficient degree of maturity to withstand the winter, and are frequently destroyed by frost. When it happens that a tree has not done well in the early part of the season, and the upright shoot is not of a suitable length or vigour at the proper period for stopping it, it is not meddled with afterwards until the winter pruning of the tree.

Second Year.—Winter Pruning.—At the middle or end of November the tree is pruned. The upright leading shoot is now shortened down to ten inches from the place where it was last stopped. The tree will now be represented by the accompanying sketch (fig. 355). The sideshoots (but which will hereafter be termed branches) are not shortened, but left their full length. If, during summer, the end of a branch should have been accidentally broken or damaged, the general consequence resulting from it is the production of several shoots or fruit-buds. If shoots (which is very generally the case) were produced, and were shortened during summer agreeably to directions for similar shoots in the treatment of the tree for the second year, they are now cut down to about half an inch in length (fig. 356). If, instead of shoots, natural fruit-buds should have been produced (these are short and stiff, from half an inch to an inch in length, and reddish at the ends), such are allowed to remain untouched, as it is on those that fruit are produced. The advantage of shortening back the upright shoot as much as is directed to be done is, that by it branches are certain to be produced at those places desired, so that no vacancy occurs. The leading upright shoot thus attended to will reach the top of a wall twelve feet high in seven years, which is as soon as the tree will be able to do, so as to support every part sufficiently.

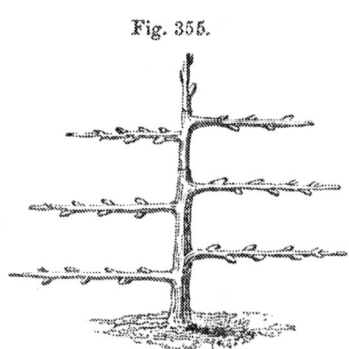

Summer Pruning.—When the buds upon that part of the leading stem which was produced last have pushed, they are all rubbed off to the three uppermost. The topmost is trained straight up the wall, for a lead to the main stem; and the two others, one on each side. The instructions given for stopping the leading shoot in summer, and shortening it back in winter pruning, &c., are attended to until the tree arrives at a few inches from the top of the wall. The sidebranches are allowed to grow without being shortened back at any time, until they have extended as far as can be permitted, when they are pruned in every winter, by cutting back each leading shoot to two buds from where it pushed the previous spring. Any shoots arising from the fore part of the main stem are taken clean away. The buds upon the wood made last year will this summer generally make fruitful ones. If, on the contrary, shoots are produced instead of fruitful buds, they are allowed to grow ten or twelve inches long, until the wood attains a little hardness towards the bottom of it, when they are cut down to about two inches in length; and at the bottom part of what remains, one or two fruit-buds are formed, so as to be productive in most cases the next year, but in others not until the second year. Although such a shoot was shortened as directed, yet it will generally push a shoot or more the same season from the top part of it. After such have grown a suitable length, they are cut back to about two inches from where they pushed. If more than one shoot were produced after the first shortening, and a bud or two is well swelled at the origin of the shoot, all the shoots are left, and shortened as directed; but if no such bud is produced, all the shoots are cut clean away, excepting one, which is treated in shortening as before directed. The latter practice will generally be found necessary, and also be more advantageous, as a greater portion of sun and air is admitted to the buds, which will be considerably strengthened and forwarded to a mature state.

Third Year.——Winter Pruning.——Such of the buds as produced wood shoots the last year, and were shortened during summer as described, are now shortened more. It frequently happens that a fruitful bud, or in some instances two, will have been formed at the lower part of the shoot (fig. 356, *a a*); such shoots are now cut off about a quarter of an inch above the uppermost of the fruitful buds (*b*): but if fruitful buds have not been produced, there will be growing buds, and then the shoots are cut down so as to leave one bud (fig. 356, *c*). On some occasions the growing buds and fruitful buds will appear but very indistinctly, and in an embryo state; when this is the case the shoots

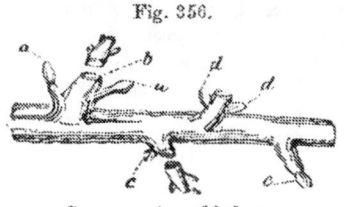

Fig. 356.

Spur-pruning, third year.

are cut down so as to leave two of these embryo buds (*d d*). There are generally some natural fruit-buds which did not push to shoots; all such are left entire (*e*). They are of a reddish colour, and are easily distinguished from growing buds, which are considerably less, and all of a dark colour.

Summer Pruning.——This summer the fruitful buds are productive. When the fruit has swelled a little, a shoot generally proceeds from the stem of the spur, just underneath the fruit; such are allowed to grow eight or ten inches long, and are then shortened back to two inches, or so as to leave three eyes upon each (fig. 357, A *a*). By shortening the shoot, strength is thrown into the fruit, and, during summer, two or more fruit-buds are generally produced at the bottom of the shoot thus cut down (fig. 357, *b b*), or, otherwise, from the lower part of the spur (fig. 357, *c*). It sometimes occurs that when the tree

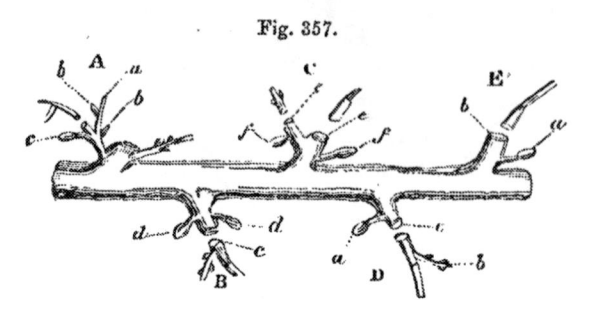

Fig. 357.

Spur-pruning, fourth year.

is very vigorous, some of the buds (fig. 357, *b b*) will push into shoots, or occasionally into bloom, during the latter end of summer. If shoots, they are allowed to grow, and are then shortened, as described for similar shoots; but, when bloom is produced, it is immediately cut off close under the blossom.

The shoots (fig. 356, *c*) produced after the third year's winter pruning are allowed to grow, and are then shortened, as already directed for similar shoots (see second year's summer pruning). The shoots which were pruned as directed last winter, and had embryo buds (fig. 356, *d d*) during this summer generally have a fruit-bud, and in some cases two, formed at their bases. The treatment of all shoots produced upon any of the spurs in future is agreeably to the previous instructions given.

Always thin the fruit, and where two are situated together, take one away; this is done when they begin to swell.

Fourth Year.—Winter Pruning.—The spurs (fig. 357, A B) which were productive last summer, and upon which a shoot was made and shortened (fig. 357, *a*, spur A), are now regulated in the following manner:—If there be two good fruit-buds formed upon the stem of the spur (fig. 357, *d d*, spur B), all that part of it above such buds is cut away, about a quarter of an inch above the uppermost (as at c); but, if there is only one good fruit-bud upon the stem, and one upon the shoot which was cut in during summer (as at *a*, spur A), then it is pruned off (as at spur C, *e e*), so that two buds only remain (as at *f f*). When there is only one fruit-bud upon the stem of the spur (as spur D, *a*), and no fruitful buds at the shoot (*b*), then the spur is pruned away (as at *c*). Sometimes the spurs that bear fruit will not have a shoot produced, but, instead of it, a fruitful bud (as spur E, *a*); it is then pruned off just above such bud (as at *b*).

Summer Pruning.—All shoots are pruned, as already directed, in the second and third years.

Fifth Year.—*Winter Pruning.*—All the spurs are allowed to retain three fruitful buds each; but as there are generally more than are required to keep, some of them are thinned away, retaining the best buds. The ripest buds are most plump and red at the ends. If such buds are situated near to the origin of the spur (as fig. 358, spur A, *a a a*), they are retained in preference to similar fruitful buds that are nigher the end of the spur (as *b b*); the spur is then cut off (as at *c c*). When there are no fruitful buds near to the origin of the spur, those are left that are further off; but always take care to preserve the bud situated nearest to

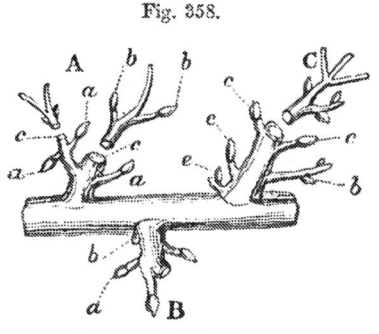

Fig. 358.

Spur-pruning, fifth year.

the branch which supports the spur, whether it be a growing or a fruitful one (as spur B, in which *a* is a fruitful bud, and *b* a growing one).

If there be a suitable supply of buds upon the old part of the spur (as c, *c c c*), they are retained in preference to those buds formed at the bases of shoots which have been pruned during summer (as *e b*); for when there is a proper supply on the old part of the spur, all such shoots are cut clean away, with the exception of one that is situated near to the origin of the spur (as *e*), when only that bud and the two next are left.

Summer pruning is performed as before directed.

Sixth Year.—*Winter Pruning.*—In order to convey a correct notion of the treatment of the spurs in future it will be necessary to point them out by numbers, as 1, 2, and 3. The enumeration will proceed from the bole of the tree, along the branch. After three spurs are thus numbered, begin again and proceed with No. 1, &c. (agreeably to fig. 359).

Every spur, No. 1, is now cut down to the lowest bud there is upon it, whether it be a fruitful bud (as *a*), or growing bud (as *b*). Every spur, No. 2, should have three fruit-buds (as *c c c*), and every spur, No. 3, four fruit-buds (as *d d d d*). When a spur, No. 1, is destitute of either a fruitful or a growing bud towards the lower part of it, such a spur is cut down so low as only to leave about one half inch remaining (fig. 359, A). There is generally an eye or embryo of a bud situated near to the origin of the spur (as *a*, spur A); from this a shoot or a fruitful bud is produced the ensuing summer, and thus a supply is obtained for that cut away.

Summer Pruning.—All shoots are shortened during summer, as before directed. Particular care is paid to the spurs No. 1, as a shoot or a fruitful bud is generally produced nearer to the base of the spur than to the bud that was left at winter pruning, and most commonly at the

538   THE APPLE.

side of the spur opposite to it. Either a shoot or a fruitful bud generally pushes from those spurs that were cut entirely down (as spur A, fig. 359); the shoots are cut down, as directed for others.

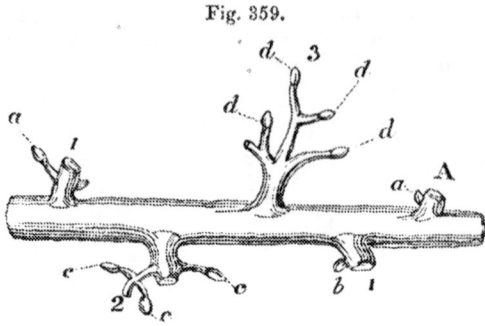

Fig. 359.

Spur-pruning, sixth year.

Seventh Year.—Winter Pruning.— The spurs No. 1 now generally have two fruit-buds each; they are allowed to retain them (as fig. 360, *a a*). If, instead of a fruitful bud, a shoot pushed (as *b*), and a fruitful bud was formed at the lower part of it; the shoot is then cut off above it (as at *c*); but if there is not a fruitful bud formed, it is cut down, so as to leave it half an inch long (as at *d*). The spurs No. 2 have four fruit-buds left upon each (as *e e e e*); the spurs, No. 3, are now cut down, so that one fruitful bud remains (as *f*).

If a fruit-bud has been produced from the spur cut entirely away (as spur A, fig. 359), it is left entire (as 360, *g*); but if a shoot, instead

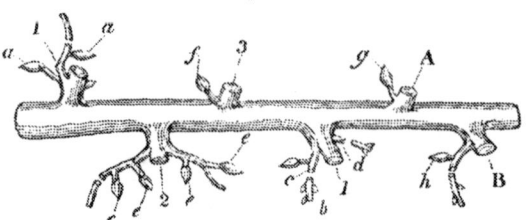

Fig. 360.

Spur-pruning, seventh year.

of a fruitful bud, it is cut off just above the lowest bud, whether a fruitful or a growing bud (as at *h*, spur B). This treatment of such spurs cut entirely down, is always pursued with similar ones in future.

Summer Pruning.—This is attended to agreeably to the foregoing directions.

Eighth Year.—Winter Pruning.—The spurs, No. 1, are allowed to retain three fruit buds each (as fig. 361, *a a a*) and the spurs, No. 2, are now cut down (as *b*); the spurs No. 3, are regulated as were the spurs Nos. 1 and 2. (See Sixth and Seventh Year's Summer Pruning.)

Summer Pruning.—This is performed as before directed.

Ninth Year.—Winter Pruning.—The spurs, No. 1, are allowed to have four fruit-buds each (as fig. 362, *a a a a*); the spurs, No. 2, to have two fruitful buds (as *b b*), and the spurs, No. 3, to have three (as *c c c*).

SPUR-PRUNING.

Summer Pruning.—Performed as before.

Tenth Year.—*Winter Pruning.*—The spurs, No. 1, are now cut down again (as fig. 363, *a*, a fruitful bud, and *b*, a growing bud). The spurs, No. 2, are pruned to three fruit-buds (as *c c c*), and the spurs, No. 3, to four fruit-buds (as *d d d d*).

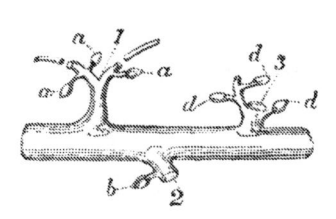

Fig. 361.

Fig. 362.

Spur-pruning, eighth year.

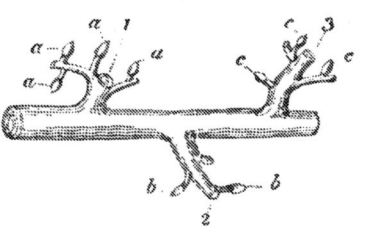

Spur-pruning, ninth year.

It will be observed that the spurs, No. 1, have now been cut down twice ; the first time in the sixth year, and the second in the tenth. Thus those spurs cut down to a fruitful bud (as fig. 359, *a*) have borne fruit four years; and those spurs cut entirely down, or to a growing bud (as A, *b*, fig. 359), would have only borne fruit three years. In these two cases always leave the spurs with three fruit-buds each this winter, and cut them down the following winter, unless they have grown very vigorous and straggling.

Fig. 363.

Spur-pruning, tenth year.

The system already detailed, of cutting down and renewing the spurs, is practised with all others as here directed. Thus, the next year, the spurs No. 3 are cut down (as in fig. 360, *f*) and the second year from this time, the spurs No. 2 (as fig. 361, *b*), and in the fourth year from the present time, the spurs No. 1 cut down (as fig. 359, *a*, and fig. 363, *a*) require to be cut down again.

These directions may appear tedious and intricate ; but it was necessary to enter into minute details, in order to illustrate the principle of this system of spur-pruning, the object of which is to obtain spurs always at a proper distance from each other, so that a suitable portion of sun and air may be admitted to them, and so that the spurs may always be kept supplied with young healthy wood and fruitful buds. This renewal of spurs may proceed during the life of the tree, and thus those long and injurious straggling spurs which are so generally seen on wall-trees and espaliers may be avoided. Modern cultivators allow of a freer growth of the top branches, and trust to root pruning more than top-cutting, to induce and maintain a fruitful state. Under this treatment and close summer pinching, but very little winter pruning is needed by apple-trees trained as espaliers, bushes, or pyramids.

Pruning, with reference to the entire tree, should have for its object to admit the light and air among the branches, to preserve the symmetry of the head by causing it to spread equally, and in the same form and manner on every side, and to eradicate branches which are diseased or decaying. In the case of espalier and wall trees it may frequently become necessary to shorten a portion of the roots in order to lessen the vigour of the branches, and throw them into a fruit-bearing state ; and the same treatment may occasionally be required for dwarfs, and conical trees on dwarfing stocks ; but it can seldom or never be either necessary or desirable for standards, which require the aid of long ramose roots to enable them to resist high winds; and their roots as well as their heads having abundant space for extension, a due equilibrium is preserved between them. Most trees and shrubs, whether fruit-bearing, ornamental, or merely useful, require a certain degree of pruning in summer, as well as in autumn or spring. The object of summer pruning, in all standards and bushes, ought to be to stop or to thin out shoots of the current year, in order the better to admit the sun and air to mature, by means of the leaves, the shoots which remain. The shoots, so stopped or removed, may either be cut or stopped to one or two buds with a view to forming spurs, or cut close off, according as there may or may not be room for the spurs to be developed. In the case of trees on walls, espaliers, or trained as dwarfs, or cones, it is not desirable to add much strength to the root, and therefore most of the summer shoots should be shortened early in the season by pinching out their points with the finger and thumb, when they are only a few inches in length, repeating this operation when the shoot, thus shortened, has again developed its last or farthest bud. At the same time, wherever shoots are wanted to complete the form or dimensions of the tree, or when it is desirable to add strength to the stem or the root, there the branches should be left at their full length to be laid in, shortened, or cut out, at the autumnal or winter's pruning, as may be found most desirable. The apple against a wall or espalier is almost always trained in the horizontal manner ; it is better adapted for dwarfs than any other fruit tree, and the mode of training these, as well as of forming cones, has been already described. Other modes of training have likewise been fully illustrated in our chapters on training espaliers, cordons, &c.

Gathering and Keeping.—All apples intended to be kept for some weeks or months, should be gathered by hand and carried to the fruit-room in baskets. Table apples should be spread out singly on shelves, or packed in sand, fern, or kiln-dried straw, or in jars with any of these materials ; but kitchen sorts may be laid in layers on shelves, or on a cool floor. The common mode of keeping, by those who grow apples in large quantities for the market, is to lay them in heaps in cool dry cellars, and cover them with abundance of straw. In some parts of England they are preserved in ridges, the apples being laid on, and covered with, green turf or straw, and the ridge finished with a foot or more of soil to keep out the frost, in the same manner as is done in keeping potatoes. By this mode they keep perfectly; but it is evidently better adapted for a market gardener who sells his produce in large quantities, than for a gentleman's gardener or amateur. For all who require small quantities of fruit almost daily, shelves or the cellar-floor are to be preferred during the winter, and jars during the spring and summer months.

The French crab, the Northern Greening, and various other long-keeping sorts, may be preserved in cellars, on a large scale, in dry sand or in ridges, or on a small scale in jars kept in cellars, for two years or upwards. The French crab may also be kept on shelves in a garret for two years; but by this mode it is always more or less shrivelled. What is termed the sweating of apples consists in covering them with short grass, aftermath hay, mats, or blankets, or any similar covering, so as to excite a degree of fermentation, the heat produced by which expands the water in the apple, and causes it to exude through the pores of the skin. This takes place sooner or later, according to the temperature of the atmosphere, but generally, in a fruit-cellar at 40°, in the course of a week or ten days, after which the apples are wiped, and being thus deprived of a portion of their moisture, it is thought they will keep better. This may be true where they are kept on shelves exposed to a change of air; but the natural moisture of the apple is no impediment to its keeping in any situation where the air and the temperature are not, or but very slightly, changed.

Diseases, Insects, Casualties, &c.—No tree is more subject to the canker than the apple, and particularly some kinds, such as the Ribston pippin, Hawthornden, &c. In practice it is wise, if possible, to avoid planting any varieties that manifest a peculiar tendency to canker. This disease may possibly be prevented, but it can hardly be cured. The most active producing causes are a bad wet subsoil, rich manures, cropping and digging round the roots, an ungenial climate, and probably fungi on the leaves or young wood, and general debility. All such predisposing causes must be avoided and their contraries secured, and canker will seldom appear, or assume a virulent form if it does. The first speck of it should be cut out as soon as it appears, as by some it is held to be infectious, and it certainly has a tendency to spread. To facilitate the ripening of the wood in a bad climate, nothing is better than to prevent the tree from making much wood to ripen; and this may be effected by keeping the soil poor rather than rich, by planting on hillocks above the surface, and by never stirring the soil over the roots more than an inch or two in depth. The woolly aphis, or American blight, is the most injurious insect that infests the apple-tree, but it is also that which is most easily destroyed. This is effected by washing the parts with diluted sulphuric acid; which is formed by mixing ¾ oz. by measure of the sulphuric acid of the shops with 7½ oz. of water. It should be rubbed into the parts affected by means of a piece of rag tied to a stick, the operator taking care not to let it touch his clothes. The same mixture applied all over the bark of the tree will effectually destroy mosses and lichens. After the bark of a tree has been washed with this mixture, the first shower will re-dissolve it, and convey it into the most minute crevice, so as effectually to destroy any insects that may have escaped. There are several species of weevil which attack the young shoots of the apple-tree, or bore into their blossom-buds before they expand in spring. There are also several species of moth, some butterflies, and the aphis and chermes mali, but very little can be done either to prevent the attacks of these insects, or to destroy them after they have made their appearance. Smoke of any kind, such as from damp straw, if the heads of the trees can be enveloped in it, will bring down caterpillars, and by destroying these the number produced next season will be lessened. Tobacco-water or strong soot-water thrown over the tree with an engine, will kill or remove the aphis and chermes. Lime-water will destroy the caterpillars of all insects that live on the leaves of plants; but neither it nor tobacco-water can be readily brought in contact with the larvæ of beetles and other insects that live in the interior of the bud or shoot (see our Chapter on Insects, and the different modes of destroying them, and also that on the Diseases and Accidents to which Plants are liable, pp. 52, 74); but the maintenance of the tree in perfect health is the most powerful antidote to insect pests, as the latter prey mostly upon debilitated plants.

The Pear.

The pear (Pyrus communis, *L.*) is a deciduous tree of a more upright and regular form than the apple-tree, and of greater duration. It is indigenous in the woods of most parts of Europe, and also in many parts of Asia; but it is not native in North America. The wild pear differs from the apple in growing on poorer soil, having a larger and more permanent tap root, and in a seedling state not coming so soon into bearing. The pear in its cultivated state is found in the gardens of all civilized countries, more especially in those of temperate climates. In Britain it forms a leading article in the dessert, from July to March, or later.

Uses.—The fruit of the pear is more esteemed in the dessert than that of the apple, but the latter is much more valuable in the kitchen. The pear is used for baking, stewing, compôtes, and marmalades. Pared and dried in the sun, the fruit will keep several years, either with or without sugar, and those sorts which are less esteemed for the table are found to answer best for this mode of drying and preserving. Perry is made from the expressed juice of the pear, fermented in the manner of cider, and when well made from the most suitable kinds of fruit, it is more highly prized than cider. The tree has not its white blossoms tinged with red, like those of the apple, but it grows to a greater height and assumes a more pyramidal shape: the leaves die off in autumn of a richer yellow or red; and the tree being of greater duration than the apple, it is from these properties better adapted for ornamental plantations. The wood is light, smooth, and compact, and much used in turnery, tool-making, for picture-frames, and for dyeing to imitate ebony. The leaves will dye yellow.

Properties of a good Pear.—Dessert pears are characterized by a sugary aromatic juice, with the pulp soft and sub-liquid or melting, as in the beurrés or butter-pears. Kitchen pears should be of large size, with the flesh firm and crisp, neither breaking nor melting, and rather austere than sweet, as in the Windsor, for instance. Perry pears may be either large or small; but the more austere the taste, the better will be the liquor. Excellent perry is made from the wild pear, which is altogether unfit either for the kitchen or the dessert.

The varieties of pear cultivated by the Romans, Pliny informs us, were numerous; in France they have long been more so than the varieties of the apple; and hence the kinds formerly cultivated in this country were obtained from France, and generally required the protection of walls. Since the Peace of 1815, however, many new and hardy varieties of pear have been introduced from Belgium, where the cultivation and improvement of this fruit has, till lately, been more attended to than anywhere else. Some excellent and very hardy varieties have also been raised by the late Mr. Knight, so that the old French varieties, with the exception of some of superior excellence, such as the Jargonelle, are rapidly disappearing from our gardens. In 1842 more than 700 sorts had been proved in the Horticultural Society's Gardens to be distinct, as appears by the Society's Fruit Catalogue. Many more have been added to our gardens since then. The following will be found a good selection, arranged in the order of their ripening.

Dessert Pears, earliest varieties, from June to September.

Jargonelle, Citron des Carmes, Doyenné d'Eté, Peach, Tyson, Autumn Bergamot, Beurré Goubault, Beurré d'Amanlis, Colmar d'Eté, Beurré Gifford, Yat, Jersey Gratioli, Beurré Superfin, Williams's Bon Chrétien, Calebasse d'Eté, d'Aremberg, Summer Beurré.

Dessert Pears in Season from September to January.

Marie Louise, Louise Bonne of Jersey, Fondante d'Automne, Duchesse d'Orleans, Duchesse d'Angoulême, Vicar of Winkfield, Crasanne, Thompson's, Passe Colmar, Glou Morceau, Beurré Léon le Clerc, Huyshe's Victoria, Forelle, Napoleon, Ligne d'Hiver, Délices d'Hardenpont, Urbaniste, Beurré Bosc, Gansel's Bergamot, Suffolk Thorn.

Dessert Pears, Second Period, from September to January.

Chaumontel, Beurré Clairgeau, White Doyenné, Aston Town, Beurré Hardy, Comte de Lamy, Prince Consort, Doyenné du Comice, Seckle, Alexander Lambré, Beurré d'Aremberg, Dumas' Honey, Beurré d'Anjou, Comte de Lamy, Comte de Flandres, Gansel's Late Bergamot, Délices de Hardenpont, Knight's Monarch, Vicar of Winkfield.

Dessert Pears from January to April.

Glou Morceau, Beurré Langelier, Beurré Duhaume, Marie Louise, Fondante de Noel, Ne plus Meuris, Winter Nélis, Josephine de Malines, Huyshe's Prince of Wales, Nouvelle Hâtive.

Dessert Pears from January to June.

Easter Beurré, Beurré de Rance, Ne plus Meuris, Doyenné d'Alençon, Susette d'Bavay, L'Inconnue, Jean de Witte, Bergamotte d'Esperen, Commissaire Delmotte, Madame Millet.

Kitchen Pears, arranged in the order of their Ripening and Keeping.

Summer Compôte Morel, Bezi d'Heri, Black Worcester, Flemish Bon Chrétien, Double de Guerre, Moul, Verulam, Catillac, Uvedale's St. Germain.

The two last are probably the best of all stewing pears, the last, however, requiring a wall to develop its full size.

The best dessert pears, and such sorts as the Vicar of Winkfield, are likewise the very best for stewing, so that fewer kitchen pears are grown than formerly..

Perry Pears, arranged in the order of their Merits.

Oldfield, Barland, Longland, Teinton Squash.

A list of pears adapted for walls of different aspects has been given in p. 389.

A list of pears for espaliers, dwarfs, or standards, trained conically or spurred in, has been given in p. 399.

A list of pears adapted for an orchard or being grown as standards, will be found in p. 404.

A selection of Pears, where the space is very limited, or for Cottage Gardens.—Jargonelle, Dunmore, Marie Louise, Beurré de Capiaumont, Beurré Diel, Louise Bonne of Jersey, Hacon's Incomparable, Glou Morceau, Easter Beurré, and Beurré de Rance. These are pears of first-rate excellence, and they will all succeed as standards in any climate where wheat can be brought to perfection, with the exception of the Jargonelle, which requires a wall or espalier, even in the best climates. Where there is only room in a cottage garden for one pear-tree, Hacon's Incomparable, which is one of the best, and almost a constant bearer, may have one branch or limb grafted with the Marie Louise, others with the Easter Beurré, Glou Morceau, and Beurré de Rance, which would thus afford a succession of fruit of first-rate excellence from October till March. The three last-named pears may be advantageously trained against the walls of a cottage, or on a trellis raised about six inches above its roof. The Jargonelle succeeds admirably against cottage walls, with any aspect, in the centre or south of England, requiring, however, a south or west aspect in the north.

Pear trees of forms adapted for Landscape Scenery.—Glou Morceau, a handsome pyramidal tree with spreading branches, hardy, a good bearer, and the fruit most excellent. Swan's-egg, a handsome pyramidal tree, and an excellent bearer, but the fruit of only secondrate merit. The Eloho, a Scotch variety, with a fastigiate head almost like that of a Lombardy poplar, but the fruit of little value; and the Beurré Diel, a handsome and somewhat fastigiate tree, a great bearer, and the fruit excellent. Such varieties as the Louise Bonne of Jersey, Maria Louise, Beurré de Capiaumont, and Colmar's Van Mons; indeed, with care almost any of the above dessert varieties may be trained into handsome conical forms for forming avenues along the central or side walks of kitchen gardens.

Fig. 364.

The propagation, nursery culture, and choice of plants are much the same for the pear as for the apple; but the pear is never propagated by cuttings, as they root with difficulty, and as it is oftener required for walls than the apple, it is more frequently flat-trained for one, two, or three years in the nursery. The pear is grafted or budded on stocks raised from seeds of the wild pear, or from any strong upright-growing kind, when the object is large and durable plants; and when dwarfs or conical trees are to be produced, the stock used is the quince, which is propagated for that purpose by layers. The mountain ash, the medlar, the wild service, the white beam, the common thorn, and the crab apple, have also been used

A pyramidal pear-tree.

as stocks for the pear; and hence, wherever there is a thorn hedge, or a wood or plantation containing white service trees, white beam trees, or the mountain ash, pear-trees may be speedily grown in abundance. Grafting on the mountain ash is said to retard the blossoming of the trees, and thus adapt them for a climate where there is danger from spring frosts; while the flesh and flavour of the pear is said not to be affected. Grafting the pear on the thorn is known to bring it into very early bearing, and to produce thriving trees on a strong clayey soil, where neither stocks of the wild pear nor the quince would thrive. The thorn stock, however, is said to render the fruit smaller and harder. When the thorn is grafted either with the apple or pear, the scions or buds require to be inserted as near the root of the stock as possible, in order that the moisture of the soil may aid in the swelling of the stock, which, notwithstanding this care, generally remains of smaller diameter than the apple or pear grafted on it, and thus acts like the operation of ringing in increasing the fruitfulness of the tree. The quince, as it grows naturally in situations within the reach of water, is evidently the best stock for moist soils, and it is also thought the best for clayey and light soft soils; while for chalky and silicious soils, and gravels of every kind, the pear stock is recommended. The pear does not unite very readily with the apple, and when it does so, is but of short duration. When grafted on a pear stock the plants have fewer fibrous roots, in proportion to the bulk and age of the plant, than the apple on a crab stock; and hence it requires more care in taking up for removal, and in the nursery requires to be more frequently transplanted than the apple. As quince stocks have more fibrous roots than pear stocks, the pear on them is transplanted without difficulty.

Soil, Situation, and Final Planting.—The pear grows naturally on a much poorer and drier soil than the apple, but to produce large crops of excellent fruit it requires like it a deep loamy soil on a dry subsoil. On a wet subsoil the pear will not thrive nor produce good fruit. The distances at which the pear ought to be planted against a wall may be somewhat greater than that for the apple, or from twenty-five to thirty feet against a wall twelve feet high. The distances for espaliers, dwarfs, cones, cordons, dwarfing stocks, and trees in orchards, have been already given, pp. 391, 400.

The mode of bearing, pruning, and training the pear is much the same as for the apple, but in most of the varieties the spurs are somewhat longer in being formed, being generally produced on two years' old wood, instead of the former year's wood. The branches of standard pears are also less liable to cross each other than those of the apple, and hence pear-trees in an orchard require comparatively little pruning. The more they are cut in, the more breast wood they make, and close spurring is apt to engender sterility. The remedy for this is summer pinching, laying in or allowing plenty of young wood to remain, and root-pruning. Any pruning that is needed in winter should be deferred until the blossoms are nearly expanded in the spring, to keep the latter as safe as possible from spring frosts.

In training the pear on walls or espaliers horizontally, the ordinary distance between the shoots is from nine inches to twelve inches, the latter distance being adopted for large-leaved pears, such as the Jargonelle; but for shy-bearing pears, which always are most prolific on young spurs, it has been proposed to have the main branches at double the distance, and to lay in laterals from them at regular intervals, as in fig. 365. These laterals in two or three years will be covered with spurs and blossom-buds, and will be more certain of producing fruit than the spurs on the main branches. They can be renewed at pleasure, by cutting them off, having previously encouraged young shoots to supply their place. In pursuit of the same object, fruitfulness, some reverse the order of the laterals, and train them down from the main shoots instead of up as in fig. 365.

On walls or espaliers the pear is apt to produce a superfluity of young shoots, but this is chiefly owing to the borders being made too deep and rich, and to their being dug deeply and cropped, by which the roots are forced down to the subsoil, where they are supplied with

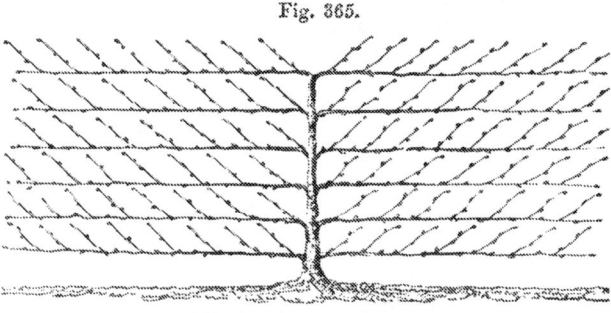

Fig. 365.

A method of training shy-bearing pears.

more moisture than is beneficial for the fruitfulness of the tree, and which consequently expends itself in young shoots. The remedies are root-pruning or disleafing, and mulching the border with litter instead of digging it. The summer shoots, which it is foreseen will not be wanted at the winter's pruning, should be stopped, as recommended for the apple.

Old standard pears may be cut in, and wall or espalier trees headed down to within a few inches of the graft; or the horizontal shoots may be cut off within a few inches of the upright stem, and a graft of a superior kind put on each. This has now become a very general mode of renovating old pear-trees that have been trained horizontally on walls or espaliers, and it affords an excellent opportunity of grafting a number of different kinds on one tree. On a wall twelve feet high there will be at least twelve horizontal branches on each side of the main stem, which will allow of grafting twenty-four different sorts on one tree, a matter of the utmost importance in small gardens.

Thinning the blossoms of pear-trees, and soaking the soil well with water at the same time, has been found to facilitate the setting of the fruit, and the practice is worth adopting not only with pear-trees but with fruit trees in general. The blossoms are sometimes thinned in the autumn or early spring, but it is the safest practice to wait till the fruit is fairly set, and then to thin the crop to the quantity that the tree can fairly finish, remembering that one fine fruit is worth three small ones.

Gathering and Keeping.—Dessert pears of the summer kinds, being softer and more tender than apples, require greater care in handling: they require to be kept but a short time before being used, and should therefore be placed in that division of the fruit-room which is devoted to summer fruits. Those which are intended to be kept for winter and spring use may be laid on open shelves, and the latest keeping kinds may be packed in jars, as recommended for apples.

The diseases, insects, and casualties to which the pear is liable, are much the same as for the apple; but the pear is less subject to canker, is seldom affected with the woolly aphis, and the tree being of more vertical growth is also less liable to be broken by winds. The brown and white scale are sometimes very troublesome; however, perhaps the best remedy is to paint the trees thoroughly over with a thick mixture of equal parts of soot, lime, and cow-dung, or to wash them with spirits of wine. The former dressing smothers, the latter kills the scale.

The Quince.

The quince (Pyrus Cydonia, L.) is a low, much-branched, crowded, and distorted deciduous tree, a native of Austria and other parts of Europe, generally in moist soil or near water, and in a somewhat shady situation. It blossoms in May or June, and ripens its fruit in October and November. The tree has been grown for its fruit since the time of the Romans. The fruit is not eaten raw but stewed, or in pies or tarts, along with apples; it is much esteemed, and it makes excellent marmalade. When apples have become flat, or have lost their flavour, a quince, or a part of one, in a pie or pudding, will add sharpness, and communicate a flavour by many preferred to that of apples alone. The fruit is large, and of a golden yellow when ripe, and its appearance on the tree bears a nearer resemblance to the orange than any other hardy fruit; and on this account, and also the beauty of its large pale-pink and white blossoms, the tree well deserves a place in the ornamental landscape. On the borders of a pond it attains the highest degree of beauty, which is doubled by its reflection in the water. The use of the quince, as a stock for dwarfing the pear, has been already mentioned.

Varieties.—These are the oblong, or pear quince; the ovate, or apple quince; and the Portugal quince. The Portugal quince has broad cordate leaves, and an oblong fruit, which is more juicy and less harsh than that of the other varieties, and is therefore the most valuable. It is rather a shy bearer, but is highly esteemed for marmalade, as the pulp has the property of assuming a fine purple tint in the course of being prepared. This is also the best sort upon which to work the pear-tree, its wood swelling more in conformity with that of the latter than the harder wood of other sorts.

Propagation, Soil, and other points of Culture and Management.— The quince is generally propagated by layers, but cuttings root without difficulty, and the Portugal quince is sometimes grafted on the pear quince, or the wild pear or thorn. In propagating for stocks, no particular care is requisite in training the plants; but for fruit-bearing trees, it is necessary to train the stem to a rod, till it has attained four feet or five feet in height, and can support itself upright. The best standards, however, are produced by grafting at the height of from five to six feet on the pear, the thorn, or the mountain ash. The quince is generally planted in the orchard, in some part where the soil is good and somewhat moist; it bears on two-years' old wood, and requires little pruning except thinning out crossing, crowded, or decaying branches. Trained against an espalier, it blossoms in May or the beginning of June, and the fruit in October or November makes a fine appearance. The fruit may be kept in the same manner as the apple, on shelves; or packed in sand, or kiln-dried straw.

The Medlar.

The medlar (Mespilus germanica, L.), a low deciduous tree, with semi-pendulous branches, a native of Europe and the west of Asia, in bushy places and woods, and said to be found wild in Kent, Sussex, and some other parts of England. It flowers in May and June, and the fruit is ripe in November. It makes a jelly, equal to guava, and is eaten raw, in a state of incipient decay, when it has a peculiar flavour and acidulous taste, relished by some but disliked by others. This tree, when it has plenty of space, is a striking and unique object in the landscape, the branches spreading wide and resting upon the ground, and leaves, flower, and fruit, all have a singular and pleasing effect.

Varieties.—The Dutch medlar has the largest fruit; the Nottingham medlar has fruit of a livelier and more poignant taste; the stoneless medlar has small obovate fruit, without stones or seeds; and the wild medlar has the leaves, flowers, and fruit smaller than in any of the other kinds except the stoneless. The Gros Monstrueux, and the Royal have recently been added to these.

Propagation, Soil, and other points of Culture and Management.— Grafting on its own species is considered the best mode of propagation for the medlar as a fruit tree; but it will root by layers, and, but with difficulty, by cuttings. The seeds, if sown as soon as the fruit is ripe, will come up the following spring, and make plants fit for grafting dwarfs in two years, and standards in three years. It requires a similar soil and situation to the quince, and the same treatment as that tree in every other respect, excepting that no attempt is made to keep the fruit longer than the period of its natural decay. It should be laid lightly on the shelves, in order that it may not be bruised, and is generally fit to eat about the end of November, and it lasts till the end of January.

The True Service.

The True Service (Sorbus domestica, L.) is a middle-sized deciduous tree, with a handsome regular head, a native of France and other parts of central Europe, and of Barbary, in the neighbourhood of Algiers; and a solitary tree of the species has been found in Wyre Forest, near Bewdley in Worcestershire. The leaves are pinnate, and closely resemble those of the mountain ash; but the fruit is much larger, and, when ripe, is of a rusty brown, tinged with yellow and red. It flowers in May, and the fruit is ripe in October. It is eaten like that of the medlar, but is deemed inferior. There is a pear-shaped variety, one apple-shaped, and a third berry-shaped; the latter being the form of the fruit in the wild plant. The tree is rarely planted for its fruit in Britain, and is now neglected on the Continent. One may be introduced in an orchard or a shrubbery for the sake of variety.

Pyrus torminalis, the griping-fruited Service-tree, is not cultivated in gardens, but it grows wild in Sussex, and the fruit is sent to Covent Garden market, and eaten in a state of incipient decay, like that of the True Service.

Pyrus Aria (var. cretica), the Cretan white beam tree, is a mealy, agreeably-tasted fruit, which is eaten when ripe, and before it has begun to decay. This tree is as well worth cultivating for its fruit as the True Service.

The Cherry.

The cherry (Cerasus sylvestris and C. vulgaris) is, in its wild state, a middle-sized deciduous tree, a native of most parts of Europe, and of part of Asia, and cultivated for its fruit from the time of the Romans. It is the first hardy fruit that ripens in the open air in Britain, and is grown in every garden and most extensively in Kent and Hertfordshire for the London market.

Use.—The fruit, besides being highly valued for the dessert, is useful in pies, tarts, and other preparations in cookery and confectionery. Steeping cherries in brandy is said to improve its strength and flavour, and brandy-cherries have long been prized; a wine may be made from the pulp, and from the pulp and kernel bruised and fermented, the German spirit *Kirschwasser* is distilled. The fruit of the Kentish cherry may be stoned, and dried, and used like raisins. The gum which exudes from the tree is said to have all the properties of gum arabic. The wood of the tree is hard, and tough, and is used by the turner, flute-maker, and cabinet-maker: and the wild cherry, as a tree, is an excellent nurse for the oak on light soils, while its fruit is a great encourager of the thrush, blackbird, and other singing birds.

Varieties.—The Romans had eight kinds of cherry, and in England, in the time of Parkinson, there were twenty-four sorts. In France and Germany the sorts were more numerous than in England before the collection made by the Horticultural Society of London. Since then the number of good cherries have rapidly increased.

Dessert Cherries.

Earliest Varieties.—Werder's Early Black Heart, Knight's Early Black, Bowyer's Early Heart, Early Black Bigarreau, Belle d'Orleans, Early Red Guigne, Waterloo, Early Lamaurée, Noir précoce de Straus, Bigarreau Jaboulay. *Second Earliest.*—Black Eagle, White Heart, Ox Heart, Governor Wood, Gloire de France, Bedfordshire Prolific, Downton, Elton, Bigarreau Napoleon, Bigarreau White.

Late Varieties.—Late Duke, Florence, Coe's Late Carnation, Late

Black Bigarreau, Late Purple Guigne, Rival, Nouvelle Royale, Planchoury, Transparent, and the latest of all, Belle Agathe.

Cherries for Preserving.—Kentish and all its varieties, Belle Magnifique, Morello.

Cherries adapted for being trained against walls of different aspects have been enumerated before.

Cherries for a Cottage Garden.—May Duke, Late Duke, Kentish, and Morello.

Cherries for the North of Scotland.—May Duke, Elton, Downton, Tilger's Redheart, Winter's Blackheart, Lundy Gean, Kentish, Morello.

Propagation, Nursery Culture, and Choice of Plants.—Budding is more frequently resorted to than grafting, because the wounds made by the latter operation are apt to gum. Stocks raised from stones of the wild cherry, or the cultivated cherry, are used when free-growing plants are required; the Morello, when the object is plants of moderate size; and the perfumed cherry (Cerasus Mahaleb), when very dwarf trees are wanted. Standard cherry trees are generally budded standard high, on free stocks of three-years' growth from the seed, which have been one year transplanted. Cherry-stones for stocks are sown in sandy soil in autumn, immediately after they have been taken from the fruit, or they are preserved in sand through the winter, the heap being two or three times turned over, and sown in spring. The plants come up the same season, and may be transplanted in autumn, in rows three feet apart, one foot distant in the row if for dwarfs, and eighteen inches if for standards. If for dwarfs, they may be budded the following summer, but if for standards, a third season's growth will be required. The dwarfs require no pruning the first year; but the second spring, if not sold, or transplanted to where they are finally to remain, they require to be cut down, and if intended for a wall, they should be flat-trained by means of a row of three or four stakes to each tree. Whatever pruning is required for the cherry should be done a little before midsummer, which, while it is found to prevent gumming, is also favourable for the healing over of the wounds the same season. The best plants for removal are those which have been one or two years worked; but as the cherry produces abundance of fibrous roots, it may be transplanted after it has been three or four years trained, more especially if growing in a loamy soil.

Soil, Situation, and Final Planting.—The cherry grows naturally in dry sandy soils, and situations rather elevated than low; but the cultivated tree requires a soil rather more loamy, which, however, must be on a dry bottom. Almost all the varieties may be grown as standards, and there is no great difference between them in regard to hardiness; but the earliest and largest fruit is produced against walls, by which the fruit is also improved in flavour. The distances at which cherry-trees may be planted against walls, espaliers, as dwarfs, and in the orchard, are given at pp. 391, 400.

Mode of Bearing, Pruning, and Training.—The fruit is generally produced on small spurs or studs, from half an inch to two inches in length, which proceed from the sides and ends of the two-year, three-year, and occasionally from the older branches; and as the new spurs continue being produced from recently formed wood, bearing branches are never shortened back where there is room for their extension. The cherry is not very prolific in wood, and the shoots do not often cross one another; therefore very little pruning is required for standards. Against walls, or espaliers, some modification of the fan or half-fan mode is the best. In summer-pruning strong-growing cherries, most of the laterals should be stopped when a few inches in length; but in the case of the Morello, a regular supply of young wood should be left all along the branches, as exhibited in Mr. Seymour's mode of fan-training, p. 330, to succeed the fruit-bearing shoots. The Morello produces a few fruit on spurs formed on two-year old wood, but scarcely ever on wood of the third year; therefore the only mode of managing this tree, to ensure a crop of fruit, is to have a regular succession of laterals, the growth of the last year, all along the shoots. In many gardens these laterals are not laid in; and though the tree by this mode does not assume such a neat appearance, yet the crop of fruit we believe is greater. After the fruit is thoroughly set, it should be carefully thinned in proportion to the strength and size of the tree, otherwise the trees will probably revenge themselves by throwing off a large portion of the fruit at the stoning period. Old or diseased cherry-trees may sometimes be renovated by cutting in or heading down, but in general the wounds necessarily made exude so much gum as to prevent their ever being entirely covered with bark, in consequence of which the stems and roots rot in the interior. To prevent this evil as much as possible the soil should always be renewed at the time of amputating.

Gathering and Keeping.—The fruit can only be gathered by hand, and care should be taken not to pull out with the foot-stalks of the fruit any of the buds which are to produce the blossoms of the succeeding year; unless, indeed, these buds should be so abundant, that the lessening their number will be advantageous rather than otherwise. Where no buds can be spared, the stalks may be cut with scissors. For the dessert the cherry is never kept longer than a day or two.

Diseases, Insects, Casualties, &c.—The gum is almost the only disease to which cherry-trees are liable; the exudation when it has once commenced is not easily checked, but if the tree is healthy in other respects, and in a suitable soil and situation, the gum will not do much injury; in an unfavourable soil it commonly brings on canker. Against a wall the cherry is liable to the attacks of the red spider, aphides, and some other insects, which may be destroyed or kept under by the usual means. Syringing the trees with tobacco-water and soft-soap, before the blossoms have expanded, will destroy every insect to which the cherry is liable, and they may be washed with clear lime-water from the time the fruit is set till it has begun to colour. The greatest enemies to ripe cherries are birds, from which they are to be protected by netting, in the case of walls and espaliers, and by the use of the gun in the case of standards. Cats may also be employed to guard the crop and protect the trees from birds.

A Dutch Cherry Garden.—In Holland and other parts of the Continent it is a favourite practice with the possessors of gardens to eat the fruit direct from the trees or plants, and there are many rural cottage gardens in Britain where such treats are offered at so much per head. In the villas of the wealthy, a small garden, in some retired part of the grounds near the house, was set apart for this purpose, and planted with summer fruits, especially cherries, gooseberries, and strawberries; and in some cases this garden was entirely covered with a roof of netting. One of the most complete gardens of this kind, in the neighbourhood of London, existed, in 1828, at Hylands, near Chelmsford. It was in the form of a parallelogram, twice as long as broad, and contained a quarter of an acre. It was surrounded by a wire fence, ten feet high, the texture being such as to exclude small birds—that is, each mesh was two inches high by one inch broad. The principal standard trees are cherries of the best early and late kinds, one or two early apples, one or two early pears, and one or two early plums. The trees are planted in quincunx, and their branches are trained in a horizontal position so as to be within reach of the hand, by being tied down to stakes. All round the margin are, first a bed of strawberries, and next a row of plants of gooseberry, currant, and raspberry. A gravel walk surrounds the whole, between the strawberry-bed and the row of fruit-shrubs, and the space among the standard trees is simply left unstirred, so that when dry every part of it may be walked on. The manner in which the roof of netting is fixed over this garden is thus:—At regular distances all through the area, wooden boxes, as sockets for posts, as at fig. 366 *b*, are fixed in the ground, and when the cherries begin to ripen a net of the kind used in pilchard-fishing, and made at Bridport, in Dorsetshire, the meshes of which are two inches wide, is drawn over the whole parallelogram, fastened to the top of the wire fence by hooks which are fixed there, and supported above the trees by the props placed in the sockets. These props are fourteen feet high at the sides, and gradually rise to the middle of the garden, and they have blunt heads, in order not to injure the netting. The netting necessary for covering this space, which is eighty feet by two hundred and twenty feet, is in two pieces, each one hundred feet by one hundred and fifty feet; it is put on in the following manner:—One piece is spread out immediately within the wire fence, and a number of men with poles carry it over the top of the trees and posts, after it is fastened to one side; then they fasten on the other, and so on till the whole is completed. The separate divisions are then joined together, which thus form one entire netted

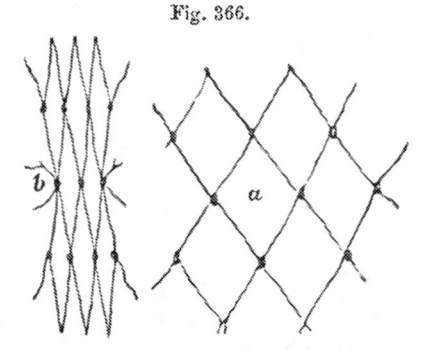

Fig. 366.

Netting for covering a cherry garden.

roof, giving the garden a very singular and agreeable appearance. During rain, or dewy evenings, the net is tightened or stretched to its utmost extent (fig. 367, *a*), and forms a grand vault over the whole cherry garden (fig. 366, *a*, and 367, *a*) ; during sunshine, or when the weather is dry, it is slackened (fig. 366, *b*), and forms a festooned vault,

Fig. 367.

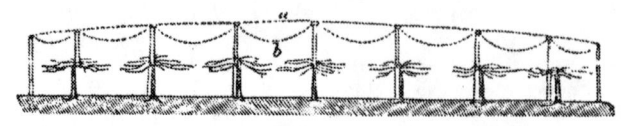

Section through a cherry garden, showing the netting tightened by rain (a), and slackened by drought (b).

supported by posts (fig. 367, *b*). It is advisable to tan the net every year with oak bark, which adds greatly to its durability. We have seen plantations of currants and gooseberries protected in a similar manner, but in these cases bunting was used in lieu of netting, to exclude wasps and flies as well as birds ; the nets for such fruit bushes and strawberries are placed from 2 to 4 feet from the ground, and in the long run it pays to elevate all nets on a wooden or iron frame to keep them off the ground. Perhaps galvanized or other iron nets would prove the most economical, as all textile fabrics speedily wear out.

Forcing the Cherry.—See p. 483.

The Plum.

The plum (Prunus insititia, L., and P. domestica, L.) is a low irregular deciduous tree, a native of most parts of Europe, and also of part of Asia and Africa, and it is either indigenous or naturalized in North America. Its culture in gardens is as universal as that of the cherry, and dates from the time of the Romans.

Use.—The plum is a delicious dessert fruit, and it is also excellent in pies, tarts, conserves, sweetmeats, and in a dried state. A wine is made from the pulp, and a powerful spirit from the pulp and kernel fermented. Raki is made in Hungary by fermenting apples ground or crushed with bruised plums, and distilling the liquor. The spirit produced is said to be very agreeable to the taste, and, though not quite so strong, much more wholesome than brandy. In the south of France an excellent spirit is obtained from the bruised pulp and kernels of plums, fermented with honey and flour, by distillation in the usual manner. Medicinally, plums are cooling and laxative, especially the dried fruit called brignoles, or French plums. The wood of the plum is used in turnery, cabinet-work, and in making musical instruments, and the tree is valued in ornamental landscape-gardening from its being one of the earliest which come into blossom.

Varieties.—The Romans had a multiplicity of sorts of plums, and the varieties have long been very numerous in France and Italy. Of late years our collections have been very much enriched by Mr. Rivers and others. The following list includes the best dessert plums.

Earliest Varieties.—Early Favourite, Early Prolific, Early Green Gage, Early Mirabelle, Cullen's Golden Gage, M'Laughlin's Gage, Imperial Ottoman, Early Orleans, Royale de Tours, Précoce de Tours, Royale Hâtive.

Second Season Dessert Plums.—Woolston's Black Gage, Coe's Golden Drop, Angelina Burdett, Jefferson, Prince Englebert, Transparent Gage, Denniston's Superb, Royale Hâtive, Green Gage, Reine Claude Bodaert, Huling's Superb, Bleeker's Yellow Gage.

Latest Dessert Plums.—Reine Claude de Bavay, Ickworth Impératrice, Reine Claude d'Octobre, St. Martin's Quetsche, Belvoir Plum, Autumn Gage, Coe's Fine Late Red, Coe's Golden Drop, Fulton, Guthrie's Late Green, Nouvelle de Dorelle, Late Black Orleans.

Most of these varieties—especially the Golden Drop, Jefferson, and the Green Gage—are likewise the very best for preserving and culinary purposes.

A selection of plums for walls of different aspects, espaliers and dwarfs, and for an orchard, have been before given.

Kitchen Select Plums.

Earliest.—Early Orleans, Early Favourite, Early Prolific, Goliath, Nectarine, Mirabelle, Royale de Tours, Dove Bank, Prince Englebert, Main Crop, Victoria, Washington, White Magnum Bonum, Pond's Seedling, Prune Damson, Diamond, Cox's Emperor, Orleans, Autumn Compôte, Fellemberg, Mitchelson's, Standard of England.

Latest Varieties.—Downton Impératrice, Winesour, New Large Bullace, White Damson, Impériale de Milan, Coe's Golden Drop.

Dessert and Kitchen Plums for a Garden of Limited Extent.—Royale Hâtive, Jefferson, Victoria, Diamond, Drap d'Or, Green Gage, Kirke's, Washington, Reine Claude Violette, Coe's Golden Drop, Coe's Fine Late Red, Early Orleans, Shropshire Damson, and White Magnum Bonum.

A Selection of Dessert Plums for a very Small Garden.—Royale Hâtive, Green Gage, Purple Gage, Coe's Golden Drop, and Orleans.

Dessert and Kitchen Plums for a Cottage Garden.—Royale Hâtive, Green Gage, Coe's Golden Drop, and Reine Claude Violette; and for the kitchen, the Shropshire Damson, Victoria, Pond's Seedling, Winesour, and White Magnum Bonum.

Propagation, Nursery Culture, and Choice of Plants.—The plum, like other stone fruit, is mostly propagated by budding, and the stocks, when the object is large and permanent trees, are the Mussel, St. Julian, Magnum Bonum, or any free-growing plum, either raised from seed, or, as is more commonly done, from layers or suckers. The dwarfing stock for the plum is the Myrobalan, or Mirabelle of the French. The common baking-plums, such as the damson, bullace, &c., are generally propagated by suckers, without being either budded or grafted. The Mussel and St. Julian plums are extensively propagated in the nurseries as stocks for the peach, nectarine, apricot, and almond. The nursery culture of the plum, and the choice of grafted or trained plants, are the same as for the cherry.

Soil, Situation, and Final Planting.—The plum naturally does not grow in so light a soil as the cherry, nor in so clayey a soil as the apple; and in a state of culture, a medium soil, on a dry subsoil, is found to be the best. Only the finer varieties are planted against walls, and none of them require a south aspect excepting in very cold exposed situations in the north, or when the object is to have an early crop. The distances adopted in final planting are given in pp. 391 and 400.

Mode of Bearing, Pruning, and Training.—All the varieties produce their blossoms on small spurs, which are protruded along the sides of the shoots of one, two, or three years' growth, generally in the course of the second and third year. These spurs, if duly thinned, and when necessary cut in, will continue bearing for five or six years, or longer, in the case of wall-trees and espaliers; and when the fruit becomes too small, it is easy to renew the branches, one at a time, by encouraging young shoots from the main stem. Standard trees require very little pruning, beyond that of occasionally thinning out the branches, and this should always be done before midsummer, to prevent the gum from appearing on the wounds. Plum-trees against walls or espaliers are generally trained in the horizontal manner. Old trees may be renovated by heading in or cutting down.

Gathering, Keeping, Packing, &c.—The fruit is generally gathered by hand, and, with the exceptions mentioned, it cannot be kept longer than three or four days without losing its flavour, or shrivelling. As the bloom of the plum is more easily rubbed off than that of any other fruit, great care is requisite in gathering it, and in packing, when the fruit is to be sent to a distance. Nettle leaves, on account of their roughness, are the best material in which to envelope the fruit, and it ought to be sent in suspended boxes. As the plums brought to market are very liable to have the bloom rubbed off, some fruiterers supply an artificial bloom, by putting the fruit in an atmosphere charged with finely calcined magnesia, as is done in giving an artificial bloom to the cucumber. At first sight it may appear surprising that a white powder should be employed to give a bloom to the green surface of the cucumber, and the purple or yellow surface of the plum; but the colour of the fruit in these and all other cases, resides under the bloom in the skin, and the bloom is merely a number of semi-transparent colourless particles, secreted by nature for some useful purpose, which are very well imitated by any very fine colourless powder.

Insects, Diseases, Casualties, &c.— The red spider and green or black fly are the common enemies of the plum against walls, and are to be kept under by frequent and abundant waterings with the syringe. The gages and all very rich plums, when nearly ripe, are attacked by wasps, which may be lured away by and caught in vessels of honeyed water, or excluded by canvas or bunting. The gum and canker are not unfrequent in the plum when it has been severely pruned, or when it has been planted too deep, or the roots subjected to vicissitudes of drought and wet.

The plum may be forced by the same treatment as the peach, but with a temperature a few degrees lower. It is generally forced in large pots, either in a peach, cherry, or orchard-house. Many of the choice varieties are higher flavoured when grown under glass, and a few pots of the later sorts placed in a cool orchard-house will furnish a supply of plums of the highest quality right through November, while by forwarding the earliest varieties in a gentle heat plums may be gathered in May.

The Gooseberry.

The Gooseberry (Ribes Grossularia, L., and R. Uva crispa, L.) is a deciduous shrub, a native of Piedmont and other Alpine regions, and long cultivated in British gardens. The fruit is of little worth in a wild state, and the shrub does not appear to have been known to the Romans, nor to have been much cultivated in any part of the world except in Britain. With us it is esteemed for pies and tarts next in value to the apple; and as a luxury for the tables of the poor, it is even more valuable than that fruit, since it can be grown in less space, in more unfavourable circumstances, and brought sooner into a state of full bearing. At the tables of the wealthy it contributes to the dessert from the end of July to the end of September, and longer by matting up or otherwise covering the bushes.

Use.—Before being ripe it is much used for tarts, pies, sauces, and creams, and when mature it is esteemed in the dessert. Unripe gooseberries are preserved in bottles, and the ripe fruit in sugar. Bruised and fermented, wines and brandies are made from the green fruit, and gooseberry champagne is often substituted for that of the grape.

Varieties.—There are now some hundreds of kinds in British nurseries, most of them raised from seed in Lancashire and Cheshire, where the weight of the berry has been raised from ten pennyweights, the usual weight of the old sorts of red and green gooseberries, to thirty-six pennyweights and upwards, the weight of the largest modern kinds that have gained prizes. Pretty extensive lists have already been given at page 401. The following are among the best and highest-flavoured sorts in cultivation:—The four varieties of Champagne, Green, Red, White, and Yellow. The Green Gage, Wilmot's Early Red, Red Warrington, Old Rough Red, Rambouillon, Golden Drop, Ironmonger, Keen's Seedling, and Early Green Hairy.

Gooseberries for a Cottage Garden.—Red Champagne and Red Warrington, Yellow Champagne and Early Sulphur, Pitmaston Green Gage, Massey's Heart of Oak and Early Green Hairy, Woodward's Whitesmith, Taylor's Bright Venus, and Crystal.

Large Lancashire Gooseberries adapted for a Cottage Garden.—*Red*: Prince Regent, Wonderful, Top Sawyer, Huntsman, Companion, London, Clayton, Lion, Lancaster Lad, Catherina, Drill. *Yellow*: Rockwood, Sovereign, Smuggler, Stockwell, Telegraph. *Green*: Niger, Greenwood, No Bribery, Peacock. *White*: Carden, Antagonist, Wellington's Glory, Whitesmith, Queen Charlotte, Eagle, Fleur-de-lis.

The most valuable red gooseberry in cultivation is perhaps the red Champagne, generally called the Ironmonger in Scotland, the fruit of which is of superior flavour, is well adapted for all the purposes to which gooseberries are applied, and by matting it may be preserved on the bush till December. The fruit of the Pitmaston Green Gage will hang on the branches till it shrivels and almost candies. The red Warrington is an excellent gooseberry, either for table or wine-making, but it is of pendulous growth, and part of the fruit is apt to be rotted in wet seasons. There is a general prejudice against the large Lancashire kinds, which, it is alleged, are deficient in flavour; but this is not the case with many of them, as we have long proved. Their great size also gives them a special value as dessert fruit.

Propagation, Nursery Culture, and Choice of Plants.—The common mode of propagation is by cuttings, which should be formed from shoots taken from healthy vigorous plants in autumn, as long and straight as they can be got. The point of the shoot should be shortened two or three inches, to where the wood is firm, and the buds mature; and the cutting, which should, if possible, be twelve or fifteen inches in length, should be planted in sandy loam, in a moist situation, shaded from the direct influence of the sun, but not covered or confined by the branches of large trees. Some of the Lancashire growers tie a little moss round the lower part of the cutting, which is said to cause it to strike stronger roots. In loamy moist soil they need not be planted above three inches deep, but in ordinary garden soil six inches will be safer; in either case the cutting must be made quite firm at its lower extremity. Where there is only one plant of a rare kind, the most certain and rapid mode of propagation is by laying down the branches along the surface of the ground, as practised by the stock-growers in propagating plum and Paradise stocks. Suckers are occasionally resorted to, but as they generally contain a greater number of adventitious buds at the lower extremities than shoots from the branches, they are apt to throw up a redundancy of suckers. Gooseberries seldom remain longer in the nursery than two years, being transplanted into rows two feet by one foot the autumn of the same season in which they are struck. No other pruning is requisite than removing suckers or shoots from the stem, so as to leave three, or at most four, divergent shoots to form the head.

Soil, Situation, and Final Planting.—The best soil is a cool marly loam, rich, deep, well-manured, and kept moderately moist, either by the situation and subsoil, or by the surface being covered by the branches of the bushes, so as greatly to lessen evaporation. The situation should be open, and by no means shaded with standard fruit trees, the gooseberries grown under which are almost always bitter. In general gooseberries and all fruit shrubs should be cultivated in plantations by themselves; but in small gardens they may be placed in rows along the borders, either as dwarfs or espaliers or pyramids, in which form they bear well, and are highly ornamental.

Mode of Bearing, Pruning, and Training.—The fruit is produced on the shoots of the preceding year, and on spurs from shoots of three or more years' growth. The largest fruit is always produced on the wood of the preceding year, and as the spurs grow old, and increase in size, the fruit becomes smaller, though it increases in quantity; which, indeed, is the case with all fruit grown on spurs. The gooseberry requires to be pruned in early summer, because in general it produces more shoots than can be allowed to remain, without depriving the fruit-bearing branches of a due share of light and air. All superfluous shoots, therefore, should be stopped with the finger and thumb when they are between one inch and two inches in length, and again stopped at the second joint, when they have made a second growth. A common fault in gardens is to allow the shoots of gooseberries and currants to grow nearly their full length before they are thinned out, in consequence of which the fruit is deprived of its due share of nourishment, light, and air, and more strength is communicated to the root than is required for the due adjustment of the root and top. Hence, in almost all gardens, we find the gooseberry and currant bushes far too luxuriant. All the training the gooseberry, treated as a bush, requires, is to stop or prune it in such a manner as to keep the bush rather open in the centre, and the branches all radiating outwards from the stem, or from the main branches; crossing one another as little as possible, and when they do cross, never touching. On espaliers they should be trained in the perpendicular manner; and if only two upright shoots are trained from every plant, the trellis or espalier rail will be the sooner covered. Where plants are in abundance, which they may in many cases be by raising them from cuttings at home, only one upright shoot may be trained from each cutting, and these being planted at one foot apart, the trellis or rail, if not more than five feet high, will be completely covered in three years. If the Champagne or Ironmonger is planted, and the plants, when cuttings, allowed to make only one vertical shoot from the terminal bud, then after they have made two years' growth against the espalier rail, they will have reached its summit, and may be spurred in afterwards from within a foot of the ground to the top of the rail. If a double espalier rail is used, a very handsome gooseberry hedge will thus be formed, which will bear abundance of fruit of the best flavour, because freely exposed to the light and air, for twelve or fifteen years.

The growers of gooseberries for prizes necessarily take much more pains in pruning and training than the gardeners of private gentlemen. The plants are raised from cuttings in the usual manner, and in the autumn of the first year they are transplanted to the soil and situation where they are to produce their fruit. This is, if possible, a deep, cool, rich, marly loam, moderately moist, at the bottom of such a slope as shall at once produce shelter from the highest winds of the locality, and ensure a certain degree of coolness, and supply of moisture, from what may be termed the insensible escape of the rain which has sunk into the soil in the upper part of the declivity. Being planted, the next step is to prepare for pruning and training, by procuring a few hooked sticks (fig. 368) and forked sticks (369); the former to hold down the branches that are inclined to grow upwards, and the latter to support those which are inclined to grow downwards. These are applied to the plant in the manner shown in fig. 370, in which, also, the roots appear regularly spread out in every direction. In the autumn of the second year these three shoots will have produced a number of side-shoots, most of which may be shortened to one eye, and the others reduced to one-half of their length. No shoots should be left either at the origin or the extremities of the branches, but only at the sides; the fewer the number of shoots, and the younger the tree, the larger will be the fruit. Thus the plant, when pruned in the November of the second year, will consist of three principal shoots, each bearing two young shoots, shortened to about seven inches of their length. These last, in the pruning of the third year, are to be left with two shoots only of new wood: these shoots being placed in such a manner as to preserve the symmetry of the plant, without crowding it in any part. The same system of pruning and thinning is continued in future years—cutting out the old wood occasionally, so as to preserve a moderate and constant supply of strong, healthy young shoots, from which alone large and fine fruit can be expected. Whenever the extremities of the branches grow more than from twenty inches to two feet from the main stem, they must be cut back; for large fruit will never be produced at the extremities of long branches. The roots of the plants must also be attended to, by cutting a trench round the plant at the distance to which the branches are limited, so as to shorten all the main roots to that length, smoothing their extremities with a knife, and filling up the trench with fresh marly loam, enriched with cow-dung. Some growers even carry the system of root-pruning so far as to lay bare the whole of the roots, and thin out and shorten the larger ones in the same manner as is done with the branches, re-covering the roots with fresh soil. The fruit

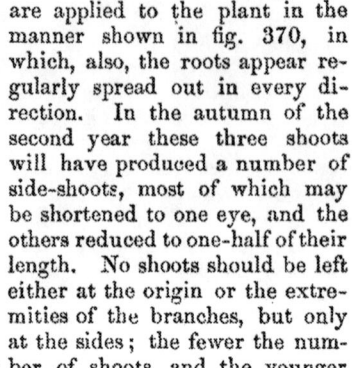

Fig. 368. 
Hooked stick for training prize gooseberry-bushes; length two feet.

Fig. 369. 
Forked stick for training prize gooseberry-bushes; length two feet.

Fig. 370. 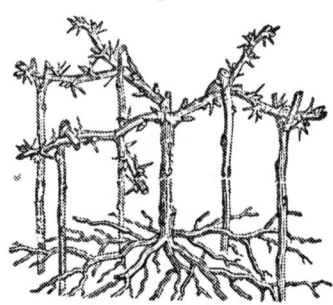
A trained prize gooseberry-bush, two years' growth from the cutting.

after being set is thinned out, as well as the branches, and not more than one or two berries are allowed to a branch when the object is prize fruit; we have, indeed, seen not more than two berries to an entire bush, the shoot being pegged down to within a few inches of the ground, and a saucer of water placed under each berry, in order, by its evaporation, to keep its surface moist and promote its swelling. The berries intended for prizes are protected from heavy rains by a cap of oiled paper, or by a bell-glass, or any other suitable contrivance; because should a slight shower fall on them at the time they are ripening, they are very apt to burst. These caps, however, must not be put on except when rain is expected, in order not to deprive the leaves of sun and air. Prize gooseberry-bushes are thought to be at their best when five or six years old from seed, and four or five years from cuttings.

Gathering and Keeping, &c.—Unripe gooseberries for tarts are in a fit state for that purpose by the end of April, and they may be thinned out from those that are to remain for ripening till the middle of July. If two-thirds of the produce of every plant is thinned out in a green state, it will add considerably to the size of those which remain. Ripe gooseberries should be gathered on the day in which they are sent to table, but both these and unripe fruit may, when necessary, be kept a week or more, by being placed in the icehouse-room or in the fruit-cellar. Gooseberries may be preserved on the trees, either by matting up each bush separately; by covering with canvas or matting both sides of an espalier or gooseberry-hedge; or by enclosing a square of bushes by pales or canvas frames six feet high; constructing the framework of a roof over this space, and covering it with canvas.

Insects, Diseases, and Casualties.—No pest is more common in gardens than the gooseberry caterpillar, by which is meant the larva of several kinds of moths, saw-flies, and some butterflies. They are all hatched on the leaves, and the great art of preventing them from injuring the plants is to watch for the appearance of the eggs, and, as soon as any are seen, commence syringing the plants powerfully with lime-water, using an inverted rose on the syringe, so as to throw the water against the under-sides of the leaves, as it is there that the eggs are deposited. Lime-water, when properly prepared and applied, will destroy, in its young state, the larva of every insect that lives on the leaves of plants; but to those who find it insufficient, we would recommend, first, to moisten the leaves by the syringe or watering-pot, and then to dust them, either with powdered quick-lime, coarse tobacco powder, or the powder of white hellebore (Veratrum album); or if either of the two last means be used, the powder may be mixed with soap-suds, and the plants watered or syringed with it; but in this case the skin of the fruit will not escape being covered with the liquor; and hellebore is less deadly in its effects than if it is applied directly to the insects in the state of powder. Dusted on in a fresh state, it kills every one that it touches. As the caterpillars are mostly under the leaves, it should be thrown up with a puff, or the finger and thumb, directly on the insects. If merely scattered over the surface of the bushes, more powder is needed, and the dressing is less effective. Unfortunately, in many gardens the caterpillars are not observed until they have attained a considerable size, and done great part of the mischief, when they are also more difficult to destroy. Hand-picking is recommended in such cases, but the mischief being already done, this only prevents the insect from attaining maturity, which, no doubt, is an advantage, by lessening the number of females for producing future broods.

Forcing.—The gooseberry has frequently been forced in Russia and Germany, and occasionally in England. A low temperature and abundance of air are the requisites to success. Plants in pots introduced into a peach house in November will ripen their fruit by the end of April, and form a pleasing variety to the dessert at that early season.

The Red and the White Currant.

The red and the white currant (Ribes rubrum, *L.* and R. r. var. album) are deciduous shrubs, the red variety indigenous in England and other parts of Europe, and the white variety produced from it by culture. The fruit in a wild state is small and very acid, but in gardens it has been increased in size and greatly improved in flavour. It contributes to the dessert from the beginning of July to September, and by matting up the fruit will hang on the trees till November or December.

Use.—The appearance of large red currants at table is brilliant, and contrasts well with dishes of white currants, and with green fruit, such as apples, pears, and plums. The taste cannot be called rich, but it is agreeably subacid and cooling. The red currant is much used for jellies, jams, wines, to acidulate punch, and for tarts; and continues longer in season, both for the table and the kitchen, than any other summer fruit.

Varieties.—The best are the White Dutch, White Champagne, Red Dutch, Knight's Sweet Red, which is less acid than the Red Dutch, Raby Castle, Grape, La Fertile, Mammoth, Berlin, Cherry, and Knight's Large Red. No selection can be better for a cottage garden, or for a garden in the coldest part of the country; but for display the Champagne currant may be added, which is large and of a very pale red.

The propagation and after treatment of the red and white currant scarcely differs from that of the gooseberry. When the fruit is required to be large, only a limited number of bunches ought to be allowed to remain on the branches, and the greater part of the summer shoots ought to be stopped several times in order to throw strength into the fruit; admit the sun and air to give it colour and flavour, and also to ripen the wood. Even in general cultivation, stopping the shoots in the end of June ought to be performed, as, by so doing, the buds at the base are enlarged. The currant is very frequently trained against a north wall, because there it ripens later, and is thought to hang longer on the tree; but its flavour in such a situation is inferior to what it is when grown in the open garden, either as a bush, an espalier, or a pyramid. The fruit should be gathered in a dry state, it should not be heaped up on a dish till it is about to be sent to table. Late in the season it is sometimes disfigured by cobwebs, dust, and particles of decayed leaves, in which case it should be washed and dried on a sieve, or by hanging up in the fruit-room before it is presented at the dessert. The currant, like the gooseberry, is attacked by the larvæ of moths, by a species of aphis, by a coccus, and when the fruit is ripe it is sometimes devoured by earwigs. The latter may be lured into bundles of bean-stalks or reeds, and shaken out of them into hot-water or lime-water; and the former may be destroyed by the usual means. The red and white currant may be forced in the same manner as the gooseberry, and the fruit will ripen in the same period.

The Black Currant.

The black currant (Ribes nigrum, L.) is a deciduous shrub common in woods throughout great part of Russia and Siberia, and occasionally found apparently wild in Britain. It is sometimes brought to the dessert, but its use is more frequently to make jams, jellies, wines, and to flavour punch, or as a gargle for sore throats. It is likewise used in puddings and tarts; and in Russia, and also in Ireland, it is put into spirits, as cherries are in England. The Russians also ferment the juice with honey, and thus form a strong and agreeable liquor. The dry leaves form an excellent substitute for green tea. The best varieties are the Black Naples, Ogden's Black or Black Grape, and Lee's Prolific. Cuttings strike readily, and other points of treatment are the same as for the red currant, excepting that the fruit of the black currant is produced chiefly on the shoots of the preceding year. Therefore the pruning consists mostly in cutting out occasionally a few old shoots to make room for new wood. Black currants require little pruning, and should not be spurred in like the gooseberry or common currant. The plant is less subject to insects than either the red currant or the gooseberry. It forces well, and in Russia this is practised for the sake of the young foliage. Ribes aureum has fruit resembling the black currant, and, with other species of the genus, might doubtless be made to contribute to the varieties, or improvement, of our gooseberries and currants.

The Raspberry.

The raspberry (Rubus Idæus, L.) is a suffruticose deciduous plant, with biennial stems, a native of Britain and other parts of Europe in moist woods, and cultivated in gardens from an unknown period. Even in a wild state the fruit is grateful to most palates, and it has been enlarged in size and greatly improved in flavour by hybridization and cultivation. The shoots which are produced from the stock during one summer produce fruit the next, and afterwards die. Technically the shoots are called canes, from the straight smooth cane-like appearance of the shoots of some of the varieties, more especially the Barnet. The fruit ranks in the dessert with the gooseberry and strawberry, but its principal uses are for jams, tarts, sauces, sweetmeats, and ices; and it is employed on a large scale in preparing cordial spirituous liquors, and cooling syrups. Raspberries are reckoned next in efficiency to the strawberry in dissolving the tartar of the teeth; they are likewise recommended to gouty and rheumatic patients.

Varieties.—These are increasing every year. The following include the best worth cultivating: The Red Antwerp, Yellow Antwerp, Fastolf, Fill Basket, Carter's Prolific, Cornwall Large Yellow. The autumn or double-bearing varieties: The October Red and Yellow, Autumn Black, Large Orange, and McLaren's Prolific.

Propagation, Soil, and other points of Culture.—The only mode of propagation is by suckers, except by seeds, which is only resorted to when new varieties are wanted. Seedlings carefully treated will produce fruit the second year. The suckers are separated in autumn, either by taking up the whole plant and dividing it, or by slipping them off from the sides and roots of the main stock. They may be planted at once where they are finally to remain in a compartment by themselves, in rows from north to south, four feet apart every way. They will grow in any good garden soil, and if on the lower part of a slope, towards the north, east, or west, the soil will be kept moderately moist by its position, and the situation will not be so much exposed to light and heat as if it sloped to the south. The raspberry grows naturally in soft, peaty, or vegetable soil, shaded by woods, and always moist; but it is most prolific in fruit, and the fruit is better flavoured, in the more substantial and drier soil, and opener situation, of the garden. In making a plantation, one or three or more suckers are allowed to each stool, and planted six inches apart. The plants will produce fruit the first year, but if this fruit can be dispensed with, the suckers for the succeeding year will be greatly strengthened by cutting the stems of the newly-planted plants down to within six inches of the ground. The plantation being established, the future treatment consists in going over the stools every year early in May, and selecting six or seven of the strongest suckers from each stool for next year's bearing wood, and destroying all the rest, unless they are wanted for a new plantation. In autumn, as soon as the fruit is gathered, the stems which have borne it should be cut down to the ground to give light and air to the suckers; but as these are sometimes liable to be injured by frost, they should not be pruned till the following March. They may then be shortened to two-thirds or three-fourths of their length, by cutting off the weak wood at the extremities of the shoots. If large fruit is wanted, but few stems (canes) should be left to each stool, and these should be tied singly to stakes placed round the stool in a circle, at about a foot distance from it, so that the canes when tied to the stakes shall be bent outwards; which position at once facilitates the development of the buds all along the canes, exposes the fruit more freely to the sun and air, and allows room for the suckers to rise upright from the stool without shading the fruit-bearing canes. Sometimes, instead of a circle of stakes round each plant, a line of rails or of iron wire, or long rods with the bark on, is placed between every alternate two rows of raspberries, supported at about three feet from the ground by stakes; and to these rails, wires, or rods, the canes from the adjoining plants are bent over and fastened by ties of matting or willow-twigs. In this way every alternate space between the rows is covered by the bearing canes which are bent over it, and the other spaces are left open for gathering the fruit. Where a large crop of fruit is wanted, without regard to the size of the berries, half the number of the canes on each plant may be bent over, so as to meet the half of those of the adjoining plant, and a foot or more of the points of the canes of each plant may be interwoven and made fast by matting. A row of raspberries thus treated will present a series of arches of fruit-bearing branches, alternately with columns of suckers; the bending of the bearing canes will cause every bud to break, the fruit-bearing laterals will be exposed to the sun and air without being crowded by the suckers, and the latter will have more room for their foliage, and hence grow stronger, and ripen their wood better. This, being the easiest and most economical mode of training the canes, is that most generally adopted in gardens. Some growers, however, prefer neither to stake nor train the canes; they simply shorten them to about thirty-one inches in length; they support themselves even when laden with fruit without inconvenience. Where very large fruit is required, the whole or the greater part of the suckers may be destroyed as fast as they appear, and the blossoms may be thinned; but this practice, by destroying the plant, requires a double plantation, one for producing suckers, and another for producing fruit; and hence it should only be adopted in gardens where there is abundance of room. To obtain a successional crop late in the season, the canes of the autumnal varieties may be cut down to the ground in winter, and the suckers, which will be produced with more than usual vigour, may be stopped in the beginning of June, which will cause the buds to break and produce fruit late in the season, generally till it is destroyed by frost. The suckers of the twice-bearing raspberry naturally produce a second crop—that is, they produce fruit the first year as well as the second; but for a full supply in the autumn, it is best to cut the whole of the old shoots out, and concentrate the entire strength of the plant into its autumnal produce. The ground between the rows should be manured and dug every year, but no attempt should be made to grow a crop between the rows after the first year. A new plantation may be made every six or seven years, or oftener, if the plants should show any symptoms of degeneracy; or if their travelling roots should grow out of bounds, which they are very apt to do from the outside suckers always being the strongest, and consequently selected for bearing in preference to the inside suckers.

Gathering.—The fruit begins to ripen in the end of June, and continues being produced till October. It should be gathered immediately after it becomes ripe, which is known by every part of it being equally high-coloured, and by the pulpy part separating readily from the conical receptacle. If allowed to remain ripe on the plant for two days, the eggs of a beetle, Byturus tomentosus, which had been deposited in it when in flower, become maggots, and render it unfit to be used. If gathered and kept two or three days, the same effect takes place; or the fruit becomes mouldy and unfit for use.

Forcing.—The raspberry forces equally well with the gooseberry and currant, either in pots or planted in the free soil of a cherry-house; or it may be planted in pits, and trained under the glass, which is the practice in Holland.

The Nootka raspberry (R. Nutkanus, 'Arb. Brit.,' vol. ii. p. 745, and 'Encyc. of Trees and Shrubs,' p. 318), produces large red fruit, which is found to make excellent tarts. If the same care were bestowed on this species which has been given to the raspberry, we have no doubt it would become one of our standard fruit shrubs. R. odoratus, a closely allied species, or perhaps, only a variety, with fragrant foliage, is said to produce yellow fruit of a large size, and a very fine flavour.

The Strawberry.

The strawberry (Fragaria, L.) is an herbaceous stoloniferous plant, of which there are several species, natives of Europe, the temperate parts of Asia and North America. The fruit has received its name from the practice, more common in former times than at present, of laying straw or litter between the rows. The fruit of the European strawberry in a wild state, gathered from the woods, has long been esteemed by the rich as well as the poor, but little or no improvement took place in its culture till the introduction of the Virginian Strawberry or Scarlet, the Pine or Surinam Strawberry, and the Chili Strawberry, which are considered by botanists as distinct species. All these sorts may be crossed indiscriminately; and thus have been produced some hundreds of sorts, many of very great excellence, and chiefly by British gardeners; for till within these few years, no other strawberry was cultivated on the Continent than the small sort common in the woods. What gives the strawberry a special value is, that like the gooseberry, it can be grown in as great perfection in the ground plot of the peasant, as in the finest walled garden of the peer.

Use.—The fruit is much valued in the dessert, of which, without the aid of glass, it may form a part from the beginning of June to November, and by the aid of the forcing pit from March till June, thus giving an eight months' season of this most delicious fruit. It is of very general use in confectionery, and is recommended medicinally in cases where acid fruits are injurious. It dissolves the tartareous incrustations of the teeth, promotes perspiration, and has many other good qualities.

Varieties.—The following list includes all the best. The earliest varieties: Black Prince, Princess Alice, Keen's Seedling, Sir Joseph Paxton, Prince Frederick William, Prince Imperial, La Bonne Marie.

Choice Dessert Strawberries. — British Queen, Dr. Hogg, Eliza, Myatt's Pine, Old Pine, La Constante, Carolina Superba, Victoria, Sir Charles Napier, Deptford Pine, White Pine-apple, Prince Arthur, Victoria, Empress Eugenie, Admiral Dundas, Ascot Pine-apple, Elton Pine, Mr. Radclyffe.

Culinary or Preserving Strawberries. — Old Scarlet, Grove End Scarlet, Black Prince, Elton Pine, Oscar, President, Prince of Wales, Sir Harry, and Eleanor. Hautbois: The Royal is far superior to all other varieties in this class.

Alpine and Wood Strawberries.—These comprehend the Fragaria semper-florens, and F. vesca of botanists. The Alpine and the Wood strawberry differ chiefly in the form of the fruit, which in the Alpines is conical, and in the Wood varieties, roundish. 1. The Red Alpine has the largest fruit of its class, and bears abundantly in light, sandy, rich soils, especially when liberally supplied with water in dry hot weather, and continues producing from June to November. 2. The White Alpine only differs from the preceding sort in having the fruit white, and the flavour somewhat more delicate. 3. The Red Wood resembles the preceding in colour and flavour; but the fruit is smaller, and the plants do not bear so long in succession. 4. The White Wood only differs from the preceding in having the fruit white. To these may be added such French varieties in this class as Blanche d'Orleans, Galland, and Brune de Gilbert.

Propagation, Soil, &c.—All the sorts are propagated by runners, but the Alpines are sometimes also increased by division and by seeds. The runner plants are taken off when their roots are two or three inches in length, which is generally the case in the last week of July, or early in August. By some they are planted where they are finally to remain, which is the best mode when there is abundance of ground and a scarcity of hands; and by others they are planted in nursery-beds, a foot apart every way, where they remain till the end of February or beginning of March following; and they should then be removed and planted with balls, by means of a trowel. When runner plants are to be transplanted without receiving any check, they are rooted in pots in the manner already described for preparing plants for forcing. The soil for all the varieties, except Alpines, should be a strong loam, well enriched with stable-dung; and the best situation for all of them is one which is open and fully exposed to the sun. For the Alpines the soil should be lighter, and if the situation is a walled border facing the east, the plants, by being kept cooler, will thrive with less watering. Nevertheless, Alpines will thrive remarkably well, and their fruit will have a higher flavour, in the most exposed and sunny situation, provided they are abundantly supplied with water.

Culture.—Though the strawberry, like most herbaceous perennials, is found chiefly in woods and waste places, yet in a state of culture it is found most productive of large high-flavoured fruit when grown in the open garden in plantations freely exposed to the sun and air. The plants are generally planted in rows, but sometimes in beds; and they are occasionally planted as edgings to gravel-walks. In this latter mode they bear well: the gravel of the walk containing moisture and its surface reflecting heat, while nutriment is obtained from the border; but the fruit in this situation is apt to be soiled by the gravel after heavy rains. In whatever way the strawberry is grown it requires to be renewed every third, fourth, or, at the latest, fifth year.

Culture in Rows.—In the ordinary mode of culture the runners are planted in rows, varying in width from eighteen inches to thirty inches. Unless the plants are very strong no fruit should be taken the first year; this will ensure a full crop for the next season. The rows should receive a good dressing of dung every winter, which may be slightly forked, but on no account dug in. Top-dressings may also be applied in autumn or winter with great advantage; and such may consist of leaves, dung, any rich compost, or even loam alone, and their own decayed foliage may also be included; of the latter, therefore, the plants should not be deprived, by previously mowing and clearing off the leaves in autumn, as is often improperly done. The strawberry being a native of woods is naturally covered with leaves every autumn, and hence a top-dressing that would smother many other kinds of plants will prove beneficial to the strawberry. All the runners should be taken off, excepting such as are wanted for a new plantation, as soon as they appear, and before the fruit has ripened. In places where large quantities of strawberries are forced it is good practice to plant out the forced plants as soon as they have done bearing into rich soil. They will yield a second crop in the autumn, and a most extraordinary crop during the next summer; they may then be dug in, or one more crop may be taken from them. They would then be succeeded by other forced plants, and thus no strawberries would be kept more than three years, and four crops would be gathered in that time. It is most unexpectedly found that neither the forcing nor the autumn bearing seems to weaken the plants, but to have a contrary effect, the heaviest crops we have ever seen having been gathered under this mode of culture.

Culture in Beds.—The large kinds are planted in rows two feet apart and eighteen inches distant in the row; each bed contains two rows, and an interval of three feet wide alternates with each bed, as an alley from which to water and gather the fruit, &c. The runners may be first planted in a nursery bed to remain from August till March, when they should be removed to the fruiting beds. There they will bear an excellent crop the first year, a very good crop the second, and a good crop the third; after which the plants should be dug down.

Another mode of growing strawberries in beds is to plant them thickly in rich beds early in August, take one crop, and destroy the plants; however, this system is now but little used, unless for Alpines or Hautbois, as all the choice sorts are grown to much greater perfection on thoroughly manured deep soils in drills, and the plants are seldom allowed to stand on the same ground for more than three or four seasons.

Mulching and Watering.—Mulching is useful both for keeping the fruit clean, and retaining moisture in the soil. If stable litter is used, and put on just before the leaves expand, it will serve also as manure; the animal matters which adhere to it will be washed in by the rains, and by the time the fruit is ripe the litter will be bleached as white as clean straw. Short grass may be used as a mulch, but it is too retentive of moisture and congenial to snails, and the same may be said of leaves. Coarse gravel requires too much labour in laying down and taking off; but flat tiles form an excellent mulch, retaining moisture, and reflecting heat among the leaves and fruit. Some persons have had tiles made of a semicircular form, each with a small semicircle, about three inches in diameter, cut out of it, so that two of these tiles cover a circular space round the plant; but not only is this a needless refinement and waste, the tiles being unfit for anything else, and a portion of the ground is left unmulched; whereas by using common roof tiles the ground can be more completely covered, no extra expense is incurred in their manufacture, and they are as fit for roofing, and a variety of other purposes, as if they had never been used for mulching. Cocoa-nut fibre refuse in a coarse state and rough tan are also good and clean material for mulching. Watering is essential to a good crop of strawberries in dry weather, and may be performed on a large scale by the watering-barrel, hose, or the common watering-pot. The best time is the evening or early in the morning, because at these seasons less is lost by evaporation; and the water should always, if possible, be of a temperature somewhat higher than that of the soil. Some amateurs grow their strawberries in beds having small open brick channels as alleys, and these and the beds being formed on a perfect level, by filling the alleys with water, it penetrates the soil of the beds on each side. Surface irrigation, however, appears preferable, because the soil being warmest there the water will carry down heat to the interior of the soil. Liquid manure or sewage should not be used after the fruit begins to colour. It is of the greatest service through all the early stages of growth; care should, however, be exercised to keep strong manure-water from direct contact with the fruit.

Retarding a Crop.—This may be done to a certain extent by planting on the north side of an east-and-west wall, or in any situation shaded from the sun, or exposed to the north; but the most effective mode of procuring a late crop is to remove all the blossoms that would have produced the first crop; and then, after allowing the plants to receive a check from the dry warm weather which usually occurs in the latter end of June, to supply water abundantly. The Elton Pine planted in clay behind a north wall will continue bearing for two months, and yield a very late crop; grown thus it is very acid, but is beautiful in form and colour, and can readily be sweetened to the palate with sugar.

Accelerating a Crop in the Open Garden.—This may be done by planting a row close along the base of a wall having a south aspect. The best variety for this purpose is the Black Prince, which has small leaves and an early habit, and which so treated may be made to ripen its fruit towards the end of May. Another mode consists in planting on the south side of an east-and-west ridge of soil. The ridge may be no larger than to admit of a single row, or it may be four feet or five feet high, so as to admit of three or four rows on the south side for accelerating a crop, and an equal quantity on the north side for retarding one. If the ground on the south side is covered with flat tiles, bricks, flints, or pebbles, they will retain moisture, conduct heat to the soil, and reflect it also among the plants. The common calculation, from a ridge at an angle of 45°, is a fortnight earlier for the south side, and eight or ten days later for the north side; so that by means of a ridge the strawberry season in the open garden is extended at least three weeks. Sometimes these ridges are built of brickwork, in steps, and sometimes they are formed of stones, in the manner of a wall built without mortar, the plants being placed in the interstices. In whichever way the ridge is formed there ought to be a gutter of three inches or four inches in width along the apex, as a channel for supplying warm water to the roots. It would be an improvement also to cover the south side of the ridge during nights with mats or canvas, supported on hoops or rods at nine inches or one foot above the plants, to check radiation. A few hand-lights or feet of Rendle's patent glass and tile plant protectors would prove a clear gain of another three weeks. Ridges of this kind require to be taken down every year after the crop is gathered, and replanted with the earliest runners that can be got. If such ridges could be furnished with the plants forced the previous year the crop would be still further accelerated. The ordinary slope of the ridge is an angle of 45°, because loose soil will remain stationary at that angle; but where the ridge is to be faced with stones or tiles, the slope may be nearly perpendicular, or at all events 70°. In the garden of a cottage which has been built on a platform, the sloping bank which supports the latter might be planted with strawberries, either with or without the addition of stones or tiles.

Gathering the fruit should take place when it is quite dry, and they should be taken to table the same day. It should always be gathered with the calyx attached, and laid singly in shallow baskets on strawberry leaves. Those of the cabbage tribe, though generally used, injure the flavour of the fruit.

Forcing.—See p. 513.

The Cranberry.

The cranberry (Oxycoccus, Pers.) is a genus of low trailing shrubs; one, O. palustris, the English cranberry, a native of Britain and the north of Europe in moist bogs; and the other, O. macrocarpus, the American cranberry, a native of swamps in the United States. The fruit of both has long been gathered from the native habitats of the plants, and used for tarts and other purposes; and it forms an article of exportation from Sweden, Russia, and North America. Both sorts may be cultivated in gardens in peat-soil, kept moist; and if it is enriched with thoroughly rotted dung the vigour of the plants will be greatly increased, and the flavour of the fruit improved. The English cranberry requires a more constant supply of moisture than the American; but the fruit of both is better flavoured when grown with much less moisture than they enjoy in their native habitats. The American cranberry has even been grown in beds of dry peat-soil, and produced a plentiful crop of excellent fruit. The plants are readily propagated by layering the shoots, or by taking off their points and striking them in sand under a hand-glass. Both species may be grown on the margin of a pond, or on moist parts of rockwork.

The Scotch cranberry (Vaccinium Vitis-idæa, L.); the whortle-berry

(V. Myrtillus, L); the great bilberry (V. uliginosum, L.); and various other species of Vaccinium, bearing edible and very agreeable cooling acid fruit, may all be grown in moist peat. When a garden is situated in a part of the country where peat soil abounds, and perhaps forms part of the garden or adjoins it, it may be worth while to attempt growing these fruits, but not otherwise.

The Mulberry.

The black or garden mulberry (Morus nigra), is a middle-sized deciduous tree, a native of Persia, and supposed to have been introduced into Europe by the Romans. It has been cultivated in England since the middle of the 16th century, for its highly aromatic fruit, which ripens in August. An agreeable wine is made from the juice, and a syrup from the unripe berries; it is also used in puddings and pies. It is readily propagated by cuttings or truncheons, and will thrive as a standard in any good garden soil in the central districts of England; but north of York, and in Scotland, it requires a south wall. As the fruit drops as soon as it is ripe, the tree is generally planted on a lawn or grass plot; but the fruit attains a larger size when the soil round the tree is kept slightly dug and well manured. In a small garden the tree may be very conveniently grown as an espalier. The fruit is produced chiefly on short shoots of the same year, which are protruded from last year's wood, and on spurs from the two-year old wood; both laterals and spurs being produced mostly at the ends of the branches. The tree being of slow growth, very little pruning is required for either espaliers or standards; though no doubt thinning out the branches would strengthen those that remain. The fruit should be gathered just when it is about to fall, and used the same day. The tree is remarkable for the great age which it attains, and for its vitality; instances being common of trees growing after remaining out of the ground for a year, or being transplanted in full leaf, and after remaining a year dormant. One, or at most two, mulberry-trees are usually sufficient for a garden, whether large or small. There is a large-fruited white sort, which may be planted for variety.

The Walnut.

The walnut (Juglans regia, L.), is a deciduous tree of large size, a native of Persia and Caucasus, and has been cultivated in England as a fruit and timber tree from the middle of the 16th century, or before. The ripe kernel is used in the dessert, and the fruit whole, in a green state, before the nut and its involucre or husk harden, forms an excellent pickle. The timber, being very light in proportion to its strength and elasticity, is much used for gun-stocks. The variety most esteemed for its fruit is the Thetford, but the large French Prolific and tender-shelled are also good sorts. They are propagated chiefly by budding on the common walnut, or by inarching; but as there is little demand for these trees, most of those which are sold in the nurseries are seedlings. The tree thrives best in a deep sandy loam, and it is generally planted in the north margin of the orchard, or on a lawn, or in a paddock. Seedlings will bear in seven years from the seed. The Prolific bears in a small state. The fruit is produced, as in most amentaceous trees, from short shoots of the current year protruded from the extremities of the preceding year's shoots. It is gathered by hand for pickling, and too frequently beaten down with rods when ripe; but as it drops of itself just before the leaves, no beating down, or gathering from the branches, is requisite. The fruit is best kept in dry sand, or slightly covered with straw. Little or no pruning is ever given to this tree, though there can be no doubt that thinning out the branches would throw more strength into the fruit of those which remain.

The Peccan-nut Hickory (Carya olivæformis), some varieties of which, Michaux says, produce fruit which is far superior to that of the European walnut (and of which Washington is said to have been so fond that during the War of Independence he had always his pockets full of them); and the Shell-bark Hickory (C. alba), may be grafted on the walnut, and treated in all respects like that tree.

The Sweet Chestnut.

The sweet chestnut (Castanea vesca, W.), is a large deciduous tree, a native of Spain and Italy, and cultivated in the south of England, more especially in Devonshire, for its fruit, as well as its timber. The nut is brought to table roasted, and eaten with salt, or with salt fish, or stewed in cream. In Spain and Italy it is used as an article of food, boiled, roasted, in puddings, cakes, and bread. In France and Italy there are a great many varieties in cultivation, and upwards of twenty have been grown in the Garden of the Horticultural Society, of which the Downton and Prolific are among the best. For a small garden, the Châtaigne exalade of the south of France deserves the preference, not only as producing the best fruit of all the varieties for the table, but on account of the tree being an abundant bearer and of small size. The varieties are propagated by grafting on the species. The fruit is produced in the same manner as that of the walnut.

The Filbert.

The filbert (Corylus Avellana, L.), in a wild state is the hazel-nut, common in woods in many parts of Europe, on loamy soils. Its use in the dessert is familiar to every one. By cultivation several varieties have been obtained, of which the best are the Red, White, Purple-leaved, Prolific, and Frizzled filbert; the Cosford, which ought to be in every collection; the Cob-nut, the Great and Red and White Prize Exhibition Cob-nut, the Downton large square nut, and the Spanish nut, on account of their large fruit. All these varieties are usually propagated by grafting on the common hazel-nut, or on the Spanish nut, which grows very fast, and differs from all the others in not sending up suckers. "The plants should be trained to a single stem, from a foot to two feet in height, and then be permitted to branch into a symmetrical head, rather open in the middle, and not of greater height than a man can conveniently reach from the ground to perform the necessary operations of pruning and gathering." The fruit is produced from the preceding year's wood, and in unpruned trees is always most abundant at the extremities of the branches, where the leaves of the preceding year have had abundance of light and air. Hence the importance of pruning so as to keep the bush open in the centre. The spring, at the time the male blossoms are shedding their pollen, is the best time for pruning, as by the shaking of the trees the pollen is diffused. The young shoots should be shortened to half their length, cutting to a female blossom, and removing all side suckers. If a plantation is to consist of a single row, the plants may be placed from eight feet to ten feet apart; but if there are to be several rows together, the intervals between them may be ten feet or twelve feet. The whole may be treated like a plantation of currants on a large scale. The usual situation for a plantation of filberts is the orchard, where single rows may be introduced, for a few years, between rows of standard fruit trees. If a separate plantation of filberts is formed, currants or gooseberries may be introduced in the intervals between the plants for four or five years—care being taken to destroy them whenever their branches are within a foot or two of the filberts. A plantation of filberts will last twenty years, and if occasionally manured, it will produce from 20 to 30 cwt. of nuts per acre annually. The nut weevil lays its eggs in the fruit in June, where it is hatched, and escapes in August. There is no practical preventive of this insect, and all that the gardener can do is to remove all the nuts that have been perforated by it. The fruit is gathered when the calyx turns brown, and at a time when it is quite dry, and it may be preserved through the winter with the husks, or in dry sand, or in air-tight vessels. Some put them into large garden-pots, sprinkling a little salt amongst them, which is said to preserve the husks from getting mouldy and rotting; the pots are turned bottom upwards on boards, and covered with earth or sand to exclude the air. The dealers subject them to the fumes of sulphur in close vessels, when newly gathered and dried, in order to improve the colour of the calyx.

The Barberry, Magellan Sweet Barberry, Nepal Barberry, Elderberry, and Cornelian Cherry.

The barberry (Berberis vulgaris, L.) is a deciduous shrub, a native of Britain in woods and hedges on dry soil, and sometimes planted in gardens for its fruit, which is not eaten raw, but is excellent when preserved in sugar, in syrup, or candied. The berries are also made into jelly and rob, both of which are not only delicious to the taste, but extremely wholesome, and they are pickled in vinegar when green as a substitute for capers. They are also used instead of lemon for flavouring punch, for garnishing dishes, and for various other purposes, independently of their medicinal properties.

The Magellan Sweet Barberry (Berberis dulcis, D. Don, syn. B. buxifolia, B. rotundifolia) has round black berries about the size of those of the black currant, which are produced in great abundance, and used in its native country, both green and ripe, as we use gooseberries, for pies, tarts, and preserves, for which it is said to be most excellent. The plant is evergreen, quite hardy, and very ornamental, flowering from March to June, and ripening its fruit in June and July.

The Nepal barberry (B. aristata, Nepal, and B. asiatica, Roxb., also from Nepal) produce purple fruit covered with a fine bloom, which in Nepal and other parts of India are dried in the sun like raisins, and, like them, brought to table. The plants are quite hardy, and fruit abundantly in English gardens, but are scarcely worth cultivating for that purpose, except by the curious.

The elder-tree (Sambucus nigra, L.) is a low deciduous tree, a native of most parts of Europe, and chiefly found near human habitations. It is highly ornamental both when in flower and in fruit. An infusion of the flowers is used to flavour some articles of confectionery, and a wine is made from the fruit by boiling it with spices and sugar. Immense quantities of fruit are grown in Kent, and other places in the neighbourhood of London, and sent to market for making this wine, which is always taken hot. The tree requires a good soil and an open airy situation, and should be kept free from suckers.

The Cornelian cherry (Cornus Mas., L.) is a low deciduous tree, a native of the middle and south of Europe, in the margins of woods, and in soils more or less calcareous; and it has been cultivated in gardens, from the time of the Romans, for its fruit, which, however, was not much esteemed by that people. It was very general in ancient gardens; its fruit being very ornamental on the tree, and also found excellent in tarts, robs, and preserved in various ways. As seedling plants of this species of Cornus bear only male blossoms for twelve or fifteen years, and some continue to do so always, it is desirable to procure plants which have been grafted, or raised by layers from fruit-bearing trees, the flowers of which are always hermaphrodite.

Half-hardy and Wall Fruits.

The wall-fruits of Britain include all those which in the central districts of England require the aid of a wall to bring them to perfection. These are the grape, peach, nectarine, almond, apricot, fig, pomegranate, love-apple, egg-plant, and Peruvian cherry.

The Grape.

Many varieties have been produced by different soils and situations on the Continent, in countries where the vine is grown for many years on the same spot for wine; and by seeds in Britain, where the fruit is grown solely for the dessert. Of late years many successful attempts have been made in crossing different varieties, and the result has been several first-class grapes of English origin.

Varieties.

Black Grapes.—We will begin with the king of them all, the

Black Hamburgh, in all its varieties of Frankenthal, Richmond Villa, Champion, Mill Hill, Victoria, &c.—the Frankenthal being the very best of them all; Alicante, Madresfield Court, Black Prince, Burchardt's Prince, Lady Downes, West's St. Peter's, Esperione, Royal Ascot, Trentham Black, and Barbarossa.

Muscat Grapes.— Muscat of Alexandria, Bowood Muscat, Mrs. Pince's Black Muscat, Muscat Hamburgh, Cannon-ball Muscat, Ingram's Prolific Muscat.

Frontignan Grapes.—Chasselas Musqué, Duchess of Buccleugh, White Frontignan, Trovéren Frontignan, Grizzly Frontignan, Black Frontignan, Purple Constantia, Tokay Frontignan, Duc de Magenta.

White Grapes.—Golden Champion, White Lady Downes, Trebbiano, Buckland Sweetwater, White Nice, Reeves' Muscadine, Royal Muscadine, Chasselas Royale, Foster's White Seedling.

Grapes for Main Crops.—Black Hamburgh, Black Prince, Muscat of Alexandria.

Grapes for Latest Crops.—Alicante, Lady Downes, White Lady Downes, Barbarossa, Muscat of Alexandria, West's St. Peter's.

Grapes for a Cool Vinery or Orchard-house.—Royal Muscadine, White Sweetwater, Black Hamburgh, Esperione, Ingram's Hardy Prolific Muscat.

Grapes for Pot Culture.—Black Hamburgh, Muscat of Alexandria, Royal Muscadine, all the Frontignans, Trentham Black, Black Prince; and for late hanging on the plants, Alicante and Lady Downes.

Varieties for Ground Vineries.—Esperione, Trentham Black, Black Hamburgh, Early Auvergne, Frontignan, Royal Muscadine Sweetwater, Cambridge Botanic Garden, Ingram's Prolific Muscat, Madeleine Royale.

Grapes with Small Leaves, and Hardy; adapted for the Rafters of a Greenhouse.—White and Black Sweetwater, and Parsley-leaved Muscadine.

Grapes with Small Leaves, less hardy than the preceding selection, and fit for the Rafters of a Plant-stove.—Chasselas Musqué, Mrs. Pince, Blue Tokay, Royal Muscadine, and Parsley-leaved grape.

Grapes for a Cottage Garden where the Climate is not very Favourable.—White Muscadine, Black July, Large Black Muscadine, and Pitmaston White Cluster.

Grapes Suitable for the Open Wall, or for Cottages in Situations where the Peach will Ripen on the Open Wall.—Esperione, Royal Muscadine, Cambridge Botanic Garden, and White Cluster. If the peach requires a flued wall, so will the grapes in this list; and when they are planted against a house, it should only be on those walls which are decidedly warm, from facing the south and from a fire always being kept in the room within, or from the wall containing a chimney-flue to a fire in constant use.

Propagation.—See p. 447.

Culture, Pruning, Training, &c.—See pp. 444, 457.

Growing Grapes for Wine-making.—Excellent wine may be made from unripe grapes and these may be produced in abundance in the central and southern districts of England, in the open garden on espaliers and on walls.

The Peach and Nectarine.

The peach and nectarine (Persica vulgaris, Dec.; and P. lævis, Dec.) are deciduous trees, under the middle size, natives of Persia, and cultivated in gardens for their fruit from the time of the Romans. The nectarine (pêche lisse, Fr.), is distinguished from the peach by having a smooth skin, while that of the peach is downy. The almond is supposed by many to be the peach in a wild state, but for convenience in treating of their culture, we have kept them apart. The peach has long been cultivated extensively in France, from whence our best varieties have been obtained; it is highly prized in India, and is common in the warmer parts of the United States as an orchard fruit.

Use.—The peach and nectarine are dessert fruits, next in estimation to the grape and the pine-apple; they also make delicious preserves, and the peach, when gathered a little before it is ripe, most excellent tarts. In the Southern States of North America, and in some parts of France, the pulp is fermented, and brandy obtained from it by distillation. A few of the green leaves put into gin or whisky give these spirits the flavour of noyau. As both the leaves and the skin of the fruit contain prussic acid, the use of the former should not be carried to excess, and the skin of the latter should always be removed before the pulp is eaten.

Properties of a good Peach or Nectarine.—Flesh firm; skin thin, of a deep or bright red colour next the sun, and of a yellowish green on the shady side; pulp yellowish, full of high-flavoured juice; the fleshy part thick, and the stone small.

Varieties.—These are naturally arranged into two divisions, peaches and nectarines. There are now a great many varieties of both in cultivation; great and splendid additions have very recently been made to our collections by Mr. Rivers, of Sawbridgeworth, many of whose seedlings are of the highest merit. The following are among the very best proved varieties up to this year:—Chancellor, Early Rivers, Early York, Raymacker's, Rivers, Early York, Alexandra, Noblesse, Dr. Hogg, Early Silver, Lady Palmerston, Princess of Wales, Grosse Mignonne, Red Magdalen, Royal George, Noblesse, Malta, Barrington, Bellegarde, Late Admirable, Salway.

Select Nectarines.—Elruge, Downton, Hardwicke Seedling, Rivers' Orange, Rivers' Pine-apple, Albert, New White, Violette Hâtive, and Pitmaston Orange.

Peaches and Nectarines for a Wall, to come in, in succession from the beginning of August to the end of October, arranged in the order of their Ripening.—Peaches: Early Rivers, Early York, Grosse Mignonne, Royal George, Noblesse, Malta, Royal Charlotte, Bellegarde, Barrington, Late Admirable, Princess of Wales, and Lord Palmerston. The best nectarines for a wall are the Elruge, Violette Hâtive, Pine-apple, and Victoria. A more extended selection of peaches and nectarines for a wall has been already given.

A Selection of Peaches for Forcing.—Bellegarde, Noblesse, Grosse

Mignonne, Royal George, Barrington, Early Rivers, Early York, Early Albert.

Nectarines for Forcing.—Elruge, Hardwicke Seedling, Pitmaston Orange, Rivers' Orange, Rivers' Pine-apple, Lord Napier, Albert Victor, Prince of Wales.

Propagation and Nursery Culture.—Budding on plum stocks is the general practice; but some of the more delicate kinds are budded on the almond, strong-growing seedling peaches, or on the apricot. On the peach stock they grow very vigorously at first, but do not long continue to thrive. For general purposes the plum stock is by far the best, as from its abundance of roots it transplants readily; while the roots of the almond and peach, being few and very remote, they transplant with difficulty. The French gardeners used the almond stock for light chalky or sandy soils, and the plum stock for clayey or loamy soils. When the plants are not removed the first year to where they are finally to remain, they are cut down in the nursery to three or four eyes, and the shoots produced trained in the fan manner already described at length. This may either be done in the open garden against a row of stakes, or the plants may be removed to a wall, which is the best mode for ripening the wood. To ensure this result the plants should in no case be placed in very rich moist soil. In the training of maiden plants, the point of the shoot produced by the bud is pinched off after it has grown six inches or eight inches in length, and only five buds are allowed to push; the five shoots produced by these buds are shortened with the finger and thumb to five inches or six inches in length, and these being disbudded, so as to admit of only two shoots from each, a complete fan-shaped tree is produced in one season. The quickest mode of proving the quality of peaches, or of the fruit of other trees raised from seed, is to take a bud from them, and insert it near the extremity of a lateral branch of a tree of the same species. Budded on the Moor-park apricot, the flavour of the peach is said to be greatly improved; on the Mirabelle or Myrobalan plum, the tree is somewhat dwarfed.

Soil, Situation, &c.—A fresh loamy soil on a dry bottom answers best, and care should be taken not to enrich the soil so much by manure as to occasion the production of longer shoots than can be properly ripened. In few situations should the peach border be more than eighteen inches or two feet in depth, and it need not be more than ten feet or twelve feet in width, even when the walls are fifteen feet in height. The peach in Britain is almost always planted against a south wall, but in some sheltered situations it will succeed on a south-east, south-west, or west aspect. Against a south-west wall the blossoms are more liable to be injured by the heavy rains from that quarter, and the shoots are apt to grow stronger, in which case they ought to be laid in more horizontally than in the case of a wall facing the south. Mr. Glendinning recommends all peach walls to be covered with horizontal copper wires, extended longitudinally at six inches or seven inches distance, and fastened to cast-iron eyes driven into the wall. The advantage is, that a man can tie two trees to the wires with bast ligaments, in the same time that he can nail one tree to the bricks. The chief advantage of wiring the walls, however, is not the saving of time, but of the face of the bricks or the mortar joints of the walls, which are disfigured and destroyed by incessant nailing. When nails and shreds are used, the latter should be of a darker colour, and narrower than are generally used, because they look neater, and they last long enough, as they are never applied a second time. Where the peach is grown only for tarts it may be tried as an espalier or standard. In the midland and southern counties such trees would ripen a crop. Where there is a choice of plants from a nursery, trees three or four years trained, if grafted on plum stocks, may be chosen, and the trees, if carefully removed in October or November, will bear a few fruit next year. In planting never dig a pit, because, by the sinking of the loose soil, the tree will in two or three years be much too deep; spread the roots carefully out on the surface of the border, and cover them three inches with soil. This is the best mode of planting all fruit trees and fruit shrubs whatever, which are planted on newly-trenched ground. Where a wall to be covered with peaches is upwards of twelve feet high, riders may be planted as before recommended, and these should always be trees which have been several years trained, the object being to cover the walls as soon as possible. Permanent dwarf trees may be planted from ten to twenty feet apart, according as the wall is twelve feet or fifteen feet in height.

Mode of Bearing, Pruning, &c.—The blossom-buds in all the different varieties of peach, nectarine, and almond are produced almost exclusively on the wood of the preceding year; and that wood seldom produces blossom a second time. There are, however, occasional small spurs produced on two-year-old wood, but these cannot be reckoned on. The great art in pruning the peach, therefore, is to produce an annual crop of young wood all over the tree, which can only be done by shortening back lateral shoots on every part of it. In the course of the spring and summer, all the shoots that are not wanted to bear the following year should be disbudded—that is, the buds entirely removed as soon as they begin to expand; and in the course of the winter pruning following, all the shoots left ought to be shortened according to their strength and situation, the weakest cut to one or two buds, the less weak to one-half or more of their length, and the strongest shortened one-fourth or one-third of their length. According to the commoner modes of fan-training, these shoots are left all over the tree, as equally as can be done by the eye, or as the shoots produced admit of; but, according to Seymour's mode of training, they are left at regular and fixed distances, and the buds being all removed between these fixed points, no laterals are produced anywhere else; so that the tree once fully formed on this system, nothing can be more regular than its future treatment. Notwithstanding these advantages, Seymour's system has not been adopted to such an extent as might have been expected, and perfectly-formed trees continue rare.

Mr. Callow's Mode of Training.—By the common fan manner of training, it is found that the lower branches soon become weak, from having been laid in at a less angle than the others, which deprives them of their due proportion of sap. By turning up the extremities of the branches, so as to give all an equal inclination and equal curvature, all parts of the tree may be maintained in equal vigour. By the adoption of this very simple and natural system of training, Mr. Glendinning, who adopted it extensively at Bicton in 1832, observes, various inexplicable failures will be avoided; such as premature decay, an unequal quantity of young wood in the centre of the tree, and the constant and grievous calamity of losing the entire under limbs, which completely disfigures the tree for ever. Hayward's mode of training is founded on the same principle—viz., that the sap will always flow in the greatest quantity to the most vertical buds.

Shortening the Young Wood of the Peach.—This is practised in all the different modes of training that are or ever have been used in Britain. The effect of shortening the shoots of the peach is not merely to throw more sap into the fruit, but to add vigour to the tree generally, by increasing the power of the roots relatively to the branches. The peach being a short-lived tree, were it allowed to expend all the power of its accumulated sap every year, it would soon exhaust itself, and die of old age; as the standard peach-trees do in a few years in the unpruned American orchards, and in those of Italy, and as the almond does in the neighbourhood of Lyons and Vienna. No tree is so apt as the peach to produce over-luxuriant shoots, technically water-shoots, or gourmands. These may always be known by the extraordinary vigour of their commencement, which is almost always from latent buds after the regular buds of the tree have been developed. These buds ought to be rubbed off immediately, and as fast as they appear, in order to throw the sap which would have been wasted by them into the other parts of the tree; or if the entire tree is too strong, the shoots may be left to grow, care being taken to disleaf them as fast as they advance, in order that no new sap may be generated. Besides these over-luxuriant shoots, others will arise not suitably situated; as when they come on the main stem, or on the fronts of the branches, technically fore-right shoots; all of which ought to be rubbed off, retaining only such as are required to bear fruit the following year, or may be wanted to supply the place of a branch which has been or is to be cut out; or to cover the upper portion of walls that are not yet furnished. What is called the summer pruning of peach-trees, commences as early in spring as the leaf-buds can be distinguished from the blossom-buds, when all that are not wanted of either should be rubbed off; and it continues till the fall of the leaf, immediately after which the winter pruning may be performed, but should not be deferred later than February. In winter pruning the rule, as in all similar cases, is to cut to a leaf-bud, and as this sometimes is situated between twin blossom-buds, care must be taken not to injure the latter, as it is in such situations that the fruit is produced with least expense of sap to the tree; the branch attracting sap to the fruit from the root, and also returning sap to it from the leaves.

In summer pruning the peach in cold, late situations, it is found that stopping the shoots, when they are an inch or two in length, facilitates the production of blossom-buds and the ripening of the wood. The French method of disbudding in spring and summer, and pinching off with the finger and thumb in the latter season, instead of leaving the young shoots to become woody, and afterwards using the knife, and also their mode of pinching off the blossom-buds, instead of allowing more blossoms than are wanted to set their fruit, and afterwards thinning it out, and of taking out all the leaf-buds not wanted as soon as they have swelled a little, so as to have very few shoots to remove, has been imitated by the cultivators of fruit trees in pots, and a modification of this pinching system would be useful on walls. A French gardener seldom uses his knife to a peach-tree in the summer season ; and, indeed, if he were to allow as much of the strength of the tree to run to waste in fruits to be thinned out, and shoots to be cut away in winter, his borders, which are narrow, shallow, and poor compared with those in British gardens, would be unable to support the tree.

Thinning the fruit must be attended to when the blossoms have not been thinned, or not thinned sufficiently : it should commence when the fruit are about the size of large peas, and be continued till the stoning season is over. Healthy trees may be allowed to ripen four peaches to every square foot. The smaller the number and the larger the size, the less will the tree be exhausted in proportion to the weight of fruit produced; for, as we have already observed, a greater exhaustion is produced by the seed and stone than by their fleshy envelope. Ten dozen of peaches, weighing 20 lbs., will exhaust a tree nearly twice as much as five dozen amounting to the same weight.

Treatment of the Peach Border.—The peach, as well as most other wall-fruit trees, is commonly planted in borders far too deep and too rich. If a good loamy soil from the surface of an old pasture-ground can be procured, and if the border is not cropped, it will require no manure for several years. If the soil is either poor at first, or becomes poor, bone manure may be applied, as decomposing slowly; or if the trees become weak, the surface may be annually mulched with stable dung. All fruit-tree borders should be occasionally forked up gently ; but no spade should ever be used for this purpose, not even among gooseberry-bushes ; for more injury is done by it than most people are aware of. No vegetables should ever be cultivated in fruit-tree borders, more especially none that require manure. Throughout the summer the peach border will require occasional watering in dry weather, but water ought to be withheld when the fruit is ripening.

Over luxuriant peach-trees may be reduced by disleafing, root-pruning, or, what is perhaps the best mode, especially if the tree has been too deeply planted, or that effect has been produced by the sinking of the tree or the raising of the border, by taking up and replanting, bringing the roots within six inches of the surface. The operation may be performed in autumn immediately after the fall of the leaf; and during next summer the surface of the border should be well mulched to retain moisture and encourage the production of fibres.

Old decaying peach-trees may sometimes be renovated by cutting them down and renewing the soil, but in general it is far better to root them out and plant young trees.

Protecting Peach-trees during Winter and Spring.—In cold elevated situations some gardeners protect the branches of their peach-trees from severe frost by tucking in among them branches of broom, spruce, fen, birch, or beech, which serve to check the radiation of heat from the wall. Others, when the branches are frozen, water them well before sunrise, which, when the vegetable tissue is not too far ruptured by frost, saves the branches from injury by thawing them more gradually than the sun would do. This mode is only useful when the trees are slightly frozen. Once the tender tissues are ruptured by the expansive energy of frost, nothing can mend them again. The great thing is to protect the trees with some resisting material or frost-proof screens. A succession of rough straw bands hung a foot from the wall has been found pretty effective. One of the best protections of this character is afforded by the leaves of common fern, tucked in along the shoots as shown in fig. 371. The stalk of the leaf

Fig. 371.

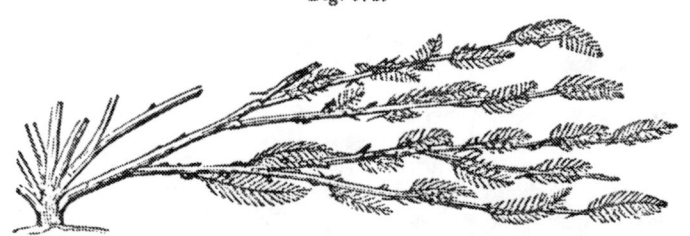

Branch of a peach-tree, with the young wood protected by fern.

is introduced in a shred at the base of the lateral shoot which is to bear the fruit, and the point of it is brought to the point of the lateral; it is there wound once or twice round the nail near the point of the shoot, taking care to reserve an inch or two of the point of the frond to be turned in between the point of the shoot and the wall, which is a sufficient fastening if properly done. As soon as the fruit is set the fern is removed.

A more efficient mode, however, of protecting the peach and all other wall-fruit trees, is by a thin canvas covering let down from a temporary wooden coping, as used in the Horticultural Society's Garden. Another very good mode is to fix iron rods horizontally to a temporary coping, from which bunting is suspended by rings; each piece of bunting is of the size of the tree; and in the day-time it is drawn from the sides to the middle, and fastened to the wall till near sunset, when it is spread out again. A very efficient mode is to cover the wall with double netting, and allow it to remain on till the fruit is fairly set. This mode dispenses with much daily labour, and, like the thin canvas, protects the blossoms from the frequently too powerful rays of the sun, which, striking against a south wall, is more than the peach, as a standard in its native country, has to bear at the blossoming period of the season. Most of these methods have now given place to glass walls, or moveable screens of glass, which have the great merit of being water-tight, and can readily be made air-proof. Glass screens in skilful hands can hardly fail to ensure a crop, and in the end are the cheapest of all protecting expedients.

Growing the Peach on a Flued Wall.—The fires should not be applied until the trees are in flower. The internal heat is most useful in resisting the frost. They likewise render good service in accelerating the ripening of the fruit and wood in autumn. The maturation of the wood may, in some cases in low wet lying localities, require the border to be thatched to throw off heavy rains, and lessen the flow of moisture to the shoots.

The acceleration of the ripening of a crop of peaches on a common wall has been effected by covering the border, to the width of five or six feet from the bottom of the wall, with tiles; the reflection of the heat from which has been found to ripen the fruit in the lower part of the wall, a fortnight before that on the upper part. The retardation of a crop may be effected by interposing a screen of canvas, or boards, or any other convenient medium between the trees and the sun. It should, however, be placed merely as a screen, and not as a preventive against the escape of radiant heat from the wall and ground, a principal object in spring covering; when retardation is required, the screen should be placed so as to intercept the sun's rays, leaving at the same time an opening at top for the escape of radiant heat.

Gathering should take place a day or two before the fruit is to be used, and before it is dead ripe, and it should be laid on clean paper in the fruit-room. Peaches may be gathered in the heat of the day without any deterioration of flavour; in this respect they are very different from such northern fruits as the gooseberry, currant, and strawberry, which should be gathered in the morning. Provision for the dropping of ripe fruit should be made by the suspension of netting, or by providing a soft bed of hay or moss, to save it from bruising.

Diseases, Insects, &c.—The peach and nectarine are liable to the honey-dew, mildew, gum, blister, and canker. The mildew may be destroyed by watering the leaves and dusting them with sulphur; but little can be done with other diseases, excepting taking care that the regimen is suitable. The blister is produced by cold when the leaves are just expanding, and it thickens and distorts them in such a manner as to prevent the proper elaboration of the sap. Nothing can be done with them but taking them off, as soon as warmer weather favours the production of healthier foliage. Lifting the trees and replanting them in fresh soil, and taking care that the shoots are annually thoroughly ripened, will check incipient canker and gum, and enable trees tainted with these diseases to continue bearing for some years longer than they otherwise would have done. The red spider, the chermes, the black and green aphis, and the coccus, attack the peach. The last should be washed off by syringing with soft-soap and water, or with clear water, and a hard brush. The chermes is the cause of the leaves rising into unsightly red blister-like tubercles, and can only be destroyed by the use of tobacco-water, which, after it has taken effect, may be washed off with clear water. For the other insects mentioned, washing abundantly with lime or soot-water, or even with common clear water, will in general keep them under. In order to destroy the eggs of insects which may be deposited on the branches, many gardeners wash them over after the spring pruning with a mixture of lime-water, so thick as to act like whitewash, and form an incrustation on the shoots, which prevents or retards the hatching of the eggs by the exclusion of air; others use a mixture of soft-soap, sulphur, lime, and soot, which destroys the eggs; and some use soft-soap and sulphur alone. In general, however, where the trees and soil are in a good state, and their treatment proper, the free use of clear water will answer the purpose of all other washes. Woodlice, earwigs, the large blue fly, and wasps, attack the fruit when it is ripening, and may be trapped by means of bundles of bean-stalks or reeds, flower-pots partially stuffed with hay, and glasses or bottles of sugared water. (See the Chapter on Insects.)

The essential points of peach-culture are :—Use a strong loam for the border; never crop it; add no manure; keep the trees thin of wood by disbudding and the early removal of useless wood; shorten each shoot according to its strength, at the spring pruning; elevate the ends of the leading branches so that they may all form the same curvilinear inclination with the horizon; and, what is of the utmost importance in the culture of the peach, at all times keep the trees in a clean and healthy state.

Forcing the Peach and Nectarine.—See p. 476.

The Almond.

The almond (Amygdalus, L.; Amandier, Fr.; Mandelbaum, Ger.), is a deciduous tree, a native of Persia and other Eastern countries, closely resembling the peach, and supposed to be that fruit in its unimproved state. There are several kinds—the common or sweet almond (A. communis, L.), and the bitter almond (A. c. amara, Dec.), also what is called the large-fruited and the thin-shelled. A white and a scarlet double flowering almond have also been lately introduced. Both kinds are cultivated in the south of Europe, and in the Levant. The kernels are much used in cookery, confectionery, perfumery, and medicine. The varieties best deserving culture are, the tender-shelled, the fruit of which is small; the sweet, which is larger; and the Jordan, which is also large and sweet. These and all the other varieties are propagated by budding on the plum, and sometimes on seedling almonds for dry situations. The trees are commonly grown as standards, and as such will ripen fruit in fine seasons as far north as York; but at Edinburgh they require a wall. In Britain, the tree is more valued for its blossoms than for its fruit; but nevertheless, in every suburban garden, where there is room, there ought to be a tree or two for the latter purpose, as well as several for the former.

The Apricot.

The apricot (Armeniaca vulgaris, Lam.) is a low deciduous tree, a native of Caucasus, very extensively distributed through the countries of the East, and cultivated in European gardens from the time of the Romans. In British gardens the apricot is the earliest wall-fruit, flowering with the sloe in March, ripening about the end of July, and supplying the dessert till the middle of September. Its uses are the same as the peach; in addition to which it makes excellent marmalades, jellies, and preserves, and tarts even when gathered green, and of the smallest size. In the Oases of Upper Egypt the fruit of a particular variety, called the Musch-Musch, is produced in great quantities and dried, so as to form an article of commerce.

Varieties.—These are much less numerous than those of the peach. The following selection includes Oullin's Early Peach, Peach, Sardinian, Alberge de Montgamet, Kaisha, Large Red, Rivers' Golden Drop, Royal, Moorpark, and Breda.

Apricots for the Walls of a Cottage.—The best is the Moorpark, which in Lincolnshire and other parts of England bears well on the gable-ends, and ripens early in consequence of the heat communicated to the wall by the flue. The fruit is thinned, and the thinnings are sent to market for tarts, and afterwards the ripe fruit, the whole producing twenty shillings or upwards. Next to the Moorpark the Breda and the Alberge de Montgamet, Sardinian, and Royal, may be taken as the hardiest, and the Red Masculine as the earliest.

Propagation, Nursery Culture, &c.—For dwarfs, the apricot is generally budded on the Mussel plum, or any other variety; but the Breda, when intended for a standard, is budded on the St. Julian plum, which produces a strong clean stem. The Moorpark is sometimes budded on an apricot stock; and when it is wanted to have very dwarf plants some recommend budding one variety on another that has been previously budded on a Mirabelle plum. As the apricot is a very early plant, budding may be commenced sooner than in the case of the peach. The nursery culture is the same as for that tree, and the plants remove equally well after being three or four years trained.

Final Planting, Pruning, &c.—In the warmer parts of the country an east or west aspect is preferred to the south, the heat of which brings forward the blossom too early, and renders the fruit mealy. Where the fruit is only wanted for tarts it may be grown as a standard or as an espalier. It would well repay to give standards a winter pruning in order to regulate the branches, and moderately shorten the young shoots to prevent their becoming naked as they elongate—a tendency which both standard apricots and peaches have in this climate. The blossom is produced chiefly on the young shoots of the last year, but partly also upon spurs which rise on the two or three years old shoots. The fan method of training is generally preferred; or the horizontal manner, with the branches elevated so as to form an angle of 25° with the horizon. In almost every other respect, what has been advanced respecting the pruning, training, and general management of the peach will apply to the apricot. The chief point of difference in the treatment required for the two trees is founded on the precocity of the apricot, which exposes the blossom to unusual danger. In consequence of the tree blooming so early, its blossoms, particularly in the case of young trees, are extremely liable to drop off in setting. This is not to be wondered at, when it is considered that the ground is frequently at the time (March) in as cold a state as at any period of the whole season, neither the sun's heat nor the warm rains having reached so far below the surface as to warm the soil in contact with the roots; and thus whilst the latter are in a medium perhaps a little above freezing, the tops, exposed to a bright sun against a wall, are at that period of the season occasionally in a temperature as high as $90°$ or $100°$ Fahr. The injurious effects of this disparity must be sufficiently obvious to every one, and the only remedy to be adopted is to have a very complete drainage below the roots, and the whole soil of the border, not retentive, but of a pervious nature. If it could also be kept perfectly dry previous to the commencement of vegetation, and then only allowed to receive the rain when warm, avoiding the cooling effects of melting snow or hail, the tree would thus be placed under circumstances comparatively more natural. Thatching the border, therefore, for the sake of the roots, and covering the branches with netting, hay ropes, &c., may very properly be adopted with the apricot, in all low, cold, moist situations. Naked stems or branches of apricot-trees trained against a wall are apt to be scorched to death in summer, and hence limbs or whole trees are sometimes lost. In order to prevent this, it is advisable to train shoots so as to protect such naked parts from the direct rays of the sun. The fruit should be gathered before it is thoroughly ripe, otherwise it is apt to become mealy. The tree is much less subject to insects than the peach, probably from the more coriaceous nature of its bark and leaves. It is impatient of heat in forcing, but fruits well in pots in cool orchard or peach houses.

The Fig.

The fig (Ficus Carica, L.) is a low deciduous tree, a native of Asia and Barbary, in situations near the sea, and naturalized in Italy and the south of Europe, where it has been cultivated since the time of the Romans, as it has been in Greece and Egypt from the earliest ages. In British gardens the fig is chiefly cultivated under glass; but it will arrive at maturity on the open wall in warm situations, and indeed wherever the grape will ripen. The fruit is of no use, except in a ripe state, when it is much prized for the dessert by many persons, while others prefer the dried figs of commerce. The fig is much cultivated in the south of France and Italy, where the varieties are numerous. Among the best of those grown in British gardens are the following: Brown Turkey, Brunswick, Marseilles, Small Brown Ischia, Black Ischia, White Ischia, Brown Prolific, Golden.

A great many figs have recently been introduced, most of them so recently that we cannot speak of their qualities from experience.

Over fifty so-called varieties have recently been received, and a large collection is grown at the gardens of the Horticultural Society at Chiswick.

Propagation, Culture, &c.—The fig roots readily from cuttings of the ripened wood, and it may be also budded or grafted, and trained in the nursery like any other fruit tree. Young plants, however, of two or three years' growth are preferable for removal, as the fig is then very abundantly furnished with fibrous roots. It requires a south wall, and a light soil thoroughly drained, to which, however, water of the same temperature as the soil must be abundantly supplied as soon as the first leaves are expanded, when the fruit is setting; for if the roots are too dry at that time, the fruit will drop off. The fan mode of training is most suitable; and as the fruit in the open air is produced on the points of last year's shoots, a number of such shoots should be preserved all over the tree. A good plan is to back a half standard against a wall, and allow it to produce a thicket of short-jointed bearing wood. Immense quantities of fruit may be ripened on such trees in warm nooks and corners. (See on this subject what has already been stated on the treatment of the fig under glass.) The ripening of the fig might be accelerated by planting it against a flued wall, and by protecting the wood by fern, spruce branches, or hay-rope netting. In some parts of the south of England the fig is grown on espaliers, and as a standard; and when the winters are mild, it bears abundantly when so treated. It succeeds remarkably well at Tarring and Lancing in a loamy soil on chalk; and in the gardens of Arundel Castle, in the same county, the standard fig-trees are as large as full-grown apple-trees. Care should be taken in gathering the fruit not to destroy the bloom, nor to crush it by laying one above another. They will keep good only for two or three days.

The Pomegranate.

The pomegranate (Punica Granatum, L.), is a low deciduous tree, in its form and mode of growth not unlike the common hawthorn. It is a native of the south of Europe and other warm countries; and has been long cultivated in the north of France as a greenhouse tree, in the same manner as the orange, for the beauty of its fruit. Its cultivation is becoming more common in England, some of the dwarf double-flowering varieties making very showy objects in pots. As it is a most ornamental fruit both on the tree and at table, and as it can be brought to maturity against a south wall in situations where the fig will ripen, we would recommend one plant to be tried wherever there is room. Plants of the cultivated pomegranate can be obtained from any nursery. It is propagated by layers and cuttings and by grafting on the common sort. It may be trained in the fan manner, taking care to leave a sufficient number of lateral spurs, on the points of the shoots proceeding from which the blossom is produced. The ripening of the fruit might be greatly accelerated by planting the tree against a flued wall, and as the tree is greatly injured by severe winters, it might be advisable to protect the wood during severe weather.

The Peruvian Cherry.

The Peruvian cherry (Physalis peruviana), is a biennial, a native of Buenos Ayres, Lima, and other parts of South America, where it grows from six feet to ten feet high. It is occasionally cultivated in British stoves and forcing-houses for its fruit, which is produced through the winter as well as during summer, and tastes exactly like that of the hardy species. It is commonly trained against a trellis, on the back of an early-forced vinery or peach-house; but, treated like the capsicum, or the love-apple, it will ripen its fruit in abundance during summer, against a south wall.

Tropical or Sub-tropical Fruits.

The fruits which we include in this section are such as require to be grown entirely or chiefly under glass—viz., the pine-apple, banana, the orange and lemon tribe, the melon and cucumber, and some fruits not in general cultivation, but which may be tried by the curious amateur.

The Pine-apple.

The pine-apple (Ananassa sativa, Lindl.), is a low evergreen shrub, a native of South America, the natural history of which having been given on p. 417, we have only here to name the varieties best worth cultivating:—Baroness Rothschild, Ripley Queen, Smooth-leaved Cayenne, Globe, New Black Jamaica, the Queen, the Moscow Queen, the Black Jamaica, the Brown Sugar-loaf, the Black Antigua, the Enville, the White Providence, the Trinidad. Among these, Queens, Smooth-leaved Cayennes, and Black Jamaicas, are by far the most useful, and of the highest quality; the Queen being looked upon as the main summer and early autumn fruit, the Jamaica and Smooth Cayenne for winter and spring.

Culture.—This is given at length at p. 418, and we shall here give a general summary. Plant in turfy, rich, but not adhesive loam; plunge the pots in tan or leaves, or some other medium that will produce and retain heat. At no period, either of winter or summer, allow the temperature of the air of the house to fall lower than 65°, but in summer let it rise as high as 80° or 85°; the bottom heat should never be under 70°, and it may rise as high as 85° when the atmosphere is at or above that temperature; in summer give air early in the morning, and shut up at three in the afternoon with a high temperature, syringing the plants overhead. Grow the Queen pines by themselves, the Black pines by themselves, as they require a higher temperature, and the large pines also by themselves, as they require more room than the other kinds. Treated in this manner pines will seldom be infested with insects; but if they should, the remedies have been already given. To cause a pine to show fruit, give it a rest and a check by withholding water for a considerable time, till the leaves have become quite lax and almost flagging, and then supply water and heat liberally.

The Banana.

The banana (Musa sapientum, L.), is a scitamineous plant, the natural history and culture of which have been already given, p. 511. Every plant throws up a single flower-stem, which flowers and fruits; after which the plant dies, and is succeeded by a sucker. The fruit of none of the varieties contains seed, and hence these suckers are the only means of propagation. There are several species or varieties, but those best worth cultivating in Britain are the M. s. Cavendishii (syn. M. s. chinensis), and the M. s. Dacca, both already noticed, and the M. s. St. Helenensis, to be afterwards described. Several other kinds have been grown in the different public and private gardens of Britain.

Musa sapientum, var. St. Helenensis, the St. Helena banana, grows to the height of fourteen feet. The usual weight of each bunch of fruit is from 60 lbs to 80 lbs.

M. s. var. Dacca, the Dacca banana, is considered by some as next in value to the St. Helena variety. Its average height of stem is seven feet, producing clusters from 10 lbs. to 20 lbs. weight. The fruit is smaller and drier than that of the St. Helena banana, but perhaps rather higher flavoured. This variety, when allowed plenty of room in a congenial climate, grows twenty feet high, with a stem measuring three feet in circumference at the base; leaves ten feet long and three feet broad. Bunches of fruit have been produced weighing above 50 lbs. The fruit is more pointed than that of M. s. Cavendishii, and is of excellent quality.

M. s. var. Cavendishii, syn. M. s. chinensis, the Duke of Devonshire's banana, is valuable on account of its fruiting at a small size, and within a year from the time the suckers are taken off. This is the most useful variety that can be grown, as it requires so much less headroom than any of the other fruiting sorts.

Culture, &c.—Twenty plants of Musa s. Cavendishii may be fruited within the year, in a pit thirty feet by fifteen feet, and the weight of fruit produced may be from 400 lbs. to 500 lbs. They also grow and fruit exceedingly well either in pots, tubs, or planted out in a common plant-stove. The summer temperature for the banana is 65° min. and 85° max., or more with sun heat. Winter temperature, 65° min. and 75° max. The bananas that ripen in winter are but little inferior to the summer fruit. They thrive best, at all seasons, with a bottom heat of from 80° to 90°, though they will grow and ripen fruit without it.

The Melon.

The melon (Cucumis Melo, L.) is a trailing or climbing tendrilled annual, the history and culture of which will be found at p. 492, and the following are the best varieties at present in cultivation.

Melons with Scarlet Flesh.—Moreton Hall, Turner's Scarlet Gem, Royal Ascot, International, Netted Scarlet, Hunt's Medium Scarlet.

Melons with Green Flesh.—Bromham Hall, Queen Emma, Wills's Pine-apple, Perkins' Hybrid, Cashmere, Golden Perfection, Dr. Hogg, Burghley Green Flesh, Bailey's Eclipse.

Water Melons.—The water melon is the Cucurbita citrullus, a trailing annual, producing a large, round, smooth, dark-green fruit, with dark seeds. It is full of watery juice, which is refreshing, but almost without flavour. It is much cultivated in Italy and other parts of the south of Europe, but very rarely in England. The foliage is very ornamental, and the shoots extend to a great length. The time for ripening melons to a high degree of perfection in Britain extends from about the middle of June to the middle or latter end of September. Ripened before or after these periods the flavour is inferior, for want of sun.

The Cucumber.

The cucumber (Cucumis sativus, L.) is a trailing or climbing tendrilled annual, of which we have already given the history and culture, p. 498. The varieties in cultivation are continually changing, but those considered the best, at the present time, are the following:—Lord Kenyon's Favourite, Telegraph, Dr. Livingstone, Long Gun, Cuthill's Black Spine, Conqueror of the West, Berkshire Champion, Barr's Winter Prolific, James Cuthill, Nichol's Prolific, Dr. Hogg, and a host of others. Of ridge cucumbers Donald Beaton and Stockwood Selected Long Ridge are the best long sorts, and the Russian the best pickling variety.

The Pumpkin and Gourd.

The pumpkin, or more properly pompion, and gourd (Cucurbita, L.) are trailing or climbing tendrilled annuals, natives of tropical climates, and long in cultivation, both in the old and new world, for the fruit. This, in some varieties, is used in a ripe state, and in others before it is fully grown, in soups, stews, pies, tarts, boiled or fried, and as a substitute for greens or spinach. In Hungary sugar has been obtained from the gourd at the rate of 100 lbs. to between 2000 lbs. and 3000 lbs. of pumpkins; and an excellent edible oil is obtained there from the seeds, at the rate of 1 lb. of oil to 5 lbs. of seeds. The tender points of the shoots may in many cases be substituted for the fruit, or used as greens or spinach. The kinds in cultivation are very numerous, but the leading sorts are as follows:—

The pumpkin, or pompion (C. Pepo, L.): Large, roundish, smooth, green, striped or blotched with white. The oldest variety in cultivation in England; tender and excellent in an unripe state as a substitute for greens, and mixed with apples in pies, but not nearly so good when fully ripe.

Spanish pumpkin: Middle size, somewhat flattened; skin green, smooth, hard; flesh firm.

The vegetable marrow (C. ovifera, var. L.): Under the middle size, oval, five inches to eight inches long; pale yellow; flesh tender till the fruit is ripe, when it becomes stringy. One of the best gourds in cultivation when used in a young state, and before the seeds begin to be matured. The sweet gourd of Brazil closely resembles this variety, both in form and properties.

There is also an excellent green variety of marrow. Hibberd's Early Prolific fruits very early, and produces a succession of delicate fruit, about the size of a turkey's egg. The Custard marrow is likewise beautiful in form and very rich in flavour.

The Mammoth Gourd, syn. American Gourd (C. maxima, Pepo, Dec.) is very large, sometimes weighing 160 lbs., and one has been grown of the enormous weight of 245 lbs., at Luscombe, in Devonshire; round, skin yellow, flesh deep yellow, solid. Used as a substitute for turnips, carrots, &c., in soups and broths, and for potatoes and other vegetables, with meat. It is only used when ripe, and in that state will keep several months, even though a portion should be cut for use every day. The Harrison pumpkin is a new American variety of the Mammoth, supposed to be the most productive known.

The Squash-melon Pumpkin, or Bush Gourd (C. Melopepo, L.) is of middle size, round, skin yellow when ripe. Chiefly used in a green state when of the size of a hen's egg. Much cultivated in America as food for men, cattle, and swine. The Early Orange Squash is mentioned by Kenrick, 'American Orchardist,' 1841, p. 370, as a new summer variety; very early, and of superior quality. The Canada Crook-neck, he says, is, without doubt, superior to any and all others for a late or main crop; the fruit, in a dry and mild temperature, will keep till the following summer.

The Turban Pumpkin, or Turk's-cap (C. Pepo, var. clypeata, L.); the Warted Gourd (C. verrucosa, L.); the Orange Gourd (C. aurantia, L.); the Bottle Gourd, or False Calabash (C. Lagenaria, L., Lagenaria vulgaris, var. turbinata, Ser.); and various other sorts to be found in nurserymen's catalogues, are cultivated chiefly as ornamental fruits. Immense numbers of curious warted and other varieties have made their appearance of late years, partly from the stimulus given by a prize offered for the best collection in 1868. The following are the varieties offered for sale by Messrs. Barr and Sugden, who took the prize on that occasion, in their Catalogue for 1871 :—

Ornamental Gourds.

Benincasa cerifera.
Cucumis Arada.
,, dipsaceus.
,, Figarei
,, flexuosus (Serpent Gourd).
,, grossularia.
,, melo chito.
,, ,, large fruited.
,, ,, odoratissimus.
,, metuliferus.
,, pancherianus globosus.
,, ,, longus.
Cucurbita moschata argyrosperma.
,, de la Floride.

Cucurbita maxima verrucosa.
,, Melopepo Hectoriana.
,, Pepo aurantiiformis.
,, ,, pyriformis.
,, ,, ,, viridi annulata.
,, ,, rouge de Crimée.
,, perennis.
,, radicans.
Involucraria Lepiniana.
Lagenaria angolensis.
,, enormis.
,, gigantea.
,, grosse pélerine.
,, hou-lo de Chine.

The fruit of the Orange gourd is bitter; and that of the Bottle gourd is said by Dr. Royle to be poisonous. The Bottle gourd is at first long and cylindrical, like a cucumber, but as it ripens it swells chiefly at the upper end, thus acquiring the form of a Venetian bottle. After being gathered, the end of the neck where it was attached to the plant is cut off, the pulp and seeds carefully taken out, and the interior repeatedly washed, so as to remove the bitter principle which constitutes the poison.

Culture.—All the sorts are propagated exclusively by seeds, which, being large, require to be covered with nearly an inch of soil. They may be sown in April, in a hotbed, under glass, or in a stove, to raise plants for transferring to the open garden, at the end of May, under a warm aspect; or for planting out in the middle of May, on a ridge of hot dung, under a hand-glass or half-shelter; otherwise sow at the beginning of May, under a hand-glass, without bottom heat, for transplanting into a favourable situation; or sow three weeks later (after the 20th) at once in the open garden, under a south wall, for the plants to remain. The smaller-fruited kinds do best trained to an upright pole or trellis. As the runners extend five feet or more, peg down at a joint, and they will take root. Water copiously whenever warm weather without showers makes the ground arid; and thin out the shoots where they are crowded. With those kinds the fruit of which is gathered green, by no means allow any to ripen, because that would stop the production of young fruit; and where the fruit is to be used ripe, or where it is allowed to ripen for the production of seed, do not allow more than one, if the kind is large, or two or three, if it is middle-sized or small, to ripen on a plant. Where the walks of a garden are covered with wire trellis-work, of the kind indicated in figs. 120 and 121, they may be covered with the smaller-fruited species, and even with cucumbers and water-melons during summer when shade is desirable for the walk; while, in winter, the trellis will be left naked to admit the sun and air to dry the gravel or flag-stone.

The Tomato, the Egg-plant, and the Capsicum.

The tomato or love-apple (Lycopersicum esculentum, Dunal) is a trailing annual, a native of South America, which when raised in a hotbed, and afterwards planted against a wall in the open air, will ripen its fruit in England. The fruit, which is an irregular red or yellow berry from one inch to four inches in diameter, is seldom eaten raw, but when ripe is used in soups and sauces, and for other purposes in confectionery and cookery; and in a green state it is pickled. The juice is made into a sauce, which is considered excellent both for meat and fish. The best variety is the Trophy Tomato, though others, such as the Large Red, the tree variety, New Giant, New Rose, and Early Prolific, are good. The Cherry-currant, and small red and yellow are likewise interesting or ornamental varieties. The seeds may be sown in a hotbed in March, and transplanted once or twice into pots, so as to be ready to transfer to the base of a south wall, or any other situation where it will enjoy the full influence reflected sun heat, about the middle or end of May, according to the situation and the season. The vacant spaces between fruit trees will answer for this purpose; or a temporary wall of boards, five feet high, may be erected; or, in warm situations, they may be trained on a steep bank, raised artificially to an angle of 45°, and covered with flat tiles. The plants have a very beautiful effect on an espalier; but they only ripen their fruit there in the warmest summers. The fruit will be increased in size, and its maturity accelerated, by stopping every shoot after it has produced one cluster of fruit, and by judiciously thinning the leaves. The fruit ripens between August and October, and if hung up in a dry airy part of the summer fruit-room, it will continue fit for use till the end of November. One ripe fruit reserved for seed will contain enough for any garden whatever: cleanse the seeds from the pulp, dry them thoroughly, and preserve them in paper till next spring.

The Egg-plant, Mad Apple, or Jew's Apple (Solanum Melongena) is an erect branchy annual, a native of Africa, and cultivated in British gardens for its fruit, partly as an ornament, and partly for its uses in cookery. The plant grows about two feet high; the fruit is oval, and about the size of a hen's egg, or larger when cultivated with extraordinary care. There are several varieties, such as the White, Black, Golden-striped, and Chinese Giants of different colours. The fruits are of different sizes as well as colours, and great quantities of them are used in Paris and other Continental cities. They are divided lengthways, and fried in oil with pepper, salt, and the crumbs of toasted bread, and in various other ways which are detailed at length in French cookery books. In the garden the plant receives the same treatment as the tomato, though it requires a greater degree of heat to ripen it, and should therefore always be trained against a south wall. The fruit hung up will keep through the winter, and therefore the seed need not be taken out till wanted for sowing.

The Capsicum, or Bird pepper (Capsicum, L.): There are three or more species in cultivation for their fruit, natives of tropical climates; the annual capsicum, the Spanish, or Guinea pepper (C. annuum, L.), a native of South America, growing in our stoves about two feet high, and producing pods, long or short, round, long, or cherry-shaped, and red or yellow, in the autumn of the same year in which the seed is sown; the Bell pepper (C. grossum, W.), a biennial, a native of India, producing large red or yellow berries, which remain on through the winter; the Bird pepper (C. baccatum, L.), and the Chilies or Cayenne pepper (C. frutescens, L.). To these the French have lately added another variety, the Tomato capsicum (Piment Tomate, Fr.), the fruit of which is round, yellow, furrowed, twisted like the tomato, and in a green state so mild as to be eaten sliced in salad. This is also the case with the Bullock's-heart variety of the common capsicum, the C. cordiforme of Miller. In the native countries of these plants there are numerous varieties which are cultivated for using green, and for pickling, and for making the well-known cayenne pepper, which is much employed in curries and other preparations. In Britain they are used chiefly for the two former purposes, and for putting into vinegar, which from the fruit being in some places called chilies, is called Chili vinegar. Medicinally, a small portion of the fruit put into a carious tooth is said to give instant relief, and Chili vinegar mixed with barley-water forms an excellent gargle. It is also, from its pungent and digestive properties, the most suitable condiment to all kinds of fish. The ripe fruit ground into powder, as cayenne pepper, is in great request as a condiment in every part of the world, and more especially in hot countries; both in a green and ripe state, it is much used as seasoning, and in the preparation of pickles, and it also forms an excellent pickle of itself. Fresh gathered in a green state, pickled, ripe, or as cayenne pepper, taken during dinner, it prevents flatulency and assists digestion. When ripe, it may be preserved on the plant for several years by hanging it up in a dry and moderately warm room. In some families the green fruit is supplied daily throughout the year, from plants kept in the pine-stove. Some of the varieties, such as the small, round, yellow, and red, make almost as showy plants as the Solanum capsicastrum and other varieties.

Culture of the Capsicum.—The seeds should be sown in March on a hotbed, and transplanted from one pot into another till the middle of June; when in warm parts of the country, the annual sorts may be transferred to a warm situation in the open garden, where they will at least produce fruit fit for pickling; and if trained against a south wall, it will ripen in many situations when the summer proves warm. In less favourable circumstances the plants should be kept in pots and under glass, either in a frame or pit, or in a greenhouse. In this state they will ripen their fruit, which will remain on the annual plants great part of the winter; and that of the biennial and frutescent kinds may be kept in the greenhouse in a fruit-bearing state for two or three years. The market-gardeners about London, who raise immense quantities of capsicums for pickling, transplant first on heat, three inches or four inches apart, and in June plant out in rows, a foot apart and six inches distant in the row. The fruit is gathered and sent to the market as soon as it has attained the proper size; and not being then above half that of the ripe fruit, an immense quantity of pods is produced during August and September. A single ripe pod will produce enough of seed for a small garden, and it need not be separated from it till wanted for sowing.

The Orange Family.

The Orange family (Citrus, L.) includes the sweet orange, bitter orange, bergamot orange, lime, shaddock, sweet lemon, true lemon, and citron. It is very doubtful how far the orange was known to the Romans, though the citron is said to have been cultivated by Palladius in the second century; and it is generally thought that the golden apples of the Hesperides either were, or bore some allusion to, this fruit. One or more of the varieties have been in cultivation as ornamental trees in the royal orangeries of France since the commencement of the fifteenth century, and in the open air in the warmest part of the south of Europe for its fruit, for at least three centuries. In Britain, at the present time, the different species and varieties are cultivated under glass, chiefly as ornamental trees, but in part also for their fruit, which from some gardens is sent regularly to table throughout the greater part of the year.

The common Orange is the C. Aurantium, L. In the year 1500, there was only one orange-tree in France, which had been sown in 1421, at Pampeluna, then the capital of the kingdom of Navarre. After having been taken from Pampeluna to Chantilly, and from Chantilly to Fontainebleau, it was, in 1684, taken to the orangery at Versailles, where it still remains, holding the first rank among the numerous trees there for its shape and beauty, under the name of the Grand Bourbon, François I., &c. From the establishment of the orangery at Versailles, the taste for orange-trees spread extensively in France, till about the middle of the eighteenth century, when it began to give way to a taste for more rare exotics. The oldest orange-trees in England were planted at Beddington, in Surrey, about the end of the sixteenth century, and here as in France it was the most popular tree, till it was supplanted by a taste for plants of other countries, and more especially the plants of the Cape. At present the taste for the orange tribe is reviving, both in France and England. The uses of the fruit of the orange in the dessert, in confectionery, and in medicine, and its flowers in perfumery, are universally known. The more remarkable varieties of the orange are the following: the China, pear-shaped; Nice, tiny-fruited, fingered, blood-red, ribbed, sweet-skinned; Mandarin, and St. Michael's. The last two are by far the best worth cultivating for their fruit. The Mandarin orange (C. nobilis) is small, oblate, with a thin rind, which separates of itself from the pulp—so much so, that when fully ripe, the latter may be shaken about in the inside like the kernels of some nuts. It is originally from China, but is now cultivated in Malta. The flesh is of a deep orange colour, and its juice and flavour superior to those of most varieties. The St. Michael's orange is also small, but the skin instead of being of an orange colour like that of the Mandarin, is of a pale yellow; the fruit is generally without seed, the rind thin, and the pulp extremely sweet. It is the most delicious of all the oranges, and the tree is a great bearer. It is in general cultivation in the Azores, from which it is shipped in large quantities. The Tangerine orange is strongly recommended by some. Mr. Rivers, who has devoted great attention to the orange, and supplies his own table with a succession of choice fruit, grows the following varieties :—

The Bigarade, Seville, or Bitter orange, has elliptic leaves, with a winged stalk, very white flowers, and middle-sized, globose, deep-yellow fruit, the pulp bitter and acid. This is the hardiest variety of the orange, and that which has the largest and most fragrant flowers, which are produced in great abundance. The fruit is chiefly used in making marmalade. The tree is that chiefly grown by the French gardeners for its flowers, to gather for nosegays. The varieties are the Horned, the Female, the Curled-leaved, the Purple, the Double-Flowered, the Seville, the Myrtle-leaved, and the Bizarre. The Curled-leaved Bigarade, has small curled leaves, and thick clusters of flowers at the ends of the branches; the plant is very hardy, and it is that most generally cultivated in France for its flowers, and in Italy and Spain, for both its flowers and its fruit. The Double-flowered Bigarade is prized on account of its fragrant double flowers, which last longer than those which are single. The plant requires a very rich soil. The Seville Bigarade, or Seville orange of the shops, has round dark fruit, with an extremely bitter rind. It is imported from Spain, and used for marmalades, bitter tinctures, candied orange-peel, and for flavouring Curaçoa. The Myrtle-leaved Bigarade, is said to be employed by the Chinese gardeners as an edging to flower-beds, in the same way as box is in this country. The Bizarre Bigarade is a lusus naturæ, with deformed leaves, purplish or white flowers, and fruit half Bigarades, and half lemons or citrons, some having the pulp sweet, and others having it acid and bitter.

The Bergamot orange (C. Bergamia, Poit.), has small flowers and pear-shaped fruit, the whole plant having a peculiar fragrance, much valued by the perfumer, who obtains from the flowers and rind of the fruit his bergamot essences. The rind, first dried and then moistened, is pressed in moulds into small boxes for holding sweetmeats, to which they communicate a bergamot flavour. There are several varieties of this species.

The Lime (C. Limetta, Poit.) has obovate leaves on a wingless stalk, small white flowers, and roundish pale-yellow fruit with a nipple-like termination. The leaves and general habit of the plant resemble those of the lemon; but the acid of the pulp of the fruit, instead of being sharp and powerful, is flat and slightly bitter. It is principally used in flavouring punch and in confectionery. Among the varieties are the Pomo d'Adamo, in which Adam is supposed to have left the marks of his teeth.

The Shaddock (C. decumana, W.) : The leaves are large and winged, and the flowers and fruit very large and roundish; the skin of the fruit is yellow, and the rind white and spongy; the pulp is juicy and sweetish. The plant forms an excellent stock for grafting other kinds upon. The fruit makes a splendid show at table, and is found cooling and refreshing. It has been grown successfully on the open wall in some gardens in Devonshire, with the protection of glass and mats during the winter months, but without artificial heat. M. Poiteau considers the "forbidden fruit" of the shops to be a variety of this species, but others make it a variety of the lemon.

The sweet Lemon (C. Lumia, Poit.) : The fruit has the leaves, the rind, and the flesh of a lemon, but with a sweet pulp. There are many varieties in Italy, but very few are cultivated either in France or England. The flowers differ from those of the lime in being red externally.

The true Lemon (C. Limonum, Poit.) : Leaves ovate-oblong, pale-green with a winged stalk, flowers red externally, fruit pale-yellow, with a juicy and very acid pulp. Unlike the other kinds of citrons, the lemon on the Continent is generally raised from seed, and hence the great difference in quality of the fruit obtained in the shops.

The Citron (C. Medica, L.): Leaves oblong, flowers purple externally; fruit yellow, large, warted, and furrowed; rind spongy and thick, very fragrant; pulp subacid. Supposed to be the Median or Persian apple of the Greeks. As an ornamental tree, it is one of the best of the genus Citrus. A delicate sweetmeat is prepared from the rind of the fruit, and the juice with sugar and water forms lemonade, and is used to flavour punch and negus, like that of the lemon. The Madras citron is the largest and best variety, and has been grown to an enormous size, both in England and Scotland.

Propagation and Culture.—All the kinds will root by cuttings, either of the young wood partially ripened, planted in sand in spring, and covered with a bell-glass; or of ripe wood put in in autumn, kept cool through the winter, and placed on heat when they begin to grow in the spring. Grafting and budding, however, are the usual and best modes of propagation, and the stocks may either be raised from seeds or cuttings; citron and shaddock stocks are esteemed the strongest, and those of the Seville orange the hardiest. For ornament the plants are generally grown in pots or boxes; but for fruit and also for ornament, when the luxuriance of the tree is an object, they will thrive best when planted in free soil in a house devoted to them; or against a flued or conservative wall, to be covered with glass in the winter season. At Beddington they were planted against a wall, and protected by a temporary structure; and in the Duke of Argyll's garden at Whitton, where, Miller informs us, the citron was grown as large and as perfectly ripe as it is in Italy or Spain, the trees were trained against a flued south wall, over which glass covers were put when the weather began to be cold. The finest oranges and lemons in Paris, some years ago, were grown against a wall like peach-trees; and in various parts of Devonshire all the kinds are grown against the open garden walls, and protected during winter, not by glass, but by wooden shutters. In the south of Devonshire, at Luscombe, orange-trees have withstood the winter in the open air upwards of a hundred years, and produced large and fine fruit. All the kinds of Citrus require a loamy soil, richly manured, well drained at bottom, and rendered pervious to water, by the soil being unsifted and mixed with fragments of freestone. When grown in pots or boxes a richer soil, better drained, is required than when the trees are planted in a border. Being evergreens, and the sap in consequence circulating during the winter, the soil, even in mid-winter, ought never to be allowed to become so dry as might be the case were the trees deciduous. When any of the sorts are grown for their fruit for the table, the best mode is to grow them against a wall or trellis, either under glass throughout the year, or against a wall to which sashes can be fitted during the winter months. They may also be grown as standards in a span-roofed house placed in the direction of north and south; and if the situation is warm and sheltered, the roof and sides of such a house may be entirely removed in the summer season, and the ground turfed over, so as to give the trees the appearance of standing on a lawn. Only tall standard trees are well adapted for this purpose. The winter temperature for the orange is 48° with fire heat; but as the season advances it may be 15° or 20° higher; and in summer it may vary between 60° and 80°. The roots should never be kept in a temperature so low as 40°; at 45° a gentle circulation will be maintained, sufficient to prevent the roots from perishing. As all the Citrus tribe grow naturally in woods, and many of them in islands near the sea, a situation somewhat shaded is preferable to one fully exposed to the sun; but a high temperature during summer is essential to the perfect ripening and luscious flavouring of the fruit. Orange-trees will bear exposure to the sun if previously in good health; but in all cases it would be advisable to place a thin canvas screen between them and the rays of the sun when the plants are first set out in summer, and especially when they are trained against a wall. With regard to such plants as are required to flower or fruit freely, exposure to direct solar light will be necessary. In the management of orange-trees in large boxes and tubs, great care is requisite to ascertain that the water reaches the roots of the plants. By using comparatively rough turfy soil, more or less mixed with fragments of stone, balls so compact as not to admit water poured on their surface can hardly occur. When orange-trees in boxes are placed in the open air in the summer season, the situation ought always to be thoroughly sheltered and partially shaded, especially when the trees are first exposed, otherwise the leaves will soon lose their deep green. Good fruit cannot, however, be gathered off trees sheltered under opaque roofs in winter, and removed out of doors in summer. Where fruit is the primary object, the treatment of the orange should be similar to that of the grape-vine.

The Guava, Lo-quat, Granadilla, and other Fruits little known in British Gardens.

The Guava (Psidium, L.) : There are several species, but that which has been found to succeed best in British stoves is Cattley's Guava (P. Cattleyanum, Lindl.), an evergreen shrub or low tree, a native of China, which produces abundance of fruit, about the size of gooseberries, of a purple colour, juicy, and flavoured somewhat like the strawberry. It fruits very well in a large pot in loamy soil, in a light airy situation, and the fruit ripens in autumn or in the winter season. It does well on the back wall of a conservatory or other cool house, is prized by some for dessert, and makes one of the best of jellies.

The Lo-quat or Japan Quince (Eriobotrya japonica, Lindl.) is an evergreen tree from Japan, of which there are some varieties that will stand the open air against a wall; but to ripen fruit they require the heat of the peach-house in summer, and of the greenhouse in winter.

The fruit is highly perfumed and delicious in flavour, and this is one of the handsomest trees for a conservative wall, on account of its fine large foliage.

The Granadilla (Passiflora, L.): There are several species of this genus, the fruit of which may be eaten—viz., the granadilla vine (P. quadrangularis, L.); the apple-fruited granadilla, or sweet calabash (P. maliformis, L.); the laurel-leaved granadilla, or water lemon (P. laurifolia, L.); the flesh-coloured granadilla, (P. incarnata, L.); the large new granadilla (P. macrocarpa); the yellow granadilla (P. glauca); and the purple granadilla (P. edulis.) The latter will ripen its fruit in a greenhouse, but the others require a stove. The fruit of most of these is highly prized for the dessert, and makes excellent ices. They are all highly ornamental twining shrubs, natives of South America or the West Indies, and require abundance of room, and to be trained close to the glass in the stove, excepting P. edulis, which may be trained under the rafter of a greenhouse.

The Indian fig, or prickly pear (Opuntia vulgaris, Haw.), is a native of Barbary, naturalized in the south of Italy, and cultivated in Virginia. The fruit is of a purplish red, with an agreeable subacid flavour. It requires a dry soil, and the protection of glass to ripen its fruit properly; but it would produce abundantly in a pit in a layer of soil on a bed of stones, which admitted of being occasionally heated by a flue.

The Pawpaw (Carica Papaya, L.) is a cucurbitaceous tree, a native of the East Indies, of rapid growth in our stoves, and soon producing a very showy fruit, larger than a lemon, and agreeable to the taste. It has been ripened and sent to table at Ripley Castle, and probably other places.

The Olive (Olea europæa, L.) is a branchy low evergreen tree which requires the protection of a greenhouse, and might be cultivated for the sake of its fruit for pickling.

Other exotic fruits which might be cultivated by the amateur, or which may be included in a select collection of stove-plants, are as follows:—The Great Indian Fig (Opuntia Tuna); the Barbadoes Gooseberry (Pereskia aculeata); the Strawberry Pear (Cereus triangularis); the Akee Tree (Blighia sapida); the Alligator Pear, or Avocado Pear (Laurus Persea); the Anchovy Pear (Grias cauliflora); the Durion (Durio zebethinus); the Jamrosade Apple, or rose-apple (Eugenia Jambos); the Malay Apple (E. malaccensis); the Bastard Guava (E. Pseudo-Psidium); the Cayenne Cherry (E. cotinifolia); the Cherimoyer (Anona Cherimolia); the Custard Apple (A. reticulata); the Alligator Apple (A. palustris); the Sweetsop (A. squamosa); the Soursop (A. muricata); the Mammee Apple (Mammea americana); the Lee-chee (Euphoria Litchi); the Long-yen (E. Longana); the Mango Tree (Mangifera indica); the Mangosteen, or Mangustin (Garcinia Mangostana). This has been very successfully fruited at Zion House, near London, and has been pronounced the most delicious of all fruits. The Cocoa-nut, (Cocos nucifera); the Bread-fruit (Artocarpus incisa); the Chinese Lemon (Triphasia aurantiola); the True Lotus (Zizyphus Lotus); the

Jujube Tree (Z. Jujuba); the Kaki (Diospyros Kaki). The last four will fruit in a greenhouse. Few of these, with the exception of the Mangosteen and the Bread-fruit, will repay the trouble of cultivation for their fruit alone, though all might be worth growing as objects of botanical or economic interest.

Remarks Applicable to Fruit Trees and Fruit-bearing Plants Generally.

Standard fruit trees occasion less trouble in managing, and are more certain in bearing, than either wall-trees or espaliers; though there are some trees, as the peach, which are too tender for being grown as standards, and others, as the vine, which are unsuitable. In standard trees, the top will generally be adjusted to the root naturally, and hence in such trees very little pruning will be requisite beyond that of thinning out crossing or crowded branches; but, in wall and espalier-trees, as the top is disproportionately small to the roots, pruning, or disbudding, &c., as a substitute, becomes necessary during the whole period of their existence. The nearest approach which a wall-tree can be made to have to a standard, is when in the case of north and south walls, one-half of the branches are trained on the east side of the wall, and the other half on the west side; or when one tree is made to cover both sides of a double espalier. Pruning may be rendered almost unnecessary by disbudding, disleafing, and stopping; but this will not always be the best course to pursue. When the root of a wall-tree is to be strengthened, more shoots should be left than are required for being laid in at the winter pruning; and when the root is to be weakened, transplantation or root-pruning is the best means of doing so.

Keeping roots near the surface, and encouraging the production of surface roots, will have a tendency to moderate the production of wood; and deep planting and stirring the surface to one foot or more in depth, will throw the roots down to a moisture stratum, and encourage the production of wood, but of an inferior quality for the future production of fruit. Dry sandy soil, not rich, will produce moderate growth and precocity, both in the fruit and the ripening of the wood, and rich deep soil the contrary; hence dry soil, comparatively poor, ought to be preferred for cold late situations, in which it is always desirable to ripen early both the fruit and the wood. As all plants require a certain period of rest, by bringing on this period sooner in autumn, by disleafing and depriving the roots of moisture, by thatching the ground over them, they will be predisposed to vegetate sooner in spring. Hence the advantage of pruning all trees, the young wood of which is not liable to be injured by frost, immediately after the fall of the leaf. All wood that is not thoroughly ripened should be protected during winter by branches, fern, hay, netting, or some other means; but as this is only applicable to wall-trees, the soil for all others should be so adjusted to the climate as to ensure their wood ripening in the open garden or orchard. As the most exhausting part of every fruit is the seed, and as the number of seeds in every fruit is limited by nature, it follows that a few fruit grown to a large size will be less injurious to a plant than the same weight of fruit produced in fruits of small size. As in plants in a state of seed-bearing, the chief energies of the plant are directed to the nourishment of the seed, so in those fruit-bearing plants in which the fruit is gathered green—such as cucumbers, gourds, capsicums, peas, beans, kidney-beans, &c.—none of the fruit should be allowed to mature any seed, so long as any of it is gathered in an unripe state. Hence the immense importance of thinning out the blossom-buds of trees before they expand, and thinning out the fruit before the embryo of the seed begins to assume that stage which in berries and pomes is called setting, and in nuts and stone-fruit, stoning.

Any check given to the head of a tree, such as disleafing, the attacks of insects, disease, overbearing, &c., has a tendency to cause the plant to throw up suckers, if it is natural to the root or stock to do so. As the leaves produced at the base of a young shoot are small and generally soon drop off, so the buds in the axils of such leaves are never blossom-buds till they have become invigorated by at least another year's growth; and hence when young wood is shortened, if blossom is the immediate object, it ought not to be cut farther back than to the first large bud. This is particularly applicable in the case of vines, roses, &c. In shortening such wood on spur-bearing trees, such as the apple and pear, only one or two of the imperfect buds are left at the base of the shoot, and these the following year generally become blossom-buds, if the tree is neither too weak nor too luxuriant. In general, winter pruning a young tree retards the period of its fruit-bearing, but greatly increases the vigour of the tree; hence delicate trees, such as the peach, require more pruning than very hardy trees, such as the apple and plum.

Summer pruning effects various objects: it exposes the fruit, where it exists, and also the embryo fruit-buds, and leaves connected with them, to the beneficial influence of light, air, and dews. Such pruning removes the mechanical obstructions to the free and full action of light and air upon the buds, flowers, or fruit. Physiologically considered, the progress of the sap is limited by summer pruning, and is directed towards the leaves and buds on the lower parts of shoots, which are in consequence invigorated, more especially as their free exposure to light, &c., enables them better to elaborate this increased supply. But although the foliage so left to act is increased in size and efficiency, yet the agency of this portion in producing roots is notwithstanding less powerful than the whole mass would be if the shoots were allowed to grow wild throughout the summer; for in proportion to the mass of healthy foliage so is the increase of roots. Hence excessive vigour is moderated by summer pruning, and this in a greater or less degree according to the time and manner of performing the operation. The longer the operation is deferred, and the less the portion cut off from the shoots, the greater will be the strength which the roots will derive; and the earlier and shorter the shoots are cut, the less will be the quantity of foliage, and proportionally so the quantity of roots. In the course of a fortnight the uppermost buds on the portion left will have commenced to push, and they must be allowed to go on for a longer or shorter time without stopping, according as there may be more or less danger of the buds at the base being also developed into shoots, instead of remaining in the character of a fruit-bud till next spring. If the roots, and, of course, the tree generally, require to be invigorated, the shoots will not be so numerous, and may be allowed to extend till after midsummer, and then only shortened for a little at first, in order that as much foliage as is consistent with the principles above explained may be left to act. It is a very prevalent notion that, in the case of an over-vigorous tree, as much wood should be retained, and as many shoots allowed to grow as is possible, in order that its vigour may be moderated by the expenditure. But it must be borne in mind that the more a young tree grows, the more it is capable of growing; for growth is not a mere evolution of parts already formed, evolved by a determinate amount of expansive power. If ten buds give rise to a hundred others, these last have the power of originating, in the same ratio, one thousand, and so on, as long as force of sap towards new formations is undiminished. But in fruit trees an exhaustive process proceeds simultaneously with growth, and one of the most effectual means of checking excessive vigour is a full crop of fruit. All shoots under half an inch in diameter, cut from the side of a stem before midsummer, will generally heal over the same season. Terminal wounds made by shortening, will not heal over till a shoot has been produced, the base of which will cover the wound.

The fruit-bearing shoots of all trees, in a natural state, are chiefly such as are lateral, while the wood of the tree is chiefly increased by the vertical shoots; hence some modification of lateral training will, in almost every case, be found preferable to training vertically. Lateral roots are also those which contribute most to fruit-bearing wood; and tap or deep-growing roots to upright and barren wood. All restraint imposed on trees, whether by training or root-pruning, if not followed up by art, will speedily end in disfiguring the tree and rendering it unfruitful, till it has assumed its natural form and habit of growth; and if the tree should be of a species so tender as not to ripen fruit in its natural form as a standard, it will by assuming that form have become useless as a fruit tree. In the case of all trees in a state of culture, and more especially such as grow in soil the surface of which is heated more than that of the general surface of the locality, as is the case of a border exposed to the reverberation of the sun's rays in front of a south wall, artificial supplies of water are necessary at particular seasons, and water therefore must be considered as much an element of culture as manure. Most of the diseases of trees may be effectually prevented or cured by judicious culture; and all insects which live on the surface of trees, may be destroyed or subdued by abundant washings with clear soot or lime-water by the syringe or engine. All fruit-bearing plants (and indeed all others) grown in pots, ought to be potted in soil which has not been sifted, and which, if not sufficiently coarse to keep it so open as to receive and part with water freely, should be mixed with fragments of bones, bricks, charcoal, or stone, for that purpose, and for retaining moisture.

CHAPTER XVIII.

CATALOGUE OF CULINARY VEGETABLES.

The culinary vegetables usually cultivated in British gardens are herbaceous plants, annuals, biennials, and perennials, with one or two suffruticose or shrubby plants.

Horticulturally and economically, the culinary plants of British gardens may be thus arranged:—

I. Esculents.—*Plants Used for their Nutritious or Pleasant Properties.*

Brassicaceous esculents, syn. cabbage tribe; comprehending the white and red cabbage, cabbage colewort, Savoy, Brussels sprouts, borecoles, cauliflower, broccoli, Kohl Rabi, and Chinese cabbage.

Leguminaceous esculents; comprehending the pea, bean, and kidney-bean.

Radicaceous esculents, syn. esculent tubers, and roots; comprehending the potato, Jerusalem artichoke, turnip, carrot, parsnip, red beet, skirret, scorzonera, salsify, and radish.

Spinaceous esculents; comprehending the garden spinach, white beet, orache, perennial spinach, New Zealand spinach, sorrel, and herb-patience.

Alliaceous esculents; comprehending the onion, leek, chives, garlic, shallot, and rocambole.

Asparagaceous esculents; comprehending asparagus, sea-kale, artichoke, cardoon, rampion, hop, &c.

Acetariaceous esculents, syn. salads; comprehending lettuce, endive, succory, celery, mustard, rape, corn-salad, garden-cress, American-cress, winter-cress, water-cress, burnet, and some of those included in other sections, as the sorrel, tarragon, Indian cress, &c.

Adornaceous esculents, syn. seasonings and garnishings; comprehending parsley, purslane, tarragon, fennel, dill, chervil, coriander, carraway, anise, Indian cress, marigold, borage, and some others.

Condimentaceous esculents, syn. plants used in tarts, and for preserving and pickling; comprehending rhubarb, Oxalis crenata, angelica, elecampane, the samphire, caper; and the Indian cress, radish, horse-radish, kidney bean, onion, red cabbage, &c., included in other sections; and among fruits, the cucumber, love-apple, egg-plant, capsicum, &c.

Aromaceous esculents, syn. sweet herbs; comprehending thyme, clary, mint, marjoram, savory, basil, pennyroyal, &c.

Fungaceous esculents; comprehending the mushroom, truffle, and morel.

II. HERBS.—*Plants used for their Fragrance, for Medicinal Purposes, or as Poisons for Vermin.*

Odoraceous herbs, syn. fragrant herbs, plants used in domestic distillation; comprehending lavender, rosemary, peppermint, and others.

Medicaceous herbs, syn. medicinal herbs, plants used in domestic medicine; comprehending chamomile, hyssop, wormwood, horehound, balm, rue, liquorice, blessed thistle, blue melilot, and some others.

Toxicaceous herbs, plants used in gardens for subduing or destroying insects; comprehending the tobacco, white hellebore, foxglove, &c.

Propagation and Seed-saving.—The greater number of culinary vegetables are annuals, or biennials, which are propagated by seeds, but a few are perennials or shrubby, and these are increased by division of the root, or by cuttings or layers. The seeds are for the most part purchased annually from the seedsman, whose business it is to procure from all quarters the best kinds, and have them grown for him by a particular class of cultivators known as seed-growers. The more select varieties are frequently grown by private gardeners for their own use; but this can only be done to a limited extent, on account of the liability of varieties of the same species or race, as of different kinds of cabbage or turnip, to become hybridized by proximity, and by their flowering at the same time. The care and labour, also, which are required for saving seeds on a small scale, are so disproportionate to the produce, that it would render the seeds much more expensive than if they were purchased, and hence the practice is seldom resorted to, except to preserve a valuable variety, and to grow a large quantity of only one or two kinds for the sake of selling to, or exchanging with, the seedsman, for small quantities of the different kinds which may be wanted.

The selection of varieties is an important part of the gardener's care, and one of more difficulty than in the case of fruit trees; because in culinary vegetables the kinds are continually changing, from the influence of soil, culture, neglect, fashion, &c.; so that a sort of pea, onion, broccoli, or cabbage, which is esteemed the best at one time, may in the course of a few years be almost forgotten. The number of synonymes of varieties is also very great, and though the Horticultural Society has at various times done good service by testing and proving them, yet from the frequent introduction of new sorts, the task would require to be undertaken yearly. We shall give a selection of the best varieties in culture at the present time, recommending the amateur and young gardener to deal only with the most respectable seedsmen, and to be guided by them in cases where he cannot profit from the information contained in books.

Some crops require to be sown where they are to remain, and others do best transplanted. Such plants as the turnip, with the exception of the Swedish, will not produce a crop when transplanted; and others, such as the beet and spinach, succeed but indifferently; while for the pea and bean, the labour, except in the case of the earliest crops, would be disproportionately great to the advantage gained. The carrot is sometimes transplanted in a prepared border for an early crop; and transplanting may be performed with tolerable success with the other sorts mentioned, if done when the plants are very young, and with proper care; but it should not be attempted unless in cases of emergency. All the cabbage tribe, and lettuce, endive, &c. transplant freely, and there is a great saving of ground by sowing them in seed-beds, instead of sowing them where they are finally to remain. For example, if the lettuce or endive plants which occupy a few square yards of seed-bed for a month, were at once sown where they are finally to remain, they would occupy, perhaps, several rods of ground one month longer than they otherwise would do. Thus a crop of peas may be coming into flower, at the time when the endive or lettuce was sown on the seed-bed, and when the lettuce or endive plants are ready to transplant, the crop of peas will have been gathered, and the crop of endive will follow it; but had the crop of endive been sown where it was finally to remain, an additional piece of ground, equal to that occupied by the peas, would have been required. As a proof of the economy of this system generally, it may be observed that it is the one followed by all the market-gardeners in the neighbourhood of London. Another advantage attendant on the transplanting system—more especially in the case of esculents, the leaves of which are the parts used—is, that the plants being deprived of a part of their tap-root, throw out a greater number of lateral roots, in consequence of which the production of radical leaves is encouraged, and the tendency to run to flower is retarded, while a more succulent growth is induced, owing to the plants being placed in newly prepared soil.

Soils.—Though garden plants grow naturally in soils very different both in their chemical constituents and mechanical properties, yet in a state of cultivation there are few or none of them that will not thrive in the soil of a garden, which is neither extremely sandy, gravelly, clayey, chalky, nor peaty, provided it has been well pulverized and drained, and manured with stable-dung. Practically, almost the only changes that can be made in garden-soil are, to render it richer by stable-dung, or other animal manure; lighter, by the addition of leaf-mould; more compact, by the addition of clay in a natural state; more open, by the addition of burnt clay or sand; more calcareous, by the addition of lime; and more sandy on the surface, for the purpose of raising seedlings to transplant, by working in a top-dressing of sand. Of these different ingredients, animal manure, sand, and leaf-mould are alone universally in request in kitchen gardens, for adding to their soils, whatever these may be.

For the proportion of each crop which under ordinary circumstances requires to be cultivated, the quantity of seed, plants, or sets, necessary for this purpose, the place of the crop in the rotation, the advantage of sowing or planting in rows, and various other points of general application, we must refer the reader back to the chapter on the Cropping and General Management of a Kitchen Garden, p. 383.

Brassicaceous Esculents, or the Cabbage Tribe.

The Cabbage tribe include the White and Red Cabbage, Savoy, Brussels Sprouts, Borecole, Cauliflower, and Broccoli. All these are considered to have sprung from Brassica oleracea, L., a cruciferous biennial, found on the sea-shore at Dover and a few other parts of Europe, on chalky or calcareous soil. At Dover the plant varies considerably in its foliage and general appearance, and in its wild state it is there used as a culinary vegetable, and found of excellent flavour ('Gard. Mag., viii. p. 54). Improved varieties have been cultivated in gardens since the time of the Romans, and probably long before. They occupy a large space among the rotation crops of every kitchen garden, because there is not a day in the year in which one or more of the kinds is not required at table. We shall first enumerate the varieties and the best sub-varieties of each, and give what is peculiar in their culture; and conclude the section with the culture and management of the Cabbage tribe generally.

The White cabbage (B. oleracea var. capitata, Dec.; Chou pommé, or cabus blanc, Fr.) is perhaps the most general vegetable in cultivation in temperate climates; it is in perfection from May to November, and the Scotch Drumhead field cabbage, or the Vanack, and Rosette Colewort, afford a supply through the winter; from the open air, when the winter is mild, and taken up and planted under cover when it is severe. The properties of a good cabbage are, a small, short stem, and a large, compact, well-formed head of succulent leaves, surrounded with but few loose leaves. The sub-varieties are now very numerous, almost every grower having his favourite. But the Early York and Battersea still hold their ground, and such varieties as the true Atkins' Matchless, Nonpareil, Early Barnes, Little Pixie, Cattel's Reliance, Wheeler's Imperial, &c., are among the best for early or general crops; the Sugarloaf is likewise a useful, tender, summer cabbage; and the Early York, for early and late crops, and the Cornish and Vanack for main crops. The Vanack cabbage is always in season; and as it sprouts freely from the stem after being cut, and the sprouts form heads as well as the summits of the plants, one plantation of this kind might serve the whole summer, and actually does so in some considerable gardens in the neighbourhood of London. The main plantation of cabbages, to come into use in May, is made about the end of October, and for this the seeds are sown in the last week of July or first week of August. Any time from the 8th to the 12th of August will do well to sow good varieties of early kinds of cabbage; and such should be as plentiful in March and April as they were in May and June, under the improved method of growing pretty little early close-headed varieties, such as Little Pixie or Vanack, on sloping banks, planted twelve to fifteen inches apart. Many of the London market-gardeners are so particular as to the time of sowing that they sow annually on the same day—viz., July 25, or as near it as circumstances will permit. The seeds are sown in an open airy situation, quite thin, and watered and shaded, if necessary. The ground for the plantation being prepared by deep digging and manuring, if it is not already rich, the early sorts, being small, are planted out in rows fifteen inches or eighteen inches apart, and about one foot distance in the row; and the Scotch cabbage, which, however, is but little cultivated in gardens, at three feet between the rows, and two feet in the row. For the Scotch cabbage to attain the largest size the seed should be sown in cold, stiff soil, about the middle of August, and the plants transplanted in the May of the following year. They will form immense heads by the middle of November. These large cabbages are less grown than formerly, as Savoys are preferred in winter. For a late summer and autumn crop, sow in the end of February or beginning of March, and transplant in May, June, or July. These two seasons of sowing and transplanting are enough for the largest garden as well as the smallest.

For a cottage garden the Early York, Battersea, Hill's Incomparable, Atkins' Matchless, and Wheeler's Imperial are among the best. With spring-planted crops in cottage gardens a Mazagan bean may be sown alternately with every cabbage plant in the same row.

The Couve Tronchuda, syn. large-ribbed cabbage (B. oleracea costata oblonga, Dec.) is a delicious vegetable, much more tender than the common cabbage. The plants may be sown in the first week in August, preserved through the winter in frames, and transplanted in spring about the same time as the cauliflower; or the seed may be sown on heat early in spring. The ribs of the outer and larger leaves, when divested of their green parts, and well boiled, make a good dish, somewhat resembling sea-kale. The heart or middle part of the plant is, however, the best for use; it is peculiarly delicate, tender, and agreeably flavoured, without any of the coarseness which often belongs to the cabbage-tribe. There is a dwarf variety known in Portugal by the name of Murciana, which is much earlier than the other, and unlike it, throws out numerous suckers from the lower part of the stem. This, when cooked, is much more delicate and tender than the other taller and coarser-ribbed variety.

Cabbage coleworts are cabbages used before they have formed hearts or become cabbaged. The seeds of any early variety are sown from the middle of June to the last week of July, and transplanted in August, September, and October, as ground becomes vacant by the removal of peas, beans, onions, &c. Cabbage coleworts are put in at from six inches to eight inches apart every way, according to the size which they are expected to attain before being gathered; and they are occasionally watered if the season is dry, so as to forward them as much as possible before winter. They are gathered (or pulled up to retain the sap in them if they are to be sent to a distance) as wanted, late in autumn, and throughout the whole of the winter, and will be found far superior to the cabbage sprouts which can be obtained at these seasons. The Rosette colewort is one of the best for this purpose. But cabbage coleworts are less grown now, as Mr. Melville, of Dalmeny Park, has succeeded in crossing the cabbage with Brussels sprouts, and raising many useful varieties, such as the Dalmeny and the Albert sprout. These, if sown in March or April, yield abundance of small cabbages on the stems throughout the winter.

The red cabbage (B. oleracea var. capitata rubra, Dec.), is chiefly used for pickling, though sometimes for sauerkraut. The seed is mostly sown in autumn, and treated in all respects like the autumn-sown white cabbage. The dwarf red is esteemed the best sub-variety.

The Savoy (B. oleracea var. bullata major, Dec.), has wrinkled leaves, but in most other respects it resembles the common cabbage, and may be cultivated in the same manner. As it is chiefly used during winter, and after it has been mellowed by frost, sow in March and April for planting out from June to August. The best varieties are the Drumheads, Dwarf Green Curled, Mitchell's Green Globe, and the New Feather-stemmed (like Brussels sprouts, with Savoys all up the stems).

Brussels sprouts (B. oleracea bullata gemmifera, Dec.; Chou de Bruxelles, or à jets, Fr.), differ from the Savoy in forming small green heads like miniature Savoy cabbages along its stem, which often grows three feet or four feet high. These miniature cabbages are used as winter greens, or with a sauce composed of vinegar, butter, and nutmeg, poured upon them hot after they have been boiled. The top, or terminal cabbage, is very delicate when dressed, and quite different in flavour from the side cabbages. The best varieties are the Imported, Scrymger's Giant, Improved Dwarf, and the two hybrids before adverted to under coleworts. Sow in February and March, and transplant into rows, eighteen inches apart every way, in June. The side leaves are sometimes taken off as the plants advance in height, to throw more sap into the buds which form the sprouts, or side cabbages; these come into use after the first frost.

Borecole (B. oleracea acephala sabellica, Dec.; Chou vert, or non pommé, Fr.). Of this variety there are many sub-varieties, but the best are the Dwarf Green Scotch kale, syns. German greens, curlies; the Tall Green Scotch kale, Scotch cabbaging or hearting asparagus kale, and Veitch's Late Green curled. For very cold late situations, there is the Jerusalem kale, syn. Ragged Jack, a dwarf sub-variety, with long, serrated leaves, which being produced close to the ground, the plants are less injured by the frost than those of the taller varieties. The Buda, syn. Russian kale, is so dwarf as scarcely to have any stem, and is very hardy. The sprouts of this kind may be blanched like sea-kale, by turning a pot over the plant early in spring. As all the borecoles are only wanted during winter and spring to supply the place of cabbage, the seeds are sown in April, or later, and the plants put out, where they are finally to remain, in June; or earlier or later, according to the situation and the ground which may become vacant. The distance of the Scotch kale may be two feet between the rows, and eighteen inches in the row; those of the Buda and Jerusalem kale may be a few inches less. Within these few years great improvements have been made by Mr. Melville and others in raising variegated varieties of borecole for garnishing desserts and filling flower beds, and some of these strains are very beautiful, and used in some gardens by the thousand for filling flower-beds or forming ribbon borders in winter.

The cauliflower (B. oleracea Botrytis cauliflora, Dec.; Chou-fleur, Fr.) is the most delicate production of the cabbage tribe, both with reference to the table and to its culture. The head of embryo flowers is the part used, and it ought to be compact, round, not broken at the edges, convex on the upper surface, and succulent throughout. There are several so-called varieties, such as the Early London Market and Frogmore Forcing, two good early sorts; and the Asiatic and Stadtholder, two fine late kinds; while the Walcheren is one of the very best for sowing at any time from February to October. It is one of the sweetest, whitest, hardiest cauliflowers at all seasons. In books an early and a late variety are mentioned, but in the seed-shops and gardens they are the same, the earliness or lateness depending on the time of sowing. As it is desirable to have cauliflower as many months in the year as possible, three sowings are made at different times— viz., between the 18th and 24th of August, for plants to stand through the winter and produce the first crop next May and June; in the end of February or beginning of March, on a moderate hotbed for transplanting in April, to produce the second crop in July and August; and in the beginning of April for transplanting in June to produce a crop from September till the first frosts; sow again in May, June, and July, and plant out in sheltered borders to pass through and come in during mild winters, affording, if needed, protection where they stand, or removing the plants into a shed or cellar.

The First Crop.—When the plants have leaves one and a-half inches broad, prick them out at three inches or four inches apart, either in the open garden, for transplanting in October, or under a wall, or in some other warm, sheltered situation, to remain through the winter and be transplanted in spring. In most parts of Britain, cauliflower requires the protection of glass through the winter, and hence the first crop is almost always planted in patches of four or five plants, placed so as to be covered by a hand-glass or bell-glass or Rendle's Plant Protector. The glass remains over the plants throughout the winter, air being admitted every fine day, either by tilting up the glass with a brick or other prop, by taking it off altogether, or, if the cover of the glass forms a separate piece from the sides, taking it off, raising it, or changing its position (fig. 76, in p. 107), according to circumstances. The patches for being covered by hand-glasses are put out in rows, about three and a-half feet or four feet apart, and about three feet patch from patch in the row; each patch being of the size of the bottom of the hand-glass, or about eighteen inches square. Put three or four plants under each glass, to allow for deaths during the winter, and for transplanting all, except two or three, into the open ground in the following April. In the last week of April or the first of May, the glasses may be removed, and put over the transplanted plants till they have taken root, and afterwards used for cucumbers, gourds, or other purposes. The soil all round the patches should now be stirred, and, if not already very rich, manure may be added, or the plants may be frequently watered with liquid manure. By keeping on some of the glasses as long as the plants can be contained under them, a part of the crop will come in earlier; and by frequently stirring the soil and supplying liquid manure, so as to retard the appearance of the flower, and keep the plants long in a growing state, a portion of the crop will be later and larger. If some of the patches have been planted in sandy soil, not very rich, the plants will be smaller and forwarder than the others, and will admit of being covered by the glasses till the crop is fit to cut, which will give a very early supply. The same objects will be effected to a certain extent by giving a similar treatment to plants which have stood out through the winter at the base of a wall, or to plants which have been sown in spring.

The Second Crop.—Prick out the plants as soon as they admit of it into beds, six inches apart every way, so as to allow of their being taken up with balls, and planted in rows, four feet by three feet, in rich soil, in the end of April or the beginning of May.

The Third Crop.—Proceed in the same manner, and transplant into rows, three feet by two feet, about the middle of July.

Succession crops throughout the summer can be treated like those of cabbages. It is a good practice to sow frequently, so as always to have a stock of plants to fill any vacant ground. A winter crop may be obtained by sowing in the middle of July, in a warm border, or on the south side of an east and west ridge, and allowing the plants to come to heads without transplanting, but taking care to thin them to twelve inches or fourteen inches apart every way. In the course of November, heads will be formed from three inches to nine inches or ten inches across, and the plants may then be removed with balls, and planted in a bed of soil, to be covered by a frame and sashes; or in a bed under an open shed, and farther protected by mats and dry hay. By this latter mode, which may be adopted where a frame cannot be had, Mr. Cockburn, in Sussex, has been able to send three dishes of cauliflower to table every week during the autumn and winter till February ('Hort. Trans.' vol. v. p. 281).

Broccoli (B. oleracea Botrytis cymosa, Dec.), differs from the cauliflower chiefly in being so much hardier as to produce a supply of heads during the winter and early spring. There are a number of excellent varieties, which may be arranged as autumn, winter, spring, and summer varieties.

The best autumn broccoli is the Walcheren, which, by planting late, may generally be had up to Christmas. Then follow Hammond's and Adams' White Cape, Grange's White Cape, and Purple Cape. For winter use, the Early Cornish is the best winter white broccoli known; Snow's White, Osborn's White, Backhouse's White Protecting are good; while for spring use, Knight's Protecting, Frogmore Protecting, Dilcock's Bride, Dalmeny Park, Osborn's New White Sprouting and the Purple-sprouting Mammoth, Portsmouth, and Veitch's Spring White. For summer use, Wilcove's Late White, Carter's Champion,

Cattell's Eclipse, Melville's Dalmeny, May's Surprise, Elliston's Mammoth, and Williams's Alexandra are good varieties.

Time of Sowing.—For the early autumn and winter varieties, sow at two or three different times from the end of April to the middle of June or July. The late winter, early spring, and summer varieties should be sown in March and April.

General Culture.—Most of the sorts may be planted in rows two and a-half by three feet; but for the dwarf varieties, such as the late Dwarf Purple, and the Spring White, eighteen inches every way will be sufficient. The routine culture consists of watering when the plants are newly planted, destroying the weeds by hoeing, stirring the soil with a fork, and earthing up the stems. The very dwarf sorts require no protection in ordinary winters; but the taller growing kinds are apt to be severely injured by frost, and should either be protected where they stand, or by removal to an open shed, as directed for cauliflower. A mulching of hay, straw, or leaves, or a number of branches with the leaves on, stuck in among the tall-stemmed sorts, is frequently found effective. Tying the leaves together over the top is often a sufficient protection; the plants are also frequently thrown half over before winter, with their heads to the north, and their stems earthed up to the leaves, as a means of protecting them from frost. Thus treated the flowers will not be so large, but a small head is better than none. In gathering the heads, they should be cut while they are compact, or as technically expressed, before the curd becomes broken, with about six inches of the stalk to each head and the stems may be left to produce sprouts.

The turnip-cabbage, or turnip borecole (B. oleracea Caulo-rapa communis, Dec.; Chou-rave, Fr.; Kohl Rabi, Ger.), is a dwarf-growing plant, with the stem swelled out so as to resemble a turnip above ground, but of a delicate green colour. It is much cultivated in Germany, and even forced for the sake of the stem or turnip, which, taken in a young state, is dressed whole and eaten with sauce, or as vegetables to meat, like turnips or potatoes. In England it is very little used. The seed is sown in early spring, and the plants treated like other borecoles; the stem or turnip part being gathered while it is quite succulent, and will boil tender. To procure a supply throughout the summer, two or three sowings would require to be made.

General Culture and Management of the Cabbage Tribe.—In the choice of sub-varieties, it will be borne in mind that the dwarf kinds come soonest into use, and retain heat and moisture better, by the covering which their leaves afford to their stems, and to the soil, than the tall-growing kinds; but that owing to the shorter period at which, in most cases, they arrive at maturity, they require a richer soil; while the ramose roots of the tall kinds extend to a greater distance, and consequently are adapted for poorer soil; and in rich soils for producing larger plants. As all the varieties are biennials, the largest crops will be produced by autumnal plantations, by which longer time is given to the plants to lay up a stock of organizable matter. An ounce of seed of any of the varieties is the usual quantity ordered from seedsmen for small or middle-sized gardens, and half an ounce will be enough where several sub-varieties are sown; as, for example, of broccoli. The seed comes up in ten days or a fortnight, according to the season. In early spring, when it is desirable to advance the plants as rapidly as possible, the seed should be sown in light rich soil in a warm situation; but in autumn, when the great object is to produce plants of firm texture that will resist the winter, a poor and rather stiff or clayey soil is preferable. The plants are mostly transplanted with the dibber as soon as they have made four or five leaves; but it is best to pick out of the seed-beds into other ground the whole tribe of such plants, placing them from three to four inches apart, and finally removing them into rows with a spade or trowel. Bury the stem of the plants up to the leaves, and compress the soil firmly round both root and stem in planting. As all the kinds have the property of rooting freely from the stems, the plants, excepting the few that are stemless, are strengthened by being earthed up; and to increase the depth of this earthing, they are planted in drills two or three inches deep. All the varieties require an open, airy situation, for no one ever found the cabbage in a wild state in hedges or woods; but it should be sheltered from high winds, as plants on the sea-shore, whether among cliffs or on the beach, generally are. A small reserve of plants should always be preserved to make up for failures or runaways. The soil can hardly be too rich and deep for these crops. The roots will run down from four to five feet. Calcareous soils and open situations yield the best results. And the whole tribe require liberal watering in dry weather, as they are greedy of water, clean or foul; they thrive admirably and produce immense weights of cheap food when treated to sewage or liquid manure. It is highly probable that the plants would be benefited by a slight sprinkling of common sea-salt given once to each crop in an early stage of its progress. The soil should always be more or less calcareous; not only as the plant grows naturally on limestone or chalky cliffs and shores, but because the finest-flavoured cabbages and broccolis in England are produced in gardens in Kent on the south bank of the Thames, made in old chalk-pits. As the leaves of all the kinds are naturally large and succulent, they present a large perspiring surface, and therefore, to maintain this succulency in long-continued droughts, the plants should be liberally supplied with water; and as they are all gross feeders, they may all be watered with liquid manure. In all the sprouting varieties, when the stem is to be preserved for this purpose, the leaves should be taken off, that the sap may be thrown into the buds; and when these do not break freely, it will be facilitated by slitting the stem from an inch or two below the top to within an inch or two of the bottom, keeping the slit open with a bit of stick or a small stone; or the same object may be effected by cutting a notch above the buds. The hearting or heading, and consequently the blanching of all the kinds, will be promoted by loosely tying up the leaves, as soon as the plants show an indication of hearting, with strands of matting; and this may be usefully practised with the earliest spring cabbages, and with the borecoles when it is wished to have the leaves blanched. The best varieties of cabbages, however, close in, and blanch themselves. Cauliflowers, in summer, can be made more white and delicate by tying the leaves over the flowers, and, as already described, the same practice may often preserve broccoli from winter or spring frost. Most of the varieties, but more especially the broccolis, are subject to the club in the root; an unnatural protuberance produced by the puncture of an insect, and the subsequent hatching of deposited eggs, and apparently producing a diseased habit, so that club roots are produced afterwards in the same plant without the intervention of an insect. When the club has once appeared on the roots of a plant, there is no remedy for it; but in soils and situations subject to this disease, the insect may be deterred from laying its eggs in the root by putting a little quicklime in the hole made by the dibber before inserting the plant. Incorporating burnt clay with the soil has also been found to check clubbing, as well as to annoy worms and slugs; but the quantity necessary for these purposes, unless it was also required for the improvement of the soil, amounts almost to a prohibition of its use. As the leaves, more especially of the common cabbage in very dry weather, are subject to be covered by aphides, and to be eaten by the larvæ or caterpillars of butterflies (Pontia sp.), as soon as the former or the eggs of the latter are observed, the plants should be liberally watered with clear lime-water and the operation repeated till every egg and caterpillar is destroyed. Even copious supplies of clear water, poured on the plants for several evenings in succession, will effectually destroy the caterpillar in every stage of its growth; and in no variety of the cabbage tribe, excepting the cauliflower when it is nearly mature, will water in the slightest degree injure the flavour. Where lime-water or water alone cannot be supplied in sufficient quantities, the eggs of the butterflies ought to be collected and destroyed; and indeed this may be done in connexion with watering. The eggs are deposited in small patches on the upper side of the leaf; and in very warm weather they will hatch in twenty or thirty hours, and soon spread over the whole surface of the leaf. Slugs and earth-worms may be effectually destroyed by lime-water; or as a convenient substitute, where quicklime is not at hand, potash and water, or a decoction of foxglove, henbane, white hellebore, or walnut leaves. In general, the routine culture of the cabbage tribe consists in destroying weeds as soon as they appear, stirring the soil as deep as the roots will admit with a fork, or a pronged hoe, and supplying water or liquid manure when the condition of the plants, or the soil, or the state of the weather, requires it. Where the stems are left to produce sprouts, deeply stirring the soil and manuring are of essential service. In gathering the crop, when sprouts are not wanted, the plants, after the head is cut off, should be pulled up by the roots and carried to the manure-heap; or, if the stems are to be left, they should be stripped of their leaves, and the whole of these removed to the dung-heap and mixed with other materials; for nothing among vegetables is more offensive than the decaying leaves of the cabbage tribe, and indeed of the Cruciferæ generally. Coleworts are generally gathered by pulling them up by the root, by which the sap is retained better than if the heads were cut off. If after gathering any of the varieties it should be suspected by the cook that the heads contain slugs, caterpillars, or earth-worms, by plunging them into salt and water for a minute or two the vermin will be driven from their hiding-places among the leaves and left in the water. All the kinds may be preserved in a growing state through the winter under an opaque roof, the sides being opened on the south side on fine days; and the heading kinds by burying in the soil. Being gathered, none of the kinds will keep fresh above two or three days; but chopped into small pieces, and put in a cask in layers, each layer sprinkled with salt, a liquor is formed, immersed in which the cabbage, turnip, and every other cruciferous plant, will keep through the winter, and thus is formed the sauerkraut of the Germans. To save seed of any variety, select the finest specimens, and take care that no other brassicaceous plant is in flower at the same time within a considerable distance of it; and the more specimens there are planted together of any one variety for the purpose of seeding, the less liable they are to become adulterated. A solitary brassicaceous plant can never be depended on unless many miles indeed remote from any other; whereas a body of fifty or so will produce the sort generally true, even although not far from other varieties. The seed will keep four or five years; but as after a year it is liable, in common with other seeds, to the attacks of the weevil (Curculio, L.), it ought to be exposed every winter during severe frost in a thin layer for an hour or two, which will completely destroy vitality both in the eggs and the insects. The place of the cabbage tribe, in a rotation of crops, may be after or before the leguminous tribe, or the Alliaceæ.

Substitutes for the cabbage tribe are to be found in the Cruciferæ generally, the tender leaves of almost all of which may be used as greens, and the embryo heads of flowers as substitutes for broccoli. Among the best substitutes are the leaves of the turnip when running to flower, the wild cabbage, and the garlic cress or sauce-alone. (Erysimum Alliaria, L.; Alliaria Adan.) The spinaceous and acetariaceous esculents may also, in general, be used as greens. Nettles are a very common substitute, and an excellent one when gathered tender.

Leguminaceous Esculents.

The leguminaceous esculents of British gardens are chiefly the pea, bean, and kidney-bean, all of which thrive best in a deep free soil. In every garden they occupy a larger space than any other rotation crop, but they do not occupy it long; the main crops arriving at maturity in from three to four months.

The Pea.

The Pea (Pisum sativum, L.) is a tendrilled climbing annual, a native of the south of Europe, but arriving at maturity in the course of the summer in British gardens. No vegetable is more highly prized than green peas, and few are more nourishing when nearly ripe, or ripe. The seeds alone are eaten in most kinds, and they are boiled with mint to correct a slight tendency which they have to flatulency; but the entire pod is eaten of the sugar pea, in the manner of that of the kidney-bean, the outside edges of the pods being stripped off previously to boiling. The inner tough film which lines the pods is wanting in this variety, which renders it very distinct. Peas gathered when partially ripe, and dried, are used in soups and stews; but it is found that after they have been kept a year they do not break, or fall well in the soup: it is also understood among dealers in peas, that those which have been grown on stiff soil, or on sandy soil, that has been limed or marled, will not fall in boiling, whether new or old. Among the best the following may be named:—

First Crop.—Carter's First Crop, Beck's Gem or Early Dwarf, Laxton's Supreme, Maclean's Advancer, Sangster's No. 1, Eley's Essex Rival, Dillistone's Prolific.

Second Crop.—Champion of England, Fairbeard's Surprise, Auvergne, Dickson's Favourite, Harrison's Glory, Harrison's Perfection, Maclean's Dwarf Prolific, Napoleon, Nonpareil, Princess Royal, Veitch's Perfection, and The Prince of Wales.

Late and General Crop.—Burbridge's Eclipse (a splendid dwarf pea), Hair's Dwarf Green Mammoth, Ringwood Marrow, Victoria Marrow, Blue Scimitar.

Late Crop.—British Queen, Knight's Tall Green Marrow, Mammoth, Ne plus Ultra, Knight's Dwarf Green Marrow, Yorkshire Hero.

Culture.—The pea, being a tendrilled climber, whenever it is to be cultivated to the greatest advantage, ought to be supported by peasticks, which are branches of trees or shrubs well furnished with spray, and of lengths suited to the height to which the plants grow. These sticks are put in in two rows with the row of peas between them, the sticks or branches in one row being opposite the intervals of those in the other row. They are placed upright, but somewhat wider apart at top than at bottom, to allow room for the branching of the stems as they ascend, and for the larger space required for the top foliage, which is larger than that below, and for the pods. To facilitate the sticking, peas are always sown in rows. They are also always earthed up, principally for the sake of keeping the plants upright, as they do not produce roots freely above the collar, like the cabbage tribe. When sticking peas is inconvenient, or impracticable, from the extent of the crop, the rows are earthed up on one side only, so as to throw the haulm to the opposite side, by which means the ground between the rows is more readily kept clean, the crop more readily gathered, and the plants not so liable to be blown about by high winds. Rows of peas which are not to be sticked may be closer together than such as are to be sticked; because the tops of the plants of one row may extend to the lower parts of the plants of the row adjoining, without doing the plants of either row any injury. Hence when peas are not to be sticked, nor to be gathered green, the greatest amount of produce is obtained when they are sown broadcast; but by this mode the soil cannot be conveniently stirred or weeded. Peas are generally sown in single drills, at the same distance apart as the plants grow high, with intervening rows of spinach, or some such secondary crop, which is gathered before the peas are matured; but for all the taller growing kinds it is better considerably to increase the distance, so as to allow abundance of light and air to the peas, by which they will be much more productive, and a crop of a more permanent kind than spinach, such as some of the cabbage tribe, or roots or tubers, obtained between. A much larger crop, and a great saving of ground is by this means obtained. It is well known that the outsides of double rows bear much more abundantly than the insides; and if only two rows in one place, and two more in another, fifteen or twenty feet distant, were sown, there would be four outsides; whereas, if they were all sown together, there would be but two outsides. Two rows in one place occupy three feet six inches in width, and two rows in another the same, making together seven feet; but if four rows were sown together, they would take up eleven feet or twelve feet of ground. Here, therefore, is a saving of ground of nearly one-half. ('Gard. Mag.,' vol. iv. p. 225.) In pea culture, there is not a greater error than that of sowing the seeds too thick in the row. We would recommend, in every case except in that of the crops sown to stand the winter, to deposit the peas singly in the same manner as beans are planted. We know some gardeners who practise this mode, and they have always a larger produce, larger pods, and larger peas in them, than those who sow thick, and do not thin out. Abercrombie, who is one of the safest of guides in matters of this kind, recommends for the early frame, three peas in the space of an inch; dwarf marrowfat, two in an inch; blue Prussian and similar sorts, three in two inches; for Knight's marrow and all similar dwarf sorts, a full inch apart; and for all the tall-growing sorts, an inch and a half or two inches apart. For the early sorts, the seeds of which are small, the drills may be an inch and a half deep; and for the larger sorts, they may be two inches deep. After covering the peas by putting back, with the hoe, the earth that came out of the drill, it should be trodden down, if the soil is in good condition as regards dryness; but if from situation, or the state of the weather, it should be otherwise, it is better only to chop the soil with the teeth of the rake, holding the handle nearly upright.

The Earliest Crops.—In the neighbourhood of London, every gardener is expected to gather peas in the first week in June, if not before. To accomplish this, the early frame should be sown in a warm border, or along the south side of an east-and-west ridge in the open garden, towards the middle or end of November; if the winter is mild, the plants will appear above ground in January, or early in February, when they must be slightly earthed up, and during hard frosts protected by haulm, fern, litter or dried branches with the leaves on. Early in May they will have shown blossoms, and then every plant must be stopped at the first joint above the blossom, so as not to have more than two pods on a plant. The whole strength of the root being thus thrown into these pods, they will grow rapidly. If there is any spare space close along the bottom of a south wall, a row of peas may be planted there in December, protected by branches of yew, or spruce fir, during severe frosts, and during every night till they come into flower; and instead of being sticked, the plants may be kept close to the wall with twine or strands of matting, and stopped at the first joint above the first flowers. Thus treated, the pods will be fit to gather a fortnight before those in the open part of the warmest border; but if the wall is covered with the branches of fruit trees to within a foot of the ground, these will be materially injured by the shade of the peas. A second sowing of the same variety on a warm border, or on the south side of a drill, may be made after the first; and a third sowing, which may be of the earliest marrow, such as Prizetaker, may be made in March. This will suffice for the early crops. The plants of the last two sowings need not be stopped, nor will they require protection.

A very convenient mode of obtaining an early crop is to sow the peas in January in shallow pots, and protect them from frost by placing them close to the glass in the front of a greenhouse, or under a frame, hand-glasses, or hoops and mats; and about the middle of March to turn them out with balls into the open air in such situations as we have mentioned. Where pots are scarce, the peas may be sown in rows on pieces of turf, or even tiles, or pieces of boards covered with soil, brought forward on a slight hotbed, and afterwards deposited in the open ground; or they may be raised in shallow pots, and afterwards separated and transplanted singly in rows. In short, there are numerous ways in which peas may be forwarded under cover, or in very gentle heat, in January and February, so as to be ready to transplant into the open ground about the middle or end of March.

Fig. 372.

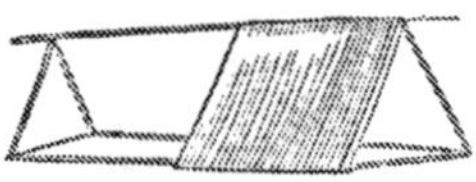

Cover for peas and other early crops.

Peas may be protected in the open garden by portable covers such as fig. 372, which is thus formed:—Two long and two short poles of larch, fir, or other straight wood, form each side; the top piece is left longer, to form handles at each end, and the sides are attached to the top with hinges, and kept apart by two removable stretchers. The whole is then covered with sugar-mats, fastened on with laths. The covers are always kept on during night, and mostly opened or taken off during the day ('Gard. Mag.' 1842, p. 187).

Portable Walls for Early Crops of Peas, &c.—As a substitute for a brick wall a portable wall might be formed of very thick boards, or of double boards; the vacuity within to be filled up with charcoal, and protected from rain by a coping, and from dropping out by a fixed bottom. Such a wall need not be above three feet in height, and to render it portable, it may be made in lengths of six feet or eight feet, with stakes to serve as strengthening piers, and for readily fixing the wall to the ground. These hurdle walls, as they may be called, would be found useful for a variety of purposes beside forwarding peas, such as ripening tomatoes, capsicums, melons, &c. Rendle's Plant Protectors, composed of tall sides and glass tops, will supersede most other expedients for protecting or forcing peas in the open ground.

The Summer and Autumn Crops.—The first sowing may be made in the middle of March, and where peas are in demand, which they are in almost every family, a sowing may be made every three weeks, till the 1st of August. Those sown in the latter period will not produce a crop unless the autumn is fine; but if this should be the case, peas may be gathered till December. For the latest as well as the earliest crops, the earliest varieties should be chosen. They should also be sown on light warm ground if possible, so as to encourage podding rather than growth. For the general crops, the ground can hardly be too rich and dark. Early and late peas are also grown in some gardens in pots. Such excellent marrows as McLean's Little Gem, or Advancer, and other early dwarfs such as Bishop's and Tom Thumb, might be sown in the first week in September, placed under glass in October, and brought on in any house with a temperature of $50°$ throughout the autumn and winter. Successional crops of dwarfs might be sown in pots or boxes like French beans, and green peas be gathered throughout the year. The chief point is to keep them close to the glass, and maintain a temperature of from $50°$ to $60°$. (See Forcing the Pea.) In sowing during summer when the ground is very dry, after being dug and the drills drawn, the bottom of the drill ought to be thoroughly soaked with water before the peas are sown, and firmly rolled after they are covered; and throughout the whole summer, whenever there is a continuance of drought, water ought to be liberally supplied. All the late crops ought to be sown in the driest soil which the garden affords, in an open, airy situation, and sticked; the last operation being essential to prevent the plants of the late crops from rotting; and as a preventive against this and mildew, the seeds should not be sown too thickly.

Gathering.—The rows should be looked over daily, and all those pods gathered that are sufficiently advanced; for if a single pod on a stem is allowed to remain so long as to begin to ripen, the production of young pods will, in a great measure, cease; whereas if they are gathered as fast as the peas are produced of an eatable size, the plants will continue to grow and to produce pods much longer than they otherwise would do. The same doctrine applies to cucumbers, kidney-beans, and all cases where fruit is gathered before it is ripe.

Diseases, Vermin, &c.—The mildew may in general be prevented by abundant waterings, which indeed is a preventive to both diseases and insects. Birds attack peas when they appear above ground early in spring, eating out the growing point; and again when the pods are beginning to ripen, and may be scared by some of the usual means. Mice are very apt to eat the peas when newly sown, to prevent which some sow chopped furze along with them; others rub the peas with powdered resin, and some cover the drills with a layer of clean, sharp sand, which it is alleged drops into the ears of the mice while they are burrowing underneath it. Wetting the peas before sowing, and dusting them over with red lead, protects them from both mice and rats; but the best mode is to attempt the destruction of such vermin, which is easily effected by a covered pit, or a covered vessel of water, or for rats good traps. With respect to birds, while they must be destroyed, especially sparrows, they are so useful in gardens in keeping down insects and eating snails, worms, &c., as well as so agreeable by their song, that we would allow them a small share of such seeds and fruits as are of easy growth. The reader is recommended to peruse on this subject the articles on birds in Waterton's 'Essays on Natural History.'

To save seed, allow a row or two, according to the quantity wanted, to ripen all their pods, previously pulling out any plants that appear to be of a different variety, or to have degenerated. Peas will grow the second year, but not often the third or fourth.

In a rotation of garden crops, the pea alternates well with the cabbage tribe, with root crops, or with perennial crops.

Forcing the Pea.—See page 520.

The Bean.

The Garden Bean (Vicia Faba, L.) is an erect annual, supposed to be a native of Egypt, and, like the pea, in cultivation from the remotest antiquity, for its seeds. These are used in soups, or dressed by themselves, and are considered very nourishing, though not of so delicate a flavour as the pea. The best varieties are, Marshall's Early Dwarf Prolific, by far the best early variety; the Early Mazagan, so named from a place in Portugal, a later-growing early variety, which comes in about a fortnight after Marshall's; the Early Longpod, a very prolific variety; the Broad Windsor, with the largest seeds, and best flavoured of all the beans, but not a good bearer, excepting in rich soils; the best varieties for a late crop are Beck's Green Gem, and Wonderful. The seed is ordered by the pint or quart, and for the small beans a pint is required for every eighty feet of row, and for the larger kinds two quarts for every 240 feet of row. The bean comes up in a week, ten days, or a fortnight, according to the season. Not less than a quart of seed will be required to produce a single gathering occasionally. The times of sowing, and the situation in the garden, for the earliest crops, are the same as for the pea; but the plants do not require sticking, nor, as the seeds are longer of coming to maturity, is it usual to sow later for an autumnal crop than the beginning of June. Marshall's Dwarf Prolific bean may be planted in rows two feet apart, and at six inches distant in the row, and the other sorts in rows two feet and a half to three feet apart; or, which will ensure a larger crop, in rows eight feet or ten feet apart, with dwarf-growing crops between, as recommended for the pea. The seeds may be deposited in drills an inch and a half or two inches deep, and covered and pressed down like the pea. Very early crops may be brought forward under cover, or by other means used in obtaining an early crop of peas. The bean transplants remarkably well, and many gardeners adopt this mode with their earliest crops.

In cottage gardens, not only in Britain but in the North of Europe generally, it is customary to plant beans in the same rows with cabbages, and also with potatoes; a bean being planted alternately with every potato set or cabbage plant. The rows of potatoes or cabbages are two feet and a half or three feet apart, according as they may be of small or large sorts; the distances in the rows are eighteen inches, and between each two plants a bean (the Longpod is the best variety for this purpose) is deposited. If the beans are transplanted, they get the start of the potatoes or cabbages, and as they come in early they will be gathered before they can do any injury to the cabbage or potato crops.

All the routine culture required for a crop of beans is, destroying weeds, slightly earthing up the stems, stirring the soil, watering in very dry weather, and stopping the plants when the first opened blossoms are beginning to set. Stopping in the case of an early crop may take place as with the pea, at the joint above the first blossom as soon as it appears; but this is only when a very early crop is more desirable than an abundant one. A very late crop of beans may be obtained by cutting over a summer crop, a few inches above the ground, as soon as the plants have come into flower. New stems will spring from the stools in abundance, and continue bearing till they are destroyed by frost. Beans for the table should be gathered before they arrive at maturity, which is known by their being black-eyed—that is, black at the hilum, or point of attachment to the pod. When this has taken place, beans are tough and strong-tasted, and much inferior for eating as a dish; though they are excellent in the soups of the cottager. For the higher classes, the beans are used when they are about one-third grown. The bean is sometimes attacked by the black aphis, which may be kept under by abundant syringing with lime or soot-water. Seed of any variety may be saved by allowing a sufficient number of plants to bring their pods to maturity; it will keep a year, and sometimes two years.

The bean is rarely or never forced, not being held in sufficient estimation for this purpose by the wealthy classes of society.

The Kidney-bean.

The Kidney-bean (Phaseolus, L.) includes two species—the common dwarf kidney-bean, syn. French bean (P. vulgaris, L.), an annual, growing twelve or eighteen inches high, a native of India; and the runner, syn. climbing kidney-bean (P. multiflorus, W.), a twining annual, attaining the height of ten or twelve feet, a native of South America. Though both sorts are too tender to endure our springs and autumn in the open air, yet so rapid is their growth during our summers, that they produce abundant crops of green pods in the open garden, from June to October, and, by forcing, these can be obtained all the year. The unripe pods both of the dwarf and twining kidney-beans, form the most delicate legume in cultivation; having no tendency to flatulency like the pea and bean, and producing abundant crops in dry hot weather, when the pea, unless abundantly watered, is withered up. The green pods, also, make an excellent pickle; and the ripe seeds are much used in cookery, especially in what are called haricots, soups, and stews. The scarlet runner, one of the twining varieties, is at once a highly ornamental plant, and eminently prolific in pods, from July till the plant is destroyed by frost; and as it is of the easiest culture, it forms one of the most valuable plants in the catalogue for the garden of the cottager. There is no vegetable from which such a large weight of excellent food can be gathered for so many months in succession as these runner beans.

Varieties.—Those of the dwarf species are very numerous; but the kinds considered best worth cultivating are the Sion House, Newington Wonder, Fulmer's Forcing, and Early Negro, for forcing, or the earliest crops; and the pale dun, long-podded Negro, dark dun, Canterbury early white, and light dun, for general crops. The best variety of the twining species (Haricot à rames, Fr.), for cultivating for its pods to be used green is the scarlet runner; though there is a large white runner, the white Dutch, and also a variegated-blossomed runner, the Painted Lady, which produce equally good pods, but the blossoms are not so ornamental. The pods of the kidney-bean are smooth, and those of the scarlet runners are rough outside. The roots of the scarlet runner, if taken up on the approach of frost and preserved through the winter, will grow again next spring, like the roots of the marvel of Peru, or the dahlia; or like them they may be protected where they stand; but as nothing would be gained by this practice, it is never adopted. Half a pint of seed will sow a row eighty feet in length, the beans being placed from two inches and a half to three inches apart in the row; and this length of row will be required for gathering a single dish at a time. The seed comes up in a week or more, according to the temperature of the soil.

Culture of the Dwarf Sorts.—The first sowing in the open garden may be made in the beginning of April, if the situation is warm, and the soil dry. The second about the middle of the month, and subsequently sowings may be made every three or four weeks till the first week in August. The rows may be two feet asunder, and the beans deposited in drills from two inches to three inches apart, and covered to the depth of one inch, or one inch and a half. The routine culture consists in watering abundantly in very dry weather, and using lime-water if, which is often the case, the plants are attacked by snails or slugs.

Culture of the Twining Sorts.—These being rather more tender than the dwarfs, are not sown till towards the end of April or the beginning of May; a second sowing may be made about the middle of May; and a third and last in the first week in June. To forward the gathering season, the first crop is often sown under glass in March, and planted out in May, when all danger of frost is over. In cottage gardens, one sowing in the beginning of May will produce plants which, if the soil is in good condition, water judiciously applied, and the green pods gathered before the seeds formed in them begin to swell, will continue bearing, from the middle of June, till the plants are destroyed by the frosts. The rows, as in every similar case, should be in the direction of north and south, for reasons already given; they should be at least four feet apart, and the beans should be placed in shallow drills, three inches asunder, and covered about two inches with soil. When the plants come above ground they may be slightly earthed up; and in another week, when they begin to form runners, they should be sticked with branches or rods, the former being preferable, of six or eight feet in length, a row being placed along each side of the plants, as in sticking peas; but instead of the stakes for runners being placed wider apart at their upper extremity, they may be made to meet there, as, contrary to the vegetation of the pea, the twining stems of the runner produce more leaves below than at their summits. In many cases, the scarlet runner may be planted where it will not only produce excellent crops, but afford shelter or shade to a walk, a seat, a grass-plot, a cucumber-bed, or a temporary arbour. Where sticks or rods are scarce, wires or even twine may be substituted, and in this way the scarlet runner may be trained against wooden walls, pales, or other fences, or made to cover the walls of a cottage. The following mode of arranging pack-thread, or hempen lines, for the support of scarlet runners, is practised in the neighbourhood

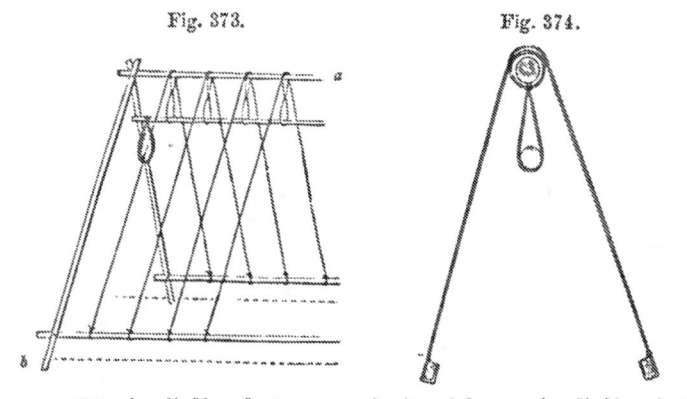

Fig. 373.   Fig. 374.

Prop for climbing plants.   *Section of the prop for climbing plants.*

of St. Petersburg. Take half-inch and two-inch-wide rods or laths, join them at top as in fig. 373, *a*, so as to leave the ends a few inches beyond the junction; stick the lower ends into the ground, just within the lines of the plants. Connect these triangles by similar rods at the bottom, as at *b*, about three inches above the soil. Take a cord, fix it firmly to the lower bar; carry it over the upper bar, which is placed in the cross formed by the long ends left, as shown in the figure. Make a loop a yard long, carry the cord again over the plank (that is, round it), and fix the other end to the lower rod on the other side. In like manner go on through the whole length, taking care to make the loops all of the same length. Through these loops suspend a long stick or bar, the section of which is shown in fig. 374; hang to this bar bags of sand, as many as may be wanted. Train the plants up the strings, and when they are well grown the whole will be covered, and when in flower the appearance will be very ornamental. By this method, the cords being fixed at the lower bars will not pull the plants out of the earth; the tension and contraction of the cords being counteracted by the bar suspended in the loops, which is raised or lowered by every change of atmospheric moisture; so much so, indeed, that it serves as an hygrometer. ('Gard. Mag.,' 1841, p. 211.) In some market gardens in the neighbourhood of London, very abundant crops of the scarlet runner are obtained without staking, by merely stopping the plants after they begin to form pods. By this treatment they also continue longer in bearing, when the pods are to be gathered green; but when seed is to be ripened, it is found best to stake the plants.

Gathering.—Care should be taken not to let any of the pods ripen, otherwise these will attract all the strength of the plant, and prevent in a great measure its future growth, for the production of young pods. The kidney-bean is sometimes attacked by the aphides, but its greatest enemies in the open garden are the snails and slugs. A few plants should be set aside for ripening seed early in the season, in order that they may be perfectly matured, while the weather is fine. The seed cannot be depended on above a year.

The Lima bean (Dolichos, L.), of which there are several species and numerous varieties, is cultivated in France and the South of Europe, but it is rather too tender for the open air in Britain.

The Common Lentil (Ervum Lens, L.); the winter lentil (E. Ervilia, L.); the Spanish lentil (Lathyrus sativus, L.; and the chick pea (Cicer arietinum, L.); and some other lentils, are annuals cultivated on the Continent, as peas are in England, for their ripe seeds, which are put in soups, or dressed as a dish in the same manner as haricots. French cooks occasionally require lentils in English gardens. They are easily cultivated. Sow in drills 18 inches or two feet apart, from the end of March to the middle of May, keep clear of weeds, and gather when fully grown, but before the seeds get hard.

The White Lupin (Lupinus albus, L.) is cultivated in some parts of Spain and Italy for its ripe seeds, which are put in soups or dressed like haricots.

Substitutes for leguminaceous esculents are few, and chiefly the field pea, which is a variety of the garden pea, and the sea pea (Pisum maritimum, L.), a perennial, a native of Britain, on the sea-shore.

Radicaceous Esculents.

The principal esculent roots cultivated in British gardens are the potato, Jerusalem artichoke, turnip, carrot, parsnip, red beet, skirret, scorzonera, salsify, and radish. All of these plants thrive best in deep sandy loam on a dry bottom, deeply trenched and well manured, and with an atmosphere moist and moderately warm. The potato, turnip, and carrot occupy a considerable space in the garden, but not the others. In a rotation of crops they all answer well for succeeding leguminous or alliaceous plants, and some of them for following the cabbage tribe.

The Potato.

The Potato (Solanum tuberosum, L.) is a solanaceous herbaceous perennial with tuber-bearing subterraneous stems, a native of the western coast of South America, and in cultivation in Europe, for its tubers, from the beginning of the sixteenth century. Its uses as a culinary vegetable and as a substitute for bread are known to every one. Potato starch, independently of its use in the laundry, when mixed with a small proportion of wheat flour, makes a most excellent light bread; and it is also manufactured into a substitute for sago, arrow-root, and tapioca; and as starch is convertible into sugar by fermentation, both a wine and a spirit can be produced from it. The tender tops are eaten as spinach in Canada and Kamtschatka, in the same manner as those of the gourd; and the unripe berries have been pickled and preserved, and when ripe dressed like those of the tomato. As potatoes, like bread, are required at table every day in the year, if the whole supply is grown in the garden, a large breadth will be required for this purpose; but the winter supplies are chiefly obtained from the field or the public market, and indeed in most gardens only the early crops are grown. The crop is more exhausting than any other, except in cases where seed is ripened, as when a gardener grows his own turnip or onion seed. In the rotation it ought either to be accompanied with, or follow, a light crop which has been grown on soil in good heart. The uses of the potato in the management of live stock, and its field culture, being foreign to this work, we shall confine ourselves to a brief notice of its culture in gardens.

Varieties.—These are now very numerous. In the 'Gardener's Chronicle' for November, 1869, one writer, Mr. Alexander Dean, says he grows 140 varieties; it is difficult among so many to choose the very best. Among early sorts, the Ash-leaved Kidney still holds its ground. We have now many varieties of it, such as Rivers' Royal, Mona's Pride, the Albion, Myatt's Prolific, Veitch's Improved Early, and the Red Ash-leaved Kidney. All of these are good, as is the Walnut-leaved, which is a dwarf and excellent variety. The Rufford Kidney, Gloucestershire Kidney, and Sheppard's Early are also good. To these might be added most of Paterson's varieties, nearly all of which are distinguished by great excellence of quality and vigour of constitution.

Paterson's Fluke is a first-rate kidney, and said to resist disease. Ditto Red Goliath is a fine pale-red kidney, and a great bearer. Ditto Rock, a large round fine potato. Ditto Early, white flesh, fine-flavoured, round. Ditto Regent, better, hardier, and more productive than any of the other Regents. Ditto Oval Blue, very fine flesh, fine flavour.

A good deal has been heard of late of American potatoes. Among these the Early Rose, Peach Blow, Early Goodrich, Calico, Late

Goodrich, American Red, Bresee's Prolific, King of Earlies, and Climax have been recommended either for form, size, earliness, or lateness. But it has been remarked that most of them are coarser in the grain than our own established sorts. As Mr. Dean, I think, puts it in the 'Gardener's Chronicle,' they smack of the backwoods, and the British grower had better confine himself to such sorts as have proved their qualities in our own climate. Floury early ripeners, late keepers, and good croppers only should be grown.

Round Early Potatoes.—Among Round Early potatoes the Wandsworth, Frame, Early Oxford, Early Coldstream, and Paterson's Victoria, are good varieties.

As intermediate kinds, there are the Huntingdon, Prince of Wales, and Milky White, among kidneys, and the Dalmahoy and Shaws among rounds. Among late sorts the following should be generally grown:—The Fluke, Lapstone, Yorkshire Hero, Taylor's Yorkshire Hybrid, The King of Potatoes, Gryff Castle, Webb's Imperial, and others. Among rounds, the Yorkshire and Scotch Regents, Red Forty-fold, Snowball, Royal Albert, Scotch Blue, and Emperor are good.

Culture.—The potato is propagated by cuttings of the tuber, technically termed "sets;" and, where new sorts are wanted, by seed. A quarter of a peck of tubers will produce from 120 to 150 sets, according to the size of the tuber; and as these should be planted at from six inches to nine inches apart in the drill, according to the kind of potato, a calculation may readily be made of the quantity of any particular kind wanted for sets. The result of many experiments in the culture of the potato by sets, made by the late Mr. Knight, the Horticultural Society, Sir G. S. Mackenzie, and others, is thus given by Dr. Lindley in the 'Gardener's Chronicle':—

"Good sets with single eyes, taken from partially ripe tubers, or small tubers undivided, furnish the best means of multiplying the potato. Large tubers have been recommended, but it has been proved experimentally that no advantage is derived from employing them, while there is a great disadvantage in consequence of the large quantity required. It has been found, too, that if the tubers are over-ripe, that is to say, have acquired all the mealiness and solidity possible, they are apt to produce the curl. It is, therefore, the practice with some growers of potatoes to take up in the autumn what they want for 'seed' before the general crop is ripe, or to select for sets the worst ripened potatoes they can pick out.

"The period of planting should be as soon after the 1st of March as circumstances will permit. 'I have uniformly found,' says Mr. Knight, 'that to obtain crops of potatoes of great weight and excellence, the period of planting should never be later than the beginning of March.' This is in order to give the potato as long a summer as possible. From experiments made some years ago in the garden of the Horticultural Society, it appeared that a crop planted in the first week of March exceeded that planted in the first week of April by about a ton and a quarter per acre. It must be obvious, however, that the propriety of planting thus early will depend upon the nature of the soil, and that it is too early for wet, heavy land, although it is the best season for light soils. In reality, land cannot be advantageously cropped with potatoes until all the superfluous moisture has been drained or evaporated.

"In all cases the plantation should be made in open places, fully exposed to light. The quality of the potato depends upon the quantity of starchy matter (mealiness) it contains. Now this starchy matter can only be formed abundantly by the action of light upon the leaves, which are the natural laboratory in which such secretions take place, and from which they are conducted by sure, though hidden, channels to the tubers, where they are stored up. To plant potatoes, then, in plantations or orchards, or under the shade of trees, is to prevent the formation of the mealiness which renders this plant so nutritious, and to cause the tubers to be watery and worthless. This is probably one reason why field potatoes are usually better than those raised in gardens.

"But the potato may suffer by its own shade as much as by the shade of other plants. When its sets are planted too close, the branches shoot up and choke each other, the leaves of the one smothering the leaves of the other; so that the more sets are planted, the smaller will be the crop of this plant. Mr. Knight was the first to point out this common error, and to show that there is a certain distance at which the sets of each variety of potato should be planted so as to ensure the greatest produce. By planting too close, the plants smother, and so injure each other; by planting at too great a distance, land is uselessly wasted. Practice and well-conducted experiments demonstrate what theory suggested, that the true distance at which potatoes should be set is to be determined by the average length of the haulm. One kind of potato is dwarf, and only grows six inches high; its rows should, therefore, be only six inches apart. Another kind grows three feet high, and its rows should be three feet asunder. The space from set to set in the rows appears to be immaterial; six or eight inches are sufficient for those which grow two feet high. An experiment formerly conducted by the writer of these observations showed that, when the Early Champion, a sort whose stems are on an average two feet long, was planted in rows two feet six inches apart, the produce was 15 tons 19 cwt. 82lbs. nett per acre; while, by reducing the distance between the rows to two feet, the produce was increased to 24 tons; but by diminishing it still further to one foot six inches, the produce was reduced to 22 tons 16 cwt. 102lbs.; and where the rows were only six inches apart, the produce fell to 16 tons 17 cwt. 110lbs. Such an experiment seems conclusive.

"The depth at which the potato should be planted is not ascertained with the same exactness, nor perhaps can it be; for much will depend upon the nature of the soil. In warm, dry land, we regard nine inches as not too deep," provided the sets are large and strong; "in cold, stiff soil, four inches would be better. Six inches is a good depth for average land," and, indeed, may be considered the best depth in most soils. Weak sets do not come up well at nine inches deep; but, on the contrary, four inches is too shallow, occasioning the tubers to be partially exposed to the light, and hence to become green. If, however, the land is so shallow as to admit of no greater depth, then more space must be allowed between the rows for earthing up. "In one of the experiments above alluded to, different depths were also inquired into, when the rates of produce were nearly as follows:—Three inches deep gave 13 tons; four inches, 14 tons; six inches, 14½ tons; and nine inches, 13 tons. At so great a depth as nine inches, sets are apt to perish, unless the soil is dry, light, and warm. The deeper, however, the sets can be safely inserted, the better, for the following reason:— Potatoes are formed on underground branches; the deeper the set, the more branches will be formed before the shoots emerge from the soil, and consequently the more ample will be the means possessed by the potato plant of forming tubers. The important practice of earthing-up is to effect the same end, by compelling the potato stem to grow as much as possible underground.

"The best method of increasing a crop of potatoes is to destroy all the flowers as they appear. The flowers and fruit of plants are formed at the expense of the secretions elaborated by the leaves; if of those secretions a part is consumed in the organization of flowers and fruit, there is so much the less to accumulate in the tubers; but if no such consumption is permitted, the tubers will become the depositories of all the nutritious matter which the plant is capable of producing."— ('Gard. Chron.,' 1842, p. 155.)

For an Early Crop.—The sets may be planted in the first week of October, in a sheltered dry situation, in light sandy soil, eight inches or nine inches deep, and the surface of the ground afterwards covered with long dry litter in such a manner as to exclude the frost and throw off rain. To facilitate the latter object, the sets are best planted in beds, the rain being conducted by the litter to the alleys; or three rows may be planted at a foot apart, leaving every third interval of the width of twelve feet. The plants will appear above ground in March, and with the usual routine culture, and nightly protection till all danger from frost is over, they will produce potatoes fit to gather in May, or early in June. A better mode is to forward the sets by laying them on dry straw in a warm loft, room, or cellar, or on the floor of a greenhouse in January, or the beginning of February; and when they have produced shoots of two inches or three inches in length, which will be the case about the middle or end of March, to plant them out in dry, warm, sheltered soil, covering them with litter at night, and exposing them to the sun during the day. Both these modes are practised in Lancashire and Cheshire, and by both young potatoes are brought to market by the first week of June, and sometimes earlier. By using whole potatoes as sets, burning out with a red-hot iron all the eyes except one, the abundant nutriment thus supplied increases the rapidity of the growth of the young shoots, and produces both an abundant and an early crop. Planting either sets, or sprouted sets, at the base of a south wall, and giving nightly protection, will produce potatoes fit to gather about the end of May; and sets planted in pots forwarded on heat, and afterwards turned out into a warm border, will effect the same object. For ordinary early crops in the open garden the Ash-leaved Kidney may be planted in rows eighteen inches apart, and six to eight inches asunder in the row, from the middle of February to the middle of April.

The Lancashire practice, in planting for an early crop, is as follows:—In the beginning of winter lay the ground up in narrow ridges, two feet and a half centre from centre, fig. 375, *a*; in March the surface of the ridges will be loose from the effects of frost, dry from its position, and warmed by its exposure to the sun to the depth of two inches or three inches; collect this dry mould in the bottom of the furrows, between the ridges, as at *b*; then lay on a little dung, and plant as at *c*; cover to the depth of two inches with dry warm mould from the top of the ridge, and when the plants begin to appear add two inches more, and again two inches when they appear a second time. This is also one of the best modes of planting a main late crop. On wet heavy soils it may be improved upon by simply placing the potatoes on the surface, placing a little burnt earth over them, and then drawing the earth from each side to cover the sets, as practised by Mr. Ingram, at Belvoir, and described in the 'Gardener's Chronicle' for 1869, page 1232.

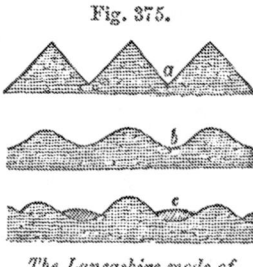

Fig. 375.

The Lancashire mode of planting potatoes.

The first gathering of early potatoes may be made by taking one or two of the largest tubers from every plant by hand, previously removing a portion of the soil with a small three-pronged fork, fig. 33, *c*, in page 88, and afterwards replacing the soil. This, especially if a good watering is given, will throw more strength into the tubers which remain; when the lower leaves begin to fade, the crop may be taken up as wanted, by digging up the plants and collecting the tubers.

Messrs. Chapman's New Spring Potatoes.—" The production of what may be termed late young potatoes, has been achieved extensively by the Messrs. Chapman, of Brentford. They employ principally for this purpose a white Kidney, not a late one, but yet none of the earliest varieties. The tubers are taken up in spring, and spread thinly on a hard dry surface, in order to prevent their springing too far before the time they require to be planted. The greening thus induced is to be regarded as an unavoidable consequence of exposure to air and light rather than an essential condition; for forwardness could be otherwise easily promoted by a few days' earlier planting, at the warm season at which it takes place, that is, the middle of July. They are then planted in the open ground in the usual way. The crop is taken up before frost and stored between layers of soil, whence the tubers, being delicately skinned, are taken only as required for use, forming, both as regards appearance and quality, a very fair substitute for forced new potatoes till the following spring. Any of the earlier varieties, such as the Ash-leaved Kidney, or Early Manly, might be planted even later, and still be in time to produce tubers before frost; and they would prove equally delicate when first taken up, but would not retain the quality of new potatoes so long afterwards as a variety which is less disposed to attain an early maturity." (N. in ' Gard. Mag.,' 1842.)

Young potatoes during winter are obtained by the following modes: —In Cornwall the sets are planted in October; they spring up a few weeks afterwards, are pretty well advanced before the frost stops their growth, and, the soil being covered with litter to exclude the frost, they are first used about the end of December, and continue in use till May, when they are succeeded by the spring-planted crops. Of late years Covent-garden market has received supplies of early potatoes from Cornwall, treated in the above manner ('Gard. Mag.,' vols. ii. v. vi.) In various parts of the country young potatoes for the table during winter are thus produced:—Large potatoes are picked out from the winter stock of any early variety, and buried in dry soil to the depth of three feet. This depth, and the circumstance of treading the soil firmly over the potatoes, so far exclude both heat and air as to prevent vegetation. About the middle of July following, take the tubers out of the pit, and pick out all the buds except a good one in the middle of the potato. Plant these potatoes in a dry border sloping to the south, the soil being in good condition, but not manured. Place the eye or bud of each potato uppermost, and, as their growth will be rapid at this season, earth them up carefully, to preserve their stems from the wind. About the end of October the young potatoes formed by the plants will average the size of pigeons' eggs, and all that is now required to be done, is to cover them well up with long litter, to preserve them from the frost. During winter they may be dug up as wanted, and their delicate waxy taste will resemble that of new potatoes ('Gard. Mag.,' vol. viii. p. 56). Mr. Knight procured a crop of young tubers by planting large ones in September; not a single shoot from these tubers appeared above the soil, but a portion of the matter of the old tuber was merely transformed into young ones, as frequently happens when potatoes are laid between layers of earth in boxes. (Ibid., p. 315.) The same thing has been effected by R. Taplin, who selects the largest potatoes he can find in spring, continues rubbing off the sprouts as fast as they appear till the month of August, when he prepares a bed of light soil, about six inches thick, in a dry, warm shed. On this bed he places his potatoes whole, and very close to each other, covering them with light soil four inches deep, giving it a moderate watering, and letting the bed remain in that state till it is time to cover it over, in order to protect it from frost. On examining the bed in December, he found an abundant crop of potatoes, without the least appearance of haulm or outward shoot from the parent root. ('Gard. Chron.,' 1841, p. 182.)

For a main or late crop, sets, containing each a single eye, are preferable. In cutting sets, enter the knife a little above the eye, slanting the section somewhat downwards: each eye will thus have a fair proportion of substance till the crown only is left of similar size to the other pieces; but here the eyes are generally too much crowded, and therefore all the eyes, except one or two, should be pared off. The sets should have been previously cut and exposed to the air for two or three days, and dusted with hot lime or burnt ashes, to dry up the moisture of the wound. They should be planted in rows two feet or two feet and a-half wide, and from six inches to eight inches apart in the row, according to the richness of the soil and the vigour of the sort, and about six inches deep. The best time in the climate of London is the first week of March, if the soil and the weather are suitable, or a week or more later if they are otherwise. They may either be planted in the Lancashire manner in drills drawn six inches deep, or in holes made by the potato dibber (fig. 17, in p. 83), the latter being the usual mode. They require no further culture than stirring the soil between the rows, keeping it clear of weeds, and drawing the earth up to the stems to the height of three inches or four inches above the general surface; not, however, in a narrow ridge, as is sometimes done, but in a broad rounded ridge, thereby providing soil for covering the tubers that may be protruded into it from the stem, and pinching off the blossom-buds as soon as they appear. The crop will be fit to gather when the leaves and the points of the shoots have begun to decay. They may either be wholly taken up and stored in a cellar, or in a ridge, or left in the ground covered with litter, and taken up through the winter as wanted. For potatoes to be used before March this is an excellent mode; but at that season they generally begin to grow, and then recourse must be had to such as have been covered, so as to retard vegetation.

Selecting and Preparing the Sets.—As the buds at the top end of the tuber, like those on the points of shoots of trees, always vegetate first, these are chosen for sets for an early crop, and they are found in the case of the Ash-leaved Kidney to produce a crop nearly a fortnight earlier than sets taken from the root end of the tuber, where the starch being more concentrated, it requires a longer period to be converted into mucilage. For a main crop the point of the tuber should be rejected whenever it contains a number of small buds, because these produce an equal number of weak stems, which, as shown above, are far inferior in productiveness to one good stem; and the root end ought to be rejected, because the buds there, especially when the potato is over-ripened, sometimes do not vegetate. Early potatoes intended for being cut into sets are found to keep better and sprout earlier when they are taken up before they are ripe, just when the outer skin peels off, and before the stalk or stem begins to wither, and exposed to the direct influence of the sun on any dry surface, till they become green. This will require a month or six weeks, when they become quite green and soft, as if frosted, and often much shrivelled. They are then put away in a cellar or pit, where they remain dry and cool till February, when they will be found sprouted and fit to cut into sets, and planted at once.

Greening potatoes for sets is practised as above stated with a view towards forwarding the crop; but, "why it does so, appears to be imperfectly understood, even by those who practise it. It is well known that tubers are not solely formed on the underground part of the stem; they are also formed upon the stem above ground in many varieties, and these formations are of course green. Though formed at the same time as those below, or later, yet they sprout directly, in the same manner, even in the case of late varieties, the underground tubers of which do not vegetate till the following spring. When, however, an underground tuber is exposed to light, it becomes green, and thereby is assimilated to the nature of the tuber produced above ground, and like it disposed to sprout earlier than those not subjected to the influence of light. It is not, however, necessary to green the sets for a general crop, for if planted in time they come up early enough to be safe from spring frosts without previous exposure, for the purpose of greening; but in the case of early plantations, with protection if necessary, greening may be of some advantage; and in the method of retarding the sets so as only to plant them in July for a late young crop, it is unavoidable, for the tubers would either grow too much or rot, if they were not spread out in a dry cool situation, and consequently one unfavourable for growth. Greening the tubers when taken up is of great importance in forwarding and strengthening the early crops.

Taking up and Preserving a Crop.—They should be carefully taken up without injury; not exposed to the sun or air, and at once stored away in frost-proof cellars or pits, in layers or ridges of moderate thickness, to prevent fermentation. If possible take them up in dry weather, and store at once. If in pits, four feet wide and three feet high will be quite enough. A turf, with the earthy side next the potatoes, might be laid on to keep the soil from mixing with them. Then one foot of earth should follow, and this in severe weather might be thatched over with litter to exclude frost. Buried in this way, potatoes will keep well without sprouting or losing their flavour.

Diseases, Insects, &c.—The potato is subject to the curl in the leaves, which, when it has once taken place, cannot be remedied, but which may, in general, be prevented by using healthy sets from the middle or top end of the tuber, and by good culture in well pulverized soil, dry at bottom. The heating and fermenting of sets, after they have been cut, often produces the curl and other diseases; and some particular soils and manures seem to be the cause of the scab in the tuber. These diseases, however, are more common in fields than in gardens. A change of variety, or of sets of the same variety from a different locality, is frequently resorted to, more especially in field culture, as a general preventive of disease in the potato. None of these methods, however, have checked the ravages of what is now so well known as the potato disease. This has hitherto baffled the power of the hybridizer and the cultivator. It created the Irish famine, and still threatens to destroy the potato crop. Though less virulent than it was, it has been occasionally very destructive in many districts. It attacks the potato in the last stages of growth in August or September. At first a few black spots, about the size of hail-stones, speck the leaves. The gangrene spreads rapidly, runs down and blotches the stem, and rots the suckers in a wholesale manner. Cutting off the branches, raising new varieties, change of soil, new modes of culture, and endless specifics, have all been tried in vain. The only chance of a sound crop is to grow early varieties, plant early, and get them safely harvested before the disease comes. When this is the case, the disease has no power over the tubers afterwards; but when once the black specks appear among them, the disease is latent in the tubers, and may break forth after they are stored.

Forcing the Potato.—See p. 518.

The Jerusalem Artichoke.

The Jerusalem Artichoke (Helianthus tuberosus, L.) is a tuberous-rooted perennial, a native of Brazil, but sufficiently hardy to thrive in the open air in Britain. Before the potato was known, the tubers of this plant were much esteemed, but they are now comparatively neglected, though in our opinion the Jerusalem artichoke is as deserving of culture as the common artichoke. The tubers are wholesome, nutritious, and in stews boiled and mashed with butter, or baked in pies with spices, they have an excellent flavour. In many families they are much used for soups. Propagation is effected by division of the tuber, or by small tubers planted in March: the soil ought to be light, sandy, and rich, and the situation open. As the stems grow from four feet to eight feet in height, the rows may be three feet or four feet apart, and the plants a foot distant in the row. The tubers may either be taken from the plants as wanted, or the crop dug up and housed in the manner of potatoes. No plant in the whole catalogue of culinary vegetables requires less care in its culture. It very seldom flowers, but by destroying the tubers as they appear, it might doubtless be made to produce seed, by means of which some improved varieties might possibly be obtained.

The Turnip.

The Turnip (Brassica Rapa, L.) is a cruciferous biennial, a native of Britain, of no value in its wild state, but so greatly changed by culture as to become one of our most useful culinary and agricultural vegetables. It was cultivated by the Romans, but was little known about London till the beginning of the seventeenth century. The use of the root in broths, soups, stews, and entire or mashed, is general in all temperate climates, and also the use of the tender radical and stem leaves, and the points of the shoots, when the plant is coming into flower, as greens. The seedling plants, when the rough leaf is beginning to appear, like those of all others of the Brassica family, are used in small salading. The earliest crop of turnips, if sown in March, comes into use about the end of May or beginning of June, and a succession is kept up throughout the summer by subsequent sowings once a fortnight till September; and turnips may be had through the winter, partly from the open garden and partly from roots stored up in the manner of potatoes. Hence a large portion of the kitchen-garden is devoted to this crop. A well-grown turnip has a large, smooth, symmetrical bulb, a small neck, and a small root or tail, with few fibres, except near its lower extremity. In the rotation the turnip follows the potato, the leguminous family, or any crop not cruciferous.

Varieties.—Early White Dutch, Red Top, American Stone, Early Snowball, Early Stone, and American Strap Leaf, are among the best and sweetest varieties. The Yellow Stone, Yellow Malta, Yellow Altringham, are good summer sorts; while for winter use no better can be sown than the Black Stone, Orange Jelly, and Jersey Navet. These should be sown on light dry soil in August or early in September to draw from the open ground throughout the winter.

Culture.—The turnip should be sown in drills from a foot to fifteen inches apart, and thinned to six inches between the plants. The seed comes up in ten days or a fortnight, according to the season. The soil should be in good heart, and well pulverized. A sowing should be made once in March, and twice in April, for the earliest crops; and afterwards at intervals of a fortnight, till the end of August, for a winter crop or for plants to stand through the winter to shoot up and supply greens in February, March, and April. The main crops of turnips should be sown in the latter end of June. All sorts should be sown in drills, as admitting of stirring the soil among the plants with less labour. The earliest and latest crops should be of the early Dutch, as coming into use sooner in autumn, and sending up sprouts soonest in spring. The routine culture consists in weeding, thinning, stirring the soil, and supplying water abundantly in very dry weather, to prevent the roots from becoming tough and stringy; taking great care, when stirring the soil, not to earth up the roots, which, on strong soils, might prevent their swelling.

In gathering the root the entire plant is necessarily pulled up, and the tops and tails taken at once to the rubbish-heap. Choose the largest, and take them from the most crowded parts of the rows, to make more room for the growth of those which remain. In gathering the tops in spring, the tenderest leaves only are taken, whether from the crowns of plants that have not yet run, or from the flower-stems. Some also gather the points of the stems, which, however, are much less delicate than the leaves, but excellent to salt beef. The leaves and tops are good from all the varieties; but sweetest from the Swedish turnip, which is seldom grown in gardens.

Preserving Turnips through the Winter.—In ordinary winters neither the yellow nor the Swedish turnip require to be covered; but as when left exposed they will begin to vegetate, in February a portion of the crop should be taken up, topped (but not tailed, which would favour the escape of sap), and preserved in sand or straw in the root-cellar, or in a ridge like potatoes; and like them so thickly thatched as to exclude both heat and rain, and maintain a degree of coolness that will prevent vegetation. Or the rows as they stand on the ground may have the leaves cut off and covered with soil, so as to form them into ridges, and after the whole mass of the ridges has been cooled down to 32° by frost, it may then be thickly covered with litter, to exclude the heating influence of the sun. As the turnip vegetates at a much lower temperature than the potato, much greater care is required to keep it in a dormant state.

To Save Seed.—One kind only can be saved in one garden in the same year. It is so cheap that it is not worth while, unless in cases of scarce or highly-valued varieties. In such cases the best-formed roots, and those which have come earliest or latest to maturity according to the variety, should be selected and transplanted in autumn, or early in spring, into a spot by themselves, and the stems tied to stakes, if there should be any danger apprehended from high winds. The seed will keep four or five years, but should be aërated once every winter, during severe frost.

Diseases, Insects, &c.—The turnip in very dry seasons is liable to the mildew, if it has not been liberally supplied with water; and also to excrescences on the root, produced by a species of cynips which deposits its eggs there. Lime, soap-boilers' waste, putrid urine, or the urine of cows, are said to render the soil offensive to the parent-fly; and when its attacks can be foreseen, this mode may be adopted, more especially as, if it fails, it will at all events manure the soil. On coming through the ground, the plants are liable to the attacks of a small jumping-beetle, called the turnip-flea (Haltica nemorum), besides five or six other insects of different kinds, the effects of which are very serious in field-culture; but in gardens they can generally be guarded against, or counteracted by watering, or by digging down and re-sowing. Dry soot or ashes is a good remedy for the fly; but the likeliest way to secure the safety of the crop is to sow on good soil, and hurry it through the first stages of growth.

Forcing the turnip for the root is seldom attempted in British gardens, though in Russia and some parts of Germany it is sown on hot-beds, as radishes are in England. The large white turnip-radish is sometimes used as a substitute for early turnips in England. The roots, more especially those of the Swedish turnip, placed close together on heat in January, will produce an abundance of delicate sprouts through February and March.

The Carrot.

The Carrot (Daucus Carota, L.) is an umbelliferous biennial, common in Britain and other parts of Europe, of no use in cookery in a wild state, but by culture rendered succulent, agreeable, and when young highly nutritive. It is excellent in a mature state as a dish, or in stews; and no vegetable is so much in demand for soups. For the latter purpose, it is required in some families throughout the year, several crops being forced, and the supply from May to October being furnished from the open garden. A considerable breadth is therefore required for this crop, which in the rotation may follow some of the cabbage tribe, or some crop that has been manured; for any manure, except what is in a liquid state, applied to the carrot, causes the roots to branch and their rind to become ulcerated.

Varieties.—Early Horn: orange, short, coming earlier to maturity than any other variety; sow this variety thickly in drills in the middle of July, to command nice young carrots all the winter; and in middle of August for early spring use. Early French Scarlet Horn: larger than the preceding, and better for a main crop. Long Orange, syn. Altringham, and Long Red Surrey: long and of good quality, excellent also for a main crop. James's Scarlet: the very best garden carrot for quality, colour, and form.

Culture.—The only mode of propagation is by seed; and as the seeds have numerous forked hairs on their edges, by which they adhere together in clusters, they should be rubbed between the hands and mixed with dry sand, in order to separate them as much as possible before sowing. For a bed four and a half by thirty feet, the plants to be thinned out to six inches every way, or for 150 feet of drill, one ounce of seed will be requisite. The seed does not come up for four or five weeks in spring, and for three or four in summer and autumn. The soil should be light and sandy, and deep and rich, in consequence of being well trenched and manured the preceding year. The first sowing of the Early Horn may be made in the middle of February, in a warm border; and if the family require a constant supply of young carrots, successional sowings may be made, as recommended for a constant supply of turnips. From the middle of March to the first week in April is the best time for sowing the main crop for taking up and preserving through the winter; and a crop of small carrots, to stand through the winter and afford roots in February, March, and April, may be sown in the first week in August. All the crops that are to be drawn young may be sown in drills, six inches apart, and the plants thinned out to three inches, but those which are intended to produce carrots of full size should be sown in drills eighteen inches apart, and the plants thinned out to from eight inches to ten inches in the row.

Gathering and Keeping.—Young carrots are drawn by hand, and full-grown ones dug up with the spade or two-pronged fork, a trench being made alongside one row after another, so as to admit of taking out the carrots without, in the slightest degree, injuring their rind. A portion of the main crop may be left in the ground, and covered with litter to be taken up as wanted; and the remainder may be preserved in cellars or in ridges by some of the modes recommended for preserving turnips. The tops should be wrung off by hand, and great care be taken in harvesting neither to mow tops nor bottoms by slicing off the leaves with knives, breaking the roots in the ground, or cutting them with the spade.

Diseases and Insects.—The root is sometimes disfigured by ulcers, supposed to be the effect of recent manure, and they are often attacked by the grub of some dipterous insect, which in its perfect state may be prevented from depositing its eggs by watering the soil after the plants have come up with some nauseous liquid-manure, such as putrid urine or spirits of tar, at the rate of about one gallon to every sixty square yards. (C. M'Intosh, in 'Gard. Chron.' for 1841, p. 53.) Grubs already in the soil cannot so readily be destroyed, unless the ground is so deep that they may be trenched down, when the want of air will kill them; but some other crop may be grown on it which the insects will not attack.

Seed Saving.—Select some of the finest specimens and transplant them in autumn, growing only the seeds of one variety in one year in the same garden. The seed, if kept dry and adhering to the stalk, will keep three or four years; but, if separated from the stalk, it will grow with difficulty the second year.

The Parsnip.

The Parsnip (Pastinaca sativa, L.) is an umbelliferous biennial, a native of Britain, on calcareous soils in open situations, and withstanding our severest winters. It has been as much changed by culture as the carrot, and like it its roots are highly valued both in horticulture and agriculture. With respect to culinary purposes, they are in season from October till March. They differ from the carrot in being only used in their mature state, and chiefly during winter; forming a dish to be eaten to meat or to salt fish; and they are used in soups, mashed, stewed, and fried. Beer and wine can be made from them, and also a powerful spirit. The parsnip is excellent food for cows, being highly nutritive, and giving to the milk a peculiarly rich and agreeable flavour, resembling that from cows that are fed on the richest old pasture. Hence it should be grown on a large scale by every cottager who has a cow. Only a moderate space is required for them in the gentleman's garden, and they come in in the rotation along with the carrot and the beet. The varieties are few; the Hollow-crowned, the Guernsey, and the Student being the best worth cultivating. There are also a turnip-rooted variety, and one with yellow flesh and a high flavour, known as the Siam parsnip.

Cultivation.—The seed required for a bed five feet by twenty feet, the plants to be thinned to eight inches' distance every way, is one ounce; and the same for a drill of one hundred and fifty feet; the seed comes up in eight or ten days. Seldom more than one crop is required, and this is sown in March, in rows eighteen inches apart, the plants being afterwards thinned out to eight inches' distance in the row. Routine culture as in the carrot. The roots are not liable to be injured by the frost, and may therefore be left in the ground to be taken up as wanted till February, when they will begin to grow. If parsnips are required after this season, a quantity of roots must be taken up in winter, and stored like those of the carrot. The parsnip is seldom attacked by diseases or by insects. Seed may be saved as in the carrot, and it generally retains its vitality only one year.

The Red Beet.

The Red Beet (Beta vulgaris, L.) is a fusiform-rooted biennial, a native of the South of Europe on the sea-coast, and cultivated in gardens for its root from the beginning of the seventeenth century, and probably long before. The roots are boiled and eaten cold, either to meat, especially mutton, by themselves, dressed as salad, or in mixture with other salad ingredients; they form a beautiful garnish, and a very desirable pickle. The thin slices dried in an oven are also used in confectionery, and the leaves may be used as spinach or greens. The roots must be washed and also boiled with all their lateral fibres, and, in short, without any part cut off except the leaves; because it is found that when the root is wounded in any part, the colour in boiling escapes through the wound. There are several varieties, among the best being Henderson's Pine-apple, Dell's Dark Crimson, Dewar's Crimson, Covent Garden Improved, Cattell's Crimson, Cattell's Short Top, Nutting's, and Pine-apple Short Top; of these the last four are about the best. One crop of beet is enough for the largest garden, and this should be sown in the middle of April. For a bed four feet and a half by twelve feet, or one hundred and fifty feet of drill, one ounce of seed is sufficient. The ground should be prepared as for the carrot, and the seed may be sown in drills at the same distances, and the same routine culture given, with this difference, that blanks when they occur may be filled up by transplanting when the plants are quite small. The plants come up in a month. The crop will be ready for use in September, and may be treated in all respects like a crop of carrots, and like them, if desirable, kept in pits from December till the September following. Great care must be taken in harvesting the crop not to break the roots, else the sap, and with it the colour of the beet, will ooze out, and the quality be destroyed.

The Skirret, Scorzonera, Salsify, and Œnothera.

Though these plants are at present but little cultivated in British gardens, yet we think a small portion of each deserves a place for the sake of variety.

The Skirret (Sium Sisarum, L.) is an umbelliferous tuberous-rooted perennial, a native of China, and in cultivation in British gardens from the beginning of the sixteenth century. The part used is the root, which is composed of fleshy tubers, about the size of the little finger, and joined together at the collar of the plant in the manner of the tubers of the ranunculus. The tubers were formerly esteemed as "the sweetest, whitest, and most pleasant of roots," either boiled and served up with sauce, or fried in various ways. The root is in season during the same period as the parsnip. There are no varieties; but when the plant is cultivated, it is generally propagated by dividing the roots. Seed, however, may be obtained, and its culture and management are in all respects the same as directed for the beet. The seed keeps four years.

The Scorzonera or Viper's-grass (Scorzonera hispanica, L.) is a chicoraceous fusiform-rooted biennial, a native of the South of Europe, in culture in British gardens since the middle of the sixteenth century. The root is straight, conical, and about the thickness of a middle-sized carrot, with a black rind. It is used boiled or stewed, in the manner of carrots or parnips; it comes into use in August, and may be taken up in November, and preserved as long as may be thought desirable. Though a perennial, it is always propagated by seed, of which an ounce will be sufficient for one hundred and fifty feet of drill. The seed comes up in three or four weeks. The routine culture is the same as for the carrot and parsnip.

The Salsify, or Purple Goat's-beard (Tragopogon porrifolius, L.) is a chicoraceous fusiform-rooted biennial, not unlike the scorzonera, to which, however, it is much to be preferred, but with much narrower leaves, at a distance resembling those of leeks, a native of England, commonly cultivated for its roots, which are used like carrots and parsnips, or more frequently served up with white sauce. The seeds may be sown in March or April, and treated in all respects like those of the scorzonera. The seed keeps two years. This is a most useful and pleasant vegetable, and is in pretty general use.

The Spanish Salsify (Scolymus hispanicus, L.) is a carduaceous biennial, a native of the south of France, where the roots of the wild plant are collected and dressed like those of salsify or scorzonera, which they closely resemble when dressed.

The Tree-primrose (Œnothera biennis, L.), an onagraceous fusiform-rooted biennial, a native of North America, is cultivated in some parts of Germany for the same purpose as the scorzonera, and the points of the shoots are used in salads. The roots of the other biennial species may doubtless be similarly applied. Seeds are readily procured from the seed-shops, and the plant grows freely in sandy soil.

The Hamburg Parsley.

The Hamburg parsley is a biennial, resembling the common parsley, but with much larger, less curled leaves, and with large fusiform roots of the same colour and texture as those of the parsnip. It is occasionally cultivated in Germany, to put in soups and stews, and also as a separate dish, like the parsnip or turnip. Its culture is in all respects the same as that of the parsnip. It is also scraped or bruised to form a cooling poultice, and applied to broken breasts or any inflammatory wound.

The Radish.

The Radish (Raphanus sativus, L.) is a fusiform-rooted cruciferous annual, said to be a native of China, in cultivation in Britain, from the earliest period of garden history, for the roots, which are eaten raw as salad, or in mixture with other ingredients. The roots are also excellent when boiled and sent to the table in the manner of asparagus. The young seedling leaves are sometimes used as small salading, and the seed-pods are frequently pickled, and used as a substitute for capers.

Varieties.—These are arranged as spring and summer radishes, turnip radishes, autumn radishes, and winter radishes. The first class are delicately acrid, the second more powerfully so, and the last strong and coarsely pungent.

Spring and Summer Radishes.—Scarlet, Short-topped Scarlet, Semi-long Scarlet, Wood's Short-top Scarlet, and the Paris little pink breakfast radish.

Turnip Radishes.—White turnip and Rose-coloured turnip.

Autumn Radishes.—White Russian, Yellow turnip, and Round brown. These three used to be grown for autumn use; now the best spring or summer varieties are mostly grown in autumn as well. The China rose is, however, a fine autumn radish.

Winter Radishes.—White Spanish and Black Spanish are the hardiest of the winter radishes; the best for a cottage garden.

The soil for all the kinds should be light, rich, and well pulverized to at least eighteen inches in depth, and the situation for an early crop sheltered and exposed to the sun. The seed should be sown in January and February for a crop to be drawn in March and April, and covered with mats, straw, or fern, nightly and during great part of the day in snowy or very cold windy weather. The seeds should be scattered so thin as not to come up thicker than one and a half inches or two inches apart. For a bed four feet six inches by twelve feet, two ounces of seed will be required. It will come up in eight or ten days. Successional sowings may be made every ten days or fortnight, till the end of May; afterwards the autumn radishes may be sown till the end of July; and the winter radishes may be sown from the beginning of July till the end of August. The autumn and winter radishes are most conveniently cultivated in rows, and as they are allowed to attain a considerable size before being used, the distance between the rows may be nine inches or a foot, and the distance in the row six inches. The winter radishes come into use in October, and being very hardy, may either be left in the open ground through the winter, which is the practice in Russia where the ground is covered with snow, and taken up as wanted; or stored up in ridges or cellars in the manner of turnips or carrots. The tender green seed-pods used in pickling are taken from plants of the early sorts that have been allowed to run to seed for that purpose in July and August. The early radishes are so short a time on the ground that they are seldom troubled with insects; but in the case of seed-bearing plants, the sparrows are very fond of the newly-formed seeds. In saving seed only one kind ought to be grown in the same garden at the same time. The seed will keep two years. A few years since an extraordinary sensation was created by the introduction of a new radish which grew up into a large bush and produced pods nearly a yard long. This vegetable wonder is called the Raphanus caudatus, or Rat-tailed radish, and the pods, which are mild and crisp when young, are eaten instead of the root. It is curious as well as useful, and a few should be grown either in pots in a house, or in a warm sheltered corner out of doors.

For forcing the radish the details have already been given at length.

Oxalis Deppei, O. crenata, and Tropæolum tuberosum.

Deppe's Oxalis (O. Deppei, B. C.), is an Oxalideous bulbous-rooted perennial, a native of Mexico, introduced in 1827, and strongly recommended for cultivation for its fusiform roots, which form a delicate vegetable dish; and for its stems, flowers, and leaves, for putting into salads. The roots, when the plant is properly cultivated, become nearly four inches in length, and above an inch in thickness, consisting of cellular matter without woody tissue or sap vessels, not unlike, in texture and nutritious properties, the tubers of the salep orchis (O. Morio, L.) The roots should be gently boiled with salt and water, after being washed and slightly peeled; they are eaten like asparagus, in the Flemish fashion, with melted butter and the yolk of eggs. They are also served up like scorzonera and endive, with white sauce. They form, in whatever way they are dressed, a tender succulent dish, easy to digest, agreeing with the most delicate stomach. The young leaves are dressed like sorrel, put in soup, or used as greens; they have a fresh and agreeable acid, especially in spring. The flowers are excellent in salad, alone, or mixed with corn salad, endive of both kinds, red cabbage, beetroot, and even with the petals of the dahlia, which are delicious when thus employed. When served at table, the flowers with their pink corolla, green calyx, yellow stripes, and little stamens, produce a very pretty effect. Propagation may be effected by the little scaly bulbs, which are found in abundance round the collar of the plant. They require a light sandy soil, enriched with decayed vegetable matter, and frequent watering in very dry weather, either with clear water or liquid-manure. The bulbs may be planted about the middle or latter end of April, when all danger from frost is over, in drills seven inches asunder, the bulbs five inches apart in the row, and covered with an inch deep of soil. The bulbs being exceedingly small, three or four of them are put down together, so as to form a group of plants. Vegetation continues till October, when the plants may be taken up, and the roots preserved through the winter in sand in a dry cellar, protected from frost. The bulbs are previously taken off the sides of the crown of the root, and preserved till the planting season, in the same manner.

Oxalis crenata, Jacq., a tuberous-rooted Oxalis from Lima, where it is used as an esculent, has been cultivated in this country since 1832, for the same purposes as Oxalis Deppei; but it is said to be inferior to that species in the flavour of the tubers. The stalks and leaves, however, are used in tarts, alone or with other vegetables or fruits. Neither of these plants are much cultivated now. There are several other bulbous or tuberous-rooted species of Oxalis from South America, which might in all probability be used in the same manner as the species mentioned.

Tropæolum tuberosum, Maund., is a tropæolaceous, tuberous-rooted, climbing perennial, growing five feet or six feet high, introduced from Peru in 1837, which has also been added to the list of our esculent roots. The tubers, when well grown, are about the size of hens' eggs, and have the flavour of sea-kale or asparagus, joined to somewhat of the hot taste of garden cress. The plant is propagated either by cuttings taken from tubers placed in heat early in the season, and treated like cuttings of dahlias so obtained, or by cuttings of the tubers, leaving one good eye in each set. These may be brought forward on heat in separate pots, and when all danger from frost is over, turned out into a light, rich, sandy soil, three feet or four feet apart every way, and either left to cover the ground with their trailing stems, by which the soil will be kept moist, or sticked like peas. The latter is the best mode in a moist season or damp soil. In October, when the leaves are beginning to decay, the plants may be taken up, and the tubers placed in a dry cellar, or in a pit or ridge, out of the reach of frost and damp, in the manner of the tubers of Oxalis, or those of the potato. ('Gard. Mag.,' 1838, p. 254.) T. edule, and other species with tuberous roots, might doubtless be used as substitutes for the Tropæolum tuberosum, L.

Spinaceous Esculents.

The only spinaceous esculents generally cultivated in British gardens are the common spinach, and the sorrel; but we have also French spinach, beet-spinach, perennial-spinach, New Zealand spinach, and Herb-patience. They are all very mild in quality, and may be used as greens by persons with whom the cabbage-tribe would disagree. In the rotation of crops, some of them, as the common spinach, are secondary; others, as the white beet, are annual; and some, as the sorrel, are stationary.

The Common Spinach.

The Common Spinach (Spinacia oleracea, L.) is a chenopodiaceous, diœcious annual, a native of the north of Asia, in cultivation from the middle of the sixteenth century, or earlier, for its succulent leaves. It is a very hardy plant, the Flanders variety particularly, withstanding the severest frost. The leaves are used boiled and mashed up as a separate dish, and in soups or stews, with or without the addition of sorrel. The leaves may be obtained from the open ground from April to November, and also to a moderate extent through the winter and spring. There are three varieties, the round-seeded, for sowing during summer; the Flanders spinach, which has also smooth seeds but larger, and very large leaves, for sowing in autumn for use in winter and spring; and the prickly-seeded, or common winter spinach. The quantity of seed required for a bed four and a half feet by thirty feet is two ounces, or for one hundred and fifty feet of drill, one ounce. The seed comes up in a fortnight or three weeks, according to the season. The best mode of sowing is in drills eight inches apart for summer spinach, and ten inches or one foot for Flanders spinach; the plants in the former case to be thinned to six inches apart, and in the latter to eight inches, as soon as they have shown a proper leaf. In order that the leaves may be succulent, and properly flavoured, the soil should be rich and the situation open and airy, more especially for the main crops. The summer crops are frequently sown alternately with rows of peas or beans; but, as the spinach is generally more or less shaded by these crops before it is fit to be gathered, it is never of so good a quality as that which is grown in the open garden. For summer spinach, the first sowing may be made in open weather in January, and sowings in succession every three or four weeks may be made till the end of July. For winter and spring use, a large sowing of the Flanders variety, and also some of the prickly-seeded, which some prefer, should be made in the first or second week of August, and a secondary one towards the end of that month. These sowings will come into use in November, and will continue to afford gatherings occasionally through the winter, and frequently in spring, till May or June. The routine culture of all the sowings consists in thinning, stirring the soil between the rows, and watering in very dry weather. In gathering, the largest leaf only, or at most a few of the largest leaves, should be taken off one plant at a time: they may either be cut or pinched off. A portion of the winter crop may be protected by hoops and mats, when a heavy fall of snow is anticipated, to admit of its being more readily gathered. Seed may be saved by leaving a portion of a row, containing both male and female plants. When the female blossoms are set, the male plants should be pulled up. The seed will keep four years.

Orache, or French Spinach.

The Orache, or French Spinach (Atriplex hortensis, L.) is a chenopodiaceous polygamous annual, growing to the height of three feet or four feet, a native of Tartary, and in cultivation as a spinach plant from the beginning of the sixteenth century. The leaves are used as in the common spinach, to mix with those of sorrel, and sometimes also the tender points of the shoots. There are several varieties, the white (syn. pale green-leaved), the green-leaved, the dark red-leaved, and Lee's Giant, by far the best of this class, possessing extraordinary productive powers, and said to be superior in flavour. An ounce of seed will sow a drill of one hundred feet in length; and it comes up in ten days or a fortnight. A dozen or two of plants placed two feet apart every way, in rich soil, in an open situation, kept moderately moist, will afford gatherings two or three times a week during the whole summer. The leaves ought to be taken while they are tender, and the blossoms pinched off as fast as they appear. The earliest crop may be sown in February, and for succession another sowing may be made in June. One plant will afford abundance of seed, which will keep two years.

New Zealand Spinach.

The New Zealand Spinach (Tetragonia expansa, H. K.) is a ficoidaceous trailing annual, a native of New Zealand, growing freely in the open garden during our summers, and suffering much less from drought than the common spinach. It has been more or less in culture as a spinach plant since the beginning of the present century; but it is of inferior quality to the common spinach, and even to the Orache, or French spinach. The seed, of which $\frac{1}{4}$ oz. will be sufficient, may be sown on a gentle heat in March; it will come up in ten days, and the plants may be transplanted into small pots and kept in a cold frame till the middle of May, when they may be turned out into the open garden, allowing each plant at least a square yard for the extension of its trailing branches. Half-a-dozen plants are enough for an ordinary-sized garden. Seed may be saved in fine seasons from plants in the open garden; and in cold wet summers by planting on dry rubbish, keeping a plant in a pot, or training one up a wall. It will keep two years.

Perennial Spinach.

The Perennial Spinach (Chenopodium Bonus Henricus, L.) is a chenopodiaceous perennial, a native of Britain, in loamy soils, and formerly cultivated in gardens for its leaves, which when grown in a rich soil on vigorous young plants, make a very succulent spinach. The plant is easily propagated by division, and it also ripens seeds. In Lincolnshire it is said to be cultivated in preference to the common spinach.

The Spinach Beet, and the Chard Beet.

The Spinach Beet, Leaf Beet, or White or Silver Beet (Beta cicla, L.) is a chenopodiaceous biennial, a native of the sea-shores of Spain and Portugal, and in cultivation in British gardens from the middle of the sixteenth century, for the leaves, which are boiled as spinach, or put into soups, and used as greens.

The Chard Beet, syn. Swiss Chard, belongs to this species; it has leaves with strong white footstalks and ribs, and these, separated from the disk of the leaf and dressed like asparagus, are thought to be nearly as good as that vegetable. There are varieties with white, yellow, and red midribs.

The advantage of using the White Beet as a spinach plant is, that it affords a succession of leaves during the whole summer; and hence it is recommended for the gardens of cottages. The same advantage also attends the use of the Sugar or Silesian Beet, the Sea-beet (Beta maritima, L.), a biennial, or imperfect perennial, a native of our shores. All the beets require similar culture to that of the beet already described. Only those grown for the leaves alone might be cultivated in a richer soil, as succulency of top and not quality of root is required. A single plant will produce abundance of seed, which will keep five or six years.

Patience Spinach.

Patience Spinach, Herb-patience, or Patience Dock (Rumex Patientia, L.) is a polygonaceous perennial, a native of Italy, formerly common in gardens as a spinach plant, but now much neglected. The leaves rise early in spring, and continue to be produced during great part of the summer; they should be gathered when quite tender, and boiled with about a fourth part of common sorrel. It may be raised from seeds, or increased by division like the perennial spinach.

The Sorrel.

The Sorrel (Rumex, L.) is a polygonaceous genus, of which two species have been long in cultivation for their leaves as salad. The French sorrel (syn. Roman sorrel), or round-leaved sorrel (R. scutatus, L.) is a perennial, a native of France and Italy; and the common garden sorrel (R. Acetosa, L.) is an indigenous perennial, common in moist meadows. The leaves of both species are used in soups, sauces, and salads; and very generally by the French and Dutch as a spinach; in the latter way it is often used along with Herb-patience, to which it gives an excellent flavour, as well as to Orache, turnip-tops, nettle-tops, and those of Jack-by-the-hedge. There are several varieties of the common sorrel, but that most esteemed is the large-leaved, de Belleville, Fr. The mild-leaved (R. montanus H. P.) is a diœcious species, of which the leaves are smaller and less acid than those of R. Acetosa. All the kinds are propagated by division or by seeds, and they may be grown in rows eighteen inches apart, and a foot distant in the row; lifting a portion of the plantation every year after the flowering season, when the plants are in a comparatively dormant state, dividing them, and replanting. If this is neglected for two or three years, the plants will become large and crowded, produce only small leaves, rot in the centre, and ultimately die off. Wherever French cookery is in demand, a considerable breadth of sorrel will be required, and to produce the leaves in a succulent state the soil ought to be rich, loamy, and kept moist.

Alliaceous Esculents.

The alliaceous esculents in cultivation in British gardens are chiefly the onion, leek, shallot, and garlic; but there are also the chive and the rocambole. They are all asphodelaceous perennials belonging to the genus Allium, L. They all require a rich, loamy soil and an open situation; the onion, shallot, and leek crops occupy a considerable proportion of every garden, and they may follow either the cabbage tribe or some of the leguminosæ; they are all more or less subject to the onion-fly, which is described under the heading of the onion.

The Onion.

The Common Onion (Allium Cepa, L.), is an asphodelaceous bulbous perennial, the native country of which is unknown, but its culture is as old as the history of the human race, and as extensive as civilization. The common onion, though treated as an annual when grown for its bulb, and as a biennial when grown for seed, is yet as much a perennial as the garlic, and, like it, produces offsets the second year, though not in such abundance. The Welsh onion, potato onion, and bulb-bearing onion, are different species, or very distinct varieties, also cultivated in British gardens, but not of such antiquity as the common onion. The onion is in universal use, when young, in salads; and when more advanced, or when mature, in soups, stews, or alone boiled or roasted.

Varieties and Species.—The silver-skinned; chiefly used for pickling. Nuneham Park, Danvers' Yellow, Bedfordshire Champion, Strasburgh, Deptford, James's Keeping, Blood-red, White Spanish, Reading, Brown Portugal, and Tripoli. The Welsh onion, or ciboule (A. fistulosum, L.), a native of Siberia, strongly flavoured, but does not bulb; very hardy, sown in autumn for drawing in spring. The underground, or potato onion (A. Cepa, var. aggregatum, G. Don), multiplies by young bulbs on the parent root, which have all the properties of the common onion, and are equally productive, but do not keep longer than February. The tree, or bulb-bearing onion, syn. Egyptian onion (A. Cepa, var. viviparum); the stem produces bulbs instead of flowers, and when these bulbs are planted they produce underground onions of considerable size, and being much stronger flavoured than those of any other variety, they go farther in cookery.

Propagation and Culture.—All the kinds, except the last two, are propagated by seeds, of which two ounces will be requisite for a bed four feet by twenty-four feet, to be drawn young; or one ounce for a bed five feet by twenty-four feet, to remain till they are full grown; two ounces of seed to sow 800 feet of drill a foot apart. The seed will come up in about a fortnight. The soil in which the onion succeeds best is a strong loam well enriched with manure, which may be of the strongest kind, such as bullocks' blood, night soil, powdered bones, &c., previously rotted. It should be well pulverized to a considerable depth. The best mode is to sow in drills, nine inches apart for the smaller kinds, and a foot for such as are larger; the plants to be thinned out when three inches high to four inches, six inches, or eight inches, according to the kind, or whether onions of large or moderate size are wished for. To produce small onions for pickling, the silver-skinned variety, or the Nocera, should be sown thick, or very thick, according to the size wanted; and to produce very large onions, the Tripoli ought to be sown thin, and the soil stirred once or twice during the summer, care being taken, in this and in every other case of stirring the soil among onions, not to earth up the incipient bulb, that being found to impede its swelling. Liquid manure may be freely applied. The time for sowing a main crop, to produce bulbs for keeping through the winter, is the beginning or middle of March; and great care is requisite not to cover the seed more than an inch, and to press the soil on it firmly by treading or rolling. Thinning and hoeing-up weeds should be performed with a two-inch hoe, and the soil may be stirred with a common Dutch or draw-hoe; or, if the plants are very close, with the sickle hoe, fig. 376. When the seeds are to be sown in drills, these may be made either singly with the drill-hoe, fig. 377, or in three or four at a time, by the drill-rake, fig. 378. The teeth of this rake, like the head, are of wood; the latter being pierced with holes an inch apart, so that the teeth, which are to form the drills, may be fixed at any convenient distance. Market-gardeners sometimes, instead of distributing the seed along the drill, drop four or five seeds together at every six or eight inches' distance, giving no

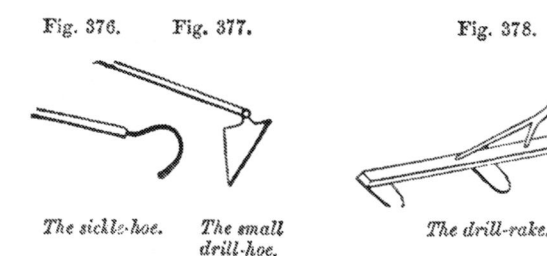

Fig. 376. Fig. 377. Fig. 378.

The sickle-hoe. *The small drill-hoe.* *The drill-rake.*

thinning afterwards, but leaving the plants to press against and push aside one another. This saves the labour of thinning; and if the soil is kept well stirred between the rows, a considerable bulk of crop will be produced, though the onions will be very irregular in point of size. In deep alluvial loam, the onion plants grow most luxuriantly, but are more apt, especially in wet seasons, to produce what are called scallions; the foliage being strong and thick at the neck, but the root is made soft and ill-ripened, and will not keep. It has been found advantageous sometimes to roll or tread such land well; but in the general run of seasons, when the climate is moist, soil of a rather clayey nature is found to suit best, and to produce the foliage small at the neck, and the bulb round, protuberated, and well ripened. A thin crop also is more apt to produce most scallions, and it is safer to have the crop rather to the thick side, as they are found to increase less in foliage and more in root, and though the onions are not so large, the weight of the crop is greater, and they keep better. Much of the tendency to produce thick necks flows, as in turnips, from not choosing the roots well in saving the seed. The plants that have small foliage, and handsome well swelled-out roots, are most likely to produce their like again from seed, and much depends on the carefulness of the person who saves the seed. Where great breadths of onions are annually sown, the seed imported from Holland from careful agents there is allowed to give the best crops. Soil that can be broken small to a fine surface requires less seed. Clayey ground intended for onions should be thrown up rough in November or December to get the frost, which converts it into a fine mould more favourable to the growth of the onion. On light dry soils, near the coast, the practice of sowing in autumn is found to succeed best, as the onions fail in the drought of summer when spring-sown. Nitrate of soda, guano, and soot are among the best manures for onions. Common salt in moderation applied to the soil has been found very beneficial. Large prize onions are frequently grown on a layer of rich manure, six inches deep, placed on a hard surface. They are transplanted on this rich feeding ground, and copiously watered with sewage or liquid-manure, and thus swell out to a great size.

An autumn and winter crop of onions, for being drawn as wanted for salads and soups, or to stand for an early crop the next summer, is procured by sowing the Strasburgh or Tripoli about the middle of August or beginning of September. These will be fit for use by Michaelmas, and will afford supplies through the winter, and in early spring till the March-sown crop for drawing comes into use; or till thinnings can be obtained from the main crop. Formerly the Welsh onion was sown to stand through the winter for a spring crop, but as it does not bulb, and is rather stronger than the common onion, it is now but little cultivated; being much hardier, however, it answers well for cold late situations. Any of the varieties of Tripoli, such as the Globe, Red Italian, and Giant Rocca, are good for standing through the winter and producing an early crop the following summer.

A transplanted crop is, by many gardeners, preferred to a sown one. The seed is sown quite thick in the last week of August, or first week of September, and transplanted into rows, the ordinary kinds nine inches wide, and six inches or eight inches apart in the row, and the larger kinds at double these distances, in the following March; the greatest care being taken to keep the whole of the bulb above ground, and only to fix the fibres in the soil. Onions thus treated attain a large size, and produce a uniform crop, without the trouble of thinning, some weeks before a crop sown in March; the only drawback is that the plants sometimes run to flower. Some persons, instead of leaving the onions in the seed-bed through the winter, sow in June, or even in April, if the soil is very poor, quite thick, take up the bulbs in September, dry them, and hang them in bags till the February following, when they are transplanted, by pressing them down with the finger and thumb, at regular distances, in rows. As the object is to prevent the bulb from being earthed up, the ground should be previously trodden or rolled, at least along the line where the plants are to be placed. The shorter the time these onions have been in the ground the preceding year the less likely will they be to run to flower. Another mode of obtaining a transplanted crop, is by sowing in February on a slight hotbed, or merely under glass, and transplanting into rows in April. Very large onions are often grown in this manner.

The potato-onion may be planted in February, in shallow drills one foot apart and six inches distant in the row, leaving the point of every bulb exposed, and pressing its lower end firmly to the soil. In Devonshire, where this onion is grown extensively, it is slightly earthed up during summer in the manner of potatoes. It is a common saying there, that it should be planted in the shortest day, and taken up in the longest; which being fully two months before the common onion is taken up, it is evident that the potato-onion does not keep so long as that variety. To prevent this onion from mildew and rot, keep the earth pulled away from the bulbs, exposing them to sun and air; they will then keep well. It is an excellent onion for the cottager, as it produces both an early and a certain crop.

The Bulb-bearing Onion.—The small bulbs are collected from the heads of the stems, and planted in shallow drills in September; or the stems, with the heads and bulbs attached, are hung up in a dry airy shed from October till February, and the bulbs are then planted rather closer together than those of the potato-onion. The crop will be fit to take up in July, or the beginning of August.

Treatment Common to all the Kinds.—When the leaves begin to decay at the points, or when any indication of running to flower appears, bend down the stem an inch or two above the bulb, in order to check the supply of sap thrown into the leaves, and thereby promote its accumulation in the bulb. This is commonly done by one person with the back of a rake, or by two, with the handle of a rake or hoe between them. If one bending has not the desired effect, repeat the operation, or bend the stem back again, or give it a twist and turn down at the same time. In very warm dry seasons, the bulbs come to maturity and the stems decay naturally, with perhaps a few exceptions; but in cold wet seasons, the operation is useful, and is generally performed about the middle of August.

Diseases, Insects, &c.—The onion in good soil is little subject to disease, but there are some insects which live on it in their grub or maggot state. When a crop has been attacked by insects, but little can be done; but when an attack is anticipated, it may perhaps be prevented by watering the ground with some fetid liquid, such as putrid urine, or thin putrid liquid manure, which by its offensive smell will deter the parent insect from depositing its eggs in the plant, and at the same time invigorate the plant and prepare it to resist their attacks. It is almost impossible to save a crop when once maggots attack it. The best remedies are deep cultivation and firm consolidation of the soil. The soil should likewise be so rich as to hurry the onion through the maggot stage, which is an early one in its growth. The maggots attack the plants at the bottom, and eat their way upwards; hence the difficulty of destroying them.

The onion-fly, an insect not unlike the common house-fly, is the most common insect which attacks the onion, the leek, and the shallot, and as it frequently occasions very serious losses, the following details respecting it by Mr. Westwood may be useful. During the summer months, and especially in June and July, the cultivator of onions is annoyed by perceiving that, here and there, in various parts of his crops, the plants appear to be in a dying state, and the leaves fallen on the ground. At first, this is observed in plants which are only just above the surface of the soil, and which are not above the thickness of a straw. These soon die, and then others, of a larger size, are observed to decay in a similar manner; this continues until the middle of July, and even until the onions are full-grown; at which time they have occasionally sufficient strength to survive the injury, with the decay of a portion only of their outer layer or root, the centre part remaining sound. In this manner whole beds are destroyed; and it seems to be of little use to sow again, as the fresh-sown plants fare no better. In light soils especially, the attacks of this insect are occasionally very annoying to the gardener. On stripping off the coats of the young onions which show evident signs of decay, it is at once perceived that it is owing to the attack of a small grub, destitute of legs, upon the vital parts of the bulb or stem of the plants, that the destruction is occasioned. On pulling up a very young onion, its interior is found to be completely devoured by a single grub at its very heart; but, in plants of larger growth, at least half-a-dozen of these grubs have been counted, varying considerably in size. In the summer season, these grubs are about a fortnight in arriving at their full growth. They generally consume the entire of the interior of the onion, the outside skin of which is alone left dry and entire, serving as a place in which they undergo their transformations, without forming any cocoon. In about another fortnight the perfect fly makes its appearance, the time varying according to the season, from ten to twenty days. To prevent the attacks of this insect, it has been recommended to sow after strawberries that have occupied the soil for four or five years, or to strew the surface of the soil with charcoal cinders, such as may be obtained from a wood where charcoal has been made; or to transplant in preference to sowing, dipping the roots or the bulbs in a puddle, consisting of three parts of earth, and one of soot. The most effective mode with a sown crop, we believe to be that first mentioned—viz., to water with any fetid liquid, such as stale soap-suds mixed with a little stale tobacco-water, from the middle of May till the beginning of July.

Gathering the Crop.—When the neck shrinks and the leaves decay, pull them up and tie in bunches while they are in the hand; hang up to rafters of shed or store-room to dry gradually; they will thus keep well, and not get so rank and strong for eating. They keep well hanging in this state for the winter. Others clear off the grosser portions of the leaves, stalks, and roots; and then spread out the bulbs in an airy loft or cool dry cellar, in which they should be turned over occasionally, and those that begin to decay picked out. Thus treated, onions will keep sound and good, all winter and spring, till May following, except the potato-onion, which with difficulty keeps beyond February. Onions are not injured by frost, unless they are moved when frozen, which, by bruising them, ruptures the tissue, and when a thaw takes place, the bruised part becomes a wound, and the bulbs begin to decay. Onions intended for market are tied by the neck round sticks, by strands of matting, or plaited into straw, and thus form what are called ropes of onions. Onions for the London market are sold by the half-sieve, sieve, or bushel. In other places they are sold by weight—by the score or hundredweight, or by the pound. Hanging up these ropes in an open airy shed is a good way of keeping them; but if they are spread out, or hung up in a close cellar, room, or loft, the temperature must be kept below 40°, or they will grow.

To save seed, select some of the finest specimens and plant them in rich soil early in spring. The seed will ripen in August, when the heads should be cut off and laid in cloths exposed to the sun till they are perfectly dry, when the seed may be thrashed out, and again exposed to the sun for a few hours, previously to being put up in bags. It will keep two years, and sometimes three. It varies considerably in price, according to the crop in this country, and also in Holland, whence much onion-seed is imported.

The Leek.

The Leek (Allium Porrum, L.) is a perennial, a native of Switzerland, in cultivation in British gardens from an unknown period. Its blanched stem is used in soups and stews, and in a dish by itself, served up on toasted bread with white sauce. The best varieties are the London, Musselburgh, Ayton Castle Giant, Henry's Hybrid Prize. For a seed-bed four feet wide by eight feet in length, one ounce of seed is sufficient, which may be sown about the middle of March, and will come up in a fortnight. The plants should be transplanted when three or four inches high, in May or June, if possible in showery weather. They require a very rich soil, and may either be planted along the bottom of drills, or on the surface in rows, ten or twelve inches apart, by six or eight inches in the row; inserting the sheathed stems nearly up to the leaves, or in default of this mode of planting, earthing them up as they grow, in order that a greater portion of the plant may be blanched. In planting, press the soil to the fibres with the dibble, but leave the stem quite loose and free, and as it were standing in the centre of a hollow cylinder, two inches in diameter, and at least six inches deep. This cylinder will afterwards be filled up by the swelling of the stem, and as the leaves are so close together, it is a much better mode than attempting to earth the plants up. Some plant in hollow drills, and earth up as in celery culture, which produces very large stems. Some form holes with a large dibble, drop the plant in, followed by as much loose earth as will just cover its fibrous roots, and afterwards water once a day, till it has taken sufficient hold of the soil. If the soil is very rich to a considerable depth, and on a dry bottom, the size of the stem, by this mode of culture, becomes enormous. The leeks will be fit for use in September, and will continue in perfection till the following April or May, when they may be taken up and placed in a cool cellar to retard vegetation, which will admit of their being used till the middle or end of May; or much later, if growth is prevented by cutting off the plate from which the roots proceed. When severe frost is anticipated, a portion of the crop may be taken up in the beginning of winter, and planted in sand, in an open shed; or it may be protected where it stands. A few plants left will produce abundance of seed, which will ripen in September, and may be treated like that of the onion. The seed will keep two or three years.

The Shallot.

The Shallot (Allium ascalonicum, L.) is a bulbous-rooted perennial, a native of Palestine, and long in cultivation for its bulbs, which separate into cloves. These are used like the bulbs of onions, in soups and stews, and in a raw state cut small, as sauce to steaks and chops; and sometimes a clove or two is put into winter salads, more especially potato salad. The best variety is the Long-keeping, which will remain good for two years. Propagation is effected by dividing the bulb into its separate cloves, and planting and managing these in all respects like the potato-onion. The soil should be rich, and particular care taken to guard against the onion-fly, by the means already indicated. Plant on the surface of firm ground, earth up a little at first, and as soon as the roots take hold, remove the soil with the hoe, and water abundantly, to check the ravages of the maggot. The bulbs, if planted in March, or, as is sometimes done, in the preceding November, will be ready for use towards the end of July, and the crop may be taken up in September and harvested like onions. A sufficient quantity of the smallest cloves ought to be selected for sets for the following year.

The Garlic.

The Garlic (Allium sativum, L.) is a bulbous-rooted perennial, a native of the South of Europe, long in cultivation for flavouring meats, and for various sauces and ragouts. In many parts of Europe, particularly in France and Spain, the peasantry rub garlic over the slices of their black bread as a seasoning, and think the bread so prepared delicious. The bulb divides into cloves like the shallot, and is cultivated exactly in the same manner. The leaves begin to wither in August, and the bulbs may be taken up in September, dried, and laid in an airy loft, or tied up in ropes.

The Chive.

The Chive (Allium Schœnoprasum, L.) is a bulbous perennial, a native of Britain, in meadows and pastures, but rare. It has been long in cultivation for its leaves, which are used in spring salads, in soups, omelets, and generally as a substitute for young onions. The bulbs are very small, and seldom applied to any culinary purpose. The plant flowers in May, and after the leaves have begun to decay in June, it may be taken up and divided, and planted in rows one foot by six inches; but as the chive is little used except in cottage-gardens, a very few plants are sufficient, and these may be planted in the herb-ground in the slip. If kept cut so as to prevent its flowering, it will succeed for several years in the same spot. No cottage-garden ought to be without the chive: it forms one of the most wholesome herbs for chopping up and mixing among the food for young chickens, ducks, turkeys—making them thrive wonderfully, and preventing that pest the gripes.

The Rocambole.

The Rocambole (Allium Scorodoprasum, L.) is a bulbous perennial, a native of Denmark, formerly cultivated for the same purposes as garlic, but now comparatively neglected. It differs from garlic in having the bulbs smaller, milder to the taste, and in producing bulbs on the joints of the stem, as well as at its base.

Substitutes for alliaceous plants are to be found in the genus Allium, of which there are several indigenous species, and a number in gardens which are natives of other countries. Three cruciferous plants, by no means rare, also taste and smell of garlic—viz., Peltaria alliacea, L., a perennial from Austria; Thlaspi alliaceum, L., a biennial from the South of Europe; and Alliaria officinalis, Andrz. (Jack-by-the-hedge), a perennial, a native of Britain. The latter is used as greens or spinach in many parts of the country.

Asparagaceous Esculents.

The asparagaceous esculents belong to various natural orders, but the principal are the Asparagus, the Sea-kale, and the Artichoke; there are a few others of less note. They are all comparatively plants of luxury, though the asparagus and sea-kale may with propriety be cultivated in the garden of the cottager, who if he does not use the produce, may sell it.

The Asparagus.

The Asparagus (Asparagus officinalis, L.) is an asphodelaceous perennial, found in light sandy soils on the sea-shore in Britain and other parts of Europe; often where it is covered by drifting sand, and watered by salt water during spring-tides. It is also found in abundance on sandy steppes in the interior of Russia. It has been in cultivation, for its stalks when they are just emerging from the ground, as a culinary esculent, from the time of the Greeks; coming into use in the open ground in May, and lasting till the middle of June, and procured by forcing during the winter and spring months. The shoots or buds, more or less blanched according to taste, are boiled and served on toasted bread with white sauce, and the smaller shoots, which are allowed to become green, are cut into pieces about the size of peas, and used as a substitute for that legume. There scarcely can be said to be any particular variety, though the preference is generally given to seed saved at Battersea, Gravesend, or Mortlake—places famous for the large size to which asparagus has been grown for the London market. Mr. Barnes (late of Bicton) says: "I have seen the asparagus growing naturally and abundantly in the county of Cornwall, more particularly in three or four places about the Lizard, near Helstone."

Soil, and Sowing or Planting the Asparagus.—Asparagus can only be grown large, and succulent, on a soil sandy, deep, and light, more especially on the surface, from vegetable matter, and well enriched with animal manure. The toughness and stringiness of much of the London asparagus are owing to the surface soil through which it sprouts being too deep, and not sufficiently light. In consequence of this the woody fibre of the sprouts has time to strengthen and harden; whereas, with no other covering than leaves or even leaf-mould, the sprouts would be quite tender throughout the greatest part of their length. From the asparagus being a sea-side plant, it may be inferred that salt water might be occasionally beneficial, and hence fresh stable-dung mixed with sea-weed has long been found the best manure for asparagus in Scotland; and night-soil the best at St. Sebastian, where the surface of the beds is only about three feet above high-water mark. From this last circumstance we are led to conclude, that if the subsoil at the depth of three feet is porous and kept moist in the growing season by the water of an adjoining river or lake, and the surface strewed over every spring with salt, there will be a union of the most favourable circumstances for growing asparagus to a large size. The soil ought to be trenched at least three feet deep, and a layer of animal manure of some kind, such as good stable-dung or night-soil, put in the bottom of the trench, and mixed with the soil throughout in trenching; and if the ground is re-trenched immediately before planting, so much the better. For the convenience of management the plants may be grown in beds four feet wide, with alleys between them two feet wide. There may be three rows of plants in each bed, the outer rows nine inches from the edge of the bed, and the centre row fifteen inches from the outer rows. To afford the means of keeping the beds of a regular width, a strong oak stake may be driven down in each corner, which will be a guide in stretching the line, when the alleys are to be dug out in autumn, and filled in from the bed in spring. The seed may be sown in drills an inch deep in March, and the plants thinned out to the distance of one foot in the July following. The fourth year the plants will afford stalks fit to cut. To save time, two-year-old plants are sometimes used instead of seeds; these are either purchased from a nursery, or raised in a seed-bed, and for a bed four and a half feet wide, by six feet long, one quart of seed will be sufficient. If sown to remain, then for three rows in a bed of fifty feet in length, half a pint of seed will be necessary. The seed will come up in three weeks. The quantity of plants required is easily calculated. They are planted in the trench manner, or in drills, in February, March, or April, keeping the crowns of the roots two inches below the surface. The quantity of ground sown or planted, even in the smallest garden, should not be less than a rod, as it requires that extent of plantation to produce a single good dish. For a large family one-eighth of an acre will be requisite; but five poles, planted with 1600 plants, will yield from six to eight score heads daily for a month.

Routine Culture.—Mr. James Barnes says: "Plant to the extent required good two-year-old plants—in rows two feet apart on well-manured, well-trenched ground—well incorporated together by frequent turnings in winter: no fear of applying too much manure, or other decayed vegetation, old decayed well-rotted leaves, sea-weed, &c., so long as it is well incorporated, tumbled over into rough ridges during the frosty days of winter, forked down level about the end of March or beginning of April; plant it carefully as soon as it has commenced, or made a start of two or three inches of growth—placing the line at two feet distance, drawing a deep drill on each side of the line—forking out the plants from your seed-bed, if any, dividing their roots, carefully placing them astride the little ridge that is left by drawing the drill each side of the line as above, covering over the roots as soon as possible to prevent checks from sun or wind. The second year each alternate sowing may be taken up as first-class plants for forcing, and a moderate cutting of fine asparagus commenced. If a tender green well-flavoured shoot is wished for, but little earthing is required; if long, white, tough-drawn sticks are the order and the fashion, earth or cover up to the desired height. Top-dressing and forking it in each autumn, leaving a rough surface to get pulverized, and always keeping the surface clear of weeds, will ensure a splendid crop of fine asparagus for many years—nay, a generation or two. Apply liberal sowings of common salt in dark, cloudy, and rainy weather."

Mr. W. P. Ayres's observations on this subject are as follow:—
"If we had a society for the prevention of cruelty to plants, we wonder how those who torture asparagus would fare? A native of the sea-coast, where it may be found in abundance in some parts of the country, nothing can exceed the barbarism to which it is subjected in many gardens, the London market-gardens not excepted. The plant is as frost-proof as the heath upon the mountain, and, though it prefers a deep, rich, and rather moist soil, will grow upon a sandhill, and fight a good fight for existence; and yet some people swathe it in a thick covering of rich manure for the winter, while the London market-gardener plants it upon a high bank and unearths the plants, leaving them as bare as the back of your hand for the same season. The London grower, however, has an object in this—to get the produce of his beds into the market as early as possible; consequently he exposes the nearly perpendicular sides of his narrow beds to the action of the sun, and as the heat accumulates daily upon the surface of the beds, the men follow late in the afternoon and cover in the manured earth with a sprinkling of soil from the path between the beds. In this way, and in bright, sunny weather, the plants in the course of a week or ten days are covered with a layer, some six inches thick, of heated earth, which adds very materially to the early growth of the plants, and gives the 'drumsticks' upon the point of which the consumable inch of asparagus is fixed. This may be a permissible system of cultivation, but certainly it is not a rational one; for to fix a plant which would grow in a ditch through the summer upon a ridge of earth at that season, and then bare its roots to the winter's blast, is anything but a commendable system of cultivation.

"Now, if really first-class rich succulent asparagus is wanted, the first point to attend to is to trench the ground at the least two feet deep, if three feet all the better, mixing intimately at the same time a thick coat of rich manure, and, if a good dressing of 'culch' or seaweed can be added, it will be so much the better; but if not, then salt, sufficient to make the surface of the ground quite white, may be used twice or thrice during the growing season. If possible, this preparation should be made in the autumn; and if up to April, the time of planting, the ground is repeatedly forked over, especially after frost, it will be a great advantage. At the time of planting, which should not be before the middle of April, banish altogether the idea of raised beds, and cultivate the plant entirely upon the flat, seeking to raise the ground in the paths between the beds, so as to make them hold a copious supply of manure-water, instead of sinking the path. In planting, we prefer two rows a foot apart, and the plants the same distance apart in the row, then a three-feet space and two more rows of plants, and so on until the ground is planted. The advantage of single or double-row planting is, that the plants in the growing season are better exposed to light, and have more room to grow. The certain way to complete success in the cultivation of this plant is a deep, rich, porous soil, plenty of manure-water through the summer and autumn, a coat of manure to cover the whole of the ground when the stems are cut down in the autumn; and, if ordinary manure cannot be had, then a few handfuls of Peruvian guano added to the salt at each dressing through the summer. In planting always prefer plants one year old.

"In cutting, never touch a stem until the third year after planting, and then only take a few stems from each root. When the plants become strong, cut every shoot up to the end of May or first week in June, then leave the strongest shoot upon each plant, and you may continue to cut for a fortnight or three weeks longer, when you must cease altogether. More beds are ruined by excessive cutting late in the season than by any other cause. We have been speaking of cutting; but when we gather asparagus for our own eating, we never cut at all, but are content to let it grow to the height of six or eight inches, and then break it off between the forefingers at the proper length; it is brittle as an icicle. It is true we have no handle to our asparagus; but what we gather we can eat, which is more than can be said for the mismanaged article sold in our markets."

Gathering.—To suit the taste of some persons, asparagus should be so far grown as to become green, but in general it is preferred more or less blanched, that is, when the shoot is three or four inches above the surface of the soil, with the terminal bud close and plump. In some parts of the Continent each particular stalk is blanched by putting a wooden or earthenware tube, eighteen inches long, and one inch in diameter within, over it; and at St. Sebastian the beds are covered, before cutting commences, to the depth of eight inches with dead leaves, which effects the same object, and keeps the soil moist. The last mode well deserves to be adopted in this country, as well as that of watering abundantly during the gathering season. In young plantations, gather only the largest stalks for two or three weeks, and then permit the whole of the others that may be produced to run to flower; but in plantations in full vigour gather all the stems that appear, whether large or small, for a month or six weeks, or till the time fixed on for leaving off gathering If, instead of gathering all the stems, some are allowed to run to flower while the gathering is going on, but few more stems will be sent up from the root, and these weak on account of the main force of the sap being spent in the flowering stem. To ensure large stalks, gathering should not be continued longer than the middle of June, or if continued to the end of the month, no cutting should take place the following year. It must be constantly borne in mind that the stalks of the coming year, culture and other circumstances alike, depend on the number of matured stalks with healthy leaves of the present year. In gathering, first scrape away a little earth from the shoot; then cut it off within the ground, with a narrow sharp-pointed knife, or small saw, about nine inches long (fig. 41, p. 91); thrusting the knife or saw down straight, close to the shoot, cutting it off slantingly, about three inches below the surface, and taking care not to wound the younger buds advancing below. The shoots are next sorted and tied in bundles of between two and three inches in diameter, and in that state sent to the kitchen or to market.

The duration of an asparagus plantation should seldom be less than ten or twelve years; but in deep sandy soils, well enriched with manure, it will last twenty or thirty years. The plants are not subject to the attacks of insects, though the asparagus beetle (Crioceris asparagi, L.) sometimes makes its appearance in spring, and ought to be deterred from laying its eggs by watering with some fetid liquid in April, or the insects, which are easily known from their bright lively colours, may be gathered by hand.

To save seed, allow the blossoms of some of the strongest stems to remain on; the fruit will ripen in October, and may either be thrashed out and kept in bags, in which state it will retain its vitality for four or five years, or it may be retained on the stems, and these being hung up in a dry place, the seed will grow at the end of fifteen or twenty years.

Forcing the asparagus in the open garden and under glass has been already treated of.

The Sea-Kale.

The Sea-kale (Crambe maritima, L.) is a cruciferous perennial, with long, strong, deeply-penetrating roots, a native of Britain, on the sea-coast in many places, and always most vigorous in a sandy soil, or a loamy subsoil, overflowed by spring tides. The young shoots and leaf-stalks, just as they come through the sand, and are blanched and tender, have been boiled and eaten by the inhabitants of the western shores of England from time immemorial; but the plant was not cultivated as a garden esculent till after the middle of the last century. It is now reckoned second in excellence to the asparagus, and to be found in every good garden, sometimes even in that of the cottager. It comes into use in the open garden in the beginning of March, and continues good till May; and by forcing it can be obtained from November throughout the whole of the winter and spring. No plant requires less care in its cultivation, or less heat to force.

Propagation and Culture.—By seed is the common mode, but it will also grow freely by cuttings of the roots. If sown to transplant, a seed-bed four feet by ten feet will require two ounces; if sown in drills to remain, the same quantity will sow one hundred and fifty feet of drill. The seed will come up in a month. It is generally grown in rows two feet apart, and the plants about the same distance in the row. Seeds, plants which have been one year in the seed-bed, or cuttings of the roots of old plants, may be used; in the latter case leaving two eyes to each cutting; or cuttings without eyes may be used, provided the upper part of the cutting be placed uppermost; or the cutting be laid on its side in a shallow drill. Sowing and planting may take place about the beginning of March. The best soil is a deep sandy loam, thoroughly enriched with manure, including seaweed, if it can be got, or if not, a sprinkling of salt once a year. The most efficient mode of culture would be to follow that recommended for asparagus. The strongest plants are produced from seeds sown where the plants are to remain. Three rows may be marked out two feet apart, leaving an interval of three feet after every third row, the centre of which, to the width of eighteen inches, is to be treated as an alley for the convenience of gathering the crop. The seeds may be dropped in patches of three or four along the drills, and the plants thinned out to one plant in a place, soon after they come up. The first winter's dressing may consist of some littery stable-manure, seaweed, and leaves, spread over the surface, which may be forked in early in the following spring. This may be repeated the second autumn, increasing the thickness, and the second spring a few stalks may be gathered. The third autumn the dressing may be repeated; or the rows may be covered with leaves alone, with sand, or with soil dug out of the alleys, to the depth of six inches. The third spring several stalks may be gathered from each plant; and the fourth spring the plantation will be in full bearing. Excepting in the first spring after sowing no spring dressing is required till May, after the crop has been gathered. The London market-gardeners plant the sea-kale in rows from four to six feet apart, and every autumn after the leaves have died down to the surface, they dig a trench between the rows, and cover the plants with soil to the depth of a foot. As the crop is gathered the ridges so formed are levelled down, and a crop planted between. By this mode the whole produce of the plant is gathered at once, every part of it being completely blanched and tender.

Gathering.—The points of the stems will appear above the leaves, or other matters with which the plants have been covered the preceding autumn, about the beginning or middle of March, according to the warmth of the situation and of the season. Remove the covering round such of the young stems as are about three inches long, and cut them over half an inch above the collar, taking care not to injure any of the buds which remain on the plant, and which will immediately begin to swell. It is a good plan to invert wide pots over the plants, as it keeps the kale clean and prevents it from contracting an earthy or dungy flavour. From four to six heads or stalks, according to the size, make a dish, and they are sent to the kitchen or the market tied together like asparagus. Three stout plants will afford five dishes in a season; and hence when the number of dishes required by any family is known, one-third added to their number will give the amount of plants required for a plantation. A plantation will afford a succession of gatherings for six weeks, after which period the plants should be uncovered, and their leaves suffered to grow, in order to strengthen the roots for the succeeding year. If very large and succulent sea-kale is required, gathering should only be made every other year, and the plants should be manured with stable-dung or nightsoil, taking care to thin the buds and young shoots at an early stage in order to secure strength for the succeeding year without undue robbery to root or bud.

To Save Seed.—Leave the blossoms on a few of the strongest plants, the seed produced by which will ripen in August, and the stalks may be collected and thrashed like those of the common cabbage. The seeds will retain their vitality for four or five years.

Forcing.—Where a crop is to be forced in the open ground, the ordinary mode is to cover the plants in autumn with sea-kale pots (fig. 66 in p. 101), or with large garden-pots, and to cover these and the whole surface of the ground with hot dung, or a mixture of hot dung and leaves. When this is done in October, kale may be gathered in November or December; and by successive applications of heat to other parts of the plantation, a supply may be obtained till it can be procured from the plants covered with soil, or leaves only. Other modes of forcing have been already noticed. The best mode is, grow plants strong and well, and take them up to force. They may be grown either from seed, crowns, or cuttings of the roots. Take them up in succession throughout autumn, winter, and early spring, and place in a cellar, mushroom-house, dark archways, under shutters, in pits or frames, and a sure crop of fine blanched sea-kale will be the result, with but little trouble, expense, or anxiety. Plant the roots again; if they are wanted they are sure to be ready again the next year. It is marvellous the quantity of fine sea-kale that may be produced by these simple means.

The Artichoke.

The Artichoke (Cynara Scolymus, L.) is a carduaceous perennial, a native of the South of Europe and North of Africa, in cultivation in British gardens from the middle of the sixteenth century. The plant is cultivated for the head of flowers, which is gathered before their expansion; and the common receptacle, and the base of the involucral scales, are the parts eaten. These are boiled, sometimes fried in butter, and they are occasionally eaten raw in salads. The receptacles, or bottoms, as they are commonly called, after being blanched in boiling water, are sometimes dried and preserved for use during winter and spring. In the North of Spain the smaller flower-heads are cut soon after they appear, and the bottoms are taken off and form a palatable ingredient in the puchera or olla, a favourite Spanish dish. Artichoke bottoms are also combined with capsicum in a sort of stew made of fowl. The first heads are ready in July, and by continuing to gather them before allowing any to expand their flowers, they will continue being produced till November; and by cutting off the heads at that season, with a foot or more of stalk attached, and inserting the stalks in moist sand, in an open shed secured from frost, they will keep fit for use till January or longer. The leaves of the artichoke may also be blanched like those of the cardoon. The varieties are, the Globe, with a globular purplish head, which is the best variety for a main crop; the French, with an oval green head, considered as having more flavour than the other and being hardier. Both sorts are propagated by rooted suckers taken from the old plants in March and April, and planted in rows four feet asunder, and two feet distant in the row. The soil ought to be deep, sandy, and rich, and sea-weed is said to be an excellent ingredient in the manure for this plant, being the manure used in the Orkney islands, where the artichoke grows stronger than anywhere else. The routine culture consists in keeping the plants clear of weeds, thinning out the shoots produced by the stools, stirring the soil, manuring once a year, in autumn or spring, and laying litter round the plants in autumn to protect the roots from frost during the winter. The plants will produce some heads the first year, and all that they produce may be gathered as soon as they attain the proper size, as the strength of the root depends on the leaves, and not on the flowers. The plantation will continue productive for six or seven years, or longer. By planting a few every year a later crop may be gathered, as the newly-planted stools will often flower right on into November. In gathering, the heads are cut off within an inch or two of the stalk attached, and half-a-dozen heads are considered as making a dish.

Culture for Producing the Chard.—This is only attempted when the artichoke plantation is to be renewed, and the old plants to be thrown away. After Midsummer, cut over the leaves within half a foot of the ground, and the stems as low as possible. Then, when the new crop of leaves, which will be produced in September or October, are about two feet high, tie them up close, first slightly with matting, and in a few days afterwards with hay or straw, and earth them up like celery, or lay litter round the stems. In a month or six weeks, the interior leaves will be found completely blanched, and fit for use. By digging up the plants before frost sets in, and planting them in sand in an open shed, they will keep till Christmas, or later.

The artichoke is seldom attacked by insects, and though generally propagated by division, slips, or suckers, yet it ripens seeds freely in September, which, sown the following spring, will produce heads in the second summer. The seed keeps three years.

The Cardoon.

The Cardoon, or Chardoon (Cynara Cardunculus, L.) is a carduaceous perennial, a native of the South of Europe and the North of Africa, closely resembling the artichoke in appearance and properties. It has long been cultivated in gardens for the midrib of the leaf, which is rendered white and tender by blanching, and is used stewed, or in soups and salads during autumn and winter, much in the same manner as celery. The flavour is that of the artichoke. It is much more in request on the Continent than in England. In France the corollas, both of the cardoon and artichoke, as well as those of several thistles, are dried and used as a substitute for rennet in curdling milk.

Cookery of the Cardoon.—" When a cardoon is to be cooked, its heart, and the solid, not piped, stalks of the leaves are to be cut into pieces, about six inches long, and boiled like any other vegetable, in pure water, not salt and water, till they are tender. They are then to be carefully deprived of the slime and strings which will be found to cover them; and having thus been thoroughly cleaned, are to be plunged in cold water, where they must remain till they are wanted for the table; they are then taken out and heated with white sauce, marrow, or any other of the adjuncts recommended in cookery books. The process just described is for the purpose of rendering them white, and depriving them of a bitterness which is peculiar to them; if neglected, the cardoons will be black, not white, as well as disagreeable."

Varieties, Propagation, &c.—There are several varieties, but the best are the cardoon of Tours, and the Spanish cardoon. The cardoon is always propagated by seed, which must not be sown too early, unless it is abundantly supplied with water in the dry season, otherwise it is apt to run to flower. In the climate of London, the end of April, or beginning of May, is found a proper time for a crop to come into use in November; but an earlier crop may be obtained by sowing in March. It should always be sown where the plants are finally to remain. Sow in patches of three or four seeds. Prepare shallow trenches a foot wide, and four feet apart, centre from centre, manuring the soil in the bottom of the trench. Sow the seed in patches in the centre of the trench twenty inches or two feet apart, and as soon as the plants come up, one only should be left in each patch. Two ounces of seed will be sufficient for fifty patches. With the usual routine culture, the leaves will be three feet or four feet long by the middle of October, when they should be first slightly tied up with pieces of matting for a few days, and afterwards closely wrapped round with haybands, so as completely to exclude the light from the root to about two-thirds of the length of the leaves. In three weeks the interior leaves will be fit for use. On the approach of winter, they may be earthed up like celery, as high as the haybands, to protect them from the frost; or they may be covered with litter and thatched hurdles, for that purpose, or taken up with balls, and placed close together in an open airy shed.

In taking the plants for use, remove the haybands and the outer leaves, and shorten those plants which are tender and blanched to the length of eighteen inches or two feet, cutting off the root. One or two plants will make a dish. Seed may be saved by protecting some plants, the leaves of which have not been blanched, through the winter, in the spot where they have grown; they will flower in the following July, and ripen seed in August, which will keep five or six years.

The Rampion.

The Rampion (Campanula Rapunculus, L.) is a campanulaceous fusiform-rooted biennial, a native of England, in gravelly soil, and formerly much cultivated in gardens for its roots as well as its leaves. The latter are excellent, eaten raw as a salad, or boiled as spinach; and the root, which has the flavour of walnuts, is also eaten raw like a radish, or mixed with salads, either raw or boiled and cold. It is always propagated by seed, which is so exceedingly small, that a sixteenth part of an ounce is sufficient for any garden. It will come up in a fortnight. As in the case of other biennials, if sown too soon, the plants will run to flower the same season. The end of May, or beginning of June, is considered the best time for a main crop; but a crop to come in early may be sown in March. The seeds may either be sown broadcast or in drills six inches apart, and from a quarter to half an inch in depth; in either case covering the seed with not more than an eighth of an inch of soil. The plants may be thinned out to three or four inches apart, and the soil among them should not be deeply stirred, lest the roots should be encouraged to branch, which they are very apt to do, and are then unfit to be sent to table. The principal point in the culture of the rampion is to sow it in a deep sandy light rich soil, which can be penetrated by the roots without difficulty, and to supply water abundantly in very dry weather. The roots may be taken up as wanted from November till April, when the plants will begin to run; but by burying the roots out of the reach of surface heat, in the manner of potatoes, they may be kept through the summer. A few plants allowed to stand the second year will produce abundance of seeds, which will keep two years.

Substitutes for Asparagaceous Esculents.

Substitutes for asparagaceous esculents are to be found in the following plants:—The hop (Humulus Lupulus, L.), the young shoots of which, when they have risen three or four inches from the root, are boiled in the hop districts, and eaten like asparagus, to which they are considered little inferior. The bladder campion (Silene inflata, H. K.), is a perennial common on sea-shores, the tender shoots of which, when not above two inches long, have a flavour which, according to Bryant, is surpassed by few garden vegetables; and it will continue producing these shoots for two months. In our opinion, it well deserves cultivation. The Virginian poke (Phytolacca decandra, L.) is a perennial from Virginia, where the points of the young shoots are used as asparagus. The willow-herb (Epilobium angustifolium, L.): the young and tender shoots are eaten as asparagus, and the leaves as greens. Solomon's seal (Polygonatum vulgare, Dec.): the young shoots are boiled and eaten as asparagus, and the roots are said to be dried, ground, and made into bread. The common comfrey (Symphytum officinale, L.): the blanched stalks form an agreeable asparagus. The black bryony (Tamus communis, L.): the blanched tops are eaten as asparagus. The burdock (Arctium Lappa, L.): the tender stalks are eaten as asparagus. Stachys palustris, L., the underground stems of which, when grown in rich moist soil, are white, crisp, and agreeable to the taste. The milk-thistle (Carduus Marianus, L.) is a biennial, a native of Britain; the young stalks, peeled and soaked in water to extract a part of their bitterness, and then boiled, are said to be an excellent substitute for asparagus. When very young the leaves are used as a spring salad; and the large leaves, blanched in autumn like those of the cardoon, form a good substitute for that vegetable, and they are also used as greens. Early in the spring of the second year, the root is prepared like skirret or salsify, and in the summer of the second year, the receptacle of the heads of flowers gathered before they expand, is pulpy, and eats like that of the artichoke. The cotton-thistle (Onopordum Acanthium, L.), is an indigenous biennial, the leaves of which were formerly blanched and used like those of the cardoon; the tender blanched stalks, peeled and boiled like asparagus, and the receptacle of the flower treated like that of the artichoke. The carline-thistle (Carlina acanthifolia, All.), a perennial, a native of Carniola; and the common species (C. vulgaris, L.), a biennial, a native of Britain, produce large heads of flowers, the receptacle of which may be used like that of the artichoke, and in all probability the flowers and leaves of most carduaceous plants might be used like those of the artichoke and cardoon. The pyramidal campanula (Campanula pyramidatus, L.), and various other species of campanula, producing fleshy roots, might doubtless be used as substitutes for the rampion, as are those of the campanulaceous plants, Phyteuma spicatum, L., in Sussex, and Canarina Campanula, L., in the Canary Islands. Ruscus aculeatus, L., for its tender young shoots in spring; Ornithogalum pyrenaicum, L. (the Bath asparagus), the flower-stems of which are brought to market at Bath, where the flowers are in a close head like an asparagus bud; the maize (Zea Mays, L.), the sweet or sugar variety of which, when the seed is immature, is much used in America, roasted, fried, or boiled.

Salads.

The salads in cultivation in gardens are numerous, but those of most importance are the lettuce, endive, and celery. They are all articles of luxury, unless we except the lettuce, which is a useful vegetable in every cottage-garden.

The Lettuce.

The Lettuce (Lactuca sativa, L.) is a succulent composite plant, annual or biennial, according to the time in which it is sown; considered by some as the Lactuca virosa in a cultivated state, and by others as a different species, of Eastern origin. It has been cultivated in British gardens from the time of Elizabeth, and by suitable management may be had all the year round. Lettuce is in universal esteem in a raw state, as a cooling and agreeable salad, and it is also used in soups and stews.

Varieties.—The varieties are very numerous, and are included under two divisions—

1. Cos lettuces, of which the best are the black-seeded green, a very hardy kind, which does not run readily to seed; the Bath Cos, which is the best for standing the winter in the open ground; the Brown Cos, the White Paris Cos, Williams' Victoria, Moor Park, London White, Alma, Carter's Giant White, Hardy Winter White, Snow's, and Gem.

2. Cabbage lettuces, the best of which are: the Brown Dutch, hardy and of good quality; the Hammersmith Hardy Green, the best for standing through the winter; the Marseilles, a large excellent summer lettuce, the Malta, Dutch Forcing, Victoria, All the Year Round, Royal Albert, Tennis Ball, Large Versailles, William Robinson, Red-Edged Victoria, and Covent Garden Long-Standard.

Propagation and Culture.—All the sorts are raised from seed, which being small and light, for a seed-bed four feet by ten feet a quarter of an ounce is sufficient, and will produce four hundred plants. It comes up in ten days or a fortnight. To grow large succulent lettuces, it is essential that the soil be deep, light, sandy, and rich, on a dry subsoil; and that it be abundantly supplied with water during the hot season. In Spain, recent nightsoil is used as a manure for the lettuce, being buried in a trench between every two rows of plants. To produce a supply of lettuce throughout the year, the first sowings may be made in the beginning of February, on a warm border, or on the south side of an east-and-west ridge, either broadcast or in drills, and of the kinds preferred by the family. Some persons dislike the cabbage-lettuce from its softness, while others prefer it for that reason. As soon as the plants have shown the third leaf, they should be thinned with a two-inch hoe, so as not to stand nearer together than six inches; or in the case of the large-growing varieties, such as the Marseilles and Malta, a foot. From this time to the beginning of August a sowing may be made every fortnight or three weeks, choosing a north border, or screening the ground from the sun, by wickerwork hurdles, in the hottest part of the season. The crop sown in the first week of August will last till it is destroyed by frost, or till October; from which time recourse must be had to the lettuces grown under glass in the manner before described. Independently of the forced crop, a sowing may be made in the third week in August, which, if the winter should be mild, will afford some plants for use during that season; and a sowing in the last fortnight of September, under the shelter of a south wall, in poor, dry, sandy soil—or in the same soil, covered by a frame and sashes—or by hoops and mats, to be taken off every fine day, will produce plants for transplanting early in spring. These, if put into light rich soil, in a warm situation, at one foot apart every way, will produce plants fit for use about the end of April, when the forcing of lettuces may be given up; and this spring-transplanted crop will be in perfection during great part of the month of May. In this way lettuces are obtained throughout the year both in private and public gardens; but the market-gardeners about London, instead of sowing the crops where they are to remain, sow in seed-beds and transplant. The plants to stand through the winter for spring-transplanting are sown in a cold frame about the middle of September, and planted out in February or the beginning of March. The first spring sowing for transplanting is made on heat, and the subsequent sowings in the open garden; always on comparatively sandy, poor soil, that the plants may form abundance of roots and comparatively rigid foliage, so as not to suffer so much from transplanting as if they had been grown on rich soil, and consequently had tender succulent leaves and roots. The routine culture consists of little more than weeding and watering; each crop being but a short time on the ground. In the beginning of summer the Cos varieties are sometimes slightly tied up with matting, to hasten their blanching. In gathering, pull up the plant, and take the outside leaves and roots at once to the rubbish-heap.

The following instructions are given by Mr. James Barnes (late of Bicton): "They should be sown in shallow frames close to the glass, on poor but sweet soil, at a sharp angle, the first week in October; air freely night and day, in order to keep the plants short, stubby, and hardy; keeping them very dry all the winter, which will keep them free from fogging, damping, shanking, or canker; keep dry dust and old dry mortar, or ceiling dust, always ready in a shed; mix together half and half of poor, dry, dusty loam and sand, and sift with a fine sieve over the plants with care, occasionally, on fine dry winter days. The return will be a batch of healthy, clean, well-rooted, stubby, hardy plants, free from all disease, and fit to plant out early in any well-cultivated garden."

By far the best system of cultivating lettuces is that pursued in the neighbourhood of Paris. The French are much more fastidious about tender, well-grown, and clean salads than we are, and the market-gardeners of Paris not only supply the wants of that city in that way, but also to a great extent in winter, and early spring, those of London and other large English cities. The winter and spring culture is mostly carried on under the cloche, described elsewhere in this book. To some of the varieties, such as the Petite Noire, no air whatever is directly given—*i.e.*, the cloches are kept firmly down during the whole period of growth, and in the case of varieties like the Cos, which it is not considered necessary to treat in this way, the custom is also to leave the cloche firmly down for many weeks during the cold season, and so far from this injuring the plants, as some might think, they are as far superior in every way to English-grown lettuces as can be conceived. The other radical differences between the French and English modes of cultivating lettuces are that the soil in the French market-gardens is of the finest, lightest, and richest nature, and the plants are cultivated from the earliest stage—*i.e.*, instead of allowing the seedlings to run together, or become drawn in the least degree, they prick them out when just broken into the seed-leaves, so that the plants at once begin to form healthy little rosettes, are again transplanted under the cloche, and rapidly grow without a check of any kind, or even a speck of dust. The sorts chiefly grown are the Petite Noire, Verte Maraichère, Laitue Gotte, Laitue de la Passion, and the Palatine.

Lettuces as small salad are produced by sowing the seed in drills, and cutting over the plants when they are in the third and fourth leaf, as is done with mustard and cress.

To save seed, a few plants which have stood through the winter and been transplanted into rich soil in spring, or some spring-sown plants, may be allowed to run, and the seed will be ripe in August, and will keep three years; but as it is very difficult to save lettuce-seed in wet seasons, it is an excellent method to grow a few plants in pots, in good soil, one in each pot, and place them in front of a south wall, moving them under glass shelter to ripen off, if the weather render it necessary. Birds are very fond of lettuce-seed; and the lettuce-fly (Anthomyia Lactucæ, Bouché) lays its eggs in the flower, the larvæ produced by which live on the seed.

Forcing.—See page 521.

The Endive.

The Endive (Cichorium Endivia, L.) is a fusiform-rooted biennial, said to be a native of China and Japan, but long cultivated in European gardens for its leaves as salad. These are blanched to diminish the bitter taste, and they are used chiefly in autumn, winter, and spring. There are two principal varieties: the Batavian, or broad-leaved, and the curled-leaved, of each of which there are a number of sub-varieties, the best of them being probably the Digswell Prize, the Moss Green, the White-curled, and the White Broad-leaved Batavian. As the season for endive is from August till March or April, the first sowing is made about the middle of June, the second about the end of that month, the third in July, and the fourth in the beginning of August. The plants are seldom raised where they are finally to remain (though in very dry weather they succeed best by that mode), but generally in seed-beds; and for a bed four feet wide by ten feet in length, half an ounce of seed is sufficient. When the plants attain three or four leaves, they should be transplanted into rich soil, at one foot apart every way; and, as they are generally earthed up, to facilitate this process, they may be planted in drills. The two latest crops for use during winter and spring should be planted in a dry, warm border, on the south side of an east-and-west ridge.

Blanching.—As the summer and autumn crops advance to maturity, a portion should have the leaves tied up every ten days or fortnight, to cause the hearts to blanch and become tender, crisp, and mild-tasted; but this ought not to be done till the plant is almost fully grown, for blanched leaves can no longer add any strength to the root. This operation ought only to be performed in dry days, and when the leaves are quite dry; and in winter, when the weather is dry without frost. The mode of performance is as follows:—When the plants are well filled up in the heart, and apparently nearly fully grown, put your fingers under the leaves which rest upon the ground, and gather the whole plant up in your hands into a conical form; then tie it round with strands of matting, loose during summer, but tighter late in autumn and in winter, when the plant grows more slowly; arranging the leaves so as to terminate in a point at the top, in order to prevent rain from falling into the heart of the plant. The curled endive, if carefully earthed up, will blanch tolerably well without being tied; but the broad-leaved variety, from its looser growth, hearts and blanches much better when bandaged. The blanching, when the weather is hot and dry, will sometimes be completed in a week; but late in autumn and during winter it will require a fortnight or a month. As soon as it is properly blanched, it should be taken up for use, as it will rot afterwards in a week or less, more especially if much rain fall. Sometimes blanching is effected by laying a flat tile on the plants; setting tiles or boards on each side of them, and bringing them together at top in the form of a ridge, so as to confine their growth and exclude the light; or covering them with garden-pots or blanching-pots, in the manner of sea-kale. In the north of Spain the blanching of endive is generally effected by covering the heart of the plant with a fragment of tile; " over this a light covering of earth is sifted. The fringed edges of the exterior leaves are carefully freed from earth, and exposed to light; having small bits of tile laid over that portion of the soil from which they protrude, to render the blanching perfect, and produce what the gardeners particularly pride themselves on—viz., a plant of endive white all over, excepting the edges of the outer leaves, which should show about two inches of green."

The best method to have fine blanched tender endive every day throughout winter, is to take up all plants sown late and planted in succession, and place them in dry frames, pits, orchard-houses, peach-houses, late vineries, or such dry places, away from frost or wet. Plant deep and thick; there will then be always plenty well blanched, without further trouble. The new Batavian, if it can be procured, is so much like a lettuce in growth and flavour, that for winter and early spring no one should be without it. Also the beautiful thick-curled moss endive, the most delicate and beautiful of all the varieties, blanches itself through its density.

A crop may be preserved through the winter either by covering it where it stands by thatched hurdles raised on props; by hoops and mats; by removing it with balls to an open airy shed; by covering it with dry litter, taking it off every fine day or, what is best of all, covering it where it stands with frames and sashes, taking the latter off every fine day. During the period that the endive is covered, tying up for blanching must go regularly on with every plant about ten days or a fortnight before it is to be gathered.

The endive is little troubled with insects; but snails and slugs attack it, as they do the lettuce, in every stage, and require to be kept under by frequent waterings with lime-water.

Seed may be saved as in the lettuce, and it will keep good four or five years.

The Succory.

The Succory, Chicory, or Wild Endive (Cichorium Intybus, L.) (Chicorée sauvage, Fr.), is a cichoraceous fusiform-rooted perennial, a native of England, in chalky soils, in open situations. It is much cultivated on the Continent for its roots, which are cut in slices, kiln-dried, and ground as a substitute for coffee; and for its leaves, which are blanched and used like those of the endive. It is also sown thick, and when quite young cut as small salad. In Flanders the roots are scraped and boiled, and eaten along with meat, or with a sauce of butter and vinegar. In British gardens it is only cultivated as a winter salad. It is sown in the end of June or beginning of July, and treated like the endive, except that it is not blanched. Instead of this process, the leaves are cut off the plants, but so as not to destroy their hearts, about the beginning of October; the roots are then dug up, shortened, and planted in pots, or portable boxes, with the dibble, very close together in rich soil, watered, and afterwards protected from the frost by a light covering of litter, taken off in the daytime, or by any other convenient means. In a week or two the plants will be established, and the pots or boxes are then removed, as the produce is wanted, into the mushroom-house, or into a cellar, or any other dark warm place where the light will be completely excluded; or into any light warm place, and covered over so as to force the production of leaves and the blanching of them at the same time. In a few days the roots will push forth leaves which will be completely blanched, and each leaf, when fully expanded, may be gathered separately till the plants cease to produce any. These leaves in Belgium, and in the North of Germany and Russia, are considered as forming the most agreeable of all winter salads; and by a sufficient number of roots, it may be had in perfection from November till May. It is not even necessary to plant the roots in pots or boxes: they may be left in the soil covered with litter, and taken up to be forced as the salad is wanted; or they may be taken up and preserved in sand; or they may be pitted in the manner of potatoes; portions being regularly taken up, potted, and forced as wanted. The roots being established in the pots before forcing is a matter of very little consequence, as the leaves are supplied, not from the soil by means of the spongioles of the fibres, but from the nutriment laid up in the roots. The temperature of the mushroom-house, or other place in which the chicory is forced, should be between 55° and 60°; but the roots will send up leaves if the temperature is a few degrees above the freezing point. No blanched production is more beautiful than succory, as the leaves become of a pure white with most delicate pencillings of crimson, when grown as above recommended in a mushroom-house. Aboard ship the roots of the succory are packed into casks of sand, with their heads protruding through numerous holes pierced in the sides of the cask, by which means a maximum of produce is procured from a minimum of space.

An excellent substitute for the succory, both as a salad and a coffee plant, may be found in the common dandelion (Leontodon Taraxacum, L., which is by many persons, and by us among the number, considered not inferior to it for both purposes.

The Celery.

The Celery (Apium graveolens, L.) is an umbelliferous biennial, a native of Britain, by the sides of wet ditches, and in marshy places, especially near the sea; and though poisonous in a wild state (when it is called smallage), yet by long cultivation it has become one of our most agreeable salads. The part used is the blanched leafstalks, and in the case of one variety the roots. Both stalks and roots are used raw in salads from August till March, and also in soups and stewed. In Italy, the points of the unblanched leaves are used to flavour soups; and in Britain, when neither stalks, leaves, nor roots can be had, the bruised seeds form a good substitute.

Varieties.—Those at present considered the best are, the Red Solid, syn. Manchester Hardy, which grows to a large size, single plants having measured four feet six inches in height, and weighed nine pounds; Seymour's Solid, very solid, and fine-flavoured; Seymour's Superb White; Cole's White Perfection; Hooly's Giant; Laing's Mammoth Red; Matchless White; and Turner's Incomparable White. The turnip-rooted, syn. celeriac, has rough irregular-shaped roots, about the size of the fist; it is generally cultivated in Germany, but in England is considered coarser than the kinds of which the blanched stalks are used. Upright or stalked celery, when well grown, has the stalks solid, and not hollow or piped, as is frequently the case—thoroughly blanched, crisp, tender, and of a delicate flavour. The roots of the celeriac should be solid, tender, and delicate. To attain these qualities both sorts require to be grown with rapidity, in very rich soil, kept very moist at the root, but dry about the leaves.

Propagation and Culture.—The celery, like other culinary biennials, is only propagated by seed, and half an ounce of the stalked or upright sorts is sufficient for a seed-bed four and a half feet by ten feet; but for celeriac, as it is a spreading plant, half the quantity of seed will suffice for the same space. The seed is long in coming up, often a month; and this is one reason why the first sowing is generally made on heat. As the celery grows naturally in marshy soil, and as such soils are always rich in vegetable matter, and when near the sea must be slightly saline, these circumstances afford a guide for its culture in the garden; in which it can never be brought to a large size, without constant and abundant supplies of water during the whole period of its growth. The flavour, however, is better when it is grown of smaller size, and with less water. In general, three crops are enough, even for a large family; the first should be sown in the end of February, to transplant in June, and to come into use in August; the second is sown in the end of March, to be transplanted in July, and to come into use in September; and the third is sown about the middle of April, to be transplanted in the first week of August, and to come into use in October or November, and last till March. The plants raised by every sowing, when about one inch high, should be pricked out into rich soil two inches or three inches apart every way, and again transplanted into a nursery plantation, also in rich soil, about six inches apart every way. Those for the earliest crop may be pricked out in a small hotbed, and transplanted into a warm border; but those for the others do not necessarily require artificial heat. As the earlier crops of celery are very apt to run to flower, and as this tendency in herbaceous plants, and especially annuals and biennials, is known to be checked and retarded by destroying the tap-root, and encouraging the production of fibrous roots, some excellent growers of celery adopt the following process with their plants :—The seed-bed, whether for an early or a late crop, is formed of fresh, dark, loamy soil, mixed with old rotten dung, half and half, and placed on a hotbed. The nursery or transplanting bed is formed with old hotbed dung, well broken, laid six inches or seven inches thick on a piece of ground which has lain some time undisturbed, or which has been made hard by compression. The situation should be sunny. The plants are set six inches apart in the dung, without soil, and covered with hand-glasses. They are watered well when planted, and frequently afterwards. By hardening the soil under the dung in which the plants are set, the root is formed into a brush of fibres; and by thus preventing the pushing of a tap-root, the plant never runs to seed before the following spring.

Transplanting into Trenches.—Where the object is to have very large celery, only one row ought to be planted in a trench; but where a moderate size is preferred, there may be two rows; or the trenches may be made four feet or six feet wide, and the celery planted in rows across the trench, at the distance of a foot from one another, and six inches apart in the row. Single trenches, when the object is to grow celery alone, may be made in the direction of north and south, three feet or four feet apart, centre from centre, and eight inches or ten inches deep; the soil dug out being formed into a ridge between the trenches. As every trench is opened, dig into the bottom a coating of five or six inches in thickness of thoroughly-rotted dung, and along the centre of the trench insert the plants with a trowel, at six inches apart. When the plants are being removed, previously to planting, all side-slips should be carefully taken off. Where celery is to be grown with other crops, as in simultaneous rotations, the trenches may be made six feet or eight feet apart centre from centre, and a row of peas for sticking, or some other crop of short duration, should be grown between every two rows of celery. Where celery is to be planted in rows across broad trenches, whatever may be the width of the trench, a similar width must be allowed between them for containing the soil dug out; and these trenches should be made in the direction of east-and-west, for the same reason that trenches for single or double rows are made in the direction of north-and-south. To save ground, the plants before they are planted in the trenches should be kept in the nursery till they are six inches or eight inches high, taken up with balls, any descending roots shortened, any suckers that may have appeared removed, so as to throw the whole strength of the plant into the central bud, or growing point.

Blanching.—Blanching weakens the plant by lessening the power of the leaves to elaborate nourishment, and return it to the root; and hence, celery which is intended to grow of large size should be nearly full-grown before it is earthed up at all. Celery has been grown averaging from 9 lbs. to 12 lbs. weight, which had not been finally earthed up more than three weeks before it was gathered, and which had only one slight earthing-up previously to the final one, which was in September. On the other hand, when celery is wished to be of small size, and tender, it ought to be earthed up in an early stage of its growth, and the process continued as it advances in height. If the plants have been liberally supplied with water, excepting during rains, they will be ready to receive the first earthing-up in three or four weeks. This is done by paring down a little soil on each side of the trench with the spade, drawing it against the plants by hand, and taking care that none of it gets into their hearts. To prevent this, each plant may be first slightly wrapped round with a strand of matting. The earthing-up may then proceed with rapidity, and when finished the matting should be removed. It is scarcely necessary to observe, that where there are two rows in a trench, both must be tied up at the same time; or that when the rows are made across a broad trench the whole must be tied before any are earthed up. The height of the soil applied may be three, four, or five inches, according to the height of the plants; and the earthings-up may take place at intervals of ten days or a fortnight, till by degrees the stalks are covered to the height of twelve inches for the earliest crop, and eighteen inches, or two feet, or more, for the later crops; always taking care to perform the operation when the plants are quite dry, and to keep the heart open and free; excepting in the last earthing before winter, when the summits of the plants may be nearly closed to exclude rain. The longer celery is allowed to grow before applying the soil the longer time does it require to blanch; but in general three weeks or a month will effect this, more especially in the early part of the season. The latest crop of celery which is to be in use through the winter will require to be protected by dry litter, or thatched hurdles, during severe frosts; or it may be taken up and preserved in sand or soil, in a shed or cellar. When celery is frozen, it begins to rot immediately after the first thaw; and therefore to prolong a crop in the open garden, protection of some sort is essential on the approach of severe frosts.

Late Spring Celery.—As celery is in great demand for soups in most families, especially during winter and spring, when other delicate vegetables are scarce, a crop may be procured till the beginning of June by the following means:—Sow on a seed-bed about the middle of May; prick out, when the plants are six weeks old, into rows six inches apart, and allow the plants to remain in this nursery till September or October, then transplant them into trenches; earth them up slightly, and protect them by litter or thatched hurdles during winter; and in February or March earth them up finally. The stalks thus produced will not always be fit to use in salads, but they will be valuable for soups and stews. No celery crop that has been blanched in autumn will keep sound longer than the end of March; but green celery which has been only slightly earthed up will stand through an ordinary winter with little or no protection.

Taking the Crop.—The plants should be dug up without being bruised, beginning at one end of a row; and afterwards, the roots and green points of the leaves being cut off, and the loose outer leaves removed, the heart of the plant in a compact state is fit for being sent to the kitchen; but if intended for market, or to be sent to a distance, the outer leaves should be kept on, and also the root, excepting the fibrous part.

Celeriac is cultivated with greater ease, and at less expense of ground and manure, than the common celery; and it may be used in the kitchen for seven or eight months in succession. The times of sowing are the same as for the other sorts, and the plants should be pricked out in a similar manner. They should be divested of all side-slips, not only before transplanting, but also during their after growth. Early in June they may be finally transplanted in rows fifteen inches apart every way, into flat beds of very rich light or sandy soil, with two-feet alleys between, to admit of watering the plants. The routine culture here consists chiefly in liberal waterings, and in slightly earthing up the roots after they have swelled to their full size in order to blanch them. The celeriac has a continual tendency to revert from the knob-rooted form to that which is natural to it; and hence, like the turnip and similar plants of culture, it will not attain any large size if much earthed up. Still the celeriac, to be eatable, requires to be blanched, and therefore must be earthed up to a certain extent, but the less the better. The roots of the celeriac may be taken up on the approach of frost, and preserved in sand or soil, like potatoes, for an indefinite period. The London market used formerly to be supplied with this root from Hamburgh.

Diseases, Insects, &c.—The celery is liable to the canker in some soils, and also to be eaten by the maggot of the celery-fly (Tephritis Onopordinis, Fab.), which is hatched in the leaves, and may be destroyed as soon as these have a blistered appearance, by cutting them off, and bruising or burning them; or fetid substances may be frequently sprinkled near the plants, as a preventive.

To Save Seed.—Select the finest specimens of the variety to be propagated, in February or March; and either remove a part of the soil with which they have been earthed up, and allow them to flower where they stand, or transplant them to a more convenient situation. The seed will ripen in September, and will keep ten years.

The Lamb's Lettuce, Burnet, the Garden Cress, Winter Cress, American Cress, and Water Cress.

The Lamb's Lettuce or Corn-salad (Valerianella olitoria, Dec.) is a valerianaceous indigenous annual, very hardy, and which requires no other culture than sowing in August, September, and February, and thinning the plants to three inches apart. The leaves should be gathered singly, like those of spinach, when of full size; except when the plant is grown as small salading, when the leaves and stems may be cut over, as in gathering the common cress or mustard. They are considered as forming, when used raw, a delicate salad, and when boiled, a good spinach.

The Burnet (Poterium Sanguisorba, L., and Sanguisorba officinalis, L.) are rosaceous perennials, the leaves of which, especially those of the second species, are put into salads, and sometimes into soups; and so much are they esteemed in Italy, that the Italians have a proverb, quoted by Evelyn, signifying that a salad without burnet is good for nothing.

The Garden Cress (Lepidium sativum, L.) is a cruciferous annual, long in cultivation for its young leaves, which have a peculiarly warm and grateful relish, either alone or with other salading. There are several varieties; the best of which are the common curled-leaved, the Normandy curled, and the broad-leaved. The Normandy curled is the hardiest and most useful variety, supplying a beautiful garnish to dishes throughout the winter. The seed, which comes up in three days, may be sown in September and October for winter and spring supply; and in March, April, and May, for summer use. These five sowings will afford a constant supply throughout the year of leaves to be gathered singly, whether for garnishings or salads; but as the cress is also used as a small salad, and for that purpose gathered in the seed-leaf, where it is in demand in that state, it should be sown once a week during winter and spring under glass, and in summer and autumn in a shaded situation, the soil being kept moist by watering, or by covering with hand-glasses or mats. The soil should always be rich, the great object being rapid growth, so as to ensure succulence and delicacy. A few plants allowed to run to flower will produce abundance of seed, which will keep two years. Half a pound of seed at least will be required where the cress is in constant demand as small salading.

The Winter Cress (Barbarea vulgaris, H. K.), and the American Cress (B. præcox, Dec.), are cruciferous perennials, natives of Britain in watery places, and by careful culture in gardens they can be made to produce their leaves throughout the year. Sow in August, or the beginning of September, in rows a foot apart, for a crop to stand through the winter, and thin the plants out to six inches in the row. If the leaves are gathered singly, and the plants protected from frost by glass, or nightly coverings, they will afford a regular supply till the following June. The plants will then run to flower, and produce seed in abundance.

The Water-cress (Nasturtium officinale, H. K.) is a cruciferous, amphibious, creeping perennial, held in general estimation in this and other countries as an antiscorbutic plant, and brought to market in immense quantities from its natural habitat in running water, or artificial plantations made there. The most favourable description of water is a clear stream, not more than an inch and a half deep, running over sand or gravel; the least favourable, deep still water on a muddy bottom. It is evident, therefore, that there are few private gardens in which the water-cress can be cultivated in running water; but fortunately it will grow luxuriantly in rich sandy soil, if watered overhead every morning and evening during the growing season; and the cresses thus produced are almost equal to those grown in clear running water. The plants may be raised from seed or obtained by division of old plants; and they may be planted early in spring, a foot apart every way. In gathering, only the points of the shoots should be taken, as the lower leaves are not only coarser, but apt to be infested by the larvæ of insects if growing in water, and by snails and slugs if on land.

For a small garden, the common Normandy and the water-cress are the only plants of the cress kind worth cultivating.

Small Salads.

Small salads are understood to be very young plants of the salad kind, sown thick, and gathered, some, as the cress, mustard, rape, radish, and some other cruciferous plants, in the seed-leaf; and others, as the lettuce, endive, succory, lamb's lettuce, and various others, when in the third or fourth leaf. In general, all rapidly-growing salad plants are fit for being used as small salads, and are so used on the Continent; but the principal small salads in England are the cress, mustard, rape, and radish, which are sown weekly all the year round on fine rich soil, kept warm, moist, and shaded, and cut in the seed-leaf, generally in about a week after they are sown. Of the small salads which are allowed to advance beyond the seed-leaf before they are cut, by far the best is the common Cos lettuce. There are two kinds of mustard which may be grown as small salading (Sinapis alba, L. and S. nigra, L.); but the former alone is grown as salading, the latter being the kind grown in fields for its seeds to be ground into the flour-of-mustard ot the shops. It is, therefore, seldom seen in gardens. The Rape (Brassica Napus, var. oleifera, Dec.) is only grown in gardens as a small salad, and as in the case of other small salads, when much in demand, one pound of seed of each kind at least will be required.

Adornaceous Esculents.

Adornaceous esculents—under which term we include chiefly the plants used as garnishes, such as the parsley, chervil, fennel, horseradish, &c.—include a great variety of plants belonging to different natural orders, and some of which, such as the Indian cress, might even have been included under acetariaceous esculents. The culture of all the plants of this class is very simple, and with the exception of the horseradish and parsley, a dry calcareous soil, poor rather than rich, is to be preferred; because such a soil is found to be most favourable for the preservation of their aromatic properties.

The Parsley.

The Parsley (Apium Petroselinum, L.) is an umbelliferous biennial, a native of Sardinia, long in cultivation as a seasoning, and also as a garnish. Eaten along with any dish strongly seasoned with onions, it takes off their smell, and prevents their after-taste; no herb is more valuable for communicating flavour to soups and stews. There are many varieties, differing only, however, in the extent of the curling of the leaves. The plain-leaved variety is scarcely grown now in gardens. Parsley-seed, of which an ounce will sow a drill 150 feet in length, requires to be sown every year in February, either broadcast or in rows, the latter being preferable. The seed will remain in the ground from forty to fifty days before it vegetates, being a longer period than is required for any other garden-seed; and, unlike most other seeds, parsley-seed that has been kept several years comes up sooner than new seed; unless, indeed, the new seed has been taken from the plant before it was fully ripe, and sown immediately. The plants should be thinned out to six inches distance in the row; and also all those plants that have not the leaves beautifully curled should be pulled up, an operation technically called roguing; because one of the principal uses of parsley is as a garnish, and the curled leaves are incomparably more ornamental than the plain ones. They should be gathered leaf by leaf; and when there is a want of young tender leaves, the plant should be cut over by the surface of the ground, when a new set of leaves will be sent up. In order that there may be a supply in the winter season a sowing should be made about May, to be covered in October with a frame and sashes, or with hoops and mats, or propped hurdles. The parsley-leaf may be preserved in a state fit for being used in soups and stews, by drying it in a Dutch oven, or in a tin roasting-screen (or hastener), and when it becomes brittle, rubbing it into a fine powder, and putting it into glass bottles till wanted for use. Seed may be saved by selecting a few plants with the most beautifully-curled leaves, and allowing them to run to flower. The seed will ripen in July, and will keep six or eight years.

The Hamburgh parsley, the roots of which are eaten like those of the parsnip; and the Naples parsley, the footstalks of the leaves of which are used like celery, are also occasionally grown and used.

The Chervil, the Coriander, Dill, Fennel, Tarragon, and Purslane.

The Chervil (Chærophyllum sativum) is an umbelliferous annual, a native of the south of Europe, and cultivated for the same purposes as the parsley; but as it runs rapidly to seed, several sowings require to be made in the course of the growing season. Sow in shallow drills six inches apart, and thin out the plants; and when gathering, take the leaves singly. They may be dried and preserved in the same manner as those of parsley. A few plants allowed to run will bear abundance of seed, which will keep six or eight years.

The Coriander (Coriandrum sativum, L.), an umbelliferous annual, a native of the south of Europe, is sometimes cultivated in gardens for the same purposes as the chervil; but more frequently, especially on the Continent, for its seeds, which are sold by the confectioners encrusted in sugar.

The Anise (Tragium sativum, Spr.) is an annual, a native of Egypt, sometimes cultivated in gardens for the same purposes as the coriander.

The Dill (Anethum graveolens, L.) is an umbelliferous biennial, a native of Spain, the leaves of which are occasionally used in soups and sauces, and to put along with pickles, especially cucumbers. Two or three plants will be enough for any family. It is easily propagated by division or by seeds.

The Fennel (Anethum Fœniculum, L.) is an umbelliferous perennial, resembling the dill, but considerably larger, a native of the south of Europe, and very generally cultivated in gardens for the stalks and leaves. The leaves, boiled, enter into many fish-sauces, and, raw, form a beautiful garnish; the tender stalks are used raw in salads; and the blanched stalks of the variety called finocchio are eaten with oil, vinegar, and pepper, as a cod-salad; and they are likewise put into soups. Three or four plants of the common fennel are sufficient for any garden. The finocchio may be grown in rows in light, rich soil, and earthed up to the height of five inches or six inches, to blanch the stalks. This blanching will be effected in ten days or a fortnight; and by cutting down a few plants at a time during summer, a succession of young shoots will be produced, which, being blanched, will afford a supply from June till December. The soil ought to be calcareous, dry, and rich, and watered in very dry weather.

The Tarragon (Artemisia Dracunculus, L.) is an anthemideous perennial, a native of Siberia, cultivated for its leaves and the points of its shoots as an ingredient in salads, soups, stews, pickles, and other compositions. By infusion, the stalks and leaves make tarragon vinegar, which is considered one of the best condiments for fish. Tarragon is propagated by division or by seed, and grown in rows eighteen inches apart, and six inches distant in the row. The soil in which it is grown should be dry and calcareous; otherwise the plants will be comparatively without flavour, and be apt to perish in a severe winter. It is easily forced by transferring a few plants to the hotbed or hothouse; and the stems may be gathered just before they are coming into flower, dried, compressed into small packets, and put up in paper.

Substitutes for the tarragon are to be found in the Achillea serrata, E. B., and the Tagetes lucida, Cav.; in the latter plant more especially. The former is much used in Nottinghamshire, under the name of sweet mace. Achillea nana, L., and several dwarf species of Artemisia are used for the same purpose in the Alps.

The Purslane (Portulaca oleracea, L.) is a portulaceous annual, with succulent leaves and procumbent stems, a native of South America, and cultivated for its young shoots and succulent leaves as ingredients in spring and summer salads, and as pot-herbs and pickles. There are two sorts, considered as distinct species, the green and the golden; the latter is more showy as a garnish, but the former is more succulent as a salad. Where a constant supply is required, the first sowing should be made on heat in February, and the others monthly, on a warm border till August. The shoots are gathered for use when they are from two inches to five inches in height, and well furnished with leaves; and if they are cut off close to the collar of the plant it will sprout out again, and afford a second supply. A few plants will produce abundance of seed, which will keep good two years.

The Indian Cress, Borage, and Marigold.

These plants are annuals, and only a very few of each are required for any garden.

The Indian cress, or Nasturtium (Tropæolum majus, L.) is a trailing or climbing annual, a native of Peru, but growing vigorously in the open air in the climate of Britain. The flowers make a beautiful garnish alone, or along with those of the borage, the marigold, oxalis, dahlia, &c.; and both the flowers and the young leaves and tender shoots are eaten in salads, having a warm taste like the common cress, whence the name Indian cress. The fruit is gathered green, and pickled like capers, for which they form so excellent a substitute that they are preferred to the true caper by many persons. The two sorts best worth cultivating are the common large, with an orange flower, and the blood-red flowered. The seed may either be sown on heat in March, and transplanted in May, or sown in May where it is finally to remain; and in order to keep the flowers and fruit quite clean, it is advisable to stake the plants in the manner of peas. The leaves, points of the shoots, and flowers, should be gathered only a few hours before using; and the fruit for pickling, while green, plump, and tender. One or two plants will ripen abundance of seed, which will keep two years.

The Borage (Borago officinalis, L.) is a boraginaceous annual, indigenous or naturalized in Britain, and generally cultivated among other plants used in garnishing for its beautiful blue flowers. The tender leaves and points of the shoots are used in salads and as pot-herbs, more especially on the Continent. The flowers and upper leaves are sometimes put in a cool tankard, which is a beverage composed of wine, water, lemon-juice, and sugar. The seed keeps four years.

The Marigold, or pot-marigold (Calendula officinalis, L.), is an annual, the double-flowered varieties of which have been long cultivated in gardens as ornamental plants, for their flowers as garnishes, and for their petals, which are occasionally used in broths and soups. A few plants are enough for any garden, and they may be raised from seed sown in February or March. The petals may be gathered, dried in the sun, and put up in paper for winter use.

The Horse-radish.

The Horse-radish (Cochlearia Armoracia, L.) is a cruciferous perennial, a native of England in marshy places, long cultivated for its roots or underground stems. These are scraped into shreds, as a garnish and a condiment to roast-beef, and also as an ingredient in winter salads and sauces; and by some persons it is eaten raw with bread-and-butter. It is propagated by cuttings, which may be either of the crown with one or two inches of the root attached, or of the root, without any visible buds, about the same length, and planted with the upper end uppermost, as in sea-kale. These cuttings may either be dropped into holes made by a dibber, fifteen or eighteen inches in depth, and about the same distance apart every way, the upper part of the hole being filled in with light soil or wood ashes; or they may be planted while the ground is being trenched, covering them to the depth of eighteen inches. March is the season for planting, and the soil should be rich, free, moist, and at least two feet deep. The roots, that is the part produced between the top of the cutting and the surface of the ground, and which may be called a blanched stem, will be fit for use at the end of the first autumn, when the leaves have decayed; but they will be much stronger at the end of the second autumn. They ought never to be allowed to remain longer than three years, nor to ripen seed, otherwise the roots become tough and disagreeable to use. A portion ought to be planted every year to come in in succession. The horizontal mode of growth has recently been adopted with great success. Instead of inserting the roots vertically, they have been laid along in rich soil, about four inches from the surface. They swell rapidly, and are easily found when wanted. In taking the crop, begin at one end of a row, and dig down as far as the roots have penetrated, so as to take up every particle of root, for the least fragment left will send up leaves the following year. For this reason many gardeners grow their horse-radish always on the same spot of ground; trenching up one-half every winter; and selecting the larger roots, and laying them up in sand, or earthing them up in a shady border, for use, and leaving the smaller roots in the bottom of the trench for next year's crop. In whichever way horse-radish is grown, the soil ought to be deep, rich, and moist, in order that the growth may be rapid and the root succulent; the flower-stems should be cut off as soon as they appear, because they deprive the root of nourishment which would otherwise be sent down to it; and the crop should not be allowed to stand more than three or four years, otherwise the roots will become filled with woody fibre, sticky, and unfit for use.

Lepidium latifolium, L., a cruciferous annual, a native of Britain on the sea-coast, has roots resembling those of the horse-radish, which may very well be used as a substitute; the leaves are excellent as greens, and not bad in salads.

Condimentaceous Esculents.

Condimentaceous esculents are such as in cookery are always used with pastry in the form of tarts, pies, puddings, &c.; or preserved in sugar, or pickled in vinegar. Though fruits are chiefly employed in these preparations, yet we have as substitutes the rhubarb and the Oxalis crenata for tarts, pies, and puddings, and the angelica for preserving in sugar, and the samphire for pickling. The principal plant belonging to this section, however, is the rhubarb, which, though scarcely known as a tart plant in the commencement of the present century, is now become generally cultivated for that purpose, even in the garden of the cottager. The other plants of this section occupy but a very small space in the herb-ground.

The Rhubarb.

The Rhubarb (Rheum, L.) is a polygonaceous perennial, a native of Tartary and other countries of the East, of which there are several species, hybrids and varieties, in culture for the petioles of the radical leaves. These are peeled, cut into small pieces, and put into tarts and pies, in the manner of gooseberries and apples, or, like them, baked whole in a dish. A wine is also made from them, and they are also pickled and preserved. There are a great many different kinds in cultivation, and every year produces some new sort; but those considered the best at the present time are: For an early crop, Linnæus, Myatt's Crimson Perfection, Scarlet Defiance, New Crimson; and for a main crop, Myatt's Victoria, which is also the best for forcing. To ensure the flavour in pies and puddings, a portion of the stalks should always be put in without being peeled.

Propagation and Culture.—By division is the most common method, and the most certain for continuing particular varieties. The flower-stems should be cut down as soon as they appear, unless seed is wanted. Some persons prefer the leaves partially blanched, and for this purpose place a sea-kale pot over each plant, but without the cover; others have grown it in chimney-pots for the same purpose, and find also an increased produce from the greater length of stalk. It can readily be forced into use even as early as January, by applying hot dung or leaves around such pots, and greatly accelerated in spring by covering each plant with a common hand-glass, or such like contrivances. In gathering the leaves, remove a little soil, bend them down, and slip them off, without injuring the buds at their base, and without bruising the stalks. The stalk is fit to use when the disk of the leaf is half expanded; but a larger produce and a fuller flavour are obtained by waiting till the leaf is fully grown. One plant allowed to run will produce abundance of seed, which ripens in August, and will keep a year.

Substitutes for the tart rhubarb may be found in every other species of the genus, not even excepting the so-called medicinal species, R. palmatum; in the stalks of the oxalis crenata, of the sorrel, and of the different species of dock, which, according to Cobbett, are sent to market for that purpose in America.

The Angelica, Elecampane, Samphire, and Caper.

The Angelica (Angelica, Archangelica, L.) is an umbelliferous biennial, a native of England, in moist situations in good soil, but rare, and cultivated in gardens for their leaves, and the tender flower-stalks, which were formerly blanched like celery. They are now chiefly candied with sugar, and in Sweden and Norway, the leaves and stalks are eaten raw, or boiled with meat and fish; and the seeds are used to flavour ardent spirits. The time for gathering the stalks is May, and if the plant be then cut down a second crop will be produced; and if the flower-stems be cut off as fast as they appear, the plant, though a biennial, will last several years. Seed is produced in abundance, and will keep three or four years.

The Elecampane (Inula Helenium, L.) is a carduaceous perennial, a native of the south of England in moist pastures. The root is fusiform, thick, and aromatic, and is candied like the stalks of the angelica, and much admired in France and Germany. The plant ought to be taken up yearly, and divided and replanted, in order that the roots may be obtained succulent and tender, and for the same reason the plant ought never to be allowed to come into flower.

The Samphire (Crithmum maritimum, L.) is an umbelliferous perennial, a native of England, on rocky cliffs by the sea, and cultivated in gardens for its seed-pods, which make a warm aromatic pickle, and its leaves, which are used in salads. It is propagated by division, or by sowing the seed in April; but in either way it is rather difficult of cultivation. It succeeds best in a gravelly soil, kept moist, and sprinkled in spring with common sea-salt. During winter it requires to be protected by a little dry litter. By this treatment it has produced an ample supply of shoots, which may be cut twice in a season. Seed may be saved, or plants procured from their native habitats on the sea-coast, as for example at Dover, Salcombe, and on the coast of Galloway and Haddington.

Substitutes for the samphire are to be found in some other plants which grow within salt-water mark; for example, the golden samphire (Inula crithmifolia, L.), a perennial, not uncommon in salt marshes; and Salicornia herbacea, L., a chenopodiaceous annual, found on muddy sea-shores throughout Europe; in Echinophora spinosa, L., an umbelliferous plant, a native of sandy shores in Lancashire and Kent; the young leaves of which make a wholesome and excellent pickle.

The Caper (Capparis spinosa, L.) is a capparidaceous trailing shrub, a native of the south of Europe, on rocks and dry stony or gravelly places, and cultivated about Marseilles, and other parts of France, for its flower-buds, which are gathered when about half the size which they attain before expanding. It might be cultivated in the south of England in the open garden, and in other parts against a conservative wall; or if it were thought necessary, a few plants under glass would supply all that would suffice for an ordinary family. It would thrive on the rocky shores of the south of Devon, or among the old stone quarries of Somersetshire.

Excellent substitutes for the caper are found in the unripe fruit of the Indian cress, and of the Euphorbia Lathyris, L.

The Ginger (Zingiber officinale, L.), a scitamineous perennial from the East Indies, is sometimes cultivated in our stoves for the roots, or creeping underground stems, to be taken when succulent, and pickled and preserved. The plants are divided when in a dormant state, and planted in rich light soil, and in a year afterwards the roots are fit to gather. Ginger, as soon as its growth is finished and fully ripe in autumn, which will be observed by the decaying of its foliage and stalks, should be stored away in dry earth or sand in a warm, dry situation, and kept without any water all the winter, to be taken up and shaken out in February, placed in shallow boxes or pans, flat and thickly placed over the surface, covered with an inch of fine sandy soil, and placed in heat, such as an early vinery or plant-stove. As soon as the buds have started, take the roots or tubers, cut or break them into small pieces, allowing one bud only to each piece; pot singly into sixty-sized pots, place in strong heat again, where they will grow freely; by April they will become sufficiently strong to turn out on a moderate hotbed, such as would suit the growth of melons. Good heavy-holding loam should be used a foot in depth. Some growers save the old pine soil with its charcoal and soot in it, and thus grow such heavy crops of this useful root as would astonish many to see; in fact, the soil by the autumn becomes entirely full of the most luxuriant large young roots or tubers, splendid for preserving or any other use.

Aromaceous Esculents.

The esculent aromatic plants, or sweet herbs, in common use, are about a dozen in number, and each should have a tiny bed to itself in the herb-garden. The soil for all of them may be dry and calcareous, with the single exception of the mint family. They are used to give flavour to soups, stews, and other dishes, and in sauces and various stuffings. The leaves and stalks of all these plants may be gathered when they are coming into flower, dried, and compressed in a shallow box by a screw-press, so as to form packets about the size of a small octavo volume, which, being put up in paper, will retain their fragrance for two or three years. Nothing can be worse than the former mode of keeping herbs, by hanging them up loose, in the back sheds, or in the seed-room, where they soon become covered with dust, and deprived of their aroma.

The Common Thyme (Thymus vulgaris, L.) is a labiaceous evergreen under-shrub, a native of Spain and Italy. The young leaves and tops are used either green or dried in soups, stuffings, stews, and sauces. It is readily increased by seeds, cuttings, or by division, and the plants should be renewed by one or other of these modes every year in spring.

The Lemon Thyme is the T. citriodorus, Pers., a trailing evergreen, used for the same purposes as the preceding species; but being less pungent it is more grateful, and therefore used as a seasoning for veal, instead of lemon peel.

The Sage (Salvia officinalis, L.) is a labiaceous evergreen undershrub, a native of the south of Europe. The leaves and tender tops are used in stuffings and sauces, for many kinds of luscious and strong meats, as well as to improve the flavour of various articles of cookery. There are several varieties: the common, red, or purple-leaved; the narrow-leaved green; and the broad-leaved green—all of equal merit. They are propagated by seeds or cuttings, and like the thyme, the plantation ought to be renewed every two or three years, otherwise it is very apt to be destroyed in the winter.

The Clary (S. Sclarea, L.) is a biennial, a native of Italy, sometimes used as a substitute for the sage.

The Common Mint, or Spear Mint, is the Mentha viridis, L., a labiaceous creeping-stemmed perennial, a native of England, in marshy places; the young leaves and tops of which are used in spring salads, and form an ingredient in soups; they are also employed to give flavour to certain dishes, as peas, &c.; being boiled for a time, and then withdrawn. Mint is much in demand about London as an ingredient in sauce for lamb. It is propagated by division of the roots before they begin to grow in spring, which are buried in shallow drills; or by the young shoots slipped off when they are three inches or four inches in length, and planted in beds a few inches apart. To produce tender stalks and leaves the plants require to be liberally supplied with water. When mint is to be dried, the stalks should be cut when they are just coming into flower, dried in a shaded place, compressed in packets, and papered, to be laid up in a drawer or herb-case till wanted for use. No plant is easier to force, and this ought always to be done in time for new lamb.

The Pennyroyal Mint (M. Pulegium, L.) is a low creeping perennial, a native of England, in wet commons, and on the margins of brooks. It is used in cookery like the common mint, and for distilling pennyroyal water. It should be planted afresh every spring. During winter the old plants have a great tendency to die off, only a few creeping shoots surviving. These should be carefully planted in a fresh bed, and the old plants destroyed. In some families this herb is in great request for flavouring black puddings, and it is apt to perish in many situations.

The Pot Marjoram (Origanum Onites, L.) is a labiaceous undershrub, a native of Sicily, but hardy enough to stand through our winters. The leaves and tender tops, green or dried, are used in soups as a substitute for those of the sweet or knotted marjoram. It is readily propagated by division of the roots, or by seeds.

The Sweet Marjoram, or Knotted Marjoram, is a biennial, a native of the south of Europe, and long cultivated in British gardens as a seasoning for soups, and for other culinary purposes. This species being somewhat tender, is commonly sown on a slight hotbed towards the end of March, or on a warm border about the middle of April; in the former case transplanting it into rows one foot apart, and the plants six inches distant in the row; and in the latter case thinning them out without transplanting. The green tops may be gathered as wanted; but those to be preserved in packets will have most flavour if gathered when just coming into blossom.

The Winter Marjoram (O. heracleoticum, L.) is a perennial, a native of the south of Europe, with leaves resembling those of the knotted marjoram, but with the flowers in spikes instead of whorls. It is used like the other marjorams, and propagated by division.

The Winter Savory (Satureja montana, L.) is a labiaceous under-shrub, a native of the south of Europe, and cultivated for its tender tops as a seasoning for soups and made dishes, and for boiling with peas, beans, &c. It is propagated by seed, cuttings, or division, like thyme, but most frequently by the latter mode.

The Summer Savory (S. hortensis, L.) is an annual, a native of Italy, with larger leaves and a more agreeable fragrance than the winter savory, to which it is generally preferred. It is sown in drills, one foot apart, in the open garden, in March or April.

The Sweet Basil, or larger Basil (Ocymum Basilicum, L.) is a labiaceous annual, a native of the East Indies, cultivated for its highly aromatic properties. The leaves and bracteæ, or leafy tops, are the parts gathered; and, on account of their strong flavour of cloves, they are often used in highly-seasoned dishes, as well as in soups, stews, and sauces; and a leaf or two leaves are sometimes introduced into salads. Sow on a hotbed in the end of March, and plant out in a warm border when all danger from frost is over, allowing the plants at least a square foot of space for each.

The Bush Basil, or least Basil (O. minimum, L.), an annual, also from the East Indies, is a much smaller plant than the former, but being equally aromatic, and rather more hardy, is frequently substituted for it.

The Tansy (Tanacetum vulgare, L.) is a perennial composite, a native of Britain, on the sandy banks of rivers, and cultivated in gardens for the young leaves, which are shredded down, and employed to flavour puddings, omelets, and cakes. There is a variety with the leaves doubly curled, which is generally preferred. No plant is more easily propagated or cultivated, and it also forces freely.

Fungaceous Esculents.

The only fungaceous vegetable cultivated in Britain is the common mushroom, though attempts have been made to bring under culture the truffle and the morel.

The Garden Mushroom (Agaricus campestris, L.) is a fungus, a native of Britain and most parts of Europe, appearing in pastures in August and September, and readily distinguished from other fungi by its fine pink or flesh-coloured gills and pleasant smell. As the natural history of the mushroom was given when treating of the mode of forcing it, and as there are no varieties to be described, we have only to notice a practice sometimes adopted of growing the mushroom, in imitation of nature, in pastures. The attempt will not succeed in every soil and situation, but it has done so in a great many instances. Take mushroom spawn, and in the beginning of July inoculate a pasture with it by simply raising one piece of turf, three inches thick, with the spade, in every square yard, inserting a small fragment of spawn beneath it, and pressing it firmly down again with the back of the spade or the foot. In all probability a crop will be produced during the latter end of August and the beginning of September; and mushrooms will appear of themselves in the same ground for a number of years afterwards. Mushroom spawn has also been planted among potatoes and other crops in the open garden, and has produced mushrooms, but no mode yet discovered is so certain as those in which artificial heat and a bed of stable-dung is employed. The best crops in the open ground have been gathered from beneath the leaves of cucumbers and vegetable marrows grown on dung-ridges. The mushroom, when cultivated in houses, is liable to the attacks of various insects, slugs, and worms, all of which may be collected by baits, or devoured by a toad or two kept on purpose.

The Truffle (Tuber cibarium, Sibth.) is a fungus, a native of Britain, and growing naturally some inches below the surface. It is very common in the downs of Wiltshire, Hampshire, Kent, and Devonshire, where dogs are trained to scent it out, and where also it is sought out and devoured by pigs—which on the Continent are used to discover the localities of this fungus, as dogs are in England. It is sent to the London market from different parts of England in a green state, and imported from the Continent sliced and dried. The most celebrated truffles are those from the oak forests of Perigord. Various attempts have been made, both in Britain and on the Continent, to cultivate the truffle, but hitherto with but little success; but it would appear that Dr. Klotzsch, of Berlin, has ascertained that the best course is to take truffles which are no longer good for the table, being over-ripe, and nearly in a state of decomposition, diffusing a disagreeable odour; to break them into pieces, and place them two inches or three inches deep in the earth, in rather raised flat places, under copse or underwood, protected from the north and east winds. Truffles in the state in which they are eaten are never ripe, and therefore are unfit for propagation ('Gard. Chron.,' 1842, p. 287). Mr. Barnes, late of Bicton, says: "The truffle grows plentifully in Devonshire, and in other parts, under large beech-trees. Their whereabouts is always known by the squirrels. These little animals seek them out by scent, no doubt, as they scratch holes exactly over them to take them out, and sit on their hind legs holding them with their two fore-paws, turning them round while they nibble and devour them, which I have seen them do many times, and if disturbed, bolt up the nearest tree with the truffle in their mouths."

The Morel (Morchella esculenta, Pers.) belongs to the same division of fungi as the truffle. It is a native of Britain in wet banks, in woods, and in moist pastures, and is in perfection in May and June. When gathered dry it will keep several months. It is used for the same purpose as the truffle, but like it has not as yet been subjected to cultivation. The morel is often found under elm-trees, in old dry sandy loam, on banks, in plantations, where the sun seldom penetrates, and under cedars of Lebanon and old white thorns.

Odoraceous Herbs.

The odoraceous herbs, or perfumery herbs, cultivated in British gardens in the present day are, with the exception of lavender and peppermint, applied to very little use.

The Lavender (Lavandula Spica, L.) is a labiaceous under-shrub, a native of the south of Europe, a few plants of which are cultivated in most gardens for their powerfully aromatic flowers. These are gathered with a portion of the stalk attached, and tied up in little bundles, dried, and placed among linen to perfume it and to deter the moth. They are also used for scenting rooms, wardrobes, and for a variety of similar purposes, and for affording lavender-water by distillation. It is propagated by seeds or cuttings, and thrives best on dry calcareous soils, in which it will last five or six years. L. latifolia, Ehrh., and L. viridis, Herit., are cultivated in some gardens instead of the common sort, or along with it.

The Rosemary (Rosmarinus officinalis, L.) is a labiaceous evergreen under-shrub, a native of the south of Europe, and, like the lavender, highly aromatic. The flowers are used like those of the lavender, and for distilling Hungary-water; and the sprigs are sometimes used as a garnish. It is readily propagated by seeds or cuttings in dry calcareous soil, and a plant will last six or seven years.

The Peppermint (Mentha piperita, L.) is a labiaceous creeping-stemmed perennial, a native of England in watery places. Its only use is for distilling peppermint-water, for which purpose it may be propagated like the mint, and planted in a soft, rich soil, moist either naturally or by art. The stalks are gathered when they are in full flower, and taken at once to distil. The plantation, from its travelling roots, requires to be renewed every four or five years.

Medicaceous Herbs.

The medicinal herbs here enumerated are still found in a number of gardens, though very little use is made of them.

The Medicinal Rhubarb (Rheum palmatum, L.) may be cultivated like the Tart Rhubarb, and after standing three or four years, the plants may be taken up and their larger roots dried for use. After taking up and cleaning the roots and cutting off the lateral fibres, cut them into sections an inch or more in thickness, make holes in them, and string them, and hang them up to dry gradually in an airy loft, laundry, or kitchen, till they are fit for being bruised into a powder, or cut into pieces about the size of peas, to be taken as pills.

The Chamomile (Anthemis nobilis, L.) is a creeping perennial, a native of England in gravelly pastures, and cultivated for its flowers, which are bitter and stomachic, and much used for chamomile tea.

The Wormwood (Artemisia Absinthium, L.) is a perennial, a native of Britain in calcareous pastures, and formerly cultivated as a vermifuge, and for other purposes in domestic medicine. It is found beneficial to poultry, and should be planted in poultry grounds; it is also used as a substitute for hops in beer. It is easily propagated by cuttings or division.

The Rue (Ruta graveolens, L.) is a rutaceous evergreen under-shrub, a native of the south of Europe, the leaves of which are sometimes eaten with bread-and-butter, and frequently given to poultry for the croup. They also make a beautiful garnish.

The Horehound (Marrubium vulgare, L.), is a labiaceous perennial, a native of Britain on dry chalky or gravelly soil, and was formerly in demand as a cure for coughs and asthmas, for which candied horehound is still a popular remedy.

The Hyssop (Hyssopus officinalis, L.), is a labiaceous evergreen under-shrub, a native of the south of Europe, the leafy tops and flowers of which are gathered and dried for making hyssop tea and other purposes.

The Balm (Melissa officinalis, L.) is a labiaceous perennial, a native of Switzerland, of which balm tea and balm wine used to be made.

The Blessed Thistle (Centaurea benedicta, L.) is a carduaceous annual, a native of the south of Europe, an infusion of the leaves of which is considered as stomachic.

The Liquorice (Glycyrrhiza glabra, L.) is a leguminous deep-rooting perennial, cultivated in fields more frequently than in gardens for its saccharine juice, which is used as an emollient in colds, fevers, &c.

The Blue Melilot (Melilotus cærulea, L.) is a leguminous annual, a native of Switzerland, Bohemia, &c., remarkable for its powerful fragrance, which is used in Switzerland to aromatize the Schabziguer cheese, and there and in other countries to perfume clothes, and afford, by distillation, a fragrant water. In a dried state, the perfume is more powerful, and it is retained for upwards of half a century.

Toxicaceous Herbs.

The poisonous plants cultivated in gardens for the purpose of destroying insects or vermin are few, and indeed the tobacco is almost the only one.

The Tobacco (Nicotiana Tabacum, L.) is a solanaceous annual, a native of South America, and cultivated to a limited extent in gardens for horticultural purposes. "It is used to fumigate hothouses; large infusions of it are put into most washes that are prepared for extirpating insects; and by drying and grinding it into the form of snuff, it is found very efficacious in destroying the green-fly on peach and rose trees out of doors." The best variety is the large-leaved Virginian.

Propagation and Culture.—Sow the seed, which is small, in shallow seed-pans in light rich soil, in March or April, on a nice hotbed with a top and bottom heat of 70°. Prick off into other seed-pans as soon as the plants can be fairly handled, and return them to the seed-pot, frame, or house. When they have grown about three inches, put them singly into three or four-inch pots, and place them again in a warm house until the pots are full of roots and the plants have reached six or eight inches in height; then gradually inure them to exposure.

They are, however, as susceptible of cold as the potato, and should not be planted out finally till the end of May.

Cultivation in the Open Ground.—The soil for growing tobacco can hardly be too rich and deep. It is a gross feeder and a rapid grower. The plants should be set in rows three or four feet apart, and eighteen inches at least from plant to plant in the rows. Here they will only require to be kept clean by frequent hoeings, and if their progress is not satisfactory, their growth may be vigorously stimulated with doses of sewage or liquid-manure. The tobacco is a plant of rapid growth, and, in three months from the time of planting, it will have reached a height of from six to nine feet, and formed an immense number of large leaves. It will now begin to flower, and at this stage it probably possesses the maximum amount of poison; this is therefore the time chosen by many for harvesting and curing the crop. The piecemeal mode of harvesting is the best:—About August, go over the tobacco and pick off all the largest leaves. Tie them in bundles, and hang them up in an airy shed or any hot dry house or closet to dry. When they begin to get crisp, they should be placed in a moist atmosphere until the leaves "come again," as it is called—that is, until they are pliable and can be rolled up without breaking. The leaves should then be laid one upon another, in bundles twenty or thirty thick, firmly pressed, and then stored away in close boxes and tubs in a dry place, and preserved for use. The drying, sweating, and pressing seem to be the great points needed to develope and preserve the essential oils of the tobacco. If dried only, as is often the case, the tobacco becomes brittle; if the sweating is carried to excess, the leaves will rot; if exposed to the air after it is cured, the strength will vanish away. The drying and sweating should, if possible, be performed in a high temperature, at least from 70° to 80°. A second or third crop of leaves will be produced, to be treated in the same manner; and finally, early in October, the entire plant should be cut over and the stalks preserved like the leaves. From their greater substance they will need more time in drying. In all other respects treat them like the leaves. By this mode excellent fumigating tobacco may be prepared.

The White Hellebore (Veratrum album, L.) is a melanthaceous tuberculous-rooted perennial, a native of Denmark, and formerly in much repute as a powerful medicine. The part employed is the root dried and powdered; and as it has lately been found more efficacious than tobacco powder in destroying the caterpillar on the gooseberry, it might be worth while to cultivate it in gardens for that purpose. The plant is not rare, and is easily propagated by seeds or by division. At two years from the seed the roots may be fit for use, and may be taken up, dried on a hothouse flue, and beaten into powder, first on a stone with a cast-iron rammer, and afterwards, if thought necessary, to a finer powder, in a mortar. A decoction of the leaves and stems might probably also be effective; or they might be treated like those of the tobacco, and afterwards used in fumigation or as snuff.

The Foxglove (Digitalis purpurea, L.) is a scrophularinaceous biennial, a native of Britain, and common in copse-woods and hedge-wastes. The whole plant is poisonous, and may be used for the same purpose, and in the same manner, as the tobacco.

The Henbane (Hyoscyamus niger, L.), and the Thorn-apple (Datura Stramonium, L.), are well known indigenous annuals, of highly narcotic properties, which, if treated like the tobacco, would probably be equally efficacious in the destruction of insects.

A MONTHLY CALENDAR OF OPERATIONS.

The nature of this work precludes the necessity of giving a copious calendar of operations; still it would be incomplete without one: we shall therefore briefly state what should be done in each month, and the reader can refer to the body of the work for the practical details.

JANUARY.

VEGETABLE DEPARTMENT.

Artichokes—secure from frost, if not yet done. *Asparagus*—plant on a hotbed twice in the month, to keep up a succession. *Carrot*—sow on a slight hotbed. *Cauliflower*—sow in a box, and place in a forcing-house, to provide plants in succession to the autumn-sowed, and to make up blanks should any of the latter have failed. *Celery*—protect during severe weather. *Cucumbers*—prepare a seed-bed for sowing next month; renew the linings of the fruiting-beds; keep them made up above the surface of the soil in the frame. *French Beans*—sow in pots for forcing a batch once a fortnight. *Mint* and other *herbs*—take up and plant in pots or boxes, and place them in a forcing-house. *Potatoes*—plant on a slight hotbed. *Radishes*—sow on a slight hotbed, or in the same frame with potatoes. *Rhubarb*—take up old roots, and plant in boxes or pots; place them in a forcing or mushroom-house; *Sea-kale* ditto; *Asparagus* ditto.

FRUIT DEPARTMENT.

Pinery—maintain a temperature in the fruiting-house of from 70° to 75° by day, and from 65° to 75° by night; succession-house, from 5° to 8° lower; nursing-pits about 60°. *Vinery*—commence forcing for fruit in June; begin with a temperature of 45°; gradually increase in the first month to 55° min. *Peach-house*—commence forcing for fruit in May; begin with a temperature of 45°. *Cherry-house*—commence forcing with a temperature of 40° min. by night. *Orchard-house*—protect fruit trees in pots from being frozen with a covering of litter. Prune, and paint the trees with a mixture of paint formed of sulphur, soot, and lime, dissolved in a strong solution of soft-soap, or Gishurst's compound; top-dress or renew the borders; plant fruit trees. *Figs*—plants in pots may now be placed in a vinery. *Strawberries*—take plants in pots into a forcing-house or pit twice in the month. *Prune* the apple, pear, plum, cherry, gooseberry, currant, and raspberry, if the weather is not severe. Nail and tie wall and espalier trees.

FEBRUARY.

VEGETABLE DEPARTMENT.

Beans—plant in boxes for turning out next month, also sow in the open ground. *Cabbage*—sow on a warm border. *Carrots*—sow on a warm border. *Cauliflowers*—prick out those sown in boxes last month on a slight hotbed; sow on a sheltered border. *Celery*—sow in boxes, and place in a forcing-house for first crop. *Cucumbers*—plant from the seed-bed, and afterwards keep the heat by night 70° to 75°, and by day 75° to 85°. *French Beans*—earth up former sowings, and sow again twice; gather as soon as fit. *Lettuce*—sow on a warm border. *Mushrooms*—make beds and spawn at 80°. *Onions*—sow in boxes, and place in a forcing-house, for planting out in April. *Peas*—sow in boxes, in slits of turf three inches wide, and in the open ground. *Potatoes*—plant on a slight hotbed and on a warm border. *Radishes*—sow on a warm border. *Sea-kale*—cover with pots for forcing. *Spinach*—sow. *Turnips*—sow.

FRUIT DEPARTMENT.

Pinery—give air in mild weather; slightly sprinkle the plants on fine mornings; give 5° more warmth. *Vinery*—increase the heat 5°; start a second house. *Peach-house*—cease syringing when the trees are in flower. *Cherry-house*—give air at every favourable opportunity. *Orchard-house*—give abundance of air in mild weather; arrange the trees for their summer growth; give a thorough soaking of water; sprinkle the trees overhead in the morning; guard against night frosts. *Fig-house*—commence forcing where the trees are planted in the borders. *Melons*—sow seed for early crop. *Strawberries*—take into the forcing-house two batches for succession. Prune and nail fruit trees. Finish planting fruit trees in open weather. Point and top-dress fruit quarters.

MARCH.

VEGETABLE DEPARTMENT.

Artichokes—make new plantations. *Asparagus*—make new beds; top-dress in the latter end of the month. *Rhubarb* and *Sea-kale*—introduce more roots into heat. *Basil*—sow. *Beans*—plant twice in the month. *Cabbage*—fill up vacancies in the autumn plantations. *Capsicums*—sow. *Carrots*—sow the early crop. *Herbs*—make new beds. *Horse-radish*—make new plantations. *Jerusalem Artichokes*—plant early in the month. *Leeks*—sow. *Lettuce*—prick out on a slight hotbed those sown last month in boxes. *Mushrooms*—make beds for summer use. *Onions*—sow the main crops. *Parsley*—sow, if neglected last month. *Parsnips*—sow the main crop. *Peas*—sow twice; earth up early crops. *Potatoes*—plant main crop. *Radishes*—sow twice. *Savoys*—sow in the beginning and end of the month. *Shallots* and *Garlic*—plant in the beginning of the month. *Spinach*—sow. *Turnips*—sow on a sheltered border.

FRUIT DEPARTMENT.

Pinery—pot succession-plants; top-dress fruiting plants; increase the temperature from 75° to 85°. *Vinery*—raise the temperature of the first house to 65° and 70°, and top and tie the shoots; keep a moist atmosphere; attend to succeeding crops; start a third house. *Peach-house*—remove all foreright shoots from the trees; when the fruit is set, syringe them. *Cherry-house*—increase the heat, after the bloom is set and stoned, to 60°; introduce more plants. *Orchard-house*—finish pruning all the trees; in frosty weather shut up early, and protect unheated house with tiffany, canvas, or mats; water freely; heat still in the morning to prevent the frost laying hold of wet surfaces. *Fig-house*—water freely, both at the root and overhead. *Melons*—plant out from last month's sowing. *Strawberries*—give air freely while in flower. *Prune* and *nail* peaches and nectarines, and afterwards protect them with nets or other covering. Finish planting fruit trees. *Graft* fruit trees. Introduce more *Strawberries* into heat; gather when ripe.

APRIL.

VEGETABLE DEPARTMENT.

Beans—plant twice, and earth up the early crop. Sow *Borecole*. *Broccoli*—sow the winter varieties. *Brussels Sprouts*—sow in the beginning of the month. *Cabbage*—prick out the February sowing. *Cardoons*—sow for early crop. Sow main crop of *Carrots*, *Beet*, *Salsify*, and *Scorzonera*. *Cauliflowers*—plant out those wintered in frames. *Celery*—prick out the early-sown on a slight hotbed. *Cucumbers*—sow to plant out on ridges. *French Beans*—sow, in the beginning of the month. *Lettuce*—fill up the autumn plantations. *Onions*—transplant the autumn sowing, and also those sown in boxes in February. *Peas*—sow twice in the month; earth up and stick early crops. *Radishes*—sow twice in the month. *Spinach*—sow in the first and third week. *Turnips*—thin, and sow in the latter end of the month. *Vegetable Marrow*—sow in the middle of the month. *Ridge Cucumber*—sow about the first of the month.

FRUIT DEPARTMENT.

Pinery—add fresh tan between the pots of fruiting-plants, and sprinkle them overhead frequently; pot suckers that have been wintered in dung-beds. *Vinery*—when the grapes are in flower, keep a dryish minimum temperature of 75°; when set, keep a very moist atmosphere, and commence thinning them immediately; push on the succession-houses; give air freely in mild weather, shutting up early in the afternoon. *Peach-house*—partially thin the fruit before stoning, afterwards thin to the quantity required to ripen off; syringe the trees daily in fine weather, and smoke them occasionally, to keep down insects. *Cherry-house*—after the fruit is stoned, give the trees a good root-watering, which will probably be sufficient till the fruit is gathered; watch narrowly for insects. *Orchard-house*—the trees will now be in full bloom; give air freely; avoid cutting draughts on cold days; keep the air dry; gently top the trees several times a day, and if the pollen sticks to the flowers, use a camel's-hair pencil to distribute it. If frost occurs it must be excluded either with coverings or fire-heat, or the crop will be endangered. *Fig-house*—when the shoots have made three or four joints, stop them to cause them to produce fruit in the autumn. *Melons*—allow several of the main shoots to reach the sides of the frame before being stopped. *Cucumbers*—stop the shoots and cut the fruit when fit. *Prune* and *nail* figs. Disbud peaches and nectarines.

MAY.

VEGETABLE DEPARTMENT.

Basil—plant on a rich sheltered border. *Beans*—top the early crops; plant twice in the month. *Beet*—thin to 15 inches apart. *Borecole*—prick out of the seed-bed. *Broccoli*—prick out those sown last month, and make another sowing of the winter kinds; also Cape, Grange's, and Walcheren the last week. *Cabbage*—plant out the February sowing. *Cauliflower*—earth up and water with liquid-manure; take off the hand-glasses. *Cucumbers*—prepare ridges for out-door crops; attend to stopping, gathering the fruit, and top-dressing those in pots or houses. *French Beans*—make sowings in the first and last weeks. Transplant *Leeks*. *Lettuce*—transplant early sowings; sow twice in the month. *Onions*—thin them to nine inches apart. *Peas*—make two sowings. *Potatoes*—earth up the early crops. *Radishes*—make two sowings. *Spinach*—sow in the middle of the month; thin former sowings. *Scarlet Runners*—sow in the beginning and middle of the month; plant out those raised in heat. *Turnips*—make a sowing, if not done in the end of last month.

FRUIT DEPARTMENT.

Pinery—give the plants manure-water occasionally, if fruit of a large size is required; keep up a high temperature during the day; sprinkle them in the afternoon; shut up early, at a temperature of 80°, allowing it to rise to 90° or 100°. *Vinery*—keep the laterals stopped to one joint; take away all useless shoots, thin bunches and berries. *Peach-house*—when the fruit begins to ripen, withhold water both at the roots and over-head; at the same time admit air freely. *Cherry-house*—raise the temperature to 65° when the fruit is swelling off. *Orchard-house*—open the house as much as possible; break the force of the wind, and exclude birds and soot, by covering the ventilating space with woollen netting of a quarter or half-inch mesh. Look out for caterpillars on apricots; destroy green-fly; disbud the trees, and pinch back all shoots but the leader to about four buds; syringe and water freely. *Fig-house*—as the first crop approaches maturity, only sufficient water should be given to prevent the second crop of fruit falling off. *Melons*—regulate the vines at an early stage of their growth; after the fruit is set, put pieces of slate beneath it; stop the shoots; set the fruit; water, air, and sow successional crops. Continue to disbud wall-trees; remove their coverings when danger from frost is over; and wash the trees with soap-suds when the fruit is set. Place the last batch of Queen strawberries into heat. Thin the fruit of the apricot, peach, plum, and pear.

JUNE.

VEGETABLE DEPARTMENT.

Asparagus—discontinue cutting. *Beans*—put in the last crop; top and earth up former crops. *Broccoli*—sow Cape, Grange's, and Walcheren. *Cabbage*—sow seeds for Coleworts. *Capsicums*—plant out on a warm border. *Carrots*—thin to two inches apart. *Celery*—transplant into trenches for an early crop. *Cucumbers*—plant under handglasses. *Endive*—sow for an early crop. *French Beans*—make a sowing in the middle of the month. Transplant *Leeks*. Transplant *Lettuce*. *Peas*—complete the sowing of the marrow varieties. *Potatoes*—earth up. *Radishes*—sow as in last month. *Savoys*—transplant for an early crop. *Scarlet Runners*—make the last sowing. *Spinach*—sow twice. *Tomatoes*—Turn out against walls. *Vegetable Marrow*—plant under hand-glasses.

FRUIT DEPARTMENT.

Vinery—pot the succession-plants and suckers; plunge in a brisk heat, and shade for a week or so; keep fruiting-house hot and dry; as the fruit ripens, cut and preserve in a warm fruit-room. *Vinery*—as the fruit approaches maturity keep a dry atmosphere; leaves may be taken off or tied on one side where they shade the fruit; see that the roots do not suffer from drought; leave air on at the top of the house all night to colour; attend to stopping, thinning leaves, and watering successional crops. *Peach-house*—suspend nets or mats beneath the trees, and place in them some soft material to catch the fallen fruit. *Cherry-house*—when the fruit is gathered, give the trees several good washings to destroy insects; the house should also be smoked. *Figs, Cherries, and Plums*—in pots must be duly supplied with water. *Orchard-house*—syringe freely twice a day, unless when early fruits, such as cherries and apricots, are ripe; water and air freely, leaving all ventilating spaces and doors open; give manure-water, or top-dress with rich soil; place some of the trees out of doors to ripen their fruit, to give a succession, and to make room; keep the house clean. *Melons*—ridge out late crops, give air freely to ripening fruit. Summer prune *Vines* against walls. Finally thin *Apricots*. Set traps for wasps. Net *Cherry-trees and Strawberries*. Plant out forced plants.

JULY.

VEGETABLE DEPARTMENT.

Borecole—transplant. Transplant *Broccoli*. Transplant *Brussels Sprouts*. *Cauliflower*—transplant from the April sowing. Sow *Walcheren Broccoli*. *Cabbage*—sow in the last week for a crop to come in in May. *Celery*—transplant into trenches; earth up; water. *Endive*—make a second sowing. *French Beans*—earth up, and make the last sowing in the latter end of the month. *Lettuce*—make a sowing in the first and last week. *Peas*—make two last sowings of early sorts. *Potatoes*—take up early sorts. *Radishes*—sow on a cool border. Plant out *Walcheren Broccoli*.

FRUIT DEPARTMENT.

Pinery—discontinue watering those plants which are ripening their fruit; keep a moist atmosphere in the succession-house. *Vinery*—carefully avoid raising a dust when the fruit is ripe; give air freely; maintain a high temperature, and a moist heat; further cut grapes, and in late houses water freely; shut up early with 90°. *Peach-house*—when the fruit is all gathered, give the trees several good washings over-head; give abundance of air till the leaves begin to decay, when the lights may be removed. *Cherry-trees* in pots should now be placed in a shady situation. *Fig-house*—when the first crop is gathered, water the trees liberally to bring forward the second crop. *Orchard-house*—attend to summer-fruiting; fumigate with tobacco-smoke, to destroy green-fly; top-dress pots with rich compost water or sewage; give abundance of air, leaving doors and ventilators open; gather ripe fruit, and remove *Cherries* and early *Apricots* out ofd oors as soon as the fruit is gathered. *Melons*—pay proper attention to the plants; stop and water freely; cut the fruit before quite ripe, to prevent it cracking; finish in a warm vinery or pine stove. Finally thin wall-fruit. *Prune*, stop, and tie espalier trees. *Bud* fruit trees. Pot *Strawberry* runners for forcing. Mat *Currants* and *Gooseberries* to preserve them. Stop the shoots of *vines against walls* two joints above the fruit. Water forced *Strawberries* that are planted out.

AUGUST.

VEGETABLE DEPARTMENT.

American Cress—sow to stand the winter. Transplant the main crops of *Borecole* and *Broccoli*. Plant out a good breadth of *Walcheren Broccoli* for winter use. *Cabbage*—sow for main spring crop; transplant for Coleworts. *Carrots*—sow to stand the winter. *Cauliflowers*—transplant to come in during the autumn; sow for the main spring crop. *Celery*—transplant into trenches, and earth up for blanching. *Endive*—make the last sowing, and transplant from former sowings. *Lettuce*—sow for standing through the winter; transplant from former sowings. *Onions*—sow for standing through the winter. *Radishes*—

sow the winter varieties. *Savoys*—transplant the main crop. *Scarlet Runners*—earth up and stick. *Spinach*—sow the main winter crop. *Turnip*—sow the winter crop.

FRUIT DEPARTMENT.

Pinery—pot the succession-plants into their fruiting-pots; plunge into a good heat, and shade till they begin to grow again. *Vinery*—syringe the vines, and give them a root-watering after the fruit is cut, to prevent the leaves decaying prematurely. *Peach-house*—the lights may be taken off the early-house, and used for the purpose of forwarding grapes against walls. *Fig-house*—syringe the trees frequently, to keep down insects. *Orchard-house*—continue side pinchings, and stop the main shoots; water and air abundantly; remove part of the *Peaches*, *Nectarines*, *and Plums* out of doors, to finish their fruit, and bring in *Pears* in pots and choice *Apples* to fill up the vacuum thus created. Make new plantations of *Strawberries*. Cut down the old canes of *Raspberries* when the fruit is gathered. Keep the shoots of *wall-trees* nailed in; displace all laterals. Stop the laterals of *Vines* to one joint. Continue to bud *fruit trees*, such as *Cherries*, *Peaches*, *Apricots*, and *Plums*. Stop all breast-wood on *Apples*, *Pears*, *Plums*, *Gooseberries*, &c., back to from four to six buds, if not done at the end of July; this gives light and air to the fruit, and developes the wood-buds at the base of the shoots into fruit-buds.

SEPTEMBER.

VEGETABLE DEPARTMENT.

Cabbage—prick out from last month's sowing. *Celery*—earth up for blanching. *Chervil*—sow for winter use. *Curled Cress*—sow for winter use. *Endive*—transplant, and tie up for blanching. *Mushrooms*—make beds for winter use. *Onions*—pull up and house them when dry. *Parsley*—cut down a portion of the spring sowing. *Potatoes*—take up the early sorts. *Purslane*—sow for winter use. *Shallots* and *Garlic* should now be taken up. *Dig* up vacant ground, and fill it with *Walcheren Broccoli* for winter use.

FRUIT DEPARTMENT.

Pinery—pot suckers that have been taken off fruiting-plants; prepare the fruiting-house for the fruiting-plants, by renewing the plunging material, if derived from leaves, tan, &c., and clean the house thoroughly. *Vinery*—the lights of the early forcing-house should now be left open night and day; or they may be taken off if repairs are required; finish thinning, tying, and stopping succession-crops. *Peach-house*—if any vacancies are to be filled up, take out the old soil and replace it with fresh ready for planting next month. *Orchard-house*—Water sparingly as the fruit ripens. In stormy weather keep the house closed. Place the ripest fruit at one end, and give more water and less air to the latest trees. Place clean hay over the surface of the pots and floor for the fruit to fall upon, and leave the house open on mild days and nights. Protect out-door grapes from wasps by bagging the bunches. Gather fruit as it ripens. Expose wall-fruit to the sun and air to give it flavour and colour. Continue to make new strawberry plantations as in last month. Protect and gather the fruit ripening on forced plants.

OCTOBER.

VEGETABLE DEPARTMENT.

Artichokes—tie up the leaves for producing the chard. *Asparagus*—cut down and winter dress. *Beet*—dig up and lay in sand. *Cabbage*—plant out for the main crop. *Cardoons*—tie up the leaves for blanching. *Carrots*—take up the main crop. *Cauliflower*—prick out under hand-glasses, and into frames. *Cucumbers*—make beds, and sow seed for early crops. *Lettuce*—plant out for the main spring crop. *Parsnips*—take up and preserve in sand. *Potatoes*—take up the main crop. *Tomatoes*—gather the unripe fruit and lay in a forcing-house. Dig and trench ground, and manure during dry weather. Protect and gather autumn *Strawberries*.

FRUIT DEPARTMENT.

Pinery—the plants intended for fruiting next season should now be got into the fruiting-house; only partially plug the pots at first; plant all the remaining suckers in spent tan or a dung-bed. *Vinery*—as soon as the leaves have fallen from the vines, prune them; take off the loose rough bark, and wash them. *Peach-house*—fill vacancies with trees from the walls in the open garden; take up and plant carefully. Pot cherry-trees for forcing. Withhold water from fig-trees when the fruit is gathered. *Orchard-house*—gather late fruit; prune the trees as the leaves fall off; dress the wood with some anti-insect compound, and pack them close together to make room for cauliflowers, Walcheren broccoli, full-grown lettuce, &c., towards the end of the month; house all fruit trees in pots. *Melons*—keep up the heat of the beds, to forward the ripening of the late fruit. Gather any remaining fruit. Plant fruit trees of all sorts. *Prune* Currants and Gooseberries, and hardy Apples.

NOVEMBER.

VEGETABLE DEPARTMENT.

Artichokes—cover the roots with litter. *Asparagus*—take up the first lot of roots for forcing. *Beans*—sow first crop. *Cauliflowers*—protect those which have formed heads from frost. *Celery*—take every favourable opportunity to earth it up. *Cucumbers*—ridge out the plants in the fruiting-beds. *Endive*—preserve from frost. *Horseradish*—dig up for winter use. *Jerusalem Artichokes*—take up for winter use. *Peas*—sow for an early crop. *Rhubarb*—begin to force.

A MONTHLY CALENDAR OF OPERATIONS.

Salsify—dig up for winter use. *Scorzonera*—dig up for winter use. *Sea-kale*—clear away the decayed stems and leaves, and take up the first lot for forcing. *Preserve* culinary vegetables from frost in pots, frames, and orchard-houses, with temporary screens of mats, &c.

FRUIT DEPARTMENT.

Pinery—water the plants cautiously at this season; those planted on a dung-bed will require none: admit air at every favourable opportunity. *Vinery*—protect the border where the vines of the early forcing-house are growing outside, with wooden shutters, thatched hurdles, or glass. *Peach-house*—prune and dress the trees as soon as the leaves have fallen. *Cherry-house*—if the lights have been taken off, they should now be replaced, but left open night and day, unless the weather is severe. The trees should now be pruned. *Orchard-house*—prune and dress the trees for the destruction of scale and other insects; keep open in mild weather; plant out trees in borders; make borders: top-dress the pots, and sow near the front of the house a row or two of early dwarf peas, and some lettuce. *Pot* Fig-trees for forcing. Continue to plant all sorts of fruit trees and bushes as in last month. Protect Fig-trees. *Prune* the Apple, Pear, Plum, Cherry, Filbert, and Gooseberry and Currant; also nail and tie those against walls and espaliers. Look over the fruit in the fruit-room. Mulch newly-planted fruit trees, to protect them from frost.

DECEMBER.

VEGETABLE DEPARTMENT.

Asparagus—take up roots for forcing. *Celery*—protect during severe frosts. *Cucumbers*—attend to the linings of the beds. *French Beans*—plant in pots for forcing. *Mushrooms*—keep a moist and steady temperature in the house. *Radishes*—sow on a hotbed for early use. *Rhubarb*—take up roots, and pot for forcing. *Sea-kale*—take up roots carefully, for forcing. *Small Salad*—keep a succession, by sowing once a week. Prepare materials for hotbeds. *Preserve* and *force* Lettuces, Radishes, &c., under hand-lights, cloches, and Rendle's Plant Protectors, or in pots and frames.

FRUIT DEPARTMENT.

Pinery—slightly increase the temperature of the fruiting-house; if there is a great declination of bottom-heat, add a little fresh tan between the pots. *Vinery*—clean and paint the house, or prune the vines; prepare for forcing. *Peach-house*—after the trees are tied to the trellis, take away a little of the loose, dry top-soil; slightly dig the border, so as not to injure the roots, and add some fresh soil. *Cherry-house*—fix the trees to the trellis, and make preparations for forcing next month. *Orchard-house*—protect the trees from frost by covering the pots with litter, and keep the house closed in severe weather. Beware of bulfinches and chaffinches, which often make a merry meal off the buds in winter. Trap these, mice, and other vermin. If aphis appear, syringe the plants with strong soot or quassia-water, or with Gishurst's Compound in the proportion of four ounces to the gallon. Wash the woodwork and glass; paint, repair, and clean, ready for the coming season. *Fig-house*—the frost should be kept out; and if the trees need any pruning, it should now be done. Continue to prune and nail in mild weather. Partially unnail the shoots of Peach and Nectarine trees. Protect Strawberries in pots, and all fruit-trees intended for forcing. Dig, point, or top-dress fruit quarters where pruning is completed.

NOVEMBER, DECEMBER, AND JANUARY.

It is hoped the young gardener will find leisure during the long evenings of the winter months to improve himself by reading, to which he should add writing and drawing, including of course arithmetic and mensuration. In these days, when the employers of gardeners are readers of gardening books, and often possess a considerable knowledge of botany, vegetable physiology, and practical horticulture, the young man who does not occupy every moment of his spare time in improving himself, has no chance whatever of getting or keeping a good situation as head gardener.

INDEX.

AIR, dry, effect of in ripening fruit, 41
,, in motion, principal effects of, 38
Almond, history and uses of the, 583
,, best varieties, 583
,, propagation, &c., 583
Angelica, uses and culture of the, 677
Anise, description and uses of, 674
Apple, history and uses of the, 526
,, properties of a good, 527
,, lists of best kinds, 528
,, best kinds for cottage-gardens, 530
,, ornamental kinds, 530
,, propagation of the, 531
,, proper soil and situation for, 532
,, pruning and training, 533
,, gathering and keeping the fruit, 540
,, diseases, insects, casualties, &c., 541
Apricot, history and uses of the, 584
,, best varieties, 584
,, propagation, culture, &c., 584
,, planting, pruning, &c., 584
,, protection in low, cold situations, 585
,, time of gathering, 585
,, forcing, 585
Artichoke, history and uses of the, 657
,, varieties, 658
,, culture of the French, 658
,, ,, ,, Jerusalem, 631
Articles of various kinds required in gardens, 129
Asparagus, history and uses of the, 651
,, culture, &c., 652
,, Mr. James Barnes's mode of growing, 652
,, Mr. W. P. Ayres's method, 653
,, gathering, 654
,, forcing, 516
,, substitutes for, 660
Asparagus-knife, 91
Atmosphere, constituent parts of the, 25
Axe, garden, best kind of, 97

"BALL," meaning of the horticultural term, 294

Banana, history of the, 511
,, culture, 512, 588
,, species or varieties, 588
Barberry, the common, 573
,, Magellan sweet, 573
,, the Nepal, 574
Barrow-engine for watering, 113
Basil, culture and uses of the sweet, 681
,, ,, ,, bush, 681
Baskets, garden, various kinds of, 106
Beam-tree, the Cretan white, 550
Bean, history and uses of the garden, 618
,, best varieties, 618
,, culture, &c., 618
,, the kidney, 619
,, the Lima, 622
Beet, history and uses of the red, 635
,, best varieties, 636
,, culture, &c., 636
,, culture of the spinach, 624
Beetles and rammers, 89
Bell-glasses, 107
,, substitutes for, 110
Birds, general remarks on, 68
,, various modes of scaring, 69
Blanching of various plants described, 357
Bleeding in plants, how to prevent, 77
,, of the vine, styptic for, 466
Blight, remarks on, 77
Boiler for a small house, best, 177
,, Perkins' double, 175
,, Weeks's patent duplex, 178
Boilers, remarks on, 171
,, estimation of heating powers of, 176
Borage, uses and culture of, 675
Borders, management of fruit-tree, 413
Brown scale in the peach, to prevent, 482
Budding, general remarks on, 265
,, uses of, 266
,, proper time for, 266
,, operations in shield, 267
,, Roses, proper season for, 269
,, ,, Belgian mode of, 269
,, various modes of shield, 269
,, flute or tube, 271
,, annular, 273
,, treatment of plants after, 273

698   INDEX.

Budding, proper time for, 267
   ,,   composition of wax for, 267
   ,,   roses, directions for, 269
Bulbs and roots, best mode of preserving, 368
Burnet, species and uses of, 671

CABBAGE, history, species, and varieties of, 605
   ,,   couve tronchuda, 606
   ,,   coleworts, 606
   ,,   red, 607
   ,,   savoy, 607
   ,,   brussels sprouts, 607
   ,,   borecole, 607
   ,,   cauliflowers, 608
   ,,   broccoli, 609
   ,,   turnip, 610
   ,,   tribe, general culture of the, 610
   ,,   substitutes for, 613
Calendar of operations, monthly, 687
Camellias propagated by buds, 226
Canker in trees, causes of, 74
   ,,   how to prevent, 74
   ,,   how to cure, 75
Canvas coverings for houses or plants, 133
   ,,   shades, apparatus for, 135
Caper, uses and culture of the, 678
   ,,   substitutes for the, 678
Capsicum, history and uses of the, 592
   ,,   culture, &c., 593
Cardoon, history and uses of the, 658
   ,,   varieties, 659
   ,,   propagation and culture, 659
   ,,   how to cook the, 659
Carrot, history and uses of the, 633
   ,,   best varieties, 634
   ,,   culture, &c., 634
   ,,   gathering and keeping, 634
   ,,   diseases, insects, &c., 634
   ,,   seed saving, 635
Celery, history and uses of, 667
   ,,   best varieties, 667
   ,,   propagation and culture, 667
   ,,   transplanted into trenches, 668
   ,,   how to blanch, 668
   ,,   late spring crop, 669
   ,,   gathering and keeping, 670
   ,,   culture of turnip-rooted or celeriac, 670
   ,,   diseases, insects, &c., 670
Chamomile, culture and uses of, 683
Charcoal in gardens, use of, 298
   ,,   how to make, 298
   ,,   used for rooting cuttings, 230
Chatsworth, ridge-and-furrow roofed house at, 157
Cherry, history and uses of the, 550
   ,,   best varieties, 550

Cherry, propagation, soil, culture, &c., 551
   ,,   gathering and keeping, 552
   ,,   diseases, insects, &c., 552
   ,,   garden, a Dutch, 552
   ,,   garden, mode of netting a, 553
   ,,   forcing the, 483
   ,,   the Peruvian, 587
   ,,   the Cornelian, 574
   ,,   culture under glass, 483
   ,,   best kinds for forcing, 484
   ,,   time of commencing to force, 484
   ,,   insects injurious to the, 485
   ,,   thinning the, 485
   ,,   treatment when taken out of the house, 486
   ,,   forcing in a temporary structure, 486
   ,,   German practice of forcing the, 487
Chervil, culture and uses of, 673
Chestnut, the sweet, 572
Chicory, history and uses of the, 665
   ,,   culture, &c., 666
   ,,   substitute for, 666
   ,,   how forced, 517
Chive, uses and culture of the, 650
Citron, description and uses of the, 595
   ,,   culture, &c., 596
Clary, description and uses of, 680
Cleft-grafting, 252
Clipping, its object and mode of performance, 204
Cloches, or French bell-glasses, 107
   ,,   in the propagating-house, 108
   ,,   where to buy, 110
Conservatory, proper temperature of the, 189
Copings for fruit-tree walls, 133
   ,,   permanent, 140
Coriander, culture and uses of the, 673
Corn-salad, culture of, 670
Coverings of canvas for houses or plants, 133
   ,,   for shade and protection, various, 358
   ,,   for pits and frames, 118
Cranberry, history and uses of the, 570
   ,,   the Scotch, 570
Cress, culture of garden, 671
   ,,   winter, 671
   ,,   water, 671
   ,,   Indian, 675
Crops, observations on rotation of, 408
Cucumber, culture of the, 498
   ,,   grown on a dung-bed, 499
   ,,   beds, linings of, 502
   ,,   grown in various sorts of pits, 504
   ,,   pit, heated by hot water, 505
   ,,   ,, description of Corbett's, 505
   ,,   ,, ,, Green's, 506

INDEX.

Cucumber, grown in pots, 507
,, house, construction of, 570
,, ,, Ayres's, 508
,, ,, treatment of plants in, 508
,, how grown for exhibition, 509
,, ,, in the open air, 509
,, and melon culture compared, 511
,, best varieties of, 589
Currant, history and uses of the, 562
,, best varieties, 562
,, propagation and culture, 562
,, insects, &c., 563
,, forcing, 563
,, various modes of planting, 400
,, list of best sorts of, 402
Cuttings, propagation by, 214
,, how to force shoots for, 232
,, how to select, 215
,, preparation of, 217
,, insertion of, 220
,, necessary conditions for success with, 231
,, of delicate plants, treatment of, 221
,, treatment of various kinds of, 223
,, Forsyth's mode of striking, 222

DAHLIA, grafting the, 259
Daisy-knife, 97
Daisy-weeder, 87
Deppe's Oxalis, uses and culture of, 639
Dew, formation of, 28
Dew-point, how to find the temperature of the, 128
Dibbers, 82
Digging, proper mode of, 197
Dill, culture and uses of, 674
Disbarking, object and practice of, 305
Disbudding, object and practice of, 305
Diseases of plants, 74
Disleafing, object and practice of, 306
Dormice, 72
Dutch cherry-garden, a, 552

EDIFICES used in horticulture, 193
Egg-plant, history and culture of the, 592
Elder-tree, the, 574
Elecampane, uses and culture of, 678
Endive, history and uses of the, 664
,, best varieties, 664
,, propagation and culture, 664
,, best mode of blanching, 665

Endive, how to preserve a crop through the winter, 665
,, succory, or wild, 665
Espalier-rails, various kinds of, 148
,, of strained wire, 395
,, how constructed, 393
Espaliers, French mode of constructing, 396
Evergreens, best season for transplanting, 284
,, packing and removing of, 289
Exotic fruits that may be grown in stoves, 598

FENNEL, culture and uses of, 674
Fig, history and uses of the, 585
,, best varieties, 585
,, propagation, culture, &c., 586
,, culture under glass, 488
,, how forced in British gardens, 489
,, ,, in pots, 490
,, winter treatment of the, 491
Filbert, best varieties of the, 572
,, propagation, 572
,, pruning and planting, 573
,, gathering and keeping, 573
,, insects, 573
Flues, plant-houses heated by, 165
Flute-budding, or tube budding, 271
Fly-trap, made with hand glasses, 64
Forcing-house, illustration of a half-span 190
,, uses of the, 189
Forcing of hardy fruit-trees, 492
,, the cherry, 483
Forks, garden, various kinds of, 88
Forster's patent orchard-house, 192
Frame, common hotbed, described, 136
French artichoke, culture of the, 657
Frogs and toads, 68
Frost, how to protect plants from, 31
,, places most liable to suffer from, 33
Frozen plants, how to treat, 33
Fruit, best mode of gathering and keeping, 368, 369, 414
Fruit-room, construction of the, 194
Fruit-trees, general remarks on, 599
,, for walls, select list of, 389
,, ,, how to plant, 391
,, for espaliers and dwarfs, 392, 399
,, for an orchard, selection of, 402
Fruit and flowers, packing and transporting of, 370
Fumigating bellows, description of, 114
Fumigating-pot, description of, 114
Furnaces, Mr. Hood's remarks on, 177

INDEX.

GARDEN, the general management of a, 379
Gardeners, remarks on the wages of, 381
  ,, useful rules for, 377
Garlic, uses and culture of, 650
Gathering fruit, proper mode of, 368
Germination, process of, 207
  ,, of various seeds, time necessary for the, 208
Ginger, culture and uses of, 678
Girdling-machine, described, 308
Girdling trees, effects of, 308
Glasses, bell, 107
  ,, hand, 107
Glazing plant-houses, best mode of, 182
Gooseberry, history and uses of the, 557
  ,, best varieties, 401, 557
  ,, propagation and culture, 558
  ,, soil, situation, and planting, 400, 558
  ,, pruning and training, 559
  ,, how grown for prizes, 559
  ,, gathering, keeping, &c., 561
  ,, insects, diseases, &c., 561
  ,, forcing, 562
Gourds, history and uses of, 589
  ,, species or varieties, 590
  ,, list of ornamental, 590
  ,, propagation and culture, 591
Grafting, fundamental principle of, 241
  ,, De Candolle's remarks on, 242
  ,, conditions essential to the success of, 243
  ,, modifications effected by, 244
  ,, various uses of, 246
  ,, materials used in, 247
  ,, clay, composition of, 248
  ,, wax, ,, ,, 248, 257
  ,, ,, best kind of, 248
  ,, by detached scions, 249
  ,, commonest mode of, 250
  ,, splice, tongue, or whip, 250
  ,, cleft, 252
  ,, saddle, 254
  ,, side, 255
  ,, the mistletoe, 256
  ,, root, 256
  ,, herbaceous, 257, 259
  ,, the pine and fir tribe, 257
  ,, the tree pæony, 258
  ,, the dahlia on its own tubers, 259
  ,, the melon, 260
  ,, succulents, 260
  ,, by approach or inarching, 261
  ,, by detached buds, 265
Granadilla, culture of the, 598
Grape, best varieties of, 575
  ,, propagation, 447

Grape culture, pruning, and training, 444, 457
Greenhouse, common form of, 187
Ground vineries, 470
Guava, culture of the, 597
Gum-disease, causes of, 76

HAMMER, garden, 90
Hand-glasses, 107
  ,, substitutes for, 132
Hares, to prevent barking trees, 73
Heat, conduction of, 26
  ,, radiation of, 27
  ,, means of counteracting the radiation of, 29
  ,, carried off by wind and evaporation, 31
  ,, in plant-houses, remarks on, 162
  ,, ,, retained by coverings, 179
Heating by hot water, ordinary mode of, 40
  ,, ,, Mr. Penn's mode of, 39
  ,, plant-houses with fermenting manure, 163
Hedgehogs useful in gardens, 72
Hellebore, culture and uses of white, 685
Henbane, culture and uses of, 686
Herbaceous grafting, 257
Hickory, the peccan-nut, 572
  ,, the shell-bark, 572
Hoeing, object and proper mode of, 200
Hoes, various kinds of, 83, 84
Honey-dew on leaves, remedy for, 77
Horehound, culture and uses of, 684
Horse-radish, culture of the, 676
  ,, substitute for the, 676
Hotbed, description of Mc Phail's, 360
  ,, frame, common, described, 136
Hotbeds, uses and construction of, 359
Hot water in pipes, cause of the circulation of, 170
  ,, ,, plant-houses heated by, 170
  ,, ,, siphon mode of circulating, 172
  ,, ,, how to calculate the quantity required, 174
House, span-roofed forcing, 153
Hygrometer, uses of, 126
Hyssop, culture and uses of, 684

IMPLEMENTS of horticulture, 78
Indian cress, culture of, 675
Indian fig, description of the, 598

Insects, transformation of, 52
,, food of, 54
,, distribution and habits of, 56
,, uses of, 57
,, natural checks against the undue increase of, 57
,, various modes of destroying, 60

JAPAN quince, culture of the, 597
Jerusalem artichoke, culture of the, 631

KIDNEY bean, history and uses of the, 619
,, varieties, 620
,, culture, &c., 620
,, how forced, 519
Kitchen garden, how to lay out a, 383
,, cropping and general management of a, 406
,, best mode of sheltering, 39
Knives for hedge-pruning, 92
,, garden, 91
Kohl Rabi, 610

LABELS, best mode of writing on, 121
,, various kinds of, 121, 122
Ladders for garden use, 124
Lamb's lettuce, culture of, 670
Lavender, culture and uses, 683
Layers, theory of propagation by, 233
,, various modes of propagating by, 235
Leaves, propagation by, 228
Leek, history and uses of the, 649
,, best varieties of, 649
,, culture, &c., 649
Lemon, description and uses of the, 595
,, culture, &c., 596
Lentil, the common, 622
Lettuce, history and uses of the, 661
,, best varieties, 662
,, propagation and culture, 662
,, French mode of growing, 663
,, grown as small salads, 663
,, forcing, 521
,, lamb's, 670
Level-garden, for adjusting box-edgings, &c., 126
Levers and crowbar, 82
Light, laws of, 43
,, and heat, point of difference between, 43
,, effects of on plants, 42
,, how affected by reflection, 43

Light, how plants may receive the greatest amount of, 45
,, transmitted and refracted, 43
,, when necessary to exclude or diminish, 45
Lime, description and uses of the, 595
,, culture, &c., 596
Liquorice, culture and uses of, 684
Lopping, various modes of, 303
Loquat, culture of the, 597
Lupin, the white, 622

MACHINES, mowing, description of, 111
,, used in horticulture, 111
Mallet, wooden, 90
Manure, general remarks on, 13
,, leaf-mould as, 13
,, green crops as, 14
,, sea weed as, 14
,, malt-dust as 14
,, rape-cake as, 14
,, straw as, 14
,, rotten tan as, 14
,, peat-soil as, 14
,, animal matters as, 15
,, sewage as, 16
,, liquid 16
,, nightsoil as, 16
,, bones as, 17
,, how to save, 18
,, lime as, 19
,, marl as, 20
,, gypsum as, 20
,, sea-shells as, 20
,, saltpetre as, 21
,, salt as, 21
,, coal-ashes as, 22
,, vegetable ashes as, 22
,, soot as, 23
,, street-sweepings as, 23
,, mixed, or composts, 24
,, application of, 24
Marigold, uses and culture of the, 675
Marjoram, culture and uses of pot, 680
,, ,, sweet, 680
,, ,, winter, 680
Mats of various kinds described, 116
,, how to arrange as coverings, 118
Mint, culture and uses of the common, 680
,, ,, pennyroyal, 680
Medicinal herbs, list of, 603
Medlar, history and uses of the, 549
,, varieties, 549
,, propagation, soil, and culture, 549
Melon, culture of the, 492
,, best varieties, 495, 588
,, seedlings, 495
,, planting out, 495

Melon, general treatment, 495
," grown in the open air, 496
," insects and diseases, 497
," water, 589
Mice, best way to trap field, 72
Mildew, in grapes, 463
," causes of, 76
," remedy for, 76
Mistletoe, grafting the, 256
Moisture, atmospheric, general remarks on, 33
," ," Dr. Lindley's remarks on, 38
," ," simplest mode of measuring, 33
," deficient in hothouses, causes of, 36
," in vineries diminished at night, 34
," in hothouses, how to maintain, 37
," in plant-houses, how supplied, 179
Moles, how to catch, 71
Monthly calendar of operations, 687
Mouse-trap, figure 4, 73
," formed with an inverted flower-pot, 71
Mowing of lawns and garden grass, 205
Mulberry, history and uses of the, 571
," propagation and culture, 571
Musa sapientum, 511
Mushroom, how forced, 523
," house described, 523
," spawn, 524
," beds, how made, 524
," grown in cellars, 524
," beds, management of, 525
," how to introduce into pastures, 681
," the truffle, 682
," the morel, 682

NAILS, cast-iron, to prevent rusting, 123
Nectarine, history and uses of the, 576
," best varieties, 576
," propagation, culture, &c., 476, 577
," forcing, 476

OFFSETS, propagation by, 240
Olive, description of the, 598
Onion, history and uses of the common, 643
," best varieties and species, 644
," propagation and culture, 644
," autumn and winter crops, 646

Onion, transplanted crops, 646
," culture of the potato, 646
," ," bulb-bearing, 647
," treatment common to all kinds of, 647
," diseases, insects, &c., 647
," fly, remedy for the, 648
," gathering and keeping, 648
Open sheds, uses of, 195
Operations, monthly calendar of, 687
Orange, history and uses of the, 593
," species or varieties, 594
," culture, &c., 596
Orangery, chief uses of, 188
Orchard, culture of the soil in an, 405
Orchard-house, Forster's patent, 192
Orchard-houses, remarks on, 191
Oxalis, uses and culture of Deppe's, 639
," crenata, 639

PACKING and transporting fruits and flowers, 370
Packing and transporting plants and seeds, 369
Parsley, history and uses of the, 672
," propagation and culture, 673
," Hamburgh, 637, 673
," Naples, 673
Parsnip, history and uses of the, 635
," best varieties, 635
," culture, &c., 635
Pawpaw, description of the, 598
Pea, history and uses of the, 613
," best varieties, 614
," culture, 614
," how to obtain an early crop, 616
," summer and autumn crops, 617
," gathering, 617
," diseases, vermin, &c., 617
," forcing, 618
," the chick, 622
," how forced, 520
Peach and nectarine, history and uses of the, 576
," properties of a good, 576
," best varieties, 576
," propagation and culture, 476, 480, 577
," soil, situation, &c., 577
," pruning and training, 478, 578
," border, treatment of the, 580
," protection in winter and spring, 581
," growing on a flued wall, 582
," mode of gathering, 582
," insects, diseases, &c., 480, 582

INDEX.

Peach and nectarine culture, essential points of, 583
,, forcing, 476
,, house, construction of, 478
,, grown in pots, 481
Pear, history and uses of the, 542
,, properties of a good, 543
,, lists of the best kinds, 543
,, best kinds for cottage-gardens, 544
,, ornamental kinds, 544
,, propagation and culture, 545
,, soil and situation, 546
,, pruning and training, 546
,, gathering and keeping the fruit, 547
,, insects and diseases, 548
Pennyroyal, culture and uses of, 680
Peppermint, culture and uses of, 683
Perforators, 82
Peruvian cherry, culture of the, 587
Picks, 83
Pincers, garden, 90
Pine and fir trees, grafting of, 257
Pine-apple, culture of the, 416
,, proper soil for the, 419
,, pits or houses for the culture of the, 421
,, times and modes of potting the, 425
,, rules to be observed in watering the, 426
,, manures for the, 427
,, proper temperature for the, 428
,, how to propagate the, 430
,, selection of varieties of, 430, 587
,, time required to fruit the, 431
,, grown in pots and open beds, 431
,, Hamiltonian system of growing the, 432
,, how to improve the quality and size of the, 432
,, how to accelerate or retard the fruiting of the, 433
,, how to preserve when ripe, 433
,, what constitutes a good, 433
,, weight to which it has been grown, 434
,, insects injurious to the, 434
,, diseases and malformations of the, 435
,, summary of monthly culture, 436
,, grown in the open air in England, 439
,, summary of culture, 587

Pipes, causes of the circulation of hot water in, 170
Pits and frames, to remove superfluous moisture from, 41
,, cold and heated, 185
,, Corbett's mode of heating, 186
Plant-box, convenient kind of, 103
Plant-houses, general remarks on, 151
,, Beard's patent metallic, 160
,, heated by fermenting manure, 163
,, heated by flues, 165
,, heated by hot water, 170
,, heated by steam, 169
,, heated from vaults, 164
,, how to glaze the roofs of, 182
,, how to supply moisture in, 179
,, materials used in building, 158
,, proper kinds of roofs for, 44
,, remarks on heat in, 162
,, ventilation of, 181
Planting and sowing, proper seasons for, 412
Planting small plants, methods of, 289
,, treatment of plants before, 293
,, in drills and trenches, 290
,, in holes and pits, 291
,, out plants grown in pots, 292
,, treatment of plants after, 292
,, summary of general rules for, 293
Plum, history and uses of the, 554
,, best varieties, 554
,, propagation, culture, &c., 555
,, soil, situation, and planting, 556
,, pruning and training, 556
,, gathering, keeping, and packing, 556
,, insects, diseases, &c., 556
,, forcing, 557
Pomegranate, history and uses of the, 586
,, propagation and culture, 586
,, training, &c., 586
Potato, history and uses of the, 623
,, best varieties, 623
,, culture, &c., 624
,, early crops, 626
,, Lancashire mode of planting, 627
,, Messrs. Chapman's New Spring, 627
,, how to raise young, in winter, 628
,, details of planting, 629
,, taking up and preserving, 630
,, diseases, insects, &c., 630
,, forcing, 518
Pot-herbs, how forced, 522

Pots, contrivance for carrying, 106
" relative sizes of, 99
" various forms of, 100, 101
Potting, general observations on, 294
" soil suitable for use in, 294
" its mode of performance, 295
" seasons and times for, 297
" treatment of plants after, 296
" of Cape Heaths and like plants, 297
" shed, contents of the, 195
Prickly pear, description of the, 598
Propagation, general remarks on, 205
" by seed, 206
" by cuttings, 214
" by joints and nodules, 226
" by bulbs, tubers, and tubercles, 227
" by bulb-bearing leaves, 228
" by leaves, 228
" by layers, 233
" by suckers and slips, 239
" by offsets, 240
" by runners, 240
" by division, 241
" by grafting and budding, 241
Props for plants, various kinds of, 119
Protectors, wickerwork, of various kinds, 131
Pruning-chisels, 92
Pruning, general observations on, 299
" various uses of, 300
" close, 301
" by shortening-in and foreshortening, 302
" by spurring-in, and heading-in, 303
" by various modes of lopping, 303
" proper seasons for, 309
" saws, 92
Pumpkins and gourds, 589
Purple Goat's-beard or salsify, 637
Purslane, uses and culture of, 674

QUINCE, history and uses of the, 548
" varieties, 548
" propagation, soil and culture, 548
" culture of the Japan, 597

RABBITS and hares, fence for, 73
" to prevent barking trees, 73
Radiation checked by coverings, 29
" by motion of the air, 30
Radish, history and uses of the, 637
" best varieties, 637
" culture, &c., 638
" forcing, 521
" the Rat-tailed, 638

Radish, horse, 675
Rafters, mode of fixing temporary, 140
Raidisseur for tightening trellis-wires, 93
Rain, effects of trees on the fall of, 35
Rakes, various kinds of garden, 89
Raking, object, and proper mode of, 201
Rampion, culture of the, 660
Raspberry, history and uses of the, 563
" best varieties, 564
" propagation, soil, and culture, 564
" gathering, 565
" forcing, 565
" the Nootka, 566
" best positions for, 401
Rearing, operations of, 274
Resting of vegetation, how effected, 364
Retarding vegetation, various modes of, 363
Rhubarb, history and uses of, 677
" best varieties of, 677
" propagation and culture, 677
" how forced. 517
" culture of the Medicinal, 683
Ridge-and-furrow roofed house at Chatsworth, 157
Rocambole, uses and culture of the, 650
Rollers, various kinds of garden, 112
Rolling, object and uses of, 202
Roofs, advantages of ridge-and-furrow, 156
Roofs of plant-houses, curvilinear, 155
" " iron, 159
" reflection of light from glass, 159
Root-cellar, 194
Root-pruning, twofold result of, 307
Rosemary, culture and uses of, 683
Roses, directions for budding, 269
" proper season for budding, 269
Rotation of crops considered, 408
Rue, culture and uses of, 683
Rust on grapes, 463

SADDLE-GRAFTING, 254
Sage, culture and uses of, 679
Salads, plants used as small, 672
Salsify, culture of the, 637
" Spanish, 637
Samphire, uses and culture of, 678
" substitutes for, 678
Savory, culture and uses of summer, 681
" " winter, 681
Sawing, its object and mode of performance, 203
Saws, various kinds of garden, 92
Scorzonera, culture of the, 636
Scrapers, 84
Screen for sifting soil, gravel, &c., 105
Scythe, garden, 97

INDEX.

Sea-kale, history and uses of the, 655
  ,, propagation and culture, 655
  ,, gathering, 656
  ,, forcing, 517, 657
Sécateur, or French pruning shears, 96
Seed-room, arrangement of the, 194
Seeds, accelerating the germination of, 211
  ,, care of newly-sown, 209
  ,, depth at which they should be sown, 209
  ,, duration of vitality in, 212
  ,, proper seasons for sowing, 213
Selecting and improving plants in culture, 371
Service-tree, the true, 549
  ,, the griping, 556
Shaddock, description and uses of the, 595
  ,, culture, &c., 596
Shades, apparatus for canvas, 135
Shallot, uses and culture of the, 649
Shanking in grapes, 463
Shears, for clipping grass verges, 97
  ,, garden, 95
  ,, pruning, 95
Shed, contents of the potting, 195
Sheds, uses of open, 195
Shield-budding, how performed, 267
Shifting or repotting, 296
Side-grafting, 255
Siphon mode of circulating hot water, 172
Skirret, culture of the, 636
Snails and slugs, 50
  ,, how to destroy, 51
Soil, origin and kinds of, 1
  ,, alluvial, 4
  ,, calcareous, 4
  ,, clayey, 3
  ,, gravelly, 3
  ,, loamy, 5
  ,, peat, 5
  ,, sandy, 2
  ,, organic matter in, 5
  ,, on the inclination of the surface of, 6
  ,, varieties of, indicated by the plants which grow on them, 7
  ,, improvement of, by draining, 7
  ,, altering the texture and composition of, 8
  ,, burning of, as a means of improving, 10
  ,, pulverizing of, necessity for the, 11
  ,, free admission of air to, 12
  ,, general remarks on the preparation of, 196
Sorrel, culture of various kinds of, 643
Sowing and planting, proper seasons for, 412
Spades, various kinds of, 85, 86
Spinach, culture of the common, 640
  ,,   ,, French, 641

Spinach, culture of, New Zealand, 641
  ,,   ,, perennial, 642
  ,,   ,, Beet, 642
  ,,   ,, Patience, 642
Splice-grafting, 250
Spud, garden, 87
Steam, plant-houses heated by, 169
Stirring the soil, advantages of, 356
Stoves for plants, various kinds of, 189
Strawberry, history and uses of the, 566
  ,, best varieties, 566
  ,, propagation and soil, 567
  ,, culture in rows, 567
  ,, culture in beds, 568
  ,, mulching and watering, 568
  ,, retarding a crop, 569
  ,, accelerating a crop, 569
  ,, gathering, 570
  ,, forcing, 570
  ,, how forced, 513
  ,, best kinds for forcing, 513
  ,, treatment after forcing, 514
  ,, the Alpine, 515
Straw mats, mode of making, 117
  ,, wisps, used as protectors, 116
Structures and edifices, garden, 130
Styptic for vine-bleeding, 466
Subsoils, importance of good, 6
Substitutes for hand-glasses, 132
Succory, chicory, or wild endive, 665
Syringe, garden, best kind of, 112

TANSY, culture and uses of the, 681
Tarragon, culture and uses of, 674
  ,, substitutes for, 674
Temperature, influence of hills on nightly, 31
  ,, of water and air for plants, 41
Tender shrubs and trees, best positions for, 32
Thermometers, best kinds of, 126
Thinning of garden-crops and plantations, 311
Thinning-out plants, general remarks on, 310
Thyme, culture and uses of the common, 679
  ,, culture and uses of the lemon, 679
Tobacco, history and uses of, 684
  ,, propagation and culture, 684
Tomato, history and uses of the, 591
  ,, best varieties, 659
  ,, culture, &c., 591
Tongue-grafting, 250
Tools, garden, how to keep, 80
  ,,   ,, various kinds of, 78
Training, general remarks on, 313
  ,, manual operations of, 314

Training of herbaceous plants in beds and pots, 316
,, of hardy flowering shrubs in the open ground, 317
,, fruit-trees, various modes of, 320
,, of dwarf fruit-trees, 321
,, the spurring-in system of, 322
,, of conical standards, or Quenouille fashion, 323
,, different stages of fan, 326
,, Seymour's mode of fan, 329
,, wavy-fan method of, 332
,, various stages of horizontal, 336
,, horizontal and fan-training combined, 337
,, perpendicular and horizontal combined, 338
,, various stages of the half-fan method of, 339
,, various stages of perpendicular, 340
,, of peach-trees at Montreuil, 341
,, of apple-trees as cordons, 341
,, as cordons, list of kinds suitable for, 346
,, instruments and materials used in, 346
,, comparative view of the different modes of, 347
Transplanted trees, modes of securing, 282
Transplanters, 88
Transplanting, general remarks on, 274
,, different modes of, 277
,, of evergreens, the, 283
,, machines for, 280, 283, 286
,, French mode of, 288
Tree-peony, grafting the, 258
Tree-primrose, shoots used in salads, 637
Trellises and lattice-work, 149
Trellis, mode of fixing galvanized-wire, 145
Trenching, object and proper mode of, 199
Tropæolum tuberosum, uses and culture of, 639
Tropical and subtropical fruits, 587
Trowels, garden, 87
Turnip, history and uses of the, 631
,, best varieties, 632
,, culture, &c., 632
,, gathering and preserving, 632
,, diseases, insects, &c., 633
,, forcing, 633
Twisting the shoots of fruit-trees, object of, 307

UTENSILS used in horticulture, 98

VARIETIES in plants, how produced, 372
Varieties in plants, how perpetuated, 374
,, observations on the permanence of, 375
Vegetable marrow, 589
Vegetables, catalogue of, 602
Vegetation, stimulants to, 211
Ventilation of plant-houses, 181
,, when most necessary in plant-houses, 41
Verge-cutters, 86, 87
Viper's-grass or Scorzonera, 636
Vine, culture of the, 440
,, bottom-heat advantageous to the, 441
,, borders, various modes of heating, 442
,, ,, construction of, 444
,, modes of propagating the, 447
,, ,, planting the, 449
,, grafting the, 451
,, budding the, 452
,, watering the, 454
,, pruning and training the, 454
,, thinning the fruit, 455
,, extension system of pruning, 458
,, diseases and pests of the, 461
,, mildew and rust on the, 463
,, adventitious roots on the, 464
,, removing the loose bark of the, 465
,, cheap and effective styptic for bleeding in the, 466
,, grown in pots, 467
,, forced in pots, 468
,, grown in ground vineries, 470
,, grown on open walls and cottages, 472
,, propagated by buds or eyes, 227
Vinery, the ground, 470

WALKS, plan of trellised, 151
Wallet, useful in nailing wall-trees, 124
Wall-fruits, 574
Wall, plan of a hollow brick, 141
,, plan of a reed, 147, 148
Walls, conservative or flued, 146
,, best colour for fruit-tree, 146
,, for fruit-trees, best kind of, 138
,, height of garden, 139
,, how to erect garden, 140
,, in gardens, 137
,, mode of arranging wires on, 143, 144

Walls, plans of brick, 141
Wall-training, a greater amount of light secured to trees by, 44
Wall-trees, protection of, 32
Walnut, history and uses of the, 571
,, propagation, culture, &c., 571
,, gathering and keeping, 572
,, pruning, 572
Wasp-trap, best form of, 64
Water-barrow, garden, 114
Water-cress, culture of, 671
Water in pipes, to prevent the freezing of, 178
Watering engines, various kinds of, 112
,, instructions for, 351
,, of plants in houses, the, 481
,, pot, French, 105

Watering-pot, best kind of, 105
Weasels, useful in gardens, 71
Weeds, various modes of destroying, 348
Wheelbarrows, garden, various kinds of, 112
Whip-grafting, 250
Wickerwork protectors of various kinds, 131
Worm, common earth, 46
,, ,, injurious in gardens, 48
,, ,, how to destroy, 49
,, ,, how to keep out of pots, 49
,, eel, 49
Worms, snails, insects, &c., 46
Wormwood, culture and uses of, 683

THE END

LONDON:
SAVILL, EDWARDS AND CO., PRINTERS, CHANDOS STREET,
COVENT GARDEN.